ENCYCLOPEDIA OF THE LEWIS AND CLARK EXPEDITION

ENCYCLOPEDIA OF THE LEWIS AND CLARK EXPEDITION

ELIN WOODGER
AND
BRANDON TOROPOV

Foreword by Ned Blackhawk

Checkmark Books®

An imprint of Facts On File, Inc.

Encyclopedia of the Lewis and Clark Expedition

Copyright © 2004 by Elin Woodger and Brandon Toropov
Maps copyright © 2004 by Facts On File, Inc.
Foreword copyright © 2004 by Facts On File, Inc.

Checkmark Books
An imprint of Facts On File, Inc.
132 West 31st Street
New York NY 10001

Library of Congress Cataloging-in-Publication Data

Woodger, Elin.
Encyclopedia of the Lewis and Clark Expedition / Elin Woodger,
Brandon Toropov ; foreword by Ned Blackhawk
p. cm.
Includes bibliographical references (p.) and index.
ISBN 0-8160-4781-2 (hc.)—ISBN 0-8160-4782-0 (pbk.)
1. Lewis and Clark Expedition (1804–1806)—Encyclopedias. 2. West
(U.S.)—Discovery and exploration—Encyclopedias. 3. West (U.S.)—
Description and travel—Encyclopedias. I. Toropov, Brandon. II. Title.
F592. 7 .W68 2004
917.804'2'03—dc21   2003006120

Text design by Erika K. Arroyo
Cover design by Semadar Megged
Maps by Dale Williams and Jeremy Eagle

Printed in the United States of America

VB FOF 10 9 8 7 6 5 4 3 2 1

This book is printed on acid-free paper

To my husband, Norman Murphy,
without whom this book would not have been possible;
and to my father, Herbert Woodger,
without whom I would not be possible.

—Elin Woodger

To Judith Burros,
whose patience and commitment to this project
are impossible to describe adequately here.

—Brandon Toropov

Note on Photos

Many of the illustrations and photographs used in this book are old, historical images. The quality of the prints is not always up to modern standards because in many cases the originals are from glass negatives or the originals are damaged. The content of the illustrations, however, made their inclusion important despite problems in reproduction.

Contents

List of Entries

Foreword

In 1800, as the contested election of Thomas Jefferson dominated the national political scene of the new U.S. republic, multiple imperial powers vied for supremacy over the American West. Far from being the only state power with designs on the trans-Mississippi West, U.S. politicians confronted British, Russian, Spanish, and French colonies and claims over western North America. The 19th-century struggle for control of the American West, then, involved a constellation of imperial, Euro-American, as well as American Indian and indigenous mixed-race métis and mestizo actors, many of whom had lived for generations in territories where English was never spoken. And as the third U.S. president assumed command over the nascent nation, a series of international as well as domestic events rapidly set in motion the factors that led to Lewis and Clark's epic journey in 1804.

In 1801 few could have imagined that the young American republic would soon dominate the North American continent. The revolutionary experiment in the United States still remained untested in international diplomacy, while the truly revolutionary experiment in France threatened to unmake all of Europe. France and its also revolutionary colony, Saint-Domingue—now Haiti—are more central to the study of Lewis and Clark than most would imagine. For it was France, not the United States, that in 1801 held territorial claim to the trans-Mississippi region of Louisiana. Recently acquired from Spain, France, under arguably the most influential person of the 19th century, Napoleon Bonaparte, held renewed visions of empire in the Americas in which Louisiana was central. Envisioning Louisiana as a breadbasket for its Caribbean plantation colonies, including Saint-Domingue, Napoleon dreamed of restoring New France in North America. In this dream Louisiana was to be the agricultural and pastoral supplier of grains, leathers, meats, and furs for the French slave Caribbean colonies. Humiliated by its loss of its North American colonies after the Seven Years' War in 1763, France longed to rebuild its empire in North America.

When interviewed in exile after his plan of a European and North American empire had disintegrated, Napoleon replied that one of his most lasting regrets was neither his invasion of Russian or his inability to overcome the British navy. He replied that he wished he had made peace with the slave rebels who had dismantled the plantation system on Saint-Domingue. Under the leadership of Toussaint Louverture, the Haitian Revolution cost France tens of thousands of soldiers, countless francs, and perhaps, as Napoleon suggested, its chances of empire not only in Europe but also in North America. Haiti had been, according to one scholar, "the centerpiece of a restored French empire encompassing the Floridas,

Louisiana, French Guiana, and the French West Indies." France's loss of Haiti, then, ended Napoleon's chances of securing a foothold in North America.

Thomas Jefferson was more than happy to take advantage of France's humiliation. Jefferson had deeply feared renewed French expansion in North America. "The day that France takes New Orleans," he warned a friend, "we must marry ourselves to the British fleet and nation." When France did indeed acquire New Orleans in 1801, Jefferson attempted to buy better access to the Gulf coast rather than attempting another turbulent marriage with Britain. New Orleans was one of the most important ports in America, especially for farmers and merchants in the trans-Appalachian West who depended upon the Ohio River and the other watersheds of the Mississippi to get their goods to market. "There is on the globe one single spot," Jefferson remarked, "the possessor of which is our natural and habitual enemy. It is New Orleans, through which the produce of three-eighths of our territory must pass to market." Ordering his ambassador in Paris to inquire about buying New Orleans, Jefferson wanted better but still limited access to the Gulf coast.

With no end in sight to the war in what became Haiti, French foreign minister Talleyrand clearly realized that much was lost for French designs in North America, and rather than agreeing simply to the sale of New Orleans, as Jefferson had intended, Talleyrand suggested the complete sale of all of Louisiana.

The Louisiana Purchase, then, resulted from the complex interplay among three revolutionary states: France, Haiti, and the United States. While Haiti lost nearly one-third of its population and France was eventually defeated by a unified Europe, the United States doubled its territory. This "unprecedented and exhilarating event," as one scholar describes the purchase, offered Jefferson far more than access to New Orleans. It opened up the enormous and largely uncharted lands of the trans-Mississippi West to American exploration and eventually settlement. Mapping, exploring, and delineating this vast territory became the task of an entire generation of American explorers, geographers, and mapmakers, the first and foremost being Meriwether Lewis and William Clark.

For the indigenous peoples of western North America, events in Washington, Paris, and Haiti were of little import. Dealing with the generations of disruptive changes ushered in by European contact remained the primary concerns for all American Indian peoples in the lands foreigners called "Louisiana." New diseases, firearms, relations of warfare, and economies of trade dominated relations among and between the native peoples of the trans-Mississippi West. Everywhere Lewis and Clark traveled, then, the influences of Europeans had already long been felt. Among the Mandan on the Missouri, for example, the Corps of Discovery repeatedly noted the effects of *variola major,* or smallpox, which had in the 1770s and 1780s struck with such rapidity and fury as to depopulate several flourishing horticultural villages.

Diseases not only killed, they also combined with larger disruptions to undermine the social fabric of entire communities. Militarily, equestrian peoples, such as the Lakota, who migrated seasonally and had fully adopted European horses and later guns, prospered at the expense of more sedentary semihorticulturalists such as the Mandan, Arikara, and Hidatsa of the upper Missouri as well as the Pawnee of the central plains. In essence driving a wedge between these Missouri villagers and dominating the region's bountiful bison and horse grasslands, equestrian Indians emerged in the 18th-century West as the premier economic, political, and military powers. Lewis and Clark understood as much and constantly noted the fear of the "Sioux" (Dakota, Lakota, Nakota) among the Missouri villagers. Contemporary students and scholars of the 19th-century West must similarly recognize the origins of such disruptions, recognizing that the peoples Lewis and Clark encountered had long-standing historical relations with one another as well as outsiders.

By reaching the Pacific by land, Lewis and Clark proved that overland travel was difficult but possible. Meticulously charting the newly acquired lands of the West, they accelerated the process of American exploration and overland travel that would characterize much of 19th-century U.S. history. Securing a foothold on the Pacific, they also set in motion a series of American claims that would lead to the creation of a continental empire.

Jefferson's dream of enlarging an agrarian nation, of removing Indian groups from the East to the newly acquired territories of Louisiana, and securing a seat for the young republic at the table of international affairs was immensely aided by the Louisiana Purchase and the accomplishments of the Corps of Discovery, whose charts, maps, and journals literally introduced much of the continent to receptive eastern audiences. The first English speakers in the Far West, Lewis and Clark helped build one of the fastest-growing empires in world history. For the Native peoples of Louisiana, incorporation into the American empire would entail continued and, eventually, overpowering challenges.

—Ned Blackhawk
Assistant Professor of History and
American Indian Studies
University of Wisconsin, Madison

Preface

While there have been many excellent books written on the Lewis and Clark Expedition, the extraordinarily wide range of their achievements has meant that there have been few truly comprehensive accounts of their journey. The delay of a hundred years before the first full publication of their journals resulted in many of their scientific discoveries being attributed to others who followed them. There are large gaps in Lewis's journals that scholars are still debating today; are there missing journals yet to be found, or did Lewis simply stop writing for some reason? Other journals known to have been written during the expedition are also missing and may still appear; Clark's field notes for the winter of 1803–04, for example, were not found until 1953.

The vast scope of the expedition's mission and the variety of their accomplishments have forced writers to concentrate on particular aspects of the journey. Thus, while Stephen Ambrose's *Undaunted Courage* (1996) is a vivid and engaging portrayal of the expedition, its primary focus is on Meriwether Lewis's role in the exploration as well as interactions with the Indian nations he and William Clark encountered. Paul Russell Cutright's excellent *Lewis & Clark: Pioneering Naturalists* (1989) provides much of the detail behind the planning and execution of the expedition in addition to covering its natural history. The title of James P. Ronda's *Lewis and Clark among the Indians* (1984) speaks for itself.

It is the aim of this encyclopedia to encompass every aspect of the Corps of Discovery's journey, from their botanical, ornithological, and zoological discoveries to the people and events connected to the expedition. Places visited, Indians encountered, and information on what they took with them or acquired along the way are also covered. Yet to include every campsite, river, landmark, animal, and Indian nation they wrote about in their journals would take an encyclopedia far longer than this one. The authors have therefore selected what they think are the most salient topics related to the expedition.

For 200 years scholars have been studying and writing about Meriwether Lewis, William Clark, and the Corps of Discovery. Inevitably, contradictions have arisen regarding dates, the particulars of certain events, and the spelling of names. In this encyclopedia the most commonly accepted versions have been used as much as possible. In addition, many place names have changed since Lewis and Clark made their journey. The authors have generally used the names given by Lewis and Clark, although modern equivalents are employed where convenience or clarification requires it. Alternate place names, tribe names, or spellings of people's or tribe's names are provided in parentheses at the head of each entry, and cross-references will assist in finding places, tribes, or people with more than one name.

In the various editions of the journals that have been published, different approaches have been taken to their editing. Many have "cleaned up" the quaint spellings and punctuation used by the journal writers, while others have been meticulous in retaining the errors exactly as they appear in the explorers' notebooks. For this book the authors have reproduced the spellings that appear in the sources they used (including on-line versions of the journals), with preference given to the original writings. Although archaic to modern eyes, they serve to bring the explorers' thoughts more vividly to the reader.

It should also be noted that Lewis and Clark copied each other's journal entries to ensure the safety of the information they gathered. It is therefore sometimes impossible to give the correct attribution of a quote to one or the other. Other journal writers have been attributed by name.

This encyclopedia has been designed to give easy access to topics in which a reader may be interested. Within each entry, cross-references to other entries are provided in small capital letters. Suggestions for further reading are listed under each entry. Subject indexes at the end provide a guide to the topics covered.

It is hoped that this book will prove a valuable resource to students of the Lewis and Clark Expedition as well as to all those who, like the authors, have found themselves fascinated by this remarkable event in the history of America.

Acknowledgments

The authors gratefully thank Lieutenant Colonel N. T. P. Murphy for his invaluable assistance in researching and writing this encyclopedia. We are also deeply indebted to Judith Burros for all the help she gave in numerous capacities, from drawing draft maps to running errands to researching photos. Thank you, Judith and Norman.

Thanks are due to Professor Ned Blackhawk of the University of Wisconsin at Madison for his support and contribution to this book, and to David Nicandri of the Washington State Historical Society, who provided us with valuable input. We are grateful as well to all the organizations who provided photographs, including the American Antiquarian Society, American Numismatic Society, American Philosophical Society, Beinecke Rare Book and Manuscript Library, Dartmouth College, Library of Congress, Missouri Historical Society, Montana Historical Society, National Archives, New-York Historical Society, Peabody Museum of Archaeology and Ethnology, Smithsonian Institution, Virginia Military Institute, and Washington State Historical Society. Several individuals were particularly helpful to us and deserve acknowledgment: Barbara Blakey, Carol Cooper, Victoria Cranner, Anne Mainman, Elaine Miller, Ellen Thomasson, Terri Tremblay, Joshua Shaw, Elena Stolyarik, and Nicole Wells. We are especially indebted to Rich Aarstad and Rebecca Kohl of the Montana Historical Society, who provided high doses of enthusiasm, support, and assistance.

Finally, we benefited greatly from the advice, guidance, and help given us by Nicole Bowen, Laura Shauger, and Seth Pauley at Facts On File. They patiently answered every question, pointed us in the right direction time and again, and otherwise proved that the publisher's support is crucial to the success of any book.

Introduction

On May 14, 1804, the most epic exploration in the history of the United States began from a small, wooded site called CAMP DUBOIS. That day a KEELBOAT and two PIROGUES bearing approximately 45 men crossed the MISSISSIPPI RIVER to the mouth of the MISSOURI RIVER and began a journey of more than 4,100 miles. Their mission, as dictated by President THOMAS JEFFERSON, was "to explore the Missouri river, & such principal stream of it, as, by it's course and communication with the waters of the Pacific ocean, whether the Columbia, Oregon, Colorado or any other river may offer the most direct & practicable water communication across this continent for the purposes of commerce." It was a mission that Captains MERIWETHER LEWIS and WILLIAM CLARK followed almost to the letter of Jefferson's incredibly detailed, wide-ranging, and farsighted instructions.

It is always difficult to imagine a world other than one's own. It needs a conscious and deliberate effort of the mind to appreciate a time without television, radio, railways, automobiles, or airplanes. The time of Lewis and Clark was one when the horse was the fastest method of travel, when the Allegheny Mountains were still the frontier in the minds of many Americans, when two-thirds of the population lived within 50 miles of the Atlantic Ocean, when it took two days to travel from Philadelphia to New York, and when three-quarters of the North American continent was still an unexplored wilderness inhabited by Indians.

It was the fifth year of the 19th century, and the United States was not quite 28 years old. The previous year the country had doubled in size when, through the LOUISIANA PURCHASE, the LOUISIANA TERRITORY was acquired from FRANCE. Until then the nation's westernmost border was the Mississippi River. Now it stretched to the ROCKY MOUNTAINS, and Jefferson, who had long been curious to know what lay out there—three times previously he had tried and failed to send an exploratory party into the West—had an even stronger reason for dispatching Lewis and Clark: to establish a U.S. presence in those lands and take advantage of the burgeoning, prof-

itable FUR TRADE with the continent's Indians. A leading figure of the 18th-century ENLIGHTENMENT, Jefferson was also a man well ahead of his time. He had a vision of the nation's future growth and greatness, and he knew full well the importance of the purchase he had just made. He foresaw that the United States would spread inexorably westward across the continent, he foresaw the benefits that sovereignty over the American hinterland would bring, and he foresaw the withdrawal of European power from North America.

Jefferson also knew that he was in a "now or never" situation. The Spanish had established empires in the south, conquering vast areas in a space of a few years. Although the French had ceded their claims in the New World, their explorers had opened up the interior of the North American continent. In the North, the British had not only settled CANADA but had established a monopoly on the fur trade—and were filtering southward into the Louisiana Territory. Most significant, in 1793 ALEXANDER MACKENZIE, an employee of the NORTH WEST COMPANY, had reached the Pacific Ocean overland through Canada, and his 1801 report of that expedition had recommended that the British establish trading posts in the Pacific Northwest, which was rich in sea OTTER furs. Mackenzie had shown that, in Canada at least, the journey across country to the Pacific was straightforward. If the British exploited this route, it would give them a good claim to the Northwest and the Pacific coastline. If the United States did not act quickly, Jefferson's vision would be no more than a pipe dream as other countries laid claim by occupation to the continent's western lands.

Lewis and Clark were to attempt what Mackenzie had done, but they had many tasks other than their primary aim of finding a NORTHWEST PASSAGE to the Pacific. A man of remarkably wide interests, Jefferson had given them a set of instructions that still impresses the reader with its remarkable range of subjects, its detail, its common sense, and its practicality. These MISSION OBJECTIVES required the leaders of the CORPS OF DISCOVERY to be botanists, ornithologists,

The Lewis and Clark Expedition has been the subject of countless paintings. This one by E. S. Paxson depicts the two captains with Sacagawea at Three Forks. The figure on the right probably represents George Drouillard, while York stands with another expedition member on the left. *(Montana Historical Society, Helena)*

ichthyologists, and zoologists for scientific studies of the western country's PLANTS, BIRDS, FISH, and ANIMALS; astronomers as they made celestial observations for purposes of NAVIGATION, establishing their position, and determining the borders of the Louisiana Territory; cartographers as they mapped the previously uncharted territory through which they passed; ethnographers and linguists as they met and studied the numerous Indian nations they met along the way; diplomats as they impressed the fact of American sovereignty and trade upon the Indians of the territory; and reporters as they wrote down their daily activities and discoveries in field notes and JOURNALS.

Furthermore, they had to lead their expedition through an unknown and dangerous region of the country. Through painstaking planning and remarkably good fortune, Meriwether Lewis and William Clark proved themselves more than equal to the task, safely taking 29 men, a woman, and her baby across the continent and back. How they did it and what they accomplished along their journey has rightly become the stuff of American legend. Their story inspires awe even today.

It was Lewis whom Jefferson decided should lead the expedition. A military man with frontier skills, Lewis also had the education to carry out the scientific aspects of his mission—an education that was enhanced when, in 1801, he became the newly elected president's private secretary. Under Jefferson's tutelage, he increased his knowledge of astronomy and botany and met many of the leading philosophers and scientists of the age. It is not known when the president told him that he was to lead the expedition into the West—the best surmise is the summer or fall of 1802—but from that moment, all of Lewis's energies were devoted to the preparation of what he realized was the feat by which he would be remembered.

The original plan envisaged a party of one officer and 12 men. Possibly this small number was decided on to ensure funding from the U.S. CONGRESS. In any event, it was successful, the appropriation of $2,500 was approved, and in January 1803 Lewis began his PREPARATIONS FOR THE EXPEDITION in earnest. He traveled to HARPERS FERRY to order FIREARMS and other SUPPLIES AND EQUIPMENT and to supervise the construction of an IRON-FRAME BOAT that he and Jefferson considered would be necessary to navigate the upper reaches of the Missouri River. He took crash courses in astronomy and surveying from ANDREW ELLICOTT in Lancaster, Pennsylvania, and ROBERT PATTERSON in PHILADELPHIA, where he was also instructed in basic medical and surgical skills by BENJAMIN RUSH; received instruction from BENJAMIN SMITH BARTON on identifying and labeling plant specimens; and learned about fossils from CASPAR WISTAR. (It is a measure of the scientific knowledge of the times that both Wistar and Jefferson thought the mastodon might still be found roaming the country of the Far West.) In Philadelphia he also ordered and packed some 2^{1}/$_{2}$ tons of supplies and equipment, which he dispatched to PITTSBURGH.

On June 19, 1803, back in Washington, Lewis wrote a historic letter, inviting William Clark to join him as a cocaptain.

This was a move that contradicted accepted military procedure, whereby a unit had only one commander, but it made sense. The expedition was not an ordinary military operation, and because of its scope, Lewis was correct in his perception that he was going to need help to carry it out. Clark was the perfect choice, a man whom Lewis knew and trusted and one who, thanks to his abundant calm and common sense, provided the necessary counterbalance to Lewis's own mercurial temperament. The two men worked so well together that, with one exception, there is no record of any discord or disagreement in the expedition's journals.

Had Clark not accepted his invitation, Lewis would have selected somebody else to act as his lieutenant (*not* as cocommander). Fortunately he did accept, and months later, when he received his commission for a lieutenancy rather than a captaincy, he still "proceeded on" for the good of the unit. Neither Lewis nor Clark informed the men that one of them was not in fact a captain, and both leaders were addressed with that title throughout and after the journey. Lewis had every opportunity to claim sole credit for the expedition, but he never did. As far as he and Clark were concerned, it was a joint operation from start to finish. Indeed, their high regard for each other along with the fortunate meshing of their personalities proved to be one of the most important factors in the expedition's success.

When Lewis set out from Washington for Pittsburgh in early July 1803, he carried Jefferson's instructions with him. He had not yet received Clark's acceptance of his invitation, and he still had much to do if he were to carry out the mission that Jefferson had given him with any degree of success. As already noted, his primary objective was to follow the Missouri River to its source and from there to find a practical route to the Pacific. In addition, Jefferson had set out a list of other tasks that are breathtaking in their scope. Lewis was to note and describe the country through which he passed and to chart all changes of course of the Missouri as well as the natural landmarks along his journey, the features of each, and the distances between them. He was to comment on the trees, plants, animals, and fish he saw and, especially, was to report on the Indian nations he encountered. Jefferson wanted information on not only their names and languages but also their way of life; the tools and weapons they used; their food, clothing, social habits, laws, and customs; and the diseases that affected them. It is doubtful

Lewis and Clark's willingness to compromise with each other and to take into account the views of those they led were just two of the factors that made them outstanding leaders and made the expedition a success. *(Library of Congress, Prints and Photographs Division [LC-USZ62-50631])*

if ever an expedition was given, before or since, such clear but varied and multitudinous tasks.

It was not until August 31, 1803, while the United States was still absorbing the news of the Louisiana Purchase, that Lewis was at last able to leave Pittsburgh on the 55-foot-long keelboat and one pirogue to begin his journey down the OHIO RIVER. He purchased a second pirogue in Wheeling, West Virginia, along the way. On October 15 he reached CLARKSVILLE in Indiana Territory, where William Clark awaited him. During the next two weeks they interviewed volunteers for the party and enlisted the NINE YOUNG MEN FROM KENTUCKY—those exceptional individuals who, along with GEORGE DROUILLARD, would be the backbone of the expedition.

On October 26 they set off again down the Ohio, reaching its junction with the Mississippi River on November 13. Here Lewis and Clark spent a week practicing their astronomical and surveying skills before setting off north against the current on November 20. It is now generally agreed that the struggle to work the keelboat up the Mississippi—it took four

It was common practice for representatives of the U.S. government to present medals as gifts to Indian leaders. This Dakota Sioux Indian named Rushing Eagle, photographed ca. 1890, is wearing a peace medal among other ornaments. *(Library of Congress, Prints and Photographs Division [LC-USZ62-131772])*

days to travel 48 miles upstream—led both captains to decide that the expedition was woefully undermanned. They therefore recruited more men from the army posts at FORT MASSAC, KASKASKIA, and Cahokia before arriving at the Wood River (near the mouth of the Missouri and about 12 miles upstream of St. Louis) on December 9. Here they built their winter quarters, which was named Camp Dubois.

Between December 1803 and May 1804, Clark trained and prepared the men for the expedition, while Lewis bought more supplies and equipment in St. Louis. Both men also sought out and questioned traders and trappers who were familiar with the lower section of the Missouri. In this way they learned what rivers they would pass and what Indian nations they would encounter on the first part of their journey.

On March 9–10 Lewis and Clark attended the formal ceremonies transferring Louisiana, first from Spain to France and then from France to the United States. Once this was done, they no longer needed permission from the Spanish to make their journey up the Missouri. However, both captains knew they needed more time and more supplies before they dared depart. It was therefore not until May 14, 1804, that the small fleet of the heavily laden keelboat and two pirogues set off up the Missouri.

The surviving journals of the party describe vividly the tremendous physical labor of the corps's journey; the occasional following wind seems to have been the only respite from the tedious, exhausting, never-ending work of forcing the boats upstream. The keelboat was an ungainly, heavy craft, which had to be towed, rowed, or dragged up a river full of shallows, snags, rocks, and floating debris. A skilled waterman—usually PIERRE CRUZATTE or FRANÇOIS LABICHE—had to be stationed in the bow all the time to watch out for obstacles ahead—and all this against a current of five to seven miles an hour. It was an ordeal that was to last for 3,000 miles.

By June 26 (six weeks into the journey), the expedition had covered 366 miles and reached the KANSAS RIVER. On July 21 (nine weeks), they were at the mouth of the PLATTE RIVER (630 miles). They were managing an average of 10 miles a day.

On August 3, at COUNCIL BLUFF near present-day Omaha, Nebraska, Lewis and Clark held the first of their COUNCILS WITH INDIANS, this one attended by chiefs of the OTOE (Oto) and MISSOURI INDIANS. It was an unsatisfactory meeting, as the Indians wanted more gifts than the captains were prepared to give, and little was achieved. It went no better on August 18 at a second meeting with some more important Otoe and Missouri chiefs, an indication of difficulties to come in carrying out the diplomatic aspects of their mission.

On August 20 Sergeant CHARLES FLOYD died, probably of peritonitis resulting from appendicitis, and was buried on a bluff near today's Sioux City, Iowa. He was the only man to die on the expedition. Two days later, in a radical change from normal military procedure, Lewis and Clark held an election to replace Floyd; PATRICK GASS was elected. It was shortly after this that Lewis first referred to the members of the expedition as "the corps of volunteers for North Western Discovery." In time they would become better known as the Corps of Discovery.

A week later, a council was held with the YANKTON NAKOTA INDIANS (Yankton Sioux) at CALUMET BLUFF, near today's Gavins Point Dam, South Dakota. As he had done with the Otoe and the Missouri, Lewis spoke of the necessity of accepting the United States as the new ruling authority, the need to trade with U.S. rather than British traders, and the importance of making peace with their neighbors. He and Clark also pronounced one of the chiefs, WEUCHE, to be "first chief." This was a continual and unfortunate error in judgment made by the captains, who were slow to appreciate that the Indians had their own system of deciding who were the most important chiefs. They also failed to understand the complex trading systems among the nations whereby HORSES and furs were traded for agricultural products and European goods, especially guns and powder. Nor did Lewis and Clark realize that the nation with the most guns could and did exert authority over its neighbors. Having reached a precarious accommodation with fellow nations, there was, in Indian eyes, little advantage in what Lewis had to offer.

On September 24, 1804, the expedition had its first encounter with the TETON LAKOTA INDIANS (then called the Teton Sioux), an encounter that might have ended in bloodshed had not Chief BLACK BUFFALO intervened and offset the aggressiveness of THE PARTISAN. This incident confirmed the warlike reputation of the Teton Lakota, and their resistance to white encroachment was to last for another 80 years.

In October, near the mouth of the Grand River, Lewis and Clark held a council with ARIKARA INDIANS, who impressed the soldiers with their BULL BOATS, coracles made from BUFFALO hide. The captains hoped to bring about a peace between the Arikara and the MANDAN INDIANS, and to that end they took an Arikara chief with them upriver to the Mandan and HIDATSA villages at the junction of the Missouri with the KNIFE RIVER. After reaching the villages on October 24, they decided to spend the winter there. They were now some 1,600 miles from their starting point at the mouth of the Missouri.

The Corps of Discovery spent the winter of 1804–05 in friendly association with the Mandan, who lived by agriculture, and the Hidatsa, who raided for horses and slaves as far west as the CONTINENTAL DIVIDE, some 600 miles away. They met traders from the North West Company and the HUDSON'S BAY COMPANY; studied the ways of life of the Mandan and the Hidatsa; and, from the latter, received valuable information on the territory that still lay ahead of them. They also enlisted TOUSSAINT CHARBONNEAU as interpreter, because they had learned that his wife SACAGAWEA (Sacajawea) was a SHOSHONE Indian whose knowledge of the Shoshone language and country would be useful to them. (By a twist of fate, she has now become the most famous member of the expedition, and there are more statues to her than to any other American woman.)

On April 7, 1805, the keelboat left FORT MANDAN to return downstream to ST. LOUIS. It was loaded with 25 boxes of pelts, animal skeletons, plant specimens, and artifacts of every description. The cargo also included a live PRAIRIE DOG, a sharp-tailed GROUSE, four magpies, and members of the temporary party who had been discharged. On the same day, the permanent party set off again up the Missouri in the two pirogues and six dugout CANOES they had made during the winter. Although they were to pass Indian fires and campsites all along their journey, it was to be more than four months before they saw another Indian—and that was to be just east of the Continental Divide.

On April 25, 1805, they reached the mouth of the YELLOWSTONE RIVER, at which point the journals began to make regular mention of the numbers of buffalo they saw. Vast herds crossing the river held up their progress, and Lewis noted they were so numerous that "the men frequently throw sticks and stones at them in order to drive them out of their way." It was just a few days later that the corps finally encountered a grizzly BEAR. Stories they had heard of the beast's ferocity had long intrigued the men; numerous frightening encounters later, Lewis would write that "I find the curiossity of our party is pretty well satisfied with rispect to this anamal."

By May 3 the expedition had traveled 2,000 miles, marked by Clark when he named a small river "2000 Mile Creek." They reached the MARIAS RIVER on June 2. For six days Lewis and Clark explored both the Marias and the next length of the Missouri to ascertain which was the main stream. Every other member of the party, including the expert waterman Pierre Cruzatte, considered the Marias to be the route to follow, but both captains were convinced the southern stream was the true Missouri. It is a measure of their LEADERSHIP qualities and the confidence the men had in them that Lewis was able to write: "They said very cheerfully that they were ready to follow us any wher we thought proper to direct but that they still thought that the other way was the river." Three days later Lewis came to the GREAT FALLS of the Missouri, proving that he and Clark had been right.

The difficult and exhausting PORTAGE around the falls and the unsuccessful attempt to construct the iron-frame boat they had carried so far took them a month. "The Experiment" was to prove the only source of irritation between Lewis, whose pet project it was, and Clark, who considered it a waste of time. When it became clear that it would not float and had to be abandoned, more canoes were constructed and, as was noted repeatedly in the journals, "we proceeded on."

The first week of August 1805 brought them into Shoshone territory, and Sacagawea began to recognize landmarks from her childhood. On August 11 Lewis and a foot party saw a Shoshone on horseback, the first Indian they had seen since leaving Fort Mandan four months before; Clark and the river party commemorated another landmark of the journey by naming an island in the river "3000 Mile Island." The following day Lewis walked over LEMHI PASS, becoming the first non-Indian American to cross the Continental Divide. From the top of the pass he saw, to the west, not the open plains and river he had hoped to find but range after range of inhospitable mountains.

On August 13, 1805, Lewis and his party at last met the Shoshone, and they were joined by Clark and the rest of the

William Clark's calculation of 4,162 miles for the expedition's east-to-west journey was based on a detailed and meticulous noting of the Missouri's twists and turns as well as the tortuous journey through the Bitterroot Mountains. Modern cartographers believe he erred by only 40 miles. *(American Philosophical Society)*

last reached the villages of the NEZ PERCE INDIANS near today's Weippe, Idaho. It had taken them 11 days to travel 160 miles.

At their camp with the Nez Perce, the party constructed canoes and set off again by water on October 7, 1805. They canoed down the CLEARWATER and SNAKE Rivers, through rapids and defiles, until they reached the COLUMBIA RIVER on October 16. As they traveled down the Columbia, they met and noted the habits and customs of numerous Indian nations. Finally, on November 7, Clark wrote: "Ocian in view! O! the joy." But it was to be another 11 days before he could carve his name on a tree at CAPE DISAPPOINTMENT with the proud words "By Land from the U. States in 1804 & 1805."

By Clark's reckoning, they had traveled 4,162 miles from their starting point of Camp Dubois. Modern cartographers now believe he was only 40 miles in error—an astonishing achievement when one remembers that his calculations had to take into account the constant twists and turns of the rivers they navigated, the portages, and the journey through the tree-and-snow-covered hills of the Lolo Trail.

To the captains' disappointment, there were no trading ships visiting that could take all or part of their group home, so they prepared to spend the winter on the West Coast. In another radical departure from the custom of the day, the captains had every member of the party vote on where they should set up their winter quarters. Even Sacagawea and YORK, Clark's slave, were allowed to have their say, and the result was a move from STATION CAMP on the north bank of the Columbia estuary to the south bank, where they built FORT CLATSOP. This was to be their home from December 1805 until March 1806.

It was a long, dreary winter, but the two captains employed it fruitfully. Lewis spent his time writing long, detailed descriptions of the fish, birds, animals, TREES, and plants they had seen along their journey, while Clark drew and redrew the MAPS that were to remain the most accurate charts of the Northwest for nearly 50 years. (He would continue to add to and refine his maps in the years following the expedition, drawing on information received from Indians, traders, and MOUNTAIN MEN.)

The expedition left Fort Clatsop on March 23, 1806. Their return journey up the Columbia was fraught with difficulties, not least of which was the petty thievery of CHINOOK INDIANS along the way. They finally succeeded in acquiring enough horses to carry their baggage back to the Nez Perce villages, where they arrived in May. However, they still had to wait until June, when enough snow had melted to allow them to travel back through the Bitterroot Mountains with the help of some INDIAN GUIDES. This time the crossing that had taken them 11 days on the way out was completed in six. They returned to Travelers' Rest on June 30, 1806.

It was here that Lewis and Clark implemented a plan that could have led to disaster. They were still 3,000 miles from home, in unknown country, but by now they had complete faith in all the members of their party and in their men's ability to carry out any task given to them. It is a tribute to the captains as leaders and to the trust their men had in them that

group two days later. At the formal council meeting, in perhaps the most dramatic twist of fate in the expedition, Sacagawea recognized the Shoshone chief, CAMEAHWAIT, as her brother. This piece of good fortune was offset by the realization that the nearby SALMON RIVER was impassable and the party would have to travel north before turning west through the mountains. With OLD TOBY, a Shoshone guide, they rode up to the BITTERROOT RIVER valley, where they met the FLATHEAD INDIANS at ROSS'S HOLE, and then north again to TRAVELERS' REST, near today's Missoula, Montana.

The party then set out on what proved to be the most dangerous and arduous part of their journey, following the LOLO TRAIL through the BITTERROOT MOUNTAINS. Making their way slowly up and down precipitous snow-covered hillsides, their food ran out and they were near starvation when they at

none of the journals record any doubts or misgivings about the decisions made at Travelers' Rest.

The plan involved a dangerous—and foolhardy—splitting of the group. While Lewis and one party would ride due east to the Great Falls, Clark would take the remainder south to CAMP FORTUNATE, where the canoes had been hidden the year before. At Great Falls, Lewis would leave one group under the charge of Sergeant Patrick Gass to dig up the CACHES of supplies they had buried there, while he took the remainder off to explore the Marias River. Clark, for his part, detached Sergeant JOHN ORDWAY and some men to take the canoes down to join the group at the Great Falls, where together they would carry out the portage. Meanwhile, he and the remainder of the party traveled farther south to the Yellowstone River. Here the party split yet again, one group (led by Clark) to build canoes and travel down to the agreed rendezvous at the mouth of the Yellowstone, and the other (led by Sergeant NATHANIEL PRYOR) to take the horses and ride 400 miles across country to the Mandan villages.

With hindsight, the two captains were taking outrageous risks. They were splitting their party into five groups, two as small as four men. Any unit would be helpless against an Indian raiding party, and they were hundreds of miles apart, spread across the whole of today's Montana. If ever a plan deserved to fail, this one did. But if ever two officers had their faith in their subordinates justified, then Lewis and Clark did.

As Lewis and three men returned from their exploration of the Marias River, they encountered a small group of BLACK-FEET INDIANS, who attempted to steal their guns and horses. In the ensuing fight, two Indians were killed, and Lewis and his men rode 100 miles with only one break before coming back to the Missouri the following morning. With great fortune they overtook John Ordway's river party an hour later, and within two more hours the combined party was joined by Sergeant Patrick Gass and his group, who had come down from the Great Falls on horseback. It was undoubtedly the most amazing of many COINCIDENCES AND CHANCE ON THE EXPEDITION.

Far to the south, Clark and his group had ridden down the Yellowstone until they found trees suitable for making canoes. He then detached Sergeant Pryor and three men to take the horses across the GREAT PLAINS to the Mandan villages, while he and the rest embarked down the Yellowstone. Two days later, all their horses were stolen by CROW INDIANS, and Pryor's group displayed the determination and ingenuity that characterized the expedition. They simply picked up their packs, walked north to the Yellowstone, shot two buffalo, skinned them, made two bull boats, and followed Clark and his party downstream. At the mouth of the Yellowstone they found a note that Clark had left for Lewis, saying that he had moved further downstream. They followed him down and caught up with him, as did Lewis and the rest of the party on August 12. In a rare expression of emotion, Patrick Gass wrote in his journal, ". . . and now (thanks to God) we are all together again in good health. . . ."

From that reunion on August 12, 1806—a year exactly since Lewis had walked westward over the Continental Divide—the corps's journey home was pleasant and uneventful. Two days later they were back at the Mandan and Hidatsa villages, where the Mandan chief BIG WHITE agreed to accompany them to St. Louis (and then on to Washington). On August 17 JOHN COLTER became the first to leave the expedition; he was to become one of the earliest legendary mountain men.

After leaving the Mandan (and Charbonneau and Sacagawea), the corps proceeded on downriver, making 70–80 miles a day where they had made only 10 miles coming upstream, and met a succession of boats coming up the Missouri. Some carried traders, others trappers; all were the direct result of the expedition: men who had heard of Lewis and Clark's mission, of their peaceful reception by the Indian nations they had met (the Teton Lakota excepted); men who had come to open up the West in their wake.

On September 23, 1806, the expedition came back in triumph to St. Louis, the beginning and end of their journey. The Corps of Discovery was disbanded immediately, Lewis and Clark were feted, there were PAYMENTS AND REWARDS for all the men, and NEWS REPORTS OF THE EXPEDITION spread quickly. But the glory soon faded as months went by, and Lewis

While the expedition used canoes for the greater portion of their journey west, horses were essential to cross the mountains between two great rivers, the Missouri and the Columbia. (Courtesy Art Today.com/IMSI)

failed to publish his and Clark's journals. In 1807 Patrick Gass published his account of the journey; it was not until 1814 that the official Lewis and Clark narrative was published in an incomplete form.

It is one of the sad ironies of their achievement that Lewis and Clark discovered so much and reported it in such detail that the sheer volume of their findings prevented publication of all of it for nearly a century. Lewis's procrastination, his suicide in 1809, the failure of Benjamin Smith Barton to edit the natural history volumes, and numerous other problems all contributed to the delays. It was not until 1904 that the journals (edited by Reuben Gold Thwaites) were published in their entirety. In the interim, other naturalists, botanists, and geographers repeated the Lewis and Clark findings and received the credit for them. Other explorers followed their ROUTE and gave new names to the rivers and landmarks they had named.

After the expedition's return, numerous portraits were painted of Lewis and Clark. This one by Charles Saint-Mémim shows Lewis wearing an ermine tippet given him by Shoshone chief Cameahwait. *(Collection of The New-York Historical Society, negative number 51322)*

As a result, their feats as explorers are remembered, but their remarkable achievements in other fields are too often overlooked.

From one point of view, the Lewis and Clark expedition was a failure in that they did not find the all-water route to the Pacific that was their primary objective. They also failed to achieve many of their diplomatic goals with the Indians. Yet from another aspect they achieved important successes that resonate even today. One of the difficulties in describing or even appreciating the Lewis and Clark Expedition is the vast range of their accomplishments. They were first and foremost explorers, but they were also superb leaders and field naturalists. What they and their group achieved as both a military unit and as a mission of peace still has lessons for soldiers today. Clark's meticulous charts and surveys still stand as a landmark in American cartography, while the importance of Lewis's detailed drawings and descriptions of the countless plants and animals then new to science is only today being properly appreciated.

Perhaps the most significant result of the expedition was the effect it had on the popular imagination and thus the future of the United States. The nation would have expanded into the West even without the trailblazing of the Corps of Discovery. But their feats helped to spur on that expansion and contributed to the growth of the U.S. fur trade, as merchants such as MANUEL LISA and, later, JOHN JACOB ASTOR set up trading posts in the West after learning of the expedition. In reaching the Pacific, Lewis and Clark also strengthened the U.S. claim to the OREGON TERRITORY and set a goal for others to follow. In fact, one lifetime would encompass their journey and the settlement of the nation from coast to coast.

Lewis and Clark took their party across the continent in the first decade of the 19th century, but they did so as men whose thinking, equipment, and aims were those of the 18th century. They made their journey as people had traveled throughout history: on horseback, on foot, and by boat. Except for the FIREARMS they carried, their equipment was on a par with that of Columbus and the Vikings before them. On their return journey, they met traders and travelers following in their wake—but Lewis and Clark were the last of their kind.

The expedition occurred at a watershed in American history. The year after the Corps of Discovery returned, Robert Fulton's steamboat was making regular runs on the Hudson River. The 19th century—the century of steam power—lay ahead of them. Twenty years after the expedition's return, the United States saw its first working steam locomotive. Before the century ended, railroads were crisscrossing the country.

The expedition also took place at a watershed in world history. The 16th century had seen SPAIN as the dominant power. The 17th century had seen the rise of France, and the end of the 18th century saw the advent of Napoleon Bonaparte, who conquered Europe but was to lose everything at Waterloo. October 21, 1805, saw the Corps of Discovery making their way down the Columbia River. It also saw Admiral Horatio Nelson winning the Battle of Trafalgar, which led to the pax Britannica,

again, an entry in the journals brings someone to life: Meriwether Lewis, the brilliant but brooding captain subject to periods of introspection; William Clark, the practical commander delighting in the antics of Pomp, Sacagawea's boy; George Drouillard, the frontiersman and tracker who keeps the expedition supplied with fresh meat for FOOD; SILAS GOODRICH, the fisherman who does the same when game is scarce; JOHN SHIELDS, the blacksmith whose skill helps feed the corps during the winter at Fort Mandan; Patrick Gass, the carpenter who builds huts as readily as he carves canoes out of cottonwood trees; Nathaniel Pryor, the resourceful sergeant who leads a small party on foot across the Great Plains to the Yellowstone River and makes bull boats to carry them to safety; HUGH MC-NEAL, who "stood with a foot on each side of this little rivulet and thanked his god that he had lived to bestride the mighty & heretofore deemed endless Missouri." And from Fort Mandan onward, there is the quiet Sacagawea, who still raises a smile as she asks to be allowed to go to see the "monstrous fish" (WHALE).

It is images like these that bring home that, unlike other explorations, the exploits that capture one's imagination today are not just those of Lewis and Clark but of the remarkable group of people they led—including a young Indian woman.

After the closing of the frontier, photographs of Indians became very popular. This picture of a Sioux Indian named Grey Eagle, taken ca. 1900, is a typical example. (Library of Congress, Prints and Photographs Division [LC-USZ62-117374])

a period of British dominance in the world that lasted for the next hundred years.

When the Louisiana Purchase transferred the Mississippi basin to the United States, it marked a crucial second stage in the withdrawal of European powers from the New World, a process that had begun with the American Revolution and was to finish with the Spanish-American War in 1898. In this period the United States expanded and acquired the strength that would later lead to its own position as a world power. Thomas Jefferson believed that it would take 50 generations before the continent could be settled. He did not appreciate, however, that the land hunger of American settlers and the concept of "manifest destiny" would populate it in five generations, not 50.

Today the population of the 11 states through which the Corps of Discovery passed is more than 39 million—seven times the total population of the 16 states that composed the United States in 1800. Every year new books about the expedition are published, continuing to fuel interest in the expedition and its accomplishments. The extant journals have recently undergone their most extensive editing yet (by Gary Moulton), and it is hoped that other missing journals may yet be discovered.

More than anything else, it is the journals that capture one's imagination, showing how the success of this epic journey rested on both the leadership of the two captains and the bravery and ingenuity of the people they commanded. Time and

Often portrayed as a guide, Sacagawea actually served mainly as an interpreter. She has become the most famous member of the Corps of Discovery, and there are more statues of her than any other American woman. (Montana Historical Society, Helena)

Chronology

For the years 1804 and 1805, the mileage from the start point of Camp Dubois has been noted in an arrow beside certain entries. These mileage indicators provide an odometer of sorts. Note that these were estimated miles in the journals; William Clark was off in his calculations by only 40 miles.

▪ PRE-EXPEDITION ▪

1578

- English explorer Sir Francis Drake travels up the Pacific coast as far as the 48th parallel.

1603

- Sailing up the Pacific coast, Spanish explorer Martín d'Aguilar becomes the first to sight what is probably the mouth of the COLUMBIA RIVER.

1670

- The HUDSON'S BAY COMPANY is established under a charter from King Charles II.

1682

- French explorer René Robert de La Salle travels the length of the MISSISSIPPI RIVER to its mouth and claims the region drained by the river for FRANCE. He names the territory Louisiana.

1738

- As French explorers and fur traders begin to travel beyond the Mississippi River, Pierre de La Vérendrye becomes the first white man to enter what is now North Dakota, meeting the MANDAN INDIANS. This same year the brothers Pierre and Paul Mallet set off into North America's interior.

1741

- Some 2,000 miles after beginning their journey, the Mallet brothers reach a mountain range at the head of the PLATTE RIVER; local Indians call these mountains the Rockies.

1743

- François and Louis-Joseph de La Vérendrye claim the area at present-day Fort Pierre, South Dakota, for France. (The lead plate they bury at the site will be discovered in 1913.)
- *April 2:* THOMAS JEFFERSON is born in Albermarle County, Virginia.

1762

- As the Seven Years' War (1756–63; French and Indian War in the United States, 1754–63) nears its end, France cedes its territories west of the Mississippi River to SPAIN. The following year France cedes its Canadian territories to England.

1764

- Fifteen-year-old René AUGUSTE CHOUTEAU, SR., starts to build a trading post on the Mississippi River, close to the mouth of the MISSOURI RIVER. It will become ST. LOUIS.

1765

- Explorer and adventurer Robert Rogers petitions King George III of Britain to send an expedition to the territory of "Oregon"—the first known use of this word. Despite the king's refusal, the following year Roberts sends Jonathan Carver of Massachusetts to conduct the exploration. Carver will be turned back by an Indian war but still makes significant explorations of the upper Great Lakes and Mississippi region.

1769

- The Spanish begin settlement of California, reaching the land by sailing up the Pacific coast.

1770

- *August 1:* WILLIAM CLARK is born in Virginia. He is the younger brother of Revolutionary War hero GEORGE ROGERS CLARK.

1774

- *August 18:* MERIWETHER LEWIS is born in Albemarle County, Virginia.

1775

- Bruno Heceta becomes the first European to stand in the Pacific Northwest when he lands at what is now Point Grenville, Washington, and claims the territory for Spain. During his journey, Heceta makes special note of what he calls "the mouth of some great river, or of some passage to another sea"—the Columbia River.

1778

- After discovering Hawaii, Captain James Cook sails up to the Alaskan coast in hopes of finding the NORTHWEST PASSAGE; he fails to do so but travels farther north than any previous European explorer. Although he dies the following year, his men return to England with news of a rich TRADE in sea OTTER furs in the Pacific Northwest.

1783

- Thomas Jefferson writes to General George Rogers Clark suggesting that Clark lead an expedition across the continent, to be funded by a party of British investors; the general politely refuses although expresses support for the idea.

1784

- As the FUR TRADE spreads westward, the NORTH WEST COMPANY is established to challenge HUDSON'S BAY COMPANY.

1786

- Jefferson supports the attempt of John Ledyard to cross the continent. Ledyard's plan is to cross the Bering Strait from Siberia and then travel from west to east. However, he is arrested in Siberia and sent to Poland.
- Jean François La Pérouse surveys the Pacific coastline between Monterey and Alaska. He tries but fails to claim the territory for France.

1787

- The Northwest Ordinance is passed, setting guidelines for settlement of the American frontier; it includes provisions on dealing with Native Americans and also prohibits slavery in western territories.

1790

- Captain ROBERT GRAY becomes the first American to circumnavigate the globe when he sails into Boston harbor; his ship carries furs obtained from Indians of the Pacific Northwest. This sets off increased trade between the two coasts and helps to establish U.S. claims to the OREGON TERRITORY.
- French explorer Jacques d'Église encounters British traders at the MANDAN INDIAN villages, proof that they are filtering down into LOUISIANA TERRITORY from CANADA.
- U.S. Secretary of War Henry Knox attempts secretly to send an expedition to the Missouri River. His idea is ill conceived and poorly planned, and the expedition never moves beyond the Mississippi River.

1792

- Captain GEORGE VANCOUVER of GREAT BRITAIN arrives at the northwest coast and for the next three years explores and charts the coastline. He will conclude that the Northwest Passage does not exist. After Robert Gray's discovery of the Columbia River on May 11, Vancouver sends a party 100 miles inland to explore and MAP the river. With information gained from Gray and Vancouver, Thomas Jefferson estimates the continent to be about 3,000 miles wide. He subsequently initiates an attempt to launch a transcontinental expedition.

1793

- North West Company employee ALEXANDER MACKENZIE becomes the first non-Indian to cross the North American continent. He travels from what is now Alberta, Canada, across the ROCKY MOUNTAINS into British Columbia, and finally down the Bella Coola River to the Pacific. Mackenzie's accomplishment establishes a British claim to the Oregon Territory. His account of the journey will be published in 1801 and will be read by Thomas Jefferson and Meriwether Lewis.

- *July:* Under the sponsorship of Jefferson and the AMERICAN PHILOSOPHICAL SOCIETY, French botanist ANDRÉ MICHAUX begins a transcontinental expedition. However, when it is revealed that Michaux is a secret agent for the French Republic, the botanist is recalled the following year, having traveled no farther west than Kentucky.

1795

- The Treaty of San Lorenzo delineates the Mississippi River as the border between the United States and Spanish territories.

1797

- North West Company partner Charles Chaboillez sets up a trading post at the crossing of the Pembina and Red Rivers in what is now North Dakota.

1800

- Through the Treaty of San Ildefonso, Spain secretly transfers the Louisiana Territory back to France but with the caveat that the territory should not be ceded or sold to an English-speaking nation.
- Thomas Jefferson is elected president. At this time the United States's westernmost border is the Mississippi River.

1801

- Meriwether Lewis becomes private secretary to President Jefferson. Jefferson still hopes to cross the continent, especially after reading Alexander Mackenzie's account of his 1793 journey. Within a year Jefferson comes to believe that Lewis is the man to lead an American expedition. Lewis subsequently begins to study and train to acquire the knowledge and skills that he will need for the journey.

■ THE EXPEDITION ■

1803

- *January 18:* President Jefferson asks CONGRESS for an appropriation of $2,500 to send an expedition across the continent by way of the Missouri River. He justifies it by citing the expanding FUR TRADE and noting the need to find out whether there is a water route across the continent to the PACIFIC OCEAN.

    Meanwhile, Napoleon Bonaparte of France has already begun secret negotiations with the United States to sell the Louisiana Territory to the young nation. If the deal goes through, there will be even stronger reasons to send an expedition to the Pacific: to explore the country's new lands and to strengthen its claims in the Northwest.

- *March 13:* Meriwether Lewis leaves Washington for HARPERS FERRY to order weapons and to supervise construction of an IRON-FRAME BOAT he has designed.
- *April:* In need of money—and in violation of the Treaty of San Ildefonso with Spain—Napoleon strikes a deal with Jefferson, selling the Louisiana Territory to the United States for $15 million. This more than doubles the size of the nation.
- *April 14:* Lewis leaves Harpers Ferry for Frederickstown, Maryland.

- *April 19:* Lewis arrives in Lancaster, Pennsylvania, to study with astronomer ANDREW ELLICOTT.
- *May 7:* Lewis leaves Lancaster for PHILADELPHIA, where he begins basic courses in medicine with Dr. BENJAMIN RUSH; botany, zoology, and American-Indian history with Dr. BENJAMIN SMITH BARTON; surveying with ROBERT PATTERSON; and paleontology with Dr. CASPAR WISTAR. He also begins to buy more SUPPLIES AND EQUIPMENT.
- *June 6 or 7:* Lewis arrives back in Washington.
- *June 19:* Lewis writes to William Clark, inviting him to join the expedition as a captain and coleader.
- *June 20:* Jefferson gives Lewis a detailed letter of instructions for the expedition.
- *July 4:* News of the LOUISIANA PURCHASE is published in the nation's newspapers.
- *July 5:* Jefferson formally sends Lewis off on his mission with detailed instructions and a LETTER OF CREDIT.
- *July 6:* In Harpers Ferry, Lewis arranges for the transportation of SUPPLIES AND EQUIPMENT to PITTSBURGH.
- *July 15:* Lewis arrives in Pittsburgh to find that the KEELBOAT he ordered is not yet ready.
- *July 29:* Lewis receives Clark's acceptance of his invitation to join the expedition. Clark will begin to recruit men for what will eventually be called the CORPS OF DISCOVERY.
- *August 31:* After repeated delays, the keelboat is finally completed and launched along with a PIROGUE. The journey begins as Lewis, a crew of 11 (including JOHN COLTER and GEORGE SHANNON) and his dog SEAMAN head down the OHIO RIVER. Lewis makes his first journal entry.
- *September 7:* The keelboat arrives at Wheeling, Virginia, to pick up SUPPLIES AND EQUIPMENT sent overland. Another pirogue is purchased.
- *October 4:* Lewis visits Bone Lick, Kentucky, to see some fossilized mastodon remains.
- *October 14:* Lewis and the boats arrive at the Falls of the Ohio.
- *October 15:* Lewis joins Clark in CLARKSVILLE, Indiana Territory. By this time the NINE YOUNG MEN FROM KENTUCKY—Colter, Shannon, WILLIAM BRATTON, JOSEPH FIELD, REUBIN FIELD, CHARLES FLOYD, GEORGE GIBSON, NATHANIEL PRYOR, and JOHN SHIELDS—have been recruited. Also joining them is YORK, Clark's slave.
- *October 26:* The expedition leaves Clarksville.
- *November 11:* They arrive at FORT MASSAC, 35 miles above the junction of the Ohio with the Mississippi River. Lewis hires GEORGE DROUILLARD as interpreter. More volunteers are recruited from the army post, including JOHN NEWMAN and JOSEPH WHITEHOUSE.
- *November 13:* They leave FORT MASSAC and reach the Ohio's confluence with the Mississippi, where they test their surveying equipment and ASTRONOMICAL OBSERVATIONS.
- *November 28:* They reach KASKASKIA, 60 miles below St. Louis. More men are recruited from the army post here, including JOHN COLLINS, PATRICK GASS, JOHN ORDWAY, JOHN ROBERTSON, JOHN B. THOMPSON, EBENEZER TUTTLE, PETER WEISER, RICHARD WINDSOR, and ALEXANDER HAMILTON WILLARD.
- *December 7:* Clark arrives in Cahokia, Illinois, with the keelboat and two pirogues; Lewis has already arrived by land.
- *December 8:* Lewis crosses the river to St. Louis to obtain Spanish permission to travel up the Missouri River. It is not forthcoming, and the captains decide to camp in the area for the winter.
- *December 12:* The men begin to clear land to set up CAMP DUBOIS alongside the Wood River.

- *December 22:* The keelboat is hauled up on land so that modifications can be made. More recruits arrive at Camp Dubois. The Corps of Discovery settles in for the winter.

1804

- *March 9–10:* Lewis and Clark attend ceremonies in St. Louis marking the official transfer of the Louisiana Territory from France to the United States. This legitimizes the LOUISIANA PURCHASE and eliminates the need for Spanish permission to travel on the river.

  By this time Clark has received the disappointing news that he has been granted only a second lieutenant's commission, not the captaincy he had been promised. He continues with the mission anyway, and Lewis always refers to him as Captain Clark. The enlisted men are never told of this.
- *March 29:* John Colter and John Shields are court-martialed for mutiny after threatening Sergeant Ordway's life. After they ask for forgiveness and promise "to doe better in future," they are forgiven.
- *May 14:* The expedition sets out from Camp Dubois in the keelboat and two pirogues, beginning the journey up the Missouri River. The party includes York, Clark's slave.

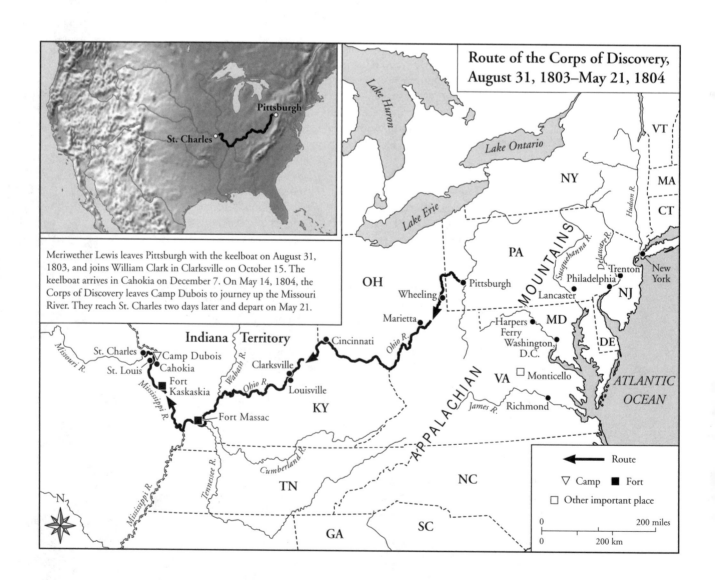

Meriwether Lewis leaves Pittsburgh with the keelboat on August 31, 1803, and joins William Clark in Clarksville on October 15. The keelboat arrives in Cahokia on December 7. On May 14, 1804, the Corps of Discovery leaves Camp Dubois to journey up the Missouri River. They reach St. Charles two days later and depart on May 21.

Route of the Corps of Discovery, August 31, 1803–May 21, 1804

Route of the Corps of Discovery, May 21–September 28, 1804

Cheyenne R.

Confrontation with Teton Lakota

MN

Bad R.

SD

White R.

James R.

Big Sioux R.

Missouri R.

Yankton

Vermillion

Calumet Bluff

Niobrara R.

Ponca

Floyd R.

Sioux City

Sergeant Floyd's gravesite

North Loup R.

NE

N. Platte R.

S. Platte R.

Platte R.

Council Bluff

IA

Camp White Catfish

Mississippi R.

Illinois R.

Big Blue

Republican R.

Independence Creek

IL

Atchison

N

MO

Kansas R.

Missouri R.

St. Charles

La Charette

KS

Osage R.

Legend

→ Route

▽ Camp

○ Present-day city (provided for reference; these did not exist at the time of the expedition)

● White settlement

□ Other important site

Note: Contemporary boundaries and state names are provided for reference.

0 — 100 miles
0 — 100 km

Confrontation with Teton Lakota

St. Charles

After leaving St. Charles, the corps passes La Charette, the last non-Indian settlement on the Missouri, on May 21. As they journey upriver, they meet the Otoe, Missouri, and Yankton Lakota Indians. On September 25 they have a confrontation with the Teton Lakota, but they stay in the area another three days before proceeding on September 28.

---

21 miles

- *May 16:* The corps arrives in ST. CHARLES, Missouri. PIERRE CRUZATTE and FRANÇOIS LABICHE join the expedition here. During the stay in St. Charles, John Collins, HUGH HALL, and WILLIAM WERNER are court-martialed for being absent without leave.
- *May 21:* The expedition leaves St. Charles.
- *May 25:* They pass the small settlement of LA CHARETTE, marking their passage beyond non-Indian civilization.

133 miles

- *June 1:* They reach the mouth of the Osage River.
- *June 3:* Lewis and Clark name their first geographical feature: Cupboard Creek. The next day they name Nightingale Creek.
- *June 12:* The expedition meets a party of trappers including PIERRE DORION, SR., who agrees to go to the Sioux villages with them.

366 miles

- *June 26:* The expedition reaches the mouth of the KANSAS RIVER.
- *June 29:* Privates Hugh Hall and John Collins are court-martialed for stealing whiskey. They are found guilty, and at 3:30 that day, Hall receives 50 lashes on his bare back, while Collins is given 100 lashes.
- *July 4:* The keelboat's cannon is fired during the first-ever Fourth of July celebration west of the Mississippi. The captains name Independence Creek, near today's Atchison, Kansas.

630 miles

- *July 12:*   Alexander Willard is court-martialed for sleeping on guard duty. He is sentenced to 100 lashes over four consecutive nights.
- *July 21:*   The corps reaches the mouth of the PLATTE RIVER.
- *July 22:*   They set up CAMP WHITE CATFISH, where they stay for a few days before proceeding.
- *August 1:*   William Clark's 34th birthday. The expedition is now in Nebraska.
- *August 3:*   At COUNCIL BLUFF (near present-day Omaha, Nebraska), Lewis and Clark meet with OTOE (Oto) and MISSOURI chiefs. Lewis makes a speech and hands out PEACE MEDALS. This is the first official parlay between U.S. representatives and western Native Americans. That night Private MOSES REED asks permission to go back for his knife. Within two days the captains realize that he has deserted the expedition.
- *August 7:*   The captains dispatch George Drouillard and three others to find Reed and bring him back. They are also instructed to find Otoe chief LITTLE THIEF.

730 miles

- *August 8:*   Lewis and Clark reach and name Pelican Island.
- *August 12:*   Members of the expedition see their first COYOTE.
- *August 18:*   Lewis's 30th birthday. Near the site of what is now Sioux City, Iowa, Drouillard and his party catch up with the expedition. They bring not only Reed but also Little Thief and the Missouri chief BIG HORSE. Reed is court-martialed immediately, sentenced to run the gauntlet four times, and discharged from the permanent party. He will be kept in the corps as a laborer until the following spring, when he will return to St. Louis.
- *August 20:*   Sergeant CHARLES FLOYD becomes the only man to die on the expedition; it is now believed that he suffered from a ruptured appendix. His body is buried on a bluff near present-day Sioux City.
- *August 22:*   In the first non-Indian democratic election held west of the Mississippi, near today's Ponco, Nebraska, the men vote on who will replace Floyd as sergeant; Patrick Gass is elected.
- *August 23:*   Private Joseph Field kills the expedition's first BUFFALO.
- *August 25:*   The captains and several of the men visit the SPIRIT MOUND near present-day Vermillion, South Dakota.
- *August 26:*   Lewis first uses the term *corps of volunteers for the North Western discovery.*
- *August 27:*   The expedition meets three young YANKTON NAKOTA INDIANS (Yankton Sioux) at the mouth of the James River, South Dakota.
- *August 30:*   At CALUMET BLUFF, near what is now Gavins Point Dam, South Dakota, Lewis and Clark hold a council with a delegation of Yankton Nakota.
- *September 4:*   The corps reaches the Niobrara River.
- *September 7:*   Expedition members are amazed by their first sighting of a town of PRAIRIE DOGS. With considerable effort they drown one out of its hole.
- *September 8:*   Clark kills his first buffalo.
- *September 10:*   Near Cedar Island, South Dakota, they discover the remains of a plesiosaur.
- *September 11:*   After being lost for more than two weeks, George Shannon rejoins the expedition, which now has only one horse left of the original four.
- *September 17:*   They come to a prairie dog village that covers nine square miles.
- *September 21:*   They reach the Big Bend of the Missouri.
- *September 25:*   A council with some TETON LAKOTA INDIANS (Teton Sioux) becomes hostile when the Indians demand to be given one of the expedition's boats. Lewis and Clark stand their ground, while Teton chief BLACK BUFFALO manages to calm the Lakota.
- *October 1:*   The corps reaches the Cheyenne River.

- *October 8:* Lewis and Clark meet the ARIKARA INDIANS near the mouth of the Grand River.
- *October 9:* The expedition sees a BULL BOAT for the first time and meets JOSEPH GRAVELINES.
- *October 10:* PIERRE-ANTOINE TABEAU brings the Arikara chiefs to a council. The corps leaves the Arikara two days later.
- *October 13:* After Private John Newman becomes mutinous, he is confined, court-martialed, and sentenced to 75 lashes on his bare back plus banishment from the permanent party. Like Reed, he is forced to become a manual laborer and will be sent back to St. Louis in the spring.
- *October 14:* The expedition enters present-day North Dakota.
- *October 20:* They encounter their first grizzly BEAR near today's Bismarck, North Dakota.

1,600 miles

- *October 27:* The corps reaches the MANDAN and HIDATSA Indian villages on the KNIFE RIVER. More than 4,500 Native Americans live here

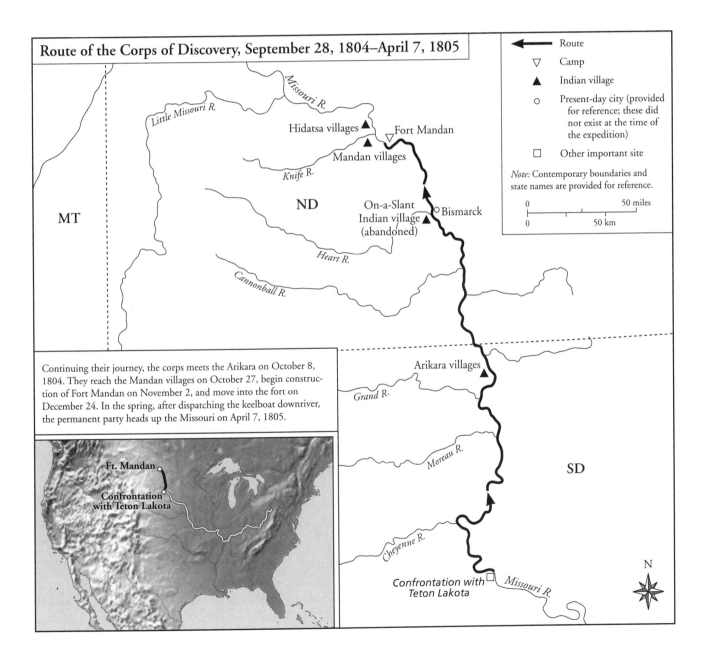

Route of the Corps of Discovery, September 28, 1804–April 7, 1805

Continuing their journey, the corps meets the Arikara on October 8, 1804. They reach the Mandan villages on October 27, begin construction of Fort Mandan on November 2, and move into the fort on December 24. In the spring, after dispatching the keelboat downriver, the permanent party heads up the Missouri on April 7, 1805.

in earth lodges—more people than were living in Washington, D.C., at that time.

- *October 30:* Lewis and Clark meet Hugh McCracken, an agent for the North West Company.
- *November 2:* The men begin construction of FORT MANDAN alongside the Missouri River, approximately six miles below the mouth of the Knife River.
- *November 4:* TOUSSAINT CHARBONNEAU, a French Canadian living among the Mandan and the Hidatsa, is enlisted as interpreter for the expedition. Lewis and Clark request that his Shoshone wife SACAGAWEA (Sacajawea) also accompany the corps.
- *December 24:* The expedition moves into Fort Mandan.

1805

- *January 1:* The men celebrate New Year's Day in the Mandan villages, amusing the Indians with their music and dancing.
- *January 3–5:* The Mandan hold a BUFFALO DANCE in which corps members take part. Just a few days later, herds of BUFFALO show up in the area, and several corpsmen join the Indians in the hunt.
- *February 10:* The last COURT-MARTIAL of the expedition tries THOMAS PROCTOR HOWARD for his recklessness in scaling the walls of the fort to get in, tempting an observant Indian to do the same. Howard is found guilty but receives no punishment.
- *February 11:* After a long and difficult delivery, JEAN BAPTISTE CHARBONNEAU is born to Sacagawea and Toussaint Charbonneau. Meriwether Lewis and RENÉ JESSAUME assist at the birth. The boy will later become a favorite of the corpsmen and acquire the nickname "Pomp."
- *April 2:* Lewis and Clark begin to pack up items to be sent back to President Jefferson with a return party on the keelboat. The shipment includes live ANIMALS, pelts, and skeletons; samples of soil, PLANTS, minerals, and INSECTS; various ARTIFACTS; TOBACCO and seed; and MAPS, LETTERS, and JOURNALS. Of the live animals, only a prairie dog and a magpie will survive the trip east.
- *April 7:* As the keelboat with its shipment returns to St. Louis under the command of Corporal RICHARD WARFINGTON, the expedition leaves Fort Mandan. A total of 31 men plus Sacagawea and Pomp form the permanent party who will proceed on to the Pacific coast in pirogues and CANOES.

> **1,693 miles**
> **1,888 miles**

- *April 11:* The expedition reaches the mouth of the Little Missouri River.
- *April 25:* They reach the mouth of the YELLOWSTONE RIVER.
- *April 27:* The Corps of Discovery passes out of North Dakota into Montana.
- *April 29:* Near Big Muddy Creek, Lewis shoots at a grizzly bear, which begins to chase him. Lewis shoots again, this time killing the bear. This same day his dog Seaman kills an ANTELOPE. Expedition members note huge herds of buffalo.

> **2,000 miles**

- *May 3:* The expedition reaches Porcupine River (now Poplar River), where Clark names its first tributary 2000 Mile Creek.

> **2,090 miles**

- *May 8:* They reach and name MILK RIVER.
- *May 11:* William Bratton shoots and then is chased by a grizzly bear; other expedition members rescue him and kill the bear.

> **2,200 miles**

- *May 14:* With Charbonneau at the helm, the white PIROGUE (so named because of its color) nearly capsizes. Sacagawea saves the day by swiftly retrieving valuable papers and other items from the waters.

> **2,260 miles**

- *May 20:* The expedition arrives at the MUSSELSHELL RIVER. Lewis and Clark name a creek after Sacagawea. This honor of having a feature named after them is eventually bestowed on all the members of the expedition.
- *May 25:* The first bighorn SHEEP is killed.

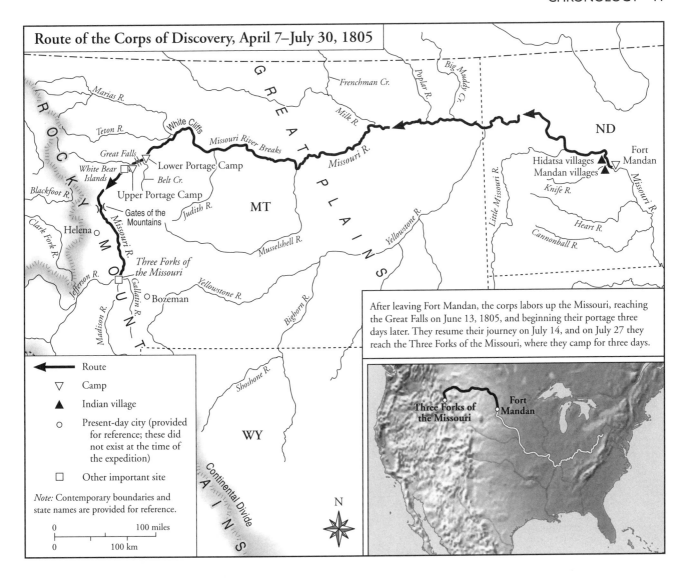

Route of the Corps of Discovery, April 7–July 30, 1805

After leaving Fort Mandan, the corps labors up the Missouri, reaching the Great Falls on June 13, 1805, and beginning their portage three days later. They resume their journey on July 14, and on July 27 they reach the Three Forks of the Missouri, where they camp for three days.

- *May 26:* The Rocky Mountains are spotted in the distance; Lewis writes an eloquent description of the sight.
- *May 29:* Clark names the JUDITH RIVER after a young woman in Virginia whom he hopes to marry. (He will in fact marry Julia "Judith" Hancock on January 5, 1808.)
- *May 31:* The expedition passes the White Cliffs of the Missouri, large and remarkable sandstone formations that remind them of a city.

2,508 miles

- *June 2–8:* When the river forks, scouting parties are sent up both branches to determine which is the true Missouri. The sergeants and privates press for taking the fork on the right, heading north, which is really the MARIAS RIVER. The captains, however, decide on the south fork.
- *June 10:* The expedition buries the red pirogue and evacuates a CACHE for stores, chisels, and blacksmith's equipment.
- *June 13:* With an advance party, Lewis discovers the GREAT FALLS of the Missouri. This tells him that he and Clark have chosen the correct river.
- *June 14:* Several in the party, including Sacagawea, are sick. While Clark camps with the group on the left side of the river (near Black Coulee, Portage, Montana), Lewis takes a small party and explores the area around the GREAT FALLS. He fights off a grizzly bear with his ESPONTOON (pike).

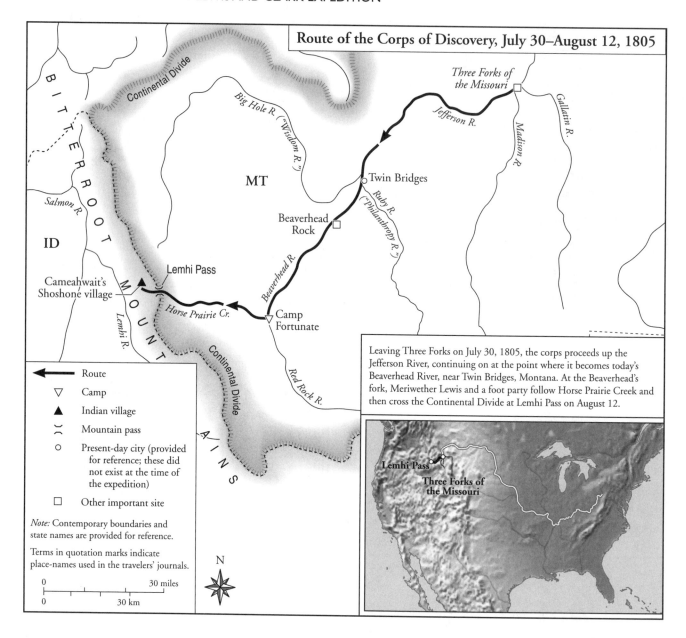

Route of the Corps of Discovery, July 30–August 12, 1805

Leaving Three Forks on July 30, 1805, the corps proceeds up the Jefferson River, continuing on at the point where it becomes today's Beaverhead River, near Twin Bridges, Montana. At the Beaverhead's fork, Meriwether Lewis and a foot party follow Horse Prairie Creek and then cross the Continental Divide at Lemhi Pass on August 12.

- *June 16–July 14:*   It takes almost a month to complete the PORTAGE of canoes, pirogues, equipment, and supplies around the Great Falls in addition to the futile attempt to assemble Lewis's iron-frame boat. The work is arduous, and several men are injured during the portage, which significantly delays the expedition.
- *July 15:*   Lewis names FORT MOUNTAIN (Square Butte today).
- *July 19:*   The expedition reaches an impressive series of cliffs that Lewis calls "the GATES OF THE MOUNTAINS."
- *July 23:*   Clark and a foot party go to look for the SHOSHONE INDIANS, whom they fail to find.
- *July 27:*   The party reaches the THREE FORKS of the Missouri River; Lewis names the three branches Jefferson's River, Maddison's river, and Gallitin's river (today's JEFFERSON RIVER, Madison River, and Gallatin River).
- *August 8:*   The captains are excited when Sacagawea recognizes a landmark named BEAVERHEAD ROCK; this tells them that they are well into Shoshone

country. They hope to bargain with the Shoshone for HORSES and guides to cross the Rockies.

3,000 miles

- *August 11:* Lewis and a foot party encounter a mounted Shoshone who rides away. The river party names 3000 Mile Island.
- *August 12:* Lewis walks across LEMHI PASS, becoming the first non-Indian American to cross the CONTINENTAL DIVIDE. He hopes to find some evidence of the Northwest Passage, but he can see only mountains.

    On this same day the expedition's shipment from Fort Mandan arrives in Washington.
- *August 13:* Lewis and his party encounter a group of Lemhi Shoshone, thus initiating that nation's first contact with white men.
- *August 17:* Near the BEAVERHEAD RIVER, Clark arrives late for a rendezvous and council with the Shoshone. Sacagawea is with him, and she joyously recognizes the Shoshone chief, CAMEAHWAIT, as her brother. The captains name this spot CAMP FORTUNATE.
- *August 18:* Clark goes off with a party to explore the SALMON RIVER. Days later he returns to report that it is impassable.
- *August 31:* The expedition proceeds north toward the BITTERROOT MOUNTAINS. They now have one mule, 29 horses, and the assistance of a Shoshone guide they name OLD TOBY.
- *September 4:* Near what is now Sula, Montana, the corps encounters the FLATHEAD INDIANS (Salish). The Flathead are friendly, and the expedition camps with them at ROSS'S HOLE.

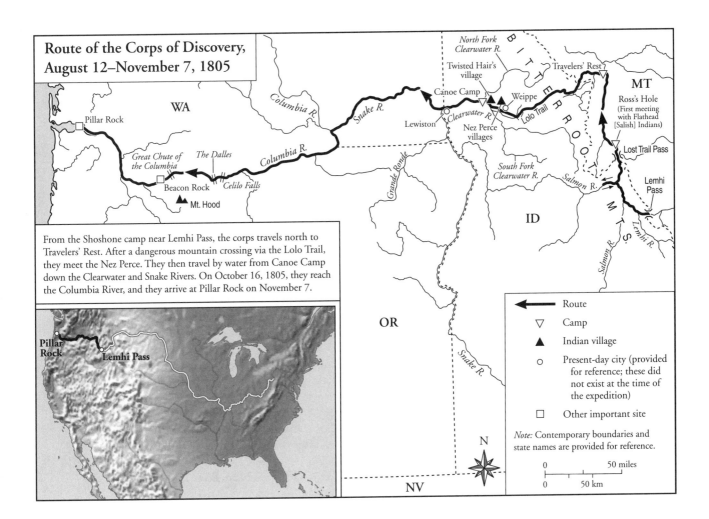

Route of the Corps of Discovery, August 12–November 7, 1805

From the Shoshone camp near Lemhi Pass, the corps travels north to Travelers' Rest. After a dangerous mountain crossing via the Lolo Trail, they meet the Nez Perce. They then travel by water from Canoe Camp down the Clearwater and Snake Rivers. On October 16, 1805, they reach the Columbia River, and they arrive at Pillar Rock on November 7.

→ Route
▽ Camp
▲ Indian village
○ Present-day city (provided for reference; these did not exist at the time of the expedition)
□ Other important site

Note: Contemporary boundaries and state names are provided for reference.

0   50 miles
0   50 km

- *September 9:* The expedition stops at TRAVELERS' REST, near today's Missoula, Montana, preparatory to turning west to cross the mountains.
- *September 11–22:* The Corps of Discovery has great difficulty making a dangerous and arduous journey over the Bitterroot Mountains. Old Toby loses the LOLO TRAIL at one point, and provisions run low; three horses must be killed for food. Weary and near starvation, they finally exit from the Bitterroots onto the WEIPPE PRAIRIE, near present-day Weippe, Idaho. Here they encounter a band of NEZ PERCE INDIANS, some of whom consider killing the white men, but an old woman named WATKUWEIS convinces the Indians to befriend them.
- *September 22:* Lewis and Clark hold a council with the Nez Perce, explaining their mission and requesting the Indians' assistance in building canoes. The Nez Perce impress the captains with their friendliness, cooperation, and culture.
- *September 26:* Suffering from dysentery, the expedition sets up CANOE CAMP at the junction of the North Fork and Middle Fork of the CLEARWATER RIVER. Here they begin to build canoes.
- *October 7:* The expedition sets out on the CLEARWATER RIVER in five canoes. Nez Perce chiefs TWISTED HAIR and TETOHARSKY accompany them.
- *October 10:* They reach the SNAKE RIVER and camp near present-day Lewiston, Idaho.
- *October 13:* They encounter more rapids, and Old Toby leaves them.
- *October 16:* Moving much more quickly now, the Corps of Discovery reaches the Columbia River, where they meet a number of PLATEAU INDIANS.
- *October 18:* Clark spies MOUNT HOOD, proof that they are nearing the Pacific Ocean. This same day he and Lewis hold a brief council with the WALLA WALLA INDIANS. They promise Chief YELLEPT to stay longer with him the following spring.
- *October 23:* The party comes to a dangerous 15-mile stretch on the Columbia from Celilo Falls to The Dalles (see CELILO FALLS AND THE DALLES). The WISHRAM village Nixluidix is a major trading center on the river.
- *November 1:* They canoe through the COLUMBIA RIVER GORGE (Great Chute of the Columbia).
- *November 2:* They pass the mouth of the Sandy River, the furthest point reached by George Vancouver's expedition in 1792.
- *November 3:* They reach BEACON ROCK, the beginning of the tidewater.
- *November 7:* Clark writes in his field journal: "Ocian in view! O! the joy." But as it turns out, they are still some 20 miles from the sea, and foul WEATHER prevents them from getting there for another 10 days.
- *November 15:* The expedition reaches the Columbia River estuary. STATION CAMP is established at Baker's (Haley's) Bay, but because of arduous weather conditions, it soon becomes apparent that they will need to find another campsite.
- *November 18:* At CAPE DISAPPOINTMENT, Clark finds the tree on which Lewis had carved his name and adds his own name plus "By Land from the U. States in 1805 & 1805." The expedition has reached the Pacific after 4,162 miles. (Clark calculates this figure using dead reckoning; he is off by only 40 miles.)
- *November 24:* Every member of the party—including, remarkably, Sacagawea and York—are given a say on where to spend the winter. They decide to move to the river's south shore, where the HUNTING will be better. The next day they start upriver to find a place to cross.
- *December 7:* The winter camp at FORT CLATSOP is established on the south bank of the Columbia estuary. It is named after the neighboring CLATSOP INDIANS.
- *December 28:* Joseph Fields, William Bratton, George Gibson, Peter Weiser, and Alexander Willard are sent to establish a SALTWORKS. Five days later they

> **3,714 miles**

> **4,142 miles**

> **4,162 miles**

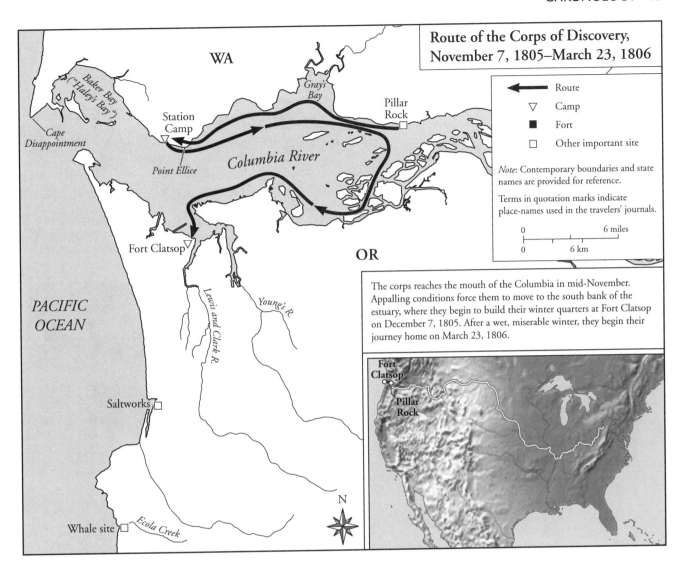

Route of the Corps of Discovery, November 7, 1805–March 23, 1806

Route
▽ Camp
■ Fort
□ Other important site

Note: Contemporary boundaries and state names are provided for reference.

Terms in quotation marks indicate place-names used in the travelers' journals.

0   6 miles

0   6 km

The corps reaches the mouth of the Columbia in mid-November. Appalling conditions force them to move to the south bank of the estuary, where they begin to build their winter quarters at Fort Clatsop on December 7, 1805. After a wet, miserable winter, they begin their journey home on March 23, 1806.

find an appropriate site approximately 15 miles southwest of Fort Clatsop. Once set up and running, the saltworks will run continuously until February 21, 1806.

- *December 30:* Fort Clatsop is completed.

1806

- *January 4:* In Washington, President Jefferson meets with a delegation of Arikara, Missouri, Otoe, and Yankton Nakota Indians who had met Lewis and Clark the previous year. The president thanks them for their help to the expedition and expresses the hope that white men and Indians will be able to "live together as one household."
- *January 6:* Clark takes a party to view a WHALE stranded on the beach to the south. When he arrives three days later, he finds that the TILLAMOOK INDIANS have already stripped it. He negotiates with them for blubber and oil.
- *March 7:* The corps has run out of both whiskey and tobacco by this time. After a long, dreary winter, all are anxious to return home.
- *March 23:* The expedition loads up the canoes, turns Fort Clatsop over to the Clatsop, and begins their homeward journey.

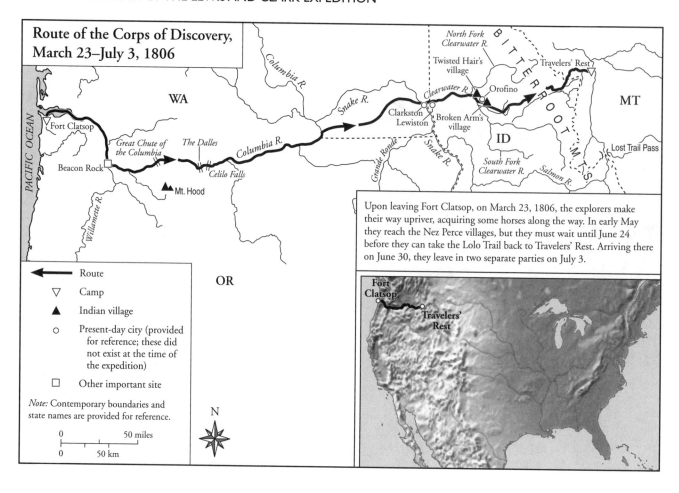

Route of the Corps of Discovery, March 23–July 3, 1806

Upon leaving Fort Clatsop, on March 23, 1806, the explorers make their way upriver, acquiring some horses along the way. In early May they reach the Nez Perce villages, but they must wait until June 24 before they can take the Lolo Trail back to Travelers' Rest. Arriving there on June 30, they leave in two separate parties on July 3.

- *April 3:*   Clark takes a party to explore the WILLAMETTE RIVER.
- *April 11:*   After a series of petty thefts are inflicted on the corps, three Indians steal Seaman, which proves to be the final straw for Lewis. He sends three men after them to demand the dog's return. Frightened, the Indians give up Seaman without a fight.
- *April 18:*   Desperate to buy horses above The Dalles, Lewis trades two large kettles for four horses. The party is now down to one small kettle per mess.
- *April 27–30:*   The WALLA WALLA INDIANS welcome the expedition and invite them to stay. Chief Yellept draws Lewis and Clark a map of the vicinity and gives them necessary items for their journey.
- *May 4:*   The expedition again meets Chief Tetoharsky, who guides them back to Nez Perce country.
- *May 9:*   Near present-day Orofino, Idaho, the corps retrieves their horses from the Nez Perce. They will stay in CAMP CHOPUNNISH near the Nez Perce until the snows on the Rocky Mountains have melted.
- *June 10:*   Although the Nez Perce advise against it, the corps leaves Camp Chopunnish and resume their journey. They turn back when they discover the snow on the Bitterroots is still too deep.
- *June 24:*   The expedition sets off again with some Nez Perce guides.
- *June 28:*   They reach LOLO HOT SPRINGS.
- *June 30:*   They arrive back at Travelers' Rest, having done 156 miles through dense forest in six days.
- *July 3:*   Lewis and Clark split the expedition into two groups to explore the Marias and Yellowstone Rivers. Lewis and nine men will ride east toward the

Missouri, while Clark and the rest of the expedition will go south to the Yellowstone to follow that river down to the Missouri.

- *July 7:* Lewis crosses the CONTINENTAL DIVIDE at what is now LEWIS AND CLARK PASS.
- *July 8:* Lewis arrives at MEDICINE RIVER (today's Sun River). Clark arrives at Camp Fortunate.
- *July 9:* Lewis's party kills its first buffalo in nearly a year. Clark's party leaves Camp Fortunate with both canoes and horses.
- *July 12:* Lewis's party arrives back at WHITE BEAR ISLANDS near the Great Falls. Clark's party splits at THREE FORKS. Six canoes and 10 men led by John Ordway go down the Missouri; Clark takes the remainder on toward the Yellowstone.
- *July 13:* At White Bear Islands, Lewis opens a cache secreted the year before but finds that the specimens he left there have been ruined by water.

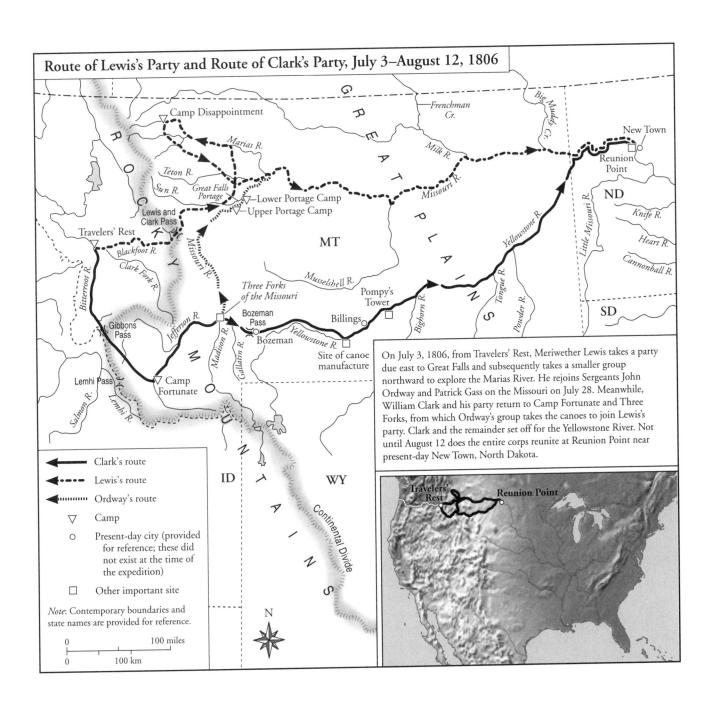

Route of Lewis's Party and Route of Clark's Party, July 3–August 12, 1806

On July 3, 1806, from Travelers' Rest, Meriwether Lewis takes a party due east to Great Falls and subsequently takes a smaller group northward to explore the Marias River. He rejoins Sergeants John Ordway and Patrick Gass on the Missouri on July 28. Meanwhile, William Clark and his party return to Camp Fortunate and Three Forks, from which Ordway's group takes the canoes to join Lewis's party. Clark and the remainder set off for the Yellowstone River. Not until August 12 does the entire corps reunite at Reunion Point near present-day New Town, North Dakota.

Clark's route
Lewis's route
Ordway's route
▽ Camp
○ Present-day city (provided for reference; these did not exist at the time of the expedition)
□ Other important site

Note: Contemporary boundaries and state names are provided for reference.

0   100 miles
0   100 km

- *July 15:* Guided by Sacagawea, Clark arrives at the Yellowstone via BOZEMAN PASS.
- *July 16:* Leaving the others behind at the Great Falls with Sergeant Patrick Gass in charge, Lewis takes George Drouillard and Joseph and Reubin Field to explore the upper part of the Marias River.
- *July 19:* Ordway's party arrives at Great Falls and unites with Gass and the others. Lewis and three men are still exploring the Marias, while Clark starts to build canoes just south of present-day Park City, Montana.
- *July 21:* Lewis reaches a fork in the Marias and follows the right branch, today's Cut Bank Creek. He and his party continue until he realizes that the river will not go as far north as he had hoped. They set up camp, where he tries but fails to make astronomical observations due to poor weather conditions. He names the site CAMP DISAPPOINTMENT.
- *July 24:* Clark finishes the canoes and sets off down the Yellowstone, sending Sergeant NATHANIEL PRYOR and three men across country with horses to the Mandan villages.
- *July 25:* Near present-day Billings, Montana, Clark comes to an impressive sandstone formation that he names POMPY'S TOWER, after Sacagawea's son. He etches his own name and the date into the rock—the only visible evidence of the expedition still extant.
- *July 26:* Lewis and his party leave Camp Disappointment and meet eight BLACKFEET warriors, with whom they set up camp for the night.
- *July 27:* Early in the morning the warriors steal the men's rifles. Joseph Field wakes up and, after a brief struggle, kills one of the BLACKFEET INDIANS. Lewis shoots and mortally wounds one of the warriors, and the others flee. The soldiers recover their rifles and make a hasty retreat, riding some 100 miles through the night. Fearful of a surprise attack by the Blackfeet, Lewis pushes on to warn the rest of the expedition of the danger.
- *July 28:* Lewis and his men and Ordway and Gass and their parties all meet within three hours of each other near present-day Loma, Montana, near the mouth of the Marias. Clark's party is now traveling down the Yellowstone, but they are plagued by mosquitoes.
- *August 3:* Clark has now traveled 837 miles to the mouth of the Yellowstone, of which 636 miles has been in two small canoes. The mosquitoes are so bad that the party proceeds down the Missouri. Meanwhile, Pryor's party, whose horses had been stolen by CROW INDIANS, are following him down in bull boats.
- *August 7:* Lewis arrives at the mouth of the Yellowstone, finds a note from Clark, and follows him down.
- *August 8:* Pryor and his party catch up with Clark on the Missouri.
- *August 11:* Lewis and PIERRE CRUZATTE go off on a hunting expedition, during which the private accidentally shoots the captain in the leg.
- *August 12:* Lewis meets two hunters from Illinois, Joseph Dickson and Forrest Hancock, who inform him that they had met Clark the day before. Lewis hurries to catch up to Clark, and they finally connect at Reunion Point, near today's New Town, North Dakota. It is exactly a year since Lewis had first crossed over the Continental Divide. The last entry in Lewis's journal describes the events of this day.
- *August 14:* The expedition arrives back at the Mandan villages.
- *August 15:* John Colter asks permission to accompany the trappers Dickson and Hancock up the Yellowstone River. The captains allow him to be honorably discharged on the condition that no other men make the same request.
- *August 17:* Colter leaves the expedition, and Charbonneau is paid and released from his duties as interpreter. Mandan chief BIG WHITE and his family agree to

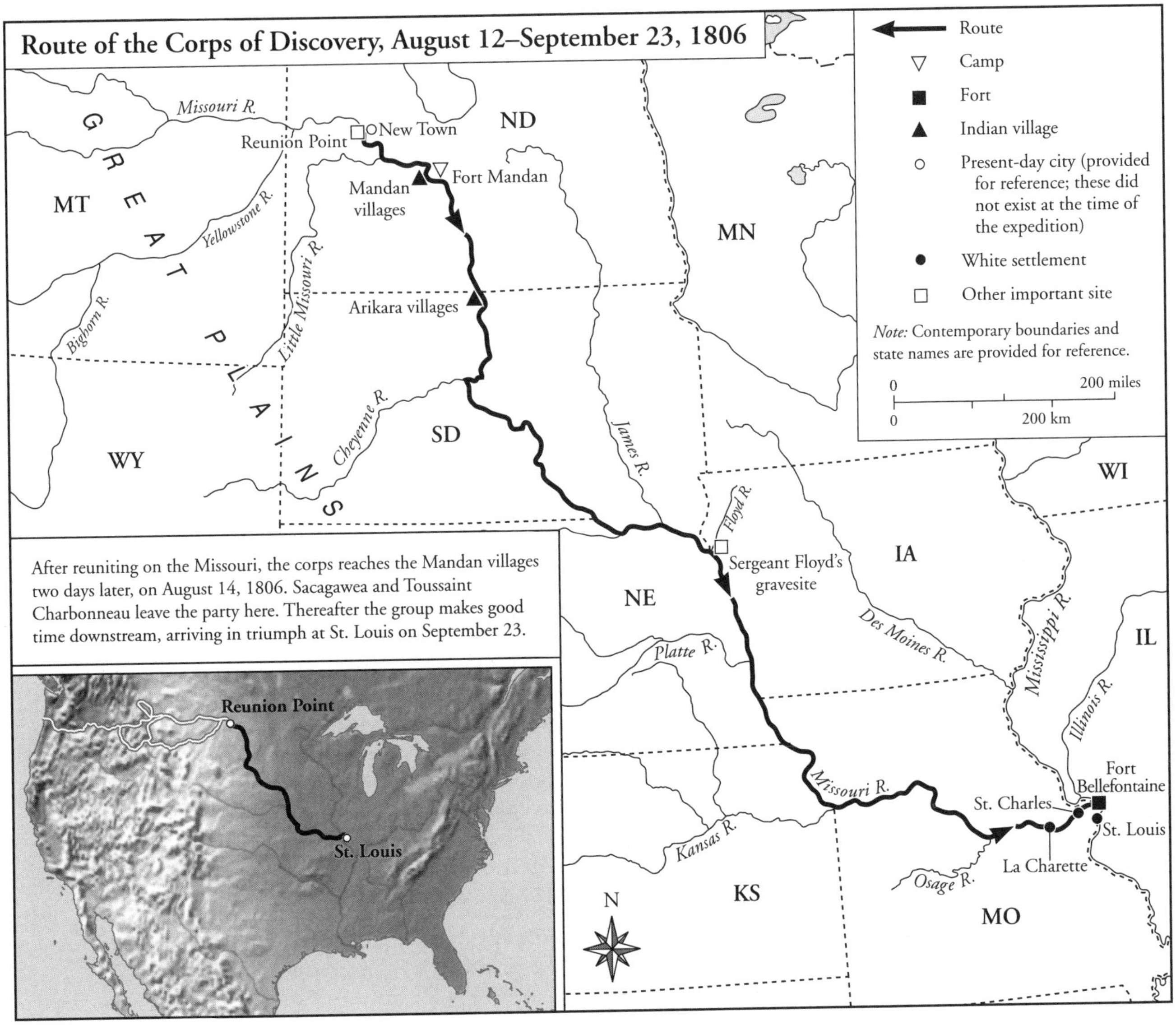

Route of the Corps of Discovery, August 12–September 23, 1806

Legend:
- ← Route
- ▽ Camp
- ■ Fort
- ▲ Indian village
- ○ Present-day city (provided for reference; these did not exist at the time of the expedition)
- ● White settlement
- □ Other important site

Note: Contemporary boundaries and state names are provided for reference.

0 — 200 miles
0 — 200 km

Map labels: Missouri R., New Town, Reunion Point, ND, Mandan villages, Fort Mandan, MT, MN, GREAT PLAINS, Yellowstone R., Little Missouri R., Bighorn R., Arikara villages, Cheyenne R., WY, SD, James R., Floyd R., Sergeant Floyd's gravesite, IA, Des Moines R., Mississippi R., Illinois R., WI, IL, NE, Platte R., Kansas R., Osage R., La Charette, St. Charles, Fort Bellefontaine, St. Louis, Missouri R., KS, MO, N

After reuniting on the Missouri, the corps reaches the Mandan villages two days later, on August 14, 1806. Sacagawea and Toussaint Charbonneau leave the party here. Thereafter the group makes good time downstream, arriving in triumph at St. Louis on September 23.

Inset map labels: Reunion Point, St. Louis

accompany the corps on the last leg of their journey and then to Washington with Lewis. They leave this day.

- *August 21:* The corps arrives back at the Arikara villages.
- *August 30:* The expedition encounters a group of 80–90 TETON LAKOTA warriors who are on the riverbank. Clark threatens to kill any Indians who approach the camp, and the Teton do not attack.
- *September 3:* They meet a trading party coming up from St. Louis.
- *September 4:* They visit and refurbish Sergeant Floyd's grave.
- *September 6:* They meet traders employed by Auguste Chouteau.
- *September 9:* At the mouth of the Platte River, they leave the Great Plains.
- *September 14:* Three keelboats traveling up the Missouri from St. Louis signal the men that civilization is imminent. They obtain liquor and FOOD from those on the keelboats and celebrate that night.
- *September 15:* The expedition passes the mouth of the Kansas River.
- *September 17:* Near what is now Brunswick, Missouri, Lewis and Clark meet Captain John McClallen, who informs them that the Spanish had been trying to locate and stop their expedition and that many in the United States had assumed they were now dead.

- *September 20:*   The expedition passes La Charette. The men cheer when they see a dead cow on the shore—proof that they are almost home. They ask permission to fire a volley in celebration.
- *September 21:*   They canoe past St. Charles.
- *September 22:*   The party stops at Fort Bellefontaine, where clothes are purchased for Big White and his family.
- *September 23:*   The arrival of the Lewis and Clark Expedition is greeted in St. Louis with tremendous cheers and celebrations, which will continue in other cities in the weeks to come.

The Corps of Discovery disbands in St. Louis. Later, as rewards, pay for all the men is doubled. Corpsmen receive 320 acres of land apiece, while the captains are each given 1,600 acres. Lewis is named governor of the Louisiana Territory. Clark becomes Indian agent for the West and is appointed brigadier general of the territory militia.

▪ POSTEXPEDITION ▪

1806

- While Lewis and Clark are returning from the Pacific coast, other exploration parties are setting out. At Jefferson's request, WILLIAM DUNBAR—who had previously explored the Ouachita (Washita) River—oversees an expedition up the Red River, headed by Thomas Freeman and Peter Custis. Their mission fails when the Spanish turn them back at Spanish Bluff.
- ZEBULON PIKE heads for Nebraska and the headwaters of the Arkansas River. On Thanksgiving Day he tries and fails to ascend the peak in Colorado that bears his name.

1807

- After celebrations in Washington and meetings with the president and others, Lewis returns to Philadelphia, where he attends to numerous postexpedition details. Although he sets wheels in motion for the publication of his and Clark's journals, he procrastinates in beginning the writing itself. He also delays in taking up his appointment as governor of the Louisiana Territory.
- A party led by Nathaniel Pryor attempts to return Mandan chief Big White to his people. They are attacked by the Arikara and forced to turn back to St. Louis. George Shannon loses a leg in the battle.
- MANUEL LISA builds a trading post at the mouth of the Bighorn River in Montana. He names it Fort Raymond.
- John Colter discovers and explores an area filled with geysers and hot springs, which becomes known as Colter's Hell; it will become part of present-day Yellowstone National Park.
- DAVID THOMPSON of the North West Company begins to survey the length of the Columbia River; it will take him five years.
- Zebulon Pike is captured and later released by the Spanish. He becomes a national celebrity after an account of his explorations is published.
- PATRICK GASS becomes the first to publish an account of the expedition: *A Journal of the Voyages and Travels of a Corps of Discovery, under the command of Capt Lewis and Capt Clarke of the Army of the United States from the mouth of the River Missouri through the interior parts of North America to the Pacific Ocean during the years 1804, 1805, and 1806.*

1808

- Lewis finally moves to St. Louis to begin his duties as Louisiana Territory's governor. He will be beset by numerous problems that will affect his state of mind.
- JOHN JACOB ASTOR establishes the American Fur Company to compete with the North West Company in the northern plains.
- The St. Louis Missouri Fur Company is formed. Its partners include Lewis, Clark, Manuel Lisa, and Auguste and PIERRE CHOUTEAU, SR. Lewis is criticized publicly for his apparent conflict of interest.

1809

- *August 21:* Big White is finally returned to the Mandan villages after three years and a cost of $20,000.
- *October 11:* While on his way from St. Louis to Washington, Meriwether Lewis dies mysteriously in Grinders Stand, a tavern south of Nashville, Tennessee. His death is apparently a suicide, although theories abound that he was murdered.

1810

- John Jacob Astor sets up the Pacific Fur Company, taking his fur-trading enterprises to the Pacific coast. The following year his employees establish Fort Astoria at the mouth of the Columbia River. (Astoria is now the oldest permanent non-Indian settlement in the Pacific Northwest.)
- George Drouillard is killed by Blackfeet Indians.

1812

- Astor employee Wilson Price Hunt completes a journey (begun in 1811) from St. Louis to Fort Astoria, using a route approximating that of the later OREGON TRAIL.
- While traveling eastward from Astoria, Robert Stuart discovers South Pass through the Rocky Mountains. Despite the ease this route provides through the mountains, it will be another 12 years before it becomes the most popular route for crossing the Rockies.
- *December 20:* Sacagawea dies at Fort Manuel. A few months later William Clark, who has already taken in her son Jean Baptiste (Pomp), arranges to care for her baby daughter LIZETTE CHARBONNEAU.

1814

- *History of the Expedition under the Command of Captains Lewis and Clark, to the Sources of the Missouri, thence across the Rocky Mountains and down the River Columbia to the Pacific Ocean* is published. Edited by PAUL ALLEN and NICHOLAS BIDDLE, the book is based on the explorers' journals and notes. Its preface is by Thomas Jefferson.

1818

- *October 20:* A 10-year joint occupation of the Oregon Territory is agreed at the Anglo-American Convention. The United States, Great Britain, Russia, and Spain all make claims. Spain will renounce its claim in 1819, Russia in 1824.

1820

- Major Stephen Long heads an expedition that goes through Kansas to the Rocky Mountains. A member of the expedition, Dr. Edwin James, successfully ascends Pike's Peak. In Long's account of the journey, published in 1823, he describes the territory as "The Great American Desert"—a description that will slow westward migration to a trickle for the next two decades.

1824

- Explorer Jedediah Smith rediscovers South Pass. From this point on, it becomes a standard corridor through the Rockies.

1826

- *July 4:* Thomas Jefferson dies.

1834

- Nathaniel Jarvis Wyeth establishes Fort Hall on the Snake River in southeast Idaho. This soon becomes an important way station on the Oregon Trail.

1838

- *September 1:* William Clark dies of natural causes in St. Louis.

1842

- The U.S. government begins to issue grants for land in the Oregon Territory.
- John C. Frémont and Kit Carson explore the length of the Oregon Trail.

1843

- A steady wave of westward migration begins as more than 1,000 pioneers follow the Oregon Trail to Washington and Oregon. The numbers of migrants grow tremendously during the years to come.

1845

- Texas is annexed from Mexico.

1846

- The Oregon Treaty sets the Oregon-Canada border at the 49th parallel from the Rocky Mountains to the Pacific Ocean.

1848

- The Treaty of San Guadalupe Hidalgo adds 500,000 square miles to the United States, including the future states of California, Nevada, and Utah.

1853

- *December 30:* The Gadsden Purchase completes the country's expansion from coast to coast by acquiring from Mexico 29,644 square miles of territory in the Southwest.

1859

- Oregon is admitted to the Union as the 33rd state.

1869

- JOHN WESLEY POWELL takes a party on a hazardous journey down the Colorado River through the Grand Canyon in one of the last explorations of the American West.

1870

- *April 2:* At the age of 98, Patrick Gass becomes the last member of the Lewis and Clark Expedition to die.

1889

- Washington is the 42nd state to be admitted to the Union.

1890

- The U.S. Census Bureau declares the frontier to be closed.

A to Z
Entries

Agency Creek   See LEMHI RIVER.

airgun   See FIREARMS.

alcohol

Alcohol and TOBACCO were second in importance only to the FIREARMS, gunpowder, and ammunition the Lewis and Clark Expedition took with them. Meat and vegetables could be procured along their route, but whiskey could not. To a party consisting primarily of mature soldiers and frontiersmen, it was a significant item. It helped morale, could be used as a reward, and provided a means of celebration when appropriate.

Although MERIWETHER LEWIS and WILLIAM CLARK both appreciated that there might be problems of drunkenness, they carried as large a quantity of whiskey as practicable. The actual amount is uncertain, but records indicate that they took with them approximately 120 gallons of whiskey. This may seem excessive, but a daily issue of a gill (a quarter of a pint) each to 32 men used up a gallon.

During the CORPS OF DISCOVERY's first winter at CAMP DUBOIS, near ST. LOUIS (1803–04), whiskey supplies were plentiful, and duties well performed were rewarded with an extra gill. Once St. Louis was behind them, however, the availability of alcohol was limited to what they could carry. It is known that this included six kegs (30 gallons) of brandy that Lewis had purchased in Philadelphia. Whether brandy or whiskey, alcohol had become a precious commodity and thus was strictly rationed. The men understood this, but sometimes

the desire to drink outweighed practicality or common sense. On the night of June 28, 1804, JOHN COLLINS, who was on guard duty, persuaded HUGH HALL to join him in tapping the whiskey reserves. The two became drunk and were court-martialed the next day for what in the eyes of their comrades was a serious crime. Collins was charged "with getting drunk on his post this morning out of whiskey put under his Charge as a Sentinel and for Suffering Hugh Hall to draw whiskey out of the Said Barrel intended for the party." Found guilty, Collins received 100 lashes, Hall 50. After their sentences were carried out, the two men were immediately put to work pulling oars in the KEELBOAT, and the expedition continued up the river.

By necessity, Lewis and Clark imposed a frugal regime during their journey. Small amounts of whiskey (a bottle or a single glass) were given to Indians when it was considered wise to do so, and Christmas Day at FORT MANDAN was celebrated with three gills per man. But their supply of alcohol had to run out eventually, and it did so on Independence Day at the GREAT FALLS in July 1805. It was not until September 6, 1806, during their return down the MISSOURI RIVER, that they were able to buy some whiskey from traders employed by AUGUSTE CHOUTEAU. Clark reported: "We purchased a gallon of whiskey and gave to each man of the party a dram which is the first spiritious licquor which had been tasted by any of them since the 4 of July 1805."

Further Reading

Ambrose, Stephen E. *Undaunted Courage: Meriwether Lewis, Thomas Jefferson, and the Opening of the American West.* New York: Simon and Schuster, 1996.

This receipt is for 30 gallons "Strong Spt. Wine" (brandy) and six kegs, which Lewis bought in Philadelphia. Whiskey, however, was the preferred drink on the expedition. *(National Archives Old Military and Civil Records [NWCTB-92-NM81E225-LEWIS 1])*

Hunt, Robert. "Gills and Drams of Consolation: Ardent Spirits on the Lewis and Clark Expedition." *We Proceeded On* 17, no. 3 (February 1991).

Moulton, Gary E., ed. *The Journals of the Lewis and Clark Expedition.* 13 vols. Lincoln: University of Nebraska Press, 1983–2001.

Allen, Paul (1775–1826) *editor, poet*

Numerous obstacles stood in the way of getting the JOURNALS of the Lewis and Clark Expedition published. While MERIWETHER LEWIS had made such arrangements as commissioning artists to illustrate his projected book, having the botanical specimens described and illustrated by FREDERICK PURSH, putting together a prospectus, and so on, he failed to produce a single word of copy before his suicide in 1809. The following year, WILLIAM CLARK contracted with NICHOLAS BIDDLE, an attorney in PHILADELPHIA, to edit the journals, write a narrative, and prepare the book for publication. By that time interest from publishers had diminished considerably, in part because the journals of Sergeant PATRICK GASS had already been published. Then Dr. BENJAMIN SMITH BARTON failed to deliver on his promise to prepare the natural history volume. Furthermore, while Biddle did his best to write, edit, and line up a publisher, his other professional commitments prevented him from completing the work. For this reason he hired Paul Allen, a writer and editor for *Port Folio,* to finish the editing and proofreading and to oversee the printing.

A native of Providence, Rhode Island, and graduate of Brown University, Allen had moved to Philadelphia in 1800 to join *Port Folio,* then the United States's leading literary magazine. In 1801 he published *Original Poems, Serious and Entertaining.* According to Paul Russell Cutright, a contemporary had once characterized him as "an ordinary looking man with a character of sluggishness, slovenly in-aptitude and moroseness Yet there is not a better fellow on earth." Biddle apparently thought highly enough of Allen to pay him $500 for his work on the Lewis and Clark journals, which were finally published in 1814 as *History of the Expedition Under the Commands of Lewis and Clark, to the Sources of the Missouri, thence across the Rocky Mountains and down the River Columbia to the Pacific Ocean: Performed during the Years 1804–5–6 by Order of the Government of the United States.* Interestingly, despite his last-minute role and the fact that the book is today referred to as the Biddle edition, it is Allen's name that appears on the title page.

Of importance to the Biddle version of the journals is the memoir of Lewis written by THOMAS JEFFERSON that follows Allen's preface. It was Allen who persuaded the former president to write this personal tribute to the explorer, there by earning him the gratitude of historians. Allen published numerous orations and produced other books, including *A History of the American Revolution; The Life of Charles Brockden Brown;* and *Noah, A Poem.* He died in Baltimore in 1826.

Further Reading

American Council of Learned Societies. "Allen, Paul." *Dictionary of American Biography.* New York: Charles Scribner's Sons, 1928.

Cutright, Paul Russell. *A History of the Lewis and Clark Journals.* Norman: University of Oklahoma Press, 2000.

Lewis, Meriwether, and William Clark. *History of the Expedition under the Command of Captains Lewis and Clark, to the Sources of the Missouri, thence across the Rocky Mountains and down the River Columbia to the Pacific Ocean: Performed during the Years 1804–5–6 by Order of the Government of the United States.* Prepared for the press by Paul Allen; in two volumes. Philadelphia: Bradford and Inskeep; New York: Abm. H. Inskeep, 1814. Reprints, New Amsterdam Book Company, New York, 1902; Lippincott, Philadelphia, 1961.

American Philosophical Society (APS)

Lewis and Clark's expedition had no greater advocate, and no greater beneficiary, than the American Philosophical Society (APS). The United States's first scientific organization and still in existence today, it was founded by Benjamin Franklin and other colonists in 1743. The society sponsored early research in agriculture, manufacturing, and transportation. By the time of the expedition, it had become the nation's de facto national library, museum, and academy of science.

One of the society's leading members was THOMAS JEFFERSON, who was elected to membership in 1780 and who himself later sponsored the election of MERIWETHER LEWIS in 1803. Jefferson also served as APS president from 1797 to 1815. In 1793 he solicited society members to finance an expedition into the West. The man he chose to lead it was ANDRÉ MICHAUX, a French botanist. Among those members who subscribed to this expedition were John Adams, George Washington, ALEXANDER HAMILTON, and JAMES MADISON, as well as Jefferson himself. Consequently, the expedition's subscription list (now in the society's archives) is the only known document signed by the first four U.S. presidents.

However, when it was learned that Michaux was an agent of the French Republic, he was recalled from the frontier, having never traveled farther than Kentucky. (It is noteworthy that the instructions that Jefferson had drawn up for Michaux at the time would later form the foundation for his instructions to Meriwether Lewis.) Despite this failure, the society's enthusiasm for Jefferson's vision of western exploration remained undiminished, and members were supportive when Lewis went to PHILADELPHIA in 1803 to receive instruction in a number of sciences. Among those who taught and counseled him were eminent physician BENJAMIN RUSH, botanist BENJAMIN SMITH BARTON, mathematician ROBERT PATTERSON, and physician CASPAR WISTAR. The society's treasurer and librarian, John Vaughan, also assisted Lewis in procuring necessary navigational instruments.

The American Philosophical Society was subsequently rewarded for its support of the Lewis and Clark expedition with many of the original JOURNALS and numerous ARTIFACTS now stored there. After his return from the Pacific coast, Lewis took advantage of his membership in the APS for the first time and attended meetings in April, June, and July 1807.

See also EXPLORATION, EARLY.

Further Reading

American Philosophical Society. "Treasures of the APS: Jefferson Proposes a Scientific Expedition." Available on-line. URL: http://www.amphilsoc.org/library/exhibits/treasures/michaux.htm. Downloaded on January 10, 2002.

Avalon Project at the Yale Law School. "Jefferson's Letter to George Rogers Clark." Available on-line. URL: http://www.yale.edu/lawweb/avalon/jefflett/let21.htm. Downloaded on January 10, 2002.

Jackson, Donald. *Thomas Jefferson & the Stony Mountains: Exploring the West from Monticello.* Norman: University of Oklahoma Press, 1993.

Wilson, Gaye. "The American Philosophical Society and Western Exploration." From *Thomas Jefferson and the Lewis and Clark Expedition.* Available on-line. URL: http://www.monticello.org/jefferson/lewisandclark/aps.html. Downloaded on January 10, 2002.

ammunition   See FIREARMS; SUPPLIES AND EQUIPMENT.

animals, new species

Although the JOURNALS of MERIWETHER LEWIS and WILLIAM CLARK are still remarkable for the accuracy of their descriptions of the flora and fauna they encountered during the expedition, they met so many new species of birds and animals that they were unable to classify them all properly. When they saw animals of one genus in a variety of different fur or skin colors, they were unable to decide whether these differences were the sign of a different species or subspecies or simply seasonal variations.

Lewis and Clark are credited with identifying 122 animals altogether; of these 57 were discovered east of the CONTINENTAL DIVIDE, and 65 were found to the west. Some 42 different species of mammals were described in their JOURNALS, of which 11 were new to science. While many had been reported by previous explorers, Lewis and Clark were the first to give them scientific descriptions. Early naturalists who described certain species include George Ord, Constantine Samuel Rafinesque, John Richardson, and Thomas Say.

Certain species that are dealt with separately (see the list at the end of this entry) are not included in this entry. It should be noted that the majority of animals listed here are subspecies of animals already known to scientists of the time. This should not detract from the importance of Lewis's and Clark's findings, as it was the first time these animals had been properly described or recorded and proved vital in future zoological research and classification, despite many errors on the parts of the amateur naturalists.

Badger *(Western badger)* This subspecies, discovered by the expedition near COUNCIL BLUFF on July 30, 1804, was unknown to American zoologists, who had thought that it was restricted to Europe. A full description of the animal was written by Lewis at FORT CLATSOP on February 25, 1806.

Bobcat *(Northern bobcat/Oregon bobcat)* The skin of a Northern bobcat was among the ARTIFACTS AND SPECIMENS shipped back to President THOMAS JEFFERSON from FORT MANDAN in April 1805. At Fort Clatsop on February 21, 1806, Lewis noted that "The tyger cat is found on the border of the plains and in the woody country lying along the PACIFIC OCEAN. . . . This is quite distinct from the Canada lynx." Lewis was right to point out the difference in appearance, but both bobcats are now classified as members of the lynx family.

Ermine *(long-tailed weasel)* Clark bought a long-tailed weasel (ermine) from a MANDAN INDIAN and wrote on November 8, 1804, that the Indian kept the tail to adorn his clothing. This is the first mention of the ermine tippets that Lewis noted later among the SHOSHONE INDIANS. On August 20, 1805, on the LEMHI RIVER with the Shoshone, Lewis reported that they "attach from one to two hundred and fifty litle roles of Ermin skin [to their tippets]." Lewis's portrait by Charles de St. Mémin shows him wearing the ermine-covered coat given to him by Shoshone chief CAMEAHWAIT.

Gopher *(Dakota pocket gopher)* On April 9, 1805, above Fort Mandan, Lewis and Clark investigated the loose hillocks of earth thrown up by these creatures, and Lewis later described "the work of an anamal of which I could never obtain a view. Their work resembles that of the salamender common to the sand hills of the States of South Carolina and Georgia. . . ."

Groundhog *(yellow-bellied marmot)* Lewis noted on April 24, 1806, that he had seen "a Moonax which the natives had tamed."

Moose Neither Lewis nor Clark seem to have seen any moose (*Alces americanus*) themselves, but Sergeant JOHN ORDWAY and Private JOSEPH WHITEHOUSE reported seeing "mooce Deer which was much larger than the common deer" on May 10, 1805, just north of the MILK RIVER. A year later, on July 7, 1806, Lewis reported that "REUBEN FIELD wounded a moos deer this morning near our camp." According to a later naturalist, the moose had no scientific standing in their day and should therefore be considered as another of the Lewis and Clark discoveries.

Mountain Goat This species was first seen by Clark on August 24, 1805, on the Lemhi River. Lewis wrote a description of it at Fort Clatsop on February 22, 1806. A single horn of a Rocky Mountain goat brought back by the expedition was bequeathed by a descendant of Clark to the Filson Club, Louisville, Kentucky.

Mountain Lion Two members of the party wounded a "panther," or mountain lion, on May 16, 1805, between the Milk and MUSSELSHELL Rivers. On August 3, 1805, on the JEFFERSON RIVER, Reubin Field killed a panther measuring 7 1/2 feet from nose to tail. At Fort Clatsop in February 1806, Clark noted that the panther of the plains of the COLUMBIA RIVER was the same as that in the Atlantic states.

Panther See mountain lion, above.

Porcupine Lewis killed a porcupine on September 13, 1804, near present-day Brule City, South Dakota. On May 3, 1805, Lewis saw many porcupines and named Porcupine River after them (now Poplar River, Montana).

Raccoon This animal was seen often by the expedition, and since they were already familiar with it, they paid it little attention except to note that it was common on the West Coast around Fort Clatsop.

Rat *(packrat/bushy-tailed woodrat)* Those rats seen by Lewis and Clark had not been recorded before and can be counted as one of their discoveries. On July 2, 1805, at GREAT FALLS, Lewis recorded that they had caught a rat larger and lighter in color than the European rat, with a tail longer than its body and covered with a fine fur that was the same color as the body.

Squirrel During their journey the CORPS OF DISCOVERY came across at least six different types of squirrel, though they sometimes became confused when distinguishing between these and prairie dogs. They were certainly the first to note that western gray squirrels (of the Columbia River area) were larger than those on the East Coast and preferred areas with a preponderance of oak trees. While at Fort Clatsop, Lewis also noted that the chickaree was similar in size to the red squirrel of the East and lodged in holes in the ground as rats do, always having its "habitation in or near the earth."

Lewis described the animal now known as Richardson's red squirrel as "a small gray squirrel common to every part of the rocky mountain which is now timbered." On April 9, 1805, near present-day Garrison Dam, Clark saw an animal that was bigger than the barking squirrel and resembled the prairie dog. Naturalists now believe that this was the Richardson's ground squirrel.

Although their description of Columbian ground squirrel, also called the whistling squirrel or the burrowing squirrel, has led to discussion that it might have been confused with the pocket gopher (see above), it is clear that the party identified this animal correctly in Idaho in May and June 1806. Lewis recorded that the meat was as well flavored as that of the gray squirrel.

Lewis reported the pale-striped ground squirrel (or 13-lined ground squirrel) in July 1805, just above the Great Falls of the Missouri. He noted that it was larger than other squirrels he had seen and also mentioned the greater number of stripes.

Other animals mentioned in the expedition's journals include the bean mouse, muskrat, lynx, marten, and leather-winged bat.

See also ANTELOPE; BEARS; BEAVERS; BIRDS, NEW SPECIES; BUFFALO; COYOTES; DEER; ELK; FISH, NEW SPECIES; FOXES; HORSES; JACKRABBITS; OTTERS; PRAIRIE DOGS; SHEEP AND GOATS; WOLVES.

Further Reading

Burroughs, Raymond Darwin, ed. *The Natural History of the Lewis and Clark Expedition.* East Lansing: Michigan State University Press, 1995.
Cutright, Paul Russell. *Lewis & Clark: Pioneering Naturalists.* Lincoln: University of Nebraska Press/Bison Books, 1989.
———. "Meriwether Lewis: Zoologist." *Oregon Historical Quarterly* 69 (June 1968).
———. "The Odyssey of the Magpie and the Prairie Dog." *Missouri Historical Society Bulletin* 23, no. 3 (1967): 215–228.
Quinn, C. Edward. "A Zoologist's View of the Lewis and Clark Expedition." *American Zoologist* 26 (1986): 299–306.
Reid, Russell, and Clell G. Gannon. "Birds and Mammals Observed by Lewis & Clark in North Dakota." *North Dakota History* 66, no. 2 (1999): 2–14. Jamestown, N.Dak.: Northern Prairie Wildlife Research Center Home Page. Also available on-line URL: http://www.npwrc.usgs.gov/resource/2000/bmam/bmam. htm. Downloaded on May 20, 2001.
Setzer, Henry W. "Zoological Contributions of the Lewis and Clark Expedition." *Journal of the Washington Academy of Sciences* 44 (November 1954).
Wilkinson, Todd, and Paul Rauber. "Lewis & Clark's America: The Corps of Discovery left us a blueprint for a wild West." *Sierra* (May/June 2002): 42–46.

antelope (pronghorn, Oregon pronghorn)

There are five subspecies of antelope in North America, of which two were reported by MERIWETHER LEWIS and WILLIAM CLARK. The pronghorn and the Oregon pronghorn are, in fact, not members of the antelope family, though the physical resemblance justifies the term commonly applied to them. They are the only representatives of a species (*Antilocapridae*) intermediate between deer and cattle and are the only mammals with a branched, hollow horn that is cast and renewed each year. Although the pronghorn antelope (*Antilocapra americana*) had been seen and described by Spanish explorers in the 16th century, Lewis and Clark were the first to record its appearance and characteristics, sending specimen skeletons and skins back to President THOMAS JEFFERSON from FORT MANDAN in April 1805.

The CORPS OF DISCOVERY first saw pronghorns—or goats, as they first called them—on September 16, 1804, above the mouth of the Niobrara River. Clark killed the expedition's first pronghorn some days later near the White River in present-day South Dakota, recording details of its size and coloring and noting that, ". . . in my walk I Killed a Buck Goat of this Countery about the height of a grown deer. . . . he is more like the Antilope or Gazella of Africa than any other species of goat." It is possibly because of this remark by Clark

that the expedition members began to use the term *antelope* for the animal, though the word *goat* continued to be used as an alternative.

The characteristic that most struck corps members was the pronghorn's fleetness of foot. Three days after Clark had shot the first specimen, Lewis attempted to track a small herd and got to within 200 yards of it before the animals fled. He noted on September 17, 1804, that when he reached the spot where the antelope had been, they were already "at a distance of about three miles on the side of a ridge." He doubted whether these could be the same group, "but my doubts soon vanished when I beheld the rapidity of their flight along the ridge before me it appeared reather the rappid flight of birds than the motion of quadrupeds. I think I can safely venture the assertion that the speed of this anamal is equal if not superior to that of the finest blooded courser."

Lewis's assertion was correct. The pronghorn is the fastest of all American animals. It can reach a speed of 60 miles an hour over short distances and can keep up a speed of 40 miles an hour for several minutes. The pronghorn can outrun any horse with ease, but they are poor swimmers, and taking them while in the water seems to have been the main means of killing them. Lewis also recorded the method the SHOSHONE INDIANS had developed to hunt pronghorn. Shoshone riders spread themselves out in a huge circle, some five or six miles in diameter. Two or three hunters then stampeded the pronghorn from one side until they reached the hunters on the other side of the circle. These in turn drove the pronghorn back the other way, while the first party rested their horses. Eventually the pronghorn became tired and slowed their pace enough to be shot with bow and arrow.

"I was very much entertained with a view of this Indian chase," wrote Lewis on August 14, 1805, while on the LEMHI RIVER. "[I]t was after a herd of about ten antelope, and about 20 hunters. It lasted about 2 hours and considerable part of the chase was in view from my tent. About 1 p.m. the hunters returned—had not killed a single Antelope."

The only mention of the Oregon pronghorn (*Antilocapra americana oregana*) was on April 16, 1806, during the return journey up the COLUMBIA RIVER, and it is only a hearsay report: "The hunters informed me they saw some Antelopes."

See also HUNTING; SHEEP AND GOATS.

Further Reading

Burroughs, Raymond Darwin, ed. *The Natural History of the Lewis and Clark Expedition.* East Lansing: Michigan State University Press, 1995.
Cutright, Paul Russell. *Lewis & Clark: Pioneering Naturalists.* Lincoln: University of Nebraska Press/Bison Books, 1989.
Knue, Joseph. *Big Game of North Dakota: A Short History.* Bismarck: North Dakota Game and Fish Dept., 1991.
Van Wormer, Joe. *The World of the Pronghorn.* Philadelphia: Lippincott, 1969.
Washington State University. "Lewis and Clark Among the Indians of the Pacific Northwest. Excerpts from the Journals of the

Expedition of the Corps of Discovery: Flora and Fauna (recorded at Fort Clatsop)." Available on-line. URL: http://www.libarts.wsu.edu/history/Lewis_Clark/LCEXP_Flor.html. Downloaded on May 20, 2001.

appropriations See CONGRESS, U.S.; COSTS OF THE EXPEDITION.

Arikara Indians (Arikaree, Ree)

The Arikara Indians were living in what is now northern South Dakota when Lewis and Clark encountered them in October 1804. They were a nation of farmers, using hoes made from animal scapulas to grow CORN, squash, and beans as well as TOBACCO, watermelon, and pumpkins. It is believed that they introduced principles of agriculture to other Indian nations on the upper MISSOURI RIVER. When crop yields were low, the Arikara supplemented their food supply by hunting BUFFALO. But agriculture was essential both for internal consumption and for trade with the TETON LAKOTA INDIANS (Teton Sioux), a

This photo of an Arikara woman was taken about 1908. The Arikara are now part of the Three Affiliated Tribes (with the Mandan and the Hidatsa) and live primarily on the Fort Berthold Reservation in North Dakota. *(Library of Congress, Prints and Photographs Division [LC-USZ62-107915])*

military power who depended on the Arikara harvests and who traded European goods and meat for their corn and HORSES. The Arikara villages were also a center for trading with other nations such as the Arapaho, Comanche, Kiowa, OSAGE, and CHEYENNE INDIANS.

Like their neighbors farther up the MISSOURI RIVER, the MANDAN and HIDATSA INDIANS, the Arikara lived in permanent earth-lodge villages. All three nations had begun to TRADE with the Spanish and others by as early as the mid-18th century. Though they shared a common economic and social life, their language and customs differed. While the Mandan and Hidatsa speak a Siouan dialect, the Arikara language is from the Caddoan linguistic group.

The Arikara are thought to be descended from the Caddo Indians and closely related to the Pawnee and the Skidi. Anthropologists believe that when Lewis and Clark met them, the Arikara were gradually moving upstream on the MISSOURI RIVER, in a long-term migration that had begun in prehistoric times. In the late 18th century, this migration was accelerated because of a series of devastating smallpox epidemics. Prior to this time, the Arikara population had been around 30,000. In 1804, however, Lewis and Clark passed by numerous abandoned Arikara sites before finding only about 2,000 Indians living in three villages: Sawa-haini on Ashley Island (now submerged by Lake Oahe) and, about four miles north, Rhtarahe and Waho-erha.

Sergeant PATRICK GASS, who was a carpenter, made note in his JOURNALS of the Arikara's round, covered earthen lodges, which the expedition had never seen before. The circular design was complex, consisting of a series of timber columns and rafters covered by willow branches, sod, and earth. A single lodge was anywhere from 40 to 70 feet in diameter. The Arikara had apparently used this design for hundreds of years.

The Corps of Discovery stayed with the Arikara, whom they called the "rickeres" or "ricaras," for five days. Communications were eased by the presence of JOSEPH GRAVELINES and PIERRE-ANTOINE TABEAU, two traders then living with the Arikara who spoke their language and thus served as interpreters. Tabeau's knowledge of the Indians was particularly important. When he had arrived at the villages the previous year, he had invited 42 of their leaders to a grand council but was scolded for overlooking dozens more. He subsequently described the population as "captains without companies," a facet of the Arikara culture that he attempted to convey to Lewis and Clark when they invited the three primary village chiefs—CROW AT REST, HAWK'S FEATHER, and HAY—to a council. Despite Tabeau's suggestion that they treat all three chiefs as equals, they insisted on making Crow at Rest the "grand chief," a gesture that initially offended the others, although they were later conciliated.

Despite their initial faux pas on their treatment of the chiefs, relations between the captains and the Arikara were mainly friendly, and there were negotiations on future trade with the United States. Like the OTOE (Oto) and MISSOURI INDIANS, the Arikara agreed to send a representative to Wash-

This Mandan Indian buffalo robe, sent back east by Lewis, depicts a battle fought by the Mandan and the Hidatsa against the Lakota and the Arikara. Thomas Jefferson had hung it in Monticello's entryway. It is now in the Peabody Museum at Harvard. *(Peabody Museum, Harvard University, N27515)*

ington to meet President THOMAS JEFFERSON. The tribal chiefs also agreed when Lewis and Clark encouraged them to make peace with their rivals the Mandan, and in a show of good faith, an Arikara chief accompanied the expedition up to the Mandan villages and engaged in conciliatory talks with chiefs there.

The friendly relations between non-Indians and the Arikara that Lewis and Clark had hoped for did not last. Ankedouchera, the Arikara chief whom they had sent to Washington, unfortunately died there soon after his arrival in summer 1806. Although his death had been from natural causes, the Arikara became deeply suspicious of the Americans, and in 1807 they used violence to stop a delegation led by NATHANIEL PRYOR that was attempting to return Mandan chief BIG WHITE to his village on the upper Missouri.

Disease and warfare with the Sioux (Dakota, Lakota, Nakota) forced the Arikara to join with the Mandan and the Hidatsa; this union was later called the Three Affiliated Tribes. In 1851 the Treaty of Fort Laramie assigned them a large reservation, which originally totaled 13.5 million acres and included parts of Montana, Wyoming, North Dakota, and South Dakota. During the next four decades, however, it was reduced to less than 930,000 acres. In 1954 another 152,300 acres of land was lost when the U.S. Army Corps of Engineers created the Garrison Reservoir, forcing the Arikara to move to the west side of the newly created Lake Sakakawae. Today the Three Affiliated Tribes maintain a museum of Indian history and artifacts on the Fort Berthold Reservation, where they hold a powwow every summer.

Further Reading

Cash, Joseph H., and Gerald W. Wolff. *The Three Affiliated Tribes (Mandan, Arikara, and Hidatsa)*. Phoenix, Ariz.: Indian Tribal Series, 1974.

Meyer, Roy W. *The Village Indians of the Upper Missouri: The Mandans, Hidatsas, and Arikaras.* Lincoln: University of Nebraska Press, 1977.

PBS Online. *Lewis and Clark: The Native Americans:* "Arikara Indians." Available on-line. URL: http://www.pbs.org/lewisandclark/native/idx_ari.html. Downloaded on May 18, 2001.

Ronda, James P. *Lewis and Clark among the Indians.* Lincoln and London: University of Nebraska Press, 1984.

Waldman, Carl. *Encyclopedia of Native American Tribes.* Revised ed. New York: Checkmark Books, 1999.

Army, U.S.

See CLARK, WILLIAM; CORPS OF DISCOVERY; COURT-MARTIALS; LEWIS, MERIWETHER; ORGANIZATION OF THE EXPEDITION PARTY.

artifacts and specimens

On April 7, 1805, the CORPS OF DISCOVERY resumed their westward journey from FORT MANDAN in six CANOES and two PIROGUES. That same day, the KEELBOAT that had taken them up the MISSOURI RIVER the previous year left to head back downriver to ST. LOUIS. On board was a small crew headed by Corporal RICHARD WARFINGTON as well as boxes, trunks, and cages destined for Washington, D.C. These contained reports, LETTERS, MAPS, some live animals, and numerous artifacts and specimens that MERIWETHER LEWIS and WILLIAM CLARK had collected during their journey up the Missouri and were now sending to THOMAS JEFFERSON. Even more material of scientific and ethnological import would be brought back a year and a half later, after the expedition had completed its journey.

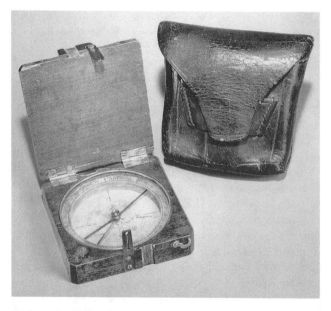

William Clark's compass is today housed at the Smithsonian in Washington. *(National Museum of American History, Smithsonian Institution Behring Center)*

The tasks the captains were given to carry out were so varied as to be bewildering. To meet their MISSION OBJECTIVES, they had to be not only explorers but astronomers, cartographers, botanists, zoologists, ornithologists, paleontologists, ethnographers, linguists, diplomats, and reporters. Their daily activities and discoveries were faithfully recorded in JOURNALS and field notes, and whenever they could, they collected specimens to be sent back east for examination, analysis, and preservation.

Because of the difficulty of transporting goods and specimens over great distances, many were buried in CACHES as the expedition traveled westward, to be retrieved on the return journey. Unfortunately, even with the use of OILCLOTH, it was impossible to adequately protect all the specimens from INSECTS and moisture. As a result, much of the material collected on the upper Missouri River and west of the ROCKY MOUNTAINS was lost. Nevertheless, much also made it back east, and the accumulated wealth of artifacts and specimens from the Lewis and Clark Expedition has provided historians, botanists, ornithologists, zoologists, and ethnologists with a tangible and fascinating record of the greatest journey in the annals of the United States.

The keelboat shipment of April 1805 included Indian CORN and TOBACCO, animal skins and skeletons, a pair of ELK's horns, soil and mineral samples, 60 PLANTS, a box of insects, four living magpies, and a live PRAIRIE DOG, as well as Indian artifacts, including buffalo robes, tools, and WEAPONS. The shipment arrived in Washington on August 12, 1805—interestingly, the same day that Meriwether Lewis became the first non-Indian American to cross the CONTINENTAL DIVIDE at LEMHI PASS. Jefferson was then at his home in MONTICELLO, but when he returned to Washington in October, he pored excitedly over the contents of the boxes. Of the ANIMALS, only the prairie dog and one magpie had survived the trip. Some of the items ended up at Monticello, where Jefferson subsequently grew Indian corn and tobacco. Plant specimens went to Dr. BENJAMIN SMITH BARTON, and many years later, long after being catalogued by FREDERICK PURSH, were deposited with the Academy of Natural Sciences in PHILADELPHIA. Today its Lewis and Clark Herbarium includes 226 plant specimens, many with their original labels, handwritten by Meriwether Lewis. These plants compose the first major scientific collection from the northwestern United States and include 94 species that were new to science at the time of the expedition. The original specimens still have uses today. In 1997, for example, a researcher measured isotopes of carbon in small pieces of leaf material at the herbarium to compare changes in the atmosphere since the Lewis and Clark Expedition.

Lewis and Clark also gathered specimens of animals, preparing bird and mammal skins and even preserving the skulls of some animals. The majority of these (as well as those collected later) were shipped to CHARLES WILLSON PEALE for his museum in PHILADELPHIA. Peale subsequently acquired many of the expedition's Indian artifacts as well, including the ermine tippet given to Lewis by the SHOSHONE chief CAMEAH-

WAIT. After Peale's museum closed, the collection was divided between the Boston Museum and P. T. Barnum's American Museum in New York, which was partially destroyed by a fire in 1865. It is believed that many Lewis and Clark artifacts were lost in this fire. Peale's "Memorandum of Specimens and Antiques," listing his acquisitions from the expedition, is now at the Historical Society of Pennsylvania in Philadelphia.

Many items have been lost during the years, and some may yet be discovered. It is not known, for example, what happened to the lists of Indian LANGUAGES that Lewis and Clark had recorded on the first leg of their journey up the Missouri in 1804. Following the expedition, in ST. LOUIS, Lewis and Clark held a public auction at which they sold off such items as their rifles, powder horns, shot pouches, axes, kettles, and tools. Historian Stephen Ambrose described this as "a dreadful disgrace." In what can only be called a tragedy, 25 boxes of artifacts from the West were lost when the ship carrying them sank in Chesapeake Bay; only some moose and wapiti horns survived the accident.

Fortunately, a number of artifacts and specimens from the expedition can still be seen in institutions around the country. The AMERICAN PHILOSOPHICAL SOCIETY of Philadelphia is home to most of the original expedition JOURNALS, including those of Sergeant JOHN ORDWAY, which were rediscovered in 1913. The Lewis and Clark journals stored there consist of 18 small notebooks, 14 of them bound in leather, four in boards covered in marbled paper. (Scholars disagree whether these were the actual field journals or rewrites after the expedition.) The Missouri Historical Society in St. Louis has five of Clark's journals, four bound in red leather and the fifth in ELK skin, as well as Clark's memorandum book of 1809–10. The Newberry Library in Chicago has Sergeant JOSEPH WHITEHOUSE's journal, and the Historical Society of Wisconsin has that of Sergeant CHARLES FLOYD.

Several other institutions in Philadelphia also hold artifacts from the expedition. These include the Athenaeum of Philadelphia, which has Lewis's telescope, reputedly carried to the PACIFIC OCEAN and back. The University of Pennsylvania Museum owns fragments of two Mandan pots, while the Library Company of Philadelphia houses the book by Antoine Simon Le Page du Pratz that had been loaned to Lewis by Dr. Benjamin Smith Barton (see BOOKS ON THE EXPEDITION). Along with the journals, the compass, Lewis's air rifle (see FIREARMS), and possibly the telescope, this book was one of the few artifacts from the expedition known to have traveled across the country and back.

The Museum of Comparative Zoology at Harvard University contains the only remaining skin of a bird brought back; appropriately it is Lewis's woodpecker. Also at Harvard, the Peabody Museum of Archeology and Ethnology contains approximately 20 ethnographic artifacts from the expedition. Yale University houses 150 maps from or related to the expedition as well as Clark's field notes from the 1803–04 winter at CAMP DUBOIS. The Library of Congress also houses a number of maps.

Some artifacts were found by chance or handed down through an expedition member's descendants. The Filson Historical Society in Louisville, Kentucky, houses the horn of a bighorn sheep that William Clark had given his sister Fanny as well as a number of LETTERS from the expedition. The Oregon Historical Society possesses a Jefferson PEACE MEDAL found in Idaho; GEORGE SHANNON's sewing kit; and Lewis's branding iron, possibly the one used to brand horses bought from the NEZ PERCE INDIANS, which was found on an island in the COLUMBIA RIVER in 1892. Perhaps the Society's most fascinating artifact is a piece of whalebone. Found at Seaside, Oregon, as late as 1967, it is inscribed "M. Lewi."

Further Reading

Academy of Natural Sciences. "The Lewis and Clark Herbarium." Available on-line. URL: http://www.acnatsci.org/lewis&clark/. Downloaded on May 17, 2001.

Burroughs, Raymond Darwin, ed. *The Natural History of the Lewis and Clark Expedition.* East Lansing: Michigan State University Press, 1995.

Cutright, Paul Russell. *Lewis & Clark: Pioneering Naturalists.* Lincoln: University of Nebraska Press/Bison Books, 1989.

———. "Meriwether Lewis: Botanist." *Oregon Historical Quarterly* 69 (June 1968): 148–170.

———. "The Odyssey of the Magpie and the Prairie Dog." *Missouri Historical Society Bulletin* 23, no. 3 (1967): 215–228.

Hawke, David Freeman. *Those Tremendous Mountains: The Story of the Lewis and Clark Expedition.* New York: W. W. Norton & Company, 1998.

Kyle, Robert. "Bargains Galore at Lewis & Clark's Yard Sale." *Maine Antique Digest,* November 1997. Available on-line. URL: http://www.maineantiquedigest.com/articles/lewi1197.htm. Downloaded on February 10, 2002.

Osgood, Ernest S. "A Prairie Dog for Mr. Jefferson." *Montana: The Magazine of Western History* 19, no. 2 (1969): 54–56.

Rasmussen, Jay. "Visual Resources and Artifacts." *Lewis & Clark on the Information Superhighway.* Available on-line. URL: http://www.lcarchive.org/visualresources.html. Updated on November 6, 2001.

Snow, Jan. "Lewis and Clark in the Museum Collections of the Missouri Historical Society." *Gateway Heritage* 2, no. 2 (1981): 36–41.

Assiniboine Indians

When in late October 1804 the Lewis and Clark Expedition reached the villages of the MANDAN and HIDATSA INDIANS, they arrived at what was the hub of a large trading network. Just a few weeks previously, the villages had been teeming with Indians from the CROW, CHEYENNE, Kiowa, Arapaho, and Assiniboine nations, in addition to traders from the HUDSON'S BAY COMPANY and NORTH WEST COMPANY. Now, however, winter was about to set in, and the scene was relatively quiet. Nevertheless, the next few months saw the captains gathering geographic and ethnographic information from fur traders and

Lewis and Clark encountered the Assiniboine during their stay at Fort Mandan. Wary of this nation's fierce reputation, they were glad not to encounter them again during their journey west. This Assiniboine named Rattlesnake was photographed ca. 1907. *(Library of Congress, Prints and Photographs Division [LC-D4-19791])*

trappers, the Mandan, and the Hidatsa. In addition, Indians of other nations who heard of their presence at the villages came to meet them. Among these were the Assiniboine.

A Siouan-speaking people, the Assiniboine Indians originally lived around Lake Superior but moved westward toward Lake Winnipeg sometime during the 1600s. Once they acquired HORSES, their range extended even further through western Manitoba, up into Saskatchewan, and down into Montana and North Dakota, establishing themselves among the PLAINS INDIANS. Nomadic hunter-gatherers, the Assiniboine traded meat and furs for the agricultural products of other nations and, once they met the French and English, for trade goods and weapons. In 1738 the French explorer Pierre de La Vérendrye visited the Mandan villages and noted the sort of merchandise most desired by the Assiniboine, including "guns, axes, kettle, powder, bullets, knives, awls."

By the time MERIWETHER LEWIS and WILLIAM CLARK arrived on the scene, the trading relationship between the Assiniboine and the Mandan had been firmly established for

years, although it was marked by pressure, even bullying, on the part of the northern Indians. The captains hoped to convince the Mandan to break from the Assiniboine and bring them into the ST. LOUIS–based trading network that the expedition was promoting. Lewis and Clark considered the Assiniboine to be scoundrels whose association with the British and violent clashes with their sworn enemies the Sioux Indians (Dakota, Lakota, Nakota) only added to the bad opinion the Americans held of them.

In November 1804 a band of Assiniboine arrived at the villages to trade and, hearing of the expedition's presence, asked to meet the white men, an introduction arranged by the Mandan chief BLACK CAT. Despite their distrust of the Assiniboine, Lewis and Clark were aware that it was necessary for the United States to deal with them and therefore welcomed Chief Chechank and others to FORT MANDAN. Because the nation was largely Canadian based and therefore technically under British protection, the captains could not perform their usual ceremony and speeches nor give out the customary PEACE

MEDALS. Clark did, however, offer a piece of gold braid as a gift, and the meeting went smoothly. Consequently, Black Cat showed some willingness to break off relations with the Assiniboine in favor of the Americans, but he was restrained from pursuing this due to his people's distrust of white men as well as threats from the Assiniboine to retaliate if the Mandan pursued a trading relationship with the United States.

By the time the CORPS OF DISCOVERY left Fort Mandan the following spring, Lewis and Clark had decided that they would be better off to avoid the Assiniboine on the GREAT PLAINS. "We do not wish to see those gentlemen just now," wrote Lewis, and although they saw many signs of Assiniboine bands on their journey, there was, fortunately, no further contact with that nation.

Further Reading

Denig, Edwin Thompson. *The Assiniboine.* Edited by J. N. B. Hewitt. Norman: University of Oklahoma Press, 2000.

Ronda, James P. *Lewis and Clark among the Indians.* Lincoln: University of Nebraska Press, 1984.

Waldman, Carl. *Encyclopedia of Native American Tribes.* Revised ed., New York: Checkmark Books, 1999.

Writers' Program, Montana. *Land of Nakoda; the story of the Assiniboine Indians. From the tales of the Old Ones told to First Boy (James L. Long), with drawings by Fire Bear (William Standing).* Helena, Mont.: State Pub. Co., 1942. Reprint, New York: AMS Press, 1975.

Astor, John Jacob (Johann Jakob Astor)
(1763–1848) *fur trader, merchant*

America's first multimillionaire was also one of the first to capitalize on the Lewis and Clark Expedition. In setting up Fort Astoria at the mouth of the Columbia River in 1811, John Jacob Astor attempted and nearly succeeded in carrying out MERIWETHER LEWIS's vision of an American FUR TRADE based on the Pacific coast.

Born Johann Jakob Astor in Waldorf, Germany, the 20-year-old Astor arrived in the United States in 1783 with $25 and almost immediately established himself in New York as a fur trader. His business operation was innovative, diversified, and tightly controlled. His agents bought furs directly from the Indians west of the Mississippi in exchange for colonial goods and ALCOHOL, but rather than sell the furs in New York, Astor shipped them to China, Europe, and Russia, where he traded them for merchandise that brought high prices in New York.

In 1808, with the support of the U.S. government—at that time concerned about the expansion of the Canada-based HUDSON'S BAY COMPANY and NORTH WEST COMPANY—Astor created the American Fur Company, which soon monopolized the fur trade in the Missouri Territory. By 1810 Astor had become the richest man in the United States. Having read about the Lewis and Clark Expedition, in 1811 he formed the Pacific Fur Company with the goal of starting a fur-trading operation at the mouth of the COLUMBIA RIVER, just as Lewis had proposed in his report to THOMAS JEFFERSON following the expedition.

Astor sent two expeditions to Oregon. The first traveled by ship around Cape Horn and established a trading post on the river, naming it Astoria. It is noteworthy that during the winter of 1805–06, the CORPS OF DISCOVERY camped not too far from the site of Astor's post, which has since become the oldest non-Indian settlement in the Northwest. (A column marking the spot of this first settlement was erected in 1926 on Coxcomb Hill.)

Astor's second group traveled overland, the first such expedition since Lewis and Clark. This group made it over the mountains, but one man died and a significant amount of supplies was lost or ruined due to a capsizing on the SNAKE RIVER. Employee Robert Stuart then led a return party to get assistance from Astor in St. Louis. During this west-east trip, Stuart discovered what was later named South Pass, a 20-mile-wide gap in the ROCKY MOUNTAINS. As this pass was suitable for wagons, it made up for the lack of an adequate water passage and in later years became a key element in American migration to the West (see OREGON TRAIL).

Astor intended to use Astoria to capitalize on the Far East market, but the War of 1812 saw the post blockaded, and he eventually sold it to the North West Company. Nevertheless, his far-flung trading operations, including the Southwest Fur Company, prospered and expanded as he set up trading posts across the country. Astor monopolized the fur trade until 1834, when he sold out his interest in the American Fur Company and turned his attention to real estate enterprises in New York. When he died in 1848, his record fortune was estimated at more than $20 million.

Further Reading

Bryce, George. *The Remarkable History of the Hudson's Bay Company, Including That of the French Traders of North-western Canada, and of the North-west XY, and Astor Fur Companies.* 2d ed. New York: B. Franklin, 1968.

Irving, Washington. *Astoria: or, Anecdotes of an Enterprise Beyond the Rocky Mountains.* 1836, Reprint edited by Edgeley W. Todd. Norman: University of Oklahoma Press, 1964.

Madsen, Axel. *John Jacob Astor: America's First Millionaire.* New York: Wiley, 2001.

Stokesbury, James L. "John Jacob Astor: A Self-Invented Money-Making Machine." Available on-line. URL: http://www.thehistorynet.com/AmericanHistory/articles/1997/12972_text.htm. Downloaded on May 15, 2001.

Astoria See ASTOR, JOHN JACOB.

astronomical observations

When MERIWETHER LEWIS and WILLIAM CLARK began their transcontinental journey, they had some specially drawn MAPS that provided what little information was then known of the territory into which they were heading. They also knew the latitude and longitude of the mouth of the COLUMBIA RIVER, their chosen destination, which had been established by Captain ROBERT GRAY in 1792. Their compasses gave them their direction of travel up the MISSOURI RIVER and across the ROCKY MOUNTAINS, and they calculated the distance by their log-line or by dead reckoning. Establishing their exact position, however, was a very different matter.

Sailors had known for centuries how to find their latitude (north or south of the equator) by measuring the height of the sun at midday. What was far more difficult was finding their longitude (east or west of the meridian). The best and easiest way of establishing longitude was to use an accurate chronometer, or timepiece. If such an instrument were available and set to Greenwich mean time, then a comparison of the local time at midday, compared with Greenwich time, enabled them to find the longitude. If, however, the chronometer was not accurate—and Lewis already knew that his was not—then other methods had to be used. These depended on astronomical observations, of which there were two main methods at that time. The more accurate was to measure the angle between the moon and the sun or a fixed star. The second relied on measuring the time of eclipse of Jupiter's satellites. Both methods entailed long and complicated calculations and reference to astronomical tables.

Lewis had already acquired some basic astronomical knowledge before spending the period of April 20–May 7, 1803 with ANDREW ELLICOTT, then the United States's leading astronomer. Ellicott taught him to use the sextant, the quadrant, and the chronometer and familiarized him with the nautical and astronomical almanacs he took with him on the expedition. Lewis then spent an additional week with mathematician ROBERT PATTERSON, who gave him further instruction in the use of his astronomical and surveying instruments. After joining his cocaptain in CLARKSVILLE, Lewis began to train Clark in what he himself had only recently learned. Probably to accustom themselves to working under field conditions, the two began by taking a series of astronomical observations during their week's stay at the mouth of the OHIO RIVER. This had the secondary advantage of being a point at which the latitude and the longitude had already been determined, enabling them to check whether their observations and subsequent calculations were correct. It was important that the chronometer be kept running, and thus one of the sergeants had the job of winding it every day at noon.

Although Lewis was the most skilled in astronomical work, Clark soon learned to use the sextant to establish the party's latitude each day. This was an important factor on its own, since the border between the United States and Canada was then still a matter of debate. The farther north Lewis and Clark traced the tributaries of the MISSOURI RIVER, then the better claim the United States would have, under the terms of the LOUISIANA PURCHASE, to the NORTHWEST TERRITORY and its FUR TRADE. It was for this reason that the report sent back to President THOMAS JEFFERSON from FORT MANDAN in April 1805 included Clark's "Summary Statement of Rivers, Creeks and Most Remarkable Places." This document listed all the landmarks from the mouth of the Missouri, the compass direction of the route between them, the distance from one to another, the total estimated distance of each landmark from the mouth of the Missouri, and the latitude of each location.

Following Jefferson's instructions to take "observations of latitude and longitude, at all remarkable points on the river," Lewis and Clark were assiduous in taking daily observations when this was possible. On June 1, 1804, at the mouth of the Osage River, they spent two days carrying out their measurements, even cutting down trees to give them a better horizon. Between 6:22 and 8:28 A.M., they took observations every three minutes, setting out their findings in tabular form. They repeated this exercise throughout the journey when circumstances allowed, in addition to their normal daily sextant reading. It is known that Lewis completed one calculation of both latitude and longitude from his own astronomical observations at the mouth of the Missouri and attempted another at Fort Mandan. Apart from these, he settled for noting the figures and measurements he and Clark obtained and bringing them back for astronomers to work out.

See also NAVIGATION.

Further Reading

Ambrose, Stephen E. *Undaunted Courage: Meriwether Lewis, Thomas Jefferson, and the Opening of the American West.* New York: Simon and Schuster, 1996.

Bedini, Silvio A. "The Scientific Instruments of the Lewis and Clark Expedition." *Great Plains Quarterly* 4, no. 1 (1984): 54–69.

Large, Arlen. "Lewis and Clark: Part Time Astronomers." *We Proceeded On* 5, no. 1 (February 1979).

Merritt, James, et al. "Shooting the Moon (and the Sun and Stars): Lewis and Clark as Celestial Navigators." *We Proceeded On* 27, no. 4 (November 2001).

Preston, Richard S. "The Accuracy of the Astronomical Observations of Lewis and Clark." *APS Proceedings,* June 2000. Available online. URL: http://www.aps-pub.com/proceedings/jun00/Preston.pdf. Downloaded on February 10, 2002.

University of Virginia. "Exploring the West from Monticello: Observations of Latitude and Longitude at All Remarkable Points." Available on-line. URL: http://www.lib.virginia.edu/exhibits/lewis_clark/home.html. Downloaded on March 27, 2002.

B

badgers   See ANIMALS, NEW SPECIES.

Bad River (Teton River)

Named the Teton River by Lewis and Clark, the Bad River flows into the MISSOURI RIVER at present-day Pierre, South Dakota. Four miles north of the rivers' junction is a column marking both the center of the state and approximate center of North America. The State Historical Museum at Pierre has a lead plate claiming the area for FRANCE that was buried by two sons of the explorer Pierre de La Vérendrye on the opposite side of the river in 1743.

It was at the mouth of the Bad River that the CORPS OF DISCOVERY had their first confrontation with the TETON LAKOTA INDIANS (Teton Sioux), an incident that could have led to the expedition's abrupt conclusion before it had gotten very far. On the evening of September 23, 1804, the party was camped a few miles below the river's mouth. Three boys from the Teton villages nearby swam over to them and took back a message asking for a meeting with the Teton leaders in two days' time. As the expedition made its way up the Missouri River to the designated meeting place, Private JOHN COLTER, who had been HUNTING, reported that his horse had been stolen by some Teton Indians, an incident that did not bode well for the corps.

The formal council with the Teton Lakota took place on September 25, 1804, on a sandbar at the mouth of the Bad River. A canvas awning was in place, a flagstaff was raised, and the meeting began at 11:00 A.M. The Teton chiefs in attendance were BLACK BUFFALO, THE PARTISAN, and Buffalo Medicine. After both sides had exchanged and eaten food, the speeches began. It was clear that the Teton Lakota wanted to extract a large tribute of gifts and goods from the expedition as the price for allowing them to proceed upriver. In an attempt to divert them from their demands, Captains MERIWETHER LEWIS and WILLIAM CLARK took them on board the KEELBOAT and entertained them there. It was only with difficulty that Clark managed to get them into the PIROGUES to take them back to land. When they reached the bank, three warriors seized the end of the rope, while another locked his arms around the mast and The Partisan told Clark the expedition could go no further. Clark drew his sword, Lewis ordered the swivel guns on the keelboat made ready, and the rest of the party cocked their rifles. In response the Indians fitted arrows to their bows and raised their muskets. Both sides would certainly have opened fire had not Black Buffalo ordered his men away from the pirogue.

The following day the expedition traveled five miles up the Missouri, carrying Black Buffalo back to his village at his request. It was to be three more days before Lewis and Clark were able to leave the Teton Lakota and the Bad River behind and continue their journey.

Further Reading

Ambrose, Stephen E. *Undaunted Courage: Meriwether Lewis, Thomas Jefferson, and the Opening of the American West.* New York: Simon and Schuster, 1996.

Moulton, Gary E., ed. *Atlas of the Lewis and Clark Expedition.* Revised ed. Lincoln: University of Nebraska Press, 1999.

Ronda, James P. *Lewis and Clark among the Indians.* Lincoln: University of Nebraska Press, 1984.

Barralet, James See PHILADELPHIA.

barter See TRADE.

Barter, Joseph (La Liberté, Liberté, Le Bartee, Jo Barter) (unknown–unknown) *private, deserter*

Confusion surrounds Joseph Barter, referred to in many sources and in the expedition's JOURNALS as La Liberté or Liberté. Some expedition rosters list him as a private; others place him among the ENGAGÉS. As he was recruited for the expedition in KASKASKIA, he was most likely a private in the temporary party whose primary responsibilities were as an oarsman on the PIROGUES and CANOES. Prior to his enlistment in the CORPS OF DISCOVERY, he had reputedly lived among the OTOE INDIANS (Oto) near Fort Gage, Canada.

Late in July 1804, as MERIWETHER LEWIS and WILLIAM CLARK were searching for the Otoe, GEORGE DROUILLARD met a MISSOURI INDIAN, one of a few who were then living with the Otoe. Because La Liberté spoke the language, he was sent back with the Missouri to invite the Otoe to a council. Several days passed, and the captains grew increasingly anxious when the private did not return. Finally, on August 2, a party of Otoe and Missouri appeared, along with a French-Canadian trader. From them Lewis and Clark learned that La Liberté had set out for their camp the previous day. He never showed up, however, and though he was initially assumed to be lost, it soon became evident that he had deserted the expedition. On August 3, MOSES REED also deserted.

After three days a search party headed by Drouillard was sent out to locate La Liberté and Reed, the latter of whom was captured and returned for punishment. According to the journals, "they had also caught Liberté, but by a trick he had made his escape." He was never seen again. There are at least two theories as to Barter's later whereabouts. One source places him near Jefferson City, Missouri, and dying under the name of Joab Barton in 1820. Another theory has him taking the name of Joseph La Liberté, a man who married an African-American woman in ST. LOUIS in 1835 and died there two years later.

Further Reading

Clarke, Charles G. *The Men of the Lewis and Clark Expedition: A Biographical Roster of the Fifty-One Members and a Composite Diary of Their Activities from All Known Sources.* 1970. Reprint, Lincoln: Bison Books, University of Nebraska Press, 2002.

Lewis, Meriwether and William Clark. *The History of the Lewis and Clark Expedition.* Edited by Elliott Coues; 4 vols., 1893, Harper. Reprinted in 3 vols., New York: Dover Publications, 1979.

Barton, Benjamin Smith (1766–1815) *botanist*

Considered the first academic botanist in America, Dr. Benjamin Smith Barton was a member of both the AMERICAN PHILOSOPHICAL SOCIETY and the Academy of Natural Sciences of PHILADELPHIA, as well as professor of medical botany at the University of Pennsylvania. In spring 1803 President THOMAS JEFFERSON sent MERIWETHER LEWIS to Philadelphia to study with Barton and several other leading scientists of the time. As a result of his instruction from Barton, Lewis was able to collect, identify, date, and preserve specimens of plants and animals discovered during the expedition.

Born in Lancaster, Pennsylvania, Barton was a nephew of the renowned astronomer David Rittenhouse. In 1785 he accompanied Rittenhouse on an expedition to survey the western borders of Pennsylvania and Maryland. While on that frontier, Barton met some Indians, sparking what would be a lifelong interest in Native American ETHNOGRAPHY. The following year he went to Edinburgh, Scotland, to study medicine, returning in 1788 to an appointment as the first professor of natural history and botany at the College of Philadelphia (shortly to become the University of Pennsylvania); he held this position for the next 24 years.

In addition to writing *Elements of Botany,* the first such textbook published in the United States, Barton issued texts on such differing topics as rattlesnakes, American Indians, and medicine. A major influence on Barton's work was William Bartram, the United States's first native-born naturalist. Evidence of Barton's dependence on Bartram's botanical knowledge can be seen in the herbarium sheets from Barton's collection now at the Academy of Natural Sciences of Philadelphia; correspondence between them is now in the American Philosophical Society's library.

In May 1807 Lewis returned to Barton for help with the natural history volume of the expedition's JOURNALS, which

Dr. Benjamin Smith Barton is considered to be America's first academic botanist. He was one of several Philadelphia scholars to advise and instruct Meriwether Lewis in spring 1803. *(Library of Congress, Prints and Photographs Division [LC-USZ62-125768])*

he was then attempting to publish. At that time he returned a book he had borrowed from Barton and taken across the country, *History of Louisiana* by Antoine Simon Le Page du Pratz. This book, with an inscription by Lewis on the flyleaf, now resides in the Library Company in Philadelphia. Lewis also showed a delighted Barton many of the plant specimens he had collected west of the MISSISSIPPI RIVER.

In 1810, when NICHOLAS BIDDLE was preparing Lewis's and Clark's account of the expedition for publication, he asked Barton to prepare the scientific volume. Although the botanist began the project, he was unable to finish it due to ill health. He died five years later, and the volume he was to prepare was never completed, as a result of which many of the plants and animals discovered and named by Lewis were rediscovered and renamed by others.

Further Reading

Ambrose, Stephen E. *Undaunted Courage: Meriwether Lewis, Thomas Jefferson, and the Opening of the American West.* New York: Simon and Schuster, 1996.

Cutright, Paul Russell. *Contributions of Philadelphia to Lewis and Clark History.* Philadelphia: Philadelphia Chapter Lewis and Clark Trail Heritage Foundation, 2001. Also available on-line. URL: http://www.lewisandclarkphila.org/philadelphiacutrightconten.html. Updated on October 15, 2001.

———. *Lewis & Clark: Pioneering Naturalists.* Lincoln: University of Nebraska Press/Bison Books, 1989.

Bates, Frederick (1777–1825) *Louisiana Territory secretary*

One of the key players in the troubled life of MERIWETHER LEWIS following the expedition was Frederick Bates, secretary for the Louisiana Territory during and after Lewis's short term as governor. Born in Belmont, Virginia, Bates began to study law at an early age but never pursued it as a career. He worked for the Quartermaster's Department of the Army of the Northeast from 1795 to 1802 and then became postmaster in Detroit. In 1804 he was appointed receiver at the Detroit Land Office and consequently also set up a business as a storekeeper. During these years he switched his political allegiance from the Federalist Party to the Republican Party. His appointment as territorial judge and land commissioner in the territory of Michigan was viewed with popular approval, as was his service on Michigan's Supreme Court from 1805 to 1808.

In 1806 family friend and president THOMAS JEFFERSON appointed Frederick Bates secretary of Louisiana Territory, a position akin to that of lieutenant governor. He was also made recorder of land titles and appointed to a board of commissioners for land claims in the territory. Bates did not want the job of secretary but felt compelled to accept it, and he arrived in ST. LOUIS in spring 1807. About that same time, Meriwether Lewis was appointed governor of the territory, but aside from the occasional letter to Bates, he did not take up his duties until a full year later. This left Bates in the role of acting governor, a task that overwhelmed him initially, due to the petty quarrel-

ing, favor seeking, and profiteering among the city's inhabitants. As he waited for Lewis, he sent out frequent appeals, imploring the governor to come to St. Louis as soon as possible.

Lewis finally arrived in March 1808, but he soon found himself unequal to the demands of governing in a city filled with corrupt and unscrupulous men—a legacy of his predecessor as governor, General JAMES WILKINSON. The territory was still young, and laws and policies were not yet clearly defined. Lewis's handling of Indian affairs was less than exemplary, earning him rebukes from Secretary of War HENRY DEARBORN, and he entered into private speculation in the FUR TRADE. He also made enemies when he fired several public office holders, including some who were friends of Bates's. On top of this, he was drinking heavily, suffering from malaria (and possibly syphilis), and had become debt ridden, causing him to borrow frequently from others, including his friend WILLIAM CLARK and Bates.

By January 1809 Lewis and Bates were at odds with each other and engaging in public rows. Bates began to endorse the concerns expressed by others that Lewis, as governor of the territory, was guilty of a serious conflict of interest by promoting the fur trade, in which he had a commercial interest, rather than encouraging settlement, a matter of greater importance to Bates. In addition, the secretary's anger was aroused when Lewis appointed Clark rather than Bates as his agent while he was away from St. Louis. Hurt by this, jealous of Lewis's fame, and genuinely disturbed by the governor's increasingly erratic actions, Bates wrote to his brother, "[L]ike an overgrown baby, he [Lewis] begins to think that everybody about the House must regulate their conduct by his caprices." In the same letter he noted, "I lament the unpopularity of the Governor, [but] he has brought it on himself by harsh and mistaken measures. . . ."

Relations between Lewis and Bates went from bad to worse, and when Lewis heard rumors that Bates was planning to denounce him to the president, he confronted the secretary. Bates denied the rumors but then upbraided Lewis for appointing Clark as the governor's agent when by law that role belonged to him, Bates. Lewis subsequently ordered him to print the laws of the territory at the expense of the secretary's office, causing Bates to write to the secretary of the Treasury to complain and to ask for recompense. He thereafter continued to send complaints about Lewis's actions to Washington, while Lewis vehemently denied Bates's accusations of misconduct. There were other public scenes, but when Clark asked Bates to mend his relationship with Lewis, the secretary refused, saying, "He has *injured* me, and he must *undo* that injury."

In August 1809, shortly after Lewis left St. Louis on his ill-fated trip to Washington, Clement Penrose, a land commissioner, accused Bates of "barbarous conduct" toward Lewis, which in his view had contributed to the latter's mental breakdown. Like many others, Penrose believed that Bates coveted Lewis's position and that the secretary's political ambitions lay behind his attacks on the governor. Bates angrily denied the allegations and later expressed sympathy for Lewis in a letter.

Beacon Rock, once known as Castle Rock, has long been a landmark for travelers along the Columbia River. For Lewis and Clark, the sight of it meant that they were nearing the Pacific Ocean. *(Washington State Historical Society, Tacoma)*

Whether Bates's attitude toward Lewis was a factor in the latter's suicide is a matter of debate. Certainly it was his opinion that Lewis's military background did not equip him to handle the politics and machinations of the governor's office properly, and in this Bates was probably correct. After Lewis's death, Bates once again became acting governor of the territory, holding the position until 1812 and then regaining it for a brief period after the War of 1812 broke out. He then became secretary of Missouri Territory, and after Missouri became a state in 1820, he acted as recorder of land until 1824, when he was elected the state's governor. His term was cut short, however, when he died of pleurisy in August 1825.

Further Reading

Ambrose, Stephen E. *Undaunted Courage: Meriwether Lewis, Thomas Jefferson, and the Opening of the American West.* New York: Simon and Schuster, 1996.

Marshall, Thomas Maitland. *The Life and Papers of Frederick Bates.* St. Louis: Missouri Historical Society, 1926.

Beacon Rock (Castle Rock)

Beacon Rock, also known as Castle Rock, is a dark rock tower rising 848 feet from its base above the COLUMBIA RIVER. With a shape like a bell jar, it lies 150 miles upstream from the river's mouth and 35 miles east of present-day Vancouver, Washington. In early November 1805, as MERIWETHER LEWIS and WILLIAM CLARK scouted the area around the Cascades, they noted an absence of rapids in the waters near the rock. This meant that they were nearing the Columbia's estuary.

Beacon Rock is the core of a long-extinct volcano. It was created when floods through the COLUMBIA RIVER GORGE during the ice age eroded the mountain's softer material, leaving the tall mass of rock standing alone. For centuries the rock had been a landmark for Indian travelers on the river, signaling the beginning of tidewater from the ocean.

The rock marked the furthest point on the river reached by Lieutenant William Broughton on a scouting expedition for Captain GEORGE VANCOUVER in 1792. Lewis and Clark were carrying MAPS produced by Vancouver following his survey of the area and were thus able to identify geographic features that Broughton had named. It does not appear, however, that Broughton had recorded Beacon Rock, so Lewis and Clark are credited with giving it its current name. Nevertheless, in 1811, before their expedition JOURNALS were published, Alexander Ross (an employee of JOHN JACOB ASTOR) dubbed the rock "Inshoack Castle." It subsequently became known as Castle Rock.

In the early 20th century, businessman Henry J. Biddle bought the property around the rock and built a trail leading up to it. The area was later turned over to the state of Washington for use as a park and was improved by the Civilian Conservation Corps (CCC) during the Great Depression of the 1930s. In 1961 the U.S. Board of Geographic Names restored the name given to the rock by Lewis and Clark, and Castle Rock Park has been Beacon Rock State Park ever since.

Further Reading

Fifer, Barbara, and Vicky Soderberg. *Along the Trail with Lewis and Clark.* Great Falls, Mont.: Montana Magazine, 1998.

Schmidt, Thomas. *National Geographic Guide to the Lewis & Clark Trail.* Washington, D.C.: National Geographic, 1998.

bears

During the course of the expedition, the CORPS OF DISCOVERY encountered three types of bear: black, cinnamon, and grizzly. The black bear (*Ursus americanus*) was already familiar to them; the first was killed on June 7, 1804, near the mouth of Good Woman's River, Missouri. Between then and June 26, when the corps reached the KANSAS RIVER, a dozen more black bears were killed. After that, however, they saw no more of that species until GEORGE DROUILLARD spotted one on February 9, 1806, near FORT CLATSOP. There MERIWETHER LEWIS, who had commented on the absence of the bears from the upper waters of the MISSOURI RIVER, learned from local Indians that the bears "are aboundant but now in their holes [hibernating]."

The classification of the cinnamon bear as a separate species is still a matter of doubt today, as it was for the expedition. Lewis and Clark were puzzled by the different-colored fur of this animal, calling it variously a brown bear or a reddish brown black bear. They knew of the variations of color in black bears brought about by age, moulting, and other factors, but so many differences in color confused them. According to the NEZ PERCE INDIANS, Lewis wrote, "the uniform redish brown black bear etc. are a speceis distinct from our black bear and from the black bear of the Pacific coast." During their return journey the party killed several cinnamon bears in May and June 1806 along the CLEARWATER RIVER.

Long regarded as a subspecies of the black bear, the cinnamon bear was classified as a separate species (*Ursus cinnamomeus*) in 1893, then reclassified again as a subspecies, and then relabeled again as a full member of the black-bear family. Its current status is that of a subspecies (*Ursus americanus cinnamomum*).

In view of the respect and awe in which the Indians held the grizzly bear (*Ursus horribilis horribilis*), it seems strange that there is no record of Lewis and Clark hearing stories of its size and ferocity before they set out on their journey. Explorers in CANADA had certainly seen and described it 20 years earlier, but Lewis and Clark were the first to provide any detailed information about its size, characteristics, and habitat. They called it by different names—white, yellow, or grizzly bear—probably based on the fur color of the animal encountered.

Expedition members survived several close encounters with bears. This illustration from the 1810 edition of Patrick Gass's journal shows William Clark and his men shooting bears. *(Library of Congress, Prints and Photographs Division [LC-USZ62-19233])*

The first mention of the grizzly in the expedition's JOURNALS is Lewis's note of September 1, 1804, when they were near Bon Homme Island: "This clift [cliff] is called White Bear Clift, one of those animals having been killed in a whole in it." Tracks of a "white bear" were seen at the mouth of the Moreau River on October 7, 1804, but the first to be encountered was on October 20, 1804, near the mouth of the Heart River. Here WILLIAM CLARK recorded that the hunters wounded a white bear, whose tracks were "3 times as large as a man's tracks."

There is no record of any more grizzlies being seen that year. Lewis noted in April 1805 that the MANDAN INDIANS had, during the winter, given him "a very formidable account of the strength and ferocity of this anamal, which they never dare to attack but in parties of six, eight or ten persons. . . ." Their stories apparently did little but stir his curiosity, and he noted that "the men as well as ourselves are anxious to meet one of these bear."

Lewis got his wish two weeks later on April 29, 1805, when he and one of his men shot a grizzly. They found that the reaction of a grizzly to a bullet was not to run away but to charge his attacker. Lewis had to run 80 yards before he was able to reload and fire a second shot. A few days later, on May 5, Clark and Drouillard shot another grizzly; Lewis wrote that it was "a most tremendious looking anamal, and extremely hard to kill notwithstanding he had five balls through his lungs and five others in various parts, he swam more than half the distance across the river to a sand bar; and it was at least twenty minutes before he died; [he] made the most tremendous roaring from the moment he was shot." Clark estimated the bear's weight at 500 pounds, Lewis at 600 pounds. They measured the beast at 8'7¹/₂" from nose to hind feet and 5'10" around the breast. His talons were 4'³/₈" in length.

The corps encountered many more grizzlies on their journey up the Missouri River in 1805 and learned to be wary of them; PIERRE CRUZATTE, WILLIAM BRATTON, and George Drouillard all had close encounters with grizzlies. On June 28, at the GREAT FALLS, Lewis wrote, "The White Bear have become so troublesome to us that I do not think it prudent to send one man alone on an errand of any kind. . . . I have made the men sleep with their arms by them as usual for fear of accidents." No more were seen, however, between THREE FORKS and the COLUMBIA RIVER. On the return journey in 1806, six were killed on the CLEARWATER RIVER and 14 more in the valleys of the YELLOWSTONE RIVER and the Missouri. The journals indicate a total of some 43 grizzlies being killed. One that was not was a white grizzly that treed Private HUGH MCNEAL for several hours near the Great Falls on July 15.

Perhaps the most appropriate tribute Lewis paid to the grizzly is the comment he made on May 6, 1805, when he and Clark had each killed one. Less than a month after he had recorded the anxiety of his men to meet one, when they saw a grizzly in the river ahead of them, he noted dryly that there was little eagerness to catch up with it: "I find the curiossity of our party is pretty well satisfied with rispect to this anamal."

Further Reading

Burroughs, Raymond Darwin, ed. *The Natural History of the Lewis and Clark Expedition.* East Lansing: Michigan State University Press, 1995.

Cutright, Paul Russell. *Lewis & Clark: Pioneering Naturalists.* Lincoln: University of Nebraska Press/Bison Books, 1989.

Furtwangler, Albert. *Acts of Discovery: Visions of America in the Lewis and Clark Journals.* Urbana: University of Illinois Press, 1993.

Hawke, David Freeman. *Those Tremendous Mountains: The Story of the Lewis and Clark Expedition.* New York: W. W. Norton & Company, 1998.

McNamee, Thomas. *The Grizzly Bear.* New York: Viking Penguin, 1990.

Schullery, Paul. *Lewis and Clark Among the Grizzlies: Legend and Legacy in the American West.* Guilford, Conn.: Globe Pequot Press, 2002.

Washington State University. "Lewis and Clark Among the Indians of the Pacific Northwest. Excerpts from the Journals of the Expedition of the Corps of Discovery: Flora and Fauna (recorded at Fort Clatsop)." Available on-line. URL: http://www.libarts.wsu.edu/history/Lewis_Clark/LCEXP_Flor.html. Downloaded on May 20, 2001.

Beaverhead River

The upper portion of what MERIWETHER LEWIS named Jefferson's River (now the JEFFERSON RIVER), today's Beaverhead River runs southwest from Twin Bridges, Montana, to the Clark Canyon Reservoir. Approximately 15 miles southwest of Twin Bridges is the massive rocky outcrop known as BEAVERHEAD ROCK, after which the river is named.

By the end of July 1805, the CORPS OF DISCOVERY had made their way past the GREAT FALLS of the MISSOURI RIVER and were approaching the ROCKY MOUNTAINS. They knew that they would soon have to leave the river and were anxious to find the SHOSHONE INDIANS, from whom they hoped to obtain HORSES to cross the mountains. The expedition arrived at THREE FORKS and, believing that they had reached the end of the Missouri, Lewis named the three tributary rivers Gallitin's, Maddison's, and Jefferson's rivers.

On July 30 the corps set off up the Jefferson, Lewis and three men going ahead on foot to look for the Shoshone while Clark and the remainder continued with the laborious task of paddling or dragging the CANOES around the river's twists and bends. On August 4 Lewis arrived at another fork in the river, just north of today's Twin Bridges. Deciding correctly that the left-hand fork was the main stream, he left a note on a stick for Clark and went on. The stick was gone when Clark arrived (a beaver had probably taken it), and he and his party traveled up the right fork, which Lewis had named the WISDOM RIVER (today's Big Hole River). Luckily, after a day they met GEORGE DROUILLARD, who was out HUNTING and told them of their mistake. They turned back and reunited with Lewis at the river junction, the spot where today the Jefferson River becomes the Beaverhead River.

Sacagawea's recognition of Beaverhead Rock reassured the expedition that they were nearing Shoshone country. *(Montana Historical Society, Helena)*

Tired and depressed as they were, the corps were encouraged by SACAGAWEA's recognition of Beaverhead Rock in the distance. The following morning, Lewis and three men set off again on foot up the Beaverhead, determined to find the Shoshone, while Clark and the remainder continued to bring the canoes up the narrow meandering river. After two days, Lewis reached the point where the Beaverhead splits into two streams, Horse Prairie Creek and Red Rock River. Neither was navigable, so Lewis left another note for Clark telling him to camp at the junction until he (Lewis) returned. Clark, however, had not yet arrived to see the note by the time Lewis finally met the Shoshone and returned to the spot with Chief CAMEAHWAIT. After a tense day's wait, Clark arrived on August 17, joining Lewis and the Shoshone at CAMP FORTUNATE, just below the river's forks. Here, in one of the COINCIDENCES AND CHANCE ON THE EXPEDITION, Sacagawea had an unexpected and joyful reunion with her brother Cameahwait. Lewis described the scene in the JOURNALS: "Capt. Clark arrived with the Interpreter Charbono, and the Indian woman, who proved to be a sister of the Chief Cameahwait. The meeting of those two people was really affecting."

It was to be nearly a year before the explorers came back to the Beaverhead River. On July 9, 1806, Clark and his party rode back to Camp Fortunate, retrieved the canoes they had hidden there, and set off on their long journey home. Camp Fortunate and the Beaverhead River now lie under the Clark Canyon Reservoir, but they will always be remembered as the spot where Sacagawea was reunited with her brother.

Further Reading

Fifer, Barbara, and Vicky Soderberg. *Along the Trail with Lewis and Clark.* Great Falls, Mont.: Montana Magazine, 1998.

Moulton, Gary E., ed. *Atlas of the Lewis and Clark Expedition.* Revised ed. Lincoln: University of Nebraska Press, 1999.

Beaverhead Rock

In the first week of August 1805, the CORPS OF DISCOVERY was making slow, agonized progress against the swift current of the BEAVERHEAD RIVER. WILLIAM CLARK was hardly able to walk due to a painful growth on his ankle, GEORGE DROUILLARD had suffered a bad fall, and the party had still seen no sign of the SHOSHONE INDIANS on whose horses they relied for crossing the ROCKY MOUNTAINS.

On August 8, however, SACAGAWEA pointed out a large, rocky outcrop ahead of them. It was Beaverhead Rock, north of present-day Dillon, Montana. That day Lewis wrote, "The Indian woman recognized the point of a high plain . . . which she informed us was not very distant from the summer retreat of her nation on a river beyond the mountains which runs to the west. This hill she says her nation called the beaver's head from a conceived resemblance of it's figure to the head of that animal. She assures us that we shall either find her people on this river or on the river immediately west of it's source; from which it's present size cannot be very distant." Encouraged by this, Lewis took three men and set out on foot across country, and two days later they met a Shoshone, the first Indian they had seen in four months.

Further Reading

Ambrose, Stephen E. *Undaunted Courage: Meriwether Lewis, Thomas Jefferson, and the Opening of the American West.* New York: Simon and Schuster, 1996.

Moulton, Gary E., ed. *Atlas of the Lewis and Clark Expedition.* Revised ed. Lincoln: University of Nebraska Press, 1999.

Ronda, James P. *Lewis and Clark among the Indians.* Lincoln: University of Nebraska Press, 1984.

beavers

The huge market for beaver pelts was one of the main incentives behind the exploration and settlement of the west. A European hunger for fur for clothing, especially hats, had already resulted in the extinction of the beaver in western Europe by the late 1500s, and the animal was nearing extinction in Scandinavia and Russia. But at the time of the Lewis and Clark Expedition, beavers ranged over most of North America, and the abundance of the animal in the Pacific Northwest was attracting European trappers and traders to that area. As a result, the commercial benefits to staking a claim in the OREGON TERRITORY lay behind President THOMAS JEFFERSON's decision to send an expedition into the West.

The largest rodent in North America, an adult beaver can grow up to four feet long and weigh more than 60 pounds. Its body fur—dark brown on the back and sides, with a light brown on its belly and chest—is virtually waterproof, providing protection and buoyancy during the time the animal spends underwater. Its hind legs are large with fully webbed feet to propel it through the water, and its flat, hairless tail resembles the end of a canoe paddle. Its primary food is bark, in particular that of young twigs and the new growth of wood found between the outer bark and the wood of tree branches and trunks. It also eats various water plants as well as CORN and other crops when obtainable.

Beavers are found in watery areas—mostly rivers, streams, small lakes, and marshes—and they dig dens and tunnels on the shores and banks. Master engineers, they are notorious for building dams across streams and river channels, within which they often create large, dome-shaped lodges out of tree limbs and other debris. The work of beavers can change the ecology

Beavers utilize every form of timber to build dams like this one—including, on one occasion, a stick on which Lewis had left a note for Clark at a fork of the Jefferson River. *(Library of Congress, Prints and Photographs Division [LC-D418-78117])*

of an area by diverting water and creating ponds and sometimes lakes.

Although they would later be severely threatened by the FUR TRADE, beavers were plentiful in many of the regions through which the CORPS OF DISCOVERY passed. In some areas they were so numerous that WILLIAM CLARK reported being kept awake at night by the loud slapping of their tails on the water. Yet they provided a good source of FOOD; roasted beaver tail was a particularly tasty treat for many of the men. The animal was also a subject of study for the expedition's amateur naturalist, MERIWETHER LEWIS, who is credited with writing the first detailed, scientific description of the mountain beaver.

An important part of the Lewis and Clark mission was to persuade the Indian nations they met to enter into a trading partnership with merchants in ST. LOUIS. GREAT BRITAIN was already enjoying a great advantage in the growing fur trade; the BLACKFEET INDIANS were among those nations that had been trading with the Canadian-based HUDSON'S BAY COMPANY and NORTH WEST COMPANY for many years, exchanging the pelts of beavers and WOLVES for alcohol, guns, and ammunition.

In part through the groundwork laid by the expedition and in part due to a spirit of adventure and competition, the trade in beaver pelts had begun to attract American trappers even before the Corps of Discovery had returned from the West; they became the first of the legendary MOUNTAIN MEN. Two such adventurers were Joseph Dickson and Forrest Hancock, who accompanied the corps part of the way on their return trip in 1806 and subsequently invited Private JOHN COLTER to go to Yellowstone with them to trap beaver. Colter thus became the first—but not the last—member of the corps to enter the beaver fur trade following the expedition. Unfortunately, subsequent commercial trapping and human encroachment nearly decimated the beaver population, particularly in the eastern and southern United States.

Further Reading

Beavers: Wetland and Wild Life. "The Beaver (Castor Canadensis)." Available on-line. URL: http://www.beaversww.org/beaver.html. Downloaded on December 10, 2001.

Calverly, Dorthea. "The Beaver: Foundation of the Fur Trade." Available on-line. URL: http://www.calverley.dawson-creek.bc.ca/Part%2002%20-%20Fur%20Trade/2-001.html. Downloaded on December 10, 2001.

Cutright, Paul Russell. *Lewis & Clark: Pioneering Naturalists.* Lincoln: University of Nebraska Press/Bison Books, 1989.

Moulton, Gary E., ed. *The Journals of the Lewis and Clark Expedition.* 13 vols. Lincoln: University of Nebraska Press, 1983–2001.

Rich, E. E. *The Fur Trade and the Northwest to 1857.* Toronto: McClelland and Stewart, 1967.

Washington State University. "Lewis and Clark Among the Indians of the Pacific Northwest. Excerpts from the Journals of the Expedition of the Corps of Discovery: Flora and Fauna (recorded at Fort Clatsop)." Available on-line. URL: http://www.libarts.wsu.edu/history/Lewis_Clark/LCEXP_Flor.html. Downloaded on May 20, 2001.

Belt Creek   See PORTAGE CREEK.

Biddle, Nicholas (1786–1844) *financier, editor*

The multifaceted Nicholas Biddle was the first to edit the expedition JOURNALS of Lewis and Clark. He later became a noted financier.

Born in PHILADELPHIA, Biddle was a prodigy who had entered the University of Pennsylvania at age 10 and graduated from the College of New Jersey (later Princeton) at age 15. He was admitted to the bar in 1809 and served in the Pennsylvania legislature in 1810–11. He also edited and contributed to *Port Folio,* the leading American literary periodical.

Following the return of the Lewis and Clark Expedition, MERIWETHER LEWIS tried but failed to publish his and WILLIAM CLARK's journals. After Lewis died in 1809, Clark asked Biddle to complete the task. Both Clark and GEORGE SHANNON helped with the work, and in the process Biddle learned that Clark had never received his captain's commission. The editor was asked, however, not to include that fact in the book, which combined notes, sections of the journal, and interviews with Clark into a narrative form. Eventually the overworked Biddle turned the manuscript over to PAUL ALLEN to complete the editing; it is Allen's name that appears on the title page, although the book is referred to as the Biddle edition. After numerous attempts to find a publisher, Biddle finally placed the manuscript with Bradford and Inskeep of Philadelphia, which went bankrupt during its printing of the book. Nevertheless, *The History of the Expedition Under the Commands of Lewis and Clark* was finally published in 1814. Biddle's edition was faithful to the original journals, but with innumerable spelling corrections that many scholars deplored.

Biddle had asked Dr. BENJAMIN SMITH BARTON to prepare the scientific volume of the journals, but Barton was unable to finish the task due to ill health. Consequently, most of Lewis's notes on plants and animals found during the expedition were omitted from the Biddle edition. From 1814 to 1904, this was the only published account of the expedition based directly on the journals of Meriwether Lewis and William Clark. As a result, many species identified and named by Lewis were rediscovered and renamed by others.

In 1893 Elliott Coues published a reprint of Biddle's work that included footnotes on geography, plants, animals, and birds. In 1904, however, the book was finally superseded by Reuben Gold Thwaites's superior edition, which included the complete journals of Lewis and Clark as well as those of CHARLES FLOYD and JOSEPH WHITEHOUSE.

Later in life Biddle became president of the Bank of the United States and of Girard College. He is famous in part for his political battle with President Andrew Jackson over the recharter of the bank, which Jackson had vetoed in the belief that the national bank had become too powerful. Consequently, the bank's charter was not renewed, and it went out of business in 1841. Biddle, however, had already resigned two years previously and retired to his estate in Delaware, where he lived for the remainder of his life.

Further Reading

Barth, Gunther. "Timeless Journals: Reading Lewis and Clark with Nicholas Biddle's Help." *Pacific Historical Review* 63, no. 4 (1994): 499–519.

Business Leader Profiles for Students. "Nicholas Biddle." Gale Research, 1999. Available on-line. URL: http://online.valencia.cc.fl.us/ckillinger/AMH2010/AMH2010.Biddlebio2.htm. Downloaded on January 10, 2002.

Furtwangler, Albert. *Acts of Discovery: Visions of America in the Lewis and Clark Journals.* Urbana: University of Illinois Press, 1993.

Govan, Thomas Payne. *Nicholas Biddle: Nationalist and Public Banker, 1786–1844.* Chicago: University of Chicago Press, 1959.

Lewis, Meriwether, and William Clark. *History of the Expedition under the Command of Captains Lewis and Clark, to the Sources of the Missouri, thence across the Rocky Mountains and down the River Columbia to the Pacific Ocean: Performed during the Years 1804–5–6 by Order of the Government of the United States.* Prepared for the press by Paul Allen; in two volumes. Philadelphia: Bradford and Inskeep; New York: Abm. H. Inskeep, 1814. Reprints, New Amsterdam Book Company, New York, 1902; Lippincott, Philadelphia, 1961.

Big Blackfoot River (Blackfoot River, River of the Road to Buffalo)

On July 3, 1806, on their return journey from the COLUMBIA RIVER, the CORPS OF DISCOVERY was at TRAVELERS' REST, just south of present-day Missoula, Montana. The party had camped here for some days while Captains MERIWETHER LEWIS and WILLIAM CLARK worked out the plan for the next stage of their journey and the routes they would take. As they had discussed at FORT CLATSOP, the expedition was to split into two. Lewis and a party of nine men would travel northeast to the GREAT FALLS of the Missouri and then turn north to explore the MARIAS RIVER before returning to the MISSOURI RIVER. Clark would travel south, cross the mountains, and then travel down the YELLOWSTONE RIVER, meeting Lewis at the junction of the Yellowstone and Missouri, some 500 miles to the east.

The two captains parted on the morning of July 3. While Clark went south, following the BITTERROOT RIVER upstream, Lewis's party and their NEZ PERCE guides went north down the river to what is now Missoula, Montana. The following day, July 4, the Indians left them, and Lewis continued east for five miles until he reached the Big Blackfoot River, now just the Blackfoot River and then called by the Nez Perce River of the Road to Buffalo.

Because of the signs of recent Indian tracks, Lewis and his party took precautions against attack, the captain noting, "much on our guard both day and night." However, the two-day journey up the river proved uneventful, and Lewis wrote that there was "much sign of beaver in this extensive bottom." On July 7 they left the river and turned up the hillside to LEWIS AND CLARK PASS, which took them down into the valley of the upper Missouri River.

Further Reading

Ambrose, Stephen E. *Undaunted Courage: Meriwether Lewis, Thomas Jefferson, and the Opening of the American West.* New York: Simon and Schuster, 1996.

Moulton, Gary E., ed. *Atlas of the Lewis and Clark Expedition.* Revised ed. Lincoln: University of Nebraska Press, 1999.

Schmidt, Thomas. *National Geographic Guide to the Lewis & Clark Trail.* Washington, D.C.: National Geographic, 1998.

Big Hole River   See WISDOM RIVER.

bighorn sheep   See SHEEP.

Big Horse (unknown–unknown) *Missouri chief*

On August 3, 1804, MERIWETHER LEWIS and WILLIAM CLARK held their first meeting with a delegation of OTOE (Oto) and MISSOURI INDIANS at COUNCIL BLUFF. Little of consequence was achieved, as the two primary chiefs for each nation—LITTLE THIEF of the Otoe and Big Horse of the Missouri—were away hunting. Determined to meet these chiefs, the captains sent GEORGE DROUILLARD and a small party out to find them. Meanwhile, the expedition continued up the MISSOURI RIVER.

On August 18 the search party returned, having successfully completed their mission of finding both the two chiefs and also a deserter, MOSES REED. After Reed was tried and punished for his offense, Lewis and Clark held an informal meeting with Big Horse and Little Thief. While the Otoe and Missouri were related nations who shared a common enemy, the OMAHA INDIANS, they had sent word ahead that they wished to make peace with the Omaha. However, when they discussed it with Lewis and Clark, they aired a list of grievances and explained the complexities of intertribal warfare. That evening the explorers shared whiskey with the Indians, and everybody danced to celebrate Lewis's birthday.

The following day a formal council was held with Big Horse, Little Thief, and a number of other lesser chiefs. It did not go well for Lewis and Clark. To their amazement, Big Horse arrived naked in an attempt to demonstrate his poverty. In his response to Lewis's speech, he referred to his nakedness and the need to obtain quality goods from the white traders, a point that Little Thief also emphasized. Yet Big Horse seemed interested not so much in TRADE as in whiskey, and he made obtaining it a condition of keeping his warriors from attacking the Omaha and Pawnee—in essence, bartering peace for ALCOHOL.

Adding to the explorers' problems was the offense that they had given Big Horse by previously giving superior gifts to Little Thief. They attempted to make up for it by giving the Missouri chief a better medal, but this only caused the lesser chiefs to complain of the quality of the gifts they had received. Unable to satisfy all or any of the chiefs, Lewis and Clark left the Missouri and Otoe without a real commitment for either trade or peace—a problem they would face again when they met other Indian nations and other chiefs like Big Horse.

Further Reading

Ronda, James P. *Lewis and Clark among the Indians.* Lincoln: University of Nebraska Press, 1984.

Big White (Sheheke) (unknown–1832) *Mandan chief*

The story of MANDAN chief Big White, or Sheheke, is considered to be by many one of the sadder outcomes of the Lewis and Clark Expedition. As a result of his connection to the CORPS OF DISCOVERY, several lives were lost, MERIWETHER LEWIS's reputation was damaged, and Big White himself became caught between the worlds of the white men and his own nation—all because he tried to assist Lewis and WILLIAM CLARK in their peacemaking and trade-building efforts.

Big White was the fat, light-skinned, and gregarious chief of Matootonha (also called Matutonka or Mitutanka), the Mandan village closest to FORT MANDAN; the location of the fort was chosen in part due to his insistence that the Mandan would be better winter neighbors for the soldiers than the HIDATSA INDIANS. The other village, Rooptahee, was led by BLACK CAT, on whom the captains initially focused their diplomatic efforts, believing him to be more powerful and useful than Big White. Big White, however, was hospitable and accommodating to the expedition as well as a frequent visitor to the fort. When a small party of corps members were attacked by some TETON LAKOTA (Teton Sioux) in February 1806, he responded to a call for help by supplying some warriors and two guns—all he could spare, since most of his village were out hunting.

Despite Big White's friendliness, it was Black Cat the captains wanted to send to Washington to meet THOMAS JEFFERSON and discuss future trading prospects with the United States. When they returned to the Mandan villages in August 1806, they tried to tempt him with promises of rich gifts and rewards and offered assurances of a quick and safe return. But Black Cat refused to go, unconvinced the U.S. government could guarantee his safety in getting past the Teton Lakota.

After another Mandan chief, Little Raven, agreed to make the trip and then changed his mind, the captains turned their attention to Big White. Initially he too refused to do it, partly out of fear of the Sioux and partly out of jealousy over the favorable treatment Little Raven had received. Finally, however, RENÉ JESSAUME convinced him to go, as long as members of his family and Jessaume went as well. It was not what Lewis and Clark wanted, but they were desperate to have a Mandan chief go to Washington, so they agreed.

On August 17 they left the Mandan villages and proceeded downriver, arriving at the villages of the ARIKARA INDIANS on August 21. Here Lewis and Clark held a council with Arikara and CHEYENNE INDIANS, still hoping to forge a peace among Indian nations of the upper Missouri. Big White did his part, offering Mandan TOBACCO for the smoking ceremony, but his presence did not smooth matters. There was too much rancor between the Mandan and the Arikara, and on August 22 he fell into a vitriolic argument with Chief One Arm, forcing Clark to

When Mandan chief Big White agreed to go to Washington, Clark bought him white men's clothing to wear. This George Catlin lithograph shows a similar costume change made by Assiniboine chief Wi-Jun-Jon (or Pigeon's Egg Head), who visited Washington about 1837. *(Library of Congress, Prints and Photographs Division [LC-USZC2-3313])*

intervene. Later both chiefs again pledged to make peace, but it was clear that it would not be readily kept.

Just before the expedition arrived back at ST. LOUIS, Clark took Big White to Fort Bellefontaine, where he bought clothing and other accoutrements. It was his first taste of how the white men lived; there was plenty more to come, first in St. Louis and then in Washington. On December 31, 1806, Big White and his Mandan delegation met President Jefferson. They stayed in Washington for several weeks, during which time the captains began to face the problem of how to get the Mandan back to their people. It had initially seemed easy enough to do, but now there were not just the Sioux to deal with on the Missouri. The Arikara, a chief of whose had died while on a visit to Washington, had also become hostile to the Americans. Getting Big White and his family back to their people had suddenly become a perilous mission.

By March 1807, shortly before his return to St. Louis, Clark had been given the authorization and funds to organize an expedition to escort the Mandan home. NATHANIEL PRYOR, now an ensign, was selected to lead the party, which also included GEORGE SHANNON. Along their way on the Missouri, they were attacked and turned back by the Arikara; three lives were lost, several were wounded, and Shannon's leg was hurt so badly it had to be amputated. Big White and his family were forced to remain in St. Louis until another solution could be found. Unfortunately his wife and son died during this period.

In 1808 the St. Louis Missouri Fur Company was formed, with Lewis and Clark among its partners. One of the company's first objectives was to assemble a large party to return the Mandan to the upper Missouri. From Washington, Jefferson sent messages castigating Lewis for not already having accomplished Big White's safe return. Finally, in 1809, with a government-supplied military escort and at a cost of $20,000, an expedition led by PIERRE CHOUTEAU succeeded where Pryor's 1807 party had failed.

On August 21, 1809, Big White arrived home at his village, slightly more than three years after he had left it. If he expected praise and adulation from his people, he did not get it. He had been away too long, and the stories he told of his travels to marvelous cities and of adventures among the whites were all met with disbelief. His prestige ruined, his wife and son dead, it was reported that he spent the rest of his life hoping to return to white civilization. One account indicates that he did so in 1812 but was killed when he returned upriver. Most sources, however, maintain that he remained in his village, where he was killed by Sioux raiders in 1832.

Further Reading

Ambrose, Stephen E. *Undaunted Courage: Meriwether Lewis, Thomas Jefferson, and the Opening of the American West.* New York: Simon and Schuster, 1996.

Foley, William E., and Charles David Rice. "The Return of the Mandan Chief." *Montana: The Magazine of Western History* 29, no. 3 (1979): 2–15.

Lewis & Clark in North Dakota. "Personal Profiles: Profile of Three Chiefs." Available on-line. URL: http://www.ndlewisandclark. com/profiles.html. Downloaded on February 2, 2002.

Ronda, James P. *Lewis and Clark among the Indians.* Lincoln: University of Nebraska Press, 1984.

birds, new species

In common with the majority of their zoological discoveries, MERIWETHER LEWIS and WILLIAM CLARK made most of their finds of birds new to science as they went further west; ornithologists of the time were already familiar with the birds that the CORPS OF DISCOVERY saw in the lower MISSOURI RIVER valley. Yet as with so many of their scientific and geographical discoveries, the credit has been given to others because of the long delay in the publication of the expedition's JOURNALS.

Although Lewis and Clark noted and accurately described more than 50 new species of birds, they tended to compare them to birds with which they were already familiar. While Lewis would give an exhaustive description of every bird he was able to examine, he often assumed that variations of marking or coloring were caused by seasonal variations or moulting.

Because of the painstaking detail he provided, however, subsequent writers have been able to identify the new species he noted so carefully.

In addition to CRANES, CURLEWS, GEESE, GROUSE, and GULLS, the two captains noted new varieties of the tern, magpie, poor-will, horned owl, jay, cormorant, crow, and quail. They noted their first new species, the least tern, on August 5, 1804, in present-day Washington County, Nebraska; and their last, Foster's tern, just above the mouth of the YELLOWSTONE RIVER on August 7, 1806.

Lewis had a gift for describing birds. His note on the least tern is more than 600 words and includes measurements of the various feathers, a description of its habits and habitat, its weight, the size and position of the eyes in its head, and the number of joints in its wing. His ending is equally detailed though less scientific: "this bird is very noysey when flying which it dose extreemly swift the motion of the wing is much like that of Kildee it has two notes like the squaking of a small pig only on reather a higher kee, and the other kit'-tee'-kit'-tee'—as near as letters can express the sound. "The beak of the female is black and the black and quaker colour of the male in her is yellowish brown mixed with dove colour."

Lewis also wrote a long and detailed description of a magpie that he had killed on September 16, 1804. Four live magpies were included in the shipment he sent back to Washington from FORT MANDAN in April 1805. Only one, however, survived the trip, having killed the other three en route.

While Lewis had hoped to bring back specimens of each new animal, bird, and plant found, many of them had to be left in CACHES along the journey and were destroyed by dampness or were eaten by INSECTS. Many, however, were brought back in September 1806, and Lewis asked the artist ALEXANDER WILSON to make drawings of the bird specimens. It is known that Wilson drew three: the Louisiana tanager, Lewis's woodpecker, and Clark's nutcracker. By naming the last two, the artist ensured credit for their discovery was properly attributed.

The original sketches Wilson made are to be seen at the Academy of Natural Sciences of PHILADELPHIA. The dead birds themselves passed through various hands, and it is now believed that of all the zoological specimens that Lewis and Clark brought back, only three still exist: an elk horn now at MONTICELLO; a mountain goat horn housed in the Filson Club, Louisville, Kentucky; and the sole remaining bird skin at Harvard's Museum of Comparative Zoology. Appropriately, it is the skin of Lewis's woodpecker, which he brought back 200 years ago.

Further Reading

Burroughs, Raymond Darwin, ed. *The Natural History of the Lewis and Clark Expedition.* East Lansing: Michigan State University Press, 1995.

Cutright, Paul Russell. *Lewis & Clark: Pioneering Naturalists.* Lincoln: University of Nebraska Press/Bison Books, 1989.

Furtwangler, Albert. *Acts of Discovery: Visions of America in the Lewis and Clark Journals.* Urbana: University of Illinois Press, 1993.

Reid, Russell, and Clell G. Gannon. "Birds and Mammals Observed by Lewis & Clark in North Dakota." *North Dakota History* 66, no. 2 (1999): 2–14. Jamestown, N.Dak.: Northern Prairie Wildlife Research Center Home Page. Also available on-line URL: http://www.npwrc.usgs.gov/resource/2000/bmam/bmam. htm. Downloaded on May 20, 2001.

Walcheck, K. C. "Birds Observed by Lewis and Clark in Montana, 1805–06." *Proceedings of the Montana Academy of Science* 29 (1969) 13–29.

bison   See BUFFALO.

bitterroot   (*Lewisia rediviva*)

The bitterroot, or rockrose, grows along rocky ridges and in thin soils of basalt flats and remains partially hidden until flowers are produced. The plant gives its name to the BITTERROOT MOUNTAINS and BITTERROOT RIVER. In honor of MERIWETHER LEWIS, German botanist FREDERICK PURSH (who catalogued many of the plant specimens brought back from the expedition) named the plant *Lewisia rediviva*.

Bitterroot was generally eaten after being peeled and boiled. During the expedition's time with the Shoshone Indians, Chief CAMEAHWAIT offered the roots to the travelers, who found it unappealing, with Lewis writing that it was "naucious to my palate."

On their return journey, on July 1, 1806, Lewis collected several specimens of the perennial bitterroot with its rose-colored flowers. He carried these by horse, boat, and stagecoach more than 3,000 miles back to PHILADELPHIA. These same plants can be seen today at the Academy of Natural Sciences in Philadelphia.

The bitterroot is now the state plant of Montana.

See also ARTIFACTS AND SPECIMENS.

Further Reading

Cutright, Paul Russell. *Lewis & Clark: Pioneering Naturalists*. Lincoln: University of Nebraska Press/Bison Books, 1989.

Bitterroot Mountains

The Bitterroot Mountains, crossed by Lewis and Clark in 1805 and 1806, are part of the ROCKY MOUNTAINS in western North America. With their steep-walled, rocky canyons, the Bitterroots are among the most impenetrable peaks in North America. The range has been referred to as "Montana's Alps."

The Rocky Mountains are generally described as having four distinct sections—the Southern, Central, Northern, and Canadian Rockies. The Bitterroot Range is in the Northern Rockies, which cover areas of northern Idaho, northeastern Washington, and western Montana. The main range runs from northwest to southeast on the Idaho-Montana state line. Mount Garfield is the highest peak at 10,961 feet.

The CORPS OF DISCOVERY spent nearly a month in and along the Bitterroot Range on its way west. The corps began its westward crossing early in September 1805. Guided by a SHOSHONE Indian named OLD TOBY, the corps went up the north fork of the SALMON RIVER and then crossed over the LOST TRAIL PASS into the Bitterroot valley, where, at what is now ROSS'S HOLE, they encountered a band of FLATHEAD INDIANS (Salish). As they proceeded up the BITTERROOT RIVER, the mountains on their left loomed large and threatening—"the most terrible mountains that I ever beheld," wrote Sergeant PATRICK GASS.

On September 9 at the mouth of Lolo Creek, near the north end of the valley, the corps made camp near the present town of Lolo, Montana; they named the site TRAVELERS' REST. Here they met three Indians (most likely NEZ PERCE) who assured them that the LOLO TRAIL to which Old Toby was leading them was passable and could be crossed in about five days. However, once the expedition set out on the trail, they found that it was blocked by fallen timber and freshly fallen snow, making it impassable in some areas. Confused, Old Toby lost his bearings, and the corps wandered, lost, for two days before finding the right path again. As the days passed, the cold, snow, hazardous terrain, and lack of FOOD plunged the party into despair. The absence of wild game forced the explorers to eat three of their HORSES. One week into the crossing, Lewis wrote, "I find myself growing weak for the want of food and most of the men complain of a similar deficiency, and have fallen off very much." Clark, meanwhile, wrote, "I have been wet and as cold in every part as I ever was in my life."

Nearing starvation on the 11th day, the corps finally descended the mountain's lower slopes and reached WEIPPE PRAIRIE. There they met a band of Nez Perce Indians, who welcomed and fed them. The crossing of the Bitterroots in 1805 was the most hazardous and arduous part of the expedition. They had to delay their return crossing in June 1806 because, as the Nez Perce had warned them, the trail was impassable with snow. They waited in the foothills for more than a week before trying again with INDIAN GUIDES, this time successfully.

At the time of the expedition, the Bitterroot Mountains were inhabited by Nez Perce, Shoshone, and Flathead Indians. In the 100 years following Lewis and Clark's historic crossing, non-Indian settlement brought significant changes, most notably after the discovery of gold in the 1860s and the beginning of logging in the 1880s. The area became national forestland when the Forest Service was created in 1907. The Bitterroot National Forest now covers about 1.6 million acres and is drained by the Selway, CLEARWATER, Bitterroot, and other rivers. Just under half of the forest is designated wilderness. Herds of ELK and DEER roam the meadows and lowlands, while moose and BEAVER live in the wetlands. There are also black bear and bighorn SHEEP. In some places in the Bitterroots, wolves are beginning to return, but the grizzly BEARS and lynx encountered by Lewis and Clark are seldom seen. It is still one of the most sparsely populated areas in the United States, and mountain tracks are still closed by snow until June.

Further Reading

Discovery Writers. *Lewis & Clark in the Bitterroot.* Stevensville, Mont.: Stoneydale Press Publishing Co., 1999.

Hawke, David Freeman. *Those Tremendous Mountains: The Story of the Lewis and Clark Expedition.* New York: W. W. Norton & Company, 1998.

Space, Ralph S. *The Lolo Trail: A History and a Guide to the Trail of Lewis and Clark.* 2d ed. Missoula: Historic Montana Publications, 2001.

Bitterroot River (Clark's River)

The Bitterroot River rises in southwest Montana and flows in a northerly direction for about 120 miles before joining the Clark Fork River near Missoula. The CORPS OF DISCOVERY literally stumbled onto the Bitterroot River on September 4, 1805. Guided by the SHOSHONE Indian known to MERIWETHER LEWIS and WILLIAM CLARK as OLD TOBY, they had traversed the LOST TRAIL PASS the previous day. Now, in fresh, heavy snow, the party fell down a steep embankment and landed near the river, which Lewis proceeded to name after Clark.

Besides the river, at what is now ROSS'S HOLE, the corps met 400 Salish, or FLATHEAD INDIANS. Old Toby did not speak their language, but his tribe were allies of the Flathead, who proceeded to help the corps by sharing their limited winter stock of roots and berries. They also exchanged several good HORSES for the worn-out specimens the explorers had acquired from the Shoshone.

After resting for two days with the Flathead, the expedition marched northward along the river, following it for three days. It is not clear why Lewis and Clark chose not to build CANOES for this part of the journey, although most likely they were anxious not to lose any more time than they already had.

Coming up the west bank of the Bitterroot, the corps made camp on September 9 at an old Indian campground at the confluence of Lolo Creek. Lewis and Clark named the camp TRAVELERS' REST, and they spent the next few days getting equipment ready for their crossing of the BITTERROOT MOUNTAINS.

Old Toby advised the captains that, although he believed the Bitterroot River might take them eventually to the COLUMBIA RIVER and the western ocean, they should instead turn westward up Lolo Creek and cross the mountains by way of the LOLO TRAIL. He said that it was the shortest route to the PACIFIC OCEAN and that it was too late in the fall to go any farther northward.

On a more disturbing note for Lewis and Clark, Toby informed them that at this point they were only four days from the MISSOURI RIVER and the GREAT FALLS. If they continued down the Bitterroot about nine miles to what is now called Clark's Fork, they could find their way back eastward across the mountains in a matter of days. The route the expedition had followed along the Missouri had taken them 53 days from the Great Falls, a significant and frustrating delay.

After wintering on the Pacific, the corps returned to Travelers' Rest on the Bitterroot River on July 3, 1806. It was here that Lewis and Clark decided to divide into two parties to explore more of the surrounding country and look for an easier pass over the CONTINENTAL DIVIDE.

Years after the expedition, in 1841, a Roman Catholic mission established in the area began to introduce agriculture. Since then there has been a slow growth in population, and today the river is best known for its excellent fishing.

Further Reading

Discovery Writers. *Lewis & Clark in the Bitterroot.* Stevensville, Mont.: Stoneydale Press Publishing Co., 1998.

Moulton, Gary E., ed. *Atlas of the Lewis and Clark Expedition.* Revised ed. Lincoln: University of Nebraska Press, 1999.

National Geographic Atlas of Natural America. Washington, D.C.: National Geographic Society, 2000.

Black Buffalo (Black Bull, Black Bull Buffalo, Untongarabar) (unknown–1813) *Teton Lakota chief*

It is generally agreed that one of the most dangerous moments on the Lewis and Clark Expedition was the CORPS OF DISCOVERY's confrontation with the TETON LAKOTA INDIANS (Teton Sioux) at the mouth of the BAD RIVER in September 1804. Their ability to proceed up the MISSOURI RIVER and complete their mission hinged on this one encounter, which might have ended disastrously were it not for the Brulé Teton chief Black Buffalo.

Even before their council with the Teton Lakota on September 25, 1804, MERIWETHER LEWIS and WILLIAM CLARK were on their guard against these Indians who, they had been told, controlled the river traffic with often violent measures. One of the expedition's horses had already been stolen, and the Lakota warriors were heavily armed. Complicating matters was an ongoing struggle for power between Black Buffalo and THE PARTISAN, two of the three chiefs of the Brulé Teton (Buffalo Medicine was the third). Furthermore, the expedition lacked an interpreter who could speak the Lakota language with any fluency, resulting in miscommunications.

After Lewis gave his standard speech and the corps had put on an impressive parade, GIFTS were presented, with the most important ones going to Black Buffalo, whom the captains had designated as first chief—the first of several slights to The Partisan. Unhappy with the quality of the gifts, all the chiefs demanded a full PIROGUE of TRADE goods as payment for the expedition being allowed to continue upriver. To divert them, Lewis and Clark invited the chiefs and some of their warriors onto the KEELBOAT, where they were given some whiskey. The trouble began when they were escorted back to shore, where three young warriors grabbed the pirogue's bow cable, another wrapped his arms around the mast, and The Partisan confronted Clark, saying that the expedition would not be allowed to pass up the river.

At this Clark drew his sword and shouted a warning, and the guns on the keelboat were loaded and aimed. An exchange of gunfire and possible loss of life seemed certain—until Black Buffalo stepped forward, took the bowline away from the Teton warriors, and ordered them to get clear of the boat. There ensued a war of words between the captain and the chief, each threatening the other, until some armed men from the keelboat arrived and the Indians backed off. Black Buffalo finally released the bowline after receiving a promise that Teton women and children could tour the keelboat.

Although an attempt by Clark to shake hands with the chiefs was rebuffed, he granted a subsequent request from Black Buffalo to sleep on board the keelboat that night with two of his warriors. The next morning the keelboat took off up the Missouri with Black Buffalo still on board. They landed five miles upriver, and the next two days were marked by numerous talks with various chiefs and elders as well as festivities that included music, dancing, and displays of Lakota power. Black Buffalo continually rejected any idea of intertribal peace and pointedly emphasized the opinion that the Americans should not enter into a trading relationship with the ARIKARA INDIANS and other nations of the upper Missouri, known enemies of the Lakota.

Another tense moment occurred on the evening of September 27, when The Partisan and one of his warriors accompanied the captains to the keelboat for the night. A cable broke as the pirogue approached the keelboat, causing both vessels to swing wildly. As Clark shouted out instructions to his men, an alarm was raised on shore, which Black Buffalo interpreted to mean an attack by OMAHA INDIANS was underway. The Lakota mobilized, and even after the error was realized, some 60 of them remained on alert throughout the night, suspicious of a trick.

Both Black Buffalo and The Partisan were determined to assert their authority over the expedition. Although Lewis and Clark were equally determined to break clear of the Lakota, on the morning of Friday, September 28, they allowed the chiefs on board the keelboat one more time before their departure. As the crew made to cast off, The Partisan's warriors again intervened, grabbing hold of the bowline. Black Buffalo attempted to defuse the situation by telling Lewis that all they wanted was TOBACCO. Lewis refused angrily, while Clark threw a carrot of tobacco onto the riverbank in disgust.

Meanwhile, The Partisan continued to make demands for gifts. Again the situation tensed and guns were made ready, and again Black Buffalo informed the captains that if they gave tobacco to the warriors holding the bow cable, the expedition would be allowed to leave. Lewis and Clark both refused; they "did not mean to be trifled with." Black Buffalo responded that he, too, was irate, "to see us stand so much for one carrot of tobacco." At last Lewis relented and tossed tobacco to the warriors, the bowline was released, and the expedition finally got underway.

Although THOMAS JEFFERSON had instructed Lewis to deal with all Indians "in a most friendly and conciliatory manner," the Lakota clearly made this difficult for them. Were it not for Black Buffalo's compromise solution, the outcome of the expedition might have been very different. The memory of the confrontation rankled the captains. Almost two years later, on August 30, 1806, as the expedition returned down the Missouri, they sighted a large band of armed Teton Lakota lining the southern bank of the river. Clark had RENÉ JESSAUME call out insults and make it clear that the expedition was not to be attacked or the Indians would suffer the consequences. Late in the afternoon, a warrior, believed to be Black Buffalo, approached the boats and invited the captains to come across the river. When they ignored him, he retreated to a nearby hilltop and struck the ground with the butt of his gun three times—"a great oath among the Indians," Clark reported. After a tense night they moved on, unmolested.

Black Buffalo continued to be a major chief of the Brulé Teton Lakota until his death in July 1813. Highly influential in the Missouri River trade, he was, as PIERRE-ANTOINE TABEAU described him, "of good character, although angry and fierce in his fits of passion"—something Lewis and Clark learned firsthand.

Further Reading

Ambrose, Stephen E. *Undaunted Courage: Meriwether Lewis, Thomas Jefferson, and the Opening of the American West.* New York: Simon and Schuster, 1996.
MacGregor, Carol Lynn, ed. *The Journals of Patrick Gass, Member of the Lewis and Clark Expedition.* Missoula, Mont.: Mountain Press Publishing Company, 1997.
Ronda, James P. *Lewis and Clark among the Indians.* Lincoln: University of Nebraska Press, 1984.
Tabeau, Pierre-Antoine. *Tabeau's Narrative of Loisel's Expedition to the Upper Missouri.* Edited by Annie Heloise Abel. Translated by Rose Abel Wright. Norman: University of Oklahoma Press, 1939.

Black Cat (Posecopsahe) (unknown–unknown)
Mandan chief

The villages of the MANDAN INDIANS and HIDATSA INDIANS lay near the junction of the MISSOURI RIVER and the KNIFE RIVER. There were two Mandan villages and three Hidatsa, and the CORPS OF DISCOVERY soon learned that, as with the ARIKARA INDIANS, each had its own principal chief. The leaders of the Mandan were BIG WHITE (Sheheke) and Black Cat (Posecopsahe), both of whom became friends and allies of the white explorers. Yet despite the chiefs' equality in stature, MERIWETHER LEWIS and WILLIAM CLARK insisted on making one of them "first chief." This honor was accorded to Black Cat, chief of the village Lewis and Clark called Rooptahee (now Nuptadi).

On October 29, 1804, having already visited the Mandan villages and their chiefs, the captains held their first formal council with the Mandan and Hidatsa; an Arikara chief was also in attendance. It was not an auspicious beginning. Despite the presence of a large number of Indians, neither Big White nor ONE EYE, the powerful Hidatsa chief, was present. Gifts were presented only to certain chiefs and elders, which offended others present. As the council got underway, the Indians exhibited obvious signs of impatience, and as with the Arikara, they listened to the captains' words and offered some response but mostly reserved their reactions until they had some time to reflect, a custom that irritated Lewis and Clark.

On October 31 Black Cat invited Clark to his lodge, where a BUFFALO robe was placed around the captain's shoulders, and according to Clark he was "Seeted on a roabe by the Side of the Chief." Black Cat then gave his response to the American proposals, telling Clark that he approved of the American desire to make peace among the Mandan, Hidatsa, and Arikara and to that end would provide men to accompany the Arikara chief back to his village. He also said that he would go to meet the "Great Father" (THOMAS JEFFERSON) the following spring. Nevertheless, he rebuked Clark for the GIFTS the expedition had brought, which had greatly disappointed his villagers (although not himself); and he indicated there was confusion about the expedition's mission, which had engendered a certain amount of ill will among some of his people. The meeting concluded with the return of some of the expedition's stolen BEAVER traps as well gifts of CORN and buffalo robes for the corps. Both Clark and Black Cat felt satisfied with the meeting.

Although wary of the ASSINIBOINE INDIANS, Lewis and Clark were anxious to meet them to get some sense of future U.S. relations with that nation. This objective was achieved in mid-November 1804 when Black Cat brought the Assiniboine chief Chechank to FORT MANDAN. The meeting went well, and the captains learned much about the northern trading routes and customs. On a subsequent visit Black Cat brought the news that there had been discussions among the Mandan about the possibility of breaking off their current trading relations with the British-associated Assiniboine and entering into the U.S.-proposed TRADE network with merchants in ST. LOUIS. While this was good news for the captains, they were still hampered by the distrust that many of the Mandan felt toward the Americans, which prevented any firm commitment being made.

Black Cat made frequent visits to Fort Mandan, bringing and receiving presents and sometimes staying in the captains' quarters. On one occasion he presented a fine Mandan bow, which was included among the ARTIFACTS AND SPECIMENS sent back to Washington in spring 1805. Lewis clearly regarded Black Cat as a friend—but also as a tool. After one of the chief's visits, the captain wrote: "This man possesses more integrity, firmness, intelligence and perspicuity of mind than any Indian I have met in this quarter, and I think with a little management he may be made a useful agent in furthering the views of our government." Black Cat served other purposes as well, assisting Lewis in ethnographic studies by providing much information about the Mandan nation and whatever he knew about other nations to the west. He also talked extensively about the

FUR TRADE in the area, of which the Mandan-Hidatsa villages were the hub.

On April 8, 1805, the day after the KEELBOAT left Fort Mandan for St. Louis, Lewis paid a final call on Black Cat, with whom he smoked a pipe and talked before joining the expedition on the river. Captain and chief would not see each other again until August 1806, when the CORPS OF DISCOVERY stopped by the villages and held further councils with the Mandan and the Hidatsa. Black Cat had bad news for Lewis and Clark: Efforts to make peace with the Arikara had failed, and there had been intertribal fighting. Furthermore, he and other chiefs would not go to Washington as long as the hostile TETON LAKOTA INDIANS (Teton Sioux) threatened them. The captains and trader-interpreter RENÉ JESSAUME pleaded and made many promises of gifts and military protection, but Black Cat was adamant. Eventually Big White was finally persuaded to make the journey, but numerous problems, including interference from the Lakota and the Arikara, prevented his return home until three years later, justifying Black Cat's fears.

Further Reading

Lewis & Clark in North Dakota. "Personal Profiles: Profile of Three Chiefs." Available on-line. URL: http://www.ndlewisandclark. com/profiles.html. Downloaded on February 2, 2002.

Ronda, James P. *Lewis and Clark among the Indians.* Lincoln: University of Nebraska Press, 1984.

Blackfeet Indians

During the Lewis and Clark Expedition's return journey in 1806, the decision was made at TRAVELERS' REST to divide the party in two (and eventually into five groups) to carry out separate explorations. While WILLIAM CLARK and his party proceeded south to the YELLOWSTONE RIVER, MERIWETHER LEWIS went north and, leaving some men to see to the PORTAGE around the GREAT FALLS, took a small party (GEORGE DROUILLARD, JOSEPH FIELD, and REUBIN FIELD) to explore the MARIAS RIVER. This was a dangerous risk to take; Lewis knew it, because he knew of the Blackfeet's fierce reputation, and he was now venturing into their territory.

The Blackfeet were (and still are) a confederacy of three independent bands: the Blackfoot proper, also known as the Siksika or North Blackfoot, who lived the furthest north, in Canada, and the Blood (Kainan) and the Piegan (Pikuni, Pigunni), who lived further south, including upper Montana. (The confederacy also included the Sarcee and Gros Ventre [Atsina].) Algonquian speakers, their name was taken from the distinctive black moccasins they wore. The Blackfeet were believed to have migrated in the 17th century from the northern Great Lakes region onto the GREAT PLAINS, where they adopted a nomadic lifestyle and began to hunt BUFFALO as well as DEER, ELK, and mountain SHEEP. By the 18th century, the Blackfeet Indians had developed a friendly trading relationship with British traders, exchanging BEAVER and wolf pelts for ALCOHOL, guns, and ammunition. In the process the armed

Two Blackfeet Indians were killed when Meriwether Lewis and three men encountered a small band at Two Medicine River in July 1806. These Blackfeet were photographed in Glacier National Park ca. 1912. *(Library of Congress, Prints and Photographs Division [LC-USZ62-124226])*

Blackfeet came to dominate their NEZ PERCE and SHOSHONE rivals.

Late in July 1806, having ascended the Marias as far as the point that he named CAMP DISAPPOINTMENT, Lewis and his men crossed overland to the southern branch of the Marias, TWO MEDICINE RIVER. On July 26, while Drouillard was ahead in the Two Medicine valley, Lewis noticed a small band of Blackfeet watching Drouillard. He immediately dispatched

Joseph Field to ride toward them with an American flag, which had the effect of flustering the Indians. One then began to gallop at Lewis, but, realizing that it was not an attack, the captain dismounted and stood his ground.

There were eight Piegan Blackfeet altogether. While one of them went with Reubin Field to bring back Drouillard and the supplies, Lewis conversed with the others in the best sign language he could manage. He also presented them with PEACE MEDALS, flags, and handkerchiefs, which apparently calmed them sufficiently to decide to camp with the soldiers that night. However, Lewis was unaware that much of what he had said to them had disturbed them greatly. On learning that they traded regularly with the HUDSON'S BAY COMPANY and NORTH WEST COMPANY, Lewis informed them of plans for a U.S. trading network that was to include many of their enemies—and worse yet, those enemies would be receiving guns from the Americans. Lewis had thought he could draw the Blackfeet into his plans for peace among the PLAINS INDIANS. Instead, he had unknowingly strengthened this band's resolve to steal the soldiers' guns.

Early on the morning of July 27, the Blackfeet took advantage of an unguarded moment and began to sneak off with the rifles of all four men. However, Joseph Field surprised them and with a shout roused his brother and Drouillard. Reubin Field immediately gave chase and caught an Indian named Side Hill Calf, whom he angrily killed with a knife. As he later described it, Side Hill Calf "drew but one breath [and] the wind of his breath followed the knife and he fell dead."

Drouillard, meanwhile, went after the Indian making off with his rifle and shot pouch. As he shouted, "Damn you let go my gun," Lewis awoke to the noise and confusion. Seeing that his own rifle was gone, he drew his pistol and began to chase the thief, who gave up the rifle. After refusing to allow the Field brothers or Drouillard to kill any more men, Lewis realized that two of the Blackfeet were taking their HORSES. He ran after them and cornered them by some rocks. As one of them, who was armed, swerved around toward him, Lewis, believing that he was about to be attacked, shot the Indian in the stomach. As the mortally wounded Piegan fell to his knees, he shot at Lewis but missed. Lewis later reported: "Being bearheaded, I felt the wind of his bullet very distinctly."

It was the only encounter of the expedition to result in the deaths of Indians, and the violence ended as suddenly as it had begun. Shaken, Lewis ordered the horses be rounded up for a speedy escape. While the men hastily packed, he put a peace medal around Side Hill Calf's neck, as a message to the Blackfeet so that "they might be informed who we were." Then, on the Indians' horses, the four men rode for a day and a night until they were safely clear of Blackfeet territory and had rejoined the party on the MISSOURI RIVER.

It has been posited that the fight at Two Medicine River and Lewis's defiant action in placing the medal around Side Hill Calf's neck was to blame for subsequent hostility between the Blackfeet and the Americans. The truth of this statement continues to be debated today. Certainly the Blackfeet were known to attack pioneers on the OREGON TRAIL, and Blackfeet war parties were responsible for the deaths of Drouillard, JOHN POTTS, and possibly also PETER WEISER. But how much of this animosity can be traced directly to the deaths at Two Medicine is a matter of conjecture.

In the years after the expedition, the size and strength of the Blackfeet was weakened by smallpox epidemics and the destruction of buffalo herds. The confederacy signed treaties ceding land to the U.S. government in 1855, 1886, and 1895; and to CANADA in 1877. Today there are an estimated 14,000 Blackfeet, of whom more than half are Piegan living on a reservation in Montana. The town of Browning is the seat of the tribal government as well as the site of the annual North American Indian Days celebration in mid-July. The three bands of Blackfeet also have rights to lands in Alberta.

Further Reading

Cutright, Paul Russell. "Lewis on the Marias 1806." *Montana: The Magazine of Western History* 18, no. 3 (1968): 30–43.

Ewers, John C. *The Blackfeet: Raiders on the Northwestern Plains.* Norman: University of Oklahoma Press, 1958.

Lewis, Meriwether, and William Clark. *The History of the Lewis and Clark Expedition.* Edited by Elliott Coues; 4 vols., 1893, Harper. Reprinted in 3 vols., New York: Dover Publications, 1979.

Ronda, James P. *Lewis and Clark among the Indians.* Lincoln and London: University of Nebraska Press, 1984.

Waldman, Carl. *Encyclopedia of Native American Tribes.* Revised ed. New York: Checkmark Books, 1999.

blunderbuss   See FIREARMS.

boat, iron-frame   See IRON-FRAME BOAT.

boats   See BULL BOATS; CANOES; IRON-FRAME BOAT; KEELBOAT; PIROGUES.

bobcats   See ANIMALS, NEW SPECIES.

Boley, John (unknown–unknown) *private in the temporary party*
Private John Boley was one of the men of the CORPS OF DISCOVERY who was recruited only for the first leg of the expedition up the MISSOURI RIVER. Originally from PITTSBURGH, he was at KASKASKIA when he enlisted for the corps. Apparently rambunctious, he was one of a small group of privates at CAMP DUBOIS—including JOHN COLTER, JOHN ROBERTSON, and PETER WEISER—who in March 1804 defied Sergeant JOHN ORDWAY and got drunk at a local whiskey shop. When Captain MERIWETHER LEWIS returned to camp from a visit to ST. LOUIS, he confined the four to quarters for 10 days.

As only a temporary participant in the expedition, Boley returned to St. Louis on the KEELBOAT in spring 1805, under the command of Corporal RICHARD WARFINGTON. That same year he joined the expedition organized by ZEBULON PIKE to find the source of the MISSISSIPPI RIVER; he also accompanied Pike to the ROCKY MOUNTAINS the following year, and he was with that part of the group that descended the Arkansas River to New Orleans. He eventually settled in Carondelet, Missouri, where he was reported to be living in October 1823, but there is no further information on him after this.

Further Reading

Clarke, Charles G. *The Men of the Lewis and Clark Expedition: A Biographical Roster of the Fifty-One Members and a Composite Diary of Their Activities from All Known Sources.* 1970. Reprint, Lincoln: Bison Books, University of Nebraska Press, 2002.

books on the expedition

Although MERIWETHER LEWIS had studied extensively with leading scholars in PHILADELPHIA to learn the basic tenets of medicine, anatomy, botany, zoology, astronomy, and American Indian history, the need to take books on the expedition was always understood. His mentor, THOMAS JEFFERSON, was an avid reader whose library at MONTICELLO (one of three that he built during his lifetime) contained the latest and the best books on history, geography, astronomy, and numerous other areas. Indeed, it was this collection that formed the nucleus of the Library of Congress when Jefferson donated it to that body in 1815. Small wonder that Lewis drew heavily on the resources at Monticello as he made his PREPARATIONS FOR THE EXPEDITION.

While at least two of the books that Lewis took on his journey had been borrowed from Jefferson, some were loaned to him by other mentors, including ANDREW ELLICOTT, ROBERT PATTERSON, and BENJAMIN SMITH BARTON. He also bought several books, including Barton's just-published *Elements of Botany*, for which he paid $6. It is uncertain exactly how many books were taken on the expedition; there were at least a dozen. Titles known to have been carried include:

Astronomy/Navigation

- *The Nautical Almanac and Astronomical Ephemeris* (London, 1781–1804), published by order of the Commissioners of Longitude.
- *A Practical Introduction to Spherics and Nautical Astronomy* (London, 1796), by Patrick Kelly.
- *Tables Requisite to be Used with the Nautical Ephemeris for Finding the Latitude and Longitude at Sea* (London, 1781), by Nevil Maskelyn.

History/Geography

- *The History of Louisiana, or the Western Parts of Virginia and Carolina* (London, 1763; 2nd ed., 1774), by Antoine Simon Le Page du Pratz.

- *Voyages from Montreal through the Continent of North America to the Frozen and Pacific Oceans in 1789 and 1793, with an Account of the Rise and State of the Fur Trade* (London ed., 1801; American ed., 1802), by Alexander Mackenzie.

Natural Sciences

- *Elements of Botany; or, Outlines of the Natural History of Vegetables* (Philadelphia, 1803), by Benjamin Smith Barton.
- *An Illustration of the Sexual System of Linneaus,* vol. 1 (London, 1779) and *An Illustration of the Termini Botanici of Linneaus,* vol. 1 (London, 1789), by John Miller.
- *Elements of Mineralogy* (London, 1784; 2nd ed., 1794), by Richard Kirwan.
- *A New and Complete Dictionary of Arts and Science* (London, 1753; 2nd ed., 1764), by a Society of Gentlemen.

The traveling library also included a four-volume dictionary, which may have been either Chambers's *Cyclopedia* or *Owen's Dictionary.* Jefferson also sent Lewis a copy of the journal written by the French-Canadian trader Jean-Baptiste Truteau, although this volume is not usually included in lists of the expedition's books.

Due to the need to travel light in the latter part of the journey, not all of Lewis's books went to the West Coast and back; some were buried in CACHES at GREAT FALLS in June 1805. Bearing in mind the countless capsizes, storms, and other mishaps over thousands of miles of river travel, it is remarkable that the JOURNALS or any of the books they took came back at all.

A book that did make the full journey can still be seen in the Library Company of Philadelphia today. It is du Pratz's *History of Louisiana,* which Dr. Barton had loaned to Lewis. After the explorer arrived back at Philadelphia in 1807, one of the first things he did was to return this book to its owner. It bears an inscription on the flyleaf:

Dr Benjamin Smith Barton was so obliging as to lend me this copy of Monsr. Du Pratz's History of Louisiana in June 1803, it has been since conveyed by me to the Pacific Ocean through the interior of North America on my late tour thither and is now returned to it's proprietor by his Friend and Obt. Servt. Meriwether Lewis Philadelphia, May 9th, 1807.

Further Reading

Coalwell, Christine. "Jefferson's Library: Exploring the Americas at Monticello." From *The Author of Our Enterprise: Thomas Jefferson and the Lewis and Clark Expedition.* Available online. URL: http://www.monticello.org/jefferson/lewisand clark/libraryofamerica.html. Downloaded on January 21, 2002.

Jackson, Donald. "Some Books Carried by Lewis and Clark." *Bulletin of the Missouri Historical Society* 16 (1959): 3–13.

Boone, Daniel (1734–1820) *frontiersman*

On May 24, 1804, when the expedition was only 10 days into its journey up the MISSOURI RIVER, they passed Boone's Settlement, a colony founded by the legendary pioneer Daniel Boone. A myth has grown up that MERIWETHER LEWIS and WILLIAM CLARK met Boone that day as he was returning from a hunting trip with a load of BEAVER skins. Myth, however, is all it is for, as far as is known, Boone was away when the expedition passed his settlement. Nevertheless, the idea of the two explorers on such a pioneering mission meeting the greatest pioneer of all tantalizes historians even today.

Daniel Boone's life was the stuff of legend. He was born the son of an English squire in Bucks County, Pennsylvania, and began to hunt game and trap for furs when he was only 12 years old. In 1750 he moved with his family to North Carolina, where he married Rebeccah Bryan six years later. Attracted to frontier life, he began to make trips to Kentucky in 1767, and in 1775 he led the first settlers to that territory as an agent for Colonel Richard Henderson of the Transylvania Company (which was then aiming to set up a colony there). In April that year he started to build a fort at the site that became known as Boonesborough, and in the fall he returned briefly to North Carolina to bring back his wife, family, and more settlers. With the arrival of the first white women in the territory, Kentucky had its first permanent non-Indian settlement.

Thereafter Boone became a hunter, surveyor, and Indian fighter around whom numerous tall tales—some true, some self-invented—began to grow. Captured by Shawnee Indians in 1778, he was adopted by Chief Blackfish but escaped after five months and returned to Boonesborough in time to help defend it against a siege by Indians and the British. In 1780 he was robbed of $20,000 he had collected from settlers to obtain land warrants from Virginia, of which Kentucky had been made a county. This was the first in a series of legal problems that eventually resulted in his losing all his holdings in Kentucky. In the meantime, he served in a number of public offices as well as in the territorial legislature. Yet despite his close association with Kentucky, which became a state in 1792, the loss of all his lands finally compelled him to move. He went first to what is now West Virginia in 1788 and then, approximately 10 years later, to present-day Missouri, where he obtained from the Spanish authorities a grant of land at the mouth of the Femme Osage Creek—the settlement that the Lewis and Clark Expedition passed. In 1800 he was appointed magistrate of the district, but when the LOUISIANA PURCHASE was finalized, he once again lost the title to his land; it was not confirmed by the U.S. CONGRESS until 1814.

Had Lewis and Clark ever met Boone, it is fascinating to imagine what they would have discussed. According to the expedition's JOURNALS, they stopped at Boone's Settlement, where they bought CORN and butter and talked to the settlers, but Boone himself was never mentioned. The following day they passed LA CHARETTE, the last settlement of non-Indians on the Missouri, to which Boone would move two years later. A few years after that, he became justice of the district of

Contrary to some accounts, Lewis and Clark did not meet the legendary Daniel Boone, although they did stop at Boone's Settlement early in their journey up the Missouri. *(Library of Congress, Prints and Photographs Division [LC-USZ62-112549])*

Femme Osage. The man who appointed him to the position was then governor of LOUISIANA TERRITORY—Meriwether Lewis.

Widowed in 1813, Boone lived out his remaining years with his son Nathan. By the time he died, he had won renown for his frontier exploits, in large part because of his fantasy-driven "autobiography," published in 1784. Three years after his death in ST. CHARLES, Missouri, the English poet Lord Byron devoted the eighth canto of *Don Juan* to Boone, further increasing his fame. While many of the Boone legends are regarded with skepticism by many historians, there is no doubt that he was a superb hunter, an uneducated but brilliant woodsman, and a courageous leader who did much for the settlement, defense, and growth of Kentucky.

Further Reading

Bakeless, John. *Daniel Boone: Master of the Wilderness.* Reprint, Lincoln: University of Nebraska Press, 1989.

Faragher, John Mack. *Daniel Boone: The Life and Legend of an American Pioneer.* New York: Henry Holt, 1992.

Van Noppen, John James, and Ina Woestemeyer Van Noppen. *Daniel Boone, Backwoodsman: The Green Woods Were His Portion.* Boone, N.C.: Appalachian Press, 1966.

Bozeman Pass

On July 13, 1806, WILLIAM CLARK wrote in his journal, "[T]he indian woman who has been of great Service to me as a pilot through this Country recommends a gap in the mountain more south which I shall cross." Previously, at TRAVELERS' REST, he and MERIWETHER LEWIS had divided the CORPS OF DISCOVERY into separate parties. SACAGAWEA was with Clark's group, and as they ventured back southward into her SHOSHONE homeland, she began to recall landmarks and trails. The most important one, an "old buffalo road," was a shortcut to the YELLOWSTONE RIVER, which was Clark's destination. On July 15 the party took this route, which would later be known as Bozeman Pass.

Other explorers may have preceded Clark. In 1802 Charles LeRaye traveled with a party of HIDATSA and CROW INDIANS to Little Goose Creek in the Big Horn Mountains and wintered with them. In 1804 the French fur trader FRANÇOIS-ANTOINE LAROCQUE, who had met Lewis and Clark at the MANDAN villages, accompanied a party of Crow to the Big Horns, and he may have gone through the same pass.

Almost 60 years after Clark's crossing, during the winter of 1862–63, John Bozeman—a gold miner, wagon master, and trail guide—traveled from Bannack, Montana, to Colorado by a route to the east of the Bighorn Mountains. This took him through land that was then reserved by treaty to the Native Americans and then through the pass that Sacagawea had identified for Clark. Both the pass and the trail he took acquired his name.

The northern spur off the OREGON TRAIL, the Bozeman Trail had several routes that began in southern Wyoming and ended at Virginia City, Montana. Several parties, including one guided by Bozeman himself, used the trail in 1864. Four wagon trains of 1,500 people departed from the North Platte River at Richard's Bridge east of present Casper, Wyoming, traveling to the Montana settlements. In 1865–66, the U.S. Army built forts Reno, Phil Kearney, and C. F. Smith to guard the trail, despite the protests of area TETON LAKOTA INDIANS (Teton Sioux) and CHEYENNE INDIANS who wished to stem the tide of new settlers on their lands. The transcontinental railroad led to the trail's obsolescence, and in 1883 the Northern Pacific Railway was built through Bozeman Pass, paralleling the Bozeman Trail, as does Interstate 90 today.

Further Reading

Frontier Heritage Alliance. "Travel the Bozeman Trail." (Includes history of the trail and pass.) Available on-line. URL: http://www.bozemantrail.org/index.htm. Downloaded on January 10, 2002.

Hebard, Grace Raymond, and E. A. Brininstool. *The Bozeman Trail: Historical Accounts of the Blazing of the Overland Routes in the Northwest, and the Fights with Red Cloud's Warriors.* Lincoln: University of Nebraska Press, 1990.

Moulton, Gary E., ed. *Atlas of the Lewis and Clark Expedition.* Revised ed. Lincoln: University of Nebraska Press, 1999.

brandy   See ALCOHOL.

brants   See GEESE AND BRANTS.

Bratton, William (Bret Bratton, Bratten)
(1778–1841)   *private in the permanent party*

One of the NINE YOUNG MEN FROM KENTUCKY, William Bratton was born in Augusta County, Virginia, on July 27, 1778; his Scotch-Irish family moved to Kentucky 12 years later. As a young man Bratton was apprenticed as a blacksmith and acquired skills as a gunsmith and a woodsman, making him one of the most useful members of the CORPS OF DISCOVERY. He was hired as a private on October 20, 1803, in Louisville, Kentucky, and among his many duties, he worked as assistant blacksmith to JOHN SHIELDS. Reportedly Bratton was a very pleasant man, nearly six feet tall, with red hair and high moral standards. His nickname was "Bret."

When MOSES REED deserted the expedition early in August 1804, Bratton was part of the four-man search team headed by GEORGE DROUILLARD to find Reed and return him to camp. They were successful, returning not only with Reed but also with OTOE (Oto) Indian chiefs LITTLE THIEF and BIG HORSE, whom Lewis and Clark had wanted to meet. Reed was punished and discharged, and the peace council with the Otoe did not go well. To make matters worse, later that month Sergeant CHARLES FLOYD died unexpectedly. Consequently, in the first election west of the Mississippi, Patrick GASS was selected to be Floyd's replacement; Bratton and GEORGE GIBSON split the runner-up votes.

A few months later, during the winter in FORT MANDAN, Bratton's skills as a blacksmith were utilized in TRADEs with the MANDAN and HIDATSA INDIANS. In exchange for dried vegetables and CORN, he, Shields, and ALEXANDER WILLARD (another trained blacksmith and gunsmith) would sharpen and repair the Indians' knives, FIREARMS, pots, and other metal implements.

Late during the afternoon of May 11, 1805, while walking along the MISSOURI RIVER in what is now northeastern Montana, Bratton encountered a grizzly bear, which he shot through the lungs. Enraged, the wounded bear chased him for nearly a half-mile before others on the river saw him running and came to his aid, finally killing the bear with two shots to the head. They subsequently skinned it and rendered the meat into cooking grease.

In November 1805, after the corps had reached the PACIFIC OCEAN, Bratton was recruited for a smaller party of 10 men, headed by Captain Clark, who made a journey approximately nine miles up the coast from their camp on the COLUMBIA RIVER. During the expedition's subsequent winter sojourn in FORT CLATSOP, he was assigned, along with JOSEPH FIELD and George Gibson, to establish a SALTWORKS approximately 15 miles south of the camp (near present-day Seaside, Oregon). By the time they finished their work in late February 1806, they had produced 20 gallons of salt, which was used to preserve meat and flavor cooked foods. Twelve gallons of salt were packed for the return journey.

In early January 1806 Bratton discovered a whale stranded on the beach. Alexander Willard and PETER WEISER hurried back to Fort Clatsop, bringing some blubber with them. A pleased WILLIAM CLARK took a party back to the beach, but by the time they arrived the TILLAMOOK INDIANS had already stripped the whale. Clark subsequently bargained with them to obtain blubber and oil.

By the time the expedition left Fort Clatsop, Private Bratton was plagued with ever-worsening health problems, primarily bouts of influenza and excruciating back pain. (Bratton's illnesses receive more mention in the JOURNALS than those of any other expedition members.) Treatment with Rush's Pills failed to help his back, and by April 1806, nearly paralyzed with pain, he was forced to ride horseback while the others walked. The following month, at the suggestion of John Shields, Clark decided to build a sweat lodge and try treating Bratton with sweat baths. Stones were heated and placed inside the lodge with the private; water was poured over the stones to make steam. After 20 minutes Bratton was taken out, plunged into cold water, and then returned to the sweat lodge. He was also given mint tea to drink. The treatments seemed to work, as he began to walk again within a day and was greatly improved by the end of June. Scholars have since theorized that his problem was either a dislocated disk or lumbago.

Bratton was honorably discharged from the expedition on October 10, 1806. He returned to Kentucky but later moved to Missouri, settling near JOHN ORDWAY. He subsequently served in the War of 1812 and reportedly saw the great Shawnee chief Tecumseh killed in the Battle of the Thames. On November 25, 1819, Bratton married Mary H. Maxwell, with whom he had eight sons and two daughters. After living for a while in Greenville, Ohio, they moved to Waynetown, Indiana, where Bratton died on November 11, 1841. He is buried in the Waynetown Pioneer Cemetery under a monument that reads: "Went with Lewis and Clark in 1804 to the Rocky Mountains."

Further Reading

Bratton, Steve. "William E. Bratton of Lewis and Clark Fame." *The Bratton Bulletin,* Vol. 5, Issue 1, October–December 1995. Available on-line. URL: http://www.gendex.com/~guest/69751/BrattonHomePage/br09011.htm. Updated on February 6, 2000.

Clarke, Charles G. *The Men of the Lewis and Clark Expedition: A Biographical Roster of the Fifty-One Members and a Composite Diary of Their Activities from All Known Sources.* 1970. Reprint, Lincoln: Bison Books, University of Nebraska Press, 2002.

Lange, Robert. "William Bratton—One of Lewis and Clark's Men." *We Proceeded On* 7, no. 1 (February 1981): 8–11.

North Dakota Lewis & Clark Bicentennial Foundation. *Members of the Corps of Discovery.* Bismarck, N.Dak.: United Printing and Mailing, 2000.

Broken Arm (Tunnachemootoolt)

(unknown–unknown) *Nez Perce chief*

On September 20, 1805, WILLIAM CLARK and a small party finally completed their hazardous crossing of the BITTERROOT MOUNTAINS and arrived on the WEIPPE PRAIRIE. Exhausted and hungry, they approached three NEZ PERCE boys, who

retreated to their village. Shortly thereafter a Nez Perce man came and invited them into a nearby TIPI, explaining that it belonged to Broken Arm, a chief who was then away on a raid. Clark and MERIWETHER LEWIS were not to meet this chief until the following spring, by which time they had already established a liking and respect for the Nez Perce. But it was Broken Arm who earned some of Lewis's greatest praise with a dramatic act of generosity.

While the Nez Perce had shown the expedition kindness and hospitality, they were also anxious to gain guns and power through TRADE with white men. As one of the few chiefs present when the CORPS OF DISCOVERY arrived in autumn 1805, TWISTED HAIR had been the first to put himself in the captains' good graces. They had not, however, encountered either Broken Arm or another chief named CUT NOSE. This was corrected during their return journey in early May 1806, when they finally met Cut Nose, who greeted them and rode with them until, two days later, they met Twisted Hair. Almost at once the two chiefs began to argue loudly, with Cut Nose accusing Twisted Hair of neglecting and abusing the expedition's HORSES. As the captains attempted to mediate, it became clear that both Cut Nose and Broken Arm had become jealous of Twisted Hair's increased prestige due to his prior association with the expedition. Lewis and Clark therefore determined not to play favorites but to show equal respect to all the chiefs.

To that end, after spending some time with Twisted Hair, the expedition set out for Broken Arm's village to formally introduce themselves. Their journey up the Columbia had been hard due to their shortage of horses and petty pilfering of their supplies by Indians along the way. In addition, the corps had previously become used to trading with the Nez Perce for even the smallest items. Broken Arm, however, proved different. When the captains asked if they might trade one of their lean horses for a fatter one that could be slaughtered for FOOD, he replied that he was "revolted at the aydea of an exchange." He then offered them as many horses as they wanted and immediately produced two fat colts they could take immediately. A pleased Lewis noted that this was "the only act which deserves the appellation of hospitality which we have witnessed in this quarter."

At a subsequent two-day council in Broken Arm's village, Lewis and Clark met all the Nez Perce chiefs together for the first time. The captains' message stressed their usual themes of promoting intertribal peace and establishing a trading relationship with U.S. merchants. The Nez Perce were interested, and on the second day of the council, the chiefs and elders openly discussed their reactions to the American proposals. Finally Broken Arm rose to make a speech. First he made a thick mush of flour made from cous roots which was then poured into "the kettles and baskets of all his people." After talking at length about the decisions the council had reached, he stated that all who accepted those decisions should eat the mush. Lewis later commented, "All swallowed their objections if any they had cheerfully with their mush."

The expedition stayed among the Nez Perce for several more weeks; yet despite the friendship the Indians felt for the soldiers, Broken Arm was wary about committing his people fully to their proposals. Lewis and Clark had hoped that a Nez Perce delegation might go to Washington, but the chief indicated that this would be unlikely. He also refused to allow any of his warriors to accompany the expedition over the LOLO TRAIL to TRAVELERS' REST—it was simply too early in the year. In early June, when the captains again tried to obtain a commitment from him, he had them speak to other Nez Perce leaders who had not been present at the council the month before, so that they might hear the American proposals. He then reaffirmed his desire to make peace with the SHOSHONE INDIANS, noting that he would do all he could to achieve this end. He still refused to give them men as guides, but his interest in their trade proposals, his willingness to discuss peace, and his gift of horses when they first met him all left a favorable memory of this open, honest, and generous chief.

Further Reading

Ronda, James P. *Lewis and Clark among the Indians.* Lincoln: University of Nebraska Press, 1984.

budget of the expedition   See COSTS OF THE EXPEDITION.

buffalo (bison)

While many legends of the American West have proved to be exaggerated, many stories that have grown up around the American bison, more commonly called the buffalo, are based on fact. Although bison were once common throughout North America, early settlers and farmers had driven them out of the eastern seaboard regions by about 1760. Thus, by the time of the Lewis and Clark Expedition, there were few buffalo left east of the MISSISSIPPI RIVER. However, those that roamed the GREAT PLAINS at the beginning of the 19th century were counted in the millions, and the expedition's JOURNALS record time and again the dependence of the PLAINS INDIANS on the beast.

Although some members of the CORPS OF DISCOVERY had seen buffalo near the mouth of the KANSAS RIVER, it was not until August 23, 1804, near present-day Vermilion, South Dakota, that JOSEPH FIELD shot the first one. MERIWETHER LEWIS took 11 men out to butcher the meat and bring in the carcass; they estimated it weighed between 1,000 and 1,500 pounds. Some of the ENGAGÉS showed the explorers the best parts for eating and the best way to skin it to make a robe.

From then until they passed the GREAT FALLS of the MISSOURI RIVER, the corps found buffalo to be so plentiful that it was noteworthy when none were to be seen. One bison alone could provide enough meat for all the men for a day, and there were so many that the expedition had a constant source of FOOD for weeks. At one point JOHN ORDWAY wrote: "Saw large gangs of buffaloe Swimming the River just before our canoes & we would not Shoot them as we had enofe meat on board." No buffalo, however, were found west of the THREE FORKS or along the JEFFERSON RIVER; this may have been due to seasonal migration. It was not until nearly a year later, on July 9, 1806, as they returned to their old camp at Great Falls that Joseph Field again became the first to shoot a buffalo.

From the Indians they met, the engagés, and personal observation, Lewis and WILLIAM CLARK learned of the many ways in which the Plains Indians depended on the buffalo. First and foremost, it provided meat, and dried buffalo meat saw many nations through the winter when the buffalo had moved elsewhere. While DEER, ELK, and other game were sources of meat as well, the buffalo provided much more, making it the true staple of life for many nations. Its hides were used to make CLOTHING, blankets, SHELTER (TIPIS), BULL BOATS, saddle cloths, and moccasins, while reins and halters were made from thongs of rawhide. The buffalo also formed the basis of trade between nomadic nations and more settled communities like the ARIKARA INDIANS. CORN and other vegetables were exchanged for buffalo meat and skins, which in turn could be passed on and bartered for TRADE goods or guns.

Both captains wrote about Indian HUNTING techniques they observed. Before the Spaniards had introduced HORSES into the American continents, buffalo were hunted on foot and, especially along the river valleys, stampeded over cliffs. One of these sites, known as pishkuns or buffalo jumps, can still be seen at present-day Ulm, Montana. Sometimes Indians would don buffalo hides and decoy herds to such precipices, relying on a crevice in the rocks to hide in or on their fleetness of foot to escape the stampede behind them.

The Plains Indians were known to hold elaborate ceremonies to attract the buffalo herds on which their lives depended. The MANDAN INDIANS held one such ceremony, called the BUFFALO DANCE, which the explorers witnessed in early January 1805, and its efficacy was proved to the Indians with the arrival of a herd within a few days. Corps members joined them on the subsequent hunt, the Indians riding bareback and using bows and arrows while the soldiers used their rifles to kill some 20 buffalo.

A more practical method of attracting buffalo was to burn off sections of the prairie in the early spring (see PRAIRIE FIRES). The new fresh growth that resulted tempted herds to the area. On March 6, 1805, at FORT MANDAN, Clark wrote: "A cloudy morning, and Smokey all Day from the burning of the plains, which was set on fire by the Minetarries for a new crop of grass, as an enducement for the Buffalow to feed on." Three weeks later he again commented on this, noting it was done "every Spring for the benefit of their horses and to induce the Buffalow to come near them."

The journals give a unique view of the life of the Plains Indians and their dependence on the buffalo. But the most remarkable aspect for today's readers must be the accounts of the richness of the wildlife on the Great Plains and the almost

At the time of the expedition, buffalo were so numerous that, according to Meriwether Lewis, "the men frequently throw sticks and stones at them to drive them out of their way." By the time this photograph was taken in the late 1800s, they had been hunted nearly to extinction. *(Dartmouth College Library)*

unimaginable numbers of animals Lewis and Clark saw there. On September 9, 1804, near the Niobrara River, Lewis wrote: "I saw at one view at least 500 buffalo, those animals have been in View all day feeding in the Plains. . . . [E]very copse of timber appear to have Elk and Deer." Eight days later, near the White River, he noted: "I do not think I exagerate when I estimate the number of Buffaloe which could be comprehended at one view to amount to 3,000." A year later, on August 29, 1806, near Big Bend, Clark wrote: "[F]rom an eminance I had a view of a greater number of buffalow than I had ever seen before at one time. I must have seen near 20,000 of these animals feeding on this plain. . . ." When buffalo were near, their noise could frighten the horses keep the corps awake at night, especially if it was mating season, when they made, as Lewis described it, "one continual roar."

After Lewis and Clark, numerous changes, including but not exclusive to the advance of non-Indians onto the plains and the resulting overhunting, combined to drive the buffalo to near extinction. By the end of the 1880s, it was estimated that only 835 bison remained in the United States. Conservation efforts saved the buffalo, and its population today is large and stable. However, never again will any human see such numbers of them as the expedition did or find them so unafraid of humans as Lewis described them on May 8, 1805:

> We saw a great quantity of game today particularly Elk and buffaloe; the latter are now so gentle that the men frequently throw sticks and stones at them to drive them out of their way.

Further Reading

Burroughs, Raymond Darwin, ed. *The Natural History of the Lewis and Clark Expedition.* East Lansing: Michigan State University Press, 1995.

Cutright, Paul Russell. *Lewis & Clark: Pioneering Naturalists.* Lincoln: University of Nebraska Press/Bison Books, 1989.

Dary, David A. *The Buffalo Book: The Full Saga of the American Animal.* Athens, Ohio: Swallow Press/Ohio University Press, 1989.

Flores, Dan. "The American Bison." From *Discovering Lewis and Clark.* Available on-line. URL: http://www.lewis-clark.org/bison/bison_flores-history.htm. Downloaded on March 21, 2002.

buffalo dance

During the CORPS OF DISCOVERY's winter among the MANDAN INDIANS in 1804–05, they had numerous opportunities to study the customs and ceremonies of that nation. Among these was the buffalo dance, an annual festival whose purpose, as WILLIAM CLARK wrote, was "to cause the buffalow to Come near So that They may kill them." The BUFFALO being a major source of food and clothing for the Mandan, a festival to honor the animal was a significant facet of their culture and signaled the start of the buffalo-hunting season. While several variations of the dance have been reported in different sources, the following is what the expedition witnessed—and some participated in—during the three nights from January 3 to 5, 1805.

The dance took place in a communal earth lodge. Onlookers from the corps stood at the back and looked on as rattles and drums began to play and the village elders, finely dressed, entered and sat together in a circle. They were followed by younger warriors and their wives, who stood behind the old men and fixed pipes for them. After a smoking ceremony, the drums became louder and there was increased chanting. A warrior would then offer his wife to one of the elders. As Clark described it, the naked wife "then takes the Old man (who verry often can Screcely walk) and leades him to a Convenient place for the business, after which they return to the lodge." If the wife was not gratified, the young warrior would offer her to the old man again, along with a buffalo robe, and would plead with the elder not to despise them.

While the primary purpose of this dance was to attract buffalo to the area, there was another objective to it as well. Age and experience had given the old men certain powers that, it was believed, could be transferred to the younger men through sexual contact with their wives, thus making better hunters of

them. Similarly, the white men of the expedition were also viewed as having "big medicine" that the warriors hoped to tap. Consequently, wives were offered to corps members, many of whom were happy to oblige. ("Sent a man to this Medisan Dance last night," wrote Clark. "[T]hey gave him 4 Girls.") A few days later, a large herd of buffalo arrived in the area, and the Mandan were rewarded for their dance with a highly successful hunt. Fur trader PIERRE-ANTOINE TABEAU reported that the Mandan gave a large portion of the credit for this happy event to the explorers, who were "untiringly zealous in attracting the cow."

See also ETHNOGRAPHY; SEX DURING THE EXPEDITION; SMOKING CEREMONIES.

Further Reading

Ambrose, Stephen E. *Undaunted Courage: Meriwether Lewis, Thomas Jefferson, and the Opening of the American West.* New York: Simon and Schuster, 1996.

Catlin, George. *Letters and Notes on the Manners, Customs, and Conditions of the North American Indians; Written during Eight Years' Travel (1832–1839).* Reprint, New York: Dover Publications, 1973.

Ronda, James P. *Lewis and Clark among the Indians.* Lincoln: University of Nebraska Press, 1984.

The buffalo dance varied among nations. This photo of a buffalo dancer was taken ca. 1926. William Clark described the ritual of the Mandan Indians' buffalo dance in January 1805. *(Library of Congress, Prints and Photographs Division [LC-USZ62-106264])*

bull boats (skin canoes)

Notwithstanding the high waves, two or three squaws rowed to us in little canoes made of a single buffalo skin, stretched over a frame of boughs interwoven like a basket, and with the most perfect composure.

The date was October 6, 1804, and this encounter with some ARIKARA women was the first time the CORPS OF DISCOVERY had seen a bull boat. Two days later, Sergeant PATRICK GASS was highly impressed when he was taken across the river in "a buffaloe skin stretched on a frame made of boughs, wove together like a crate or basket for that purpose."

The circular skin boat (coracle) is common across the world—there are still some in Wales, Iraq, and northern India—especially where timber is not available for normal boat building. The Arikara, for example, lived on a treeless plain and were dependent for firewood on the trees and branches that swept down the MISSOURI RIVER.; thus the need for boats made of other materials.

Captain WILLIAM CLARK wrote a typically precise description of a bull boat's construction:

2 Sticks of 1¼ inch diameter is tied together so as to form a round hoop of the size you wish the canoe, or as large as the Skin will allow to cover, two of these hoops are made one for the top or brim and the [other] for the bottom the deabth you wish the canoe then Sticks of the same size are crossed at right angles and fastened with a thing to each hoop and also where each Stick crosses each other, then the Skin when green is drawn tight over this fraim and fastened with thongs to the brim or outer hoop so as to form a perfect bason.

As both Clark and MERIWETHER LEWIS noted, this vessel was a common form of transport on the rivers of the treeless GREAT PLAINS. Called skin CANOES at that time, the term *bull boat* came into use much later, when it was realized the Indians usually used the green (i.e., uncured) hide of the bull BUFFALO rather than that of a cow.

After meeting the Arikara, although the explorers themselves used wooden canoes and PIROGUES for much of the journey up the MISSOURI RIVER and canoes thereafter, they clearly appreciated the advantages of bull boats. On the return journey, when the captains had split the party into two, Lewis and his group reached their old camping ground above the GREAT FALLS on July 11, 1806. "Here," Patrick Gass reported, "our hunters, in short time, killed five buffaloe; and we saved the best of the meat; and of the skins made two canoes to transport ourselves and baggage across the river." While following the MANDAN INDIAN technique for making one of these bull boats, the other, according to Lewis, was constructed "on a plan of our own," although he never explained the American design.

This craft was made from a single buffalo skin, with branches forming the spars. Expedition members first saw a bull boat at the Arikara villages and were impressed by the ease of its construction. *(Montana Historical Society, Helena)*

The most dramatic use of bull boats was made by Sergeant NATHANIEL PRYOR and his small party on the return journey. By July 24, 1806, while Lewis and his men were far to the north, Clark and his men had reached the YELLOWSTONE RIVER (near modern Billings, Montana) and found timber to construct canoes. On that date, while he and his group paddled off downstream, Pryor set off with GEORGE SHANNON, RICHARD WINDSOR, and HUGH HALL to take a string of HORSES across country to the villages of the Mandan Indians, some 200 miles to the east. On the second night of their journey, probably in the area of present-day Hardin, Montana, Indians (most likely CROW) stole all of their horses.

The four men were stranded in unknown country with hostile Indians nearby and the knowledge that the rest of the expedition was far away and days ahead of them. They reacted with courage, ingenuity, and resourcefulness. With their baggage on their backs, they walked 30–40 miles north to the Yellowstone River, reaching it near POMPY'S TOWER. There they killed two buffalo, skinned them, made two bull boats, and followed Clark's party down through the shallows and rapids. On August 8 they caught up with Clark and the others some 150 miles downstream, just below the mouth of the Yellowstone. Patrick Gass's journal records their exploit in a single laconic sentence:

On the second day after the sergeant and his party had started for the Mandan village, the Indians stole the whole of his horses, and the party were obliged to descend the river in skin canoes.

Further Reading

Ambrose, Stephen E. *Undaunted Courage: Meriwether Lewis, Thomas Jefferson, and the Opening of the American West.* New York: Simon and Schuster, 1996.

MacGregor, Carol Lynn, ed. *The Journals of Patrick Gass, Member of the Lewis and Clark Expedition.* Missoula, Mont.: Mountain Press Publishing Company, 1997.

Mussulman, Joseph. "Bull Boats: Float Craft on the Middle Missouri." From *Discovering Lewis and Clark: Clark on the Yellowstone.* Available on-line. URL: http://www.lewis-clark.org/CLARK-YELLOWSTONE/YELLOWSTONE/in_bull-boat.htm. Downloaded on March 1, 2002.

bullets   See FIREARMS; SUPPLIES AND EQUIPMENT.

caches

While MERIWETHER LEWIS and WILLIAM CLARK knew that ships called at the mouth of the COLUMBIA RIVER and that they hoped to return home by that means, both realized that they might have to return overland. They also appreciated that they might not reach the PACIFIC OCEAN at all; hostile Indians, impassable mountains, and lack of HORSES were all factors they had to take into account. Any of these would force them to turn back.

Furthermore, as the expedition proceeded up the MISSOURI RIVER, it was clear they could not continue to carry the rapidly growing collection of specimens and artifacts they had gathered. By concealing these at various places along their route, they reduced the weight of baggage in the PIROGUES and CANOES. Also, by burying gunpowder, ammunition, and kegs of such dried foods as pork and flour as well as TOBACCO, they could set up an emergency supply system for their journey home.

It was PIERRE CRUZATTE who showed the others how to build caches (from the French word *cacher,* meaning "to hide"), a method developed by hunters and trappers to hide their furs and supplies from Indians. Digging a cache began with removing sods of grass to leave a circle of bare earth. This was then dug out vertically, after which the bottom was excavated sideways to produce a bottle-shaped hole (described as kettle-shaped by the captains) up to six or seven feet deep. The floor was covered by a layer of brushwood and twigs with rawhide on top to keep the cached stores dry. These were then further protected from damp by inserting more rawhide or brushwood between them and the walls of the chamber. Finally, more skins were placed over the stores, the hole was filled in, and the grass sods were carefully replaced. All the surplus earth was then disposed of to hide any trace of the cache.

The first cache was dug at the mouth of the MARIAS RIVER on June 10–11, 1805, to lighten the load the expedition was carrying. Sergeant JOHN ORDWAY wrote that they put into it their blacksmith's bellows and tools, two rifles, some axes, BEAVER pelts, and kegs of parched CORN and pork. Two separate caches were dug for 24 pounds of powder in lead kegs. Sergeant PATRICK GASS estimated that they buried 1,000 pounds of stores.

Another cache was dug on June 18, 1805, at PORTAGE CREEK, at the foot of the GREAT FALLS; this time some of WILLIAM CLARK's MAPS, MERIWETHER LEWIS's writing desk, books, more pork, flours, and ammunition were buried. The failure of Lewis's IRON-FRAME BOAT led to another cache being dug at the top of the falls. The dugout CANOES they had to make to replace it were too small to carry the load they had originally planned for the iron-frame boat. Thus, into this cache they put botanical specimens, BEAR hides, and Clark's chart of the MISSOURI RIVER as well as the rough wheels and frame they had constructed to pull the canoes along the 18-mile PORTAGE around the falls. The iron-frame boat was also buried here; perhaps understandably, there is no record of any attempt being made to recover it on the way back a year later.

Another cache was dug in the area of CAMP FORTUNATE in August 1805 when the men transferred their baggage from the canoes to the horses they had bought from the SHOSHONE INDIANS. The last known cache was dug in early October that year when they transferred their equipment back into their newly made canoes beside the CLEARWATER RIVER at CANOE CAMP.

The chain of caches left along the expedition's route was remarkably successful. On their return journey in 1806, corps members seem to have recovered most of the important items they had buried, although their botanical specimens were nearly all badly damaged by damp. Yet each report of digging up caches notes that the dried goods, powder, and maps and charts were in good order; for practical purposes, these were far more important. On July 8, 1806, Clark's party reached the cache where they had left their canoes in August 1805. He noted that the men "scarcely gave themselves time to take of their saddles before they were off to the deposit" for the tobacco they had gone without for six months.

It is known that at the Marias River (June 1805) and Canoe Camp (October 1805) caches, powder had been buried separately. At Canoe Camp, for example, the main cache was dug for the saddles that they hoped to use on the way back. In an attempt to keep their powder secure, the explorers buried two canisters of it at a separate location in the middle of the night. The expedition's JOURNALS have the melodramatic note that the canisters were to be found "a short distance from the river at 2 feet 4 inches N. of a dead toped pine tree." It is a nice irony that the precaution proved unnecessary. Seven months later, on May 7, 1806, Patrick Gass reported: "At this lodge the natives found two canisters of ammunition which we had buried last fall on our way down, and which they took care of and returned to us safe."

Further Reading

Cutright, Paul Russell. *Lewis & Clark: Pioneering Naturalists.* Lincoln: University of Nebraska Press/Bison Books, 1989.

Fritz, Harry. "Store Room." From *The Lewis & Clark Expedition: A Western Adventure—A National Epic.* Available on-line. URL: http://www.lewis-clark.org/te_cache.htm. Downloaded on February 21, 2002.

MacGregor, Carol Lynn, ed. *The Journals of Patrick Gass, Member of the Lewis and Clark Expedition.* Missoula, Mont.: Mountain Press Publishing Company, 1997.

Cahokia   See RECRUITING.

Calumet Bluff

On August 27, 1804, as the CORPS OF DISCOVERY passed the mouth of the James River on their way up the MISSOURI RIVER, they were met by three Indian boys, two of them YANKTON NAKOTA INDIANS (Yankton Sioux) and the other an OMAHA. The boys told them of a large Yankton camp not very far up the James. Sergeant NATHANIEL PRYOR and interpreter PIERRE DORION accompanied the boys back to the village with instructions to arrange a formal meeting. The two men were welcomed warmly and lodged in TIPIS made "of a Conic form Covered with Buffalow Roabs."

The site chosen for the council with the Yankton Nakota was named Calumet Bluff after the French word for the Indian peace pipe. It was located on the west side of the Missouri, just downstream from present-day Gavin's Point Dam, Nebraska. The council took place on August 30, with Yankton chiefs WEUCHE, White Crane, and Half Man in attendance, among others. Both sides took pains to impress the other. The Yankton brought four musicians who sang and played as their delegation arrived, and Captains MERIWETHER LEWIS and WILLIAM CLARK had the bow swivel gun on the KEELBOAT fired in reply.

The meeting went on for two days, during which the Yankton made clear that they wanted better access to TRADE goods both for their own use and to increase their importance among other Indian nations. They did agree to the captain's request to organize a delegation from other nations in the area. Half Man, however, warned the expedition that they would not be well received by other Sioux (Dakota, Lakota, Nakota) farther up the river, saying, "I fear those nations above will not open their ears, and you cannot I fear open them." As the council ended, it was agreed that Dorion would stay with the Yankton for the winter and attempt to make peace between them and other nations.

Like many sites of the Lewis and Clark Expedition, Calumet Bluff can no longer be seen today. It was destroyed during construction of Gavin's Point Dam.

Further Reading

Fifer, Barbara, and Vicky Soderberg. *Along the Trail with Lewis and Clark.* Great Falls, Mont.: Montana Magazine, 1998.

Moulton, Gary E., ed. *Atlas of the Lewis and Clark Expedition.* Revised ed. Lincoln: University of Nebraska Press, 1999.

Ronda, James P. *Lewis and Clark among the Indians.* Lincoln: University of Nebraska Press, 1984.

camas root (*Camassia quamash*)

The diet of many Pacific coastal Indian tribes was heavily dependent on fish, acorns, and camas root. The camas is a member of the lily family, growing up to 2 feet high, with a cluster of six or more white petals, green stamens, and narrow, grasslike leaves. The food is found in the onionlike root.

In September 1805, after the expedition had finally descended from the BITTERROOT MOUNTAINS and encountered the NEZ PERCE INDIANS, they were given FOOD to eat that included dried fish and the camas root. Their initial reaction to the change in diet was to develop dysentery (possibly from bacteria in the fish). In time, though, their stomachs became accustomed to the camas, finding it preferable to the BITTERROOT as it had a "sort of sweetish taste, and much the consistency of a roasted onion." MERIWETHER LEWIS also observed that the camas root—which he called the quaw-mash—was "much the greatest portion of [the Nez Perce] subsistence." This did not, however, mean that he himself found it appealing. Although he wrote 1,500 words about it and how the Nez Perce prepared it, he was of the personal opinion that

"This root is pallateable but disagrees with me in every shape I have ever used it."

Indian villages established camps in flood plains when the camas root was ready to be harvested; for the Nez Perce this was usually about mid-July. It was eaten either raw, boiled, or baked. About the size of a hen's egg, it was odorless and tasteless when eaten in its raw state. The usual method of cooking was to steam the roots in a specially prepared pit. The Indians preserved the cooked or sun-dried bulbs by pressing them into cakes called pasheco, which were sometimes added to boiling salmon to give them flavor. Camas soup was also made.

Many artifacts relating to the camas have been found by archaeologists. It is thought that the Kalispel nation used camas ovens in the floodplain of the Pend Oreille River of Washington State. Some earthen ovens used for cooking and drying the camas have been carbon dated at about 4,000 years old.

Although Lewis and Clark returned with a number of camas roots that ended up in the Philadelphia Museum of CHARLES WILLSON PEALE, it is unclear what has since happened to them; it is possible that they were lost in the 1865 fire at P. T. Barnum's American Museum.

Further Reading

Cutright, Paul Russell. *Lewis & Clark: Pioneering Naturalists.* Lincoln: University of Nebraska Press/Bison Books, 1989.

Cameahwait (One Who Never Walks)

(unknown–unknown) *Shoshone chief*

In August 1805, as the CORPS OF DISCOVERY approached the ROCKY MOUNTAINS, they became increasingly anxious to find the Lemhi SHOSHONE INDIANS who lived in the area. MERIWETHER LEWIS and WILLIAM CLARK were in need of HORSES and intelligence, and they were counting on the Shoshone to provide both. On August 13, Lewis and a few men riding ahead of the main party finally met a group of Shoshone. Among them was their chief, whose name was Cameahwait (One Who Never Walks).

After determining that the strangers were friendly, Cameahwait brought them back to his Shoshone village, where they were treated as honored guests. Lewis had GEORGE DROUILLARD communicate with the chief by sign language, and in this way they were able to convey that more white men were coming. Although he and his warriors were anxious to proceed to a planned BUFFALO hunt at THREE FORKS, Cameahwait agreed to accompany Lewis's group back across the CONTINENTAL DIVIDE to the BEAVERHEAD RIVER to meet Clark and the rest. Unfortunately, when they arrived at the meeting point, they found that the others had not yet arrived, which caused some suspicious Shoshone warriors to accuse Lewis of leading them into a trap. The captain defused the situation by giving Cameahwait his hat and gun and by donning a Shoshone cape.

On August 17 Clark and his party finally arrived, and negotiations with the Shoshone began. First, however, they all witnessed a scene which, in a different century, could have only been created by Hollywood. Shortly after Sacagawea joined the men and began to translate (see INTERPRETATION), she began to stare at the chief—and in him recognized her own brother, whom she had not seen in years. "She instantly jumped up," wrote Clark, "and ran and embraced him, throwing over him her blanket, and weeping profusely."

It was an emotional scene, and if Cameahwait had had any doubts about Lewis and Clark, they were dispelled by the presence of his sister. Once he was also assured of their willingness to provide guns to the Shoshone, negotiations for horses and information proceeded smoothly. Consequently, the captains named the site CAMP FORTUNATE.

In the process of talking to Cameahwait, Lewis and Clark learned much about the terrain and were disappointed when he informed them that the route they had hoped to take down the SALMON RIVER to the COLUMBIA RIVER was impassable. While Clark and some men reconnoitered the river to verify this, Lewis stayed on at Camp Fortunate and studied the Shoshone (see ETHNOGRAPHY). He made detailed notes about all aspects of the nation's life, including its clothing; he described an ermine tippet that Cameahwait had given him as "the most eligant peice of Indian dress I ever saw."

During this time when the corps was separated, Cameahwait decided that he had waited long enough to go to the buffalo hunt and prepared to leave. Lewis learned of the Shoshone's impending departure from TOUSSAINT CHARBONNEAU, and he quickly moved to stop them, fearing that they would leave before the expedition had all the horses it needed for the journey across the mountains. After berating and threatening the Shoshone chiefs, Lewis listened as Cameahwait apologized and explained that his people were hungry but that they would stay until the white men were on their way.

Once the corps was prepared to move on, Cameahwait allowed them to take along OLD TOBY, a Shoshone who would guide them across the BITTERROOT MOUNTAINS. They did not meet the chief again on their return journey. Cameahwait was later killed during a battle with the HIDATSA INDIANS, although the date is not known.

Further Reading

Ambrose, Stephen E. *Undaunted Courage: Meriwether Lewis, Thomas Jefferson, and the Opening of the American West.* New York: Simon and Schuster, 1996.

Duncan, Dayton, and Ken Burns. *Lewis & Clark: The Journey of the Corps of Discovery.* New York: Alfred A. Knopf, 1998.

Ronda, James P. *Lewis and Clark among the Indians.* Lincoln and London: University of Nebraska Press, 1984.

Camp Chopunnish (Long Camp)

When the CORPS OF DISCOVERY arrived at WEIPPE PRAIRIE in late September 1805 after a long and dangerous journey over the BITTERROOT MOUNTAINS, they were kindly received by the NEZ PERCE INDIANS. They stayed with the Nez Perce for the next few weeks while they recovered from a bout of dysentery and built CANOES for the next stage of their journey. On October 16 they left CANOE CAMP and set off down the CLEARWATER RIVER to the SNAKE RIVER and from there to the COLUMBIA RIVER. They were accompanied part of the way by two Nez Perce chiefs, TWISTED HAIR and TETOHARSKY.

The following spring, as the corps was returning back up the SNAKE RIVER, they met Tetoharsky, who took them to Twisted Hair's village. Along the way they met two more chiefs, CUT NOSE and BROKEN ARM, and mediated a dispute between Cut Nose and Twisted Hair over the latter's care of the expedition's HORSES during the winter. They were also told that any passage back over the Bitterroots would be impossible until the snows had melted, at least not for another month. The expedition thus had no choice but to make camp with the Nez Perce. Their stay from May 14 to June 10 was one of the longest they were to remain in one place; only the encampments at FORT MANDAN and FORT CLATSOP exceeded it. This is why some historians refer to it as Long Camp. Other sources, however, call it Camp Chopunnish, after MERIWETHER LEWIS's and WILLIAM CLARK's name for the Nez Perce. (The JOURNALS never actually named the camp.)

Camp Chopunnish was situated on the north bank of the Clearwater River (across from present-day Kamiah, Idaho), a site that offered good grazing for their horses. Relations with the Nez Perce were generally excellent, and the journals refer often to their honesty. The Indians had found the saddles the explorers had hidden the previous year and moved them to a safer spot. One had also found the two canisters of powder that had been carefully buried and returned them to the corps.

There was, however, one problem: FOOD. There was some game in the woods, but this proved insufficient, and the river proved empty of salmon. Sergeant PATRICK GASS recorded incidents of corps members and Nez Perce helping each other to catch and kill game, and as another means of obtaining food, Captain Clark dispensed MEDICINE AND MEDICAL TREATMENT. On their westward journey the year before, he had used massage and liniment to cure an elderly Indian, as a result of which his medical expertise was in constant demand. A hot/cold water treatment that greatly helped an old chief who had been paralyzed for three years confirmed his reputation. Clark soon found himself dealing with as many as 40 patients a day, and in return the expedition was paid in roots, dried fish, and sometimes with a horse or a dog.

Even with this resource, food was scarce, and the explorers had to barter the very few TRADE goods they had left to procure more to eat. When it was discovered that brass buttons from uniform coats were in demand, these were promptly brought into service, and Lewis proudly noted that the buttons from his and Clark's dress coats brought in three bushels of roots "not less pleasing to us than the return of a good cargo to an east India merchant." (It should be remembered that the Nez Perce were as hungry as the explorers, something that all the corps members appreciated.)

Although their relationship with their Indian hosts was good, helped by relaxation in the form of friendly horse and foot races and shooting matches, the captains' anxiety to get back over the mountains overrode all else. Thus, on June 10, 1806, after nearly a month at Camp Chopunnish, the party moved on up to Weippe Prairie. There was an initial attempt to transit the LOLO TRAIL unaided; this failed, but two weeks later, with the help of five Nez Perce guides, the expedition finally succeeded in crossing back over the Bitterroots.

When they at last bade farewell to the Nez Perce who had guided them over the Lolo Trail, Patrick Gass recorded the gratitude the corps felt: "We . . . waited here some time in order to have a morning hunt, as our guides intend to return, and we wish to give them a plentiful supply of provisions to carry back over the mountains. . . . We were able to furnish them with two DEER and a half from those we killed yesterday, We then gave them some presents and took a friendly leave of them. . . . After taking our farewell of these good hearted, hospital and obliging sons of the west, we proceeded on. . . ."

Further Reading

Ambrose, Stephen E. *Undaunted Courage: Meriwether Lewis, Thomas Jefferson, and the Opening of the American West.* New York: Simon and Schuster, 1996.

Cutright, Paul Russell. *Lewis & Clark: Pioneering Naturalists.* Lincoln: University of Nebraska Press/Bison Books, 1989.

Camp Disappointment

The northernmost point of the LOUISIANA TERRITORY reached by MERIWETHER LEWIS was the site he named Camp Disappointment. It lies about 12 miles north of present-day Browning, Montana.

On July 3, 1806, during their return journey from the PACIFIC OCEAN, the expedition split their party at TRAVELERS' REST. While WILLIAM CLARK was to take a party south to find and follow the YELLOWSTONE RIVER down to the MISSOURI RIVER, Lewis would go northeast to the GREAT FALLS, down the Missouri, and then turn north up the MARIAS RIVER to chart its course. If the river went as far north as he hoped—into CANADA—then the United States could lay claim to the area as part of the LOUISIANA PURCHASE and thus have a means of diverting some of the lucrative Canadian FUR TRADE.

Accompanied by GEORGE DROUILLARD, JOSEPH FIELD, and REUBIN FIELD, Lewis reached the Marias on July 18 and followed it north for three days to the junction of TWO MEDICINE RIVER and Cut Bank Creek. He then followed Cut Bank Creek, the more northern of the two rivers, for two days before realizing the river turned west into the mountains. "I thought it unnecessary to proceed further," he wrote, "and therefore encamped resolving to rest ourselves and HORSES for a couple of days at this place and take the necessary observations. . . . I now have lost all hope of the waters of this river ever extending to N. Latitude 50."

The party stayed at the site for four unpleasant days. The WEATHER having turned to heavy rain and winds, ASTRONOMICAL OBSERVATIONS were impossible, and the hunters were unable to find any game to eat except for some pigeons. Little wonder that Lewis named the place Camp Disappointment. They gladly left it on the morning of July 26 and had their first encounter with the BLACKFEET INDIANS that afternoon.

Further Reading
Cutright, Paul Russell. *Lewis & Clark: Pioneering Naturalists.* Lincoln: University of Nebraska Press/Bison Books, 1989.
Ronda, James P. *Lewis and Clark among the Indians.* Lincoln: University of Nebraska Press, 1984.

Camp Dubois (Camp Wood)

Now known as Camp Wood, Illinois, Camp Dubois lay at what was then the junction of the MISSISSIPPI RIVER and Wood River (called the Dubois River by the French), about 12 miles north of ST. LOUIS. Usually accepted as the starting point of the Lewis and Clark Expedition, the CORPS OF DISCOVERY arrived at this site and started to clear land for their winter camp on December 12, 1803.

Although the U.S. CONGRESS had approved the expedition in January 1803, it was not until August 31 that MERIWETHER LEWIS was able to take the KEELBOAT down the OHIO RIVER to the Mississippi. He had spent the interim period receiving tuition in basic medicine and surgery, botany, and astronomical studies as well as buying SUPPLIES AND EQUIPMENT, acquiring WEAPONS, and seeing to the design and building of the keelboat and the collapsible IRON-FRAME BOAT.

Lewis met WILLIAM CLARK in Clarksville, Indiana Territory, and with him officially recruited the NINE YOUNG MEN FROM KENTUCKY for the expedition. However, the journey down the Ohio with the cumbersome keelboat had put doubts in both their minds as to the size of the corps—doubts that were decisively confirmed when they turned upstream against the flow of the Mississippi. The exhausting effort to make even one mile an hour against the current made it clear that more men would be required, and a decision was made to expand the party from 15 to 45. Thus, further RECRUITING took place at KASKASKIA and FORT MASSAC as they proceeded upriver, and three squads were formed, each headed by a sergeant.

Hit by a snowstorm almost as soon as they arrived, the expanding corps set up Camp Dubois on the banks of the Mississippi in an area near the Wood River that was filled with cottonwood, maple, and oak TREES. The camp consisted of an assortment of log huts that comprised sleeping quarters for the men, a cabin for the captains, a blacksmithy, and a storehouse to which goods from the keelboat were transferred. Once building was complete, the winter was spent training and drilling the men, refurbishing and making alterations to the keelboat, and combating boredom. Clark attempted to relieve some of the tedium by holding regular shooting matches between men of his party and challengers who lived in the area, with a silver dollar as the prize. Although the country men enjoyed initial success, by spring 1804 the woodsmen of the expedition were beating all comers.

Fighting, drinking, and DISCIPLINE problems were rampant, and Clark was continually devising punishments to keep the men in line, usually some form of hard labor. Occasionally COURT-MARTIALS were necessary to deal with particularly bad breaches of military conduct. Good behavior was rewarded with extra gills of whiskey. During their first Christmas together, Clark noted, "The men frolicked and hunted all day." Lewis, meanwhile, was in St. Louis, where he—and occasionally Clark—spent a lot of time buying more supplies and equipment for the larger-size expedition and also gathering information on what lay ahead of them up the Missouri. With the help of fur trader PIERRE CHOUTEAU, they also hired ENGAGÉS to help bring the PIROGUES up the Missouri.

By spring 1804 the men of the Corps of Discovery had been sorted into two groups: the permanent party, who were to go all the way to the PACIFIC OCEAN, and the smaller, temporary party, who were to go only as far as the MANDAN INDIAN villages on the upper Missouri and then return to St. Louis with the keelboat in spring 1805. Although it had originally been their intention to leave Camp Dubois on April 18, 1804, the captains decided to delay another month to procure more supplies and to test the trim of the loaded keelboat. With a load that included some seven tons of FOOD alone, Clark, who was an experienced waterman, saw this to be a vital factor. While Lewis continued to comb St. Louis for supplies, Clark spent three days supervising trials of the keelboat, shifting and reshifting its load until the right balance was achieved. Not until May 14, 1804, did the expedition's keelboat and two pirogues pull away from Camp Dubois and set out on its epic journey.

The original site of Camp Dubois no longer exists, due to the Mississippi's propensity to change its course over time. Although located at the time on the Illinois shore, the campsite is now thought to be in Missouri. The mouth of the Missouri River, once close to the camp, is now 2½ miles south of the site.

Further Reading
Ambrose, Stephen E. *Undaunted Courage: Meriwether Lewis, Thomas Jefferson, and the Opening of the American West.* New York: Simon and Schuster, 1996.
Applemen, Roy E. "The Lost Site of Camp Wood: The Lewis and Clark Winter Camp, 1803–04." *Journal of the West* 7, no. 2 (1968): 270–274.
Lankiewicz, Donald P. "The Camp on Wood River: A Winter of Preparation for the Lewis and Clark Expedition." *Journal of the Illinois State Historical Society* 75, no. 2 (1982): 115–120.
Mayer, Robert W. "Wood River, 1803–1804." *Journal of the Illinois State Historical Society* 61, no. 2 (1968): 140–149.
Schmidt, Thomas. *National Geographic Guide to the Lewis & Clark Trail.* Washington, D.C.: National Geographic, 1998.

Camp Fortunate

By August 11, 1805, the Lewis and Clark Expedition had passed the THREE FORKS of the MISSOURI RIVER and come to what they knew was a critical point in their journey: the passage across the CONTINENTAL DIVIDE. All in the party were tired, several were injured, much of the SUPPLIES AND EQUIPMENT were wet and damaged, and FOOD supplies were uncertain. Most significant of all, the expedition had no HORSES, and without these any crossing of the ROCKY MOUNTAINS was dangerous at best and impossible at worst.

Three days earlier, on August 8, SACAGAWEA had recognized the landmark of BEAVERHEAD ROCK and assured MERIWETHER LEWIS and WILLIAM CLARK that the SHOSHONE INDIANS would be found nearby. The captains had therefore decided that Lewis should go on ahead on foot with GEORGE DROUILLARD, HUGH MCNEAL, and JOHN SHIELDS. These four followed the BEAVERHEAD RIVER until it split into two forks and then, after leaving a note for Clark, began to travel overland. On August 11 they encountered a Shoshone scout, who retreated before they could establish any contact. The next day, following the Indian westward, Lewis and his men crossed the Continental Divide at LEMHI PASS. Two days later they finally met a band of Shoshone and Chief CAMEAHWAIT. The Indians welcomed the soldiers, and the rest of the day and that night was spent in cheerful comradeship, during which time Lewis learned much of what he needed to know about obtaining horses and crossing the mountains.

The next morning, however, the Shoshone balked at Lewis's request that they accompany him back east over Lemhi Pass to meet Clark and the remainder of the party. Cameahwait persuaded his warriors to go, but when the party reached the forks on the Beaverhead River, there was no sign of Clark and the others. The suspicious Shoshone suspected a trap, and it was only by turning over his rifle and exchanging clothing with Cameahwait that Lewis barely convinced them that he could be trusted.

After a tense delay of 24 hours, Clark finally arrived, and thereafter relations with the Shoshone were much improved. Enhancing the situation was the discovery that Sacagawea and Cameahwait were sister and brother, leading to an emotional family reunion that Lewis described as "really affecting." While Clark went on to conduct a reconnaissance of the SALMON RIVER, Lewis stayed for the next six days at the site below the river's forks, which was named Camp Fortunate. During this time he conducted ethnographic studies of the Shoshone while also caching supplies, gathering information, and bartering for horses and guides. He departed the camp on August 24, and a week later the expedition finally left the Shoshone for the next stage of their journey over the BITTERROOT MOUNTAINS.

On the return journey in 1806, after recrossing the Bitterroots and stopping at TRAVELERS' REST, the captains decided to split the party in two. While Lewis took some men northeast to explore the MARIAS RIVER, Clark and the rest went back along their old route south, reaching Camp Fortunate on July 8, 1806. They stayed there for two days before descending the BEAVERHEAD RIVER and JEFFERSON RIVER. The site of Camp Fortunate is now covered by the Clark Canyon Reservoir, 20 miles southwest of Dillon, Montana.

Further Reading

Ambrose, Stephen E. *Undaunted Courage: Meriwether Lewis, Thomas Jefferson, and the Opening of the American West.* New York: Simon and Schuster, 1996.

Ronda, James P. *Lewis and Clark among the Indians.* Lincoln: University of Nebraska Press, 1984.

Schmidt, Thomas. *National Geographic Guide to the Lewis & Clark Trail.* Washington, D.C.: National Geographic, 1998.

Camp White Catfish

The site of Camp White Catfish lies across the MISSOURI RIVER from modern Bellevue, Nebraska. By July 21, 1804, the expedition had reached the PLATTE RIVER, where they hoped to make contact with the OTOE INDIANS (Oto) and Pawnee. Because there were so few TREES at the mouth of the Platte, the party pressed on some 12 miles up the Missouri to find a suitable campsite with trees for shade and firewood. Finding the ideal location the next day, they stopped and made camp. Lewis noted that "The hunters have found game scarce in this neighborhood; they have seen DEER, turkeys and GROUSE; we have also an abundance of wild grapes; and one of our men caught a white catfish, the eyes of which were small, and its tail resembling that of a dolphin." Consequently, their campsite was named after the strange-looking fish, which had been caught by Private SILAS GOODRICH.

While the party rested, hunted, dressed skins, and refurbished their equipment, Privates GEORGE DROUILLARD and PIERRE CRUZATTE set off to invite the Otoe and Pawnee chiefs to a council. However, they returned two days later with the news that the Indian villages were empty, since the tribes were away hunting BUFFALO. The expedition left Camp White Catfish on July 27, 1804, and continued on their way upriver to what was to be their first formal meeting with Otoe chiefs a few days later.

Further Reading

MacGregor, Carol Lynn, ed. *The Journals of Patrick Gass, Member of the Lewis and Clark Expedition.* Missoula, Mont.: Mountain Press Publishing Company, 1997.

Ronda, James P. *Lewis and Clark among the Indians.* Lincoln: University of Nebraska Press, 1984.

Camp Wood   See CAMP DUBOIS.

Canada

At the time THOMAS JEFFERSON and MERIWETHER LEWIS were planning the expedition into the West, British companies were using the young nation's neighbor to the north, Canada, as a base for extensive fur trading. The United States was naturally eager to share in that profitable business.

Explorers from FRANCE and GREAT BRITAIN had long searched Canadian rivers for the fabled NORTHWEST PASSAGE to China and India. In the process, they built a number of posts—the French mostly along the St. Lawrence River, the Great Lakes, and as far south as the Mississippi River; the British around Hudson Bay and along the Atlantic coast, including the future United States.

Although the French and British explorers never found a route to Asia, they discovered valuable fish and game, including fur-bearing BEAVER, fox, and BEAR. Permanent French settlement began in the early 17th century, but the colonies remained economically dependent on the FUR TRADE and were kept under tight control by France.

In 1763 the Treaty of Paris assigned all French territory east of the Mississippi River to Britain, except for the islands of Saint Pierre and Miquelon off Newfoundland. The population in the British territory included 65,000 French-speaking Quebeçois. In 1774 the British Parliament passed the Quebec Act, granting recognition of French civil laws and guaranteeing religious and linguistic freedom. The act also aroused indignation in the American colonies by extending the Quebec border down to the OHIO RIVER, which effectively annexed the Ohio Territory to Canada.

After the American Declaration of Independence in 1776, many loyalists moved north to Canada, primarily into Nova Scotia and New Brunswick and along the Great Lakes. The increase in English-speaking population led the British to create Upper Canada (now Ontario) in 1791, with representative governing bodies similar to those of Quebec, or Lower Canada.

In 1778 the English explorer Captain James Cook sailed along the Pacific coast, discovering the sea OTTERS that would subsequently be the basis for a lucrative FUR TRADE. This trade was one of the motives for Britain, France, SPAIN, Russia, and the new United States to assert claims on the ORE-GON TERRITORY.

Many French- and English-speaking Canadians trappers and traders ventured south into what later became U.S. territory. By the 1790s, traders in Canada had formed the NORTH WEST COMPANY to develop the fur trade in western Canada. ALEXANDER MACKENZIE, a member of the company, led an overland expedition across Canada to the Pacific Ocean in 1793. His route included a half-mile portage over the CONTINENTAL DIVIDE (much shorter, but much farther north, than the PORTAGE Lewis and Clark would face a decade later). In 1798 DAVID THOMPSON, a cartographer with the North West Company, went far enough south to map part of the upper Missouri River—seven years before Lewis and Clark got there.

By 1800, when Thomas Jefferson was elected president, the North West Company and other Canada-based interests had a monopoly over much of the fur trade in the LOUISIANA TERRITORY. Jefferson resolved to secure this for the United States, and the Lewis and Clark Expedition had this as one of its major objectives.

Most of western Canada at that time was ungoverned territory. A confederation of Canadian provinces from the Atlantic to the Pacific did not come about until the mid-19th century—nor independence from Britain until the 20th century.

Further Reading

Pathfinders and Passageways: The Exploration of Canada. Available on-line. URL: http://www.nlc-bnc.ca/2/24/index-e.html. Updated on December 7, 2001.
Wood, W. Raymond, and Thomas D. Thiessen. *Early Fur Trade on the Northern Plains: Canadian Traders Among the Mandan and Hidatsa Indians, 1738–1818.* Norman: University of Oklahoma Press, 1985.

candles

One of the impressive aspects of the journey of the CORPS OF DISCOVERY is the planning and preparation that both MERIWETHER LEWIS and WILLIAM CLARK put into it. In this regard their forethought on bringing and later making candles helped to produce the JOURNALS, MAPS, and field notes on plant and animal life then new to science—and on one occasion even provided FOOD for the men.

Among the supplies Lewis and Clark took with them from CAMP DUBOIS were at least two tin "Lanthorns" (lanterns), two tin lamps, and two boxes of candles as well as a bag of candlewick. Perhaps two cases of candles might be more accurate, since Clark's careful memorandum of "Articles in Readiness for the Voyage" notes that the boxes weighed 60 pounds each. The candles were most likely made of tallow (animal fat) or beeswax. These lanterns and candles enabled the two captains and other journal writers to make their entries at the end of each day, but it is probable that lanterns and lamps were lost or broken along the way.

Stephen Ambrose notes that by September 18, 1805, when the expedition was in the BITTERROOT MOUNTAINS, the only provisions the party had left comprised "a skant proportion" of portable soup, some bear oil, and about 20 pounds of candles. It has been related that they resorted to eating these, including the candles, in addition to killing some of their HORSES, to help alleviate their intense hunger (see SOUP, PORTABLE).

Throughout the winter of 1805–06 at FORT CLATSOP, the two captains spent much of their time writing and updating their findings. While Clark worked on his charts and observations, Lewis wrote lengthy descriptions of BIRDS, PLANTS, FISH, and the habits and clothing of the nearby Indian nations. On January 13, 1806, he wrote: "This evening we exhausted the last of our candles, but fortunately had taken the precaution to bring with us moulds and wick, by means of which and some Elk's tallow in our possession we do not yet consider ourselves destitute of this necessary article."

As a result, among the activities devised to keep the men busy during their stay at Fort Clatsop was candle making. Knotted wicks were hung down into the candle molds and tied to sticks at the top. The tallow was then heated and poured into the molds and left to set. When it had cooled, the wick knots were trimmed at the bottom and excess tallow trimmed before removing the candles from the molds. The length of time they burned depended on the type of animal fat used for tallow. The men usually mixed beeswax into their tallow to allow the candles to burn better.

The CLATSOP INDIANS had a very ingenious way of making candles, although it was not mentioned by Lewis or Clark in their journals. The eulachon, which was prized by the corps as a tasty fish to eat, could also serve as candles when wicks were drawn through their fattened bodies. It is for this reason that they are called candlefish.

Further Reading

Cutright, Paul Russell. *Lewis & Clark: Pioneering Naturalists.* Lincoln: University of Nebraska Press/Bison Books, 1989.

Fort Clatsop National Memorial. "Candle Making." Available on-line. URL: http://www.nps.gov/focl/candles3.htm. Posted on April 30, 1999.

Canoe Camp

From September 11 to 22, 1805, the CORPS OF DISCOVERY struggled to make their way over the BITTERROOT MOUNTAINS, a crossing that nearly cost them their lives. When they finally descended the western slopes onto WEIPPE PRAIRIE, they met a band of NEZ PERCE INDIANS, who received them hospitably and offered the starving explorers dried fish and CAMAS ROOT. Unfortunately the change in diet, combined with the possibility of bacteria in the fish, resulted in severe gastrointestinal distress for the soldiers. On September 24, though most of the men were still in distress, Nez Perce chief TWISTED HAIR and two of his sons took WILLIAM CLARK to look for a suitable site where he and his men could build canoes for the next stage of their journey.

The site they chose was on the south side of the CLEARWATER RIVER, opposite the junction with its north fork (about four miles northwest of present-day Orofino, Idaho). Here on September 26 the party established what they called Canoe Camp and set to work. Although they were able to fell several ponderosa pines, the process of hollowing out the interiors was laborious and slow. On the advice of the Nez Perce, the men adopted the slower but easier method of burning out a section of the trunk, then chipping away the charcoal that was left. With many of the men still sick, the work took some 10 days to complete, so it was not until October 7 that the expedition gave their HORSES to the Nez Perce for safekeeping, cached the saddles and some ammunition, and were able to set off in five dugout canoes down the Clearwater, their first journey by water on the rivers west of the CONTINENTAL DIVIDE. It was to be another month down the Clearwater River, the SNAKE RIVER, and the COLUMBIA RIVER before they were to reach their goal, the PACIFIC OCEAN at the mouth of the Columbia.

Further Reading

MacGregor, Carol Lynn, ed. *The Journals of Patrick Gass, Member of the Lewis and Clark Expedition.* Missoula, Mont.: Mountain Press Publishing Company, 1997.

Ronda, James P. *Lewis and Clark among the Indians.* Lincoln: University of Nebraska Press, 1984.

Schmidt, Thomas. *National Geographic Guide to the Lewis & Clark Trail.* Washington, D.C.: National Geographic, 1998.

canoes

The popular image of a canoe is that of a slim, fragile craft, pointed at each end and light enough to be easily carried overland. While light, birchbark canoes of this type, known as Algonquian canoes, were indeed in widespread use in the Northeast and on the Great Lakes, the most common canoe in use across North America was the dugout canoe.

In 1804 the Lewis and Clark Expedition made its way from CAMP DUBOIS on the MISSISSIPPI RIVER up the MISSOURI RIVER to the villages of the MANDAN INDIANS in North Dakota on the KEELBOAT and two PIROGUES. It was MERIWETHER LEWIS's intention to send all three back to Camp Dubois and proceed westward by canoe alone, but the amount of baggage, Indian GIFTS, and TRADE goods forced him to take the two pirogues upriver. Thus, when the expedition left FORT MANDAN on April 7, 1805, they did so in the two pirogues and six dugout canoes they had made. (The Mandan do not seem to have used canoes. Instead, they crossed the river in BULL BOATS, extremely light and useful craft for short journeys but too unsuitable for the expedition's needs.)

Sergeant PATRICK GASS, the best carpenter in the party, was responsible for the canoes' construction. His journal entry for February 28, 1805, reads: "Sixteen of us went up the river about six miles where we found and cut down trees for four canoes." The next day he wrote: "The same party encamped out to make the canoes, and continued until six were made." Three weeks later he reported: ". . . we carried them to the river about a mile and half distant: There I remained with two men to finish them, and to take care of them, until the 26th [March], when some men came up from the fort, and we put the canoes in the water."

The expedition's JOURNALS do not give the dimensions of the canoes, but historians estimate that each one weighed about 1,000 pounds and was between 22 and 28 feet long. They were carved out of cottonwood TREES, the only ones that grew to any size in that part of the GREAT PLAINS, and were built for strength rather than speed. (The journey up the Missouri had made the explorers very familiar with the snags, rocks, and rapids of the river.)

Despite the canoes' sturdiness, though, they were not perfect. Lewis recorded on March 27, 1805: "We had all our canoes brought down, and were obliged to cauk [caulk] and pitch very attentively the cracks so common in cottonwood." WILLIAM CLARK made the same comment: "Had all the canoes corked pitched and tined [tinned] in and one the cracks and windshakes, which is universally in the cotton wood."

Despite these flaws, the canoes served the explorers well, taking the expedition up the river for four months until they reached CAMP FORTUNATE below the CONTINENTAL DIVIDE in August 1806. Two months previously, in June, they had hidden their one remaining pirogue (the other had been left downstream) below the GREAT FALLS, the intention being to replace it with the IRON-FRAME BOAT. When this proved a failure, the explorers had had to go miles upstream to find cottonwoods. They were lucky enough to find two suitable trees in a small grove, and in five days they had constructed two more canoes, both 3 feet wide; one was 25 feet and the other 33 feet long.

Although Lewis and Clark had hoped to find a route by water from LEMHI PASS down to the PACIFIC OCEAN, the SALMON RIVER proved impassable, and it was not until they reached the CLEARWATER RIVER in late September 1805 that they were once again able to take to the water. Near today's Orofino, Idaho, they set up CANOE CAMP on September 26. After they cut down some ponderosa pine trees, the NEZ PERCE chief TWISTED HAIR showed them how to save labor by burning out the centers of the logs rather than chipping them out. On October 7 the expedition set off downriver in five canoes, reaching the mouth of the COLUMBIA RIVER a month later.

The expedition found that CELILO FALLS AND THE DALLES on the Columbia was a boundary between the upland Indians and those living downstream of the falls. The SHOSHONE, Nez Perce, and FLATHEAD INDIANS (Salish) were horse-owning nations. As the expedition moved down the Clearwater, SNAKE, and Columbia Rivers, they found Indians who used both HORSES and canoes. Downstream of The Dalles, however, there were few, if any, horses to be seen, and canoes were the normal method of travel.

In the same way that they had admired the horsemanship of the Shoshone and Nez Perce, the explorers were impressed by the canoes used by the CHINOOK nations around the mouth of the Columbia. In the JOURNALS they reported Indians making long, elaborate canoes, painted and decorated, that had carved heads at the bow and stern. The soldiers envied the Chinook their ability to take their canoes into the roughest tidal water and the ingenuity they used in their boat making. Some of the canoes Lewis and Clark observed were as much as 50 feet in length and could carry 20–30 people. (It is worth noting that even more elaborate canoes were made by the Haida Indians who lived on Queen Charlotte's Island. Their seagoing canoes were almost 100 feet long and 7 feet wide and could carry 60 people.)

After losing two of the expedition's canoes, washed away by a high tide, Lewis had to buy a canoe from the Chinook and was forced to steal another. With these and three they had made on the Clearwater, the expedition made its return journey upstream in 1806. Leaving FORT CLATSOP on March 23, it reached Celilo Falls on April 21, disposed of three of the canoes there, and discarded the last two above the falls on April 24. By that time the members had acquired enough horses to carry their baggage until they reached the Nez Perce, where they had left their own horses months before.

To travel the rivers along their route, the Lewis and Clark Expedition used dugout canoes, as favored by Indians of the West. They greatly admired the long, graceful models fashioned by the Chinook Indians, such as this one in a photo taken near Celilo Falls on the Columbia River in 1897. *(Library of Congress, Prints and Photographs Division [LC-USZ62-101331])*

The expedition rode to TRAVELERS' REST, where it split into two parties on July 3, 1806. Lewis and one group rode east to explore the MARIAS RIVER, while Clark and the remainder rode south back to Camp Fortunate. There Clark left some men to retrieve the canoes that had been hidden nearly a year before while he took another group across country to the YELLOWSTONE RIVER. Here he had to ride some days before finding cottonwood trees big enough to make canoes. Even then they were so narrow—less than two feet wide—that he had to lash them together for stability.

Five weeks after leaving Travelers' Rest, the expedition reunited on August 12, about 30 miles upstream of the mouth of the Little Missouri. They arrived back at ST. LOUIS on September 23. Of the dugout canoes in which they returned in triumph, five had taken them from Fort Mandan up to the Continental Divide, then brought them safely back thousands of miles to St. Louis. One wonders whether Lewis or Clark recalled then the words they had written so many months before about the cracks and windshakes "so common in cottonwood."

Further Reading

Ambrose, Stephen E. *Undaunted Courage: Meriwether Lewis, Thomas Jefferson, and the Opening of the American West.* New York: Simon and Schuster, 1996.

Boss, Richard C. "Keelboat, Pirogue, and Canoe: Vessels Used by the Lewis and Clark Corps of Discovery." *Nautical Research Journal* 38, no. 2 (1993): 68–87.

Cutright, Paul Russell. *Lewis & Clark: Pioneering Naturalists.* Lincoln: University of Nebraska Press/Bison Books, 1989.

MacGregor, Carol Lynn, ed. *The Journals of Patrick Gass, Member of the Lewis and Clark Expedition.* Missoula, Mont.: Mountain Press Publishing Company, 1997.

Cape Disappointment

Cape Disappointment, the northern headland of the COLUMBIA RIVER estuary, lies just south of present-day Illwaco, Washington. It had been given its name by British captain John Meares in 1788 when he had concluded, erroneously, that there was no great river (and thus no NORTHWEST PASSAGE) at this

Lewis and Clark arrived at Cape Disappointment and carved their names on a tree there in November 1805. Finding no trading ships in the area, they prepared to spend the winter on the Pacific coast. *(Washington State Historical Society, Tacoma)*

location on the Pacific Coast. In 1792, when Captain ROBERT GRAY discovered the Columbia, he named it Cape Hancock, but Meares's name for the cape stuck in future generations.

On November 7, 1805, the expedition reached what they had hoped would be their final destination: the mouth of the Columbia River. They camped at the head of the estuary on the northern bank, near modern Dahlia, Washington, and WILLIAM CLARK wrote: "Great joy in camp we are in View of the Ocian, this great Pacific Ocean which we had been so long anxious to See."

While the party was happy to have reached the estuary, they found the conditions appalling. The seemingly continuous rain chilled and depressed them, and the north shore of the estuary was bleak and inhospitable. They found it difficult even to find a flat campsite on the rocky shore. From November 10 to 15, they took shelter on the eastern side of POINT ELLICE but found that even their CANOES were not safe from the storms and waves. On November 15 they moved around the point to STATION CAMP on Baker's Bay, near Chinook Point (called Haley's Bay by Lewis and Clark). Although this site was more comfortable, this was only because they were able to make crude SHELTERs from boards they had found in an abandoned Indian village.

MERIWETHER LEWIS then set out to fulfill the final part of his orders from THOMAS JEFFERSON: "On your arrival on that coast, endeavor to learn if there be any port within your reach frequented by the sea vessels of any nation. . . ." With a small party, he walked northwest around Baker's Bay to the headland on the Pacific. Clark had determined that this bay was the usual place for trading vessels to lie at anchor, but Lewis saw none. He went on to the cape and then turned north up the coast for several miles just in case some other harbor existed. He found nothing but did have the satisfaction of carving his name on a tree on Cape Disappointment. A few days later, on November 18, Clark and 11 men also went to see the ocean, and he added his name to Lewis's on the tree, proudly adding the line "By Land from the U. States in 1805 & 1805." (In this he was following the example of ALEXANDER MACKENZIE, who had painted his name and achievement on a rock by the Pacific after crossing the continent in 1793.)

By November 24 it was clear that the expedition had to find a home for the winter, and the captains put the matter to a vote in which both YORK and SACAGAWEA took part. The following day they turned back up the estuary to find a spot where they could cross to the southern shore and build what would be their home for the next three months: FORT CLATSOP.

Cape Disappointment was appropriately named, according to JOSEPH WHITEHOUSE, "on account of not finding Vessels there." As the captains may have suspected when they carved their names on the tree, it was the westernmost point of their journey. The cape lies west of the 124th meridian, while Fort Clatsop is well east of that line. When Clark and his party climbed the 150-foot headland, he wrote: "The men appear much Satisfied with their trip, beholding with astonishment, the high waves dashing against the rocks & this emence

Ocean." Cape Disappointment is now part of the Fort Canby State Park.

Further Reading

Fifer, Barbara, and Vicky Soderberg. *Along the Trail with Lewis and Clark.* Great Falls, Mont.: Montana Magazine, 1998.

MacGregor, Carol Lynn, ed. *The Journals of Patrick Gass, Member of the Lewis and Clark Expedition.* Missoula, Mont.: Mountain Press Publishing Company, 1997.

Carson, Alexander   See ENGAGÉS.

cartography   See MAPS.

Cascade Mountains

The Cascade Mountain Range, west of the ROCKY MOUNTAINS, runs from CANADA across Washington and Oregon into northern California. Dozens of Cascade volcanoes, both dormant and active, are visible from the Pacific coast as well as from the COLUMBIA RIVER, and it was from the Columbia that Lewis and Clark first sighted the mountain range in October 1805.

More than a decade before the Lewis and Clark Expedition, the English explorer GEORGE VANCOUVER surveyed the Pacific coast and made note of the Cascades, naming MOUNT HOOD and MOUNT ST. HELENS, among others. The highest peak in the range is Washington's Mount Rainier, which rises to 14,410 feet. Once they reached the Columbia River, MERIWETHER LEWIS and WILLIAM CLARK began to search for landmarks on Vancouver-produced maps that they carried with them. On October 15 Lewis walked onto a plain some distance from the river and spotted the Cascade Range on the horizon. Three days later Clark spotted what he believed to be one of the peaks recorded by Vancouver as Mount St. Helens; it would later prove to be Mount Adams. Nevertheless, seeing the peaks of the Cascades reassured the explorers that they were nearing the PACIFIC OCEAN.

The Cascades consist of two volcanic regions. The severely eroded Western Cascades are much older than the more prominent High Cascades, whose snow-packed peaks were seen by the explorers. With the ocean only 100 miles to the west, weather systems produce a large amount of humid air condensing into rain or snow.

Further Reading

Harris, Stephen L. *Fire and Ice: The Cascade Volcanoes.* Revised ed. Seattle: The Mountaineers, Pacific Search Press, 1980.

National Geographic Atlas of Natural America. Washington, D.C.: National Geographic Society, 2000.

Cascades   See COLUMBIA RIVER GORGE.

The Cascade Mountain range, west of the Rocky Mountains, runs south from Canada into northern California. Meriwether Lewis first saw them on October 15, 1805. This view of the Cascades includes Lake Chelan in Washington State. *(Library of Congress, Prints and Photographs Division [LC-PAN US GEO—Washington, no. 35])*

Castle Rock   See BEACON ROCK.

Caugée, Charles   See ENGAGÉS.

Celilo Falls and The Dalles

One of the most impressive but dangerous stretches of water the expedition had to navigate was Celilo Falls and The Dalles, a series of falls and turbulent rapids on the CO-LUMBIA RIVER covering approximately 15 miles, in the course of which the CORPS OF DISCOVERY also had to pass through the Short Narrows and Long Narrows. In October 1805 the corps had already made their way past the fast and dangerous rapids on the CLEARWATER RIVER and the SNAKE RIVER when, on the 16th, they reached the Columbia. Here they were warmly greeted by the YAKAMA (Yakima) and WANAPAM INDI-ANS who had built bankside FISHING villages of mat lodges at the junction of the Snake and Columbia Rivers. Each village was congested by scaffolds for drying the FISH they caught.

As the corps canoed down the Columbia, they encountered the WALLA WALLA and UMATILLA INDIANS and finally, on October 22, 1805, the Tenino Indians at Celilo Falls, the first major barrier on the river. The falls were located just downstream of the Deschutes River and some 100 miles upstream from present-day Portland, Oregon. These and The Dalles, downstream from it, were the center of a vast Indian trading network in addition to being a major gathering place for numerous Indian nations to catch salmon. The explorers were struck immediately by the numbers of Indians who lived along the banks to catch salmon in the same way the PLAINS INDIANS congregated to hunt BUFFALO.

The Celilo Falls area was a major salmon-fishing site surrounded by lodges, but they were clearly impassable except by PORTAGE. A number of Tenino were recruited to help carry the boats and baggage downstream, and although the Indians proved helpful, their constant pilfering of supplies caused the explorers considerable annoyance. It took a full day (October 23) to complete the portage, during which expedition members suffered badly from the fleas that infested the area, feeding off the fish skins that lay everywhere. Once below Celilo Falls they met the WISHRAM AND WASCO INDIANS, with whom MERIWETHER LEWIS traded the expedition's smallest canoe for one of theirs.

The following day the party set off again downriver and to the amazement of watching Indians shot through, first, the Short Narrows of the Columbia—just 45 yards wide and a quarter-mile long—and then the Long Narrows, which was 200 yards wide and 5 miles long. WILLIAM CLARK wrote of their passage through the Narrows that "the water was agitated in a most Shocking manner. . . ." Indeed, the waters were so treacherous that Indians lined the riverbanks expecting to see men killed. Once through, the corps arrived at The Dalles, another series of shorter falls and rapids that served as the border between the Shaptian-speaking Indians and the Chinookan-speaking nations of the western coast. They then set up camp at the mouth of Mill Creek, the site of today's city of The Dalles, Oregon. (The area's name was taken from a French-Canadian term that trappers used to describe the nearby rock formations.)

Archaeological digs in the mid-20th century indicated that Celilo Falls had been the site of Indian villages for at least 11,000 years. As recently as the 1930s, there were still hundreds of Indian fishing stations in and around

Celilo Falls. Taking advantage of the vast numbers of salmon that came up the river, the fishers built gantreys, or scaffolds, overhanging the water and, securing themselves to the scaffolds with ropes, dipped in hand nets to catch the salmon as they swam upstream. Such scenes are no more, however, due to the construction of the Dalles Dam in 1957, which created Lake Celilo and thus buried Celilo Falls along with the Short and Long Narrows under many feet of water.

Further Reading

Moulton, Gary E., ed. *Atlas of the Lewis and Clark Expedition.* Revised ed. Lincoln: University of Nebraska Press, 1999.

Ronda, James P. *Lewis and Clark among the Indians.* Lincoln: University of Nebraska Press, 1984.

Schmidt, Thomas. *National Geographic Guide to the Lewis & Clark Trail.* Washington, D.C.: National Geographic, 1998.

chain of command   See ORGANIZATION OF THE EXPEDITION PARTY.

The Corps of Discovery had to portage their canoes around Celilo Falls, a major salmon-fishing site on the Columbia River. At that time the falls were surrounded by hundreds of Native American fishing lodges. *(Library of Congress, Prints and Photographs Division [LC-USZ62-107043])*

Charbonneau, Jean Baptiste (Pomp, Pompey)
(1805–1866) *mountain man*

The youngest member of the Lewis and Clark Expedition was born to SACAGAWEA and TOUSSAINT CHARBONNEAU at FORT MANDAN on February 11, 1805. The birth of Jean Baptiste Charbonneau was not easy; Sacagawea endured tremendous pain during a long labor, causing a worried MERIWETHER LEWIS to investigate ways to assist her. On the advice of RENÉ JESSAUME, he crushed the rings of a rattlesnake, mixed it with water, and then gave her the potion. He recorded the result in his journal: "Whether this medicine was truly the cause or not I shall not undertake to determine, but . . . she had not taken it more than ten minutes before she brought forth."

That the infant would accompany the CORPS OF DISCOVERY out west was taken for granted; both Lewis and WILLIAM CLARK considered his mother's presence essential to maintaining peace with the Native Americans whom they would encounter, in addition to needing her as a translator with the SHOSHONE. That he would, in later years, mix with European royalty and become a renowned mountain man could not have been foreseen—certainly not when the expedition set out from Fort Mandan on April 7, 1805, with 55-day-old Jean Baptiste snug in a cradleboard on his mother's back.

As he grew during the journey and turned into an alert and lively toddler, the young Charbonneau became a favorite of the corps members, and particularly of Clark. The boy soon acquired the nickname of "Pomp," the Shoshone word for "leader," most likely bestowed by his mother (although many sources indicate that it was a doting Clark who had bestowed the name on the "dancing little boy"); he was also called Pompy or Pompey. Although his mother twice saved him from falling overboard on the MISSOURI RIVER, he caused only one moment of real concern during the expedition. In spring 1806, as the corps prepared to traverse the LOLO TRAIL through the BITTERROOT MOUNTAINS, Pomp came down with a high fever as well as a swollen neck and throat, most likely the result of mumps or tonsillitis (although it has also been suggested he had an abscess on his neck). Wild-onion poultices were applied to his neck, "as hot as he could stand it," according to Clark, as was a salve "made of the rozen of the long leaf pine, Beaswax and bears oil mixed." Whether it was the result of this concoction or simple natural healing, the boy recovered slowly over the next three weeks.

Several weeks later, in July 1806, after the expedition had split into two groups, Clark and his party came to a sandstone rock formation standing beside the south shore of the YELLOWSTONE RIVER. Clark promptly named it POMPY'S TOWER; today it is called Pompeys Pillar. A nearby stream was named Baptiests Creek, also for young Pomp.

Clark's affection for Pomp was so strong that he wanted to bring up the boy after he was weaned. He wrote to Toussaint Charbonneau, "I will educate him and treat him as my own child." First, however, the youngster accompanied his mother and father back to Fort Mandan and then to ST. LOUIS. In March 1811, six-year-old Pomp was finally turned over to Clark, and Charbonneau and Sacagawea went back up the Missouri. The next year Clark and his wife also took in Pomp's sister LIZETTE CHARBONNEAU following their mother's death.

Once in Clark's charge, young Jean Baptiste began his schooling in St. Louis. At the age of 16, however, he went back to the frontier, where he put both innate and learned skills to good use. Little is known about his relations with Clark after this. In 1823, at age 18, he met German prince Paul Wilhelm, who brought him back to Europe and introduced him to the aristocracy and German court life. Six years later, Charbonneau—who by now spoke four languages and had become highly sophisticated—returned to the United States and immediately resumed his frontier ways, becoming an explorer and fur trapper for some 15 years. He quickly developed a reputation for his resourcefulness, quick wittedness, and bravery. He knew or associated with other well-known explorers and MOUNTAIN MEN, including Jim Bridger, Joe Meek, Jim Beckwourth, Kit Carson, and John C. Frémont, and his importance as a fur trader is mentioned in George Frederick Ruxton's book *Life in the Far West.*

However, due to the increasing scarcity of BEAVERS, by the early 1840s the FUR TRADE had diminished to the point that it was no longer profitable. Turning to other pursuits, Charbonneau became a guide for groups traveling west. One such group was a sporting expedition led by Sir William Drummond Stewart; included in the party was Jefferson Kearny Clark—William Clark's son. Charbonneau also acted as a guide for army colonel Philip St. George Cooke and the Mormon Battalion when they journeyed from New Mexico to California in 1846–47. Eventually he became *alcalde,* or magistrate, of San Luis Rey Mission in California, but he soon resigned this post, in part out of disgust over the treatment of the Indians there and in part because he wanted to try his luck at gold mining. Having heard of the gold strike at Sutter's Mill in 1848, he was among the first to rush to the site. Although he experienced no luck in his mining efforts, he stayed in northern California for the next 17 years. By 1861 he had become a hotel clerk in Auburn, California. Five years later he started out for the gold fields in Montana, but he contracted pneumonia along the way. He died at Inskip's station in Oregon on May 16, 1866, and was subsequently buried in a cemetery in Danner, Oregon. In March 1973 Jean Baptiste Charbonneau's gravesite was recorded in the National Register of Historic Places.

Further Reading

Anderson, Irving W. "A Charbonneau Family Portrait: Profiles of the American West." *American West* 17, no. 2 (1980): 4–13, 58–64.

Mussulman, Joseph. "My Boy Pomp: About That Name." From *Discovering Lewis and Clark: Clark on the Yellowstone.* Available on-line. URL: http://www.lewis-clark.org/CLARK-YELLOWSTONE/POMPSTOWER/yr_pomp1.htm. Downloaded on February 28, 2002.

Sonneborn, Liz. *Pomp: The True Story of the Baby on the Sacagawea Dollar.* Available on-line. URL: http://pompstory.home.mindspring.com/. Downloaded on May 22, 2001.

Tinling, Marion. *Sacagawea's Son: The Life of Jean Baptiste Charbonneau.* Missoula, Mont.: Mountain Press Publishing, 2001.

Charbonneau, Lizette (Lisette Charbonneau)

(1812–unknown) *Sacagawea's daughter*

Reputedly the daughter of SACAGAWEA, Lizette Charbonneau is believed to have been born at Fort Manuel, South Dakota, in August 1812. Her existence was recorded by John Luttig, a clerk, who in December that year wrote that "the Wife of Charbonneau, a Snake Squaw, died of a putrid fever . . . aged abt 25 years she left a fine infant girl." Most scholars agree that Luttig was referring to Sacagawea, although some believe that this was in fact another of TOUSSAINT CHARBONNEAU's wives and that Sacagawea lived until 1884.

Two months after Luttig recorded Sacagawea's death, Fort Manuel was attacked by Native Americans. It was originally believed that Charbonneau was among the 15 men killed in the attack, although this proved incorrect. Nevertheless, a month later Luttig traveled to ST. LOUIS with the baby Lizette, and early in August 1813 he filed a petition with the Orphans Court to become guardian to "Sacagawea's Lizette," as he called her, and a 10-year-old boy he named "Tousant." (This was probably another of Toussaint Charbonneau's children and not JEAN BAPTISTE CHARBONNEAU, Lizette's older brother, who had already been taken into WILLIAM CLARK's care.) It is thought that Luttig (who died in 1815) may have been too ill to take care of the children, as the court records were very soon altered, and on August 11, 1813, William Clark became the guardian of "Tousant Charbonneau, a boy about ten years old, and Lizette Charbonneau, a girl about one one year old."

Surprisingly, little to nothing is known of Lizette Charbonneau after this. Some sources indicate that William and Julia Clark adopted both Jean Baptiste and Lizette Charbonneau (with no mention of the boy named Tousant), although this seems unlikely, given that Toussaint Charbonneau was still alive and the law of the time required both parents to be dead to legalize an adoption. Clark apparently left no information on what became of the little girl, and one source even records her as dead in 1813. A baptismal record in Westport, Missouri, for a girl named Victoire names her parents as Joseph Vertifeuille and Elizabeth Carboneau, whom some genealogists believe to be Lizette Charbonneau, although this appears doubtful.

Further Reading

Butterfield, Bonnie. "Spirit Wind-Walker." *Sacagawea: Captive, Indian Interpreter, Great American Legend: Her Life and Death.* 1998, 2000. URL: http://www.geocities.com/CollegePark/Hall/9626/NativeAmericans.html. Downloaded on March 15, 2002.

Clark, Ella E., and Margot Edmonds. *Sacagawea of the Lewis and Clark Expedition.* Berkeley: University of California Press, 1979.

Howard, Helen Addison. "The Mystery of Sacagawea's Death." *Pacific Northwest Quarterly* 58, no. 1 (1967): 1–6.

Charbonneau, Toussaint (ca. 1758–ca. 1843)

expedition interpreter

Fur trader, interpreter, coward, and wife beater—this is how most historians sum up Toussaint Charbonneau. While he proved himself to be a competent translator for the CORPS OF DISCOVERY (despite speaking no English), he is probably better known now for being the husband of SACAGAWEA, the SHOSHONE woman whose importance to the expedition far eclipsed his.

While the exact dates of his birth and death are not known, most sources indicate that Charbonneau was born somewhere near Montreal in either 1758 or 1759 and that he was in his 80s when he died, in about 1843, the year his will was probated. Another suggested birth date is March 22, 1767, in Boucherville, Quebec; and a gravestone with Charbonneau's name found at the Church of Saint Stephen's in Richwoods, Missouri, provides birth and death dates of March 1, 1781–February 19, 1866. However, despite the claims of presumed Charbonneau descendants in Richwoods, most scholars believe that this cannot be Lewis and Clark's interpreter, since accounts from the time indicate that he was well into his 40s at the time he was hired, making him the oldest member of the expedition.

Charbonneau's earliest history is unknown. Sometime in the late 1700s he began to work as an *engagé* (laborer) for the NORTH WEST COMPANY. He was mentioned several times in a journal maintained by fellow employee John MacDowell, who reported on May 30, 1795, that Charbonneau had been stabbed by the mother of a woman he had been raping. He survived the attack and subsequently set out to become an independent fur trader. His travels frequently brought him to the MANDAN and HIDATSA villages on the upper MISSOURI RIVER (near present-day Bismarck, North Dakota). By 1797–98 he had begun to live among the Indians on a permanent basis. He eventually acquired a working knowledge of the Hidatsa language, which enabled him to find occasional work as a competent though not outstanding interpreter.

After Sacagawea and another young Shoshone, probably named Otter Woman, were taken prisoner by a Hidatsa raiding party, Charbonneau bought and subsequently married them. By the time the Corps of Discovery reached the Mandan villages in October 1804, Sacagawea (only 15 or 16 at the time) was pregnant with his son. Despite her youth and condition, MERIWETHER LEWIS and WILLIAM CLARK were anxious to have somebody who spoke Shoshone on the expedition. Thus, when Charbonneau signed on as an interpreter with the expedition on November 7, 1804, it was with the understanding that Sacagawea would accompany them as well. However, Charbonneau would also be required to engage in manual labor and guard duty, like the other privates—terms that did not suit him too well.

After FORT MANDAN was completed, Charbonneau and both his wives moved in. He appears not to have been present for the birth of his son, JEAN BAPTISTE CHARBONNEAU, on February 11, 1805. Instead, Meriwether Lewis and RENÉ JESSAUME assisted Sacagawea at the delivery, which was long and exceedingly difficult.

As the time for departure from Fort Mandan drew near, Charbonneau began to chafe at the idea of his extra duties. He had also come to realize just how much Lewis and Clark needed Sacagawea. On March 11, 1805, he submitted demands that the captains found untenable. They ejected him from the fort and hired JOSEPH GRAVELINES as interpreter instead. Apparently Charbonneau thought better of his demands, and on March 17, after he had apologized for his behavior and agreed to the required duties, he was readmitted to the corps.

It was during the first part of the expedition that Charbonneau acquired his reputation as a coward and a wife beater. Although he could not swim and was not a boatsman, he was nevertheless given the helm of one of the PIROGUES and almost lost control of it when a sudden wind hit and he panicked; GEORGE DROUILLARD managed to save them from disaster. Despite this incident, a month later, when the expedition's white pirogue nearly capsized, he again needed the crew to correct his ineptness at the helm. Meanwhile, his calm and clear-headed wife acted swiftly to retrieve many valuable papers and other items from the waters.

On August 14, 1805, Charbonneau struck Sacagawea during an argument; disgusted, Clark ordered him to stop at once. Although this is the only reported incident of his hitting his wife, he often tended to behave brutishly toward women. Later, when Sacagawea became ill, Clark apparently blamed Charbonneau for it, although the reason why is not given in the JOURNALS.

Aside from his role as an interpreter, Charbonneau appears to have made no great impact on the expedition. When necessary, Sacagawea would translate from Shoshone into Hidatsa, Charbonneau from Hidatsa into French, and FRANÇOIS LABICHE from French into English. Interestingly, the official translator George Drouillard usually played no role in this cumbersome but effective system of INTERPRETATION.

Following the expedition's return, Charbonneau and Sacagawea took their leave of Lewis and Clark at the Hidatsa-Mandan villages. PATRICK GASS reported in his journal that the captains gave the Frenchman the expedition's blacksmith tools as a parting gift, "supposing they might be useful." For his services, Charbonneau was paid $500.33⅓ and was given 320 acres of land. He and Sacagawea also agreed to turn young Jean Baptiste (called Pomp) over to Clark after the boy was weaned; Clark had become attached to Pomp and wanted to provide for his education. The transfer of guardianship took place five years later, and for a short period of time Charbonneau tried to farm his Missouri acreage. However, he was unsuited to the work, and after selling his land to Clark for $100, he returned to the Hidatsa with Sacagawea. He resumed fur trading for a while, striking up an association with MANUEL LISA. There is no indication of whether he was with Sacagawea when she died at Fort Manuel, South Dakota, in December 1812, shortly after giving birth to her daughter LIZETTE CHARBONNEAU, nor whether he mourned her death.

An unimpressed Lewis described Toussaint Charbonneau as "a man of no peculiar merit." Clark's opinion was not quite as negative, and his support of his former interpreter helped to offset Charbonneau's general unpopularity. From 1811 on, thanks to Clark, he worked occasionally as a translator for the Indian Bureau at the Upper Missouri Agency. He was incorrectly presumed killed during an Indian attack on Fort Manuel in 1813. He engaged in diplomatic errands for the U.S. government during the War of 1812 and was captured and imprisoned by the Spanish for a short time in 1815. These years also saw him working for Manuel Lisa's Missouri Fur Company as well as the American Fur Company owned by JOHN JACOB ASTOR, with no loyalty to either. His work as an interpreter ceased after Clark's death in 1838.

Charbonneau's predilection for wedding young Indian women apparently did not abate in his old age. At 80 years old, he was reported to have married a 14-year-old ASSINIBOINE girl, presumably his fifth Indian wife, although there may have been others. His last appearance in any official records was in 1839, when he arrived in St. Louis to claim back salaries owed him by the Indian Bureau. It is believed that he died in or before 1843, the year his son Jean Baptiste settled his estate.

Further Reading

Ambrose, Stephen E. *Undaunted Courage: Meriwether Lewis, Thomas Jefferson, and the Opening of the American West.* New York: Simon and Schuster, 1996.

Anderson, Irving W. "A Charbonneau Family Portrait: Profiles of the American West." *American West* 17, no. 2 (1980): 4–13, 58–64.

Hebard, Grace Raymond. *Sacagawea: Guide and Interpreter of Lewis and Clark.* Reprint, Mineola, N.Y.: Dover Books, 2002.

Ottoson, Dennis R. "Toussaint Charbonneau, a Most Durable Man." *South Dakota History* 6, no. 2 (1976): 152–185.

PBS Online. *Lewis and Clark: Inside the Corps of Discovery:* "Toussaint Charbonneau." Available on-line. URL: http://www.pbs.org/lewisandclark/inside/tchar.html. Downloaded on May 18, 2001.

Cheyenne Indians

The Cheyenne Indians were one of many nations involved in a complex Indian trading network around the MISSOURI RIVER. Of importance to MERIWETHER LEWIS and WILLIAM CLARK was their connection to the ARIKARA INDIANS, who supplied HORSES and agricultural goods to the Sioux Indians (Dakota, Lakota, Nakota). The captains' hope was to convince the Arikara to sever their trade connections with the Sioux and enter into the ST. LOUIS–based trading network that they were trying to establish. Given the tense relations between the Cheyenne and the Sioux, it seemed possible the Cheyenne could be enlisted as allies. Thus, the captains were happy to have the opportunity to meet representatives of this nation during the expedition's return journey in 1806.

The name *Cheyenne* was that given them by the Sioux; their own native name translates as "beautiful people" or "our people." An Algonquian-speaking people, the Cheyenne were originally farmers who lived in the eastern prairies of what is now Minnesota. In the late 1600s they began to migrate into the GREAT PLAINS, settling along the Missouri River in what is now North and South Dakota. After they acquired HORSES in the late 1700s, they abandoned their roles as farmers and began

Lewis and Clark met some Cheyenne in August 1806 during their return journey. This photo taken ca. 1891 in Montana shows the Cheyenne's great Omaha powwow dance. *(Library of Congress, Prints and Photographs Division [LC-USZ62-101168])*

a nomadic existence as BUFFALO hunters. Although some Cheyenne were still living in settlements along the Missouri in the early 1800s, it was around that time that the Sioux began to push them south to the region of the North PLATTE RIVER in eastern Wyoming and western Nebraska.

Like the Sioux, the Cheyenne depended heavily on the Arikara for agricultural products, especially corn. They also came to the Arikara for guns and powder, which were exchanged for Cheyenne horses, meat products, and skin clothing. It was an arrangement that suited both nations very well, and the proposed U.S. trading network was unlikely to upset it. Lewis and Clark were nonetheless persistent. Although they had talked to a few Cheyenne during their winter among the MANDAN INDIANS in 1804–05, the opportunity to hold any sort of formal council did not occur until August 21, 1806, when the expedition returned to the Arikara villages. There Clark spoke to an assembled group of Arikara and Cheyenne chiefs, with the Mandan chief BIG WHITE by his side. It did not go well, as the Arikara, while acknowledging that the Sioux were a "bad people," continued to reject any notion of changing the trading system they currently enjoyed with that nation or with any others.

That same afternoon, a Cheyenne chief invited Clark to talk to him in his TIPI. They smoked together, but when Clark offered him a PEACE MEDAL, the chief refused it. According to Clark, "He knew that all white people were medecine and was afraid of the medal or anything that white people gave them." It took the captain some time to convince the chief that in fact gifts such as medals and flags were a significant honor and would not harm him in any way. The next day, before the expedition left the Arikara villages, some Cheyenne chiefs approached Clark to say they would be glad if American traders could be sent to them to teach their people techniques of trapping. It was a rare positive moment in an otherwise gloomy encounter. Big White did not help matters when he attempted to pick an argument with a Cheyenne chief, but apart from that, the expedition left the Cheyenne hopeful that more negotiations with that nation were possible.

In the years following the expedition, the Cheyenne initially maintained peaceful relations with the U.S. government. After 1832, they separated into two groups: the Northern Cheyenne, who in time became allies of the Sioux; and the Southern Cheyenne, who in 1840 formed an alliance with the

Comanche and the Iowa (Ioway). Both groups also allied with the Northern and Southern Arapaho.

Like other Indian nations, the Cheyenne suffered from continued U.S. incursions into their lands. Eventually a cholera epidemic and the continued violation of treaties by migrating settlers resulted in pockets of Cheyenne resistance that were met with the full weight of U.S. retaliation. On November 29, 1864 at Sand Creek, Colonel John Chivington led a brutal massacre of a band of peaceful Cheyenne, killing more than 150, over half of them women and children. Inevitably this led to increased Indian resistance and some epic battles on the Plains as well as the rise of the Cheyenne Dog Soldiers, a warrior society that attacked white settlements.

The Northern and Southern Cheyenne battled on for several years but were finally defeated in 1876 and removed to Indian Territory. In September 1877 the great Northern Cheyenne chief Dull Knife led a large band out of this region in an attempt to return to their homeland in Wyoming. They eluded federal forces for weeks before being caught; among those who were killed was Dull Knife's daughter. It was not until 1884 that the nation was finally given reservation lands in Montana. Today the Northern Cheyenne Reservation is located in Lame Deer, Montana, while the Southern Cheyenne live alongside the Southern Arapaho on federal trust lands in Oklahoma.

In October 2000 the U.S. CONGRESS passed a bill to establish the Sand Creek Massacre National Historic Site to protect the graves of massacre victims from artifact poachers. The bill was sponsored by Colorado senator Ben Nighthorse Campbell, a Northern Cheyenne whose wife's great-grandfather was a survivor of the massacre.

Further Reading

Grinnell, George Bird. *The Cheyenne Indians: Their History and Ways of Life.* Reprint, Lincoln: University of Nebraska Press, 1972.

Jablow, Joseph. *The Cheyenne in Plains Indian Trade Relations, 1795–1840.* New York: J. J. Augustin, 1951.

Ronda, James P. *Lewis and Clark among the Indians.* Lincoln: University of Nebraska Press, 1984.

Stands in Timber, John, and Margot Liberty. *Cheyenne Memories.* 2d ed. New Haven: Yale University Press, 1998.

Waldman, Carl. *Encyclopedia of Native American Tribes.* Revised ed. New York: Checkmark Books, 1999.

Chinook Indians

Chinook is the name applied to the Indians the CORPS OF DISCOVERY met on the middle and lower COLUMBIA RIVER as well as the immediate coastal area around the river's mouth. They were not a single nation but a group of similar peoples sharing a similar way of life. The CLATSOP INDIANS, near whom the Corps of Discovery wintered at Fort Clatsop in 1805–06, were Chinook, as were the SKILLOOT, WATLALA, and WISHRAM AND WASCO INDIANS.

The Chinook were fishers who lived off the vast numbers of salmon, sturgeon, smelt, and other FISH that swam up the Columbia and its tributaries. They were also the center of an extensive coastal and inland trading system centered around CELILO FALLS AND THE DALLES. They lived in plank houses or mat shelters, depending on the season, and had a social structure that was apparently not tribal but family centered. Expert water people, some Chinook built large, sturdy CANOES that could hold great numbers of people; MERIWETHER LEWIS and WILLIAM CLARK described and admired both the boats and how they were handled.

There were several dialects of Chinook language, as Lewis and Clark discovered when they attempted to take vocabularies. These are more correctly described as separate LANGUAGES, with some common words and phrases that resulted from their roles as middlemen in trade between Indians of the Northwest Coast and PLATEAU INDIANS.

Lewis and Clark found an abandoned Chinook fishing village when they arrived near the mouth of the Columbia in November 1805; American explorer Captain Robert Gray had noted this same village on his 1792 map of the area. It was unoccupied because it was used for fishing only during the summer; in the winter months the Chinook of that village moved farther north. In the expedition's time, there were dozens of Chinook winter villages strung along both banks of the lowest 200 miles of the Columbia River plus 25 miles up the WILLAMETTE RIVER and about 20 miles north and south along the Pacific coast.

This profile of an elderly Chinook woman (ca. 1910) gives some idea of the distinctive flattened foreheads that Lewis and Clark both noted. *(Library of Congress, Prints and Photographs Division [LC-USZ62-99364])*

The Clatsop were the expedition's nearest neighbors; Lewis and Clark estimated their population at about 300. Other Chinookians in the region included the Cathlamet, Clackamas, Clowwewalla, Multnomah, Shahala, Shoalwater, Skilloot, Tlakluit, Wahkiacum, Wishram, Wasco, Watlala, and White Salmon. Chinook living along the Columbia and coastal region were known by outsiders as Lower Chinook or Chinook Proper. Because of their extensive contact with British and American traders, they developed a trade jargon, based on the Chinook language, which was in use as a lingua franca as late as 1900.

By the 1840s the influx of white settlers had begun to affect the Chinook population adversely. Those who survived the diseases introduced by non-Indians were eventually relocated through treaties with the United States, and by 1900 most of the original Chinook groupings were no longer discernible. Many joined unrelated Indian nations on reservations in Washington and Oregon. Those Chinook descendants who stayed to fish along the Columbia were displaced in the 20th century when the U.S. Army Corps of Engineers dammed the river.

Further Reading

Drucker, Philip. *Indians of the Northwest Coast.* New York: McGraw-Hill, 1955.

Ray, Verne F. "The Chinook Indians in the Early 1800s." In *The Western Shore: Oregon Country Essays Honoring the American Revolution.* Edited by Thomas Vaughan. Portland: Oregon Historical Society, 1976, pp. 121–150.

Ronda, James P. *Lewis and Clark among the Indians.* Lincoln and London: University of Nebraska Press, 1984.

Ruby, Robert H., and John A. Brown. *The Chinook Indians: Traders of the Lower Columbia River.* Norman: University of Oklahoma Press, 1976.

Waldman, Carl. *Encyclopedia of Native American Tribes.* Revised ed. New York: Checkmark Books, 1999.

Chopunnish Indians　See NEZ PERCE INDIANS.

Chouteau, Auguste, Sr. (1749–1829)
fur trader, cofounder of St. Louis

When MERIWETHER LEWIS and WILLIAM CLARK arrived in ST. LOUIS in December 1803, one of their first tasks was to purchase SUPPLIES AND EQUIPMENT needed for the expedition. Inevitably, they conducted the majority of their business with Auguste and PIERRE CHOUTEAU, fur-trading brothers who only recently had held a near-monopoly on commercial goods in the city. René Auguste Chouteau, born in New Orleans, had assisted his stepfather, Pierre Laclede, in the founding of St. Louis in 1764; although then only 15 years old, he supervised the workers who built the city's foundations. A shrewd trader, he established friendly relations with the local OSAGE INDIANS, and until the arrival of MANUEL LISA, he monopolized all trade with the Osage and throughout the area for some eight years. Meanwhile, his half brother Pierre joined him in his business, eventually becoming as wealthy and influential as Auguste.

Lewis and Clark, the latter of whom already knew Chouteau from a 1797 visit to St. Louis, bought provisions and supplies from the Chouteaus and from Lisa. It was either Pierre or Auguste Chouteau who arranged for the ENGAGÉS needed for the next leg of the journey. As Lewis conducted most of the business, he spent the most time in St. Louis, usually staying at Auguste Chouteau's home. He also asked innumerable questions, gaining information about the territory, its Indians, and the fur trade from Chouteau and others. A few months later, in spring 1804, Lewis and AMOS STODDARD recommended two of Chouteau's sons for appointment to the new military academy at West Point; both were successfully enrolled and later graduated with army commissions, even though one of them, Lorimier Chouteau, was half Indian.

In May 1804 Auguste Chouteau was among a small party of friends to see Lewis, Clark, and the CORPS OF DEPARTURE off from ST. CHARLES. Two and a half years later, as the expedition returned down the MISSOURI RIVER, they encountered a Chouteau trading party from whom they purchased the first whiskey they had had since the Fourth of July the previous year. As they proceeded downriver, they met more trading parties, some of them representing Chouteau, others new trading interests; this was just the first wave of WESTWARD EXPANSION that was already following on the heels of the expedition.

Two years later, Lewis and Clark joined forces with the Chouteaus, Lisa, REUBEN LEWIS, Benjamin Wilkinson (brother of General JAMES WILKINSON), and others to form the St. Louis Missouri Fur Company. After returning the MANDAN chief BIG WHITE to his people, the company's plans were to set up a fur-trading monopoly at the mouth of the YELLOWSTONE RIVER. Although this was a gross conflict of interest for Lewis, by then governor of LOUISIANA TERRITORY, their plans went forward and the company prospered, even after Lewis's death.

Auguste Chouteau represented the U.S. government in the negotiation of several treaties with Native Americans, served as a territorial judge for Louisiana Territory, and became the first chairman of St. Louis's board of trustees when the city incorporated in 1809. With the decline of the FUR TRADE, he began to branch out into real estate and banking; at his death he was the largest and wealthiest landholder in St. Louis. Described as "a man of incorruptible integrity," Chouteau's family continued to prosper through succeeding generations.

Further Reading

Ambrose, Stephen E. *Undaunted Courage: Meriwether Lewis, Thomas Jefferson, and the Opening of the American West.* New York: Simon and Schuster, 1996.

Foley, William E. "The Lewis and Clark Expedition's Silent Partners: The Chouteau Brothers of St. Louis." *Missouri Historical Review* 77, no. 2 (1983): 131–146.

Foley, William E., and C. David Rice. *The First Chouteaus: River Barons of Early St. Louis.* Urbana: University of Illinois Press, 2000.

Chouteau, Pierre, Sr. (Jean-Pierre Chouteau)
(1758–1849) *fur trader*

Like his half brother, AUGUSTE CHOUTEAU, Pierre Chouteau was an enterprising and ambitious fur trader who profited immensely from his association with the Lewis and Clark expedition. Born Jean-Pierre Chouteau in New Orleans, he first began to work in the FUR TRADE for his brother Auguste but eventually expanded their business. In 1796 he founded the first permanent non-Indian settlement at Salina in Oklahoma Territory. By the time MERIWETHER LEWIS and WILLIAM CLARK arrived in ST. LOUIS in December 1803, Pierre and Auguste Chouteau had become the city's most prominent and wealthiest citizens, more than ready to do business with the new U.S. government after years of skillfully handling the Spanish governors of LOUISIANA TERRITORY.

From the Chouteaus as well as from MANUEL LISA, Captains Lewis and Clark purchased the provisions and other SUPPLIES AND EQUIPMENT needed for the expedition, as well as the ENGAGÉS for the boats. They established particularly good relations with both Chouteau brothers, who provided them with a wealth of information on what was then known about the territory and its Native American inhabitants, in particular the OSAGE INDIANS. Pierre Chouteau subsequently agreed to accompany a delegation of Osage to Washington to meet President THOMAS JEFFERSON. This party left St. Louis on May 19, 1804, just as the CORPS OF DISCOVERY was beginning its northward journey on the MISSOURI RIVER. Chouteau carried with him and duly delivered a package for the president, containing a report from Lewis as well as a number of MAPS and ARTIFACTS AND SPECIMENS.

The delegation reached Washington in July 1804, meeting Jefferson as well as numerous other officials. Chouteau acted as interpreter and took the opportunity to pursue his own interests as well. In a meeting with Secretary of the Treasury ALBERT GALLATIN, he requested a monopoly on trade with Indians west of the Mississippi. Gallatin refused to make any firm commitment, astutely realizing that Chouteau "seems well disposed, but what he wants is power and money." The delegation returned to St. Louis that fall, and Chouteau subsequently delivered news of the expedition's progress to President Jefferson as he picked it up from Indians.

When the corps arrived back in St. Louis in September 1806, both Lewis and Clark took up residence in Chouteau's home to write their reports and enjoy the hospitality of both Chouteau brothers. Two months later the captains left the city to go to Washington with a group that included MANDAN chief BIG WHITE and another delegation of Osage Indians led by Pierre Chouteau. In Washington the following January, Chouteau and Big White accompanied Lewis to a celebratory ball.

When Meriwether Lewis returned to St. Louis in March 1808, it was to take up his position as governor of Louisiana Territory. Once again he depended on the Chouteaus for assistance, and after sharing a house with William and Julia Clark for a brief period, he moved in with Pierre Chouteau. Such was his friendship with both Chouteau brothers that he saw no problems in setting up the St. Louis Missouri Fur Company with them, Clark, his brother REUBEN LEWIS, and others, with the purpose of establishing a fur-trading monopoly at the mouth of the YELLOWSTONE RIVER.

When trouble broke out with the Osage Indians, Lewis turned to his friend Chouteau to mediate. In November 1808 Chouteau arranged a treaty that ceded Osage land to the U.S. government while allowing them to maintain lands west of a certain line. Chouteau continued to be involved in treaty making for years thereafter. Meanwhile, he was also put in charge of an armed expedition formed by their new company to return Big White to his people on the upper Missouri (previous attempts had failed due to resistance from the ARIKARA INDIANS)—at the expense of the U.S. government. After this mission was completed, their commercial venture was to begin. A public outcry over Lewis's obvious conflict of interest in this concern was spearheaded by the territory's secretary, FREDERICK BATES, but the partners carried on with their plans and Chouteau's party set out in the middle of May 1809. Chouteau also had explicit instructions from Lewis on how to handle any hostile Indian action and was also to act as his agent in the renewing of licenses for fur traders he would encounter along the way. He succeeded in his mission, and Big White was finally returned safely to his people.

After Lewis's death, Chouteau carried on with his trading enterprises and eventually retired to a plantation outside St. Louis. Two of his sons joined him in his business. Auguste Pierre graduated from West Point in 1806 and served a year before leaving the army and later joining the St. Louis Missouri Fur Company. Meanwhile Pierre Jr. became even more successful than his father through his investments in railroads and mining. Pierre Chouteau's son thus enhanced his legacy by becoming one of the most powerful figures in the settlement of the West.

Further Reading

Ambrose, Stephen E. *Undaunted Courage: Meriwether Lewis, Thomas Jefferson, and the Opening of the American West.* New York: Simon and Schuster, 1996.

Foley, William E. "The Lewis and Clark Expedition's Silent Partners: The Chouteau Brothers of St. Louis." *Missouri Historical Review* 77, no. 2 (1983): 131–146.

Foley, William E., and C. David Rice. *The First Chouteaus: River Barons of Early St. Louis.* Urbana: University of Illinois Press, 2000.

Clark, George Rogers (1752–1818)
American general

General George Rogers Clark was the older brother of WILLIAM CLARK, cocommander of the Lewis and Clark Expedition. A

Revolutionary War hero with numerous claims to fame, Clark himself had been asked by his good friend, THOMAS JEFFERSON, to lead an expedition into the West. He never did, but he later recommended his younger brother for such a task and was present when MERIWETHER LEWIS and William Clark met prior to the start of their historic journey.

Born in Virginia in 1752 to John and Ann Rogers Clark, George Rogers Clark was 18 years old when his brother William was born. Altogether there were six brothers and four sisters, of whom George was the second son. As an adult, he stood more than 6 feet tall and was a handsome man with red hair. He was also considered to be a charismatic and persuasive leader.

Between the French and Indian War (1754–63) and the American Revolution (1775–83), the British laid claim to a large stretch of the western frontier across the Allegheny Mountains from the American colonies. Although they forbade American settlement in this area, many young men from Virginia were crossing over to Kentucky looking for land; Clark was one of them. He had learned surveying from his grandfather, and in 1772 he went west on a surveying trip. After finding land for himself and his family and friends, he stayed on in Kentucky as a guide for settlers.

Enforcing its antisettlement proclamation, Britain began to send Indian war parties against colonial settlers, including those in Kentucky. Clark, in turn, organized the Kentucky militia to resist the raids. Rather than wait for more attacks, he planned a major offensive, leading a force of frontiersmen into the Illinois country to strike at the source of the Indian attacks.

In 1774 Clark fought in Lord Dunmore's War, in which Shawnee and Ottawa Indians were soundly defeated and forced to make territorial concessions. Nevertheless, Indians continued to attack colonial settlements, and he continued to lead military actions against them and against British forces until the end of the Revolutionary War in 1783. In the process he became known as the conqueror of the Old Northwest. Following the war, he was named surveyor of public lands for Virginia military veterans and headed the Board of Commissioners, which supervised the allotment of land in Illinois to former soldiers. He held this latter position until 1813. In addition, he was often consulted on Indian affairs throughout the Ohio Valley and earned the respect of both Indians and non-Indians.

Not long after the end of the Revolutionary War, Clark's longtime friend THOMAS JEFFERSON wrote to him:

> I find they have subscribed a very large sum of money in England for exploring the country from Missisipi to California. They pretend it is only to promote knolege. I am afraid they have thoughts of colonizing into that quarter. Some of us have been talking here in a feeble way of making the attempt to search the country. But I doubt whether we have enough of that kind of spirit to raise the money. How would you liked to lead such a party?

Clark agreed with Jefferson that an expedition should be undertaken, but he advocated a small party—three or four young men, a dozen at most. He also demurred on participating himself, citing pressing business affairs, and Jefferson subsequently pursued other avenues.

Twenty years later, on October 15, 1803, Meriwether Lewis met his partner William Clark at George Rogers Clark's home overlooking the Falls of the Ohio in Clarksville, Indiana. It was the first time the two had seen each other since 1796, and it was in nearby Louisville that they officially enlisted the NINE YOUNG MEN FROM KENTUCKY, who would become the core of the permanent party to the PACIFIC OCEAN. Thus, the beginnings of the CORPS OF DISCOVERY took place with George Rogers Clark as a witness. The following year, just before the expedition set out from its quarters near ST. LOUIS, William Clark received the gratifying news that his brother had recovered from a near-fatal illness.

George Rogers Clark continued to suffer physically, suffering a stroke in 1809 that led to the amputation of his right leg. He also experienced tremendous financial problems. Like many military leaders of the period, Clark had assumed personal responsibility for some of the expenses incurred in his campaigns and never received full repayment from Virginia or the U.S. government. He was in debt to the end of his life.

Following the amputation of his leg, Clark moved in with his sister Lucy and her husband, near Louisville, Kentucky. He died there in 1818. In 1869 his body was moved to Cave Hill Cemetery in Louisville, where it rests today.

Further Reading

Avalon Project at the Yale Law School. "Jefferson's Letter to George Rogers Clark." Available on-line. URL: http://www.yale.edu/lawweb/avalon/jefflett/let21.htm. Downloaded on January 15, 2002.

Bakeless, John E. *Background to Glory: The Life of George Rogers Clark.* Lincoln: University of Nebraska Press, 1992.

Thwaites, Reuben G. *How George Rogers Clark Won the Northwest and Other Essays in Western History.* New York: Arno Press, 1978.

Clark, William (1770–1838) *expedition cocommander*

On June 19, 1803, MERIWETHER LEWIS paused from working on plans for the expedition he would lead into the West and wrote a letter to his friend and former army superior officer, William Clark. In it he described the proposed journey and its purpose, concluding, "If . . . there is anything under those circumstances in this enterprise, which would induce you to participate with me in it's fatigues, it's dangers and it's honors, believe me there is no man on earth with whom I should feel equal pleasure in sharing them as with yourself." A month and a half later, Lewis received Clark's reply: "This is an undertaking fraited with many dificulties, but My friend I do assure you that no man lives with whome I would perfur to undertake Such a Trip & c. as yourself."

In inviting Clark to share the LEADERSHIP of what would be a great and dangerous adventure, Lewis made an ideal, even inspired, choice. A man of physical and moral strength as well as courage, Clark's personality both complemented and balanced Lewis's. He also had the frontier and military experience that made him eminently qualified to lead a corps of men across the continent and back.

Like his friend Lewis and the president, THOMAS JEFFERSON, William Clark hailed from a Virginia plantation family. He was born in Caroline County on August 1, 1770, the youngest of six sons and the ninth of 10 children of John and Ann Rogers Clark. His older brother, General GEORGE ROGERS CLARK—William's senior by 18 years—distinguished himself in battle on the western frontier during the American Revolution, becoming one of the heroes of that war. Coincidentally, when Thomas Jefferson first proposed sending an expedition into the West in 1783, it was George he asked to lead it (see EXPLORATION, EARLY). Clark turned Jefferson down but some years later recommended his younger brother William, who was, he noted, "as well qualified for almost any business."

In 1785 14-year-old William moved with his family to a new plantation named Mulberry Hill, near Louisville, Kentucky. There his brother George instructed him in frontier skills as well as natural history. His formal education, however, was not very extensive, which is evident in his JOURNALS of the expedition. Nevertheless, he had a good innate intelligence, and despite a recurring stomach complaint, he was strong and hardy, growing to more than six feet tall. He had red hair, an even temperament, and was described as being "brave as Caesar."

In 1789, at the age of 19, Clark joined the Kentucky Militia and participated in expeditions against the Ohio Valley Indians who were then raiding white settlements. Two years later he enlisted in the regular army and was commissioned a lieutenant. In 1794, under the command of General "Mad Anthony" Wayne, he fought in the Battle of Fallen Timbers, a significant victory that led to the eventual eviction of Native Americans in the valley.

By 1795 Clark had become captain of the Chosen Rifle Company. Late that year a young ensign was assigned to his command: Meriwether Lewis. The two struck up an immediate friendship, but it was short-lived, since Clark resigned his commission the following year. His reasons for leaving the army involved both his chronic stomach ailment and the need to attend to family plantation business, which included helping to sort out his brother George's complicated financial affairs. This left him little time to correspond with his friend Lewis, and it appears communication between the two men was sparse—until Lewis's letter of June 19, 1803, arrived.

Clark was then living in Clarksville, Indiana Territory, and apparently was ready for a change, for he readily accepted Lewis's invitation. One problem arose, however, after the trip had already begun. Lewis had offered Clark a position on the expedition as a commissioned army captain, but this had not been authorized by Secretary of War HENRY DEARBORN,

Meriwether Lewis's choice of William Clark (above) as his cocaptain was vital to the expedition's success. Unlike Lewis, Clark enjoyed a happy and successful postexpedition career. *(Library of Congress, Prints and Photographs Division [LC-USZ62-10609])*

Lewis's de facto superior. When the commission arrived at CAMP DUBOIS, however, it was for a second lieutenant only. Disappointed, Clark still chose to proceed. (He later informed NICHOLAS BIDDLE, "I did not think myself very well treated.") Lewis, who never told the men what had happened, unfailingly referred to him as "Captain Clark" and both regarded and treated his friend as equal in command. Even after they returned to white civilization, Lewis worked to rectify the error, and it was he who dubbed the journey "The Lewis and Clark Expedition."

Lewis's regard and admiration for his cocommander was equaled only by Clark's for him. The two men trusted each other implicitly, and there is no indication that they ever seriously disagreed or countermanded each other's orders throughout the expedition. They frequently talked over decisions, coming to agreement without rancor. They also learned from each other; Lewis taught Clark astronomy, for instance, and Clark taught Lewis watermanship.

Both men were physically fit frontiersmen as well as strong, level-headed leaders. They shared responsibility for RECRUITING men who were of the strength and caliber the journey required, but otherwise they divided responsibilities between them. During the journey up the MISSOURI RIVER, Clark spent most of his time managing the men on the KEEL-

BOAT, while Lewis supervised those on shore. Clark was the corps's cartographer, producing detailed MAPS of the areas they passed through, while Lewis recorded details of the animals and plant life. Their approach to ETHNOGRAPHY was also balanced; where Lewis was far more descriptive in his depictions of the Native Americans they encountered, Clark was likely to analyze a nation's organization, customs, and rituals. Although Lewis was the corps's primary doctor, Clark looked after his friend, nursed SACAGAWEA when she became ill shortly after the expedition set out from FORT MANDAN in spring 1805, and bartered his services as physician to the NEZ PERCE INDIANS in exchange for FOOD. He also sometimes took a hand in the medical treatment of corps members, particularly the long-suffering private WILLIAM BRATTON. (See MEDICINE AND MEDICAL TREATMENT.)

Like Lewis, Clark was well rewarded for his achievement, even though he did not get his captain's commission nor the promised compensation for that rank. In addition to receiving double pay and 1,600 acres of land, he was granted two appointments, as brigadier general of militia and as superintendent of Indian affairs for the Territory of Upper Louisiana. Unlike the unfortunate Lewis, he was successful and well respected in his career after the expedition. He became a business partner in the St. Louis Missouri Fur Company, capitalizing on the booming FUR TRADE. On January 5, 1808, he married Julia Hancock, after whom he had named the JUDITH RIVER, and the two named their oldest son Meriwether Lewis Clark. Clark and his wife later also took SACAGAWEA's children, JEAN BAPTISTE CHARBONNEAU and LIZETTE CHARBONNEAU, into their home.

In August 1809 Clark met Lewis in ST. LOUIS, to discuss the publication of their journals as well as Lewis's financial problems. Lewis was in deep trouble due to his own conflicted interests with the St. Louis Missouri Fur Company and other controversies that had arisen during his term as governor of the LOUISIANA TERRITORY. Clark had often loaned his friend money and was distressed to see how much Lewis had declined. They agreed to meet again in PHILADELPHIA, but this was the last time they would see each other. On October 11, Lewis died in a roadhouse in Tennessee, an apparent suicide. Five years later Clark finally succeeded in getting their journals published (see BIDDLE, NICHOLAS).

In 1813 Clark was appointed governor of the Missouri Territory, a position he held until Missouri was admitted to the Union in 1820. He ran for election as the first state governor but lost; his wife Judith died that same year. Reappointed superintendent of Indian affairs at St. Louis in May 1822, he became renowned for his fair treatment of Native Americans while also earning the respect of non-Indians. In 1825 he was one of the negotiators for the Treaty of Prairie du Chien, as a result of which a number of Indian nations ceded their lands to the United States. In his later years he also continually updated his maps of the American West with information brought to him from traders, fur trappers, and Native Americans. His personal life, however, became marred by tragedy

when three of his seven children died during a 10-year period, and his second wife, Harriet Radford, died on Christmas Day 1831.

On September 1, 1838, William Clark died of natural causes in St. Louis, where he was buried. On his gravestone is the inscription, "His life is written in the history of his country." On January 17, 2001, he was finally promoted to captain.

Further Reading

Ambrose, Stephen E. *Undaunted Courage: Meriwether Lewis, Thomas Jefferson, and the Opening of the American West.* New York: Simon and Schuster, 1996.

Bakeless, John E. *Lewis & Clark: Partners in Discovery.* Mineola, N.Y.: Dover, 1996.

Clark, William, and Jonathan Clark. *Dear Brother: Letters of William Clark to Jonathan Clark.* New Haven, Conn.: Yale University Press, 2002.

Duncan, Dayton, and Ken Burns. *Lewis & Clark: The Journey of the Corps of Discovery.* New York: Alfred A. Knopf, 1998.

Hawke, David Freeman. *Those Tremendous Mountains: The Story of the Lewis and Clark Expedition.* New York: W. W. Norton & Company, 1998.

———. "William Clark and the Mapping of the West." *Gateway Heritage* 10, no. 3 (1989–90): 4–13.

Jones, Landon Y. "Iron Will." *Smithsonian* 33, no. 5 (August 2002): 96–107.

Loos, John L. "William Clark: Indian Agent." *Kansas Quarterly* 3, no. 4 (1971): 29–38.

Steffen, Jerome O. *William Clark: Jeffersonian Man on the Frontier.* Norman: University of Oklahoma Press, 1977.

Clark's River   See BITTERROOT RIVER.

Clarksville

Clarksville, Indiana—billed as the "Oldest American Town in the Northwest Territory" as well as the place that many consider to be the true starting point of the Lewis and Clark Expedition—was chartered in 1783. In this area in 1778–79, Revolutionary War general GEORGE ROGERS CLARK conducted assaults on British forces. So successful were his campaigns in the area that after the war he and other veterans were granted 150,000 acres on the land north of the OHIO RIVER. Of this, 1,000 acres were set aside for the town of Clarksville, located by the Falls of the Ohio in what was then Indiana Territory.

In 1803 Clark's younger brother WILLIAM CLARK was living with him in Clarksville when MERIWETHER LEWIS's letter of June 19 arrived, inviting William to join his expedition as cocommander. Once the matter was settled, Clark set to work at once finding men for what would become the CORPS OF DISCOVERY. During the next several months the two men corresponded frequently, agreeing to meet in Clarksville later in the year. In that time Lewis bought supplies and equipment and readied the KEELBOAT and his custom-designed IRON-FRAME BOAT for the journey. In PITTSBURGH he met GEORGE SHANNON and JOHN COLTER, who joined him on the keelboat when it set off down the Ohio. Meanwhile, Clark wrote that he had recruited seven fine young men, subject to Lewis's approval.

On October 14, 1803, Lewis and a party of 11 men brought the keelboat and PIROGUES through the passable passage on the north bank of the Ohio and tied up at Clarksville. There the two captains had a happy reunion; they had not seen each other since 1796. They subsequently spent two weeks talking, planning, and defining their respective responsibilities for what was to be the greatest feat of exploration in the United States. During their time at Clarksville, they also spent time interviewing volunteers for the expedition, eventually selecting Colter and Shannon as well as the seven men Clark had already found. The NINE YOUNG MEN FROM KENTUCKY were subsequently sworn in at a ceremony in nearby Louisville, Kentucky, attended by General Clark.

On October 26 the captains and their new recruits left Clarksville to begin the first stage of their journey up the MISSISSIPPI RIVER. Years later, at the Falls of the Ohio, a plaque was erected to mark the moment when the expedition began: "Near this site on October 26, 1803, Meriwether Lewis and William Clark with the nucleus of the Corps of Discovery together set off down the Ohio River on their epic journey to explore the LOUISIANA PURCHASE and Pacific Northwest."

Further Reading

Ambrose, Stephen E. *Undaunted Courage: Meriwether Lewis, Thomas Jefferson, and the Opening of the American West.* New York: Simon and Schuster, 1996.

Town of Clarksville, Indiana. "Clarksville History." Available on-line. URL: http://town.clarksville.in.us/home/history.html. Downloaded on February 13, 2002.

Clatsop Indians

In November 1805 the Lewis and Clark Expedition finally arrived at the mouth of the COLUMBIA RIVER and the PACIFIC OCEAN. They were disappointed, however, when they failed to find any trading vessels on which all or part of the CORPS OF DISCOVERY could be taken home. This meant they would have to spend the winter on the coast and return the way they had come, over land. After scouting the area, they decided to build their winter camp on the south side of the Columbia. They named it FORT CLATSOP after their nearest neighbors, the Clatsop Indians, although this winter would differ in many ways from the one spent with the MANDAN INDIANS in 1804–05.

About 300–400 strong when MERIWETHER LEWIS and WILLIAM CLARK met them, the Clatsop Indians were a band of the larger group of Native Americans called the CHINOOK INDIANS. These Chinookian-speaking peoples also included the WISHRAM AND WASCO, Cathlamet, Clackamas, and Multnomah Indians. There were three Clatsop villages; the captain

and corps members usually visited the nearest one, Lä't'ap, situated about seven miles southwest from the fort. Consisting of three large houses with 12 families, this was probably the home of Chief COBOWAY, who visited the fort often and became a good friend of the expedition. A larger village, Neahkeluk—never visited by the expedition—stood north of this settlement and contained eight wooden houses. The farthest village was located at the mouth of the Necanicum River and had seven houses, of which three contained Clatsop while the rest were home to some TILLAMOOK INDIANS.

While the corps met a number of different Chinook during their months on the West Coast, it was the Clatsop with whom they became best acquainted. Like other Indians in the area who had had extensive contact with white men since ROBERT GRAY sailed into the mouth of the Columbia in 1792, the Clatsop, while friendly, had become very opportunistic and looked for ways they could profit from the expedition. While Lewis found them and other Chinook to be "very loquacious and inquisitive," he also noted that they were "much more illy formed then the Indians on the Missouri and those of our frontier; they are generally cheerfull but never gay. With us their conversation generally turns upon subjects of trade, smoking, eating and women."

The Clatsop advised the expedition where to find ELK for HUNTING and provided other assistance, but they were also shrewd traders who were able to assess what the corps needed in the way of FOOD and other supplies and consequently struck some hard bargains. It was not long before the captains began to complain that "those people ask generally double and tribble the value of what they have to sell, and never take less than the real value of the article in such things as is calculated to do them service." Before the winter was half gone, Lewis was noting that the few TRADE goods they had left had been "reduced to a mear handful." But at least the Clatsop were not thieves, which made them more trustworthy than other Chinook in the area who were prone to constant pilfering.

The Clatsop had much to recommend them in other ways as well. Both captains remarked on the speed and skill with which CANOES were built and utilized; some were up to 50 feet long and could carry 30 people or five tons of goods. Clark called them "the best canoe navigators I ever Saw." The Indians were also, not surprisingly, excellent fishers, and they not only sold FISH to the expedition but also showed the soldiers how to prepare the eulachon, or candlefish. Their craftsmanship was equally impressive; Lewis and Clark so admired a certain type of waterproof hat that they hired a Clatsop women to make it for all the soldiers. Lewis subsequently wrote that "the woodwork and sculpture of these people as well as these hats and their waterproof baskets evince an ingenuity by no means common among the Aborigenes of America."

By mid-March 1806, after a long, dreary winter at Fort Clatsop, the expedition was anxious to leave sooner than originally planned. To make the trip back up the Columbia, they needed more canoes, but they had almost nothing to trade by this time. One canoe was finally purchased at the cost of Lewis's uniform coat, but a Clatsop with whom he was bargaining for another vessel stubbornly refused to sell. Finally, in desperation, Lewis resorted to stealing a canoe, justifying his action by noting that it was "in lue of the six Elk which they stole from us in the winter." In fact the Clatsop had paid for those elk with dogs, thus making Lewis a liar as well as a thief. It was one of the few moments on the expedition when his standing as an honest man and diplomat faltered.

Lewis's ethnographic studies of the Clatsop and other Chinook during the winter at Fort Clatsop have proved invaluable to historians. The Indians of the region had already been severely depleted by two smallpox epidemics. In 1825–26 a malaria epidemic almost completely wiped them out. What few remained became absorbed into the increasing white population, and consequently the cultures that Lewis and Clark observed had nearly vanished within a generation.

Further Reading
Ambrose, Stephen E. *Undaunted Courage: Meriwether Lewis, Thomas Jefferson, and the Opening of the American West.* New York: Simon and Schuster, 1996.

Drucker, Philip. *Indians of the Northwest Coast.* New York: McGraw-Hill, 1955.

Ronda, James P. *Lewis and Clark among the Indians.* Lincoln: University of Nebraska Press, 1984.

Waldman, Carl. *Encyclopedia of Native American Tribes.* Revised ed. New York: Checkmark Books, 1999.

Clearwater Forest

In September 1805 the CORPS OF DISCOVERY undertook a long and arduous trek across the BITTERROOT MOUNTAINS, taking them through what is now the Clearwater National Forest. The forest covers 1.8 million acres from the Bitterroots in the east to the canyons and hills of the Palouse Prairie in the west. Ridges between the deep canyons here have provided corridors across the mountains for centuries, and these were used by the NEZ PERCE INDIANS long before Lewis and Clark arrived. Even today the area provides habitat for ELK, moose, DEER, black BEAR, cougar, and other animals.

It was in the Clearwater Forest that the Corps of Discovery, with help and advice from the Nez Perce, cut Ponderosa pines to make CANOES for the trip down the CLEARWATER RIVER and onward to the COLUMBIA RIVER. The corps used the Indian method of burning rather than hewing the wood to make their canoes.

Although they suffered terrible hardships during their crossing of the Bitterroots, both MERIWETHER LEWIS and WILLIAM CLARK were impressed and somewhat intimidated by the view beyond the forest. Lewis wrote that he "could observe high rugged mountains in every direction as far as I could see," and Clark said they "were entirely surrounded by those mountains from which to one unacquainted with them it would have seemed impossible ever to have escaped."

Further Reading
Space, Ralph S. *The Clearwater Story: A History of the Clearwater National Forest.* Missoula, Mont.: Forest Service, ISDA; Orofino, Idaho: Clearwater Historical Society, 1980.

USDA Forest Service. "Clearwater National Forest, Idaho." URL: http://www.fs.fed.us/r1/clearwater/. Updated on February 27, 2002.

Clearwater River (Kooskooskee River)

The Clearwater is a 190-mile river rising in the BITTERROOT MOUNTAINS on the border between Idaho and Montana and flowing west to join the SNAKE RIVER at today's Lewiston, Idaho, on the border with Oregon. Draining about 9,645 square miles, it was called the Kooskooskee by the NEZ PERCE INDIANS (as was the LOCHSA RIVER).

After the CORPS OF DISCOVERY made their arduous, 11-day crossing of the Bitterroots by way of the LOLO TRAIL, they came down to WEIPPE PRAIRIE and met the Nez Perce on September 20, 1805, in the valley of the Clearwater River. MERIWETHER LEWIS wrote of "the pleasure I now felt in having triumphed over the rockey Mountains and descending once more to a level and fertile country. . . ." The Nez Perce made the explorers welcome and fed them with fish and CAMAS ROOTs, which caused problems for the party, who suffered severe stomach disorders from the change in diet (and possibly bacteria in the fish).

On September 26 the expedition arrived at the Clearwater River near today's Orofino, Idaho. Here they set up CANOE CAMP and built the CANOES that would take them down to the COLUMBIA RIVER and the PACIFIC OCEAN. On October 7 the canoes were finished, and the party set off down the Clearwater. They had a rough passage due to the rapids in the river and nearly lost one canoe, but with the current behind them, they soon reached the junction with the Snake River at today's Lewiston.

The expedition returned to the Clearwater in May 1806, hoping to return over the Bitterroot Mountains as soon as possible. The snows were too deep, however, and from May 14 to June 10, the party stayed beside the Clearwater at CAMP CHOPUNNISH. Leaving camp on the 10th, they found the snows still made the mountains impassable, and they were forced to return to Weippe Prairie. Not until June 23, 1806, did the expedition leave the Clearwater valley behind.

Further Reading
Dryden, Cecil. *The Clearwater of Idaho.* New York: Carlton Press, 1972.

Fifer, Barbara, and Vicky Soderberg. *Along the Trail with Lewis and Clark.* Great Falls, Mont.: Montana Magazine, 1998.

Moulton, Gary E., ed. *Atlas of the Lewis and Clark Expedition.* Revised ed. Lincoln: University of Nebraska Press, 1999.

Simon-Smolinski, Carol. "The Corps of Discovery on the Clearwater River." *Idaho's Northwest Passage.* Available on-line. URL: http://www.idahonwp.org/togo/bmc/lc_clear.htm. Downloaded on February 10, 2002.

clothing

The clothing of the Lewis and Clark Expedition falls into two categories: their everyday clothing during the journey and the uniforms they wore as U.S. soldiers. With hindsight, some might question whether the CORPS OF DISCOVERY need ever have carried dress uniforms over 4,000 miles to the PACIFIC OCEAN and back again. However, it should be remembered that, besides being a unit of the U.S. Army on an expedition of exploration, they were also on a diplomatic mission. They were, among other tasks, to make official and friendly contact with the Indian nations who lived along their route and to persuade them to accept the United States as their new protecting power. Dress uniforms and the pomp and ceremony of close-order drills were intended to make the status of the expedition clear.

Uniforms were worn during the parades and councils held for the Indian nations the corps met along the MISSOURI RIVER, up to and including the MANDAN INDIANS. A typical journal entry, dated October 29, 1804, records of the council with the Mandan: "That the impression might be more forcible, the men were all paraded, and the council was opened by a discharge from the swivel [gun] of the boat."

After this council, there is no record of the corps having donned their uniforms again. The uniforms did, however, still have a useful purpose to serve. On the return journey in 1806, when the expedition left FORT CLATSOP in late March, their stock of TRADE goods was minimal. Lewis had already traded his frock coat for a CANOE they needed to take them back up the COLUMBIA RIVER. They reached the WALLA WALLA INDIANS on April 27, and when Chief YELLEPT gave WILLIAM CLARK a fine horse, the captain had to give him his sword plus some balls and powder in exchange.

When the expedition reached the NEZ PERCE INDIANS and realized they still had weeks to wait before the snows had melted enough to allow them to return over the mountains to the GREAT PLAINS, their trade goods were practically nonexistent. They needed FOOD, and the Nez Perce wanted something in return for the FISH and roots they could provide. While Clark's medical skills were in great demand and could be exchanged for some food, there was little else the expedition had to offer. Then, in late May 1806, the soldiers discovered the brass buttons on their uniforms were "an article of which these people are tolerably fond."

The two captains were happy to follow their men's example. They cut the buttons off their dress coats, and these brought in three bushels of roots. MERIWETHER LEWIS was delighted, writing, "A successful voyage not much less pleasing to us than the return of a good cargo to an East India merchant."

It is known that Lewis obtained shirts, coats, wool overalls, stockings, and shoes at the army's public store, but only for the one officer, a sergeant, and 12 men originally authorized by CONGRESS. It is fair to assume that when the numbers were doubled in December 1804, he was able to obtain the additional supplies of needed clothing from the army garrisons at Cahokia or KASKASKIA.

Some historians believe that members of the expedition bought buckskins and moccasins from the traders they met on the river soon after leaving CAMP DUBOIS in May 1804. What is more likely is that the ENGAGÉS showed them how to dress and cut skins to make clothing from DEER hide. Whichever is correct, it was after the expedition left FORT MANDAN in April 1805 that the JOURNALS begin to include comments on the party curing skins and making moccasins and clothing out of them.

On June 19, 1805, below the GREAT FALLS and with a tremendous PORTAGE ahead of the expedition, the Lewis and Clark journals note: "All our people are making mockasons to go through the prairie." When the portage was completed and they were preparing to set off toward the ROCKY MOUNTAINS, Sergeant PATRICK GASS wrote on July 4 that many of the expedition were "dressing skins for clothing." Sergeant JOHN ORDWAY, however, noted that "mockasons will not last more than two days." This slightly depressing statement was clearly the result of the period spent dragging the canoes over the rough ground on the portage and the ever-present PRICKLY PEAR against which deer hide was little protection.

When their uniforms wore out or proved unsuitable for the conditions, the Corps of Discovery adopted clothing made from animal skins, similar to that worn by this Southern Paiute Indian. *(National Archives Still Pictures Branch [NWDNS-111-SC-103737])*

When they reached THREE FORKS two weeks later, the expedition rested for a couple of days, and Lewis reported that "all [the men] are leather dressers and taylors." Private JOSEPH WHITEHOUSE seems to have been the most skillful in the party, and he is often mentioned as a "hide-curer" and "tailor" who made and repaired clothes for his comrades. During the stay at Three Forks, it is noted that he made "leather clothing" for the men. The following month, on August 22, 1805, he is recorded as making leather shirts and overalls for the party. For Christmas that year at Fort Clatsop, he made a pair of moccasins for Clark as a present.

When the soldiers were preparing for the return journey, Gass made a surprisingly formal note in his journal for March 13, 1806: "I this day took an account of the number of pairs of mockasons each man in the party had; and found the whole to be 338 pairs. This stock was not provided without great labour, as the most of them are made of the skins of ELK." He also noted that each man "has also a sufficient quantity of patch-leather."

According to one estimate, a single elk skin could be made into 12 pairs of moccasins and a deer skin into five or six pairs. They were also used to make coats and trousers, though detailed information is sketchy on the methods employed.

Probably because lack of time did not allow the corpsmen to cure skins properly, the shortcomings of their clothing efforts were evident. When they were well on their way home on August 8, 1806, Gass wrote that the party stopped "to repair the pirogue, and to dress some skins to make ourselves clothing."

On September 6, 1806, on the last lap of their triumphant journey home, the expedition met a trader from ST. LOUIS coming upstream. Lewis promptly bought whiskey, which his men had not tasted for over a year. It is recorded that the other items the party bought were linen shirts to replace the deer and elk skin they had worn for so long.

Further Reading

Cutright, Paul Russell. *Lewis & Clark: Pioneering Naturalists.* Lincoln: University of Nebraska Press/Bison Books, 1989.

Gottfried, J. "The Well-Dressed Explorer." Available on-line. URL: http://www.northwestjournal.ca/sample.html. Downloaded on February 28, 2002.

Jefferson National Expansion Memorial. "The Lewis and Clark Journey of Discovery: What did the men who went west with Lewis and Clark wear?" Available on-line. URL: http://www.nps.gov/jeff/LewisClark2/CorpsOfDiscovery/Preparing/Clothing/Clothing.htm. Downloaded on April 11, 2002.

MacGregor, Carol Lynn, ed. *The Journals of Patrick Gass, Member of the Lewis and Clark Expedition.* Missoula, Mont.: Mountain Press Publishing Company, 1997.

National Geographic. "Lewis and Clark Expedition Supplies." Available on-line. URL: http://www.nationalgeographic.com/lewisandclark/resources.html. Downloaded on May 18, 2003.

Rogers, Ken. "Heart and Sole: Expedition members placed one tender foot in front of the other." *The Bismarck Tribune.* Available on-line. URL: http://www.ndonline.com/tribwebpage/features/lewisclark/2001/sole.html. Downloaded on February 21, 2002.

Coboway (Comowooll, Conia)

(unknown–unknown) *Clatsop chief*

While the CORPS OF DISCOVERY came to know many of the CHINOOK INDIANS in the area around FORT CLATSOP during the winter of 1805–06, it was the CLATSOP whom they met most often. This nation numbered 300–400 when the expedition knew them, but there are very few chiefs mentioned in the JOURNALS of MERIWETHER LEWIS and WILLIAM CLARK. One exception was Coboway, a frequent and highly regarded visitor to the fort whose goodwill they would eventually betray.

On December 12, 1804, while Fort Clatsop was still being built just a few miles away from his village, Coboway came to visit. He was presented with a medal and must have perceived at once that the expedition was lacking in TRADE goods. Nevertheless, like all of his people, the chief was an expert trader, and he sold them roots and skins in exchange for some fishhooks and TOBACCO. It was the first of many trading sessions that became increasingly difficult as the expedition ran out of goods with which to barter.

According to historian James Ronda, Lewis and Clark never established the same type of rapport with Coboway and other Chinook chiefs as they had with the MANDAN chiefs. This may have been due partly to problems in communication, since nobody in the corps could speak or understand Chinookian and there were no white interpreters available to them as there had been at FORT MANDAN. Yet the captains acknowledged that Coboway and his people were friendly and hospitable, and they found much to admire in the Clatsop's skills in building and navigating CANOES as well as other crafts.

Unlike other Chinook Indians, the Clatsop did not have a reputation for thieving, but in early February 1806, they took six ELK from the place where GEORGE DROUILLARD had stored them. After Lewis and Clark complained to Coboway about it, he arranged to have three dogs brought to the fort as payment for the elk. The following month, however, the incident was used as an excuse for Lewis to commit theft of his own. Anxious to get started on their return journey, the poverty-stricken expedition needed canoes, but the prices the Indians were asking were too dear. On March 18, in an act of desperation, Lewis had four of his men steal and then hide one of the Clatsop canoes. Conveniently forgetting the payment of the dogs, he noted that the canoe had been taken "in lue of the six elk which they stole from us in the winter."

That same day Coboway came to visit at the fort. While feeling "a little awkward" about what he had done, Lewis made a point of giving him "a cirtificate of his good conduct and the friendly intercourse which he has maintained with us during our residence at this place." Further trying to mitigate his own behavior, the captain also presented the chief with a list of names of men in the Corps of Discovery. Four days later, as the corps was preparing to leave, Coboway paid a final visit, and Lewis, in a final gesture, presented the chief with the fort and its contents. The captain wrote of his Indian friend, "He has been much more kind an hospitable to us than any other Indian in this neighbourhood." He apparently missed the irony in this statement as he departed the next day in a canoe that belonged by right to the Clatsop.

While Lewis and Clark never returned to the Columbia River, in the years after the expedition, Coboway and his people were to see white traders move into the area, beginning the transformation that would bring about an end to their culture. By 1814 the British NORTH WEST COMPANY had taken over Fort Astoria, and on May 21 that year, Chief Coboway visited Alexander Henry, a trader for North West. He proudly carried with him the list of names Lewis had given him back in 1806. With great disdain, Henry threw the paper into the fire and replaced it with a British document; a sad and discourteous ending to what had been a gesture of friendship years before.

Further Reading

Mussulman, Joseph. "A Neighborly Gift." From *Discovering Lewis and Clark*. Available on-line. URL: http://www.lewis-clark.org/FTC-COLUMBIA/fc_ngift.htm. Downloaded on March 19, 2002.

Ronda, James P. *Lewis and Clark among the Indians*. Lincoln: University of Nebraska Press, 1984.

———. *Finding the West: Explorations with Lewis and Clark*. Albuquerque: University of New Mexico Press, 2001.

coincidences and chance on the expedition

The Latin tag translated as "Fortune favors the brave" was never more appropriate than when considering the significant events of the 1804–06 journey that rested on chance alone—an aspect of the Lewis and Clark Expedition often overlooked but crucial to their success.

The CORPS OF DISCOVERY was an extremely efficient, brave, and resourceful but small body of men crossing an area of the continent in which they were sure to encounter hostile Indians or Indians who had never before seen white men. They were carrying goods and equipment, especially rifles, that would be coveted by almost every Indian they met. Yet on just about every day of the long journey, one or two men, sometimes more, were sent out on their own to kill meat for the expedition. Often they were away for days on end, but they always returned safely; GEORGE SHANNON, who became lost, is one notable example of this. Their HORSES might be stolen, their kills might be eaten by WOLVES, they might have close encounters with grizzly BEARS, but they always managed to rejoin the party.

On April 7, 1805, the expedition left FORT MANDAN in two PIROGUES and six CANOES and proceeded up the MISSOURI RIVER. They had been warned repeatedly by white traders and by their hosts, the MANDAN INDIANS, to watch out for the BLACKFEET and ASSINIBOINE INDIANS, whose war parties were known to frequent the prairie the expedition was to pass through. Yet despite these warnings, the captains saw no

reason not to continue sending out small HUNTING and scouting parties when it seemed convenient. In the subsequent weeks, hunters and scouts continually reported seeing Indian fires, abandoned camp sites, and recent traces of Assiniboine hunting parties. Yet when MERIWETHER LEWIS at last met a SHOSHONE warrior on August 11, 1805, it was the first Indian any expedition member had seen in more than four months. Even though Indians had been all around them for all that time, the expedition had made their way openly up one of America's largest rivers, seemingly unobserved.

While SACAGAWEA's recognition of her brother CAMEAH-WAIT is often, understandably, considered to be the most dramatic coincidence of the journey, it should not be forgotten that her inclusion in the party was also by pure chance. Before their arrival at Fort Mandan, Lewis and Clark certainly had not considered the possibility that they would meet a young Shoshone woman so many hundreds of miles from her homeland, to which they were headed, but they were quick to take advantage of it. Consequently, Sacagawea's presence had the welcome effect of reassuring the Indians they met that the explorers were not hostile, a significant factor in their good fortune.

When in September 1805 the NEZ PERCE INDIANS first became aware of the expedition's arrival in their land, they considered attacking the party to obtain their goods and firearms. The warriors were dissuaded from this by WATKUWEIS, a Nez Perce woman who had been treated kindly by whites and now urged her people to return the kindness. While this was a small incident, it was another chance event that helped the expedition on its way.

The happiest and most dramatic coincidence of all must surely be that of July 28, 1806, during the homeward journey. For their return, Meriwether Lewis and WILLIAM CLARK made plans that, in retrospect, must be called dangerous if not downright foolhardy. Although it went against prudence as well as military principle, they decided to split the expedition into five parties. Whether they assumed that the prairies would be as empty of Indians as they were on the outward journey or whether they simply accepted the risk they were taking will never be known. It is clear, though, that the captains had the utmost faith in the courage and ingenuity of their men—a faith that turned out to be justified.

On July 3, 1806, Lewis and nine men left TRAVELERS' REST and headed east toward the GREAT FALLS of the Missouri. That same day, Clark and the remainder rode due south back to CAMP FORTUNATE. The plan was for Lewis to leave Sergeant PATRICK GASS with some men at Great Falls to begin unpacking the CACHES and preparing for the PORTAGE. Lewis and three men would then go north to explore the MARIAS RIVER and rejoin Gass's party at the mouth of the Marias on August 5.

Meanwhile, Clark and his party picked up the canoes left at Camp Fortunate and traveled by water down to THREE FORKS. There Sergeant JOHN ORDWAY and nine men were detached to take the canoes down the MISSOURI RIVER to the Great Falls, where they would join Gass's party in making the portage around the falls before going on to meet Lewis. With Ordway and his company off, Clark headed south on horseback with the remaining 11 men to the YELLOWSTONE RIVER. Here they made two narrow canoes that were lashed together for stability to continue their journey by water. In the meantime, Sergeant Pryor and three men were detached—the fifth split—to travel across country on horseback to the Mandan villages.

A glance at the map shows that Clark was now some 350 miles away from Lewis, who was, in turn, more than 100 miles away from Sergeant Gass and his party. The plan could have been a disaster and nearly was had it not been for ingenuity and chance. After Pryor and his men suffered the theft of all their horses, they simply picked up their rifles and baggage and walked 30–40 miles north to the Yellowstone. There they killed two BUFFALO, made two BULL BOATS, and followed Clark downstream.

To the north, Lewis and his party had a hostile encounter with some BLACKFEET INDIANS in which they killed two warriors. The captain led his men south on a ride of 100 miles in a day, and the following morning (July 28), after another 20 miles, they arrived at the Missouri well west of the Marias rendezvous point. They turned downstream and, just eight miles later, Lewis "had the unspeakable satisfaction to see our canoes coming down" with Sergeant Ordway. Some two to three hours later, there was another reunion when they were joined by Sergeant Gass and his group, who were riding across country to the Marias. After 25 days and hundreds of miles apart, the three groups had reunited—a week earlier than planned. They would catch up with Clark and his party more than 400 miles downstream 14 days later.

Of the events of July 28, Patrick Gass, that most laconic of writers, simply noted:

> At about one o'clock [we] came to the point at the mouth of Maria's river, where we met with the party who had come down from the falls by water, and who had just arrived; and also unexpectedly with Captain Lewis and the three men who had gone with him. They had joined the party this forenoon, after riding one hundred and twenty miles since yesterday morning. . . .

"Unexpectedly" is a masterly understatement for the last of the fortunate coincidences that played such an important part in the expedition's success.

Further Reading

Ambrose, Stephen E. *Undaunted Courage: Meriwether Lewis, Thomas Jefferson, and the Opening of the American West.* New York: Simon and Schuster, 1996.

Cutright, Paul Russell. *Lewis & Clark: Pioneering Naturalists.* Lincoln: University of Nebraska Press/Bison Books, 1989.

MacGregor, Carol Lynn, ed. *The Journals of Patrick Gass, Member of the Lewis and Clark Expedition.* Missoula, Mont.: Mountain Press Publishing Company, 1997.

Moulton, Gary E., ed. *The Journals of the Lewis and Clark Expedition.* 13 vols. Lincoln: University of Nebraska Press, 1983–2001.

Collin, Joseph   See ENGAGÉS.

Collins, John (unknown–1823) *private in the permanent party*

Originally from Frederick County, Maryland, Private John Collins enlisted in the CORPS OF DISCOVERY on January 1, 1804. His chief role on the expedition was that of cook, but he was also one of the corps's best hunters, along with JOHN COLTER, GEORGE DROUILLARD, and JOSEPH and REUBIN FIELD. In addition to HUNTING for FOOD, the five obtained hides for CLOTHING and SHELTER and helped gather specimens of the wildlife to send back to Washington.

Although Collins acquitted himself well in the latter part of the expedition, he was prone to irresponsibility in the beginning. In May 1804, while the corps laid over in ST. CHARLES, he and privates HUGH HALL and WILLIAM WERNER went absent without leave. Tried and convicted by COURT-MARTIAL, Hall and Werner were given 25 lashes each on their bare backs. The charges against Collins were more serious; in addition to being AWOL, he was also found guilty of "behaveing in an unbecoming manner at the ball last night" and "Speaking in a language after his return to camp tending to bring into disrespect the orders of the Commanding officer." Because of these additional offenses, he received 100 lashes.

This experience apparently had no effect on Collins's and Hall's behavior. During the evening of June 28, 1804, while Collins was on sentry duty, he began to help himself to whiskey out of a barrel and was soon encouraging Hall to do the same. The two were arrested the following morning and tried immediately. Collins was found guilty of "getting drunk on his post this morning out of whiskey put under his Charge as a Sentinel and for Suffering Hugh Hall to draw whiskey out of the Said Barrel intended for the party." His punishment was 100 lashes to his back; Hall received 50 lashes. The sentence was carried out that afternoon, and both were back pulling oars in the evening.

Following the expedition, Collins chose not to keep his grant of land and sold it to Drouillard for $300. He subsequently became a trapper, working for fur trader William Ashley. He and 11 other Ashley employees were killed in a fight with ARIKARA INDIANS in North Dakota on June 2, 1823.

See also DISCIPLINE.

Further Reading

Clarke, Charles G. *The Men of the Lewis and Clark Expedition: A Biographical Roster of the Fifty-One Members and a Composite Diary of Their Activities from All Known Sources.* 1970. Reprint, Lincoln: Bison Books, University of Nebraska Press, 2002.

North Dakota Lewis & Clark Bicentennial Foundation. *Members of the Corps of Discovery.* Bismarck, N.Dak.: United Printing and Mailing, 2000.

Colter, John (John Coalter, John Coulter)

(ca. 1775–1812) *private in the permanent party, mountain man*
One of the more unusual members of the CORPS OF DISCOV-
ERY was John Colter, a quick-witted and courageous individual who chose not to return to civilization with the expedition
but instead returned to the West, where his exploits made him
the first and one of the greatest of the legendary MOUNTAIN
MEN. Colter was born in Augusta County, Virginia, and moved
with his family to Kentucky when he was about five years old.
He grew into an outstanding hunter and frontiersman, one
who stood 5'10" tall and reportedly had strikingly blue eyes
and a pleasant if somewhat shy manner.

After meeting MERIWETHER LEWIS in PITTSBURGH and
accompanying him to Louisville, Kentucky, on the KEELBOAT,
Colter was officially enrolled in the expedition on October
15, 1803, as one of the NINE YOUNG MEN FROM KENTUCKY.
However, he did not get off to an auspicious start with the
captains. In February 1804 he was among those who defied
orders not to go to a local whiskey shop while Lewis was away
in ST. LOUIS. Upon his return, Captain Lewis confined all
the men to their quarters for 10 days. The following month
Colter and JOHN SHIELDS got into separate disputes with
JOHN ORDWAY, both making threats on the sergeant's life.
The two were accused of mutiny and court-martialed on
March 29 (see DISCIPLINE). When they begged forgiveness for
their insubordination and made promises to behave themselves in the future, they were released from confinement
and subsequently readmitted as permanent members of the
expedition.

Aside from these transgressions, Colter was a reliable
corpsman. Quick-witted and resourceful, he was frequently
chosen for scouting and search parties. On August 26, 1804, he
was sent to look for GEORGE SHANNON, who had not returned
from a HUNTING trip. Neither Colter nor GEORGE DROUIL-
LARD, who was dispatched to search the next day, had any success, however, and the expedition moved on. Colter was again
sent out on September 3 but still failed to find Shannon, who
had apparently traveled ahead of the expedition by this time.
The lost and near-starving private was finally recovered on
September 11.

Nearly a year later, in August 1805, Colter was chosen to
accompany Captain WILLIAM CLARK on a scouting expedition
up the north fork of the SALMON RIVER (in present-day Idaho)
to see if it provided a way through the ROCKY MOUNTAINS. It
did not, and Colter was sent back to Lewis and the main party
with a horse and Clark's message that they should take the
advice of OLD TOBY, their SHOSHONE guide, and attempt to
cross by way of the LOLO TRAIL. The party eventually did so,
albeit with great difficulty. Three months later, when the expedition had reached the PACIFIC OCEAN, Colter and nine other
men went with Clark up the north coast of what is now Washington State to scout out the area.

In August 1806, after the returning expedition had split
into two parties of exploration, Lewis and his group encountered two fur trappers named Joseph Dickson and Forrest Hancock. Even though the expedition had not yet made it home,
the American FUR TRADE was already spreading into the West,
and the two were heading to the Yellowstone area. They accompanied the corps back to the HIDATSA and the MANDAN villages, during which time they asked Colter to join them on
their fur-trapping ventures. His enlistment was not due to
expire until October 10, but Colter agreed to their proposal,
conditional on obtaining the captains' permission, which was
granted. Thus, on August 17, 1806, John Colter became
the first man to be honorably discharged from the Corps of
Discovery.

With Dickson and Hancock, Colter returned to the
THREE FORKS area of the upper MISSOURI RIVER, and they
trapped together for about six weeks. However, the three got
into disputes, and Colter finally set out on his own. In 1807
he began to work for MANUEL LISA. On Lisa's behalf, he
traveled some 500 miles that winter, making contact with
various Indian nations for trading purposes. During this time
he discovered the area that would become known as Jackson's
Hole as well as some strange geological wonders never before
seen by white men: thermal springs and spouting geysers
of mud and steam. After he returned to St. Louis, many listened in disbelief to his descriptions of these amazing sights,
which came to be called "Colter's Hell." However, William
Clark included the information that Colter provided in MAPS
that he later made of that area and other places that the
mountain man described to him. In time it was realized that
Colter had in fact discovered what is now Yellowstone
National Park.

By autumn 1809 Colter was working as a trapper for fur
trader Andrew Henry, and another former expedition member, JOHN POTTS, had joined him. When the two men were
attacked by a party of BLACKFEET INDIANS, Potts was killed
and butchered. Colter expected to be tortured to death, but
instead the Blackfeet stripped him naked and made him run for
his life while they gave chase. Through amazing endurance
and ingenuity he managed to escape the Indians, killing one in
the process, and then spent the next 7–11 days (accounts vary)
wandering through the wilderness with only a blanket to cover
himself until he reached Fort Raymond (also called Lisa's Fort)
on the Roche Jaune River. He was again attacked when he went
back later to retrieve his traps but escaped more easily that time.
In 1810, after yet another Blackfeet attack during an expedition
for the St. Louis Missouri Fur Company, Colter finally left the
West and returned to Missouri for good.

At this point information about him begins to conflict. He
settled near Charette, Missouri, and was married, but the name
of his wife varies widely, depending on the source: Sallie, Sally,
Sarah, and Jane have all been suggested, with Sally or Sallie
being the likeliest. It is known he had a son named Hiram (who
later fathered eight children), and it is possible he also had a
daughter named Evalina.

Conflict surrounds Colter's death. Older sources claim
that he died of jaundice on November 22, 1813, and for some
time it was believed that his remains became lost when a railroad track went through the cemetery near Dundee, Missouri,
where he was said to be buried. However, more recent research

carried out by one of his descendants indicates that he served with Nathan Boone's Mounted Rangers in the War of 1812 and died (still of jaundice) on May 7, 1812. Colter is in fact buried on private land near New Haven, Missouri. In 1988 a group called the Tavern Bluff Party set up a stone marker at his grave.

Further Reading

Colter-Frick, Ruth. "Forty-Four Years with John Colter: Colter, U.S. Mounted Ranger." *Yellowstone Net Newspaper.* Available on-line. URL: http://www.yellowstone.net/newspaper/news090998. htm. Posted on September 9, 1998.

———. "Forty-Four Years with John Colter: John Colter's Estate." *Yellowstone Net Newspaper.* Available on-line. URL: http:// www.yellowstone.net/newspaper/news100998.htm. Posted on October 9, 1998.

Harris, Burton. *John Colter: His Years in the Rockies.* Lincoln: University of Nebraska Press, 1993.

Johnston, Ed. "The Life and Times of John Colter." Available on-line. URL: http://www.edjohnston.com/edsci/colter1.htm. Downloaded on September 16, 2001.

Moring, John. *Men with Sand: Great Explorers of the North American West.* Helena, Mont.: Twodot Books, 1998.

Mountain Men and the Fur Trade (Research Center): "Accounts of John Colter's Escape from the Blackfeet." From various contemporary sources. Available on-line. URL: http://alt.xmission. com/~drudy/mtman/html/colter.html. Downloaded on May 20, 2001.

Columbia River

The Columbia River flows from Columbia Lake in southeastern British Columbia to the PACIFIC OCEAN at the Oregon-Washington border, a length of more than 1,200 miles draining an area of approximately 259,000 square miles. At the time of the expedition, THOMAS JEFFERSON, MERIWETHER LEWIS, and WILLIAM CLARK had all hoped it would form part of an all-water TRADE route from the eastern half of the continent to the Pacific.

Spanish explorer Martín d'Aguilar was most likely the first to locate the Columbia River near the 42nd parallel in 1603. It began to appear on European maps as "River of the West" in the early 17th century. In 1775 the Spaniard Bruno Heceta described a river estuary at the Columbia's latitude, confirming the river's location. At the time he wrote of it, "These currents and eddies of water cause me to believe that the place is the mouth of some great river, or of some passage to another sea."

Seven years later, in May 1792, the American captain ROBERT GRAY sailed across the dangerous Columbia bar and into the mouth of the river, which he then named after his ship. In October that same year, the British explorer GEORGE VANCOUVER, who had previously failed in an attempt to cross the Columbia bar, sent his lieutenant, William Broughton, to reconnoiter the area. Broughton explored slightly more than 100 miles and created the first detailed map of the lower river, which Lewis and Clark subsequently used on their own exploration.

Celilo Falls was just one of the obstacles the expedition encountered on the Columbia River. *(Washington State Historical Society, Tacoma)*

After the CORPS OF DISCOVERY crossed the BITTERROOT MOUNTAINS in September 1805, they arrived at the CLEARWATER RIVER, from which they were able to proceed by water to the SNAKE RIVER before finally reaching the Columbia. They arrived at the Pacific Ocean in November and built FORT CLATSOP (after the nearby CLATSOP INDIANS), where they spent the winter. The expedition began its return up the Columbia in March 1806. Along the way, both coming down and returning back up the river, they encountered numerous CHINOOK and PLATEAU INDIANS, including the WISHRAM AND WASCO, UMATILLA, TILLAMOOK, WATLALA, WANAPAM, WALLA WALLA, and YAKAMA (Yakima).

Although the Columbia was to remain a port of call for ships for some years, it was the establishment of Fort Astoria by JOHN JACOB ASTOR in 1811 that saw the first permanent settlement of non-Indians in the Pacific Northwest.

Further Reading

Dietrich, William. *Northwest Passage: The Great Columbia River.* Seattle: University of Washington Press, 1996.

Lang, William L., and Robert C. Carriker, eds. *Great River of the West: Essays on the Columbia River.* Seattle: University of Washington Press, 1999.

Moulton, Gary E., ed. *Atlas of the Lewis and Clark Expedition.* Revised ed. Lincoln: University of Nebraska Press, 1999.

Schwantes, Carlos A. *Columbia River: Gateway to the West.* Moscow: University of Idaho Press, 2000.

Columbia River Gorge

Generally the term *Columbia River Gorge* is used to describe the stretch of river that runs 80 miles downstream from the CELILO FALLS to the western side of the CASCADE MOUNTAINS. Strictly speaking, however, it describes the western section of that stretch of water where the COLUMBIA RIVER passes through the Cascade Mountains.

By late October 1805, the Lewis and Clark Expedition had come down the CLEARWATER and SNAKE rivers to the Columbia and then negotiated the Celilo Falls and the rapids of the Short and Long Narrows, finally arriving at The Dalles. As they proceeded down the Columbia, they reached the mouth of a river they named after Private FRANÇOIS LABICHE (today's Hood River). Here WILLIAM CLARK wrote of the local Indians, "Those people are friendly, gave us to eate fish Beries, nuts bread of roots and Drid beries and we Call this the friendly village."

Clark and MERIWETHER LEWIS had already noticed the difference between the PLAINS INDIANS and those who lived west of the ROCKY MOUNTAINS. It was at the Columbia River Gorge, where they arrived on October 29, that they noticed there was an equally significant difference between the nations upstream of the gorge and those below it. While they had been welcomed by the Indians further up the Columbia, many of whom had never before seen white men, things were very different in this lower section of the river. Although all were part of the CHINOOK tribal grouping, the Indians downstream spoke a different language and had evolved a different way of life, reflecting the different landscape which they inhabited. Above the gorge are semiarid, grassy hills; below it the country is a rain-soaked area of small valleys full of ferns, thickly timbered slopes, and waterfalls. The Chinook of this region also had experience of white men and had traded with visiting ships for at least 30 years.

On October 30 the expedition reached the eight-mile series of rapids known as the Cascades, or the "Great Chute of the Columbia." With the waters too dangerous to float their SUPPLIES AND EQUIPMENT, they chose to PORTAGE around the Cas-

This photograph taken ca. 1906 shows the Middle Cascades, part of the Columbia River Gorge, which the expedition portaged in late October 1805. *(Library of Congress, Prints and Photographs Division [LC-USZ62-123513])*

cades and to pull their CANOES through on long lines. The process took two days. On October 31 Sergeant PATRICK GASS wrote, "We unloaded our canoes and took them past the rapids, some part of the way by water, and some over rocks 8 or 10 feet high. It was the most fatiguing business we have been engaged on for a long time, and we got but two over all day, the distance about a mile and the fall of the water about 25 feet in that distance." They went through the same performance the following day, and it was not until November 3 that they reached clear water again, at the spot where BEACON ROCK stands. At this point they saw the first signs of tides affecting the Columbia's current and knew they were near the PACIFIC OCEAN.

In 1937 the Bonneville Dam was built, flooding the valley where the expedition had labored so hard to pass. In The Dalles, Oregon, the modern Columbia Gorge Discovery Center and Wasco County Historical Museum offers exhibits on the area, its wildlife, Indians, and the expedition's passage through the gorge.

Further Reading

MacGregor, Carol Lynn, ed. *The Journals of Patrick Gass, Member of the Lewis and Clark Expedition.* Missoula, Mont.: Mountain Press Publishing Company, 1997.

Schmidt, Thomas. *National Geographic Guide to the Lewis & Clark Trail.* Washington, D.C.: National Geographic, 1998.

compensation   See PAYMENTS AND REWARDS.

Congress, U.S.

The First Congress under the new Constitution of the United States convened in New York City on March 4, 1789. There

were 95 senators and representatives. Of these, 59 were Revolutionary War veterans and 17 were signers of the Constitution. By 1804, when the Lewis and Clark Expedition began its journey, there were 175 members of the U.S. Congress. Today there are 535 voting members.

Until 1794 there were no well-defined national POLITICAL PARTIES in any branch of the U.S. government. Neither George Washington nor his vice president, John Adams, had any party affiliation. However, a two-party structure began to emerge during the Adams presidency. The Federalist Party, led by ALEXANDER HAMILTON, sought to strengthen national power over the states. Members of that party favored a national bank and the assumption of national debt, as well as a standing army. Among the influential Federalists were Hamilton, John Jay, and Charles Cotesworth Pinckney.

The opposition Democratic-Republicans were led by Congressman JAMES MADISON and Secretary of State THOMAS JEFFERSON. Before Jefferson's election to the presidency in 1800, his party was in the minority. The Federalists held majorities in both houses of Congress. The Sixth Congress, in session 1799–1801, was divided thus:

Senate: 13 Democratic-Republicans, 19 Federalists

House: 42 Democratic-Republicans, 64 Federalists

Totals (both houses): 55 Democratic-Republicans, 83 Federalists

This changed dramatically with the 1800 election. The Seventh Congress, in session 1801–03, swung to Jefferson's Democratic-Republicans:

Senate: 18 Democratic-Republicans, 14 Federalists

House: 69 Democratic-Republicans, 36 Federalists

Totals (both houses): 87 Democratic-Republicans, 50 Federalists

With the Eighth Congress, in session 1803–05, the Federalists continued to decline:

Senate: 25 Democratic-Republicans, 9 Federalists

House: 102 Democratic-Republicans, 39 Federalists

Totals (both houses): 127 Democratic-Republicans, 48 Federalists

Ironically, when Jefferson became president, federal-government expenditures increased, and the executive branch increased in power relative to Congress. An early example of Jefferson's aggressive executive behavior occurred in 1801 when the Barbary States resumed raids on U.S. shipping. With Congress in recess, Jefferson sent a navy squadron to Tripoli on his own authority. Even his cabinet questioned the legality of this, but Jefferson stood firm, setting a precedent for responding to aggression without prior congressional approval.

When Congress reconvened later in the year, it approved the naval expedition.

In January 1803 Jefferson formally requested an appropriation from Congress in the amount of $2,500 for an expedition to the Missouri and Columbia Rivers. While one of his motivations was scientific curiosity about the West, he had sound geopolitical and commercial reasons as well, as he concluded in his confidential letter to Congress:

> While other civilized nations have encountered great expense to enlarge the boundaries of knowledge by undertaking voyages of discovery, and for other literary purposes, in various parts and directions, our nation seems to owe to the same object, as well as to its own interests, to explore this, the only line of easy communication across the continent, and so directly traversing our own part of it. The interests of commerce place the principal object within the constitutional powers and care of Congress, and that it should incidentally advance the geographical knowledge of our own continent, cannot be but an additional gratification. The nation claiming the territory, regarding this as a literary pursuit, which is in the habit of permitting within its dominions, would not be disposed to view it with jealousy, even if the expiring state of its interests there did not render it a matter of indifference. The appropriation of two thousand five hundred dollars, "for the purpose of extending the external commerce of the United States," while understood and considered by the Executive as giving the legislative sanction, would cover the undertaking from notice, and prevent the obstructions which interested individuals might otherwise previously prepare in its way.

Initially, Congress was not that impressed, as only one week previously Jefferson had asked for an appropriation of nearly $10 million to buy New Orleans from FRANCE (the subsequent LOUISIANA PURCHASE cost $15 million). Nevertheless, the Democratic-Republican–controlled Congress soon approved both of Jefferson's requests, and before long the expedition was underway.

Following the return of the CORPS OF DISCOVERY from the Pacific coast, on February 19, 1806, Jefferson submitted a report to Congress on the findings of the expedition. Meanwhile, a special committee had been formed to consider PAYMENTS AND REWARDS for members of the expedition. MERIWETHER LEWIS lobbied the president, Secretary of War HENRY DEARBORN, and Congress to ensure that WILLIAM CLARK—who had never received the captain's commission he had been promised—received his due share of the acclaim and honors that might have been Lewis's alone. In fact, Congress rewarded both captains and nearly all the members of the permanent party with double pay and grants of land.

Further Reading

Jefferson, Thomas. Jefferson's Confidential Letter to Congress. From *Thomas Jefferson and the Lewis and Clark Expedition.* Available on-line. URL: http://www.monticello.org/jefferson/lewisand clark/l&c_congress_letter.html. Downloaded on January 10, 2002.

Lewis & Clark in North Dakota. "Report to Congress." Available on-line. URL: http://dorgan.senate.gov/lewis_and_clark/message. html. Downloaded on May 17, 2001.

Continental Divide (Great Divide)

The Continental Divide, or Great Divide, is the height of land running from northern CANADA down to Mexico and Central America that separates waters draining into the Pacific from those draining into the Atlantic or Gulf of Mexico. It is difficult today to appreciate the significance of the Continental Divide to Americans at the time of the Lewis and Clark Expedition. While the LOUISIANA PURCHASE had given the United States sovereignty over a vast area, the boundaries of the LOUISIANA TERRITORY were not known. Only by traveling up the tributaries of the MISSISSIPPI RIVER could these be defined. The land to the west of those tributaries was claimed by SPAIN.

The Spanish had already established many settlements up the Pacific coast, and under the international agreements then in effect, Spain had a better claim to western territories than the United States did. Meanwhile, the somewhat recent feat (1793) of ALEXANDER MACKENZIE in reaching the PACIFIC OCEAN overland through Canada had alarmed many Americans—in particular THOMAS JEFFERSON—who foresaw that the British could use this achievement to expand southward down the Pacific coast and thereby prevent the United States from claiming the territory.

Furthermore, an intense interest in the then-unknown vast areas of the American hinterland was common among scientists and men of the ENLIGHTENMENT such as Jefferson, in addition to traders, trappers, and businessmen. The markets of China could only be reached by the long sea journey around South America, and for 20 years ships had been making that extended trip to trade for furs in the OREGON TERRITORY and then taking them on to China. Traders and trappers were already reporting that many Indian nations in the hinterland had formed strong trading connections with the HUDSON'S BAY COMPANY and NORTH WEST COMPANY of Canada. Jefferson and others feared the inevitable British expansion into the North American interior.

Finally, it must be remembered that, until the railways came, rivers were the best and often the only means of travel or communication. The existence of the ROCKY MOUNTAINS was known, but no one knew if they could be traversed easily. If a passage could be found across the Continental Divide to a navigable waterway on the other side, it would immediately alter the entire trading strategy and political prospects of the United States.

On August 11, 1805, MERIWETHER LEWIS, GEORGE DROUILLARD, JOHN SHIELDS, and HUGH MCNEAL were walking ahead of the main party to find the SHOSHONE INDIANS. Lewis and WILLIAM CLARK knew that the rivers would soon become impassable in the high ground they were now approaching, and they needed HORSES to cross the mountains before winter set in. From present-day Dillon, Montana, Lewis and his men set off southwest, following the JEFFERSON RIVER until they came to the junction of Horse Prairie Creek and Red Rock River. About six miles west of today's Clark Canyon Reservoir, Lewis finally saw a mounted Shoshone but was chagrined when the man galloped away after he was approached. All the small party could do was to follow in the Indian's tracks westward.

The next day they arrived at a hillside and ascended to the top. This was LEMHI PASS—their passage over the Continental Divide. Lewis and his men thus became the first Americans to cross the divide. At the top, the captain was disappointed to see nothing but mountains in the west, and he perceived at once that a water passage through the Rockies would probably not be found. On August 13 he finally met a band of Shoshone, who enabled the expedition to cross over the BITTER-ROOT MOUNTAINS by foot some three weeks later. However, that crossing would prove a far more difficult one than their transit over the Continental Divide.

On the return trip in 1806, after the expedition was split into two, Clark and his party crossed the divide at Gibbons Pass. Lewis, meanwhile, took his party northward, and they made their crossing at LEWIS AND CLARK PASS—an ironic name, since Clark himself never saw it.

Further Reading

Fifer, Barbara, and Vicky Soderberg. *Along the Trail with Lewis and Clark.* Great Falls, Mont.: Montana Magazine, 1998.

Moulton, Gary E., ed. *Atlas of the Lewis and Clark Expedition.* Revised ed. Lincoln: University of Nebraska Press, 1999.

National Geographic Atlas of Natural America. Washington, D.C.: National Geographic Society, 2000.

Cook, James (Captain)   See EXPLORATION, EARLY.

corn (maize, *Zea mays*)

Corn was first introduced to European colonists by North American Indians. It was an especially important crop for the people of the Northeast woodlands, being one of their main foods. The corn came in many varieties—white, blue, yellow, and red—and some was dried to preserve it for the winter months. Dried corn could be made into hominy and was also ground into corn meal, using wooden mortars and pestles.

All parts of the plant were used for a variety of purposes besides eating. Corncobs could be used for fuel or to make darts for a game and sometimes were tied onto sticks to serve as rattles for ceremonies. Husks were braided and woven to make baskets, moccasins, sleeping mats, masks, and cornhusk dolls.

During its winter with the MANDAN INDIANS, the CORPS OF DISCOVERY consumed hundreds of bushels of Indian corn. Corn and other dried produce was often brought to FORT MANDAN by Indian women, who traded with individual expedition members for small manufactured items such as awls. Medical treatments of Indians, generally performed by MERIWETHER LEWIS, were reciprocated with gifts of corn.

Corn and other agricultural products were key to the development of the ARIKARA and Mandan-HIDATSA villages as trading centers on the upper MISSOURI RIVER. As a staple in intertribal networks, it became central to the burgeoning TRADE between Indian villages and French and British traders during the 18th century. During the 19th century, American trading posts along the Missouri became dependent on Indian corn, routinely shipping it from post to post.

Corn was often presented to Lewis and Clark during formal ceremonies and was also purchased outright from the Indians. Throughout the winter of 1804–05, expedition members traded metal and metalworking skills for the villagers' corn. These resources became increasingly important as the winter deepened and meat supplies were exhausted. Were it not for the Mandan corn, it is unlikely that the expedition would have survived the winter.

Among the artifacts and specimens that Lewis and Clark collected and sent back east were Arikara and Mandan corn and TOBACCO. THOMAS JEFFERSON grew the plants in his garden at MONTICELLO.

Further Reading

Ambrose, Stephen E. *Undaunted Courage: Meriwether Lewis, Thomas Jefferson, and the Opening of the American West.* New York: Simon and Schuster, 1996.

Emerson, William Dana. *Indian Corn.* Wilmington, Del.: Scholarly Resources, 1978.

Fussell, Betty. *The Story of Corn.* New York: Knopf, 1992.

Ronda, James P. *Lewis and Clark among the Indians.* Lincoln: University of Nebraska Press, 1984.

Corps of Discovery

Corps of Discovery was the name given to the exploratory expedition headed by MERIWETHER LEWIS and WILLIAM CLARK. Although it was not an official title, it succinctly described the men's mission and reflected the team's largely military makeup. The phrase was first used after the death of Sergeant CHARLES FLOYD, when PATRICK GASS was elected as his replacement. On August 26, 1804, Meriwether Lewis appointed Gass "Sergeant in the corps of volunteers for North Western Discovery." In later accounts of the expedition, this was shortened to Corps of Discovery.

Rosters of the Corps of Discovery usually list the 33 individuals who journeyed across the continent and back again, otherwise known as the permanent party of the expedition. Yet some in the permanent party joined the corps well after what many scholars consider to be the expedition's official start date of May 14, 1804 (setting out from CAMP DUBOIS), while others enlisted in or associated with the expedition made significant contributions even if they did not go all the way to the PACIFIC OCEAN. One man died; two deserted; some were discharged; and many, such as the ENGAGÉS, were hired only for a specified period of time. Consequently, upward of 50 people could be considered members of the Corps of Discovery.

The permanent party of the expedition comprised:

Captains: Meriwether Lewis, William Clark

Sergeants: Patrick Gass, JOHN ORDWAY, NATHANIEL PRYOR (Sergeant Charles Floyd is often listed as a permanent party member, even though he did not reach the Pacific.)

Privates: WILLIAM BRATTON, JOHN COLLINS, JOHN COLTER, PIERRE CRUZATTE, JOSEPH FIELD, REUBIN FIELD, ROBERT FRAZIER, GEORGE GIBSON, SILAS GOODRICH, HUGH HALL, THOMAS PROCTOR HOWARD, FRANÇOIS LABICHE, JEAN-BAPTISTE LEPAGE, HUGH McNEAL, JOHN POTTS, GEORGE SHANNON, JOHN SHIELDS, JOHN B. THOMPSON, PETER WEISER, WILLIAM WERNER, JOSEPH WHITEHOUSE, ALEXANDER HAMILTON WILLARD, RICHARD WINDSOR

Civilian Personnel: GEORGE DROUILLARD, TOUSSAINT CHARBONNEAU, SACAGAWEA, JEAN BAPTISTE CHARBONNEAU, YORK

Floyd, Pryor, Bratton, Colter, the Field brothers, Gibson, Shannon, and Shields were the first to be recruited, in August and October 1803; referred to as the NINE YOUNG MEN FROM KENTUCKY, they formed the core of the permanent party, and remarkably, none of them seemed to have had military experience prior to enlisting. Colter and Shannon had met Lewis in PITTSBURGH and had accompanied him on the KEELBOAT down the OHIO RIVER to Louisville, where they were approved by Clark. Apart from the 11 men (a pilot; seven soldiers recruited from the army post at Carlisle, Pennsylvania; and "three young men on trial" who included Colter and Shannon) who had labored to get the keelboat and pirogues from Pittsburgh to Louisville, other volunteers for the expedition came from army forts at South West Post (Tennessee), FORT MASSAC, and KASKASKIA. Many of the men hired were "on trial"—that is, if they wished to be chosen for the permanent party, they had to prove themselves. Others were enrolled in the temporary party, accompanying the corps only as far as the upper portion of the MISSOURI RIVER and then returning to ST. LOUIS. Most of those chosen in either category were not placed on the expedition's payroll until January 1, 1804, or later.

The expedition was organized into three squads, each headed by a sergeant. It is not certain how many volunteers spent the winter of 1803–04 at CAMP DUBOIS on the Wood River, near St. Louis, but by the spring Captains Lewis and Clark had dismissed some and sorted the rest into permanent and temporary expedition members. In addition, they hired a number of engagés, or boatmen, to help propel the PIROGUES up the river (the KEELBOAT would be handled solely by members of the permanent party). The head engagé was BAPTISTE DESCHAMPS.

The party consisted of 45 men when it left Camp Dubois in May 1804. During the first leg of the journey, at least three were discarded from the corps. Private JOHN ROBERTSON was sent back to St. Louis in June 1804, dismissed for disorderly conduct. Two months later, MOSES REED deserted the expedition; he was found, court-martialed, and discharged but kept on as a laborer. In October that year, JOHN NEWMAN was also court-martialed (for making mutinous remarks), discharged, and relegated to laborer. Both men spent the winter of 1804–05 at FORT MANDAN with the corps and were returned to St. Louis on the keelboat in April 1805. Reed's place in the permanent party was assumed by Private Robert Frazier, Newman's by fur trader Jean-Baptiste LePage, who was hired at Fort Mandan. Another deserter, Private JOSEPH BARTER (known as La Liberté), was apparently not replaced after he disappeared in late July 1804.

Most of the members of the Corps of Discovery were already military men or enlisted in the army when they joined the expedition. One exception to this was George Drouillard, who was hired as the corps's civilian interpreter. Other interpreters were occasionally needed, however, and two hired in this capacity on a temporary basis were PIERRE DORION, SR. and JOSEPH GRAVELINES. At Fort Mandan, another civilian, Toussaint Charbonneau, was hired for the same purpose; at 47 he became the oldest member of the corps. With Charbonneau came his wife, the SHOSHONE Sacagawea, and their baby son Jean Baptiste, both of whom are usually counted by historians as members of the party. Sacagawea was the only woman on the expedition, and Jean Baptiste—nicknamed "Pomp" or "Pompy"—was its youngest participant, being only 55 days old when the explorers left Fort Mandan for the Pacific in April 1805.

York, Clark's slave, was treated by the other men as a full member of the unit in every respect, taking his turns as sentry and hunter. The member of the expedition not usually listed on its rosters was the only four-legged one: SEAMAN, Lewis's Newfoundland dog, who made the trip from Pittsburgh to FORT CLATSOP and back to St. Louis, a journey matched only by Lewis and George Shannon.

Three out of the 12 hired engagés apparently left the expedition prior to their arrival at the MANDAN and HIDATSA villages in November 1804; the remainder were dismissed thereafter, and three joined the return party on the keelboat to St. Louis in April 1805. In addition to these men, the disgraced Reed and Newman, and the interpreter Gravelines, who also acted as pilot, the return party included the temporary members of the corps: Corporal RICHARD WARFINGTON, who commanded the keelboat; and Privates JOHN BOLEY, JOHN DAME, EBENEZER TUTTLE, and ISAAC WHITE.

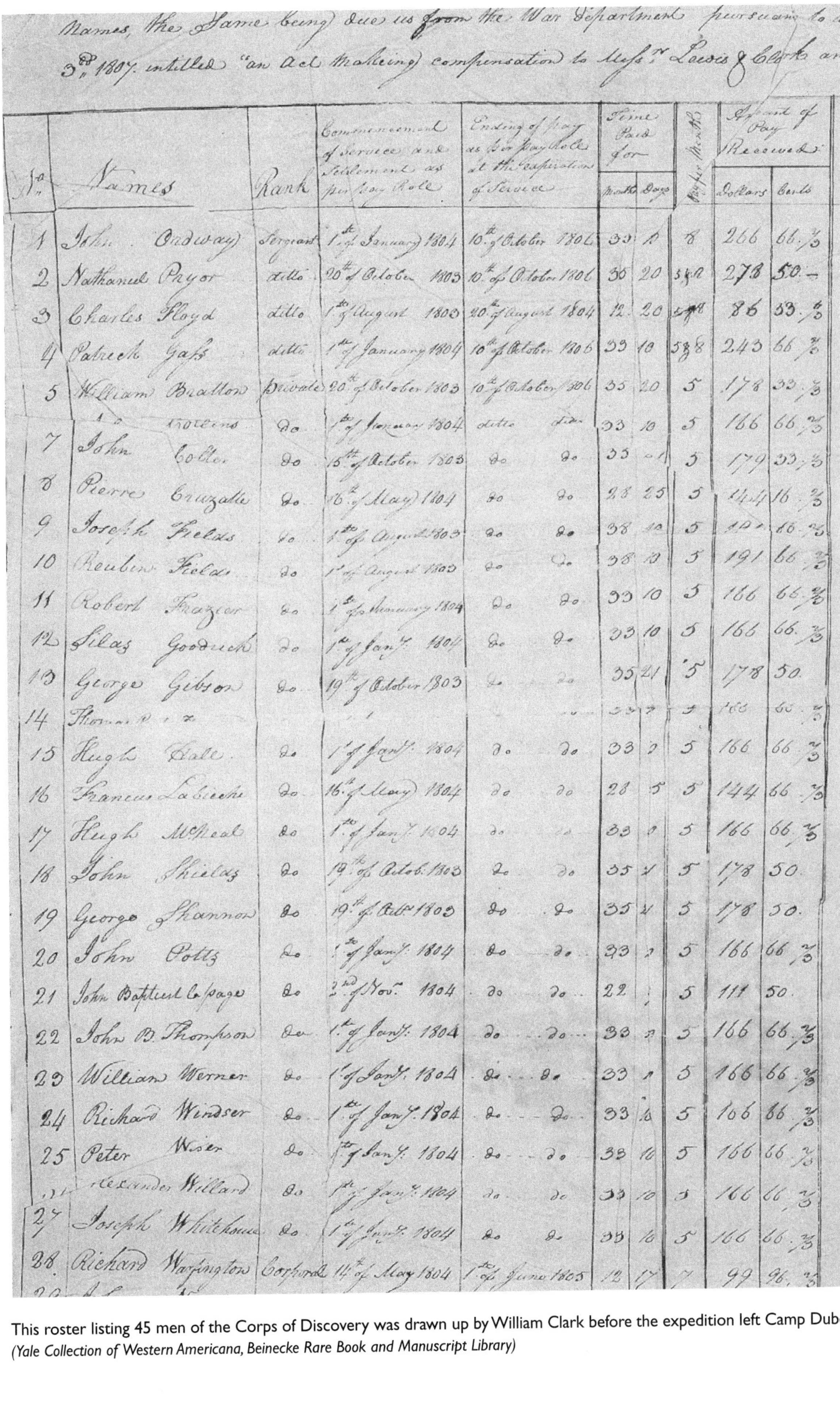

No.	Names	Rank	Commencement of Service and Settlement as per Pay Roll	Ending of pay as Pr Pay Rolls at the expiration of Service	Time Paid for		Pr Month	Amount of Pay Received	
					month	Days		Dollars	cents
1	John Ordway	Sergeant	1st of January 1804	10th of October 1806	33	10	8	266	66 ⅔
2	Nathaniel Pryor	ditto	20th of October 1803	10th of October 1806	36	20	5 & 8	278	50 —
3	Charles Floyd	ditto	1st of August 1803	20th of August 1804	12	20	5 & 8	86	53 ⅓
4	Patrick Gass	ditto	1st of January 1804	10th of October 1806	33	10	5 & 8	243	66 ⅔
5	William Bratton	private	20th of October 1803	10th of October 1806	35	20	5	178	33 ⅓
6	... Crocens	Do	1st of January 1804	ditto	ditto	33	10	5	166	66 ⅔
7	John Colter	Do	15th of October 1803	Do	Do	35		5	179	33 ⅓
8	Pierre Cruzatte	Do	16th of May 1804	Do	Do	28	25	5	144	16 ⅔
9	Joseph Fields	Do	1st of August 1803	Do	Do	38	10	5	191	66 ⅔
10	Reubin Fields	Do	1st of August 1803	Do	Do	38	10	5	191	66 ⅔
11	Robert Frazier	Do	1st of January 1804	Do	Do	33	10	5	166	66 ⅔
12	Silas Goodrich	Do	1st of Jany 1804	Do	Do	33	10	5	166	66 ⅔
13	George Gibson	Do	19th of October 1803	Do	Do	35	21	5	178	50
14	Thomas P. ...				33		5	166	66 ⅔
15	Hugh Hall	Do	1st of Jany 1804	Do	Do	33	10	5	166	66 ⅔
16	Francis Labiche	Do	16th of May 1804	Do	Do	28	5	5	144	66 ⅔
17	Hugh McNeal	Do	1st of Jany 1804	Do	Do	33	10	5	166	66 ⅔
18	John Shields	Do	19th of Octob 1803	Do	Do	35	4	5	178	50
19	George Shannon	Do	19th of Octr 1803	Do	Do	35	4	5	178	50
20	John Potts	Do	1st of Jany 1804	Do	Do	33	10	5	166	66 ⅔
21	John Baptist Lepage	Do	2nd of Nov 1804	Do	Do	22		5	111	50
22	John B. Thompson	Do	1st of Jany 1804	Do	Do	33	10	5	166	66 ⅔
23	William Werner	Do	1st of Jany 1804	Do	Do	33	10	5	166	66 ⅔
24	Richard Windsor	Do	1st of Jany 1804	Do	Do	33	10	5	166	66 ⅔
25	Peter Weiser	Do	1st of Jany 1804	Do	Do	33	10	5	166	66 ⅔
26	Alexander Willard	Do	1st of Jany 1804	Do	Do	33	10	5	166	66 ⅔
27	Joseph Whitehouse	Do	1st of Jany 1804	Do	Do	33	10	5	166	66 ⅔
28	Richard Warfington	Corporal	14th of May 1804	1st of June 1805	12	17	7	99	96 ⅔

This roster listing 45 men of the Corps of Discovery was drawn up by William Clark before the expedition left Camp Dubois.
(Yale Collection of Western Americana, Beinecke Rare Book and Manuscript Library)

Following the return of the expedition, all of the military members of the permanent party were rewarded with double pay and grants of land. Some sold their land warrants; others attempted to make livings as farmers. Some remained in the military, and some entered the FUR TRADE, while some drifted into obscurity. John Colter and George Drouillard, who became renowned MOUNTAIN MEN, had separate encounters with BLACKFEET INDIANS. Drouillard was killed, but Colter, in a party that was ambushed, managed to escape; another former corps member, John Potts, was killed in the same ambush. It is also likely that Peter Weiser was killed by Blackfeet. George Shannon, the youngest enlisted man, lost a leg in a fight with the ARIKARA INDIANS but went on to a distinguished career in the law and politics. Many corps members died relatively young; William Clark attempted to keep track of the members of the permanent party and listed many as dead by 1825–28. Only Patrick Gass and Alexander Willard lived to advanced ages. Willard was 87 when he died in 1865, and Gass passed away in 1870 at the age of 98, the last of the Corps of Discovery to go.

See also COURT-MARTIALS; DEMOCRACY ON THE EXPEDITION; DISCIPLINE; ORGANIZATION OF THE EXPEDITION PARTY; PAYMENTS AND REWARDS; RECRUITING; SKILLS ON THE EXPEDITION.

Further Reading

Archambault, Alan, and Marko Zlatich. "Corps of Volunteers for North Western Discovery, 1804–1806." *Military Collector and Historian* 44 (winter 1992): 176.

Clarke, Charles G. *The Men of the Lewis and Clark Expedition: A Biographical Roster of the Fifty-One Members and a Composite Diary of Their Activities from All Known Sources.* 1970. Reprint, Lincoln: Bison Books, University of Nebraska Press, 2002.

Duncan, Dayton, and Ken Burns. *Lewis & Clark: The Journey of the Corps of Discovery.* New York: Alfred A. Knopf, 1998.

Jefferson National Expansion Memorial. "The Lewis and Clark Journey of Discovery: Corps of Discovery—The Others." Available on-line. URL: http://www.nps.gov/jeff/LewisClark2/CorpsOfDiscovery/TheOthers/Others.htm. Downloaded on April 11, 2002.

Large, Arlen. "'Additions to the Party': How an Expedition Grew and Grew." *We Proceeded On* 16, no. 1 (February 1990): 4–11.

North Dakota Lewis & Clark Bicentennial Foundation: *Members of the Corps of Discovery.* Bismarck, N.Dak.: United Printing and Mailing, 2000.

Yater, George H. "Nine Young Men from Kentucky." *We Proceeded On,* Publication No. 11, May 1992, Lewis and Clark Trail Heritage Foundation, Inc., p. 3.

costs of the expedition

On January 18, 1803, President THOMAS JEFFERSON sent a confidential letter to the U.S. CONGRESS requesting an appropriation of $2,500 "for the purpose of extending the external commerce of the United States"—that is, to fund what came to be known as the Lewis and Clark Expedition. This figure had been drawn up by MERIWETHER LEWIS, whom Jefferson had chosen to lead the journey across the continent. Although Congress approved the request, it should be noted that Lewis originally planned for an expedition consisting of one officer and up to a dozen men, who were to be taken from army posts and were expected to make the trip to the PACIFIC OCEAN and back in less than two years. The final party consisted of 31 men, including the two captains; the PREPARATIONS and the journey itself took more than 3½ years to accomplish; and in the end, the cost of the expedition was more than 15 times the amount originally budgeted.

The sum Congress had approved was quickly spent. By June 1803 Lewis had already spent more than the original $2,500, and expenditures continued daily. President Jefferson and Secretary of War HENRY DEARBORN abetted in the overspending, the former giving Lewis what has been called the most liberal LETTER OF CREDIT ever issued, the latter writing to the superintendent of the federal armory at HARPERS FERRY with orders that Lewis be supplied with whatever he needed. (This included the construction of a special IRON-FRAME BOAT that Lewis had designed.) Dearborn continued to authorize extra expenditures, such as the addition of an officer to the expedition, although he would later refuse to give WILLIAM CLARK a commission as captain, as Lewis had wanted.

During Lewis's time in PHILADELPHIA in May–June 1803, he spent freely, acquiring 2½ tons of SUPPLIES AND EQUIPMENT for the expedition. In some cases he did manage to limit outlays to those originally envisaged. For instance, he had estimated spending $696 on GIFTS for Indians but actually disbursed $669.50. Because he acquired many of his supplies from army stores, his final cost of $117.67 was nearly $140 less than he had estimated. His access to the federal armory enabled him to keep costs low on FIREARMS and WEAPONS, for which only $81 had been budgeted, and his famous air rifle was bought with his own funds. But frugality was rare. Not only did he run over his original budget, but he overspent heavily on items for which he had made no previous allowance. He disbursed $412.95, more than twice his original estimate, on surveying and navigational equipment; his chronometer alone was $250. The $289.50 he paid for 193 pounds of PORTABLE SOUP was the largest amount spent on any provision.

The spending continued from the East Coast to ST. LOUIS, where Lewis used his letter of credit to buy additional supplies needed to accommodate the increased size of the expedition. Many costs could be borne by a multitude of U.S. Army branches, and pay for the enlisted men in the CORPS OF DISCOVERY was low; privates were paid $5 per month, corporals $6, and sergeants $8. However, not all the men added to the party were military personnel. GEORGE DROUILLARD, the expedition's interpreter, was paid $25 a month, and other interpreters would be hired as the expedition proceeded. Through the St. Louis trader PIERRE CHOUTEAU, Lewis hired a number of ENGAGÉS to help move the KEELBOAT and PIROGUES up the MISSOURI RIVER to the villages of the MANDAN

INDIANS. More expenses were incurred when he arranged for Chouteau to take a delegation of OSAGE INDIANS to visit Jefferson in Washington; other Indian delegations would follow, further increasing costs.

After the expedition's return, corps members received double pay and land warrants as rewards for their service. The amount approved by Congress for compensations came to $11,000. Lewis, meanwhile, had the unenviable task of settling the expedition's accounts. When he had finished adding everything up, it amounted to 1,989 items totaling $38,722.25. Some scholars have speculated the actual expenses may have run as high as $60,000.

While Lewis's failure to produce receipts may reflect carelessness in accounting, this was not always the case. How, for example, could he report items that had been traded to Indians in exchange for FOOD or other necessities? His description of one such transaction reflects the difficulties he faced: "One Uniform Laced Coat, one silver Epaulet, one Dirk, & belt, one hanger & belt, one pistol & one fowling piece, all private property, given in exchange for Canoe, Horses &c. for public service during the expedition—$135."

See also PAYMENTS AND REWARDS.

Further Reading

Ambrose, Stephen E. *Undaunted Courage: Meriwether Lewis, Thomas Jefferson, and the Opening of the American West.* New York: Simon and Schuster, 1996.

Hawke, David Freeman. *Those Tremendous Mountains: The Story of the Lewis and Clark Expedition.* New York: W. W. Norton & Company, 1998.

Lange, Robert. "$2,500.00 Vs. $38,722.25—The Financial Outlay for the Historic Enterprise." *We Proceeded On* 1, no. 2 (February 1975): 17–18.

cottonwood   See TREES.

Council Bluff

By the last week of July 1804, the Lewis and Clark Expedition had passed the KANSAS RIVER and PLATTE RIVER and had come to the GREAT PLAINS. They were anxious to make contact with the OTOE (Oto) and the MISSOURI INDIANS, and although they had passed many deserted campsites, they had not seen a single Indian since they had left ST. CHARLES two months before. GEORGE DROUILLARD and PIERRE CRUZATTE had gone up the Platte to look for them but reported that the Indians were off hunting BUFFALO elsewhere.

On July 28, as the expedition was passing the site of today's Omaha, Nebraska, the hunters came back with a Missouri Indian, one of a party of Otoe buffalo hunters nearby. A meeting with his people was arranged, and, as Sergeant PATRICK GASS described it, the expedition proceeded upstream until they "came to some timberland at the foot of a high bluff and encamped there in order to wait for the Indians." The chosen location was on the west bank of the MISSOURI RIVER, just north of present-day Fort Calhoun. Two days after arriving there, Gass reported, "This place we named Council-Bluff."

At sunset on August 2, six Otoe and Missouri headmen and their retinue arrived at the camp, accompanied by a Frenchman who acted as interpreter. As custom required, the captains presented them with TOBACCO, pork, flour, and meal, while the Indians returned the courtesy with some melons. The following morning a formal council was held. Despite the absence of the two chiefs, LITTLE THIEF of the Otoe and BIG HORSE of the Missouri, MERIWETHER LEWIS knew it was time to impress their visitors. Both he and WILLIAM CLARK wore their dress uniforms, as did their soldiers. A parade was held and the soldiers drilled, marching past in review and firing a volley from their rifles. Lewis then spoke on the aims of the expedition. It was a speech he was to give often along the journey to the PACIFIC OCEAN in numerous COUNCILS WITH INDIANS. He stressed the cession of the LOUISIANA TERRITORY by the Spanish and French to the United States and the goodwill of the United States toward the Indians. He spoke of the need for peace among Indian nations and the advantages this would bring. He also indicated that such a peace would bring benefits in the way of trading posts and Americans eager to buy the furs and skins that the Indians possessed. He concluded with an invitation to the chiefs to travel to Washington and then handed out GIFTS and PEACE MEDALS to his audience. The Otoe and Missouri chiefs listened and expressed their agreement, then asked for and were given some powder and whiskey. The expedition continued on its way the same afternoon.

Though there were no important consequences of the meeting at Council Bluff, it was a significant incident in the Lewis and Clark Expedition. They had come more than 600 miles on their journey, and the Otoe and Missouri headmen were the first Indians they had met. The council was the first between PLAINS INDIANS and representatives of the U.S. government. It also gave both Lewis and Clark the chance to practice their roles as diplomats and information gatherers, roles they would have to exercise continually during the months ahead.

Council Bluff itself—that is, the hill below which that first council was held—later became the site of Fort Atkinson, built in 1819. A reconstruction of the fort stands on the hill today. The city of Council Bluffs, across the river from Omaha, takes its name from the site of Lewis and Clark's first Indian council.

Further Reading

Fifer, Barbara, and Vicky Soderberg. *Along the Trail with Lewis and Clark.* Great Falls, Mont.: Montana Magazine, 1998.

MacGregor, Carol Lynn, ed. *The Journals of Patrick Gass, Member of the Lewis and Clark Expedition.* Missoula, Mont.: Mountain Press Publishing Company, 1997.

Moulton, Gary E., ed. *Atlas of the Lewis and Clark Expedition.* Revised ed. Lincoln: University of Nebraska Press, 1999.

Ronda, James P. *Lewis and Clark among the Indians.* Lincoln: University of Nebraska Press, 1984.

councils with Indians

Although the primary motives of the Lewis and Clark Expedition were scientific and commercial, the diplomatic element was very important. With the LOUISIANA PURCHASE, the United States had doubled in size and gained thousands of new citizens, most of whom were American Indians. That the Indians did not in fact have official citizenship status was irrelevant. They were now living within U.S. territory and had therefore become an even more significant factor in the expedition than they had been previously. THOMAS JEF-FERSON wanted to ensure not only that the Indians accepted the new sovereignty but that they would transfer their trading connections from the British and French to the United States. Thus, in his MISSION OBJECTIVES, Jefferson devoted much attention to the Indians, specifying how they were to be treated and what Lewis was to learn from and about them. Further, Lewis was to invite their chiefs to go to Washington to meet Jefferson.

Lewis's cocommander, WILLIAM CLARK, a soldier and surveyor, had already had significant contact with Indians on what was then the American frontier and had become a friend and confidant to many. In addition, having witnessed the negotiation of the Treaty of Greenville in 1795, Clark knew the protocol involved. He and Lewis planned to hold formal meetings with the chiefs of each nation they met east of the ROCKY MOUNTAINS (the demarcation line of the Louisiana Purchase). Once they were over the mountains and into non-U.S. territory, their objectives would change.

Their first council was with chiefs of the OTOE (Oto) and MISSOURI INDIANS on August 3, 1804. Since the two most important chiefs of those nations were absent, this was in effect a rehearsal for future councils. First, GIFTS for the chiefs were specially prepared in individual bundles. Then an awning was made out of the KEELBOAT's main sail, a flagstaff erected, and a flag raised. The captains and their men wore full-dress uniforms, and once the Indians had gathered under the awning, the sergeants put their men through a review drill, complete with volleys from their FIREARMS. There is no record of how much any of this impressed the Indian witnesses, but it was all just a prelude to the main event: Lewis's speech.

Lewis and Clark had spent much time preparing what they would say in their councils with Indians. Speeches were long and made even longer by the INTERPRETATION process. It was Lewis who normally spoke, and in most councils he emphasized the same message. The Indians, usually addressed as "children," were first told of the change in government and that they had a new "father" (Jefferson) who was the "great chief of the Seventeen nations." They were then told that the expedition had come to make "a road of peace" and of the benefits and prosperity their new American father would bring them. They were also instructed to make peace with their neighbors and TRADE with the merchants in ST. LOUIS. If they did this, then trading posts would be built, enabling them to "obtain goods on much better terms than . . . before." If, however, they followed the "bad birds" (British traders), then they would suffer. Finally, they were invited to send a delegation to

This illustration from the 1810 edition of Patrick Gass's journal shows Captains Lewis and Clark holding a council with Indians. *(Library of Congress, Prints and Photographs Division [LC-USZ62-17372])*

Washington. In this way they would see the riches of their new nation and receive numerous gifts and honors. Lewis concluded by telling them that the United States was "the only friend to whom you can now look for protection."

In the case of the first Otoe and Missouri council, the response of the chiefs was immediate. In later councils the captains were told that the chiefs would respond in a day or two. There followed a presentation of gifts, which Lewis had carefully prepared months previously; the distribution of PEACE MEDALS; and a demonstration of Lewis's airgun, which never failed to impress the Indians.

In the months to come, there would be variations in detail, dependent on the audience. For example, many councils were preceded by SMOKING CEREMONIES, while others included a firing of the keelboat's swivel gun to make a strong impression on the Indians. The basic elements, though, remained the same. Whether these meetings were the diplomatic success Lewis and Clark hoped for is a matter for debate. There was much that the captains did not understand about the PLAINS INDIANS, their complex system of trading, and their intertribal politics. Similarly, the Indians rarely understood fully what the captains were trying to say and do. After the first council with the MANDAN INDIANS on October 29, Clark complained that "those nations know nothing of reagular Councils, and know not how to proceed in them, they are restless &c." He and Lewis were also continually irritated by the Indians' custom of waiting before they gave their replies to the American speeches.

One prime example of the captains' attempts to impose an American attitude on the Indians was their insistence on designating one chief as the "grand chief" or "first chief." This not only ignored the Indians' own hierarchy but also ran the risk of offending those who were deemed "lesser" chiefs in their eyes. This was an important factor in their encounter with the TETON LAKOTA INDIANS (Teton Sioux) in September 1804, but by the time they met the NEZ PERCE INDIANS, they had learned to treat all chiefs with equal respect.

While the captains managed to elicit some positive responses from certain Indians regarding the new American trading scheme, their proposal had a number of flaws. First, for many of the nations to whom they talked, it was not with whom they were trading that mattered so much as the quality and availability of the goods. The Americans would therefore have to back up their words with actions before the Indians would express wholehearted approval of the plan.

Second, as Lewis and Clark discovered, it was naïve to ask Indians to break a long-established pattern of trade. There was a complex trading interdependency that worked on both a commercial and a political level, and the Indians saw no good reason to disrupt the pattern without a guarantee that they would gain rather than lose from doing as the Americans asked. The ARIKARA, for example, depended on the Teton Lakota for European goods and BUFFALO meat, which were traded for Arikara CORN and HORSES. If they broke off relations with the Lakota, those Indians would retaliate. It was therefore safer to keep things as they were.

Finally, many nations wanted guns and ammunition to resist nations like the Teton Lakota, who already had firearms and had driven them from their hunting grounds. Until they had a ready supplier of those crucial items, whatever else the Americans had to offer was of little interest, particularly if it was more of what the captains had offered as gifts and trade goods.

Lewis and Clark were most unsuccessful in their efforts to negotiate peace agreements. They wanted the Otoe to reconcile with the OMAHA, the Arikara to be neighborly with the Mandan, the Nez Perce to make peace with the SHOSHONE, and so on. Perhaps more than anything else, this demonstrated their ignorance of Indian ways, for as historian Stephen Ambrose writes, "The terms 'peace' and 'war' as understood by the Americans had no meaning to the Indians." While many chiefs agreed that peace with their neighbors was desirable, they realized what the captains did not: it would be fleeting. Conflicts between nations was an integral part of Plains Indian culture; the honor of warriors usually depended on their achievements in battle, and chiefs were chosen from the best warriors. Furthermore, peace depended on cooperation from all nations, but the Teton Lakota, the ASSINIBOINE, and others were never likely to cooperate.

While Lewis and Clark's diplomatic mission failed on many levels, they did succeed in fulfilling one element of Jefferson's instructions. As a result of their efforts, many Indians came to Washington, and Jefferson met with representatives from several nations. He gave them the same message that Lewis had done: that he wished his "children" to live in peace and harmony and that they would benefit from trading with their new friend and protector, the United States. It was trade and only trade, not land, that the Americans wanted, said Jefferson. Little did he realize that in less than 50 years it would be the American greed for land that would completely destroy not only the Indians' trading networks but their entire way of life.

Further Reading

Ambrose, Stephen E. *Undaunted Courage: Meriwether Lewis, Thomas Jefferson, and the Opening of the American West.* New York: Simon and Schuster, 1996.
Ronda, James P. *Lewis and Clark among the Indians.* Lincoln: University of Nebraska Press, 1984.

court-martials

One of the necessary ways by which commanders of any military unit maintain DISCIPLINE is to convene court-martials. These were and are courts of military law usually presided over and impaneled by officers. In the case of the CORPS OF DISCOVERY, however, trials were conducted by the soldiers themselves, acting as a jury of peers, with either or both of the captains overseeing the proceedings. A usual court consisted of one sergeant and four privates, although the numbers sometimes varied. In some cases more than one man was tried.

Between November 1803, when the corps set up CAMP DUBOIS near Wood River, and April 1805, when the permanent expedition set out from FORT MANDAN, the captains convened seven court-martials. The first took place on March 29, 1804. In separate incidents, Privates JOHN COLTER and JOHN SHIELDS had defied orders and threatened Sergeant JOHN ORDWAY's life. They were tried together for mutiny, and both "asked the forgivness &c & promised to doe better in future." The captains decided on this occasion to let the matter go, and both men were readmitted to the corps without punishment.

In mid-May 1804 at ST. CHARLES, three enlisted men were tried for being absent without leave. Privates WILLIAM WERNER and HUGH HALL were sentenced to "twenty-five lashes on their bear backs," and Private JOHN COLLINS, who was guilty of additional offenses, received 50 lashes. Collins and Hall were tried again the following month for getting drunk while Collins was on sentry duty. Hall was given 50 lashes, while Collins, again the bigger offender, received 100 lashes.

During the night of July 11–12, 1804, Private ALEXANDER WILLARD committed the cardinal sin of falling asleep while on guard duty. This was a crime that could be punishable by death, and for that reason the court-martial was carried out by the captains alone. Willard pled guilty to lying down but not guilty to falling asleep. He was found guilty of both charges and sentenced to 100 lashes a day for four successive days.

In August 1804, following the corps's first meeting with the OTOE (Oto) INDIANS, Private MOSES REED deserted the expedition after receiving permission to go back and retrieve a knife he had supposedly left behind. After three days, according to the journal of PATRICK GASS, "four of our people were dispatched to the Oto nation of Indians after the man who had not returned on the 4th, with orders to take him, dead or alive, if they could see him." Ten days later the search party, headed by GEORGE DROUILLARD, returned with Reed. Clark noted that they "only Sentenced him to run the Gantlet four times through the Party & that each man with 9 Swichies Should punish him." Reed was thereupon expelled from the corps and put to work as a laborer on the PIROGUES. In October a similar punishment was meted out to JOHN NEWMAN, whom Reed had incited into making verbal attacks on the captain that they considered mutinous. Subjected to 75 lashes and expelled from the corps, Newman also became a laborer. Both he and Reed were returned to ST. LOUIS on the KEELBOAT the following spring.

The last court-martial of the expedition was also the only one held at Fort Mandan. On February 9, 1805, Private THOMAS PROCTOR HOWARD returned to the fort after dark and foolishly scaled the walls to enter. Seeing this, a Mandan Indian entered the fort the same way—a tremendous breach of security that could have had serious consequences for the expedition if less friendly Indians were to try it. Howard was arrested, court-martialed, and sentenced to 50 lashes. However, given that he had merely been thoughtless, Captain Lewis took the advice of the court and forgave Howard, sparing him a lashing. Howard remained with the permanent party.

To modern eyes, the rough-and-ready punishments of these court-martials seem brutal. However, it is clear that, given the circumstances, such trials and their attendant consequences were the only sanctions available to enforce army discipline, apart from execution. Certainly the men of the CORPS OF DISCOVERY accepted the necessity of court-martials and the carrying out of harsh sentences—and this acceptance reflects great credit on the LEADERSHIP of Lewis and Clark as well as on the men they led.

Further Reading

Ambrose, Stephen E. *Undaunted Courage: Meriwether Lewis, Thomas Jefferson, and the Opening of the American West.* New York: Simon and Schuster, 1996.

Hunt, Robert R. "Crime and Punishment on the Lewis and Clark Expedition." *Military Collector and Historian* 41 (summer 1989): 56–65.

coyotes (prairie wolves, *Canis latrans latrans*)

Although MERIWETHER LEWIS and WILLIAM CLARK were not the first to describe the coyote (*Canis latrans latrans*), they were certainly the first to record its appearance and habits. On August 12, 1804, northwest of present-day Whiting, Iowa, Clark wrote, "A Prarie Wolf came near the bank and Barked at us this evning, we made an attempt but could not get him, the animale Barkes like a large ferce dog." The following month, on September 18, 1804, near the mouth of the White River in South Dakota, he recorded, "I killed a Prarie Wolf, about the Size of a Gray fox, bushy tail, head and ears like a Wolf, Some fur, Burrows in the ground and barks like a Small Dog. What has been taken heretofore for a Fox was those Wolves and no Foxes has been seen. . . ."

The expedition referred to coyotes as "prairie wolves" throughout the journey, and this is still the alternative name for these members of the wolf family. The term *coyote* has been traced back to Mexican Spanish, circa 1759. The animal is smaller than the wolf and resembles the jackal. Its length is about 40 inches, and the general color is tawny mingled with black, with white above and a whitish shade below. Coyotes live in burrows on the plains and hunt in packs at night, making yapping cries as they gallop. Hares, chipmunks, and mice are their main food, supplemented with fawns of DEER and pronghorn ANTELOPE, sage hens, and other game birds. They dig burrows for themselves or will take possession of burrows already dug by badgers and PRAIRIE DOGS. If no meat is available, they will eat juniper berries and other wild fruits.

Coyotes are found on the plains on either side of the ROCKY MOUNTAINS, from Canada down to Guatemala. At FORT CLATSOP on February 20, 1806, Lewis noted that "the large [gray wolf] and small wolves [coyotes] of the plains are the inhabitants principally of the open country and the woodlands on their borders, and resemble in their habits and appearance those of the plain of the Missouri precisely. They are not abundant in the plains of the Columbia because there is but little game on which for them to subsist."

Further Reading

Burroughs, Raymond Darwin, ed. *The Natural History of the Lewis and Clark Expedition.* East Lansing: Michigan State University Press, 1995.

Cutright, Paul Russell. *Lewis & Clark: Pioneering Naturalists.* Lincoln: University of Nebraska Press/Bison Books, 1989.

Washington State University. "Lewis and Clark Among the Indians of the Pacific Northwest. Excerpts from the Journals of the Expedition of the Corps of Discovery: Flora and Fauna (recorded at Fort Clatsop)." Available on-line. URL: http://www.libarts.wsu.edu/history/Lewis_Clark/LCEXP_Flor.html. Downloaded on May 20, 2001.

cranes

The expedition noted two types of cranes on its journey: the whooping crane (*Grus americana*) and the sandhill crane (*Grus canadensis*). The whooping crane had been described in 1772 and classified by biologist Carolus Linnaeus in 1776, but they were rarely seen on the eastern seaboard. On April 11, 1805, on the stretch of the MISSOURI RIVER now covered by Lake Sakakawea, North Dakota, MERIWETHER LEWIS noted: "Saw some large white cranes pass up the river. These are the largest bird of the genus common to the country through which the Missouri and Mississippi pass. They are perfectly white except the large feathers of the first two joints of the wing which is black." WILLIAM CLARK made on a note on October 26, 1805, when the party was near The Dalles, Oregon, that they "saw a great number of white cranes flying in Different Directions very high."

Because the whooping crane does not adapt itself to human activity or association, it is now an endangered species. It is known there were tremendous flocks in the Midwest in the first half of the 19th century, but by 1874 it was already being noted that these had diminished considerably. It is believed there are only 30 or so whooping crane surviving today.

The sandhill crane was first recorded by Lewis, who clearly recognized it on July 21, 1805, near the GATES OF THE MOUNTAINS in Montana: "Saw several of the large brown or Sandhill crain today with their young, the young Crain is as large as a turkey and cannot fly; they are of a bright red bey colour, or that of the common DEER at this season. This bird feeds on grass principally and is found in the river bottoms."

A week later, near THREE FORKS, the hunters brought in a live young sandhill crane, of which Lewis wrote: "This young animal is very fierce and strikes a severe blow with its beak; after amusing myself with it I had it set at liberty apparently much pleased with being relieved from his capativity." Later, west of the CONTINENTAL DIVIDE, sandhill cranes were seen again, and some were killed for food. On November 16, 1805, Sergeant PATRICK GASS noted that the hunters had returned with "2 deer, 9 brants, 2 geese, 1 crane."

Although the numbers of the sandhill crane are now much reduced, several breeding colonies still exist.

Further Reading

Burroughs, Raymond Darwin, ed. *The Natural History of the Lewis and Clark Expedition.* East Lansing: Michigan State University Press, 1995.

Cutright, Paul Russell. *Lewis & Clark: Pioneering Naturalists.* Lincoln: University of Nebraska Press/Bison Books, 1989.

Washington State University. "Lewis and Clark Among the Indians of the Pacific Northwest. Excerpts from the Journals of the Expedition of the Corps of Discovery: Flora and Fauna (recorded at Fort Clatsop)." Available on-line. URL: http://www.libarts.wsu.edu/history/Lewis_Clark/LCEXP_Flor.html. Downloaded on May 20, 2001.

credit, letter of   See LETTER OF CREDIT.

Crow at Rest (Kakawissassa, Lighting Crow)

(unknown–unknown) *Arikara Indian chief*

On October 8, 1804, the CORPS OF DISCOVERY met the ARIKARA INDIANS at their villages by the MISSOURI RIVER, just north of present-day Mobridge, South Dakota. There were three villages: Sawa-haini on Ashley Island (now submerged by Lake Oahe) and, about four miles north, Rhtarahe and Waho-erha. Crow at Rest was chief of Sawa-haini, and it was he whom MERIWETHER LEWIS and WILLIAM CLARK treated as the "grand chief" of all the Arikara, despite the advice of French trader PIERRE-ANTOINE TABEAU to treat the three chiefs as equals. This caused some tension with HAY and HAWK'S FEATHER, who initially resisted attending a council with the explorers but finally agreed to do so.

On October 10 the captains held a formal meeting with the three chiefs. Lewis spoke on the need for peace with the MANDAN INDIANS upstream, the benefits of trade with the United States, and the advantages of breaking the Arikara's association with the TETON LAKOTA INDIANS (Teton Sioux). The three chiefs retired to consider what he said, though they welcomed the explorers into their villages. That night William Clark, with YORK, Sergeant PATRICK GASS, and several others, crossed over to Ashley Island, where they were warmly greeted.

The following day, Crow at Rest gave his formal response to Lewis's speech. He assured them the Arikara would let them travel on in peace and that peace with the Mandan was desirable. He also expressed an interest in trading BUFFALO skins with the merchants in ST. LOUIS. Later that day, Crow at Rest and a nephew went with the expedition up to the next village, where the second chief, Hay, was to meet the party.

In 1806 the explorers again met Crow at Rest near the end of their return journey. He told them that he had handed over his chieftainship to a younger man named Grey Eyes. Although Grey Eyes welcomed the explorers and endorsed their views on peace among the Indian nations, he later led an attack on a U.S. trading party in 1823.

Further Reading

MacGregor, Carol Lynn, ed. *The Journals of Patrick Gass, Member of the Lewis and Clark Expedition.* Missoula, Mont.: Mountain Press Publishing Company, 1997.

Ronda, James P. *Lewis and Clark among the Indians.* Lincoln: University of Nebraska Press, 1984.

Crow Indians

Among the Indians who frequently came to trade at the villages of the MANDAN INDIANS were the Crow. While the Lewis and Clark Expedition appear to have had no direct contact with the Crow, they were well aware of them and knew these Indians could be a factor in the course of the journey through the GREAT PLAINS.

Siouan speakers, the Crow are PLAINS INDIANS who at that time occupied the area around the YELLOWSTONE RIVER and its tributaries. Those who lived in the valleys of the Powder, Wind, and Bighorn Rivers came to be called River Crow, while whose who were further upriver, at the foot of the ROCKY MOUNTAINS, were known as Mountain Crow. Prior to 1700, the Crow had been affiliated with the HIDATSA INDIANS, but they moved westward after a dispute over BUFFALO; they were probably also lured by the trade in HORSES with the Spanish. Nomads who lived in TIPIS, by 1740 they had become middlemen for TRADE between the Hidatsa and the SHOSHONE INDIANS in Idaho.

Crow life revolved around the horse and buffalo, which provided them with food, clothing, tipi covers, sinew thread, and shields. They also grew TOBACCO, which had been given to them to overcome their enemies, according to Crow legend. Tobacco was often used in ceremonial occasions, and they had a special society that revolved around it. While women tended to the crops and home, men engaged in war parties, primarily to raid other nations for horses. They grew their hair very long, often as far as the ground, and because of this they were known to some traders as the long-haired Indians.

From the Hidatsa MERIWETHER LEWIS and WILLIAM CLARK learned about the size and location of the Crow groups. They may also have obtained information from the French trader FRANÇOIS-ANTOINE LAROCQUE, whom they met at the Mandan-Hidatsa villages and who was known to trade with the Crow. In addition to including them in the "Estimate of the Western Indians" (see ETHNOGRAPHY), Clark also drew "the war path of the Big Bellies [Crow]" on his map of the region. Signs of Crow were later seen on their journey westward, but the party never met them, perhaps because at that point they were traveling by water and had no horses.

It was a different story on the return journey in 1806. After the expedition had split into two parties, Sergeant NATHANIEL PRYOR and a small party were given the mission of taking a number of their horses back to the Mandan villages and from there to deliver a letter to the trader HUGH HENEY. Pryor and his men left Clark at the Yellowstone River to travel cross-country. Along the way, however, all of their horses were stolen by the Crow, forcing the soldiers to return to the Yel-

The Crow, who depended on the horse and buffalo for survival, stole most of the expedition's horses during the return journey in 1806. This photograph taken ca. 1905 shows two Crow Indians on horseback in Montana. *(Library of Congress, Prints and Photographs Division [LC-USZ62-106885])*

lowstone, construct BULL BOATS, and follow Clark and the others down the Yellowstone. Clark, meanwhile, had also lost 24 horses to the Crow at BOZEMAN PASS.

In 1808 former expedition member JOHN COLTER joined Crow and FLATHEAD INDIANS in a battle against the BLACKFEET INDIANS. During the Wars for the West later in the century, the Crow allied with the U.S. Army against several other nations, including the Sioux (Dakota, Lakota, Nakota) and the NEZ PERCE INDIANS. This made no difference, however, in their treatment by the U.S. government as settlers invaded their territory and brought their way of life to an end. In 1868 they accepted a reservation on former tribal lands in southern Montana. The size of their reservation was reduced in the 1950s when the Yellowtail Dam was built in Bighorn Canyon. By the late 20th century, the Crow population had reached about 5,000.

Further Reading

Lowie, Robert H. *The Crow Indians.* Lincoln: University of Nebraska Press, 1983.

Ronda, James P. *Lewis and Clark among the Indians*. Lincoln and London: University of Nebraska Press, 1984.

Waldman, Carl. *Encyclopedia of Native American Tribes*. Revised ed. New York: Checkmark Books, 1999.

———. "Wars for the West." In: *Atlas of the North American Indian*. Revised ed. New York: Checkmark Books, 1999, pp. 147–182.

Cruzatte, Pierre (unknown–unknown)

private in the permanent party

Private Pierre Cruzatte was a member of the CORPS OF DISCOVERY who was of French and OMAHA INDIAN extraction. An expert riverman recruited for his navigational skills and his command of the French and Omaha languages, he was small and wiry and had the use of only one eye, which was nearsighted. His father was probably a descendant of the Cruzatte family, early settlers of ST. LOUIS. His mother was an Omaha Indian.

Cruzatte, whose nickname among other corps members was "St. Peter," enlisted with Lewis and Clark on May 16, 1804, at ST. CHARLES. He had previously been a trader for the fur merchants PIERRE CHOUTEAU and AUGUSTE CHOUTEAU on the MISSOURI RIVER and had traveled up as far as the PLATTE RIVER. This had enabled him to gain extensive geographical knowledge of the area, which would prove useful to the corps. It was also Cruzatte who showed the captains how to make CACHES to lighten their loads along the way.

Because of his proficiency as a riverman, Cruzatte was assigned along with FRANÇOIS LABICHE to man the bow in the KEELBOAT, in addition to setting the pace on the oars; the two men alternated these responsibilities. Cruzatte was in the bow on one occasion when TOUSSAINT CHARBONNEAU lost control of the PIROGUE he was helming. According to MERIWETHER LEWIS, as Cruzatte shouted instructions from the keelboat, he "threatened to shoot him [Charbonneau] instantly if he did not take hold of the rudder and do his duty. . . ." Charbonneau finally regained his composure, while SACAGAWEA had coolly retrieved many of the items that had fallen into the water.

Cruzatte also played the fiddle, reportedly with great exuberance, and this had a positive effect on the explorers' morale. His music frequently boosted spirits during periods of low activity, as well as during the holidays. On New Year's Day 1805, Cruzatte and 17 other corps members carried "a fiddle & a Tambereen & a Sounden Horn" [tin, with a brass reed] across the river to the MANDAN village, delighting the Indians with their music, singing, and dancing. Indeed, Cruzatte's playing often provided a means of establishing trust and good will with the Indian nations whom the expedition encountered.

Because of his fluency in the Omaha language and skills in sign language, Cruzatte sometimes played a role at Indian councils and during encounters with the nations on the lower MISSOURI RIVER. Unfortunately, he could be helpful only minimally during their tense meeting with the TETON LAKOTA INDIANS (Teton Sioux) in September 1804. Unable to speak more than a few simple words of the Lakota language, neither Cruzatte nor official interpreter GEORGE DROUILLARD, speaking in sign language, were unable to convey the captains' message to the Indians, who included among their party a number of Omaha prisoners. Disappointed with the GIFTS that had been presented to them, and unimpressed by a visit aboard the keelboat, the Teton became belligerent, seizing one of the expedition's pirogues and demanding more gifts. After a brief standoff, the captains and the Indians made an uneasy peace. The next day, however, Cruzatte spoke to some of the Omaha prisoners and learned that the Teton were planning to rob the expedition and keep it from continuing up the Missouri. A sleepless night ensued, but after another standoff the following day, the expedition was finally able to break free of the Lakota.

On October 20, 1804, Cruzatte was the first member of the expedition to encounter a grizzly BEAR. He shot the beast but succeeded only in wounding it and then running, leaving behind his gun and tomahawk, which he later retrieved. Not long after this he shot and wounded a BUFFALO, which chased him into a ravine.

Cruzatte's poor markmanship almost had dire consequences for the expedition. On August 11, 1806, while he and Lewis were hunting ELK, the captain was shot in the "left thye," or buttocks. Believing that BLACKFEET INDIANS were attacking, Lewis ran, calling to Cruzatte to retreat. Only later was it realized that the one-eyed Cruzatte had mistaken Lewis for an elk and accidentally shot his captain. The private denied this, but as the bullet was army issue, there seemed no doubt of his guilt. A gracious Lewis let the matter pass.

With the other enlisted men, Cruzatte was awarded extra pay and a land warrant for 320 acres after the expedition's return. He may have been with John McClallan's expedition to the ROCKY MOUNTAINS in 1807. WILLIAM CLARK had listed him as killed by 1825 or 1828.

Further Reading

Clarke, Charles G. *The Men of the Lewis and Clark Expedition: A Biographical Roster of the Fifty-One Members and a Composite Diary of Their Activities from All Known Sources*. 1970. Reprint, Lincoln: Bison Books, University of Nebraska Press, 2002.

North Dakota Lewis & Clark Bicentennial Foundation. *Members of the Corps of Discovery*. Bismarck, N.Dak.: United Printing and Mailing, 2000.

PBS Online. *Lewis and Clark: Inside the Corps of Discovery:* "Private Pierre Cruzatte." Available on-line. URL: http://www.pbs.org/lewisandclark/inside/pcruz.html. Downloaded on May 18, 2001.

curlews (*Numenius americanus americanus*)

On April 17, 1805, MERIWETHER LEWIS reported that WILLIAM CLARK had seen a curlew, a bird with long legs and a long, curving bill that is related to the sandpiper and the snipe. It is now thought that Clark's bird was the first scientific sighting of the long-billed curlew (*Numenius americanus americanus*).

Some weeks later, on June 23, 1805, Lewis reported at GREAT FALLS, Montana, that he "Saw quantities of little birds and the large brown curlew; the latter is now setting; it lays its eggs which are of a pale blue with black specks, on the ground without any preparation of a nest."

At FORT CLATSOP on March 5, 1806, Lewis wrote: "I have not seen the . . . large brown Curloo so common to the plains of the Missouri, but believe that the latter is an inhabitant of this country during summer from Indian information." It is now believed that Lewis's references to the "Jack Curloo" referred to the Western Willet and the mountain plover, providing an instance where he was confusing a species due to similarities in appearance and color.

See also BIRDS, NEW SPECIES.

Further Reading

Burroughs, Raymond Darwin, ed. *The Natural History of the Lewis and Clark Expedition.* East Lansing: Michigan State University Press, 1995.

Cutright, Paul Russell. *Lewis & Clark: Pioneering Naturalists.* Lincoln: University of Nebraska Press/Bison Books, 1989.

Washington State University. "Lewis and Clark Among the Indians of the Pacific Northwest. Excerpts from the Journals of the Expedition of the Corps of Discovery: Flora and Fauna (recorded at Fort Clatsop)." Available on-line. URL: http://www.libarts.wsu.edu/history/Lewis_Clark/LCEXP_Flor.html. Downloaded on May 20, 2001.

Cut Nose (Neeshneparkkeook)

(unknown–unknown) *Nez Perce chief*

On May 4, 1806, as the CORPS OF DISCOVERY was making its return journey up the SNAKE RIVER, they met the NEZ PERCE chief TETOHARSKY, who had helped to guide them down the COLUMBIA RIVER the previous autumn. Low on provisions, they gladly accepted his offer to take them to the village of TWISTED HAIR, another Nez Perce chief who had provided invaluable assistance and had promised to care for the expedition's HORSES during the winter. Four days later, on May 8, the corps came to the lodge of Chief Cut Nose, whose name was the result of a wound received during a battle with the SHOSHONE INDIANS. Reputedly a more important chief than Twisted Hair, Cut Nose had been away on a raid during the previous time the expedition had spent with the Nez Perce. Although he did not impress MERIWETHER LEWIS or WILLIAM CLARK greatly, they presented him with a medal. Fortunately, there was a Shoshone prisoner in his band, who was immediately enlisted to assist in the expedition's complicated chain of INTERPRETATION.

Cut Nose joined the party as they traveled east along the Clearwater, and two days later they met Twisted Hair. Almost at once, the two chiefs began to engage in a loud, almost violent argument that lasted for some time. It was later revealed that Cut Nose had accused Twisted Hair of failing to care properly for the expedition's horses, a responsibility that should have

been his by right, since he was the greater chief. According to Twisted Hair, both Cut Nose and BROKEN ARM, another important chief, were jealous of his increased importance due to his association with the expedition. After listening attentively to the two chiefs' arguments, Lewis and Clark offered a diplomatic solution that mollified them both, with Twisted Hair receiving only partial payment for his services until he had produced all the horses and was able to show that they had been well tended. (In fact, Cut Nose's charges that Twisted Hair had allowed his warriors to ride some of the horses too hard appeared to be true.)

The expedition went on to meet Broken Arm, in whose lodge a council with all the Nez Perce chiefs was held on May 11 and 12. Nothing is known of Cut Nose's contribution to these talks, although the chiefs and elders present took turns expressing their reactions to the Lewis and Clark proposals regarding peace with the Shoshone and trade with the United States. After a few weeks' stay with the Nez Perce, the expedition prepared to travel back over the BITTERROOT MOUNTAINS. This was against the Indians' advice, and Broken Arm flatly refused to lend the corps warriors to lead them over the LOLO TRAIL, saying that it was too soon and that the snows needed to melt more. But the bored and frustrated corps wanted to move on and prepared to leave on June 10.

That day they received word from Cut Nose that he would send two of his warriors to act as guides. This cheered the captains, and with the assurance they would shortly have assistance, they moved on to WEIPPE PRAIRIE. Here the expedition camped for four days and nights, anxiously awaiting Cut Nose's men, who never showed up. Finally, on June 15 they set off for the mountains without the INDIAN GUIDES. They soon found, however, that there was truth in what the Nez Perce had warned them about the snow on the mountain; it was impassable, and they had to turn back. On June 18 GEORGE DROUILLARD and GEORGE SHANNON headed back to the Indian villages to bargain for assistance. While they were gone, two teenage Nez Perce heading for the Lolo Trail showed up at camp and were convinced to stay on with the expedition until Drouillard and Shannon had returned.

It was an anxious wait of several days, but finally the privates came back with three guides, including a brother of Cut Nose. With these and the two boys, the expedition could finally cross the mountain, leaving Cut Nose and the Nez Perce behind forever.

Further Reading

Ambrose, Stephen E. *Undaunted Courage: Meriwether Lewis, Thomas Jefferson, and the Opening of the American West.* New York: Simon and Schuster, 1996.

Ronda, James P. *Lewis and Clark among the Indians.* Lincoln: University of Nebraska Press, 1984.

Cutssahnem   See WANAPAM INDIANS.

Dalles, The   See CELILO FALLS AND THE DALLES; WISHRAM AND WASCO INDIANS.

Dame, John (1784–unknown) *private in the temporary party*
Originally from Pallingham, New Hampshire, Private John Dame was among those recruited in KASKASKIA, Illinois, for the first part of the expedition only. He stood 5′9″ tall and was described as being of a fair complexion, with light hair and blue eyes. Although not a permanent member of the party, his killing of a pelican on August 7, 1804, earned him a mention in the expedition's JOURNALS.

Further Reading
Clarke, Charles G. *The Men of the Lewis and Clark Expedition: A Biographical Roster of the Fifty-One Members and a Composite Diary of Their Activities from All Known Sources.* 1970. Reprint, Lincoln: Bison Books, University of Nebraska Press, 2002.

dancing   See RECREATION ON THE EXPEDITION.

dead reckoning   See NAVIGATION.

Dearborn, Henry (1751–1829) *U.S. secretary of war*
Henry Dearborn, soldier and political leader, was the country's secretary of war at the time of the Lewis and Clark Expedition and thus, technically, the man to whom the captains reported. Fort Dearborn in Chicago was named after him, as was the DEARBORN RIVER.

Born in North Hampton, New Hampshire, Dearborn was a doctor in that state when the American Revolution erupted. After the Battle of Lexington and Concord in April 1775, he led a militia company to Cambridge, Massachusetts, and joined the colonial army. His company became part of John Stark's First New Hampshire Regiment and fought at the Battle of Bunker Hill.

Dearborn went to Quebec with Colonel Benedict Arnold later that year. Captured with some of his men during the attack there, Dearborn was later paroled and, after being exchanged, became a major in the Third New Hampshire Continental Regiment. He fought at the battles of Ticonderoga and Saratoga and was subsequently promoted to lieutenant colonel.

In June 1781 Dearborn was named assistant quartermaster general of the U.S. Army. He served in this capacity until 1782, when he assumed active command of the First New Hampshire Regiment. He was discharged from the army in July 1783 after having served more than eight years.

Dearborn represented the District of Maine in the U.S. CONGRESS from 1793 to 1797. When THOMAS JEFFERSON was elected president, Dearborn joined his cabinet as secretary of war, serving from 1801 to 1809. In this capacity he assisted in plans to remove Native Americans to lands beyond the Mississippi River. He also was the direct supervisor of the Lewis and Clark Expedition, in the process causing some considerable headaches for MERIWETHER LEWIS.

Their relationship was initially fine. In March 1803, when Lewis arrived at the U.S. armory and arsenal at HARPERS FERRY, WEST VIRGINIA, he carried with him a letter from Dearborn to the superintendent that instructed, "You will be pleased to make such arms & Iron work, as requested by the bearer Captain Meriwether Lewis and to have them completed with the least possible delay." Lewis was thus able to obtain the FIREARMS and hardware that would meet the requirements of his expedition.

Dearborn also provided the authorization for Lewis to hire an interpreter and to choose up to 12 noncommissioned privates and officers for the expedition, these men to be selected from army garrisons at FORT MASSAC and KASKASKIA, Illinois. He ordered commanding officers at these posts to cooperate with Lewis, but at Kaskaskia, Captain Russell Bissell refused to allow Lewis to recruit Sergeant PATRICK GASS. Using the carte blanche that Dearborn had given him, Lewis took Gass anyway. (In the end the permanent party was made up of 31 men; see CORPS OF DISCOVERY; RECRUITING.)

When Lewis invited WILLIAM CLARK to colead the expedition with him, he promised that Clark would receive a captain's commission. Dearborn, however, only authorized a lieutenant for Lewis and thus made Clark a second lieutenant in the Corps of Artillerists. When the commission arrived in ST. LOUIS, Lewis was dismayed and embarrassed, and Clark was extremely disappointed. Dearborn wrote that Clark would still receive appropriate compensation, but this was not enough for Lewis, and after the expedition's return he unsuccessfully lobbied the secretary to amend the wrong and make Clark a captain. He also requested that Dearborn ensure that Clark was compensated for his service on a level equal to Lewis. Dearborn refused, although Congress later authorized double pay for Clark and all the men, and Clark received a land warrant for 1,600 acres, the same as Lewis.

In July 1805, after Lewis and Clark had completed their PORTAGE of the GREAT FALLS of the Missouri, Lewis and a party riding ahead of the others came to two rivers. One he named for Jefferson's navy secretary Robert Smith. The other he named Dearborn's River. Meriwether Lewis noted in his journal that it was a "handsome bold and clear stream."

As required, Lewis reported to Dearborn at the end of the expedition. The two often clashed, however, for not only did the secretary refuse the captain's request to promote Clark, he also challenged many of Lewis's accounts. These encounters continued during Lewis's short, sad term as governor of LOUISIANA TERRITORY. Miscommunications resulting from the slowness of the postal service caused Dearborn to criticize Lewis's actions and refuse to sanction some of his decisions, particularly in regard to Indian policy.

Following his service as secretary of war, Dearborn became collector for the port of Boston. At the outbreak of the War of 1812, President JAMES MADISON appointed him a major general of the U.S. Army. By this time, however, age and illness were affecting his decision-making capacity. He planned but failed to execute attacks on the British, and his inaction was responsible for the U.S. loss at the battle of Detroit. Although he captured York in April 1813 and Fort George the following month, his incompetency in other sectors resulted in significant losses for U.S. forces. He was relieved of command in August 1813 but was later given command of New York City. He was honorably discharged in 1815.

Dearborn served as minister to Portugal from 1822 to 1824, upon which he retired to Roxbury, Massachusetts. Married and widowed twice, his third wife and a son by his second marriage survived him when he died in 1829.

Further Reading

Ambrose, Stephen. *Undaunted Courage: Meriwether Lewis, Thomas Jefferson, and the Opening of the American West.* New York: Simon and Schuster, 1996.
Dictionary of American Biography. "Henry Dearborn." Available on-line. URL: http://www.hampton.lib.nh.us/hampton/biog/henrydearborn1.htm. Updated on December 22, 1999.
Erney, Richard Alton. *The Public Life of Henry Dearborn.* Reprint, New York: Arno Press, 1979.

Dearborn River (Dearborn's River)

Scouting up the Upper Missouri in west-central Montana on July 18, 1805, MERIWETHER LEWIS came upon two rivers. He described the one on the right as a "beautiful river" meandering "through a most lovely valley." Impressed by, among other things, the clarity of the water, he spent some time exploring this river. According to Lewis's journal entry for that day,

At the distance to 2.5 miles we passed the entrance of a considerable river on the Stard. side; about 80 yds. wide being nearly as wide as the Missouri at that place. Its current is rapid and water extremely transparent; the bed is formed of small smooth stones of flat rounded or other figures. Its bottoms are narrow but possess as much timber as the Missouri. The country is mountainous and broken through which it passes. It appears as if it might be navigated but to what extent must be conjectural. This handsome bold and clear stream we named in honor of the Secretary of War calling it Dearborn's River.

It is now called the Dearborn River.

The Dearborn's source is at Scapegoat Mountain, north of Lincoln, Montana, in what is now called the Lewis and Clark Range. It flows in an east-southeasterly direction for 67 miles, partly through former BLACKFEET hunting grounds, before discharging into the MISSOURI RIVER. Had Lewis and Clark not been set on their course of following the Missouri to its source and instead followed the Dearborn, they would have come to what is now called LEWIS AND CLARK PASS over the CONTINENTAL DIVIDE. This would have brought them to the BIG BLACKFOOT RIVER and then the Clark Fork River, which flows into the COLUMBIA RIVER—a shorter journey than the one they ultimately took.

Further Reading

Fifer, Barbara, and Vicky Soderberg. *Along the Trail with Lewis and Clark*. Great Falls, Mont.: Montana Magazine, 1998.
Moulton, Gary E., ed. *Atlas of the Lewis and Clark Expedition*. Revised ed. Lincoln: University of Nebraska Press, 1999.

deaths on the expedition   See BLACKFEET INDIANS; FLOYD, CHARLES.

deer

Although the Lewis and Clark Expedition set off in May 1804 with some seven tons of nonperishable FOOD, they relied on the country through which they passed to provide fresh meat for their daily consumption. Of all the animals and birds killed for food during the course of the expedition, deer were by far the most numerous. While the thousands of animals taken by the hunters may seem excessive to modern minds, their need for meat justified it, as WILLIAM CLARK wrote: "It requires 4 deer, or an ELK and a deer, or one BUFFALO to supply us for 24 hours." It has been calculated that about 1,000 deer were killed by the party between May 1804 and September 1806. This works out at just a deer per day, not excessive in view of Clark's remark.

While deer were to be found along most of the expedition's ROUTE, the hunters found few in the BITTERROOT MOUNTAINS or along the upper reaches of the COLUMBIA RIVER. It is noteworthy that they were only able to kill 17 deer between November 1805 and March 1806, though it is probable that the topography of scrub land and trees were major factors in making deer HUNTING difficult.

In terms of deer species, MERIWETHER LEWIS and William Clark were the first to identify and name the mule deer and the first to describe the Columbian black-tailed deer as well as to classify it as a separate subspecies. The most common deer was the white-tailed deer, also called the Virginia deer or the red deer, with which all the explorers were familiar. The expedition found it all the way up the lower MISSOURI RIVER, although they noticed that the deer they saw on the upper stretches differed in appearance, and Clark called it a "fallow deer." Apparently neither Lewis nor Clark considered the difference in appearance sufficient enough to classify it as a new subspecies, but such is how the Oregon white-tail deer are recognized today.

Clark first wrote about the Columbian black-tailed deer on November 19, 1805, just north of CAPE DISAPPOINTMENT, Washington: "The Deer of this coast differ materially from our Common deer in as much as they are much darker, deeper bodied, shorter legged, horns equally branched from the beam, the top of the tail black from the rute [root] to the end. Eyes larger, and do not lope but jump." This deer is still the most plentiful in western Oregon, where its preference for dense forests and brushland has enabled it to evade its natural enemies.

The mule deer was first noted by Clark on September 17, 1804, near present-day Chamberlain, South Dakota: "Colter [JOHN COLTER] killed . . . a curious kid of Deer of a Dark gray colour—or more so than common, hair long and fine, the eyes large and long, a small recepticle under the eyes like the Elk, the tail about the length of the Common Deer, round (like a cow) a tuft of black hair about the end, this Species of Deer jumps like a goat or Sheep." On May 10, 1805, near modern Fort Peck, Montana, Lewis wrote a long and detailed description of the animal and coined the term by which it is now known:

There are several essential differences between the Mule deer and the common deer as well in form as in habits. They are fully a third larger in general and the male is particularly large. . . . The ear and tail of this anamal when compared with those of the common deer, so well comported with those of the mule when compared with the horse, that we have by way of distinction adapted the appellation of the mule deer, which I think more appropriate.

As they continued on to the PACIFIC OCEAN after crossing the Bitterroots, Lewis noted that they had seen no mule deer since leaving the LOLO TRAIL. He concluded that there were no such deer west of the ROCKY MOUNTAINS. However, common red deer were to be found in the area, with only one characteristic distinguishing them from the eastern counterparts: a longer tail, which Lewis found in one case to be 17 inches long.

Further Reading

Burroughs, Raymond Darwin, ed. *The Natural History of the Lewis and Clark Expedition*. East Lansing: Michigan State University Press, 1995.
Cutright, Paul Russell. *Lewis & Clark: Pioneering Naturalists*. Lincoln: University of Nebraska Press/Bison Books, 1989.
Knue, Joseph. *Big Game of North Dakota: A Short History*. Bismarck: North Dakota Game and Fish Dept., 1991.
Washington State University. "Lewis and Clark Among the Indians of the Pacific Northwest. Excerpts from the Journals of the Expedition of the Corps of Discovery: Flora and Fauna (recorded at Fort Clatsop)." Available on-line. URL: http://www.libarts.wsu.edu/history/Lewis_Clark/LCEXP_Flor.html. Downloaded on May 20, 2001.

Degie, Phillipe   See ENGAGÉS.

democracy on the expedition

Although the Lewis and Clark Expedition is popularly viewed as a mission of exploration and discovery conducted by deerskin-clad frontiersmen, in fact the members of the CORPS OF DISCOVERY were soldiers of the U.S. Army on a military mission. As such, they were organized according to strict army regulations. Soldiers drilled, did sentry duty, wore their dress uniforms when conducting COUNCILS WITH INDIANS, obeyed orders, and suffered the consequences for any breach of DISCIPLINE. Most of all, they did not question or challenge the decisions of their superiors.

Yet the nature of the corps's organization and mission was such that it invited certain exceptions to the rules. It should not be forgotten that 11 members of the permanent party were not regular soldiers but civilians when they enlisted: the NINE YOUNG MEN FROM KENTUCKY, FRANÇOIS LABICHE, and PIERRE CRUZATTE. Although required to function as soldiers as well, TOUSSAINT CHARBONNEAU and YORK were actually civilian personnel; GEORGE DROUILLARD was the only man exempted from military duties. The party also included two highly unusual members for a military mission: SACAGAWEA and her baby, JEAN BAPTISTE CHARBONNEAU. Further, there were the ENGAGÉS and temporary corpsmen who accompanied the expedition only as far as the MANDAN villages. The permanent party that left FORT MANDAN totaled 33 members, and as their journey continued they became a close-knit company whose members knew and relied on each other completely.

There were other features that distinguished the expedition from other military units. First of all, the objectives of their mission were peaceful. Second, all members of the party were encouraged to keep JOURNALS; the captains, all the sergeants, and at least two of the privates did so. Finally, the command was an uncommon one in that it was shared by two men, MERIWETHER LEWIS and WILLIAM CLARK. This went against all normal military procedure, which ordinarily called for a single commander and a distinct chain of command. Yet the sergeants and privates accepted without reservation the equal authority of their two captains.

Such was the LEADERSHIP of Lewis and Clark that they recognized the exceptional circumstances of their mission as well as the remarkable capabilities of their men. Because of this, they did something military commanders rarely do. When deemed appropriate, they invited opinions and discussion on important decisions, and on two occasions they even held elections. It can therefore be said that the most unusual aspect of the expedition was that democratic principles were allowed— and worked successfully.

On August 20, 1804, Sergeant CHARLES FLOYD died, making it necessary to select a replacement for him. Lewis and Clark would normally have made this decision themselves, but instead they left it to the men. An election was held, and PATRICK GASS was chosen to succeed Floyd as sergeant; WILLIAM BRATTON and GEORGE GIBSON were the runners-up. It was the first democratic election west of the MISSISSIPPI RIVER.

In early June the following year, as the expedition was traveling up the MISSOURI RIVER, they came to a fork in the river. Now a decision had to be made: Which fork was the true Missouri? The captains had reason to believe that the left fork was the one to take. For one thing, the waters of the right-hand fork were muddy, which should not have been the case if the river drained from the ROCKY MOUNTAINS. More important, the

At the junction of the Marias and Missouri Rivers, the captains and the men debated which river to follow. According to Lewis, the men "said very cheerfully that they were ready to follow us any wher we thought proper to direct but that they still thought the other was the river." This painting by Robert F. Morgan is entitled *Decision*. (Montana Historical Society, Helena)

right fork appeared to go in a northerly direction, which did not seem right. Lewis and Clark asked for opinions, and the men unanimously selected the right fork. Uncertain, the captains opted to conduct a reconnaissance of both forks.

On June 4 Lewis and Clark each took a small party to explore the two branches of the Missouri. Lewis took the north fork, going as far up as 60 miles before turning back, firmly convinced that he and Clark were right. He named the river Maria's River (later the MARIAS RIVER) before rejoining Clark and the others at the junction on June 8. Again they discussed the situation, but to a man all but the captains were "fully persuaded that this river was the Missouri." Even Pierre Cruzatte, an experienced waterman, believed the Marias to be the true Missouri. In this case, however, no vote was taken. The captains settled the matter by having Lewis and a small party walk on ahead along the southern fork while Clark and the others brought the boats along behind them. The decision made, Lewis noted that the men "said very cheerfully that they were ready to follow us any wher we thought proper to direct but that they still thought the other was the river." As it happened, the captains were proved correct in their decision when Lewis came to the GREAT FALLS on June 13.

A notable instance of democracy took place in late November 1805. After arriving at the estuary of the COLUMBIA RIVER, the corps spent a miserable, rain-soaked week by POINT ELLICE before moving around to STATION CAMP in present-day Baker Bay, where conditions were only mildly better. Some game was available for HUNTING, but the campsite was too often flooded. With no trading ships in the area to take any of the party home, the corps was faced with three choices. First, they could move further upriver until they found adequate SHELTER. Second, they could stay on the north side of the river, although they found the CHINOOK INDIANS there were too avaricious. Third, they could cross the river to the south bank and set up camp near the friendly CLATSOP INDIANS in an area where they had a better chance of finding DEER and ELK.

On November 24 a vote was taken at Station Camp. All members of the expedition, including YORK and SACAGAWEA, were allowed to have their say (although some historians believe that Sacagawea did not officially get to "vote.") Sacagawea expressed a preference for the south bank because of the WAPATO she enjoyed; the meat-eating majority of the men agreed with her. Shortly thereafter they moved across the river to the south bank, where on December 10 they began to build FORT CLATSOP alongside what is now the Lewis and Clark River, four miles southwest of today's Astoria, Oregon.

See also ORGANIZATION OF THE EXPEDITION PARTY.

Further Reading
Allen, John Logan. "Lewis and Clark on the Upper Missouri: Decision at the Marias." *Montana: The Magazine of Western History* 21, no. 3 (1971): 2–17.

Ambrose, Stephen E. *Undaunted Courage: Meriwether Lewis, Thomas Jefferson, and the Opening of the American West.* New York: Simon and Schuster, 1996.

Duncan, Dayton, and Ken Burns. *Lewis & Clark: The Journey of the Corps of Discovery.* New York: Alfred A. Knopf, 1998.

Nicandri, David. "The Independence Hall of the West." Washington State Historical Society. Available on-line. URL: http://www.wshs.org/lewisandclark/independence_hall.htm. Downloaded on July 12, 2002.

Democratic-Republicans   See POLITICAL PARTIES.

Deschamps, Baptiste (Jean-Baptiste Deschamps, Jean-Baptiste Dechamps) (unknown–unknown)
boatman, private in the temporary party
Private Baptiste Deschamps was recruited for the first part of the expedition from CAMP DUBOIS to FORT MANDAN. He was named *patron,* or head, of the French ENGAGÉS on May 14, 1804, and in this capacity commanded one of the PIROGUES up the MISSOURI RIVER. After the boatmen were discharged in November 1804, Deschamps and three others built a hut adjacent to Fort Mandan and remained there for the winter under the expedition's protection. The following spring, Deschamps was among those who took the KEELBOAT back down the river to ST. LOUIS, under the command of Corporal RICHARD WARFINGTON.

Further Reading
Clarke, Charles G. *The Men of the Lewis and Clark Expedition: A Biographical Roster of the Fifty-One Members and a Composite Diary of Their Activities from All Known Sources.* 1970. Reprint, Lincoln: Bison Books, University of Nebraska Press, 2002.

desertion   See BARTER, JOSEPH; REED, MOSES.

diplomacy   See COUNCILS WITH INDIANS.

disbursements   See PAYMENTS AND REWARDS.

discipline
As a military unit, the CORPS OF DISCOVERY employed military measures to deal with problems of discipline—which became an issue before the expedition had even begun to travel up the MISSOURI RIVER. During the winter of 1803–04 at Wood River, Illinois, there were more men in CAMP DUBOIS than would go on to the Pacific coast. In effect, the men were on trial to see how they would work together as a group. Fostering unit cohesion involved eliminating intraservice rivalries (artillery versus infantry, for example), integrating old army personnel with new civilian volunteers, and ensuring that all the men accepted the strict discipline that such a venture required.

Excessive indulgence in ALCOHOL often resulted in the captains having to take disciplinary action. In addition to their regular gill of whiskey each day, the men were getting extra liquor from enterprising locals who had set up a grog shop nearby. Consequently, drunkenness and fighting was common. Thefts in camp of public and personal property were also common occurrences.

To maintain order among the men, WILLIAM CLARK developed some creative punishments at Wood River. For instance, after Privates JOHN POTTS and WILLIAM WERNER engaged in a fistfight, they were ordered to labor together, building a hut for the laundress. There was no shortage of hard labor to be accomplished, and work could be handed out as a punishment. The banks of Wood River were caving in and had to be shored up. The KEELBOAT had to be improved; it was modified with, among other things, special lockers along the sides. When tasks like these ran out, however, and the men had little to do, the drinking and fighting resumed.

MERIWETHER LEWIS was perhaps less creative than Clark in dealing with problems of discipline. In March 1804, during a period while the captains were away from camp, Privates JOHN COLTER, JOHN BOLEY, JOHN ROBERTSON, and PETER WEISER had flouted the authority of Sergeant JOHN ORDWAY and had gotten drunk at a local whiskey shop. When he returned, Lewis confined the four to quarters for 10 days.

Constant drills and training—probably irksome for the independent-minded NINE YOUNG MEN FROM KENTUCKY—kept the men busy, and they were expected to shave at least once every three days. The U.S. Army had already forbidden queues (long, tied ponytails) on men in uniform. The expedition JOURNALS do not reveal just how scrupulously these regulations were observed as the corps moved farther and farther away from non-Indian civilization, although it is well nigh certain that the rules were relaxed on practical grounds.

Incidents requiring disciplinary measures continued even after the expedition was underway, and sometimes COURT-MAR-TIALS were necessary. The most common forms of punishment imposed by court-martial were flogging with a cat-o'-nine-tails and running the gauntlet. The former was a rope divided into nine strands, each tied off at the end with a simple knot. A man could receive up to 100 lashes, according to U.S. Army regulations. In most cases, 100 lashes would not be inflicted in one day, as it might threaten the life of the soldier. Thus, normally the punishment was meted out over a number of successive days, reopening wounds and making a bloody mess out of a man's back.

Running the gauntlet could be equally brutal. The soldiers of a company were lined up in two lines facing each other, all holding switches or, in some cases, the iron ramrods of their muskets. The convicted man had to walk between the double files of his comrades, and as he walked he was beaten on the back with the switches or ramrods. To prevent him from running and getting off lightly, another soldier preceded him with a loaded musket and bayonet. The man holding the musket walked slowly backward, ensuring that the culprit received a slow, painful punishment. With characteristic understatement, Clark observed that "we have always found the men verry ready to punish" others for their crimes.

Although such punishments may seem barbaric by today's standards, they were in fact the only practical way for the captains to maintain discipline, especially on the frontier. The men accepted the necessity of court-martials and the carrying out of harsh sentences, which often had the desired effect. For example, although twice put on trial, Private JOHN COLLINS later proved himself one of the best members of the permanent expedition party. On the other hand, Private MOSES REED was expelled from the corps after being found guilty of desertion, and Private JOHN NEWMAN was banished for mutiny. Both men were forced to become laborers and were returned to ST. LOUIS on the keelboat in April 1805.

As might be expected of volunteers for an exploration, the men were either too high-spirited or too bored to be models of military decorum. As the expedition progressed, however, they began to coalesce into a close-knit unit, fully recognizant of their dependence on each other. Consequently, there were no court-martials after the winter of 1804–05 at FORT MANDAN, and as the expedition traveled westward, the need for any disciplinary measures lessened.

Thomas Jefferson wrote of Meriwether Lewis that he was "careful as a father of those committed to his charge, yet steady in the maintenance of order and discipline." Together, Lewis and Clark's remarkable LEADERSHIP ensured that the Corps of Discovery would make its way safely through thousands of miles of dangerous, uncharted territory and return home as a cohesive, disciplined group.

Further Reading

Ambrose, Stephen E. *Undaunted Courage: Meriwether Lewis, Thomas Jefferson, and the Opening of the American West.* New York: Simon and Schuster, 1996.

Hunt, Robert R. "Crime and Punishment on the Lewis and Clark Expedition." *Military Collector and Historian* 41 (summer 1989): 56–65.

dogs   See FOOD; SEAMAN.

Dorion, Pierre, Sr. (unknown–unknown)
interpreter, trapper

Pierre Dorion, Sr., was a French fur trapper who had known GEORGE ROGERS CLARK during the Revolutionary War. Author Washington Irving had described Dorion as "one of those French creoles, descendants of the ancient Canadian stock, who abound on the western frontier, and amalgamate or cohabit with the savages. He had sojourned among various tribes, and perhaps left progeny among them all; but his regular, or habitual wife, was a Sioux squaw. By her, he had a hopeful brood of half-breed sons. . . ."

Dorion, who was working for RÉGIS LOISEL, met the westbound CORPS OF DISCOVERY when he was heading down the MISSOURI RIVER in June 1804. He had with him two PIROGUES full of furs and other items for sale in ST. LOUIS. Having lived intermittently with the YANKTON NAKOTA INDIANS (Yankton Sioux) for some 20 years, he was fluent in their language as well as in French and English. MERIWETHER LEWIS and WILLIAM CLARK, who needed an interpreter who could speak the Siouan LANGUAGE as well as somebody to escort a delegation of Indians to Washington, offered Dorion the job. They also bought 300 pounds of buffalo grease from him (to be used as repellent for INSECTS).

When the expedition entered Yankton Nakota territory in late August, Lewis and Clark sent Dorion and Sergeant NATHANIAL PRYOR to invite the Indians to a council at CALUMET BLUFF. The two returned with about 70 Yankton warriors, in addition to Dorion's son, Pierre, Jr. In the ceremonies that followed, Dorion translated MERIWETHER LEWIS's speech, assisted with certain rituals, and suggested that the soldiers throw gifts to the Indian dancers. The Yankton were a poor but peaceful nation, and their chiefs had much to say. A few indicated their willingness to travel to Washington if Dorion would accompany them. This was what Lewis had hoped to hear. It was subsequently decided that Dorion would stay with the Yankton Nakota and work with them to make peace with other Indian nations, in addition to putting together a delegation to send to Washington.

Because he had stayed with the Yankton, Dorion was not available to assist the expedition in its confrontation with the Bois Brulé TETON LAKOTA INDIANS (Teton Sioux) the following month. This was unfortunate, as communication problems led to a stand-off between the soldiers and the Indians that nearly resulted in violence, and a good interpreter might have allayed the situation.

As arranged, Dorion subsequently accompanied a delegation of Indians to Washington meet President THOMAS JEFFERSON. He returned to the West with instructions from the president to escort another expedition interpreter, JOSEPH GRAVELINES, past the Teton Lakota and encourage more Indian chiefs to travel east to meet their "great white father." The two men encountered the returning expedition on the MISSOURI RIVER in September 1806. During the time that Dorion spent with the expedition, he also helped Lewis document ethnographic data about the Yankton Nakota culture (see ETHNOGRAPHY).

Further Reading

Ambrose, Stephen E. *Undaunted Courage: Meriwether Lewis, Thomas Jefferson, and the Opening of the American West.* New York: Simon and Schuster, 1996.

PBS Online. *Lewis and Clark: Inside the Corps of Discovery:* "Pierre Dorion." Available on-line. URL: http://www.pbs.org/lewisandclark/inside/pdori.html. Downloaded on May 18, 2001.

Drouillard, George (George Drewyer, George Drewer) (ca. 1775–1810) *interpreter, permanent expedition member, mountain man*

One of the few civilian members of the CORPS OF DISCOVERY, George Drouillard was the son of Pierre Drouillard, a French Canadian who had served as an interpreter for General GEORGE ROGERS CLARK. His mother was a Shawnee Indian. Although his date of birth is not known positively, several accounts of the expedition indicate that he was 28 years old when he joined the expedition. By then he was already a highly capable frontiersman and scout. Fluent in French, English, and two Indian languages, he was also proficient in the sign language of the PLAINS INDIANS.

Captain Lewis—who usually referred to Drouillard as "Drewyer" in his JOURNALS—first met the Frenchman in November 1803 during a RECRUITING trip to FORT MASSAC. He was immediately impressed by Drouillard's skills and confidence and hired the woodsman to be the expedition's inter-

preter; the pay was $25 a month, although Lewis later lobbied unsuccessfully to have it raised to $30. Drouillard accepted on a provisional basis, wanting to be certain of both the mission and its captains before he committed himself. His first assignment was to go to South West Post, Tennessee, to retrieve eight soldiers who had volunteered for the expedition and bring them to the winter quarters near ST. LOUIS. He and the volunteers arrived at CAMP DUBOIS on December 16. By late that month he had made up his mind to join the expedition, and he was put on the payroll as of January 1, 1804.

Throughout the subsequent journey, the captains relied heavily on Drouillard, a superlative hunter, and they trusted his bravery and judgment. He was usually the first man Lewis picked for hunting and scouting missions, and he was frequently called upon for translating services. Unfortunately, he could do little to help during the corps's encounter with the TETON LAKOTA INDIANS (Teton Sioux) in September 1804. He was unable to speak their language, and they could not—or would not—understand his sign language. The ensuing miscommunications led to a confrontation that nearly ended in violence but was defused by WILLIAM CLARK's diplomatic skills.

This close call led to the captains' decision to hire another interpreter, TOUSSAINT CHARBONNEAU, after they had encamped at FORT MANDAN for the winter. Thereafter a complicated chain of INTERPRETATION was established in which Charbonneau's wife, SACAGAWEA, spoke in Hidatsa to him and he translated into French for Drouillard, PIERRE CRUZATTE, or FRANÇOIS LABICHE, who then translated into English for Lewis and Clark.

In February 1805, Clark sent Drouillard, ROBERT FRAZIER, SILAS GOODRICH, and JOHN NEWMAN out from FORT MANDAN to retrieve some carcasses left behind after a HUNTING expedition. The four men were attacked by a party of Teton Lakota who made off with two sleighs and two knives. That the soldiers survived the attack was remarkable, given that they were vastly outnumbered.

The following July Drouillard survived another nasty encounter, this time with a grizzly BEAR. As one of the expedition's best hunters, he accompanied Lewis on a foray to find and kill as many bears as they could. As Lewis wrote, "We found only one, which made at Drewyer and he shot him in the brest at the distance of about 20 feet, the ball fortunately passed through his heart, the stroke knocked the bear down and gave Drewyer time to get out of his sight. . . ." The bear died a few minutes later.

In August Drouillard was one of the men accompanying Lewis on an advance party across the CONTINENTAL DIVIDE and was therefore present at their first encounter with SHOSHONE INDIANS. This time his sign language was understood, and they were able to communicate adequately with the Indians until Clark arrived with Charbonneau and Sacagawea. They achieved similar success when they met the NEZ PERCE INDIANS, although Sacagawea could no longer be useful in the chain of translation and the captains had to rely almost exclusively on Drouillard's signing.

In 1806, after the expedition split into two parties during their return journey, Drouillard was chosen to accompany Lewis, as had become usual. The men split even further, with Lewis taking Drouillard, JOSEPH FIELD, and REUBIN FIELD on an exploration of the MARIAS RIVER. On July 26 Drouillard was riding ahead when Lewis spotted a band of BLACKFEET INDIANS studying the Frenchman from a distance. To divert their attention, Lewis and the Field brothers moved forward with a flag and signaled a desire to parlay. There ensued a meeting at TWO MEDICINE RIVER that seemed to go well, with the Indians willing and able to converse in sign language through Drouillard. Early the following morning, however, several Blackfeet attempted to steal the soldiers' rifles and HORSES. In the confrontation that followed, Reubin Field killed one Indian with a knife and Lewis shot another through the belly, although he had initially forbidden Drouillard and the Fields to shoot another of the Indians. The four men quickly saddled up and ran from the area, riding nonstop for several hours until they were certain they had put enough distance between themselves and the Blackfeet.

One of Drouillard's last tasks for the expedition was to post the captains' LETTERS and initial report to THOMAS JEFFERSON. Although he was awarded double pay, he did not receive the salary of $30 monthly that Lewis had wanted to give him. Following his discharge he lived briefly at Cape Girardeau, Missouri. He bought the land warrants of JOHN COLLINS and JOSEPH WHITEHOUSE, which, with other land, he sold on April 3, 1807, for $1,300.00. He subsequently made a return trip to the ROCKY MOUNTAINS and gave WILLIAM CLARK a great deal of additional topographical data that Clark incorporated into his MAPS of the Northwest.

Making a name for himself as one of the best known of the early MOUNTAIN MEN, Drouillard also became a fur trader for MANUEL LISA. In 1807 Lisa ordered him to find a deserter named Antoine Bissonnette and bring him back to St. Louis, dead or alive. Drouillard chose the former course, and consequently he was put on trial for murder. Due to mitigating circumstances, the jury acquitted him. However, his luck ran out three years later, when, in the THREE FORKS region of the upper Missouri, Drouillard and other members of a Lisa party were attacked by Blackfeet Indians, and he was killed.

In his report to Secretary of War HENRY DEARBORN in 1807, Meriwether Lewis wrote that George Drouillard was a

> *man of much merit; he has been peculiarly usefull from his knowledge of the common language of gesticulation, and his uncommon skill as a hunter and woodsman; those several duties he performed in good faith, and with an ardor which deserves the highest commendation.*
>
> *It was his fate also to have encountered, on various occasions, with either Captain Clark or myself, all the most dangerous and trying scenes of the voyage, in which he uniformly acquited himself with honor.*

Further Reading

Ambrose, Stephen E. *Undaunted Courage: Meriwether Lewis, Thomas Jefferson, and the Opening of the American West.* New York: Simon and Schuster, 1996.

Clarke, Charles G. *The Men of the Lewis and Clark Expedition: A Biographical Roster of the Fifty-One Members and a Composite Diary of Their Activities from All Known Sources.* 1970. Reprint, Lincoln: Bison Books, University of Nebraska Press, 2002.

Lange, Robert. "George Drouillard (Drewyer)—One of the Two or Three Most Valuable Men on the Expedition." *We Proceeded On* 5, no. 2 (May 1979): 14–16.

PBS Online. *Lewis and Clark: Inside the Corps of Discovery:* "George Drouillard." Available on-line. URL: http://www.pbs.org/lewisandclark/inside/gdrou.html. Downloaded on May 18, 2001.

Skarsten, M. O. *George Drouillard: Hunter and Interpreter for Lewis and Clark and Fur Trader, 1807–1810.* Glendale, Calif: A.H. Clark Co., 1964.

Dubois River   See CAMP DUBOIS.

dugouts   See CANOES.

Dunbar, William (ca. 1750–1810) *naturalist, explorer*

Even as the Lewis and Clark Expedition was underway, President THOMAS JEFFERSON began to send more explorers into other areas of the recently acquired LOUISIANA TERRITORY. One of these was William Dunbar, a fellow member of the AMERICAN PHILOSOPHICAL SOCIETY who undertook a reconnaissance of the Ouachita (Washita) River during the winter of 1804–05 and subsequently directed the failed RED RIVER EXPEDITION of 1806.

Originally from Morayshire, Scotland, Dunbar was a graduate of King's College in Aberdeen. In 1771 he emigrated to Philadelphia, where he formed a partnership with another Scotsman, John Ross, in 1773; he later moved to Natchez, Mississippi. Dunbar applied scientific principles to growing crops on the plantations he established with Ross in West Florida and near Natchez. He also served as surveyor general in the Natchez area, and in 1799 he recorded the first meteorological observations in the Mississippi Valley.

In 1804 Jefferson asked Dunbar, then in his 50s, to conduct an exploratory expedition to find the source of the Red River, with the intention of making not only scientific observations but also MAPS of the regions through which the river passed. "We shall delineate with correctness," wrote Jefferson, "the great arteries of this great country . . ."—this with a view to forming alliances with Indians in the Southwest and finding a resolution to the dispute with SPAIN over the western boundary of the LOUISIANA PURCHASE.

Before committing himself to the Red River expedition, Dunbar decided to make a preliminary run up the Ouachita

River, taking with him his friend and fellow scientist, Dr. George Hunter. Accompanied by 16 men, the two men began their journey on October 14, 1804. They eventually arrived at the Ozark Mountains, near what is now Hot Springs, Arkansas. Here Dunbar recorded his observations on animal and plant life, fossils, and Indian sign language, in addition to astronomical data. He also became the first to write a scientific report on the activity of the hot springs. By the time he and Hunter returned the following spring, however, both men had resolved not to go on what would be a more grueling exploration up the Red River. Dunbar subsequently set to work planning that expedition with Secretary of War HENRY DEARBORN, choosing an experienced scientist, Thomas Freeman, and a budding naturalist, Peter Custis, to lead it. Unfortunately, three months after the Red River party left Natchez in late April 1806, Spanish military forces intercepted the explorers and ordered them to turn back.

Information regarding the Ouachita and Red River expeditions was combined with preliminary news from Lewis and Clark and reports on Louisiana Territory from JOHN SIBLEY and published in a communiqué from President Jefferson in 1806. Dunbar later became a member of the Mississippi Territorial Legislature as well a chief justice the Mississippi Court of Quarter Sessions. He died in Mississippi on October 16, 1810. In 1904 his journal of the Ouachita exploration was published as *Documents Relating to the Purchase and Exploration of Louisiana.*

Further Reading

DeRosier Jr., Arthur H. "William Dunbar, Explorer." *Journal of Mississippi History* 25 (July 1963).

Dunbar, William. *Documents Relating to the Purchase and Exploration of Louisiana.* Boston: Houghton, Mifflin & Co., 1904.

Flores, Dan K. "Red River Expedition." Handbook of Texas Online. URL: http://www.tsha.utexas.edu/handbook/online/articles/view/RR/upr2.html. Downloaded on February 6, 2002.

Jefferson, Thomas. *Message from the President of the United States Communicating Discoveries Made in Exploring the Missouri, Red River and Washita, by Captains Lewis and Clark, Doctor Sibley, and Mr. Dunbar: with a statistical account of the countries adjacent.* Washington, D.C.: A. & G. Way, printers, 1806.

early expeditions   See EXPLORATION, EARLY.

Ecola Creek   See WHALE.

effects and influences of the expedition

Although the CORPS OF DISCOVERY was not the first expedition to execute a transcontinental crossing along the northern tier of the region that is now the United States of America (that honor belongs to ALEXANDER MACKENZIE), the corps was certainly responsible for the most influential journey in the country's early history. How the American West would have evolved without MERIWETHER LEWIS, WILLIAM CLARK, and their companions is a question that probably cannot be answered. Yet the expedition's impact on that evolution, however, and on the growing country's vision of itself is inestimable.

In evaluating the consequences of the remarkable journey, four areas in particular are worth understanding.

Relations with Indian Nations

The Corps of Discovery gathered vast amounts of new information on more than 50 Indian nations, information that was of extraordinary importance in the later U.S. expansion into the West. Unlike many of those who followed them, Lewis and Clark made every effort to maintain good relations with the native groups they encountered. Yet the expedition's promises of benevolent, long-term governmental protection in exchange for an American trading presence, however earnestly expressed, were not fulfilled. What did come about was a new and fateful phase of the European influence in North America as Lewis and Clark continued a process that had started with the arrival of the Spanish in the 16th century—a process of white cultural expansion that would culminate in the virtual eradication of the traditional Indian ways of life in the late 19th century. The cautious sincere diplomacy of the Corps of Discovery notwithstanding, this white cultural expansion was eventually carried out at the expense of American Indian civilization.

Science

Although Lewis and Clark discovered many new ANIMALS and PLANTS, formal credit for many of these finds was not forthcoming because of long delays in publishing their work. Among the countless animals they identified were the BUFFALO, the PRAIRIE DOG, and the grizzly BEAR. The expedition's contributions to the geographical understanding of what would eventually become the American West cannot be overstated; the countless MAPS, measurements, and journal entries they completed brought understanding of the North American continent to a new level. One of many notable intellectual results was the expedition's conclusion that the supposed water route to the Pacific—the fabled NORTHWEST PASSAGE—did not exist. Today's understanding of the physical features of the American landscape is a given; much of this knowledge is attributable to the Corps of Discovery, and in particular to the mapmaking skills of William Clark and the writers of the JOURNALS, especially the two captains.

Commerce

Although the journey proved that the long-sought commercial shipping route to the PACIFIC OCEAN was a fantasy, the expedition's additions to the knowledge of North America's rivers proved an exceptional boon to American commerce. The Corps of Discovery also laid the groundwork for commercial relationships with numerous Indian nations. In doing so, it made possible an American trading presence that countered the British and French influence and set the stage for the extraordinary economic development that would follow in the West.

Nationalism

By the 1840s, a belief known as manifest destiny had taken hold in many American circles; it held that the United States was fated to expand from one end of the North American continent to the other. This belief was an important doctrine in the development of a distinctly American brand of nationalism, and it was supported in many ways by the hold on the popular imagination that WESTWARD EXPANSION in general and the Lewis and Clark Expedition in particular had exerted on Americans. The expansionist impulse that accompanied the notion of manifest destiny had enormous influence in the conflicts with the Indian peoples and the controversy over slavery, during which northern and southern political factions each sought to admit new states to the Union that would support their policies. In the late 19th century, the philosophy of manifest destiny was used to justify American intervention in the Pacific and the Caribbean. This expansion-based vision of the United States was rooted in a deeply felt sense that the vast central expanse of the continent was and ought to be American. People of the 19th century were inspired by the struggles and triumphs of the Corps of Discovery, and they regarded the expedition as the first campaign in the effort to develop a continental nation.

Further Reading

Ambrose, Stephen E. *Undaunted Courage: Meriwether Lewis, Thomas Jefferson, and the Opening of the American West.* New York: Simon and Schuster, 1996.

Botkin, Daniel B. *Our Natural History: The Lessons of Lewis & Clark.* New York: Putnam, 1995.

Fields, Wayne D. "The Meaning of Lewis and Clark." *Gateway Heritage* 2, no. 2 (1981): 2–7.

Goetzmann, William. *Exploration and Empire: The Explorer and the Scientist in the Winning of the American West.* New York: Alfred A. Knopf, 1966.

Montgomery, M. R. *Jefferson and the Gun-Men: How the West Was almost Lost.* New York: Crown Publishers, 2000.

Wallace, Anthony F. C. *Jefferson and the Indians: The Tragic Fate of the First Americans.* Cambridge, Mass.: Harvard University Press, 2001.

Young, F. G. "The Higher Significance in the Lewis and Clark Expedition." *Quarterly of the Oregon Historical Society* 6, no. 1 (March 1905).

In the years following the expedition, the U.S. government subjugated Native Americans, who were forced into a state of dependency. This lithograph (ca. 1855) shows an encampment of Assiniboine at Fort Union, North Dakota, waiting for provisions. *(Library of Congress, Prints and Photographs Division [LC-USZC4-6872])*

elk (*Cervus elaphus*)

The elk, a large member of the deer family, was a major FOOD source for the CORPS OF DISCOVERY. The men also used elk skins to make CLOTHING and tents. Elk antlers were among the ARTIFACTS AND SPECIMENS returned to President THOMAS JEFFERSON following the expedition's winter sojourn at FORT MANDAN in 1804–05.

Elk cows weigh up to 500 pounds and the bulls 700 pounds. Males grow antlers annually; the natural purpose of the antlers is sometimes for defense but primarily to display dominance. The elk's predators include humans, BEARS, mountain lions, WOLVES, and COYOTES. Some Indians used their antlers for bows.

In accordance with the scientific aspects of their MISSION OBJECTIVES, MERIWETHER LEWIS and WILLIAM CLARK studied the elk whenever they had the opportunity and made frequent notes about the animals in their journals. In March 1806, for example, Clark noted, "The horns of some of the Elk have not yet fallen off and those of others have Grown to a length of six inches, the latter are in the best order, from which it would seem that the pore Elk retain their horns longer." Both captains also commented extensively on the uses certain Indian nations made of the various parts of the elk.

On the westward journey no elk were killed and very few were spotted until the expedition had reached the GREAT PLAINS. After that point, there were elk in abundance, and many were killed by expedition hunters. Two were killed at TRAVELERS' REST in September 1805, but none were seen thereafter until the corps had reached the mouth of the COLUMBIA RIVER. In fact, it was a report from CHINOOK INDIANS on where elk could be found in abundance that led the corps to build FORT CLATSOP on the south side of the river. Between then and their departure in March 1806, the men killed 131 elk, in the process depleting the stock of elk in the vicinity of the fort. Once they returned to the Great Plains, HUNTING resumed.

Usually only the best hunters were sent out to shoot elk. In August 1806, however, a near-disaster occurred when Private PIERRE CRUZATTE, who had only one eye, mistook the buckskin-clad Lewis for an elk and shot him in the buttocks. Lewis was not badly injured, although he suffered from the pain for some time.

Up to the 1800s, elk ranged throughout North America, except in Alaska and Florida. The elk population may have been about 10 million before the arrival of Europeans on the continent. Overhunted or killed as pests, the greatest reduction of the population came from the conversion of their habitat to agricultural lands. Today the elk population in North America is about 1 million.

Further Reading

Burroughs, Raymond Darwin, ed. *The Natural History of the Lewis and Clark Expedition.* East Lansing: Michigan State University Press, 1995.

Knue, Joseph. *Big Game of North Dakota: A Short History.* Bismarck: North Dakota Game and Fish Dept., 1991.

Ellicott, Andrew (1754–1820) *astronomer, mathematician, surveyor*

PREPARATIONS FOR THE EXPEDITION involved much more than obtaining SUPPLIES AND EQUIPMENT and RECRUITING men. MERIWETHER LEWIS also had to prepare himself to acquire necessary skills and knowledge that would enable him to act as navigator, doctor, botanist, zoologist, ethnographer, and natural historian throughout the journey. To this end, President THOMAS JEFFERSON sent him to PHILADELPHIA to be tutored by many of the leading scientists and intellectuals of the day. First, though, Lewis stopped in Lancaster, Pennsylvania, where he met Andrew Ellicott, a mathematician and surveyor who was also the nation's premiere astronomer.

Born in Bucks County, Pennsylvania, Ellicott had taught mathematics at Baltimore Academy and also served with distinction during the American Revolution. Following the war, he surveyed large areas where borderlines were still being established, including those of western and northern Pennsylvania and southwestern New York. In 1784 he helped to complete the delineation of the Mason-Dixon line between Pennsylvania and Maryland. In 1789, while surveying the lands between Pennsylvania and Lake Erie, he made the first topographical study of the Niagara River and its falls, recording measurements that stood for the next 80 years. Between 1791 and 1793 he surveyed the "Federal City"—the current-day District of Columbia—and redrew Pierre L'Enfant's design for what would become Washington, D.C. In 1792 he was appointed surveyor general of the United States. In 1796, at George Washington's request, he surveyed the boundary between the United States and Florida, traveling to the area by way of the OHIO RIVER and MISSISSIPPI RIVER. MAPS and observations that he collected during this trip were later used by NICHOLAS KING in preparing a map of North America that Secretary of the Treasury ALBERT GALLATIN commissioned for the expedition.

A member of the AMERICAN PHILOSOPHICAL SOCIETY and supporter of the LOUISIANA PURCHASE, Ellicott also had knowledge of the frontier and experience in dealing with Native Americans, all of which made him ideally suited to provide instruction for Lewis. He had been appointed secretary of the Pennsylvania Land Office and was settled in Lancaster when President Jefferson wrote to request his assistance in training Lewis in the principles of ASTRONOMICAL OBSERVATIONS and surveying. Ellicott was willing but noted that the skills Lewis needed to acquire could "only be obtained by practice." By April 20, 1803, he had set to work with his pupil, teaching the use of the sextant, the chronometer, and other instruments for recording celestial movements and applying them to techniques of NAVIGATION. The practice sessions took longer than anticipated, and it was not until May 7 that Lewis was able to move on to Philadelphia and his studies with other scientists. In that time, however, he learned much, and he was

Mathematician Andrew Ellicott was one of the most respected scientists of his time. At President Jefferson's request, he taught Meriwether Lewis how to make astronomical observations. *(Library of Congress, Prints and Photographs Division [LC-USZ62-98345])*

later able to impart many of his newly acquired skills to WILLIAM CLARK.

Ellicott continued to consult on the expedition's preparations even after his time with Lewis. As a result of Ellicott's advice and with additional input from ROBERT PATTERSON, Lewis wrote to Jefferson that he had purchased "two Sextants, an artificial horizon or two; a good Arnold's watch or chronometer, a Surveyor's compass with a ball and socket and two pole chain, and a set of plotting instruments." One of the artificial horizons had been specially developed by Ellicott to enable Lewis to take more accurate measurements in unfamiliar terrain.

In 1808 Ellicott was dismissed as secretary of the Pennsylvania Land Office, a move that was politically motivated and brought him into conflict with Governor Simon Snyder and General JAMES WILKINSON. He continued to accept surveying commissions, including that of Georgia's northern border in 1811–12 but was seldom rewarded adequately for his work and suffered continual financial problems. In 1813 he accepted a post as professor of mathematics at the still-young West Point Academy. Four years later he went to Montreal to record celestial observations in accordance with terms of the Treaty of Ghent. He died in West Point on August 20, 1820, at age 66, leaving behind his wife and nine children.

Further Reading

Ambrose, Stephen E. *Undaunted Courage: Meriwether Lewis, Thomas Jefferson, and the Opening of the American West.* New York: Simon and Schuster, 1996.

Davis, Nancy M. "Andrew Ellicott: Astronomer . . . Mathematician . . . Surveyor." Lewis and Clark Heritage Trail Foundation, Philadelphia Chapter. Available on-line. URL: http://www.lewisandclarkphila.org/philadelphiaellicott.html. Downloaded on February 7, 2002.

Mathews, Catherine Van Cortland. *Andrew Ellicott: His Life and Letters.* Alexander, N.C.: WorldComm, 1997.

engagés (voyageurs) *rivermen, temporary members of the expedition*

In November 1803, as the expedition's PIROGUES and KEELBOAT struggled up the MISSISSIPPI RIVER toward ST. LOUIS—averaging little more than a mile an hour against tough currents—it became apparent to MERIWETHER LEWIS and WILLIAM CLARK that they were severely undermanned. Although more men were recruited at KASKASKIA, they knew that what they really needed were strong, experienced watermen to get the boats to the upper reaches of the MISSOURI RIVER. The solution was provided in St. Louis by PIERRE CHOUTEAU and AUGUSTE CHOUTEAU, fur-trading brothers who sold the captains many of the supplies and provisions that the expedition would need for the next stage of its journey. After a deal with MANUEL LISA fell through, the Chouteaus recruited a number of rivermen, mostly French Canadians, called engagés or voyageurs, who paddled the pirogues and canoes from St. Louis to the MANDAN and the HIDATSA villages.

Although indications are that the Chouteaus hired eight engagés, there is some confusion about their total number and identities, probably because they included some men who had been recruited at Kaskaskia. It is undoubtedly for this reason that JOSEPH BARTER, known as La Liberté, is sometimes listed as an engagé, sometimes as a private. Conversely, some engagés—in particular Jean-Baptiste La Jeunnesse—are listed on some expedition rosters as privates. The head waterman, BAPTISTE DESCHAMPS, straddled both categories and, with the rank of private, commanded one of the pirogues. Some sources indicate there were nine engagés, others 11, but if Deschamps is included, the number is actually 12. The names of Phillipe Degie and E. Cann are included on some lists of engagés. According to Charles G. Clarke, Degie attached himself to the expedition in October 1804, but he does not appear to have been a paid crewman. Cann is probably Alexander Carson.

Many of the engagés proved useful to the corps in ways other than just providing extra manpower. Most were already familiar with the river going up to the Mandan villages and were able to prepare the captains for what lay ahead in the way of terrain, flora, and fauna. Some who had Indian blood or had married Indian women occasionally provided translation services. All strong men, they labored against the fierce Missouri currents and were sometime given sentry and HUNTING duties in addition to paddling or rowing. Only two engagés returned to St. Louis on the keelboat in spring 1805. It is not clear what happened to the others, although it is also possible that at least one returned to St. Louis in June 1804 with dismissed private JOHN ROBERTSON. Nine engagés were discharged in November 1804, of whom four built a hut adjacent to FORT MANDAN and spent the winter of 1804–05 there.

Following is a list of the engagés and what is known of them. (See also BAPTISTE DESCHAMPS and JOSEPH BARTER.)

Carson, Alexander
(E. Cann, Carr, Cane, Carrn, etc.)

Although grouped with the French engagés, Carson was born about 1775 in Mississippi, the son of an American. He is said to have been a cousin of legendary frontiersman "Kit" Carson. He was one of the engagés who went back to St. Louis on the keelboat in April 1805, and he may also have been a member of the party who successfully escorted the Mandan chief BIG WHITE back home to his people in 1810. A gunsmith, he worked for the HUDSON'S BAY COMPANY in 1820–21, later becoming one of the earliest settlers in OREGON TERRITORY. He was killed by Indians in 1836.

Caugée, Charles

Nothing is known about this engagé.

Collin, Joseph

A French Canadian, Collin was, according to Sergeant PATRICK GASS, a former employee of the NORTH WEST COMPANY. Collin may have traveled only as far as the ARIKARA INDIAN villages. He was living among the Arikara when the expedition returned there in August 1806, and with the captains' permission accompanied the corps back to St. Louis.

Hebert, Charles (Hebert dit Cadien)

Born in Prairie de la Madeleine, Canada, Hebert married a St. Louis woman, with whom he had 11 children. He was among those discharged at Fort Mandan in November 1804; nothing else is known of him.

La Jeunesse, Jean-Baptiste
(La Junesse, Le Guness, Le Jueness)

Perhaps a private on the expedition (sources are unclear), La Jeunesse was born in Quebec, married in St. Louis to Elisabeth Malbeuf (a half sister of Étienne Malboeuf, below), and was the father of three children, one of them born after his death, which is presumed to be in late 1806. A nephew, Basil Le Vasseur, accompanied explorer John Charles Frémont on expeditions to the West in 1842–43.

Malboeuf, Étienne (Mabbauf, Malbeuf, Mallat)

Presumed born about 1775, Malboeuf was originally from Lac de Sable, Canada, and married to a CROW INDIAN woman. His half sister Elisabeth, the daughter of a MANDAN woman, married Jean-Baptiste La Jeunesse, above. Hired in Kaskasia, Malboeuf was paid for his services on October 4, 1805. Nothing is known of him after that.

Pinaut, Peter (possibly Charles Pineau)

Pinaut was born probably about 1776, the son of a Frenchman named Joseph Pineau and a MISSOURI INDIAN woman. He enlisted with the expedition in May 1804, and it is possible he returned to St. Louis just a month later on the same raft that took back dismissed private JOHN ROBERTSON.

Primeau, Paul (Paul Primaut)

Originally from Chateauguay, Canada, and recruited at Kaskaskia, Primeau was one of the expedition's married men; he and his wife Pelagie had 10 children. Later a trader, he was reported in 1807 as being in debt to GEORGE DROUILLARD and MANUEL LISA for the amount of $292.05, which was repaid the following year.

Rivet, François

Born in Montreal in 1757 and recruited in Kaskaskia, Rivet's claim to fame in the expedition's JOURNALS was his talent for dancing on his hands. He had a varied career after his service with the expedition. In April 1805 he and Philippe Degie built a canoe and accompanied the keelboat back down the Missouri as far as the ARIKARA INDIAN villages. When the expedition returned to the MANDAN INDIAN villages in 1806, Rivet was there, probably as a trader. He was later reported to be among the FLATHEAD INDIANS in 1810 and served as an interpreter for explorer Alexander Ross in 1824. Reputedly he also worked for the HUDSON'S BAY COMPANY. Late in life he lived in Willamette Valley, Oregon, where he died in 1852 at the age of 95.

Roi, Peter (Pierre Roy, Le Roy, etc.)

Nothing is known about this engagé.

"Rokey" (Ross, Rocque)

The full name of this engagé is not known. JOHN ORDWAY referred to him as "Ross," but Rocque was most probably his last name; Rokey seems to have been the nickname by which he was better known. After the engagés were discharged, he remained on the upper Missouri and was living among the Arikara when the expedition returned to those villages in August 1806. He went back to St. Louis with the corps. It is possible he was later employed by the Hudson's Bay Company.

Further Reading

Clarke, Charles G. *The Men of the Lewis and Clark Expedition: A Biographical Roster of the Fifty-One Members and a Composite Diary of Their Activities from All Known Sources.* 1970. Reprint, Lincoln: Bison Books, University of Nebraska Press, 2002.

Rogers, Ken. "The Engages: Who were the unnamed French watermen?" *The Bismarck Tribune.* Available on-line. URL: http://www.ndonline.com/tribwebpage/features/lewisclark/2001/engages.html. Downloaded on February 16, 2002.

Enlightenment, Age of

The Enlightenment is a term applied to a movement that attracted many philosophers and thinkers during the late 17th and 18th centuries—a period of time that Thomas Paine called the Age of Reason. It was also in many ways a conflict between religion and the mind, which seeks to understand through reason based on evidence and proof. The Lewis and Clark Expedition comprised one aspect of Enlightenment thinking and curiosity.

Basic values of Enlightenment thinkers were a commitment to reason, a trust in the emerging physical sciences to solve problems and even control nature, a commitment to the idea of progress in material wealth, and a desire for individual self-determination. The movement revived and gave new life to the ideas of the ancient Greek philosophers and the Renaissance scholars, as well as scientific discoveries of the late Middle Ages. Noting a regularity in the natural world's cycle, ancient philosophers had decided that the reasoning mind could understand and explain this regularity. Intellectual discoveries and scientific revolution thus ended the dominance of the Christian church's view of the world.

One name that stands out as an exponent of the Enlightenment in the revolutionary new world of 18th-century America is THOMAS JEFFERSON. He read widely in the sciences and corresponded with like minds worldwide. His home, MONTICELLO, was filled with devices for observing, measuring, and recording natural phenomena. Influenced by thinkers such as Isaac Newton, Jefferson believed that a rational system governed the natural world and that by applying these rules of science the condition of man could be improved.

Jefferson was particularly interested in such sciences as astronomy, which could be studied and expressed mathematically. As secretary of state, Jefferson established America's decimal system of currency and argued—unsuccessfully—for the adoption of a decimal system of weights and measures. He was president of the AMERICAN PHILOSOPHICAL SOCIETY for 17 years and the only American of his time to be elected as a foreign associate of the Institute of France. Known internationally as a man of learning, Jefferson is recognized today not only as a politician, political theorist, and architect but also as a pioneer in paleontology, ethnology, geography, and botany.

Jefferson and his colleagues in the American Revolution were Enlightenment thinkers almost by definition, placing importance on the rational individual. PHILADELPHIA was a center of botany and other research, and the scientific community there was eager to be recognized by the European and British scientific societies.

Influenced by the botanical collections and other academic resources in Philadelphia, Jefferson had MERIWETHER LEWIS spend several weeks there, studying and consulting with leading scientists before the expedition. His detailed instructions to Lewis, which included specific directions on recording PLANTS and herbs the Indians used for FOOD and medicine, combined so many aspects of scientific and commercial concerns with geographic discovery and political need that it can be said to exemplify current Enlightenment thinking.

The Lewis and Clark Expedition can be viewed as a journey of exploration, a search for a new TRADE route, or even simple imperialism. It was all of these, but the influence of the Enlightenment movement, the quest for knowledge for its own sake, and the improvement of the human condition were inherent factors that should not be overlooked.

Further Reading

Haycox, Stephen W., et al. *Enlightenment and Exploration in the North Pacific 1741–1805.* Seattle: University of Washington Press, 1995.

Ronda, James P. "'A Knowledge of Distant Parts': The Shaping of the Lewis and Clark Expedition." *Montana: The Magazine of Western History* 41, no. 4 (1991): 4–18.

Seelye, John. "Beyond the Shining Mountains: The Lewis and Clark Expedition as an Enlightenment Epic." *Virginia Quarterly Review* 63, no. 1 (1987): 36–53.

equipment   See SUPPLIES AND EQUIPMENT.

ermines   See ANIMALS, NEW SPECIES.

espontoon (spontoon)

I selected a fat buffaloe and shot him very well, through the lungs; while I was gazing attentively on the poor anamal . . . a large white, or reather brown bear, had perceived and crept on me within 20 steps before I discovered him; in the first moment I drew up my gun to shoot, but at the same instant recolected that she was not loaded . . . there was no place by means of which I could conceal myself from this monster until I could charge my rifle; . . . I ran about 80 yards and found he gained on me fast, I then run into the water the idea struk me to get into the water to such debth that I could stand and he would be obliged to swim, and that I could in that situation defend myself with my espontoon; accordingly I ran haistily into the water about waist deep, and faced about and presented the point of my espontoon, . . . the moment I put myself in this attitude of defence he sudonly wheeled about as if frightened, declined the combat on such unequal grounds, and retreated with quite as great precipitation as he had just before pursued me.

—Meriwether Lewis, June 14, 1805

The six-foot espontoon (called a spontoon today) carried by MERIWETHER LEWIS and WILLIAM CLARK was a development of the pike carried by foot soldiers until muskets became standard issue. A formal mark of military rank in the early U.S. Army, during the expedition Lewis and Clark demonstrated its effectiveness as a walking staff, a rifle rest, and, in the last resort, as a WEAPON of self-defense.

Around 1760, junior officers in the British army were issued with espontoons instead of the short muskets they had previously carried. Though they generally fought with sword and pistol, the espontoon was a sign of rank which, in an emergency, could be used for personal protection. The custom was adopted in the young American army, many of whose senior officers had served in British regiments before the Revolutionary War. General Anthony Wayne, under whom both Lewis and Clark had served, was noted for the espontoon he carried.

Unlike the long infantry pike carried in the 17th century, the espontoon was six feet long, with a short, strong blade at one end and a metal ferrule at the other. A common variation was a short crossbar just below the blade. Although this might seem an unnecessary item to take on an exploratory mission, it should be remembered that Lewis, Clark, and their men were a unit of the U.S. Army. They took uniforms with them, which the captains retained and wore with their swords when they felt it appropriate.

Both the captains put their espontoons to practical, sometimes surprising use. On May 29, 1805, the expedition was in present-day Montana, roughly halfway between the MUSSELSHELL RIVER and the MARIAS RIVER. At the point where Arrow Creek comes in from the south, near the water's edge, they found innumerable carcasses of BUFFALO that had drowned when the river ice had melted. Packs of WOLVES were scavenging, and one was so satiated that Clark was able to kill it with his espontoon.

Ten days later, on June 7, Lewis and a small party were returning down the banks of the Marias River, back toward the MISSOURI RIVER. As he made his way along a muddy path on the side of a high bluff, "I sliped at a narrow pass of about 30 yards in length and but for a quick and fortune recovery by means of my espontoon I should have precipitated into the river down a craggy pricipice of about ninethy feet. I had scarcely reached a place on which I could stand with tolerable safety even with the assistance of my espontoon."

A week after this incident, near the mouth of the MEDICINE RIVER, Lewis encountered the grizzly that might have killed him in the river were it not for his quick thinking and his espontoon. (The site of this incident is commemorated in West Bank Park, Great Falls, Montana.) Later that same day, he spotted a catlike animal (probably a wolverine) and noted that he took careful aim at it, using his espontoon as a rest. He was mortified, however, to see it escape into a burrow.

Further Reading

Ambrose, Stephen E. *Undaunted Courage: Meriwether Lewis, Thomas Jefferson, and the Opening of the American West.* New York: Simon and Schuster, 1996.

Hunt, Robert R. "The Espontoon: Captain Lewis's Magic Stick." *We Proceeded On* 16, no. 1 (February 1990): 12–18.

Rogers, Ken. "A Life Saver: Espontoon: Lewis' trusty pike." *The Bismarck Tribune.* Available on-line. URL: http://www.ndonline.com/tribwebpage/features/lewisclark/2001/saver.html. Downloaded on February 21, 2002.

ethnography

You will therefore endeavor to make yourself acquainted, as far as a diligent pursuit of your journey shall admit, with the names of the nations & their numbers; the extent & limits of their possessions; their relations with other tribes of nations; their language, traditions, monuments; their ordinary occupations in agriculture, fishing, hunting, war, arts, & the implements for these; their food, clothing, & domestic accommodations; the diseases prevalent among them, & the remedies they use; moral & physical circumstances which distinguish them from the tribes we know; peculiarities in their laws, customs & dispositions; and articles of commerce they may need or furnish, and to what extent.

—Thomas Jefferson to Meriwether Lewis,
June 20, 1803

One unusual aspect of the Lewis and Clark Expedition is the remarkable number and variety of tasks THOMAS JEFFERSON gave to MERIWETHER LEWIS in his MISSION OBJECTIVES. The president wanted information on the geography of the Northwest and the discovery of an easy route to the PACIFIC OCEAN, if one existed; he wanted a report on the rivers, geology, minerals, ANIMALS, BIRDS, FISH, and plant life the expedition saw on the way; and he also wanted as much information as possible on the Native Americans they met during their 4,100-mile journey to the Pacific.

From the very beginning of the expedition, during the winter of 1803–04 at CAMP DUBOIS, both Lewis and WILLIAM CLARK acquired as much information as they could about the Indians they knew they would meet along the MISSOURI RIVER. All the way up the Missouri to the MANDAN INDIANS, with whom they would spend the winter of 1804–05, they took account of, noted, and recorded every aspect of the Indian nations they met. They even took with them blank vocabulary sheets to collect and preserve Indian words and phrases. When they sent the KEELBOAT back down to ST. LOUIS from FORT MANDAN in April 1805, its shipment included 14 lists of Indian words that Lewis and Clark had collated during the 11 months they had been away.

The keelboat also brought back their "Estimate of the Eastern Indians." This remarkable document is still one of the most comprehensive studies of American Indian nations in American ethnography. The two captains set out the information they had gathered on nearly 50 nations and bands of Indians. Under 19 separate heads, Lewis and Clark wrote what they had learned of the names of Indian nations, their LANGUAGES, the number of villages and lodges in each, their warriors, where they lived, and where and what they traded. The "Estimate" finished with the identification of "The Countrey in which they usially reside, and the principal water courses on or near which the Villages are Situated, or the Defferant Nations & tribes usially rove & *Remarks.*"

The "Estimate" is all the more remarkable because it was accompanied by Clark's meticulously detailed MAP of the

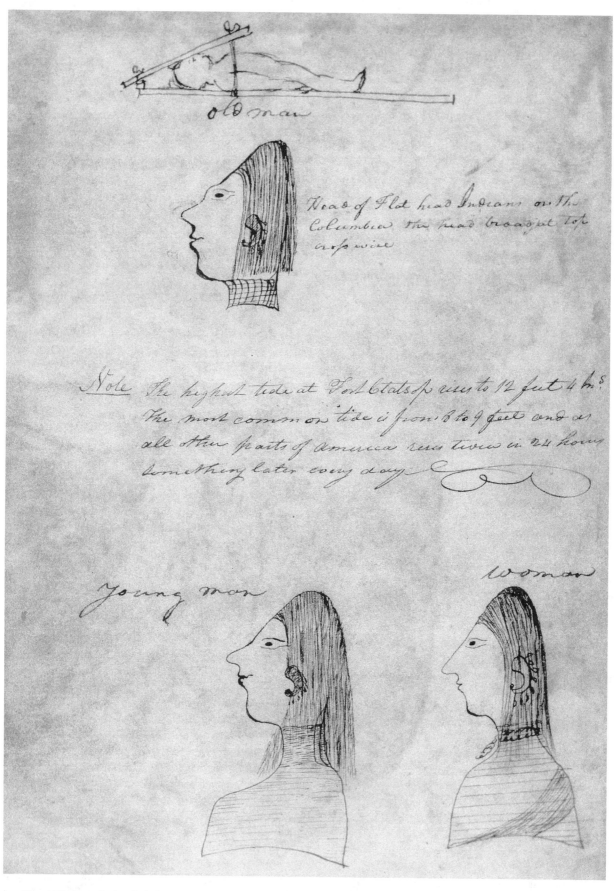

old man

Head of Flat head Indians on the Columbia the head broad at top crosswise

Note The highest tide at Fort Clatsop rises to 12 feet 4 Ins. The most common tide is from 8 to 9 feet and as all other parts of america rises twice in 24 hours something later every day—

Young man

woman

Lewis and Clark made detailed observations of Indian life and culture. This page from the journals shows the Chinook's method for flattening the heads of their babies. *(William Clark Papers, Missouri Historical Society, St. Louis)*

twists and turns of the Missouri River as well as Lewis's voluminous notes on the new species of animals, birds, and fish they had seen—plus some live specimens. It is clear from their JOURNALS that while Lewis was a better botanist, zoologist, and observer of natural phenomena, Clark was the better waterman, surveyor, and mapmaker. Similarly, Lewis wrote more graphic descriptions of the Indians they met, while Clark wrote the better account of their organization, customs, and rituals.

Elliott Coues gives a good example of the captains' work in his edited record of July 22–26, 1804. Writing of the OTOE INDIANS (Oto), the journals say:

Five leagues above them, on the same side of the river resides the nation of Pawnees. . . . They now consist of four bands; the first [the Grand Pawnee] is the one just mentioned, of about 500 men, to whom of late years have been added to the second band, who are called Republican Pawnees, from their having lived on the Republican branch of the Kansas River, whence they emigrated to join the principal band of Pawnees; the Republican Pawnees amount to nearly 250 men. The third are the Pawnee Loups, or Wolf Pawnees, who reside on the Wolf fork of the Platte, about 90 miles from the principal Pawnees, and number 280 men. The fourth band originally resided on the Kansas and Arkansas, but in their wars with the Osages were so often defeated that they at last retired to their present position on the Red river, where they form a tribe of 400 men. All these tribes live in villages, and raise corn; but during the intervals of culture rove in the plains in quest of buffalo.

Lewis and Clark remained fervent ethnographers throughout the expedition. Other members of the expedition also made important observations of the Indians of the time, describing their appearance, manners, and customs. PATRICK GASS, the expedition's carpenter, frequently commented on the form and construction of Indian housing, but it was NICHOLAS PRYOR who, after meeting the YANKTON NAKOTA Sioux, was the first to describe the classic Plains TIPI, which "was handsum made of Buffalow Skins Painted different Colour, all compact & handSomly arranged, their Camps formed of a Conic form Containing about 12 or 15 persons each and 40 in number."

On October 16, 1805, the expedition reached the junction of the SNAKE RIVER and COLUMBIA RIVER. For the first four months after leaving the Mandan villages, they had, surprisingly, encountered no Indians until meeting the SHOSHONE in August. Since then they had met the FLATHEAD and NEZ PERCE. Now, at the junction of the Snake and Columbia, the riverbanks were lined with Indian villages, and they met numerous bands of different nations, as Gass noted: "We found here a number of natives, of whom we have not yet found out the names. We encamped on the point between the two rivers. . . ."

The expedition stayed at this point for two days while Lewis and Clark, mindful of Jefferson's instructions, did their research. On October 18 Gass wrote: "In the forenoon our Commanding Offices were employed in getting specimens of the language of the natives, there being three, or part of three, different nations here. They are almost without clothing, having no covering of any account, except some skin robes and a few leggins to cover their nakedness. The women have scarce sufficient to cover their nakedness."

The three nations were the Palouse, YAKAMA (Yakima), and WANAPAM, all of whom appear in the "Estimate of the Western Indians" Lewis and Clark brought back with them. This document and the "Estimate of Eastern Indians," now in the possession of the AMERICAN PHILOSOPHICAL SOCIETY of PHILADELPHIA, record their important contributions to American ethnography.

Lewis and Clark never really appreciated the intricacies of the tribal and trade alliances of the nations they met, but they made an invaluable addition to the knowledge, if not the understanding, of the American Indians of that time. Much has happened since then to change and destroy the relationship between Indian nations and white Americans. However, it is worth noting that Lewis and Clark at least are still kindly remembered in the legends of some of the nations whom they visited and questioned so long ago.

See also RELIGION.

Further Reading

Ambrose, Stephen E. *Undaunted Courage: Meriwether Lewis, Thomas Jefferson, and the Opening of the American West.* New York: Simon and Schuster, 1996.

Catlin, George. *Letters and Notes on the Manners, Customs, and Conditions of the North American Indians; Written during Eight Years' Travel (1832–1839).* Reprint, New York: Dover Publications, 1973.

Furtwangler, Albert. *Acts of Discovery: Visions of America in the Lewis and Clark Journals.* Urbana: University of Illinois Press, 1993.

Jefferson National Expansion Memorial. "The Lewis and Clark Journey of Discovery: Native Peoples." Available on-line. URL: http://www.nps.gov/jeff/LewisClark2/TheJourney/NativePeoples.htm. Downloaded on April 11, 2002.

Lewis, Meriwether, and William Clark. *The History of the Lewis and Clark Expedition.* Edited by Elliott Coues; 4 vols., 1893, Harper. Reprinted in 3 vols., New York: Dover Publications, 1979.

Nichols, William. "Lewis and Clark Probe the Darkness." *American Scholar* 49, no. 1 (1979/80): 94–101.

Peabody Museum of Archeology and Ethnology, Harvard University. "The Ethnography of Lewis and Clark." Available on-line. URL: http://www.peabody.harvard.edu/Lewis_and_Clark/default.html. Downloaded on March 22, 2002.

Ray, Verne F., and Nancy O. Lurie. "The Contributions of Lewis and Clark to Ethnography." *Journal of the Washington Academy of Sciences* 44 (1954): 358–370.

Ronda, James P. *Lewis and Clark among the Indians.* Lincoln: University of Nebraska Press, 1984.

Sappington, Robert Lee. "Lewis and Clark Expedition Among the Nez Perce Indians: The First Ethnographic Study in the Columbia Plateau." *Northwest Anthropological Research Notes* 23 (1989): 1–33.

eulachon   See FISH, NEW SPECIES.

Evans, John (1770–1799) *trader, explorer, mapmaker*
During the winter of 1804–05, as the expedition wintered at CAMP DUBOIS, MERIWETHER LEWIS and WILLIAM CLARK spent a lot of time in nearby ST. LOUIS, among other things gathering information about the MISSOURI RIVER and the Indian nations living along it. Among the men they met was JAMES MACKAY, a Scotsman who had spent many years trading with the Indian nations they would meet. Furthermore, Mackay had lived with the OMAHA INDIANS and had sent his colleague John Evans to the MANDAN INDIAN villages upstream. Evans had not only spent the winter of 1796–97 among the Mandan and written a journal about his experiences but had also drawn a map of the upper Missouri and its tributaries—an invaluable resource that the expedition took with them up the river.

The son of a Methodist minister from Carnavonshire, North Wales, Evans was recruited in Britain in 1791–92 to investigate the possibility of the Mandan being the legendary WELSH INDIANS. He arrived in Baltimore, Maryland, in 1792 and remained there until spring 1793 and then made his way on foot to St. Louis, where he was imprisoned by Spanish authorities. It is not known when he was released, but by 1795 he was out of prison and working for Mackay. Mackay was then employed by the Spanish-controlled Missouri Company, which was trying to wrest the Indian trade up the river from the NORTH WEST COMPANY of CANADA. Evans traveled with Mackay up the Missouri in 1795 and, the following year, went on to the Mandan villages, where he spent the winter of 1796–97.

It has been claimed that Mackay commissioned Evans to find a way across the continent to the PACIFIC OCEAN, but this has not been confirmed. What seems certain is that Evans ran out of supplies at the Mandan villages and in 1797 was forced to return downriver to St. Louis. There he promulgated the view that the Mandan were not in fact the Welsh Indians, an opinion that some historians think was written to please his Spanish employers. Certainly when Lewis and Clark conducted their inquiries in St. Louis, this was the commonly accepted view. Evans, however, could not be questioned, having died in New Orleans in 1799.

There is still some doubt whether the map of the upper Missouri that was said to be drawn by Evans was in fact done entirely by him or whether he merely added information to one already sketched by Mackay. Whichever it was, a copy had come into the possession of the governor of Indiana Territory, who had sent it to THOMAS JEFFERSON. Jefferson in turn sent it to Lewis at Camp Dubois. The Evans map, as it is usually known, was the most accurate the expedition was to take with them, and the captains found it invaluable along the first part of their journey. Comprising seven sheets depicting the course of the Missouri, the map marked the locations of the Omaha, Ponca, ARIKARA, Mandan, and HIDATSA villages. It also provided a remarkably accurate outline of what the corps would meet afterward, depicting as it did the multiple-ridge structure of the ROCKY MOUNTAINS and noting the locations of the YELLOWSTONE RIVER and the GREAT FALLS of the Missouri. While the Lewis and Clark Expedition would probably have succeeded without the Evans map, it gave them valuable insight into the unknown territory ahead of them.

Further Reading
Kimberly, Howard. "John Evans—Waunfawr—Explorer, 1770–1799." Madoc 1170 website. Available on-line. URL: http://www.madoc1170.com/jevans.htm. Updated on February 7, 2001.
Williams, David. *John Evans and the Legend of Madoc, 1770–1779.* Cardiff: University of Wales Press, 1963.
Wood, W. Raymond. "The John Evans 1796–97 Map of the Missouri River." *Great Plains Quarterly* 1 (1981): 39–53.
———. *Prologue to Lewis & Clark: The Mackay and Evans Expedition.* Norman: University of Oklahoma Press, 2003.

Experiment, The   See IRON-FRAME BOAT.

exploration, early
Although Indians were the first to inhabit the American continents, by the mid- to late 1500s several European countries—primarily GREAT BRITAIN, FRANCE, and SPAIN—were sending explorers to lay claim to the lands there. The French and British had begun to colonize CANADA and the northeast coast of North America, while Spain had conquered Mexico and Central America as well as much of South America. Exploratory missions by all these countries had largely been confined to the east coasts (and in Spain's case also to the Gulf of Mexico and Caribbean islands), until in 1539 the Spanish began to send expeditions up the California coast. Bartolomé Ferrolo is believed to have reached the 42nd parallel in 1543, and in 1592 Juan de Fuca discovered the straits that are now named for him. In 1603 Martín d'Aguilar became the first to sight what was probably the mouth of the COLUMBIA RIVER.

In 1578 the English explorer Sir Francis Drake also reached the Northwest coast, going as far as the 48th parallel in southern Oregon. His hope had been to find a water route from the Pacific to the Atlantic that would enable European traders to reach the markets of the Far East without going around the tip of South America. Other explorers followed, and by the 1700s the race was on to find a NORTHWEST PASSAGE across northern Canada. In 1728 Vitus Bering, a Danish explorer sailing for Russia, discovered the strait and sea now

Captain James Cook explored America's northwest coast in 1778. He died the following year, but his men returned to England with reports of the trade in sea otter fur, encouraging British interest in the Pacific Northwest. *(Library of Congress, Prints and Photographs Division [LC-USZ62-100822])*

named for him, and in 1741 he claimed Alaska for Russia and became the first to trade with Indians of that area.

In 1765 Major Robert Rogers petitioned King George III to explore the territory in the Northwest, which he called Oregon (see OREGON TERRITORY); his petition was refused, but interest in the area remained high. The Spanish remained especially keen explorers, and in 1774 Juan Pérez reached the coast of British Columbia. The following year Bruno Heceta sailed up the Pacific coastline and landed at what is now Point Grenville, Washington. Claiming the region for Spain, Heceta and his lieutenant became the first Europeans recorded as standing on land in the Pacific Northwest. Along his journey he noted the Columbia River, writing, "These currents and eddies of water cause me to believe that the place is the mouth of some great river, or of some passage to another sea." Others, including THOMAS JEFFERSON, would later share his feeling that the Columbia might be the key to the Northwest Passage.

In 1778 the great English explorer Captain James Cook sailed from the Hawaiian Islands up to the northwest coast and became the first European to land on Vancouver Island, British Columbia. He continued further north, going through the Bering Strait and into the Arctic Ocean. Along the way he discovered and named King George's Sound, now known as Nootka Sound. Cook was killed in Hawaii the following year,

but his men returned to England with news of a lucrative trade in sea OTTER fur.

In 1788 Estevan José Martínez, sailing for Spain, led an expedition to Nootka, where he discovered Russian intentions to settle there. The Spanish at once claimed the region and began to build their own settlements. Martínez seized three British ships at Nootka, an incident that foreshadowed the future rivalry for control of the Pacific Northwest.

The French also attempted to lay claim to the region. In 1786 Jean François La Pérouse surveyed the coastline between Monterey and Alaska, although his attempts to establish French sovereignty failed. By then the primary contenders for the area were Russia, Spain, and Great Britain. In 1788 Captain John Meares strengthened the British claim when he built a trading post on Nootka Sound; however, this post and his ships were seized by the Spanish the following year.

By 1792 hopes for a Northwest Passage were fading, but many retained the belief that an all-water route was still possible by a series of connecting rivers. The English commander GEORGE VANCOUVER, who had sailed with Cook, was one of these, and in 1791 he set out for the Pacific Northwest, arriving there the following year. Although he surveyed and mapped the coastline as far north as Vancouver Island and Puget Sound, surprisingly he missed the mouth of the Columbia River. It was only when he learned of Captain ROBERT GRAY's discovery of this river that he turned back and sent an exploratory party some 100 miles up the Columbia. His MAPS would later be used during the expedition of MERIWETHER LEWIS and WILLIAM CLARK.

Captain Gray's establishment of the latitude and longitude of the Columbia's mouth in May 1792 was significant because it became the basis for the first American claim on the Oregon Territory. The following year, however, ALEXANDER MACKENZIE, a Scottish-Canadian fur trader and partner in the NORTH WEST COMPANY, bolstered Britain's claim when he became the first non-Indian to cross the North American continent. After he arrived at an inlet off the Pacific Ocean, he inscribed a message in vermilion on a rock: "Alexander Mackenzie, from Canada, by land, the twenty-second of July, one thousand seven hundred and ninety-three." Less than 10 years later Thomas Jefferson would read Mackenzie's account of his journey and be spurred to send his own expedition west.

By that time European claims had been established on territory in the interior of the American continent. While the Spanish had moved into the Southwest from Mexico, the French had descended southward from Canada. In 1669–70 René-Robert Cavalier, sieur de La Salle, explored the region south of Lake Erie into present-day Ohio. In 1673 Père Jacques Marquette and Louis Joliet went down the Wisconsin River into the MISSISSIPPI RIVER and passed the mouths of the MISSOURI, OHIO, and Arkansas Rivers before turning back. Finally, in 1682 La Salle traveled the length of the Mississippi to its mouth and claimed the region drained by the river for France, naming it Louisiana.

While French colonization efforts went slowly, they made significant advances in establishing contact with the Indians of the GREAT PLAINS. In the late 1720s and into the early 1740s the French-Canadian trader Pierre de La Vérendrye conducted searches with three of his sons for an overland Northwest Passage to the Pacific (then called the Western Sea). They discovered and explored the Saskatchewan, Assiniboine, and north Red Rivers as well as the upper Missouri, and in 1738 they became the first explorers to meet the MANDAN INDIANS. In 1742–43, two of La Vérendrye's sons made a famous journey westward that apparently took them as far as present-day Pierre, South Dakota. There they buried a lead plate (found in 1913), claiming the area for France.

Other traders and explorers followed La Vérendrye. In 1739 the Frenchmen Pierre and Paul Mallet journeyed from the Missouri River across the plains to Santa Fe. The following year they descended the Canadian River through the Texas Panhandle to the Arkansas and Mississippi Rivers. They continued their explorations in this area, and in 1741, at the head of the PLATTE RIVER, they reached a mountain range that the Indians called the Rockies. In 1750 Pierre Mallet ascended the Red River, preceding ZEBULON PIKE and the later RED RIVER EXPEDITION by more than 50 years.

In 1766 Robert Rogers, having failed to receive permission from King George III to send an expedition to the Pacific Northwest, hired Jonathan Carver of Massachusetts to carry out the mission anyway. Carver first traveled up the Mississippi River to a location north of today's Minneapolis and then went to Prairie du Chien (Wisconsin). However, his party was halted by a war between the Sioux (Dakota, Lakota, Nakota) and Chippewa Indians, forcing them to turn north instead, up the Chippewa River and then over to Lake Superior. He went on to publish the first English account of the Upper Great Lakes and Mississippi region, *Travels through the Interior Parts of North America* (1778), a book read by Thomas Jefferson. Another book Jefferson studied was Antoine Simon Le Page du Pratz's *History of Louisiana, or the Western Parts of Virginia and Carolina* (London, 1763; 2nd ed., 1774), which Lewis carried with him during his journey west (see BOOKS ON THE EXPEDITION).

In 1790 Jacques d'Église reached the Mandan villages and discovered that British traders were now filtering down into the area from Canada. By this time Spain held sovereignty over the LOUISIANA TERRITORY, and they began to take steps to explore the upper Missouri with the formation of the Missouri Company in 1793. Among the explorers the Spanish sent into the region were Jean-Baptiste Truteau and JAMES MACKAY.

By now Jefferson had become determined to send an American expedition to the Pacific Northwest, something he had attempted three times already. In 1783 he asked GEORGE ROGERS CLARK to lead an expedition into the West. Clark agreed it ought to be done but declined to take on the assignment. In 1784, while serving as minister to France, Jefferson met John Ledyard, an American explorer who proposed traveling to the western coast of North America by way of Siberia and then journeying across the continent from west to east. Jefferson supported the plan, but it failed when Ledyard was arrested in Russia and sent back to Europe.

Finally, in 1793—the year Alexander Mackenzie made his epic journey across Canada to the Pacific—Jefferson convinced fellow members of the AMERICAN PHILOSOPHICAL SOCIETY to sponsor an expedition led by the French botanist ANDRÉ MICHAUX. The purpose of the expedition was to "find the shortest & most convenient route of communication between the U.S. & the Pacific Ocean." Unfortunately, due to the political scheming of French minister Edmund Genêt, this mission was halted before Michaux got further west than Kentucky. It was to be another 10 years before Jefferson at last realized his ambition by sending American soldiers across the continent to the Pacific.

Further Reading

Allen, John Logan. *Passage Through the Garden: Lewis and Clark and the Image of the American Northwest.* Urbana: University of Illinois Press, 1975. Reprint, New York: Dover Publications, 1991.

Barclay, Donald A., James H. Maguire, and Peter Wild, eds. *Into the Wilderness Dream: Exploration Narratives of the American West, 1500–1805.* Salt Lake City: University of Utah Press, 1994.

Brebner, John B. *The Explorers of North America 1492–1806.* New York: Macmillan, 1933.

Carver, Jonathan. *The Journals of Jonathan Carver and Related Documents, 1766–1770.* Edited by John Parker. St. Paul: Minnesota Historical Press, 1976.

Delgado, James P. *Across the Top of the World: The Quest for the Northwest Passage.* New York: Checkmark Books, 1999.

The Illustrated Lower Columbia Handbook. "Exploration." Available on-line. URL: http://www.lowercolumbiahandbook.com/explorers.cfm. Downloaded on March 25, 2002.

Maritime Museum of British Columbia. "European Exploration on the Northwest Coast." Available on-line. URL: http://mmbc.bc.ca/source/schoolnet/exploration/ee_nwc.html. Downloaded on April 10, 2002.

Nasatir, A.P., ed. *Before Lewis and Clark: Documents Illustrating the History of the Missouri, 1785–1804.* 2 vols. St. Louis: St. Louis Historical Documents Foundation, 1975.

Pethick, Derek. *First Approaches to the Northwest Coast.* Vancouver: J. J. Douglas, 1976.

Schwantes, Carlos, ed. *Encounters with a Distant Land: Exploration and the Great Northwest.* Moscow: University of Idaho Press, 1994.

University of Virginia. "Exploring the West from Monticello." Available on-line. URL: http://www.lib.virginia.edu/exhibits/lewis_clark/home.html. Downloaded on March 27, 2002.

Walker, Dale. *Pacific Destiny: The Three Century Journey to Oregon Country.* New York: Forge Books, 2000.

Wood, W. Raymond. *Prologue to Lewis & Clark: The Mackay and Evans Expedition.* Norman: University of Oklahoma Press, 2003.

exploration, later

When the LOUISIANA PURCHASE doubled the size of the United States in 1803, President THOMAS JEFFERSON was finally able to realize his long-held dream of sending an exploration party across the continent. The mission of the Lewis and Clark Expedition had many facets, among which were mapping part of the newly acquired LOUISIANA TERRITORY, finding a viable route to the PACIFIC OCEAN, and establishing a valid U.S. claim to the OREGON TERRITORY. But there were other areas of the territory to explore as well; Jefferson wanted to know what was out there, and he wanted it all mapped. As he explained in a letter to the naturalist WILLIAM DUNBAR: "We shall delineate with correctness the great arteries of this great country: those who come after us will extend the ramifications as they become acquainted with them, and fill up the canvas we begin."

Jefferson had already put the wheels into motion with the Lewis and Clark Expedition. Before the CORPS OF DISCOVERY had even returned from the West Coast, other expeditions were being sent out. In the winter of 1804–05, while the Corps of Discovery was preparing for its journey at CAMP DUBOIS, William Dunbar undertook a survey of the Ouachita (Washita) River as a trial run for an exploration of the Red River that Jefferson wanted him to lead. Dunbar, Dr. George Hunter, and a party of 16 men went as far as the Ozark Mountains, near present-day Hot Springs, Arkansas, and there wrote the first report on the activity of the hot springs in addition to collecting other valuable scientific data. He subsequently declined to lead the RED RIVER EXPEDITION (the first to be conducted by civilians) but oversaw its planning and selected its leaders, Thomas Freeman and Peter Custis. That expedition set out from Natchez in April 1806, but three months later they were intercepted and turned back by Spanish forces.

The most famous military expedition besides Lewis and Clark was led by Lieutenant ZEBULON PIKE. In 1806, after failing to find the source of the MISSISSIPPI RIVER in his first mission, Pike took a party of 20 men later that year to explore the southwestern region of the Louisiana Territory, specifically the areas along the Red and Arkansas Rivers. In Colorado he sighted what later became known as Pike's Peak. Pike and his party were eventually captured by the Spanish in New Mexico, ending their mission. (The Spanish were still disputing the border of the Louisiana Territory.)

Further important military explorations were conducted in 1820 and 1823 by Major Stephen Long of the Army Corps of Topographical Engineers. In 1817 Long had surveyed the Fox and Wisconsin Rivers and explored the upper MISSISSIPPI RIVER. In June 1820 he took a party of 19 men to explore the headwaters of the PLATTE, Arkansas, and Red Rivers. Reaching the ROCKY MOUNTAINS in Colorado, he discovered the peak that bears his name today, and on July 14, three men in his party made the first successful ascent of Pike's Peak. Ten days later he divided the party in two, leaving Captain John Bell to follow the Arkansas while he proceeded to the Red River. As he later discovered, however, he had mistakenly followed the Canadian River. Long's 1823 expedition was to explore the sources of the Minnesota and Red Rivers in the north as well as the U.S.-Canadian boundary west of the Great Lakes. In his account of the 1820 expedition, he described the Southwest as

"The Great American Desert," which did much to discourage WESTWARD EXPANSION for another two decades.

Nevertheless, by the time the Corps of Discovery returned to ST. LOUIS in September 1806, movement into the West, led by fur traders and MOUNTAIN MEN, had already begun. The mountain men were particularly important in opening up routes to the West, and some of these included former corps members such as GEORGE DROUILLARD and JOHN COLTER. In 1807 these two each explored regions of present-day Montana and Wyoming; Colter became famous for discovering what is now Yellowstone National Park.

Between 1807 and 1812, DAVID THOMPSON of the NORTH WEST COMPANY traveled and surveyed the length of the COLUMBIA RIVER. Meanwhile, in 1811 JOHN JACOB ASTOR set up a trading post near the mouth of the Columbia, the first settlement in the Pacific Northwest (today's Astoria, Oregon). Astor's employees played a large role in blazing paths to the West that others would follow. In 1811–12 Wilson Price Hunt traveled from St. Louis to Fort Astoria, using a route that almost matched the OREGON TRAIL of later years. In 1812, on a return trip from Astoria, Robert Stuart discovered South Pass through the ROCKY MOUNTAINS, a point that became a vital part of numerous trails to the West after famed mountain man Jedediah Smith led a party through it in 1824.

In 1826–28 Smith earned his place in the history books when he carried out life-threatening explorations of the Mojave Desert, the Great Basin, the Sierra Nevada, and the Great Salt Desert. In addition to being the first non-Indian explorer of the Great Basin, he was also the first white American to travel to and from California overland.

Another great American explorer was John C. Frémont, a lieutenant in the U.S. Topographical Corps who became known as The Pathfinder. In 1842, with the legendary Kit Carson as his guide, Frémont explored the length of the Oregon Trail. In subsequent years he and Carson surveyed the route from Kansas City to Oregon and surveyed the central Rockies and Great Salt Lake region. In 1845 he crossed the Sierra Nevada in California. The following year he was in the Sacramento Valley in California when he incited American settlers to rebel against Mexican rule in the controversial Bear Flag Revolt. Found guilty of mutiny and insubordination in a court-martial, Frémont was forced to resign from the service, but he continued to conduct expeditions into the West, where he surveyed routes for the transcontinental railroad.

In 1850 the African-American frontiersman James Pierson Beckwourth discovered Beckwourth Pass in the Sierra Nevada, which opened a route to the Sacramento Valley. When the Gadsden Purchase was signed in 1853, the United States acquired the American Southwest from Mexico and in so doing now extended from coast to coast. Further exploration was to come, notably the expedition of JOHN WESLEY POWELL down the Colorado River through the Grand Canyon in 1869. The canvas of the American interior was filling fast, only a half-century after the Lewis and Clark Expedition—far sooner than Jefferson had ever imagined.

Further Reading

Coues, Elliott, ed. *The Explorations of Zebulon Montgomery Pike.* 3 vols. New York: Harper, 1895.

Flores, Dan K., ed. *Jefferson and Southwestern Exploration: The Freeman and Custis Accounts of the Red River Expedition of 1806.* Norman: University of Oklahoma Press, 1984.

Goetzmann, William. *Army Exploration in the American West.* 2d ed. Lincoln: University of Nebraska Press, 1979.

Jefferson, Thomas. *Message from the President of the United States Communicating Discoveries Made in Exploring the Missouri, Red River and Washita, by Captains Lewis and Clark, Doctor Sibley, and Mr. Dunbar: with a statistical account of the countries adjacent.* Washington, D.C.: A. & G. Way, printers, 1806.

Montgomery, M. R. *Jefferson and the Gun-Men: How the West Was almost Lost.* New York: Crown Publishers, 2000.

Schwantes, Carlos, ed. *Encounters with a Distant Land: Exploration and the Great Northwest.* Moscow: University of Idaho Press, 1994.

Utley, Robert M. *A Life Wild and Perilous: Mountain Men and the Paths to the Pacific.* New York: Henry Holt and Co., 1997.

F

Falls Mountain See MOUNT HOOD.

Federalists See POLITICAL PARTIES.

Field, Joseph (Joseph Fields) (1774–1807) *private in the permanent party*

Joseph Field—also listed as Fields in some sources—was one of the first three men recruited for the CORPS OF DISCOVERY in August 1803; the other two were his brother REUBIN FIELD and Sergeant CHARLES FLOYD. These three and six others were referred to as the NINE YOUNG MEN FROM KENTUCKY. Along with his brother, Joseph Field became among the most valued members of the expedition, taking part in one its most harrowing moments.

Joseph was one of four boys born in Culpeper County, Virginia, to Abraham and Elizabeth Field, pioneers who moved their family to Jefferson County, Kentucky, in 1784. The region around the Falls of the Ohio had only recently been settled by a military expedition led by WILLIAM CLARK's brother GEORGE ROGERS CLARK, and Louisville was then the westernmost American settlement. There is a possible connection between the Field and Clark families, although it is unclear exactly how William Clark and the Field brothers were related.

As an outstanding woodsman and hunter, Field is mentioned repeatedly in the JOURNALS of MERIWETHER LEWIS and WILLIAM CLARK as an important contributor to the expedition's success. Like his brother Reubin, he was trusted highly by the captains, to the extent that he was sent to explore the lower YELLOWSTONE RIVER during the outward journey.

On July 4, 1804, Field was bitten by a snake. Lewis, the corps's de facto doctor, drew out the poison with a poultice, and there seemed to be no ill effects. The following month Field shot and killed a BUFFALO, the first one seen by most of the men on the expedition. The carcass was brought back to camp, and the corps dined on buffalo for the first time.

In June 1805 Field was among the party whom Lewis selected to accompany him in a search by land for the GREAT FALLS of the MISSOURI RIVER. Lewis became extremely ill during the trip and treated himself with an improvised tea made of twigs. After he recovered, the party went on and finally found the falls on June 13. The following day Lewis sent Field back to the expedition with a letter for Clark advising the location of the Great Falls.

According to Clark's journal, during the construction of FORT CLATSOP in late 1805, Joseph Field built writing desks for the captains out of rough-hewn boards. Both Lewis and Clark worked at these to document and chart the outbound journey. That winter one of the tasks assigned to Field was that of setting up and running the expedition's SALTWORKS. It is a reasonable assumption that Joseph had picked up some knowledge from his older brother Ezekiel, who was a salt maker.

Joseph and Reubin Field and GEORGE DROUILLARD were the men Captain Lewis chose to accompany him on an exploration of the MARIAS RIVER in July 1806. Early on the morning of the 26th, the soldiers surprised some BLACKFEET INDIANS who were attempting to steal their guns and HORSES. In the skirmish that followed, Reubin stabbed an Indian to death, and Lewis mortally wounded another warrior.

In his January 1807 report to Secretary of War HENRY DEARBORN, Meriwether Lewis wrote of Joseph and Reubin Field that they were "two of the most active and enterprising young men who accompanied us. It was their peculiar fate to have been engaged in all the most dangerous and difficult scenes of the voyage, in which they uniformly acquitted themselves with much honor."

After his discharge in October 1806, Field returned to Kentucky. Like others on the expedition, he received double pay for his service and a land warrant for 320 acres. He apparently died in 1807, since late that year his father deeded his right in Joseph's estate to Reubin Field. Joseph Field lies in an unmarked grave in Jefferson County, Kentucky.

Further Reading

Appleman, Roy E. "Joseph and Reubin Field, Kentucky Frontiersmen of the Lewis and Clark Expedition and Their Father, Abraham." *Filson Club Quarterly* 49, no. 1 (1975): 5–36.

Clarke, Charles G. *The Men of the Lewis and Clark Expedition: A Biographical Roster of the Fifty-One Members and a Composite Diary of Their Activities from All Known Sources.* 1970. Reprint, Lincoln: Bison Books, University of Nebraska Press, 2002.

Field, Eugene A., and Lucie C. Field. "The Ancestry of Joseph and Reubin Field of The Lewis and Clark Expedition The Corps of Discovery." Available on-line. URL: http://www.luciefield.net/ancjr.html. Updated on January 5, 2001.

Lange, Robert. "The Expedition's Brothers—Joseph and Reuben Field." *We Proceeded On* 4, no. 3 (July 1978): 15–16.

North Dakota Lewis & Clark Bicentennial Foundation. *Members of the Corps of Discovery.* Bismarck, N.Dak.: United Printing and Mailing, 2000.

Field, Reubin (Reuben Fields) (ca. 1772–ca. 1822)
private in the permanent party

Born in Culpeper County, Virginia, to Abraham and Elizabeth Field, and raised in Kentucky, Reubin Field was, along with his brother JOSEPH FIELD, one of the first three men to be recruited to the CORPS OF DISCOVERY, in August 1803. As one of the NINE YOUNG MEN FROM KENTUCKY, Field was one of the corps's best hunters and was considered among the most trusted members of the Lewis and Clark Expedition.

It did not start out that way. In February 1804, while MERIWETHER LEWIS and WILLIAM CLARK were away from the corps's winter camp on Wood River, Field and fellow private JOHN SHIELDS defied the orders of Sergeant JOHN ORDWAY and refused to mount guard duty. Upon his return, Lewis expressed himself to be "mortified and disappointed" at their conduct and issued orders emphasizing that when the captains were away, the sergeant in charge must be obeyed at all times. No punishment for this offense was imposed on Field and Shields (see DISCIPLINE).

In September 1805, as the corps struggled over the BITTERROOT MOUNTAINS, Clark took six men, including Field, and pressed on ahead of the others. On the 20th, this small group found their way down to WEIPPE PRAIRIE, where they met the NEZ PERCE INDIANS. Two days later, Lewis and the others were met by Field, who gave them FOOD and brought them back to the Nez Perce village.

In July 1806 the Field brothers, together with GEORGE DROUILLARD, were the men Lewis selected to join him on a dangerous side exploration of the MARIAS RIVER. They traveled north from the GREAT FALLS of the Missouri to the Marias and then followed the Marias River in a northwesterly toward the eastern slopes of the ROCKY MOUNTAINS. It was on this excursion that the most northerly point of the entire mission was reached at what Lewis called CAMP DISAPPOINTMENT. As they returned along the TWO MEDICINE RIVER, they had a skirmish with a band of BLACKFEET INDIANS, during which two Indians were killed—one stabbed by Reubin Field—and the soldiers barely escaped with their lives.

In his January 1807 report to Secretary of War HENRY DEARBORN, Meriwether Lewis wrote of Reubin and Joseph Field that they were "two of the most active and enterprising young men who accompanied us. It was their peculiar fate to have been engaged in all the most dangerous and difficult scenes of the voyage, in which they uniformly acquitted themselves with much honor."

After the expedition, Captain Clark recommended Reubin Field for a lieutenancy in the army, leading some historians to believe that he was older than his brother Joseph, although other sources list him as a year younger. Reubin received a warrant for land in Missouri but instead returned to Kentucky. In 1808 he married a woman named Mary Myrtle. Childless, Reubin and Mary acquired land south of present-day Louisville and became farmers. Reubin died in 1822 or 1823 in Jefferson County, Kentucky, where he is buried. His last name is listed as Fields in some sources.

Further Reading

Appleman, Roy E. "Joseph and Reubin Field, Kentucky Frontiersmen of the Lewis and Clark Expedition and Their Father, Abraham." *Filson Club Quarterly* 49, no. 1 (1975): 5–36.

Clarke, Charles G. *The Men of the Lewis and Clark Expedition: A Biographical Roster of the Fifty-One Members and a Composite Diary of Their Activities from All Known Sources.* 1970. Reprint, Lincoln: Bison Books, University of Nebraska Press, 2002.

Field, Eugene A., and Lucie C. Field. "The Ancestry of Joseph and Reubin Field of The Lewis and Clark Expedition The Corps of Discovery." Available on-line. URL: http://www.luciefield.net/ancjr.html. Updated on January 5, 2001.

Lange, Robert. "The Expedition's Brothers—Joseph and Reuben Field." *We Proceeded On* 4, no. 3 (July 1978): 15–16.

North Dakota Lewis & Clark Bicentennial Foundation. *Members of the Corps of Discovery.* Bismarck, N.Dak.: United Printing and Mailing, 2000.

firearms

It is no exaggeration to say that the success—as well as the safety—of the Lewis and Clark Expedition depended on the firearms they carried. Their rifles enabled them to kill animals

Meriwether Lewis purchased his air rifle, which required no gunpowder to fire it, from Isaiah Lukins of Philadelphia. Demonstrations of the rifle were given at every council with Indians. *(Virginia Military Institute Museum, Lexington, VA)*

for FOOD, to defend themselves if they had to, and to impress the Indians they met with the accuracy of their WEAPONS.

Because firearms were such a commonplace part of life on the American frontier at that time, there is no specific listing of all the weapons carried by the expedition. However, the JOURNALS and other sources do note that the CORPS OF DISCOVERY took the following with them on their journey:

1. A one-pounder bronze cannon mounted on a swivel on the KEELBOAT. This could fire a one-pound ball but was more effective firing grapeshot, a generic term that involved loading the cannon with musket balls, nails, or even pebbles—all of which could be devastating at close range.
2. Four blunderbusses, two mounted on swivels on the keelboat and one each mounted on the two PIROGUES. These were smooth-bore weapons designed to discharge a quantity of grapeshot. Inaccurate over any distance, they were very effective at close quarters.
3. Fifteen rifles from the HARPERS FERRY Armory. It is generally believed these were prototype Model 1803 rifles. Soon to become standard issue in the U.S. Army, they were muzzle-loading flintlocks of .54 caliber with a 33-inch rifled barrel. Accurate up to 100 yards, a skilled rifleman could get off two aimed shots in a minute. Sometimes loosely called the Kentucky (more accurately the Philadelphia) rifle, the Harpers Ferry model had a slightly shorter barrel than its civilian equivalent. It has been claimed that the Model 1803 rifles Lewis took with him did not have sling swivels, but it seems close to certain that those Lewis procured were equipped with this facility. It would be pointless to set off on such a journey as the expedition undertook without being able to slip a weapon over one's shoulder.
4. Further rifles procured at Lancaster, Pennsylvania. The number and type is unknown, but it is possible these were "Philadelphia" rifles, similar to the Harpers Ferry models but with a longer barrel. It is believed that both MERIWETHER LEWIS and WILLIAM CLARK carried rifles of this type.
5. A number of the 1795 issue musket, which was carried by some members of the expedition. Of .69 caliber, its smooth bore meant it was less accurate than a rifle, but it could fire either ball or birdshot, an advantage when hunting small game.
6. Clark's squirrel rifle—his so-called Small rifle, which it is now believed referred to its maker, John Small.
7. Trade guns—that is, small, light, smooth-bore muskets for GIFTS or trading. Guns were not normally given to Indians, although an exception was made in the case of the NEZ PERCE, who had been particularly helpful to the expedition.
8. Pistols carried by some members of the party. These were probably the 1799 Model flintlock, which had an 8½-inch barrel and the same .69 caliber as the musket. Lewis also had a pair of pocket pistols, and it is probable that others in the party had these as well.
9. An air rifle.

This last item, made by Isaiah Lukins of Philadelphia, was .31 caliber, had its air reservoir in the stock, and is reported to have achieved a pressure equivalent in power to a light musket charge. This seems an unusual weapon to take on such an enterprise, though it proved useful in demonstrations to Indians, who were impressed by its relative quietness of firing and the fact that no powder was needed. It seems likely, however, that Lewis realized his plan to use rivers wherever possible brought with it the danger of gunpowder becoming wet and useless. If this occurred, the airgun would be his only useable firearm.

Fortunately, this did not happen. All members of the party were fully aware of the need to keep their gunpowder dry, and along with the journals, their weapons and gunpowder were the most carefully protected items. In retrospect, one of the noteworthy facts of the expedition is that its members not only carried enough ammunition and powder to last them through their 28-month journey but managed to bring a good supply back with them.

One factor often overlooked is the ingenious method Lewis employed to carry some of his powder. In addition to the normal barrels and other containers, he had 52 lead canisters made to hold 176 pounds of powder. In addition to keeping the powder dry, the canisters were designed to be melted down for bullets and, equally cleverly, were so made that the weight of lead produced the number of balls the powder inside them would fire.

Further Reading

Ambrose, Stephen E. *Undaunted Courage: Meriwether Lewis, Thomas Jefferson, and the Opening of the American West.* New York: Simon and Schuster, 1996.

Lentz, Gary. "Captain Lewis's Air Rifle." *Washington State Chapter Lewis and Clark Trail Heritage Foundation January 2000 Newsletter.* Available on-line. URL: http://www.lcarchive.org/wa_n0100.html. Downloaded on January 10, 2002.

Lewis & Clark on the Information Superhighway. "Firearms of the Lewis & Clark Expedition." Available on-line. URL: http://www.lcarchive.org/firearms.html. Downloaded on May 20, 2001.

Russell, Carl P. *Firearms, Traps & Tools of the Mountain Men.* Albuquerque: University of New Mexico Press, 1977.

———. "The Guns of the Lewis and Clark Expedition." *North Dakota History* 27 (1960): 25–34.

fish, new species

Although the number of new fish species discovered on the expedition is small compared to the numbers of ANIMALS and BIRDS, the list is still an impressive one. The JOURNALS mention some 31 varieties of fish, but many were already known to the explorers. There is now general agreement among ichthyologists that MERIWETHER LEWIS and WILLIAM CLARK were the first to give scientific descriptions of 12 species, beginning with the channel catfish caught on the MISSOURI RIVER on July 24, 1804.

Lewis was a skilled and observant naturalist, but he had little time for FISHING on the expedition. Luckily, among the SKILLS ON THE EXPEDITION was the fishing expertise of SILAS GOODRICH, whose name is constantly mentioned whenever Lewis describes a new fish in his journals. The entry of July 24, 1804, is typical: "This evening Guthrege caught a White catfish, its eyes small and tale much like that of a Dolfin."

On June 11, 1805, above the mouth of the MARIAS RIVER, Lewis wrote: "Goodrich who is remarkably fond of fishing caught several douzen fish of two species—one about 9 inches long of a white colour, round in form and fins resembling the white chub . . . this fish has a smaller head than the chubb. [This was the northern mooneye] . . . the other species is precisely the form and about the size of the well known hickory shad or oldwife, with the exception of the teeth . . . we have seen none untill we reached that place and took them in the Missouri above its junction with that river. [This was a sauger.]"

East of the ROCKY MOUNTAINS, the expedition can be credited with the discovery or the first detailed description of the channel catfish, the blue catfish, the northern mooneye, the sauger, the cutthroat trout, and the mountain sucker. Once

they crossed the CONTINENTAL DIVIDE and began their journey down to the COLUMBIA RIVER, they were in a country where the salmon was the staple food source.

Although salmon can be found on the East Coast, its range is mainly in the Canadian waters, and neither Lewis nor Clark had ever seen one. When Lewis met Chief CAMEAHWAIT of the SHOSHONE INDIANS on August 13, 1805, the Indian gave him dried cakes of choke cherries, ANTELOPE, and a piece of salmon. Lewis wrote: "This was the first salmon I had seen and perfectly convinced me that we were on the waters of the PACIFIC OCEAN."

At FORT CLATSOP during the winter of 1805–06, Lewis described three of the five salmon species to be found along the Columbia River: the king salmon (which Lewis called the common salmon), the sockeye or blueback salmon, and the silver salmon. Neither he nor Clark mentioned hump-backed or dog salmon. They recorded how the salmon was caught, cooked, dried, preserved, and sold as well as the incredible numbers that came up the Columbia. They also noted that salmon were to be found in the smallest tributaries 1,000 miles upstream.

In common with many observers before and since, Lewis and Clark occasionally became confused by the differences between salmon and trout. On October 24, 1805, beside The Dalles, Lewis noted "a salmon trout of a silvery white colour on the belly and sides, and a bluish light brown on the back and head. . . ." This was the steelhead trout. Two days later Clark noted that a "white salmon trout" fried in bear's oil was the finest fish he had ever tasted. This was the silver or coho salmon.

Lewis exhaustively described the salmon, trout, and other fish he saw along the Columbia, including the starry flounder, the Columbia River chub, the northern squawfish, and the sturgeon. But he and Clark agreed the eulachon was the best-tasting fish of their time in the Pacific Northwest. According to Clark, they were introduced to it on February 24, 1806, by Chief COBOWAY of the CLATSOP INDIANS, who came to Fort Clatsop to sell "a species of small fish which now begin to run, and are taken in great quantities in the Columbia R. about 40 miles above us by means of skimming or scooping nets." He went on to say that the fish were best eaten roasted "on a wooden spit without any previous preparations whatever. They are so fat they require no additional sauce, and I think them quite superior to any fish I ever tasted."

It is not known whether the Clatsop told the captains of the eulachon's other use, which gives it its better known name of candlefish. At the beginning of their run upriver, the eulachon is so fat that, when dried and a wick is drawn through the body, it can be used as a CANDLE. If he had known this, Clark surely would have mentioned it.

The rest of the party shared this appreciation of the eulachon, even though they normally preferred meat to any other diet. On February 25, 1806, PATRICK GASS wrote: "They [Indians] brought us yesterday a number of small fish of a very excellent kind, resembling a herring, and about half the size." The

of small fish which now begin to run an, are
taken in great quantities in the Columbia R.
about 40 miles above us by means of skiming
or scooping nets. on this page I have drawn
the likeness of them as large as life; it
as perfect as I can make it with my
pen and will serve to give a
general idea of the fish. the
rays of the fins are boney but
not sharp tho' somewhat pointed.
the small fin on the back
next to the tail has no
rays of bone being a
bonaceous pellicle.
to the gills have
each. those of the
eight each, those
are 20 and 2
that of the back
the fins are of
is of a bleuish
the the lower
is of a silve=
part. the
behind the
second of
the pieple
a silver
and
like

thin mem
the fins next
eleven rays
abdomen have
of the pinnaani
haff formed in front.
has eleven rays. all
a white colour. the back
duskey colour and that of
part of the sides and belly
ony white. no spots on any
first bone of the gills next
eye is of a bleuis cast, and the
a light gaald colour nearly white
of the eye is black and the iris of
white. the under jaw exceeds the uper;
the mouth opens to great extent, folding
that of the herring. it has no teeth.
the abdomen is obtuse and smooth; in this
differing from the herring, shad anchovy;
&c of the Malacopterygious Order & Class
Clupea

Meriwether Lewis drew this picture of a eulachon, or candlefish. Roasted whole on a spit, the eulachon were "superior to any fish I ever tasted," according to Lewis. *(American Philosophical Society)*

next day he confirmed the eulachon's popularity when he wrote: ". . . three men went in search of those small fish which we had found very good eating."

Further Reading

Burroughs, Raymond Darwin, ed. *The Natural History of the Lewis and Clark Expedition.* East Lansing: Michigan State University Press, 1995.

Cutright, Paul Russell. *Lewis & Clark: Pioneering Naturalists.* Lincoln: University of Nebraska Press/Bison Books, 1989.

Moring, J. R. "Fish Discoveries by the Lewis and Clark and Red River Expeditions." *Fisheries* 21 (July 1996): 6–12.

Fish Creek   See SALMON RIVER.

fishing

Though the expedition combined HUNTING for FOOD with scientific examination of the many ANIMALS and BIRDS they encountered, they made few references to FISH. Without SILAS GOODRICH in their party, it is likely that some of the species of fish MERIWETHER LEWIS described would never have appeared in the JOURNALS. It is difficult to ascertain whether he was responsible for catching all the new species east of the CONTINENTAL DIVIDE that Lewis described, but the journals show he certainly caught three of them.

The men of the expedition were voracious meat eaters, consuming amounts that seem astonishing to modern eyes. WILLIAM CLARK recorded that the corps ate four DEER or one BUFFALO a day, and the other game and birds they killed for food seem to have been shot for the occasional change in diet. Fish also provided some variety.

On August 13, 1804, the party encamped near today's Dakota City, Nebraska, hoping to meet the chiefs of the OMAHA INDIANS. For a week they waited in vain, and, probably to give the men some diversion, Lewis took two parties out fishing. The journals record: "They made a kind of drag with small willows and bark and swept the creek. The first company brought 318 fish, the second upward of 800, consisting of pike, bass, fish resembling salmon-trout, redhorse, buffalo-fish, rock-fish, one flat-back, perch, catfish, a small species of perch called on the Ohio silver-fish, a shrimp of the same size, shape and flavor of those about New Orleans and the lower part of the Mississippi; we also found very fat muscles. . . ." On August 25, 1804, PATRICK GASS wrote: "Two of our men last night caught nine catfish, that would together weigh three hundred pounds. The large catfish are caught in the Missouri with hook an line."

Once the expedition crossed the Continental Divide, fishing became a necessity rather than a diversion. Apart from the SHOSHONE, FLATHEAD, and NEZ PERCE INDIANS who rode east to the GREAT PLAINS to hunt buffalo, the nations whom the expedition met on their way down to the mouth of the COLUMBIA RIVER depended on fish for their staple diet. Though ELK, deer, ducks, and GEESE were to be found in the

forests, the vast number of salmon and other fish who swarmed into the Columbia River and its tributaries formed the basis of life for dozens of nations.

On August 22, 1805, only 10 days after they had crossed over the LEMHI PASS and were making their way along the LEMHI RIVER, Patrick Gass recorded: "Game is scarce and we killed nothing since the 18th but one deer; and our stock of provisions is exhausted." This is presumably the reason Lewis wrote that same day: "late in the evening I made the men form a bush drag, and with it in about 2 hours they caught 528 very good fish, most of them large trout. . . ."

Above the CELILO FALLS AND THE DALLES, the explorers began to appreciate the importance of salmon to the CHINOOK INDIANS in the area. They saw salmon jumping out of the water and could also see them crowded in the water down to depths of 20 feet. Indians lined the banks, catching the fish with spears, with simple scoops, or in fish weirs (traps). As part of their ethnographic studies, Lewis and Clark wrote detailed descriptions and made numerous drawings of the Indians' weirs and gigging (spearing) techniques. Lewis also recorded the Chinook's method of drying and packing salmon. The villages on the riverbanks were packed with fish scaffolds covered in drying fish, while Indian women sat beside vast stacks of newly caught fish, preparing them for drying. Lewis and Clark were astonished to find that timber was in such short supply that Indians were "drying fish & Prickley pares to Burn in winter."

Even though necessity made fish an important part of their diet during the winter at FORT CLATSOP, the party never became reconciled to it. They relied on the elk their hunters could kill and such geese and birds as they could shoot. Not until July 9, 1806, when they had crossed back over the Continental Divide were they able to eat the buffalo meat they had been without for nearly a year.

Further Reading

Burroughs, Raymond Darwin, ed. *The Natural History of the Lewis and Clark Expedition.* East Lansing: Michigan State University Press, 1995.

Cutright, Paul Russell. *Lewis & Clark: Pioneering Naturalists.* Lincoln: University of Nebraska Press/Bison Books, 1989.

Stewart, Hilary. *Indian Fishing: Early Methods on the Northwest Coast.* Seattle: University of Washington Press, 1977.

Flathead Indians (Salish)

The Flathead Indians, also known as Salish (meaning "people"), were originally PLATEAU INDIANS who lived between the CASCADE MOUNTAINS and ROCKY MOUNTAINS in Montana. Their name was a misnomer, since it actually applied to Salishan-speaking nations on the northwest coast who had the custom of flattening the foreheads of babies. The term began to be used for the Salishan speakers in the interior as well. Another reason for the name may have been the Indians' custom of wearing their hair "standing up," cut flat on top.

The Flathead were hunters and fishers who also gathered BITTERROOT, mosses, CAMAS ROOT, wild onions, and Indian

Originally Plateau Indians, the Flathead, or Salish, moved onto the Great Plains after acquiring horses and adopting the ways of the Plains Indians, including the use of portable tipis. Lewis and Clark met a large band of Flathead in September 1805. These Salish women were photographed ca. 1910. *(Library of Congress, Prints and Photographs Division [LC-USZ62-100822])*

potatoes. In late summer and fall, the men hunted ELK, DEER, and small game. During the winter they trapped animals and used the food that they had stored over the summer. In these cold months they lived in permanent lodges built of cedar planks and beams, while in the summer they built small shacks made of straw mats to be used wherever they were FISHING or gathering.

Around 1730 the Flathead acquired HORSES, probably from the Spanish. With these they could hunt BUFFALO on the GREAT PLAINS, and many moved east for this purpose, adopting some of the customs of the PLAINS INDIANS, including the use of portable TIPIS. However, in the early 1800s they were driven into western Montana by their enemies, the BLACKFEET INDIANS. As a defensive measure, they frequently joined forces with the Shoshone on buffalo hunts. It was while they were on their way to do this that a large band of Flathead met the Lewis and Clark Expedition in September 1805.

Prior to their trek across the BITTERROOT MOUNTAINS, the CORPS OF DISCOVERY met a band of Flathead at the site that is now ROSS'S HOLE on September 4. WILLIAM CLARK's journal noted that these Flathead consisted of 33 lodges, 440

people, and 500 horses. Their speech was so guttural as to cause MERIWETHER LEWIS to wonder if they might be descendants of the fabled WELSH INDIANS. A Shoshone boy who lived with the band entered the INTERPRETATION process, and a deal was soon transacted wherein the captains bought 13 horses from the Flathead and traded some of sadder models they had obtained from the Shoshone for better horses. Despite having few provisions of their own, the Flathead also shared roots and berries with the corps, leading Private JOSEPH WHITEHOUSE to write that they were "the likelyest and honestst Savages we have ever yet Seen." On September 6, while the Flathead rode east to join the SHOSHONE INDIANS for their annual BUFFALO hunt, the corps rode northward along the BITTERROOT RIVER. Ahead of them lay TRAVELERS' REST and the LOLO TRAIL.

Peace between the Flathead and the Blackfeet did not come about until the mid-1840s. In 1855 the Flathead ceded most of their lands in Montana and Idaho to the U.S. government. After losing even more land in 1872, what remained became the Flathead Reservation, located near Dixon, Montana. About 4,000 members of the Confederated Salish and

ly live on the reservation, while another

dians. Norman: University of Oklahoma

_____. Lewis and Clark Among the Sayleesh Indians: Ross Hole, September 4–5, 1805." *Northwest Discovery* 7, no. 32–33 (1987): 126–246.

Ronda, James P. *Lewis and Clark among the Indians.* Lincoln and London: University of Nebraska Press, 1984.

Waldman, Carl. *Encyclopedia of Native American Tribes.* Revised ed. New York: Checkmark Books, 1999.

Flathead River   See LOCHSA RIVER.

fleas   See INSECTS.

Floyd, Charles (1782–1804) *sergeant in the permanent party*

The only member of the CORPS OF DISCOVERY to die during the expedition, Sergeant Charles Floyd was also one of the NINE YOUNG MEN FROM KENTUCKY. He was born on the frontier near Louisville, Kentucky, the son of Captain Charles Floyd, who had served with General GEORGE ROGERS CLARK. Floyd and his family lived near Clark's younger brother, WILLIAM CLARK, and some sources indicate he was possibly related to the Clarks. He was also a cousin of NATHANIEL PRYOR.

Floyd was one of the first to enlist in the CORPS OF DISCOVERY, joining on August 1, 1803, along with JOSEPH FIELD and REUBIN FIELD; this was well ahead of the other "nine young men," who were not officially enlisted until October. Captain Clark considered Floyd to be a "man of much merit" and assigned him to command one of the expedition's three squads of men. At CAMP DUBOIS, the sergeant was placed in charge of the officer's quarters and supplies.

Like several other members of the expedition, Floyd maintained a journal, replete with spelling errors. He started his on May 14, 1804, when the corps set out from Camp Dubois. He seldom if ever mentioned his companions on the expedition. Instead, his journal focused on the surrounding geography and scenery and occasionally on events. He paid particular attention to topography and soil conditions. However, on July 31 he wrote, "I am verry Sick and Has ben for somtime but have Recoverd my helth again."

Not long afterward, Floyd was again showing signs of illness. His last journal entry, on August 18 (MERIWETHER LEWIS's birthday), reported that the expedition had been visited by the grand chief of the OTOE INDIANS (Oto). Clark, meanwhile, wrote in his own journal that Floyd was "dangerously ill." Two days later, wracked with pain, Floyd told Clark that he

was "going away" and asked the captain to write to his family. He died shortly after noon on August 20; Clark noted that he passed away "with a great deal of composure." Although Lewis and Clark attributed his death to a "bilious colic," historians now generally agree that Floyd had probably suffered a ruptured appendix and died of the resulting peritonitis. Clark wrote in tribute: "This man at all times gave us proofs of his firmness and determined resolution to doe service to his country and honor to himself." Following Floyd's death, PATRICK GASS was elected to replace him as sergeant.

Charles Floyd was buried on a bluff by a river, both of which were named for him; Floyd's River has retained its name to this day. His comrades also erected a small cedar post with his name and death date as a marker. In September 1806, during the expedition's return journey, they stopped by his gravesite, which had become partly uncovered. The grave was cleaned up and the marker replaced before the corps moved on. In later years the town of Sergeant Bluff would rise nearby.

In 1857 it was realized that erosion from the river had eaten into the bluff, and as a result some of Floyd's remains were lost; his skull was found by the river's shore. What was left was disinterred and reburied about 600 feet away from the original site, on a high bluff in Sioux City. After his journal was published in 1894, curiosity seekers flocked to Floyd's Bluff, trampling the grave and stealing its wooden markers. He was again reburied, this time on August 20, 1895, and a marble slab was placed on the site. This eventually gave way to a 100-foot-high sandstone obelisk, begun in August 1900 and completed in May 1901. His remains were then moved for the fourth time, to the base of the monument. The first National Registered Landmark in the United States, this monument is also the largest marker erected to any member of the expedition—ironic, since Charles Floyd had traveled the shortest distance of them all.

There is a touching postscript. William Clark had kept Floyd's pipe tomahawk to return to his parents. It traveled through the ROCKY MOUNTAINS but was stolen by a WATLALA Indian on November 4, 1805, on the COLUMBIA RIVER. On April 9, 1806, during the return journey, JOHN COLTER found it in one of the Indians' lodges. One can only hope that the tomahawk was indeed returned to Floyd's parents, having made the journey that their son was unable to make.

Further Reading

Butler, James Davie, ed. *The New Found Journal of Charles Floyd, a sergeant under Captains Lewis and Clark.* Worcester, Mass.: Press of Charles Hamilton, 1894.

Everley, Steve. "Web Site Dedicated to the History and Memory of Sgt. Charles Floyd 1782–1804." Available on-line. URL: http://www.sgtfloyd.com/default.htm. Updated on October 2, 2001.

Moulton, Gary, ed. *The Journals of the Lewis and Clark Expedition: The Journals of John Ordway, May 14, 1804–September 23, 1806, and Charles Floyd, May 14–August 18, 1804.* Lincoln: University of Nebraska Press, 1996.

PBS Online. *Lewis and Clark: Inside the Corps of Discovery:* "Sergeant Charles Floyd." Available on-line. URL: http://www.pbs.org/ lewisandclark/inside/cfloy.html. Downloaded on May 18, 2001.

Thwaites, Reuben G., ed. *Original Journals of the Lewis and Clark Expedition, 1804–1806; . . . and the journals of Joseph Whitehouse and Charles Floyd.* New York: Dodd, Mead, 1904–05.

Floyd's Bluff   See FLOYD, CHARLES.

food

One of the many risks faced by the CORPS OF DISCOVERY during their epic journey was a shortage of food. As frontiersmen, they knew that game would be plentiful along much of their journey and that their rifles would provide fresh meat. However, in his PREPARATIONS FOR THE EXPEDITION, MERIWETHER LEWIS made provision for game being scarce or unavailable in some areas. Thus, when the expedition set off up the MISSOURI RIVER in May 1804, they carried some fresh food on the KEELBOAT as well as an estimated seven tons of nonperishable staples. These included 20 barrels of flour, 14 barrels of parched corn meal, sugar, coffee, salt, preserved dried apples, lard, biscuits, and 193 pounds of the dried portable soup that Lewis had purchased in PHILADELPHIA. (See SOUP, PORTABLE.) They also had a large supply of a mixture of lard, deer tallow, and bear fat, called voyagers grease.

While carrying these stores upriver must have been tedious, the party were glad of the provisions whenever game for HUNTING was scarce—as, for example, when they reached the CONTINENTAL DIVIDE. After Lewis, GEORGE DROUILLARD, JOHN SHIELDS, and HUGH MCNEAL made their way over LEMHI PASS on August 12, 1805, Lewis noted, "As we had killed nothing during the day we now boiled and eat the remainder of our pork, having yet a little flour and parched meal." Three days later, in the company of SHOSHONE chief CAMEAHWAIT, Lewis told McNeal to divide the last two pounds of flour and to cook one-half mixed with berries. "On this new fashioned pudding four of us breakfasted, giving a pretty good allowance also to the Chief who declared it the best thing had tasted for a long time."

As well as hunting, the expedition came to depend on FISHING, the generosity of the Indians they met, and the skills of SACAGAWEA, who found edible roots and plants of which the party had no previous knowledge. However, corps members greatly preferred fresh meat; each man consumed about eight pounds of meat a day, and Clark reported, "It requires 4 deer, or an elk and a deer, or one buffalow to supply us for 24 hours." On the GREAT PLAINS they found an abundance of ELK, DEER, ANTELOPE, GROUSE, and other game. Roasted BEAVER tail became a special treat, and when there was BUFFALO to be found, it could provide up to nine pounds of meat per man each day. Over the course of the expedition, they also tried bighorn SHEEP, BEAR, raccoon, coyote, jackrabbit, and PRAIRIE DOG. Variations in the menu were often tried, and some men took turns as cook. TOUSSAINT CHARBONNEAU impressed the corps with a dish he called *boudin blanc*—stuffed buffalo intestine. Lewis himself once made suet dumplings from boiled buffalo meat as a way to reward the men. No part of an animal was wasted, and whatever could not be used for food and CLOTHING was rendered in some other way—turned into mosquito repellent or CANDLES, for instance.

FISH was also eaten, both fresh and dried, and over time the corps consumed a tremendous variety, including catfish, trout, sturgeon, and salmon. The eulachon, or candlefish, was especially delicious, with Lewis reporting, "I think them superior to any fish I ever tasted." On the west coast, the men even tried whale blubber.

Sometimes, however, the corps had to resort to other sources of meat, including DOGS. While this may seem barbaric today, frontiersmen of that time frequently feasted on dog meat, and on occasion the corps refused Indian offers of roots and berries in favor of roasting a dog. While most corps members enjoyed it—Lewis called it "an agreeable food"—Clark was one who did not, writing, "I have not become reconciled to the taste of this animal as yet."

HORSES, too, were consumed when necessary; three were killed and eaten during the onerous crossing of the BITTERROOT MOUNTAINS in September 1805. The men found fresh meat to be equally scarce when they at last descended to WEIPPE PRAIRIE and found no herds of elk or buffalo.

It was on occasions like this that Indians often came to their rescue, although not always with happy results. NEZ PERCE INDIANS fed the starving strangers upon the corps's arrival on the western slopes of the Bitterroots, but all they could offer were roots and dried fish, a change of diet that caused severe health problems for the soldiers. Roots were often offered to the explorers. The BITTERROOT lived up to its name—Lewis found it "naucious to my palate"—but the CAMAS ROOT was quite edible. More often than not, the food they were given was enough to satisfy the men's hunger or at the very least to give them new taste sensations. In addition to several different kinds of roots, they ate berries, beans, dried squash, hominy, and seedcakes. Among the foods Sacagawea was able to find were onions, currants, and wild licorice.

When the corps arrived at the COLUMBIA RIVER basin, hunting parties obtained bear, deer, and elk for meat. Elk in particular became a staple of the diet at FORT CLATSOP. For breakfast, lunch, and dinner, it was eaten roasted, boiled, dried, and jerked. Throughout the winter of 1805–06, 128 elk and 18 deer were killed. Yet despite these numbers, there was never enough to feed all the men, and as the winter wore on, the hunters needed to travel further from the fort to find fresh game. The corps consequently tried to avert hunger by procuring dried fish, roots, and dogs from the CLATSOP INDIANS.

Little enamored of their Oregon camp and its limited winter menu, the expedition departed Fort Clatsop on March 24, 1806. Food soon became even more scarce, and in June they threw themselves into an early, hungry crossing of the snowbound Bitterroots. Although it was a quicker trip (by a few days) than the westbound crossing, Clark reported in his journal that they "descended the mountain to Travellers' Rest leaving these tremendous mountains behind us, in passing of which we have experienced cold and hunger of which I shall ever remember." Thereafter, as the corps moved back into the Great Plains with its abundance of fresh game, they fared much better. By the end of their journey they had eaten a variety of meats, fish, roots, berries, and fruits, much of which had never before been consumed by non-Indians.

Further Reading

Burroughs, Raymond Darwin, ed. *The Natural History of the Lewis and Clark Expedition.* East Lansing: Michigan State University Press, 1995.

Duncan, Dayton and Ken Burns. *Lewis & Clark: The Journey of the Corps of Discovery.* New York: Alfred A. Knopf, 1998.

Furtwangler, Albert. *Acts of Discovery: Visions of America in the Lewis and Clark Journals.* Urbana: University of Illinois Press, 1993.

Hawke, David Freeman. *Those Tremendous Mountains: The Story of the Lewis and Clark Expedition.* New York: W. W. Norton & Company, 1998.

Jefferson National Expansion Memorial. "The Lewis and Clark Journey of Discovery: Food." Available on-line. URL: http://www.nps.gov/jeff/LewisClark2/CorpsOfDiscovery/Preparing/Food/Food.htm. Downloaded on April 11, 2002.

Stein, Joel. "Have You Ever Tried Ashcakes?" *Time* (July 8, 2002): 74–76. Available on-line. URL: http://www.time.com/time/2002/lewis_clark/lcuisine.html. Downloaded on July 11, 2002.

Fort Clatsop

In November 1805 the CORPS OF DISCOVERY reached the estuary of the COLUMBIA RIVER after a journey of more than 4,100 miles from their starting point, CAMP DUBOIS. Suffering from unpleasant WEATHER conditions, they followed the northern bank of the river to a site on the eastern side of POINT ELLICE and spent a miserable week there before moving on to present-day Baker Bay, where they established STATION CAMP. While the corps was encamped on the north side of the river, MERIWETHER LEWIS and WILLIAM CLARK led separate exploratory parties along the coastline of the PACIFIC OCEAN and visited CAPE DISAPPOINTMENT. After determining that there were no trading ships in the area that might take all or part of the expedition back to the East Coast, on November 24 the captains held a vote on where the expedition should camp for the winter. A majority of the corps voted for the south bank of the estuary, and consequently they left Station Camp the following day in search of their new campsite. After working their way back along the north bank of the Columbia, they crossed to the south bank, and at last, on December 7, they arrived at the site where they would build Fort Clatsop. The new campsite was located two miles up what is now the Lewis and Clark River and some four miles southwest of today's Astoria, Oregon.

Clark called the chosen site "certainly the most eligible Situation for our purpose of any in its neighborhood." In contrast to their previous winter home, FORT MANDAN, which had stood in a mainly treeless prairie, Fort Clatsop was built in the middle of a dense forest of giant evergreen trees, 300 yards back from the river and 30 feet above high tide. At Fort Mandan they had experienced a dry, biting cold. Here the constant element was rain.

While Sergeant PATRICK GASS, a carpenter, planned and supervised the clearing of the ground and the felling of timber for the fort, Clark took a group south to find a site for a SALT-WORKS. The foundations were dug on December 10, and by the 12th Gass was able to write: "We finished 3 of our cabins, all but the covering; which I expect will be a difficult part of the business, as we have not yet found any timber which splits well; two men went out to make some boards, if possible for our roofs."

On the 14th he had better news to report: "We finished the building of our huts, 7 in number, all but the covering, which I now find will not be so difficult as I expected; as we have found a kind of timber in plenty, which splits freely and makes the finest puncheons I have ever seen. They can be split 10 feet long and 2 broad, not more than an inch and a half thick." (This was either Douglas fir or Sitka spruce.)

By December 24 all the huts were covered, and the party moved into its new accommodation on Christmas Day. Because of problems with smoke, more work was needed on the chimneys, and not until December 30 was Gass able to report, "This evening we completely finished our fortification."

From a sketch in Clark's notebook, it is known that the fort comprised two long buildings facing each other, each 50 feet long and 15 wide. One was divided into three rooms for the sergeants and the men. The other consisted of four rooms, one for TOUSSAINT CHARBONNEAU, SACAGAWEA, and their baby (JEAN BAPTISTE CHARBONNEAU), the next for Lewis and Clark, a third for York and an orderly, and the fourth to be used as a storeroom. Two palisades filled the gap at each end, with a gate in one of them.

The winter was an uncomfortable one. The constant rain and damp meant wood was permanently wet, which meant in turn that cooking and curing meat was difficult. The chimneys smoked badly, and to their irritation the expedition found, even on January 1, 1806, that "the ticks, flies and other INSECTS are in abundance, which appears to us very extraordinary at this season of the year." The situation was not helped by the fleas visiting Indians brought with them. Clark wrote that the party had to "kill them out of their blankets every day."

The expedition seemed to have regarded their stay at Fort Clatsop with a mixture of resigned acceptance and exasperation. FOOD was sometimes short but was always available in some form, whether it was the perpetual ELK, which was the only game available, or the FISH and BIRDS with which they varied their diet. They exhausted their stock of CANDLES but found elk tallow answered the purpose well enough.

Relations with the CLATSOP INDIANS nearby were friendly, though never approaching the close relations that had been enjoyed with the MANDAN INDIANS. There were enough sexual liaisons with the local Indian women for the captains to be concerned about attacks of venereal disease among the men. Lewis, meanwhile, used the long winter at Fort Clatsop to write up long and detailed notes on the flora and fauna he and Clark had observed on the journey west as well as those in the immediate vicinity.

The expedition left the fort without regret on March 23, 1806. Clark summed up their stay: "At this place we wintered and remained from the 7th of Decr. 1805 to this day and have lived as well as we had any right to expect, and we can say that we were never one day without 3 meals of some kind a day either pore elk meat or roots, notwithstanding the repeated fall of rain which has fallen almost constantly." (Of the 141 days spent at Fort Clatsop, only 12 were without rain, and of these only six had clear skies.)

When Lewis and Clark left Fort Clatsop, they posted a list of the members of the expedition in one of the huts and presented the fort as a gift to the Clatsop chief COBOWAY. It is understood the chief and his family lived there for some time, and in 1899 his grandson led historians to the site. A reproduction, the Fort Clatsop National Memorial, has been built beside the original site.

Further Reading

Ambrose, Stephen E. *Undaunted Courage: Meriwether Lewis, Thomas Jefferson, and the Opening of the American West.* New York: Simon and Schuster, 1996.

Cutright, Paul Russell. *Lewis & Clark: Pioneering Naturalists.* Lincoln: University of Nebraska Press/Bison Books, 1989.

Henrikson, Stephen E. "This Place of Encampment." *American History Illustrated* 20, no. 5 (1985): 22–33.

MacGregor, Carol Lynn, ed. *The Journals of Patrick Gass, Member of the Lewis and Clark Expedition.* Missoula, Mont.: Mountain Press Publishing Company, 1997.

Rasmussen, Jay. "Report on the 1997 Archaeological Excavations at Fort Clatsop." *Lewis and Clark on the Information Superhighway.* Available on-line. URL: http://www.lcarchive.org/fcexcav.html. Downloaded on February 10, 2002.

Ronda, James P. *Lewis and Clark among the Indians.* Lincoln: University of Nebraska Press, 1984.

Fort Kaskaskia   See KASKASKIA.

Fort Mandan

On November 3, 1804, WILLIAM CLARK wrote in his journal: "We commence building our cabins." This was the start of Fort Mandan, which was to be the expedition's home from then

This illustration from the 1810 edition of Patrick Gass's journal shows Captain Clark and his men building a line of huts at Fort Mandan. *(Library of Congress, Prints and Photographs Division [LC-USZ62-19230])*

until April 7, 1805—the longest stay at any of their three winter posts.

The CORPS OF DISCOVERY had arrived at the villages of the MANDAN INDIANS on October 25, 1804. The Mandan and the HIDATSA INDIANS lived near the junction of the MISSOURI RIVER and KNIFE RIVER, north of today's Bismarck, North Dakota. The onset of winter and the friendly reception the corps received from the Mandan chief BIG WHITE prompted the captains to set up camp on the north bank of the Missouri, across the river from the chief's village and some seven miles downstream of today's Stanton, North Dakota. Further up the Missouri lay the other Mandan village, while the three Hidatsa villages lined the banks of the Knife River.

Construction began the day before Clark's journal entry, November 2, with Sergeant PATRICK GASS, the expedition's carpenter, planning and supervising the work. Using the cottonwood and elm TREES in the area for their lumber, Gass and his men built two long huts, coming together at an angle at one end. The open end was protected by a stockade so that the completed fort formed a triangle. Each hut had four rooms and a sloping roof. A ceiling of planks inserted at a height of seven feet was covered with grass and clay for insulation in addition to providing storage space below the roof.

By November 12 ice was forming on the Missouri, and the corps moved into the unfinished buildings. The expedition's JOURNALS record that the huts were finished on November 20. Gass, however, reported that the roofs were not finished until a week later. On December 1 he wrote that they had begun to cut and carry pickets "to complete our fort"—that is, the stockade across the open angle. The stockade was not completed until Christmas Eve, probably due to the difficulty in digging the posts into the frozen ground.

Gass had clearly been right to insert insulation in the roof. By December 7 the river had frozen, and the thermometer registered below zero. The next day it dropped another 10 degrees, and several cases of frostbite were reported. On December 17 the journals noted WEATHER "colder than any we had yet experienced, the thermometer at sunrise being 45 degrees below zero." The captains ordered that the sentry be relieved every 30 minutes.

Apart from the cold, the stay at Fort Mandan was a happy one. There were constant and friendly visits from and with the Mandan; the soldiers went to dances and feasts in the villages, sometimes staying all night. The party's hunters went out with the Indians to kill BUFFALO and DEER, and from the Mandan, the Hidatsa, and other Indians the captains learned much about the geography and Indians in the country ahead of them. FOOD was in short supply, but JOHN SHIELDS's skills as a blacksmith brought in CORN from Indians for whom he made tools and axes. Even pieces of sheet-iron from an old stove proved of value. Shaped and sharpened into small squares for scraping hides, each piece was traded for eight bushels of corn.

At the end of February 1805, the party found cottonwood trees suitable for CANOES, and Gass supervised their construction. March saw them collecting provisions and making preparations for their journey. On April 7, having seen the KEELBOAT set off back to ST. LOUIS, the expedition set off upstream with the two PIROGUES and six canoes. They had come 1,900 miles; they still had more than 2,000 miles to go before they reached the PACIFIC OCEAN.

The corps returned to Fort Mandan 16 months later, on August 14, 1806, and spent three days with the Mandan, though not at their old fort. JOHN COLTER, TOUSSAINT CHARBONNEAU, and SACAGAWEA left them here, and Chief Big White agreed to accompany them to visit THOMAS JEFFERSON in Washington. They left the villages on August 17 with a short pause at the fort—"the old works"—but much of it had been burnt down.

The site of Fort Mandan has long since been swept away by a change in the course of the Missouri. A reproduction has been built about 12 miles downstream, on the north bank, just west of present-day Washburn, North Dakota.

Further Reading

Hawke, David Freeman. *Those Tremendous Mountains: The Story of the Lewis and Clark Expedition.* New York: W. W. Norton & Company, 1998.

Large, Arlen. "Fort Mandan's Dancing Longitude." *We Proceeded On* 13, no. 1 (February 1987).

MacGregor, Carol Lynn, ed. *The Journals of Patrick Gass, Member of the Lewis and Clark Expedition.* Missoula, Mont.: Mountain Press Publishing Company, 1997.

Rogers, Ken. "Fort Mandan Winter: on the banks of a river of ice." *The Bismarck Tribune.* Available on-line. URL: http://www.ndonline.com/tribwebpage/features/lewisclark/2001/winter.html. Downloaded on January 29, 2002.

Ronda, James P. *Lewis and Clark among the Indians.* Lincoln: University of Nebraska Press, 1984.

———. "A Most Perfect Harmony: Life at Fort Mandan." *We Proceeded On* 14, no. 4 (February 1987).

Woolworth, Alan R. "New Light on Fort Mandan: A Wintering Post of the Lewis and Clark Expedition to the Pacific, 1804–1806." *North Dakota History* 55, no. 3 (1988): 3–13.

Fort Massac

On July 2, 1803, as MERIWETHER LEWIS was about to depart for the West, Secretary of War HENRY DEARBORN gave him an authorization to recruit up to 12 men from the army posts at Forts Massac and KASKASKIA. With this in hand, he set out from PITTSBURGH on August 31, 1803, traveling down the OHIO RIVER with the KEELBOAT and one PIROGUE. It was to be more than two months before he reached the first of the forts, at Massac, Illinois.

Fort Massac stands on the Ohio River a few miles downstream from the point where the Tennessee River enters from Kentucky. FRANCE had built a small wooden fort there in 1757, but it was burned down by Chickasaw Indians after the French and Indian War (1754–63). Although it then passed into British possession, it was not rebuilt or garrisoned by them. It is believed that General GEORGE ROGERS CLARK raised the first American flag in Illinois when he landed at the site with his men in 1778. In 1794 President George Washington ordered the fort to be rebuilt, and this was the one Lewis came to in 1803.

On giving Lewis the authorization to recruit men at Massac and Kaskaskia, Secretary Dearborn also sent letters to the commanding officers of both garrisons to reinforce the point. Realizing that no officer likes to lose good men, he left them in no doubt as to what was required: "If any [man] in your Company should be disposed to join Capt. Lewis . . . you will detach them accordingly."

Lewis had already begun to recruit members of the expedition in Pittsburgh, where the keelboat was built. In addition to a pilot for the boat, he had been given seven soldiers from the army post at Carlisle, Pennsylvania, to take it down the Ohio and then up the MISSISSIPPI RIVER to ST. LOUIS. They were then to be detached and sent down the Mississippi to Fort Adams. He also brought with him from Pittsburgh three young volunteers whom he allowed to travel with the party on a trial basis; two of these are believed to have been JOHN COLTER and GEORGE SHANNON.

The keelboat and two pirogues arrived at CLARKSVILLE on October 15, where WILLIAM CLARK awaited them with seven volunteers he had selected. The seven, along with Colter and Shannon, were then officially sworn in as soldiers. These became known as the NINE YOUNG MEN FROM KENTUCKY. Leaving Clarksville on October 26, 1803, the group moved downriver to Fort Massac, arriving there on November 11.

Lewis had been expecting to receive from Captain Daniel Bissell eight soldiers who had volunteered to join from South West Point, an army post on the Clinch River, near Knoxville, Tennessee, but they had not arrived. Lewis therefore hired GEORGE DROUILLARD, then employed as interpreter, to go and collect them and bring them to St. Louis. He then interviewed volunteers from the company at Fort Massac and selected two: JOSEPH WHITEHOUSE and JOHN NEWMAN. On November 13 the party left Fort Massac to fight their way upstream against the Mississippi current to Kaskaskia.

Fort Massac remained an army garrison until 1861. In 1903 it was decided the site should be preserved, and 22 acres were purchased to form Illinois's first state park. A reconstruction of the fort was completed in 1973.

See also RECRUITING.

Further Reading
Ambrose, Stephen E. *Undaunted Courage: Meriwether Lewis, Thomas Jefferson, and the Opening of the American West.* New York: Simon and Schuster, 1996.
Illinois Department of Natural Resources. "Fort Massac History: Chronology." Available on-line. URL: http://dnr.state.il.us/lands/landmgt/PARKS/R5/from_history.htm. Available on-line. Downloaded on January 26, 2002.

Fort Mountain (Square Butte)
On July 15, 1805, the CORPS OF DISCOVERY had just completed its long, weary PORTAGE around the GREAT FALLS and were following the MISSOURI RIVER southwest. MERIWETHER LEWIS, walking ahead on the south bank with two of his men, came to the mouth of what he named Smith's River (today's Smith River), after Secretary of the Navy Robert Smith.

Looking northwest across the Missouri, Lewis was able to admire the dramatic rocky outcrop he had first seen a month before from the other side of the Great Falls. The volcanic tower of rock reared some 700 feet up from the prairie floor and, with its flat top, resembled a fortress. Because of its appearance, Lewis named it Fort Mountain. Today this rock tower is called Square Butte. It stands a few miles west of present-day Ulm, Montana.

Further Reading
Ambrose, Stephen E. *Undaunted Courage: Meriwether Lewis, Thomas Jefferson, and the Opening of the American West.* New York: Simon and Schuster, 1996.
Fifer, Barbara, and Vicky Soderberg. *Along the Trail with Lewis and Clark.* Great Falls, Mont.: Montana Magazine, 1998.

Fort Rock Camp
Late in October 1805, the CORPS OF DISCOVERY made their way down the COLUMBIA RIVER, passing CELILO FALLS and running their CANOES through the river's Short Narrows and then the Long Narrows. (These three features were submerged by the erection of the Dalles Dam in 1957.) On the evening of October 25, they set up camp by a rock, named Fort Rock, where the Mill Creek joins the Columbia at the present-day city of The Dalles, Oregon. Here they stayed for two days to repair their canoes and dry out their baggage.

On their first day at the site, the hunters brought in six DEER and some squirrels, and the party was visited by two chiefs from neighboring Indian fishing villages. MERIWETHER LEWIS and WILLIAM CLARK received them formally and gave out medals they carried for such occasions. That night they entertained the Indians, with PIERRE CRUZATTE playing his fiddle as YORK danced.

The following day, October 27, the wind was still blowing strongly from the west, so the corps took advantage of it to spend another day at the site and kill more game. On the 28th they left Fort Rock Camp to make their way downstream to the PACIFIC OCEAN.

Nearly six months later, on their return journey from FORT CLATSOP, the expedition reached their old camp site. Sergeant PATRICK GASS wrote: "About three o'clock in the afternoon we came to Rock Camp where we stayed two days as we went down. Some hunters went out in the evening and killed a deer."

While the site had been a layover to rest and hunt on their way downstream, this second stop on their way back had a more serious purpose. The captains knew from their westward journey how difficult it would be to travel upstream by canoe and were anxious to procure HORSES, enabling them to travel by land to the NEZ PERCE INDIANS and the mountains ahead of them. They had already tried to obtain horses two days previously but with no success. Now Clark crossed the river to try again while Lewis remained with the main party at Fort Rock Camp, preparing pack saddles.

It took Clark three days to persuade the SKILLOOT and Eneeshur Indians to part with five horses, and it was with this small number that the expedition left the camp on April 18. They still had to travel by water, but at least this time they had horses to carry some of the baggage over the long portages.

As the MANDAN INDIAN villages were for the upper MISSOURI RIVER area, the fishing villages beside this area of the Columbia River were the center of an extensive Pacific–Plateau trading system where the dried fish of the Columbia was bartered with upcountry Indian nations for other foods, furs, and TRADE goods. The site of Fort Rock Camp was on the borders of two tribal groupings. The physical barriers of the Celilo Falls and the Short and Long Narrows divided the Chinookan nations of the coast, a fish-eating people who traveled on foot or by canoe, from the Sahaptian speakers upriver who traveled on horseback. A short note by Patrick Gass the day before the corps reached their old camp makes the point: "[April 14, 1806] At 10 o'clock we continued our voyage, and at 1 came to a new settlement of the natives on the north side, where we saw some horses, the first we have seen since October last."

Further Reading

MacGregor, Carol Lynn, ed. *The Journals of Patrick Gass, Member of the Lewis and Clark Expedition.* Missoula, Mont.: Mountain Press Publishing Company, 1997.

Ronda, James P. *Lewis and Clark among the Indians.* Lincoln: University of Nebraska Press, 1984.

foxes

Most books on the natural history of the expedition separate the types of fox seen by MERIWETHER LEWIS and WILLIAM CLARK into two species: the kit fox and the red fox, or bushy-tailed fox. On July 6, 1805, near the GREAT FALLS, Lewis noted that the party had been unable to catch "a remarkable small fox which associate in large communities and burrow in the prairies something like the small wolf." Two days later Clark managed to kill one, and Lewis noted its resemblance to "the common small fox of this country commonly called the kit fox." During the return journey a year later, on July 26, 1806, Lewis again commented on the kit fox: "It is about the size of the domestic cat and burrows in the ground."

The classification of the other fox noted by the expedition has been the subject of discussion among scientists for years. Lewis called it simply "the Red Fox," although it is sometimes called the bushy-tailed fox. During the winter of 1805–06 at FORT CLATSOP, he wrote: "The common red fox or gray fox of the United States is also found in the woody country on this coast nor does it appear to be altered in respect to its fur colour or any other particular." However, he also noted, "Of the foxes, we have seen several species." He then listed several types or subspecies: the large red fox of the plains, the common red fox, the black fox (which he stated was an expert in climbing, capable of chasing raccoon from tree to tree), and the silver fox, which, Lewis stated, "is an animal very rare, even in the country he inhabits" and that he had "never seen more than the Skins of this anamal."

While naturalists today classify all these, except for the kit fox, as one species, it was believed until recently that Lewis was right in his general belief that there were three main subspecies: the red fox, the silver fox, and the cross fox, which is intermediate between the other two. Red-fox skins were among the ARTIFACTS AND SPECIMENS sent back to President THOMAS JEFFERSON in spring 1805.

Further Reading

Burroughs, Raymond Darwin, ed. *The Natural History of the Lewis and Clark Expedition.* East Lansing: Michigan State University Press, 1995.

Cutright, Paul Russell. *Lewis & Clark: Pioneering Naturalists.* Lincoln: University of Nebraska Press/Bison Books, 1989.

Washington State University. "Lewis and Clark Among the Indians of the Pacific Northwest. Excerpts from the Journals of the Expedition of the Corps of Discovery: Flora and Fauna (recorded at Fort Clatsop)." Available on-line. URL: http://www.libarts.wsu.edu/history/Lewis_Clark/LCEXP_Flor.html. Downloaded on May 20, 2001.

France

The relationship between the United States and France at the time of the Lewis and Clark Expedition was a complicated one. When THOMAS JEFFERSON was born in 1743, the French were considered a hostile power whose land holdings surrounded the British colonies in North America. To the north, CANADA, though thinly settled, was firmly held by the French, and the vast basin of the MISSISSIPPI RIVER, called Louisiana, had been claimed for France by explorer René Robert de La Salle. To the south, French New Orleans, founded in 1718, controlled the traffic and TRADE from the American hinterland into the Gulf of Mexico. In the Caribbean, France had sufficient islands under its control to base ships and soldiers there.

At the end of the French and Indian War (1754–63), France was no longer a major threat, having lost Canada and then ceding the vast LOUISIANA TERRITORY to SPAIN in 1769. The American Revolution then saw France as an American ally, as it provided money, weapons, ships, and soldiers to help the colonies achieve independence from GREAT BRITAIN. The result of this French-American alliance was that the news of the French Revolution of 1789 was greeted with fervent enthusiasm by many U.S. citizens. To them the upheaval in France, which was to plunge the whole of Europe into war for 26 years, was the logical result of the example the Americans had set in throwing off despotism.

As the excesses of the French revolutionaries became more widely known, however, some began to view it with deepening concern. Jefferson, strongly pro-French in sympathy, was forced to moderate his views, especially when the European war meant that both French and British ships attacked and captured neutral U.S. vessels. However, it should be noted that when American ships were captured by Royal Navy vessels, the British government paid compensation. The French government saw no need to do so.

The result was that the United States began to build a navy, and in 1799, four engagements were fought with French naval ships, of which two were captured. Further, Britain and the United States came to an agreement during this undeclared war that is often forgotten. Under the terms of this agreement, the Royal Navy protected U.S. merchant ships on transatlantic crossings, while the U.S. Navy gave similar protection to British ships in the Gulf of Mexico.

In addition, the Americans learned of French plans to restore its old empire in North America. France's minister to the United States, Edmund Genêt, had already stirred up a number of intrigues, including a plan to foment rebellion against Spain among the settlers of the Mississippi valley that brought an abrupt end to the western exploration of French botanist ANDRÉ MICHAUX in 1793. Furthermore, a French general traveled down the Mississippi selecting sites for forts, and French Canadians were encouraged to take up arms. Additional fears of French expansion were aroused when, thwarted from an eastern empire by the Battle of the Nile in 1798, Napoleon Bonaparte sent a force to Hispaniola (the island that now contains Haiti and the Dominican Republic) in the Caribbean to suppress the republic there in 1801.

Even Jefferson, Francophile though he was, saw the possible consequences of a French army in New Orleans, which, with the rest of Louisiana, had been ceded by Spain back to France in 1800. Reluctantly, he came to the conclusion that such an event would necessitate joining Britain in fighting France. As George Washington had pointed out, it was sometimes necessary to have "temporary alliances for extraordinary emergencies."

As events turned out, disease destroyed much of the French force in Hispaniola, and it is now thought this was the basic reason for Napoleon's decision to sell Louisiana to the United States. He had no troops to garrison the territory; saw little future in such an undeveloped, faraway country; and needed more soldiers to continue the war in Europe, something for which the LOUISIANA PURCHASE helped to pay.

In Napoleon's eyes, he gained as much by the sale as the United States did. He is quoted as saying, "Sixty million francs for an occupation [New Orleans] that will not perhaps last a day!" But another remark attributed to him shows surprising prescience: "The sale assures forever the power of the United States, and I have given England a rival who, sooner or later, will humble her pride."

See also EXPLORATION, EARLY.

Further Reading

Brebner, John B. *The Explorers of North America 1492–1806.* New York: Macmillan, 1933.

DeConde, Alexander. *This Affair of Louisiana.* New York: Charles Scribner, 1976.

Morison, Samuel Eliot. *Oxford History of the American People.* New York: Oxford University Press, 1965.

Frazier, Robert (Robert Frazer, Robert Frasure)

(unknown–1837) *private in the permanent party*

Originally enlisted on January 1, 1804, as a temporary member of the CORPS OF DISCOVERY, Private Robert Frazier (spelled Frazer in some sources and occasionally Frasure in the JOURNALS) was transferred to the permanent party on October 8 that same year. Born in Augusta County, Virginia, it is unclear where and when he was recruited for the expedition, but he quickly proved himself a valuable addition to the party. Thus, a few weeks following MOSES REED'S COURT-MARTIAL for desertion, MERIWETHER LEWIS and WILLIAM CLARK chose Frazier to replace Reed; he was assigned to Sergeant PATRICK GASS's squad.

In February 1805 Frazier, JOHN NEWMAN, and SILAS GOODRICH were sent out with GEORGE DROUILLARD to retrieve some BUFFALO and ELK meat that had been prepared by another HUNTING party and deposited some 24 miles away from FORT MANDAN down the MISSOURI RIVER. They were ambushed by a large group of TETON LAKOTA INDIANS (Teton Sioux), and though they managed to fight off their attackers (despite being badly outnumbered), the Indians managed to get away with two sleds as well as two knives.

In May 1806, when the expedition fell short of provisions, men were sent out to TRADE with the Indians for FOOD. In the process they used up what little they had left in the way of trade goods. Sent to negotiate with the NEZ PERCE INDIANS, Frazier returned to camp to report that there was an interest in brass uniform buttons. Consequently, buttons disappeared from clothing to use for barter. The journals of Sergeants JOHN ORDWAY and PATRICK GASS relate that Frazier also engaged in some unusual trading with a Nez Perce woman, offering her "an old razor" in exchange for two Spanish coins. According to Lewis and Clark scholar James P. Ronda, both probably came away from the deal feeling that they had gotten the best of the bargain, and this incident points up the vast differences between Indian and non-Indian cultures of the time.

Frazier was one of the few privates to keep a journal, and following the expedition he put together a prospectus for its publication, initially with the permission of MERIWETHER LEWIS. The captain, however, was not pleased by the prospectus, which made claims of providing "an accurate description of the Missouri . . . of the Columbia . . . of the face of the Country in general . . . of the several Tribes of Indians . . . [and] of the vegetable, animal and mineral productions discovered." This not only competed with Lewis and Clark's own anticipated book but purported an expertise in natural history that the captain felt Frazier did not have. Yet despite this, Frazier joined the party that accompanied Lewis and MANDAN chief BIG WHITE to Washington in November 1806. He also maintained friendly enough relations to borrow money from Lewis and to be entrusted to deliver Clark's commission as brigadier general of militia as well as to take a dispatch to FREDERICK BATES in ST. LOUIS.

When in March 1807 the prospectus for the publication of Patrick Gass's journal was announced, and word of Frazier's book began to circulate as well, Lewis attacked both men in the press for their "unauthorized" and "spurious publications." The captain's fears, however, were needless, as Frazier's journal never appeared and was subsequently lost; scholars hope it may yet show up in somebody's attic. However, like Captain Clark, Frazier drew a map of the West, which is presently located in the Library of Congress.

Frazier subsequently served with the Louisiana Militia and was called to testify in the trial of Robert Westcott, one of the Burr conspirators. He later moved to St. Louis, where he apparently got into trouble with the law on several occasions, and from there he went to settle near the Gasconade River in Missouri. He died in Franklin County, Missouri, in 1837.

Further Reading

Clarke, Charles G. *The Men of the Lewis and Clark Expedition: A Biographical Roster of the Fifty-One Members and a Composite Diary of Their Activities from All Known Sources.* 1970. Reprint, Lincoln: Bison Books, University of Nebraska Press, 2002.

North Dakota Lewis & Clark Bicentennial Foundation. *Members of the Corps of Discovery.* Bismarck, N.Dak.: United Printing and Mailing, 2000.

PBS Online. *Lewis and Clark: Inside the Corps of Discovery:* "Private Robert Frazer." Available on-line. URL: http://www.pbs.org/lewisandclark/inside/rfraz.html. Downloaded on May 18, 2001.

French Canadians   See CANADA; CORPS OF DISCOVERY; ENGAGÉS; EXPLORATION, EARLY.

fur trade

It is difficult today to appreciate the importance of the fur trade in North America at the beginning of the 19th century. While TOBACCO produced wealth for landowners on the eastern seaboard, the forests of CANADA and the West Coast produced wealth in the form of furs. With BEAVER hats in great demand in Europe, it was for furs that FRANCE had colonized southern Canada and the reason the HUDSON'S BAY COMPANY had been established more than a century before.

When the LOUISIANA PURCHASE gave the United States sovereignty over the American hinterland, the immediate advantage this gave, from a commercial point of view, was access to the lucrative fur trade. The Hudson's Bay Company and the NORTH WEST COMPANY of Canada had long been trading for furs with Indian nations along the MISSOURI RIVER. Now that the LOUISIANA TERRITORY was part of the United States, President THOMAS JEFFERSON was anxious to secure that trade for American merchants. Further, the recent voyages

of ROBERT GRAY had shown that there was a fruitful source of furs on the PACIFIC OCEAN; those of the sea OTTERS were recognized as being particularly valuable. Since getting to the Pacific Northwest involved a journey around South America via Cape Horn—in effect, a circumnavigation of the American continents—the need for a practicable (i.e., much shorter) NORTHWEST PASSAGE or even a land route to the West Coast was even more pressing.

Although Jefferson was a visionary, he was also a practical man, and he looked for practical benefits from the expedition. An extract from his MISSION OBJECTIVES to Lewis make the point, leaving the explorer in no doubt on his primary purpose: "The object of your mission is to explore the Missouri river, & such principal streams of it, as by it's course . . . may offer the most direct & practicable water communication across the continent *for the purposes of commerce.*"

Later, in the same instructions, Jefferson added: "Should you reach the Pacific ocean inform yourself of the circumstances which may decide whether the furs of those parts may not be collected as advantageously at the head of the Missouri (convenient as it supposed to the waters of the Colorado & Oregan or Columbia) as at Nootka sound, or any other point of that coast; and that trade be consequently conducted through the Missouri & U.S. more beneficially than by the circumnavigation now practiced."

It was furs that drew men to the western rivers, and it was the fur trade that was the basis of wealth west of the MISSISSIPPI RIVER. Early in the young nation's history, the government recognized this as well as the importance of Native Americans in accessing that wealth. Furthermore, British traders filtering down into Louisiana Territory from Canada were a clear threat to the United States. For these reasons, in 1795 an experimental "factory system" was established by which the government could (in theory) exert control over the American fur trade and the Indians. Factories, or trading houses, were set up to provide quality merchandise to the Indians in exchange for furs. The idea was to make the Indians dependent on this network of factories—and thus on the U.S. government.

When, early in their journey, the CORPS OF DISCOVERY met a trading party coming downstream on June 8, 1804, Clark estimated that the furs the three trappers had with them were worth about $900. They would sell for 10 times that amount when they got to New York and 10 times more again when they were sold in China.

From the expedition's JOURNALS, it is clear the two captains regarded the fur trade as having paramount importance. The comments and notes on the availability of timber, game, or minerals were all subsidiary to this end. In their COUNCILS WITH INDIANS, they urged chiefs to forsake the British/Canadian companies with whom they had been trading and instead deal with merchants in ST. LOUIS. The captains noted places along the MISSOURI RIVER where trading posts could be established. Lewis wrote that such a post at the junction of the YELLOWSTONE RIVER and the Missouri would "afford our citizens the benefit of a most lucrative fur trade [and] might be made to hold in check the views of the British N. West Company. . . ."

In the same report after the expedition had returned home, Lewis wrote the sentence that can be compared to the announcement more than 40 years later that gold had been found in California: "The Missouri and all it's branches from the Cheyenne upwards abound more in beaver and Common Otter, than any other streams on earth, particularly that proportion of them lying within the Rocky Mountains."

Lewis made it clear to Jefferson that he had not found an easy route across the ROCKY MOUNTAINS, but he did suggest a scheme that at the time must have seemed breathtaking. "We view this passage across the Continent as affording immence advantages to the fur trade," he wrote. He then proposed a chain of trading that took furs over the mountains westward, not eastward, on NEZ PERCE and SHOSHONE horses to the mouth of the COLUMBIA RIVER, where they could be shipped direct to the lucrative China market. The current British system was to collect furs in the West, take them east to Montreal and then down the St. Lawrence River and on to London. From here they were shipped around Africa to the Orient. Shipping straight across the Pacific from a base on the West Coast would save both a year of time and heavy transport costs.

Jefferson may or may not have approved of the idea, but within five years JOHN JACOB ASTOR had followed through on it and established a fur-trading post at the mouth of the Columbia. Although later occupied by the British for a period after the War of 1812, Astoria, Oregon, was the first permanent non-Indian settlement in the American Northwest. By this time the government-controlled factory system had fallen into hard times financially and was losing ground to businessmen such as Astor. In 1822 it was abolished, and the fur trade became the province of independent American merchants.

Further Reading

Alwin, John A. "Pelts, Provisions, and Perceptions: The Hudson's Bay Company Mandan Indian Trade, 1795–1815." *Montana: The Magazine of Western History* 29 (1979): 16–27.

Ambrose, Stephen E. *Undaunted Courage: Meriwether Lewis, Thomas Jefferson, and the Opening of the American West.* New York: Simon and Schuster, 1996.

Bryce, George. *The Remarkable History of the Hudson's Bay Company, Including That of the French Traders of North-western Canada, and of the North-west XY, and Astor Fur Companies.* 2d ed. New York: B. Franklin, 1968.

Haycox, Stephen W., et al. *Enlightenment and Exploration in the North Pacific 1741–1805.* Seattle: University of Washington Press, 1995.

Mackenzie, Sir Alexander. *Voyages from Montreal through the Continent of North America to the Frozen and Pacific Oceans in 1789 and 1793, with an Account of the Rise and State of the Fur Trade.* 2 vols.; reprint ed., New York: AMS Press, 1973.

Newman, Peter C. *Caesars of the Wilderness.* Markham, Ontario: Viking, 1987.

Oglesby, Richard E. *Manuel Lisa and the Opening of the Missouri Fur Trade.* Norman: University of Oklahoma Press, 1963.

Rich, E. E. *The Fur Trade and the Northwest to 1857.* Toronto: McClelland and Stewart, 1967.

Scofield, John. *Hail, Columbia: Robert Gray, John Kendrick and the American Fur Trade.* Portland: Oregon Historical Society, 1993.

Walker, Dale. *Pacific Destiny: The Three Century Journey to Oregon Country.* New York: Forge Books, 2000.

Wood, W. Raymond, and Thomas D. Thiessen. *Early Fur Trade on the Northern Plains: Canadian Traders Among the Mandan and Hidatsa Indians, 1738–1818.* Norman: University of Oklahoma Press, 1985.

G

Gallatin, Albert (1761–1849) *secretary of the treasury, diplomat, economist*

Albert Gallatin was honored by the Lewis and Clark Expedition when one of the rivers of the THREE FORKS of the MISSOURI RIVER was named for him in July 1805. The other two were named for THOMAS JEFFERSON and Secretary of State JAMES MADISON, who would succeed Jefferson as president. Gallatin served both presidents—and the nation—as secretary of the treasury from 1801 to 1814.

Born and educated in Switzerland, Gallatin immigrated to the United States in 1780. Ten years later he was elected to the Pennsylvania state legislature, and in 1793 he was elected to the U.S. Senate. However, he was forced to leave a year later when his political opponents argued that he had not been a citizen long enough to qualify for a U.S. Senate seat (even though he had already gained legal citizenship under the terms of the Articles of Confederation of 1781). Later in 1794, he was elected to the U.S. House of Representatives. Seven years later President THOMAS JEFFERSON appointed him secretary of the treasury, in which capacity he worked to eliminate the national debt.

Throughout his 60-year career, Gallatin advocated free public education, universal suffrage, and the abolition of slavery. He was a key figure in the implementation of Jefferson's design for the young and growing republic. He organized the financial details of the LOUISIANA PURCHASE and resolved the constitutional issues involved with the transaction. Like Jefferson, he was a keen student of geography and Indian cultures and thus not only supported the Lewis and Clark Expedition but helped to plan it.

Secretary of the Treasury Albert Gallatin gave his full support to the expedition and commissioned a special map for it. *(Library of Congress, Prints and Photographs Division [LC-USZ62-110017])*

Gallatin's assistance with the expedition began in December 1802 when President Jefferson had him review a draft of a planned message to Congress that included a request for an appropriation of $2,500 for the expedition. Gallatin suggested that the appropriation request be made in a separate, confidential document. Jefferson took his advice and consequently submitted a secret message to Congress on January 18, 1803. Shortly thereafter, Gallatin asked NICHOLAS KING to draw a new map of western North America, incorporating features of the most recent MAPS by GEORGE VANCOUVER, ALEXANDER MACKENZIE, DAVID THOMPSON, and other contemporary explorers. Lewis and Clark apparently carried this map at least as far as the MANDAN and the HIDATSA villages on the MISSOURI RIVER, where Lewis annotated in brown ink additional intelligence he had obtained from fur traders.

Jefferson had circulated his instructions to Lewis among his cabinet, and several responded with suggestions for additions or changes. Gallatin hoped that Lewis would be able to obtain information about Spanish posts in LOUISIANA TERRITORY as well as what the British were doing on the frontier. Aware that U.S. settlers would be moving into the new territory, he also wanted to ensure that the land was suitable for agriculture. Jefferson incorporated Gallatin's suggestions into his instructions, although he gave them lesser importance than other concerns that were dearer to his heart.

Following the expedition's return, Jefferson consulted with Gallatin regarding a post for Lewis. Gallatin supported the notion of making Lewis governor of the Louisiana Territory but warned that the newly returned hero had numerous things to do, not least of which was getting his and Clark's JOURNALS published and that it might be some time before he was able to take up his post. Consequently, Jefferson appointed FREDERICK BATES to be secretary of the territory, a position similar to that of lieutenant governor. Bates later came to be at odds with Lewis, and some historians believe their stormy relationship to be a factor in Lewis's suicide.

In 1807, during fighting then going on between GREAT BRITAIN and FRANCE, the U.S. CONGRESS put an embargo on foreign trade. The reason for this was to maintain American neutrality, but the restrictions—and, later, the War of 1812—had a disastrous effect on the American economy, preventing any debt reduction and frustrating Gallatin. In 1813 he took a leave of absence from his Treasury post to become minister to Russia; he officially resigned as Treasury secretary in 1814. That same year he helped negotiate the Treaty of Ghent, which ended the War of 1812. He subsequently served as minister to France from 1816 to 1823 and as minister to Britain in 1826–27.

From 1831 to 1839, Gallatin was president of the new National Bank in New York. At the age of 70, he wrote an anthropological treatise describing all the known American Indian nations and later founded the American Ethnological Society. Albert Gallatin died in 1848. A man never fully appreciated by the country he adopted, he has been described as "America's forgotten statesman."

Further Reading

Allen, John Logan. *Passage Through the Garden: Lewis and Clark and the Image of the American Northwest.* Urbana: University of Illinois Press, 1975. Reprint, New York: Dover Publications, 1991.

Ambrose, Stephen E. *Undaunted Courage: Meriwether Lewis, Thomas Jefferson, and the Opening of the American West.* New York: Simon and Schuster, 1996.

Stevens, John Austin. *Albert Gallatin: An American Statesman.* New York: AMS Press, 1998.

Gallatin's River　See THREE FORKS.

games　See RECREATION ON THE EXPEDITION.

Gass, Patrick (1771–1870) *sergeant in the permanent party*

Patrick Gass began the expedition with the rank of private and ended it as a sergeant. He is notable on at least three counts. First, on the death of Sergeant CHARLES FLOYD, Gass was elected to replace him in the first democratic election west of the Mississippi. Second, his was the first of the expedition JOURNALS to be published, seven years before Lewis and Clark's book was finally issued. Finally, unlike many other members of the expedition, he lived well into old age, becoming the last surviving member of the CORPS OF DISCOVERY.

Born June 12, 1771, at Falling Springs, Pennsylvania, the rough-spoken Gass was of Irish descent, with dark hair and skin, gray eyes, a barrel chest, and a short, burly stature. An experienced carpenter, boat builder, and woodsman, Gass had served in a Ranger Company in 1792 and enlisted in the 10th U.S. Infantry at Carlisle, Pennsylvania, in 1799. When he volunteered for the corps, he was then a sergeant under the command of Captain Russell Bissell in the First Infantry at KASKASKIA, Illinois. Although Secretary of War HENRY DEARBORN had instructed commanding officers to cooperate with MERIWETHER LEWIS in his RECRUITING efforts, Bissell refused to give up Gass. A determined Lewis used his orders from Dearborn to override Bissell, and Gass officially joined the expedition as a private on January 1, 1804.

Gass was promoted to sergeant following the death of Charles Floyd on August 20, 1804. The promotion was not conferred on him by the captains but rather by all the expedition members as the result of an unusual election, which Gass won with 19 votes; WILLIAM BRATTON and GEORGE GIBSON received the remainder of the votes.

The sergeants were all encouraged to keep journals, and Gass was diligent in writing his, even though he indicated that had never learned to read or write until his adulthood. He reported events as they occurred and provided descriptions of the scenery and of the Indian nations the corps met along the journey. It was Gass who depicted the BITTERROOT MOUNTAINS as "the most terrible mountains I ever beheld," a quote widely used in books on the expedition.

Gass does not appear to have been one of the expedition's striking personalities, but he was undoubtedly solid, dependable, and trustworthy. He was the corps's head carpenter,

Patrick Gass was the first to publish an account of the expedition in 1807. This illustration of a canoe striking a tree was one of six woodcuts included in the 1810 edition published by Mathew Carey of Philadelphia. *(Library of Congress, Prints and Photographs Division [LC-USZ62-100822])*

and in that capacity he supervised the construction of CANOES and of the quarters at CAMP DUBOIS, FORT MANDAN, and FORT CLATSOP. Writing of Gass in his report to Henry Dearborn, Captain Lewis commented on the sergeant's "fortitude with which he bore the fatigues and painful sufferings."

In 1807, when news began to circulate that Gass and ROBERT FRAZIER were about to publish their journals, a letter written by Lewis appeared in the *National Intelligencer* attacking the upcoming "unauthorized" and "spurious publications" (despite his having already given his permission to Frazier to publish). Under pressure to get his and Clark's account of the expedition published, Lewis perceived that his procrastination had cost him dearly, as any other expedition-related books were sure to affect his own sales. Furthermore, a prospectus of Gass's book implied that the captains had seen, corrected, and approved the material that was about to be published, which was not the case.

A Journal of the Voyages and Travels of a Corps of Discovery, under the command of Capt Lewis and Capt Clarke of the Army of the United States from the mouth of the River Missouri through the interior parts of North America to the Pacific Ocean during the years 1804, 1805, and 1806, by Patrick Gass, was published later that year. Edited by a PITTSBURGH bookstore owner named David McKeehan, the book was subsequently published in London, France, and Germany. It was also published by Mathew Carey of Philadelphia in 1810, 1811, and 1812; these editions included a number of whimsical illustrations, which seemed to lend a fablelike aspect to the expedition's story. An embarrassed Lewis continued to procrastinate on his own book, and after his death in 1809, his cocaptain, WILLIAM CLARK, hired NICHOLAS BIDDLE to finish the official account, which was not published until 1814.

Gass later served in the War of 1812. In March 1813 he was at FORT MASSAC, Kentucky, and then at Bellefontaine, Missouri. In 1814 he went up the OHIO RIVER to Pittsburgh and then on to Fort Erie. In June 1815, as the War of 1812 was ending, he lost his left eye at Fort Independence. He was discharged that same month and granted a pension for his disability. He settled in Wellsburg, West Virginia, and in 1831, at the age of 60, he married 20-year-old Maria Hamilton, with whom he had six children. When the Civil War broke out, he was 90 years old, which did not prevent him from volunteering. Patrick Gass passed away in West Virginia on April 2, 1870. Almost 99 years old, he was the last member of the Corps of Discovery to die.

Further Reading

Forrest, Earle E. "Patrick Gass, Carpenter of the Lewis and Clark Expedition." *Bulletin of the Missouri Historical Society* 4 (July 1948): 217–222.

Jacob, John G. *The Life and Times of Patrick Gass, Now Sole Survivor of the Overland Expedition to the Pacific, under Lewis and Clark, in 1804–5–6.* Wellsburg, Va.: Jacob & Smith, 1859.

MacGregor, Carol Lynn. "The Role of the Gass Journal." *We Proceeded On* 16, no. 4 (November 1990): 13–17.

———, ed. *The Journals of Patrick Gass, Member of the Lewis and Clark Expedition.* Missoula, Mont.: Mountain Press Publishing Company, 1997.

Smith, James S., and Kathryn Smith. "Sedulous Sergeant, Patrick Gass: An Original Biography by Direct Descendants." *Montana The Magazine of Western History* 5, no. 3 (summer 1955): 20–27.

Gates of the Mountains (Gates of the Rocky Mountains)

By July 15, 1805, the CORPS OF DISCOVERY had completed their lengthy and laborious PORTAGE around the GREAT FALLS and were following the MISSOURI RIVER south toward THREE FORKS. They knew from SACAGAWEA that the SHOSHONE INDIANS should be somewhere in front of them and were anxious to contact that nation to procure HORSES for the crossing over the mountains to come.

On August 18, WILLIAM CLARK and three men walked overland to explore ahead while MERIWETHER LEWIS and the remainder made their way up the river in CANOES. The next day the river party came to the narrow gorge that is situated just north of present-day Helena, Montana. Lewis described it vividly:

This evening we entered the most remarkable clifts that we have yet seen. These clifts rise from the waters edge on either side perpendicularly to the height of [about] 1200 feet. Every object here wears a dark and gloomy aspect. The towering and projecting rocks in many places seem ready to tumble on us. This rock is of black granite below and appear to be of a much lighter colour above and from the fragments I take it to be flint of a yellowish brown and light creem coloured yellow. From the singular appearance of this place I called it the gates of the rocky mountains.

Though the 1918 Holter Dam has raised the level of the Missouri River, the Gates of the Mountains, as they are now named, are still as awe-inspiring and impressive as they were when Lewis gave them their name.

Further Reading

Fifer, Barbara, and Vicky Soderberg. *Along the Trail with Lewis and Clark.* Great Falls, Mont.: Montana Magazine, 1998.

Schmidt, Thomas. *National Geographic Guide to the Lewis & Clark Trail.* Washington, D.C.: National Geographic, 1998.

geese and brants

One of the more confusing aspects of the expedition's natural history as rendered in the JOURNALS has been differentiating

The awe-inspiring Gates of the Mountains on the Missouri River still retain the name given them by Meriwether Lewis.
(Montana Historical Society, Helena)

between geese and brants. Because these two birds are so similar in appearance and habit, and because they tend to congregate together and fly in mixed flocks, MERIWETHER LEWIS, WILLIAM CLARK, and other members of the expedition used the two words interchangeably. Furthermore, classification of geese and brants during the last 200 years has often been indecisive, and present-day terminology can only add to the confusion. One naturalist described the two birds as major subspecies, geese and brant geese, with the comment that the species *Brant* are normally black, while the species *Anser* are normally brown. Because of this, it is often difficult to clarify which birds the explorers saw during the expedition.

In October 1804, north of modern Pierre, South Dakota, Lewis and Clark named a stream White Brant Creek because they saw so many white brants and geese flying over them. At FORT CLATSOP in March 1806, Lewis gave a detailed description of what he called "the white brant." This is now generally accepted as being the lesser snow goose.

On April 13, 1805, near the Little Missouri River, the explorers were surprised to find Canada geese nesting in trees. Because the habit of such geese is normally to nest on the ground, many doubted their report, but it was subsequently confirmed by other naturalists. The following month, near Fort Peck, Montana, Lewis "[s]aw great numbers of white brant also the common brown brant, geese of the common kind and a small species of geese which differ considerably from the Canadian goose." The "small species of geese" are now known as Hutchins's goose. The "common brown brant" could have been either the black brant or the brown brant, since their migratory patterns overlap. The majority of black brant winter on the Pacific coasts, while a minority winter on the Atlantic coast. The brown brant does the reverse, with only a small number wintering on the Pacific.

The following year, on March 8, 1806, at Fort Clatsop, Lewis wrote: "The small goose of this country is rather less than the brandt. . . . I have now no hesitation in declaring them a distinct species." Accepted as a separate species for many years, the lesser Canada goose is now classified as a subspecies of Canada goose. Also while at Fort Clatsop, Lewis wrote on March 15 of "a third type of brant in the neighborhood of this place which is about the size and much the form of the pided [pied] brant." He went on to give a detailed description of what is now called the white-fronted goose.

Further Reading

Burroughs, Raymond Darwin, ed. *The Natural History of the Lewis and Clark Expedition.* East Lansing: Michigan State University Press, 1995.
Cutright, Paul Russell. *Lewis & Clark: Pioneering Naturalists.* Lincoln: University of Nebraska Press/Bison Books, 1989.
Washington State University. "Lewis and Clark Among the Indians of the Pacific Northwest. Excerpts from the Journals of the Expedition of the Corps of Discovery: Flora and Fauna (recorded at Fort Clatsop)." Available on-line. URL: http://www.libarts.wsu.edu/history/Lewis_Clark/LCEXP_Flor.html. Downloaded on May 20, 2001.

Gibson, George (unknown–1809) *private in the permanent party*

One of the NINE YOUNG MEN FROM KENTUCKY, Private George Gibson was among the first members of the CORPS OF DISCOVERY to be recruited in Louisville, on October 19, 1803. Born in Mercer County, Pennsylvania, and raised in Kentucky, Gibson possessed strong HUNTING skills and was an expert horseman and woodsman. One of the first references to him in WILLIAM CLARK's JOURNALS was a mention of Gibson's accuracy in shooting. He was also, like PIERRE CRUZATTE, a fiddle player who often provided music on the expedition.

Gibson had a basic proficiency in sign language and on occasion was called on to interpret, which (according to Sergeant JOHN ORDWAY) sometimes caused friction with the expedition's official interpreter, GEORGE DROUILLARD. In August 1804 he was sent to look for JOSEPH BARTER, one of the ENGAGÉS who had apparently deserted and was thought to be among the OTOE INDIANS. There is no indication, however, of whether he was successful in his mission. Later that same month, following the death of Sergeant CHARLES FLOYD, an election was held to name his replacement. Gibson and WILLIAM BRATTON were the two runners-up to PATRICK GASS.

The following year, in June 1805, Gibson was chosen for a scouting party to locate the GREAT FALLS of the Missouri, and he was with MERIWETHER LEWIS when it was sighted for the first time. During the winter of 1805–06 at FORT CLATSOP, Gibson, Bratton, and JOSEPH FIELD were selected to set up and run a SALTWORKS some 15 miles away from the fort. They finished their task in late February 1806, producing 20 gallons of salt for preserving meat and flavoring cooked foods. Twelve gallons of salt were packed for the return journey. In July that year, as he rode along the YELLOWSTONE RIVER, Gibson was thrown from his horse and landed in a thick snag that cut into his leg, injuring him so badly that he was unable to walk for some time afterward. This accident resulted in Clark's decision to build emergency CANOES that would take their party down the Yellowstone.

Little is known about Gibson's life following the expedition. According to Charles G. Clarke, he may have been one of the party headed by Sergeant NATHANIEL PRYOR that attempted in 1807 to return the MANDAN chief BIG WHITE to his home but were attacked by the ARIKARA INDIANS. Gibson died in ST. LOUIS two years later.

Further Reading

Clarke, Charles G. *The Men of the Lewis and Clark Expedition: A Biographical Roster of the Fifty-One Members and a Composite Diary of Their Activities from All Known Sources.* 1970. Reprint, Lincoln: Bison Books, University of Nebraska Press, 2002.
North Dakota Lewis & Clark Bicentennial Foundation. *Members of the Corps of Discovery.* Bismarck, N.Dak.: United Printing and Mailing, 2000.
PBS Online. *Lewis and Clark: Inside the Corps of Discovery:* "Lesser Known Members of the Corps." Available on-line. URL: http://www.pbs.org/lewisandclark/inside/lesser.html. Downloaded on May 18, 2001.

gifts

A crucial list among those that MERIWETHER LEWIS drew up as he made his PREPARATIONS FOR THE EXPEDITION was the gifts that he would present to the Indian nations they would encounter. These gifts had two purposes: to placate those peoples who might be hostile to the expedition's passage through their territories and to impress them with the quality of goods they could obtain through TRADE with the Americans. Consequently, with the help of ISRAEL WHELAN in PHILADELPHIA, Lewis bought 26 bags of gifts, which were taken on the journey. These included beads, buttons, axes, scissors, TOBACCO, and whiskey—any items that might be of interest to the Indians along the route.

The giving of gifts was a traditional courtesy between strangers for whom communication might be difficult and who therefore might not know the nature of the other's intentions. A typical example of gift giving occurred in October 1804 when the expedition met a community of about 2,000 ARIKARA INDIANS on the MISSOURI RIVER. Lewis and Clark invited the chiefs of the villages to a council and, after explaining the expedition's purposes, presented the contents of a gift bag that had been specially prepared for the Arikara. It included needles, cloth, beads, scissors, knives, razors, tomahawks, paint, pewter mirrors, and other manufactured items. Extra items, which included U.S. flags, military clothing, and medals, were given to chiefs, and the important ones received specially minted Jefferson PEACE MEDALS.

Beads were important items, and the expedition carried several types. A written inventory recorded:

5 pounds of white wampum

5 pounds of glass beads, mostly small

20 pounds of red glass beads, assorted

5 pounds of yellow or orange beads, assorted

2 cards of beads

3 pounds of beads

73 bunches of beads, assorted

8½ pounds of red beads

2 bead necklaces for young women

10 maces of white round beads for girls

2 maces of sky blue round beads for girls

3 maces of yellow round beads for girls

3 maces of red beads for girls

14 maces of yellow round seed beads for girls

5 maces of mock garnets

According to WILLIAM CLARK, the blue or white beads brought the highest value in trading with Indians for HORSES and supplies. On a couple of occasions, red beads, so popular in the Northeast, were flatly refused. Most of the beads were monochrome glass, and many of them were seed beads. The "mock garnets" may have been Bohemian or even Venetian. Although more common among Indian cultures of the East,

wampum—consisting of polished shells strung in strands, belts, or sashes—was also included. Whiskey was often asked for and sometimes given, although the Arikara admonished the captains for offering "a liquor which would make them act like fools."

In return, Lewis and Clark received gifts that were often valuable or practical and timely. Gifts of FOOD were welcome and sometimes led to bartering for more food. HORSES were only rarely offered as gifts. More common were samples of Indian craftsmanship, BUFFALO skins, and clothing. Lewis especially treasured an ermine tippet given to him by SHOSHONE chief CAMEAHWAIT; he described it as "the most eligant peice of Indian dress I ever saw." It later ended up in the museum of CHARLES WILLSON PEALE.

Further Reading

Ambrose, Stephen E. *Undaunted Courage: Meriwether Lewis, Thomas Jefferson, and the Opening of the American West.* New York: Simon and Schuster, 1996.

The Bead Site. "The Beads of Lewis and Clark." Available on-line. URL: http://www.thebeadsite.com/FRO-LaC.htm. Downloaded on February 10, 2002.

Cutright, Paul Russell. "Lewis and Clark Indian Peace Medals." *Missouri Historical Bulletin* 24, no. 2 (1968): 160–167.

Jefferson National Expansion Memorial. "The Lewis and Clark Journey of Discovery: Indian Presents and Trade Goods." Available on-line. URL: http://www.nps.gov/jeff/LewisClark2/CorpsOf Discovery/Preparing/Gifts/Gifts.htm. Downloaded on April 11, 2002.

gnats See INSECTS.

goats See ANIMALS, NEW SPECIES; SHEEP AND GOATS.

Goodrich, Silas (Silas Guthrich)

(unknown–unknown) *private in the permanent party*

A native of Massachusetts, Silas Goodrich appears only occasionally in the expedition's JOURNALS. Officially enlisted for the expedition on January 1, 1804, he was the principal fisherman for the CORPS OF DISCOVERY, often catching FOOD for the men when game for HUNTING was scarce. He also served on the panel for the October 1804 COURT-MARTIAL of JOHN NEWMAN for mutiny. A few months later, he was among the small party that was sent out from FORT MANDAN in February 1805 to retrieve some meat left behind by a hunting party. Goodrich, Newman, GEORGE DROUILLARD, and ROBERT FRAZIER were attacked by TETON LAKOTA INDIANS (Teton Sioux), barely escaping with their lives.

Like other expedition members, Goodrich had a landmark named for him. In his case it was an island in the MISSOURI RIVER in the state of Montana that the expedition passed on May 25, 1805. Three weeks later, he was chosen by Captain MERIWETHER LEWIS for a scouting party to locate the GREAT FALLS of the Missouri, which they reached on June 13, 1805.

Indian Presents

5 <u>lb</u> White Wampum
5 <u>lb</u> White Glass Beads mostly Small
20 <u>lb</u> Red D°: D° Asorted
5 <u>lb</u> Yellow or Orange D°. D° Asorted.
30 Calico Shirts
12 Pieces of East India muslin Hanchuchiefs striped or check'd with brilliant Colours.

12 Red Silk Hanchuchiefs
144 Small cheap looking Glasses
100 Burning Glasses
4 Vials of Phosforous
288 Steels for striking fire
144 Small cheap scizors
20 Pair large D°
12 Groces Needles Asorted N° 1 to 8 Common points
12 Groces D° Asorted with points for Sewing leather
288 Common brass thimbles — part W. office
10 <u>lb</u> Sewing Thread asorted
24 Hanks Sewing Silk
8 <u>lb</u> Red lead
2 <u>lb</u> Vermillion . at War office
288 Knives Small such as are generally used for the Indian trade, with fix'd blades & handles inlaid with brass

Purchasing gifts for the Indians whom the expedition would meet was an essential part of Lewis's preparations. This is only a partial list of what he bought. *(National Archives Old Military and Civil Records [NWCTB-92-NM81E225-LEWIS3])*

Goodrich subsequently went FISHING and caught the first cut-throat trout ever seen by non-Indians.

During the expedition's winter in FORT CLATSOP (1805–06), Private Goodrich was treated for a disease that was for many of the men an inevitable outcome of their isolation and boredom. On January 23, 1806, Captain Lewis recorded in his journal that "Goodrich has recovered from the Louis veneri [syphilis] which he contracted from an amorous contact with a Chinnook damsel." As he did with all cases of venereal disease, Lewis administered mercury, the standard treatment of the day. Nevertheless, six months later Goodrich and HUGH MCNEAL both began to show signs of the disease's secondary stage. By this time they had returned to the Great Falls, where Lewis left them while he went off with Drouillard and the Fields brothers to explore the MARIAS RIVER. During that time Goodrich and McNeal took mercury again and, with THOMAS PROCTOR HOWARD, began to disinter CACHES in preparation for the PORTAGE around the falls.

Although he reenlisted in the army after the expedition's return, little else is known about Silas Goodrich. WILLIAM CLARK listed him as dead by 1825–28.

See also FISH, NEW SPECIES.

Further Reading

Clarke, Charles G. *The Men of the Lewis and Clark Expedition: A Biographical Roster of the Fifty-One Members and a Composite Diary of Their Activities from All Known Sources.* 1970. Reprint, Lincoln: Bison Books, University of Nebraska Press, 2002.

North Dakota Lewis & Clark Bicentennial Foundation. *Members of the Corps of Discovery.* Bismarck, N.Dak.: United Printing and Mailing, 2000.

PBS Online. *Lewis and Clark: Inside the Corps of Discovery:* "Lesser Known Members of the Corps." Available on-line. URL: http://www.pbs.org/lewisandclark/inside/lesser.html. Downloaded on May 18, 2001.

gophers   See ANIMALS, NEW SPECIES.

Gravelines, Joseph (unknown–unknown)
fur trader, interpreter

On October 8, 1804, the Lewis and Clark Expedition met the ARIKARA INDIANS, who were then living in three villages on a large island in the MISSOURI RIVER, near the mouth of the Grand River. Among them was a French-Canadian fur trader named Joseph Gravelines, who had been living with the Arikara for the past 13 years. His presence delighted MERIWETHER LEWIS and WILLIAM CLARK, since he spoke English, French, Arikara, and Sioux with ease and also proved to be a good source of information about the upper Missouri. After conversing with him for some time, Lewis hired Gravelines as interpreter for the upcoming council with the Arikara.

Gravelines was not the only multilingual trader at the villages. Also present was PIERRE-ANTOINE TABEAU, who had been on a previous expedition up the Missouri and was, like Grave-

lines, an employee of RÉGIS LOISEL, a partner in the Missouri Company. Both traders put themselves at the captains' disposal, although it was Gravelines who acted as primary interpreter during their council with the Arikara and who joined the expedition as it continued up the Missouri. From him Lewis and Clark learned more about the trading network in the northern Plains, of which the villages of the MANDAN and the HIDATSA INDIANS were the hub. An Arikara chief also accompanied them and joined in councils with the Mandan and the Hidatsa, the object of which was to forge a peaceful alliance between the Arikara and the Mandan-Hidatsa. The meetings went well, and afterward Gravelines went back downriver, leaving a hopeful Lewis and Clark at FORT MANDAN.

Gravelines's usefulness as an interpreter and as an intermediary with the Indians brought him back within the explorers' orbit during the ensuing winter of 1804–05. Lewis and Clark corresponded with both Gravelines and Tabeau in an attempt to maintain watch on Arikara and TETON LAKOTA INDIANS (Teton Sioux) activities. The Sioux's status as enemies of the Mandan and the Hidatsa made a peaceful relationship with the Arikara all the more important. Thus, after some members of the expedition were attacked by the Sioux, the explorers wrote to Tabeau and Gravelines, asking them to talk to the Arikara. Late in February 1805, Gravelines arrived at Fort Mandan with a letter from Tabeau advising that the Arikara were amenable to friendly relations with the Mandan and the Hidatsa and were in fact even considering moving north to the KNIFE RIVER region. While this was welcome news, the captains were nonetheless uneasy about peace being maintained, particularly because of the Sioux. Gravelines told them several bands of the Teton Lakota regarded the soldiers as "bad medicine" and were planning an attack on Fort Mandan in the spring. This attack never took place, but Lewis and Clark never doubted the gravity of the trader's information and remained on their guard.

Gravelines stayed on at Fort Mandan, and during his time with the CORPS OF DISCOVERY he demonstrated the methods used by the Arikara to make glass beads. A fascinated Lewis not only studied the process but later wrote a detailed description of it, yet another ethnographical legacy of the expedition.

During the winter at Fort Mandan, Lewis and Clark had hired TOUSSAINT CHARBONNEAU as interpreter for the expedition, but he was balked at having to take on the duties of an enlisted man. Knowing the importance the captains attached to his wife SACAGAWEA's also coming on the journey, in March 1805 he tried in effect to blackmail them by submitting terms for his employment. His demands were firmly rejected, and Gravelines was hired as interpreter instead. Charbonneau subsequently backed down and was rehired. Given his attitude and general incompetence, it may seem strange that Lewis and Clark preferred Charbonneau over the clearly more capable Gravelines, but their need to have Sacagawea along must have outweighed other considerations.

In any event, Gravelines, whom Lewis described as "an honest, discreet man, and an excellent boatman," was needed for another purpose: to pilot the KEELBOAT from Fort Mandan back downriver to ST. LOUIS. His skills as an interpreter made his addition to the keelboat party important, and Lewis had also asked him and PIERRE DORION to escort one of the Arikara chiefs to Washington. Gravelines took his leave of Lewis and Clark on April 7, 1805. Well more than a year later, on September 12, 1806, he and Dorion had returned from Washington and were traveling upriver when they met the expedition. They had instructions from THOMAS JEFFERSON to relay the bad news that the Arikara chief had died; Gravelines had the onerous task of passing this news to the Arikara and expressing Jefferson's regrets. Little more is known of his career.

Further Reading

Ambrose, Stephen E. *Undaunted Courage: Meriwether Lewis, Thomas Jefferson, and the Opening of the American West.* New York: Simon and Schuster, 1996.

Graveline, Paul. "Joseph Gravelines and the Lewis and Clark Expedition." *We Proceeded On* 3, no. 4 (October 1977): 5–6.

Ronda, James P. *Lewis and Clark among the Indians.* Lincoln: University of Nebraska Press, 1984.

Gray, Robert (1755–1806) *explorer*

Captain Robert Gray was a renowned American sailor and explorer who, in 1792, found the mouth of what he named the COLUMBIA RIVER. Two years previously he had become the first American to circumnavigate the globe, and when he arrived in Boston with a shipload of OTTER furs, he set off a flurry of increased trade with the Indians of the Pacific Northwest.

In 1778 the famous English explorer Captain James Cook sailed along the coast of the Pacific Northwest. Although he failed to find the Columbia, he discovered a very profitable sea otter trade, which sparked a heated competition among GREAT BRITAIN, SPAIN, FRANCE, Russia, and the newly independent United States for a foothold on the West Coast. There ensued a wave of exploration, and by 1800 the Northwest coastline had been surveyed and mapped. Eventually the United States would win the battle for the OREGON TERRITORY, which began with the discoveries of Cook, GEORGE VANCOUVER, ALEXANDER MACKENZIE—and Robert Gray, who established the U.S. claim to the area.

Gray's exploration was a crucial component in the beginnings of the Lewis and Clark expedition. He first sighted the river from aboard his ship, SS *Columbia Rediviva,* in April 1792 but was unable to enter due to the sandbars and violently shifting shoals at its mouth. On April 29, the *Columbia* encountered HMS *Discovery,* captained by George Vancouver. Gray informed Vancouver that he was going to make another attempt to enter the river. He arrived back near the river's mouth on May 7 and observed an entrance between the sandbars, which the ship then crossed. Having safely reached the harbor between two capes, which he named Adams and Hancock (the latter is more commonly known as CAPE DISAPPOINTMENT), he named the river after his ship and began to trade with Indians who had come to greet him. On May 11 he sailed up the harbor, over another sandbar, and into the river's estuary. After traveling about 20 miles up the river, he turned around. It was enough to lay an American claim to the river.

Gray fixed the latitude and longitude of his position, and by this THOMAS JEFFERSON was able to estimate the width of the continent to be 3,000 miles. Shortly thereafter Jefferson made a third attempt to send an expedition to the Pacific, but it failed (see MICHAUX, ANDRÉ). Nevertheless, the die was cast, and 12 years later the Lewis and Clark expedition would set off on its historic journey.

See also EXPLORATION, EARLY.

Further Reading

Pethick, Derek. *First Approaches to the Northwest Coast.* Vancouver: J. J. Douglas, 1976.

Scofield, John. *Hail, Columbia: Robert Gray, John Kendrick and the American Fur Trade.* Portland: Oregon Historical Society, 1993.

Walker, Dale. *Pacific Destiny: The Three Century Journey to Oregon Country.* New York: Forge Books, 2000.

Great Britain

From the first planning of the Lewis and Clark Expedition, it was clear that THOMAS JEFFERSON was anxious about the threat the British in CANADA could pose to his long-term vision of a United States occupying and developing the then-unknown vast hinterland west of the MISSISSIPPI RIVER. Although the young nation had won its independence by force of arms, it was still only 25 years old, its borders were uncertain, and its judicial and political institutions were still new and untried. The HUDSON'S BAY COMPANY and the NORTH WEST COMPANY were trading with Indian nations well south of the Canadian border, and ALEXANDER MACKENZIE had crossed the northern ROCKY MOUNTAINS to reach the PACIFIC OCEAN by land in 1793.

While the Lewis and Clark JOURNALS reflect the eagerness of Jefferson and the two captains to supplant the Canadian supremacy in the northern fur trade, the president knew he had far more to fear from two other European powers, FRANCE and SPAIN. The French Revolution of 1789 had plunged Europe into war, and the widespread sympathy for France in the United States had been stifled by the excesses of the revolutionaries and their establishment of puppet regimes across Europe. By 1797 Great Britain, Russia, and the United States were the only major powers who had not acquiesced to French demands. Further, news of French designs to invade the Mississippi valley and French attacks on American shipping had forced the U.S. CONGRESS to create a Department of the Navy.

Thus, by the end of 1798, the United States and Great Britain had reached an agreement by which the American navy protected British vessels in the Caribbean. In 1799 the new American navy fought several engagements with French naval ships, even though no formal hostilities had been declared.

By 1802 Jefferson was unwilling to commit the United States to open conflict but still feared an invasion by the French force that had arrived in the Caribbean. On April 18 that year, he wrote, "The day that France takes possession of New Orleans . . . we must marry ourselves to the British fleet and nation." The following year the LOUISIANA PURCHASE removed the threat from France and in so doing also reduced any similar threat from Britain. Napoleon Bonaparte's intention was to use the money paid for the LOUISIANA TERRITORY to renew his war against the island nation, and with such a prospect ahead of them, the British were fully occupied in Europe. Thus, U.S. claims to the Missouri valley or the OREGON TERRITORY were of secondary concern to them at that time. Any border or trading disputes so far away could be settled by diplomacy or negotiation in due course—as most of them were. Jefferson had little to fear from Britain after all.

See also EXPLORATION, EARLY.

Further Reading

Morison, Samuel Eliot. *Oxford History of the American People.* New York: Oxford University Press, 1965.

Great Chute of the Columbia   See COLUMBIA RIVER GORGE.

Great Divide   See CONTINENTAL DIVIDE.

Great Falls

In June 1805 the expedition was approaching what it knew (from Indian information) would be a large waterfall on the MISSOURI RIVER. On June 10, while WILLIAM CLARK and the rest continued by water, MERIWETHER LEWIS took a small party ahead by land to locate the falls. Three days later he heard "a roaring too tremendous to be mistaken for any cause short of the great falls of the Missouri." Shortly thereafter he climbed some rocks and found himself looking upon a waterfall that stretched nearly 90 feet—"the grandest sight I ever beheld."

Unfortunately, just upriver he found another four waterfalls in succession. From start to finish, the falls dropped the Missouri nearly 400 feet. In his journal, Lewis called the Great Falls a "truly magnifficent and sublimely grand object which has from the commencement of time been concealed from the view of civilized man." However, the expedition would have to PORTAGE around this.

WILLIAM CLARK and the rest of the group arrived on June 16. Clark reconnoitered a portage route and found that the best course would be an 18-mile route on the south bank. This was much longer than they had expected, and it presented one of the biggest obstacles that the expedition would face. Lewis and Clark had thought the falls would delay them a week at most. In fact, it was nearly a month before they were able to leave.

At this point in the expedition, the corps had six dugout CANOES and a larger PIROGUE to carry, plus all the baggage. The solution involved building two wagons to carry the canoes. Slabs from a cottonwood tree were cut to make wheels, and the men were rigged with harnesses to pull the wagons. The pirogue was hidden, and some of the gear was stored in CACHES near the bottom of the falls.

Sails were rigged atop the dugouts. When the wind was favorable, it helped, but the route was 18 miles of rutted buffalo trail covered with PRICKLY PEARS. Shod in moccasins, the harnessed men trudged through prairie that was infested with INSECTS, SNAKES, and grizzly BEARS. Rough WEATHER included hail and gale-force winds, which had to be endured through four round-trips.

The party stayed at the head of the falls for another week assembling one of Lewis's pet projects, the 36-foot collapsible IRON-FRAME BOAT he had designed and commissioned at HARPERS FERRY in 1803. The original plan had been to navigate the single large KEELBOAT up the Missouri as far as the ROCKY MOUNTAINS. The expedition would then portage over the mountains to navigable waters on the western side, assemble the iron-frame boat, and sail down the COLUMBIA RIVER to the sea.

However confident Lewis had been about it, nothing seemed to work with the radical iron-frame "Experiment," as it was dubbed. About 30 large skins were needed to form the hull, and there was a shortage of animal hides. Even then the men did not have the right kind of needles to sew the hides together, and they were unable to find any pine pitch. Consequently, the iron-frame boat had to be abandoned. In its place they built two more cottonwood dugouts, which meant that more baggage had to be cached at the upper portage camp. The delay at the Great Falls at least gave the hunters and fishermen time to prepare large quantities of dried FISH and meat for FOOD, since the HIDATSA and the MANDAN had warned them that game would be scarce when they reached the mountains.

The Great Falls was the scene of a number of the expedition's ILLNESSES AND INJURIES, starting with Lewis himself, who came down with a "violent pain in the intestens" and a fever shortly after his arrival in the area. He treated himself with an herbal remedy made of twigs from a choke cherry tree boiled in water and was soon well enough to resume his work. However, during the corps's portage around the falls, he had to make time to attend to Sacagawea, who had developed what modern doctors now think was a gonorrheal infection. In addition, there were the cuts, bruises, and near fatalities caused by the long and dangerous portage. The following year, during the return journey, Private HUGH MCNEAL came close to being killed by a grizzly BEAR, causing Lewis to comment in his journal that "there seems to be a sertain fatality attached to the neighboururhood of these falls, for there is always a chapter of accidents prepared for us during our residence at them."

The Filson Historical Society collection in Louisville, Kentucky, includes Wilson Price Hunt's letter from ST. LOUIS reporting information from the explorers about the Great Falls. Today little can be seen of the Great Falls of the expedition's time because of the Ryan Dam, one of five dams that have changed the Missouri River in the area.

Further Reading

Ambrose, Stephen E. *Undaunted Courage: Meriwether Lewis, Thomas Jefferson, and the Opening of the American West.* New York: Simon and Schuster, 1996.

Lewis and Clark had been told that they would come to a great waterfall on the Missouri. They did not expect a series of five spectacular falls that dropped the river nearly 400 feet. This photograph was taken in 1880 before damming of the river obliterated the Great Falls. *(Haynes Foundation Collection, Montana Historical Society, Helena)*

Furdell, William J., and Elizabeth Lane Furdell. *Great Falls: A Pictorial History.* Norfolk, Va.: Donning Co., 1987.

Howard, Ella Mae. *Lewis and Clark's Exploration of Central Montana.* Great Falls, Mont.: Lewis and Clark Interpretative Association, 1993.

Moulton, Gary E., ed. *Atlas of the Lewis and Clark Expedition.* Revised ed. Lincoln: University of Nebraska Press, 1999.

Great Plains

The Great Plains is an area lying west of the MISSISSIPPI RIVER that stretches from Alberta and Manitoba in Canada 2,400 miles south into Mexico, and from the ROCKY MOUNTAINS 1,000 miles east to Indiana. It is characterized by an absence of TREES, a generally level surface, and a subhumid-to-arid climate. It is normally described as comprising two areas. The Mississippi Valley region, with 20–40 inches of rain a year producing luxuriant tall grass, is known as the prairie plains, or simply the prairie. The area stretching west to the Rockies, where there is much less rainfall and therefore shorter, sparser grass, is known as the high plains.

When MERIWETHER LEWIS and WILLIAM CLARK saw it, the Great Plains was home to ANTELOPE, DEER, ELK, BEARS, WOLVES, and—most important to the Indians who made it their home—the BUFFALO. The expedition reached the high plains in September 1804 near present-day Niobrara, Nebraska. It was the absence of trees that the party noted in particular, as Sergeant PATRICK GASS wrote: "There is no timber in this part of the country; but continued prairie on both sides of the river. A person by going on one of the hills may have a view as far as the eye can reach without any obstruction, or intervening object; and enjoy the most delightful prospects."

During the next two weeks, as they traveled upstream to the BAD RIVER, Lewis and Clark were busy recording animal species that had never before been reported or examined. It was during this stage of their journey across the Great Plains that they encountered PRAIRIE DOGS, COYOTES, JACKRABBITS, the prairie sharp-tailed GROUSE, the pronghorn ANTELOPE, and the mule DEER.

Further Reading

Licht, Daniel S. *Ecology and Economics of the Great Plains.* Lincoln: University of Nebraska Press, 1997.

Nichols, Roger L. "The Army and Early Perceptions of the Plains." *Nebraska History* 56, no. 1 (1975): 121–135.

At the time of the expedition, the vast, rolling Great Plains were inhabited solely by Plains Indians, such as these three Sioux (Dakota, Lakota, or Nakota) on horseback. *(Library of Congress, Prints and Photographs Division [LC-USZ62-105381])*

Webb, Walter Prescott. *The Great Plains.* Lincoln: University of Nebraska Press, 1981.

groundhogs   See ANIMALS, NEW SPECIES.

grouse

During their expedition MERIWETHER LEWIS and WILLIAM CLARK described seven types of grouse, a ground-dwelling game bird, of which six were hitherto unknown species. They noted the plains sharp-tailed grouse, already classified by naturalists, near the mouth of the Grand River, South Dakota, on October 7, 1804, and recorded seeing flocks of them on the sandbars at FORT MANDAN in February 1805. On May 22 that year, Lewis wrote: "Passed the entrance of Growse Creek 20 yards wide, affords but little water. this creek we named from seeing a number of the pointedtail prairie hen near its mouth, these are the first we have seen in such numbers for days." At FORT CLATSOP in March 1806, he noted the differences between the plains sharp-tailed grouse and the Columbian sharp-tailed grouse, correctly identifying the latter as a subspecies.

The sage grouse, largest of the North American grouse, was first noted by Lewis near the MARIAS RIVER on June 5, 1805; he recorded it then as a "mountain cock" and subsequently as "cock of the plains." Two months later, at LEMHI PASS on August 12, he wrote that "we also saw several of the heath cock with a long pointed tail and a uniform dark colour, but could not kill one of them." At Fort Clatsop the following year, he noted that the bird was to be found on the upper reaches of the MISSOURI RIVER, up to and across the ROCKY MOUNTAINS, and in the COLUMBIA RIVER basin.

The expedition first identified the dusky grouse (or Richardson's blue grouse) while they were ascending the JEFFERSON RIVER on August 1, 1805. Seeing "a flock of black or dark brown pheasants," they managed to kill one of them, and Lewis noted that "this bird is fully a third larger than the common phesant of the Atlantic states." It is from his detailed description that naturalists now classify it as the dusky grouse.

When on April 16, 1806, one of the Field brothers brought Lewis a grouse near the Deschutes River in Oregon, Lewis thought it was "a black pheasant" similar to the dusky grouse he had seen on the upper Missouri the previous year. Based on the notes he made, it has now been identified as the sooty grouse.

The last species, the Oregon ruffed grouse, was recorded by Lewis at Fort Clatsop in February 1806: "Fields brought with him a phesant which differed but little from those common to the Atlantic States; its brown is reather brighter and more of a redish tint. . . . [T]he two tufts of long black feathers on each side of the neck most conspicuous in the male of those of the Atlantic states is also observable in every particular." Despite his notes on the similarity of this grouse to the ruffed grouse of the southern Alleghenies, naturalists have classified this as a separate subspecies.

Further Reading

Burroughs, Raymond Darwin, ed. *The Natural History of the Lewis and Clark Expedition.* East Lansing: Michigan State University Press, 1995.

Grouse
are
about
short
and eye.
Cock
cock
which
on the
and
hood
Mountains
to the Mountain
the Columbia
the Great falls
they go in large
or singularly
hide hide remarkably close when pursued.
short flights &c.

the feathers about its head
pointed and stiff Some hairs
the base of the beak. feathers
fine and stiff about the ears.
This is a faint likeness of the
of the plains or Heath
the first of those fowls
we met with was
Missoure below
in the neighbour
of the Rocky
and from
which passe
between
ans Rapids
Gorgues
and
make

The large Black & White Pheasant is peculiar
to that portion of the Rocky Mountains watered by
the Columbia River. at least we did not see them untill
we reached the waters of that river, nor since we have
left those mountains. they are about the size of a
well grown hen. the cantour of the bird is much
that of the redish brown Pheasant common to
our country. the tail is proportionably as long and is
composed of 18 feathers of equal length. of a uniform
dark brown tiped with black. the feathers of the
body are of a dark brown black and white. the black

William Clark drew the sage grouse shown here. Lewis described it variously as a "mountain cock," "heath cock," and "cock of the plains." *(William Clark Papers, Missouri Historical Society, St. Louis)*

Cutright, Paul Russell. *Lewis & Clark: Pioneering Naturalists.* Lincoln: University of Nebraska Press/Bison Books, 1989.

Washington State University. "Lewis and Clark Among the Indians of the Pacific Northwest. Excerpts from the Journals of the Expedition of the Corps of Discovery: Flora and Fauna (recorded at Fort Clatsop)." Available on-line. URL: http://www.libarts.wsu.edu/history/Lewis_Clark/LCEXP_Flor.html. Downloaded on May 20, 2001.

gulls

It is claimed by some naturalists that MERIWETHER LEWIS's descriptions of the gulls seen by the expedition are insufficient to allow definite classification. Nevertheless, what he wrote has been taken up by later scientists who believe he described three types of gull. On March 6, 1806, Lewis made the following notes:

> "1st a small species the size of a Pegion; white except some black spots about the head and a little brown on the butt of the wing." This describes the Bonaparte's gull.
>
> "... the 2nd species somewhat larger of a light brown colour, with a mealy coloured back." This is the glaucous-winged gull.

> "3rd the large Grey gull, or white larus with a grayish brown back, and the light grey belly and breast, about the size of a well grown pullet. . . ." This last is the western gull.

Further Reading

Burroughs, Raymond Darwin, ed. *The Natural History of the Lewis and Clark Expedition.* East Lansing: Michigan State University Press, 1995.

Cutright, Paul Russell. *Lewis & Clark: Pioneering Naturalists.* Lincoln: University of Nebraska Press/Bison Books, 1989.

Washington State University. "Lewis and Clark Among the Indians of the Pacific Northwest. Excerpts from the Journals of the Expedition of the Corps of Discovery: Flora and Fauna (recorded at Fort Clatsop)." Available on-line. URL: http://www.libarts.wsu.edu/history/Lewis_Clark/LCEXP_Flor.html. Downloaded on May 20, 2001.

gunpowder   See FIREARMS; SUPPLIES AND EQUIPMENT.

Hall, Hugh (ca. 1772–unknown) *private in the permanent party*

Private Hugh Hall was, according to WILLIAM CLARK's journal, one of the more "adventuresome" members of the CORPS OF DISCOVERY. Born about 1772 in Carlisle, Pennsylvania, Hall joined the army in 1798. In 1803 he was recruited for the expedition from Captain John Campbell's Second Infantry Company; he was officially enrolled in the corps on January 1, 1804. Hall stood 5'8'' tall and had gray eyes, fair hair, a sandy complexion, and, according to Clark, a propensity for drink.

Because of his fondness for ALCOHOL, Hall also had a propensity for trouble. In May 1804 at ST. CHARLES, he and fellow privates WILLIAM WERNER and JOHN COLLINS were absent without leave to visit a local whiskey shop. The three were court-martialed, and Hall and Werner were sentenced to "twenty-five lashes on their bear backs," while Collins received 50 lashes.

On the night of June 28, 1804, Collins, who was on guard duty, convinced Hall to join him in tapping the whiskey reserves. By dawn they were both drunk—and under arrest. That same day a COURT-MARTIAL was convened, presided over by Sergeant NATHANIEL PRYOR and Privates JOHN COLTER, JOHN NEWMAN, PATRICK GASS, and JOHN THOMPSON. Collins was charged "with getting drunk on his post this morning out of whiskey put under his Charge as a Sentinel and for Suffering Hugh Hall to draw whiskey out of the Said Barrel intended for the party." Both were found guilty, with Collins was sentenced to 100 lashes and Hall to 50. The sentences were carried out that afternoon, and the expedition resumed its

journey—with Hall and Collins among the oarsmen in the KEELBOAT.

Hall's offenses were never so bad as to eject him from the corps. In October that same year, he experienced the other side of a court-martial when he sat on the panel that tried JOHN NEWMAN for mutiny. Newman was found guilty and discharged from the permanent party.

Hall was last seen in ST. LOUIS in 1809 when he borrowed some money from Lewis. He was apparently still living in 1828, but his whereabouts after that are unknown.

Further Reading

Clarke, Charles G. *The Men of the Lewis and Clark Expedition: A Biographical Roster of the Fifty-One Members and a Composite Diary of Their Activities from All Known Sources.* 1970. Reprint, Lincoln: Bison Books, University of Nebraska Press, 2002.

North Dakota Lewis & Clark Bicentennial Foundation. *Members of the Corps of Discovery.* Bismarck, N.Dak.: United Printing and Mailing, 2000.

PBS Online. *Lewis and Clark: Inside the Corps of Discovery:* "Lesser Known Members of the Corps." Available on-line. URL: http://www.pbs.org/lewisandclark/inside/lesser.html. Downloaded on May 18, 2001.

Hamilton, Alexander (1755–1804) *lawyer, politician, statesman*

Alexander Hamilton is one of the most important figures in American history for his role in the founding of the nation, as well as his contributions to its political and financial development. Other than Benjamin Franklin's, his is the only nonpresidential face to appear on American paper currency. He was also a supporter of the Lewis and Clark Expedition.

Born on the island of Nevis in the West Indies, Hamilton was the illegitimate son of James Hamilton and Rachel Faucett Levine, daughter of a Nevis planter and estranged wife of a Danish businessman. In 1772 he emigrated to America, where he received a bachelor's degree from King's College in New York City in 1774. Quick to side with the colonists in the American Revolution, Hamilton became known for his bravery and leadership in battle, playing significant roles in the Battle of White Plains and the Battle of Monmouth. In March 1777 he was promoted to lieutenant colonel and became aide-de-camp to George Washington.

Even before the war had ended, Hamilton's attention began to focus on politics. In letters to colonial leaders, he strongly criticized the new Confederation and advocated a strong, centralized government. As the war ended in 1783, he was admitted to the New York bar and opened an office on Wall Street. He served in the U.S. CONGRESS from 1782 to 1783 and founded the Bank of New York in 1784. In 1787–88, Hamilton, John Jay, and JAMES MADISON wrote *The Federalist Papers,* a series of letters defending the new Constitution. A classic commentary on U.S. constitutional law and the principles of government, approximately three-quarters of the papers

are attributable to Hamilton, who also secured New York's ratification of the Constitution.

After George Washington was elected president, Hamilton became the first secretary of the Treasury. In accordance with his vision of a centralized federal administration, he set to work increasing the government's coffers by imposing an excise tax on whiskey—the very sort of action against which he had only recently fought. When farmers in western Pennsylvania rebelled and began to attack tax collectors, Washington called for a militia to be formed to put down the Whiskey Rebellion. MERIWETHER LEWIS was one of those who responded to the call, beginning a military career that would eventually lead to the expedition of 1804–06.

As treasury secretary, Hamilton brought the postwar debt under control, saving the country from bankruptcy, and established himself as a notable economist with such publications as *Report on a National Bank* (1790), which led to the creation of the First Bank of the United States, and *Report on Manufacturers* (1791), which was the first significant counter to Adam Smith's *Wealth of Nations* (1776).

Hamilton left the Treasury in 1795 to return to his law practice and thereafter became one of the leaders of the Federalist Party, later advising cabinet members in President John Adams's administration. He was a vigorous opponent of THOMAS JEFFERSON, and the two often clashed. However, as a supporter of a strong national government and economic expansion, he approved of two of Jefferson's most important acts—the LOUISIANA PURCHASE and the congressionally funded Lewis and Clark Expedition. In fact, Hamilton had been one of the major financial supporters of Jefferson's previous proposal for an overland expedition sponsored by the AMERICAN PHILOSOPHICAL SOCIETY in 1793.

Although Hamilton and Jefferson were political opponents, Hamilton's main rival in politics and law was Aaron Burr. Hamilton was instrumental in thwarting Burr's aspirations to the presidency and to the governorship of New York. Burr challenged Hamilton to a duel, which was fought on July 11, 1804. Hamilton was mortally wounded and died the next day at the age of 49. His death was such a major event of the time that one of the first bits of news reported to Lewis and Clark on their return to ST. LOUIS was, "Mr. Burr & General Hamilton fought a duel; the latter was killed."

Further Reading

Brookhiser, Richard. *Alexander Hamilton, American.* New York: The Free Press, 1999.

McDonald, Forrest. *Alexander Hamilton: A Biography.* New York: W. W. Norton, 1982.

Although a political opponent of Thomas Jefferson, Alexander Hamilton supported the Louisiana Purchase and the Lewis and Clark Expedition. News of his 1804 death in a duel startled the Corps of Discovery on their return in 1806. *(Library of Congress, Prints and Photographs Division [LC-USZ62-91098])*

Harpers Ferry (Harper's Ferry)

Standing at the junction of the Shenandoah and Potomac Rivers in West Virginia, the arsenal and armory established in 1796 at Harpers Ferry played an important part in the Lewis and Clark Expedition. On March 16, 1803, MERIWETHER

The federal armory at Harpers Ferry supplied the expedition with firearms and Lewis's specially designed iron-frame boat. This engraving published ca. 1874 shows Harpers Ferry by moonlight. *(Library of Congress, Prints and Photographs Division [LC-USZ62-51189])*

LEWIS arrived there with a letter from Secretary of War HENRY DEARBORN, instructing the superintendent, Joseph Perkins, to "make such arms & iron work, as requested by the Bearer Captain Meriwether Lewis . . . with the least possible delay."

In addition to 15 new US Model 1803 rifles, Lewis procured powder horns, bullet moulds, extra rifle locks, gunsmith's repair tools, two dozen pipe tomahawks, and two dozen large knives. Although the explorer and many of his party preferred the longer "Pennsylvania" rifles, the Harpers Ferry model gave him the advantages of standardization. Bullets and bullet moulds, spare locks, and fittings were all interchangeable, an obvious advantage for the long journey ahead.

Most of the items that Lewis obtained at Harpers Ferry were standard issue, but it is likely that the armory staff had to exercise their ingenuity on such items as the pipe tomahawks. They certainly had to do so on Lewis's favorite project, the IRON-FRAME boat. Determined to have it made exactly to his specifications, he stayed at Harpers Ferry until mid-April to supervise its construction. As he wrote to THOMAS JEFFERSON, "my greatest difficulty was the frame of the canoe, which could not be completed without my personal attention to such portions of it as would enable the workmen to understand the design perfectly."

Returning to the armory on July 7, 1803, Lewis collected the equipment he had ordered and left with it on a wagon for PITTSBURGH the following day. He wrote to Jefferson: "I shot my guns and examined the several articles which had been manufactured for me at this place; they appear to be well exe-

cuted." The only problem he would later have would be with the iron-frame boat, which failed due to the lack of proper caulking materials in the wilderness. Otherwise Harpers Ferry had served the expedition well.

See also FIREARMS.

Further Reading

Ambrose, Stephen E. *Undaunted Courage: Meriwether Lewis, Thomas Jefferson, and the Opening of the American West.* New York: Simon and Schuster, 1996.

Hawke, David Freeman. *Those Tremendous Mountains: The Story of the Lewis and Clark Expedition.* New York: W. W. Norton & Company, 1998.

Jeffrey, Joseph D. "Meriwether Lewis at Harpers Ferry." *We Proceeded On* 20 (November 1994).

Hat Rock

On October 16, 1805, the expedition reached the junction of the SNAKE RIVER and COLUMBIA RIVER near present-day Pasco and Kennewick, Washington. There they met the Yakama (Yakima) and the WANAPAM INDIANS before proceeding down the Columbia. On October 19 they arrived at the point on the river where it bends west at the mouth of the Walla Walla River. Here they met Chief YELLEPT of the WALLA WALLA INDIANS.

In his journal for that day, Sergeant PATRICK GASS noted: "In the whole country around, there are only level plains, except for a few hills on some parts of the river." WILLIAM CLARK was more specific about one of those hills, a distinctive stone outcropping passed a few miles before reaching modern Umatilla, Oregon: "14 miles to a rock in a Lard. resembling a hat just below a rapid." Appropriately, he bestowed the name of Hat Rock on this landmark, marking the spot on his map with a dot and the word *hat*. Unlike many geographical features named by Lewis and Clark, Hat Rock retained its name and is now part of Hat Rock State Park in Heriston, Oregon. The section of the Columbia the expedition paddled is now Lake Wallula, which was formed in 1953 by the McNary Dam.

Further Reading
Fifer, Barbara, and Vicky Soderberg. *Along the Trail with Lewis and Clark.* Great Falls, Mont.: Montana Magazine, 1998.
Peterson, Nick. "Umatilla County's Hat Rock a significant site on Lewis and Clark's route." *East Oregonian.* Available on-line. URL: http://www.eastoregonian.com/stories/99/apr/01/story1. html. Posted on April 1, 1999.

Hawk's Feather (Piahito) (unknown–unknown)
Arikara Indian chief

When the CORPS OF DISCOVERY met the ARIKARA INDIANS in October 1804, the nation was then living in three villages just north of present-day Mobridge, South Dakota. Each village was jealous of its independence, and each had its own chief. The northernmost of the three, Waho-erha—or "the third village," as MERIWETHER LEWIS and WILLIAM CLARK called it—had Hawk's Feather for its chief. Although located close to the other two villages, the Arikara in Waho-erha spoke a different language, and it is now believed that they were remnants of other nations who had joined the Arikara for protection. One significant factor was that the village of Hawk's Feather had not been involved in the war with the MANDAN INDIANS a few years previously.

After the explorers' initial formal meeting with all three chiefs on October 10, during which Lewis had spoken of the need for peace with other Indian nations and the advantages of trade with the United States, Hawk's Feather and the other two chiefs, HAY and CROW AT REST, withdrew to consider their individual replies. Hawk's Feather gave his views to Lewis and Clark on October 12, telling them bluntly that he did not think peace between the Mandan and the Arikara was likely. He also warned them not to give too much credence to the optimistic statements of the other chiefs. Despite his own pessimism, he was willing to go, or to send one of his head men, with the expedition to the Mandan villages further up the MISSOURI RIVER.

Whether it was Hawk's Feather himself who accompanied the corps to the Mandan villages is still a matter for conjecture. It is known that he spoke of trusting the other two chiefs, Crow at Rest and Hay, to look after his village while he was away; yet the expedition's journals specifically state that the man who went with them was Anketahnasha, a "Chief of the

Town." One explanation is that Hawk's Feather simply accompanied them part of the way. Another is that, since Hawk's Feather's village spoke a different language from the other two, he may have been called Piahito in their villages but known as Anketahnasha in his own. Regardless of whether it was Hawk's Feather or his emissary who traveled with the expedition, he was the sole Arikara to give Lewis and Clark practical help in promoting peace with the Mandan.

Further Reading
Ronda, James P. *Lewis and Clark among the Indians.* Lincoln: University of Nebraska Press, 1984.

Hay (Pocasse) (unknown–unknown) *Arikara Indian chief*

On October 8, 1804, the CORPS OF DISCOVERY reached the villages of the ARIKARA INDIANS, just north of present-day Mobridge, South Dakota. A tense meeting with the TETON LAKOTA INDIANS (Teton Sioux) was behind them, and they were hoping for better relations with the Arikara, who were then allied in a trading partnership with the Sioux. On October 9, MERIWETHER LEWIS and WILLIAM CLARK had a short meeting with the three Arikara chiefs—Hay, CROW AT REST, and HAWK'S FEATHER—and arranged for a formal council the following day. However, because the two captains had accorded Crow at Rest the role of "grand chief," Hay and Hawk's Feather attended only reluctantly.

At the council, after Lewis had spoken on the need for peace among Indian nations and the advantages of trading with the United States, the usual GIFTS were given. The three chiefs then said they would give their answers on the next day, a development that Lewis and Clark had been warned would happen but did not appreciate. Since each of the Arikara villages guarded its independence jealously, each chief insisted on dealing with the explorers separately.

That night Sergeant JOHN ORDWAY and another member of the corps were Hay's guests at his village, named Rhtarahe. His wife served them bowls of beans and CORN and three other unnamed dishes, and Ordway found them "very friendly to us and seemed desirous to talk with us and scarcely kept their eyes off us."

On October 11 the party moved four miles upstream to Hay's village where, now conscious of his sensitivity as an independent chief, Lewis and Clark arranged a formal meeting with him the following day. Appeased, Hay reaffirmed the friendship of his village to the explorers, agreed that peace with the MANDAN INDIANS was desirable, and indicated the possibility of his visiting THOMAS JEFFERSON in Washington. He was doubtful, however, about the explorer's proposal to cut off Arikara trade connections with the Sioux, pointing out that the expedition could do little, if anything, to support them if the Sioux retaliated. "After you set out," he said, "many nations in the open plains may come to make war against us, we wish you to stop their guns and prevent it if possible." The captains could not help him, nor he them, and when they left the Arikara, much was still unresolved regarding the nation's future relationship with the United States.

Further Reading

Moulton, Gary E., ed. *The Journals of the Lewis and Clark Expedition: The Journals of John Ordway, May 14, 1804–September 23, 1806, and Charles Floyd, May 14–August 18, 1804.* Lincoln: University of Nebraska Press, 1996.

Ronda, James P. *Lewis and Clark among the Indians.* Lincoln: University of Nebraska Press, 1984.

Hay, John (unknown–unknown) *merchant, fur trader*

John Hay's name is not often mentioned in accounts of the Lewis and Clark Expedition, but he made a valuable contribution to its success. During the winter of 1803–04, while the CORPS OF DISCOVERY was at CAMP DUBOIS, MERIWETHER LEWIS spent a great deal of time in ST. LOUIS, seeking information on the MISSOURI RIVER from the town's merchants and traders. Among those he met was Hay, who had been a fur trader on the Red River. Hay was happy to pass on information to Lewis, including distances beginning "at the discharge of the Ottertail Lake, which forms the source of the Red River to his [Hay's] winter station on the Assinneboin River."

Hay was also the first interpreter employed by the expedition. When Lewis procured the journal written by JAMES MACKAY and JOHN EVANS about their time at the villages of the MANDAN INDIANS, he found that it was written in French. In a letter of December 28, 1803, he wrote to THOMAS JEFFERSON that the journal "is at present in the hands of Mr Hay who has promised to translate it for me." A translation of at least part of the journal accompanied the letter. Hay provided further help as an interpreter in persuading the Spanish officials at St. Louis to copy MAPS in their offices.

Although some references say Hay was the postmaster at Cahokia, Illinois, when he first met Lewis in winter 1803, there is some doubt about this. It is known that Lewis later recommended him for a federal post and that Hay did become postmaster at Cahokia, although when this was and whether it was because of Lewis's recommendation is not known.

Hay also gave some practical advice to WILLIAM CLARK. At the end of April 1804, Clark was supervising the packing and stowage of the expedition's baggage and SUPPLIES AND EQUIPMENT. A list shows that the FOOD alone weighed more than seven tons, and to this had to be added the camp equipment, kegs of whiskey, powder, and ammunition as well as long lists of Indian GIFTS. Based on his experience on the Red River, Hay advised Clark to disperse the equipment among different bales and packages. If a bale was lost overboard, then only a portion of the goods would be lost, whereas if it contained all of just one item, then the expedition would lose all they had. On this basis, it is known that, for example, one bale of "necessary stores" comprised four blankets, three cloth jackets, six flannel shirts, three pairs of overalls, four shirts, 200 flints, two gim-lets (a small tool for making holes), 12 pairs of socks, memorandum books, a half-pound of colored thread, three sets of rifle locks, and a screwdriver.

Hay's advice was good, and Clark took it, dispersing the Indian gifts into different bags in the same way. One of the gifts packed, not normally mentioned in the lists of Indian presents, probably seems bizarre to modern eyes: six and one-half-dozen Jew's harps. If this was a suggestion of Hay's he was right to make it. On August 30, 1804, JOSEPH WHITEHOUSE wrote of the meeting with the YANKTON NAKOTA INDIANS (Yankton Sioux): "The Indians after the goods were divided, was very merry; they play'd on the Jews harps & danced for us. . . ."

When the expedition returned in triumph to St. Louis on September 23, 1804, Lewis sent an immediate short letter to Jefferson announcing their arrival. Three days later he sat down to write a fuller report, a lengthy document that took him four days to write. It was to Hay that he gave the letter for copying and distribution.

Further Reading

Allen, John Logan. *Passage Through the Garden: Lewis and Clark and the Image of the American Northwest.* Urbana: University of Illinois Press, 1975. Reprint, New York: Dover Publications, 1991.

Hawke, David Freeman. *Those Tremendous Mountains: The Story of the Lewis and Clark Expedition.* New York: W. W. Norton & Company, 1998.

Hebert, Charles   See ENGAGÉS.

Heceta, Bruno   See EXPLORATION, EARLY; OREGON TERRITORY.

Heney, Hugh (Hugh Hené) (unknown–unknown) *fur trader*

When MERIWETHER LEWIS and WILLIAM CLARK arrived at the MANDAN villages in October 1804, as well as the Mandan and the HIDATSA INDIANS, they met fur traders, most of whom were associated with the NORTH WEST COMPANY. One of these was Hugh McCracken, and although it has not been confirmed that he was a Nor'Wester, it is known that he agreed to take a letter from them to Charles Chaboillez, a senior partner of the company. This letter explained the scientific nature of their expedition and invited Chaboillez to visit them. Chaboillez refused politely, although he offered his men and the resources of his company to obtain supplies if required. His reply was delivered by Hugh Heney in December 1804.

It remains unclear whether Heney, whose name is spelled Hené in some sources, was an agent for the North West Company at that time, although the JOURNALS imply that he was. It is known that he had previously led an expedition from ST. LOUIS up the Missouri and had been a partner of RÉGIS LOISEL in 1800. He is also recorded as being an employee for the HUDSON'S BAY COMPANY around 1807. It is possible that he was a freelancer of sorts, hiring out his services as needed. What is known for certain is that Lewis and Clark both liked him, pronouncing him to be "a Verry sensible, intelligent man," and found him an invaluable source of information as he was one of the few non-Indians who knew something about the country between the Mandan villages and the ROCKY MOUNTAINS. He also knew more about the Sioux (Dakota, Lakota, Nakota) than anyone they had met before. Another trader, FRANÇOIS LAROCQUE, noted in his journal that the captains "Enquired a great deal of Mr. Heney, concerning the sioux Nation, & Local Circumstances of that Country & lower part of the Missouri, of which they took notes." In addition to helping them with their ETHNOGRAPHY, he also gave them some snakebite medicine.

Such was their esteem for Heney that the following year, during the return journey, Lewis wrote a letter to him asking him to assist them in their peacekeeping efforts with the TETON LAKOTA INDIANS (Teton Sioux) and offering him the post of Indian agent for the United States. Specifically, Lewis and Clark wanted Heney to convince important Sioux chiefs to go to Washington to meet their "great white father," THOMAS JEFFERSON, as part of their plan to bring them into the ST. LOUIS–based trading network they were proposing. In his letter Lewis also provided details of the expedition, knowing that Heney would pass the news of its success on to others—presumably the North West Company—and thus make the British aware that the U.S. claim on OREGON TERRITORY had just been strengthened.

The letter was very long, carefully worded—and never delivered. At the YELLOWSTONE RIVER, Sergeant NATHANIEL PRYOR had been given the task of taking the letter to Heney, with additional instructions to give the trader three HORSES if he accepted the mission offered him. However, as Pryor and his party began their journey across country, their horses were stolen by CROW INDIANS, forcing them to turn back to the Yellowstone. There is no record of any further attempt to contact Heney after that.

Further Reading

Ambrose, Stephen E. *Undaunted Courage: Meriwether Lewis, Thomas Jefferson, and the Opening of the American West.* New York: Simon and Schuster, 1996.

Gottfred, A. "Lewis & Clark: A Canadian Perspective." *Northwest Journal.* Vol. XI, pp. 1–13. Available on-line. URL: http://www.northwestjournal.ca/XI1.htm. Downloaded on February 27, 2002.

Moulton, Gary E., ed. *The Journals of the Lewis and Clark Expedition.* 13 vols. Lincoln: University of Nebraska Press, 1983–2001.

Ronda, James P. *Lewis and Clark among the Indians.* Lincoln: University of Nebraska Press, 1984.

Hidatsa Indians (Minitaree Indians)

At the time MERIWETHER LEWIS and WILLIAM CLARK met them, the Siouan-speaking Hidatsa lived in three villages along the KNIFE RIVER in present-day North Dakota. They and their neighbors, the MANDAN INDIANS, were the center of a trading network in the upper regions of the MISSOURI RIVER that attracted European and Indian traders every year. Although they were called Gros Ventre (Atsina) by early French traders, they were not associated with that nation. In their JOURNALS, Lewis and Clark often referred to the Hidatsa by their alternate name, the Minitaree, meaning "willows." The name *Hidatsa* means "rows of lodges," which faintly described their villages of earthen lodges clustered irregularly around a central plaza. A protective log wall surrounded the villages.

According to tribal legend, the Hidatsa originally lived near Devil's Lake in North Dakota but were pushed southward by the Sioux (Dakota, Lakota, Nakota). Like the Mandan, they were primarily farmers who also hunted BUFFALO, but unlike the Mandan they were known to travel farther west, tracking buffalo herds into what is now Montana and South Dakota and raiding as far as the CONTINENTAL DIVIDE.

In November 1804 the CORPS OF DISCOVERY built FORT MANDAN by the Missouri, near the Hidatsa and the Mandan villages. In addition to their councils, Lewis and Clark interviewed chiefs of the two nations for information on the territory and Indians to the west. It was the Hidatsa who provided the most crucial data to the captains, giving them firsthand knowledge of what the expedition would face during the next thousand miles of their journey.

It was also at the Hidatsa villages that Lewis and Clark met SACAGAWEA, the young SHOSHONE woman who would become one of the most important members of the CORPS OF DISCOVERY. Captured by the Hidatsa a few years earlier, she was now the wife of TOUSSAINT CHARBONNEAU, a French-Canadian fur trader who had been living among the Indians and had bought her from them. Lewis and Clark knew that both would be invaluable as interpreters when the corps reached the Shoshone Indians and so hired Charbonneau on the condition that his wife accompany him.

In November 1804 the ASSINIBOINE INDIANS came to the Hidatsa and the Mandan villages and learned of the CORPS OF DISCOVERY encamped nearby. The Mandan chief BLACK CAT arranged for several prominent Assiniboine to meet the white explorers. In a period of several days, Lewis and Clark worked to facilitate peaceful relations among the Mandan, the Hidatsa, and the Assiniboine, but the latter would prove unwilling to cooperate.

As game became scarce during the winter of 1804–05, the soldiers at Fort Mandan were barely able to feed themselves. Members of the expedition began to barter with the Mandan and the Hidatsa for CORN and other dried vegetables. Using TRADE goods to buy FOOD would have quickly depleted the corps's stock, leaving no means of bartering for HORSES, food, or goodwill on the journey to the Pacific. The problem was solved when Private JOHN SHIELDS, a gunsmith and blacksmith, built a forge adjacent to the fort. With the help of WILLIAM BRATTON and ALEXANDER WILLARD, who built a kiln to make charcoal for the forge, Shields constructed war axes, arrowheads, and hide scrapers out of scrap iron, while also

The Hidatsa traveled as far as the Rocky Mountains on their raids. During the winter of 1804–05 at Fort Mandan, Lewis and Clark learned much from them about the country that lay to the west. This photo of a Hidatsa standing in a field was taken ca. 1908. *(Library of Congress, Prints and Photographs Division [LC-USZ62-96188])*

repairing the Indians' tools and weapons. In this way he exchanged his services for corn, which helped to get the expedition through the winter.

The corps briefly visited the Hidatsa and the Mandan again in August 1806, as the expedition was returning to ST. LOUIS. Here they took their leave of Charbonneau and Sacagawea, and the captains held a council with some of the chiefs. Unfortunately, they found that relations between their friends and the Assiniboine had only worsened.

Lewis and Clark spent more time in the area of the Hidatsa and the Mandan villages than anywhere else on the trip; one-fifth of the 862-day expedition was spent at the confluence of the Knife and MISSOURI RIVERS. Thirty years later, in 1837, the Hidatsa were devastated by a smallpox epidemic that forced them to regroup into a single village. In 1845 they moved to the area of Fort Berthold in North Dakota, where a large reservation for the Hidatsa, the Mandan, and the Arikara was established in 1870. These nations are now known as the Three Affiliated Tribes. At the Knife River Indian Villages National Historic Site, what little remains of the Hidatsa villages has

been preserved and protected. From a bluff above the river, shadowed depressions give evidence of where earthen lodges once stood.

See also ONE EYE.

Further Reading

Cash, Joseph H., and Gerald W. Wolff. *The Three Affiliated Tribes (Mandan, Arikara, and Hidatsa).* Phoenix: Indian Tribal Series, 1974.
Meyer, Roy W. *The Village Indians of the Upper Missouri: The Mandans, Hidatsas, and Arikaras.* Lincoln: University of Nebraska Press, 1977.
Ronda, James P. *Lewis and Clark among the Indians.* Lincoln: University of Nebraska Press, 1984.
Stewart, Frank Henderson. "Hidatsa Origin Traditions Reported by Lewis and Clark." *Plains Anthropologist* 21, no. 72 (1976): 89–92.
Waldman, Carl. *Encyclopedia of Native American Tribes.* Revised ed. New York: Checkmark Books, 1999.
Wood, W. Raymond, and Thomas D. Thiessen. *Early Fur Trade on the Northern Plains: Canadian Traders Among the Mandan and Hidatsa Indians, 1738–1818.* Norman: University of Oklahoma Press, 1985.

holidays   See RECREATION ON THE EXPEDITION.

horses

Although the CORPS OF DISCOVERY traveled most of their way by water, horses were essential to the expedition's success. Captains MERIWETHER LEWIS and WILLIAM CLARK knew the animals would be needed to carry equipment and baggage across the mountains of the West and relied upon them for HUNTING and scouting along much of their journey.

When the expedition left ST. CHARLES on May 21, 1804, they took with them four horses. These were used by the hunters who were sent out each day to act as scouts for the party as well as to chase game for FOOD and, perhaps more important, to carry game killed back to the river party. Since four deer were needed to feed the expedition each day, the horses filled an important packhorse role.

Unfortunately, by the time the explorers reached the TETON LAKOTA INDIANS (Teton Sioux) in September 1804, they had lost three of their horses; finally they lost the fourth, which may have been stolen by the Sioux. For the remainder of their journey up the MISSOURI RIVER, the party seemed to have used water transport alone, and when PORTAGE was required, they manhandled the loads themselves. Not until they met the SHOSHONE INDIANS beyond LEMHI PASS in August 1805 were they able to purchase and ride horses again.

The following month, during the treacherous crossing of the BITTERROOT MOUNTAINS, at least one packhorse was lost and three had to be sacrificed for food. Once the crossing was completed, however, they left their remaining horses with the

NEZ PERCE INDIANS and set off by canoe once more, down the CLEARWATER RIVER on their way to the COLUMBIA RIVER. It is doubtful whether they saw or used horses at all during the winter of 1805–06, and not until April 1806, on their return journey up the Columbia, did they start to bargain for sufficient horses to carry their SUPPLIES AND EQUIPMENT up the mountains. Later they rejoined the Nez Perce and collected the horses they had left the previous fall. During their time with the Nez Perce, Lewis studied that nation's technique for gelding horses and concluded that it was "preferable to that practiced by ourselves."

One of the factors rarely mentioned in the expedition's JOURNALS is the large number of horses involved in the return journey. When the party divided at TRAVELERS' REST, Clark took some 15 men and about 50 horses south up the valley of the BITTERROOT RIVER. This implies that each member of the party rode one horse and led two more. While every member of the party would have grown up with horses since childhood, the ability of each corps member to ride or lead any horse they came across is impressive. Only rarely is there an account of a horse throwing its rider, normally only when the animal had slipped or been frightened in some way.

Of the horses that went with Clark's party, all were stolen by Indians at various points in the journey. This prevented NATHANIEL PRYOR from carrying out his mission to take the horses to the MANDAN INDIAN villages and deliver an important letter for Lewis to the fur trader HUGH HENEY. Meanwhile, Lewis and some men had taken horses up the MARIAS RIVER and, after their harrowing encounter with BLACKFEET INDIANS, were forced to steal some horses themselves to escape. The journals do not indicate what happened to these horses after the expedition reunited on the Missouri, but it is assumed that they were released into the wilderness.

Further Reading

Burroughs, Raymond Darwin, ed. *The Natural History of the Lewis and Clark Expedition.* East Lansing: Michigan State University Press, 1995.

Cutright, Paul Russell. *Lewis & Clark: Pioneering Naturalists.* Lincoln: University of Nebraska Press/Bison Books, 1989.

Washington State University. "Lewis and Clark Among the Indians of the Pacific Northwest. Excerpts from the Journals of the Expedition of the Corps of Discovery: Flora and Fauna (recorded at Fort Clatsop)." Available on-line. URL: http://www.libarts.wsu.edu/history/Lewis_Clark/LCEXP_Flor.html. Downloaded on May 20, 2001.

Horses were an essential part of the Plains Indians' way of life. They were also crucial to the expedition as a means of crossing the Bitterroot Mountains and returning up the Columbia River. Lewis and Clark had to buy horses from several Indian nations in autumn 1805 and spring 1806. This photograph taken by Frank S. Balster shows Ute chief Ignacio Standing beside a horse in about 1904. *(Library of Congress, Prints and Photographs Division [LC-USZ62-112572])*

hostile encounters

The letter written by THOMAS JEFFERSON to MERIWETHER LEWIS setting out the expedition's MISSION OBJECTIVES was detailed and explicit with regard to encounters with Indian nations. Among other things, Jefferson wrote: "In all your intercourse with the natives, treat them in the most friendly & conciliatory manner which their own conduct will admit . . . As it is impossible for us to foresee in what manner you will be received by those people, whether with hospitality or hostility, so is it impossible to prescribe the exact degree of perseverance with which you are to pursue your journey. . . . To your own discretion therefore must be left the degree of danger you risk . . . we wish you to err on the side of your safety, and to bring back your party safe. . . ."

The CORPS OF DISCOVERY subsequently traveled more than 4,100 miles westward through unknown territory and met numerous Native Americans. Remarkably, there were very few hostile encounters, and relations with most nations were as friendly as Jefferson had hoped they would be. On occasion, however, the expedition had to face situations that threatened to undo all their diplomatic efforts. The two most significant incidents by coincidence occurred toward the beginning and then the end of their journey.

Late in September 1804, as they traveled up the MISSOURI RIVER, the expedition reached the mouth of the BAD RIVER, where they met the TETON LAKOTA INDIANS (Teton Sioux). A council was held on September 25, but since it did not go as well as Lewis and WILLIAM CLARK had hoped, they invited some of the chiefs on board the KEELBOAT. As Clark returned the chiefs to shore, three Teton warriors grabbed a PIROGUE's bowline, and another locked his arms around the boat's mast. One of the chiefs, THE PARTISAN, then demanded more GIFTS before allowing the expedition to continue upriver. At this, Clark drew his sword, and Lewis had the guns on the keelboat made ready to fire. The Indians likewise prepared their bows and arrows and aimed their muskets. An ugly situation seemed certain to erupt until Chief BLACK BUFFALO defused it by ordering the warriors away from the pirogue, although he continued to argue with Clark for some time afterward.

The expedition spent two more days with the Teton Lakota, during which there were festivities and demonstrations of Teton power. On the evening of September 27, another tense moment occurred when a boat cable broke as the pirogue containing The Partisan was approaching the keelboat. In the resulting confusion, armed Teton lined the riverbanks, convinced that they were being attacked by OMAHA INDIANS. The following morning, as the expedition prepared to leave, once again The Partisan stopped them to demand gifts while his warriors detained the pirogue. When Black Buffalo suggested that TOBACCO would placate them, Lewis and Clark at first refused but then relented, throwing some tobacco at the warriors holding the bowline. Only then was the expedition able to make its way upstream.

Thereafter the expedition's encounters with Indians were mostly peaceful, with only minor moments that could be described as dangerous. One of these took place the night of January 9, 1806, when Private HUGH MCNEAL was nearly killed by a TILLAMOOK Indian who wanted his blanket. A CHINOOK woman who knew McNeal saved his life by raising an alarm, although in the commotion that followed, his attacker escaped.

If anything tested Lewis's instructions to be "friendly and conciliatory" toward the native peoples, it was the Chinook Indians along the COLUMBIA RIVER, who relentlessly pilfered the expedition's dwindling supplies. As the corps was returning up the river, the increasing thefts enraged Lewis. The WATLALA INDIANS were so troublesome to the expedition that at one point JOHN SHIELDS had to draw his knife on some who were threatening to rob him. Then, on April 11, 1806, three Watlala stole Lewis's dog SEAMAN. It was the final straw, and, disregarding his instructions from Jefferson, Lewis sent some men after the thieves with instructions to kill if necessary. As soon as the Indians realized their danger, however, they released the dog. Thereafter the captains issued standing orders to shoot any Indians attempting to steal expedition property. The incidents of petty theft continued, however, until the expedition was free of The Dalles. The final one occurred on April 22, when TOUSSAINT CHARBONNEAU's saddle pad was stolen. Lewis threatened to torch a nearby Indian village unless it was returned, and

although he did not carry this out, he noted, ". . . I am quite disposed to treat them with every severyty, their defenseless state pleads forgiveness so far as respects their lives."

The expedition's final hostile encounter was the only one in which a fatality occurred. Late in July 1806, after an unsuccessful exploration of the MARIAS RIVER, Lewis, GEORGE DROUILLARD, JOSEPH FIELD, and REUBIN FIELD reached the TWO MEDICINE RIVER, where they met a small band of BLACKFEET INDIANS. Although aware of the Blackfeet's reputation for fierceness, the soldiers camped with the Indians by the riverbank. The following morning Lewis was awakened by a shout and saw Reubin Field attempting to wrestle his gun away from one of the Blackfeet. Lewis's and Drouillard's rifles had also been stolen. A scuffle ensued, and although the rifles were retrieved, Field fatally stabbed one of the Indians. Meanwhile, Lewis went after two Blackfeet who were trying to steal their horses. When one aimed a musket at him, Lewis shot the Indian in the stomach. The soldiers then grabbed their own horses and four of the Blackfeet's and rode south as fast as they could, traveling more than 100 miles before finally stopping for the night. The next day they continued riding for nearly 30 miles before meeting other members of the expedition at the Missouri River. Only then did they consider themselves safe.

This was the final and most alarming hostile encounter on the expedition. However, there was to be one more meeting with the Teton Lakota, albeit at a distance. On August 30, 1806, Lewis and Clark sighted a large band of armed Teton lining the southwest bank of the Missouri River. Clark made it clear by word and gesture that the soldiers would respond violently if the Indians attacked. Later in the afternoon, he and Lewis pointedly refused an invitation from a warrior (believed to be Black Buffalo) to come and parlay. From a nearby hilltop, the warrior struck the ground with the butt of his gun three times, a formal sign of anger, but nothing untoward followed. When the expedition arrived back at ST. LOUIS, Lewis and Clark could claim proudly that they had carried out Jefferson's instructions and brought their party home safely.

Further Reading
Ambrose, Stephen E. *Undaunted Courage: Meriwether Lewis, Thomas Jefferson, and the Opening of the American West.* New York: Simon and Schuster, 1996.
Ronda, James P. *Lewis and Clark among the Indians.* Lincoln: University of Nebraska Press, 1984.

Howard, Thomas Proctor (ca. 1779–unknown)
private in the permanent party
Private Thomas Howard's only claim to fame on the Lewis and Clark Expedition was to have been the last member of the CORPS OF DISCOVERY to be tried by COURT-MARTIAL. Other than this, he is rarely mentioned in the JOURNALS and appears to have been a steady but undistinguished participant in the historic journey. He was born in Massachusetts, enlisted in the U.S. Army in 1801, and officially joined the expedition late on January 1, 1804..Surprisingly, he never got into trouble for

drinking (as several others of the men did), even though Captain WILLIAM CLARK had wryly noted, "Howard never Drinks water."

He did, however, get into serious trouble the night of February 9, 1805, when he returned late to FORT MANDAN and rashly decided not to call the guard to let him in. Instead, he scaled the wall of the fort, an action that was observed and then followed by a MANDAN INDIAN. The two captains were appalled; if less-friendly Indians also climbed over the walls to get in, it could have dire consequences for the corps. MERIWETHER LEWIS first dealt with the Indian, ensuring that he would not repeat what he had done and sending him away with a piece of tobacco. Howard, however, was tried and found guilty of "Setting a pernicious example to the Savages." He was sentenced to received 50 lashes, but the court then recommended mercy and Howard was spared the lashing. This proved to be the last court-martial of the expedition.

Another mention of Howard occurs in July 1806 during the portion of the return journey when the corps had been split into smaller parties. Howard was part of the group under Sergeant JOHN ORDWAY whose mission was to travel down the JEFFERSON RIVER and then the MISSOURI RIVER to the GREAT FALLS. On July 13 the private was injured when he fell between one of the CANOES and a log, but he apparently made a quick recovery.

Howard stayed in the army following the expedition and later married a Genevieve Roy in ST. LOUIS; their son Joseph entered the FUR TRADE. The date and place of Howard's death are unknown.

Further Reading

Clarke, Charles G. *The Men of the Lewis and Clark Expedition: A Biographical Roster of the Fifty-One Members and a Composite Diary of Their Activities from All Known Sources.* 1970. Reprint, Lincoln: Bison Books, University of Nebraska Press, 2002.

North Dakota Lewis & Clark Bicentennial Foundation. *Members of the Corps of Discovery.* Bismarck, N.Dak.: United Printing and Mailing, 2000.

PBS Online. *Lewis and Clark: Inside the Corps of Discovery:* "Lesser Known Members of the Corps." Available on-line. URL: http://www.pbs.org/lewisandclark/inside/lesser.html. Downloaded on May 18, 2001.

Hudson's Bay Company

At the time of the Lewis and Clark Expedition, the Hudson's Bay Company was one of the most powerful participants in the expanding FUR TRADE. The company received its charter from King Charles II of England in 1670, giving them a monopoly on trade in the territory along all rivers flowing into the Hudson Bay. The charter also gave them executive, judicial, and legislative authority over the same vast area. The rights of the company were resisted by the French, who claimed that CANADA belonged to them. When FRANCE gave up its claim in 1763, French traders continued to seek furs and moved into areas where the Hudson's Bay Company had no jurisdiction.

These rival traders eventually combined to form the NORTH WEST COMPANY of Montreal.

In a power struggle for the lucrative fur trade, both companies used every means to persuade the Indian nations of Canada and the northern United States to trade exclusively with them. The methods they employed—including offers of money, guns, and whiskey—reflect little credit on either organization. The struggle came to a conclusion in 1821, when they amalgamated. The combined company lost its monopoly over the western fur trade in 1859, and most of its land holdings were surrendered to the Canadian government in 1869.

President THOMAS JEFFERSON fully realized the adverse effect on the United States caused by the Hudson's Bay Company's and North West Company's influence and trade in the northern areas of the newly acquired LOUISIANA TERRITORY. For one thing, it strengthened British claims on the U.S.-Canadian border since Indian nations looked to the British for trading goods. He also appreciated that the United States's claim to sovereignty over the area would carry little weight among those nations as long as the only organized trading groups with whom they came into contact were British. This is why, in his letter to MERIWETHER LEWIS outlining the MISSION OBJECTIVES of the expedition, Jefferson specifically stated that "[s]ome account too of the path of the Canadian traders from the Mississippi . . . to where it strikes the Missouri & of the soil and rivers in its course, is desirable."

Lewis knew from traders and trappers that the villages of the MANDAN INDIANS were the center of a vast trading network that attracted Indians from all over the northern plains as well as representatives of the North West Company and the Hudson's Bay Company, who were then the main source of TRADE goods for the Mandan and their allies. This was something Jefferson and Lewis wanted to change, and Lewis began the process at his first conference with the Mandan chiefs when he encouraged them to join in a trading relationship with the United States. In July 1806, when Lewis met the BLACKFEET INDIANS on TWO MEDICINE RIVER, he learned that they too relied on the Canadian companies, who would give them guns, whiskey, and blankets in exchange for wolf and BEAVER skins.

Although trappers and traders soon followed Lewis and Clark up the MISSOURI RIVER, it was some time before the Hudson's Bay Company lost its position among the northern Indian nations. In 1808 MANUEL LISA and others formed the St. Louis Missouri Fur Company, with Lewis and Clark as original partners in the enterprise. JOHN JACOB ASTOR formed the American Fur Company in 1808 and the Pacific Fur Company in 1811, and William Henry Ashley began the Rocky Mountain Fur Company in 1822. All of these finally broke the grip of the amalgamated Hudson's Bay and North West Company on the western fur trade.

Further Reading

Alwin, John A. "Pelts, Provisions, and Perceptions: The Hudson's Bay Company Mandan Indian Trade, 1795–1815." *Montana: The Magazine of Western History* 29 (1979): 16–27.

Bryce, George. *The Remarkable History of the Hudson's Bay Company, Including That of the French Traders of North-western Canada, and of the North-west XY, and Astor Fur Companies.* 2d ed. New York: B. Franklin, 1968.

MacKay, Douglas. *The Honourable Company: A History of the Hudson's Bay Company.* Freeport, N.Y.: Books for Libraries Press, 1970.

Newman, Peter C. *Caesars of the Wilderness.* Markham, Ontario: Viking, 1987.

Rich, E. E. *The Fur Trade and the Northwest to 1857.* Toronto: McClelland and Stewart, 1967.

Wood, W. Raymond, and Thomas D. Thiessen. *Early Fur Trade on the Northern Plains: Canadian Traders Among the Mandan and Hidatsa Indians, 1738–1818.* Norman: University of Oklahoma Press, 1985.

Hungry Creek   See LOLO TRAIL.

hunting

Given the scope of the journey they were to undertake, it was impossible for the CORPS OF DISCOVERY to take all the provisions they would need on the expedition. It was therefore necessary to procure FOOD as they traveled, and this was done largely by hunting. The corps's best hunters included GEORGE DROUILLARD, JOSEPH FIELD, REUBIN FIELD, JOHN COLTER, and JOHN COLLINS.

Early in the trip up the lower MISSOURI RIVER, Drouillard began to lead three- or four-man hunting parties. Entries in the expedition's JOURNALS frequently made note of their successes or failures. A June 1804 entry reported seven DEER killed in one day; on another day a deer, an ELK, and an ANTELOPE were taken.

As the corps entered the GREAT PLAINS, they found elk, deer, and BEAVER in great abundance, as well as GEESE, cranes, pheasant, ducks, and other birds. On August 23, 1804, Joseph Field excitedly reported killing the expedition's first BUFFALO; there would be many more. The hunters also killed BEARS, and in present-day North Dakota they encountered their first grizzly. This was dangerous prey for the men; a wounded grizzly could attack before the hunter's rifle was reloaded. Indeed, WILLIAM BRATTON was nearly killed by an enraged grizzly he had shot before others came to his assistance.

Preparing to winter near the MANDAN INDIAN villages, the explorers welcomed the advice and assistance of the native hunters, joining them for a buffalo hunt. The Indians rode bareback and used bows and arrows. The visitors used their rifles, killing 20 buffalo.

The party came to rely on as much as eight pounds of fresh meat per person per day. That all changed when the corps began the most trying part of the journey, the passage through the BITTERROOT MOUNTAINS. Very little game was available, and they were forced to eat three of their HORSES. Even with that, the members of the corps were near starvation by the time they reached the CLEARWATER RIVER, west of the mountains.

The Plains Indians had several different methods of hunting buffalo. In this 1908 painting by Frederic Remington, hunters disguise themselves with buffalo hides. *(Library of Congress, Prints and Photographs Division [LC-D4-90473])*

The winter camp of 1805–06 at FORT CLATSOP on the Oregon coast was a culinary disappointment for the explorers. There were elk and deer, but nowhere near as plentiful as on the plains, particularly in the latter part of their sojourn. The men ended up procuring roots, dried fish, and dog meat from the nearby CLATSOP INDIANS. Only when they had returned east to the Great Plains were they able to once again satisfy their hunger with elk, deer, and buffalo.

Further Reading

Burroughs, Raymond Darwin, ed. *The Natural History of the Lewis and Clark Expedition.* East Lansing: Michigan State University Press, 1995.

Johnson, Morris D., and Joseph Knue. *Feathers from the Prairie: A Short History of Upland Game Birds.* 2d ed. Bismarck: North Dakota Game and Fish Dept., 1989.

Knue, Joseph. *Big Game of North Dakota: A Short History.* Bismarck: North Dakota Game and Fish Department, 1991.

I

illnesses and injuries

In the course of the journey to the Pacific coast and back, members of the CORPS OF DISCOVERY suffered a variety of illnesses and infections and an assortment of wounds. Given the state of medical knowledge in the early 19th century, the absence of a trained doctor, and the often treacherous terrain, it is remarkable that the expedition suffered only one fatality, that of CHARLES FLOYD on August 20, 1804, from what appears to have been a ruptured appendix.

Injuries during the expedition were inevitable. As early as July 4, 1804, Clark's journal noted that "Jos: Fields got bit by a Snake, which was quickly doctered with Bark by Cap Lewis." Other medical problems included cuts, boils, sore feet, strained backs, inflamed joints, broken limbs, and numerous infections. Sergeant NATHANIEL PRYOR suffered from a dislocated shoulder that popped out three times during the expedition; the first time this happened, it took four tries to get the shoulder back in place. Clark developed a growth on his ankle, causing him much pain. In some cases, however, a corps member's disability was called into doubt. Early in August 1805, Sergeant PATRICK GASS reported himself in great pain due to an accident and thus unable to paddle a canoe. Lewis archly noted in his journal, however, that Gass "could march with convenience."

Too many illnesses were genuine and sometimes delayed the expedition from continuing. In June 1805, as the corps prepared for its first PORTAGE on the upper MISSOURI RIVER, SACAGAWEA broke into a fever and experienced irregular breathing and a weak pulse, as well as twitching in her arms and fingers. (It has since been surmised that a gonorrheal infection may been the cause of her symptoms.) After bleeding failed to help her (indeed, it might have exacerbated her condition), Lewis prescribed "two dozes of barks and opium" as well as plenty of sulphur water. The treatment worked, and she was soon well enough to continue the journey. (See SACAGAWEA SPRING.)

The captains were, by default, the expedition's doctors, with Lewis bearing the greater responsibility for the corps's medical care. He had in fact studied with Dr. BENJAMIN RUSH in PHILADELPHIA to learn basic tenets of MEDICINE AND MEDICAL TREATMENT prior to the start of the expedition. But Clark also did his share of tending to the ill and injured, and he and Lewis looked after each other throughout the journey. Both captains relied, perhaps a little too heavily, on Rush's Pills—dubbed "Rush's Thunderbolts" by the men. These were a cure-all purgative devised by Rush that often did more harm than good, particularly after their life-threatening crossing of the BITTERROOT MOUNTAINS in September 1805. Tired, cold, and hungry, the explorers eagerly ate roots, berries, and dried fish that were generously supplied by the NEZ PERCE INDIANS. It was a sudden change of diet from the game they were used to, and there may have been bacteria in the fish. Soon almost everyone in the party was suffering from dysentery. Clark decided that a course of Rush's Pills would help; he could not have been more wrong. On September 24 Lewis reported, "Several men [were] So unwell that they were Compelled to lie on the Side of the road for Some time." Lewis himself was unable to supervise the construction of CANOES for the descent to the COLUMBIA RIVER. Clark rashly continued to prescribe the Thunderbolts, sometimes combined with other purgatives.

It was only after their departure down the CLEARWATER RIVER on October 7 that the party finally began to recover.

Private WILLIAM BRATTON is mentioned most often in the expedition's journals for the number of illnesses he suffered. In February 1806, while working at the SALTWORKS on the Oregon coast, he became so ill that Lewis's notes for March 21 indicate an uneasiness about whether he would recover: "[T]he pain of which he complains most seems to be seated in the small of his back and remains obstinate. I believe that it is the rheumatism." Bratton's condition worsened and became so bad that when the party left FORT CLATSOP late in March, he traveled by canoe and horseback, while the rest of the party walked. A month later, as the expedition waited for the snow to melt in the higher elevations of the BITTERROOT MOUNTAINS, Clark and JOHN SHIELDS took Bratton's treatment in hand. A sweat lodge was built wherein heated stones were placed. Water was then poured over the stones to make steam. After 20 minutes inside the lodge, Bratton was taken out, plunged into cold water, and then returned to the sweat lodge. He was also given mint tea to drink. The treatments seemed to work, as he began to walk again within a day and was greatly improved by the end of June. Scholars have since theorized that his problem was either a dislocated disk or lumbago.

Later, on the return trip along the YELLOWSTONE RIVER, Private GEORGE GIBSON was thrown from his horse. He landed on a thick snag that cut two inches into his thigh. The next day, he was in terrible pain from his hip down to his knee. It was more than a week before Gibson was able to walk.

Perhaps the most embarrassing injury—and the only gunshot wound—was suffered by Captain Lewis. On August 11, 1806, Lewis and Private PIERRE CRUZATTE were hunting for elk, and while they were separated, Lewis was shot in the buttocks. The one-eyed Cruzatte denied having shot his captain, but as the bullet was army issue, it was evident that he was the guilty party. For some time thereafter as they traveled, Lewis was forced to lie on his stomach in a PIROGUE.

Further Reading

Ambrose, Stephen E. *Undaunted Courage: Meriwether Lewis, Thomas Jefferson, and the Opening of the American West.* New York: Simon and Schuster, 1996.

Chuinard, Eldon G. *Only One Man Died: The Medical Aspects of the Lewis and Clark Expedition.* Glendale, Calif.: A. H. Clark Co., 1979.

Paton, Bruce C. *Lewis and Clark: Doctors in the Wilderness.* Golden, Colo.: Fulcrum Publishing, 2001.

Peck, David J. *Or Perish in the Attempt: Wilderness Medicine in the Lewis & Clark Expedition.* Helena, Mont.: Farcountry Press, 2002.

Will, Drake W. "Lewis and Clark: Westering Physicians." *Montana: The Magazine of Western History* 21, no. 4 (1971): 2–17.

Indian guides

Always confident—sometimes overconfident—MERIWETHER LEWIS and WILLIAM CLARK led their expedition across the continent by following rivers, referring to MAPS of what was then known of the LOUISIANA TERRITORY, and making ASTRONOMICAL OBSERVATIONS to help navigate their way. Popular folklore has SACAGAWEA guiding the CORPS OF DISCOVERY across the ROCKY MOUNTAINS to the PACIFIC OCEAN. In truth, however, the SHOSHONE woman's primary function was as an interpreter and as a token of peace for the Indian nations whom the expedition encountered along its journey. Nevertheless, on occasion even Lewis and Clark had to accept they needed help, and that was when the explorers turned to Indian guides. Sometimes they hired Indians to get them through a section of country or to pilot them through certain areas on a river; other times they needed assistance on a larger scale.

In September 1805 they faced the daunting task of crossing the BITTERROOT MOUNTAINS. The previous month the corps had met the Shoshone Indians, with whom they had negotiated for HORSES to make the crossing. But they also needed a guide who would be able to take the expedition across the mountains. This was particularly important because of the difficulties of which Chief CAMEAHWAIT had warned them. The man chosen for the task was OLD TOBY, who, with his son, took the expedition over the LOLO TRAIL. Even with his guidance, the crossing was far more dangerous and took much more time than any of them had anticipated. This was due in large part to the snow and the amount of debris that covered the path, factors that contributed to Toby's losing his way and leading the corps astray for two days until he found the trail again. Finally, 11 days after they had started, the exhausted and starving expedition descended onto WEIPPE PRAIRIE, where they met the NEZ PERCE INDIANS.

Lewis and Clark had intended that Old Toby continue with them on the next stage of the journey, down the CLEARWATER RIVER and the SNAKE RIVER, but before they had gone very far, he and his son left the expedition surreptitiously, without being paid for their services. It is thought that fear of both the rapids and the Indians downriver were behind their abrupt departure. In any event, the captains had acquired two Nez Perce guides, chiefs TWISTED HAIR and TETOHARSKY. Because the route involved a straight river passage, they were not so much guides as messengers who went ahead of the expedition to advise nations like the WALLA WALLA INDIANS that white men with peaceful intentions were on the way. Twisted Hair and Tetoharsky filled their roles of "advance men" well and accompanied the expedition a significant distance down the COLUMBIA RIVER before turning back.

During the return journey, in early May 1806, the expedition again encountered Tetoharsky, who led them to Twisted Hair's village. During the next several weeks, the captains attempted to hire some Nez Perce to take them back over the Bitterroot Mountains, but Chief BROKEN ARM refused to cooperate, stating that none of his warriors would cross the mountains until the snows had melted sufficiently. In June the expedition attempted to make the crossing without guides but soon found that the chief was right; the Lolo Trail was impassable. They set up camp, and GEORGE DROUILLARD and GEORGE SHANNON went back to the Nez Perce villages to bargain for guides. While they were gone, two young Nez Perce met the expedition and were persuaded to stay with them for a few days. When Drouillard and Shannon finally returned with three Indians, making five guides in all, the safety of the corps was assured.

The subsequent crossing, while still difficult due to the snow, was much easier than the first had been due to the expertise of the Nez Perce. After seven days, on June 30, the expedition arrived at TRAVELERS' REST, where they set up camp and discussed what to do next. The decision was made to split the expedition into two, with the five Indian guides to accompany Lewis and his party for another day, going north along the BITTERROOT RIVER. On July 4, when they finally took their departure, Lewis wrote, "These affectionate people our guides betrayed every emmotion of unfeigned regret at separating from us." It was an emotion he undoubtedly shared.

While Sacagawea did not serve as a guide throughout the journey, she did prove enormously valuable to Clark and his party once they reentered her Shoshone homeland in July 1806. Familiar with the territory, she was able to make suggestions for the route to take to the YELLOWSTONE RIVER. On July 13 Clark wrote: "The indian woman, who has been of great Service to me as a pilot through this Country, recommends a gap [later to become BOZEMAN PASS] in the mountain more South, which I shall cross." It was the last recorded instance of the many contributions she made to the success of the expedition, which ensured her place in American legend.

Further Reading

Ambrose, Stephen E. *Undaunted Courage: Meriwether Lewis, Thomas Jefferson, and the Opening of the American West.* New York: Simon and Schuster, 1996.

Ronda, James P. *Lewis and Clark among the Indians.* Lincoln: University of Nebraska Press, 1984.

influence of the expedition   See EFFECTS AND INFLUENCES OF THE EXPEDITION.

ink

When MERIWETHER LEWIS was preparing for the expedition, one thing he made sure he had plenty of was ink; in fact, he brought along enough for two trips. The reason was simple: They needed ink to write LETTERS and, even more important, the JOURNALS they had been charged with keeping as record of the expedition and the scientific discoveries they made along the way. Both captains, all of the sergeants, and some of the privates kept journals. Ink was therefore a very necessary supply.

The ink used by Lewis and Clark was similar to that used by the Chinese as early as the second or third century A.D. The Egyptians and Chinese began to use liquid ink with reeds and brushes as much as five centuries before. Those early inks were probably made from carbon that was suspended in vegetable oil or animal glue. About 1,700 years ago, the Chinese developed solid ink—lampblack ground with a solution of glue or

gums—in the form of sticks or cakes. The user could scrape or shave bits of the solid ink and mix it with water whenever it was needed.

Lewis and Clark had a similar procedure, carrying ink in powdered form contained in papers. This was especially advantageous for traveling since in dry form the weight and volume of the ink were much less. Nevertheless, care had to be taken in mixing the powder with the right amount of water, and the WEATHER could affect the ink's consistency. On August 21, 1805, the morning air was so cold that Lewis wrote, "the ink freizes in my pen."

By the time of the expedition, ink technology was beginning to change. In 1772 a patent was issued in England for making colored inks. By the mid-19th century, there were new ink formulas using ammonia-based aniline dyes. These modern inks were less corrosive and could be used in the newly developed fountain pens.

Further Reading

Carvalho, David N. *Forty Centuries of Ink.* New York: B. Franklin, 1971.

Lewis-Clark.org. "Portable Inkwell." From *Discovering Lewis and Clark.* Available on-line. URL: http://www.lewis-clark.org/FTCLVIRTUAL/te_inkwl.htm. Downloaded on March 10, 2002.

insects

The MISSION OBJECTIVES of the Lewis and Clark Expedition encompassed a wide range, from interactions with Indians to the study of the natural environment. THOMAS JEFFERSON was specific in every respect, writing, for instance: ". . . worthy of notice will be . . . times of appearance of particular birds, reptiles or insects." However, while MERIWETHER LEWIS and WILLIAM CLARK made studies of numerous new species of animals, their mentions of insects were confined to expressions of annoyance and sometimes distress. In short, there was no need for them to seek out insects, for the insects found them all too often—especially the mosquitoes.

While science had not yet discovered the connection between mosquitoes and malaria (that would not happen for another hundred years), the members of the CORPS OF DISCOVERY knew that these insects were going to be an irritation along much of their journey. Lewis himself had already had plenty of experience with mosquitoes during his time as an army paymaster in the OHIO RIVER area. For this reason, when he was purchasing supplies for the expedition in 1803, he took particular care to buy "Muscatoe Curtains," eight parcels of cat gut (for repairing the mosquito curtains), and 200 pounds of tallow mixed with 50 pounds of hog's lard, to be used as an insect repellent.

Gnats and ticks would also prove to be a nuisance, but the mosquitoes would be the worst, beginning to plague the expedition even before it left CAMP DUBOIS. On March 25, 1804, Captain Clark wrote: "The musquetors are verry bad this evening." By June 1804, as they neared the KANSAS RIVER, the plague of both mosquitoes and gnats had become even worse, attacking eyes, ears, and every exposed part of the body. Smudge fires and the application of grease to every patch of bare skin had little effect. Not until the cool WEATHER of October 1804 arrived did the party get its first respite from the pest. However, their departure from FORT MANDAN in April 1805 coincided with the beginning of the warm weather and the renewal of mosquito attacks that were to continue until they reached the CONTINENTAL DIVIDE.

On July 24, 1805, at the THREE FORKS of the MISSOURI RIVER, Lewis wrote: "Our trio of pests still invade and obstruct us on all occasions. These are the musquetoes, eye knats and prickley pears, equal to any three curses that ever poor Egypt laiboured under, except the Mahometant yoke." Yet when the explorers at last reached the PACIFIC OCEAN, they found another pest awaiting them. They had noted the FISHING villages they had passed were infested with fleas but had escaped most of these by traveling in CANOES. It was different at FORT CLATSOP, where Clark wrote on December 26, 1805, that fleas had allowed him little sleep for two nights, and the men had "to kill them out of their blankets every day."

Sergeant PATRICK GASS speculated that occasionally the fleas proved too much even for the Indians nearby. On April 15, 1806, on the return journey up the COLUMBIA RIVER, he noted that a village they had passed on the way downstream only months before "has been lately torn down, and again erected at a short distance from the old ground where it formerly stood. The reason for this removal I cannot conjecture, unless to avoid the fleas, which are more numerous in this country than any insects I ever saw."

Once back over the Continental Divide, at the GREAT FALLS in July 1806, Lewis was forcibly reminded of the perpetual annoyance of the expedition's greatest pest: "Musquetoes excessively troublesome insomuch that without the protection of my musquetoe bier I should have found it impossible to wright a moment." He added a note that was, incidentally, the last mention of SEAMAN in the JOURNALS: "[M]y dog howls with the torture he experiences."

In retrospect, it is easy merely to sympathize with the annoyance and irritation that mosquitoes caused the expedition. The corps members' suffering can be better appreciated from the events of August 1806, after Lewis and Clark had split up the party. While Lewis had gone northeast to explore the MARIAS RIVER, Clark had gone south to travel down the YELLOWSTONE RIVER. In early August he and his party arrived at the agreed rendezvous point at the mouth of the Yellowstone. He had no idea where Lewis and his men were, nor did he know whether Patrick Gass and JOHN ORDWAY had, with their separate groups, even reached the Missouri River safely. Yet despite his anxiety and that of his men to see their friends again, mosquitoes caused them to change their plan.

After a night and a day, still with no news, Clark reluctantly took his party downstream, leaving a note for Lewis to say they had moved on due to a lack of game and abundance

of mosquitoes. In his journal he wrote that mosquitoes denied even sleep to his men "who had no bears [biers] to kep them off at night and nothing to Screen them but their blankets which are worn and have maney holes." Not until August 7 did they stop, and he was able to write, "[T]he air was exceedingly Clear and Cold and not a misquetor to be Seen, which is a joyfull circumstance."

Further Reading

Ambrose, Stephen E. *Undaunted Courage: Meriwether Lewis, Thomas Jefferson, and the Opening of the American West.* New York: Simon and Schuster, 1996.

Cutright, Paul Russell. *Lewis & Clark: Pioneering Naturalists.* Lincoln: University of Nebraska Press/Bison Books, 1989.

Hunt, Robert. "The Blood Meal: Mosquitoes and Agues on the Lewis and Clark Expedition." *We Proceeded On* 18, no. 3 (May and August 1992).

MacGregor, Carol Lynn, ed. *The Journals of Patrick Gass, Member of the Lewis and Clark Expedition.* Missoula, Mont.: Mountain Press Publishing Company, 1997.

instructions   See MISSION OBJECTIVES.

interpretation

As MERIWETHER LEWIS was preparing to leave Washington and begin his journey west, Secretary of War HENRY DEARBORN gave him authorization to recruit up to 12 men as well as a sergeant and one interpreter. However, just as the number of personnel in the CORPS OF DISCOVERY later increased, so did the number of interpreters Lewis and WILLIAM CLARK would need. Indian LANGUAGES differed from nation to nation, and not all could understand sign language. Consequently, interpretation became one of the captains' overriding concerns as they proceeded west.

Only two interpreters, GEORGE DROUILLARD and TOUSSAINT CHARBONNEAU, were hired on a permanent basis. The remainder—a dozen and perhaps more—were either traders who happened to be on the spot when the expedition arrived at a particular Indian village or other corpsmen (usually ENGAGÉS) who knew particular languages. Drouillard, who also possessed other outstanding frontier skills, was the first to be hired. His specialty was the sign language of the PLAINS INDIANS, which was of little help once the corps reached the PACIFIC OCEAN. Private GEORGE GIBSON also had a basic understanding of sign language and was called on to help when needed.

Along the MISSOURI RIVER, Lewis and Clark had the additional benefit of on-site interpreters. In June 1804 they met PIERRE DORION, a trader who had lived among the YANKTON NAKOTA INDIANS (Yankton Sioux) for 20 years and knew their language as well as French and English; he readily agreed to accompany the expedition upriver. The first group of Indians they met, the OTOE (Oto) and MISSOURI in early August 1804, were accompanied by a French trader identified in the JOUR-NALS only as "Fairfong" who acted as interpreter in the subsequent council. Later that month the expedition came to the Yankton Nakota, who greeted them warmly and seemed receptive to the idea of sending a delegation to Washington. They had one caveat, though: Pierre Dorion must accompany them. The captains agreed to this and left Dorion with the Yankton when they proceeded upriver.

This was unfortunate because their next meeting, with the TETON LAKOTA INDIANS (Teton Sioux), went badly, in part because they lacked a good interpreter. Drouillard's sign language was largely ineffective with the Teton, and PIERRE CRUZATTE could speak only a few words of Sioux. How much these interpretation problems affected the corps's difficult meeting with the Teton is a matter of conjecture.

At the villages of the ARIKARA INDIANS, Lewis and Clark met PIERRE-ANTOINE TABEAU and JOSEPH GRAVELINES, two French traders who knew both the Arikara and Sioux languages. Both men proved helpful, with Gravelines serving as interpreter during the meetings with Arikara chiefs. He later joined the expedition for a period at FORT MANDAN and was nearly hired to accompany the expedition to the PACIFIC OCEAN but instead piloted the KEELBOAT downstream when it returned to ST. LOUIS in spring 1805.

At the villages of the MANDAN and the HIDATSA INDIANS, the captains met two traders, RENÉ JESSAUME and Toussaint Charbonneau, who had been living among those nations for a number of years. Both were hired as interpreters, and both assisted not only in translating but in Lewis's efforts to record the Mandan and the Hidatsa vocabularies (a process made more difficult by the two interpreters' arguments over the meanings of certain words). Jessaume served as translator during the first council with the Mandan and the Hidatsa and in subsequent meetings both before the expedition departed FORT MANDAN in April 1805 and after they returned in August 1806. It was Charbonneau, though, who was asked to go with the expedition to the Pacific because he had something Jessaume did not: his Shoshone wife SACAGAWEA. The expedition would need a translator when they reached the territory of the SHOSHONE INDIANS, from whom they hoped to purchase HORSES. Sacagawea was therefore an ideal addition to the party.

As the expedition proceeded farther west, George Drouillard's sign language proved to be of little use. Instead, starting with the Shoshone, a complex chain of interpretation was established whereby Sacagawea translated into Hidatsa for Charbonneau, who translated into French for FRANÇOIS LABICHE (or, on occasion, PIERRE CRUZATTE or George Drouillard), who then translated into English for the captains. The process was reversed when the captains spoke to the Indians.

Technically Sacagawea's role as interpreter should have ended after they left the Shoshone, but fortune sometimes intervened. When, on September 4, 1805, the expedition met a band of FLATHEAD INDIANS, it was discovered that they had a Shoshone boy with them who spoke Flathead. Another link was added to the chain: the boy to Sacagawea to Charbonneau to Labiche to the captains and back again. Similarly, on the return journey in 1806, their stay with the WALLA WALLA INDIANS was made easier by the presence of a female Shoshone prisoner who was added to the interpretation chain.

During the expedition's stay with the NEZ PERCE INDIANS in October 1805, they had to rely exclusively on Drouillard's sign language, which the Nez Perce understood only partially but apparently well enough to communicate. In another twist in the interpretation process, when the Nez Perce chiefs TWISTED HAIR and TETOHARSKY accompanied the expedition down to the COLUMBIA RIVER, they acted as translators for the explorers with the Indians on the upper part of that river. How effectively they translated a message that they barely understood themselves, though, is anybody's guess.

The following spring, when the corps returned upriver, fortune again came to their aid: A Shoshone prisoner of the Nez Perce enabled Lewis and Clark to talk directly to the chiefs through their chain of interpreters. It was a cumbersome system, however, and slowed down the speechmaking in councils considerably.

Lewis and Clark probably experienced their most testing moments of communication during the winter months among the CHINOOK INDIANS on the West Coast in 1805–06. Here there was minimal understanding of Drouillard's signs and no white traders on hand who understood the Chinookian language. While the Chinook had learned some words of English, they did not know enough to communicate effectively. Without a reliable interpreter, the captains were continually frustrated, and Lewis repeatedly complained, "I cannot understand them sufficiently to make any enquiries."

When Lewis and the Fields brothers first encountered the BLACKFEET INDIANS near the TWO MEDICINE RIVER on July 26, 1806, George Drouillard was scouting ahead down in the valley. Without Drouillard's skills in sign language, Lewis had great difficulty in making himself understood. Only when he managed to make it clear that he would stay with the Blackfeet while REUBIN FIELD and an Indian went down to bring Drouillard back was some confidence established and a parley held. However, the Blackfeet's hostility became apparent early the next morning when they attempted to steal the small party's guns and horses. After a skirmish in which one Indian was killed and another mortally wounded, Lewis and his men fled for their lives. It was the last major incident of the expedition, one in which no interpreter would have made a difference.

Further Reading
Ambrose, Stephen E. *Undaunted Courage: Meriwether Lewis, Thomas Jefferson, and the Opening of the American West.* New York: Simon and Schuster, 1996.
Kartunnen, Frances. *Between Worlds: Interpreters, Guides and Survivors.* New Brunswick, N.J.: Rutgers University Press, 1994.

Kawashime, Yasuhide. "Forest Diplomats: The Role of Interpreters in Indian-White Relations in the Early American Frontier." *The American Indian Quarterly* 13, no. 1 (winter 1989): 1–14.

Keogh, Xavier F. "The American Federal Interpreter and How the West Was Won." *Proteus* VII: 3 (summer 1998). Available online. URL: http://www.najit.org/proteus/keogh.html. Downloaded on May 23, 2001.

Ronda, James P. *Lewis and Clark among the Indians.* Lincoln: University of Nebraska Press, 1984.

iron-frame boat (iron canoe, "The Experiment")

Along with MERIWETHER LEWIS's airgun (see FIREARMS), the iron-frame boat that he designed represented modern technology of the time. The idea of a portable, collapsible boat had an obvious attraction for an expedition based on the exploration of the longest river in North America. Lewis and THOMAS JEFFERSON discussed the advantages of such a vessel in January and February 1803, during the expedition's initial planning stages. By mid-March Lewis had completed his design and taken it to be constructed at the HARPERS FERRY armory. Anxious to ensure that it was made to his exact specifications, he spent three weeks there supervising the work. He reported to Jefferson that the frame, when covered in skins, would be able to carry some 1,770 pounds of freight.

The iron framework went up the MISSOURI RIVER on the KEELBOAT to FORT MANDAN. In spring 1805 it was transferred to one of the PIROGUES. When the expedition arrived at the GREAT FALLS in June 1805, Lewis decided the time had come to make use of it. The boat was among the first load to be carried on the laborious 12-mile PORTAGE to the head of the falls, and beginning on June 22, Lewis and some of his men devoted the next 12 days to its construction.

The idea behind Lewis's design had been to assemble the boat's basic frame, find suitable wood to make into thin cross-struts to keep its shape in the water, make an outer covering of dressed ELK and BUFFALO skins sewn together, and make the whole boat waterproof with an outer sealing of pine wood resin. The iron frame itself—36' long, 4$\frac{1}{2}$' wide and 2'2" deep—was assembled on June 23. Lewis had already sent out hunters to procure and dress elk and buffalo skins for the cover. Two other men were set to find suitable wood to cut into lengths to act as shaping struts for the carcass.

On July 1 Lewis and his boat builders began to sew the 28 elk and four buffalo skins together, but they found the needles made too large a hole. This made the outer sealing compound even more important, which presented them with their biggest problem. Accustomed to the heavily wooded land of the eastern states, Lewis had based his design on finding some adhesive water-resistant substance such as resin from pine trees. Since no pine trees were to be found, he was forced to try a substitute based on a mixture of charcoal, beeswax, and buffalo tallow. This had proved effective in caulking leaks in the wooden CANOES, and in any event these were the only materials he had on hand. While the boat and its covering skins were set to dry out and cure over small fires, he and GEORGE DROUILLARD rendered down about 100 pounds of buffalo tallow. After trying various combinations, they applied the first coats to the sewn skins on July 7.

At last, on July 9, the boat, which the men had named "The Experiment," was put on the water and at first was found to float very well, with Lewis reporting that "she lay like a perfect cork in the water." As they were putting their supplies into it, though, a storm sprang up, and the height of the waves forced them to take it out again hastily. Even that short time in the water had pulled the coating off the skins, leaving exposed seams through which water was pouring. It was apparent, even to Lewis, that it was useless without a more effective coating.

In his journal Sergeant PATRICK GASS reported, "Therefore for want of tar or pitch we had, after all our labour, to haul our new boat on shore, and leave it at this place." Lewis's final comment was, "But it was now too late to introduce a remedy and I bid a dieu to my boat and her expectd services."

The idea of the collapsible boat was an inspired one, and if pine trees had been available, Lewis would certainly have been able to demonstrate its effectiveness. A boat that could be lifted and carried easily by five men and could carry a ton of SUPPLIES AND EQUIPMENT would have been a very efficient means of transport. While the records of the expedition show remarkable ingenuity and invention in many areas, the iron-frame boat is one of the few instances where circumstances defeated them.

Further Reading

Ambrose, Stephen E. *Undaunted Courage: Meriwether Lewis, Thomas Jefferson, and the Opening of the American West.* New York: Simon and Schuster, 1996.

Hawke, David Freeman. *Those Tremendous Mountains: The Story of the Lewis and Clark Expedition.* New York: W. W. Norton & Company, 1998.

MacGregor, Carol Lynn, ed. *The Journals of Patrick Gass, Member of the Lewis and Clark Expedition.* Missoula, Mont.: Mountain Press Publishing Company, 1997.

jackrabbits

The term *jackrabbit* is a misnomer coined by later travelers who originally called it a jackass rabbit from the length of its ears. MERIWETHER LEWIS and WILLIAM CLARK, however, correctly recognized it as a member of the hare family.

The white-tailed jackrabbit, another of the expedition's discoveries, was first noted when the party was near present-day Oacoma, South Dakota, below the mouth of the White River. When JOHN SHIELDS killed one on September 14, 1804, Clark wrote, "Shield's killed a Hare like the mountain hare of Europe, weighing 6^1/2 pounds (although pore), his head narrow, its ears large i.e. 6 Inches long and 3 Inches Wide, one half of each White, the other and out part a lead gray, from the toe of the hind foot to toe of the fore foot is 2 feet 11 inches, the hith [height] is 1 foot 1 Inch and ^{3}/4. his tail long and thick and white."

The expedition members were to see and kill many white-tailed jackrabbits thereafter until their journey down the LEMHI RIVER valley in August 1805. At FORT CLATSOP on February 28, 1806, Lewis wrote a detailed and accurate description of the animal, recording its seasonal change of colour, noting the length of its leaps—"commonly from 18 to 22 feet"—and observing that "they never burrow or take shelter in the ground when pursued."

Neither Lewis nor Clark made any specific note of the black-tailed jackrabbit, and such is the accuracy of their observations that it is probable they never saw one since their route was at the northern edge of its range.

Further Reading

Burroughs, Raymond Darwin, ed. *The Natural History of the Lewis and Clark Expedition.* East Lansing: Michigan State University Press, 1995.

Cutright, Paul Russell. *Lewis & Clark: Pioneering Naturalists.* Lincoln: University of Nebraska Press/Bison Books, 1989.

Washington State University. "Lewis and Clark Among the Indians of the Pacific Northwest. Excerpts from the Journals of the Expedition of the Corps of Discovery: Flora and Fauna (recorded at Fort Clatsop)." Available on-line. URL: http://www.libarts.wsu.edu/history/Lewis_Clark/LCEXP_Flor.html. Downloaded on May 20, 2001.

Jefferson, Thomas (1743–1826) *third president of the United States*

Thomas Jefferson was author of the Declaration of Independence, president of the United States, and founder of the University of Virginia. Probably the best-known American exponent of the ENLIGHTENMENT, Jefferson became not just a lawyer, politician, and statesman but also an amateur scientist, architect, philosopher, historian, and educator. He has also been called America's first great westerner, despite having never traveled west of the Blue Ridge Mountains. Were it not for Jefferson's ideas and vision, the Lewis and Clark Expedition would never have taken place; WILLIAM CLARK referred to him as "the Author of our Enterprise."

He was born the eldest son of Peter and Jane Jefferson on April 2, 1743, at Shadwell in the County of Goochland, now Albemarle County, Virginia. His father was a successful planter

It was Thomas Jefferson's vision for the future of the United States that led to the Lewis and Clark Expedition. William Clark called him "the Author of our Enterprise." *(Library of Congress, Prints and Photographs Division [LC-USZ62-117117])*

and surveyor; his mother was from one of Virginia's most illustrious families, the Randolphs. Jefferson attended local schools and finished his formal education at William and Mary College in Williamsburg, Virginia.

After his graduation, Jefferson practiced law and served in local government as a magistrate, county lieutenant, and member of the House of Burgesses. At the age of 26, he began to build MONTICELLO on his estate in Virginia. This became his home for the rest of his life, and he spent his spare time for years making alterations to the house and landscaping the grounds. He married Martha Wayles Skelton in 1772, and the couple had six children, of whom only two daughters reached adulthood; Martha died in 1782, to his great grief.

In 1776, as a Virginia delegate to the Continental Congress in PHILADELPHIA, Jefferson drafted the Declaration of Independence. After he left Congress that same year, he returned to Virginia and served in the state legislature before his election as governor, in which role he served from 1779 to 1781. During the brief, private period following his governorship, he wrote *Notes on the State of Virginia,* which Lewis and Clark later used as a model for their report of the expedition.

Jefferson reentered public service in 1784, going to FRANCE as the U.S. trade commissioner in France and later becoming ambassador to that country, succeeding Benjamin Franklin. Throughout the time he lived in France, he immersed himself in European thought and culture, and when he returned to Monticello he was preceded by dozens of books, works of art, architectural drawings, botanical specimens, scientific instruments, and other items he had collected.

In 1790 Jefferson became secretary of state under President George Washington. During this time POLITICAL PARTIES came into being, and there was increasing friction between the Federalists, led by ALEXANDER HAMILTON and John Adams, and the Republicans (later the Democratic-Republicans), led by Jefferson. Nominated as the Republican presidential candidate in 1796, he lost to John Adams by three electoral votes and became vice president. Four years later he defeated Adams for the presidency.

Jefferson's intellectual curiosity had already attracted him to the 300-year-old quest to find a route across North America to Asia, commonly known as the NORTHWEST PASSAGE. A skilled surveyor and cartographer, for years he had methodically collected explorers' reports, charts, geographic works, and MAPS for his personal library; for years he had wanted the West explored, and prior to Lewis and Clark he had tried three times to see it done. His interest was in large part scientific; he wished to know more about the flora and fauna, about the landscape and the Indian nations who inhabited it, and whether such creatures as the mammoth and the giant ground sloth might still populate the lands west of the Mississippi. However, since explorers ROBERT GRAY, GEORGE VANCOUVER, and ALEXANDER MACKENZIE had charted large sections of the Pacific Northwest in the 1790s, Jefferson was also increasingly anxious about the need to establish a firm U.S. claim on the area, for both political and commercial reasons connected to the burgeoning FUR TRADE.

Jefferson's three previous attempts at exploration of the West occurred in 1783, when General GEORGE ROGERS CLARK refused his offer to lead an expedition; in 1786, when he supported a failed effort by American explorer John Ledyard to reach OREGON TERRITORY by way of Siberia and then travel east across the continent; and in 1793, when he persuaded fellow members of the AMERICAN PHILOSOPHICAL SOCIETY to sponsor an expedition led by French botanist ANDRÉ

MICHAUX, who was later revealed to be an agent of the French republic and was recalled before he had left Kentucky. As president, however, Jefferson was in a better position to put the resources of the federal government behind an expedition that he could personally supervise.

He had known Captain MERIWETHER LEWIS for years, and when, after his election as president, he asked Lewis to become his secretary, he probably already had the expedition in mind. However, with SPAIN then in control of the LOUISIANA TERRITORY, obtaining permission to pass through their land presented a major difficulty. Fortune assisted Jefferson by making possible the other great achievement of his first term as president: the LOUISIANA PURCHASE. In 1801 he learned that France had secretly reacquired Louisiana Territory from Spain, and shortly thereafter he began to negotiate trading rights. The following year he made an offer to Napoleon Bonaparte to buy New Orleans and West Florida; his representatives were authorized to bid up to $10 million. To his surprise, the emperor, in need of funds, made a counteroffer: The United States could have all of Louisiana Territory for $15 million. With this the size of the United States was more than doubled—and a major obstacle to the expedition was removed. A week after the president had submitted his appropriation request to the U.S. CONGRESS for the purchase of New Orleans, he submitted another for $2,500 to fund Lewis's journey.

The expedition had been in Jefferson's mind for a long time, and he had definite views on what he wanted the CORPS OF DISCOVERY to accomplish. Early in 1803 he arranged for Lewis to study with leading savants of the time in Philadelphia and to go to HARPER'S FERRY for SUPPLIES AND EQUIPMENT. In the meantime, he developed his instructions for Lewis, with input from cabinet members, members of the American Philosophical Society, and Lewis himself. When his letter containing the MISSION OBJECTIVES was finished, it encompassed a wide yet detailed range of political, geographical, commercial, and scientific goals that reflected Jefferson's Enlightenment thinking.

The expedition, an unqualified triumph, was to become a highlight of Jefferson's presidency. His second term was less successful, with numerous problems at home and abroad. His efforts to keep the United States from becoming involved in the war between GREAT BRITAIN and France resulted in a trade embargo that seriously damaged the U.S. economy and may have also been a factor in the nation's conflict with Britain in 1812. He hand-picked his friend and secretary of state, JAMES MADISON, to succeed him as president in 1809, the year Meriwether Lewis committed suicide. Jefferson later wrote a memoir of Lewis, the friend and protégé who had proved himself so worthy of the great task placed upon him by his president.

After he retired, Jefferson lived at Monticello, which he continued to modify and where many ARTIFACTS AND SPECIMENS from the expedition had been sent. He was 76 when he undertook what he considered the greatest accomplishment of his life: founding the University of Virginia. He died at the age of 83 on July 4, 1826, just hours before his old friend and political opponent John Adams. Ironically, both men passed away on the 50th anniversary of the signing of the Declaration of

Independence. Jefferson's image, along with those of George Washington, Abraham Lincoln, and Theodore Roosevelt, is depicted on Mount Rushmore in South Dakota—land that might never have been part of the United States were it not for his determination to claim the West for the nation.

Further Reading

Ambrose, Stephen E. *Undaunted Courage: Meriwether Lewis, Thomas Jefferson, and the Opening of the American West.* New York: Simon and Schuster, 1996.

Jackson, Donald. *Thomas Jefferson & the Stony Mountains: Exploring the West from Monticello.* Norman: University of Oklahoma Press, 1993.

Jefferson, Thomas. *Jefferson: Writings: Autobiography/Notes on the State of Virginia/Public and Private Papers/Addresses/Letters.* New York: Library of America, 1984.

McDonald, Forrest. *The Presidency of Thomas Jefferson.* Lawrence: University Press of Kansas, 1998.

Ronda, James P. *Thomas Jefferson and the Changing West.* St. Louis: Missouri Historical Society Press, 1997.

Wallace, Anthony F. C. *Jefferson and the Indians: The Tragic Fate of the First Americans.* Cambridge, Mass.: Harvard University Press, 2001.

Wilson, Gaye. "Jefferson's Long Look West." From *Thomas Jefferson and the Lewis and Clark Expedition.* Available on-line. URL: http://www.monticello.org/jefferson/lewisandclark/l&c_essay. html. Downloaded on January 10, 2002.

Jefferson River (Jefferson's River)

When the CORPS OF DISCOVERY spent the winter of 1804–05 in the villages of the MANDAN INDIANS, MERIWETHER LEWIS and WILLIAM CLARK learned from the HIDATSA INDIANS that they would come to place where the MISSOURI RIVER split into THREE FORKS. The most northern of these three rivers, they told Lewis, "is navigable to the foot of a chain of high mountains, being the ridge which divides the waters of the Atlantic from those of the PACIFIC OCEAN."

The Hidatsa were right. When Clark arrived at Three Forks on July 25, 1805, he took his small group up the northernmost (southwest) fork, encamped there that night, then turned in a southeasterly direction to investigate the middle fork. Late the next day they met Lewis and the main party in CANOES, and the entire group spent the following two days at the junction of the three rivers before taking the northernmost fork, as the Hidatsa had advised them.

It was several days before Lewis and Clark named the three rivers at Three Forks. The southeast (southernmost) fork was named after ALBERT GALLATIN, then secretary of the treasury; the middle fork was named after JAMES MADISON, secretary of state; and the southwest (northernmost) fork was named "Jefferson's River in honor [of] that illustrious personage THOMAS JEFFERSON President of the United States." It is now simply the Jefferson River.

The expedition set off up the Jefferson on July 30, 1805. They were anxious to find the SHOSHONE INDIANS, from whom they hoped to procure HORSES to cross the ROCKY MOUNTAINS. Lewis went ahead on his own the next day, spent the night on the riverbank, and, after consultation with Clark, agreed to take PATRICK GASS, GEORGE DROUILLARD, and TOUSSAINT CHARBONNEAU with him on August 1 since a dispersed group had a better chance of finding the Shoshone.

Gass's journal records that they took a difficult route over a mountain (today's Tobacco Root Mountains) on the northern side of the river, made 11 miles the first day, 24 miles the second, and 22 the third. The next day, August 4, they arrived at more forks on the Jefferson near today's Twin Bridges, Montana. After exploring three, they decided (correctly) that the right fork was a false trail; Lewis named this the WISDOM RIVER (today's Big Hole River). At the rivers' junction, he left a note on a stick telling Clark they were proceeding up the middle fork.

The river party led by Clark found Jefferson's River difficult. The river was fast and shallow, with rapids at intervals. As Lewis wrote:

> *At those places, they are obliged to drag the canoes over the stone there not being enough to float them, and betwen the riffles the current is so strong that they are compelled to have recourse to the cord; and being unable to walk on the shore for the brush wade in the river along the shore and hawl them by the cord . . . their feet soon get tender and soar by wading and walking over the stones.*

At the Jefferson's forks, there was no sign of Lewis's note (it was concluded that a beaver had taken the stick), and Clark's party dragged their canoes up the wrong branch for 10 miles before Drouillard met them and turned them around. When the party reunited at the forks of the Jefferson on August 7, Clark wrote: "Men much fatigued from their excessive labours in hauling the Canoes over the rapids &c verry weak being in the water all day." The following day the expedition left the forks and traveled up what is now the BEAVERHEAD RIVER to their eventual meeting with the SHOSHONE INDIANS five days later.

Further Reading

Fifer, Barbara, and Vicky Soderberg. *Along the Trail with Lewis and Clark.* Great Falls, Mont.: Montana Magazine, 1998.

MacGregor, Carol Lynn, ed. *The Journals of Patrick Gass, Member of the Lewis and Clark Expedition.* Missoula, Mont.: Mountain Press Publishing Company, 1997.

Moulton, Gary E., ed. *Atlas of the Lewis and Clark Expedition.* Revised ed. Lincoln: University of Nebraska Press, 1999.

Jessaume, René (René Jusseaume)

(unknown–unknown) *trader, interpreter*

On October 24, 1804, the CORPS OF DISCOVERY arrived at the villages of the MANDAN INDIANS on the upper MISSOURI RIVER in present-day North Dakota. Here they met René Jessaume, a mulatto trader who had been living among the Mandan for 15 years. Jessaume was married to a Mandan woman, with whom he had two sons. He initially did not make a good impression on WILLIAM CLARK, who doubted Jessaume's claim that he had been a spy for GEORGE ROGERS CLARK and described the trader as "Cunin artfull an insoncear."

Nevertheless, it soon became apparent that Jessaume could be useful as an interpreter, thus helping Lewis and Clark establish good relations with the Mandan. Despite his name, Jessaume spoke French badly, and his English was even worse, but he still managed to make himself understood to the captains, and he spoke Mandan. Consequently, in early November he and his wife moved into FORT MANDAN. Shortly thereafter, Lewis and Clark met TOUSSAINT CHARBONNEAU, a French-Canadian trader who lived with the nearby HIDATSA INDIANS along with his pregnant SHOSHONE wife SACAGAWEA, who spoke a little Hidatsa. Charbonneau, Sacagawea, and Jessaume all entered a complicated chain of INTERPRETATION in which, typically, Indian spoke to translator, who spoke to another translator, who translated into English for Lewis and Clark. Sometimes yet another translator, such as GEORGE DROUILLARD, entered the process. On occasion arguments broke out between Jessaume and Charbonneau as they disagreed on how a particular word was to be translated.

Jessaume proved himself useful in other ways as well. On February 11, 1805, Sacagawea went into labor, which Clark reported was "tedious and the pain violent." Concerned, MERIWETHER LEWIS consulted with Jessaume on how best to help her. The trader recommended a potion made from part of a rattlesnake's rattle, which was crumbled and mixed with water. The concoction was duly administered, and Sacagawea delivered a son, JEAN BAPTISTE CHARBONNEAU, within 10 minutes.

During their winter at Fort Mandan, Lewis and Clark had worked to achieve a peace among the Mandan, Hidatsa, and ARIKARA. Unfortunately, when they returned to the villages in August 1806, they learned to their distress that intertribal fighting continued and that the Hidatsa had attacked and killed some Shoshone Indians. Furthermore, the chiefs refused the captain's invitation to come with them to Washington, most being afraid to pass through TETON LAKOTA INDIANS (Teton Sioux) territory. Jessaume interceded, and finally BIG WHITE agreed to make the trip if Jessaume and his family accompanied them. This was done, and the Mandan delegation met President THOMAS JEFFERSON on December 30, 1806. (It took more than two years before Big White was finally returned to his people.)

In a footnote to the expedition, just as Clark had assumed the raising and education of Charbonneau's and Sacagawea's children, so did Lewis attempt to care for Jessaume's son Toussaint, whom he brought to ST. LOUIS in 1808. There is no record of what happened to Toussaint after Lewis's death the following year.

Further Reading

Ambrose, Stephen E. *Undaunted Courage: Meriwether Lewis, Thomas Jefferson, and the Opening of the American West.* New York: Simon and Schuster, 1996.

journals

When President THOMAS JEFFERSON wrote his letter to MERIWETHER LEWIS detailing the expedition's MISSION OBJECTIVES, he made only one reference to journals. There was no need to order Lewis and his cocommander, WILLIAM CLARK, to maintain journals or logs of the expedition; it was understood that they would do so. Unusually, however, others in the party also wrote journals, as Lewis wrote to Jefferson: "We have encouraged our men to keep journals, and seven of them do so, to whom in this respect we give every assistance in our power." Of the seven Lewis mentioned, six are known to modern historians: Sergeants CHARLES FLOYD, PATRICK GASS, JOHN ORDWAY, and NATHANIEL PRYOR; and Privates ROBERT FRAZIER and JOSEPH WHITEHOUSE. It is also possible that ALEXANDER HAMILTON WILLARD kept a journal, although it has never been located.

The first entry in the Lewis and Clark journals was written shortly after Captain Lewis left PITTSBURGH aboard the KEELBOAT on August 31, 1803. After describing his departure, a demonstration that he had given of his airgun (see FIREARMS), and the boat's troublesome passage down the OHIO RIVER, he ended that he was "much fatiegued after labouring with my men all day. Gave my men some whiskey and retired to rest at 8 Oclock." Thereafter he filled numerous journals, giving accounts of his RECRUITING and disciplinary actions, providing vivid depictions of the country through which the expedition was passing, drawing and cataloguing botanical specimens, recording scientific observations, and making extensive notes on the Indian nations they had met. His journals are considered a masterpiece of writing on exploration and discovery, conveying a gripping tale that comes alive for readers even today.

Surprisingly, there are numerous gaps in Lewis's journals in which no entries were made. These encompass the periods of September 19 to November 11, 1803; May 14, 1804, to April 7, 1805; August 26, 1805, to January 1, 1806; and August 12 to the end of September 1806. The reason for these gaps remains a mystery today, as there is no indication that Lewis ever lost any journals. Some historians have ascribed the omissions to episodes of melancholia, to which Lewis was prone.

Although Clark was not as well educated as Lewis and peppered his journals with awkward phrasings and misspellings ("mosquito" is rendered 19 different ways), they are equally enjoyable to read. Unlike Lewis, Clark was a consistent and faithful journalist, and he provided more detail than his cocaptain about the progress of the expedition.

Between the time the expedition was formed and their departure from FORT MANDAN in April 1805, the captains sent LETTERS and updated journals back east at every opportunity. William Clark's journals from the winter layover in Wood River (1803–04) remained in ST. LOUIS after the corps headed up the MISSOURI RIVER. After wintering at the Mandan villages in 1804–05, a dozen men went back downriver aboard the keelboat, which was loaded with journals, letters, and ARTIFACTS AND SPECIMENS, all of which were sent on to Washington.

Since one of the goals of the expedition was to record the natural history and ETHNOGRAPHY of the LOUISIANA TERRITORY, the journals' safekeeping was paramount, and the fragile notebooks were sealed in tin boxes to protect them from the elements. There was also an abundance of PAPER and INK brought along, enough for two journeys. Some historians believe that Lewis and Clark took rough notes compiled on a daily basis and periodically transcribed those notes in a more polished form into their hardbound volumes. Generally all the journal writers included drawings of anything from fish and animals to plants and Indian artifacts. Clark, the corps's official cartographer, also drew numerous MAPS.

On dangerous segments of the journey, the journals, along with WEAPONS, scientific instruments, and botanical specimens, were given special care and, when necessary, were portaged on land rather than floated down rapids. When they reached the PACIFIC OCEAN, Lewis and Clark had planned to send their journals and numerous artifacts and specimens back by ship, but throughout the winter of 1805–06, no ship arrived, and they were forced to carry their precious cargo back across the continent.

Technically, the journals were the property of the U.S. government, but Lewis had apparently reached an agreement with Jefferson that he would take responsibility for their publication and subsequently receive the royalties. Unfortunately, despite the president's anxiety to see an account of the expedition published, Lewis found himself unequal to the task of preparing the manuscript and finding a publisher. He was therefore embarrassed when, in 1807, Patrick Gass became the first expedition member to publish his journals. (That same year it was announced that Robert Frazier would also be issuing his journals, but they never appeared and have since vanished. Meanwhile, John Ordway—the only expedition member to write an entry every single day of the journey—had sold his journal to Lewis for $300.)

Shortly before his death in 1809, Lewis had hoped to go to PHILADELPHIA to see to the publication of the journals. Clark later went himself and hired NICHOLAS BIDDLE to finish the job. Even then there were delays, and Biddle himself turned the manuscript over to PAUL ALLEN to complete the editing. The first printer failed, and others refused the commission, but finally Bradford and Inskeep took on the publication, although they went bankrupt during the printing. At last, five years after Lewis's death and 10 years after the start of the expedition, the Biddle edition (so-called even though Biddle's name appears nowhere in it) went on sale on February 20, 1814, at $6 a copy. However, the amount of time that had passed, combined with the previous appearance of the Gass book, resulted in little interest and slow sales. There were other problems as well: Out of a print run of 2,000, 583 were defective or missing, and many lacked the large folding map that should have been included in the frontispiece.

Historians have criticized the two-volume Biddle edition for its approach, which corrected the misspellings in the original journals and combined notes, sections of the journals, and interviews with Clark into narrative form. The book contained

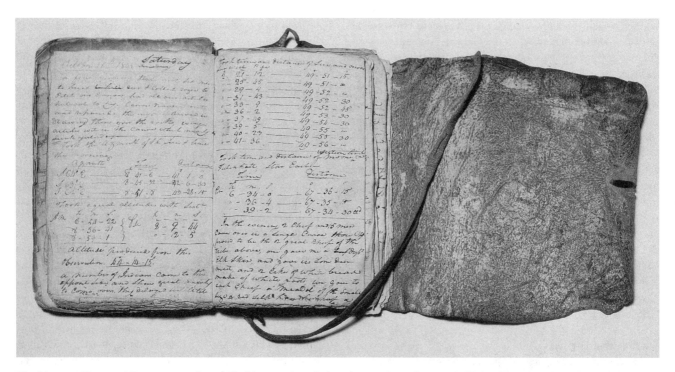

The Missouri Historical Society owns five of Clark's journals, including this one bound in rough elkskin. The pages show his field notes for October 26, 1805. *(Clark Family Collection, William Clark Papers, Missouri Historical Society, St. Lewis)*

none of the illustrations that Lewis had commissioned by prominent artists, nor did it include the work done on the botanical specimens by FREDERICK PURSH. Although it included a map by Clark, Lewis's natural history notes were not included, as a result of which many of the new species of animals and landmarks that he had discovered and named were rediscovered and renamed by others. This error was rectified in part in 1893 when the volumes were republished with annotations on the science by naturalist Elliott Coues. Nevertheless, from 1814 to 1904, Biddle's was the only official account of the expedition.

In 1894 the journal of Sergeant Charles Floyd—the expedition's only casualty—was published, exciting renewed interest in the expedition. Ten years later, to mark the 100th anniversary of the expedition, Reuben Gold Thwaites published an eight-volume edition of the Lewis and Clark journals that restored the misspellings and much of the original narratives and included the journals of Charles Floyd and Joseph Whitehouse. John Ordway's journal was published in 1916. Other editions of the Lewis and Clark journals have since been published, including the set edited by Gary Moulton and published between 1983 and 2001, which many historians consider the best.

Most of the original journal books written by members of the Corps of Discovery, including all of those by Lewis and Clark themselves, survive today. In addition to a number of loose pages and rough notes, the AMERICAN PHILOSOPHICAL SOCIETY in Philadelphia has in its collection 18 small notebooks used by the officers. Each book, of a type commonly used by surveyors of the time, measures approximately 4-by-6 inches. Thirteen of the notebooks are bound in red morocco leather, four are in boards covered with marbled paper, and one is in plain brown leather. The journals are in such good condition that some historians have speculated they are not the actual field books but copies made by Lewis after the expedition's return.

The Missouri Historical Society is home to five of William Clark's journals, four of which are bound in red leather and the fifth in elk skin. In 1953 Clark's field notes from the 1803–04 winter camp at Wood River were discovered in an attic; they are now at the Yale University Library. The Newberry Library in Chicago has Sergeant Joseph Whitehouse's journal, and the Historical Society of Wisconsin has that of Sergeant Charles Floyd. Still missing are the journals of Nathaniel Pryor and Robert Frazier, and the whereabouts of Patrick Gass's original journal are unknown.

Further Reading

Abrams, Rochonne. "A Song of the Promise of the Land: The Style of the Lewis and Clark Journals." *Missouri Historical Society Bulletin* 32, no. 3 (1976): 141–157.

Bergon, Frank, ed. *The Journals of Lewis and Clark.* Reprint, New York: Penguin, 1995.

Bolas, Deborah W. "Books from an Expedition: A Publications History of the Lewis and Clark Journals." *Gateway Heritage* 2, no. 2 (1981): 30–35.

Cutright, Paul Russell. *A History of the Lewis and Clark Journals.* Norman: University of Oklahoma Press, 2000.

Furtwangler, Albert. *Acts of Discovery: Visions of America in the Lewis and Clark Journals.* Urbana: University of Illinois Press, 1993.

Jones, Landon Y. *The Essential Lewis and Clark.* New York: The Ecco Press, HarperCollins, 2000.

Lewis, Meriwether, and William Clark. *History of the Expedition under the Command of Captains Lewis and Clark, to the Sources of the Missouri, thence across the Rocky Mountains and down the River Columbia to the Pacific Ocean: Performed during the Years 1804–5–6 by Order of the Government of the United States.* Prepared for the press by Paul Allen; in two volumes. Philadelphia: Bradford and Inskeep; New York: Abm. H. Inskeep, 1814. Reprints, New Amsterdam Book Company, New York, 1902; Lippincott, Philadelphia, 1961.

———. *The History of the Lewis and Clark Expedition.* Edited by Elliott Coues; 4 vols., 1893, Harper. Reprinted in 3 vols., New York: Dover Publications, 1979.

Lewis, Meriwether, et al. *The Journals of Lewis and Clark.* Edited by Bernard Devoto. Boston: Mariner Books, 1997.

MacGregor, Carol Lynn, ed. *The Journals of Patrick Gass, Member of the Lewis and Clark Expedition.* Missoula, Mont.: Mountain Press Publishing Company, 1997.

Moulton, Gary E. "The Missing Journals of Meriwether Lewis." *Montana: The Magazine of Western History* 35, no. 3 (1985): 28–39.

———, ed. *The Journals of the Lewis and Clark Expedition.* 13 vols. Lincoln: University of Nebraska Press, 1983–2001.

Quaife, Milo M., ed. *The Journals of Captain Meriwether Lewis and John Ordway: Kept on the Expedition of Western Exploration, 1803–1806.* Madison: State Historical Society of Wisconsin, 1916.

Thwaites, Reuben G., ed. *Original Journals of the Lewis and Clark Expedition, 1804–1806; printed from the original manuscripts in the library of the American philosophical society and by direction of its committee on historical documents, together with manuscript material of Lewis and Clark from other sources, including notebooks, letters, maps, etc., and the journals of Charles Floyd and Joseph Whitehouse, now for the first time published in full and exactly as written.* 8 vols. New York: Dodd, Mead, 1904–05.

Judith River (Judith's River)

The Judith River flows in a northerly direction in west central Montana, discharging into the MISSOURI RIVER in the 149-mile stretch known as the MISSOURI BREAKS. The expedition arrived here in May 1805. On May 28 MERIWETHER LEWIS wrote that they had come to

a handsome river which discharged itself on the larboard side. I walked on shore and ascended this river about 1½ miles in order to examine it.

I found this river about 100 yards wide from bank to bank, the water occupying about 75 yards. The bed was formed of gravel and mud, with some sand. It appeared to contain much more water than the Musselshell River; was more rapid, but equally navigable.

There were no large stones or rocks in its bed to obstruct the navigation. The banks were low, yet appeared seldom to overflow. The water of this river is clearer, much, than any we have met with.

The hills and river cliffs which we passed . . . exhibit a most romantic appearance . . . it seemed as if those scenes of visionary enchantment would never end.

William Clark explored the river farther than Lewis and must have been similarly enchanted. The next day he "thought proper to call it Judith's River" in honor of a girl back in Virginia whom he hoped to marry. The lady, Julia ("Judy") Hancock, justified the compliment by marrying him in 1808.

In January 2001 President Bill Clinton established The Upper Missouri River Breaks National Monument, 377,346 acres of federal land including portions of the Judith River. The Breaks is the only major portion of the Missouri River to be protected and preserved in its natural, free-flowing state. It is part of the Lewis and Clark National Historic Trail.

See also NOMENCLATURE, GEOGRAPHICAL.

Further Reading

Fifer, Barbara, and Vicky Soderberg. *Along the Trail with Lewis and Clark.* Great Falls, Mont.: Montana Magazine, 1998.

Moulton, Gary E., ed. *Atlas of the Lewis and Clark Expedition.* Revised ed. Lincoln: University of Nebraska Press, 1999.

Kakawissassa See CROW AT REST.

Kansas River (Kaw River)

The Kansas River flows from its headwaters at Junction City, Kansas, to meet the MISSOURI RIVER near present-day Kansas City. The Lewis and Clark Expedition reached the mouth of the Kansas River on June 26, 1804, having taken 44 days to travel the 366 miles from CAMP DUBOIS on the Wood River.

While the men repaired the PIROGUES, Captains MERIWETHER LEWIS and WILLIAM CLARK fixed the location of the river junction on their MAPS and measured the width of the two rivers. The Kansas was found to be 230 yards wide, while the Missouri measured 500 yards. Lewis also weighed measures of water from the rivers and found the Missouri water to be heavier—that is, carrying more mud. Clark noted the great number of DEER along the banks and wrote, "The Countrey about the mouth of this river is verry fine." He also "observed a great number of Parrot queets this evening." (These were Carolina parakeets, now extinct.)

It was during their stop at the Kansas River that, on the night of June 28, Privates JOHN COLLINS and HUGH HALL stole and drank enough of the expedition's whiskey to make them both drunk. A COURT-MARTIAL was convened, with Sergeant NATHANIEL PRYOR presiding and four privates on the panel. They found both men guilty and sentenced Collins to receive 100 lashes, while Hall received 50.

Further Reading

Fifer, Barbara, and Vicky Soderberg. *Along the Trail with Lewis and Clark.* Great Falls, Mont.: Montana Magazine, 1998.

Moulton, Gary E., ed. *Atlas of the Lewis and Clark Expedition.* Revised ed. Lincoln: University of Nebraska Press, 1999.

Kaskaskia (Fort Kaskaskia)

When MERIWETHER LEWIS brought the KEELBOAT down the OHIO RIVER in the late summer and early autumn of 1803, he carried with him a letter from Secretary of War HENRY DEARBORN, authorizing him to select volunteers for the expedition from western army garrisons. Standing some 55 miles south of ST. LOUIS, the fort at Kaskaskia, Illinois, was then a frontier post of the United States situated near a peninsula across the MISSISSIPPI RIVER from the Spanish/French-owned LOUISIANA TERRITORY. The French had established a settlement on the peninsula, which came into British hands after the French and Indian War (1754–63). It was captured by General GEORGE ROGERS CLARK in 1778, and the town quickly became a springboard for settlers moving west.

Lewis and WILLIAM CLARK arrived here on November 28, 1803, having had great difficulty bringing the keelboat and two PIROGUES up against the Mississippi stream. It was this struggle to make headway against the current that convinced both Lewis and Clark that they needed far more men than the one officer, one sergeant, and 12 privates originally authorized by the U.S. CONGRESS.

Knowing how reluctant commanders were to lose good men, Secretary Dearborn had also written to the captains of the

The town of Kaskaskia was destroyed by the Mississippi River in 1881. The ruins of the fort, shown here, can still be seen in Ellis Grove, Illinois. *(Library of Congress, Prints and Photographs Division [HABS, ILL,79-FORGA,2-1])*

garrisons at FORT MASSAC and Fort Kaskaskia: "If any [man] in your Company should be disposed to join Capt. Lewis . . . you will detach them accordingly." There were two army units at Kaskaskia: an infantry company commanded by Captain Russell Bissell (who may have been related to the Captain Daniel Bissell at Fort Massac) and an artillery company commanded by Captain AMOS STODDARD. It is believed that Lewis and Clark selected 12 volunteers from the troops at Kaskaskia, among whom was PATRICK GASS. Because of Gass's skills as a carpenter, Captain Bissell was unwilling to release him, but Gass persisted in his application and, with Lewis's intervention, Bissell was forced to let him go. On December 4 the boats left Fort Kaskaskia.

At the time Lewis and Clark visited Kaskaskia, the town had close to 500 residents. In the years that followed, the Mississippi began to eat away at the banks of the peninsula, and in 1881 it broke through, destroying the town and turning the peninsula into an island. The ramparts and dry moat of Fort Kaskaskia in today's Ellis Grove, Illinois, can still be seen.

See also RECRUITING.

Further Reading

Clarke, Charles G. *The Men of the Lewis and Clark Expedition: A Biographical Roster of the Fifty-One Members and a Composite Diary of Their Activities from All Known Sources.* Glendale, Calif.: Arthur H. Clark Co., 1970.

Taylor, Troy. "Curse of Kaskaskia: The Strange Fate of the First State Capitol of Illinois." *History and Hauntings of Illinois.* Available on-line. URL: http://www.prairieghosts.com/kaskaskia.html. Downloaded on April 5, 2002.

keelboat

As preparations for the westward journey got underway, one of the most important considerations was transportation. The hope was to make as much of the trip on water as possible—that is, to find a river route through the formidable ROCKY MOUNTAINS. In this regard, MERIWETHER LEWIS had ideas that he eagerly shared in his letter inviting WILLIAM CLARK to join the expedition: "My plan is to descend the Ohio in a keeled boat thence up the Mississippi to the mouth of the Missourie, and up that river as far as it's navigation is practicable with a keeled boat, there to prepare canoes of bark or raw-hides, and proceed to it's source, and if practicable pass over to the waters of the Columbia or Oregon River and by descending it reach the Western Ocean." This was an ambitious plan, and the keelboat was crucial to its success or failure.

Throughout the 19th century, keelboats were a common sight on America's rivers and canals, as they were one of the most convenient methods of transporting freight and supplies between cities and frontier settlements. A typical vessel was generally nothing more than an enlarged flatboat with a keel, anywhere from 30 to 70 feet long, with a pointed nose and stern and a roofed-over deck. While flatboats could only be floated downriver, keelboats had the advantage of being able to go upriver as well, albeit only through the application of tremendous muscle power. The boats were either poled through the water by the men on board or pulled along by rope from shore (a process known as cordelling). This latter method, however, was usually made difficult by any heavy brush or trees encountered during the journey. The men who operated keelboats had to be especially strong and tough, as were those recruited for the CORPS OF DISCOVERY's mission.

In addition to the keelboat, Lewis planned to make extensive use of CANOES. It seemed at first that they would use the smaller craft exclusively, as the Elizabeth, Pennsylvania (near PITTSBURGH), builder with whom they had contracted to con-

struct their keelboat failed to deliver it on time and, due to drunkenness and incompetence, put them through one delay after the next. The boat had been designed by Meriwether Lewis himself. When finished, it was 55 feet long, 8 feet wide in the middle, and—unusual for a keelboat—had a 32-foot-high mast, jointed at the base, which could accommodate two sails. The hold, which was 31 feet long, was capable of carrying up to 12 tons of cargo. On the deck were 11 benches, making it possible to row the boat in addition to sailing and the usual methods of poling and pulling.

The boat had barely been completed early on the morning of August 31, 1803, when an anxious Lewis had it fully loaded and started on its way down the OHIO RIVER. By that time the river was so low that he was forced to purchase two PIROGUES, one before he left Pittsburgh and one downstream

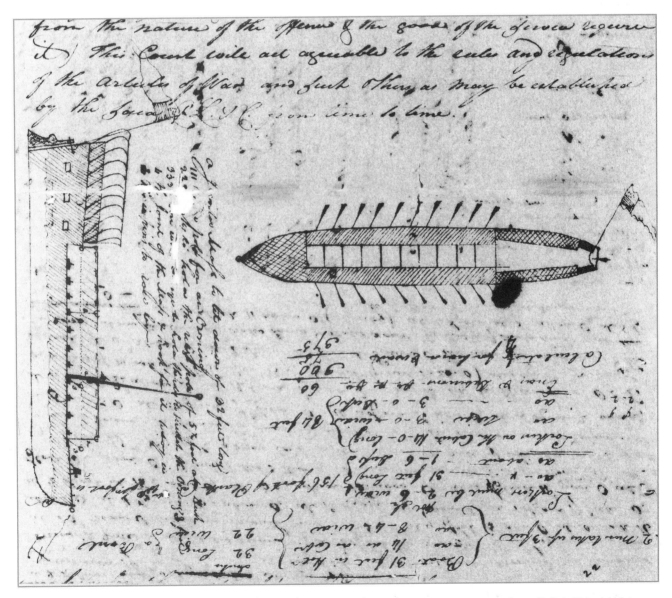

Lewis designed the keelboat and had it built in Elizabeth, Pennsylvania. Clark made modifications to it at Camp Dubois. This sketch is from Clark's field notes. *(Yale Collection of Western Americana, Beinecke Rare Book and Manuscript Library)*

in Wheeling, Virginia, to help lighten the keelboat's load. Once the expedition had set up CAMP DUBOIS on the Wood River, the boat was pulled up on land and modifications were made under Clark's supervision. Among these were the installation of lockers along the side, which had several uses in addition to storage. When the lids were raised, they created a shield for the men behind them, and when closed they provided catwalks for those poling the boat.

Most important, Clark added FIREARMS to the boat: a bronze cannon mounted on a swivel, allowing it to be fired in any direction, and two blunderbusses, also on swivels. Two additional blunderbusses were installed on the pirogues. After the expedition set out from Camp Dubois in May 1804, Clark took charge of the keelboat, staying on board for most of the journey up the MISSOURI RIVER. The boat was manned by the members of the permanent expedition. The three sergeants kept watch in the bow, midship, and stern. Privates PIERRE CRUZATTE and FRANÇOIS LABICHE, the two most experienced watermen, shared responsibility for setting the pace on the oars and manning the bow to guide it through the various river obstacles.

Throughout the journey, the team found the keelboat both a convenience and a hardship. When weather and river conditions were right, the vessel moved along at a good pace. When, however, the elements were against them, the boat frequently became stuck in low water, and horses were required to pull it free. Occasionally, too, they would have to shift their gear and cargo to achieve a proper balance. Nevertheless, it generally made good time, and its crew quickly became skilled at working in unison to keep it balanced and moving. They referred to it, appropriately, as "the barge."

On May 24 the barge hit a sandbar and nearly sank but for the quick thinking of the hands, as Clark described it: "The Swiftness of the Current Wheeled the boat, Broke our Toe rope, and was nearly over Setting the boat, all hands jumped out on the upper Side and bore on that Side untill the Sand washed from under the boat and Wheeled on the next bank. . . . By the time she wheeled a third time [we] got a rope fast to her stern and by means of Swimmers [she] was carried to shore." As a consequence of this incident, he noted, "This place I call retragrade bend as we were obliged to fall back 2 miles."

By November 1804 the expedition had reached FORT MANDAN on the upper MISSOURI RIVER, where the majority were to spend the winter. As the weather grew increasingly cold, nobody thought to remove the keelboat from the water until it had become stuck in ice. It took several weeks of chopping away at the ice before, in late February 1805, the boat was freed and up on land, where it was then overhauled for repairs. It was launched again in early April, when the westward journey resumed. But while canoes and pirogues took the expedition on the next leg of its journey up the Missouri, the larger boat headed south to ST. LOUIS, bearing the corps's temporary and expelled members. Also on board were flora and fauna, ARTIFACTS AND SPECIMENS, LETTERS, drawings, reports, and other papers intended for President THOMAS JEFFERSON and others.

The keelboat's last mission for the expedition, therefore, was to carry the news of its journey and discoveries thus far to an eagerly waiting world east of the Mississippi (see NEWS REPORTS OF THE EXPEDITION). No information is available on what happened to the keelboat when its job was done.

Further Reading

Ambrose, Stephen E. *Undaunted Courage: Meriwether Lewis, Thomas Jefferson, and the Opening of the American West.* New York: Simon and Schuster, 1996.

Boss, Richard C. "Keelboat, Pirogue, and Canoe: Vessels Used by the Lewis and Clark Corps of Discovery." *Nautical Research Journal* 38, no. 2 (1993): 68–87.

Duncan, Dayton, and Ken Burns. *Lewis & Clark: The Journey of the Corps of Discovery.* New York: Alfred A. Knopf, 1998.

Fanning, Susan. "Keelboats once king of river." American Local History Network. Available on-line. URL: http://www.usgennet.org/usa/wi/county/eauclaire/history/ourstory/vol3/keelboats.html. Updated on April 27, 2000.

Hawke, David Freeman. *Those Tremendous Mountains: The Story of the Lewis and Clark Expedition.* New York: W. W. Norton & Company, 1998.

King, Nicholas (1771–1812) *surveyor, cartographer*

Early in 1803, as MERIWETHER LEWIS made his PREPARATIONS FOR THE EXPEDITION, THOMAS JEFFERSON called on members of his cabinet for input and advice. Among these was Secretary of the Treasury ALBERT GALLATIN, a keen supporter of Lewis's mission who recognized that MAPS would be essential. As there was then no map of the entire stretch of the LOUISIANA TERRITORY through which the expedition would travel, in March 1803 Gallatin commissioned Nicholas King to create one based on what was then known of the region, drawing on maps by others.

King, an Englishman, was born to the job; his family had long been surveyors and cartographers. In 1794 he emigrated to Philadelphia, where he became a surveyor, and in 1796 and 1797 he served as the first surveyor of Washington, D.C. His assignment from Gallatin was quite specific; he was, as Gallatin wrote to Jefferson, "to project a blank map to extend from 88° to 126° West longitude from Greenwich & from 30° to 55° north latitude; which will give us the whole course of the Mississippi and the whole coast of the pacific ocean within the same latitudes together . . ." King was then to insert details on the map, incorporating features from other maps drawn by ANDREW ELLICOTT, Aaron Arrowsmith, James Cook, GEORGE VANCOUVER, ALEXANDER MACKENZIE, Jean-Baptiste d'Anville, Guillaume Delisle, and John Mitchell.

King's final result was as complete and accurate as could be expected based on information available at the time. Most of it was essentially a copy of Arrowsmith's 1802 map of North America, with modifications. King correctly located the mouth and the big bend of the MISSOURI RIVER as well as the site of the MANDAN and the HIDATSA villages, in addition to detailing the lower COLUMBIA RIVER. However, much of what lay in between was still a blank; contemporary exploration and mapping did not allow him to be any more detailed other than sketching some rivers and their tributaries, an indication of the ROCKY MOUNTAINS, and features already noted by other mapmakers. There were several flaws. The Rockies were depicted as a much shorter range with considerable gaps, a southern branch of the Columbia River was shown reaching the southern end of the mountains, and the source of the Rio Grande was placed near that of the Columbia.

Whether King's map was completed in time for Lewis to see it before he left for the West has been the subject of debate among historians. There is no mention of it in the explorers' LETTERS and field JOURNALS, nor is there any evidence that it had been sent on to Lewis in ST. LOUIS before the expedition departed. Yet there are annotations on the map in Lewis's handwriting, indicating corrections that had been made in the field.

Among the items sent back from FORT MANDAN on the KEELBOAT in spring 1805 was a map WILLIAM CLARK had drawn of the Missouri valley. Jefferson had King reduce and redraw this map so that an engraving could be made and distributed. This is considered to be the first major cartographic contribution of the Lewis and Clark Expedition. King later prepared maps in connection with other explorers' work, including WILLIAM DUNBAR and ZEBULON PIKE. He served as surveyor of Washington, D.C., from 1803 until his death in 1812.

Further Reading

Allen, John Logan. *Passage Through the Garden: Lewis and Clark and the Image of the American Northwest.* Urbana: University of Illinois Press, 1975. Reprint, New York: Dover Publications, 1991.

Knife River (Minah, Meenah Wakpa, Couteau River)

The Knife River, so-called by MERIWETHER LEWIS and WILLIAM CLARK from its French name Couteau River, was called Minah or Meenah Wakpa by the Indians. It runs roughly parallel to a north-south stretch of the MISSOURI RIVER for some nine miles before turning eastward and joining the Missouri just below today's Stanton, North Dakota. At the time of the expedition, this junction was the center of five Indian villages, two of them MANDAN and the other three HIDATSA.

In October 1804, the expedition reached this settlement of Indian villages after having traveled nearly 1,600 miles from the mouth of the Missouri. They met the Mandan chief BIG WHITE on October 24 and arrived at the first of the Mandan villages three days later. After councils with the Mandan and the Hidatsa chiefs, the expedition began to build their winter quarters, FORT MANDAN, on November 2, 1804. The fort was erected on the northern bank of the Missouri, seven to eight miles downstream from the mouth of the Knife River. One mile upstream on the opposite shore was Big White's village. The Mandan village led by Chief BLACK CAT was located some

The Hidatsa Indians were nearly wiped out by a smallpox epidemic in 1837. Those who survived moved to the Fort Berthold Reservation in 1845. The remains of their villages can be seen today at the Knife River Indian Villages National Historic Site. Shown here, in a 1908 photo by Edward Curtis, is the site of an abandoned village. *(Library of Congress, Prints and Photographs Division [LC-USZ62-96184])*

three to four miles upstream on the northern bank, nearly at the mouth of the Knife. Some three miles up the Knife lay the first of the three Hidatsa villages, which extended up that river.

The five Indian villages around the mouth of the Knife River were the center of a vast trading network where the PLAINS INDIANS came to trade BUFFALO hides and HORSES for CORN and other crops and Europeans came from CANADA to trade in furs. It is now a National Historic Site where the remains of the three Hidatsa villages can still be seen in addition to a reproduction of an earth lodge of their time.

Further Reading

Cutright, Paul Russell. *Lewis & Clark: Pioneering Naturalists.* Lincoln: University of Nebraska Press/Bison Books, 1989.

Fifer, Barbara, and Vicky Soderberg. *Along the Trail with Lewis and Clark.* Great Falls, Mont.: Montana Magazine, 1998.

Moulton, Gary E., ed. *Atlas of the Lewis and Clark Expedition.* Revised ed. Lincoln: University of Nebraska Press, 1999.

National Park Service. "Knife River Indian Villages: National Historic Site." Available on-line. URL: http://www.nps.gov/knri/overview.htm. Downloaded on April 14, 2002.

Kooskooskee River   See CLEARWATER RIVER; LOCHSA RIVER.

L

Labiche, François (Francis Labiche, William La Buche, William La Beiche) (unknown–unknown)
private in the permanent party

Recruited to the CORPS OF DISCOVERY at ST. CHARLES on May 16, 1804, Private François Labiche became one of the key members of the expedition. This was due not only to his skills as a waterman but also because he spoke several Indian languages as well as English and French, making him an important participant in the complex chains of INTERPRETATION that marked most encounters with Native Americans. Nothing is known of Labiche's life prior to the expedition, although he and PIERRE CRUZATTE had been traders up the MISSOURI RIVER previously and had met MERIWETHER LEWIS and WILLIAM CLARK in KASKASKIA several months before their recruitment. Both were of OMAHA INDIAN and French extraction; it has been suggested that Labiche was also part African.

Although they were not army regulars as most men of the corps were, Labiche and Cruzatte were sworn in as privates and consequently given the primary positions of responsibility in the keelboat, manning the bow and setting the pace on the oars. In August 1804 Labiche was assigned to the party (headed by GEORGE DROUILLARD) charged with finding the deserter MOSES REED and bringing him back to camp. On August 17 Labiche rode into camp a day ahead of the search party, announcing success not only in finding Reed but also in locating the OTOE (Oto) chief LITTLE THIEF, whom the captains had been anxious to meet. In the council that followed, Little Thief asked for Labiche's assistance in making a peace between the Otoe and the Skiri Pawnee. Captain Lewis, however, refused this request, being in more need of Labiche himself.

When the expedition finally met the SHOSHONE INDIANS a year later, Lewis was able to converse with their chief, CAMEAHWAIT, by way of a string of interpreters. First SACAGAWEA translated from Shoshone into Hidatsa; then her husband, TOUSSAINT CHARBONNEAU, translated Hidatsa into French for Labiche (or occasionally Cruzatte or Drouillard), who provided the final translation for the captains in English. While it was laborious, the system worked well and was used in other variations during encounters with other Indian nations.

Lewis had great admiration and respect for Labiche, for whom a tributary of the COLUMBIA RIVER was named in October 1805 (it is now Hood River). In late November 1805, Labiche was among the men the captain picked to accompany him on a scouting party to find a location for their winter camp near the PACIFIC OCEAN. Finally, early in December, they found a good site on a bluff a short distance up what is now the Lewis and Clark River. Here they built FORT CLATSOP (near present-day Astoria, Oregon, which was founded six years later).

After the expedition's return, Labiche remained in the army briefly, and he was one of the party chosen in late 1806 to accompany Lewis and the MANDAN chief BIG WHITE to Washington, along with a shipment of ARTIFACTS AND SPECIMENS. Lewis valued Labiche so highly that he requested extra compensation for the man who "has rendered me very essential services as a French and English interpreter, and sometimes also as Indian interpreter." When he finally left the army, Labiche settled in ST. LOUIS, where he was reported to be living around 1828. However, his later whereabouts and date of death are unknown.

Further Reading

Clarke, Charles G. *The Men of the Lewis and Clark Expedition: A Biographical Roster of the Fifty-One Members and a Composite Diary of Their Activities from All Known Sources.* Glendale, Calif.: Arthur H. Clark Co., 1970.

North Dakota Lewis & Clark Bicentennial Foundation. *Members of the Corps of Discovery.* Bismarck, N.Dak.: United Printing and Mailing, 2000.

PBS Online. *Lewis and Clark: Inside the Corps of Discovery:* "Private Francois Labiche." Available on-line. URL: http://www.pbs.org/lewisandclark/inside/flabi.html. Downloaded on May 18, 2001.

La Charette

At 3:00 P.M. on May 14, 1804, WILLIAM CLARK and the men of the CORPS OF DISCOVERY took the KEELBOAT and two PIROGUES out of CAMP DUBOIS, pulled across the MISSISSIPPI RIVER, and entered the mouth of the MISSOURI RIVER to begin their epic journey. Two days later the boats reached ST. CHARLES, where MERIWETHER LEWIS joined them, having concluded final financial arrangements and other details in ST. LOUIS. The boats remained at St. Charles until May 21, when they left with Lewis onboard.

On May 25 Clark reported that they came "To a Small French village called La Charatt of five families only. This is the Last Settlement of Whites." Sergeant PATRICK GASS referred to this village as St. John's in his journal. According to John Logan Allen in his book *Passage Through the Garden: Lewis and Clark and the Image of the American Northwest,* it was here at La Charette that Lewis and Clark met RÉGIS LOISEL, a fur trader who had conducted expeditions up the Missouri and was able to give them some useful information for their journey. (Further up the river they would encounter two of his employees, who would also provide valuable assistance to the expedition: PIERRE-ANTOINE TABEAU and JOSEPH GRAVELINES.)

At the time, La Charette stood across the river from present-day Washington, Missouri, but shifts in the Missouri's course have now washed away the settlement completely. It was a small group of seven houses, whose inhabitants eked out a precarious living. The party camped a quarter of a mile above it that night, and Clark recorded the one incident for which La Charette earned its place in the JOURNALS: "The people at this Vilage is pore, houses Small, they sent us milk & eggs to eat."

It is pleasant to imagine that the party seems to have remembered this small act of kindness. When the expedition at last came home in triumph after more than two long years away, they reached La Charette on September 20, 1806. On that day the journals record that the men asked permission to fire their guns, "which was allowed & they discharged 3 rounds with a harty Cheer which was returned."

Further Reading

Fifer, Barbara, and Vicky Soderberg. *Along the Trail with Lewis and Clark.* Great Falls, Mont.: Montana Magazine, 1998.

Moulton, Gary E., ed. *The Journals of the Lewis and Clark Expedition.* 13 vol. Lincoln: University of Nebraska Press, 1983–2001.

La Jeunesse, Jean-Baptiste   See ENGAGÉS.

Lakota Indians   See TETON LAKOTA INDIANS.

La Liberté   See BARTER, JOSEPH.

languages

There were two aspects to languages that concerned the expedition: One was a matter of simple communication; the other had to do with ETHNOGRAPHY. During the course of their journey, the CORPS OF DISCOVERY met many Indians of different cultures and many languages, some of which were related and others vastly different. These languages included Algonquian, Caddoan, Chinookian, Sahaptian, Salishan, Siouan, and Shoshone (Uto-Aztecan); and there were often separate dialects within a language grouping. How to communicate with Indians was a continual problem for MERIWETHER LEWIS and WILLIAM CLARK. Much of the time they had to rely on GEORGE DROUILLARD, who was proficient in the sign language of the PLAINS INDIANS.

On August 14, 1805, Lewis wrote of a council with the OTOE (Oto) and the MISSOURI INDIANS: "The means I had of communicating with these people was by way of Drewyer [Drouillard] who understood perfectly the common language of jesticulation or signs which seems to be universally understood by all the Nations we have yet seen. It is true that this language is imperfect and liable to error but is much less so than would be expected. The strong parts of the ideas are seldom mistaken." To a certain extent, signs were universal, and both Lewis and Clark eventually picked up enough basic knowledge to be able to communicate without Drouillard if they had to, but these occasions were rare.

As the expedition moved farther west, they came to rely less on Drouillard and more on a chain of INTERPRETATION, usually involving SACAGAWEA, who would translate from Shoshone into the Siouan-based Hidatsa language. TOUSSAINT CHARBONNEAU would then translate from Hidatsa into French, and FRANÇOIS LABICHE, PIERRE CRUZATTE, or Drouillard from that language into English. It was a cumbersome system, but it was effective.

Surprisingly, although Lewis and Clark had brought Sacagawea along specifically for the help she could give with the SHOSHONE INDIANS, when Lewis and a small party went ahead of the expedition to search for the Shoshone, he did not take Sacagawea with him. Instead, he asked her (or possibly Charbonneau) to provide a word or phrase meaning "white man." No such word existed, and he was given the closest approximation she could think of: *tab-ba-bone.* This was actually the Shoshone word for "stranger," which was meaningless and potentially dangerous when shouted, as Lewis did several times, at a Shoshone who had never seen a white man before.

Among THOMAS JEFFERSON's instructions regarding the Indians whom the explorers would meet, he listed a number of things that he wanted Lewis to learn about them, including their languages. A longtime student of Native Americans, Jefferson believed it would be possible to trace their origins by examining the roots of their language. To that end, he gave Lewis a large supply of blank vocabulary sheets on which to record words and phrases of the different Indian nations. Both Lewis and Clark tackled the task with considerable zeal, compiling word lists at every opportunity. Their work went far beyond any other Indian vocabularies that had been collected up to that time. As James Ronda notes, "the Lewis and Clark vocabularies represent an attempt to gather information useful to men of science, government, and business."

Lewis's painstaking recording of the HIDATSA language (Siouan) was observed by the British trader CHARLES MACKENZIE, who reported the process in his journal. It involved a chain of translation similar to that which used in the field. A Hidatsa would give a word to Sacagawea, who translated it for Charbonneau, who gave it in French to RENÉ JESSAUME, who then rendered it in English. However, Charbonneau and Jessaume frequently argued heatedly over the meaning of a word, which not only slowed the process down but also annoyed the Indians, who failed to understand why the explorers were recording their language and, according to Mackenzie, "concluded that the Americans had a wicked design on their country."

By the end of the winter at the FORT MANDAN, Lewis and Clark had compiled 14 word lists that were included in the shipment that went back downriver on the KEELBOAT in spring 1805. Unfortunately, those lists, reflecting hours of work, have become lost. The vocabularies they recorded of the nations west of the MANDAN INDIANS remain extant.

Eventually the explorers' ears became so attuned to the nuances of Indian speech that they were able to identify differences in languages and sometimes dialects. For example, before crossing the BITTERROOT MOUNTAINS, the expedition met a band of FLATHEAD INDIANS who spoke with such a strange guttural sound that Lewis wondered whether they might be the fabled WELSH INDIANS (they were not). Arriving at WEIPPE PRAIRIE some two weeks later, Clark met the NEZ PERCE INDIANS, who in appearance and manner seemed similar to the Flathead—but for the language, which he immediately realized was different. He was right. The Flathead were Salishan speakers; the Nez Perce spoke Sahaptian.

When the expedition later canoed down to the COLUMBIA RIVER, two Nez Perce chiefs accompanied them to speak on their behalf with the Indians on the upper part of that river. These included the YAKAMA (Yakima), the WANAPAM, and the WALLA WALLA INDIANS, who were, like the Nez Perce, Sahaptian speakers. Although the dialects were different, Lewis's study of their vocabularies revealed their common origin.

The expedition experienced their greatest language difficulties with the CHINOOK INDIANS, who were unable to understand Drouillard's sign language. Without an interpreter, communication was nearly impossible; yet Lewis still managed to assemble a number of Chinookian vocabularies. While the JOURNALS do not reveal how he accomplished this, it is safe to assume that by this time he and Clark had acquired sufficient linguistic abilities and diplomatic skills to assemble the word lists they were looking for.

Further Reading

Ambrose, Stephen E. *Undaunted Courage: Meriwether Lewis, Thomas Jefferson, and the Opening of the American West.* New York: Simon and Schuster, 1996.

Clark, W. P. *The Indian Sign Language.* Lincoln: University of Nebraska Press, 1982.

Criswell, Elijah H. *Lewis and Clark: Linguistic Pioneers.* Columbia: University of Missouri Press, 1940.

Furtwangler, Albert. *Acts of Discovery: Visions of America in the Lewis and Clark Journals.* Urbana: University of Illinois Press, 1993.

Gasque, Thomas J. "Lewis and Clark's Onomastic Assumptions." *Midwestern Folklore.* 21 (Spring–Fall 1995): 30–38.

Ronda, James P. *Lewis and Clark among the Indians.* Lincoln: University of Nebraska Press, 1984.

Saindon, Bob. "The Lost Vocabularies of the Lewis and Clark Expedition." *We Proceeded On.* 3 (1977): 4–6.

La Page, Baptiste   See LEPAGE, JEAN-BAPTISTE.

Larocque, François-Antoine (1784–1869)
fur trader, explorer

During the winter of 1804–05 at FORT MANDAN, MERIWETHER LEWIS and WILLIAM CLARK met and talked with a number of trappers and traders who came to the area frequently to TRADE with the MANDAN INDIANS. One of these who not only recorded his interactions with the expedition in a journal but also had some parallel experiences was François-Antoine Larocque, a French-Canadian employee of the NORTH WEST COMPANY.

At the time Lewis and Clark met him, Larocque was 20 years old. Born in Quebec and educated in the United States, he had only recently started to work as a clerk for the North West Company when he was given the task of taking a supply of trade goods to the Mandan and the HIDATSA villages. He arrived there in mid-December 1804 with HUGH HENEY, and Lewis subsequently invited him to visit Fort Mandan. Later, when a member of Larocque's party began to question the expedition's true mission, apparently to incite discontent among the Indians, relations between the trader and the captains soured for a time. When they heard that Larocque was dispensing flags and medals to the Indians, they sternly instructed him not to do so. "As I had neither flags nor medals," wrote Larocque in his journal, "I ran no risk of disobeying these orders, of which I assured them."

A dedicated journalist, Larocque listed occasions when the captains made ASTRONOMICAL OBSERVATIONS and recorded many of their conversations. Lewis, who liked Larocque and once spent a whole day fixing the latter's compass, spoke of his "very grand plan" to make peace among Indian nations and seemed convinced of his ability to set up a U.S trading network with the Native Americans. Larocque was understandably dubious about this.

Late in January 1805 Larocque made a request to join the expedition. He claimed to be moved by a spirit of adventure, and given his youth this was probably true. Nevertheless, the captains turned him down, unwilling to give a representative of the North West Company—and thus the British government—access to their discoveries. Although they seemed willing to discuss with Larocque where they were going and what they hoped to accomplish on their mission, they stressed that the expedition was "purely scientific and literary, and in no way concerning trade." Their main hope, they said, was "to settle the boundary line between the British and the American territories."

In February 1805 Larocque returned to his headquarters at Fort Assiniboine in Manitoba, and in June he set out on another journey, this time for the ROCKY MOUNTAINS on "a voyage of discovery"—a phrase he undoubtedly adopted from the CORPS OF DISCOVERY. His mission was to meet the CROW INDIANS and, if possible, to teach them to trap and preserve BEAVER pelts for trade. He stopped briefly at the Mandan villages, where the chiefs warned him against the Indians of the Rockies; then, with two associates, he joined a band of Crow who had been trading at the villages and were heading home. After traveling all summer overland—during which time the Canadians witnessed the Crow killing and butchering some enemies—they arrived at the YELLOWSTONE RIVER, near modern Billings, Montana, on September 13, 1805. Larocque and his companions left the Indians the next day with the promise to return to trade with them the following year (a promise they never fulfilled).

Some 10 months before William Clark would reach the same area, Larocque's party—traveling by horse and on foot—followed the Yellowstone downstream. On September 15 they camped by the large sandstone formation that Clark would name POMPY'S TOWER; the following day they reached the mouth of the Bighorn River. By September 17 they had reached country so rocky that they were forced to unload the HORSES and carry their own baggage for safety's sake. It took them the entire day to travel only 9 miles, and Larocque subsequently referred to the area as "a most abominable Country." Fearful of Indian attacks, the men never lit any campfires and traveled by night as much as possible. Further down the Yellowstone, the going became easier, and on September 30 they arrived at the junction of the Yellowstone with the MISSOURI RIVER, having averaged about 20 miles a day. The following year Clark and his party averaged 36 miles a day along the same route—but entirely by water. Larocque arrived at the Mandan villages on October 9 and was back at Fort Assiniboine by November 18.

In 1806 Larocque moved back to Montreal. He never again returned to the West, but his journal of his time there is rich with valuable historical information, not only for the time he spent with Lewis and Clark but also for his descriptions of the territory through which he traveled as well as of its Indians.

Further Reading

Larocque, François. *The Journal of François Larocque.* Reprint, Fairfield, Wash.: Ye Galleon Press, 1981.

Mussulman, Joseph. "François-Antoine Larocque." From *Discovering Lewis and Clark: Clark on the Yellowstone.* Available on-line. URL: http://www.lewis-clark.org/CLARK-YELLOWSTONE/LAROCQUE/am_laroc-mmenu.htm. Downloaded on February 28, 2002.

Ronda, James P. *Lewis and Clark among the Indians.* Lincoln: University of Nebraska Press, 1984.

Wood, W. Raymond, and Thomas D. Thiessen. *Early Fur Trade on the Northern Plains: Canadian Traders Among the Mandan and Hidatsa Indians, 1738–1818.* Norman: University of Oklahoma Press, 1985.

La Vérendrye, Pierre de   See EXPLORATION, EARLY.

leadership

Both MERIWETHER LEWIS and WILLIAM CLARK had served in the U.S. Army, as had most of the permanent expedition party. The army of that time was based on a regime almost incomprehensible today, one that consisted of repetitive training, rigid DISCIPLINE, constant drilling, and stiff punishments for offenses. As far as the expedition was concerned, a different form of discipline was required, and it is clear that both Lewis and Clark realized this. In RECRUITING their men, they looked for those who had the specialized skills to make the party independent of normal army supply and organization.

The captains needed men who could be relied on to act with intelligence in an emergency, who could work as a unit and yet also act independently toward a common aim in a hostile and unknown environment. The line between independence of mind and lack of discipline is a fine one, and it is a tribute to Lewis and Clark that, after the early stages of the expedition, it was rarely crossed.

Many of the measures they took seem commonplace today, but they were revolutionary for their time. From the beginning, Lewis and Clark emphasized that they were leaders rather than just commanders. To create a unity of purpose, a bond of common endeavor that they knew was essential, they did not appoint a replacement when Sergeant CHARLES FLOYD died; they held an election for the post. (Many commentators have noted that this was the first non-Indian election west of the MISSISSIPPI RIVER.) Clark's slave, YORK, was not only trusted with a musket and the duties and privileges of all the other members of the party, but he was allowed to vote on where the corps would build FORT CLATSOP (SACAGAWEA was also asked for her opinion).

After some disciplinary problems in the early days of the expedition, it is remarkable how closely knit the members of the expedition became. Small, independent parties and even individuals were sent to hunt for food, scout for new routes, or take responsibility for PORTAGE of SUPPLIES AND EQUIPMENT. Each member of the corps came to know what his role and responsibilities were, and he carried out his appointed tasks willingly.

One facet of their leadership often overlooked is the way Lewis and Clark involved their men in the scientific side of the expedition. PATRICK GASS's journal records the variety of Indian dwellings that he saw, how they were built, and TREEs of the northwest. SILAS GOODRICH, a keen fisherman, soon learned to bring to Lewis any FISH he did not recognize, and Lewis credited him with this in his report on the new species the party discovered.

Both Lewis and Clark looked to their men's comfort whenever possible. On May 14, 1805, near today's Fort Peck, Montana, when six of his men had a dangerous encounter with a grizzly BEAR and the white PIROGUE nearly capsized, Lewis wrote, "we thought it proper to console ourselves and cheer the sperits of our men and accordingly took a drink of grog and gave each man a gill of sperits."

The captains imbued their men with their own enthusiasm, and their habit of naming features of the landscape is indicative of the way they did it. Every member of the expedition had a creek, river, or bluff named after him along the journey. Each naming made the man concerned more closely associated with the enterprise; he saw his contribution acknowledged, his work recognized.

When they arrived at the MARIAS RIVER in June 1805, no one in the party knew which was the main branch of the MISSOURI RIVER and which the tributary. They sent out two parties to examine the first 10 miles of each. The reports were conflicting, so Lewis and Clark went to examine each themselves. On their return they agreed that the south stream was the main river. Every man in the party—including PIERRE CRUZATTE, the most experienced waterman—disagreed with them. The captains stood firm; the expedition would take the south stream. The JOURNALS record: "they said very cheerfully that they were ready to follow us any wher we thought proper to direct but that they still thought that the other was the river." (Three days later, the captains were proved right.)

All the men were volunteers—not idealistic youths but, with the odd exception, experienced men in their late 20s. Some were frontiersmen, skilled in hunting or in watermanship; others were blacksmiths or carpenters. From the journals it is clear that they came to accept the necessity of protecting their comrades as well as themselves and to work together for the common good. These are the attributes of any good army unit, but to instill them into men in a project that took them thousands of miles into unknown territory to suffer hardship, hunger, and danger needs leadership of the highest order.

See also DEMOCRACY ON THE EXPEDITION; SKILLS ON THE EXPEDITION.

Further Reading

Ambrose, Stephen E. *Undaunted Courage: Meriwether Lewis, Thomas Jefferson, and the Opening of the American West.* New York: Simon and Schuster, 1996.

Duncan, Dayton, and Ken Burns. *Lewis & Clark: The Journey of the Corps of Discovery.* New York: Alfred A. Knopf, 1998.

Jones, Landon Y. "Leading Men: Commanding, cooperative, confident, complementary—Why Lewis and Clark were perfectly cast as co-CEOs" *Time* (July 8, 2002): 54–57. Available on-line. URL: http://www.time.com/time/2002/lewis_clark/lcaptains.html. Downloaded on July 11, 2002.

LeBorgne   See ONE EYE.

Lemhi Pass

Lemhi Pass—a rounded, saddle-shaped pass 7,323 feet above sea level in the Beaverhead Mountains of the Bitterroot Range—lies along the CONTINENTAL DIVIDE between Montana and Idaho. The pass was a major route for SHOSHONE and NEZ PERCE INDIANS who used it for their annual journey to hunt BUFFALO on the GREAT PLAINS. Although it was the highest point reached on the Lewis and Clark Expedition, its transit was easy compared with the later, lower, but far more difficult passage over the BITTERROOT MOUNTAINS.

On August 11, 1805, desperate to make contact with the Shoshone Indians, from whom he hoped to procure HORSES, MERIWETHER LEWIS and three men were approaching the Continental Divide. They saw ahead of them a single Shoshone, who, as they approached, wheeled his horse and rode away. Bitterly disappointed, all Lewis and his group could do was to follow him. The next day, on August 12, 1805, when they walked over Lemhi Pass, Lewis and his men became the first non-Indian Americans to cross the divide.

Lewis saw before him "immence ranges of high mountains still to the West of us with their tops partially covered with snow." Disheartened not to see the great river through the ROCKY MOUNTAINS that he had hoped to find running due west, he continued down into the valley with his men. Lemhi Pass, previously a point of hope and expectation, became instead a point of great disappointment.

The following day, on August 13, Lewis and his men encountered the Lemhi Shoshone Indians. Once the Shoshone were convinced that the soldiers posed no threat, they agreed to accompany Lewis's party back over the pass and to assist the expedition, even though they were themselves on their way to a planned buffalo hunt. With winter now only weeks away, the entire corps had grown anxious about reaching the Pacific coast. They knew their goal was closer, however, when the Shoshone offered them salmon to eat, their first such fish. During their stay in the area, the corps went over the pass several times. On the return trip, after the expedition split into two parties at TRAVELERS' REST, Lewis and his men crossed the divide at LEWIS AND CLARK PASS, while

This painting, *At Lemhi,* by Robert F. Morgan, depicts Meriwether Lewis, George Drouillard, John Shields, and Hugh McNeal, the first non-Indian Americans to cross the Continental Divide at Lemhi Pass. *(Montana Historical Society, Helena)*

Clark's group, further south, crossed at Gibbons Pass. Neither saw Lemhi Pass again.

Some 60 years after the expedition, during the gold rush, a road was built over Lemhi Pass to carry stagecoach and freight wagon traffic. This became a county road in Montana in 1887, but it ceased to have any importance as a traffic route in 1910, with the completion of the Gilmore and Pittsburgh Railroad. Today evidence of mining and prospecting can still be seen along the road. Lemhi Pass was designated a National Historic Landmark in 1960 for the role it played in the Lewis and Clark Expedition.

Further Reading

Fifer, Barbara, and Vicky Soderberg. *Along the Trail with Lewis and Clark.* Great Falls, Mont.: Montana Magazine, 1998.

Schmidt, Thomas, and Jeremy Schmidt. *National Geographic Guide to the Saga of Lewis & Clark into the Uncharted West.* New York: DK Publishing, 1999.

USDA Forest Service. "Beaverhead–Deerlodge National Forest Southwest Montana: Lemhi Pass National Historic Landmark." Available on-line. URL: http://www.fs.fed.us/r1/bdnf/virtualtours/lemhi-pass/virtual-lemhi-pass.html. Downloaded on May 20, 2001.

Lemhi River

The Lemhi River rises in southeast Idaho, below the BITTER-ROOT MOUNTAINS, and runs northward into the SALMON RIVER at today's Salmon, Idaho. It is named for Chief Lemhi of the Lemhi Mountain SHOSHONE, an Indian nation who may have occupied the area for more than 8,000 years. The Shoshone had given the name *Ag-gi-pa,* meaning "fish water," to both the Lemhi and the Salmon Rivers.

By August 11, 1805, the CORPS OF DISCOVERY had reached the foot of the CONTINENTAL DIVIDE. They had made their way up the MISSOURI RIVER, the JEFFERSON RIVER, and the BEAVERHEAD RIVER and knew they had no chance of reaching the PACIFIC OCEAN without the HORSES that they hoped to procure from the Shoshone. SACAGAWEA had assured them they were in country frequented by her people, but it was not until August 11 that MERIWETHER LEWIS and a small advance party encountered one.

Lewis and three men were walking ahead of the CANOE party when they saw a single Indian ahead of them. Before they could establish contact, he wheeled his horse around and rode away. All Lewis could do was to follow him over the divide at LEMHI PASS where, less than a mile down the other side, on August 12, Lewis "first tasted the water of the great Columbia river." This was Agency Creek, which runs downhill to the Lemhi River.

The next day, August 13, Lewis and his group turned north along the Lemhi at today's Tendoy, Idaho. After about two miles, they met Chief CAMEAHWAIT and the Shoshone. The initial friendly meeting, further cemented by Sacagawea's recognition of Cameahwait as her brother, led to several days spent by the explorers and the Shoshone transporting the expedition's baggage west over the divide to the Lemhi River valley.

Anxious to find a direct route to the Pacific Ocean, WILLIAM CLARK took a party along the Lemhi to its junction with the Salmon River, but he found that the Salmon was impassable. The captains therefore decided to take the Shoshone's advice—ride north, and follow the LOLO TRAIL. On August 29 the Shoshone rode out of the Lemhi River valley east to hunt BUFFALO, while the expedition, led by OLD TOBY, rode north out of the valley over the LOST TRAIL PASS.

Today, about a mile north of Tendoy, Idaho, beside the Lemhi River, a monument has been erected to Sacagawea, who was born in this river valley.

Further Reading

Moulton, Gary E., ed. *Atlas of the Lewis and Clark Expedition.* Revised ed. Lincoln: University of Nebraska Press, 1999.

Schmidt, Thomas. *National Geographic Guide to the Lewis & Clark Trail.* Washington, D.C.: National Geographic, 1998.

Lemhi Shoshone   See SHOSHONE INDIANS.

LePage, Jean-Baptiste (Jean-Baptiste La Page, Baptiste Lepage, Jean-Baptiste Lapage)

(unknown–ca. 1809) *private in the permanent party*
While it is certain that Private Jean-Baptiste LePage was among those members of the CORPS OF DISCOVERY who traveled to the PACIFIC OCEAN and back, his name does not always appear on published rosters of the expedition. This may have been because he was not originally part of the permanent party, or perhaps because he was confused with Jean-Baptiste La Jeunnesse, one of the ENGAGÉS who is listed as a private on some rosters. A French-Canadian fur trader, LePage was enlisted for the expedition on November 2, 1804, at FORT MANDAN, replacing JOHN NEWMAN, who had been dismissed from the corps after being court-martialed for mutiny.

LePage is rarely mentioned in the expedition's JOURNALS and was regarded by MERIWETHER LEWIS as "Entitled to no

peculiar merit." He was assigned to the occasional scouting party and was among those who labored at the SALTWORKS during the winter of 1805–06 on the West Coast. While making the treacherous crossing over the BITTERROOT MOUNTAINS in September 1805, Lepage lost one of the packhorses and was sent to find it. When he failed to do so, two others were dispatched to locate the horse instead. He was similarly unlucky several months later, when in May 1806 he and TOUSSAINT CHARBONNEAU were sent to TRADE with the NEZ PERCE INDIANS. First their packhorse fell into the CLEARWATER RIVER, resulting in the loss of valuable (and by now scarce) trade goods; then a raft containing Indian roots for the expedition capsized, also losing its contents to the waters.

After the expedition's return to ST. LOUIS, LePage was discharged from the corps on November 10, 1806. He did not receive the bonus pay others did because, as Lewis noted, "he did not perform the labors incident to the summer of 1804." LePage died sometime before the end of 1809.

Further Reading

PBS Online. *Lewis and Clark: Inside the Corps of Discovery:* "Lesser Known Members of the Corps." Available on-line. URL: http://www.pbs.org/lewisandclark/inside/lesser.html. Downloaded on May 18, 2001.

letter of credit

A letter of credit is an instrument whereby a bank or financial institution authorizes another to advance money to the bearer, thereby allowing him or her to obtain funds and make purchases up to a specified amount. A circular letter of credit is not addressed to any specific correspondent and requires that as each payment is made, the letter is endorsed by the payer so that other banks may know how much of the total credit has been used. Issuers of such letters were usually so well known that any bank would honor the credit after asking for identification. Letters of credit, which were mainly used by travelers, simplified business transactions, especially on the frontier. Today's travelers' checks are a modern form of a letter of credit.

As MERIWETHER LEWIS bought SUPPLIES AND EQUIPMENT for the expedition, he carried with him what has been called the most liberal letter of credit ever issued. It was signed by President Thomas Jefferson, and it authorized Lewis to obtain anything he needed from any U.S. government agency as well as "the Consuls, agents, merchants & citizens of any nation," who were called upon "to furnish you with those supplies which your necessities may call for." It also guaranteed payment for the explorers' return by sea via any American or foreign merchant ship they might find in the Columbia River estuary. The expedition did not return by sea, but Lewis used the letter freely for innumerable purchases, leading to a final expedition cost of $38,722.35–far exceeding the budget of $2,500.

See also COSTS OF THE EXPEDITION.

Dear Sir

Washington. U.S. of America. July 4. 1803.

In the journey which you are about to undertake for the discovery of the course and source of the Missouri, and of the most convenient water communication from thence to the Pacific ocean, your party being small, it is to be expected that you will encounter considerable dangers from the Indian inhabitants. should you escape those dangers and reach the Pacific ocean, you may find it imprudent to hazard a return the same way, and be forced to seek a passage round by sea. in such vessels as you may find on the Western coast. but you will be without money, without clothes. & other necessaries; as a sufficient supply cannot be carried with you from hence. your resource in that case can only be in the credit of the U.S. for which purpose I hereby authorise you to draw on the Secretaries of State, of the Treasury, of War & of the Navy of the U.S.. according as you may find your draughts will be most negociable, for the purpose of obtaining money or necessaries for yourself & your men. and I solemnly pledge the faith of the United States that these draughts shall be paid punctually at the date they are made payable. I also ask of the Consuls, agents, merchants & citizens of any nation with which we have intercourse or amity, to furnish you with those sup- plies which your necessities may call for, assuring them of honorable and prompt retribution. and our own Consuls in foreign parts where you may happen to be, are hereby instructed & required to be aiding & assisting to you in whatsoever may be necessary for procuring your return back to the United States. And to give more entire satisfaction & confidence to those who may be disposed to aid you, I Thomas Jefferson, President of the United States of America, have written this letter of general credit for you, with my own hand, and signed it with my name.

Th Jefferson

To
Cap. Meriwether Lewis.

With this letter of credit signed by Thomas Jefferson, Meriwether Lewis was able to obtain anything he needed at the expense of the U.S. government. He used the letter liberally. *(Missouri Historical Society, St. Louis)*

Further Reading

Ambrose, Stephen E. *Undaunted Courage: Meriwether Lewis, Thomas Jefferson, and the Opening of the American West.* New York: Simon and Schuster, 1996.

Hawke, David Freeman. *Those Tremendous Mountains: The Story of the Lewis and Clark Expedition.* New York: W. W. Norton & Company, 1998.

letters

In an era lacking telephones, faxes, and e-mails, letters were the only form of long-distance communication possible. At the time of the Lewis and Clark Expedition, educated gentlemen such as MERIWETHER LEWIS and THOMAS JEFFERSON wrote voluminously, and even less-educated men such as WILLIAM CLARK wrote letters on an almost daily basis. The correspondence of these and others reveal much about the expedition—its mission, its progress, and its successes and failures—as well as the thoughts and feelings of the personalities associated with it.

When in early March 1801 Meriwether Lewis received a letter from President Thomas Jefferson inviting him to become the president's secretary, he evidenced his delight in a letter that he wrote to a fellow officer: "I cannot withhold from you my friend the agreeable intelligence I received on my arrival at this place [PITTSBURGH] by way of a very polite note from Thomas Jefferson . . . signifying his wish that I should except the office of his private Secretary; this unbounded as well as unexpected confidence, confered on me by a man whose virtue and talents I have ever adored, . . . I must confess did not fail to raise me somewhat in my own estimation."

Letters were not always personal missives; sometimes they were official documents. President Jefferson's instructions to Lewis regarding the expedition's MISSION OBJECTIVES were contained in the form of a letter dated June 20, 1803. Two weeks later, as Lewis prepared to leave the nation's capital for the West, he wrote to his mother, LUCY MERIWETHER LEWIS MARKS, "The charge of this expedition is honorable to myself, as it is important to my Country." His letters home thereafter would continue to reflect his pride while also reassuring his family that he was safe.

Probably the most important letter of the expedition was written on June 19, 1803. It was from Lewis to William Clark, and it began: "From the long and uninterupted friendship and confidence which has subsisted between us I feel no hesitation in making to you the following communication." He went on to describe in detail his mission to lead an expedition across the continent and how he proposed to go about it, then concluded: "Thus my friend you have a summary view of the plan, the means and the objects of this expedition. If therefore there is anything under those circumstances, in this enterprise, which would induce you to participate with me in it's fatigues, it's dangers and it's honors, believe me there is no man on earth with whom I should feel equal pleasure in sharing them as with yourself."

In *Thomas Jefferson & the Stony Mountains,* Donald Jackson describes this letter as "one of the most famous invitations to greatness the nation's archives can provide." Nearly as famous is the reply from Clark that Lewis received in Pittsburgh on July 29: "The enterprise &c. is Such as I have long anticipated and am much pleased with and . . . I will cheerfully join you in an 'official Charrector' as mentioned in your letter, and partake of the dangers, difficulties, and fatigues, and I anticipate the honors & rewards of such an enterprise. . . . This is an undertaking fraited with many dificulties, but My friend I do assure you that no man lives with whome I would perfur to undertake Such a Trip &c. as yourself."

While the CORPS OF DISCOVERY spent the winter of 1803–04 at CAMP DUBOIS, Jefferson and Lewis kept in constant touch, although they were hampered by the slowness of the mails. (For example, it took a month for Lewis's letter of invitation to reach Clark.) Jefferson commented on and occasionally criticized Lewis's reports, reminding the explorer frequently of the mission objectives. He would revise his instructions by letter as developments dictated. When the LOUISIANA PURCHASE was finalized, he gave Lewis additional directives regarding what to say to the Indians in the LOUISIANA TERRITORY now that they were under U.S. sovereignty. The president also kept Lewis informed on the political situation, writing on January 13, 1804, "The enquiries are perpetual as to your progress. The Feds [Federalists], alone still treat it as philosophism, and would rejoice in it's failure. . . . I hope you will take care of yourself, and be the living witness of their malice and folly."

Prior to their departure from FORT MANDAN on April 7, 1805, the explorers took the opportunity to write letters home. Their correspondence described many of the details of their existence and sometimes gave indications of the decisions being made. From the MANDAN villages, Lewis wrote to his mother: "The near approach of winter, the low state of the water, and the known scarcity of timber which exists on the Missouri for many hundreds of miles . . . determined my friend and companion Capt. Clark and myself to fortify ourselves and remain for the winter in the neighborhood of the Mandans. . . ."

Once the expedition left Fort Mandan, there was no communication to or from them until they returned in September 1806, leading to an agonizing wait for news back East. Because letters written during the winter of 1804–05 would not be posted until the KEELBOAT arrived back in ST. LOUIS in the spring, the president and others relied for word of the expedition's progress via trappers and Indians who met them along the MISSOURI RIVER. Jefferson often passed on to Lewis's family whatever he had heard. On July 10, 1805, having delayed a trip to MONTICELLO to wait for "the Western mail" to arrive, Jefferson wrote to REUBEN LEWIS, enclosing a newspaper report and noting of the expected letters, "It is probable they are coming on by a special messenger who travels slow."

On September 23, 1806, the expedition arrived back in St. Louis to great acclaim. Lewis's first action was to inquire when the next post left. Learning that it had just gone, he sent

to the Senate & House of Representatives of the United States.

In pursuance of a measure proposed to Congress by a message of Jan. 18. 1803. and sanctioned by their appropriation for carrying it into execution, Capᵗ Meriwether Lewis of the 1ˢᵗ regiment of infantry was appointed, with a party of men, to explore the river Missouri, from it's mouth to it's source, & crossing the highlands by the shortest portage, to seek the best water communication thence to the Pacific ocean: & Lieutᵗ Clarke was appointed second in command. they were to enter into conference with the Indian nations on their route, with a view to the establishment of commerce with them. they entered the Missouri May 14. 1804. and on the 1ˢᵗ of Nov. took up their winter quarters near the Mandan towns, 1609 miles above the mouth of the river, in Lat. 47° 21′ 47″ North, & Long. 99° 24′ 45″ West from Greenwich. on the 8ᵗʰ of April 1805. they proceeded up the river in pursuance of the objects prescribed to them. a letter of the preceding day Apr. 7. from Capᵗ Lewis, is herewith communicated. during his stay among the Mandans, he had been able to lay down the Missouri according to courses & distances taken on his passage up it, corrected by frequent observations of Longitude & Latitude; & to add to the actual survey of this portion of the river, a general map of the country between the Mississippi & Pacific, from the 34ᵗʰ to the 54ᵗʰ degrees of Latitude. these additions are from information collected from Indians with whom he had opportunities of communicating, during his journey & residence with them.

This 1806 letter from Thomas Jefferson contained news of the Lewis and Clark Expedition as well as the Red River expedition. *(National Archives [NWL-46-PRESMESS9AE2-2])*

a messenger to the postmaster at Cahokia, Illinois, asking him to hold the post until the next day. He then sat down and wrote a letter to Jefferson providing his initial report of the expedition. It arrived in Washington a month later, on October 24.

Meanwhile, aware that newspapers often got their information from letters and that articles were copied from one newspaper to another, Lewis and Clark prepared to publicize the expedition. On September 26 Lewis began to write a letter that provided a gripping account of the expedition. Intended for publication, it took him four days to write and was 32,000 words long.

Anxious, however, to get something into print quickly and knowing that the nearest newspaper was in Frankfort, Kentucky, the captains decided to write to Clark's brother GEORGE ROGERS CLARK first, before Lewis wrote his long account. As Clark did not feel confident in his writing skills, Lewis drafted the letter, which Clark then copied, signed, and sent to his brother. On October 11 the letter appeared in the Frankfort *Western World;* by October 28 it had been published in the Pittsburgh *Gazette,* and it appeared in Washington's *National Intelligencer* on November 3. Donald Jackson has noted that "the initial fame of the expedition rests largely upon this communication, which spread throughout the country as rapidly as the means of the day would allow."

See also NEWS REPORTS OF THE EXPEDITION.

Further Reading

Ambrose, Stephen E. *Undaunted Courage: Meriwether Lewis, Thomas Jefferson, and the Opening of the American West.* New York: Simon and Schuster, 1996.

Clark, William, and Jonathan Clark. *Dear Brother: Letters of William Clark to Jonathan Clark.* New Haven, Conn.: Yale University Press, 2002.

Jackson, Donald. *Letters of the Lewis and Clark Expedition, with Related Documents, 1783–1854.* Urbana: University of Illinois Press, 1979.

———. *Thomas Jefferson & the Stony Mountains: Exploring the West from Monticello.* Norman: University of Oklahoma Press, 1993.

Lewis, Meriwether (1774–1809)

expedition cocommander

The man to whom President THOMAS JEFFERSON entrusted the daunting task of leading an expedition across the American continent was a brilliant, complex individual whose short life continues to be the subject of study and debate. Although he was later to serve a disastrous term as governor of Louisiana and to die under mysterious circumstances, his achievements during the years 1803–06 made him, in the view of many historians, the greatest explorer in the history of the United States.

Born on August 18, 1774, near Charlottesville, Virginia, Meriwether Lewis was the first son and the second of three children of a Virginia planter family; his younger

brother was REUBEN LEWIS. His father, William Lewis, was a lieutenant in the Continental army as well as a neighbor and friend of Thomas Jefferson. William died in November 1779, and six months later his widow, Lucy Meriwether Lewis, married Captain John Marks, with whom she had two more children.

When Meriwether was about nine, the family moved to northeastern Georgia, which was then frontier country. Physically fit, quick of mind, and self-possessed, Lucy's oldest son reveled in his life there and, with his mother's encouragement, developed a keen interest in botany and geology. At the age of 13 he returned to Virginia and began his formal education in preparation for taking over the family plantation, Locust Hill. When his newly widowed mother returned to Virginia in spring 1792, he abandoned his studies and took up his responsibilities as head of the family.

That same year Lewis heard of Jefferson's attempt to send an expedition across the continent, under the sponsorship of the AMERICAN PHILOSOPHICAL SOCIETY. The 18-year-old applied, but Jefferson turned him down and hired instead a French botanist named ANDRÉ MICHAUX. (Michaux, a secret agent for the French Republic, would be recalled by the French government before reaching Kentucky.) For the next two years Lewis applied himself to Locust Hill, but adventure beckoned in 1794, when farmers in western Pennsylvania, angry about an excise tax on whiskey, began to attack federal tax collectors. To put down what came to be known as the Whiskey Rebellion, President George Washington called for a militia to be formed. Lewis consequently joined the Virginia volunteer corps, leaving his mother to manage the plantation.

After his enlistment expired in May 1795, Lewis joined the U.S. Army as an ensign, resisting family entreaties to return home. In November that year he was court-martialed for challenging a fellow officer to a duel while intoxicated. Acquitted, he was transferred to the Chosen Rifle Company, whose captain was WILLIAM CLARK, four years his senior. Clark left the army just six months later, but in that time the two became friends.

During the next four years Lewis became a Mason, established himself as a Jeffersonian Republican, conducted plantation business from a distance, and traveled widely through the western frontier. Promoted to lieutenant in March 1799, he was posted the following year to Detroit, where he became regimental paymaster and earned a reputation for efficiency and honesty. He was promoted to captain in December 1800. Two months later his family friend Thomas Jefferson was elected president, and shortly thereafter Lewis was invited to become Jefferson's private secretary. It is probable that Jefferson already had in mind that Lewis would lead an expedition west, for in his letter of invitation he referred to Lewis's "knolege of the Western country."

During the next two years, Lewis met many leading politicians, scientists, artists, and writers. With these and Jefferson as his teachers, he made significant advances in his education. When Jefferson raised again the idea of sending an expedition across the continent, he chose Lewis to lead it. This time the president was in a better position to see that a proper expedition was mounted with federal support. Shortly after he requested from Congress an appropriation of funds for the expedition, the LOUISIANA PURCHASE of 1803 more than doubled the size of the United States. The appropriation was granted, and Lewis, who had already begun to make PREPARATIONS FOR THE EXPEDITION, left Washington to go to PHILADELPHIA for intensive studies with leading savants of the time (see BARTON, BENJAMIN SMITH; PATTERSON, ROBERT; RUSH, BENJAMIN; WISTAR, CASPAR). Along the way he arranged for SUPPLIES AND EQUIPMENT, designed the KEELBOAT that would carry the corps for the first part of the journey, and studied the principles and instruments of NAVIGATION with ANDREW ELLICOTT. In Philadelphia he learned the basics of medicine, anatomy, botany, zoology, surveying, and American Indian history. By June 1803 he was back in Washington to finalize his instructions from the president (see MISSION OBJECTIVES) and to complete lists of supplies and men.

On June 19 Lewis wrote to William Clark, inviting him to colead the expedition; Clark's letter of acceptance arrived a month and a half later. By the time the two met in CLARKSVILLE, Indiana Territory, in mid-October, both had begun to recruit men for what came to be known as the CORPS OF DISCOVERY. By December the assembled expedition had settled for the winter at CAMP DUBOIS, near ST. LOUIS. In May 1805 they set out from Camp Dubois and proceeded up the MISSOURI RIVER on the first leg of their historic journey.

Brilliant and mercurial, Meriwether Lewis carried out his mission for President Jefferson with superb leadership skills and painstaking attention to detail. His life following the expedition, however, was clouded by tragedy. *(Library of Congress, Prints and Photographs Division [LC-USZ62-105848])*

Lewis's education, army training, frontier skills, and superb physical condition served him well throughout the arduous trek across the country and back. He was a fair and wise leader, quick to discipline when necessary but willing to perform many of the same tasks as his subordinates. He also served as the corps's primary doctor, attending at the birth of SACAGAWEA's son and attending to wounds and sicknesses (see ILLNESSES AND INJURIES; MEDICINE AND MEDICAL TREATMENT). Fully aware that his mission was not just scientific but political, he served as his country's ambassador to the Native Americans whom they encountered, offering GIFTS and laying the groundwork to establish the authority of the U.S. government in LOUISIANA TERRITORY.

Lewis's JOURNALS and LETTERS provide detailed and descriptive observations that bring the journey to life for readers. Gaps in his written records are ascribed by many historians to his tendency to melancholia, complicated by excessive drinking. Jefferson had noted this tendency in both Lewis and his father and later wrote that when Lewis had lived with him in Washington, he had "observed at times sensible depressions of mind." It is possible that when these dark moods were upon him, Lewis made no entries in his journals, creating frustrating gaps in an otherwise absorbing account of the expedition. Another reason for the gaps may be that Lewis was leaving the bulk of the journal writing to Clark, since he tended to write more when separated from his cocommander.

Lewis and Clark returned as heroes and were rewarded for their accomplishments, each receiving double pay and 1,600 acres of land. Lewis was also named governor of the Territory of Upper Louisiana as of March 1807. However, it was a full year before he went to St. Louis to assume his duties in person. During that time he made a desultory effort to publish his and Clark's journals; twice tried and failed to marry; and had increased episodes of hypochondria, melancholy, and drinking, the latter of which adversely affected his relationship with Jefferson.

His term as governor was in sad contrast to his years as an explorer. Unequal to his responsibilities as an administrator, unable to handle the growing rancor between Native Americans and non-Indians in the territory, and beset by challenges to his authority (see BATES, FREDERICK), Lewis slowly crumbled. Financial problems plagued him as well, as he had been saddled with debts that the War Department refused to cover, and he was also mired in controversy due to his handling of government funds and charges of conflict of interest due to his investment in the St. Louis Missouri Fur Company. In late September 1809, Lewis left St. Louis for Washington, in an effort to clear his name. Depression overtook him during the trip, and he reportedly tried to kill himself twice before arriving at Grinder's Stand, a roadhouse along the Natchez Trace in Tennessee. There, according to commonly accepted accounts, the 35-year-old Lewis finally succeeded in killing himself on the night of October 10–11, shooting himself in the forehead and chest and also cutting himself with a razor.

In the early 1960s, historian Vardis Fisher published a controversial book suggesting that Lewis had not in fact committed suicide but rather had been murdered, with a number of suspects posited. This view was taken up by other scholars, and in the late 1990s an effort to exhume Lewis's body to prove he was murdered was finally halted by a Tennessee judge, but Arkansas senator Frank H. Murkowski revived the exhumation request in February 2002 with apparently no success. There was no doubt, however, in the minds of either William Clark or Thomas Jefferson that Lewis had taken his own life.

Lewis's journals were published posthumously (see BIDDLE, NICHOLAS). He was buried near the site of his death, and a monument to him was erected in 1846. But it was Jefferson who summed up his former secretary's life with the eloquent words, "[He was] of courage undaunted, possessing a firmness & perseverance of purpose which nothing but impossibilities could divert from it's direction. . . ."

See also MARKS, LUCY MERIWETHER LEWIS.

Further Reading

Ambrose, Stephen E. *Undaunted Courage: Meriwether Lewis, Thomas Jefferson, and the Opening of the American West.* New York: Simon and Schuster, 1996.

Bakeless, John E. *Lewis & Clark: Partners in Discovery.* Mineola, N.Y.: Dover, 1996.

Brown, D. Alexander. "The Mysterious Death of a Hero." *American History Illustrated* 5, no. 9 (1971): 18–27.

Dillon, Richard. *Meriwether Lewis: A Biography.* Reprint, Santa Cruz: Western Tanager, 1988.

Fisher, Vardis. *Suicide or Murder? The Strange Death of Governor Meriwether Lewis.* Denver, Colo.: Alan Swallow Co., 1962; Reprint, 1993.

PBS Online. *Lewis and Clark: Inside the Corps of Discovery:* "Captain Meriwether Lewis." Available on-line. URL: http://www.pbs.org/lewisandclark/inside/mlewi.html. Downloaded on May 18, 2001.

Wagner, Chad, and Denny Wesney. "Meriwether Lewis: A Portrait of an American Explorer and Hero." Available on-line. URL: http://www.wfu.edu/Academic-departments/History/newnation/lewis/lewisdex.htm. Downloaded on January 10, 2002.

Woodhouse, Leighton. "Who Killed Meriwether Lewis?" Salon Ivory Tower. Available on-line. URL: http://www.salon.com/it/feature/1999/03/22feature.html. Posted on March 22, 1999.

Lewis, Reuben (1777–1844) *Meriwether Lewis's brother, Indian agent*

Although MERIWETHER LEWIS left his plantation, Locust Hill in Albermarle County, Virginia, at the age of 20, he remained close to his family for the rest of his life. A regular correspondent with his mother LUCY MERIWETHER LEWIS MARKS, older sister Jane, younger brother Reuben, half brother John Marks, and half sister Mary Marks, he took it upon himself to look after their interests from a distance and did all he could to further his younger siblings' educations. Meanwhile, his mother took over the management of Locust Hill, although Meriwether wrote to her, "I would wish Rubin to amuse himself with ucefull books. If he will pay attention he may be adiquate to the task [running the plantation] the ensuing year." It was

with some reluctance that Reuben Lewis took the role thus thrust on him, and though he met the challenge, eventually he joined his older brother on the frontier.

The last child of William and Lucy Meriwether Lewis, Reuben was only two years old when his father died and, six months later, his mother married Captain John Marks. About 1783 the family moved to northeastern Georgia but returned to Locust Hill after Lucy was again widowed in spring 1792. By this time Meriwether had taken up his responsibilities as head of the family, but when adventure beckoned in the form of the Whiskey Rebellion two years later, he left to join the militia. His absence distressed both his mother and Reuben, who wrote entreating him to return home. He never did so but was always full of advice and instructions regarding the plantation and his family, telling Lucy Marks to "Incourage Rubin to be industrious and be attentive to business."

On January 4, 1805, while the expedition was wintering in FORT MANDAN, President THOMAS JEFFERSON, a friend of the Lewis family, wrote to Reuben with news of his brother Meriwether. It was welcome news for the family, who, like the rest of the country, had no way of knowing what was happening to the explorers in the wilderness. Jefferson continued to pass on such reassuring information to them as and when he obtained it. On July 10, 1805, Jefferson wrote to Reuben saying he was waiting for LETTERS from the West, but "[I]t is probable they are coming on by special messenger who travels slow." With that message he enclosed a newspaper report concerning what was known of the expedition's journey to the MANDAN INDIANS.

After the return of the CORPS OF DISCOVERY, Meriwether reunited with his family at Locust Hill, and he and Reuben made plans for the younger Lewis to go to ST. LOUIS and enter the FUR TRADE. The older Lewis, who had problems with depression, became closer to Reuben during this time, and after they were settled in St. Louis he attempted to get his mother and half brother John to join them there. When Lewis, Clark, and several important fur traders formed the St. Louis Missouri River Fur Company, Reuben was brought in as one of the partners. Meriwether's position in the company was criticized due to his role as governor of Louisiana Territory, a clear conflict of interest.

It is not clear how long Reuben stayed in the fur trade, but after Meriwether died in 1809, he became an Indian agent in the territory, dealing with the Mandan and the Cherokee Indians. He eventually returned to Virginia, where he married Mildred Meriwether Dabney in December 1822. He died three days after his 67th birthday in Albemarle County, Virginia, where he had been born.

Further Reading

Ambrose, Stephen E. *Undaunted Courage: Meriwether Lewis, Thomas Jefferson, and the Opening of the American West.* New York: Simon and Schuster, 1996.

Jefferson, Thomas. "President Jefferson writes to Reuben Lewis." Lewis & Clark in North Dakota. Available on-line. URL: http://dorgan.senate.gov/lewis_and_clark/jef1.html. Downloaded on January 17, 2002.

Lewis and Clark Pass

After the expedition had crossed back over the BITTERROOT MOUNTAINS during its return journey in 1806, Captains MERIWETHER LEWIS and WILLIAM CLARK decided to split the expedition into two parties. Departing from TRAVELERS' REST on July 3, Clark took the larger group and headed south on the BITTERROOT RIVER, following for some distance the route they had taken westward. Meanwhile, Lewis, nine soldiers, and five NEZ PERCE guides headed north along the Bitterroot to the Clark Fork River, following a route often taken by the Indians to get to their BUFFALO hunts.

Lewis and his men took their leave of the Nez Perce the next day and headed east, through the site of today's Missoula, Montana, until they arrived at the BIG BLACKFOOT RIVER. This they followed for the next two days, noting signs of a HIDATSA track as they proceeded as well as increasing evidence of BEAVER and DEER. On July 7, still following the Nez Perce trail, they ascended a slope that led to a pass over the CONTINENTAL DIVIDE. From here they crossed the DEARBORN RIVER and finally arrived at the MEDICINE RIVER, where they camped for the night.

The pass by which the party crossed the divide is today called Lewis and Clark Pass, and if the explorers had found it the previous year, it could have saved a considerable amount of time for the expedition. Coming up the MISSOURI RIVER on July 18, 1805, during their western journey, Lewis had found and named Dearborn's River. After spending some time exploring the mouth of the Dearborn, the CORPS OF DISCOVERY had continued up the Missouri. Had they decided to follow the Dearborn instead, they would have approached Lewis and Clark Pass and found a shortcut across the mountains to the Big Blackfoot River valley—and to the SHOSHONE INDIANS who would prove so useful to them. Ironically, William Clark never saw the pass which today bears his name.

Further Reading

Moulton, Gary E., ed. *Atlas of the Lewis and Clark Expedition.* Revised ed. Lincoln: University of Nebraska Press, 1999.

Schmidt, Thomas. *National Geographic Guide to the Lewis & Clark Trail.* Washington, D.C.: National Geographic, 1998.

Lewis and Clark Trail

The Lewis and Clark National Historic Trail is a 3,700-mile route that starts near Wood River, Illinois (the general site of CAMP DUBOIS), and passes through Missouri, Kansas, Iowa, Nebraska, South Dakota, North Dakota, Montana, Idaho, Oregon, and Washington. The trail follows the route of the CORPS OF DISCOVERY as closely as possible. Overseen but not owned by the National Park Service, numerous organizations and individuals are responsible for trail stewardship in cooperation with the Lewis and Clark National Historic Trail office. Historic landmarks and sites along the route include the FORT CLATSOP National Memorial in Oregon as well as other attractions such as the Museum of Westward Expansion at ST. LOUIS. The Lewis and Clark Trail Heritage Foundation in Great Falls, Montana, provides state and local information about the modern-day trail. In June 2003 a bill was introduced in CONGRESS to extend the trail "to include additional sites associated with the preparation or return phase of the expedition."

Further Reading

Appleman, Roy E. *Lewis and Clark: Historic Places Associated with Their Transcontinental Expedition (1804–06).* Washington, D.C.: U.S. Department of the Interior, National Park Service, 1993.

Fifer, Barbara, and Vicky Soderberg. *Along the Trail with Lewis and Clark.* Great Falls, Mont.: Montana Magazine, 1998.

Schmidt, Thomas. *National Geographic Guide to the Lewis & Clark Trail.* Washington, D.C.: National Geographic Society, 1998.

Lewis's River   See SALMON RIVER.

Liberté   See BARTER, JOSEPH.

Lighting Crow   See CROW AT REST.

Lisa, Manuel (1772–1820) *fur trader*

One of the best-known fur traders and entrepreneurs in the early history of the West was Manuel Lisa, with whom MERIWETHER LEWIS and WILLIAM CLARK negotiated for provisions and other necessary supplies as they prepared for their historic journey. Although relations between Lisa and captains were not always ideal, they entered into business together following the expedition, and it was largely because of the Lewis and Clark journey that Lisa subsequently set up an extensive network of trading posts, earning him a reputation as the founder of Old Nebraska and the man who had the greatest effect on the growth of the FUR TRADE.

Lisa was born and grew up in New Orleans, where he began to hustle and trade at an early age. In 1798 he moved north, first to the OHIO RIVER valley and then to ST. LOUIS, where AUGUSTE CHOUTEAU, SR., and his half brother PIERRE CHOUTEAU, SR., then enjoyed a monopoly on trade with the OSAGE INDIANS. This soon changed, however, with Lisa's arrival on the scene. With his Spanish background he was able to curry favors with the Spanish authorities and was granted a license to trade, thus breaking the Chouteaus' monopoly.

Lisa was a shrewd operator who, with his partner Francis Benoit, took advantage of any opportunity to make money. When Lewis and Clark arrived in St. Louis, he and the Chouteaus were their primary supplier of provisions and other SUPPLIES AND EQUIPMENT. Lisa wasted no time in visiting their campsite on Wood River to see what they needed that he could supply. He tried to put together a canoe crew for the corps, and though the captains were initially interested, the deal apparently fell through. Lisa eventually came to feel that he was not getting enough business from Lewis and complained to the Louisiana authorities. Lewis expressed his rage in a letter to Clark: "I think them [Lisa and Benoit] great scoundrels, and they have given me abundant proofs of their unfriendly dispositions towards our government and its measures."

Nevertheless, Lewis may have been among those who subscribed to an expedition up the MISSOURI RIVER that Lisa put together almost immediately after the CORPS OF DISCOVERY's return in 1806. Excited by the reports he had heard, he realized the potential for great wealth that lay in the fur trade to the West and set about staking his claim, sending numerous trading parties up the river in the years that followed. He also went upriver himself, making at least one trip a year for the next 12 years, traveling more than 25,000 miles altogether. In 1807 he built a fort by the YELLOWSTONE RIVER at the mouth of the Bighorn River. This was Montana's first trading post and one of many he would build.

Among those Lisa hired as traders and trappers were former expedition members, including JOHN COLTER, GEORGE DROUILLARD, TOUSSAINT CHARBONNEAU, JOHN POTTS, and PETER WEISER. Late in 1808 he entered into partnership with Lewis, Clark, and the Chouteau brothers among others, forming the St. Louis Missouri Fur Company. Although the company eventually failed, in a period of several years, Lisa successfully set up trading posts along the Missouri River, most notably Fort Lisa (also called Fort Raymond and Fort Manuel) in Nebraska. In 1812 he reorganized the former joint venture, renaming it the Missouri Fur Company and becoming its president. Around this time he became a subagent for Native American nations along the Missouri River and succeeded in preventing western Indians, particularly the TETON LAKOTA INDIANS (Teton Sioux), from siding with the British during the War of 1812. Also in 1812 he founded a second Fort Lisa near what is now Omaha, Nebraska; this fort soon became one of the most important trading posts in the region. The following year he was among the investors who incorporated the Bank of St. Louis.

Following the war, in 1815 Lisa helped to negotiate several treaties with Indians and further extended his fur-trading empire. He also traded heavily in commercial goods with Native Americans. Although already married, during one of his trading expeditions in Nebraska, he took an OMAHA woman to wife and with her had a daughter, Rosalie, and a son, Raymond. After his first wife died, he married another white woman, Mary Hempstead Keeney, whom he brought to Fort Lisa in 1819. Mary Lisa thus probably became the first non-Indian woman to settle in Nebraska.

Lisa died in St. Louis on August 12, 1820, leaving provisions for his two Indian children to be educated. His wife Mary outlived him by another 50 years, becoming known to fur traders and Indians as "Aunt Manuel." She is buried beside him in Bellefontaine Cemetery in St. Louis.

Further Reading
Douglas, Walter Bond. *Manuel Lisa. With hitherto unpublished material, annotated and edited by Abraham P. Nasatir.* New York: Argosy-Antiquarian, 1964.
Oglesby, Richard E. *Manuel Lisa and the Opening of the Missouri Fur Trade.* Norman: University of Oklahoma Press, 1963.
Rich, E. E. *The Fur Trade and the Northwest to 1857.* Toronto: McClelland and Stewart, 1967.

Little Thief (unknown–unknown) *Otoe Indian chief*
Little Thief was the primary chief of the OTOE INDIANS (Oto), the first nation encountered by MERIWETHER LEWIS and WILLIAM CLARK on the lower MISSOURI RIVER. It was early August 1804 in present-day Nebraska before the expedition met their first Indians, as all the tribes of the lower Missouri had been away hunting BUFFALO while the KEELBOAT was moving upriver. On August 2, however, the CORPS OF DISCOVERY was approached by a small party of Otoe and MISSOURI INDIANS, and the following day, at COUNCIL BLUFF, Lewis and Clark had the first of what was to be many COUNCILS WITH INDIANS.

This historic council, however, was attended by only a few lesser Otoe chiefs. Lewis and Clark were anxious to meet Little Thief, and after Private MOSES REED deserted the expedition, the captains sent GEORGE DROUILLARD and a small party on a twofold mission: to find and arrest Reed and to find and bring back Little Thief. The search party succeeded in both missions, and on August 18, while the expedition was camped near present-day Sioux City, Iowa, Drouillard returned with Reed and a delegation of Otoe, headed by Little Thief.

Lewis and Clark dealt with the deserter first, and when Little Thief learned that Reed was to be punished by running the gauntlet, he was horrified and asked that the private be spared. Once he understood that there would be no pardon, he and other Otoe watched as the sentence was carried out.

The following day a council was held with Little Thief and the Missouri chief BIG HORSE. It did not go well, as the Indians had expected more in the way of GIFTS, and Big Horse was especially unhappy when his requests for whiskey were refused. Lewis explained their goal of achieving intertribal peace among the nations of the Missouri, and Little Thief agreed that such an outcome was desirable. The chief noted the friendly relationship that the Otoe had always had with white traders and stressed the need to obtain quality trade goods at a good price. He then requested that FRANÇOIS LABICHE assist in making peace with the Pawnee, a suggestion that the captains refused. Both they and the Otoe left the council feeling dissatisfied with its outcome. Nevertheless, Little Thief had agreed to be part of an Indian delegation to Washington the following spring, so one diplomatic goal had been attained. Little Thief and other Indians subsequently met President THOMAS JEFFERSON in Washington in January 1806.

Further Reading
Ronda, James P. *Lewis and Clark among the Indians.* Lincoln: University of Nebraska Press, 1984.

Lochsa River (Flathead River, Kooskooskee River)

The Lochsa River and its tributaries flow westward more than 100 miles in a semicircle across modern Idaho from the border with Montana to today's Kooskia, Idaho. It flows into the CLEARWATER RIVER, and both rivers are attributed with the Indian name of Kooskooskee. In his journal entry for September 14, 1805, WILLIAM CLARK wrote ". . . this river we call the Flat Head River." The Lochsa properly begins at the junction of today's Whitesand Creek and Crooked Fork Creek, just southwest of the Lolo Pass. It was a mistake in finding this junction that caused at least one day's delay in the CORPS OF DISCOVERY's difficult and dangerous crossing of the BITTERROOT MOUNTAINS along the LOLO TRAIL.

After the expedition guided by OLD TOBY crossed westward over Lolo Pass on September 13, 1805, they made their way southwest along a high ridge, with Glade Creek on their left. At the end of the ridge, they should have turned half-right (due west), crossed Crooked Fork Creek, and then proceeded west again on the next mountain ridge across the valley. Unfortunately, Old Toby took instead a half-left turn in the valley bottom and followed Crooked Fork Creek south to the mouth of Whitesand Creek. This was (and is) the point where the two creeks joined to become the Lochsa River, which the expedition followed downstream before camping for the night on September 14.

With the benefit of hindsight, the error seems a stupid one, but such a judgment makes no allowance for the conditions in which the corps found themselves. There was no well-trodden path to follow; there were only steep slopes and precipices, all covered with brushwood, fallen trees, and snow. Riding was impossible, and progress was made only by leading the HORSES carefully through and over fallen timber and brush. They were making their way through woodland that was dense enough to prevent any opportunity of judging distance or, more important, direction. It was not until the expedition had gone another 4 miles down the river the next day that they realized they were on the wrong route. It then took them nearly the rest of the day to make their way up the snowy, rocky, tree-strewn mountainside back to the Lolo Trail.

Sergeant JOHN ORDWAY calculated that it took them at least 10 miles to get back to the ridge. The slopes were so steep that the only possible route was to wind to and fro in a slow zigzag that William Clark noted grimly was "as bad as it can possibly be to pass." Even with such a tortuous route, they still had to leave behind two horses that were unable to make the climb up the steep slopes that border the Lochsa River.

Further Reading
Cutright, Paul Russell. *Lewis & Clark: Pioneering Naturalists.* Lincoln: University of Nebraska Press/Bison Books, 1989.

Moulton, Gary E., ed. *Atlas of the Lewis and Clark Expedition.* Revised ed. Lincoln: University of Nebraska Press, 1999.

Loisel, Régis (unknown–unknown) *trader, explorer*

On May 25, 1804, as the CORPS OF DISCOVERY moved up the MISSOURI RIVER, WILLIAM CLARK reported that they came "To a Small French village called La Charatt of five families only. This is the Last Settlement of Whites." Here they met Régis Loisel, the first in a number of traders along the river who provided valuable help to the expedition.

Loisel was a French Canadian, born in Montreal, who was an experienced fur trader and, when Clark and MERIWETHER LEWIS met him, may have been a partner in the Missouri Company. (He apparently had several trading connections, including Clamorgen, Loisel & Co., formed in 1796.) He was then traveling downriver from his trading post at Cedar Island after conducting business with the YANKTON NAKOTA INDIANS (Yankton Sioux) and ARIKARA INDIANS. According to the JOURNALS, Loisel gave the captains "a good Deel of information," presumably in regard to the geography and Indians of the upper Missouri, although this is not known for certain.

Loisel was undoubtedly the right man to question on what lay ahead of them since he had taken an expedition up the Missouri only the previous year. One of his employees (perhaps a partner), PIERRE-ANTOINE TABEAU, later wrote an account of the expedition. According to James Ronda, Loisel may also have suggested the explorers look for help from Tabeau and one of his partners at the Cedar Island post, Joseph Garreau.

Shortly after meeting Loisel, in June 1804, the expedition encountered a party of his employees, traders who were heading downriver with two PIROGUES of furs. The group included PIERRE DORION, who had lived among the Yankton Nakota for at least 20 years and had been Loisel's interpreter on a number of occasions. Learning of this, Lewis and Clark immediately hired him to accompany the expedition upriver for their expected meeting with the Yankton Sioux.

The captains continued to meet Loisel employees along the river. However, on September 22, 1804, when they reached his fort at Cedar Island—"Situated in the Country of the Scioux," about 7 miles below Chapelle Creek—they found it empty. Nearby, however, they discovered the remains of a plesiosaur (an aquatic dinosaur). Lewis and Clark subsequently met Pierre-Antoine Tabeau and JOSEPH GRAVELINES farther up the river at the villages of the Arikara Indians; they too would prove to be extremely helpful to the expedition.

During the return journey the party arrived at Loisel's fort on August 26, 1806, but again found it deserted. Loisel's Cedar Island post burned down in 1810, after which it became a trading fort for the St. Louis Missouri Fur Company run by MANUEL LISA.

Further Reading

Allen, John Logan. *Passage Through the Garden: Lewis and Clark and the Image of the American Northwest.* Urbana: University of Illinois Press, 1975. Reprint, New York: Dover Publications, 1991.

Ronda, James P. *Lewis and Clark among the Indians.* Lincoln: University of Nebraska Press, 1984.

Tabeau, Pierre-Antoine. *Tabeau's Narrative of Loisel's Expedition to the Upper Missouri.* Edited by Annie Heloise Abel. Translated by Rose Abel Wright. Norman: University of Oklahoma Press, 1939.

Lolo Creek   See LOLO TRAIL; TRAVELERS' REST.

Lolo Hot Springs

Early in September 1805, after spending more than two weeks with the SHOSHONE INDIANS, the CORPS OF DISCOVERY prepared to cross the BITTERROOT MOUNTAINS. The Shoshone had advised them that the only practicable route over the mountains was the LOLO TRAIL, and so they proceeded this way, with OLD TOBY as their guide. They arrived at TRAVELERS' REST on September 9 and spent two days there before starting off on what they knew would be a difficult journey westward through the mountains.

On September 11 the expedition left Travelers' Rest, initially following Lolo Creek. Two days later they came to a spot where hot water gushed out from the rocks: what is now called Lolo Hot Springs. Sergeant PATRICK GASS described the sight: "When we had gone 2 miles, we came to a most beautiful warm spring, the water of which is considerably above the blood-heat and I could not bear my hand in it without unpleasantness." The urgency of tackling the mountains ahead of them prevented the expedition from staying at the springs, so it was not until their return journey that Gass was able to write: "[June 29, 1806] . . . in the evening we arrived at the warm spring; where we encamped for the night, and most of us bathed in its water."

Now a popular holiday resort, the Lolo Hot Springs are located southwest of present-day Missoula, Montana.

Further Reading

Cutright, Paul Russell. *Lewis & Clark: Pioneering Naturalists.* Lincoln: University of Nebraska Press/Bison Books, 1989.

Moulton, Gary E., ed. *Atlas of the Lewis and Clark Expedition.* Revised ed. Lincoln: University of Nebraska Press, 1999.

Peebles, John J. "On the Lolo Trail: Route and Campsites of Lewis and Clark." *Idaho Yesterdays* 9, no. 4 (1965): 2–15; and 10, no. 2 (1966): 16–27.

Schmidt, Thomas. *National Geographic Guide to the Lewis & Clark Trail.* Washington, D.C.: National Geographic, 1998.

Lolo Trail (Nez Perce Trail)

The Lolo Trail is an old Indian track that runs for more than 100 miles across the BITTERROOT MOUNTAINS from present-day Lolo, Montana, to Weippe in Idaho. At the time of the Lewis and Clark Expedition, it was referred to as the Nez Perce Trail since it was most commonly used by the NEZ PERCE INDIANS.

On September 9, 1805, the CORPS OF DISCOVERY camped at TRAVELERS' REST, just west of what is now Lolo, Montana. They had crossed the CONTINENTAL DIVIDE a month earlier at LEMHI PASS, procured HORSES from the SHOSHONE INDIANS, and had hoped to make their way directly west down the SALMON RIVER. A lengthy reconnaissance by WILLIAM CLARK had shown this to be impracticable, and the captains had decided to take the advice of their Indian hosts and travel due north to find the Lolo Trail, which led west through the mountains.

With OLD TOBY as their guide, the party left Travelers' Rest on September 11 and followed the twisting Lolo Creek up into the mountains, arriving at LOLO HOT SPRINGS on September 13. A few miles further on, they crossed the divide over or near Lolo Pass and came again to what JOHN ORDWAY described as "the head Spring of the waters running West." Though they did not yet know it, they were on Packer Creek, one of the tributaries that join to make the LOCHSA RIVER. It was the beginning of the most miserable part of their journey, with little FOOD, little game to kill, and snow on its way.

The Lolo Trail, for much of its course, runs along the mountain ridges, roughly parallel with the Lochsa River. This did not mean, however, that they rode along a clear, open ridge. As Shoshone chief CAMEAHWAIT had warned them, "the road was a very bad one . . . [and travelers] suffered excessively on the rout being obliged to subsist for many days on berries alone as there was no game in that part of the mountains which were broken rockey and so thickly covered with timber that they could scarecely pass."

All of Cameahwait's forebodings proved correct. The mountains and precipitous valleys between them were everywhere covered in dense brush and fallen trees, making progress unbearably slow. The mountains dropped haphazardly into creeks and gullies, limiting visibility to the next hillside or a glimpse of the river to the south.

On September 14 the corps finished what meat they had in the morning and spent the night on the Lochsa River with PORTABLE SOUP as their only sustenance. A colt was killed to provide some meat, and when they set off the next day they found that Old Toby had made a mistake in the route. They had to make their way up the snow-covered hillside again on a slope so steep it took them 10 miles of winding, tree-covered tracks to reach the top. So severe was it that two horses had to be left behind. That night snow fell again to cover the trail, and they had to kill another colt for food.

The next day, September 17, was even worse since the horses had scattered to find forage and the party managed to travel only 10 miles in the day. In the evening the third and last colt was killed for food. It was clear that something had to be done before they perished from hunger or cold.

This picture of the Lolo Trail gives some indication of the deep ravines and tree-covered slopes that made this the most difficult part of the Corps of Discovery's journey. Snow and other hazardous conditions mean that even today the Lolo Motorway is open only from mid-July to September. *(Montana Historical Society, Helena)*

On the morning of the 18th, Clark and six of the best hunters rode west in a desperate attempt to find the plains they knew were in front of them and where food might be found. From the top of what is now named Sherman Peak, they saw open country a long way ahead, a much-needed encouragement. They spent that night by a small creek, now named Hungry Creek, without food of any sort. Finding a stray Indian horse the next day, they promptly killed it, leaving half for the main party behind them.

Another night was spent in the mountains before, on the 20th, Clark and his party at last arrived at WEIPPE PRAIRIE some 15 miles later. After another five miles or so, they made contact with the NEZ PERCE INDIANS. Private REUBIN FIELD was then sent back to the main party with a packhorse loaded with roots, berries, and dried salmon. Two days later MERIWETHER LEWIS and the others arrived. Their journey had been long and arduous, and their hunger can be measured by their supper on September 18, which is recorded as

being composed of portable soup made with water from a stream, which they had to go down a precipice to reach, along with a small amount of BEAR oil and, as one account has it, some CANDLES. It is little wonder that Lewis recorded: "The pleasure I now felt in having tryumhed over the rockey Mountains and descending once more to a level and fertile country . . . can be more readily conceived than expressed . . ."

On their return journey in June 1806, with Nez Perce guides, the expedition took only seven days to traverse the Lolo Trail back to Travelers' Rest, a crossing that had taken them 11 terrible days the year before. Some indication of the difficulties the explorers met are reflected in the warnings given to modern-day motorists traversing what travel guides say is "still wild and often deserted country." It is advised to check weather conditions, high-clearance vehicles are recommended, and "fallen trees still stop and trap travelers unequipped with saws."

Further Reading

Ambrose, Stephen E. *Undaunted Courage: Meriwether Lewis, Thomas Jefferson, and the Opening of the American West.* New York: Simon and Schuster, 1996.

Cutright, Paul Russell. *Lewis & Clark: Pioneering Naturalists.* Lincoln: University of Nebraska Press/Bison Books, 1989.

Peebles, John J. "On the Lolo Trail: Route and Campsites of Lewis and Clark." *Idaho Yesterdays* 9, no. 4 (1965): 2–15; and 10, no. 2 (1966): 16–27.

Space, Ralph. *The Lolo Trail: A History and a Guide to the Trail of Lewis and Clark,* 2d ed. Missoula, Mont.: Historic Montana Pub., 2001.

Long Narrows   See CELILO FALLS AND THE DALLES.

Long Camp   See CAMP CHOPUNNISH.

Lost Trail Pass

By August 30, 1805, the Lewis and Clark Expedition had reached the CONTINENTAL DIVIDE, crossing it at LEMHI PASS, and had met the SHOSHONE INDIANS, from whom they had obtained the HORSES they needed for the next stage of their journey. Still to the west of them, however, lay numerous mountain ranges, and a decision needed to be made: Which route should they take to get to the COLUMBIA RIVER and from there to the PACIFIC OCEAN?

Captains MERIWETHER LEWIS and WILLIAM CLARK had three options. They could go south, but from the sparse information the Shoshone had given them, they feared it would lead them into Spanish territory. The SALMON RIVER ran to the west, and although the Shoshone had advised against using it, Clark spent August 21–29 reconnoitering its possibilities. He found it not only impassable by CANOES but also so rocky that PORTAGE was out of the question. Thus, by August 30 it seemed the only route left to them was to the north, where the captains were told the NEZ PERCE INDIANS had a trail over the BITTERROOT MOUNTAINS (see LOLO TRAIL). That day they set out, following the Boyle Creek up into the mountains that divided the Salmon River valley from that of the BITTERROOT RIVER.

Clark described their journey up through the hills as "the worst road (if road it can be called) that was ever travelled." The slopes were steep and the rocks so slippery that the packhorses often lost their footing and tumbled down the hill, spilling and scattering their loads. After two wearying days, the party reached the top of the ridge at (or near) Lost Trail Pass, continuing northward for another day before turning down into the valley now known as ROSS'S HOLE, where they met a large party of FLATHEAD INDIANS.

It is still a matter of dispute among historians as to whether Lewis and Clark actually crossed the Lost Trail Pass at all; some suggest they may have used Chief Joseph Pass. Although it is likely their Shoshone guide OLD TOBY would have known of it, the severity of the WEATHER and difficulty of making their way up the mountains may have induced him simply to take whatever route to the top of the ridge was easiest. This question mark of the expedition will probably never be answered satisfactorily. Today the Lost Trail Pass lies just north of Gibbonsville, Montana.

Further Reading

Allen, John Logan. *Passage Through the Garden: Lewis and Clark and the Image of the American Northwest.* Urbana: University of Illinois Press, 1975. Reprint, New York: Dover Publications, 1991.

Ambrose, Stephen E. *Undaunted Courage: Meriwether Lewis, Thomas Jefferson, and the Opening of the American West.* New York: Simon and Schuster, 1996.

Schmidt, Thomas. *National Geographic Guide to the Lewis & Clark Trail.* Washington, D.C.: National Geographic, 1998.

Lost Tribes of Israel

Among MERIWETHER LEWIS's tutors in PHILADELPHIA in May 1803 was the eminent physician Dr. BENJAMIN RUSH, who instructed him in basic principles of medicine. President THOMAS JEFFERSON had also asked Rush and others to review and comment on his instructions to Lewis and to add anything of interest or importance to the MISSION OBJECTIVES. Rush, who had a keen interest in ETHNOGRAPHY, had a long list of questions about the Indians Lewis would meet, particularly with reference to their hygiene and social habits. One of his questions was: "What Affinity between their religious Ceremonies & those of the Jews?"

Along with many others of his time, Dr. Rush believed that among the then-unknown Indian nations of the interior would be found traces of the fabled Lost Tribes of Israel. The legend of the "10 lost tribes" has aroused curiosity and speculation for at least 500 years. Its origin lies in the Bible (2 Kings 17:6): "In the ninth year of Hoshea the king of Assyria took Samuria, and carried Israel away into Assyria, and placed them in Halah and in Habor by the river of Gozan, and in the cities of the Medes." Later, verse 18 of the same chapter reads: "Therefore the Lord was very angry with Israel, and removed them from his sight; there was none left but the tribe of Judah only."

From the beginning of the age of exploration in the 15th century, there have been speculations that some "newly discovered" tribe, race, or people might be one of the 10 lost tribes of Israel. In the early 16th century, Spanish missionary Bartolomé de Las Casas was convinced that the Indians of the West Indies and Peru were the lost tribes. In the 17th century the Portuguese traveler Antonio Montezinos claimed, "There is a Jewish Indian tribe living beyond the mountain passes of the Andes. . . . I myself heard them recite the She'ma and saw them observe Jewish rituals."

Whether or not these theories have any validity is a continuing subject for debate. Many, however, are eager to believe in them due to the widely held tradition that when the 10 lost tribes are found and reunited in the Holy Land, then the messianic age will follow. Perhaps this is why claims have been and are still being made that the Pathans of Afghanistan, certain tribes in central Africa, the Aztec, and the Welsh and Irish Celts of the United Kingdom are all descended from the Lost Tribes of Israel. Evidence that North American Indians may be among these descendants is scanty, and there is no indication in the expedition's JOURNALS that Lewis and Clark ever followed up on Dr. Rush's query.

Further Reading

Ambrose, Stephen E. *Undaunted Courage: Meriwether Lewis, Thomas Jefferson, and the Opening of the American West.* New York: Simon and Schuster, 1996.

Even, Charles. *The Lost Tribes of Israel: or, The First of the Red Men.* Reprint, New York: Arno Press, 1977.

Nova Online. "Lost Tribes of Israel." PBS Companion Website. Available on-line. URL: http://www.pbs.org/wgbh/nova/israel/. Created February 2000; downloaded on February 20, 2002.

Louisiana Purchase

The Louisiana Purchase of April 30, 1803, more than doubled the size of the United States, giving it sovereignty in theory, if not in fact, over all the land between the MISSISSIPPI RIVER and the ROCKY MOUNTAINS from New Orleans in the south to the Canadian border in the north. When the purchase was finalized, it also gave new meaning and a deeper urgency to the Lewis and Clark Expedition.

Prior to 1803, the enormous area known as the LOUISIANA TERRITORY had been under Spanish suzerainty; FRANCE had ceded the land to SPAIN via the Treaty of Fontainebleau (1762) just before the end of the French and Indian Wars. With the loss of CANADA and its thriving FUR TRADE in 1760, France had little interest in the remote and unknown area to the south. By 1800 less than 1 percent of the area had been settled, and it is estimated that the total population, comprising Creoles and their slaves, was about 40,000. These lived mainly along the lower reaches of the Mississippi, with a few trading posts and small garrisons further north, up to ST. LOUIS.

On October 1, 1800, under the secret Treaty of San Ildefonso, France regained its sovereignty over Louisiana Territory. One factor in this transfer was undoubtedly the dream of some French politicians to recover such a vast, if remote, expanse of territory. Another was the introduction of sugarcane and cotton into the Mississippi Valley from the West Indies and the consequent increase in the importance of New Orleans as a port of transit. The major factor, however, was Napoleon Bonaparte's ambition to create a new empire in the West with New Orleans and the Mississippi River as the main line of communication. It is also likely that he feared British incursions south from Canada, which the then new—and comparatively weak—United States would be unable to counter.

To implement his grand design, Napoleon sent troops to Hispaniola (Haiti) to suppress Toussaint Louverture's rising there. Meanwhile, in 1802 the Spanish governor of Louisiana, then still in office, withdrew permission for American traders to pass through New Orleans. U.S. president THOMAS JEFFERSON, who had learned of the secret treaty of 1800, found himself dealing with the domestic outcry this action caused, as well as the danger of a French army arriving on the American mainland. He therefore sent James Monroe to Paris to join the resident minister, Robert Livingston, in negotiations with the French.

The instructions given to Monroe and Livingston were that they should offer up to $10 million to buy New Orleans and West Florida. Failing that, they should offer $7.5 million for New Orleans alone. If that offer was refused, they were to press for permanent right of transit through New Orleans. If this in turn were to fail, then Monroe and Livingston were to open "confidential communications" with the British government. As Jefferson wrote to Livingston on April 18, 1802, "The day that France takes possession of New Orleans . . . we must marry ourselves to the British fleet and nation."

All this took place during a period of quiet in Europe brought about by the Peace of Amiens (March 1802–April 1803), a respite in the wars between the British and the French. When Monroe arrived in Paris, he made little progress, but events were suddenly to fall in his favor. The French campaign in Hispaniola had been a disaster, and without that island, Napoleon's plan could not succeed. He therefore decided to abandon the scheme, especially since it had become clear that the British navy had such superiority that France would never be able to maintain communications with the West Indies or, indeed, anywhere on the other side of the Atlantic. In any event, he needed funds to recommence his European war and pursue his planned invasion of GREAT BRITAIN.

Consequently, on April 11, 1803, the French minister Talleyrand asked Livingston whether the United States would be willing to buy not just New Orleans but the whole of Louisiana. Monroe and Livingston immediately agreed in principle and passed on the offer to Jefferson for confirmation. Subsequent negotiations produced agreement on a price of approximately $15 million for more than 800,000 square miles of territory. (The actual purchase arrangements comprised three separate agreements: a treaty of cession signed by Napoleon and two documents covering the transfer of monies. Copies of these are held in the National Archives and Records Administration.)

Although the U.S. CONGRESS authorized the funds for the purchase, there were still several questions left unsettled. The territory was in theory French but in practice was governed by Spain. Furthermore, Napoleon had promised Spain that Louisiana would not be disposed of to a third power, and the French constitution stated that no alienation of national territory could be enacted without a vote in the legislature. In addition, there were those in the United States who believed the president had no constitutional right to increase the national domain by treaty, much less the right to promise incorporation into the Union by people outside of its original national boundaries.

Despite these problems, the eagerness of the French to rid themselves of what they saw as an encumbrance, the equal eagerness of many Americans to acquire new land, and the

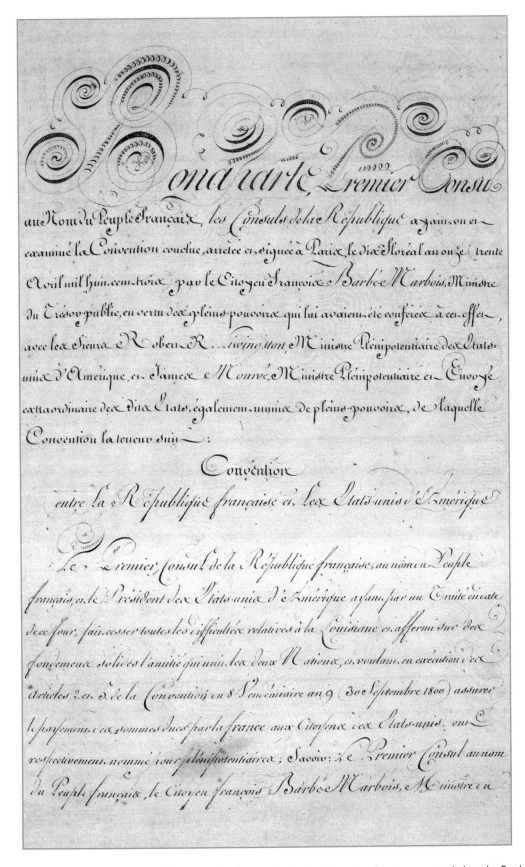

With the Louisiana Purchase, the United States's western border, previously the Mississippi River, was extended to the Rocky Mountains. This photo shows a page from the treaty covering the payment of sums from France to the United States. *(National Archives Old Military and Civil Records [NWCTB-11-ITAP1159E9-TS(EX)86B])*

inability of the Spanish to influence matters either way meant that, on November 30, 1803, in New Orleans, Louisiana Territory was formally handed over from the Spanish governor to a French official. Three weeks later the territory was transferred to the United States.

The immediate result for the expedition was that there were no longer any political obstacles to the CORPS OF DISCOVERY's exploration of the upper MISSOURI RIVER and beyond. On March 9, 1804, MERIWETHER LEWIS and WILLIAM CLARK attended ceremonies in St. Louis marking the formal transfer of Upper Louisiana to the United States. Two months later, they set out from CAMP DUBOIS to begin their ascent of the Missouri River.

The importance of the Louisiana Purchase cannot be overestimated. It is a mark of Jefferson's statesmanship that he saw the long-term benefits it would bring to his country and overrode concerns (including his own) about its constitutionality to see it through. It was an unexpected opportunity to acquire a vast territory not by war but by simple, straightforward purchase, and he was not a man to miss such a chance. By doubling the size of an emerging nation, the Louisiana Purchase established the doctrine of implied powers in the Constitution and assured the dominance of the United States in North America. Consequently, as President Jefferson noted, the purchase "increased infinitely the interest we felt in the expedition."

Further Reading

Avalon Project at the Yale Law School. "The Louisiana Purchase, 1803 and Associated Documents." Available on-line. URL: http://www.yale.edu/lawweb/avalon/diplomacy/france/fr1803m.htm. Updated on February 1, 2002.

DeConde, Alexander. *This Affair of Louisiana.* New York: Charles Scribner, 1976.

Dunbar, William. *Documents Relating to the Purchase and Exploration of Louisiana.* Boston: Houghton, Mifflin & Co., 1904.

Hitchcock, Ripley. *The Louisiana Purchase & the Exploration Early History and Building of the West.* Reprint, Scituate, Mass: Digital Scanning, Inc., 2001. Also available on-line. URL:http://www.usgennet.org/usa/topic/preservation/history/louis/cover.htm. Downloaded on March 13, 2002.

Kukla, Jon A. *A Wilderness So Immense: The Louisiana Purchase and the Destiny of America.* New York: A. A. Knopf, 2003.

Shoemaker, Floyd. "The Louisiana Purchase, 1803." *Missouri Historical Review* 48 (October 1953).

Louisiana Territory

The Louisiana Territory is commonly taken to mean the area of land lying between the MISSISSIPPI RIVER and the ROCKY MOUNTAINS from the Canadian border in the north to New Orleans in the south. It should be noted, however, that its boundaries were never clearly defined. SPAIN, FRANCE, and GREAT BRITAIN all laid claim to the area at one time or another, each basing its argument on different national precedents.

One such precedent commonly accepted in the early days of European exploration of the Americas was that the discovery of a river mouth gave the finder nation sovereignty over the inland area drained by it. It was on this basis that Spain could have staked their claim to the region because Alonso Alvarez de Pineda is considered the first to have discovered the mouth of the Mississippi in 1519. Some years later Hernando de Soto died on the banks of the river as he was exploring the southern region, and the survivors of his party sailed down to the river's mouth in 1542. Despite this, the Spanish, preoccupied by their colonies in Central and South America, laid no formal claim to the area, even though they had occupied and claimed present-day Florida and the coastal strip to New Orleans.

The first formal bid for sovereignty came when René Robert de La Salle traveled down the entire length of the Mississippi in 1682 and claimed the whole vast area of the river basin and its tributaries for France, naming it Louisiana. In 1684, after attempting to settle a colony at the mouth of the river, La Salle landed in present-day Texas, where he was killed by some of his followers in 1687. In 1712 French king Louis XIV gave a grant for the entire area to Antoine Crozat, who in turn ceded his rights to the French "Western Company." The company held the grant until 1731, when it reverted to the French Crown.

It was in 1762 that France (which by then had lost CANADA) secretly ceded to Spain Louisiana—that is, the area drained by the Mississippi and all its tributaries. The following year the Treaty of Paris granted land east of the Mississippi to Great Britain, in theory reducing the size of the Louisiana Territory. While this had little practical effect, it did mean that when the United States came into being, they saw the Mississippi as an opportunity for TRADE and expansion. In 1795 the United States and Spain signed the Treaty of San Lorenzo, which granted the United States rights of navigation down the river and the right to use New Orleans as a port (although Spain would renege on this seven years later).

In 1789 the United States had passed its first Tariff Act as a trade measure and a means of raising money. This act set duties on certain goods landed in its ports, with one rate for American, British, and French ships and a higher rate for all others. Although the British saw this as a sign of friendship, the French complained that they did not get preferential treatment. The French minister to the United States advised his government to recover the Louisiana Territory from Spain so that they would be better able to keep pressure on the new republic. The French took some time in following his advice, but it resulted in the Treaty of San Ildefonso of 1800, under which the territory reverted to French control. It was therefore with France that the United States negotiated the LOUISIANA PURCHASE in 1803.

It should be noted that the boundaries of the territory were always subject to dispute. In the Southwest, Spain claimed a frontier for Texas that the United States refused to accept. The Spanish wanted Natchitoches as the border, while the Americans insisted on the Sabine River. To the north, the Canadian border was to be a matter of dispute for more than 40 years; and the Oregon Territory, outside the Louisiana Territory, was claimed by the United States, Britain, France, Spain, and Russia. While the Spanish settlements on the West Coast were not yet considered a problem, their possessions in West Florida abutted onto New Orleans.

It required many years of diplomacy, and a good measure of bloodshed, to settle all of these and other disputes over land and borders. Nevertheless, the acquisition of the Louisiana Territory is one of the decisive steps in American history and eventually gave the Union the states of Louisiana, Arkansas, Oklahoma, Kansas, Missouri, Nebraska, Iowa, North Dakota, South Dakota, and Montana, as well as much of Minnesota, Colorado, and Wyoming.

Further Reading

Allen, John Logan. "Geographical Knowledge and American Images of the Louisiana Territory." *Western Historical Quarterly* 2 (April 1971).

DeConde, Alexander. *This Affair of Louisiana.* New York: Charles Scribner, 1976.

DiLeo, Juliet, et al. "Government and the Louisiana Territory." Available on-line. URL: http://www.artsci.wustl.edu/~lschwarz/finalhome.html. Downloaded on March 3, 2002.

Marshall, Thomas Maitland. *A History of the Western Boundaries of the Louisiana Purchase, 1819–1841.* Berkeley: University of California Press, 1914.

Mackay, James (ca. 1759–1822) *fur trader, explorer*
During the winter of 1803–04, while the CORPS OF DISCOVERY drilled and trained for the expedition at CAMP DUBOIS, MERIWETHER LEWIS and WILLIAM CLARK spent time in nearby ST. LOUIS, both to buy SUPPLIES AND EQUIPMENT and to gather information. St. Louis was then a center for trade and the starting point for fur trappers heading up the MISSOURI RIVER. Here the captains met men who were able to describe the country upriver and provide important data regarding its Indians. One of these was James Mackay, who has been described by one historian as "perhaps the most widely travelled of the many traders Lewis and Clark met during the Camp Dubois winter."

Born in Kildonan, Scotland, Mackay emigrated to CANADA in 1776. He was in the employ of the NORTH WEST COMPANY when, during the 1780s, he explored the Assiniboine and the Mouse Rivers and visited the villages of the MANDAN INDIANS on the upper Missouri. He then moved south into LOUISIANA TERRITORY, sometime between 1792 and 1794. In 1795, now in the employ of the Spanish-controlled Missouri Company, based in St. Louis, Mackay explored the basin of the lower Missouri, seeking to persuade the Indian nations in that area to look to St. Louis for TRADE rather than northward to his formerly employers, the North West Company.

Mackay spent the winter of 1796–97 among the OMAHA INDIANS and sent JOHN EVANS upstream to live with the Mandan. It is believed that he had envisaged sending Evans to look for a route to the Pacific, but these plans apparently fell through, for in 1797 both of them were back in St. Louis. In that year, probably in recognition of his exploration work, the

Spanish authorities gave Mackay a grant of 330 acres of land in the area. The site later became the home of Ulysses and Julia Grant (now the Ulysses S. Grant National Historic Site).

On January 10, 1804, Mackay visited William Clark at Camp Dubois, where he relayed helpful information on what lay up the Missouri River. Unfortunately, Clark made no record of their conversation, although he apparently told the captain that "a beautiful country" lay ahead. Meanwhile, Lewis reported to THOMAS JEFFERSON that he had obtained copies of Evans's and Mackay's journals from their previous expeditions that both he and Clark found of great value. It is known that among the documents the captains took with them on their journey was Mackay's "Notes on Indian Tribes," based on his early experiences with the Mandan and the BLACKFEET INDIANS. They also took with them a copy of the map Evans (and possibly Mackay) had drawn of the Missouri, at that time the most accurate description of the upper area of the river and its tributaries. It showed the GREAT FALLS, which no white men had yet seen; indicated the course of the YELLOWSTONE RIVER; and, based on Indian accounts, showed the ROCKY MOUNTAINS as a continuous set of ridges rather then the single ridge for which Lewis and Clark were hoping.

Further Reading

Allen, John Logan. *Passage Through the Garden: Lewis and Clark and the Image of the American Northwest.* Urbana: University of Illinois Press, 1975. Reprint, New York: Dover Publications, 1991.

Wood, W. Raymond. *Prologue to Lewis & Clark: The Mackay and Evans Expedition.* Norman: University of Oklahoma Press, 2003.

Mackenzie, Alexander (1764–1820) *explorer*

Contrary to popular belief, MERIWETHER LEWIS and WILLIAM CLARK were not the first white men to reach the PACIFIC OCEAN after a treacherous journey across the North American continent. This distinction belongs to Alexander Mackenzie, a Scottish-Canadian fur trader who accomplished the feat some 12 years earlier and in so doing spurred THOMAS JEFFERSON to make a U.S. expedition one of the first priorities of his presidency.

In 1774, when he was 10 years old, Mackenzie and his family emigrated from Scotland to New York, and less than five years later he was sent to work for a fur-trading firm in Montreal, CANADA. Within another five years he had moved to Grand-Portage. In 1787 his company and others merged to form the NORTH WEST COMPANY, and he was offered both a partnership and supervision of the Athabasca region (in northern Alberta), an important fur-trading area that brought with it the chance to find the fabled NORTHWEST PASSAGE across the continent. It was then believed that a river (later named for Mackenzie) whose headwaters were at the Great Slave Lake could be followed to the Pacific Ocean, then called the Western Sea. In 1789 Mackenzie led a party to pursue this possibility, but before long the river turned north, taking him to the Arctic instead. Although he mapped a significant area during this trip, he remained fixed on his original goal.

Four years later, Mackenzie put together a party of nine men, including two Indians, and set out on a second expedition, this time following the Peace River and its tributary, the Parsnip River, to the CONTINENTAL DIVIDE. After portaging easily across the divide, they traveled a short distance down the Fraser River before Mackenzie realized that it was not, as he had thought, a tributary of the COLUMBIA RIVER. Taking the advice of area Indians, the party proceeded overland and came to the Blackwater River, which they followed to the coast ranges, crossing over to the Bella Coola River. Descending this last river in a canoe borrowed from some Indians, they arrived at an inlet off the Pacific Ocean. From local Indians Mackenzie learned that GEORGE VANCOUVER had been in the area a little more than six weeks earlier. The next day Mackenzie used vermilion and grease to paint a message on a rock near the river: "Alexander Mackenzie, from Canada, by land, the twenty-second of July, one thousand seven hundred and ninety-three."

With this message, and by noting the latitude and longitude of his position, Mackenzie laid claim for the British to the Northwest Territory. He then turned back, his route fully mapped, completing his round trip just 117 days after he had started out. For various reasons, however, his book describing the expedition, *Voyages from Montreal,* was not published until 1801, in London. A year later President Jefferson received a copy and immediately read it through with his secretary, Meriwether Lewis. The book had a galvanizing effect on both of them. First and foremost, they perceived the need to establish a U.S. claim on the territory by getting a U.S party out to the area as soon as possible. Second, Mackenzie's accomplishment had brought home the realization that they probably could find a route over the ROCKY MOUNTAINS. Finally, even if Macken-

zie had not found an all-water route himself, in their view such a possibility still existed in the lands south of where he had explored. Jefferson was also alarmed by Mackenzie's recommendation that the British develop his overland route to the Pacific to open up the FUR TRADE there and thus claim the area for Britain. The commercial as well as political implications of this did not escape the president, and not long after reading Mackenzie's book he and Lewis began to lay the groundwork for the historic U.S. expedition.

Mackenzie made no further explorations but gained considerable fame after his book was published, and he was knighted in 1802. In 1798 he formed his own fur-trading enterprise, called the XY Company; this was amalgamated with the North West Company in 1804. In 1805 he was elected to the Legislative Assembly of Lower Canada, but three years later he returned to Scotland, where he married, had three children, and lived comfortably until his death in January 1820. Some historians have pointed out that his 1793 expedition was noteworthy not just because he was the first non-Indian to cross the continent but because he did it in less time and with fewer men than Lewis and Clark. There was one other detail, though, that Lewis probably appropriated from Mackenzie. The Scot took a dog along on his journey, and the American followed his example (see SEAMAN).

Further Reading

Bryce, George. *The Remarkable History of the Hudson's Bay Company, Including That of the French Traders of North-western Canada, and of the North-west, XY, and Astor Fur Companies.* 2d ed. New York: B. Franklin, 1968.

Daniells, Roy. *Alexander Mackenzie and the North West.* Toronto: Oxford University Press, 1971.

Mackenzie, Sir Alexander. *Voyages from Montreal through the Continent of North America to the Frozen and Pacific Oceans in 1789 and 1793, with an Account of the Rise and State of the Fur Trade.* 2 vols.; Reprint, New York: AMS Press, 1973.

Pathfinders and Passageways: The Exploration of Canada. "Alexander Mackenzie Reaches the Pacific." Available on-line. URL: http://www.nlc-bnc.ca/2/24/h24-1630-e.html. Updated on December 7, 2001.

MacKenzie, Charles (Charles McKenzie)

(unknown–unknown) *fur trader*

While encamped at FORT MANDAN during the winter of 1804–05, MERIWETHER LEWIS and WILLIAM CLARK met and talked with a number of trappers and traders, many of them employees of HUDSON'S BAY COMPANY or the NORTH WEST COMPANY. One of their most frequent visitors was Charles MacKenzie (spelled McKenzie in some sources), a North West clerk who, like his fellow Northwester FRANÇOIS-ANTOINE LAROCQUE, maintained a journal of his time at the Mandan-Hidatsa villages and his observations of Lewis, Clark, and the CORPS OF DISCOVERY.

While little is known about MacKenzie himself, his record of the corps's winter among the MANDAN and the HIDATSA

INDIANS provides fascinating insight into the lives of the captains at that time and their relationships with Indians and traders. The relatively dull conditions at Fort Mandan encouraged comradeship and conversation, as MacKenzie noted: "Mr. Larocque and I having nothing particular claiming attention, we lived contentedly and became intimate with the gentlemen of the American expedition. . . ." He indicated that Lewis "could speak fluently and learnedly on all subjects, but his inveterate disposition against the British stained, at least in our eyes, all his eloquence." On the other hand, he found Clark far more pleasant in manner.

Early in December 1805, members of the corps joined a Mandan BUFFALO hunt, with considerable success. "Hunting and eating were the order of the day," wrote MacKenzie. He noted the captains' attitude toward the Indians, which was clearly patronizing yet also full of scientific interest. He observed at separate occasions when Lewis and Clark attempted to record the Hidatsa and the Mandan LANGUAGES. The process was fraught with problems due to the complicated chain of INTERPRETATION in which a native speaker spoke a word to SACAGAWEA, who translated it for TOUSSAINT CHARBONNEAU, who put it into French for RENÉ JESSAUME, who then rendered it in English for the captains. The chance for errors being made was magnified by Jessaume's poor English as well as frequent arguments with Charbonneau about the meaning of a word. Furthermore, MacKenzie noted, "As the Indians could not well comprehend the intention of recording their words, they concluded that the Americans had a wicked design on their country."

MacKenzie made numerous visits to the Mandan-Hidatsa villages in the course of his work for the North West Company. During the expedition's return journey in 1806, Clark noted in his journal that the ASSINIBOINE INDIANS, who had turned against the Northwesters, were planning to kill MacKenzie. Whether MacKenzie himself also got word of the planned ambush is unknown, but in any event he was an active fur trader for another 40 years.

Further Reading

Ambrose, Stephen E. *Undaunted Courage: Meriwether Lewis, Thomas Jefferson, and the Opening of the American West.* New York: Simon and Schuster, 1996.

Gottfred, A. "Lewis & Clark: A Canadian Perspective." *Northwest Journal* 11: 1–13. Available on-line. URL: http://www.north-westjournal.ca/XI1.htm. Downloaded on February 27, 2002.

Ronda, James P. *Lewis and Clark among the Indians.* Lincoln: University of Nebraska Press, 1984.

Wood, W. Raymond, and Thomas D. Thiessen. *Early Fur Trade on the Northern Plains: Canadian Traders Among the Mandan and Hidatsa Indians, 1738–1818.* Norman: University of Oklahoma Press, 1985.

Madison, James (1751–1836) *secretary of state, fourth president of the United States*

On July 27, 1805, MERIWETHER LEWIS and a party of men in CANOES came around a bend in the MISSOURI RIVER to a point where it divided into THREE FORKS. The expedition pulled over, and Lewis got out and ascended to the top of a cliff, where he "commanded a most perfect view of the neighboring country" and three magnificent rivers. He subsequently named them: The southwest fork became Jefferson's River (now the JEFFERSON RIVER), after President THOMAS JEFFERSON; the southeast fork was named "Gallitin's river" in honor of Secretary of the Treasury ALBERT GALLATIN; and the middle fork became "Maddison's river" for Secretary of State James Madison, who would succeed Jefferson as president in less than four years.

Born in Port Conway, Virginia, Madison graduated from the College of New Jersey (later Princeton University) in 1771. At the Virginia Convention of 1776, he helped to write the Virginia Constitution and Declaration of Rights, and in 1780 he became a delegate to the Continental Congress, serving there until December 1783. He was subsequently a leader in the Virginia House of Delegates from 1784 to 1786. In 1787 he joined the Virginia delegation to the Constitutional Convention in PHILADELPHIA, where he became one of the primary architects of the new U.S. Constitution. He then worked tirelessly for its ratification, joining ALEXANDER HAMILTON and John Jay in writing *The Federalist Papers,* a series of letters defending the proposed constitution. Ratification was assured once Madison agreed to append a Bill of Rights to the document, which he did after his election as a U.S. congressman (1789–97). He has thus been called as the "Father of the Constitution"—a title of which he never publicly approved.

Despite strong Federalist thinking earlier in his career, Madison eventually adopted the Republican views of his friend Thomas Jefferson and came to oppose the policies of Hamilton, secretary of the Treasury during George Washington's presidency. In 1801 Jefferson was elected president and Madison was named secretary of state, a post in which he served throughout Jefferson's administration. When he first learned of Jefferson's plans to send an expedition across the continent, he was doubtful of its success, noting that it would take U.S. explorers into foreign-owned territory. However, the LOUISIANA PURCHASE soon settled that objection.

When Meriwether Lewis was named governor of LOUISIANA TERRITORY following the expedition, he reported to Madison as secretary of state. Although he did not go out to ST. LOUIS to take up his responsibilities until 1808, Lewis sent a bill to Madison on June 28, 1807, charging the State Department for his salary from March 3 to June 30, 1807, an amount of $666.66. Madison authorized the payment, but the department deducted an overcharge of $5.55.

In 1809 Madison succeeded Jefferson as president. Lewis's increasing problems as territorial governor were coming to a head, and Madison was not inclined to be as patient with the former hero as Jefferson had been. On September 16, while on his way to Washington to plead his case, Lewis wrote a letter to the president explaining his reasons for traveling by land rather than sea and also indicating what he was bringing with him to Washington for his defense. It was his

The captains named one of the Three Forks of the Missouri River "Maddison's river" (above) after James Madison, then secretary of state to President Thomas Jefferson. The other two forks were named after Jefferson and Secretary of the Treasury Albert Gallatin. *(Library of Congress, Prints and Photographs Division [LC-USF33-003083-MI])*

last communication with Madison; while still in transit, Lewis killed himself the night of October 10–11.

James Madison's two terms as president are not considered distinguished by historians, and his handling of the events that led to the War of 1812, as well as his leadership during that war, have been described as inept. Nevertheless, he became a well-liked president, due in part to the popularity of his wife Dolley and in part also to General Andrew Jackson's victory in New Orleans at the close of what has been called the Second War for Independence. The nation had been kept intact, and its international influence and authority had been much strengthened by the war. During his administration, the states of Louisiana and Indiana were admitted to the Union, and increased exploration and trade in the West brought in its train prosperity for many and the dawn of an era that would see the nation expand from the East Coast to the West.

In March 1817 Madison retired to Montpelier, his estate in Virginia. His last political act was to serve at the Virginia Constitutional Convention in 1829. During his retirement he also worked on his notes from the 1787 Constitutional Convention (published in 1840 as *Journal of the Federal Convention*). He spoke out against the incipient states' rights movement that was threatening to disrupt the Union. In "Advice to My Country," written shortly before his death in 1836, he expressed the hope "that the Union of the States be cherished and perpetuated."

Further Reading

Ketcham, Ralph. *James Madison: A Biography.* Charlottesville: University of Virginia Press, 1990.

Madison's River   See THREE FORKS.

magpies   See ARTIFACTS AND SPECIMENS; BIRDS, NEW SPECIES.

Malboeuf, Étienne   See ENGAGÉS.

Mandan Indians

With the possible exception of the NEZ PERCE INDIANS, no Native American nation played a more important role in the Lewis and Clark Expedition than did the Mandan. MERIWETHER LEWIS had already anticipated their usefulness when he planned for the CORPS OF DISCOVERY to spend the winter of 1804–05 near their villages along the upper MISSOURI RIVER, just below the mouth of the KNIFE RIVER. In many respects, this area was the edge of the wilderness. White traders had been visiting the Mandan and the HIDATSA villages for years, but few had gone any farther west, as Lewis and WILLIAM CLARK were planning to do. Furthermore, the villages were the hub of a vast trading network, which meant that the captains could, in one spot, meet representatives of many Indian nations in addition to British traders. When they arrived at the Mandan villages in October 1804, therefore, they built FORT MANDAN nearby and settled in for the winter.

A Siouan-speaking, light-skinned people, the Mandan were one of the earliest among the PLAINS INDIANS to inhabit the GREAT PLAINS, moving up the Missouri River sometime before 1400. For well more than 200 years it has been suggested that they might be descendants of the legendary WELSH INDIANS, a theory popular at the time of the expedition. Once a large nation, the Mandan had been devastated by a smallpox epidemic in 1781–82, and their seven villages had been reduced to two by the time Lewis and Clark met them. To protect themselves from the TETON LAKOTA INDIANS (Teton Sioux), they had formed an alliance with the Hidatsa Indians, moving from the Heart River to the confluence of the Missouri and Knife Rivers in the late 1700s.

The Mandan resided in round, earth lodges, with each lodge holding several families. Although they hunted BUFFALO and other game, they were largely farmers, growing CORN, beans, squash, TOBACCO, and other agricultural goods which they traded to other Indian nations for HORSES, guns, and buffalo hides. They also served as middlemen between those nations and white traders, an arrangement that began not long after the French explorer Pierre de La Vérendrye became the first non-Indian to meet them in 1738. It was La Vérendrye who noted of them: "They are sharp traders, and clean the ASSINIBOINE out of everything they have in the way of guns, powder, ball, kettles, axes, knives, and awls." They would be equally

astute with the French and British traders who came to them in the following years with the hope of gaining control over their lucrative TRADE—a hope that Lewis and Clark shared.

The two Mandan villages were called Matootonha (now Mitutanka), or the "lower village," located on the west bank of the Missouri; and Rooptahee (now Nuptadi), or the "upper village," located on the river's east bank, about seven miles upstream. Like other Plains Indians, the Mandan had numerous chiefs, but Lewis and Clark designated BLACK CAT of Rooptahee as Grand Mandan Chief. The other chief they saw most often was BIG WHITE of Matootonha, which lay just across the river from Fort Mandan and was therefore the village closest to the expedition. Farther north, the Hidatsa villages were situated along the banks of the Knife River.

The Mandan trading relationship with other nations, such as the Assiniboine and Cree, as well as with traders from the NORTH WEST COMPANY and the HUDSON'S BAY COMPANY was complex and poorly understood by the explorers. Nevertheless, as they had attempted to do with the Teton Lakota and the ARIKARA INDIANS, Lewis and Clark spoke at great length to the Mandan about changing their current connections and entering into a commercial relationship with the ST. LOUIS merchants. While they were interested in trading with the Americans, and although some Mandan chiefs were willing to consider breaking off with the British-associated Assiniboine, they were slow to take any real action to disrupt what had always been a highly satisfactory arrangement for them.

Also important to the captains was a peace agreement between the Arikara and the Mandan-Hidatsa alliance, which in their view would lessen the threat posed by the Sioux and the Assiniboine. To that end they had brought with them an Arikara chief who attended the first council with the Mandan and Hidatsa on October 29, 1804. Although they had been very dissatisfied with the GIFTS Lewis and Clark had given

This Mandan earth lodge was photographed around 1908. Note the bull boat by the doorway. *(Library of Congress, Prints and Photographs Division [LC-USZ62-114582])*

them, the Mandan were willing to discuss peace and to consider the captains' proposal that Chief Black Cat travel to Washington to meet President THOMAS JEFFERSON.

During the long winter at Fort Mandan, a friendly and mutually beneficial relationship developed between the explorers and the Mandan. They traded frequently, and JOHN SHIELDS provided blacksmith services, making and repairing tools and WEAPONS for the Mandan in exchange for FOOD. Indians came to the fort often, many staying the night; on only one occasion—Christmas Day 1804—were they asked to stay away from the fort. Soldiers, meanwhile, paid equally frequent visits to the villages, especially Matootonha; many formed attachments to Mandan women (see SEX DURING THE EXPEDITION). The corps also accompanied the Indians on buffalo hunts and in January 1805 took part in the ritual Mandan BUFFALO DANCE.

The captains had ample opportunity to study the lives and customs of the Mandan and the Hidatsa (see ETHNOGRAPHY), and the Indians willingly provided information on the country and Indian nations north and west of the villages. By April, though, any hope the captains had for peace with those further south on the Missouri had been considerably diminished by reported Sioux and Arikara attacks on Mandan hunters. Black Cat informed them that as long as the Lakota were a threat, he would make no trip to Washington for them. Promises of U.S. protection failed to reassure him.

In early April 1805, the expedition left the Mandan villages on its westward journey. They returned more than a year later, in August 1806, and the Mandan "were extreamly pleased to see us," reported Clark. However, he and Lewis were disheartened to learn that all peacemaking efforts with the Arikara had failed. Given the continued Sioux threat, Black Cat flatly refused to even consider accompanying them to Washington. After extensive persuasion and promises of rewards, Chief Big White agreed to make the trip. It would take three years, the loss of several lives, and $20,000 to get him back home, justifying Black Cat's forebodings.

In the years following the expedition, the Mandan continued to maintain friendly relations with Americans as well as with British traders. In 1837, however, a smallpox epidemic nearly wiped them out; it is believed that only 125 of 1,600 Mandan survived. The remaining few moved with the Hidatsa to Fort Berthold in western North Dakota, where they were joined by the Arikara Indians in 1862. In 1870 a permanent reservation was created at Fort Berthold for the Three Affiliated Tribes, as they are known today.

Further Reading

Alwin, John A. "Pelts, Provisions, and Perceptions: The Hudson's Bay Company Mandan Indian Trade, 1795–1815." *Montana: The Magazine of Western History.* 29 (1979): 16–27.

Cash, Joseph H., and Gerald W. Wolff. *The Three Affiliated Tribes (Mandan, Arikara, and Hidatsa).* Phoenix, Ariz.: Indian Tribal Series, 1974.

Jones, Gene. "The Mandan Indians, Descendants of the Vikings." *Real West* 9, no. 47 (May 1966): 31–32.

Meyer, Roy W. *The Village Indians of the Upper Missouri: The Mandans, Hidatsas, and Arikaras.* Lincoln: University of Nebraska Press, 1977.

Ronda, James P. *Lewis and Clark among the Indians.* Lincoln: University of Nebraska Press, 1984.

Waldman, Carl. *Encyclopedia of Native American Tribes.* Revised ed. New York: Checkmark Books, 1999.

Wood, W. Raymond, and Thomas D. Thiessen. *Early Fur Trade on the Northern Plains: Canadian Traders Among the Mandan and Hidatsa Indians, 1738–1818.* Norman: University of Oklahoma Press, 1985.

maps

From one aspect, maps and mapping can be considered the main purpose of the Lewis and Clark Expedition. THOMAS JEFFERSON, a man of foresight, knew that the United States would inevitably expand into the territory west of the MISSISSIPPI RIVER. In 1802 any American exploration of the area was bound to meet opposition from the French and the Spanish, but the LOUISIANA PURCHASE eradicated that problem. It was no longer just a matter of exploration; it was to be an expedition to establish the boundaries and chart the details of land now owned by the United States as well as a diplomatic mission to promulgate its authority over the area and the Indian nations over whom it now claimed sovereignty.

In 1802–03, when Jefferson and MERIWETHER LEWIS worked on their PREPARATIONS FOR THE EXPEDITION, maps were an essential factor. They knew the latitude and longitude of the mouth of the COLUMBIA RIVER from ROBERT GRAY's voyage of 1792. They knew that ALEXANDER MACKENZIE had reached the PACIFIC OCEAN overland through CANADA in 1793. They also knew that there was a mountain range running down the west coast—and they knew that it had been reported that the MISSOURI RIVER rose in those mountains. But that was all they knew. It was to be the task of Lewis and Clark to find and map a route across America to the Columbia, by way of the Missouri.

As an essential part of the planning, Jefferson had collected the best geographical information he could, including Mackenzie's account of his 1793 journey, which was not published until 1801. Mackenzie claimed to have crossed the CONTINENTAL DIVIDE at a point where it was only 3,000 feet high and gave an easy descent to the Pacific on the other side. If such a crossing and access could be found further south, it would be of inestimable advantage to the United States.

In March 1803 ALBERT GALLATIN, also an enthusiastic supporter of the expedition, commissioned NICHOLAS KING to collate the most recent cartographic information onto one map. Based on maps drawn by such explorers as James Cook, GEORGE VANCOUVER, and Mackenzie as well as those by the surveyor ANDREW ELLICOTT and Aaron Arrowsmith, an English cartographer whom Jefferson admired, King assembled and drew a map that depended largely on Arrowsmith for the western section and Ellicott for the Mississippi.

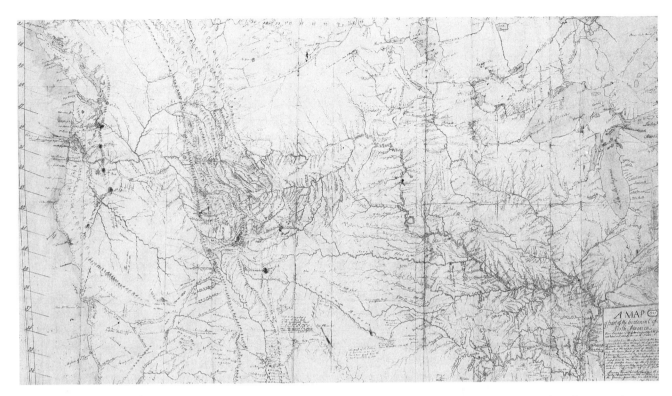

This map of the West by Clark reflects his meticulous work and incorporates information not just from the expedition's journey but from many other sources. *(Yale Collection of Western Americana, Beinecke Rare Book and Manuscript Library)*

King's map was certainly the most accurate of its time, and it is known that Lewis saw it and annotated it. What is still in doubt, surprisingly, is whether he actually took it with him on the expedition. One theory is that his amendments were made from information he gathered at ST. LOUIS during the winter of 1803–04 from JOHN HAY, JOHN EVANS, and JAMES MACKAY. Another claim is that he must have taken it along since some of his corrections could not have been made until he reached the villages of the MANDAN INDIANS. What is not in doubt is that Lewis spent much of the winter at St. Louis collecting information from the traders, trappers, and explorers who used the Missouri and knew the Indians who lived along it. While their interest was commercial, based on a search for furs, they had acquired data that Lewis and WILLIAM CLARK needed.

On January 7, 1804, during the winter at CAMP DUBOIS, Clark wrote: "I drew a Map for the purposes of Correcting from the information which I may get of the Countery to the N.W." In May 1804, before they left to begin their ascent of the Missouri, Lewis sent this map to Jefferson, describing it as "A Map of a part of Upper Louisiana, compiled from the best information that Capt. Clark and myself could collect, from the Inhabitants of Saint Louis, haistily corrected by the information obtained from the OSAGE INDIANS lately arrived at this place. . . ."

Of the two captains, Clark was undoubtedly the better surveyor and cartographer. Reading the expedition's JOURNALS, one is struck time and again by his meticulous entries. No matter what the circumstances—cold, wet, or blinding heat—the distances, descriptions, and changes of direction or compass course are always there. His map sent from St. Louis was the first cartographic product of the expedition; it was to be followed by many others as Clark measured widths of rivers, estimated heights of mountains, and drew and sketched his way across the continent. The result was the collection of nearly 150 maps drawn by Clark now in the possession of Yale University.

It was during the winter of 1805–06 at FORT CLATSOP that Clark assembled his notes, sketches, and field notebooks into the map that was to remain the most accurate depiction of the Northwest for nearly 60 years. Working from his daily notes of distances and compass bearings, from drawings he had made of maps drawn in the dirt or on skins by Indians he had met along the journey, he was the first to show the width of the ROCKY MOUNTAINS and the twisting course of the rivers that ran through them. Then, on February 14, 1806, he wrote: "I compleated a map of the Countrey through which we have been passing from the Mississippi at the Mouth of the Missouri to this place. . . ."

When the expedition was completed, Lewis wrote to Jefferson from St. Louis, announcing their safe return. Not until December 28, 1806, however, did he return to Washington, and it is believed that he and Jefferson did not discuss the findings of the expedition until after New Year's Day 1807. There is no record of what they said, but from a later letter of Jefferson's, it is known that they spread Clark's map on the floor and got down on their hands and knees to examine it.

The map Lewis and Jefferson examined so closely is now in the possession of the William Robertson Coe Collection of Western Americana, Yale University Library.

Further Reading

Allen, John Logan. *Passage Through the Garden: Lewis and Clark and the Image of the American Northwest.* Urbana: University of Illinois Press, 1975. Reprint, New York: Dover Publications, 1991.

Ehrenberg, Ralph. "Mapping on the Trail." *Route Mapping on the Lewis and Clark Expedition.* Available on-line. URL: http://www.edgate.com/lewisandclark/mapping_on_trail.html. Downloaded on March 1, 2002.

Hawke, David Freeman. "William Clark and the Mapping of the West." *Gateway Heritage* 10, no. 3 (1989–90): 4–13.

Plamondon, Martin. *Lewis and Clark Trail Maps: A Cartographic Reconstruction.* Pullman: Washington State University Press, 2000.

Ronda, James P. "'A Chart in His Way': Indian Cartography and the Lewis and Clark Expedition." *Great Plains Quarterly* 4, no. 1 (1984): 43–53.

Salter, Cathy Riggs. "Lewis and Clark's Lost Missouri: A Mapmaker Re-creates the River of 1804 and Changes the Course of History." *National Geographic* 201, no. 4 (April 2002): 89–97.

University of Virginia. "Exploring the West from Monticello: Observations of Latitude and Longitude at All Remarkable Points." Available on-line. URL: http://www.lib.virginia.edu/exhibits/lewis_clark/home.html. Downloaded on March 27, 2002.

Wood, W. Raymond. "William Clark's Mapping in Missouri, 1803–1804." *Missouri Historical Review* 76, no. 3 (1982): 241–251.

Marias River (Maria's River)

The Marias River, in northwestern Montana, is a northern tributary of the MISSOURI RIVER. It flows east and then south to discharge into the Missouri at present-day Loma, Montana. When the expedition first came to the Marias in June 1805, most of the soldiers were convinced that it was the main branch of the MISSOURI RIVER and that they should go that way. Captains MERIWETHER LEWIS and WILLIAM CLARK were equally convinced that it was the wrong route, primarily because of its northerly direction and muddy waters. Nevertheless, Lewis led a small party to explore the river. After they had gone about 60 miles, he wrote in his journal: "I now became well convinced that this branch of the Missouri had it's direction too much to the North for our rout to the Pacific."

Certain that this was not the correct path to follow, Lewis and his men turned back. He named the waterway "Maria's River," in honor of "that lovely fair one." Eventually the apostrophe was dropped, and it became Marias River. Years later editor Elliott Coues researched Lewis's genealogy and concluded that Lewis's fair lady was his cousin, Maria Wood.

The Marias figured heavily in the expedition's return from the west coast in 1806. At TRAVELERS' REST in early July, Captains MERIWETHER LEWIS and WILLIAM CLARK decided to split the CORPS OF DISCOVERY into two parties (which were later split again), take different routes across the CONTINENTAL DIVIDE, and reunite at a designated point on the Missouri River. Clark went south, while Lewis took nine men across LEWIS AND CLARK PASS. Leaving six men to handle the PORTAGE at the GREAT FALLS, he took GEORGE DROUILLARD, JOSEPH FIELD, and REUBIN FIELD with him to explore the Marias River.

Lewis's intention was "to ascend Maria's river with a view to explore the country and ascertain whether any branch of that river lies as far north as Latd 50, and again return and join the party who are to decend the Missouri, at the entrance of Maria's river." This decision was risky since it divided their already small group in the wilderness, narrowing the odds of a successful reunion, and also led Lewis and the others into the territory of the BLACKFEET INDIANS, who might well be hostile to them. Lewis nonetheless hoped to establish a trade relationship with the Blackfeet, although his primary motivation behind his scouting party was to determine how far north the Marias ran. The terms of the LOUISIANA PURCHASE had essentially given the United States all land drained by the Missouri River. If that drainage extended far enough north, it would include Canadian land in which GREAT BRITAIN maintained strong commercial interests.

Unfortunately, Lewis found that the Marias went north for only a few miles before turning west. They continued to follow the river for several days, but on July 21 they came to a fork. Still hoping, Lewis decided to go up the northern branch, Cut Bank Creek, and they traveled for another day before he finally came to the conclusion that they would not attain the 50th parallel. They finally stopped to rest for a few days at the point that he named CAMP DISAPPOINTMENT, and on the 26th they began their return, crossing overland to the southern branch of the Marias, TWO MEDICINE RIVER.

That evening Lewis and his men encountered a small band of Blackfeet warriors, who, after some hesitation, decided to camp with the soldiers. Lewis attempted to parlay with the Indians but alarmed them when he revealed that a promise had been made to the SHOSHONE and the NEZ PERCE INDIANS to supply them with guns. Early the following morning Lewis was awakened by shouts: Drouillard and the Field brothers had surprised some warriors in the act of stealing the men's guns and HORSES. In the fight that followed, Reubin Field killed a warrior and Lewis mortally wounded another one. Taking some of the Indians' horses, the soldiers made a hasty escape and did not stop riding until they felt themselves clear of the Blackfeet. This was the only battle of the expedition—and the first time blood had been shed in a confrontation between western Indians and U.S. soldiers.

See also DEMOCRACY ON THE EXPEDITION.

Further Reading

Allen, John Logan. "Lewis and Clark on the Upper Missouri: Decision at the Marias." *Montana: The Magazine of Western History* 21, no. 3 (1971): 2–17.

Cutright, Paul Russell. "Meriwether Lewis and the Marias River." *Montana: The Magazine of Western History* 18, no. 3 (1968): 30–43.

Lewis, Meriwether, and William Clark. *The History of the Lewis and Clark Expedition.* Edited by Elliott Coues; 4 vols., 1893, Harper. Reprinted in 3 vols., New York: Dover Publications., 1979.

Moulton, Gary E., ed. *Atlas of the Lewis and Clark Expedition.* Revised ed. Lincoln: University of Nebraska Press, 1999.

Ronda, James P. *Lewis and Clark among the Indians.* Lincoln: University of Nebraska Press, 1984.

Marks, Lucy Meriwether Lewis (1752–1837)

Meriwether Lewis's mother, herb doctor

Of the people who made indirect but important contributions to the success of the Lewis and Clark Expedition, one often overlooked is Lucy Meriwether Lewis Marks. The mother of MERIWETHER LEWIS was a talented and resourceful woman who in many ways shaped her son to become the extraordinary man THOMAS JEFFERSON would choose to lead a party of men across the continent.

The daughter of Thomas Meriwether and Elizabeth Mary Thornton, Lucy Meriwether was born in Albermarle County, Virginia, and grew up at Cloverfields, the family plantation. She was described as being slight of build, with light brown hair, hazel-blue eyes, and a "stern and Spartan" personality. On August 31, 1769, she married her cousin William Lewis, and a year later they had a daughter, named Jane. Their older son Meriwether was born in 1774, and a year later Thomas enlisted in the Virginia militia. When the American Revolution broke out, he became a lieutenant in the Continental army. In 1777 Lucy gave birth to his second son and youngest child, REUBEN LEWIS.

In November 1779, after a visit with his family, William Lewis died of pneumonia. The Lewis family history relates that before he passed away he encouraged Lucy to marry Captain John Marks, which she did, on May 13, 1780. With Marks she had two more children, John Hastings Marks in 1785 and Mary Garland Marks in 1788.

Although apparently something of an autocrat, Lucy Marks was also, according to a family history, "a devoted Christian and full of sympathy for all sickness and trouble." With a deep knowledge of herbs, wild plants, and their medicinal properties, she became renowned for her herbal doctoring. More significant for the health of the expedition years later, she passed on what she knew to her son Meriwether. After the family moved to Georgia (ca. 1783–84), he began to display a keen interest in plants and wildlife, which his mother encouraged, answering his questions and helping him learn. In 1787 she sent him back to Virginia for a more formal education. This early maternal instruction in natural history and herbal medicine would later serve the expedition well.

Lucy Marks returned to Virginia in 1792 after her second husband died. Two years later Meriwether left to join the Virginia militia and, subsequently, the U.S. Army. On his departure, Lucy and then Reuben took over the running of Locust Hill, the Lewis family plantation. Although they continually appealed to Meriwether to return, he never did, except for short visits, including some made after the expedition. He remained devoted to his mother, however, and wrote LETTERS to her often, reassuring her of his safety, telling her of his activities, relaying instructions to his siblings, and discussing family news. Many of the letters survive today and tell much not only of their warm and loving relationship but also some of Lewis's thoughts and feelings as he prepared for the greatest journey of his life.

On July 2, 1803, from PITTSBURGH, Lewis wrote to reassure her: "The nature of this expedition is by no means dangerous, my rout will be altogether thorough tribes of Indians who are perfectly friendly to the United States, therefore consider the chances of life just as much in my favor on this trip as I should conceive them were I to remain at home." She could scarcely conceive the extent of his mission and the part she inadvertently played in it. Lewis's excellent understanding of botany was grounded in his early years under his mother's tutelage; and as the CORPS OF DISCOVERY's doctor, he employed what she had taught him about herbal remedies on more than one occasion. He even treated himself when he was felled by "violent pain in the intestens" as well as a fever at the GREAT FALLS in June 1805. Taking some stripped and chopped twigs from a choke cherry tree, he boiled them in water until there was "a strong black decoction of an astringent bitter taste," which he then consumed at regular intervals until he recovered less than 24 hours later.

It has been suggested that Lewis's close relationship with his strong-minded mother may have contributed to his inability to attract a wife. His tendency to depression and fits of temper (to which his father had also been subject) may have been another factor. In any event, it is known that on September 11, 1809, shortly after leaving ST. LOUIS to travel to Washington, Lewis wrote his last will and testament, in which he left his entire estate to his mother, after his debts were paid. One month later he was dead, killed by his own hand.

Lucy Marks must have been devastated at the loss of her son, but she carried on with her plantation business and doctoring well into her old age. Late in life she was described by someone who knew her as having "refined features, a fragile figure, and a masterful eye." Another admirer, Georgia governor George Gilmer, rightly linked her and her famous son when he said, "Meriwether Lewis inherited the energy, courage, activity, and good understanding of his admirable mother."

Further Reading

Ambrose, Stephen E. *Undaunted Courage: Meriwether Lewis, Thomas Jefferson, and the Opening of the American West.* New York: Simon and Schuster, 1996.

Jackson, Donald. *Letters of the Lewis and Clark Expedition, with Related Documents, 1783–1854.* Urbana: University of Illinois Press, 1979.

McCracken, Hugh   See NORTH WEST COMPANY.

McNeal, Hugh (Hugh Neel, Hugh Niel, Hugh O'Nall) (unknown–unknown) *private in the permanent party*
Among the steady but nearly anonymous members of the CORPS OF DISCOVERY is Private Hugh McNeal, who is perhaps best known for having straddled the MISSOURI RIVER. Born in Pennsylvania, he was a soldier in the U.S. Army prior to his recruitment and apparently remained in the army after the corps's return, but little else is known about his life either before or after the expedition. He was officially enrolled in the corps on January 1, 1804, and was transferred to the permanent party on April 1.

McNeal was with MERIWETHER LEWIS's small party in August 1805 when they went ahead of the others to search for the SHOSHONE INDIANS. On August 10 Lewis named a tributary of the BEAVERHEAD RIVER near present-day Dillon, Montana, "McNeal's Creek." The following day McNeal stayed with Captain Lewis while Privates JOHN SHIELDS and GEORGE DROUILLARD were sent out on separate forays. Lewis had made no plans beforehand regarding what to do once they met the Shoshone and gave no instructions to the privates. Thus, when he finally encountered a young warrior, McNeal was made to stay behind with the rifles while the captain carefully approached the Indian. Drouillard and Shields, however, alarmed the Shoshone when they continued to walk forward. Drouillard stopped on a signal from Lewis, but Shields foolishly continued on, scaring the Indian away and potentially endangering their mission. McNeal subsequently neglected to retrieve a telescope that Lewis had given him, and the angry captain sent Shields and Drouillard back after it.

On August 12, as the small group approached LEMHI PASS, they reached Prairie Creek, the dwindling end of the Missouri River. Lewis wrote of the moment: "Two miles below McNeal had exultingly stood with a foot on each side of this little rivulet and thanked his god that he had lived to bestride the mighty & heretofore deemed endless Missouri." Shortly after this they finally made contact with the Shoshone, and McNeal stayed with his captain until WILLIAM CLARK and the others finally caught up with them. At Lewis's direction, the private divided what little FOOD they had with the Shoshone.

During the winter of 1805–06 at FORT CLATSOP, corps members often took advantage of the sexual offers of local Indian women. Early in January 1806, Clark took a party south down the coast to see a beached whale. This was the neighborhood of the TILLAMOOK INDIANS, whom PATRICK GASS described as "a ferocious people." On the night of January 9, a Tillamook man took McNeal on what he thought was to be a romantic assignation. However, it transpired that the Indian's actual intention was to kill him for his blanket and other items. A CHINOOK woman who knew him and was aware of the Tillamook's plan first tried to help the unsuspecting McNeal then raised an alarm in the village. Hearing the commotion across the Necanicum River and discovering that McNeal was missing from the party, WILLIAM CLARK sent Sergeant NATHANIEL PRYOR and four men to provide assistance. The private returned safely, although his Tillamook attacker escaped. Clark subsequently named the Necanicum "McNeal's Folly Creek."

On July 15, 1806, while Lewis and his men were portaging around the GREAT FALLS, McNeal had a close encounter with a white grizzly bear. His frightened horse threw him to the ground, right at the bear's feet, and McNeal barely had time to leap up and club the bear over the head with his musket, which broke at the breach. With the bear temporarily stunned, the private was able to climb a nearby willow tree, where he waited until the bear finally left.

Several of the men contracted venereal disease during the expedition, but McNeal and SILAS GOODRICH were probably the worst affected. Lewis dosed them repeatedly with mercury, but by the time they reached the Great Falls in June 1806, both were showing signs of the secondary stages of syphilis. It is possible that the disease contributed to the early deaths of both men; Clark listed McNeal as dead by 1825–28.

Further Reading
Clarke, Charles G. *The Men of the Lewis and Clark Expedition: A Biographical Roster of the Fifty-One Members and a Composite Diary of Their Activities from All Known Sources.* 1970. Reprint, Lincoln: Bison Books, University of Nebraska Press, 2002.

North Dakota Lewis & Clark Bicentennial Foundation. *Members of the Corps of Discovery.* Bismarck, N.Dak.: United Printing and Mailing, 2000.

PBS Online. *Lewis and Clark: Inside the Corps of Discovery:* "Lesser Known Members of the Corps." Available on-line. URL: http://www.pbs.org/lewisandclark/inside/lesser.html. Downloaded on May 18, 2001.

medals   See PEACE MEDALS.

medicine and medical treatment
Shortly after noon on August 20, 1804, Sergeant CHARLES FLOYD passed away after several days of enduring what MERIWETHER LEWIS described as a "bilious colic." Today medical experts generally agree that Floyd had suffered a ruptured appendix and had died from the resulting peritonitis. At the time, however, neither Lewis nor WILLIAM CLARK knew what was wrong with Floyd or how to treat him.

Under the circumstances, it was remarkable that only one man died during the entire expedition. The CORPS OF DISCOVERY made its 28-month journey through unfamiliar, treacherous terrain, innumerable miles away from non-Indian civilization, without a trained doctor on hand to treat the inevitable ILLNESSES AND INJURIES. This was almost not the case. In September 1805 at Wheeling, Virginia, Lewis met Dr. William Patterson, son of the mathematician ROBERT PATTER-

SON, with whom Lewis had studied in PHILADELPHIA. The doctor expressed enthusiasm for the expedition and asked to go along. Lewis was willing to let him come, if only for the pharmacy he could bring with him, but on the day of departure, Patterson never arrived at the KEELBOAT, and Lewis left without him. As he was known to be a drunkard, this was probably the best thing for the expedition.

The absence of a qualified doctor on the expedition meant that the responsibility for the corps's medical care fell on the captains—and chiefly on Lewis, who had briefly studied the basics of medicine with Dr. BENJAMIN RUSH in Philadelphia. Rush had put together a medical kit for Lewis and instructed him on how to use it. Chief among these instructions was the technique of bloodletting, which at that time was the favorite medical treatment for numerous ailments. Lewis also purchased a large supply of Rush's Pills, which consisted of a powerful combination of mercury, chlorine, calomel, and jalap and was used as a purgative. Such medicine would be regarded today as quackery, but Rush was a respected doctor in his time, and his pills were considered state-of-the-art medicine. Unfortunately, they were often prescribed freely to the men by both Lewis and Clark, and they frequently did more harm than good. Such was the pills' unpopularity that the soldiers called them "Rush's Thunderbolts." They were also referred to as the "Bilious Pills."

Among the corps's SUPPLIES AND EQUIPMENT there was a traveling pharmacy that Lewis acquired before and during the expedition. In addition to Rush's Pills, this pharmacy included ALCOHOL, astringent, camphor, castile soap, chocolate drink, diuretics, emetic, laudanum, lead acetate, laxatives, liniment, mineral water, essence of peppermint, jalap, mercury, potassium bitartrate, potassium nitrate, purgatives, saltpeter, salve, sulphuric acid, zinc sulphate, and various types of bark. Even gunpowder was used—Lewis's preferred treatment for snakebite was to apply a poultice made from bark and gunpowder, although he also acquired some snakebite medicine from HUGH HENEY.

As an amateur doctor, Lewis had another resource at his disposal: his mother. As an expert in the uses of herbs, LUCY MERIWETHER LEWIS MARKS had taught her son much about herbal healing. It was thanks to her training that Lewis was able to treat himself when he became sick at the GREAT FALLS in June 1805. Beset by "violent pain in the intestens" and a fever, and lacking his medical kit, he had his men strip the leaves off some twigs from a choke cherry tree, cut up the twigs, and boil them in water until there was "a strong black decoction of an astringent bitter taste." Lewis then consumed a pint of the mixture at sunset and another pint an hour later. Shortly thereafter he began to improve, and the following morning, after taking another pint, he was able to get on with his work.

Lewis was frequently called into service as a doctor, although Clark also took a hand in treatments. The medical problems they had to face included abscesses, ague, boils, colds, colic, conjunctivitis, diarrhea, dysentery, fever, food poisoning, frostbite, goiter, influenza, intestinal infection, malaria, pleurisy, rheumatism, seasickness, snakebite, snowblindness, sore and inflamed joints, sunburn, sunstroke, temporary paralysis, and toothaches, among other things.

The captains had some favorite sovereign remedies. Inflamed eyes were quite common and were treated with Lewis's special eyewash, "a solution of white vitriol [zinc sulphate] and the sugar of lead [lead acetate] in the proportion of 2 grs. Of the former and one of the latter to each ounce of water." Venereal disease was an especially big problem as the men often took advantage of the attentions of Indian women (see SEX DURING THE EXPEDITION). This was treated with mercury, the usual remedy for syphilis and gonorrhea at that time.

Both men treated Indians as well as soldiers. During the winter of 1804–05 at FORT MANDAN, Lewis amputated the frostbitten toes of a MANDAN boy and dispensed Rush's Pills for everything from fever to gastrointestinal problems. On February 11, 1805, when SACAGAWEA went into a long and painful labor, he found himself at a loss to help her. Trader RENÉ JESSAUME recommended she be given a solution of crushed rattlesnake rings in water. A skeptical Lewis did so, and whether or not this mixture was the cause, Sacagawea gave birth to a healthy boy within 10 minutes.

Clark, meanwhile, acquired a reputation among the Indians for his healing powers, and during the expedition's return in 1806, they were able to capitalize on this with the NEZ PERCE INDIANS, exchanging his services for HORSES and FOOD until they could make their next crossing of the Bitteroots. Some days he seemed to operate walk-in clinics as streams of patients came to him for help. He lanced boils, dispensed liniment and eyewash, set broken limbs, treated bad backs, and tended to an

This photograph of a Nez Perce sweat lodge was taken ca. 1910. A similar structure was used to treat William Bratton's bad back in 1806. *(Library of Congress, Prints and Photographs Division [LC-USZ62-111290])*

assortment of minor ailments. He also took charge of WILLIAM BRATTON in June 1806 when the private developed a back problem so severe that he became partially paralyzed. Clark's system of sessions in a sweat lodge followed by plunges into cold water seemed to work, as Bratton gradually recovered and eventually was able to walk without pain. The captain applied a similar treatment to an old Nez Perce chief who had become paralyzed, and to his delight the chief soon regained the use of his arms and legs.

Like Lewis, Clark liked to dispense Rush's Pills as a panacea for whatever ailed somebody. When almost all of the men became violently ill following their crossing of the BITTERROOT MOUNTAINS in September 1805—caused by a combination of food poisoning and an abrupt change in diet—Clark's remedy was to have them take the Thunderbolts, which only worsened matters. Nor did combining the pills with other purgatives help. Most of the men, including Lewis, were so sick as to be barely able to move for almost two weeks, and their recovery was very slow.

Clark had more success with Sacagawea's son, JEAN BAPTISTE CHARBONNEAU (Pomp). Prior to the return crossing of the Bitterroots in June 1806, young Pomp developed a painful swelling on his neck in addition to a sore throat and high fever—possibly mumps or tonsillitis. Poultices of wild onions were applied to his neck, which was also treated with a salve made of pine resin, beeswax, and BEAR lard. Pomp made a full recovery within weeks.

Further Reading

Ambrose, Stephen E. *Undaunted Courage: Meriwether Lewis, Thomas Jefferson, and the Opening of the American West.* New York: Simon and Schuster, 1996.

Chuinard, Eldon G. *Only One Man Died: The Medical Aspects of the Lewis and Clark Expedition.* Glendale, Calif.: A. H. Clark Co., 1979.

Fent, Cindy. "Some Medical Aspects of the Lewis and Clark Expedition." *North Dakota History* 53, no. 1 (1986): 24–28.

Jefferson National Expansion Memorial. "The Lewis and Clark Journey of Discovery: Medical Supplies of the Lewis and Clark Expedition." Available on-line. URL: http://www.nps.gov/jeff/LewisClark2/CorpsOfDiscovery/Preparing/Medicine/Medicine.htm. Downloaded on April 11, 2002.

Paton, Bruce C. *Lewis and Clark: Doctors in the Wilderness.* Golden, Colo.: Fulcrum Publishing, 2001.

Peck, David. *Or Perish in the Attempt: Wilderness Medicine in the Lewis & Clark Expedition.* Helena, Mont.: Farcountry Press, 2002.

Will, Drake W. Lewis and Clark: "Westering Physicians." *Montana: The Magazine of Western History* 21, no. 4 (1971): 2–17.

———. "The Medical and Surgical Practice of the Lewis and Clark Expedition." *Journal of the History of Medicine and Allied Sciences* 14, no. 3 (1959): 273–297.

Medicine River (Sun River)

Today called the Sun River, the Medicine flows east to join the Missouri just west of Great Falls, Montana. It was the BLACK-FEET INDIANS who had named it Medicine River, presumably because its banks contained mineral deposits that had medicinal properties.

By June 13, 1805, the Lewis and Clark Expedition had passed the mouth of the MARIAS RIVER and were traveling southwest along the MISSOURI RIVER, hoping to come to the GREAT FALLS. Following their usual practice, MERIWETHER LEWIS was making his way along the riverbank with three hunters while WILLIAM CLARK brought the CANOES and PIROGUE upstream. Lewis started walking ahead of his companions and arrived at the foot of the Great Falls around noon. He camped there with the hunters that night, and the following day he walked on to discover that there were five separate waterfalls, which meant the PORTAGE around them would be much longer than he or Clark had envisaged.

Looking for a suitable portage route, Lewis went on two more miles until he arrived at the mouth of the Medicine River. Here he shot a BUFFALO and then turned to find a grizzly BEAR advancing on him. With no time to reload, he took the only course open to him and ran back to the Missouri, where he plunged into the water, turned, and faced the monster with his ESPONTOON. Fortunately, the bear "sudonly wheeled about as if frightened, declined the combat on such unequal grounds, and retreated with quite as great precipitation as he had pursued me."

Some three miles past the junction of the Medicine with the Missouri, the CORPS OF DISCOVERY established their upper portage camp at WHITE BEAR ISLANDS. During the next fortnight, the explorers labored on the slow, 18-mile portage of canoes and baggage around the Great Falls while Lewis, PATRICK GASS, and two other men worked to assemble the IRON-FRAME BOAT. ELK skins were needed to cover the boat, so hunters were sent up the Medicine River three times to find them. Unfortunately, the project failed due to lack of proper resin or pitch caulking, and the boat had to be abandoned. On August 14, a month after they had first seen it, the expedition left the Medicine.

Nearly a year later, Lewis and nine men returned to the Medicine. Having split the expedition at TRAVELERS' REST, Lewis's party had ridden due east across the CONTINENTAL DIVIDE at today's LEWIS AND CLARK PASS, crossed the DEARBORN RIVER, and arrived at the Medicine near present-day Augusta, Montana, on July 8, 1806. They followed it down, stopping halfway to camp at today's Simms, Montana. On the following day Patrick Gass reported that one of the hunters "had killed a large buffaloe;" it was the first fresh buffalo meat they had eaten in a year. Two days later, on July 11, they arrived back at the Missouri and their old camp at White Bear Islands. It was the last they were to see of the Medicine River.

In 1913 the Gibson Dam was built, blocking the river's flow. From this dam, today's Sun River flows 101 miles to Great Falls, although a large diversion dam interrupts it. As a result, only 97 miles of the once mighty Medicine River remain free flowing.

Further Reading

Fifer, Barbara, and Vicky Soderberg. *Along the Trail with Lewis and Clark.* Great Falls, Mont.: Montana Magazine, 1998.

Moulton, Gary E., ed. *Atlas of the Lewis and Clark Expedition.* Revised ed. Lincoln: University of Nebraska Press, 1999.

Michaux, André (1746–1802) *botanist, explorer*

There were several preludes to the Lewis and Clark Expedition. THOMAS JEFFERSON had long wanted to explore the regions that lay beyond the MISSISSIPPI RIVER, but the closest he came to success was in 1793, when he chose French botanist André Michaux to lead a scientific exploration under the sponsorship of the AMERICAN PHILOSOPHICAL SOCIETY. Political controversy soon aborted the mission, however, and not until 10 years later would a rejected volunteer for the 1793 expedition, MERIWETHER LEWIS, be chosen to lead the CORPS OF DISCOVERY across the continent.

Born into a farming family in Versailles, FRANCE, Michaux seemed to have a gift for growing plants from an early age. After his wife Cecile died a few days following the birth of their son François André in 1770, the devastated Michaux began studies under the greatest botanists of the age with a view to exploring other areas of the world. Early in 1782 he went to Persia, setting off on a round of adventures in the Middle East for three years. During this time he collected and classified an abundance of plant specimens and so impressed his superiors in France that they decided to send him on a scientific mission to North America. His primary objective was to find new species of trees that would help rebuild the depleted forests of France.

Michaux, who had met Thomas Jefferson in Paris, arrived in the United States with his young son François in 1785. From then on, he traveled throughout the country, collecting botanical specimens, conducting detailed studies of the flora in different regions, and eventually shipping thousands of seeds and specimens back to France. He also formed a friendship and collaboration with renowned U.S botanist William Bartram and set up nurseries in South Carolina and New Jersey, the latter including a garden of 30 acres. He not only named hundreds of previously unclassified plants on the American continent, but he also introduced new plant species to its shores.

In summer 1792 Michaux explored the Champlain Valley, during which time he recorded 175 plants. Later that same year, with Jefferson's support, he offered a proposal to the American Philosophical Society that he lead an expedition across the continent to the PACIFIC OCEAN. Michaux, who had already traveled throughout the American frontier and into Florida and CANADA, seemed to Jefferson—by then the country's secretary of state—the ideal candidate to take on such a mission. Numerous society members subscribed to the proposal, including John Adams, George Washington, ALEXANDER HAMILTON, and JAMES MADISON, although only $128.25 was raised.

Despite the meager financial support, Michaux began his journey west in July 1793, armed with detailed guidelines from Jefferson regarding his mission to explore "the interior of North America from the Mississippi along the Missouri, and Westwardly to the Pacific ocean." (These instructions would form the basis for the MISSION OBJECTIVES that Jefferson gave to Meriwether Lewis 10 years later.) By this time the French Revolution had taken place and a new republican government was installed in France, one that hoped to uproot the Spanish influence in North America. For this reason French minister Edmund Genêt convinced Michaux to take on another, secret mission as he carried out his scientific exploration: to foment rebellion against the Spanish among settlers in the Mississippi Valley.

After other political machinations failed, Genêt was replaced as minister but wisely did not return to France, settling in America. Jefferson, feeling that Michaux had played only a minor part in the Genêt affair, continued to urge support for the expedition, but Washington and the society refused to give it. Consequently, Michaux was recalled from the frontier in spring 1794, having traveled no farther west than Kentucky. He nevertheless continued his botanical studies, in particular recording the plant life of the Carolina Piedmont, before finally returning to France in 1796.

Thereafter Michaux's fortunes suffered a severe downturn. During his return voyage he was shipwrecked on the coast of Holland, losing innumerable seeds and plants. When he arrived back in France, it was to considerable acclaim but no money, the republican government being unwilling to fund his work as the monarchy had done. Living frugally, he set to work with his son writing *History of the Oaks of North America,* published in 1801; and *Flora Boreali and America,* published in 1803. The latter book, which described more than 1,500 American plant species, was still unfinished when he decided to join an expedition to the South Seas in 1800. Leaving the ship at Mauritius, he elected to settle on Madagascar to study the island's plant life but died there of a tropical fever in 1802. Michaux's son finished his last book and later returned to North America to conduct and publish an extensive study of its forest trees of North America, thus carrying on his father's legacy to the United States.

Further Reading

American Philosophical Society. "Treasures of the APS: Jefferson Proposes a Scientific Expedition." Available on-line. URL: http://www.amphilsoc.org/library/exhibits/treasures/michaux.htm. Downloaded on January 10, 2002.

Daniel Stowe Botanical Garden. "André Michaux: Explorer, Collector, Botanist." Available on-line. URL: http://www.michaux.org. Downloaded on January 20, 2002.

Kuralt, Charles. "Tribute to the Noted French Botanist Andre Michaux." *Grandfather Mountain* (August 28, 1994). Available on-line URL: http://www.grandfather.com/museum/michaux/CKmichaux.htm. Downloaded on January 20, 2002.

Savage Jr., Henry, and Elizabeth J. Savage. *André and François André Michaux.* Charlottesville: University of Virginia Press, 1986.

migration   See WESTWARD EXPANSION.

Milk River (The River Which Scolds at All Others)

The first week of May 1805 saw the expedition making their way westward across the present state of Montana on the MISSOURI RIVER in their two PIROGUES and six CANOES. They had left the villages of the MANDAN INDIANS a month before, passed the mouth of the YELLOWSTONE RIVER (which WILLIAM CLARK was to explore a year later), and were, as far as they knew, farther west than any white American had been before. They had met and killed their first grizzly BEAR and were passing lands so rich in BUFFALO that they had to push the beasts out of their way.

On May 8, just east of present-day Fort Peck, Montana, they reached the river coming in from the north that the HIDATSA INDIANS had told them was called "The River Which Scolds at All Others." MERIWETHER LEWIS walked up this river for three miles and decided it was navigable, at least by CANOES. He wrote: "From the quantity of water furnised by this river it must water a large advantageous communication with the Saskashiwn river. . . . The water has a peculiar whiteness, such as might be produced by a table-spoonful of milk in a dish of tea, and this circumstance induced us to call it Milk river."

In one respect, the Milk River was an opportunity missed. Lewis had been told that it ran far to the north, and one of his MISSION OBJECTIVES was to ascertain whether tributaries of the Missouri reached into Canada. Since the border was still in dispute, such evidence would be useful in determining and expanding the area understood to be covered by the LOUISIANA PURCHASE. He made a point of exploring the MARIAS RIVER in 1806 with this in view and found that it turned to the west. A similar exploration up the Milk River would have taken him well past the 49th parallel.

In his journal for May 8, 1805, Sergeant PATRICK GASS noted: ". . . at 2 we passed a handsome river on the North side about 200 yards wide called the Milk river. . . . Our distance today was about twenty-seven miles. . . ." It is an indication of the force of the Missouri current that when the expedition returned down the river a year later, he wrote that they "passed the mouth of the Milk river, which was very high and the current strong. Having proceeded 88 miles we encamped for the night."

The stretch of the Missouri upstream of the Milk River is now covered by Fort Peck Lake, formed by the Fort Peck Dam. The lake, some 60 miles in length, extends up the shallow creeks running into this stretch of the Missouri. The result is a lake that, as the National Geographic Society map notes, "has more shoreline than California."

Further Reading

Fifer, Barbara, and Vicky Soderberg. *Along the Trail with Lewis and Clark*. Great Falls, Mont.: Montana Magazine, 1998.

MacGregor, Carol Lynn, ed. *The Journals of Patrick Gass, Member of the Lewis and Clark Expedition*. Missoula, Mont.: Mountain Press Publishing Company, 1997.

Saindon, Bob. "The River Which Scolds at all Others: An Obstinate Blunder in Nomenclature." *Montana: The Magazine of Western History.* 26, no. 3 (1976): 2–7.

mission objectives

20 June 1803
To Meriwether Lewis esq. Capt. Of the 1st regimt. of infantry of the U. S. of A.

Your situation as Secretary of the President of the U. S. has made you acquainted with the objects of my confidential message of Jan. 18, 1803 to the legislature; you have seen the act they passed, which, tho' expressed in general terms, was meant to sanction those objects, and you are appointed to carry them into execution.

Early in 1803, as MERIWETHER LEWIS began his PREPARATIONS FOR THE EXPEDITION, the man who had chosen him to lead it, President THOMAS JEFFERSON, began work on the instructions that would specify the expedition's mission objectives. After weeks of revision that incorporated the instructions that he had put together for the failed mission of ANDRÉ MICHAUX 10 years earlier with additional ideas of his own and suggestions from others, Jefferson presented his directive to Lewis in a letter dated June 20, 1803.

The final document was breathtaking in its scope. Jefferson had sought input from scholars in PHILADELPHIA to whom he had sent Lewis for training in the natural sciences, and he had also received advice from members of his cabinet, including Levi Lincoln, JAMES MADISON, and ALBERT GALLATIN. It was Lincoln who suggested that Jefferson stress the education of Indians in his instructions to give the expedition more appeal to the country's religious leaders. Lincoln also provided valuable suggestions regarding how the document was worded, in an attempt to allay any Federalist outcries about the mission and its costs. Gallatin, meanwhile, emphasized the geopolitical aspects, anxious to obtain more information about Spanish posts and influence in the area drained by the MISSOURI RIVER, an important component in the terms of the LOUISIANA PURCHASE as well as in Gallatin's vision of migration and settlement in the West.

Jefferson, however, was most concerned about the United States's ability to gain a foothold in the growing FUR TRADE of the Pacific Northwest and thus gave priority to finding an all-water route to the PACIFIC OCEAN: "The object of your mission is to explore the Missouri river, & such principal stream of it, as, by it's course and communication with the waters of the Pacific ocean, whether the Columbia, Oregon, Colorado or any other river may offer the most direct & practicable water communication across this continent for the purposes of commerce." Lewis was also to learn as much as he could about British trade routes and practices and to make suggestions for American advancement in the fur trade.

Lewis was further instructed to make MAPS of the areas he passed through, noting latitude and longitude as well as important landmarks "with great pains & accuracy." Jefferson's instructions were so explicit that he even told Lewis to make multiple copies of his maps and navigational calculations, with one copy to be "on the paper of the birch, as less liable to injury from damp than common paper." (This instruction was not followed, however, as birch was not available along the expedition's ROUTE.)

Other points covered in Jefferson's instructions:

- Lewis was to learn all he could about the Indian nations he would encounter: their names, numbers, languages, customs, ways of life, and relations with other nations, as well as such details as their food, clothing, housing, monuments, medical care, religious activities, laws, and, most importantly, "articles of commerce they may need or furnish, & to what extent." Historian Stephen Ambrose describes this aspect of the instructions as "an ethnographer's dream-come-true set of marching orders."

- The explorer was also to establish friendly relations with the Indians and invite some of Jefferson's "Indian children" to visit him in Washington. In the event that the expedition was stopped by hostile Indians, there was to be no resistance, and Lewis was "to bring back your party safe even if it be with less information."

- Lewis was also to act as botanist and natural historian on the journey. Jefferson instructed him to study and record the PLANTS and ANIMALS he would see, to make special note of those previously undiscovered, and to look for "the remains or accounts of any which may be deemed rare or extinct." Although Jefferson also mentioned "mineral productions of every kind," he was not referring to gold or silver but to saltpetre, pit coal, and limestone. Geographical features were also to be recorded, as were the WEATHER and "the dates at which particular plants put forth or lose their flower, or leaf, times of appearance of particular birds, reptiles or insects."

- As Gallatin had wanted, information was to be gathered on the areas drained by the Missouri River through which the expedition would pass. Jefferson noted that "Some account too of the path of the Canadian traders from the Missisipi . . . is desirable."

- On reaching the Pacific Ocean, Lewis was to assess the practicality of establishing an American presence in the Northwest for trading purposes. Should any ships be in the area, all or part of the expedition could return to the East Coast by that means.

- Jefferson was also aware that Lewis would be in need of money and supplies and to that end specified that he would provide a LETTER OF CREDIT that would be good "in any part of the world."

In *Thomas Jefferson & the Stony Mountains: Exploring the West from Monticello,* Donald Jackson provides the best summation of Jefferson's instructions to Lewis: "They embrace years of study and wonder, the collected wisdom of his government colleagues and his Philadelphia friends; they barely conceal his excitement that at last he would have facts, not vague guesses, about the Stony Mountains, the river courses, the wild Indian tribes, the flora and fauna of untrodden places."

Further Reading

Ambrose, Stephen E. *Undaunted Courage: Meriwether Lewis, Thomas Jefferson, and the Opening of the American West.* New York: Simon and Schuster, 1996.
Cutright, Paul Russell. "Jefferson's Instructions to Lewis and Clark." *Bulletin of the Missouri Historical Society* 22, no. 3 (1966): 303–320.
Hawke, David Freeman. *Those Tremendous Mountains: The Story of the Lewis and Clark Expedition.* New York: W. W. Norton & Company, 1998.
Jackson, Donald. *Letters of the Lewis and Clark Expedition, with Related Documents, 1783–1854.* Urbana: University of Illinois Press, 1979.
———. *Thomas Jefferson & the Stony Mountains: Exploring the West from Monticello.* Norman: University of Oklahoma Press, 1993.
Lewis & Clark Tours Bicentennial. "Letter from President Thomas Jefferson." Available on-line. URL: http://www.larsoncentury ranch.com/lct_Jefferson.html. Downloaded on March 2, 2002.
Tobin-Schlesinger, Kathleen. "Jefferson to Lewis: The Study of Nature in the West." *Journal of the West* 29, no. 1 (1990): 54–61.

Mississippi River

The Mississippi, North America's greatest river, takes its name from the Ojibway Indian word meaning "big river." Held by many to be the most important natural feature of the United States, it was in turn a legend for early European explorers, a goal for those who came after them, an essential trade route, an international boundary, and a theater of war from 1861 to 1865. Prior to the LOUISIANA PURCHASE, it was also the westernmost border of the United States, in whose history it has long played a vital role.

The largest river (though not the longest) in North America, the Mississippi rises at Lake Itasca, Minnesota, and runs 2,300 miles south to the Gulf of Mexico, draining some 30 states as the second largest river basin in the world. The part of the river north of Cairo, Illinois, where the OHIO RIVER runs in to join it is known as the Upper Mississippi. The section running from there down to New Orleans and the Gulf of Mexico is the Lower Mississippi.

In 1682 French explorer René Robert de La Salle traveled down the Mississippi to its mouth. News of its extent and of its many tributaries spread quickly, and early explorers, trappers, and traders began to use the river as a means of transit to the unknown area west of the Allegheny Mountains. Its size and importance as both a trade route and a means of communication soon made it a natural, easily defined boundary between the English colonies of the East Coast and the vast hinterland claimed by the French.

The first settlements along the banks of the Mississippi were French: Cahokia and KASKASKIA were founded around 1700 and New Orleans in 1718. The river was officially accepted as the boundary between British and French territory after the Treaty of Paris in 1763, although the French had already secretly ceded the LOUISIANA TERRITORY west of the river to Spain a year previously. When the United States came into being, they took over the same demarcation line.

It was their initial passage north on the Mississippi that made MERIWETHER LEWIS and WILLIAM CLARK appreciate the difficulties of taking heavily laden boats upstream against the current. While bringing their boats and supplies down the Ohio River to join the Mississippi at Cairo had been easy, their subsequent passage from there to ST. LOUIS, was a very different matter. With both the KEELBOAT and PIROGUES undermanned, it took them from November 20 to December 7, 1803, to reach Wood River near St. Louis and the mouth of the MISSOURI RIVER. On the way, they stopped at the U.S. Army fort at Kaskaskia, where Lewis secured the services of at least a dozen more men to help in the physical labor of rowing and pulling the boats against the flow of the Mississippi; some of these men would also join the permanent party of the CORPS OF DISCOVERY. Five months later, after wintering at CAMP DUBOIS, the expedition turned their backs on the Mississippi and began their journey up the Missouri.

While the Mississippi River played an apparently minor part in the Lewis and Clark Expedition, it was the underlying basis of THOMAS JEFFERSON's geopolitical plan to claim the lands west of its shores for the United States. Ever since the first explorers had crossed the Alleghenies and traveled down numerous rivers that emptied into the mighty stream running to the Gulf of Mexico, the hope and expectation was that the Mississippi had equally major tributaries to the west. It was these tributaries that Jefferson and many others hoped would furnish an easy transit by water to the Pacific coast and the trade markets of the Far East. It is one of the ironies of history that as the nation's first transcontinental expedition struggled against the river current to reach St. Louis and the start of their journey, Robert Fulton was building his first experimental steamboat—and in less than 10 years his invention would be steaming up the Mississippi.

Further Reading

Ellet, Charles. *The Mississippi and Ohio Rivers*. New York: Arno Press, 1970.

Larson, Ron. *Upper Mississippi River History: Fact, Fiction, Legend*. Revised ed. Winona, Minn.: Steamboat Press, 1998.

Moulton, Gary E., ed. *Atlas of the Lewis and Clark Expedition*. Revised ed. Lincoln: University of Nebraska Press, 1999.

National Geographic Atlas of Natural America. Washington, D.C.: National Geographic Society, 2000.

Missouri Breaks

The Missouri Breaks is a stretch of the MISSOURI RIVER, about 150 miles in length, that sweeps in a rough semicircle from the head of the modern Fort Peck Dam to today's Fort Benton, Montana. The name is now popularly applied to both the breaks along the eastern section and the White Cliffs of the western stretch.

On May 25, 1805, while looking for the GREAT FALLS of the MISSOURI RIVER, the expedition came to a rocky, barren area. MERIWETHER LEWIS described it: "The country on each side is high, broken and rocky; the rock being either a soft brown sandstone, covered with a thin stratum of limestone, or else a bare black rugged granite . . . the river low grounds are narrow, and afford scarcely any timber; nor is there much pine on the hills."

Sergeant PATRICK GASS agreed: "These hills are very much washed in general; they appear like great heaps of clay, washing away with every shower; with scarcely any herbs or grass on any of them." The next day he added: "We set out early in a fine morning, and passed through desert country; in which there is no timber in any part except a few scattered pines on the hills."

On May 27 Gass still saw little to admire: "We have now got into a country which presents little to our view, but scenes of bareness and desolation; and see no encouraging prospects that it will terminate." Lewis, however, took a more optimistic view since, on May 26, from a hill above Cow Creek (40 miles northwest of today's US 191 bridge), he saw what be believed to be the snow-topped ROCKY MOUNTAINS in the distance: ". . . when I reflected on the difficulties in which this snowey barrier would most probably throw in my way to the Pacific . . . it in some measure counterballanced the joy I had felt in the first moment in which I gazed on them. . . ."

On May 31 the expedition reached the White Cliffs stretch of the river, and Lewis depicted the scene in a way that could be written today:

> *These hills and river-cliffs exhibit a most extraordinary and romantic appearance. They rise in most places nearly perpendicular from the water, to the height of between 200 and 300 feet, and are formed of a very white sandstone, so soft as to yield readily to the impression of the water. . . . In trickling down the cliffs, the water has worn the soft sandstone into a thousand grotesque figures, among which, with a little fancy, may be discerned elegant ranges of freestone buildings, with columns variously sculptured, and supporting long and elegant galleries, while the parapets are adorned with statuary.*

The Missouri Breaks have been designated by Congress a Wild and Scenic River. The area is still nearly as sparse and open as when the expedition saw it, and the White Cliffs, only visible from the river, are as remarkable as Lewis described them two centuries ago. It is one of the very few stretches of the Missouri still unchanged from that time.

Further Reading

MacGregor, Carol Lynn, ed. *The Journals of Patrick Gass, Member of the Lewis and Clark Expedition.* Missoula, Mont.: Mountain Press Publishing Company, 1997.

Moulton, Gary E., ed. *The Journals of the Lewis and Clark Expedition.* 13 vols. Lincoln: University of Nebraska Press, 1983–2001.

Missouri Indians (Missouria Indians)

In late July 1804, as the CORPS OF DISCOVERY traveled up the MISSOURI RIVER, they were surprised by the complete absence of Indians in the countryside around them. After passing the PLATTE RIVER, a reconnaissance by GEORGE DROUILLARD and PIERRE CRUZATTE revealed that the Missouri, the OTOE (Oto), and the OMAHA INDIANS whom they had expected to find were away hunting. While there were frequent signs of Indian parties, it was not until July 28 that Drouillard finally met a lone Missouri, one of a small band that had joined the Otoe. After talking to him, Captains MERIWETHER LEWIS and WILLIAM CLARK sent the engagé JOSEPH BARTER back with the Indian to invite the Missouri and the Otoe chiefs to a council. They then proceeded upriver, set up camp at the site of COUNCIL BLUFF (present-day Fort Atkinson, Nebraska), and waited. After several anxious days, during which Barter deserted the expedition, on August 2 a number of Otoe and Missouri arrived, and the following day the captains held their first formal council with an Indian delegation.

The Missouri (today called Missouria) were a Siouan-speaking nation originally from the Great Lakes region. When they first moved west, they retained their farming culture until they acquired HORSES, after which they took on the characteristics of other PLAINS INDIANS, becoming seminomads and BUFFALO hunters. Their first encounter with non-Indians had been with the French explorer Jacques Marquette in 1673. At that time they were living at the confluence of the Missouri with the Grand River, but some 100 years later they were attacked and scattered by the Fox and Sac Indians. With their numbers further reduced by a smallpox epidemic, many of the Missouri survivors attached themselves to their relatives the Otoe, and it was some of these that Lewis and Clark met in August 1804.

The council of August 3 gave the captains their first exercise in diplomacy. After speeches that announced the new U.S. sovereignty and the advent of American TRADE into the area, GIFTS were presented, followed by a full-dress parade and demonstrations of the expedition's FIREARMS. Lewis then made what was to become a standard request, asking that a delegation of Otoe and Missouri chiefs go to Washington to meet their new "great white father," THOMAS JEFFERSON. The response from the Indians was generally positive; they especially hoped for good things to flow from the new trading system that Lewis was proposing. However, without the Otoe chief LITTLE THIEF and the Missouri chief BIG HORSE present at the council, he and Clark could not consider it a success. They subsequently sent a parcel of gifts to Little Thief, although it is unclear why they did not also do so for Big Horse.

Shortly after this council, Private MOSES REED deserted, and a few days later the captains sent out Drouillard with a small party to find and bring back Reed as well as Little Thief and Big Horse, if possible. Meanwhile, the expedition continued upriver. The search party was successful with both missions, and on August 18 they arrived at camp with the deserter and the chiefs. After dealing with Reed, the captains got down to business with Little Thief, Big Horse, and the other warriors in attendance. During the meeting that followed, the captains learned much about the conflicts between the chiefs' nations and the Omaha and Pawnee nations. The next day a formal council was held, and talk focused on trade with the Americans, about which the Indians were ambivalent; and efforts to make peace with the Omaha and the Pawnee, for which they asked to have translator FRANÇOIS LABICHE act as mediator, a suggestion that Lewis and Clark rejected.

The presentation of gifts followed, and Big Horse was given a medal equal to the one already given Little Thief. Overall, however, the Missouri and Otoe were insulted by the quality of their gifts. More were given, but still they were dissatisfied, and they lingered to demand whiskey and additional goods. This discontent with the presents the expedition gave to Indian chiefs was to be a recurrent factor in the future. However, the captains did succeed in persuading them to send a delegation to Washington. There was one Missouri Indian in the delegation.

The Missouri continued to suffer attacks from hostile nations, especially the OSAGE INDIANS. In 1829 they allied with the Otoe permanently, and by 1882 both nations had moved to Indian Territory. Today they are known as the Otoe-Missouria Tribe and hold trust lands in the Red Rock region of Oklahoma.

Further Reading

Edmunds, R. David. *The Otoe-Missouria People.* Phoenix: Indian Tribal Series, 1976.

Ronda, James P. *Lewis and Clark among the Indians.* Lincoln: University of Nebraska Press, 1984.

Waldman, Carl. *Encyclopedia of Native American Tribes.* Revised ed. New York: Checkmark Books, 1999.

Missouri River

The Missouri River is the longest in North America, flowing more than 2,500 miles to its mouth on the MISSISSIPPI RIVER. Its true headwaters rise on the border between Montana and Idaho. These headwaters—Red Rock River—become the BEAVERHEAD RIVER, which in turn becomes the JEFFERSON RIVER (so named by MERIWETHER LEWIS and WILLIAM CLARK), which meets the Madison and Gallatin Rivers at THREE FORKS, an important juncture on the expedition's journey. At this point it becomes the Missouri.

Rumors of a great tributary running northwest from the Mississippi had circulated among trappers and traders for many years before its existence was confirmed by explorers Père Marquette and Louis Joliet on their journey down the Mississippi

This 1939 photo shows a quiet stretch of the upper reaches of the Missouri River in Broadwater County, Montana. This image is in sharp contrast to the wide and often treacherous waters the Corps of Discovery had to navigate further downstream. *(Library of Congress, Prints and Photographs Division [LC-USF34-027232-D])*

in 1673. French fur traders soon began to travel up the Missouri's lower reaches, and in 1764 ST. LOUIS was established as a trading depot near its mouth.

Based on the knowledge of the time, the Missouri was the obvious route to take in exploring the unknown territory to the west, and it held the tantalizing possibility of leading to the hoped-for NORTHWEST PASSAGE to the PACIFIC OCEAN. Perhaps this is best appreciated by the fact that when Lewis began his journey, all the world knew was the width of the continent (established by Captains ROBERT GRAY and GEORGE VANCOUVER on their surveys of the west coast in 1792), the location of the mouth of the COLUMBIA RIVER, and that there were mountains inland from the west coast. Thus, the best MAP that could be produced before the expedition began showed what was known of the lower reaches of the Missouri up to the villages of the MANDAN INDIANS in what is now North Dakota, some rough drawings of mountains to the west, and an estimated course of the Columbia River. There were only three firm positions marked: the mouth of the Columbia, the Mandan villages, and St. Louis.

It was based on this slender evidence and Indian accounts of the Missouri that caused Jefferson to specify Lewis's route in his letter of instructions dated June 20, 1803:

> *The object of your mission is to explore the Missouri river, & such principal stream of it, as, by it's course and communication with the waters of the Pacific*

> *ocean, whether the Columbia, Oregon, Colorado or other river may offer the most direct & practicable water communication across the continent for the purpose of commerce.*

The expedition began its voyage up the Missouri River on May 14, 1804. It did not reach Three Forks until July 27, 1805. With the river's strong currents, floods, snags, sandbars, rapids, and falls, the journey upstream was far harder and more difficult than the most pessimistic had expected. The going was particularly difficult on the portion of the journey between St. Louis and FORT MANDAN, when the CORPS OF DISCOVERY had to maneuver the large and unwieldy KEELBOAT upstream against a strong current. Furthermore, there were often difficult decisions to be made when the river forked, as was the case at the MARIAS RIVER, which the men of the corps believed to be the true Missouri. The captains, however, were correct in their decision to take the fork that ultimately led to the GREAT FALLS. A similar decision had to be made at Three Forks, when the Jefferson River proved to be the way to take.

Not until 1819 did the first steamboat appear on the Missouri, and this was the main means of transport until 1859, when the railway to St. Joseph, Missouri, was completed. Up to the 1930s, the river was navigable to Fort Benton, 2,285 miles above the mouth. It was then that the U.S. Army Corps of Engineers began the vast program of channeling that now includes six dams, as a means of taking barges up to Sioux City, Iowa. A third of the Missouri River today is still free flowing, while the other two-thirds have been pooled or channeled.

It should be remembered, however, that the Missouri, like the Mississippi, has changed its course often since the days of Lewis and Clark. Modern historians believe that CAMP DUBOIS and Fort Mandan are both now under water, and the many dams along the river have submerged forever the river valleys along which the expedition struggled.

Further Reading

Allen, John Logan. "Lewis and Clark on the Upper Missouri: Decision at the Marias." *Montana: The Magazine of Western History* 21, no. 3 (1971): 2–17.

Botkin, Daniel B. *Passage of Discovery: The American Rivers Guide to the Missouri of Lewis and Clark.* New York: Berkley Publishing Group, 1999.

Discovery Writers. *Lewis & Clark on the Upper Missouri.* Stevensville, Mont.: Stoneydale Press Publishing Co., 2000.

Erickson, Vernon. "Lewis and Clark on the Upper Missouri." *North Dakota History* 40, no. 2 (1973): 34–37.

Moulton, Gary E., ed. *Atlas of the Lewis and Clark Expedition.* Revised ed. Lincoln: University of Nebraska Press, 1999.

Nasatir, A. P., ed. *Before Lewis and Clark: Documents Illustrating the History of the Missouri, 1785–1804.* 2 vols. St. Louis: St. Louis Historical Documents Foundation, 1975.

Salter, Cathy Riggs. "Lewis and Clark's Lost Missouri: A Mapmaker Re-creates the River of 1804 and Changes the Course of History." *National Geographic* 201, no. 4 (April 2002): 89–97.

Vestal, Stanley. *The Missouri.* Lincoln: University of Nebraska Press, 1996.

Wood, W. Raymond, and Gary E. Moulton. "Prince Maximilian and New Maps of the Missouri and Yellowstone Rivers by William Clark." *Western Historical Quarterly* 12 (1981): 372–386.

moccasins   See CLOTHING.

Monticello

In their book *Lewis & Clark: Journey of the Corps of Discovery,* Dayton Duncan and Ken Burns describe President THOMAS JEFFERSON's home, Monticello, as the "Mission Control" of the Lewis and Clark Expedition. Indeed, it was Monticello where the president and MERIWETHER LEWIS spent time planning the expedition, where Jefferson received reports of the corps's progress and heard the news of Lewis's death in 1809, and where some of the ARTIFACTS AND SPECIMENS sent back from the journey came to stay. In this sense it was the both the launching pad and the final stop of the expedition.

Son of a distinguished Virginia planter family, Jefferson was 24 years old when he first wrote down the name *Monticello.* Two years later he began to erect his personal "essay in architecture" on a hilltop near Charlottesville. Even after the house was built, he spent the rest of his life redesigning and rebuilding it as new ideas came to him. Monticello also became a salon of ENLIGHTENMENT thinking where Jefferson entertained U.S. and foreign philosophers, politicians, and scientists.

Designed by Thomas Jefferson, Monticello was both his home and a center for Enlightenment thought. It was here that he and Meriwether Lewis spent much time planning the journey west and where some of the expedition's artifacts and specimens were kept. *(Library of Congress, Prints and Photographs Division [LC-USZ62-122242])*

The plantation on which the house stood covered 5,000 acres, included four farms, and was an agricultural and industrial center. It was home not only to Jefferson and his family but also to large numbers of workers, including 130 slaves, some of whom lived and worked along Mulberry Row, south of the main house. Named for the trees planted along it, this road was the hub of plantation activity from the 1770s until Jefferson's death. Jefferson also took great pride in his gardens, where he planted Indian CORN that Lewis and Clark had sent to him.

Jefferson loved his home, writing, "All my wishes end, where I hope my days will end, at Monticello." He died there on July 4, 1826, leaving debts totaling more than $100,000. His unfortunate heirs were forced to sell land and possessions—and finally, in 1831, the house itself. Its first buyer allowed Monticello to fall quickly into a state of disrepair, but in 1834 a U.S. Navy lieutenant named Uriah Phillips Levy bought it and immediately began to make improvements. Except for a brief period during and following the Civil War—when it was again allowed to decay—Monticello belonged to the Levy family for the next 89 years. Yet despite the amount of money the Levys had poured into their excellent care of the house, pressure from both the government and the public forced Jefferson Monroe Levy to turn Monticello over to the Thomas Jefferson Memorial Foundation in 1923. The foundation has maintained the house, now a national landmark and tourist attraction, ever since. Currently Monticello is the only U.S. house on the United Nations' World Heritage List.

See also BOOKS ON THE EXPEDITION.

Further Reading

Jackson, Donald. *Thomas Jefferson & the Stony Mountains: Exploring the West from Monticello.* Norman: University of Oklahoma Press, 1993.

Leepson, Marc. *Saving Monticello: The Levy Family's Epic Quest to Rescue the House that Jefferson Built.* New York: Free Press, 2001.

McLaughlin, Jack. *Jefferson and Monticello: The Biography of a Builder.* Reprint, New York: Henry Holt, 1990.

Stein, Susan R. *The Worlds of Thomas Jefferson at Monticello.* New York: Harry N. Abrams, 1993.

Monumental Rock   See SHIP ROCK.

moose   See ANIMALS, NEW SPECIES.

mosquitoes   See INSECTS.

Mount Adams (Klickitat, Pahtoe)

Mount Adams is a stratovolcano that rises to 12,276 feet in the CASCADE MOUNTAINS of Washington state, east of MOUNT ST. HELENS. In October 1805, as the expedition moved down the COLUMBIA RIVER to the PACIFIC OCEAN, MERIWETHER LEWIS and WILLIAM CLARK began to search for landmarks that they could identify from MAPS published by GEORGE VANCOUVER, who had sent a party up the Columbia 13 years earlier. Finally, on October 18, from a cliff overlooking the Columbia, Clark

Mount Adams in the Cascade Mountains, sighted by Clark on October 18, 1805, was mistaken by the party for Mount St. Helens. *(Washington State Historical Society, Tacoma)*

spotted "a high mountain covered with snow." He concluded that it was Mount St. Helens, based on Vancouver's information, but modern geographers believe it was more likely Mount Adams. More important, it was the first sighting of a peak in the CASCADE MOUNTAINS, confirming for Lewis and Clark that they were nearing their destination.

At the beginning of April 1806, during the return journey, Clark again spotted—and this time named—Mount Adams, the Indian names for which were Klickitat and Pahtoe. While the main party was hunting ELK, Clark took a few men on an exploratory side trip and came to the WILLAMETTE RIVER, which they had missed on the westward journey due to three small islands obscuring its mouth. It was during this excursion up the Willamette that, on April 2, Clark sighted both Mount Adams and Mount St. Helens. He thus became to be the first non-Indian to ascertain that there were two volcanoes in the Cascades at that vicinity (latitude 46.2° north); in 1792 Captain ROBERT GRAY had sighted only one.

Composed of lava flows and fragments of basaltic andesite, Mount Adams is second only to Mount Shasta in eruptive volume among volcanoes of the Cascades. Its last eruption probably took place 1,000–2,000 years ago, although there are frequent small debris avalanches; a major debris avalanche occurred on the southwest flank in 1921. Because it has erupted since the Ice Age, and because weak fumes can still be detected in the summit area, geologists believe that Mount Adams may erupt again someday.

Further Reading

Harris, Stephen L. *Fire and Ice: The Cascade Volcanoes.* Revised ed. Seattle: The Mountaineers, Pacific Search Press, 1980.

mountain goats   See ANIMALS, NEW SPECIES.

mountain lions   See ANIMALS, NEW SPECIES.

mountain men

Even before the Lewis and Clark Expedition had returned from the PACIFIC OCEAN in 1806, trappers had begun to move into the West to hunt BEAVERS and trade with Indians. Innumerable legends—many of them true—have grown up around the mountain men, as these trappers/explorers came to be known. Their daily lives were fraught with the dangers posed by extreme heat or bitter cold, starvation or dehydration, animal attack or Indian ambush. Tough, brave, and resourceful, some mountain men became guides and scouts who explored previously uncharted areas of the LOUISIANA TERRITORY and found new routes across the ROCKY MOUNTAINS to the Pacific coast.

The typical mountain man had a horse, a saddle, and a bridle; six beaver traps plus bait; a gun and ammunition; a knife; tobacco; and implements for making fires. He dressed in clothes made from animal skins and usually carried an extra pair of moccasins. His way of life was dictated by the calendar, the elements, and the Indians. Trapping began in the spring and lasted until the quality of the beaver pelts deteriorated in the warmer weather, then began again in the fall.

Until 1825, trappers normally brought their furs to trading posts set up by ST. LOUIS merchants such as MANUEL LISA of the Missouri Fur Company and William Ashley of the Rocky Mountain Fur Company. That year, however, Jedediah Smith persuaded Ashley to organize a rendezvous at Henry's Fork on the Green River, whereby supplies were brought from St. Louis and exchanged for the trappers' pelts. Similar to the exchange system set up by the NORTH WEST COMPANY in Canada years earlier, it proved a successful and efficient way for traders and trappers to meet and conduct their business, in addition to providing an opportunity to socialize. Every year thereafter, from 1825 until 1840, at varying locations, a month-long rendezvous was held in which trappers, traders, Indians, French Canadians, women, and children participated. In time it evolved into a carnival that included singing, dancing, horse races, foot races, shooting competitions, heavy gambling, and even heavier drinking. They were "as crazy a set of men I ever saw," wrote one easterner who witnessed a typical rendezvous.

After the summer gathering, it was back to the mountains and the fall trapping, followed by the tedium of long and sometimes treacherous winters. Contrary to their popular image (depicted by Robert Redford in his film *Jeremiah Johnson*), most mountain men were not solitary trappers but traveled and camped together in groups of 40–60 men who subsequently separated into smaller parties to trap. With a normal trapping party of only two or three men, these were the times when they were most likely to be attacked by hostile Indians. During the winter, the men read, played games, sang, and engaged in physical contests—anything to stave off the boredom until spring, when they could begin to trap again.

While mountain men were a fixture of the American West throughout the first half of the 19th century, their heyday lasted only a short time, usually considered to be from 1820 to 1835. They were usually recruited by the St. Louis merchants through newspaper advertisements. An ad placed by William H. Ashley in the *Missouri Gazette and Public Advertiser* of January 18, 1823, offered $200 per annum for men "to ascend the Missouri to the Rocky Mountains, There to be employed as Hunters."

Several members of the CORPS OF DISCOVERY became mountain men, though some were to die violently. JOHN COLLINS was killed by the ARIKARA INDIANS in 1823, while JOHN NEWMAN died at the hands of the YANKTON NAKOTA INDIANS (Yankton Sioux) in 1838. GEORGE DROUILLARD was killed by the BLACKFEET INDIANS at THREE FORKS in 1810, and it is thought that PETER WEISER lost his life in the same incident. JOHN POTTS was trapping with JOHN COLTER on the YELLOWSTONE RIVER in 1809 when they and others were attacked by the Blackfeet. Potts was butchered, but Colter was stripped naked and made to run for his life. He succeeded in outrunning the Indians and in so doing created a legend.

The sight of the snow-capped peak of Mount Hood on the southwest horizon confirmed for the explorers on the Columbia River that they were nearing the Pacific Ocean. *(Library of Congress, Prints and Photographs Division [LC-USF34-070356-D])*

John Colter is considered the first and one of the most important of the mountain men, having discovered the areas now known as Jackson's Hole and Yellowstone National Park, among other exploits. When he left the Lewis and Clark Expedition at the MANDAN and the HIDATSA villages on August 17, 1806, he became the forerunner of James Beckwourth, Jim Bridger, Kit Carson, Jedediah Smith, and other men who were to leave an indelible mark on the history of the American West. In 1810 Colter returned to Missouri, married, and settled down—a course not often followed by the typical adventure-seeking mountain man.

See also EXPLORATION, LATER; WESTWARD EXPANSION.

Further Reading

Maguire, James H., Peter Wild, and Donald A. Barclay, eds. *A Rendezvous Reader: Tall, Tangled, and True Tales of the Mountain Men, 1805–1850.* Salt Lake City: University of Utah Press, 1997.

Mountain Men and the Fur Trade (Research Center): "Accounts of John Colter's Escape from the Blackfeet." From various contemporary sources. Available on-line. URL: http://alt.xmission.com/~drudy/mtman/html/colter.html. Downloaded on May 20, 2001.

Russell, Carl P. *Firearms, Traps & Tools of the Mountain Men.* Albuquerque: University of New Mexico Press, 1977.

Utley, Robert M. *A Life Wild and Perilous: Mountain Men and the Paths to the Pacific.* New York: Henry Holt and Co., 1997.

Zimmerman, Emily. "The Mountain Men: Pathfinders of the West." University of Virginia American Studies Project. Available on-line. URL: http://xroads.virginia.edu/~HYPER/HNS/Mtmen/home.html. Downloaded on March 14, 2002.

mountain sheep   See SHEEP AND GOATS.

Mount Hood (Falls Mountain; Timm Mountain; Wy'East)

In October 1805, as the expedition traveled down the COLUMBIA RIVER, they spotted a snow-covered mountain on the southwest horizon. MERIWETHER LEWIS and WILLIAM CLARK called it Falls Mountain or Timm Mountain, *Timm* being an Indian name for a region of falls on the Columbia River. However, this is now believed to be their first sighting of Mount Hood, today the highest and best-known mountain in Oregon. The Native American name for Mount Hood at that time was Wy'East.

This was not the first time a non-Indian had seen Mount Hood. In 1792 the British captain GEORGE VANCOUVER had sent a small party, led by Lieutenant William Broughton, on a scouting mission up the Columbia. Broughton charted the area he explored, and near the mouth of the WILLAMETTE RIVER he saw a volcano, which he named after a British naval officer,

Admiral Hood. It was the MAPS from that survey that Lewis and Clark used once they reached that area, and it was the sightings of MOUNT ADAMS and Mount Hood that confirmed the expedition was almost at the PACIFIC OCEAN.

There has been some debate among historians whether the mountain Clark saw and wrote about in his journal on October 18 was in fact Mount Hood. It was believed to be impossible to see the mountain from the corps' location on that date and that he had actually seen it on a different date, when they were in the area of HAT ROCK. However, historians Gary Lentz and David Nicandri have determined that Clark's sighting on that day was probably correct.

The fourth-highest peak in the range known as the CASCADE MOUNTAINS, Mount Hood lies 22 miles south of the Columbia River in present-day Oregon and can be seen from Portland. The Cascades themselves stretch from Mount Garibaldi in British Columbia to Mount Lassen in northern California. With a summit at 11,235 feet above sea level, Mount Hood's base spreads over 92 square miles. It is considered a dormant volcano, although there were minor eruptions in 1804, 1853, 1854, 1859, 1865, and 1907, and scientists believe that it could have a significant eruption sometime before 2075.

Further Reading

Harris, Stephen L. *Fire and Ice: The Cascade Volcanoes.* Revised ed. Seattle: The Mountaineers, Pacific Search Press, 1980.
Nicandri, David, and Gary Lentz. "Lewis & Clark and the Mountain of Mystery." Washington State Historical Society. Available online. URL: http://www.wshs.org/lewisandclark/mountain-of-mystery.htm. Downloaded on July 12, 2002.

Mount Jefferson

Mount Jefferson is another feature named by MERIWETHER LEWIS and WILLIAM CLARK after President THOMAS JEFFERSON (the JEFFERSON RIVER at THREE FORKS is another). A stratovolcano reaching 10,495 feet in height, the mountain was sighted and named in October 1805 while the CORPS OF DISCOVERY camped near the confluence of the COLUMBIA and WILLAMETTE Rivers.

Mount Jefferson lies approximately 71 miles southeast of Portland, Oregon. Located in the Mount Jefferson Wilderness area and the Warm Springs Indian Reservation, it is one of 13 major volcanic centers in the CASCADE MOUNTAINS range, although it is not itself an active volcano. Debris flows occurred in 1934 and 1955, but the most recent eruption took place more than 15,000 years ago. Even so, Mount Jefferson was apparently an explosive volcano at one time; an eruption that occurred between 35,000 and 100,000 years ago caused the spread of ash over great distances, falling as far away as southeast Idaho. Most of the upper 3,300 feet of the cone is less than 100,000 years old, which is fairly young in geological terms. For this reason Mount Jefferson is considered dormant but not yet extinct.

Further Reading

Harris, Stephen L. *Fire and Ice: The Cascade Volcanoes.* Revised ed. Seattle: The Mountaineers, Pacific Search Press, 1980.

Mount St. Helens   (Loowit)

On October 18, 1805, on a cliff above the COLUMBIA RIVER, WILLIAM CLARK saw a high, snow-covered mountain and assumed it was Mount St. Helens, which had been previously charted and named by a lieutenant in Captain GEORGE VANCOUVER's exploration party of 1792. However, it is now believed that he had really sighted MOUNT ADAMS, another volcano in the CASCADE MOUNTAINS range. During the return journey, however, there was no doubt of the identity of the mountain that he and Lewis saw on March 30, 1806. As MERIWETHER LEWIS wrote: "[W]e had a view of mount St. helines . . . the most noble looking object of it's kind in nature . . . a regular cone." Three days later Clark was able to determine that both Mount St. Helens and Mount Adams were in the same latitude (46.2° north).

Rising to 8,364 feet, Mount St. Helens is a stratovolcano in Washington State, located 34 miles west of MOUNT ADAMS. At the time Lewis and Clark saw it, however, Mount St. Helens stood 9,677 feet high, and both explorers believed it to be the tallest mountain in America. When Lewis viewed it, he described its shape as "a regular cone . . . completely covered in snow." In later years, it was called the "Fuji of America" because of its strong similarity in shape to Japan's Mount Fuji. None of these descriptions apply any longer, however, due to a deadly eruption in May 1980 that both reduced the height of the mountain and changed its shape.

The Indian name for Mount St. Helens was *Loowit.* Its present name honors British diplomat Alleyne Fitzherbert (1753–1839), whose title was Baron St. Helens. The volcano

Mount St. Helens had been named in 1792 during a British exploratory expedition led by George Vancouver. Lewis and Clark were thus able to identify it clearly in their journals. *(Library of Congress, Prints and Photographs Division [LC-USZ62-118696])*

was and continues to be active; an eruption had occurred just a few years before Lewis and Clark arrived, and there would be six in the 19th century, in addition to the 1980 eruption. Still one of the biggest mountains in the nation, the base of Mount St. Helens is about six miles across and sits approximately 4,000 feet above sea level.

Further Reading

Harris, Stephen L. *Fire and Ice: The Cascade Volcanoes.* Revised ed. Seattle: The Mountaineers, Pacific Search Press, 1980.

mule deer   See DEER.

Multnomah River   See WILLAMETTE RIVER.

music and musical instruments   See RECREATION ON THE EXPEDITION.

Musselshell River (Muscleshell River, Mahtush-ahzhah)

On May 20, 1805, the Lewis and Clark Expedition reached what is now the western edge of Fort Peck Lake, Montana, 120 miles upstream from the mouth of the YELLOWSTONE RIVER. As they had been told by the HIDATSA INDIANS at FORT MANDAN, they came to a river on the south bank, which they named the Muscleshell (Musselshell) River, the English translation of the Indian name *Mahtush-ahzhah*. The party explored it for some 5 miles and named a creek running into it from the west SACAGAWEA RIVER (now Crooked Creek).

The Musselshell rises in the Little Belt Mountains near today's White Sulphur Springs, Montana, and flows east parallel to the Yellowstone River until it turns due north to run the last 60 miles of its 230-mile course into the MISSOURI RIVER. The area where it branches off from the Missouri is now the location of the Fort Peck Reservoir.

In his journal for May 20, Sergeant PATRICK GASS wrote: "About 11 came to the mouth of the Muscle-shell river, a hand-some river that comes in on the South side. The water of the Missouri is becoming more clear. . . . The Missouri here is 222 yards wide, and the Muscle-shell 100 yards. The water of the latter is of a pale colour, and the current is not rapid; its mouth is 660 miles above Fort Mandan."

Captain MERIWETHER LEWIS described the events of that day more fully:

> . . . *After making seven miles we reached by eleven o'clock the mouth of a large river on the south and camped for the day at the upper point of its junction with the Missouri.*
>
> *This stream, which we supposed to be that called by the Minatarees [Hidatsa] the Muscleshell river, empties into the Missouri 2,270 miles above the mouth of the latter river, in latitude 47 0'6/10" north. It is 110 yards wide, and contains more water than streams of that size usually do in this country; its current is by no means rapid, and there is every appearance of its being susceptible of navigation by canoes for a considerable distance. . . .*
>
> *If this be, as we suppose, the Muscleshell, our Indian information is that it rises in the first chain of the Rocky mountains not far from the sources of the Yellowstone, whence in its course it waters a high broken country, well timbered, particularly on its borders, and interspersed with handsome fertile plains and meadows. . . . about five miles abe [above] the mouth of [the Mussel-] Shell river a handsome river of about fifty yards in width dishcarged itself into the Shell river on the Stard. or upper side; this stream we called Sâh-câ-gee-me-âh or bird woman's River, after our interpreter the Snake woman."*

Further Reading

Cutright, Paul Russell. *Lewis & Clark: Pioneering Naturalists.* Lincoln: University of Nebraska Press/Bison Books, 1989.

Fifer, Barbara, and Vicky Soderberg. *Along the Trail with Lewis and Clark.* Great Falls, Mont.: Montana Magazine, 1998.

Moulton, Gary E., ed. *Atlas of the Lewis and Clark Expedition.* Revised ed. Lincoln: University of Nebraska Press, 1999.

Nakota Indians   See YANKTON NAKOTA INDIANS.

naming of sites   See NOMENCLATURE, GEOGRAPHICAL.

Native American cultures   See ETHNOGRAPHY.

navigation

Both MERIWETHER LEWIS and WILLIAM CLARK had to become sufficiently skilled in navigation techniques to lead their men safely across the continent and back. Furthermore, when the LOUISIANA PURCHASE was finalized, they were additionally instructed to map the country's newly acquired LOUISIANA TERRITORY. For these reasons President THOMAS JEFFERSON included in his letter of instructions that Lewis was to "take observations of latitude & longitude."

In the early 1800s, establishing latitude and longitude was still difficult to do, especially out on the frontier. Fixing the latitude was possible with a certain amount of work, but longitude presented challenges that was still vexing navigators the world over. It could be estimated by knowing exactly what time it was at a certain location when it was high noon in Greenwich, England, but this required an accurate chronometer, or clock, that could withstand the rigors of a long journey by land or sea. For this reason Lewis and Clark needed to rely more heavily on celestial reckoning, or tracking the moon's movement against a fixed point in the sky.

Lewis was already well familiar with the night sky and its stars, but he needed training in how to make and record the necessary observations. To this end, during the course of his PREPARATIONS FOR THE EXPEDITION, he spent three weeks studying under the eminent astronomer and surveyor ANDREW ELLICOTT. Among other things, Ellicott taught him how to use a sextant to mark distances in angle between the moon and whatever star he would use as his fixed point, in addition to the use of other instruments.

Clark, meanwhile, was already well versed in surveying and mapmaking, and as they journeyed up the OHIO RIVER in October 1803, Lewis began to teach his cocaptain what he himself had only recently learned from Ellicott so that the two of them could share the task of observing and making notes on their positions throughout the journey. The exact latitude and longitude would not, however, be determined until after their return, when charts comparing their figures to the clock time in Greenwich could be used for more precise calculations.

In addition to celestial reckoning, Lewis and Clark engaged in "ground truthing," or checking Indian data against their own observations. Throughout the journey they carried with them an impressive array of the latest scientific instruments for navigation, including spirit and telescopic levels, several compasses, a sextant, a "Hadley's quadrant" (octant), rods and chains, telescopes, artificial horizons, drafting instruments, a measuring tape, and a chronometer (clock). These instruments saw almost daily use, even when the expedition was camped in one location for a long period.

The captains also carried the best available MAPS of the region, an Astronomical Ephemeris and Nautical Almanac,

Practical Introduction to Spherics and Nautical Astronomy, and tables for rougher estimates of latitude and longitude. As the elevation of the terrain above sea level was not generally known and a clear horizon not always available to them, they often had to use an artificial horizon in their observations. In addition to calculating latitude and longitude, they also had to figure and record their direction, course, and time and distance of travel.

Clark would determine the expedition's course by comparing magnetic variations in compass readings of north to the true north, which was itself established by taking a bearing of the North Star. By knowing the magnetic variation, he could plot his course relative to true north. By timing a log chip dropped in the river, he could determine the speed of the boat. These were crude methods according to modern standards; their navigation had an inherent error of at least a degree, and Clark's estimates of speed and distances may have erred by 5–10 percent. All the same, when, using only dead reckoning, he calculated how far they had traveled from their starting point at the mouth of the MISSOURI RIVER to the PACIFIC OCEAN, he came up with a figure of 4,162 miles—only 40 miles off the actual distance.

Despite the problems inherent in the captains' methods, modern navigators admire their achievements, especially because of the state of navigation knowledge at that time and the terrain over which they had to carry their equipment. The extensive preparation for the expedition, the use of the best available maps of the region, the creation of maps and charts en route, and the painstaking recording of data made it possible for Lewis and Clark to fill Jefferson's directives and give the United States a basis for claims on lands even beyond the Louisiana Territory.

See also ASTRONOMICAL OBSERVATIONS.

Further Reading

Ambrose, Stephen E. *Undaunted Courage: Meriwether Lewis, Thomas Jefferson, and the Opening of the American West.* New York: Simon and Schuster, 1996.

Bedini, Silvio A. "The Scientific Instruments of the Lewis and Clark Expedition." *Great Plains Quarterly* 4, no. 1 (1984): 54–69.

Large, Arlen. "Lewis and Clark: Part Time Astronomers." *We Proceeded On* 5, no. 1 (February 1979).

Merritt, James, et al. "Shooting the Moon (and the Sun and Stars): Lewis and Clark as Celestial Navigators." *We Proceeded On* 27, no. 4 (November 2001).

University of Virginia. "Exploring the West from Monticello: Observations of Latitude and Longitude at All Remarkable Points." Available on-line. URL: http://www.lib.virginia.edu/exhibits/lewis_clark/home.html. Downloaded on March 27, 2002.

William Clark used dead reckoning to calculate the total distance the expedition had traveled from the mouth of the Missouri to the Pacific Ocean. Remarkably, he erred by only 40 miles. *(Yale Collection of Western Americana, Beinecke Rare Book and Manuscript Library)*

Newman, John (ca. 1785–1838) *private in the temporary party*

A promising but headstrong member of the Lewis and Clark Expedition was Private John Newman, who but for the stubbornness of MERIWETHER LEWIS would have been part of the permanent party to the PACIFIC OCEAN. Born in Pennsylvania, he was recruited for the CORPS OF DISCOVERY at KASKASKIA but was not made a member of the permanent party until May 14, 1804. In October 1804, during the trip up the MISSOURI RIVER, he apparently listened too closely to MOSES REED, a former private and malcontent who had been expelled from the corps for desertion. Following Reed's example, Newman began to speak out against the two captains, as a result of which he was arrested and court-martialed.

The charge against Newman was that he had "uttered repeated expressions of a highly criminal and mutinous nature. . . ." Newman pled "not guilty," but his peers on the court found him "guilty of every part of the charge exhibited against him." He was sentenced to receive 75 lashes, and after being "discarded" from the corps, he was put to work as a laborer. The lashing was carried out on October 14, after which ROBERT FRAZIER was selected to take his place in the permanent party.

Newman sincerely regretted what he had done and did his best to make up for it by working hard and volunteering for the most rigorous of assignments. In February 1805, while Newman, Frazier, GEORGE DROUILLARD, and SILAS GOODRICH were a good distance from FORT MANDAN collecting some meat left by hunters, they were attacked by approximately 100 TETON LAKOTA INDIANS (Teton Sioux). Although the soldiers managed to escape with their lives, the Sioux got away with two sleds of meat and two knives.

Newman's good behavior made a strong impression on his peers, and many encouraged Captain Lewis to allow him back into the permanent party. Lewis held firm, however, and refused to readmit Newman to the corps. Consequently, the former private joined the group on the KEELBOAT that returned to ST. LOUIS in April 1805. During that trip, he continued to conduct himself well and provided valuable assistance to the keelboat's commander, Corporal RICHARD WARFINGTON. Lewis later gave Newman a positive commendation in his report to Secretary of War HENRY DEARBORN after the expedition's return from the West Coast and requested that Newman receive the same rewards as the members of the permanent expedition.

In later years, Newman became a trapper on the Missouri River. He was married in July 1832 to Olympia Debreuil and in 1834 became a trader on the upper Missouri. In spring 1838 Newman was killed by the YANKTON NAKOTA INDIANS (Yankton Sioux).

Further Reading

Clarke, Charles G. *The Men of the Lewis and Clark Expedition: A Biographical Roster of the Fifty-One Members and a Composite Diary of Their Activities from All Known Sources.* 1970. Reprint, Lincoln: Bison Books, University of Nebraska Press, 2002.

news reports of the expedition

At the time of the Lewis and Clark Expedition, newspapers were the fastest medium of communication—faster even than the postal service. Americans were anxious for news of the expedition, and newspapers were eager to supply it. However, with the explorers away in the wilderness, clearly news was hard to come by.

Reporting on the expedition began well before it got underway. On April 1, 1803, *The New England Palladium,* published in Boston, noted on page two, "It is reported, that Capt. Lewis, the president's private secretary, is about to proceed to our south-western frontier on political business." At the time, MERIWETHER LEWIS was arranging for supplies at the federal armory in HARPERS FERRY, Virginia. Surprisingly, President THOMAS JEFFERSON initially tried to conceal the extent of the expedition, telling the press that Lewis and a small company were only going to explore the upper MISSISSIPPI RIVER.

Nevertheless, by September 23 the *Palladium,* now in possession of more information, published the following news dispatch from Louisville:

An expedition is expected to leave this place shortly, under the direction of Capt. William Clark and Mr. Lewis, (private secretary to the President), to proceed through the immense wilderness of Louisiana, to the Western of Pacific Ocean. The particular objects of this undertaking are at present matters of conjecture only: But we have good reason to believe that our government intend to encourage settlements and establish sea-ports on the coast of the Pacific Ocean.

The same paper reported in another dispatch from Louisville on October 29 that Lewis and Clark had in fact left from there

. . . on their expedition to the Westward. We have not been enabled to ascertain to what length this rout will extend, as when it was first set on foot by the President, the Louisiana country was not ceded to the U. S. and it is now likely it will be considerably extended—they are to receive further instructions at Kahokia. It is, however, certain that they will ascend the main branch of the Missisippi as far as possible; and it is probable they will then direct their course to the Missouri, and ascend it. They have the iron frame of a boat, intended to be covered with skins, which can, by screws, be formed into one or four, as may best suit their purposes. About 60 men will compose the party.

Lewis corresponded regularly with President THOMAS JEFFERSON during the 1803–04 preparatory period in ST. LOUIS and CAMP DUBOIS, but the earliest significant release of information in the press occurred after the winter of 1804–05 at FORT MANDAN. As the CORPS OF DISCOVERY departed in CANOES and PIROGUES up the Missouri, the keelboat was sent back downriver to St. Louis, carrying reports, LETTERS, MAPS,

By the last Mails.

MARYLAND.   BALTIMORE, OCT. 29, 1806.

A LETTER from *St. Louis* (Upper *Louisiana*), dated *Sept.* 23, 1806, announces the arrival of Captains LEWIS and CLARK, from their expedition into the interior.—They went to the *Pacific Ocean ;* have brought some of the natives and curiosities of the countries through which they passed, and only lost one man. They left the *Pacific Ocean* 23d March, 1806, where they arrived in November, 1805 ;—and where some American vessels had been just before.—They state the Indians to be as numerous on the *Columbia* river, which empties into the *Pacific*, as the whites in any part of the U. S. They brought a family of the Mandan indians with them. The winter was very mild on the *Pacific*.— They have kept an ample journal of their tour ; which will be published, and must afford much intelligence. ————

Mr. ERSKINE, the new British Minister to the United States, is warmly attached to the U. States. He married, about seven years since, an American lady, daughter of Gen. CADWALLADER, of *Pennsylvania*. He has a daughter now in the U. States.

Newspaper reports were the surest method of spreading information. This excerpt is from an article on the expedition published in Boston's *Columbian Centinel* on November 5, 1806. *(Courtesy American Antiquarian Society)*

and ARTIFACTS AND SPECIMENS. By July that same year, *The Connecticut Courant,* published in Hartford, was able to publish a one-column story on the expedition. The July 31 issue reported that "Letters have been received from captains Lewis and Clark, by express sent by them to the commandant at St. Louis, with dispatches for the president of the United States. These enterprising young men set out from St. Louis in May 1804 to ascend and explore the Missouri river to its source and from thence to proceed to the Pacific Ocean. . . ."

The Corps of Discovery then disappeared up the Missouri River, spending much more time away than expected. Lack of news caused many, including President Jefferson, to fear that the explorers had met their demise. When the expedition belatedly reached the Pacific coast in November 1805, they hoped to meet one or more trading ships at the mouth of the COLUMBIA RIVER, which would enable some or all of the party to return to the East Coast with their JOURNALS as well as artifacts and specimens collected during the journey. They waited throughout their long winter at FORT CLATSOP, but when no ships appeared, the entire party was forced to return overland. Thus, a nation hungry for news had to wait until the corps arrived back in St. Louis in September 1806, when reporting to President Jefferson was Lewis's first priority.

There was, however, a sure method for getting the news out: LETTERS. Lewis and Clark knew that newspapers often got their information from letters and that articles were copied from one newspaper to another. They also knew that the nearest newspaper office was in Frankfort, Kentucky. For these reasons Lewis wrote a letter, which was copied and signed by his cocaptain, to Clark's brother GEORGE ROGERS CLARK in CLARKSVILLE, Indiana Territory, providing preliminary news of the expedition. By October 11 the letter had been published in the Frankfort *Western World,* by October 28 in the Pittsburgh *Gazette,* and by November 3 in Washington's *National Intelligencer.* Donald Jackson has noted that "the initial fame of the expedition rests largely upon this communication, which spread throughout the country as rapidly as the means of the day would allow."

Another Hartford newspaper, *The American Mercury,* published a three-column story about the expedition in their issue of November 13, 1806. It began, of course, with the basic news that Lewis and Clark had returned and then gave an overview of the expedition. In addition to the news article, there was a two-column letter from William Clark to his brother Jonathan, also providing details of the journey.

The following summer, *The Aurora and General Advertiser*—a PHILADELPHIA paper founded by Benjamin Franklin's grandson—published a prospectus on its back page for "a book and map of Lewis and Clark's explorations to the Pacific that is to be published by Meriwether Lewis in the near future." They promised a book in three volumes and a separate map measuring 3'10" by 5'8". Although thousands were eager to read his account of the expedition, Lewis never carried through on publication. Instead, Sergeant PATRICK GASS published his own journal, and Lewis entered into a tumultuous term as governor of the Louisiana Territory, during which time the controversies of his administration became far more newsworthy than his failure to publish his journals.

On October 20, 1809, *The Democratic Clarion,* a newspaper in Nashville, reported Lewis's apparent suicide:

> *In the death of Governor Lewis, the public behold the wreck of one of the noblest men. He was a pupil of the immortal Jefferson, by him he was reared, by him he was instructed in the tour of sciences, by him he was introduced to public life when his enterprising soul, great botanical knowledge, acute penetration and personal courage soon pointed him out as the most proper person to command a projected exploring party to the Northwest Coast of the American Continent.*

Further Reading

Clark, William, and Jonathan Clark. *Dear Brother: Letters of William Clark to Jonathan Clark.* New Haven, Conn.: Yale University Press, 2002.

Jackson, Donald. *Letters of the Lewis and Clark Expedition, with Related Documents, 1783–1854.* Urbana: University of Illinois Press, 1979.

———. *Thomas Jefferson & the Stony Mountains: Exploring the West from Monticello.* Norman: University of Oklahoma Press, 1993.

Jefferson, Thomas. *Message from the President of the United States Communicating Discoveries Made in Exploring the Missouri, Red River and Washita, by Captains Lewis and Clark, Doctor Sibley, and Mr. Dunbar: with a statistical account of the countries adjacent.* Washington, D.C.: A. & G. Way, printers, 1806.

Rasmussen, Jay, comp. "Old Newspaper Accounts Regarding Lewis and Clark." *Lewis and Clark on the Information Superhighway.* Available on-line. URL: http://www.lcarchive.org/newspapers. html. Updated on May 24, 2000.

Nez Perce Indians (Chopunnish Indians; Nimiipu Indians; Sahaptin Indians)

In September 1805, after an exceptionally dangerous crossing, the CORPS OF DISCOVERY descended, cold and starving, from the BITTERROOT MOUNTAINS to the WEIPPE PRAIRIE. There they met a number of Indians who brought them back to their villages by the CLEARWATER RIVER and gave the soldiers SHELTER, FOOD, and, eventually, more assistance than any other Indians they would meet. These were the Nez Perce, at that time the biggest nation in the Pacific Northwest, as well as the most powerful.

Prior to this moment, most of the Nez Perce had never met white men, and those who had just come off the Bitterroots were in such poor shape that it would have been an easy matter to kill them and take their HORSES and WEAPONS. Nez Perce oral tradition has it, however, that a woman named WATKUWEIS ("Returned from a Far Country")—who had at one time been kidnapped by BLACKFEET INDIANS and subsequently rescued by a white trader—stopped the warriors, telling them, "These are the people who helped me. Do them no hurt." In the end, the Nez Perce did the expedition nothing but good.

The Nez Perce called themselves the Nimiipu, meaning "the people." Lewis and Clark referred to them as the Chopunnish. The name *nez percé*—meaning "pierced nose"—was bestowed on the nation by French fur traders, even though few of the Indians wore nose pendants. The current name caught on, however, with the pronunciation of "nezz purse" being more commonly used today. The Nez Perce of the region visited by Lewis and Clark were fishers and hunter-gatherers who followed a seasonal subsistence cycle, with women generally digging for roots and wild vegetables while men traveled to the SNAKE and COLUMBIA rivers for salmon. Berries, pine nuts, sunflower seeds, and black moss were also gathered for winter storage. Big-game hunting took place in the summer and included DEER, ELK, moose, BEAR, mountain goats, and SHEEP. After the introduction of horses in the 18th century, the Nez Perce joined the FLATHEAD (Salish) to hunt BUFFALO and ANTELOPE on the GREAT PLAINS.

Before they began their journey, MERIWETHER LEWIS and WILLIAM CLARK knew little to nothing of the Nez Perce and so did not realize that their first encounter with this nation was at TRAVELERS' REST in September 1805. Just prior to the Bitterroots crossing, three Indians came to the soldiers' camp and gave them information regarding the LOLO TRAIL. The captains assumed that they were Flathead Indians, but they were more likely Nez Perce as they were from the other side of the mountains and the Lolo was known to be a Nez Perce trail.

Following their harrowing crossing of the mountains, the corps rested and tried to recoup from dysentery brought on by their recent experience combined with an abrupt change in diet. The Nez Perce had generously shared with them roots and fish, but the latter may have been infected with bacteria, and the soldiers were more accustomed to meat. This, however, was the only downside of the corps' association with a nation whom Lewis would later describe as an "affectionate people." With extraordinary willingness, the Nez Perce helped the corps build CANOES, and Chief TWISTED HAIR agreed to look after the expedition's horses until its return the following spring. Twisted Hair and another chief, TETOHARSKY, also accompanied the expedition down the Clearwater and Snake Rivers to act as intermediaries with their relatives along the upper regions of the Columbia.

In May 1806 the expedition returned to Twisted Hair's village, setting up camp nearby and staying for more than a month as they waited for the snows on the Bitterroots to melt. During this time they met CUT NOSE, another Nez Perce chief, who was at odds with Twisted Hair. After mediating a peace between the two, the captains held a two-day council with all the Nez Perce chiefs. They asked the Indians to consider moving to the other side of the ROCKY MOUNTAINS to be more accessible to the U.S. trading network and to make peace with the SHOSHONE INDIANS. In addition, they asked for a delegation to travel to Washington to meet President THOMAS JEFFERSON. The Nez Perce response, as expressed by Chief BROKEN ARM, was that while they were definitely interested in trading with white men (they especially hoped to obtain guns) and were willing to discuss peace with the Shoshone, they preferred to be cautious and were not ready to send a delegation to Washington.

Despite their disappointment at not achieving their full diplomatic aims as well as Broken Arm's refusal to lend them guides over the Bitterroots until the snows had melted, Lewis and Clark's stay among the Nez Perce was successful. Above all, they had established friendly relations with the Indians, with whom they enjoyed games and races during those weeks (see RECREATION ON THE EXPEDITION). But they were anxious to leave, and, against the advice of the Indians, the expedition set out for the Bitterroot Mountains on June 15. It was not long, however, before Lewis and Clark realized that the Indians were right; the mountains were still impassable. They set up camp to wait and sent GEORGE DROUILLARD and GEORGE SHANNON back to the Nez Perce to obtain guides. A few days later the men returned with three INDIAN GUIDES, including a brother of Cut Nose. Bargaining for the guides had cost the expedition two rifles—a rare instance of the captains giving away FIREARMS to Indians—but Lewis considered it well worth the price, especially as two more Indians had joined them in the meantime.

Lewis and Clark called the Nez Perce the Chopunnish. Their hospitality and assistance in autumn 1805 and spring 1806 were essential factors in the expedition's success. This 1911 photograph shows a group of Nez Perce and Yakama chiefs in traditional dress. *(Library of Congress, Prints and Photographs Division [LC-USF34-070356-D])*

With their guides, the corps finally made it over the Bitterroots safely, and from Travelers' Rest (where the expedition split into two parties) the Indians took Lewis and his men along a trail commonly used for their buffalo hunts. The Nez Perce finally took their leave of Lewis on July 4, 1806, parting from the expedition just before the soldiers crossed the CONTINENTAL DIVIDE at LEWIS AND CLARK PASS. It was a parting tinged with sadness, for a grateful Lewis now regarded the Nez Perce with tremendous respect and affection.

At the time the Corps of Discovery met them, the Nez Perce were living in groups of extended families in small villages along streams and rivers, and their large nation covered about 27,000 square miles across Oregon, Washington, and Idaho. Following the expedition's visit, fur traders and missionaries began to descend on the Nez Perce, and as happened to other Indian nations, they were eventually forced off their lands and onto reservations, a removal that they resisted—quietly at first. Although they had always been proud of their friendly relations with whites, in 1877 a Nez Perce effort to effect a truce erupted into violence, and war followed. Chief Joseph then led his people on a flight to Canada that failed 30 miles short of the border when they were captured by U.S. troops. Ironically, among those arrested were some old men and women who had been children when Lewis and Clark stayed in their village in 1805 and 1806. Today about 1,800 Nez Perce live on a reservation in west central Idaho, while some 1,300 live elsewhere.

See also CAMP CHOPUNNISH; CANOE CAMP.

Further Reading

Josephy, Alvin M., Jr. *The Nez Perce Indians and the Opening of the Northwest.* New Haven: Yale University Press, 1965.

McBeth, Kate. *The Nez Perces Since Lewis and Clark.* Reprint, Moscow: University of Idaho Press, 1993.

Ray, Verne F. *Lewis and Clark and the Nez Perce Indians.* Washington, D.C.: The Westerners, 1971.

Ronda, James P. *Lewis and Clark among the Indians.* Lincoln: University of Nebraska Press, 1984.

Sappington, Robert Lee. "Lewis and Clark Expedition Among the Nez Perce Indians: The First Ethnographic Study in the Columbia Plateau." *Northwest Anthropological Research Notes* 23 (1989): 1–33.

Waldman, Carl. *Encyclopedia of Native American Tribes.* Revised ed. New York: Checkmark Books, 1999.

Nez Perce Trail   See LOLO TRAIL.

nine young men from Kentucky

When MERIWETHER LEWIS and WILLIAM CLARK began to plan their expedition, a crucial aspect was RECRUITING the right men for what they knew would be a long and grueling journey. Members of the CORPS OF DISCOVERY were therefore chosen as much for their toughness and endurance as for any other qualification. For this reason many of those recruited were frontiersmen with strong wilderness survival

skills. At that time, Kentucky was at the edge of the frontier, so it was perhaps no surprise that the first nine men to be recruited were all Kentuckians or enlisted in Kentucky. The nine young men from Kentucky, as they came to be called, consisted of sergeants CHARLES FLOYD and NATHANIEL PRYOR and privates WILLIAM BRATTON, JOHN COLTER, JOSEPH FIELD, REUBIN FIELD, GEORGE GIBSON, GEORGE SHANNON, and JOHN SHIELDS. Of these, Shannon and Colter were recruited by Lewis, the remainder by Clark.

Floyd and the Field brothers were the first to be put on the payroll; they were enlisted as of August 1, 1803. Colter and Shannon met Captain Lewis in PITTSBURGH and accompanied him on the KEELBOAT to Louisville, Kentucky, where they were officially enrolled on October 15 and 19, respectively. Gibson and Shields were also enlisted on October 19, and the following day Bratton and Pryor were added to the party. These men thus formed the core of the permanent party going to the PACIFIC OCEAN; no others would be officially added to the roster until January 1, 1804.

Of the nine, only Floyd was a Kentuckian by birth. Pryor, Colter, Bratton, Shields, and the Fields brothers were all originally from Virginia and had moved to Kentucky as boys or young men. Gibson and Shannon had been born in Pennsylvania but like the others had later emigrated to the frontier with their families—in Shannon's case to Ohio. Following Lewis and Clark's recruiting guidelines, they were, for the most part, "stout, healthy, unmarried men, accustomed to the woods, and capable of bearing bodily fatigues to a considerable degree."

There were exceptions. Pryor and Shields were both married, and given Floyd's apparent health problems from the beginning (he would die on the first part of the journey), his selection for the corps now seems surprising. Otherwise all the nine young men fitted the desired qualifications for corpsmen, and several brought other qualifications as well. Shields and Bratton, for instance, were both gunsmiths and blacksmiths; Shields especially had a gift for improvisation and thus became the company's resident "mechanic." Colter and Gibson were accomplished hunters; Colter in particular had extraordinary survival instincts that would benefit the corps during the expedition and proved vital after he was discharged and returned west to become a fur trapper. Shannon, the youngest and least experienced of the nine, became lost at least twice during the journey; on the first occasion, in August–September 1804, he was alone in the wilderness for over two weeks and yet managed to keep himself from starvation. Overall, the nine young men from Kentucky would prove themselves among the best of the best in the Corps of Discovery.

Further Reading

Clarke, Charles G. *The Men of the Lewis and Clark Expedition: A Biographical Roster of the Fifty-One Members and a Composite Diary of Their Activities from All Known Sources.* 1970. Reprint, Lincoln: Bison Books, University of Nebraska Press, 2002.

Yater, George H. "Nine Young Men from Kentucky." *We Proceeded On.* Lewis and Clark Trail Heritage Foundation Publication No. 11, May 1992, p. 3.

nomenclature, botanical   See PLANTS, NEW SPECIES; PURSH, FREDERICK.

nomenclature, geographical

From the start of the expedition, both MERIWETHER LEWIS and WILLIAM CLARK adopted a pragmatic, almost prosaic approach to the naming of geographical features along their route. Sometimes their nomenclature commemorated the animals they found at a site, sometimes an incident, sometimes an outstanding aspect of the feature, such as an unusual rock formation (i.e., HAT ROCK). Butter Island was so called because the expedition consumed the last of their butter there. After Lewis's dog SEAMAN chased away a buffalo bull that had emerged from a river, the river was dubbed Bull Creek. Lewis named MILK RIVER so because its waters seemed to be the color of tea with milk in it. On it went, as features were given whatever name seemed appropriate at the time.

It was Clark who named their first feature on May 24, 1804, after the crew nearly lost control of the KEELBOAT below LA CHARETTE: "This place I call retragrade bend as we were obliged to fall back 2 miles." On June 3 Cupboard Creek was so named because Clark thought the rock at its mouth looked like a cupboard. On July 4, 1804, one inlet was named Fourth of July Creek, the next Independence Creek (near Atchison, Kansas), and the prairie where JOSEPH FIELD was bitten by a snake was promptly given the name Joseph Field's Snake Prairie. Sometimes, however, nomenclature just came to the captains, as in the creek that Clark called "Roloje, a name given me last night in my sleep."

Later in the journey, a sense of their mission as representatives of the United States prevailed—hence the Jefferson, Madison, Gallatin, Dearborn, and Smith Rivers. Sometimes personal feelings came into play. The Big Muddy Creek near Culbertson, Montana, was originally named Martha's River by Clark "in honor to the Selebrated M.F.," while the JUDITH RIVER in Montana was named after the woman Clark was to marry. The MARIAS RIVER upstream commemorates Lewis's cousin Maria Wood. Lewis later drew on his Masonic principles when he named the Philosophy, Philanthropy, and WISDOM RIVERs.

Just about every member of the CORPS OF DISCOVERY had one or more geographical features named after him or her, including SACAGAWEA. Returning down the Yellowstone in 1806, Clark adopted this method for at least nine creeks and streams. Between July 16 and August 2, JOHN SHIELDS, WILLIAM BRATTON, NATHANIEL PRYOR, GEORGE SHANNON, HUGH HALL, FRANÇOIS LABICHE, and YORK all had creeks or rivers named after them, as did Sacagawea's little boy, JEAN BAPTISTE CHARBONNEAU, for whom Baptiests Creek and POMPY'S TOWER were named.

Based on the Thwaites edition of the expedition's JOURNALS (1904), MERIWETHER LEWIS and WILLIAM CLARK named at least 265 places along their route to the COLUMBIA RIVER and back again. Today only about 50 retain the nomenclature given to them during 1804–06. While it is to be regretted that so many of the names marking the progress of the United States's greatest exploration have now fallen into disuse, there are several factors to account for this.

First, because a complete edition of the journals was not published until 1904, there was no public record of the names Lewis and Clark had given to the places they passed. The result was that when new explorers and settlers poured into the western plains in the 19th century, they gave their own names to the places they found and the landmarks they saw.

Second, because the greater part of the expedition's journey was by water, the majority of names assigned by Lewis and Clark applied, understandably, to side creeks, islands, and landmarks along the river banks. Since the MISSOURI RIVER and Columbia River have now both been extensively dammed, many of the creeks and islands they saw are now submerged. The Missouri's constant changes of course also destroyed many of their riverside campsites.

A third factor is that the first part of their journey (up the lower reaches of the Missouri) was through areas familiar to French traders and trappers who had already identified most of the landmarks along the river, so no new names were necessary. The same was to occur on the lower reaches of the Columbia where, in addition to the river itself, some features, including MOUNT HOOD, had already been discovered and identified by GEORGE VANCOUVER's exploration of 13 years before. Furthermore, Lewis and Clark occasionally preferred to retain an Indian name for a river, which later travelers found too difficult to pronounce.

There has been a revival of interest in the names Lewis and Clark bestowed on sites along their epic journey, and some have been reinstated. It should be noted, however, that sometimes the explorers themselves could not agree. The present Spring River in Campbell County, South Dakota, appears as Bordache Creek on some maps and as Bourbeuse River on others. Expedition members, however, called it Stoneidol Creek (Lewis), Stone Idol Creek (Clark), Pond River (PATRICK GASS), and Spring or Hermaphrodite Creek (JOHN ORDWAY).

A further difficulty in recognizing Lewis and Clark's nomenclature is the subsequent renaming of various sections of a river. For example, they gave the name Jefferson's River (now the JEFFERSON RIVER) at THREE FORKS to a section of the MISSOURI RIVER and continued to use this name to the CONTINENTAL DIVIDE. Today's maps show that the Missouri becomes the Jefferson River at Three Forks; this becomes the BEAVERHEAD RIVER at Twin Bridges; and this in turn becomes Horse Prairie Creek, the final stretch of water below the LEMHI PASS.

Further Reading

Cutright, Paul Russell. *Lewis & Clark: Pioneering Naturalists.* Lincoln: University of Nebraska Press/Bison Books, 1989.

Duncan, Dayton, and Ken Burns. *Lewis & Clark: The Journey of the Corps of Discovery.* New York: Alfred A. Knopf, 1998.

Large, Arlen J. "All in the Family: The In-House Honorifics of Lewis and Clark." *Names* 42, no. 4 (1994): 269–277.

Lewis, Meriwether, and William Clark. *The History of the Lewis and Clark Expedition.* Edited by Elliott Coues; 4 vols., 1893, Harper. Reprinted in 3 vols., New York: Dover Publications, 1979.

Saindon, Bob. "The River Which Scolds at All Others: An Obstinate Blunder in Nomenclature." *Montana: The Magazine of Western History* 26, no. 3 (1976): 2–7.

Thwaites, Reuben G., ed. *Original Journals of the Lewis and Clark Expedition, 1804–1806; printed from the original manuscripts in the library of the American philosophical society and by direction of its committee on historical documents, together with manuscript material of Lewis and Clark from other sources, including notebooks, letters, maps, etc., and the journals of Charles Floyd and Joseph Whitehouse, now for the first time published in full and exactly as written.* 8 vols. New York: Dodd, Mead, 1904–05.

Wesselius, Allen "Doc." "A Lasting Legacy: The Lewis and Clark Place Names of the Pacific Northwest." *Columbia* Magazine: Part I, 15:1 (spring 2001); Part II, 15:2 (summer 2001); Part III, 15:3 (fall 2001); Part IV, 15:4 (winter 2001). Available on-line. URL: http://wshs.org/lewisandclark/lc-articles.htm. Downloaded on July 12, 2002.

North West Company (Northwest Company)

One of the greatest concerns behind President THOMAS JEFFERSON's initiation of a transcontinental expedition was the hold that GREAT BRITAIN then had on the lucrative FUR TRADE in North America. Should the power and influence of such businesses as HUDSON'S BAY COMPANY and the North West Company extend into the Pacific Northwest, the tenuous U.S. claim on that region would be weakened. Furthermore, the Hudson's Bay and North West companies enjoyed a near-monopoly on trade with the Indian nations of the newly acquired LOUISIANA TERRITORY—trade that Jefferson and others wanted for the United States. One of the expedition's MISSION OBJECTIVES therefore became to invite Indian nations to join in a new trading network with the United States, thereby diminishing the influence of the British companies.

When King Charles II of England gave the Hudson's Bay Company its charter in 1670, FRANCE had already claimed CANADA and established colonies along the St. Lawrence River. Because of the distance between them, the French claims had little adverse effect on England's company, which established a series of posts around Hudson Bay and traded for the furs the Indians brought to them. After FRANCE gave up its claims to Canada in 1763, Hudson's Bay Company could have expanded its activities throughout the territory but was slow in doing so. The opportunity they missed was quickly taken up by others. The French trappers and traders of southern Canada continued their activities and were joined by Scotsmen who initiated important changes in how business was transacted. Taking advantage of Hudson's Bay's passive policy of static depots to which Indians brought furs, the new competitors went directly to the Indians and in so doing began to develop their activities westward and south into the Louisiana Territory.

Soon, however, the French and Scottish traders began to compete among themselves as well as with Hudson's Bay, leading first to conflict and then to a loose agreement on joint interests in 1779. In the winter of 1783–84 this was formalized with the founding of the North West Company, a partnership of Montreal traders in the east and Scottish and French fur traders in the West. Under the leadership of Simon McTavish, the new organization developed effective links with Indian nations and trappers across Canada and south into the GREAT PLAINS. An efficient system for transporting furs was set up whereby traders from the West met supply canoes from Montreal at Fort William on the western edge of Lake Superior. Here they spent several days exchanging furs for trade goods and supplies before turning around and heading back to their starting points. (The MOUNTAIN MEN of the United States would later set up similar rendezvous camps.)

The company also encouraged exploration by men such as ALEXANDER MACKENZIE, the first North American to reach the PACIFIC OCEAN by land in 1793. His example was followed by others, including DAVID THOMPSON, who, after leaving the Hudson's Bay Company and joining the North West Company, surveyed the source of the MISSISSIPPI RIVER in 1798 and the whole length of the COLUMBIA RIVER in 1811.

Although the Hudson's Bay Company fought to win back its trading base by sending representatives to the villages of the MANDAN INDIANS on the upper MISSOURI RIVER, it was the North West Company whom MERIWETHER LEWIS and WILLIAM CLARK found to enjoy the preponderance of Indian trade. When they arrived at the Mandan villages in October 1804, they were met by Hugh McCracken, a regular visitor to the area who was probably a North West employee. Through him they sent a letter to a senior partner of the company, Charles Chaboillez, in which they explained that they were on a government-sponsored expedition "for the purpose of exploring the river Missouri, and the western parts of the continent of North American with a view to the promotion of general science." While they did not mention their ulterior motives, they did stress a U.S. policy of free trade within the territory and invited Chaboillez to come and meet them. Chaboillez replied in a letter delivered by HUGH HENEY (who was apparently associated both with North West and with RÉGIS LOISEL of the Missouri Company). While unwilling to accept their invitation, Chaboillez put the resources of his company at their disposal to obtain trade goods and provisions, an offer the captains declined, perhaps out of national pride. All the same, a number of company traders came to see them, including FRANÇOIS LAROCQUE and CHARLES MACKENZIE, both of whom recorded their visits in journals.

Some years after the expedition, when JOHN JACOB ASTOR established Fort Astoria at the mouth of the COLUMBIA RIVER in 1811, traders from the North West Company were already there. With his post blockaded by the British during the War of 1812, Astor sold it to the rival company in 1814. Meanwhile, under new leadership the Hudson's Bay Company fought hard to regain its old power, and the rivalry became ever more bitter and violent. In 1816, at the Red River Colony in south Manitoba, matters came to a head in a battle in which 22 people were killed. Forced into action, the British government made the two companies amalgamate in 1821. This was clearly the best solution, and, probably because of its historic charter, it was agreed the older Hudson's Bay Company would give its name to the new company. The North West Company was no more.

Further Reading

Bryce, George. *The Remarkable History of the Hudson's Bay Company, Including That of the French Traders of North-western Canada, and of the North-west, XY, and Astor Fur Companies.* 2d ed. New York: B. Franklin, 1968.

Davidson, Gordon Charles. *The North West Company.* New York: Russell & Russell, 1967.

Gottfred, A. "Lewis & Clark: A Canadian Perspective." *Northwest Journal.* Vol. 11: 1–13. Available on-line. URL: http://www.northwestjournal.ca/XI1.htm. Downloaded on February 27, 2002.

Newman, Peter C. *Caesars of the Wilderness.* Markham, Ontario: Viking, 1987.

O'Meara, Walter. *The Savage Country.* Boston: Houghton Mifflin, 1960.

Rich, E. E. *The Fur Trade and the Northwest to 1857.* Toronto: McClelland and Stewart, 1967.

Northwest Passage

For centuries, even before Christopher Columbus made his first attempt to sail westward to Asia and landed on an island in the Caribbean, European powers had hoped to find a direct water route from Europe to the Far East and India without having to take long and dangerous sea voyages around Africa or South America. That there might be a Northeast Passage—either over the North Pole or north of Europe and Asia—was considered, but far more preferable to the minds of many was a route westward through the Northern Hemisphere. There was, however, an obstacle in the way: the American continent. The primary object of the earliest explorers was to find the hoped-for channel from the Atlantic Ocean across northern CANADA to the PACIFIC OCEAN. This dream water route came to be called the Northwest Passage.

In planning the exploration of LOUISIANA TERRITORY and beyond, THOMAS JEFFERSON and MERIWETHER LEWIS also hoped to find an all-water route to the Pacific. Their desired Northwest Passage was one that could be easily navigated through the country, with a limited PORTAGE at the ROCKY MOUNTAINS, and thus prevent having to sail around the tip of South America to reach the west coast. Jefferson's instructions were specific in this regard; Lewis was "to explore the MISSOURI RIVER, and such principal streams of it, as, by it's course and communication with the waters of the Pacific ocean, whether the Columbia, Oregon, Colorado, or any other river, may offer the most direct and practicable water-communication across the continent, for the purposes of commerce." The president's hope was that such a passage by inland rivers, undertaken by shallow-draft transportation, would replace the sea passage, although this was already clearly unlikely.

As it happened, Lewis and Clark failed to find an acceptable water route, although they did succeed in other aspects of their MISSION OBJECTIVES. A possible Northwest Passage was not found in the Arctic until the mid-19th century, nor was it finally traveled until 1969 by a U.S. ice-breaking tanker, the SS *Manhattan.* Meanwhile, in the years following the expedition, the transcontinental railroad was built, and in the early 1900s the Panama Canal created a shortcut for ships traveling from the Atlantic to the Pacific. The Northwest Passage was thus no longer needed; Americans had found their own way.

See also EXPLORATION, EARLY.

Further Reading

Allen, John Logan. *Passage Through the Garden: Lewis and Clark and the Image of the American Northwest.* Urbana: University of Illinois Press, 1975. Reprint, New York: Dover Publications, 1991.

Canadian Arctic Profiles. "Exploration of the Northwest Passage." *Arctic Canada,* Volume 1, Third Edition, 1982. Available on-line. URL: http://collections.ic.gc.ca/arctic/explore/intro.htm. Downloaded on January 25, 2002.

Delgado, James P. *Across the Top of the World: The Quest for the Northwest Passage.* New York: Checkmark Books, 1999.

Wells, Merle. "Lewis & Clark's Water Route to the Northwest: The Exploration That Finally Laid to Rest the Myth of a Northwest Passage." *Columbia* Magazine 8:4 (Winter 1994/95). Available on-line. URL: http://www.wshs.org/lewisandclark/water_route.htm. Downloaded on July 12, 2002.

Ohio River

The head of the Ohio River (so named by the Iroquois Indians) is at the point in PITTSBURGH, Pennsylvania, where the Allegheny and Monongahela Rivers converge. It flows nearly a thousand miles before joining the MISSISSIPPI RIVER at Cairo, Illinois. While the Lewis and Clark Expedition is normally held to have started from CAMP DUBOIS on the Mississippi, it could be argued that the distinction also belongs to Pittsburgh.

On MERIWETHER LEWIS's orders, the expedition's KEEL-BOAT was built at Elizabeth, Pennsylvania, near Pittsburgh. This not only gave him the fastest route to the West but also enabled him to transport the large quantity of SUPPLIES AND EQUIPMENT he had procured in PHILADELPHIA and HARPERS FERRY. The choice of Pittsburgh was sensible. When Lewis and THOMAS JEFFERSON began to plan the expedition, the Ohio was the most important highway in the new United States. It took three days for a coach to travel the 175 miles between New York and Boston along the best roads in the country. It took two days for a coach to do the 100 miles between New York and Philadelphia. South of Washington, D.C., there were no roads available for coaches at all. Travel by water was simple and, with a good current, often the fastest method. For example, on their return journey down the MISSOURI RIVER, PATRICK GASS recorded that the CORPS OF DISCOVERY made up to 90 miles a day in dugout CANOES.

After enduring exasperating delays in the keelboat's completion, Lewis and the seven soldiers who made up its initial crew left Pittsburgh on August 31, 1803, along with the first of two PIROGUES Lewis would purchase. The journey down the Ohio was not an easy one. The lower section of the river was still then frontier country (Ohio achieved statehood on March 31, 1803), and at that time of the year the waters were very low and therefore difficult for the keelboat to navigate as it became caught on snags and sandbanks. On the first day alone, Lewis had to go over the side three times with the rest of the crew and drag the keelboat into clear water. They made only 10 miles that day. The next day the same thing occurred often, and Lewis was forced to hire a farmer's oxen to haul it free. On the third day, the water level was sometimes only six inches deep, and he had to hire more oxen. Not until he reached Wheeling, Virginia (where he bought a second pirogue) on September 9 did things improve, and the party began to average 20–25 miles a day.

At the end of September, Lewis and his crew arrived at Cincinnati, where they stayed a week before moving on. On October 14 they reached the Falls of the Ohio, a 20-foot drop over a two-mile-long series of limestone ledges. These had to be negotiated by hiring local pilots who took the boats through. Thereafter the river gave them no further problems, and the next day they arrived at Clarksville, where Lewis met WILLIAM CLARK and the NINE YOUNG MEN FROM KENTUCKY were enlisted. The now-larger party left Clarksville on October 26, and on November 11 they picked up more recruits at FORT MASSAC, arriving at Cairo and the Mississippi River the same day.

The Ohio does not figure prominently in the story of the Lewis and Clark Expedition, although it had an important part to play. Lewis, Clark, and thousands of other Americans regarded it as the principal highway to the West, a position it was not to lose until the building of the Erie Canal in 1823.

The Ohio River provided the first test of the newly built keelboat. At the time of the expedition, the Ohio was the main highway to the West. *(Library of Congress, Prints and Photographs Division [LC-USW3-030407-D])*

Further Reading

Ambrose, Stephen E. *Undaunted Courage: Meriwether Lewis, Thomas Jefferson, and the Opening of the American West.* New York: Simon and Schuster, 1996.

Ellet, Charles. *The Mississippi and Ohio Rivers.* New York: Arno Press, 1970.

Hulbert, Archer Butler. *Waterways of Western Expansion: The Ohio River and Its Tributaries.* New York: AMS Press, 1971.

Reid, Robert L. *Always a River: The Ohio River and the American Experience.* Bloomington: Indiana University Press, 1991.

oilcloth (oilskin)

Oilcloth (or oilskin) is a generic term for several kinds of cloth treated with oil or other substances to make them waterproof. The Chinese made oilcloth 2,000 years ago, using canvas treated with flaxseed oil. At the time of the Lewis and Clark Expedition, oilcloth was a common component of frontier clothing and traveling gear; it was used for fishermen's and sailors' clothing as well as tarps and covers. For heavy-duty uses, oilcloth would be made of strong material such as canvas or burlap and treated with glue and multiple coats of oil paint. Between each application of paint, the material was rubbed down with pumice.

MERIWETHER LEWIS included oilcloth sheets and bags in his original supply list for the expedition. The sheets of oiled linen were 8 × 12 feet and could serve as both sails during the day and tent covers for SHELTER at night. The CORPS OF DISCOVERY used both the larger sheets and the oilskin bags to protect valuables such as NAVIGATION and other scientific instruments as well as papers and personal supplies from the damaging effects of moisture. They were also used for protection when the captains hid supplies in CACHES along the MISSOURI and other rivers.

Oilcloth eventually became an essential household material, used for such items as tablecloths, rain gear, and carrying bags. Synthetic waterproof materials are more commonly used today for the same purposes, but oilcloth is still made and used for many purposes.

Further Reading

Cutright, Paul Russell. "Lewis has successfully outfitted the Expedition." From *Contributions of Philadelphia to Lewis and Clark History.* Available on-line. URL: http://www.lewisandclarkphila.org/philadelphiacutright37.html. Updated on August 13, 2001.

Old Toby (Toby, Swooping Eagle)

(unknown–unknown) *Shoshone guide*

While SACAGAWEA is often given credit as the Indian who led the Lewis and Clark Expedition across the ROCKY MOUNTAINS to the Pacific coast, in fact she acted as guide only when the expedition passed through her old homeland on the return journey. To cross the Rockies, the CORPS OF DISCOVERY was assisted by Old Toby, a trustworthy and capable Lemhi SHOSHONE Indian who was familiar with the terrain and better equipped to guide them. Some historians, in fact, maintain that the expedition would never have completed its mission without Old Toby.

His full Shoshone name meant "Swooping Eagle," but MERIWETHER LEWIS and WILLIAM CLARK dubbed him Toby, which was an abbreviation of one of his names whose meaning was "furnished . . . white-man brains." Because of his age, he became better known as Old Toby. His presence on the expedition (as well as that of his son) was part of the bargain made with the Shoshone chief CAMEAHWAIT, Sacagawea's brother, from whom the captains also obtained HORSES and geographical information in August 1805. They had reached a crucial stage in the journey and were hoping to take their CANOES down the SALMON RIVER canyon through the mountains to the Columbia River. Old Toby dissuaded them from this and convinced them to follow a better route across the BITTERROOT MOUNTAINS by way of the LOLO TRAIL. To get there, they first had to travel along the north fork of the Salmon River and then cross the LOST TRAIL PASS into the Bitterroot valley, where they met a friendly band of FLATHEAD (Salish) INDIANS at the location that is now ROSS'S HOLE. They then went north along the BITTERROOT RIVER until they arrived at TRAVELERS' REST. Here Old Toby shared some interesting—and dismaying—information: If they traveled due east from this point, they would reach the GREAT FALLS and the MISSOURI RIVER in just four days' time. The route the expedition had followed had taken 53 days. Were it not for this loss of valuable time, the crossing of the Bitterroots might have proven easier.

At Travelers' Rest the corps encountered three Indians (thought by Lewis and Clark to be Flathead, but probably NEZ PERCE INDIANS) who assured them the Lolo Trail across the Bitterroot Mountains could be traversed in a matter of six days. However, when the corps finally made the crossing, it nearly killed them. The trail itself was covered with thick brush and fallen timber, obscuring both the route and Old Toby's memory. Lost, nearly frozen by the cold and snow, and weak with hunger, the company was driven to kill and eat three of their horses. On September 20 Clark and a small group of men riding ahead of the others descended the mountain onto the WEIPPE PRAIRIE, where they met a band of Nez Perce Indians. Two days later the rest of the expedition, including Lewis and Old Toby, followed them safely down. The trek had taken 11 days.

With the Nez Perce now providing assistance in building CANOES and offering guidance for the next part of the journey, Old Toby apparently decided not to continue with the expedition. His decision to leave may also have been prompted by his fear of the rapids on the CLEARWATER RIVER. About October 8 he and his son left quietly, without saying goodbye or collecting his pay. Much later Lewis and Clark would learn that two, or possibly three, other trails across the mountains would prob-

ably have been less arduous. Yet despite the tremendous difficulty of their crossing, Old Toby's advice had been basically sound, and the captains were indebted for his role in the expedition's ultimate triumph. As Lewis later wrote, " . . . we attempted with success those unknown formidable snow clad Mountains on the bare word of a Savage, while 99/100th of his Countrymen assured us that a passage was impracticable."

See also INDIAN GUIDES.

Further Reading

Ronda, James P. *Lewis and Clark among the Indians.* Lincoln and London: University of Nebraska Press, 1984.

Wells, Merle. "The Importance of 'Old Toby.'" From *Lewis & Clark in Idaho.* Available on-line. URL: http://idptv.state.id.us/lc/old-toby.html. Downloaded on May 25, 2001.

Omaha Indians

When MERIWETHER LEWIS prepared for his westward expedition, he packed numerous bags of GIFTS for the Native American nations he expected to encounter. One such bag was earmarked for the Omaha Indians, whom he hoped to bring into the ST. LOUIS-based TRADE network that he was setting up. On August 12, 1804, the expedition passed the gravesite of a renowned Omaha chief named Blackbird, near present-day Macy, Nebraska. Sergeant JOHN ORDWAY was dispatched with a small party of men to find the Omaha and invite them to a council. When they entered the village of Tonwantonga, however, it was empty; the Omaha were away hunting BUFFALO (as were other Indian nations in the area). This was a great disappointment to Lewis and Clark, who had also wanted to broker a peace between the Omaha and the OTOE (Oto) INDIANS. This would now be impossible.

When they did finally meet some Omaha, it was under unexpected circumstances. Several weeks later the CORPS OF DISCOVERY encountered a band of TETON LAKOTA INDIANS (Teton Sioux). Among this band were a number of Omaha prisoners, mostly women and children—"a retched and Dejected looking people," wrote Clark. "The Squars appear low & Corse but this is an unfavorable time to judge of them." Failing in his attempt to get the Teton to release the prisoners, he sent PIERRE CRUZATTE, who spoke Omaha, to talk to them. In this way the captains learned that the Teton were planning to rob the expedition, which put the corps on their guard. They were eventually able to break free of the Teton and continue up the Missouri.

The Omaha were in fact a prouder people than those Clark had seen. *Omaha* means "those who go upstream" or "against the current." In the centuries prior to the expedition's arrival, the nation had migrated west from the OHIO RIVER valley, and bands of Omaha ended up in Minnesota, Missouri, Nebraska, Iowa, and the Dakotas. By the time of Lewis and Clark, however, most Omaha were to be found in the area of Nebraska where they also met the Otoe and MISSOURI INDIANS. The Omaha were once a large and strong nation, but a smallpox epidemic in 1800–01 had greatly reduced their numbers. They were frequently at war with the Sioux (Dakota, Lakota, Nakota), and it was following one of their battles that Lewis and Clark had met the Omaha prisoners.

Primarily farmers and fishers, the introduction of HORSES allowed the Omaha to become hunters of game as well. They had a structured class system that included chiefs, priests, physicians, and commoners, and there were many societies, both open and exclusive, that retained responsibilities for various tribal functions and sacred objects. During the winter hunting season, the nation lived in TIPIS made of BUFFALO skins and cedar poles. In the summer their housing was earthen lodges that stood about 8 feet high and had dome-shaped roofs.

In 1854 the Omaha ceded land east of the Missouri to the U.S. government and settled on a reservation in northeastern Nebraska. They sold the northern part of the reservation in 1865 for the use of the Winnebago, and today they still reside on the 31,148-acre Omaha Reservation.

Further Reading

Ronda, James P. *Lewis and Clark among the Indians.* Lincoln: University of Nebraska Press, 1984.

Waldman, Carl. *Encyclopedia of Native American Tribes.* Revised ed. New York: Checkmark Books, 1999.

One Eye (Le Borgne, LaBorge) (unknown–unknown)
Hidatsa Indian chief

Late in October 1804, the CORPS OF DISCOVERY arrived at the villages of the MANDAN and the HIDATSA VILLAGES, near the confluence of the MISSOURI RIVER with the KNIFE RIVER. There were three Hidatsa villages, of which the most remote was also the largest, containing more than 130 earth lodges and 450 warriors. Called Menetarra, it was led by a formidable chieftain named One Eye.

The Hidatsa were a more aggressive nation than were the Mandan, and their fierceness was exemplified in One Eye (or Le Borgne, as he is called in some sources). In his edition of the Lewis and Clark JOURNALS, scholar Gary Moulton writes: "Traders' and travelers' accounts agree in describing him as ugly, brutal, lecherous, bad-tempered, and homicidal, while generally acknowledging his leadership ability and prowess in war." According to James Ronda, stories of One Eye's brutality may have been exaggerated, although there was never any doubt about his military capabilities and innate shrewdness.

On October 29 Captains MERIWETHER LEWIS and WILLIAM CLARK had the first of their councils with the Mandan and the Hidatsa. Although several chiefs from both nations were in attendance, two of the most important were not: BIG WHITE of the Mandan and One Eye of the Hidatsa, who was then out HUNTING. The Hidatsa were well represented by another chief, Caltarcota, but it was clear that antagonism between the Mandan-Hidatsa and the Arikara was going to

threaten the peace and the trading network that Lewis and Clark were trying to establish. Following the council, the Hidatsa never responded to the U.S. proposals, making further contact necessary. Consequently, on November 25 Lewis rode out from FORT MANDAN with RENÉ JESSAUME and TOUSSAINT CHARBONNEAU. Yet when they arrived at Menetarra, Lewis tried to speak to two of the lesser chiefs and made no effort to seek out either One Eye or Caltarcota, an action that historians find strange.

While both Mandan and Hidatsa were welcome at the fort throughout the corps' winter there, visits from the Hidatsa were rare. Lewis and Clark felt frustrated by their inability to establish diplomatic relations with One Eye, who had openly expressed his contempt for them and stated that he would come to the fort only if he received the captains' largest flag. However, on March 9, 1805, he finally paid a call. Lewis was his host, showing him around the fort and allowing him to examine his airgun, spyglass, and quadrant—all "Great Medicine" to the chief. When Lewis learned that One Eye had not received GIFTS that had been sent to him the previous October, the captain bestowed a number of special presents, including a flag. The chief later spotted YORK and, astonished, attempted to rub the slave's blackness off his skin. This scene was later recorded on canvas by the artist Charles M. Russell.

Despite One Eye's friendly visit, Lewis's hope to establish cordial relations with the Hidatsa and bring them into the U.S. trading network proved fruitless. The powerful chief showed no interest in discussing matters of diplomacy, and it appears that his call at the fort was largely a social one, made out of curiosity. Matters seemed to change, though, when the explorers returned to the Mandan-Hidatsa villages in August 1806. Another council was convened with a number of chiefs—and this time One Eye appeared. By this time, according to James Ronda, the powerful chief had realized that "some accommodation might be necessary with the persistent strangers from downriver." One Eye listened attentively as Clark presented the American proposals for peace and trade but noted that any idea of an American-brokered peace among nations along the Missouri was made dubious by the presence of the TETON LAKOTA INDIANS (Teton Sioux), who were unlikely to abandon their raids and would continue to kill Mandan and Hidatsa. Indeed, it would not be until the Teton Lakota were suppressed that any Hidatsa chief would consider a visit to Washington to meet THOMAS JEFFERSON.

On August 16, 1806, when One Eye arrived uninvited at the expedition's camp, Clark made one more effort to convert him to the American cause by giving him one of the expedition's swivel guns. Though delighted with the gift, the chief still made no commitment to the captains, who were finally forced to accept the failure of their diplomatic efforts with the Hidatsa.

In 1813 One Eye's power in his village ended, and he was forced out. Although he attempted to establish another Hidatsa community, he was killed by the Hidatsa chief Red Shield.

Further Reading

Lewis & Clark in North Dakota. "Personal Profiles: Profile of Three Chiefs." Available on-line. URL: http://www.ndlewisandclark.com/prfiles.html. Downloaded on February 2, 2002.

Moulton, Gary E., ed. *The Journals of the Lewis and Clark Expedition.* 13 vols. Lincoln: University of Nebraska Press, 1983–2001.

Ronda, James P. *Lewis and Clark among the Indians.* Lincoln: University of Nebraska Press, 1984.

Ordway, John (ca. 1775–ca. 1817) *sergeant in the permanent party*

Unlike many others in the CORPS OF DISCOVERY, Sergeant John Ordway was from New England and had benefited from a good education prior to joining the U.S. Army. He was recruited for the expedition from the army post at KASKASKIA, Illinois. Although he was not officially placed on the payroll until January 1, 1804, he began his duties before that date, helping in the organization of the corps's winter camp on Wood River.

As a sergeant, Ordway held responsibility for one of the expedition's three squads, in addition to being placed in charge of the men at CAMP DUBOIS whenever MERIWETHER LEWIS and WILLIAM CLARK were absent. Although highly trusted by the captains, Ordway's authority was not always respected by the privates, particularly JOHN COLTER and JOHN SHIELDS, both of whom refused to obey his orders and threatened his life in separate incidents. This happened not long after a previous occasion when Colter and three others had defied Ordway's orders to sneak off to a whiskey shop to get drunk. At that time they were confined to quarters for 10 days, but the threats against the sergeant were a more serious matter. Consequently, Colter and Shields were court-martialed for mutiny but then forgiven and allowed back into the corps. They gave Sergeant Ordway no further trouble after that.

Once the expedition was underway, Ordway's responsibilities increased to include the meting out of each squad's provisions on a daily basis. He also participated some of the corps's COURT-MARTIALS. It was Ordway who caught ALEXANDER WILLARD sleeping at his post and turned in the private for disciplinary action; and it was Ordway who subsequently stated the charge against Willard: "Lying down and Sleeping on his post whilst a Sentinal." The private was found guilty and sentenced to 100 lashes a day for four days. Ordway later presided over the trial of JOHN NEWMAN for mutiny.

Like the other sergeants, Ordway kept a journal during the expedition, and as an educated man he was able to provide well-written, vivid descriptions of the journey. He was the only member of the expedition who wrote every single day of the journey. Aware of the expedition's importance, he wrote to his parents beforehand, "If we make Great Discoveries as we expect, the united States, has promised to make us Great Rewards more than we are promised, &c." His depictions of the Native Americans whom they encountered provide important ethnographic details of the Indians of that time, including descriptions of their customs, foods, LANGUAGES, and even games. He was often approving of Indian warriors and women, commenting in his journal on their appearance, manners, and helpfulness to the corps.

Ordway was also a faithful recorder of the WEATHER as well as of ANIMALS seen by the expedition. In September 1804 they encountered a new species of mammal that lived in burrows underground. It was given various names by the journalists, but Ordway called it a PRAIRIE DOG, the name by which it is known today. After leaving the villages of the MANDAN and the HIDATSA INDIANS, he wrote of his astonishment at the sight of the GREAT PLAINS and the abundance of good HUNTING they found there: "The Game is gitting so pleanty and tame in this country that Some of the party clubbed them out of their way."

During the return trip in 1806, at TRAVELERS' REST the captains decided to split the expedition into smaller parties, primarily for purposes of exploration. Ordway was placed in charge of 10 men whose mission was to descend the JEFFERSON RIVER and MISSOURI RIVER in CANOES to GREAT FALLS, where they were to meet three others left there by Captain Lewis and assist with the repair and PORTAGE of canoes and supplies that had been cached by the falls the previous year. He carried out his mission successfully and subsequently met Lewis and three other men—who had gone off to explore the MARIAS RIVER—at almost the exact time they had planned to meet.

Following the expedition, Ordway, Sergeant PATRICK GASS, and Privates ROBERT FRAZIER and FRANÇOIS LABICHE were among the party that accompanied Lewis and MANDAN chief BIG WHITE to Washington for celebrations. He later sold his journal to Lewis and Clark for $300 and, leaving the army, returned home to New Hampshire briefly to visit his parents. He then moved to Missouri, where he married and farmed the land near New Madrid that he had earned as a reward for his service. He also acquired the land warrants of WILLIAM WERNER and JEAN-BAPTISTE LEPAGE and subsequently became quite prosperous. By 1817 both he and his wife Grace were dead, leaving no children. Ordway's journal was lost for some time, but it was found and published in 1916.

Further Reading

Clarke, Charles G. *The Men of the Lewis and Clark Expedition: A Biographical Roster of the Fifty-One Members and a Composite Diary of Their Activities from All Known Sources.* 1970. Reprint, Lincoln: Bison Books, University of Nebraska Press, 2002.

Moulton, Gary, ed. *The Journals of the Lewis and Clark Expedition: The Journals of John Ordway, May 14, 1804–September 23, 1806, and Charles Floyd, May 14–August 18, 1804.* Lincoln: University of Nebraska Press, 1996.

North Dakota Lewis & Clark Bicentennial Foundation. *Members of the Corps of Discovery.* Bismarck, N.Dak.: United Printing and Mailing, 2000.

PBS Online. *Lewis and Clark: Inside the Corps of Discovery:* "Sergeant John Ordway." Available on-line. URL: http://www.pbs.org/lewisandclark/inside/jordw.html. Downloaded on May 18, 2001.

Oregon Territory

When MERIWETHER LEWIS and WILLIAM CLARK made their epic journey, the name *Oregon Territory* had not yet been officially adopted for the area drained by the COLUMBIA and SNAKE Rivers—an area that now comprises the states of Washington, Oregon, Idaho, and part of British Columbia. The phrase *Oregon Territory* was first used by the soldier and adventurer Major Robert Rogers in 1765 when he proposed an expedition to the Northwest Coast; the name was apparently adapted from the Indian word *Ouragon*. Rogers had heard, probably through Indian contacts, of a great river (the Columbia) running west into the Pacific and adopted the term to described the territory around it. It was not until well into the 19th century, when SPAIN, Russia, GREAT BRITAIN, and the United States all laid claim to the territory that the name came to be used officially; it was also called Oregon Country.

While it is known that the Spanish explorer Bartolomé Ferrolo had sailed up the coast in 1543, probably as far as the 42nd parallel, little was made of his journey. In fact, not until 1775 did another Spaniard, Bruno Heceta, land at Point Grenville (100 miles north of the Columbia) and claim it for Spain. Three years later the English sailor Captain James Cook sailed up the 48th parallel, but it was American trade that aroused international interest and claims to the region. Soon after the American Revolution, American ships sailed around Cape Horn to trade cloth and trinkets with the Indians of the Pacific Northwest for OTTER pelts and other furs. They then sailed to China to exchange these for tea and other luxury goods.

It was while engaged in such trade that the American captain ROBERT GRAY sailed into the mouth of the Columbia River in 1792. While this gave the United States some claim to the region, it was countered by ALEXANDER MACKENZIE's expedition the next year—the first overland expedition to cross the North American continent. The LOUISIANA PURCHASE gave the United States a common boundary with Oregon Territory, but this was of little practical value if it could not be reached by land. It was the fact that the British had already done so that made a U.S. expedition so important to President THOMAS JEFFERSON.

In the years following Lewis and Clark's journey, Britain and the United States shared the exploration and development of Oregon Territory. In 1811 DAVID THOMPSON surveyed the Columbia River for Britain, the same year that JOHN JACOB ASTOR set up his trading post at Astoria. In 1818 the Anglo-American Convention agreed to a 10-year joint occupation of the territory, and claims were made by the United States, Britain, Spain, and Russia. The latter two countries dropped their claims in 1819 and 1824, respectively. However, with the arrival of American settlers in the territory, starting with the Great Migration of 1843, negotiations began to set a border between the United States and British Columbia that was agreeable to both countries. The Oregon Treaty of 1846 finally settled the dispute, and the present border was fixed at the 49th parallel. In 1859 Oregon was admitted to the Union as the nation's 33rd state; Washington followed in 1889.

Further Reading

Ross, Alexander. *Adventures of the First Settlers on the Oregon or Columbia River.* 1849. Reprint edited by Milo M. Quaife. Chicago: Lakeside Press, 1922.

Walker, Dale. *Pacific Destiny: The Three Century Journey to Oregon Country.* New York: Forge Books, 2000.

Oregon Trail

Even before MERIWETHER LEWIS and WILLIAM CLARK returned from their historic expedition, further exploration and westward migration had begun. Aside from explorers such as ZEBULON PIKE, the first to follow Lewis and Clark were MOUNTAIN MEN such as Jedediah Smith and traders sent by businessmen such as JOHN JACOB ASTOR, all seeking to capitalize on the rapidly growing FUR TRADE. By the 1840s, however, farmers and others seeking new lives began to move west in ever increasing numbers. The route many of them took was known as the Oregon Trail.

Stretching for 2,000 miles from the Missouri River to Oregon's Willamette Valley, the trail was not a clearly defined road so much as a general route to the West, with many alternate cut-offs and parallel trails. Portions of it overlapped with other trails, most notably the easternmost section of the Santa Fe Trail. From its starting point in Independence, Missouri, the Oregon Trail followed the PLATTE and North Platte Rivers through Kansas, Nebraska, and Wyoming and then proceeded through South Pass in the ROCKY MOUNTAINS and into Idaho. At Fort Hall, Idaho, pioneers had to choose whether to continue northwest on the Oregon Trail or west on the California Trail. Those who selected Oregon as their destination followed the SNAKE RIVER to the Blue Mountains, from which they turned west to Fort Walla Walla and finally down to the Willamette Valley by way of the COLUMBIA RIVER. The end of the Oregon Trail is usually accepted to be Oregon City. The trip could take as long as six months for most pioneers, and for all it was a journey that tested their strength and endurance.

The route of the Oregon Trail was not the same as that taken by Lewis and Clark. However, expedition veterans JOHN COLTER and GEORGE DROUILLARD were among those mountain men who explored other areas of the West and Northwest, blazing trails that others would follow. In 1812 Astor employee Robert Stuart discovered South Pass, which eventually became the most popular passage through the Rockies. About the same time, another Astor employee, Wilson Price Hunt, traveled from St. Louis to Astoria, Oregon, using a route that closely followed what was to become the Oregon Trail.

In 1824 Jedediah Smith led a party through South Pass. By 1830 he and other mountain men had begun to lead larger expeditions into the West. In 1836 missionaries Marcus and Narcissa Whitman were the first pioneers to follow the trail to Oregon, sending home reports that attracted other settlers from the East. The first organized wagon train to pass over the trail arrived in Oregon in 1842, and by the following year, the "Great Migration" had begun. In 1843 some 1,750 pioneers traveled the route; the following year that figure jumped to 3,000, and with the discovery of gold in the late 1840s thousands upon thousands traveled along the trail. The heaviest period of migration occurred throughout the 1850s and continued into the 1860s, until the advent of railroads—a quicker and easier way to travel—made the Oregon Trail obsolete. By the 1870s the trail had largely become abandoned, although some continued to use it and promote it. The last wagon passed over the trail in 1914. Today some parts of the trail survive, with the ruts of wagon wheels still bearing testament to a wave of westward movement that began with Lewis and Clark.

See also EXPLORATION, LATER; WESTWARD EXPANSION.

Further Reading

Hill, William E. *The Oregon Trail: Yesterday and Today.* Caldwell, Idaho: Caxton Press, 1987.

Parkman, Francis J. *The Oregon Trail.* Edited by David Levin. Reprint, New York: Viking Press, 1989.

Rollins, Philip Ashton, ed. *The Discovery of the Oregon Trail: Robert Stuart's Narratives of His Overland Trip Eastward from Astoria in 1812–13.* New York: Edward Eberstadt, 1935.

Trinklein, Mike, and Steve Boettcher. "The Oregon Trail." Available on-line. URL: http://www.isu.edu/~trinmich/Oregontrail.html. Downloaded on January 15, 2002.

organization of the expedition party

By March 31, 1804, members of the CORPS OF DISCOVERY's permanent and temporary parties had been chosen and organized into three squads, each headed by a sergeant. The following day Captains MERIWETHER LEWIS and WILLIAM CLARK drew up detachment orders: "The commanding officers did yesterday proceed to take the necessary inlistments, and select the Detachment destined for the Expedition through the interior of the Continent of North America, and have accordingly selected the persons herein after mentioned, as those which are to Constitute their Permanent Detachment." The orders then went on to list the members of each squad, as follows.

First Squad: Sergeant NATHANIEL PRYOR; Privates JOHN COLLINS, GEORGE GIBSON, HUGH HALL, THOMAS PROCTOR HOWARD, GEORGE SHANNON, JOHN SHIELDS, PETER WEISER, JOSEPH WHITEHOUSE.

Second Squad: Sergeant CHARLES FLOYD; Privates JOSEPH FIELD, REUBIN FIELD, ROBERT FRAZIER, PATRICK GASS, HUGH McNEAL, JOHN NEWMAN, JOHN B. THOMPSON, RICHARD WARFINGTON (actually a corporal), RICHARD WINDSOR.

Third Squad: Sergeant JOHN ORDWAY; Privates JOHN BOLEY, WILLIAM BRATTON, JOHN COLTER, SILAS GOODRICH, JOHN POTTS, MOSES REED, JOHN ROBERTSON, WILLIAM WERNER, ALEXANDER HAMILTON WILLARD (listed as Williams on the detachment orders).

The orders further divided each squad "into two Messes, at the head of one of which the commanding Sergeant Shall

Preside." The above list should not, however, be regarded as final. Rather, it was designed for administrative purposes to set out the expedition's initial organization and to establish proper military order and DISCIPLINE, in keeping with the corps's role as a unit of the U.S. Army. On May 26, 1804, further detachment orders outlined the specific roles of the sergeants and other members of the party. They also specified that "The guard shall hereafter consist of one sergeant and six privates and engagés" and noted arrangements for the distribution of provisions.

Additions and changes to the party over time were inevitable, and thus the detachment orders were subject to change. Consequently several other men not mentioned in the orders were among the party that left CAMP DUBOIS on May 14, 1804. Warfington, Frazier, and Boley were actually members of the temporary party who, along with Privates JOHN DAME, EBENEZER TUTTLE, and ISAAC WHITE, were intended to go only as far as the villages of the MANDAN and the HIDATSA INDIANS, returning to ST. LOUIS with the KEELBOAT in spring 1805. A number of ENGAGÉS were hired for the same purpose, and PIERRE CRUZATTE and FRANÇOIS LABICHE were recruited at ST. CHARLES, just two days after the corps left Wood River.

When Moses Reed deserted the expedition in August 1805, Frazier was appointed to his place in the permanent party, while later that month Patrick Gass was elected to replace Charles Floyd as sergeant after the latter died. In October, when John Newman was discharged, fur trader JOHN-BAPTISTE LEPAGE was enlisted at FORT MANDAN to take his place.

The expedition also included civilian personnel. Clark's slave YORK and GEORGE DROUILLARD, the party's interpreter, had been with the corps from the start, while another interpreter, TOUSSAINT CHARBONNEAU, joined them at FORT MANDAN. York and Charbonneau were treated as military personnel and required to perform guard duty and other chores; as the expedition's primary hunter, Drouillard was exempt from such duty. Charbonneau also brought with him his wife SACAGAWEA and their baby son JEAN BAPTISTE CHARBONNEAU, often listed on expedition rosters as corps members.

While the nature of their mission allowed for some flexibility (see DEMOCRACY ON THE EXPEDITION), the captains still maintained the routine of a military unit. Squads ate with their own messes, while the captains ate separately with Drouillard, Charbonneau, and Sacagawea. The latter two also slept in the captains' tent so as to keep the sole woman separate from the men.

Once the expedition entered the wilderness of the LOUISIANA TERRITORY, the corps's organization became fluid, based on the specialized skills and abilities of each individual. The unit often split into small groups, very different from the original organization, based on the circumstances in which they found themselves. Some men were better hunters or fishermen, some were carpenters or blacksmiths, and others were skilled watermen or scouts. Though employed on a variety of tasks by day, they returned to their own mess in camp at night; cooked, ate, and slept with their own squads; and did guard duty as they would in any other unit in the U.S. Army. Even when the expedition had subdivided into five parties during the return journey, each man knew what was expected of him and executed his role accordingly. The basis of sound military routine, coupled with the captains' remarkable LEADERSHIP, was an essential element of the expedition's success.

See also SKILLS ON THE EXPEDITION.

Further Reading

Ambrose, Stephen E. *Undaunted Courage: Meriwether Lewis, Thomas Jefferson, and the Opening of the American West.* New York: Simon and Schuster, 1996.

Clarke, Charles G. *The Men of the Lewis and Clark Expedition: A Biographical Roster of the Fifty-One Members and a Composite Diary of Their Activities from All Known Sources.* 1970. Reprint, Lincoln: Bison Books, University of Nebraska Press, 2002.

Hawke, David Freeman. *Those Tremendous Mountains: The Story of the Lewis and Clark Expedition.* New York: W. W. Norton & Company, 1998.

Large, Arlen. "'Additions to the Party': How an Expedition Grew and Grew." *We Proceeded On* 16, no. 1 (February 1990): 4–11.

National Park Service. "Lewis and Clark at Wood River 1803–1804, Part II." Available on-line. URL: http://www.nps.gov/jeff/L&cWood2.htm. Downloaded on September 14, 2001.

Osage Indians

After the transfer of LOUISIANA TERRITORY had taken place, President THOMAS JEFFERSON wrote to MERIWETHER LEWIS with additional instructions for the expedition. Lewis was to make clear to all Indian nations he met that they had a new father—Jefferson—who now held sovereignty over them. Lewis was also to invite the chief of the Osage Indians to come to Washington to meet this new father. Lewis proceeded to make the arrangements for that trip, inviting several Osage chiefs and enlisting fur trader PIERRE CHOUTEAU to accompany the delegation.

After numerous delays, Chouteau and 14 Osage finally set off from ST. LOUIS on May 19, 1804, arriving in Washington on July 11. There Jefferson greeted them, pronounced them "the finest men we have ever seen," and pressed upon them the message that Lewis and Clark were beginning to urge on other Indians further west: that they were now Jefferson's "children" and would do well to enter into TRADE and peaceful coexistence with their white brothers.

Though they did not realize it at the time, the Osage Indians were the first to hear what was in essence a forecast of U.S. imperialism to come, even though Jefferson had said, "No wrong will ever be done to you by our nation." The Indians were treated like royalty while they were in Washington, and when they returned home to Missouri in the fall, they were full of self-importance and, for the time being, of praise for their white father in Washington.

The Osage Indians were a seminomadic people who lived in western Missouri in two primary groupings: the Great Osage along the Osage River and the Little Osage along the MISSOURI RIVER. Primarily gardeners and foragers, they also hunted BUF-

FALO and other game at various times throughout the year. While the men hunted, the women butchered the animals, dried or smoked the meat, prepared the hides, gathered wild plants, and tended gardens of CORN, beans, squash, and pumpkins. Surplus goods, including meat and hides, were exchanged with other Indian nations or to European traders. As a result of such trade, during the 18th century the Osage acquired guns and HORSES.

Osage communities were organized into two divisions called the Sky People and the Earth People. Villages were laid out with houses that sheltered several families on either side of a main road running east and west. Clans of the Sky People lived on the north side of the road, while those of the Earth people lived on the south side. A council called the Little Old Men made the laws and settled tribal disagreements.

Following the expedition, Meriwether Lewis had further dealings with the Osage while he was governor of the LOUISIANA TERRITORY. In 1808 the Great Osage, rebelling against increasing encroachment on their lands, began to raid property, killing cattle, burning homes, and otherwise flouting the authority of the U.S. government. Lewis's first action was to encourage other nations to fight the Great Osage and to request men and ammunition to send a force against them. However, Secretary of War HENRY DEARBORN believed Lewis was overdramatizing the situation and forbade him to raise such a force. Problems with the Osage only intensified after that, and eventually Lewis enlisted Pierre Chouteau to negotiate a new treaty with them. Agreement was finally reached on land for the Osage and trade relationships. The treaty was adopted on November 10, 1808, and ratified by the U.S. Senate the following April.

Further Osage land cessions were made in 1818, 1825, 1839, and 1865. In 1870 an Osage reservation was established in former hunting grounds near what is now Pawhuska, Oklahoma. After oil was discovered on the reservation in 1896 and attempts by non-Indians to gain control of mineral rights were successfully fought off, many Osage acquired wealth and prestige. Others, however, continued to farm their lands for a living. There are now about 10,000 Osage listed on the tribal roll.

Further Reading

Chapman, Carl H. *The Origin of the Osage Indian Tribe.* New York: Garland Pub., Inc., 1974.

Ronda, James P. *Lewis and Clark among the Indians.* Lincoln: University of Nebraska Press, 1984.

Waldman, Carl. *Encyclopedia of Native American Tribes.* Revised ed. New York: Checkmark Books, 1999.

Otoe Indians (Oto Indians)

In late July 1804, after the Lewis and Clark Expedition had passed the mouth of the PLATTE RIVER, they began to search for the Indians whom they had been told inhabited that region around the MISSOURI RIVER. On July 23 GEORGE DROUILLARD and PIERRE CRUZATTE were sent to locate the Otoe (Oto) and Pawnee Indians, but they found only empty villages; the

Indians were all away hunting BUFFALO. However, on July 28 Drouillard met a MISSOURI INDIAN, one of a small band that had attached itself to the Otoe; this Indian was sent back to invite the Missouri and the Otoe chiefs to a council. The CORPS OF DISCOVERY then continued upriver and set up camp at COUNCIL BLUFF (just north of today's Fort Calhoun), where they waited to hold the first of their COUNCILS WITH INDIANS.

The Otoe Indians had once been part of a larger nation living in the Great Lakes region that included the Winnebago, the Ioway, and the Missouri Indians. Several splits had taken place as bands moved in a southwesterly direction toward the Missouri River. According to tribal legend, the final split occurred when the son of one chief seduced the daughter of another. The band led by the boy's father moved northward up the Missouri, settling south of the Platte River in what is now southeastern Nebraska. Because of the boy's behavior, this band was called the Otoe (which Lewis and Clark as well as some historians have spelled *Oto*), meaning "lechers." The band of the girl's father stayed where they were and became the Missouri (now Missouria) Indians.

Originally farmers, the Otoe retained some of their agricultural habits and maintained permanent villages, although they also took on some characteristics of the PLAINS INDIANS and became seminomadic BUFFALO hunters. Their earliest contact with white explorers was in 1673, when they met Jacques Marquette and Louis Joliet. By the time the CORPS OF DISCOVERY met them, they were well accustomed to dealing with French and British traders, but Lewis and Clark brought them news of changes to come.

Toward sunset on August 2, 1804, the captains received a party of Indians that included six Otoe and Missouri headmen as well as a French interpreter (identified by Clark only as "Fairfong"). After welcoming the Indians, Lewis and Clark gave them some roasted meat and other foods and then invited them to a council the next day. Missing from the delegation were Otoe chief LITTLE THIEF and Missouri chief BIG HORSE, who were still away hunting. Nevertheless, the council of August 3 gave Lewis and Clark a chance to practice the diplomacy that they were to exercise numerous times throughout the journey.

To begin, the soldiers, attired in full dress uniform, put on a parade for the Indians, complete with military drills and firing of rifles. Lewis then addressed the Otoe and the Missouri, telling them of the new American sovereignty in the LOUISIANA TERRITORY and advising them they had a "great chief" in Washington (THOMAS JEFFERSON) who would "now form one common family with us." After explaining what the expedition was doing, he then counseled them to make peace with their OMAHA and Pawnee neighbors and to enter into trade with the merchants in ST. LOUIS, stressing the benefits of doing so. He concluded by inviting the chiefs to travel to Washington and handed out GIFTS and medals.

According to PATRICK GASS, those headmen in attendance seemed "well pleased" with the news of the change in government. They were apparently hopeful that the St. Louis merchants would be a more reliable source of trade goods than the French or the British traders had been. Although Clark

declared himself unimpressed with the headmen's replies, he and Lewis both left the council feeling confident that the Otoe could be brought into the trading system that they were proposing.

Eager to meet Little Thief, Lewis made up a special bag of presents and had it sent to the chief along with a copy of his speech. After Private MOSES REED deserted the expedition, the captains sent GEORGE DROUILLARD and a small party out on a twofold mission to find and bring back both Reed and Little Thief. They did so, returning to camp on August 18 with Reed, Little Thief, and Big Horse. After attending to Reed, who was court-martialed and made to run the gauntlet, the captains held a council with the chiefs, repeating what had been said in the previous council. If they had hoped for a positive response, it was not forthcoming. The Otoe were interested more in the goods they could obtain from the expedition than in discussing peace with the Omaha—they preferred to leave that to the white men—and they were extremely unhappy with the gifts they were given. Not even a demonstration of the expedition's FIREARMS impressed them. The only concession the captains managed to obtain was Little Thief's agreement to go to Washington the next spring.

The captains' council with the Otoe and Missouri set the pattern for those they were to have with other Indian nations. They hoped for acceptance of and compliance with the schemes for trade and peace that they were proposing, whereas the Indians were expecting better gifts and higher quality trade goods. Their interests thus diverging, they could only talk at cross purposes, and both sides departed unhappy with the results of the council.

With the increased migration of settlers into the West, the Otoe were forced off their lands, like so many other nations. After joining permanently with the Missouri in 1829, they subsequently ceded thousands of acres in Nebraska, Missouri, and Iowa. In the mid-1850s they received a tract of land in Kansas, of which they sold the western part in 1876 and 1879 and finally the remainder in 1881 when they moved to the Indian Territory. Today the combined Otoe-Missouria Tribe holds trust lands in the Red Rock region of Oklahoma, where they sponsor a major powwow every July.

Further Reading

Edmunds, R. David. *The Otoe-Missouria People.* Phoenix: Indian Tribal Series, 1976.
Jackson, Donald. "Lewis and Clark among the Oto." *Nebraska History* 41 (1960): 237–248.
Ronda, James P. *Lewis and Clark among the Indians.* Lincoln: University of Nebraska Press, 1984.
Waldman, Carl. *Encyclopedia of Native American Tribes.* Revised ed. New York: Checkmark Books, 1999.

otters (sea otters)

Otters in the context of the Lewis and Clark Expedition refer to sea otters, which are found in the North PACIFIC OCEAN up to the Bering Straits. Larger and more heavily built than the

European otter, a sea otter is unlike any other marine mammal in possessing no blubber to keep it warm. It relies instead on a remarkably thick fur coat, which led to its becoming the skin most sought after by 18th- and 19th-century fur traders. First found and caught by Russians in the 1740s off Bering Island, news of the quality of its fur quickly spread, and it was hunted to extinction in the Aleutian Islands and the Bering Straits by 1792.

It is difficult to appreciate today the greed for furs that dominated much of the world's trade in the 18th and much of the 19th centuries. When MERIWETHER LEWIS and WILLIAM CLARK met three trappers coming down the MISSOURI RIVER at the start of their expedition in 1804, the trappers' single PIROGUE held furs that the captains estimated to be worth $900. The same furs would be sold for $9,000 in New York and 10 times as much again in China. The whole civilized world wanted furs, and the Pacific Northwest was the major source of what they wanted. And of all these furs, that of the sea otter was among the most valuable.

The expedition came across sea otter pelts during their winter at FORT CLATSOP (1805–06), and their JOURNALS make it clear that the CHINOOK INDIANS fully realized their value.

The prices the Indians asked for sea otter furs were far higher than for any other skins. Another possible reason for the high price, even then, may have been the otters' growing scarcity. Although Lewis and Clark saw many skins and bought some to bring home with them, there is no record of their seeing a live sea otter.

By the beginning of the 20th century, the sea otter had been hunted nearly to extinction. In 1912 it became a protected species by international treaty, and the current population is estimated to be more than 5,000.

Further Reading

Burroughs, Raymond Darwin, ed. *The Natural History of the Lewis and Clark Expedition.* East Lansing: Michigan State University Press, 1995.

Jameson, Ronald J. "Translocated Sea Otter Populations off the Oregon and Washington Coasts." Available on-line. URL: http://biology.usgs.gov/s+t/SNT/noframe/pn175.htm. Downloaded on April 14, 2001.

Nickerson, Roy. *Sea Otters: A Natural History and Guide.* San Francisco: Chronicle Books, 1989.

P

Pacific Ocean (Western Sea)

Great joy in camp we are in view of the Ocian, this great Pacific Ocean which we been so long anxious to see. And the roreing or noise made by the waves brakeing on the rockey shores (as I suppose) maybe heard distictly.

　　　　　　　　　　　—William Clark, November 7, 1805

Although it was not actually the Pacific Ocean the expedition was hearing but a bay several miles inland, the excitement of the CORPS OF DISCOVERY at reaching it was understandable. For more than 4,000 miles, they had traveled through unknown territory with just one goal: to reach the Pacific Ocean. Now that goal was in sight at last. In his field notes, WILLIAM CLARK recapitulated his feelings when he wrote: "Ocian in view! O! the joy." His enthusiasm for the ocean would, however, change during the long, miserable stay at FORT CLATSOP: "I have not Seen one pacific day Since my arrival in its vicinity, and its waters are . . . tempestous and horiable."

The Pacific Ocean, also known in the expedition's time as the Western Sea, is the largest body of water in the world, occupying a third of the Earth's surface (69.4 million square miles). In 1513 Spanish conquistador Vasco Núñez de Balboa became the first European to reach the Pacific overland when he crossed Central America. Subsequently, Ferdinand Magellan was the first European to sail its waters during his circumnavigation of the world in 1519–22.

While Dutch ships sailed around Africa and India to the East Indies in the late 16th and early 17th centuries, the west coast of North America remained largely unexplored. The Spaniard Bartolomé Ferrolo sailed up past modern California in 1543, as did the British captain Francis Drake on his circumnavigation of 1577–80. However, although many Spanish settlements were established on the Pacific coast throughout the 18th century, it was not until after the American Revolution that trading became common on the western shore.

Part of the reason for this was the lack of a convenient way to get from Europe or the East Coast of North America to the Pacific Ocean. Ships were forced to go around the tip of South America, a journey that could take months. For centuries, therefore, explorers hoped to find a NORTHWEST PASSAGE above or through the continent, taking them more easily to the Pacific. Finding this route became even more urgent after the explorations of ROBERT GRAY and GEORGE VANCOUVER in 1792 opened the Pacific Northwest to the lucrative FUR TRADE. It was President THOMAS JEFFERSON's hope that the COLUMBIA RIVER was a part of the longed-for Northwest Passage, and so finding a water route to the Pacific became one of the main goals of the Lewis and Clark Expedition. Although they failed in this, they had shown that it was possible to reach the West Coast by land and river, paving the way for future exploration and, eventually, a United States that truly stretched "from sea to shining sea."

See also EXPLORATION, EARLY.

Further Reading

Lower, J. Arthur. *Ocean of Destiny: A Concise History of the North Pacific, 1500–1978.* Vancouver: University of British Columbia Press, 1978.

Moulton, Gary E., ed. *Atlas of the Lewis and Clark Expedition.* Revised ed. Lincoln: University of Nebraska Press, 1999.

Naval Meteorology and Oceanography Command. "Pacific Ocean." Available on-line. URL: http://oceanographer.navy.mil/pacific.html. Updated on May 30, 2001.

Pethick, Derek. *First Approaches to the Northwest Coast.* Vancouver: J. J. Douglas, 1976.

panther   See ANIMALS, NEW SPECIES.

paper

In planning what the expedition would need for SUPPLIES AND EQUIPMENT, MERIWETHER LEWIS made certain that they would never run out of two very important items: INK and paper. Whether it was for scientific notes, field drawings, celestial and navigational observations, LETTERS, or JOURNALS, Lewis and others in the CORPS OF DISCOVERY would be writing throughout the journey and would therefore need an abundance of paper and ink. Such was Lewis's foresight that the explorers returned from the West Coast with enough for a second expedition. The ink was in powder form and was mixed with water as they needed it, writing on what was then rag paper.

Paper of one kind or another has been in use for centuries. The Egyptians used papyrus, a woven and pounded mat of reeds, from about 4,000 B.C. onward, while the Greeks developed a form of papyrus made from animal skins. In A.D. 105 a Chinese court official, Ts'ai Lun, invented a type of paper very similar to that which is used today. Ts'ai mixed mulberry bark, hemp, and rags with water; mashed it to a pulp; and then pressed out the liquid. The product that remained was paper.

The first paper mill in the Americas was built by the Spanish in Mexico in 1680. Ten years later a German immigrant named William Rittenhouse built North America's first paper mill at PHILADELPHIA and joined forces with printer William Bradford to monopolize the paper-making trade for some time. At that time paper was made from linen and cotton rags, and this was what Meriwether Lewis, WILLIAM CLARK, and their men used on the expedition. According to James Holdberg at the Filson Historical Society, some of their letters were written on paper made by John Whatman in the mid-1790s.

As early as 1719, there were advocates for the development of a wood-based paper, but it was not until later in the 19th century that a process for making it was perfected in Europe and North America. Since then all paper has been made of wood pulp.

Further Reading

History of Paper. Available on-line. URL: http://www.mead.com/ml/docs/facts/history.html. Downloaded on April 14, 2002.

Wheelock, Mary E. *Paper: Its History and Development.* Chicago: American Library Association, 1928.

Partisan, The (Tortohongar) (unknown–unknown)
Teton Lakota (Teton Sioux) chief

Among the instructions that THOMAS JEFFERSON gave to MERIWETHER LEWIS was the directive to deal with the Indian nations he met "in a most friendly and conciliatory manner." Neither Jefferson nor Lewis, however, could foresee this order being tested early in the expedition by the erratic and hostile behavior of the TETON LAKOTA INDIANS (Teton Sioux), and particularly that of one of its chiefs, called The Partisan. Of him, French trader PIERRE-ANTOINE TABEAU wrote that he could be "seen in the selfsame day faint-hearted and bold, audacious and fearful, proud and servile, conciliator and firebrand."

Late in September 1804, the CORPS OF DISCOVERY had its first encounter with the Teton Lakota and agreed to a council on September 25th on a sandbar at the mouth of the BAD RIVER. Things went badly from the start, as the three chiefs—BLACK BUFFALO, Buffalo Medicine, and The Partisan—made it plain that they were unimpressed by the captains' speeches, the corps's parade in full uniform, and the GIFTS they had been given. Lewis and WILLIAM CLARK had also erred in designating Black Buffalo as "first chief" and giving him better presents, which offended The Partisan. What they did not know was that the two chiefs were then engaged in a power struggle and were both seeking to use the expedition to serve their own ends. However, while Black Buffalo maintained a certain sense of diplomacy, The Partisan's tactics were confrontational throughout the corps's stay with the Teton Lakota.

Following the council, during which a Teton demand for a full PIROGUE of gifts was refused, Lewis and Clark invited the three chiefs aboard the KEELBOAT and gave them each a quarter-glass of whiskey. They were, according to Clark, "exceedingly fond of it, they took up an empty bottle, Smelted it, and made maney Simple jestures and Soon began to be troublesom." When he and some men attempted to bring the chiefs back to shore, The Partisan, feigning drunkenness, became belligerent and three of his warriors grabbed the pirogue's bowline, while another wrapped his arms around the mast. The Partisan declared that he would not allow the expedition to proceed up the river until he had received a canoe full of presents. Incensed, Clark drew his sword and called out to Lewis and the others to get the guns ready. In the tense moments that followed, Indians and soldiers faced each other armed and ready to fire until Black Buffalo defused the situation by taking the bowline and ordering the warriors away from the boat.

Thereafter the captains dealt primarily with Black Buffalo, but The Partisan continued his troublemaking. Both chiefs attempted over the next two days to impress upon Lewis and Clark that the Lakota were a powerful nation and that any efforts the Americans made to form trading alliances with the ARIKARA INDIANS or other nations of the upper Missouri would displease them. On the evening of September 27, The Partisan and one of his warriors came to spend the night on the keelboat, but as their pirogue approached, a cable broke, causing both vessels to swing wildly. As Clark called out orders to bring the boats back under control, The Partisan began to shout that the OMAHA INDIANS were attacking. In the resulting confusion, the Teton lined the river's shore, prepared to fight. Even after the mistake was explained, though, the tension remained, with Clark writing, "All prepared on board for any thing which might happen, we kept a Strong guard all night in the boat. No Sleep."

The Partisan was still on the keelboat when the corps prepared to leave the morning of September 28. He chose that moment to make more demands. Once again, some of his warriors grabbed the bowline, and he declared they would not let go until he had been given a flag and some TOBACCO. Clark contemptuously threw a carrot of tobacco on the riverbank and then prepared the keelboat's swivel gun for firing. Once again, Black Buffalo intervened, noting that if tobacco were given to the men holding the bowline, they would withdraw. Lewis and Clark at first refused and then relented, throwing some tobacco to the warriors. With that, and with all Indians now on shore, they took off up the river.

They had not proceeded very far and were still close to the Teton Lakota the following morning. From the riverbank, The Partisan demanded a ride up to his village along with two of his warriors. The captains refused and moved on, "Stateing verry Sufficint reasons and was plain with them on the Subject." Not until The Partisan and his Teton warriors were well behind them did the expedition relax their vigilance.

The Partisan continued to be a powerful spokesman for the Teton Lakota in the years following the expedition. It is thought that he may have met ZEBULON PIKE in September 1805, and he undoubtedly took part in a conference arranged by MANUEL LISA at Prairie du Chien in July 1815.

Further Reading

Ambrose, Stephen E. *Undaunted Courage: Meriwether Lewis, Thomas Jefferson, and the Opening of the American West.* New York: Simon and Schuster, 1996.

MacGregor, Carol Lynn, ed. *The Journals of Patrick Gass, Member of the Lewis and Clark Expedition.* Missoula, Mont.: Mountain Press Publishing Company, 1997.

Ronda, James P. *Lewis and Clark among the Indians.* Lincoln: University of Nebraska Press, 1984.

Tabeau, Pierre-Antoine. *Tabeau's Narrative of Loisel's Expedition to the Upper Missouri.* Edited by Annie Heloise Abel. Translated by Rose Abel Wright. Norman: University of Oklahoma Press, 1939.

Patterson, Robert (1743–1824) *mathematician*

When the expedition was in its planning stages, THOMAS JEFFERSON wrote to several scientists in PHILADELPHIA, asking them to provide assistance and instruction to MERIWETHER LEWIS. One of these was the president's friend and fellow member of the AMERICAN PHILOSOPHICAL SOCIETY, the mathematician Robert Patterson. Jefferson told Patterson that although Lewis had certain frontier skills and "has been for some time qualifying himself for taking observations of longitude & latitude to fix the geographical points of the line he will pass over," he needed further help to improve his knowledge

and competence in NAVIGATION. The mathematician gladly took on the task.

Born near Hillsborough, Northern Ireland, Patterson emigrated in 1768 to Philadelphia, where he taught navigation and mathematics at a number of institutions. When the American Revolution broke out, he enlisted in the colonial cause, becoming an instructor as well as a soldier. In 1779 he was appointed professor of mathematics at the College of Philadelphia (later the University of Pennsylvania), becoming its vice provost some years later. He was elected to the American Philosophical Society in 1783—he would eventually serve as its president—and it was around that time that he met Jefferson. The two became friends and regular correspondents, and both served on the advisory committee for the museum established by CHARLES WILLSON PEALE.

Prior to meeting Patterson in May 1803, Lewis had spent time with the astronomer and mathematician ANDREW ELLICOTT. From both men he learned much about the use of the scientific instruments he would need for his exploration of the frontier, and both agreed that the delicate theodolite would be of little use to him. Despite Ellicott's training, Patterson decided Lewis needed still further instruction and urged him to stay in Philadelphia a while longer, to which the explorer agreed, even though he had already been considerably delayed. During their time together, Lewis and Patterson—with input as well from Ellicott—determined what instruments should be taken on the trip. These included "two Sextants, an artificial horizon or two; a good Arnold's watch or chronometer, a Surveyor's compass with a ball and socket and two pole chain, and a set of plotting instruments." The chronometer he selected and bought with Patterson's help was sent to Ellicott to be regulated.

Some months after training with Patterson, as he was heading toward CLARKSVILLE, Lewis met the mathematician's son, Dr. William Patterson, in Wheeling, Virginia. The younger Patterson came very close to joining the expedition as its physician but failed to show up by the time the KEELBOAT left Wheeling. The elder Patterson, meanwhile, continued his scientific correspondence with Jefferson and held his position at the University of Pennsylvania until 1814. In 1805 he became director of the U.S. Mint, an appointment he retained until his death in 1824.

Further Reading

Ambrose, Stephen E. *Undaunted Courage: Meriwether Lewis, Thomas Jefferson, and the Opening of the American West.* New York: Simon and Schuster, 1996.

Cutright, Paul Russell. *Contributions of Philadelphia to Lewis and Clark History.* Philadelphia: Philadelphia Chapter Lewis and Clark Trail Heritage Foundation, 2001. Also available on-line. URL: http://www.lewisandclarkphila.org/philadelphia/philadelphiacutright conten.html. Updated on October 15, 2001.

payments and rewards

On April 8, 1804, Sergeant JOHN ORDWAY wrote to his parents from CAMP DUBOIS, telling them of the upcoming journey to the PACIFIC OCEAN. He added: "We expect to be gone 18 months or two years. We are to Receive a great Reward for this expedition, when we Return. I am to Receive 15 dollars pr. month and at least 400 ackers of first Rate land, and if we make Great Discoveries as we expect, the United States has promised to make us Great Rewards more than we are promised."

It may have been due to rumors of "Great Rewards" that many men clamored to enlist in the expedition, but MERIWETHER LEWIS and WILLIAM CLARK set high standards in their RECRUITING efforts. The first to be officially enrolled in the expedition were the NINE YOUNG MEN FROM KENTUCKY, who were given enlistment bounties. As soldiers in the U.S. Army, they and other corps members, whether in the permanent or temporary party, were paid at normal army rates: $5 per month for privates, $7 for corporals, and $8 for sergeants. (John Ordway's figure of $15 monthly may have been the double pay he expected.) Exceptions to this were the expedition's two interpreters, GEORGE DROUILLARD and TOUSSAINT CHARBONNEAU, who were paid $25 a month for their services. Lewis thought so highly of Drouillard that he later attempted but failed to get him $30 a month. The SHOSHONE woman SACAGAWEA and Clark's slave YORK received nothing.

The basic pay for captains was $40 a month plus a small subsistence allowance. However, due to bureaucratic intransigence, Clark was commissioned as a second lieutenant rather than a captain. Secretary of War HENRY DEARBORN assured Lewis that Clark would still be paid a captain's salary, and for all intents and purposes Clark was regarded as a captain throughout the expedition. Despite Dearborn's promise, though, he was eventually paid only a lieutenant's salary of $30 a month plus a subsistence allowance for both himself and York.

More than three months after the expedition returned, on January 2, 1807, the House of Representatives convened a special committee, chaired by Willis Alston, Jr., of North Carolina, to consider compensation for the corps members. Dearborn recommended that all the men receive double pay and land warrants—320 acres for each enlisted man, Drouillard, and Charbonneau; 1,000 acres for Clark; and 1,500 acres for Lewis. Lewis protested the inequity and insisted that Clark's compensation be equal to his own; Dearborn refused. Lewis also made his own formal recommendations for the enlisted men, singling out several who had gone above the call of duty in addition to two who had not made the full journey, Corporal RICHARD WARFINGTON and Private JOHN NEWMAN. Ever loyal to the men who had been so loyal to him, Lewis wrote that they had his "warmest approbation and thanks; nor will I suppress the expression of a hope, that the recollection of services thus faithfully performed will meet a just reward in an ample remuneration on the part of our Government."

On January 23 Alston submitted a bill to CONGRESS that requested double pay for the 31 men of the permanent party plus Newman and Warfington, 320 acres to the enlisted men, and 1,600 acres each to Lewis and Clark. Lewis failed, however, to get the extra compensation he had requested for Drouillard, FRANÇOIS LABICHE, JOHN SHIELDS, JOSEPH FIELD, and REUBIN FIELD. It took the House more than a month of debate to pass the bill; the Senate passed it without comment in one day.

Payments to members of the permanent party were based on the length of service from the date of enlistment in the corps to the date of discharge. Some confusion surrounds Clark's period of service and rate of pay. Although he is considered to have started on August 1, 1803, other sources put his official start date in mid-October that year, while his lieutenant's commission from Dearborn was dated March 26, 1804. Joseph Mussulman states that Clark received a total of $2,113.74 (including $823.74 subsistence) for a total of 43 months' service, while Lewis was paid $2,776.22 (including $893.64 subsistence) for 47 months and two days. Stephen Ambrose provides different figures for Lewis: $3,360 for the period of April 1, 1803, to October 1807 plus $702 in ration money, for a total of $4,062, not including the value of his land warrants ($3,200). Ambrose does not provide totals for Clark.

Lewis and Clark were to be rewarded for their services in other ways as well. On the recommendation of President THOMAS JEFFERSON, Lewis was appointed governor of the LOUISIANA TERRITORY, a post in which he proved to be much less successful than he had been as captain of his historic expedition. Clark, meanwhile, was made brigadier general of Militia and superintendent of Indian Affairs for the Territory of Upper Louisiana. In 1813, four years after Lewis's suicide, he was appointed governor of the Missouri Territory.

On January 17, 2001, one of President Bill Clinton's last acts was to confer on Clark his long-delayed commission as captain. In addition, Sacagawea and York were honored for their services to the expedition by being given the title of Honorary Sergeant, Regular Army.

See also COSTS OF THE EXPEDITION.

Further Reading

Ambrose, Stephen E. *Undaunted Courage: Meriwether Lewis, Thomas Jefferson, and the Opening of the American West.* New York: Simon and Schuster, 1996.

Jackson, Donald. *Letters of the Lewis and Clark Expedition, with Related Documents, 1783–1854.* Urbana: University of Illinois Press, 1979.

Large, Arlen. "'Additions to the Party': How an Expedition Grew and Grew." *We Proceeded On* 16, no. 1 (February 1990): 4–11.

Mussulman, Joseph. "Worth Their Salt." From *Discovering Lewis and Clark: The Extent of Our Journey.* Available on-line. URL: http://www.lewis-clark.org/ftccolumbia/cd_salry.htm. Downloaded on March 20, 2002.

peace medals

On August 17, 1805, reporting the first council with the SHOSHONE INDIANS, MERIWETHER LEWIS wrote:

We next inquired who were chiefs among them. Cameahwait pointed out two others whom he said were

Chiefs. We gave him a medal of the small size with the likeness of Mr. Jefferson, the President of the U' States, in relief on one side and clasped hands with a pipe and tomahawk on the other. To the other Chiefs we gave each a small medal . . . which were struck in the Presidency of George Washington, Esqr. We also gave small medals of the last description to two young men whom the 1st Chief informed us were good young men and much respected among them.

When Lewis was gathering GIFTS to be given to the Indian nations he expected to meet on the expedition, medals—especially peace medals—were essential items. Prior to that time it had been common for the British, French, and Spanish to present silver medals to Indian leaders during treaty signings and other ceremonial occasions. They were intended to act as tokens of peace and allegiance, as THOMAS JEFFERSON wrote in 1793: "The medals are . . . marks of friendship to those who come to see us, or who do us good offices, conciliatory of their good will towards us, and not designed to produce a contrary disposition towards others. . . ." For this reason the United States continued the tradition.

From the War Department Lewis obtained a good supply of different types of medals, of which the largest was reserved for the most important chiefs they would meet and the smaller ones for lesser chiefs. One of the smaller models was left over from George Washington's presidency; Lewis called these the "sowing medals," as they depicted a farmer sowing grain. Another type of medal portrayed domestic animals. The most important medals were the silver Jefferson Peace Medals, cast in three sizes and ranging from two to four inches in diameter. On one side was a picture of Jefferson surrounded by the inscription: "TH. JEFFERSON PRESIDENT OF THE U.S. A.D. 1801." The reverse side depicted two hands clasping under a crossed tomahawk and peace pipe and the words "PEACE AND FRIENDSHIP."

The Americans and the Indians had different perceptions of the peace medals. The Indians took the medals at face value, as a gift from one nation to another. The Americans put a more symbolic importance on them, in that the Indians' acceptance of the medals was an acceptance of American sovereignty. This was clear in the instructions that Lewis and WILLIAM CLARK gave to the OTOE (Oto) and MISSOURI INDIANS in August 1804. Now that they had accepted the American gifts and medals, they should send back "all the flags and medals which you may have received from your old fathers the French and Spaniards. . . . It is not proper since you have become the children of the great chief of the Seventeen great nations of America, that you should wear or keep

Lewis and Clark gave the Jefferson peace medals only to those Indians they deemed to be important chiefs. Lesser head men received other medals. *(The American Numismatic Society, New York)*

those emblems of attachment to any other great father but himself."

The following year Missouri chiefs were among the delegation of Indians who visited Jefferson in Washington. They proudly displayed their Jefferson peace medals, and the governor of Massachusetts (who was present) gave them silver chains on which to hang the medals. It is recorded that, in the years following the expedition, other Indians showed off the medals Lewis and Clark had given them.

On July 26, 1806, when Lewis and a small party met a band of BLACKFEET INDIANS, he gave them a medal, a flag, and a handkerchief. Early the following morning, the Blackfeet were caught trying to steal the soldiers' FIREARMS and HORSES. In the skirmish that followed, one Indian was killed and another mortally wounded. Just before Lewis and his men made their escape, he put the medal he had given out the previous night around the neck of the dead Indian, "that they might be informed who we were." It is a sad irony that a symbol of peace and unity was used to mark the most violent encounter of the expedition.

Further Reading

Cutright, Paul Russell. "Lewis and Clark Indian Peace Medals." *Missouri Historical Bulletin* 24, no. 2 (1968): 160–167.

Jefferson National Expansion Memorial. "The Lewis and Clark Journey of Discovery: Peace Medals." Available on-line. URL: http://www.nps.gov/jeff/LewisClark2/CorpsOfDiscovery/Preparing/PeaceMedals/PeaceMedals.htm. Downloaded on April 11, 2002.

Prucha, Francis Paul. *Indian Peace Medals in American History.* Norman: University of Oklahoma Press, 1995.

Stanton, Lucia C. "Jefferson Indian Peace Medal." *Monticello* (Resources). Available on-line. URL: http://www.monticello.org/resources/interests/peace_medal.html. Updated on April 27, 2001.

peace pipe   See SMOKING CEREMONIES.

Peale, Charles Willson (1741–1827) *artist, naturalist, inventor*

In April 1807 MERIWETHER LEWIS returned to PHILADELPHIA, where, four years earlier, he had studied with leading scientists preparatory to his transcontinental journey. Now he had postexpedition business to attend to—among other things, finding a publisher for the expedition's JOURNALS and seeing to the disposition of many of the ARTIFACTS AND SPECIMENS he and WILLIAM CLARK had brought back from the West. As he visited with old friends and new, he spent the most time with Charles Willson Peale, one of the country's leading portrait painters and proprietor of Peale's Philadelphia Museum.

Born in Queen Anne's County, Maryland, Peale began his adult life as a saddler in Annapolis but taught himself other trades as well, including watchmaking, silversmithing, and sign painting. After a brief period in Boston working with John Sin-

gleton Copley, he returned to Annapolis and began to paint portraits; then he went to London in 1766 to study with Benjamin West. Within 10 years he had established himself as a portrait painter in Philadelphia. His most famous subject was George Washington, of whom Peale produced numerous portraits; other leading figures of the day painted by Peale included Benjamin Franklin, John Adams, ALEXANDER HAMILTON, and THOMAS JEFFERSON.

Elected to the Pennsylvania legislature in 1779, Peale's political activities were soon superseded by a growing interest in natural history. In 1784, in the studio of his home, he founded "Peale's Museum," later moving it to the AMERICAN PHILOSOPHICAL SOCIETY's Philosophical Hall and then, in 1802, to the State House (later Independence Hall). The museum displayed numerous Peale portraits, including several by his son Rembrandt Peale, but—more important—it was the first to present mounted animal and bird specimens in an environment approximating to their natural surroundings in the wild. The animals were stuffed by Peale, who had taught himself the art of taxidermy. His collection included close to 200 stuffed animals and specimens of thousands of birds, insects, minerals, and fish. He also collected and displayed relics of Native American cultures and made waxwork figures of prominent American personages.

In 1801 Peale exhumed a mastodon's skeleton from a farm in Ulster County, New York, and reassembled it for his museum, the first time in the young country's history that such a major scientific project had been undertaken. He also became an inventor, collaborating on a polygraph with Jefferson and inventing new kinds of eyeglasses as well as a velocipede. As Peale's scientific interests expanded, so did his museum and its prestige—the more so when it acquired the jewels of the Lewis and Clark Expedition.

Meriwether Lewis spent a good portion of the weeks between April and July 1807 with Peale, mainly to have his portrait painted but also to discuss the expedition's artifacts and specimens. (Peale later painted William Clark's portrait as well, and the two paintings are the most often reproduced in all the books on Lewis and Clark.) Peale took the opportunity to also make a waxwork of Lewis, which was displayed in his museum with an ermine tippet around the mock Lewis's shoulders—the very tippet that had been given to the explorer by the SHOSHONE chief CAMEAHWAIT. The artist wrote to Jefferson that his aim was "to give a lesson to the Indians who may visit the Museum, and also to show my sentiments respecting wars."

Peale enthusiastically agreed to Lewis's and Jefferson's request to exhibit articles from the expedition, and he created a special Lewis and Clark Room to do so. This exhibition of zoological and ethnological specimens and artifacts represented everything brought back from the expedition excepting those items Jefferson, Lewis, and Clark chose to retain for themselves. At Lewis's request Peale also painted several portraits of animals in the collection, apparently with the intention of their being published in the journals. Four of these portraits have survived and are now in the possession of the American Philosophical Society. The whereabouts of the remainder are unknown.

Many of the artifacts from the expedition were displayed in the museum of Charles Willson Peale, seen here in a famous self-portrait. *(Library of Congress, Prints and Photographs Division [LC-USZ62-109708])*

Peale had a hard time keeping his museum afloat and eventually had to search for ways to attract visitors. He began to display scientific curiosities and to add such elements as music and entertainment, concepts that P. T. Barnum would later exploit to better effect. After Peale's death in 1827, the museum was moved to the Arcade Building at Ninth and George Streets and then moved again in 1838 to a building at Ninth and Sansom Streets. In 1846 the struggling museum sold off many of its contents, retaining only the natural history collection. This was finally sold in 1850, with half going to P. T. Barnum and the other half to the Boston Museum. In 1865 Barnum's American Museum in New York City was partially destroyed in a fire. It is believed that many artifacts from the expedition were lost, including possibly Lewis's ermine tippet robe.

Further Reading

American Philosophical Society. "Treasures of the APS: Lewis and Clark's Specimens as Sketched by Charles Willson Peale." Available on-line. URL: http://www.amphilsoc.org/library/exhibits/treasures/pealecw.htm. Downloaded on March 1, 2002.

Brigham, David R. *Public Culture in the Early Republic: Peale's Museum and Its Audience.* Washington, D.C.: Smithsonian Institution Press, 1995.

Cutright, Paul Russell. *Lewis & Clark: Pioneering Naturalists.* Lincoln: University of Nebraska Press/Bison Books, 1989.

Hawke, David Freeman. *Those Tremendous Mountains: The Story of the Lewis and Clark Expedition.* New York: W. W. Norton & Company, 1998.

Sellers, Charles Coleman. *Charles Willson Peale.* New York: Scribner, 1969.

———. *Mr. Peale's Museum: Charles Willson Peale and the First Popular Museum of Natural Science and Art.* New York: Norton, 1980.

pelts   See BEAVERS; FUR TRADE; OTTERS.

permanent expedition party   See CORPS OF DISCOVERY; ORGANIZATION OF EXPEDITION PARTY.

petit chien   See PRAIRIE DOGS.

Philadelphia

As a center of literary, scientific, political, and philosophical thought, Philadelphia at the beginning of the 19th century could well be described as the Athens of America. It was here that the Declaration of Independence was written and a new nation was born, here that Benjamin Franklin lived and published, and here that the U.S. capital was located until 1800. As it was also the home of many of the country's leading scientists and academics, it was natural that it was to Philadelphia that MERIWETHER LEWIS would go when he needed instruction and assistance before beginning his historic journey into the West.

Then a city of approximately 45,000 inhabitants, the largest in the young nation, Philadelphia was home to many institutions promoting higher learning. Among these was the AMERICAN PHILOSOPHICAL SOCIETY, of which President THOMAS JEFFERSON was a member. Early in 1803, after the U.S. CONGRESS had appropriated funds for the expedition, Jefferson wrote to several of his associates in the society, asking them to meet Lewis to provide instruction and guidance as well as to review and comment on his MISSION OBJECTIVES. In April 1803, after spending three weeks at HARPERS FERRY working on his IRON-FRAME BOAT and purchasing some FIREARMS, Lewis set out for Lancaster, Pennsylvania, where he studied instruments and techniques of ASTRONOMICAL OBSERVATIONS under the nation's leading astronomer, ANDREW ELLICOTT. From there he traveled to Philadelphia, arriving sometime around May 8.

Once in the city, Lewis began an intensive round of studies with physician BENJAMIN RUSH, who taught him basic principles of MEDICINE AND MEDICAL TREATMENT; botanist

BENJAMIN SMITH BARTON, who instructed him in identifying, dating, and preserving plant specimens; mathematician ROBERT PATTERSON, who gave him further training in making celestial observations for purposes of NAVIGATION; and physician CASPAR WISTAR, the nation's premiere paleontologist, with whom Lewis discussed fossils and the possibility of finding PREHISTORIC ANIMALS on the GREAT PLAINS.

In addition to his studies, Lewis spent much of his time in Philadelphia visiting ISRAEL WHELAN, the purveyor of public supplies, who was busy locating and purchasing many of the SUPPLIES AND EQUIPMENT needed for the journey. These included medical supplies, TRADE goods, TOBACCO, PAPER and INK, pencils and "Creyons," CLOTHING, sewing supplies, tools, FISHING tackle, surveying and other scientific equipment, knives, OILCLOTH, gunpowder, lead canisters, mosquito netting, GIFTS for Indians, and provisions such as PORTABLE SOUP. When Lewis had collected all he had ordered, it amounted to $2^1/2$ tons of supplies and equipment, which were packed onto a five-horse wagon and dispatched under military supervision to Pittsburgh via Harpers Ferry about two weeks before he returned to Washington in June.

Philadelphia's involvement in the Lewis and Clark Expedition did not end with the explorer's departure from the city. Many of those with whom he had consulted continued to send information and advice to Jefferson even after Lewis had gone, and once the CORPS OF DISCOVERY left CAMP DUBOIS in May 1804, Philadelphians joined the rest of the country in eagerly awaiting NEWS REPORTS OF THE EXPEDITION. In August 1805 Jefferson received the shipment of reports, maps, and ARTIFACTS AND SPECIMENS that Lewis had sent back east from FORT MANDAN. The following October some of the specimens were sent on to Philadelphia for display in CHARLES WILLSON PEALE's museum.

After the expedition's return, in April 1807 Lewis went back to Philadelphia, where over the next four months he met again with many of the scholars who had advised him, made numerous new and influential new friends, and attended parties in his honor. He also had his portrait painted by Peale, to whom he entrusted a majority of the artifacts he had brought back for display in the Philadelphia Museum, and hired FREDERICK PURSH to catalog and classify the expedition's botanical specimens. A mathematician at the West Point Military Academy, Ferdinand Rudolph Hassler (1770–1843), was hired to go over the statistics he had collected on latitude and longitude and to make the necessary corrections to the figures. Meanwhile, Lewis started preparations for the publication of the expedition's JOURNALS and also attended meetings of the American Philosophical Society, to which he had been elected while he was away.

Other postexpedition details included settling accounts and arranging for artists to record aspects of the journey and its discoveries on canvas. Peale was asked to paint some of the animals, in addition to his portraits of Lewis and WILLIAM CLARK. John James Barralet (1747–1815) was engaged to depict the GREAT FALLS, while the French-born Charles Saint-Mémim (1770–1852) did drawings of the OSAGE and the MANDAN INDIANS who had come east with Lewis, as well as a portrait of the explorer himself. The Scottish artist and naturalist ALEXANDER WILSON, known today for his masterwork *American Ornithology*, painted four birds discovered by the expedition: Lewis's woodpecker, Clark's nutcracker, the western tanager, and the back-billed magpie. Surprisingly, none of the pictures Lewis commissioned were ever used in the book published five years after his death.

During this time in Philadelphia, Lewis also conducted business in connection with his new duties as governor of LOUISIANA TERRITORY—an appointment that unfortunately had unhappy consequences. Two years later, when on his way back east to Washington and Philadelphia, he killed himself in October 1809. The following year Clark went to Philadelphia and hired NICHOLAS BIDDLE to take on the editing and publication of the journals, which were finally published in 1814—in Philadelphia. Thus the city became both the beginning and the end of the Lewis and Clark Expedition.

Today researchers with the Lewis and Clark Trail Heritage Foundation have identified 71 sites in Philadelphia that are associated with the expedition in one way or another. Of these, 23 structures are still standing. In addition, a row of orange Osage trees found in the cemetery of St. Peter's Episcopal Church—where Charles Willson Peale and Nicholas Biddle are buried—were grown from cuttings that Lewis had sent back east in 1804. It is just one of the many ties that connect Philadelphia, a city of the East, to the country's greatest exploration of the West.

Further Reading

Ambrose, Stephen E. *Undaunted Courage: Meriwether Lewis, Thomas Jefferson, and the Opening of the American West.* New York: Simon and Schuster, 1996.

Cutright, Paul Russell. *Contributions of Philadelphia to Lewis and Clark History.* Philadelphia: Philadelphia Chapter Lewis and Clark Trail Heritage Foundation, 2001. Also available on-line. URL: http://www.lewisandclarkphila.org/philadelphia/philadelphiacutright conten.html. Updated on October 15, 2001.

Jackson, Donald. *Thomas Jefferson & the Stony Mountains: Exploring the West from Monticello.* Norman: University of Oklahoma Press, 1993.

Muhly, Frank. "Firm Foundations in Philadelphia: The Lewis and Clark Expedition's Ties to Philadelphia." Lewis and Clark Heritage Trail Foundation, Philadelphia Chapter. Available on-line. URL: http://www.lewisandclarkphila.org/philadelphia/philadelphia frankmuhly.html. Downloaded on February 7, 2002.

Piahito   See HAWK'S FEATHER.

Piegan Indians   See BLACKFEET INDIANS.

Pike, Zebulon (1779–1813) *army officer, explorer*

Even before the Lewis and Clark Expedition returned from its historic journey, the U.S. Army began to send out more explorers to chart other areas of LOUISIANA TERRITORY. Perhaps the most famous of these was Zebulon Pike, for whom a mountain in Colorado was named.

Born in New Jersey, Pike was commissioned an army lieutenant in 1799, and in 1805 General JAMES WILKINSON ordered him to find the headwaters of the MISSISSIPPI RIVER. In addition to this mission, he was also charged with establishing sites for military posts and, like MERIWETHER LEWIS and WILLIAM CLARK, told to make contact with Native American nations and inform them of their new "father," the U.S. government. Pike left ST. LOUIS with a party of 20 men (including former Lewis and Clark private JOHN BOLEY) and traveled upriver some 2,000 miles on foot and by boat. They reached Leech Lake, in northern Minnesota, during the winter of 1805–06, and, mistakenly believing that he had found the river's headwater, Pike returned from there the following spring. (The true source of the Mississippi is Lake Itasca).

Later in 1806, Wilkinson sent Pike on a second mission, this time to explore the Red and Arkansas Rivers in the southwestern area of the LOUISIANA PURCHASE. This brought him into what is now Colorado and New Mexico as well as over the then-disputed boundaries with Spanish territory. Once again, John Boley was among the men who accompanied him. On November 23, 1806, Pike sighted a peak in Colorado that he later tried—and failed—to climb. (He predicted that no man would ever be able to reach the mountain's summit, but in 1820 three members of Stephen Long's expedition successfully climbed Pike's Peak, and there have been many ascents since then.)

Pike subsequently moved south and crossed the Sangre de Cristo Mountains into New Mexico and Spanish territory, where he built a fort on a branch of the Rio Grande. Before long he and his men were captured, charged with illegal entry by Spanish authorities, and held in Chihuahua for several months. Eventually the party was escorted through Santa Fe, across Texas, and released on the Spanish-American border in Louisiana. However, all of Pike's maps, notes, and papers were confiscated by the Spanish.

Without these resources, Pike was forced to write about the expedition entirely from memory. His account is said to have discouraged American settlement for many years because, as he wrote, "These vast plains of the Western Hemisphere may become in time equally celebrated as the sandy deserts of Africa." This, in combination with Major Stephen Long's description of it as the "great American desert" in 1820, did the territory a great disservice, and it was years before settlement of the area began in earnest. However, Pike's reports of the Spanish weaknesses in Santa Fe and the lucrative markets to be found in Mexico aroused American political and commercial interest in Texas, leading in time to its annexation.

Zebulon Pike was rewarded for his achievements with a series of promotions, and when the War of 1812 broke out, he

Zebulon Pike was captured by the Spanish in February 1807 before he completed his exploratory mission in the southwestern area of the Louisiana Purchase. The Spanish had also attempted but failed to intercept Lewis and Clark. *(Library of Congress, Prints and Photographs Division [LC-USZ62-128057])*

was made a brigadier general. In April 1813, in the Battle of York, he led a successful assault on what is now Toronto but died in a powder-magazine explosion.

Further Reading

Coues, Elliott, ed. *The Explorations of Zebulon Montgomery Pike.* 3 vols. New York: Harper, 1895.

Hart, Stephen Harding, and Archer Butler Hulbert, eds. *Zebulon Pike's Arkansaw Journal: In Search of the Southern Louisiana Purchase Boundary Line (interpreted by his newly recovered maps). Edited, with bibliographical resumé, 1800–1810.* Reprint, Westport, Conn.: Greenwood Press, 1972.

Jackson, Donald. *The Journals of Zebulon Montgomery Pike with Letters and Related Documents.* 2 vols. Norman: University of Oklahoma Press, 1966.

Montgomery, M. R. *Jefferson and the Gun-Men: How the West Was almost Lost.* New York: Crown Publishers, 2000.

Terrell, John Upton. *Zebulon Pike: The Life and Times of an Adventurer.* New York: Weybright and Talley, 1968.

Pinaut Peter   See ENGAGÉS.

pirogues

While MERIWETHER LEWIS used the words *pirogue* and *canoe* interchangeably, the two pirogues used by the expedition were very different from its dugout CANOES. Bigger, broader, and flat-bottomed, these boats were capable of carrying up to eight tons of cargo and a crew of six or more.

Although the two pirogues were to play an important role in the journey of the CORPS OF DISCOVERY, they were probably not in Lewis's original plan, and their purchase was forced on him by circumstances. When he commissioned the construction of the KEELBOAT at PITTSBURGH, it had been agreed that it would be completed by July 20, 1803. The boat builder was dilatory, however, and it was not finished until August 31. The delay infuriated Lewis, who considered canceling the contract and was driven to purchase a pirogue in an attempt to get some of his SUPPLIES AND EQUIPMENT down the OHIO RIVER before the water level dropped too far. When he did at last leave Pittsburgh, the keelboat was so heavily loaded that he was forced to load the pirogue with some of its cargo. He then had to buy a second pirogue on September 4 to carry the wagonload of equipment that he had arranged to meet at Wheeling, Virginia.

It is now evident that, although the pirogues were bought as a temporary measure, they proved their value as maneuverable load carriers as the keelboat party struggled upstream to ST. LOUIS against the fierce current of the MISSISSIPPI RIVER. The two pirogues were therefore retained, and on May 14, 1804, they set out from CAMP DUBOIS to ascend the MISSOURI RIVER along with the keelboat. Each pirogue was identified by its color. The white pirogue was slightly the smaller of the two, probably about 29 feet long and 8 feet wide, and carried a crew of six. The red pirogue had a crew of seven, and each boat was equipped with a mast, a sail, and a mounted swivel gun (blunderbuss).

After the keelboat was sent back downriver from the villages of the MANDAN INDIANS in April 1805, the expedition began the next leg of its journey up the Missouri in the two pirogues plus six canoes they had made during the winter. The white pirogue, though smaller, became the flagship of the party, since it was more stable. It carried the captains' scientific instruments, medicine, TRADE goods, and the JOURNALS and was also the boat in which WILLIAM CLARK, SACAGAWEA, TOUSSAINT CHARBONNEAU, and the baby JEAN BAPTISTE CHARBONNEAU usually traveled. The white pirogue had six paddlers, including the three nonswimmers in the party.

On June 10, 1805, two months after leaving the Mandan villages, the party reached the mouth of the MARIAS RIVER. Since they knew the GREAT FALLS were ahead of them, they decided to leave the red pirogue hidden on an island in the middle of the river and deposit baggage and supplies in a CACHE nearby. Eight days later, at the foot of the Great Falls, the white pirogue, far to heavy to be portaged, was also hauled out of the water and hidden near PORTAGE CREEK.

The explorers were not to see the white pirogue again until exactly a year later, when Lewis and his party returned to the falls. On July 18, 1806, Sergeant PATRICK GASS wrote: ". . . I went down with three of the men to the lower end of the portage to examine the periogue and deposit there and found all safe." Nine days later, with the PORTAGE of the canoes and baggage around the falls complete, the party set off again in the five canoes and the white pirogue. Two days' travel found them back at the mouth of the Marias, where Gass wrote, "We this day took the articles out of the place of deposit, and examined the large red pirogue we left there, and found it too rotten to take down the river. We therefore took what nails out of it we could, left our HORSES on the plains and proceeded down the river."

Thus, although they may have been bought on the Ohio River as a temporary stopgap, the pirogues gave the party invaluable load-carrying capacity for hundreds of miles of their journey and fully justified their purchase.

Further Reading

Ambrose, Stephen E. *Undaunted Courage: Meriwether Lewis, Thomas Jefferson, and the Opening of the American West.* New York: Simon and Schuster, 1996.

Boss, Richard C. "Keelboat, Pirogue, and Canoe: Vessels Used by the Lewis and Clark Corps of Discovery." *Nautical Research Journal* 38, no. 2 (1993): 68–87.

Cutright, Paul Russell. *Lewis & Clark: Pioneering Naturalists.* Lincoln: University of Nebraska Press/Bison Books, 1989.

MacGregor, Carol Lynn, ed. *The Journals of Patrick Gass, Member of the Lewis and Clark Expedition.* Missoula, Mont.: Mountain Press Publishing Company, 1997.

Moulton, Gary E. "A Note on the White Pirogue." *We Proceeded On* 12, no. 2 (May 1986): 22.

Pittsburgh

Although the official point of departure for the Lewis and Clark Expedition is considered to be CAMP DUBOIS, Illinois, cases can be made for two other locations. One is CLARKSVILLE, Indiana Territory, where MERIWETHER LEWIS met WILLIAM CLARK in mid-October 1803 and recruited the NINE YOUNG MEN FROM KENTUCKY, the backbone of the CORPS OF DISCOVERY. Six weeks earlier, however, Lewis and 11 men had left Pittsburgh, Pennsylvania, aboard the KEELBOAT, and three miles into the journey down the OHIO RIVER, he wrote his first JOURNAL entry. For many this moment marks the true start of the expedition on August 31, 1803.

At the beginning of the 19th century, Pittsburgh—now the second largest city in Pennsylvania—was the gateway to the western frontier. Standing at the junction of the Allegheny, the Monongahela, and the Ohio Rivers, 260 miles west of PHILADELPHIA, its population in 1800 was 1,565 and growing. Its position on the OHIO RIVER, then the country's most important water highway, made Pittsburgh one of the key cities in the young nation.

Pittsburgh can claim to be the birthplace of the expedition in more than one way. It was in here in early March 1801 that Captain Meriwether Lewis received a letter from President THOMAS JEFFERSON inviting him to become Jefferson's secretary. Two years later, having been given the responsibility of leading a corps of men across the continent and back, Lewis began to make PREPARATIONS FOR THE EXPEDITION that included Pittsburgh out of necessity. He had an ambitious plan, as he described it in a letter to WILLIAM CLARK: "My plan is to descend the Ohio in a keeled boat thence up the Mississippi to the mouth of the Missourie, and up that river as far as it's navigation is practicable. . . ." Pittsburgh was the logical starting point because of its position on the Ohio and the fact that it was the westernmost point where such a keelboat could be built. To that end he contracted with a boat builder in nearby Elizabeth to construct the vessel according to his design and specifications. (Located on the banks of the Monongahela River southeast of Pittsburgh, Elizabeth is now part of the Pittsburgh metropolitan area.)

While this was being done, Lewis attended to other preparations. In April, at the federal armory in HARPERS FERRY, he purchased FIREARMS and ammunition and also arranged for the building of a specially designed IRON-FRAME BOAT. In early May he went to Philadelphia, where he was tutored in basic sciences and where he purchased the necessary SUPPLIES AND EQUIPMENT that he would need for the journey. When he was done, Lewis had accumulated 2^1/2 tons of items, which he packed onto a five-horse wagon and dispatched to Harpers Ferry with the intention of having it pick up the guns and the iron-frame boat then proceed to Pittsburgh. In June he returned to Washington.

On July 5 Lewis started out for Pittsburgh. Along the way he learned that the driver of the supply wagon had found the additional equipment at Harpers Ferry too heavy and had gone on without it. After arranging for somebody else to transport those supplies and the iron-frame boat, Lewis went on to Pittsburgh, arriving there on July 15; the wagon from Harpers Ferry arrived a week later. With recruits to navigate the boat all arranged, Lewis was ready to go—but the keelboat was not. Although he had contracted with the boat builder to have it completed by July 20, he was chagrined to discover it was nowhere near ready. The builder proved to be a drunkard and procrastinator, but it was too late to hire anybody else for the job, so Lewis could do no more than harass him into finishing the work. Each deadline came and went, however, with no end in sight.

In the meantime, on July 29 the post brought some welcome news: William Clark had accepted his invitation to cocommand the expedition. This was followed a few days later by a letter discussing the RECRUITING that Clark had already begun. Now the two captains began to correspond in earnest, making plans to meet at Clarksville.

To Lewis's exasperation, the keelboat was not completed until August 31. The last nail was barely in before he had it (and a PIROGUE he had purchased) fully loaded and on its way down the Ohio, manned by "11 hands 7 of which are soldiers, a pilot and three young men on trial . . ."; these included JOHN COLTER and GEORGE SHANNON. Also on board was an additional purchase Lewis had made in Pittsburgh: his dog SEAMAN. Because the water level was now so low, making it necessary to "get out all hands and lift the boat" time and again, the journey was exceedingly long and laborious. Finally, on October 15 he arrived at Clarksville, met Clark, and began the next phase of their historic expedition.

Pittsburgh's connection with the CORPS OF DISCOVERY did not end with Lewis's departure on the keelboat. In 1807 *A Journal of the Voyages and Travels of a Corps of Discovery* by Sergeant PATRICK GASS was published. Edited by a Pittsburgh bookstore owner and produced by a Pittsburgh publisher, Gass's book was the first about the expedition to be brought into print.

Further Reading

Ambrose, Stephen E. *Undaunted Courage: Meriwether Lewis, Thomas Jefferson, and the Opening of the American West.* New York: Simon and Schuster, 1996.

Baldwin, Leland D. *Pittsburgh: The Story of a City, 1750–1865.* Pittsburgh: University of Pittsburgh Press, 1970.

Lorant, Stefan. *Pittsburgh: The Story of an American City,* 5th ed. With contributions by Henry Steele Commager et al. Pittsburgh: Esselmont Books, 1999.

Plains Indians

With an area of more than a million square miles, the GREAT PLAINS (also known as the High Plains or simply the Plains) was home to more than two dozen Indian nations before white settlers displaced them. The Great Plains extends from the MISSISSIPPI RIVER to the ROCKY MOUNTAINS and from Manitoba, Saskatchewan, and Alberta, CANADA, down to modern central Texas. It was largely semiarid, grassland country with some wooded areas along river valleys and in the hills. Prior to non-Indian settlement, this habitat supported large herds of DEER, ANTELOPE, and BUFFALO, sources of food for the Plains Indians who shared the territory. Numerous other species of animals were also common.

As the Great Plains was part of the territory included in the LOUISIANA PURCHASE, MERIWETHER LEWIS and WILLIAM CLARK planned for encounters with its Native American inhabitants. Among the expedition's MISSION OBJECTIVES was the instruction to engage as many nations as they could in a trading network with the United States as well as to bring the Indians the news that they were now under the authority of the U.S. government. But there was still the overriding element of the unknown: Who else was out there? Would they be friendly or hostile? What were their languages and customs? Some information regarding the nations of the Great Plains was already known to them, thanks to reports from traders and trappers who had gone up the MISSOURI RIVER before them, but there was much more to learn.

As it turned out, the CORPS OF DISCOVERY met only a fraction of the nations inhabiting the Plains at that time, generally those closest to the Missouri who were not away hunting when the soldiers passed through their lands. These included the ARIKARA, the BLACKFEET, the CHEYENNE, the HIDATSA, the MANDAN, the MISSOURI, the OSAGE (who lived near ST. LOUIS), the OTOE (Oto), and the YANKTON NAKOTA (Yankton Sioux), and TETON LAKOTA (Teton Sioux) Indians. They had hoped to meet the OMAHA, but except for an encounter with some prisoners held by the Teton Lakota, they failed to do so.

Although they met an ASSINIBOINE chief during their winter at FORT MANDAN in 1804–05, Lewis and Clark chose to avoid that nation while in their territory, believing them to be hostile to the expedition's mission. Others they might have met at Fort Mandan at a different time of year included the Arapaho, the Cheyenne, the CROW, and the Kiowa, who, with the Assiniboine, came regularly to the Mandan villages to trade with representatives of the NORTH WEST COMPANY.

Nations who lived in other areas of the Great Plains included the Comanche, the Cree, Gros Ventre (Atsina), the Ioway, the Kaw, the Kiowa-Apache, the Ojibway, the Ponca, the Quapaw, the Santee Dakota, the Sarcee, the Wichita, and the Yanktonai Nakota. From the helpful Mandan and Hidatsa Indians, Lewis and Clark learned much about the nations they were most likely to encounter, covering everything from location to customs. By the time the expedition left Fort Mandan in the spring of 1805, the Plains Indians had become less of a mystery to the captains, and they had compiled a great deal of important ethnographic information.

Some of the Plains nations had inhabited the area for centuries; others were relative newcomers who had migrated from the East or been driven onto the Plains by fiercer nations. Their languages, customs, clothing, lodgings, and lifestyles were rich in diversity. Almost all Plains Indians, however, were nomadic or seminomadic, due largely to the introduction of HORSES into the area by the Spanish, making it possible to hunt BUFFALO and other games over a wider area.

The period from the mid-18th to the end of the 19th century, although often regarded as a time that exemplified the "traditional" way of life for the Plains Indians, was actually an era of change. Horses, firearms, shifting migration patterns, diseases (especially smallpox), and other influences of European

For many Americans, this warrior on horseback, a Blackfoot Indian, typifies the Plains Indians. *(Courtesy Art Today.com/IMSI)*

contact brought changes that eradicated their historic lifestyle. After a period of resistance known as the Wars for the Great Plains, or Plains Indian Wars, by 1870 most of the Plains Indians had been removed to reservations.

Further Reading

Andrist, Ralph K. *The Long Death: The Last Days of the Plains Indians.* Norman: University of Oklahoma Press, 2001.

Ewers, John C. "Plains Indian Reactions to the Lewis and Clark Expedition." *Montana: The Magazine of Western History* 16 (January 1966): 2–12.

Hagen, Cecil. "Liberated Women? . . . Not Those Lewis and Clark Met on Their Way." *Pacific Northwesterner* 25, no. 2 (1981): 17–25.

Ronda, James P. *Lewis and Clark among the Indians.* Lincoln: University of Nebraska Press, 1984.

———. "Exploring the Explorers: Great Plains Peoples and the Lewis and Clark Expedition." *Great Plains Quarterly* 13, no. 2 (1993): 81–90.

Waldman, Carl. *Encyclopedia of Native American Tribes.* Revised ed. New York: Checkmark Books, 1999.

plants, new species

While the number of plants or plant species noted by the expedition is still a matter of controversy, 180 or more is accepted by most naturalists, of which 148 were new discoveries. Because some specimens were damaged in the CACHES at the GREAT FALLS, there were probably many others. Although MERIWETHER LEWIS and WILLIAM CLARK made numerous zoological and botanical discoveries during their journey, other aspects of the expedition have tended to overshadow their achievements as natural historians. Yet within the MISSION OBJECTIVES that President THOMAS JEFFERSON had given Lewis was the note that "Other objects worthy of notice will be . . . the dates at which particular plants put forth, or lose their flower or leaf. . . ." This was an instruction that the explorers carried out with remarkable diligence and success, given the harsh terrain and difficult circumstances of their journey as well as the myriad other objectives they also had to accomplish.

A man of the ENLIGHTENMENT, Jefferson was an enthusiastic and skilled geographer and astronomer but preeminently a naturalist who could hold his own with any botanical academic of his time. This was undoubtedly one of the reasons he chose Lewis, also a keen naturalist, to lead the expedition. Lewis had grown up in the countryside; knew and studied animals and plants; and from LUCY MERIWETHER LEWIS MARKS, his mother and a skilled herb doctor, had learned the therapeutic properties of many plants. In 1803, on Jefferson's recommendation, the explorer spent time in PHILADELPHIA with Dr. BENJAMIN SMITH BARTON, author of the first botanical textbook written in the United States. It was Barton who augmented Lewis's education on the identification and classification of plants, in particular how to draw and label them and how to preserve specimens. Lewis took a copy of Barton's *Elements of Botany* on the expedition as well as two volumes on the Linnean method of botanical classification.

Lewis usually began his note of a plant with an easily recognizable title—that is, "a species of bryer"—and continued his lengthy description with a comparison to a similar species in the East. This was then followed by a detailed, scientific description on which botanists still rely to make the correct classification. Perhaps from his own knowledge, or perhaps from Barton's book, Lewis used some 200 technical botanical terms; *radix, palmate, procumbent, pellicle,* and *carinated* are a few examples. Because of this mastery of terminology, some scholars have expressed surprise that he did not use the Linnean method of classification: genus term in Latin, followed by the species name, followed by a third name to distinguish a particular subgroup. It is likely, however, that he chose not to do so out of modesty. By relating what he saw to a species he knew in the East and following it with as accurate a description as he could, he was leaving the formal identification to others better qualified than himself. In this regard, his botanical work received greater recognition than the list of geographical place names that he and Clark had coined during their journey (see NOMENCLATURE, GEOGRAPHICAL).

Although Lewis is generally acknowledged to be the expedition's botanist, Clark had a keen eye as well. It was he who discovered and described the currantlike buffaloberry, convincing Lewis to preserve it; it was later found to be new to science.

Plant specimens collected along the lower MISSOURI RIVER were sent back east via the KEELBOAT in spring 1805. Thomas Jefferson sent the dried plants to the AMERICAN PHILOSOPHICAL SOCIETY in Philadelphia, where they were examined by Dr. Barton, while the seeds and cuttings were passed on to the horticulturalist William Hamilton. More than two years later, when Lewis returned in September 1806, he brought at least 173 dried specimens with him and took them to Philadelphia, where he put them into the care of Bernard McMahon, a well-known seedsman and florist. McMahon had in his employ a brilliant botanist, FREDERICK PURSH, whom Lewis hired to catalogue, describe, and sketch the plants. However, by the time Lewis died in October 1809, Pursh had left for New York, taking some of the plant specimens with him without the knowledge or consent of either MacMahon or Clark; he later took them to England. In 1856 the specimens he had appropriated were bought by an American botanist, returned to the United States, and presented to the Academy of Natural Sciences of Philadelphia. Amazingly, it was not until 1896 that a search was made for the specimens left behind in Philadelphia more than 80 years previously; these were then reunited with those Pursh had taken.

Although he had been paid for his work on the Lewis and Clark plants, Pursh's drawings and descriptions were not used in the subsequent publication of the expedition's JOURNALS. Despite this, and despite his illegally taking some of the specimens, Pursh did acknowledge fully the important part Lewis and Clark had played in botanical history. In 1814 he published *Flora Americae Septentrionalis,* in which he described 124 plants collected by Lewis and Clark, giving them full credit for their discoveries (noting each with the legend *"v.s. in Herb. Lewis"*), and included 13 of their specimens in the illustrations. He named three new subspecies after Lewis and gave both the explorers' names to two completely new genera: the *Clarkia* (an herb) and the *Lewisia* (bitterroot).

Many of the seeds and cuttings that Lewis brought back were bred successfully, including flax, two forms of gooseberry, and the snowberry. It is from these discoveries of 200 years ago that gardeners around the world can now enjoy Lewis's wild flax and Lewis's syringa, as well as the red-flowering currant, prairie apple, Osage orange, Clarkia (ragged robin), and Lewisia (BITTERROOT). Although the Clarkia is the better known of the two, the English name-form of the Lewisia has now been given to the BITTERROOT MOUNTAINS and the BITTERROOT RIVER.

While Meriwether Lewis is best remembered as an explorer, his botanical enthusiasm shines through his journals. On August 12, 1806, his party reunited with Clark's on the Missouri River after spending five weeks apart. Suffering from a gunshot wound accidentally inflicted on him by PIERRE CRUZATTE, and knowing that they were on the homeward stretch, he wrote, "I shall desist until I recover and leave to my friend Capt. C. the continuation of our journal." Nevertheless, he could not resist making one more page-long entry: "I must notice a singular Cherry. . . . The leaf is peteolate, oval acutely pointed at it's apex, from one and a $1/4$ to $1 1/2$ inches in length and from $1/2$ to $3/4$ of an inch in width, finely or minutely serrate, pale green and free from bubessence." Today, in the Lewis and Clark Herbarium at the Academy of Natural Sciences of Philadelphia, one can still see the plant he described so long ago.

See also TREES.

Further Reading
Academy of Natural Sciences. "The Lewis and Clark Herbarium." Available on-line. URL: http://www.acnatsci.org/lewis&clark/. Downloaded on May 17, 2001.

Burroughs, Raymond Darwin, ed. *The Natural History of the Lewis and Clark Expedition.* East Lansing: Michigan State University Press, 1995.

Chisholm, Colin. "Undaunted Botany." *Sierra.* (May/June 2002): 47–49.

Cutright, Paul Russell. *Lewis & Clark: Pioneering Naturalists.* Lincoln: University of Nebraska Press/Bison Books, 1989.

———. "Meriwether Lewis: Botanist." *Oregon Historical Quarterly* 69 (June 1968): 148–170.

Meehan, Thomas. "The Plants of Lewis and Clark's Expedition Across the Continent, 1804–1806." *Proceedings of the Academy of Natural Sciences of Philadelphia.* January–March 1898.

Phillips, H. Wayne. *Plants of the Lewis and Clark Expedition.* Missoula, Mont.: Mountain Press Publishing, 2003.

Rossi, Linda, and Alfred E. Schuyler. "The Iconography of Plants Collected on the Lewis and Clark Expedition." *Great Plains Research* 3, no. 1 (1993): 39–60.

Plateau Indians

The Plateau Indians were those who lived within the broad region of highlands now called the Columbia Plateau. This area extended from west to east between the CASCADE MOUNTAINS and the ROCKY MOUNTAINS and north to south from the Fraser River in British Columbia down to northern Oregon and Idaho, with a small strip reaching into northern California. Through this region flows the 1,200-mile-long COLUMBIA RIVER, in addition to innumerable rivers and streams fed by the drainoff from the flanking mountains. Tall, coniferous trees grow in the mountains and river valleys, while the flat plains and rolling hills in between are covered with grasses and sagebrush.

The Plateau Indians lived by the seasons, going wherever they would find food most abundant. With access to very little big game but many rivers, they were primarily fishers who supplemented their diets by hunting small game and by gathering roots, berries, and wild vegetables. In warm weather they built temporary, bulrush-mat-covered lodges alongside the rivers and on the plains. In cold weather they lived near the rivers in earth-covered, sunken pithouses.

Nations living in the eastern region of the Columbia Plateau (primarily the NEZ PERCE and FLATHEAD (Salish) INDIANS) owned large herds of HORSES that they used to cross the CONTINENTAL DIVIDE to hunt BUFFALO in the GREAT PLAINS. By contrast, the Indians in the western area were watermen whose main transport was the canoe, which they used to trade down to the coast. The rivers of the region, especially the Columbia, were a means not only of subsistence but also of trade and social intercourse among the Indians. A huge trading network was centered around CELILO FALLS AND THE DALLES, which teemed with Indians from numerous nations whenever the salmon were running.

There were two main language families, Sahaptian and Salishan, as well as other dialects. The CORPS OF DISCOVERY met many Sahaptian speakers, including the Klickitat, the Nez Perce, the Palouse, the Tenino (Warm Springs), the UMATILLA, the WALLA WALLA, the WANAPAM, and the YAKAMA (Yakima). Of the Salishan speakers, apparently only the Flathead had any interaction of note with the corps. Other Salishans include the Coeur d'Alene (Skitswish), the Columbia, the Colville, the Kalispel, the Lake, the Shuswap, the Spokan, and the Wenatchee, among others. The Cayuse, the Klamath, the Modoc, the Kootenai, and the Stuwihamuk spoke different dialects, while the Chinookian-speaking WISHRAM are also grouped with the Plateau Indians.

The expedition's dealings with the Plateau Indians they met were uniformly friendly. Many of the nations had never before encountered white men; yet they greeted the explorers warmly, traded with them, shared FOOD, and provided valuable assistance in the form of information or guides. When MERIWETHER LEWIS characterized the Walla Walla as "the most hospitable, honest, and sincere people that we have met," he could well have applied this description to many of the other Plateau Indians who helped to make the expedition a success.

Further Reading

Oregon Blue Book. "Oregon History—Columbia Plateau." Available on-line: URL: http://bluebook.state.or.us/cultural/history/history03.htm. Downloaded on April 4, 2002.

Pioneer Middle School. "The Wenatchee Valley Plateau Indian Culture." Available on-line. URL: http://pio.wsd.wednet.edu/SAMMgrant/NativeAm/homepage.shtml. Updated on September 14, 2001.

Ronda, James P. *Lewis and Clark among the Indians.* Lincoln: University of Nebraska Press, 1984.

Waldman, Carl. *Encyclopedia of Native American Tribes.* Revised ed. New York: Checkmark Books, 1999.

Platte River

On July 21, 1804, as the CORPS OF DISCOVERY was proceeding up the MISSOURI RIVER, they arrived at the mouth of the Platte River, just south of present-day Omaha, Nebraska. Here they hoped to make contact with the OTOE (Oto) and MISSOURI INDIANS, but those nations were away hunting BUFFALO; the captains would not meet them until a week later, further up the river at COUNCIL BLUFF.

As was their custom, MERIWETHER LEWIS and WILLIAM CLARK surveyed the mouth of the Platte River and calculated it to be 600 yards wide, with a current that Lewis estimated to be eight miles an hour. They went up the Platte in a PIROGUE for about a mile and found that it had a wide, sandy course broken by channels up to six feet deep. Although that was the only firsthand knowledge they had of the river, Lewis was to write a long report about it at FORT MANDAN. Based on what he had learned from Indians, he described its course from its headwaters in Colorado and listed the nations living along it, including the Otoe (Oto), the Missouri, four groups of Pawnee, the Kite, the Wetapahato (Comanche), the Kiowa, the Castahana (Comanche), the Cataka, and the Dotami.

Because the shallowness of its water made navigation close to impossible, the Platte was not investigated by early explorers, although it later became a vital section of the OREGON TRAIL. However, Lewis's long report reflects the importance that Americans placed on the Platte in the opening years of the 19th century. It was a recognized, if unofficial, boundary between the accepted limits of American/French-Indian trading and the unknown. Considered by many to be the beginning of the GREAT PLAINS, it also marked the point where the Lower Missouri became the Upper Missouri.

Several reference books mention French traders who regarded passing the mouth of the Platte as equivalent to crossing the equator. For centuries it has been the custom at sea that sailors or passengers crossing the equator for the first time undergo some sort of light-hearted initiation ceremony, usually involving a ceremonial shaving. Similarly, Elliott Coues's edition of the JOURNALS has a note quoting Perrin du Lac on passing the mouth of the Platte: "The river Platte is regarded by navigators of the Missouri as a point of as much importance as the equinoctial line amongst mariners. All those who had not passed it before were required to be shaved, unless they could

Lewis and Clark explored a section of the Platte River when they came to it in July 1804. The river later became an important part of the Oregon Trail. *(Library of Congress, Prints and Photographs Division [LC-USZ62-128883])*

compromise the occasion by a treat. Much merriment was indulged on the occasion."

Perhaps it is appropriate to remember this river by the description given to it by the French explorers Paul and Pierre Mallet, who traveled from Illinois to Sante Fe in 1739. They described the Platte as "a thousand miles long and six inches deep."

Further Reading

Cutright, Paul Russell. *Lewis & Clark: Pioneering Naturalists.* Lincoln: University of Nebraska Press/Bison Books, 1989.

Johnsgard, Paul A. *The Platte: Channels in Time.* Lincoln: University of Nebraska Press, 1984.

Lewis, Meriwether, and William Clark. *The History of the Lewis and Clark Expedition.* Edited by Elliott Coues; 4 vols., 1893, Harper. Reprinted in 3 vols., New York: Dover Publications., 1979.

Mattes, Merrill J. *The Great Platte River Road: The Covered Wagon Mainline via Fort Kearney to Fort Laramie.* Lincoln: Nebraska State Historical Society, 1969.

Moulton, Gary E., ed. *Atlas of the Lewis and Clark Expedition.* Revised ed. Lincoln: University of Nebraska Press, 1999.

Pocasse   See HAY.

Point Ellice (Point Distress, Stormy Point)

Point Ellice, near present-day Megler, Washington, is a cape on the north bank of the COLUMBIA RIVER estuary, eight miles upstream from the open sea. On November 7, 1805, the expedition was still upriver from this point when they reached the estuary and realized the PACIFIC OCEAN could not be far away. The fog lifted when they were just west of today's Skamokawa, Washington, there was a shout from the party, and WILLIAM CLARK reported exultantly, "Ocian in view! O the joy!"

Probably because of the many islands on the south side of the estuary, the expedition followed the northern bank as far as today's Gray's Bay, reaching it on November 8. Unskilled at working their CANOES in the waves and swells of the coastal waters, they kept well in toward shore and camped for the night on the western corner of the bay below Gray's Point ("Dismal Point" to the explorers). Bad WEATHER, a heavy swell, and the wind kept them there for another day before they were able to paddle westward on November 10 to a beach directly below the eastern side of Point Ellice.

The next five days were spent in acute discomfort, causing the corps to refer to the spot as "Point Distress." Unable to get off the beach because of the cliffs above them, they had to construct a makeshift camp among the driftwood at the water's edge. With no SHELTER from the rain, they spent a miserable first day there and had to move their baggage before the high tide swept over it. The next two days were equally unpleasant as the waves continued to crash below them and the rain poured down. Desperate to find a better campsite, the captains sent JOHN COLTER, ALEXANDER WILLARD, and GEORGE SHANNON around Point Ellice on November 13, after the weather had calmed. Colter returned by land the next day to report that the bay on the other side of Point Ellice had a good beach, calmer waters, and some game available inland. However, it was not until the afternoon of the 15th that they were able to work all the canoes around the point and camp below today's Chinook Point on the eastern side of what they called Haley's Bay (today's Baker's Bay). They named this location STATION CAMP.

On November 12, Clark had written, "It would be distressing to a feeling person to See our Situation at this time all cold and wet with our beding &c. also wet, in a Cove Scarcely large enough to Contain us . . . canoes at the mercy of the waves & driftwood . . . robes & leather Clothes are rotten." Not surprisingly, the corps was delighted to leave their old campsite and move to their new camp west of Point Ellice, where they were able to build shelters from the timbers of an abandoned Indian village and find game to kill.

From this campsite Lewis and Clark led separate parties to CAPE DISAPPOINTMENT, the headland on the Pacific, and up the coast. They had hoped to find trading ships in the area that might take all or part of the party back to the East, but none were to be seen. Clark, however, took some consolation in adding his name to Lewis's on a tree at Cape Disappointment and adding the suffix "By Land from the U. States in 1804 & 1805."

On November 24, after a vote in which all members of the party including SACAGAWEA and YORK were asked for their opinion, it was decided to find a campsite on the south side of the river. The next day they made their way back up the estuary to a point where they were able to cross to the southern bank and find the spot where they built what was to be their home for the winter: FORT CLATSOP.

Further Reading

Fifer, Barbara, and Vicky Soderberg. *Along the Trail with Lewis and Clark.* Great Falls, Mont.: Montana Magazine, 1998.

MacGregor, Carol Lynn, ed. *The Journals of Patrick Gass, Member of the Lewis and Clark Expedition.* Missoula, Mont.: Mountain Press Publishing Company, 1997.

Mussulman, Joseph. "Ocean in View." From: *Discovering Lewis and Clark: The Extent of Our Journey.* Available on-line. URL: http://www.lewis-clark.org/FTCCOLUMBIA/fc_stac1.htm. Downloaded on March 10, 2002.

political parties

Although the founding fathers had made no provision for political parties when framing the Constitution, inevitably differences of opinion among the nation's leaders led to the formation of opposing, like-minded groups. The first two political parties, the Federalists and Anti-Federalists, coalesced during George Washington's presidency. Although theoretically apolitical, Washington held Federalist views, and his successor, John Adams, was the first and only Federalist to be elected president. The Anti-Federalists became the Republicans and subsequently the Democratic-Republicans; this party was led by THOMAS JEFFERSON, who in 1801 succeeded Adams as president in the nation's first peaceful transfer of power between parties.

The United States has essentially been a two-party nation ever since, despite several attempts to change the system. Although the Federalists eventually died away, they were superseded by the Whigs, precursors to today's Republican Party. Meanwhile, with Jefferson's election to the presidency, the Democratic-Republicans held executive power for the next 28 years. By the time of Andrew Jackson's presidency they had become today's Democratic Party, retaining power for another 12 years.

In Lewis and Clark's time, the differences between the Federalists and Democratic-Republicans were epitomized by the views of the parties' leaders, ALEXANDER HAMILTON and Thomas Jefferson, respectively. In the early 1790s, Hamilton, then secretary of the Treasury, promoted fiscal programs founded on a strong, centralized federal government. He actively sought to assume the Revolutionary War debts of both the old Confederation and the states; to create a national bank; to implement federal tariffs for the support of manufacturing; and, perhaps most controversially, to impose internal excise taxes to raise funds for the Treasury. Hamilton's goal was to firmly establish the new national government as a facilitator of business and financial progress. As president, John Adams also supported this goal and encouraged close economic ties with GREAT BRITAIN. However, ideological differences between the two eventually weakened the Federalist Party.

The Federalists were clearly favorable to the landed elite of the Northeast. Opposition to their policies soon began to emerge among farmers, traders, and southern plantation owners, who favored stronger state governments to offset the power of the federal government. Consequently, they opposed a national bank, a standing army, close ties with Britain, and other federal proposals. These views were supported by then Secretary of State Thomas Jefferson and by Hamilton's onetime coauthor of *The Federalist Papers,* JAMES MADISON. Jefferson promoted simplicity and frugality in government and upheld states' rights as preferable to an overly intrusive federal government.

It is therefore surprising that one of his first actions as president was to urge the purchase of the LOUISIANA TERRITORY, a distinctly Federalist move that served to strengthen the power of the executive branch. Equally surprising, the Federalists protested the LOUISIANA PURCHASE, calling it costly and wasteful. When the expedition was wintering in CAMP DUBOIS, Jefferson wrote to Lewis often and kept him informed on the political situation in Washington. On January 13, 1804, he noted: "The enquiries are perpetual as to your progress. The Feds [Federalists], alone still treat it as philosophism, and would rejoice in it's failure. . . . I hope you will take care of yourself, and be the living witness of their malice and folly."

The Federalists were indeed chastened by the success of the expedition, and that in combination with the addition of more than 800,000 square miles to the nation only increased Jefferson's popularity with the electorate. As a result of this and other factors, the Federalist Party ceased to be a force in American politics after the election of 1804.

Further Reading

Aldrich, John. *Why Parties? The Origin and Transformation of Political Parties in America.* Chicago: University of Chicago Press, 1995.

Pomp (Pompy)   See CHARBONNEAU, JEAN BAPTISTE.

Pompeys Pillar   See POMPY'S TOWER.

Pompy's Tower (Pompeys Pillar)

Pompy's Tower is a flat-topped outcrop of sandstone located 28 miles east of what is now Billings, Montana. Rising nearly 128 feet from its base near the YELLOWSTONE RIVER, it is an obvious vantage point over the surrounding countryside.

In July 1806, after the expedition had split into smaller groups, WILLIAM CLARK and his party were returning down the valley of the Yellowstone, while Lewis and the remainder had gone to explore the MARIAS RIVER and its upper reaches. The first part of Clark's journey was by horseback since the turbulence of the upper stretches of the river had made it unsafe for building makeshift BULLBOATS and there were no trees suitable for building CANOES. Finally, near present-day Park City, Montana, he found cottonwood TREES of sufficient size, and on July 24 he set off downstream in two canoes lashed together. He took with him six men, SACAGAWEA, and her little boy, JEAN BAPTISTE CHARBONNEAU (nicknamed Pomp and Pompey or Pompy). Left behind were Sergeant NATHANIEL PRYOR and three other men, who were to take the HORSES across country to the MANDAN INDIAN villages.

The journey downstream was fast and easy, and Clark traveled 69 miles on the first day. It was on the next day, July 25, that they reached "a remarkable rock Situated in an extensive bottom, on the Stard. [starboard, or south] Side of the river & 250 paces from it." He measured its circumference to be around 400 paces, or 1,200 feet, and estimated its height to be 200 feet (he was off by some 70 feet). Clark climbed to the top, noted what he could see—a "most extensive view in every direction"—and carved his name and the date ("W Clark July 25 1806") on the soft sandstone, alongside the many pic-

Clark named Pompy's Tower, also known as Pompeys Pillar, after Sacagawea's little boy, Jean Baptiste (Pomp) Charbonneau. The inscription he left in the soft sandstone can still be seen today. *(Montana Historical Society, Helena)*

tographs that Indians had carved there before him. He named the rock "Pompy's Tower" after the little boy who had captured his affection.

Meanwhile, south of Clark, Sergeant Pryor and his men found themselves on foot after some CROW INDIANS stole their horses on the second night of their journey. They made their way back to the Yellowstone, reaching it at Pompy's Tower, where they constructed two BULLBOATS and followed Clark down the river, catching up with him 12 days later.

Clark's inscription on Pompy's Tower—the only extant physical trace the expedition left along their journey—can still be seen. The rock is now a National Historic Landmark. Today it is called Pompeys Pillar. The view of it from the river that Clark once had is now obscured by tall growths of cottonwood trees.

Further Reading

Clawson, Roger. *Pompeys Pillar: Crossroads of the Frontier.* Billings, Mont.: The Prose Works, 1992.

Moulton, Gary E., ed. *Atlas of the Lewis and Clark Expedition.* Revised ed. Lincoln: University of Nebraska Press, 1999.

Mussulman, Joseph. "Pompy's Tower." From *Discovering Lewis and Clark: Clark on the Yellowstone.* Available on-line. URL: http://www.lewis-clark.org/CLARK-YELLOWSTONE/POMPSTOWER/yr_pomp-remarkable.htm. Downloaded on February 28, 2002.

Schmidt, Thomas. *National Geographic Guide to the Lewis & Clark Trail.* Washington, D.C.: National Geographic, 1998.

porcupines   See ANIMALS, NEW SPECIES.

portable soup   See SOUP, PORTABLE.

portage

According to Merriam Webster's dictionary, *portage* is defined as "the labor of carrying or transporting." The term today evokes a picture of buckskin-clad trappers unloading furs from a canoe, which was then lifted onto their shoulders and taken along the riverbank. This is not entirely inaccurate because it was commonly done by the French-Canadian trappers around the Great Lakes. However, they were using the slim, light, birch-bark CANOES of the area.

The dugout canoes used by the CORPS OF DISCOVERY were a very different matter. On their way up the MISSOURI RIVER to the MANDAN villages, the explorers had run into sandbanks, rocks, TREES floating downstream, and snags of every sort. The canoes they hacked out of cottonwood trees at FORT MANDAN were built for strength rather than speed. Further, the SUPPLIES AND EQUIPMENT that they were carrying meant portage involved far more labor than carrying a birch-bark canoe and some furs overland.

It has been calculated that each of the expedition's canoes weighed at least 1,000 pounds. They also had thousands of pounds in equipment and baggage. Their first—and worst—portage around the GREAT FALLS took them from June 22 to July 2, 1805. It was an 18-mile drag from PORTAGE CREEK to WHITE BEAR ISLANDS over rough, rocky ground covered in PRICKLY PEARS, which soon tore their shoes to shreds. Even with the aid of two crude, wheeled "wagons" PATRICK GASS had constructed from a cottonwood tree, it needed every man pulling and struggling to get two canoes along. WILLIAM CLARK wrote that "those not employed in repairing the course, are asleep in a moment, many limping from the soreness of their feet, some become faint for a few moments."

Reading the accounts of this portage, one can appreciate why the captains made a point of hiding the rough wheels they had made for their "wagons." There were no other trees of sufficient size within 20 miles, and the wheels would come in useful on the return journey.

The next major portage for the party lay far ahead on the other side of the CONTINENTAL DIVIDE. Having met the SHOSHONE INDIANS in the LEMHI RIVER valley and procured HORSES from them, the party hid their canoes at CAMP FORTUNATE and rode northward beside the Lemhi on August 30, their supplies now carried on packhorses. After 11 days of misery and near-starvation on the LOLO TRAIL, they met the NEZ PERCE INDIANS, and after spending some 10 days making

Right: The double dotted line in the lower left of Clark's map shows the 18-mile portage around the Great Falls. While Clark oversaw the portage, Lewis attempted to build his iron-frame boat. These tasks kept the expedition in the Great Falls area for a month. *(American Philosophical Society)*

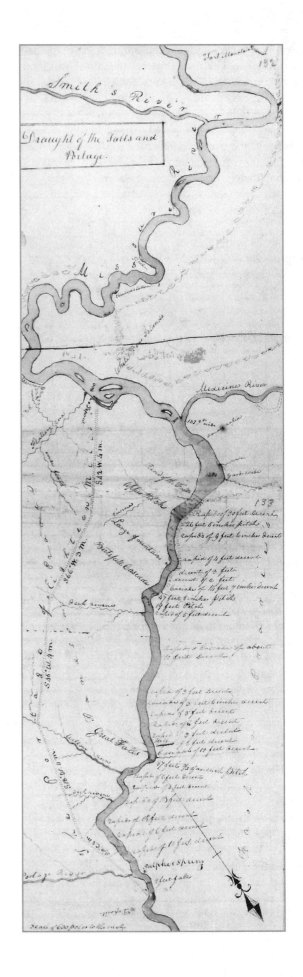

canoes at CANOE CAMP, they set off down the CLEARWATER RIVER on October 7.

Their journey down the Clearwater and SNAKE RIVERS to the COLUMBIA RIVER was eventful. The rapids were fierce—the journal writers mention them almost daily—and canoes were sunk, upset, overturned, and battered by rocks. Yet never does there seem to have been any suggestion of portaging the canoes around the many rapids that they encountered. There are several possible reasons why they did not do so. They had spent long months fighting their way upstream against the Missouri current. Now, at least, they had the current with them. They also knew they were nearing the end of their journey to the PACIFIC OCEAN and, adventurous young men that they were, they were eager to reach it.

It is also evident that they had become better boat handlers. PIERRE CRUZATTE and FRANÇOIS LABICHE had both been employed initially as skilled watermen, but by this time that could be said of every man on the expedition. Finally, the memory of the exhausting portage around the Great Falls may still have been in their minds.

On October 22, 1805, the expedition came to what they knew would be the most difficult stretch of the Columbia: the 55 miles of water from CELILO FALLS through the Short Narrows, the Long Narrows, The Dalles, and the Cascades (see COLUMBIA RIVER GORGE). Although they had to pull the heavy canoes out of the water to portage them around the falls, they only had to drag them some 450 yards, and Indians with horses were hired to make the task a light one. When they came to the Short Narrows, the captains took a long look at the turbulent water. They put the most valuable items on shore to be carried along the riverbank by the soldiers who could not swim; then they took all five canoes through the rapids, watched in amazement by the Indians on the bank. They repeated the process at the Long Narrows, three miles downstream, again before a large Indian audience.

When they came to their last obstacle, the Cascades, Patrick Gass made an unusual entry in his journal: "We unloaded our canoes and took them past the rapids, some part of the way by water and some over rocks 8 or 10 feet high. It was the most fatiguing business we have been engaged in for a long time, and we got but two over all day. . . ." Most historians accept that this comment implied the canoes were taken overland, thus making it the last portage of their westward journey. Below the Cascades they were in tidal waters and could canoe the rest of the way to the Pacific.

The expedition spent the worst of the winter at FORT CLATSOP at the mouth of the Columbia and began their return journey up the river on March 23, 1806. Aware of the waterfalls and rapids ahead of them up the river, the captains resolved to procure horses at The Dalles, the nearest place where these were available. They came back to the Cascades on April 9, and, after the baggage was unpacked the canoes were pulled upstream by men walking on the bank. It took them three days to complete the passage, during which they lost a canoe. Realizing they would have difficulty in taking their large dugouts further up the river, they destroyed them and managed to pro-

cure smaller, lighter craft from Indians in a nearby village. With some horses they had managed to buy, they portaged around Celilo Falls on April 21, and after obtaining more horses, they left the river on April 24.

Ahead of them lay their last portage, back past the Great Falls of the Missouri. This began on July 21, 1806. Lewis was away to the north, exploring the MARIAS RIVER, while Clark was far to the south, traveling down the YELLOWSTONE RIVER. The portage around the falls was carried out by Patrick Gass, JOHN ORDWAY, and a team of men, who completed the task in six days. The previous year it had taken the entire party twice as long, but this time the smaller group had four horses to help pull Gass's "wagons."

On July 27 they left Portage Creek behind. From then on, only the Missouri lay between the explorers and ST. LOUIS.

Further Reading

Ambrose, Stephen E. *Undaunted Courage: Meriwether Lewis, Thomas Jefferson, and the Opening of the American West.* New York: Simon and Schuster, 1996.

Gill, Larry. "The Great Portage: Lewis and Clark's Overland Journey Around the Great Falls of the Missouri River." *We Proceeded On* 1, no. 4 (fall 1975): 6–9.

Hawke, David Freeman. *Those Tremendous Mountains: The Story of the Lewis and Clark Expedition.* New York: W. W. Norton & Company, 1998.

MacGregor, Carol Lynn, ed. *The Journals of Patrick Gass, Member of the Lewis and Clark Expedition.* Missoula, Mont.: Mountain Press Publishing Company, 1997.

Moulton, Gary E., ed. *The Journals of the Lewis and Clark Expedition.* 13 vols. Lincoln: University of Nebraska Press, 1983–2001.

Portage Creek (Belt Creek)

Portage Creek—or Belt Creek, as it is known today—runs into the MISSOURI RIVER some 12 miles northeast of present-day Great Falls, Montana. On June 17, 1805, three days after MERIWETHER LEWIS had first seen the GREAT FALLS of the Missouri, the main party camped just below the mouth of Portage Creek. Here they hid one of the two PIROGUES, which was far too heavy to be dragged across country, and dug a CACHE in which they hid pork, ammunition, and flour, as well as some of WILLIAM CLARK's MAPS and Lewis's writing desk. To reduce the length of the PORTAGE around the falls, half of the corps took the CANOES and baggage 1 1/2 miles up Portage Creek while others began to cut TREES to make the crude wagons on which they would pull the canoes along the portage route. It was not until July 1 that they left Portage Creek behind.

More than a year later, on the return journey, PATRICK GASS and JOHN ORDWAY supervised the 14 men who hauled the canoes and baggage back down the portage route, completing their task on July 26, 1806. Of their last trip down, Gass wrote: "It is with the greatest difficulty we can get along with the canoe; though in the evening, after a hard day's labour, we got her safe to Portage river, and the men run her down to the lower landing place, where we encamped."

Today, Salem Bridge on Belt Creek stands at the start of the portage across country. Salem Road follows the first two miles of the route that the explorers followed.

Further Reading

Fifer, Barbara, and Vicky Soderberg. *Along the Trail with Lewis and Clark.* Great Falls, Mont.: Montana Magazine, 1998.

MacGregor, Carol Lynn, ed. *The Journals of Patrick Gass, Member of the Lewis and Clark Expedition.* Missoula, Mont.: Mountain Press Publishing Company, 1997.

Schmidt, Thomas. *National Geographic Guide to the Lewis & Clark Trail.* Washington, D.C.: National Geographic, 1998.

Posecopsahe   See BLACK CAT.

Potts, John (ca. 1776–ca. 1809) *private in the permanent party*

Born in Dillenburg, Germany, Private John Potts immigrated to the United States. It is not known when he arrived, but what is known is that he enlisted in the U.S. Army in 1800 and was serving in Tennessee when he volunteered for the expedition in November 1803; he was officially enrolled on January 1, 1804. Previously a miller by trade, Potts was described as having black hair, blue eyes, and a fair complexion.

Although little mentioned in the expedition's JOURNALS, Potts was apparently a trusted member of the CORPS OF DISCOVERY. On June 29, 1804, he was called on to serve as judge advocate at the COURT-MARTIAL of Privates JOHN COLLINS and HUGH HALL. The two were subsequently found guilty of breaking into the corps's supply of whiskey and getting drunk while Collins had been on night guard duty.

Following the expedition, Potts went to work for MANUEL LISA, joining a trapping party to the Upper MISSOURI RIVER in 1807. At Fort Raymond the following year, he signed a promissory note in the amount of $424.50, payable to Lisa, apparently for trapping supplies. Two other men, including fellow expedition member PETER WEISER, also signed this note. Potts later went to work for fur trader Andrew Henry, and in 1808 or 1809 (the date varies in different sources), he met JOHN COLTER, now a trapper and mountain man, at THREE FORKS on the Missouri. When their party was ambushed by BLACKFEET INDIANS, Colter managed to escape, but Potts was killed and mutilated. After his death, Lisa and the Missouri Fur Company sued his estate for past debts totaling $1,000.

Further Reading

Clarke, Charles G. *The Men of the Lewis and Clark Expedition: A Biographical Roster of the Fifty-One Members and a Composite Diary of Their Activities from All Known Sources.* 1970. Reprint, Lincoln: Bison Books, University of Nebraska Press, 2002.

North Dakota Lewis & Clark Bicentennial Foundation. *Members of the Corps of Discovery.* Bismarck, N.Dak.: United Printing and Mailing, 2000.

PBS Online. *Lewis and Clark: Inside the Corps of Discovery:* "Lesser Known Members of the Corps." Available on-line. URL: http://www.pbs.org/lewisandclark/inside/lesser.html. Downloaded on May 18, 2001.

Powell, John Wesley (1834–1902) *explorer*

American exploration west of the Mississippi can be said to have started with Lewis and Clark in 1804 and ended with John Wesley Powell in 1871. Born in Mount Morris, New York, Powell was a self-taught student of botany, zoology, and geology. At age 22 he made a solo trip by rowboat from the Falls of St. Anthony to the mouth of the MISSISSIPPI RIVER, collecting botanical and geological specimens on the way. In subsequent years he made similar trips down the OHIO and Illinois Rivers and up the Des Moines River.

Powell volunteered for the Union during the Civil War, serving as an officer with the 20th Illinois Volunteers and losing his right arm at the Battle of Shiloh. After the war he became professor of geology and curator of the museum at Illinois Wesleyan University. He continued to make field trips out West, leading geological expeditions into Colorado in 1867 and Utah in 1868. He eventually formulated a project to explore the Grand Canyon and the Colorado River. In May

A self-taught student of the natural sciences, John Wesley Powell is considered to be the last explorer of the American West. *(Library of Congress, Prints and Photographs Division [LC-USZ62-20230])*

1869 he and nine men set out from Green River, Wyoming, down the Green River. Three months later, Powell and five of his men emerged at a point downstream from the Grand Canyon now flooded by Lake Mead. They had floated or portaged countless rapids and falls on the Colorado; four of the men had deserted the dangerous expedition.

Returning to Illinois, Powell immediately began to raise money for another expedition in 1871 to produce a map and more scientific observations. Powell's writing on the arid regions of the United States, based in part on his two Colorado River expeditions, was published in 1878. It advocated restraint in the settlement of the West and warned of the danger of scarce natural resources.

Powell became director of the U.S. Geological Survey in 1881, serving until 1894. He died in 1902 and is buried in Arlington Cemetery.

Further Reading

Moring, John. *Men with Sand: Great Explorers of the North American West.* Helena, Mont.: Twodot Books, 1998.

Powell, John Wesley. *The Exploration of the Colorado River and Its Canyons.* Reprint, Washington, D.C.: National Geographic Books, 2002.

Worster, Donald. *A River Running West: The Life of John Wesley Powell.* New York: Oxford University Press, 2001.

prairie dogs

On April 7, 1805, the expedition's KEELBOAT left FORT MANDAN to make its return trip down the MISSOURI RIVER to ST. LOUIS. On board were boxes filled with items destined for President THOMAS JEFFERSON, including ARTIFACTS AND SPECIMENS, reports, MAPS, LETTERS, and copies of JOURNALS. Also on board were some live ANIMALS previously unknown to science: four magpies, a prairie GROUSE hen, and a prairie dog. Of these only one magpie and the prairie dog made it to Jefferson alive in mid-August that year.

The rodent known as the black-tailed prairie dog (*Cynomys ludovicianus*) incited great interest and comment from members of the CORPS OF DISCOVERY. It is often confused with the ground squirrel. MERIWETHER LEWIS sometimes called it a burrowing squirrel, but JOHN ORDWAY gave it the name by which it is known today—prairie dog. On September 7, 1804, about 25 miles above the Niobrara River in what is now Boyd County, Nebraska, the corps came across their first colony of prairie dogs, a species hitherto unreported. WILLIAM CLARK wrote that as they came down the side of a hill they "discovered a Village of Small animals that burrow in the grown (those animals are called by the French, Petite Chien) Killed one and Caught one a live by poreing a great quantity of Water in his hole. . . ." It had taken the better part of the day to flood out this one animal, which they kept in a cage and sent back to Washington the following spring.

As would be the case for those who came after the expedition, Clark was struck by the size of the prairie-dog villages:

[T]he Village of those animals Covered about 4 acres of Ground on a gradual decent of a hill and Contains great numbers of holes on the top of which those little animals Set erect, make a Whisteling noise and whin alarmed Step into their hole. we por'd into one of the holes 5 barrels of water without filling it. Those Animals are about the Size of a Small Squirrel. . . .

Using the term *barking squirrels,* the expedition often noted seeing prairie-dog villages up the course of the Missouri, including a note by Lewis on June 3, 1805, just below the mouth of the MARIAS RIVER: "In this plain and from one to nine miles from the river or any water, we saw the largest collection of the burrowing or barking squirrels that we had ever yet seen; we passed through a skirt of the territory of this community for about 7 miles." While wintering over at FORT CLATSOP, he noted that "the barking squirrel and handsome ground squirrel of the plains or the East side of the ROCKY MOUNTAINS are not found in the plains of the Columbia."

On July 1, 1806, near present-day Lolo, Montana, Lewis wrote:

The little animal found in the plains of the Missouri which I have called the barking squirrel weighs from 3 to 3^{1}/2 pounds, it's form is that of the squirrel . . . these squirrels burrow in the ground in the open plains usually at a considerable distance from water yet are never seen at any distance from their burrows, six or eight usually reside in one burrow to which there is never more than one entrance. these burrows are of great debth. I once dug and pursued a burrow to the debth of ten feet and did not reach it's greatest debth. . . .

The vast area of the prairie dog villages might seem remarkable to modern eyes, but in 1905 Vernon Bailey, employed by the U.S. Biological Survey, reported that he had found a prairie dog village in Texas measuring approximately 25,000 square miles and estimated that it contained as many as 400 million prairie dogs.

The prairie dog that survived the trip back to Washington was later sent to CHARLES WILLSON PEALE. It was known to be still alive on April 5, 1806, when Peale wrote to Jefferson that he would attempt to draw it "when it becomes more animated, as it must be soon, as the spring becomes warmer, at present it stirs but little." Nothing more is known of it after this date, and no drawings of it have ever been found.

Further Reading

Burroughs, Raymond Darwin, ed. *The Natural History of the Lewis and Clark Expedition.* East Lansing: Michigan State University Press, 1995.

Cutright, Paul Russell. "The Odyssey of the Magpie and the Prairie Dog." *Missouri Historical Society Bulletin* 23, no. 3 (1967): 215–228.

———. *Lewis & Clark: Pioneering Naturalists.* Lincoln and London: University of Nebraska Press, 1969.

Graves, Russell A. *The Prairie Dog: Sentinel of the Plains*. Lubbock: Texas Tech University Press, 2001.

Osgood, Ernest S. "A Prairie Dog for Mr. Jefferson." *Montana: The Magazine of Western History* 19, no. 2 (1969): 54–56.

prairie fires

On August 15, 1804, the CORPS OF DISCOVERY was just south of present-day Dakota City, Nebraska, looking for the OMAHA INDIANS, whom they knew inhabited the area. In his journal for that day, MERIWETHER LEWIS wrote: "In the morning some men were sent to examine the cause of a great smoke from the north-east, which seemed to indicate that some Indians were near; but they found that a small party, who had lately passed that way had left some small trees burning. . . ." Two days later, still seeking to arrange a conference with the Omaha, he wrote:

> This nation having left their village, that desirable purpose cannot be effected; but in order to bring in any neighboring tribes, we set the surrounding prairies on fire. This is the customary signal made by traders to apprise the Indians of their arrival; it is also used between different nations as an indication of any event which they have previously agreed to announce in that way, and as soon as it is seen collects the neighboring tribes, unless they apprehend that it is made by their enemies.

WILLIAM CLARK's comment was more succinct: "Set the Praries on fire to bring the Mahars and Soues if any wer near, this being the useal signal." On September 23, 1804, the party saw a cloud of smoke from the southwest and inferred, correctly, that it was an indication the TETON LAKOTA INDIANS (Teton Sioux) were nearby. They met the Lakota two days later.

While firing a section of prairie to make smoke had obvious advantages as a means of passing information or warnings across the wide, empty plains, it was also employed as a basic form of animal husbandry. Both Lewis and Clark reported that the PLAINS INDIANS burned stretches of prairies in the spring to encourage new grass growth, which attracted BUFFALO and ELK. Early in 1805, during their stay at FORT MANDAN, Clark wrote: "[A] cloudy morning & Smokey all day from the burning of the plains, which was set on fire by the Minnetarries [HIDATSA INDIANS] for an early crop of Grass, as an enducement for the Buffalow to feed on." The technique is still used today for ecological reasons in many parts of the world, including the United states.

Lewis believed this deliberate burning of the prairie grass was the reason for so few TREES on the open plains: "This want of timber is by no means attributable to a deficiency in the soil to produce it, but owes its origin to the ravages of the fires, which the natives kindle in these plains at all seasons of the year." This view has long been the subject of scientific argument, and many now believe the lack of timber on the high plains is simply the result of low rainfall and the shallowness of the soil.

There was an obvious danger of prairie fires starting by lightning strikes or by accident due to carelessness. Once lit, the fires could move as fast as 600 feet per minute, with temperatures up to 700°F. On June 5, 1804, near modern Jefferson City, Missouri, the expedition met two French traders returning from the Kansas territory where they "had caught great quantities of BEAVER, but had lost much of their game by fires from the prairies." On October 29, 1804, just after their arrival at the MANDAN INDIAN villages, Lewis and Clark saw just how dangerous a prairie fire could be, as noted in the Coues edition of the JOURNALS:

> In the evening the prairie took fire, either by accident or design, and burned with great fury, the whole plain being enveloped in flames. So rapid was its progress that a man and a woman were burnt to death before they could reach a place of safety; another man with his wife and child were much burnt, and several other persons narrowly escaped destruction. Among the rest a boy of the half-white breed escaped unhurt in the midst of the flames. His safety was ascribed to the great medicine spirit, who had preserved him on account of his being white. But a much more natural cause was the presence of mind of his mother, who, seeing no hope of carrying off her son, threw him on the ground and, covering him with the fresh hide of a buffalo, escaped herself from the flames. As soon as the fire had passed, she returned and found him untouched, the skin having prevented the flame from reaching the grass on which he lay.

In the captains' laconic account lies the factual origin of an incident that was to feature in many western stories thereafter, including James Fenimore Cooper's *The Prairie* (1827).

Further Reading

Cutright, Paul Russell. *Lewis & Clark: Pioneering Naturalists*. Lincoln: University of Nebraska Press/Bison Books, 1989.

Lewis, Meriwether, and William Clark. *The History of the Lewis and Clark Expedition*. Edited by Elliott Coves; 4 vols., 1893, Harper. Reprinted in 3 vols., New York: Dover Publications, 1979.

Schafer, Shaun. "Prairie Fires Designed to Help Nature." IMDiversity Daily News, Associated Press. Available on-line. URL: http://www.imdiversity.com/Article_Detail.asp?Article_ID=6612. Downloaded on February 28, 2002.

prairie wolves See WOLVES.

prehistoric animals

In his remarkably detailed and specific MISSION OBJECTIVES, President THOMAS JEFFERSON told MERIWETHER LEWIS that "Other objects worthy of notice will be: . . . the animals of the country generally, & especially those not known in the U.S. the remains or accounts of which may be deemed rare or extinct. . . ." This comment stemmed from Jefferson's wide range of interests. An enthusiastic astronomer, meteorologist, and botanist, he was also a keen paleontologist and proud of his famous collection of fossils, especially the bones of a creature found in Greenbrier County, West Virginia. Dr. CASPAR WISTAR correctly identified this as a giant ground sloth (a prehistoric animal about the size of an ox) and named it *Megalonyx jeffersoni*.

Because of his interest in fossils, Jefferson arranged for Lewis to spend some time with Dr. Wistar in PHILADELPHIA. Like the president, Wistar believed that mastodons and giant ground sloths might still be found in the unknown territory to the west, and it was he who advised Lewis to inspect recent finds at Cincinnati, Ohio.

Consequently, during his journey down the OHIO RIVER, Lewis stopped at Cincinnati on September 28, 1803, and inspected the fossils that Dr. William Goforth had found at Big Bone Lick some 20 miles away. Lewis wrote a long letter to Jefferson on what he saw, which included several "mammoth" bones. He also noted variations among the many scythe-shaped tusks there and wondered whether they were "acknowledged tusks of the mammoth" or were of another species. Goforth allowed him to send some specimens to Jefferson, but these never arrived. (After the expedition, WILLIAM CLARK visited the same site and sent a leg bone and the jaws of the *Mastodon americanus* to Jefferson; these are now at MONTICELLO.)

On September 10, 1804, Sergeant PATRICK GASS reported from what is now Gregory County, South Dakota: "On the top of these bluffs we found the skeleton or back bones of a FISH, 45 feet long, and petrified: part of these bones were sent to the City of Washington." Lewis also described the find: "Just below this island [Cedar Island] on a hill to the south, is the backbone of a fish 45 feet long, tapering toward the tail and in a perfect state of petrifaction, fragments of which were collected and sent to Washington." It is now thought this was not a fish but a plesiosaur (aquatic dinosaur). The sections Lewis and Clark sent back are now in the Smithsonian Institution.

On July 25, 1806, Clark and his party were descending the YELLOWSTONE RIVER while Lewis and his men explored the headwaters of the MARIAS RIVER. About 25 miles east of present-day Billings, Montana, they halted, and Clark climbed to the top of the outcrop he named POMPY'S TOWER (now called Pompeys Pillar). After descending, he camped a couple of miles downstream, shot two bighorn SHEEP for FOOD, and noted: "[D]ureing the time the men were getting the two big horns which I had killed to the river I employed myself in getting pieces of the rib of a fish which was Semented within the face of the rock this rib is about 3 inches in Secumference about the middle it is 3 feet in length tho part of the end appears to have been broken off. . . . I have several pieces of this rib." The site still yields dinosaur remains, and it is now thought that Clark was describing part of a dinosaur rib. Unfortunately, the pieces have been lost, but there seems little doubt that William Clark was the first American to describe the excavation of a dinosaur fossil.

Further Reading

Brooklyn College, City University of New York. "Dinosaur History: William Clark." Available on-line. URL: http://academic. brooklyn.cuny.edu/geology/chamber/clark.html. Downloaded on February 26, 2002.

Cutright, Paul Russell. *Lewis & Clark: Pioneering Naturalists.* Lincoln: University of Nebraska Press/Bison Books, 1989.

preparations for the expedition

On May 14, 1804, the CORPS OF DISCOVERY began its journey up the MISSOURI RIVER, setting out from CAMP DUBOIS in a KEELBOAT and two PIROGUES. Ahead of them lay unknown territory, friendly and hostile Indians, new species of PLANTS and ANIMALS to record, mountains to cross, and perils they could then only imagine. Behind them were months of planning, traveling, organizing, and preparing on the part of the corps's two captains, MERIWETHER LEWIS and WILLIAM CLARK.

The first stage of preparations for the expedition was entirely Lewis's responsibility. In January 1803, as soon as the U.S. CONGRESS had approved THOMAS JEFFERSON's request to appropriate $2,500 to fund the expedition, Lewis began to draw up lists of the SUPPLIES AND EQUIPMENT that he would need and to make plans for what he had to accomplish in the coming months. Jefferson, meanwhile, began to draft the instructions that would form Lewis's MISSION OBJECTIVES and wrote to scientific colleagues in PHILADELPHIA, asking them to advise and instruct Lewis in certain fields, including NAVIGATION, astronomy, medicine, and botany. He also arranged for French and British passports for Lewis (the Spanish had refused to cooperate).

Lewis had to cover many areas but sometimes got bogged down in the details. At HARPERS FERRY in March, he arranged for the purchase of FIREARMS and ammunition as well as the construction of the framework for an IRON-FRAME BOAT that he had designed. His idea was to transport the boat's frame to the upper regions of the Missouri River, where it would be completed using wood and animal skins. So important was this pet project that he delayed his departure from Harpers Ferry to oversee it, causing considerable concern to Jefferson, who was anxious for him to begin his tutelage in Philadelphia.

Lewis's scientific education had already been supplemented considerably during his two years as Jefferson's private secretary. Thanks to the library at MONTICELLO as well as his association with the president, which had brought him into contact with some of the greatest thinkers of the age, Lewis was well versed in many scientific fields. The time he spent in Philadelphia with several leading scientists allowed him to develop the specific skills and knowledge that he would need for the journey, particularly in regard to NAVIGATION and ASTRONOMICAL OBSERVATIONS. As he pursued his studies, he also purchased navigational instruments, provisions, Indian GIFTS, tools, medical supplies, and other necessary equipment; much of this was procured for him by ISRAEL WHELAN, the purveyor of public supplies. In all, Lewis collected for the expedition some 2½ tons of items, which were loaded onto a five-horse wagon and dispatched to PITTSBURGH under military supervision in late May.

A Memorandom of Articles in readiness for the Voyage

14 Bags of Parchmeal of 2 bu each about — 1200
9 do Common do do N6 do — 800
11 do Corn Hulled do do — 1000
30 half Barrels of flour } (gross 3900 w) do — 3400
3 Bags do do }
7 do of Biscuit } (gross 6500) do — 560
4 Barrels do do }
7 Barrels of Salt of 2 bu each x (870) do — 750
50 Kegs of Pork (gross 4500) do — 3705
2 Boxes of Candles (one of which has 50 lb) do — 170
1 Bag of Candle-wick do — 8
1 do Coffee do — 50
1 do Beens & Pees do — 100
2 do Sugar do — 112
1 Keg of Hogs Lard do — 100
4 Barrels of Corn Hulled 1650 do — 600
1 do of Meal 170 do — 150

600 lb Grees
40 bushels Meal
24 do. Natches corn Hulled
21 Bales of Indian Goods
Tools of every Description &c &c.

our party

2 Capts 4 Sergeants, 3 Intptrs, 22 Ams 9 or 10 French, & York
also 1 Corpl & Six in a Perogue with 40 Days provision
for the party as far as these provisions last

During the Corps of Discovery's preparations at Camp Dubois, William Clark drew up this list of "Articles in Readiness for the Voyage."
(Yale Collection of Western Americana, Beinecke Rare Book and Manuscript Library)

When his business in Philadelphia was completed, Lewis returned to Washington, where he and Jefferson went through his final instructions. He also gathered more data, studied MAPS, and made all the final arrangements for his departure. Chief among these was writing to William Clark, inviting him to cocommand the expedition. Lewis also chose a replacement in case Clark did not accept: Lieutenant Moses Hooke (who would not have shared command as Clark did). Finally, on July 5, 1803, he left Washington, stopping at Harpers Ferry along the way to arrange for the transport of the guns and iron-frame boat to Pittsburgh, where he arrived on July 15. He had expected by that time to find the construction of the keelboat (which he had designed) nearly completed, but to his dismay the boat builder proved to be extremely dilatory. As each deadline for completion passed, and the water level of the OHIO RIVER dropped lower, Lewis grew increasingly desperate. While he was waiting, he purchased a PIROGUE.

There was one bright spot. On July 29 Clark's letter accepting the cocommand arrived in Pittsburgh, and the two began to correspond immediately on the issue of RECRUITING. It was agreed that Clark would wait for Lewis in CLARKSVILLE, Indiana, and in the meantime he would begin to select men for the expedition. Lewis already had recruits from the army post at Carlisle ready to man the keelboat. He also made one more addition to the team: his dog SEAMAN, purchased for $20.

The keelboat was no sooner finished than it and the pirogue were loaded and launched with a crew of 11 men on August 31, 1803. With the water level so low, they had an excruciatingly difficult task, and they often had to get out and lift the keelboat over the shallowest stretches. A stop was made at Wheeling, Virginia, to pick up supplies Lewis had sent ahead; he also purchased another pirogue. All told, it took the party six weeks to struggle down to the Falls of the Ohio and Clarksville, where they arrived on October 15. Here Lewis and Clark officially recruited the NINE YOUNG MEN FROM KENTUCKY and probably discussed how they would share their command. They left Clarksville on October 26 and made a stop at FORT MASSAC to pick up some more recruits. Then, on the night of November 13, they reached the Ohio's junction with the MISSISSIPPI RIVER.

Congress had originally authorized a party of up to 12 privates plus the captain and a sergeant. When the keelboat turned northward onto the Missouri River on November 20, however, it became apparent that more men were going to be needed. The decision was made to double the size of the party, and on November 28 Lewis and Clark stopped at the army post at KASKASKIA, where they recruited more soldiers into the expedition. Sixty miles later, after another RECRUITING stop at Cahokia, they arrived at ST. LOUIS.

While Clark saw to the establishment of the company's winter quarters at CAMP DUBOIS and the drilling of the men, Lewis attended to business in St. Louis. With the corps now considerably larger, the supplies and equipment he had bought would not be sufficient. More would be needed, and traders such as AUGUSTE CHOUTEAU, PIERRE CHOUTEAU, and MANUEL LISA were more than happy to supply them. The Chouteaus subsequently arranged for additional ENGAGÉS to help navigate the boats upriver as far as the MANDAN villages.

There was also information to be gathered. Both Lewis and Clark met with traders and trappers who gave them valuable data about the upper Missouri—its country, its Indians, and the game that could be hunted for FOOD, among other things. They studied MAPS and read published accounts by other explorers of the Missouri. They practiced making ASTRONOMICAL OBSERVATIONS, selected the men for the permanent party, and sent reports and a map back to Washington. As the time of departure neared, Lewis arranged for Captain AMOS STODDARD to act as his agent while he was away.

As a result, when the expedition set off from Camp Dubois in May 1804, they were well stocked with provisions; well supported with strong, capable men; and as well prepared as they could be for whatever lay ahead of them.

See also BARTON, BENJAMIN SMITH; ELLICOTT, ANDREW; HAY, JOHN; PATTERSON, ROBERT; RUSH, BENJAMIN; WISTAR, CASPAR.

Further Reading
Ambrose, Stephen E. *Undaunted Courage: Meriwether Lewis, Thomas Jefferson, and the Opening of the American West.* New York: Simon and Schuster, 1996.
Cutright, Paul Russell. *Contributions of Philadelphia to Lewis and Clark History.* Philadelphia: Philadelphia Chapter Lewis and Clark Trail Heritage Foundation, 2001. Also available on-line. URL: http://www.lewisandclarkphila.org/philadelphia/philadelphiacutright conten.html. Updated on October 15, 2001.
———. "Meriwether Lewis Prepares for a Trip West." *Bulletin of the Missouri Historical Society* 23, no. 1 (October 1966).
Hawke, David Freeman. *Those Tremendous Mountains: The Story of the Lewis and Clark Expedition.* New York: W. W. Norton & Company, 1998.
Jeffrey, Joseph D. "Meriwether Lewis at Harpers Ferry." *We Proceeded On* 20 (November 1994).
Large, Arlen. "'Additions to the Party': How an Expedition Grew and Grew." *We Proceeded On* 16, no. 1 (February 1990): 4–11.
Loos, John Louis. "William Clark's Part in the Preparation of the Lewis and Clark Expedition." *Bulletin of the Missouri Historical Society.* (July 1954).

prickly pears (Indian cactus)

The prickly pear, a small, ground-hugging cactus sometimes called the Indian cactus, was to prove a severe annoyance to the expedition for much of their journey. It was clearly familiar to them, since neither MERIWETHER LEWIS nor WILLIAM CLARK recorded it as a separate or new species. The references they did make to it were most often complaints of the irritation it gave them and their men.

On September 19, 1804, at the beginning of the Great Bend of the MISSOURI RIVER, Lewis wrote: "Opposite is a creek on the south about ten yards wide, which waters a plain where there are great numbers of the prickly pear, which name we gave to the creek [Prickley Pear Creek]." The following day,

Clark noted the "great quantities of the Prickly Piar which nearly ruin my feet."

From June 22 to July 2, 1805, the CORPS OF DISCOVERY engaged in the laborious, back-breaking toil of portaging all their equipment and CANOES around the GREAT FALLS of the Missouri. This task was aggravated by the prickly pear, which covered the ground along the PORTAGE route. Where it was not present, the ground was churned up into hardened clay ridges from the BUFFALO who watered there and destroyed the grass, creating conditions that allowed prickly pears to flourish. Consequently, the expedition found it well-nigh impossible not to tread on the little cacti against which their soft, thin moccasins were no defense. Even adding an extra insole of buffalo skin afforded little protection since the spines of the cacti still pierced their ankles and the sides of their feet. Each day ended with the painful business of pulling cactus spines from their sore and tired feet.

Early in July Lewis wrote, "Our trio of pests still invade and obstruct us on all occasions, these are Musquetoes, eye knats, and prickly pears, equal to any three curses that ever poor Egypt laboured under, except the Mohometant yoke." Later that month, below THREE FORKS, he noted that "[t]he prickley pear is now in full bloom and forms one of the beauties as well as the greatest pests of the plains." The explorers noticed that the cacti seemed to increase in density the further up the Missouri they went. Lewis recorded that one night, on the river bank, prickly pears were so prevalent he "could scarcely find room to lye."

After the expedition crossed the CONTINENTAL DIVIDE and made their way down along the valley of the SNAKE RIVER, they found the flat lands between the ROCKY MOUNTAINS and the CASCADE MOUNTAINS treeless, and the dominant plant was again the prickly pear. At the junction of the Snake and the COLUMBIA RIVERS, Clark noted it was "much worst thn I have before seen."

Only once during the entire journey did the explorers indicate the prickly pear had some practical use. Along the Columbia valley between the Snake River and CELILO FALLS, Sergeant PATRICK GASS wrote on October 20, 1805, "We could not get a single stick of wood to cook with; and had only a few small green willows." The JOURNALS emphasized this lack of fuel when they recorded that the next day Lewis and Clark observed Indians by the river "drying fish & Prickley pares" to burn during the winter.

Further Reading

Cutright, Paul Russell. *Lewis & Clark: Pioneering Naturalists.* Lincoln: University of Nebraska Press/Bison Books, 1989.

Primeau, Paul See ENGAGÉS.

pronghorns See ANTELOPES.

provisions See FOOD; SUPPLIES AND EQUIPMENT.

Pryor, Nathaniel (1772–1831) *sergeant in the permanent party*

Sergeant Nathaniel Hale Pryor was, like his cousin CHARLES FLOYD, one of the NINE YOUNG MEN FROM KENTUCKY. Born in Virginia, he was 11 years old when he moved with his parents, John and Nancy Pryor, to Kentucky, which was then frontier country. In 1798 he married Peggy Patton; although MERIWETHER LEWIS and WILLIAM CLARK had intended to recruit only single men for the expedition, they made an exception in Pryor's case, no doubt due to his superior skills as a woodsman and hunter. He officially joined the CORPS OF DISCOVERY on October 10, 1803, and was later made a sergeant in command of one of the corps's three squads.

Captain Lewis called Pryor "a man of character and ability," and he was apparently a reliable and resourceful soldier, often chosen for special missions or scouting parties. Nevertheless, before the expedition had gotten very far, he managed to become lost. On November 22, 1803, as the KEELBOAT moved along the OHIO RIVER toward the MISSOURI RIVER, Pryor went out HUNTING. When he failed to return, Lewis sounded a horn and had the guns fired several times over the next two days. Finally, on November 24, Pryor appeared and rejoined the crew; Lewis reported that "he was much fatiequed with his wandering and somewhat indisposed."

In June 1804 Pryor presided at the court-martial of privates JOHN COLLINS and HUGH HALL, who were charged and found guilty of drinking while on duty. Two months later, on August 20, his fellow sergeant and cousin, Charles Floyd, died of a ruptured appendix. In recognition of their relationship, Floyd's personal effects were given to Pryor.

In September that same year Sergeant Pryor was delegated to lead a small party to invite the YANKTON NAKOTA INDIANS (Yankton Sioux) to a council at CALUMET BLUFF. Their mission was embarrassingly successful for Pryor, as the Indians mistakenly believed he was the soldiers' leader and carried him into their camp on a painted buffalo robe. Pryor subsequently became the first American to describe a TIPI of the PLAINS INDIANS, reporting that it "was handsum made made of Buffalow Skins Painted different Colour, all compact & handSomly arranged, their Camps formed of a Conic form Containing about 12 or 15 persons each and 40 in number."

During the expedition's return in 1806, the decision was made at TRAVELERS' REST to split the corps into smaller parties, each with its own mission. Sergeant Pryor was to accompany Captain Clark's group to the YELLOWSTONE RIVER and from there he and three privates (Hugh Hall, GEORGE SHANNON, and RICHARD WINDSOR) were to take the HORSES across country back to the MANDAN villages. In addition, Pryor was charged with seeing to the delivery of an important letter from Captain Lewis to HUGH HENEY, an agent with the NORTH WEST COMPANY. Unfortunately, along the way some CROW INDIANS stole the horses Pryor and his men had been riding, thus making it impossible for them to complete their mission—and also leaving them without any means of transportation. The resourceful Pryor, however, built BULL BOATS, which they used to float down the Yellowstone and rejoin Clark.

All corps members had a landmark named for him or her, and in Pryor's case it was a mountain in Montana. (Pryor River in Oklahoma and the towns of Pryor in Montana and Oklahoma are also named after him.) He was promoted to ensign following the expedition, and in 1807 he was ordered to lead a party to escort the Mandan chief BIG WHITE back to his homeland after a long visit to Washington, D.C. The party was stopped, however, by hostile ARIKARA INDIANS; in the ensuing battle four men were killed, and former expedition member GEORGE SHANNON, also in the escort party, had to have a leg amputated. It was not until two years later that Big White finally made it home safely under an escort from the St. Louis Missouri Fur Company.

Pryor resigned from the army in 1810 to take part in the burgeoning FUR TRADE on the Upper Missouri. He rejoined the army in 1813, becoming a captain in 1814 and serving in the Battle of New Orleans in January 1815. After his discharge, Pryor set up a trading post on the Arkansas River, and in 1820 he married an Osage woman with whom he had several children. They lived among the OSAGE INDIANS until his death in 1831. He is buried in a cemetery near Pryor, Oklahoma. Although Pryor had kept a journal throughout the historic expedition, it has never been found.

Further Reading

Clarke, Charles G. *The Men of the Lewis and Clark Expedition: A Biographical Roster of the Fifty-One Members and a Composite Diary of Their Activities from All Known Sources.* 1970. Reprint, Lincoln: Bison Books, University of Nebraska Press, 2002.

Mussulman, Joseph. "Nathaniel Pryor's Mission." From *Discovering Lewis and Clark: Clark on the Yellowstone.* Available on-line. URL: http://www.lewis-clark.org/CLARK-YELLOWSTONE/PRYOR/yr_pryor-mmenu.htm. Downloaded on February 28, 2002.

North Dakota Lewis & Clark Bicentennial Foundation. *Members of the Corps of Discovery.* Bismarck, N.Dak.: United Printing and Mailing, 2000.

PBS Online. *Lewis and Clark: Inside the Corps of Discovery:* "Sergeant Nathaniel Pryor." Available on-line. URL: http://www.pbs.org/lewisandclark/inside/npryo.html. Downloaded on May 18, 2001.

punishment   See DISCIPLINE.

Pursh, Frederick (Frederick Pursch) (1774–1820)
botanist, explorer

Although MERIWETHER LEWIS had received instruction from Dr. BENJAMIN SMITH BARTON on identifying, labeling, dating, and preserving botanical specimens collected on the expedition, he lacked the training to classify and describe them using the approved Linnaean method. Specimens that had been shipped back east from FORT MANDAN were already in the care of Dr. Barton, but the elderly botanist seemed disinclined to classify them, perhaps due to ill health. Thus, Lewis was

delighted when Bernard McMahon, a PHILADELPHIA seed merchant and florist to whom both Lewis and THOMAS JEFFERSON had sent seeds, wrote to him:

> . . . *I would wish you to be here before the 20th inst. [April 1807] as there is at present a young man boarding in my house who, in my opinion, is better acquainted with plants, in general, then any man I ever conversed with on the subject. . . . He is a very intelligent and practical Botanist, would be well inclined to render you any service in his power. . . .*

The young man was Frederick Pursh (spelled Pursch in some sources), a German botanist who was collecting plants for Dr. Barton. McMahon's confidence in him was not misplaced, and after viewing Pursh's drawings and scientific descriptions, Lewis gladly placed the expedition's plant specimens into the botanist's hands, paying a total of $70 in advance.

Pursh was born in Grossenhain, Saxony, Germany, in 1774 and came to the United States in 1799 as a protégé of Dr. Barton. In 1806 and 1807, on Barton's behalf, he made two trips through the eastern United States that proved significant for their botanical discoveries. The second of these journeys took place shortly after he met Meriwether Lewis, but once he returned to Philadelphia in October 1807, Pursh applied himself to the task of classifying and naming the expedition's specimens with enthusiasm and exactitude. As Pursh's expertise was in plants, not in animals or minerals, he was not asked to work on the natural history volume of the JOURNALS, but it was intended that his drawings and descriptions would be used for the book; they were not.

Pursh labored on the Lewis and Clark plants for well more than a year, describing more than 100 western plants then new to science. However, by spring 1809, with no instructions received from Lewis in months, he was forced to look for other employment. By the time he heard of Lewis's suicide in October 1809, he was working for Dr. David Hosack at the Elgin Botanic Gardens in New York. Bernard McMahon, who had grown numerous new plants from seeds of the original specimens, wrote to Jefferson in December, asking what should be done with the plants he had and mentioning that Pursh still had drawings and descriptions and would "expect a reasonable compensation for his trouble." What McMahon did not know was that Pursh, without permission, had taken several of the dried plant specimens, as well as parts of others, with him to New York. When Clark arrived in Philadelphia in January 1810, he assumed responsibility for the work on the journals that Lewis had never completed. Because of this, he paid Pursh for and received the completed drawings and descriptions, but he too did not know that some of the original specimens were still in the botanist's possession.

In 1811 Pursh went to London, where he spent most of his time writing *Flora Americae Septentrionalis,* published in 1814. This two-volume work was the first to detail the flora of America north of Mexico and contained 124 plants discovered by Lewis and Clark. Some of the book's illustrations also included 13 plants from the expedition's collection. Indebted to the two explorers for the scientific opportunity they had given him, he reflected his gratitude by creating the genera *Lewisia* and *Clarkia* in addition to naming three species after Lewis: *Linum lewisii* (Lewis's wild flax), *Mimulus lewisii* (Lewis's monkey flower), and *Philadelphus lewisii* (Lewis's syringa).

Pursh's work on the Lewis and Clark plants cannot be underestimated. Because the natural history volume of the journals was not published, much of what the explorers discovered and named was rediscovered and renamed by others. This fate might have met the plants they collected were it not for Pursh, who had been careful to acknowledge Lewis and Clark as the specimens' discoverers, even though he had appropriated some of the plants for himself. He later wrote that of all their plants, all but a dozen or so were "either entirely new [to science] or but little known."

Pursh died in Montreal in 1820, and a journal of his 1806–07 expeditions was published posthumously. Meanwhile, the Lewis and Clark plant specimens that he had appropriated came into the possession of A. B. Lambert, an English botanist and vice president of the Linnaean Society who had been Pursh's patron in London. When Lambert died in 1842, his botanical specimens were sold at an auction, and the Lewis and Clark plants were acquired by an American botanist named Edward Tuckerman. In 1856 Tuckerman presented the specimens to the Academy of Natural Sciences of Philadelphia, where they reside today.

See also PLANTS, NEW SPECIES.

Further Reading

Cutright, Paul Russell. *Lewis & Clark: Pioneering Naturalists.* Lincoln: University of Nebraska Press/Bison Books, 1989.

Pursh, Frederick. *Journal of a Botanical Excursion in the Northeastern Parts of the States of Pennsylvania and New York during the year 1807.* Edited by William M. Beauchamp. Port Washington, N.Y.: I. J. Friedman, 1969.

Reveal, James L. "Frederick Traugott Pursh (1774–1820)." From *Discovering Lewis and Clark: A Nomenclatural Morass.* Available online. URL: http://www.lewis-clark.org/REVEAL/bo_purs1.htm. Downloaded on March 1, 2002.

R

---

rabbits See JACKRABBITS.

raccoons See ANIMALS, NEW SPECIES.

rain See WEATHER.

rats See ANIMALS, NEW SPECIES.

rattlesnakes

The rattlesnake is so called because of the loose-fitting, horny shells on its tail which, when vibrated, can be heard 20 yards away. It kills its prey by injecting it with venom. If disturbed, it will try to retreat, but its distinctive rattle acts as an unmistakable warning of its presence, and it will attack when feeling threatened.

Although MERIWETHER LEWIS made accurate descriptions of the appearance, size, and characteristics of the rattlesnakes he encountered, he did not distinguish between the two species later naturalists classified as the prairie rattlesnake and the Pacific rattlesnake. In his journal entry for March 11, 1806, at FORT CLATSOP, Lewis noted that he did not know whether the rattlesnakes in the area were "either of the four species found in different parts of the United States, or of that species before mentioned peculiar to the upper part of the Missouri and its branches."

The expedition's JOURNALS mention rattlesnakes frequently, beginning in September 1804, when the CORPS OF DISCOVERY saw their first PRAIRIE DOG village. They killed one prairie dog, caught another, and, while digging, found a rattlesnake with a prairie dog inside it. From then on, rattlesnakes are often mentioned in the journals, up to August 4, 1806, when Lewis examined a large rattlesnake his men had killed. He noted that it was 5 feet long, with 176 scutae (plates) on the abdomen and 25 on the tail.

On May 17, 1805, Lewis noted that WILLIAM CLARK had "narrowly escaped being bitten by a rattlesnake in the course of his walk." A snake similar to it was killed that day, and Lewis described it: "This snake is smaller than those common to the *Middle Atlantic States*, being about 2 feet 6 inches long. It is of a yellowish-brown color on the back and sides, variegated with one row of oval spots of a dark-brown color lying transversely over the back from the neck to the tail, and two other rows of small circular spots of the same color which garnish the sides along the edge of the scuta. Its belly contains 176 scuta on the belly and 17 on the tail."

The most dramatic incident involving rattlesnakes was the birth of SACAGAWEA's baby on February 11, 1805. Her labor was long and painful, causing Lewis to consult with RENÉ JESSAUME, a French trader who had been living among the MANDAN INDIANS for 15 years. Jessaume said it was the local custom in such cases to administer a broken-up portion of a snake's rattle. Lewis did as Jessaume advised, breaking a rattle into small pieces and mixing it with water, then giving it to Sacagawea to drink. He later recorded: "Wether this medicine was truly the cause or not I shall not undertake to determine, but she had not taken it more then ten minutes when she brought forth." He added: "This remedy may be worthy of future experiment, but I must confess I want faith as to it's efficacy."

Further Reading

Burroughs, Raymond Darwin, ed. *The Natural History of the Lewis and Clark Expedition.* East Lansing: Michigan State University Press, 1995.

Cutright, Paul Russell. *Lewis & Clark: Pioneering Naturalists.* Lincoln: University of Nebraska Press/Bison Books, 1989.

Washington State University. "Lewis and Clark Among the Indians of the Pacific Northwest. Excerpts from the Journals of the Expedition of the Corps of Discovery: Flora and Fauna (recorded at Fort Clatsop)." Available on-line. URL: http://www.libarts.wsu.edu/history/Lewis_Clark/LCEXP_Flor.html. Downloaded on May 20, 2001.

recreation on the expedition

While the CORPS OF DISCOVERY's journey was most often one of backbreaking paddling, forced marches, and life-threatening situations, there were periods of idleness, boredom, and festivity as well. Whether it was to mark a holiday, to celebrate an occasion with Indians, or simply to relax, the expedition did have some recreation.

On some occasions inactivity led to tedium, which threatened morale. This was certainly the case during the winter of 1803–04 at CAMP DUBOIS. Once the camp was built and modifications to the KEELBOAT had been made, there was little for the men to do apart from military drills. Consequently, there were many instances of drunkenness and brawling, forcing Captain WILLIAM CLARK to devise ways of occupying their time. Mostly these entailed manual labor, but there was entertainment as well in the shooting matches he arranged between corpsmen and local residents. In the first of these matches, Clark offered a silver dollar as a prize to the winner, but to his chagrin, "the country people won the dollar." Thereafter betting was done among the contestants, and some weeks later, Clark could proudly report that the local competitors "all git beet and Lose their money."

Singing and dancing were the usual forms of recreation; the expedition's JOURNALS mention up to 30 such occasions. There were two fiddlers in the party: GEORGE GIBSON and, more famously, PIERRE CRUZATTE. Cruzatte is mentioned most often for his playing, which entertained not only corps members but often Indians as well. The journals also mention Indian tambourines, and there were at least 43 jew's harps, which were given as presents to Indians, who "Received them verry thankfully." The party also carried four tin "sounden horns," which had been bought for signaling but came in handy as noisemakers at the holidays.

The expedition celebrated Christmas Day 1804 at FORT MANDAN by firing a salute, enjoying glasses of brandy, and dancing. JOSEPH WHITEHOUSE reported: "Half past two another gun was fired to assemble at the dance, and So we kept it up in a jov[ia]l manner untill eight o'c[lock] at night. . . ." Christmas Day at FORT CLATSOP a year later was not quite so merry, due to the dank and miserable WEATHER and absence of alcohol. Nevertheless, guns were fired and presents were exchanged.

On New Year's Day 1805 at Fort Mandan, Sergeant JOHN ORDWAY reported that the men "went up to the 1st village of Mandans to dance as it had been their request, carried with us a fiddle & a Tambereen & a Sounden horn, as we arrived at the entrence of the vil[lage] we fired one round. then the music played. loaded again. then marched to the center of the village [and] fired again. then commenced dancing. . . . So we danced in different lodges until late in the afternoon. then a part of the men returned to the fort. the remainder Stayed all night in the village." The music and frolicking delighted the Mandan, and they were especially taken with one of the ENGAGÉS, François Rivet, who danced on his hands, as well as with YORK, who, Captain Clark reported, "amused the croud verry much and Some what astonished them, that So large a man Should be so active."

The corps observed three Independence Days, each one marking a different stage of the expedition. That of 1804 was the first celebrated west of the MISSISSIPPI RIVER. Guns were fired to start the day, Independence Creek was named, and extra gills of whiskey were passed out in the evening. In 1805 the men had just completed their PORTAGE around the GREAT FALLS and celebrated by drinking the last of the whiskey. Cruzatte played his fiddle while the men danced, and despite a thunderstorm, Clark reported that they "continued their mirth with songs and festive jokes and were extreemly merry untill late at night." In sharp contrast, there was no mention of celebrations in 1806, since the expedition had split up for the return journey. (See COINCIDENCES AND CHANCE ON THE EXPEDITION.)

Corps members were both observers of and participants in Native American festivals, such as the Mandan BUFFALO DANCE in January 1805. Even the TETON LAKOTA INDIANS (Teton Sioux), who so nearly stopped the expedition from going up the MISSOURI RIVER, impressed them with lavish feasting and dancing, including the SCALP DANCE, in which scalps taken from their enemies were displayed proudly. John Ordway described their music as "delightful."

In spring 1806 the expedition's tedious weeks with the NEZ PERCE INDIANS waiting for the snows on the BITTERROOT MOUNTAINS to melt gave them the chance to enjoy friendly competitions with their hosts. A shooting match was won by Lewis, but the Indians showed their prowess with bows and arrows, hitting moving targets from galloping horses. There were several horse races and footraces as well as games of quoits and an Indian game called prison base. On June 8, 1806, shortly before the expedition left the Nez Perce, there was a festival of races and games followed by an evening of song and dance, with Cruzatte as always providing the music.

The last cause for celebration occurred as the expedition neared the end of their long journey, when ST. LOUIS was just a week away. On September 14 they met a party of traders who gave them whiskey and some provisions. That night, with thoughts of home in their minds, they enjoyed their whiskey "and Sung Songs untill 11 oClock at night in the greatest harmoney."

Further Reading

Ambrose, Stephen E. *Undaunted Courage: Meriwether Lewis, Thomas Jefferson, and the Opening of the American West.* New York: Simon and Schuster, 1996.

Hunt, Robert R. "Merry to the Fiddle: The Musical Amusement of the Lewis and Clark Party." *We Proceeded On* 14, no. 4 (November 1988).

Mussulman, Joseph. "In Greatest Harmony: 'Medicine Songs' on the Lewis and Clark Trail." *We Proceeded On* 23, no. 4 (August 1997).

———. "Music on the Trail." From *Discovering Lewis and Clark.* Available on-line. URL: http://www.lewis-clark.org/MUSIC/mu _mmenu.htm. Downloaded on March 19, 2002.

Slosberg, Daniel. "Instruments of the Expedition." *Cruzatte! Study Guide.* Available on-line. URL: http://www.cruzatte.com/study guide/5_instruments.html. Downloaded on February 19, 2002.

recruiting

When in July 1803 WILLIAM CLARK accepted MERIWETHER LEWIS's invitation to cocommand the expedition, he at once began to play his part in the PREPARATIONS. Lewis was then in PITTSBURGH attending to the construction of the KEELBOAT and the packing of SUPPLIES AND EQUIPMENT, and he began to exchange LETTERS with Clark on the issue of recruiting. On July 24, 1803, Clark wrote: "Several young men (Gentlemens sons) have applyed to accompany us, as they are not accustomed to labour and as this is a verry essential part of the services required of the party, I am causious in giving them any encouragement."

He added: "A judicious choice of our party is of the greatest importance to the success of this great enterprise." Lewis replied in a similar vein. Their success "must depend on a judicious scelection of our men; their qualyfcations should be such as perfectly fit them for the service, otherwise they will reather clog than further the objects in view."

Lewis knew the sort of men he wanted. To keep the expedition fed, for example, he knew they would have to rely on game they killed, so he needed hunters among other things. As he put it, they should have "some good hunters, stout, healthy, unmarried men, accustomed to the woods, and capable of bearing bodily fatigue in a pretty considerable degree." Other SKILLS would also be needed.

Clark had no difficulty in recruiting; it was simply a matter of choosing the right applicants. Word of the expedition had spread like wildfire, and many young men came forward. It was adventure, it was excitement, it promised glory, and it was rumored that successful applicants would receive a grant of land for their services when they returned, as had been done for the veterans of the Revolutionary War. Consequently, when Clark finally met Lewis at CLARKSVILLE on the OHIO RIVER

on October 15, he had with him seven of "the best young woodsmen & Hunters in this part of the Countrey."

Lewis for his part had already had three applicants before he left Pittsburgh with the keelboat on August 31, 1803. By the time he met Clark, he had agreed to let two of them, JOHN COLTER and GEORGE SHANNON, join the expedition. Along with the seven men Clark had brought with him, they were sworn in as soldiers of the U.S. Army and gained the soubriquet the NINE YOUNG MEN FROM KENTUCKY.

For the remaining men he needed, Lewis took advantage of a letter Secretary of War HENRY DEARBORN had given him, authorizing him to draw recruits from western army garrisons. Aware that Lewis might meet resistance, Dearborn had also written to the garrisons' commanders, instructing them to cooperate. Lewis chose two men from the applicants at FORT MASSAC, where he had also expected to meet eight volunteers from South West Point, an army post on the Clinch River, near Knoxville, Tennessee. They had not arrived, so Lewis hired an interpreter at the fort, GEORGE DROUILLARD, to find the missing eight and bring them to ST. LOUIS. Drouillard, who was also a hunter and a woodsman, brought them in December, and Lewis selected four of the eight to join the expedition in addition to engaging Drouillard as interpreter and hunter. Unlike the others, however, Drouillard enrolled in the party as a civilian rather than a soldier and received a higher rate of pay.

As Lewis and Clark proceeded up the MISSISSIPPI RIVER on their way to St. Louis, they stopped at Fort KASKASKIA, where they selected about 12 more men—the exact number is in doubt—including PATRICK GASS. Gass was eager to go, but his commander, Captain Russell Bissell, was equally anxious that he should not. Lewis had to use Dearborn's authorization to secure Gass's services.

More army volunteers were interviewed and accepted at Cahokia, Illinois, across the river from St. Louis. During the winter of 1803–04 at CAMP DUBOIS, recruits were drilled and evaluated, then sorted into permanent and temporary expedition members. After the expedition was underway and had arrived at ST. CHARLES, the two captains engaged two voyageurs, PIERRE CRUZATTE and FRANÇOIS LABICHE, both of whom enlisted as privates in the army.

While recruiting volunteers for the expedition was easy, choosing the right men was more difficult. At least two men, NICHOLAS PRYOR and JOHN SHIELDS, were exceptions to the rule that the men be unmarried, and CHARLES FLOYD's health was apparently questionable before the expedition set out. Of all those whom Lewis and Clark recruited, though, only MOSES REED and JOHN NEWMAN failed them and were sent back to St. Louis from FORT MANDAN; another, JOSEPH BARTER, deserted. Apart from these three, the men fully justified their inclusion in the CORPS OF DISCOVERY and demonstrated the wisdom of the captains' selections.

Further Reading

Ambrose, Stephen E. *Undaunted Courage: Meriwether Lewis, Thomas Jefferson, and the Opening of the American West.* New York: Simon and Schuster, 1996.

Clarke, Charles G. *The Men of the Lewis and Clark Expedition: A Biographical Roster of the Fifty-One Members and a Composite Diary of Their Activities from All Known Sources.* Glendale, Calif.: Arthur H. Clark Co., 1970.

Hawke, David Freeman. *Those Tremendous Mountains: The Story of the Lewis and Clark Expedition.* New York: W. W. Norton & Company, 1998.

Large, Arlen. "'Additions to the Party': How an Expedition Grew and Grew." *We Proceeded On* 16, no. 1 (February 1990): 4–11.

Red River Expedition

Planned as the southern counterpart to the Lewis and Clark Expedition, the Red River Expedition of 1806 was also the first exploration of the LOUISIANA PURCHASE to be planned and executed by civilian scientists, albeit with military assistance. As with the CORPS OF DISCOVERY, President THOMAS JEFFERSON was the force behind sending other parties to explore the southwestern area of LOUISIANA TERRITORY, and his motivations were commercial and geopolitical as much as they were scientific. By finding the source of the Red River, he hoped to also find a waterway to Santa Fe, by which the United States could form alliances with southwestern Indians and gain leverage in the dispute with SPAIN over the territory's western border.

The prelude to the 1806 expedition occurred during the winter of 1804–05, when WILLIAM DUNBAR, a scientist and plantation owner from Natchez, Mississippi, went up the Ouachita (Washita) River with Dr. George Hunter, going as far as present-day Hot Springs, Arkansas, and making numerous important scientific observations. Dunbar subsequently worked with Secretary of War HENRY DEARBORN to plan the expedition up the Red River, for which the U.S. CONGRESS appropriated $5,000 in 1805. Although he did not himself go on the mission that Jefferson had dubbed the "Grand Excursion," Dunbar recruited two civilians to lead it: Thomas Freeman, a surveyor and astronomer who was the team's primary leader; and Peter Custis, a medical student and protégé of BENJAMIN SMITH BARTON who would act as ethnographer and naturalist. A military escort of 45 men as well as Indian and French guides were also hired, ballooning expenses to $11,000 by the time the party left Natchez in late April 1806.

They entered the Red River on May 2 and had traveled 615 miles when their mission was aborted due to the political scheming of Aaron Burr and General JAMES WILKINSON. Seeking to create an international incident, Wilkinson had informed the Spanish of the American expedition, resulting in New Spain's sending two military forces to stop Freeman and Custis. One of these forces intercepted the expedition on July 28, by which time they had arrived in what is now Bowie County, Texas. Ordered to turn back, the Red River party had no choice but to do so; this turning point has retained its name of Spanish Bluff to the present day. (The Spanish had also attempted to intercept and stop the Corps of Discovery but failed to find them.)

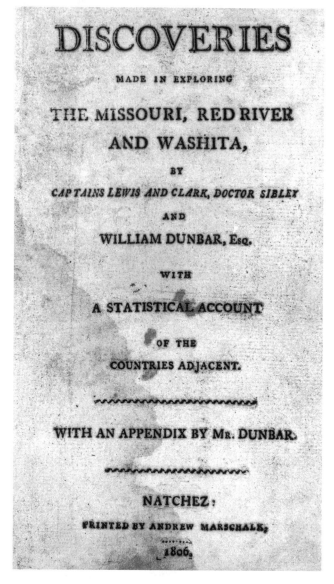

Before Lewis and Clark had returned from the West Coast, President Jefferson had published news of the expedition's early discoveries as well as those of William Dunbar and the Red River Expedition. *(Yale Collection of Western Americana, Beinecke Rare Book and Manuscript Library)*

Not long after the expedition's return, President Jefferson published a report of the Red and Ouachita River explorations, combined with preliminary news from Lewis and Clark and information on Louisiana Territory reported by JOHN SIBLEY. However, the Red River failure could by no means be considered one of the triumphs of his administration, and the political problems it caused led to the cancellation of a planned expedition up the Arkansas River. On the other hand, Burr and Wilkinson failed to ignite a war with the incident, as they had hoped to do, and Spain eventually became more amenable to allowing American traders into the Southwest. Years later, in 1852, a military exploration of the Red River was undertaken that proved more successful in meeting its objectives. However, the 1806 expedition did provide lasting positive effects in the reports generated by Freeman and Custis on the natural history and Indian cultures in the areas along the Red River that they did manage to explore.

See also EXPLORATION, LATER.

Further Reading
Flores, Dan K. "Red River Expedition." Handbook of Texas Online. URL: http://www.tsha.utexas.edu/handbook/online/articles/view/RR/upr2.html. Downloaded on February 6, 2002.
———, ed. *Jefferson and Southwestern Exploration: The Freeman and Custis Accounts of the Red River Expedition of 1806.* Norman: University of Oklahoma Press, 1984.
Jefferson, Thomas. *Message from the President of the United States Communicating Discoveries Made in Exploring the Missouri, Red River and Washita, by Captains Lewis and Clark, Doctor Sibley, and Mr. Dunbar: with a statistical account of the countries adjacent.* Washington, D.C.: A. & G. Way, printers, 1806.

Ree Indians   See ARIKARA INDIANS.

Reed, Moses (Moses Reid) (unknown–unknown)
private, deserter
Although MERIWETHER LEWIS AND WILLIAM CLARK had taken care in their RECRUITING to select good men for the expedition, one bad apple was Moses Reed. Originally selected for the permanent party, he was not an outstanding soldier and became increasingly unhappy as the CORPS OF DISCOVERY traveled up the MISSOURI RIVER. On the night of August 3, 1804, after a council earlier that day with some chiefs of the OTOE (Oto) INDIANS, Reed informed the captains that he had left his knife behind. He was given permission to go back for it, but when he did not return after three days, Lewis and Clark decided that he had deserted and sent out a party headed by GEORGE DROUILLARD to find him and bring him back, with the caveat that "if he did not give up Peaceibly to put him to Death; &c." They were also to look for JOSEPH BARTER (La Liberté), who had deserted as well.

The search party was gone 10 days while the expedition continued moving up the river. They had arrived near what is now Sioux City, Iowa, when Drouillard and company returned with both Reed and LITTLE THIEF, an Otoe Indian chief whom the captains had wanted to meet. Reed was immediately court-martialed; after pleading guilty to desertion and admitting that he had also stolen a rifle and ammunition, he asked for leniency. Though he could have been shot for his offense, Clark later wrote that "we only Sentenced him to run the Gantlet four times through the Party & that each man with 9 Swichies Should punish him." In effect, he received about 500 lashes. As the Otoe did not practice corporal punishment themselves, they were horrified by the severity of the punishment. Little Thief asked that the private be pardoned, but the sentence was carried out, and Reed was discharged from the CORPS OF DISCOVERY.

It was impossible to send Reed back to ST. LOUIS at that time, so he stayed on with the corps as a common laborer. He remained discontented and attempted to sow dissension among the other men. One who listened too closely to Reed's words was Private JOHN NEWMAN, who one day spoke out harshly against the captains himself. As a result, both Reed and Newman were arrested; the latter was court-martialed for mutiny and subsequently also dismissed from the corps. While Newman later made up for his behavior, Reed did not and was a malcontent throughout the journey.

In April 1805 Reed joined the party on the KEELBOAT that returned to St. Louis. There is no record of his whereabouts after that.

Further Reading
Clarke, Charles G. *The Men of the Lewis and Clark Expedition: A Biographical Roster of the Fifty-One Members and a Composite Diary of Their Activities from All Known Sources.* 1970. Reprint, Lincoln: Bison Books, University of Nebraska Press, 2002.

religion
Throughout the expedition, notes on religious practices in the JOURNALS applied more to Native Americans than to the explorers themselves. Nevertheless, although THOMAS JEFFERSON had instructed MERIWETHER LEWIS to observe and record "what knolege you can of the state of morality, religion, & information among them [Native Americans]," Lewis and WILLIAM CLARK, as well as other journal writers, accorded little importance to Indian religious practices.

This may seem surprising, given the explorers' dutiful descriptions of the SCALP DANCE, BUFFALO DANCE, SMOKING CEREMONIES, and other spiritual observances. Moreover, the journals describe such sacred places as the SPIRIT MOUND, which the corps visited in August 1804, and burial mounds for Indian dead. On July 12, 1804, by the Nemaha River on today's Kansas-Nebraska border, Clark found "several artificial mounds or graves . . . the mounds being certainly intended as tombs." He further records: "On a sandstone bluff about 1/4 of a mile from its mouth on the lower side, I observed some Indian marks."

Lewis and Clark were zealous in their ETHNOGRAPHY, and their journals have provided an invaluable record of the lives of the Native Americans they met. However, the expedition's aim was not just the acquisition of knowledge; more important to the captains was establishing American authority in the LOUISIANA TERRITORY. As historian James Ronda puts it, "Lewis and Clark's ethnography was never an end in itself, but was always intended for the service of government policy or commercial expansion." The spiritual practices of Native Americans therefore did not receive the close attention that Lewis and Clark devoted to those other aspects of Indian life they considered more important to their ultimate objectives.

This is probably why the explorers often misunderstood or misinterpreted much of what they observed. At FORT MANDAN, when one of the expedition's hunters placed a BUFFALO head on the KEELBOAT's bow, an Indian paused to smoke to the head. When asked, he indicated that the ritual was necessary because the buffalo was his medicine. As Ronda notes, "The Americans did not sense the connection Indians made between living things and those apparently dead." To the explorers, the Indians' attitudes were little more than superstitious nonsense. PATRICK GASS expressed his scorn when he saw a MANDAN INDIAN offering food to a buffalo head, writing, "Their superstitious credulity is so great, that they will believe by using the head well the living buffalo will come and that they will get a supply of meat."

The explorers made little sense of Native American spiritual practices unless it was in a context they could understand. On May 6, 1805, just past the mouth of the YELLOWSTONE RIVER, Gass wrote that the hunters in the party had "found some red cloth at an old Indian camp, which we suppose has been offered and left as a sacrifice; the Indians having some knowledge of a supreme being and this their mode of worship." The journals of Lewis, JOHN ORDWAY, and JOSEPH WHITE-HOUSE all mention this find in the same terms. It is ironic that the journal writers, who rarely referred to God themselves, dismissed so lightly these peoples for whom spiritual ceremonies and practices were vitally important.

Not surprisingly, in a group consisting mainly of young men, religious sentiment among the explorers appears to have been the exception rather than the rule. The journals make few references to the Almighty, and the only religious ceremony mentioned is the Mass attended by 20 members of the expedition at ST. CHARLES on May 20, 1804. Joseph Whitehouse wrote: "Several of the party went to church, which the French call mass, and sore [saw] their way of performing &c."

Christmas 1804 at Fort Mandan was marked by asking the Mandan and the HIDATSA INDIANS not to visit, "as it was one of our great medicine days." No religious observances are mentioned, although the journals record that "the best provisions

we had were brought out, and this, with a little brandy, enabled them [the men] to pass the day in great festivity."

Christmas at FORT CLATSOP the following year produced reflective comments from Clark and Whitehouse. The captain wrote of being awakened by a gunfire salute from the men and of the presents members of the party gave each other, concluding: "we would have Spent this day the nativity of Christ in feasting, had we any thing either to raise our Sperits or even gratify our appetites, our Dinner concisted of por Elk, so much Spoiled that we eat it thro' mear necessity, Some Spoiled pounded fish and a fiew roots."

Whitehouse wrote: "We had no ardent spirit of any kind among us: but are mostly in good health, a blessing, which we esteem more, than all the luxuries this life can afford, and the party are all thankful to the Supreme Being, for his goodness towards us, hoping he will preserve us in the same, & enable us to return to the United States again in safety."

A similar tribute was made by Patrick Gass in the journals' last noteworthy religious comment. For five weeks during the return journey, the expedition had been split; at one time there had been as many as five separate parties, two with only four men each, scattered all over today's Montana. By skill, ingenuity, or chance, they were all reunited on the MISSOURI RIVER (see COINCIDENCES AND CHANCE ON THE EXPEDITION). Appreciating how lucky they had been, Gass wrote on August 12, 1806: "The two men with the small canoe, who had been some time absent, came down and joined us at the place where we met with the two strangers; and now (thanks to God) we are all together again in good health. . . ."

Further Reading

MacGregor, Carol Lynn, ed. *The Journals of Patrick Gass, Member of the Lewis and Clark Expedition.* Missoula, Mont.: Mountain Press Publishing Company, 1997.

Moulton, Gary E., ed. *The Journals of the Lewis and Clark Expedition.* 13 vols. Lincoln: University of Nebraska Press, 1983–2001.

Paper, Jordan. *Offering Smoke: The Sacred Pipe and Native American Religion.* Moscow: University of Idaho Press, 1988.

Ronda, James P. *Lewis and Clark among the Indians.* Lincoln: University of Nebraska Press, 1984.

Republicans   See POLITICAL PARTIES.

rifles   See FIREARMS; WEAPONS.

Rivet, François   See ENGAGÉS.

Robertson, John (John Robinson)

(ca. 1780–unknown) *private in the temporary party*
Private John Robertson (recorded in some sources as Robinson) of New Hampshire was recruited for the CORPS OF DISCOV-

Lewis and Clark recorded evidence of many Native American spiritual practices. Clark found these petroglyphs on a limestone cliff near the Nemaha River (Nebraska-Kansas border) on July 12, 1804. *(National Archives Still Pictures Branch [NWDNS-412-DA-14665])*

ERY in KASKASKIA. A shoemaker, he and several others were cited for disorderly conduct during the expedition's stay in CAMP DUBOIS. Less than a month after the corps had started its journey, on June 12, 1804, Robertson was dismissed, apparently for drinking while on duty. He was sent back to St. Louis, and it is assumed that he rejoined his old infantry unit. His whereabouts after this are uncertain until about 1825, when he showed up as a fur trader, an occupation he pursued for the next 40 years. It is not known when or where he died.

Further Reading

Clarke, Charles G. *The Men of the Lewis and Clark Expedition: A Biographical Roster of the Fifty-One Members and a Composite Diary of Their Activities from All Known Sources.* 1970. Reprint, Lincoln: Bison Books, University of Nebraska Press, 2002.

Rocky Mountains

A physical geographical map of the United States will show that the land west of a line from Minnesota south to Austin, Texas, is much higher than that to the east. Rather than a single chain or ridge of hills, there is a complex system of mountain ranges interrupted by stretches of rolling plateaus, which together form the central spine of this higher western area. The name *Rocky Mountains* has been given to this irregular spine together with the mountain ranges and hills that join it on either side. For most of their course from Alaska down to Mexico, the Rockies carry the watershed of the continent: the CONTINENTAL DIVIDE.

While the group of associated mountains making up the Rockies in Utah and Colorado is some 300 miles wide, the range narrows to some 100 miles in the north, where MERIWETHER LEWIS and WILLIAM CLARK crossed them. The COLUMBIA RIVER–SNAKE RIVER valley cuts deeply into their western border.

Today the travel books write of the Lewis and Clark Expedition "entering" the Rocky Mountains on July 16, 1805. This was just west of present-day Cascade, Montana, two days after they had completed their PORTAGE around the GREAT FALLS of the MISSOURI RIVER. Although they were still well downstream of the rocky gorge that was named by Lewis GATES OF THE MOUNTAINS, July 16 was the day that the expedition realized they were moving out of the GREAT PLAINS. Sergeant PATRICK GASS's journal entry of that day notes this: "In the afternoon we continued our voyage, and the water continued very rapid. We got about 3 miles into the first range of the Rock mountains, and encamped on the north side of the river on a sand beach."

An indication of the variation in height of the Continental Divide running along the central ridge of the Rockies can be seen in Gass's journal entries for the next month. He wrote constantly of passing between and below mountains and of mountains that were all around them (today's Little Belt, Big Belt, Anaconda, and Tobacco Root Mountains). Yet when he eventually reached the LEMHI PASS on August 19, he described it

simply as "the dividing ridge." Crossing the Continental Divide was easy. As the expedition was to discover, though, the journey on the other side through the BITTERROOT MOUNTAINS would be far more difficult.

From the reports of ROBERT GRAY and GEORGE VANCOUVER, Lewis and THOMAS JEFFERSON knew that there were mountains bordering the Pacific coast. From Gray they also knew the latitude and longitude of the mouth of the Columbia River, which helped them determine the width of the continent. What Jefferson and Lewis did not know was the extent of the mountain barrier of the west. Along with other Americans of the time, they had assumed it would be similar to the Alleghenies or the Blue Ridge Mountains. They also believed that all the rivers in the West flowed from a single ridge. Further, from reading about ALEXANDER MACKENZIE's experience in 1793, they had hoped to find that, like him, they would be able to cross "over the height of Land [only 700 yards broad] that separates those Waters, the one empties into the Northern [Atlantic] Ocean and the other into the Western."

With hindsight, therefore, it is easy to appreciate Lewis's disappointment when he first walked over the Lemhi Pass and saw the "immence ranges of high mountains still to the West of us with their tops partially covered with snow." He knew then that these seemingly endless ranges of the Rocky Mountains still barred his way, and the all-water route to the Pacific that he and Jefferson had envisaged did not exist.

Further Reading

Hawke, David Freeman. *Those Tremendous Mountains: The Story of the Lewis and Clark Expedition.* New York: W. W. Norton & Company, 1998.

MacGregor, Carol Lynn, ed. *The Journals of Patrick Gass, Member of the Lewis and Clark Expedition.* Missoula, Mont.: Mountain Press Publishing Company, 1997.

Moulton, Gary E., ed. *Atlas of the Lewis and Clark Expedition.* Revised ed. Lincoln: University of Nebraska Press, 1999.

National Geographic Atlas of Natural America. Washington, D.C.: National Geographic Society, 2000.

Roi, Peter   See ENGAGÉS.

Rokey   See ENGAGÉS.

Ross's Hole

Hole was a term used by trappers for a broad, flat valley surrounded by mountains. Ross's Hole lies northeast of modern Sula, Montana, with the east fork of the BITTERROOT RIVER running through it.

By August 29, 1805, the Lewis and Clark Expedition had crossed the CONTINENTAL DIVIDE, met the SHOSHONE INDIANS, and traded for 29 HORSES from them, although, as WILLIAM CLARK noted, the horses had "nearly all sore backs, and several pore and young." From the Shoshone camp just north and west of LEMHI PASS, the CORPS OF DISCOVERY still had hundreds of miles to travel before they reached the PACIFIC OCEAN and a series of mountain ranges to cross to do so. The route south was unknown and, they feared, would take them into Spanish territory. The obvious route was due west, down the SALMON RIVER, but this had been explored by Clark, who found it impassable either by water or on foot. The only other option was to go north to the territory of the NEZ PERCE INDIANS and follow the route west from there.

Led by the Shoshone named OLD TOBY, the expedition made its way due north along the north fork of the Salmon River before leaving it to travel northeast up and over LOST TRAIL PASS, where the Continental Divide twists westward. They then came down into the BITTERROOT RIVER valley, which runs due north, arriving on September 4 in the valley that is now called Ross's Hole, near present-day Sula, Idaho. There they met a large party of FLATHEAD (Salish) INDIANS, who were a curiosity to the corps in some ways. They spoke a different language from the Shoshone, language so unusual that Sergeant JOHN ORDWAY wondered in his journal whether these were the legendary WELSH INDIANS.

The expedition stayed in Ross's Hole for two days, during which the Flathead generously shared some FOOD and gave them 12 good horses in exchange for the poor specimens that MERIWETHER LEWIS and Clark had brought with them. On September 6 both parties left the valley. The Flathead went south and east to hunt BUFFALO, while the corps kept on their northern journey, crossing the low mountain (Sula Peak) on the west side of the hole to ride down along the east fork of the Bitterroot River. Still to come were the worst three weeks of their journey crossing the LOLO TRAIL through the BITTERROOT MOUNTAINS.

It was to be 10 months before any of them saw Ross's Hole again. On July 3, 1806, on the return journey, Lewis and Clark parted at TRAVELERS' REST. While Lewis and one group rode east toward the THREE FORKS of the MISSOURI RIVER, Clark and his party rode south down through the Bitterroot valley. On July 5 they came back into Ross's Hole but only passed through it before continuing east over the Continental Divide at Gibbons Pass.

Further Reading

Fifer, Barbara, and Vicky Soderberg. *Along the Trail with Lewis and Clark.* Great Falls, Mont.: Montana Magazine, 1998.

Majors, Harry M., ed. "Lewis and Clark Among the Sayleesh Indians: Ross Hole, September 4–5, 1805." *Northwest Discovery* 7, no. 32–33 (1987): 126–246.

Moulton, Gary E., ed. *Atlas of the Lewis and Clark Expedition.* Revised ed. Lincoln: University of Nebraska Press, 1999.

Schmidt, Thomas. *National Geographic Guide to the Lewis & Clark Trail.* Washington, D.C.: National Geographic, 1998.

roster of the expedition   See CORPS OF DISCOVERY.

route of the expedition

Many books on the Lewis and Clark Expedition make a point of referring to the shortcuts they could have taken, the opportunities they missed, and the routes that would have been far easier for them on their journey across the continent to the PACIFIC OCEAN. With hindsight, observations like these are easy to make, but they ignore one simple fact: MERIWETHER LEWIS and WILLIAM CLARK did not have any choice.

When the expedition set out from CAMP DUBOIS in May 1804 to take the KEELBOAT and two PIROGUES up the MISSOURI RIVER, the route they were to follow had been firmly decided by THOMAS JEFFERSON. The MISSION OBJECTIVES left no room for doubt: "The object of your mission is to explore the Missouri river, & such principal stream of it, as, by it's course and communication with the waters of the Pacific ocean . . . may offer the most direct & practicable water communication across this continent. . . ."

Words like these allow for little misunderstanding. When Jefferson told them to follow "such principal stream of it"— that is, to follow the Missouri's main tributary to its source— that is exactly what Lewis and Clark tried to do, regardless of the possible alternatives.

From May 1804 they made their way upstream against the Missouri current, working their way westward for six weeks across what is now the state of Missouri to today's Kansas City before following the river northwest along its border with Kansas. Another six weeks took them up the stretch of river that now serves as the boundary between Iowa and Nebraska and into South Dakota. It was not until late October that they passed today's Bismarck, North Dakota, and met the MANDAN INDIANS by the river's junction with the KNIFE RIVER. By this time they had traveled 1,600 miles and were still only some 500 miles west of ST. LOUIS, although they were a good 600 miles north of it.

When they left FORT MANDAN on April 7, 1805, the Missouri still took them northwest until, at last, it began to turn west at the mouth of the YELLOWSTONE RIVER on North Dakota's border with Montana. In mid-July they finally arrived at the GREAT FALLS, where nearly a month was spent in the arduous labor of portaging their heavy dugout CANOES and baggage around the falls and trying to assemble the IRON-FRAME BOAT.

From what the HIDATSA INDIANS had told them at Fort Mandan, Lewis and Clark knew that the ROCKY MOUNTAINS were now not far ahead. The Hidatsa, however, traveled on horseback and rode straight across the plains, whereas the expedition was tied to the twisting river, and they had no HORSES. They might well have learned of easier routes across the Rockies from other Indians they encountered—but this was not the case. It is one of the odd aspects of the expedition that in the four months between leaving Fort Mandan and arriving at the CONTINENTAL DIVIDE, they did not see a single Indian. They saw tracks, passed deserted villages, and saw campfires still warm, but the single SHOSHONE Lewis saw below LEMHI PASS was the first Indian encountered since leaving the Mandan.

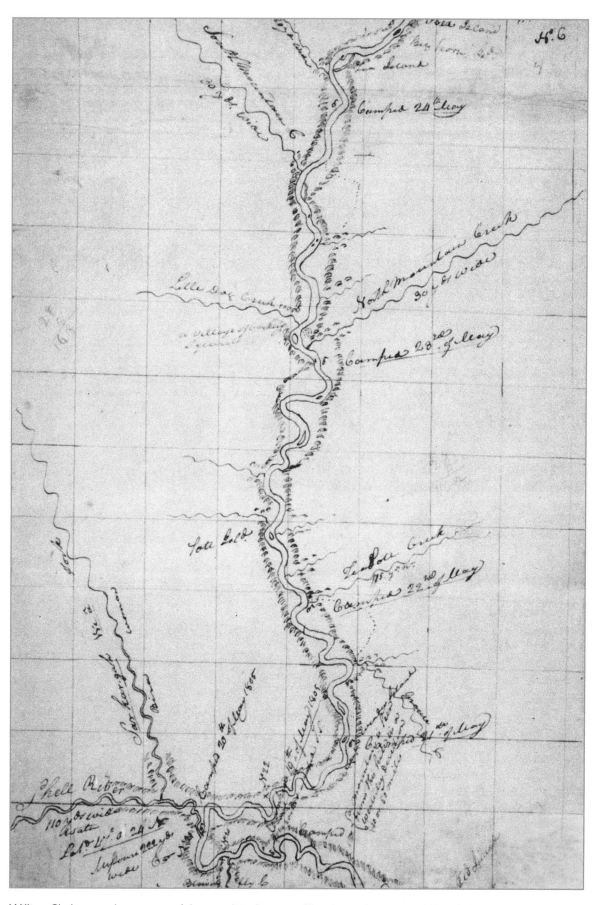

William Clark mapped every part of the expedition's journey. This shows their route of May 19–25, 1805, passing the Musselshell River. *(Yale Collection of Western Americana, Beinecke Rare Book and Manuscript Library)*

It took the expedition from July 15 to August 12, 1805, to travel from the Great Falls to Lemhi Pass. During that time they had come to the THREE FORKS of the Missouri, where it was decided (correctly) to take the northernmost branch, now called the JEFFERSON RIVER. This led them to Shoshone country, and on August 12 Lewis walked over the 7,372-foot-high pass, becoming the first non-Indian American to cross the divide on today's boundary between Montana and Idaho.

Here, for the first time, Lewis and Clark were unable to follow Jefferson's instructions to the letter. They had followed the Missouri, they had followed its principal tributary, and, as the Hidatsa had told them, there was a river that ran westward to the PACIFIC OCEAN. Unfortunately, the SALMON RIVER was impossible to travel on foot or by water. The expedition procured horses from the Shoshone, asked their advice on the best route to the west, and took it. With OLD TOBY as their guide, they began their journey of 500 miles to the coast by traveling due north to today's Missoula, Montana, before turning west on the LOLO TRAIL. (Even today this mountainous area is one of the most sparsely populated areas of the United States.) They spent 11 dangerous days of semistarvation on the trail before they at last came down to WEIPPE PRAIRIE, near today's Kamiah, Idaho, arriving there on September 22, 1805.

At CANOE CAMP, near present-day Orofino, Idaho, the corps built dugout canoes from ponderosa pines and set off on October 7 down the CLEARWATER RIVER. After two days they reached the SNAKE RIVER at Lewiston, Idaho–Clarkston, Washington. Traveling down the Snake, they arrived at the COLUMBIA RIVER at today's Pasco-Kennewick on October 16. With stops to visit Indians and delays due to portaging, it was not until November 15, 1805, that they came at last to the PACIFIC OCEAN at CAPE DISAPPOINTMENT.

By Clark's reckoning, they had traveled 4,162 miles. He was off by only 40 miles.

The explorers spent the winter of 1805–06 at FORT CLATSOP, near today's Astoria, Oregon. They left on March 23, 1806, and followed the Columbia back to its junction with the Snake River, where they procured horses and rode across country to the junction of the Snake and the Clearwater on the Idaho-Washington border. Returning to Weippe Prairie, they made their way back over the Lolo Trail to TRAVELERS' REST near Missoula, Montana. Here, on July 3, 1806, they split the party.

They had followed Jefferson's instructions on the journey west. Now, going home, they could be more flexible. Lewis therefore would go and explore the MARIAS RIVER while Clark would go south to make his way down the Yellowstone River. Each captain took parties who were subsequently detached into smaller groups headed by the sergeants: PATRICK GASS to start the portage around the Great Falls; JOHN ORDWAY to take the canoes from Three Forks down to the Great Falls, joining Gass there; and NATHANIEL PRYOR to take the horses across country to the Mandan villages (a mission that failed when their horses were stolen, forcing Pryor and his men to make BULL BOATS and follow Clark down the Yellowstone instead).

It was to be five weeks before the two captains met again on the Missouri, below the mouth of the Yellowstone, on August 12, a year to the day since Lewis had walked over the Continental Divide at Lemhi Pass. From that point it took the reunited expedition only two days to reach the Mandan villages. They left there on August 17, traveling downriver, and arrived back at St. Louis on September 23, 1806. The same journey upstream two years before had taken them five months to complete.

To modern eyes the expedition's route might appear laborious and haphazard. However, it cannot be stressed too strongly that they were army officers following the specific instructions of the president of the United States. Jefferson had told them to follow the Missouri as far as they could—and they did. The result was to take them to the worst place to attempt a crossing of the Rockies, but that was not their fault, nor Jefferson's. They still came through the Lolo Trail safely, and their experience was invaluable to those who came after them.

Cape Disappointment is only 1,800 miles in a direct line from St. Louis. Lewis and Clark traveled 4,162 miles to get there. They proved what could be done; they showed what should not be done. One can comment on the errors they made, but, remembering that they traveled mostly on foot and by dugout canoe, a moment's reflection suggests they and their men deserve nothing but respect for their achievement.

Further Reading

Appleman, Roy E. "Lewis and Clark: The Route 160 Years After." *Pacific Northwest Quarterly.* LVII (January 1966).

Cavan, Seamus. *Lewis and Clark and the Route to the Pacific.* New York: Chelsea House, 1991.

Fifer, Barbara, and Vicky Soderberg. *Along the Trail with Lewis and Clark.* Great Falls, Mont.: Montana Magazine, 1998.

Peebles, John J. "On the Lolo Trail: Route and Campsites of Lewis and Clark." *Idaho Yesterdays* 9, no. 4 (1965): 2–15; and 10, no. 2 (1966): 16–27.

———. "Rugged Waters: Trails and Campsites of Lewis and Clark in the Salmon River Country." *Idaho Yesterdays* 8, no. 2 (1964): 2–17.

———. "Trails and Campsites in Idaho." *Lewis and Clark in Idaho.* Boise: Idaho Historical Series No. 16 (December 1966).

Salter, Cathy Riggs. "Lewis and Clark's Lost Missouri: A Mapmaker Re-creates the River of 1804 and Changes the Course of History." *National Geographic* 201, no. 4 (April 2002): 89–97.

Rush, Benjamin (1746–1813) *physician*

Although his invention of Rush's Pills might have marked Dr. Benjamin Rush as a quack, in fact he was a highly respected physician of his time whose brief, intensive medical training of MERIWETHER LEWIS made it possible for the explorer to act as doctor for the expedition under extraordinary circumstances. As a signer of the Declaration of the Independence, an advocate for women's education and the abolition of slavery, and a pioneer in the treatment of the mentally ill, Rush was also one of the early nation's leading public figures.

Rush was born near PHILADELPHIA, where he lived all his life, although he pursued his education and medical training elsewhere. In 1760, after graduating at age 15 from the College of New Jersey (later Princeton University), his uncle Samuel Finley convinced him to study medicine, and for the next six years he served an apprenticeship with Dr. John Redmond of Philadelphia. In 1766 he went to study in Edinburgh, Scotland, where he received his M.D. two years later. While in Scotland he persuaded John Witherspoon to accept an appointment as president of the College of New Jersey.

After a year of travel, Rush returned to Philadelphia in 1769, becoming America's first professor of chemistry at the College of Philadelphia (later the University of Pennsylvania). He also set up practice as a doctor and began his resistance to the slave trade, helping to organize an abolitionist society. He became politically active as well; a staunch patriot, he encouraged Thomas Paine to write a tract on American independence and even provided the title: *Common Sense.* A few months after marrying Julia Stockton in January 1776, Rush, his father-in-law Richard Stockton, and John Witherspoon—all delegates to the Continental Congress—signed the Declaration of Independence.

During the American Revolution, Rush served as surgeon-general of the Middle Department of the Army. He resigned his commission after losing a protest on maladministration that he had lodged against the director-general, Dr. William Shippen, Jr., and for a brief period he supported a plot to replace George Washington as the army's commander, which he later regretted. Returning to Philadelphia, he resumed his old activities, becoming one of the country's leading teachers of medicine; in time he would train more than 3,000 medical students. He was also among the leaders at the Pennsylvania convention to ratify the U.S. Constitution. In 1792 Rush was appointed professor of the institutes of medicine and clinical practice at the newly named University of Pennsylvania; he became its professor of theory and practice in 1796.

Early in 1803, President THOMAS JEFFERSON wrote to Rush, a fellow member of the AMERICAN PHILOSOPHICAL SOCIETY, advising him of the impending expedition and the man who had been chosen to lead it and asking the physician ". . . to prepare some notes of such particulars as may occur in his journey & which you think should draw his attention and inquiry." Rush was happy to do even more. As Lewis wrote to Jefferson, during their brief time together in May 1803, "Dr. Rush . . . favored me with some abstract queries under the several heads of Physical History, medicine, Morals and Religeon of the Indians, which I have no doubt will be servicable in directing my inquiries among that people." He assembled a medical kit for Lewis and gave instructions for its use, in particular demonstrating the technique of bloodletting, a favorite treatment of the time for most medical problems. Rush's advice to Lewis was generally sensible and to the point: "When you feel the least indisposition, do not attempt to overcome it by

Renowned physician Dr. Benjamin Rush gave Lewis intensive training in basic medicine. He also supplied 50 dozen of his patent pills, dubbed "Thunderbolts" by the corpsmen. *(Library of Congress, Prints and Photographs Division [LC-USZ62-97104])*

labour or marching. *Rest* in a horizontal posture." He also advocated fasting and diluting drinks as a way of warding off fevers and, when necessary, purging the bowels with pills he had designed for that purpose.

Despite Rush's brilliance, the science of medicine was then fraught with outdated and flawed approaches to treatment—bloodletting, for instance—to which he held firmly. He had employed the practice of purging to great extent during Philadelphia's yellow-fever epidemic of 1793, and historians have since noted a correlation between his treatment and a high mortality rate. Nevertheless, based on the medical knowledge of the time, Rush's Pills were considered cutting-edge technology by both their inventor and their users. A formidable combination of mercury, chlorine, calomel, and jalap, the pills were thought to cure the body's illnesses by clearing the bowels. (Used frequently on the expedition, the men referred to them as "Thunderbolts" or "Thunderclappers.") Rush's belief in the pill's efficacy was unshaken, and he had Lewis purchase 50 dozen, along with large quantities of other drugs and medical supplies. He also recommended stocking Peruvian bark, then and still today a treatment for malaria because of the quinine in it. In his lifetime Rush came close to discovering that mosquitoes were the cause of that disease, but the culprits—which often plagued the expedition—would not be determined until after his death.

In addition to instructing Lewis, Rush prepared a questionnaire regarding the Indians the expedition would encounter. He wanted to learn about Indian diseases and daily habits, cycles of menstruation, how they raised their children, whether they took baths, disposal of their dead, and so on. He also asked about their religious ceremonies, attempting to find a connection between PLAINS INDIANS and the LOST TRIBES OF ISRAEL. Greatly impressed by Lewis, Rush wrote to Jefferson, "His mission is truly interesting. I shall wait with great solicitude for its issue."

From 1797 to until his death in 1813, Rush served as treasurer of the U.S. Mint. During his lifetime he founded the Philadelphia Dispensary for the relief of the poor as well as Dickinson College, and during a period of 30 years he served as senior physician at the Pennsylvania Hospital, where he made tremendous advances in the care and treatment of the mentally ill. His book *Inquiries and Observations upon the Diseases of the Mind* became the first American textbook on psychiatry, and his work in the field led the American Psychiatric Association to dub him the "Father of American Psychiatry." It is for his achievements in this area as well as his other contributions to the young United States that he is rightly ranked among the leading figures of his time.

See also MEDICINE AND MEDICAL TREATMENT.

Further Reading

Ambrose, Stephen E. *Undaunted Courage: Meriwether Lewis, Thomas Jefferson, and the Opening of the American West.* New York: Simon and Schuster, 1996.

Chuinard, Eldon G. *Only One Man Died: The Medical Aspects of the Lewis and Clark Expedition.* Glendale, Calif.: A. H. Clark Co., 1979.

Paton, Bruce C. *Lewis and Clark: Doctors in the Wilderness.* Golden, Colo.: Fulcrum Publishing, 2001.

Peck, David J. *Or Perish in the Attempt: Wilderness Medicine in the Lewis & Clark Expedition.* Helena, Mont.: Farcountry Press, 2002.

Rush, Benjamin. *The Autobiography of Benjamin Rush; His "Travels through life" Together with his Commonplace Book for 1789–1813.* Edited with introduction and notes by George W. Corner. Princeton, N.J.: Published for the American Philosophical Society by Princeton University Press, 1948.

Rush's Pills (Thunderbolts) See RUSH, BENJAMIN.

Russia See EXPLORATION, EARLY; OREGON TERRITORY.

S

Sacagawea (Sacajawea, Sakakawea)

(ca. 1789–1812) *Shoshone interpreter*

Apart from the two captains, the young SHOSHONE woman Sacagawea has become the best-known member of the Lewis and Clark Expedition. Fact and fiction have combined to make her a legendary figure whose name constantly appears in lists of the country's most-admired women. There are more statues to her than to any other American woman.

Despite her fame, Sacagawea remains an obscure figure. Little is known of her origins or life after the expedition, and controversy surrounds her death. Even her HIDATSA-derived name is the subject of academic debate. Some pronounce the middle syllable with a hard *g,* others with a soft *g* (accounting for the spelling variant that uses a *j*). MERIWETHER LEWIS and WILLIAM CLARK themselves spelled it 14 different ways in their JOURNALS; in naming the SACAGAWEA RIVER, Lewis indicated a pronunciation of *sah-ca-gah-we-ah,* a word meaning "bird woman." The Shoshone have claimed the *Sacajawea* spelling is correct, although this changes the meaning to "boat launcher"; and some North Dakota Hidatsa have advocated *Sakakawea,* a spelling not found in the journals.

It is known that Sacagawea was the daughter of a Lemhi Shoshone chief and lived with her people in an area of the ROCKY MOUNTAINS in today's Idaho. When she was 10 or 12 years old, she was captured by a raiding party of Hidatsa Indians somewhere near the THREE FORKS of the MISSOURI RIVER and, with another Shoshone girl, taken to one of the Hidatsa villages on the upper Missouri, hundreds of miles to the east. There, near what is now Bismarck, North Dakota, they were bought from the Hidatsa by the French-Canadian fur trap-per TOUSSAINT CHARBONNEAU, who took them both as wives.

In October 1804 the CORPS OF DISCOVERY reached the MANDAN villages where they were to spend the winter. They met Charbonneau on November 4, and on November 11 Clark wrote: "We received the visit of two squaws [Sacagawea and another], prisoners from the Rock [Rocky] Mountains, purchased by Chaboneau." The captains engaged Charbonneau as interpreter and, realizing her value when they reached the Shoshone Indians, requested that Sacagawea accompany them.

On February 11, 1805, Lewis delivered Sacagawea of "a fine boy." Named JEAN BAPTISTE CHARBONNEAU but later dubbed "Pomp," the baby traveled in a cradleboard on his mother's back when the expedition left Fort Mandan in April 1805. Sacagawea soon proved her usefulness to the party. Only two days after they left the Mandan villages, with game scarce and little meat available, she provided an addition to the corps's diet, as Lewis noted: "When we halted for dinner the squaw busied herself in searching for the wild artichokes. . . . Her labour soon proved successful, and she procured a good quantity of these roots." Her knowledge of edible roots and plants would provide not only much-needed FOOD on occasion but medicine as well.

The presence of a young woman in an all-male expedition could easily have caused problems, but the captains circumvented them by sharing their TIPI with Charbonneau, Sacagawea, Pomp, and GEORGE DROUILLARD. It is likely that such precautions were unnecessary since there is no mention in the extant journals of the men annoying Sacagawea in any way.

This photograph taken in 1910 shows an Indian woman dressed to represent Sacagawea. On her back is a cradleboard like the one Sacagawea used to carry her baby son Pomp across the continent. *(National Anthropological Archives, Smithsonian Institution)*

Perhaps they saw her and Pomp as mascots, or perhaps, like Clark, they respected her for sharing their hunger, hardship, and danger without complaint.

In May 1805, when Charbonneau's poor boatmanship nearly capsized the PIROGUE he was helming, it was Sacagawea who had the presence of mind to retrieve vital papers from the water, earning a compliment from Lewis on her "fortitude and resolution." The following month, as the party camped near GREAT FALLS, Sacagawea became seriously ill, and both Clark and Lewis nursed her until she was well enough to travel. In August, on the last long stretch of the Missouri, Sacagawea encouraged the corps by recognizing such landmarks as BEAVER ROCK—signs that they were nearing the Shoshone country of her childhood.

It was on August 17, 1805, that she entered American legend in one of the most dramatic COINCIDENCES AND CHANCE ON THE EXPEDITION. Having already had an emotional reunion with a childhood friend, Sacagawea was summoned to translate at the captains' first formal council with the Shoshone chief CAMEAHWAIT. As the council began, she paused and peered closely at Cameahwait—and, recognizing him as her brother, "she jumped up, ran & embraced him, & threw her blanket over him and cried profusely."

While Sacagawea's relationship to Cameahwait proved fortunate for the corps, her value as an interpreter continued after they left the Shoshone (see INTERPRETATION). Her very presence on the expedition played a crucial role in its success. As Clark noted on October 13, 1805, "The Wife of Shabono our interpreter We find reconciles all the Indians, as to our friendly intentions. A woman with a party of men is a token of peace."

Sacagawea and her baby endured the arduous crossing of the BITTERROOT MOUNTAINS and the long journey down the CLEARWATER, SNAKE, and COLUMBIA Rivers to the PACIFIC OCEAN. At STATION CAMP on November 24, 1805, when the captains took a vote to decide where the corps should spend the winter, Sacagawea and YORK voted as well, although Sacagawea's vote was not counted in the final tally.

During the long, rainy winter at FORT CLATSOP, Sacagawea provided one of the expedition's most touching moments. When the news arrived that a WHALE had been found on the beach 12 miles south of the camp, a party set off to salvage its meat. Sacagawea went with them since, as Lewis noted, she was "very importunate to be permitted to go, and was therefore indulged." For once the journals noted she had a complaint, and the captain's entry brings the quiet Indian girl to life: "She observed that She had travelled a long way with us to See the great waters, and that now that monstrous fish was also to be Seen, She thought it very hard that She could not be permitted to See either (She had never yet been to the Ocian)."

It was during the return journey in 1806 that Sacagawea earned her legend as the woman who guided Lewis and Clark across the continent and back. After the company split to pursue separate missions, she went south with Clark's party to travel down the YELLOWSTONE RIVER. She guided them through her homeland, and it was she who showed Clark "a large road passing through a gap in the mountains" (known later as BOZEMAN PASS).

Charbonneau and Sacagawea left Lewis and Clark after arriving back at their Hidatsa village on the upper Missouri in August 1806. Although her husband was awarded $500.33 and 320 acres of land for his services, Sacagawea was given nothing.

There are conflicting accounts of Sacagawea's life after the expedition. Most indicate that she accompanied Charbonneau on a trip to ST. LOUIS, where William Clark took charge of the young Pomp, of whom he had become extremely fond. She and her husband then returned to the upper Missouri and his life as a fur trapper. In 1812 at Fort Manuel (in present-day South Dakota) she gave birth to a daughter, LIZETTE CHARBONNEAU. Sacagawea died there later that year, on December 12. Reports vary on the cause of her death; some historians attribute it to an epidemic of "putrid fever," while others feel she died of a lifelong medical condition complicated by Lizette's birth. It has been reported that Clark legally adopted both Pomp and Lizette eight months after her death, although this has not been verified.

Another theory has it that Sacagawea had left Charbonneau to return to her Shoshone people and that the woman who died at Fort Manuel was one of Charbonneau's other wives. Shoshone legend and some scholars have maintained that Sacagawea actually died in 1884 and was buried on the Wind River Indian Reservation in Wyoming. Later investigation, however, indicates that this woman could not have been the one of whom, in a letter to Charbonneau, William Clark wrote that she "diserved a greater reward for her attention and services on that rout than we had in our power to give her."

Sacagawea was twice honored by Lewis and Clark when they named SACAGAWEA RIVER and SACAGAWEA SPRING. She is commemorated today by several sites, including Sacagawea Park, Washington; the Sacagawea Monument near Tendoy, Montana; Lake Sakakawea in North Dakota; and the Sacagawea Memorial Campground at LEMHI PASS, Montana. In the year 2000, her image appeared on the new U.S. silver dollars, and on January 17, 2001, President Bill Clinton named her honorary sergeant, regular army.

Perhaps the most appropriate epitaph for Sacagawea was the explorer Henry Marie Brackenridge's description of her in his 1811 journal: "We had on board a Frenchman named Charbonet, with his wife, an Indian woman of the Snake* nation, both of whom had accompanied Lewis and Clark to the Pacific, and were of great service. The woman, a good creature, of a mild and gentle disposition, greatly attached to the whites. . . ."

See also COUNCILS WITH INDIANS; INDIAN GUIDES; WOMEN ON THE EXPEDITION.

Further Reading

Anderson, Irving W. "The Sacagawea Mystique: Her Age, Name, Role and Final Destiny." *Columbia* Magazine 13, no. 3 (fall 1999). Available on-line. URL: http://www.wshs.org/lewisandclark/sacagawea.htm. Downloaded on July 12, 2002.

Butterfield, Bonnie. "Spirit Wind-Walker." "Sacagawea: Captive, Indian Interpreter, Great American Legend: Her Life and Death." ©1998, 2000. Available on-line. URL: http://www.geocities.com/CollegePark/Hall/9626/NativeAmericans.html. Downloaded on March 15, 2002.

Chuinard, E. G. "The Actual Role of the Bird Woman." *Montana: The Magazine of Western History.* 26, no. 3 (1976): 18–29.

Clark, Ella E., and Margot Edmonds. *Sacagawea of the Lewis and Clark Expedition.* Berkeley: University of California Press, 1979.

Dawson, Jan C. "Sacagawea: Pilot or Pioneer Mother?" *Pacific Northwest Quarterly* 83, no. 1 (1992): 22–28.

Hebard, Grace Raymond. *Sacagawea: Guide and Interpreter of Lewis and Clark.* Reprint, Mineola, N.Y.: Dover Books, 2002.

Howard, Helen Addison. "The Mystery of Sacagawea's Death." *Pacific Northwest Quarterly* 58, no. 1 (1967): 1–6.

Hunsaker, Joyce Badgley. *Sacagawea Speaks: Beyond the Shining Mountains with Lewis & Clark.* Helena, Mont.: Falcon Publishing Co., 2001.

————. "Who Was Sacagawea?" *Time,* July 8, 2002, 56–57.

Kessler, Donna J. *The Making of Sacagawea: A Euro-American Legend.* Tuscaloosa: University of Alabama Press, 1996.

Nielsen, Quig. "Sacagawea of the Lewis and Clark Expedition." Available on-line. URL: http://www.thehistory.net.com/WildWest/articles/1999/1299_text.htm. Downloaded on May 23, 2001.

Talbot, Margaret. "Searching for Sacagawea." *National Geographic* 203, no. 2 (February 2003): 68–85.

Sacagawea River (Crooked Creek)

Now known as Crooked Creek, the Sacagawea River runs into the MUSSELSHELL RIVER near its junction with the MISSOURI RIVER in central Montana. It was named by MERIWETHER LEWIS and WILLIAM CLARK to honor SACAGAWEA after she helped to save the expedition from near disaster.

By May 14, 1805, the expedition had passed the mouth of the YELLOWSTONE RIVER and the MILK RIVER and were just west of present-day Fort Peck, Montana. On that day both captains were walking on shore, a break from their normal routine (one usually stayed in the boats). On the river, the white-colored PIROGUE was being steered by TOUSSAINT CHARBONNEAU, about whom Lewis later wrote: "[He] cannot swim and is perhaps the most timid waterman in the world." As wind caught the pirogue's sail, Charbonneau turned the rudder in the wrong direction, and the boat went over on its side. Waves washed in, and the vessel would have gone down if PIERRE CRUZATTE had not shouted to Charbonneau to turn the rudder the other way. The baggage on board was completely soaked, and much would have been swept away if Sacagawea had not calmly retrieved articles from the water.

In their JOURNALS, both captains expressed their relief at the outcome. Clark wrote: "This accident had like to have cost us dearly." Lewis expanded on this theme, writing that "we had been . . . terrified by an accident of a different kind. This was the narrow escape of one of our canoes, containing all our papers, instruments, medicine, and almost every article indispensable for the success of our enterprise." He then added a note of his gratitude to Sacagawea: "The Indian woman, to whom I ascribe equal fortitude and resolution with any person on board at the time of the accident, caught and preserved most of the light articles which were washed overboard."

The expedition's arrival at the mouth of the Musselshell River enabled Lewis to acknowledge her presence of mind. "About five miles abe [above] the mouth of the [Mussell]Shell river a handsome river of about fifty yards in width discharged itself into the Shell river on the upper side; this stream we called Sah-ca-gee-mea-ah or bird woman's River, after our interpreter the Snake woman."

Further Reading

Ambrose, Stephen E. *Undaunted Courage: Meriwether Lewis, Thomas Jefferson, and the Opening of the American West.* New York: Simon and Schuster, 1996.

Fifer, Barbara, and Vicky Soderberg. *Along the Trail with Lewis and Clark.* Great Falls, Mont.: Montana Magazine, 1998.

---

* Traders in the area often collectively called the Northern Shoshone, Northern Paiute (Numa), and Bannock the Snake. Contemporary writings on Sacagawea often refer to her as Snake.

Lewis, Meriwether, and William Clark. *The History of the Lewis and Clark Expedition.* Edited by Elliott Coues; 4 vols., 1893, Harper. Reprinted in 3 vols., New York: Dover Publications, 1979.

Sacagawea Spring (Sulphur Springs)

In mid-June 1805, the CORPS OF DISCOVERY reached the GREAT FALLS of the MISSOURI RIVER and discovered they had not one but five waterfalls to pass before they could resume their westward journey. MERIWETHER LEWIS, who had gone ahead of the expedition and reached the falls before them, was anxious to organize a reconnaissance along both riverbanks to find the best PORTAGE route. First, however, he had a medical problem to resolve.

When SACAGAWEA had shown signs of sickness at the camp at the mouth of the MARIAS RIVER the week before, WILLIAM CLARK had followed the standard medical practice of bleeding her. When she showed no sign of improvement the next day, he bled her again. By June 16, when Lewis returned to the main party some six miles below the falls, it had become clear that the SHOSHONE woman was very ill indeed, being in great pain and having an almost imperceptible pulse. Lewis examined her and administered a basic form of quinine and sedative: "two doses of barks and opium." This brought her some relief, upon which Lewis remembered that he had seen a sulphur spring across the river. He sent a man over to collect some of the water, gave it to her to drink, and then applied a poultice to her pelvic region.

Modern medical opinion is that Sacagawea was probably suffering from a chronic pelvic inflammation and that the poultices and sulphur water may well have brought about her cure. By June 19 she had recovered enough to go for a walk, during which she gathered a considerable quantity of apples, eating them raw with some dried fish. Lewis, who had given her strict instructions on what to eat, was furious and rebuked TOUSSAINT CHARBONNEAU for letting her do it. Then he "gave her broken doses of diluted nitre until it produced pespiration and at 10 P.M. 30 drops of laudanum which gave her a tolerable nights rest." The next morning he was relieved to report that Sacagawea was "quite free from pain and fever and appears to be in a fair way for recovery, she had been walking about and FISHING."

On Clark's map of the portage around the Great Falls, he had marked the "Sulpher springs" opposite PORTAGE CREEK (today's Belt Creek). The great majority of place names allotted by Lewis and Clark are long gone (see NOMENCLATURE, GEOGRAPHICAL), but here at least the subsequent replacement name Sacagawea Spring commemorates the expedition. The spring can be found on the north bank of the Missouri River, just below the Morony Dam east of Great Falls, Montana.

Further Reading

Fifer, Barbara, and Vicky Soderberg. *Along the Trail with Lewis and Clark.* Great Falls, Mont.: Montana Magazine, 1998.

Schmidt, Thomas. *National Geographic Guide to the Lewis & Clark Trail.* Washington, D.C.: National Geographic, 1998.

sacred pipe   See SMOKING CEREMONIES.

St. Charles

Although May 14, 1804, is generally considered to be the official start date of the Lewis and Clark Expedition, an argument can be made for May 21, the day they left St. Charles. More than a year had been spent in making preparations, including building and later refurbishing the KEELBOAT, buying SUPPLIES AND EQUIPMENT, RECRUITING and training men for the journey, studying MAPS, and gathering crucial information. In the days prior to their departure, while MERIWETHER LEWIS attended to final details in ST. LOUIS, WILLIAM CLARK supervised the loading of the keelboat, which he took out into the MISSISSIPPI RIVER several times, testing its balance and shifting its load until he was satisfied. Finally, on May 13, he sent a message to Lewis indicating they would be on their way the next day, with the intention of making a trial run up as far as St. Charles.

It was on the 14th that the expedition really began, when the keelboat and PIROGUES of the CORPS OF DISCOVERY entered the mouth of the MISSOURI RIVER and began their laborious journey northward. They reached St. Charles two days later. Meanwhile, Lewis finished his business in St. Louis and, on May 20, accompanied by a group of friends, left the city on horseback and headed overland to meet Clark and the expedition at St. Charles, some 22 miles away.

Located on the north bank of the Missouri, St. Charles was a village of approximately 450 inhabitants living in wooden houses that Lewis called "small but illy constructed." It had been founded by French-Canadian trader Louis Blanchette in 1769, five years after the founding of St. Louis; he called his settlement Les Petites Cotes ("The Little Hills"). Later renamed St. Charles, it was by no means as impressive as its name. Lewis expressed a low opinion of the village's population, calling them "miserably poor, illiterate, and when at home excessively lazy." Clark's opinion was slightly better; he described the people as "pore, polite & harmonious." Theirs was not a community of farmers; the men made their livings primarily by hunting and hiring out as ENGAGÉS.

Indian blood had mingled with the mostly French-Canadian lineage of St. Charles, and among these of mixed heritage were PIERRE CRUZATTE and FRANÇOIS LABICHE, who had apparently been recommended for the expedition by fur trader AUGUSTE CHOUTEAU. Skilled watermen, they impressed Lewis at once, and he enlisted them as privates in the expedition. Both would justify his choice throughout the journey. Other members of the expedition already hired, however, would prove less impressive. It was during the corps's stay in St. Charles, awaiting Lewis's arrival, that Privates WILLIAM WERNER, HUGH HALL, and JOHN COLLINS went absent without leave, an offense for which they were court-martialed and punished.

Though small and poor, St. Charles had a Catholic chapel and a priest, and 20 men in the CORPS OF DISCOVERY asked for a mass before the expedition got underway. This was carried out on the morning of May 21, 1804. That afternoon, at 3:30 P.M., the keelboat and pirogues moved off to the cheers of onlookers from the riverbank, including Captain AMOS STODDARD, who later wrote to Secretary of War HENRY DEARBORN: "His [Lewis's] men posses great resolution and they are in the best health and spirits." They would not see St. Charles again until September 21, 1806, when Lewis wrote, "the inhabitants of this village appear much delighted at our return and seem to vie with each other in their politeness to us all."

When Missouri became a state, St. Charles served as its capital from 1820 to 1826. In 1849 it was incorporated as a city.

Further Reading

Ambrose, Stephen E. *Undaunted Courage: Meriwether Lewis, Thomas Jefferson, and the Opening of the American West.* New York: Simon and Schuster, 1996.

St. Louis

Late in November 1803, MERIWETHER LEWIS, WILLIAM CLARK, and the first recruits of the CORPS OF DISCOVERY were laboring up the MISSISSIPPI RIVER on the KEELBOAT. Their destination was St. Louis, then the largest town on the American frontier in what is now Missouri. Located on the west bank of the Mississippi some 200 miles above its junction with the OHIO RIVER and about 20 miles below the mouth of the MISSOURI RIVER, St. Louis was then still under the control of SPAIN, although it would soon pass to the United States as part of the LOUISIANA PURCHASE. Its importance to the expedition was manifold for its key location, the TRADE goods that could be bought there, and the opportunities it provided for obtaining essential information on what lay ahead for the expedition.

By the time the expedition arrived at St. Louis, the town contained close to 1,000 inhabitants (some 1,400 more lived on outlying farms) and had become the hub of the growing FUR TRADE throughout the territory drained by the Missouri. Populated mostly by French Canadians, the town had been named in honor of French king Louis XV by its founder, Pierre Laclede, who in 1762 had obtained an exclusive license to trade with the OSAGE INDIANS. On February 14, 1764, a party of workmen arrived at the site Laclede had chosen for his trading post; originally it was called Pain Court (French for "short bread"). The crew was supervised by his 15-year-old stepson, AUGUSTE CHOUTEAU, now considered a cofounder of the town and a key player in its later incorporation as a city. When the LOUISIANA TERRITORY came under Spanish control, Laclede and Chouteau adapted easily, retaining their monopoly on trade on the area. They were eventually joined in business by Chouteau's half brother, PIERRE CHOUTEAU. Although the town's growth was slow, it was steady, and the Chouteau brothers prospered. In 1798 MANUEL LISA arrived and broke the Chouteaus' monopoly when he obtained his own trading license from the Spanish authorities. It was with Lisa and the Chouteaus that Lewis and Clark principally dealt during their time in St. Louis.

While Lewis had originally hoped to travel well beyond St. Louis on the first leg of the expedition's journey, by the time they reached St. Louis in early December 1803 it was clear that they would have to winter in the vicinity. There were several reasons for this aside from the obvious WEATHER-related issue. First, until the official transfer of Upper Louisiana took place, permission from the Spanish was needed to proceed up the Missouri, and it was not forthcoming from the Spanish lieutenant governor, Colonel Carlos Dehaul Delassus. Second, the journey up the Mississippi had made it manifest that more men—and thus more SUPPLIES AND EQUIPMENT—were going to be needed. Time was needed to train and evaluate their volunteers as well as to determine what else they had to purchase to properly equip themselves for the journey. Finally, obtaining information on the river, the territory, and its Indians was essential, and St. Louis was a home base to fur traders and trappers who could provide such crucial data. As a result, a site for the corps's winter encampment was found about 12 miles north of the town, near the mouth of the Wood River.

During the five-plus months that the corps spent at CAMP DUBOIS, both captains, especially Lewis, visited the town often to purchase supplies and gather information. Their chief contacts and hosts were, of course, the two Chouteau brothers and Lisa, who vied for the expedition's custom and brought them additional recruits. Their chief military contact was Captain AMOS STODDARD, soon to become acting governor of the Louisiana Territory as well as Lewis's agent in St. Louis while the expedition was out West. The captains also gathered data from such sources as the journals of JAMES MACKAY and JOHN EVANS, who had recently spent time among the MANDAN INDIANS, and visits from Mackay himself as well as other traders. They learned about the river, the territory, and the game that could be hunted for FOOD. They also learned as much as they could about the river's Indians—what they were like, what kinds of GIFTS should be offered, protocol for council meetings with the chiefs, and other helpful facts.

On March 9, 1804, St. Louis was the site of the formal transfer of Upper Louisiana from Spain to France and then, on the following day, from France to the United States. Lewis and Clark attended the ceremonies at which Captain Stoddard took possession of the territory, but even though they no longer needed Spanish permission to ascend the Missouri, their business in St. Louis was not yet finished. More supplies needed to be purchased, a team of ENGAGÉS had to be hired (arranged by the Chouteaus), and reports to President THOMAS JEFFERSON had to be written, all as they continued to gather information. It was not until May 14, 1804, that the expedition left Camp Dubois.

The following year the town saw the arrival of the KEELBOAT from FORT MANDAN, carrying reports, MAPS, and numerous ARTIFACTS AND SPECIMENS to be sent on to Jefferson in Washington. In September 1806 the expedition returned to a triumphant welcome in St. Louis. During the 2$\frac{1}{2}$ years they had been gone, the town had grown as Americans began to move west in increasing numbers and the fur trade entered a boom period. During that period as well, the District of Louisiana came briefly under the control of Indiana Territory but was then established officially as the Territory of Louisiana, with St. Louis as its seat of government.

In 1808 St. Louis was incorporated as a city, and the *Louisiana Gazette* began publication as the first newspaper west of the Mississippi. That same year Meriwether Lewis returned to take up his duties as governor of the Louisiana Territory. It was an unhappy time for him, however, and in October 1809, shortly after leaving on a trip to Washington, he killed himself at a roadhouse on the Natchez Trace. St. Louis, which had played such a crucial role in his expedition, would continue to occupy a central position in the fur trade for years to come and eventually became one of the major cities of the United States.

Further Reading

Ambrose, Stephen E. *Undaunted Courage: Meriwether Lewis, Thomas Jefferson, and the Opening of the American West.* New York: Simon and Schuster, 1996.

Billon, Frederic. *Annals of St. Louis in Its Early Days under the French and Spanish dominations, 1764–1804.* Reprint, New York: Arno Press, 1971.

DiLeo, Juliet, et al. "Government and the Louisiana Territory. Part One: St. Louis." Available on-line. URL: http://www.artsci.wustl.edu/~lschwarz/finalstlouis.html. Downloaded on March 3, 2002.

Foley, William. "St. Louis: The First Hundred Years." *Bulletin of the Missouri Historical Society.* Vol. XXXIV, No. 4, Pt. 1 (July 1978).

Saint-Mémim, Charles   See PHILADELPHIA.

salaries   See PAYMENTS AND REWARDS.

Salish Indians   See FLATHEAD INDIANS.

salmon   See FISH, NEW SPECIES.

Salmon River (Lewis's River)

On August 12, 1805, MERIWETHER LEWIS became the first non-Indian American to cross the CONTINENTAL DIVIDE at LEMHI PASS. He and his three companions were following the trail of a single SHOSHONE Indian they had seen the day before, and as they crossed the ridge, Lewis wrote of his delight in drinking from "a handsome bold runing creek of cold Clear water. Here, I first tasted the water of the great Columbia river." He was right. The stream from which he drank (today's Agency Creek) flowed into the LEMHI RIVER and from there to the Salmon River, then to the SNAKE RIVER, and finally to the COLUMBIA RIVER—which, however, Lewis would not reach until two months later.

The Salmon River is one of the two main tributaries of the Snake River, the other being the CLEARWATER RIVER. Both the Salmon and the Clearwater follow a long and tortuous course, threading their ways through a series of mountain ranges in Idaho. The Salmon rises some 100 miles southwest of Lemhi Pass, below today's Ryan Peak, Idaho. It runs northwest toward the Continental Divide before turning due north at present-day Salmon, Idaho. Here it is joined by the Lemhi River and turns due west before turning northwest again to join the Snake.

After finally making contact with the Shoshone, Lewis quizzed their chief CAMEAHWAIT on the geography of the area. Cameahwait drew a wavy line on the ground to represent the Salmon River and then piled sand on both sides of the line to show "the vast mountains of rock eternally covered with snow through which the river passed." He also described "perpendicular and even juting rocks so closely hemned in the river that there was no possibilyte of passing along the shore. . . . the whole surface of the river was beat into perfect foam as far as the eye could reach." The mountains, too, were "inaccessible to man or horse."

Nevertheless, the captains were so anxious to find a river route to the Columbia to avoid portaging over the mountains that WILLIAM CLARK decided to investigate the Salmon himself. On August 18, leaving Lewis behind to organize the building of the CACHE at CAMP FORTUNATE, Clark and 11 men set off. After crossing Lemhi Pass, they turned north and followed the Lemhi River to its junction with the Salmon. The following day they arrived at the junction of the Salmon with its north fork, which Clark named Fish Creek, and turned west on the main stream, leaving the north fork on their right. A short journey of some 12 miles made it clear to Clark that Cameahwait had been right.

Sergeant PATRICK GASS described what they found: "The river at this place is so confined by the mountains that it is no more than 20 yards wide, and very rapid. . . . They found it was not possible to go down either by land or water, without much risk and trouble. The water is so rapid and the bed of the river so amazingly high, steep and rocky, that it seems impossible to go along the river by land."

The Salmon River clearly justified its nickname "River of No Return." Both Lewis and Clark were disappointed that they would be unable to use it, since this now meant that they would be forced to travel by land over the BITTERROOT MOUNTAINS. That route—north up to the BITTERROOT RIVER then west along the LOLO TRAIL—was dangerous and difficult, but the Salmon River route would have been impossible.

Clark named it Lewis's River. The Shoshone gave the name *Ag-gi-pa*, meaning "fish water," to both the Salmon and Lemhi rivers.

Further Reading

Ambrose, Stephen E. *Undaunted Courage: Meriwether Lewis, Thomas Jefferson, and the Opening of the American West.* New York: Simon and Schuster, 1996.

The peaceful headwaters of the Salmon River seen here give no indication of its tortuous route downstream through the mountains. Lewis and Clark had hoped to use the Salmon River but found it impassable. *(Library of Congress, Prints and Photographs Division [LC-USF34-074026-D])*

MacGregor, Carol Lynn, ed. *The Journals of Patrick Gass, Member of the Lewis and Clark Expedition.* Missoula, Mont.: Mountain Press Publishing Company, 1997.

Moulton, Gary E., ed. *Atlas of the Lewis and Clark Expedition.* Revised ed. Lincoln: University of Nebraska Press, 1999.

saltworks

By the end of December 1805, the CORPS OF DISCOVERY had nearly finished building their winter quarters at FORT CLATSOP, some two miles up the Lewis and Clark River and a few miles southwest of present-day Astoria, Oregon. Here they had timber for building and ELK for HUNTING but little else to eat apart from the FISH and dogs they procured from the CLATSOP INDIANS. In the constant wet weather, meat rotted quickly, and the party needed salt both to improve the flavor of the fresh meat that they ate as well as to cure any that they wanted to store.

The expedition had started out from CAMP DUBOIS in May 1804 with 750 pounds of salt, but this had long been exhausted. As long as elk were plentiful, they could eat fresh elk meat, but the arduous journey down from the ROCKY MOUNTAINS had made clear to both captains the need to preserve and cure as much food as they could for the return trip. As the winter passed, this became even more important as the elk became more scarce. (The party killed 128 elk during their four months at Fort Clatsop, roughly one each day.)

On December 28, 1805, before the building of the huts had been completed, five members of the corps were sent out to determine a suitable site to build a saltworks. They found the right location five days later on the PACIFIC OCEAN, 15 miles southwest of Fort Clatsop, at present-day Seaside, Oregon. There was sufficient timber to keep a fire going and, initially at least, enough game available to feed the detached party.

The three men assigned to be saltmakers were WILLIAM BRATTON, JOSEPH FIELD, and GEORGE GIBSON. ALEXANDER WILLARD and PETER WEISER assisted them in setting up the site and there was occasional relief from the fort, but otherwise it was Bratton, Field, and Gibson who made most of the salt during the winter of 1805–06.

The method of salt production was crude but effective. A large oblong oven was built of stones and a fire lit inside. Five brass kettles full of sea water were then placed on top and boiled until the liquid evaporated, leaving a deposit of salt behind. To keep a fire going continuously meant constant cutting of timber and chopping it to firewood lengths, as well as nonstop monitoring to ensure that the fire was burning well for 24 hours a day.

In their JOURNALS of January 5, 1806, MERIWETHER LEWIS and WILLIAM CLARK noted that the saltmakers could produce from three quarts to a gallon of salt per day. It is now estimated that this was based on their boiling some 40 gallons of seawater. Lewis recorded that the first batch of salt brought back was "excellent, fine, strong & white."

On February 10, 1806, Sergeant PATRICK GASS wrote: "In the afternoon two men came from the saltworks, with information that two others were sick and a third had cut his knee so badly he could scarcely walk." From the reports, it now seems clear that Gibson had influenza and that Bratton had a severe form of rheumatism, both conditions brought on by the exposed location of the saltworks by the ocean. The third man, possibly Alexander Willard, had cut his knee badly with a tomahawk. Bratton continued to suffer crippling back pain for weeks.

On February 19 the captains decided that the corps had enough salt and sent a group to bring back the equipment and the rest of the salt. They closed down the oven the next day and returned to the fort on the 21st. The following month the expedition began its journey home. While the saltworks had been a minor factor in their story, it demonstrated once again the ingenuity of Meriwether Lewis, William Clark, and their men in making every possible use of the scant resources available to them.

Nearly a century after the corps's winter on the Pacific coast, Jenny Michel, a Clatsop born in 1816, pointed out the pile of rocks that her mother had told her was the site of the saltworks. It has been reconstructed at its old location beside the ocean and is now part of the Fort Clatsop National Memorial.

Further Reading

MacGregor, Carol Lynn, ed. *The Journals of Patrick Gass, Member of the Lewis and Clark Expedition.* Missoula, Mont.: Mountain Press Publishing Company, 1997.

National Parks Service. "A moment in history: The Salt Works, Seaside, Oregon." Available on-line. URL: http://www.seasurf.com/~kirkham/saltwork.html. Downloaded on February 28, 2002.

scalp dance

Among the ceremonial rites of many PLAINS INDIANS was the scalp dance, a celebration of victory and superiority over one's enemies. Some historians believe that Europeans introduced the practice of scalping to Indians of the Northeast, who then took it with them onto the prairie and high plains when they moved west. While this cannot be verified, it is known that scalping—usually taking the skin and hair just above the eyes to below the ears—had a different meaning in the two cultures. Europeans used it as a way of collecting bounties, whereas for many Indians there was a religious significance to the taking of scalps. Since hair represented the soul, a scalped person was held to earth and could not enter the afterlife to take revenge on the victorious Indian's ancestors.

In many Indian nations, scalps were stretched on a hoop and then displayed on a pole, which was carried in the scalp dance. The scalps were then given to female relatives or sometimes added to medicine bundles. Some bands planted scalp poles at the graves of slain warriors, where they were left to disintegrate.

The form of the scalp dance varied from nation to nation but usually involved the display of recently taken scalps. Such was the case with the dance put on by the TETON LAKOTA INDIANS (Teton Sioux), which the expedition witnessed on the night of September 26, 1804. The Lakota had recently defeated a band of OMAHA INDIANS in battle, killing and scalping 65 warriors and taking 48 women and children as prisoners. WILLIAM CLARK had appealed to Chief BLACK BUFFALO to release the prisoners, but instead the scalp dance began. Clark later described it:

A large fire made in the Center, about 10 musitions playing on tamberins made of hoops & skin stretched. long sticks with Deer & Goats Hoofs tied So as to make a gingling noise and many others of a Similar kind, those men began to Sing & Beet on the temboren, the women Came forward highly Deckerated in theire way, with the Scalps and Trofies of war of ther father Husbands Brothers or near Connection & proceeded to Dance the war Dance. Women only dance—jump up & down. . . . Every now and then one of the men come out & repeat some exploit in a sort of song— this taken up by the young men and the women dance to it.

It was apparently the only scalp dance the expedition was to see. Private JOSEPH WHITEHOUSE noted that "they took the 65 of the Mahars [Omaha] sculps and had them hung on Small poles, which their women held in their hands when they danced." The soldiers tossed presents to the dancers and singers, and JOHN ORDWAY later said the dance was performed "with great Chearfullness."

Further Reading

Ambrose, Stephen E. *Undaunted Courage: Meriwether Lewis, Thomas Jefferson, and the Opening of the American West.* New York: Simon and Schuster, 1996.

scientific observations   See ANIMALS, NEW SPECIES; ASTRONOMICAL OBSERVATIONS; BIRDS, NEW SPECIES; ETHNOGRAPHY; PLANTS, NEW SPECIES.

Seaman (Scannon) *Newfoundland dog*

Not all members of the CORPS OF DISCOVERY had two legs. Another to make the journey across the ROCKY MOUNTAINS and back was MERIWETHER LEWIS's dog Seaman. A New-foundland purchased for $20 in PITTSBURGH prior to the start of the expedition, Seaman was characteristic of his breed: large (most stand about 28 inches tall and weigh up to 150 pounds), intelligent, strong, and a good swimmer. Newfoundlands were often used aboard ships because they were strong swimmers and had the reputation of saving drowning sailors—hence the name *Seaman.* He receives numerous mentions in Lewis's JOURNALS and LETTERS, although the writing and spelling was such that for many years the dog's name was erroneously reported as *Scannon.* (It was renowned scholar Donald Jackson who discovered and corrected the error.)

Seaman was brought on the expedition as a working dog, and one of Lewis's first mentions of him, on September 11, 1803, reports his catching squirrels, which "were fat and I thought a plesant food." On November 16 some impressed Shawnee Indians offered Lewis three BEAVER skins in exchange for Seaman, but the captain, by now firmly attached to his dog, noted, ". . . of course there was no bargain." After this

exchange, Seaman disappears from Lewis's journals for some time and receives only brief mention in the writings of CHARLES FLOYD and WILLIAM CLARK. He reappears on April 22, 1805, and is present in the journals for several months thereafter. Lewis's feelings for him are apparent in the entry for April 25: ". . . my dog had been absent during the night, and I was fearfull we had lost him altogether, however, much to my satisfaction he joined us at 8 Oclock this morning."

Among other Seaman feats reported was his capture of an ANTELOPE near the mouth of the YELLOWSTONE RIVER; killing it midstream, he then dragged it to shore. In May 1805 Seaman went after a beaver that one of the men had shot, and the wounded animal bit him in the hind leg, cutting an artery. Because of the severe loss of blood, Lewis feared the dog would die, but Seaman recovered quickly and was soon back to hunting for FOOD and providing warnings for the men. On the night of May 28, once again proving his worth, he diverted a BUFFALO that had begun to trample through the camp and prevented the beast from doing too much damage.

In mid-April 1806, as the expedition proceeded back up the COLUMBIA RIVER, local CHINOOK INDIANS plagued them with a series of thefts. On April 11, near the Cascades, three

This painting by British artist Anne Mainman shows the three unpaid members of the Lewis and Clark Expedition: Sacagawea, her baby Pomp, and Lewis's Newfoundland dog Seaman. *(Courtesy Anne Mainman, painted in 2000)*

WATLALA INDIANS stole Seaman. In a rage, Lewis sent three men after the thieves with orders to kill, if necessary. Detecting their pursuers, the Indians released the dog. Shortly after this incident, Seaman again disappeared from the journals for a while, but on July 5, 1806, Lewis noted that his dog had been accorded an honor bestowed on all expedition members at various points during the journey: He had a landmark named after him. In Seaman's case, it was a stream in Montana that is today called Monture Creek. After this the dog received only two more mentions, the last on July 15, reporting that Seaman, like other expedition members, was being tortured by the biting mosquitoes. Thereafter he disappears from the expedition's records, and his whereabouts following the journey remain unknown. It is noteworthy, however, that only Lewis and Private GEORGE SHANNON matched Seaman's feat of making the trip from PITTSBURGH to the PACIFIC OCEAN and back to ST. LOUIS.

Further Reading

Jackson, Donald. "Call Him a Good Old Dog, but Don't Call Him Scannon." *We Proceeded On* 11, no. 3 (1985).

Osgood, Ernest Staples. "Our Dog Scannon—Partner in Discovery." *Montana: The Magazine of Western History* 26, no. 3 (1976): 8–17.

PBS Online. *Lewis and Clark: Inside the Corps of Discovery:* "Seaman." Available on-line. URL: http://www.pbs.org/lewisandclark/inside/seaman.html. Downloaded on May 18, 2001.

Pringle, Lawrence. *Dog of Discovery: A Newfoundland's Adventures with Lewis and Clark.* Honesdale, Penn.: Boyds Mills Press, 2002.

sea otters   See OTTERS.

settlement   See WESTWARD EXPANSION.

sex during the expedition

The journey of the CORPS OF DISCOVERY took 28 months to complete and covered more than 8,000 miles. During that time the corpsmen lived in the wilderness, well away from the comforts of home—and from the company of women. It was therefore almost inevitable that they would turn to Indian WOMEN for sexual gratification when opportunity offered, and the JOURNALS record numerous instances of their doing so.

Often the availability of women for sex was dependent on the culture of the particular Indian nation that the expedition was visiting. Many of the PLAINS INDIANS were practitioners of polygamy, and warriors would hospitably offer their wives to visitors. The concept of *medicine*—the wisdom or special powers with which a person may be imbued—was also important. Many warriors believed that by sharing their wives with, for example, an experienced older warrior, that person's medicine would be transferred to them. As a black man, YORK was perceived to be Big Medicine and consequently was often in demand as a sexual partner. On at least one occasion a warrior even stood guard while York gratified his wife.

In January 1805 at FORT MANDAN, the MANDAN INDIANS invited the soldiers to observe their ritual BUFFALO DANCE, in which young wives were offered to the tribe's elders. The purpose of the dance was to attract BUFFALO to the area and give strength and courage to the younger men for the hunt. Hoping to gain the white men's medicine, many warriors offered their wives to the soldiers, who readily accepted the invitations. The highly successful buffalo hunt that followed was credited in no small part to their participation in the dance.

To modern eyes, the idea of women being given to others may seem like prostitution, but the Indians in question—male and female—did not view it this way. Women fully understood and accepted their roles and were often as eager to engage in sexual relations as the soldiers were. Sex, in fact, was an integral part of the Plains hospitality; to refuse to have sex with an Indian woman could be viewed as an insult. When the expedition were with the TETON LAKOTA INDIANS (Teton Sioux) WILLIAM CLARK noted that "a curious custom with Souix as well as the rickeres [ARIKARA] is to give handsom squars to those whome they wish to Show some acknowledgements to." He and MERIWETHER LEWIS were both offered bed partners but refused. This did not help their already uneasy relations with the Teton Lakota, as Clark noted: "They again offered me a young woman and wish me to take her & not Dispise them, I wavered the Subject."

Nevertheless, not all Indians were willing to share their wives with the soldiers, as Sergeant JOHN ORDWAY discovered at Fort Mandan. When Clark attempted to settle a violent marital squabble between a Mandan couple, he was told that Ordway had slept with the wife, whom the husband now wanted to kill. Ordway was ordered to give the man some trade goods, but Clark claimed that his men had not slept with any married women in the Mandan villages. Both captains lectured their men on sex, telling them to give Indian men "no cause of jealousy by having connection with their women without their knowledge."

As the expedition traveled further west, they noticed a subtle change in the Indian men's attitude toward their women, who, increasingly, were treated no better than slaves. This was certainly true of the SHOSHONE INDIANS, but Lewis and Clark saved their sharpest comments for the CHINOOK INDIANS during the winter at FORT CLATSOP. Here women prostituted themselves freely, a result of their decade-long association with white traders. Indeed, the Chinook women had become better traders than the men, and business arrangements were often sealed with an offer of sex. It was this that caused Clark to comment that they were "lude and carry on sport publickly." PATRICK GASS, misunderstanding the difference between this behavior and that of the Plains Indian women, wrote of the Chinook: "The women are much inclined to venery, and like those on the Missouri are sold to prostitution at an easy rate."

The wife of the Chinook chief Delashelwilt became known as "the old baud" for her habit of bringing young women to the expedition's camp and subsequently to Fort Clatsop, making them available to the soldiers. Clark wryly commented that "The young females are fond of the attention of our men"—but at such a price that the expedition's already lean supply of trade goods was becoming depleted, forcing the captains to put a brake on the proceedings. They subsequently "divided some ribbon between the men of our party to bestow on their favorite Lasses, this plan to save the knives and more valuable articles."

Lewis and Clark were well aware before the expedition set out from CAMP DUBOIS that their men would be engaging in sexual liaisons during the course of the journey, and they were also aware of the possible consequences. Lewis therefore included among his medical supplies provisions for treating venereal disease, in particular tincture of mercury, the most common treatment at that time. By mid-January 1805 symptoms of "the pox" were being noted in the journals. Just before they left Fort Mandan, Clark reported that the men were "generally healthy except Venerials complaints which is very common among the natives." (Many modern historians believe the Indians probably contracted the disease from white traders, and even possibly from expedition members, but when Lewis studied the matter he concluded, "I think it most probable that these disorders are original with them." There is no conclusive proof either way.)

In September 1805, during the crossing of the BITTER-ROOT MOUNTAINS, Lewis noted that in addition to being sick with dysentery, many of the men were suffering from "irruptions of the Skin," most likely signs of venereal disease contracted from Shoshone women. Throughout the winter at Fort Clatsop, Lewis dispensed mercury often, but most often to two men, HUGH MCNEAL and SILAS GOODRICH. On January 27, 1806, Lewis wrote, "Goodrich has recovered from the Louis veneri which he contracted from an amorous contact with a Chinnook damsel. I cured him as I did Gibson [GEORGE GIBSON] last winter by the uce of murcury." But mercury was hardly a cure for the disease. On the return journey, by the time the expedition reached the GREAT FALLS in June 1806, Goodrich and McNeal were showing secondary symptoms of syphilis. Clark later reported both men dead by 1825–28, and it is suspected that the mercury as much as the syphilis probably contributed to their early demises.

While there are numerous mentions of the sergeants and privates having sex with Indian women, the captains themselves appear to have abstained. In the journals, Clark talks of refusing offers of bed partners, in one instance noting that "the female part appeared to be highly disgusted at our refuseing of their favours &c." Amorous encounters are recorded with most Indian bands with whom the expedition spent time, yet the journals are strangely silent on the subject of sexual relations with the Nez Perce. Intriguingly, some 70 years after the expedition, a photographer named William Jackson met and photographed a blue-eyed, sandy-haired Nez Perce man who claimed to be the son of William Clark. When the Nez Perce War concluded in 1877 with the surrender of Chief Joseph, among those taken prisoner was this same man. Clark is, in fact, rumored to have fathered a number of Indian children. Although this is certainly possible, no conclusive evidence has emerged connecting Clark (or Lewis) amorously to any women encountered on the expedition.

Further Reading

Ambrose, Stephen E. *Undaunted Courage: Meriwether Lewis, Thomas Jefferson, and the Opening of the American West.* New York: Simon and Schuster, 1996.

Hagen, Cecil. "Liberated Women? . . . Not Those Lewis and Clark Met on Their Way." *Pacific Northwesterner* 25, no. 2 (1981): 17–25.

MacGregor, Carol Lynn, ed. *The Journals of Patrick Gass, Member of the Lewis and Clark Expedition.* Missoula, Mont.: Mountain Press Publishing Company, 1997.

Moulton, Gary E., ed. *The Journals of the Lewis and Clark Expedition.* 13 vols. Lincoln: University of Nebraska Press, 1983–2001.

Ronda, James P. *Lewis and Clark among the Indians.* Lincoln: University of Nebraska Press, 1984.

Shannon, George (1785–1836) *private in the permanent party*

Private George Shannon, one of the NINE YOUNG MEN FROM KENTUCKY, was also the youngest enlisted man in the expedition. He was born in Pennsylvania, moved with his family to Ohio when he was 15, and just three years later enlisted for the CORPS OF DISCOVERY. Related to Kentucky's governor Shannon, he was reportedly a good singer as well as a strong horseman. He was perhaps best known, however, for getting lost.

In 1803, while still in school in PITTSBURGH, Shannon met MERIWETHER LEWIS, who was there attending to the construction of the KEELBOAT. He must have made a good impression, for he ended up accompanying Lewis on the keelboat to Louisville, where he gained WILLIAM CLARK's approval. He enlisted in the CORPS OF DISCOVERY at Louisville on October 19 and was subsequently chosen for the permanent party going to the PACIFIC OCEAN. He was assigned to Sergeant NATHANIEL PRYOR's squad, and despite his youth he was appointed to be in charge of the squad during a period in spring 1804 that Pryor was sick.

Late in August 1804, as the expedition worked its way up the MISSOURI RIVER, Shannon was ordered to find two packhorses that had strayed from camp during the night. He succeeded in finding the HORSES but failed to find the corps, whom he assumed had gotten ahead of him up the river. In fact, they were behind him, sending out men to look for him while he continued northward in search of the others for 16 days. On September 11 the keelboat turned a bend in the river, and the nearly starved Shannon was found sitting by the bank. Having run out of bullets, he had had to improvise to find FOOD in the wilderness, relying mainly on grapes and berries. Weakened from hunger, he had decided to give up and hoped to catch a trading boat going downstream. Clark subsequently wrote, "Thus a man had like to have Starved to death in a land of Plenty for the want of Bullitts or Something to kill his meat."

A month later, Shannon was selected to serve on the court-martial of Private JOHN NEWMAN, who was charged with and found guilty of mutiny; Newman was subsequently dismissed from the corps. Shannon, however, would prove himself to be one of the most reliable and trustworthy privates on the expedition, despite his talent for getting lost. He also had his share of ILLNESSES AND INJURIES, in one instance cutting his foot with an adz while constructing dugout CANOES early in March 1805.

Private Shannon receives frequent mention in the expedition's JOURNALS, and whenever the corps broke into smaller parties, he was often among the men under Captain Clark's command. It was during one of these sorties, in early August 1805, that he once again became lost, albeit for a shorter period. Clark sent him to up the WISDOM RIVER, a tributary of the JEFFERSON RIVER, to do some HUNTING. Some time later, when Shannon had not returned, Clark sent GEORGE DROUILLARD out to look for him, but there was no sign of the private. Shannon finally returned three days later, on August 9, having gone some 25 miles up the river before turning back. He brought back three DEER skins and the news that the Wisdom River could not be navigated by canoes.

In mid-November that year, Shannon, JOHN COLTER, and ALEXANDER WILLARD joined Captain Lewis to explore various tidewater inlets near the COLUMBIA RIVER. While on a separate hunting foray, Shannon and Willard met and camped with five CHINOOK INDIANS who then stole their rifles. As the two privates argued with the Indians, Lewis and some others arrived on the scene and forced the Chinook to return the rifles. Lewis then had Shannon escort them to Clark, who chastised them severely for their theft. Shannon was subsequently picked again for a small scouting party to help Lewis choose a spot for their winter camp. They eventually settled on a bluff overlooking the present-day Lewis and Clark River, where they built FORT CLATSOP.

In June 1806, when the corps's first attempt to cross the BITTERROOT MOUNTAINS failed due to heavy snows, Lewis sent Drouillard and Shannon back to the NEZ PERCE INDIANS to bargain for a guide. It took them several days, but when they finally returned to the expedition, they brought three guides, to the relief of both captains. A few weeks later, Shannon received an honor already accorded to many others in the corps: Shannon's Creek, a tributary of the YELLOWSTONE RIVER, was named for him.

Following the expedition, Shannon was one of the party under Nathaniel Pryor charged with escorting the MANDAN chief BIG WHITE back to his people on the upper Missouri. The group was attacked by the ARIKARA INDIANS, and during the fight Shannon was badly wounded in the leg, which subsequently had to be amputated. This ended his military career, but he was awarded a pension from the U.S. CONGRESS. In October 1809, he was accompanying Clark to Washington when word was received of Lewis's suicide. The following year, while he was studying law, he assisted NICHOLAS BIDDLE in preparing the expedition's journals for publication. He refused an offer from Clark to join a fur-trading enterprise, choosing instead to practice law in Kentucky and later serving in that state's legislature. He was married in 1813, and he and his wife Ruth had seven children. They subsequently moved to Missouri, where he became a U.S. senator as well as a lawyer. George Shannon died on August 31, 1836, and was buried in Palmyra, Missouri; his grave, however, was not marked and has never been identified.

Further Reading

Clarke, Charles G. *The Men of the Lewis and Clark Expedition: A Biographical Roster of the Fifty-One Members and a Composite Diary of Their Activities from All Known Sources.* 1970. Reprint, Lincoln: Bison Books, University of Nebraska Press, 2002.

Lange, Robert. "Private George Shannon: The Expedition's Youngest Member—1785 or 1787–1836." *We Proceeded On* 8, no. 3 (July 1982): 10–15.

North Dakota Lewis & Clark Bicentennial Foundation. *Members of the Corps of Discovery.* Bismarck, N.Dak.: United Printing and Mailing, 2000.

PBS Online. *Lewis and Clark: Inside the Corps of Discovery:* "Private George Shannon." Available on-line. URL: http://www.pbs.org/lewisandclark/inside/gshan.html. Downloaded on May 18, 2001.

sheep and goats

Both MERIWETHER LEWIS and WILLIAM CLARK used what are now considered incorrect terms in their descriptions of ANIMALS. Constantly encountering new species, they understandably related what they saw to animals with which they were already familiar. For example, they both described the pronghorn ANTELOPE as a goat when they first saw it. A similar confusion arose in their description of the bighorn sheep and the mountain goat, an error justified by an entry on sheep in the 1927 edition of *Encyclopaedia Britannica*: "Sheep belong to the family of hollow-horned ruminants or Bovidae. Practically they form a group impossible of definition, as they pass imperceptibly into the goats."

Although an employee of the NORTH WEST COMPANY had already killed a bighorn sheep and sent a specimen to London, where it was classified and named in 1803, Lewis and Clark first heard of it on October 1, 1804, at the mouth of the Cheyenne River. Clark reported that Jean Valle, a French trader, had told them that there were "no BEAVER on Dog river, on the Mountains great numbers of goat [antelope] and a kind of anamale with circular horns, this animale is nearly the size of a Small Elk, White bears is also plentiful."

Although Lewis purchased four horns of the "Mountain Ram or big horn" at the villages of the MANDAN INDIANS and sent them back to THOMAS JEFFERSON in April 1805, the first sighting of them was not until April 26, 1805. At the mouth of the YELLOWSTONE RIVER, Clark reported that JOSEPH FIELD "saw several of the bighorned animals in the course of his walk; but they were so shy that he could not get a shot at them; he found a large horn of one of these animals which he brought with him."

On May 25, 1805, above the MUSSELSHELL RIVER, Sergeant PATRICK GASS reported that "some of the party killed three of what the French and natives call mountain sheep; but they very little resemble sheep, except in the head, horns and feet. . . . Captain Clarke calls them the Ibex, and says they resemble that animal more than any other."

Lewis wrote a lengthy and detailed description of the bighorn shot that day and noted that the horns were used by Indians to make bows, "watercups, spoons and platters of it." He added that the horns would make "elegant and useful hair combs." Both Lewis and Clark seem to have referred to the sheep subsequently as "the Bighorn animal" and found it all the way up the MISSOURI RIVER from the Yellowstone to the Beaverhead Mountains.

On August 24, 1805, Lewis observed that some of the skins worn by the SHOSHONE INDIANS "have almost every appearance of the common sheep." He also learned from them that it lived "on high mountains" and concluded, "I am now convinced that the sheep as well as the bighorn exist in these mountains." At FORT CLATSOP on February 2, 1806, he wrote:

> The sheep is found in various parts of the ROCKY MOUN-TAINS, but most commonly in those parts which are timbered and steep. they are also to be found in greater abundance on the chain of mountains which form the commencement of the woody country on this coast and which pass the Columbia between the GREAT FALLS and the rapids. we have never met with this anamal ourselves but have seen many of their skins in possession of the natives. . . .

There is no record of the bighorn sheep being seen west of the CONTINENTAL DIVIDE, and Lewis made no mention of it until he regained the Missouri below the MARIAS RIVER on July 29, 1806. Clark saw some as he crossed the divide on the return journey on July 4, 1806, near Gibbons Pass, and he found them again on cliffs all the way down the Yellowstone River.

It is now thought that none of the expedition ever saw a mountain goat, although they were shown its skins in Indian villages and had its appearance and habits described to them. Clark may have seen one at a distance on August 24, 1805, in the LEMHI RIVER valley, but since he used the term *goat* to cover the pronghorn antelope as well, this is in doubt. In their accounts of the mountain goat, both Lewis and Clark refer to it as a sheep, which, given what they heard of it, is understandable. It is also worth noting that in 1789 ALEXANDER MACKEN-ZIE had listed it among the animals of the MacKenzie River valley as a "White Buffalo."

Further Reading

Burroughs, Raymond Darwin, ed. *The Natural History of the Lewis and Clark Expedition.* East Lansing: Michigan State University Press, 1995.

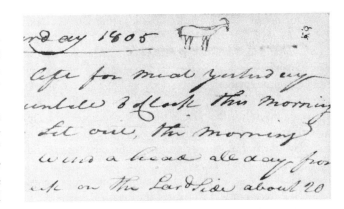

William Clark made this sketch of a bighorn sheep on May 25, 1805, near the Musselshell River. *(Clark Family Collection, William Clark Papers, Missouri Historical Society, St. Louis)*

Cutright, Paul Russell. *Lewis & Clark: Pioneering Naturalists.* Lincoln: University of Nebraska Press/Bison Books, 1989.

Knue, Joseph. *Big Game of North Dakota: A Short History.* Bismarck: North Dakota Game and Fish Dept., 1991.

Monson, Gale, and Lowell Sumner, eds. *The Desert Bighorn: Its Life History, Ecology, and Management.* Tucson: University of Arizona Press, 1980.

Toweill, Dale, and Valerius Geist. *Return of Royalty: Wild Sheep of North America.* Missoula, Mont.: Boone and Crockett Club, 1999.

Sheheke   See BIG WHITE.

shelter

Throughout the JOURNALS of the Lewis and Clark Expedition, two phrases constantly recur: "We proceeded on" and "We encamped on the south [or north] side." While the statement "we encamped" is clear, surprisingly little detail is given of what it implied. Readers of the journals are told of sentries standing guard, of the meals that were eaten, and whether the night was cold or wet. But only rarely does one learn of the forms of shelter the expedition employed.

During the 28 months of their journey, the expedition brought, found, or made all types of shelter, ranging from the log houses of CAMP DUBOIS, FORT MANDAN, and FORT CLAT-SOP to tents, OILCLOTH awnings, TIPIS, brushwood shanties, and abandoned Indian huts. Tents were probably the most commonly used shelters for their weeks in the wilderness, especially during the first part of their journey. When MERIWETHER LEWIS brought the KEELBOAT down the OHIO RIVER in 1803, it is known that the SUPPLIES AND EQUIPMENT he had bought included "1 Common Tent" and "8 Tents, Oil Treated." This would certainly have been appropriate for the party originally authorized by CONGRESS: an officer, a sergeant, and 12 men. However, it was clearly insufficient for the two officers and 29 men who were to become the permanent party of the CORPS OF DISCOVERY, in addition to SACAGAWEA and her boy Pomp.

During the winter of 1803–04 at Camp Dubois, both Lewis and WILLIAM CLARK spent much of their time buying more supplies and equipment in ST. LOUIS. At that time this was a small frontier town accustomed to supplying trappers and traders, and its merchants would certainly have been able to provide basic camp equipment. Whether these included tentage is doubtful. It is more likely that the two captains bought quantities of the nearest equivalent: sheets of oilcloth. Similar to today's tarpaulins, these cloths could be used for groundsheets, as awnings to keep off rain, and as protection for their baggage, and they could be easily converted into simple tents.

On November 2, 1804, after the decision was made to build Fort Mandan, Sergeant PATRICK GASS noted: "We pitched our tents and laid the foundation of one line of huts." While not confirmed in the journals, it is likely that they took their tents with them when they left the villages of the MANDAN INDIANS in April 1805. In addition, the captains used a tipi that was bought from TOUSSAINT CHARBONNEAU, probably because Sacagawea and her baby had now joined them. He wrote, "Capt. Clark, myself, the two Interpretters, the woman and child sleep in a tent of dressed skins."

There is no record of how far the explorers took their tents, and it is possible that some were left in the CACHES they built along their route. By November 1805 they had reached the COLUMBIA RIVER and were camping in extreme discomfort on the shore by POINT ELLICE. On November 11, 1805, Patrick Gass wrote that they "built large fires and made our situation as comfortable as possible, but still bad enough, as we have no tents, or coverings to defend us, except our blankets and some mats we got from the Indians, which we put on poles to keep off the rain."

The implication from this is that their supply of oilcloth sheeting was also exhausted, probably replaced by dressed DEER or BUFFALO skins. Some of the party kept their skins through the winter at Fort Clatsop. On their return journey up the Columbia in 1806, Gass wrote on April 18, "Several of the men went up to the village with their buffalo robes, to dispose of them for HORSES."

A month later, when it was clear they would have to wait at CAMP CHOPUNNISH for the snows to clear before they could cross the BITTERROOT MOUNTAINS, Gass gave a vivid picture of the party's accommodation: "[May 15, 1806] This was a fine morning, and some hunters went out early. The rest of the party were engaged making places of shelter, to defend them from the stormy WEATHER. Some had small sails to cover their little hovels, and others had to make frames and cover them with grass."

This sort of improvisation would continue throughout the latter part of their journey. It seems probable, in fact, that in the last stages the expedition came to rely for shelter, as the Indians did, on the deer and buffalo around them.

Further Reading

MacGregor, Carol Lynn, ed. *The Journals of Patrick Gass, Member of the Lewis and Clark Expedition.* Missoula, Mont.: Mountain Press Publishing Company, 1997.

Moulton, Gary E., ed. *The Journals of the Lewis and Clark Expedition.* 13 vols. Lincoln: University of Nebraska Press, 1983–2001.

Rogers, Ken. "Roughing It: Give me shelter." *The Bismarck Tribune.* Available on-line. URL: http://www.ndonline.com/tribweb-page/features/lewisclark/2001/rough.html. Downloaded on February 16, 2002.

The only tipi on the expedition was one that Lewis and Clark bought from Toussaint Charbonneau, similar to those seen in this 1922 photograph. *(Library of Congress, Prints and Photographs Division [LC-USZ62-115455])*

Shields, John (1769–1809) *private in the permanent party*

One of the NINE YOUNG MEN FROM KENTUCKY, Private John Shields played a crucial role in the expedition's survival thanks to his skills as a blacksmith, gunsmith, and mechanic. Born in Augusta County, Virginia, Shields had moved to Tennessee with his family while he was still a boy and then later moved to Kentucky. He was recruited for the expedition in Louisville on October 19, 1803; at 34 he was the oldest member of the corps aside from TOUSSAINT CHARBONNEAU. He and NATHANIEL PRYOR were the exceptions to Lewis's and Clark's rule that only unwedded men be recruited for the expedition; Shields had married in 1790 and had a daughter with his wife Janet.

While he became a valued member of the expedition, during the corps's months at CAMP DUBOIS, Shields was not always a model soldier. He blatantly refused to take orders from Sergeant JOHN ORDWAY, and late in March he stated his desire to go home and then threatened Ordway's life. JOHN COLTER had also made threats against the sergeant; consequently, the two privates were court-martialed for mutiny. Both Shields and Colter begged forgiveness, which was granted to them, and they were admitted into the permanent party.

Shields, WILLIAM BRATTON, and ALEXANDER WILLARD were the expedition's blacksmiths. Shields in particular had an ability to improvise with metalwork, using a makeshift forge and bellows to create objects such as arrowheads, battle-axes, and hide scrapers for TRADE with the Indians, for whom he also mended hoes and other implements. The three men's combined efforts made it possible to obtain sustenance, especially CORN, from Indians in exchange for the products of their labors, but it was Shields whom Lewis and Clark singled out for particular praise. As gunsmith he also looked after the corps's FIREARMS and made bullets from the lead canisters that held their gunpowder.

Shields made other contributions to the expedition as well, acting when needed as both hunter and scout. On May 20, 1805, MERIWETHER LEWIS noted in his journal that the private had discovered a freshwater spring near the mouth of the YELLOWSTONE RIVER, a significant discovery since most springs in the area "without exception are impregnated with the salts [minerals] which abound in this country."

Early in August 1805, Captain Lewis took Shields, GEORGE DROUILLARD, and HUGH MCNEAL with him on a scouting party to locate the SHOSHONE INDIANS. Their first encounter with a Shoshone warrior ended badly. As Lewis approached the Indian from one direction, Drouillard and Shields began to walk in from different directions. Drouillard saw and obeyed Lewis's signal to stop; Shields did not, and his continued approach finally frightened the Indian into riding away. Lewis was furious, especially with Shields.

The following year Shields assisted in the medical treatment of William Bratton, who had become nearly paralyzed from back pain. While the corps camped near the NEZ PERCE INDIANS in March 1806, Shields suggested that Bratton might benefit from a sweathouse, and Captain WILLIAM CLARK agreed, directing him to construct it. He did so by digging a large hole in which a fire was built, and stones were placed on top. A tent made of willow poles and blankets was then placed over the hole, atop which a seat had been placed for Bratton, and water was sprinkled on the stones to create steam. After 20 minutes inside the sweathouse, during which he also drank a strong mint tea, Bratton was taken out and dunked in the icy CLEARWATER RIVER; then he was made to repeat the whole procedure several times over. The treatment worked, and Bratton was soon walking unassisted.

Shields had not one but two rivers named for him. The first is now called Highwood Creek, a tributary of the MISSOURI RIVER located near GREAT FALLS. The second was a tributary of the YELLOWSTONE RIVER flowing out of the Crazy Horse Mountains near BOZEMAN PASS in present-day Montana. Shields River is one of the few landmarks that has retained the name given it by Lewis and Clark to the present day.

The captains thought very highly of John Shields, and in his report to Secretary of War HENRY DEARBORN, Lewis lauded the private and recommended that he be given extra pay for his service: "Nothing was more peculiarly useful to us, in various situations, than the skill and ingenuity of this man as an artist, in repairing our guns, accoutrements, &c. and should it be thought proper to allow him something as a artificer, he has well deserved it." However, apparently nothing extra was awarded to Shields or other men whom Lewis believed deserved special consideration.

Shields did receive the double pay and land warrant of 320 acres awarded to most of the men of the permanent party. After his discharge on October 10, 1806, he spent some time fur-trapping in Missouri and Indiana with DANIEL BOONE, who was apparently a relative. He subsequently settled in Indiana, where he died in December 1809.

Further Reading

Clarke, Charles G. *The Men of the Lewis and Clark Expedition: A Biographical Roster of the Fifty-One Members and a Composite Diary of Their Activities from All Known Sources.* 1970. Reprint, Lincoln: Bison Books, University of Nebraska Press, 2002.

Lange, Robert. "John Shields: Lewis and Clark's Handyman: Gunsmith–Blacksmith–General Mechanic for the Expedition." *We Proceeded On* 5, no. 3 (July 1979): 14–16.

North Dakota Lewis & Clark Bicentennial Foundation. *Members of the Corps of Discovery.* Bismarck, N.Dak.: United Printing and Mailing, 2000.

PBS Online. *Lewis and Clark: Inside the Corps of Discovery:* "Private John Shields." Available on-line. URL: http://www.pbs.org/lewisandclark/inside/jshie.html. Downloaded on May 18, 2001.

Ship Rock (Monumental Rock)

Mid-October 1805 saw the Lewis and Clark Expedition making their way by canoe down the CLEARWATER RIVER and SNAKE RIVER to join the COLUMBIA RIVER. On October 10 they reached the junction of the Snake and the Clearwater (at present-day Lewiston on the Idaho-Washington border) and made their way down past FISHING settlements of the NEZ PERCE and the FLATHEAD INDIANS. Though they encountered several rapids, most of these were negotiated successfully. Their most serious problem was the lack of FOOD and timber. While the generosity of the Indians along the riverbanks had provided plenty of FISH and, occasionally, dogs to eat, cooking them was done with difficulty over small fires of willow twigs, the only fuel available.

Sergeant PATRICK GASS wrote of the fishing settlements: "Their summer lodges are made of willow and flags, and their winter lodges of split pine, almost like rails, which they bring down on rafts to this part of the river where there is no timber." On October 14, while on the Snake, downstream from modern Ayer, Washington, the CORPS OF DISCOVERY came to two more sets of rapids. The first they passed successfully, but the second capsized one of the canoes and left four men marooned on a rock until the others could rescue them. Sergeant Gass noted that "all the men got safe to shore; but the baggage was wet, and some articles were lost. We halted on an island to dry the baggage having come 14 miles."

It is unclear whether the rock on which the party dried the baggage was the one they called Ship Rock, from its resemblance to a ship's hull. It may have been, though the name was changed by later travelers to Monumental Rock. This at least is commemorated by the Lower Monumental Dam, which has now submerged the rapids through which the expedition struggled.

Further Reading

Ambrose, Stephen E. *Undaunted Courage: Meriwether Lewis, Thomas Jefferson, and the Opening of the American West.* New York: Simon and Schuster, 1996.

Fifer, Barbara, and Vicky Soderberg. *Along the Trail with Lewis and Clark.* Great Falls, Mont.: Montana Magazine, 1998.

MacGregor, Carol Lynn, ed. *The Journals of Patrick Gass, Member of the Lewis and Clark Expedition.* Missoula, Mont.: Mountain Press Publishing Company, 1997.

Short Narrows   See CELILO FALLS AND THE DALLES.

Shoshone Indians (Shoshoni Indians, Snake Indians)

Native Americans played crucial roles in the success of the Lewis and Clark Expedition. Many gave FOOD to the explorers when they were hungry; others provided MERIWETHER LEWIS and WILLIAM CLARK with information on the rivers, country, and nations ahead of them on their journey; others guided them over difficult terrain. The Shoshone filled all these roles for the expedition, although they sometimes had to be shamed into assisting the explorers and they extracted a heavy price for their help.

In the early 1800s the Shoshone lived on both sides of the ROCKY MOUNTAINS. There were three distinct groups, each with a unique dialect and way of life according to the area in which they lived. The Western Shoshone occupied what is now central and eastern Nevada, eastern California, and northwestern Utah; the Northern Shoshone were located in present-day southeastern Idaho and northern Utah; and the Eastern Shoshone (an offshoot of the Northern Shoshone) were found in the western part of modern Wyoming. Some bands also extended into parts of western Montana. Traders and others often called the Northern Shoshone, Northern Paiute (Numu), and Bannock collectively the Snake Indians.

Those Shoshone whom the explorers met were a Northern Shoshone band called the Lemhi who had once lived on the plains of Montana but had moved to the area of the LEMHI RIVER in eastern Idaho many years previously . The Lemhi subsisted largely by FISHING and collecting wild roots and berries; they hunted BUFFALO when they could, but they were often attacked and driven off the plains by their enemies,

Lewis and Clark were the first white men the Shoshone had seen. This picture of a Shoshone, which is clearly of a later period, shows how they adopted elements of white men's dress. *(Courtesy Art Today.com/IMSI)*

the Gros Ventre (Atsina), the BLACKFEET, and the HIDATSA INDIANS.

Having learned of the Lemhi Shoshone from the Hidatsa during their stay at FORT MANDAN (1804–05), Lewis and Clark knew that they would be the best source for HORSES to cross the mountains. Because of this they needed a Shoshone translator, and by coincidence one was found living in one of the Hidatsa villages: SACAGAWEA, the teenage (and pregnant) wife of TOUSSAINT CHARBONNEAU, the expedition's newly hired interpreter. It was therefore arranged that Sacagawea would accompany the expedition.

In early August 1805, as they made their way up the JEF-FERSON RIVER, the search for the Shoshone began in earnest. They knew they were getting close when Sacagawea recognized BEAVERHEAD ROCK on August 8. Three days later Lewis and a small party traveling ahead of the expedition on foot encountered a lone Shoshone warrior but inadvertently frightened him away. Following him, they crossed LEMHI PASS the next day, and on August 13 they encountered a small group of Shoshone WOMEN. After Lewis had reassured them that they would not be harmed, a party of about 60 Shoshone warriors arrived, led by Chief CAMEAHWAIT. Lewis presented them with GIFTS, upon which Cameahwait welcomed them and brought them back to his village.

Although the Shoshone had been about to go down to the plains to hunt buffalo, Cameahwait acceded to Lewis's request that they accompany him back to the BEAVERHEAD RIVER to meet Clark and the rest of the party. When they arrived at the location, however, Clark was nowhere in sight, and Lewis had to give Cameahwait his gun as reassurance that he was being honest. When Clark finally arrived on August 17, they had their first formal council with the Shoshone. There followed one of the most remarkable COINCIDENCES AND CHANCE ON THE EXPEDITION as Sacagawea suddenly recognized Cameahwait as her brother. The captains took the ensuing emotional reunion as a good sign and subsequently named the location CAMP FORTUNATE.

Things were not so fortunate for the Shoshone, who had recently suffered some severe losses in a battle with the Blackfeet. One of the reasons for which they welcomed the explorers was their need for guns—a need that became a recurring theme in their talks with the captains. As Cameahwait told Lewis, "If we had guns, we could live in the country of the buffaloe and eat as our enimies do, and not be compelled to hide ourselves in these mountains and live on roots and berries as the bear do." Lewis assured him that they would get guns when the white traders came.

Despite their poverty and hunger, the Shoshone were a generous people who shared what they had in the way of roots and berries. The expedition reciprocated as much as possible by sharing meat whenever the hunters managed to shoot some game. Lewis noted of the Shoshone, "Notwithstanding their extreem poverty they are not only cheerful but even gay, fond of gaudy dress and amusements. . . ."

Negotiations for horses went well, although as the Indians realized how desperate the expedition's need was, their prices went up. Cameahwait gave the captains much helpful information about the mountains and the country to the west. Despite his advice that the SALMON RIVER was impassable, Clark went to see for himself. While he was gone, Lewis conducted ethnographic studies of the Shoshone and supervised the building of CACHES. He was still negotiating for more horses when he learned from Charbonneau that the Shoshone were about to leave for their long-delayed buffalo hunt.

Lewis angrily reproached Cameahwait and the other chiefs, reminding them of their promises to help and insisting that they stay until his business with them was concluded.

According to Lewis, Cameahwait admitted he had been at fault "but that he had been induced to that measure from seeing all his people hungary, but as he had promised to give me his assistance he would not in future be worse this his word." Lewis acknowledged in his journal that the condition of the Shoshone was "really distressing," but he was determined to make them stay until he had obtained all the horses he needed. It was also arranged that OLD TOBY would guide them over the BITTER-ROOT MOUNTAINS by way of the LOLO TRAIL.

The Shoshone continued to set high prices for the horses; Clark was forced to give his pistol, a knife, and 100 rounds of ammunition for one horse alone. When the expedition at last parted from the Shoshone, they did so with what were mostly castoff horses—"nearly all Sore Backs [and] several Pore, & young," wrote Clark. In the end, wrote James Ronda, "The Shoshonis had proven to be better Yankee Traders than the Americans."

During the next 70 years, the Lemhi Shoshone experienced both good and bad relations with U.S. traders and soldiers. When the government began to assign all Shoshone to reservations in the 1860s, there was a period of Lemhi resistance that ended when they were moved onto the Lemhi Valley Reservation near Fort Lemhi in 1875. However, the land was infertile, and promised rations from the government never came. In 1880 the starving Lemhi sent a delegation to Washington to petition the government to allow them to move to the Fort Hall Reservation, where a number of Northern Shoshone and Bannock Indians had already been moved. The request was granted, and by 1907 the relocation had been completed. A few years later, however, a few Lemhi moved back to their old homeland near the Lemhi River, where some of their descendants still live today.

Further Reading

Madsen, Brigham D. *The Lemhi: Sacagawea's People.* Caldwell, Idaho: Caxton Printers, 1979.

Rees, John E. "The Shoshoni Contribution to Lewis and Clark." *Idaho Yesterdays* 2 (1958): 2–13.

Ronda, James P. *Lewis and Clark among the Indians.* Lincoln: University of Nebraska Press, 1984.

Trenholm, Virginia and Maurine Carley. *The Shoshonis: Sentinels of the Rockies.* Norman: University of Oklahoma Press, 1964.

Waldman, Carl. *Encyclopedia of Native American Tribes.* Revised ed. New York: Checkmark Books, 1999.

Sibley, John (1757–1837) *physician, explorer*

In 1806, before the Lewis and Clark Expedition arrived back in ST. LOUIS, President THOMAS JEFFERSON published a message providing sketchy but important information about explorations of the LOUISIANA TERRITORY. The sources for his communiqué were reports received from MERIWETHER LEWIS (sent from FORT MANDAN in spring 1805), preliminary data from the recent RED RIVER EXPEDITION, and letters from Dr. John Sibley, a resident of Natchitoches, Louisiana. Sibley, who would later become a brief participant in Major Stephen Long's explorations of the territory, was a prolific correspondent with Jefferson and other leading figure of the day, providing invaluable information on the LOUISIANA PURCHASE and its inhabitants.

A native of Sutton, Massachusetts, Sibley studied medicine before serving in the American Revolution as a surgeon's mate. He later moved with his wife to Fayetteville, North Carolina, where he set up practice and founded the Fayetteville *Gazette.* Widowed in 1790, he remarried the following year, but in September 1802 he moved, alone, to Natchitoches. In March 1803, he traveled some distance up the Red River, acquiring extensive knowledge about the region's Indians as well as Spanish Texas. A year later he began to correspond with Jefferson, who subsequently named him contract surgeon to the U.S. Army at Natchitoches. From 1805 to 1814 he served as Indian agent for the Orleans territory, succeeding in acquiring the friendship of numerous Indian nations and the enmity of Spanish officials.

Sibley's voluminous correspondence with Jefferson, Louisiana governor W. C. C. Claiborne, and others reported on not just on the territory and its Indians but also on its people and events. He thus became an important source of information on Louisiana for U.S. officials in the East. Sibley also wrote articles about Spanish Texas for newspapers around the country, helping to shape public perceptions of that area. Dismissed as Indian agent in 1814, he went on to become a militia captain, parish judge, and state senator in Louisiana. In 1819 he accompanied the military exploration of the Southwest headed by Stephen Long, but before long he returned to his home and his third wife. He died in Natchitoches 18 years later.

Further Reading

Connor, Seymour V. "Sibley, John (1757–1837)." Handbook of Texas Online. URL: http://www.tsha.utexas.edu/handbook/online/articles/view/SS/fsi2.html. Downloaded on February 6, 2002.

Jefferson, Thomas. *Message from the President of the United States Communicating Discoveries Made in Exploring the Missouri, Red River and Washita, by Captains Lewis and Clark, Doctor Sibley, and Mr. Dunbar: with a statistical account of the countries adjacent.* Washington, D.C.: A. & G. Way, printers, 1806.

sign language   See LANGUAGES.

singing   See RECREATION ON THE EXPEDITION.

Skilloot Indians

In late October 1805, prior to reaching the area of CELILO FALLS AND THE DALLES on the COLUMBIA RIVER, the CORPS OF DISCOVERY found the Indians whom they met to be welcoming, friendly, and helpful. As they proceeded downriver, however, the atmosphere began to change. The UMATILLA INDIANS regarded the explorers with tremendous fear until they

were reassured they would not be killed. Then, at Celilo Falls and The Dalles, the corps met large numbers of CHINOOK INDIANS, whose reaction to them proved quite different from that of the PLATEAU INDIANS. This was a large center for FISHING and trading, and the river Indians guarded their territory jealously. Suspicious, even hostile toward strangers, many of the Chinook of this region saw the expedition as intruders. This included the Skilloot Indians.

The Skilloot lived along both sides of the Columbia River below The Dalles, between Oregon's Washougal and Cowlitz Rivers, although they had some settlements beyond these boundaries as well. On November 4, 1805, the expedition visited a large Skilloot village with 25 houses near the mouth of the WILLAMETTE RIVER. By this time MERIWETHER LEWIS and WILLIAM CLARK had already begun to notice European goods and influences, a result of trading at the mouth of the Columbia. The Skilloot were the river's middlemen between that area and The Dalles, and one of the first things the captains noticed was how well armed they were. Their clothing was a combination of both American Indian and European dress, and they seemed friendly initially. Lewis and Clark had earlier hired a Skilloot to help pilot them down a stretch of the river, and this man now invited them into his lodge, where they ate WAPATO roots.

The expedition then moved several miles downriver and set up camp for their noon meal. At that point several CANOES of well-dressed, well-armed Skilloot appeared; the captains smoked with them and invited them to join the corps at lunch. Soon, however, the Indians became "assumeing and disagreeable." Clark reported: "during the time we were at dinner those fellows Stold my pipe Tomahawk which they were Smoking with, I immediately serched every man and the canoes, but could find nothing of my Tomahawk, while Serching for the Tomahawk one of those Scoundals Stole a cappoe [coat] of one of our interperters, which was found Stuffed under the root of a tree, near the place they Sat, we became much displeased with those fellows, which they discovered and moved off on their return home to their village."

The explorers, too, moved off, even staying in their canoes for an hour after it got dark "with a view to get clear of the natives who [were] constantly about us, and troublesom." They would be equally troublesome on the expedition's return journey the following spring. The worst offenders were the WATLALA INDIANS, who harried and stole from the corps throughout their PORTAGE around the Cascades. (Coincidentally, in a Watlala lodge JOHN COLTER discovered the pipe tomahawk that the Skilloot had stolen from Clark.) By mid-April 1806, Lewis and Clark had decided they would need HORSES, and the Skilloot (who had set up temporary fishing lodges around The Dalles for the spring salmon runs) seemed the best possibility for obtaining them.

While Lewis oversaw the portaging, Clark set up a makeshift trading post and sent some men out to drum up business. Only GEORGE DROUILLARD succeeded, finding a Skilloot chief who seemed interested in trading and who invited Clark's party to his village that night. Things seemed hopeful as PIERRE CRUZATTE played his fiddle and the men danced. Trading, however, went poorly, although Clark tried hard to attract the Indians to the few goods he had left to offer. The Skilloot were largely uninterested, and those few who came to him demanded prices for their horses that he could ill afford. Over a period of two days, he finally managed to obtain three horses from the Skilloott and two from some Eneeshur Indians, but the experience exasperated him, and both he and Lewis were glad when they finally cleared The Dalles.

The Skilloot and others kept their tight control over the region for several years until the effects of white migration drastically reduced their population and destroyed their way of life. By midcentury the few remaining Skilloot had been settled on reservations in Washington and Oregon.

Further Reading

Ronda, James P. *Lewis and Clark among the Indians.* Lincoln: University of Nebraska Press, 1984.

skills on the expedition

One of the most remarkable aspects of the Lewis and Clark Expedition was the ingenuity and skills of its members, beginning with its captains. The term *polymath* is misused often today but can be properly and correctly applied to MERIWETHER LEWIS. An army officer, he was an excellent shot, a hunter who could kill and dress game, an inspiring leader, an astronomer, a navigator, a botanist, a zoologist, and an ethnographer; and his medical skills are recounted throughout the expedition's JOURNALS.

WILLIAM CLARK justified every hope Lewis had placed in him. He was a meticulous navigator and cartographer; a compassionate and understanding officer who knew the men he commanded better than they knew themselves; a skilled waterman; and, as he proved among the NEZ PERCE INDIANS, an excellent albeit intuitive doctor. Together, Lewis and Clark were prime examples of outstanding LEADERSHIP.

The skills of the men the captains chose for the CORPS OF DISCOVERY fully validated their methods of RECRUITING. They looked for men who could undertake hard physical labor; for hunters and watermen; and for men skilled in ironwork, carpentry, and surveying. Time and again in reading the journals, one has to admire the choices they made. After the initial weeks of the journey, the captains came to rely on their men, and their trust was justified. It would be tedious to list all the talent they had at their command, but some examples illustrate the point.

GEORGE DROUILLARD, employed as an interpreter, was highly proficient in the sign language of the PLAINS INDIANS. He soon also proved his worth as a guide, a hunter, and a tracker. Lewis made sure Drouillard accompanied him whenever encounters with Indians were likely and knew that if any game were to be found, Drouillard would find it.

Sergeant PATRICK GASS was a soldier and a skilled carpenter. His journal looked at the expedition across the continent from a practical aspect. He planned and supervised the building of FORT MANDAN and FORT CLATSOP. He knew which TREES were suitable for making CANOES, found them, and built the vessels the expedition needed.

JOHN SHIELDS, the blacksmith, repaired and tested rifles throughout the 28 months of the journey. With ALEXANDER WILLARD and WILLIAM BRATTON, his skill and inventiveness kept the expedition supplied with FOOD during the winter of 1804–05, as he repaired iron tools and made axes for the MANDAN INDIANS in exchange for CORN. When salt was required during the winter of 1805–06 at Fort Clatsop, it was Bratton, JOSEPH FIELD, and GEORGE GIBSON who extracted it from sea water at the SALTWORKS.

Throughout the journals, there are notes on the making of CLOTHING and moccasins from DEER and BUFFALO hide. This was the special province of JOSEPH WHITEHOUSE, who was expert as a "hide-curer" and "tailor." If there were FISH to be caught, then SILAS GOODRICH came into his own, catching fish for food or often as a new scientific discovery, for which the journals gave him due credit. A typical entry (June 11, 1805) reads: "Goodrich who is remarkably fond of FISHING caught several douzen fish of two species—one about 9 inches long of a white colour, round in form and fine resembling the white chub."

TOUSSAINT CHARBONNEAU was, as Lewis wrote, "perhaps the most timid waterman in the world" and "a man of no peculiar merit," but he proved an excellent cook, producing a superb white pudding of chopped buffalo meat and kidneys stuffed into an intestine. His wife, SACAGAWEA, gathered vegetables, fruits, and roots unknown to the expedition and helped to vary their diet. She also, perhaps unknowingly, acted as the best symbol of peace the two captains could have had in their encounters with unknown Indian nations, by virtue of her very presence on the expedition.

When there was a new skill to be acquired, it was acquired quickly. The party learned to build CACHES from PIERRE CRUZATTE who, like FRANÇOIS LABICHE, was originally employed for his skill as a waterman. Patrick Gass and JOHN ORDWAY saw how the Mandan Indians constructed BULL BOATS from buffalo skins. Gass's journal entry of July 11, 1806, written at WHITE BEAR ISLANDS, notes: ". . . our hunters killed five buffaloes; and we saved the best of the meat; and of the skins made two canoes to transport ourselves and baggage across the river."

That same month, when Sergeant NATHANIEL PRYOR and his party had their HORSES stolen as they were riding across country from the YELLOWSTONE RIVER to the Mandan villages, they picked up their packs and walked 30–40 miles north to the Yellowstone. There they killed two buffalo, made bull boats out of the skins, and followed Clark and his party down the river, catching up with them nearly a fortnight later.

Often the factors that helped the expedition on its way were unplanned. The color of YORK's skin was a source of wonder to Indians who had never seen a black man before, while Pierre Cruzatte's fiddle was a constant source of enjoyment and RECREATION ON THE EXPEDITION. In the Mandan villages, Clark noted on January 1, 1805: "In the morning we permitted the 16 men with their music to go up to the first village where they delighted the whole tribe with their dances, particularly with the movements of one of the Frenchmen, who danced on his head." This was one of the ENGAGÉS, FRANÇOIS RIVET, who danced on his hands.

It should also be noted that all four of the sergeants and at least two privates in the party wrote journals at the captains' suggestion. One cannot but wonder how many army units of 29 men could do such a thing today.

When the expedition returned home, Lewis sought the reward for his men that he knew was their due. He wrote that they had won "my warmest approbation and thanks; nor will I suppress the expression of a hope, that the recollection of services thus faithfully performed will meet a just reward in an ample remuneration on the part of our Government." Never was such a tribute better deserved, and rarely, if ever, has such a small military unit demonstrated such ingenuity or variety of talent.

Further Reading

Ambrose, Stephen E. *Undaunted Courage: Meriwether Lewis, Thomas Jefferson, and the Opening of the American West.* New York: Simon and Schuster, 1996.

Clarke, Charles G. *The Men of the Lewis and Clark Expedition: A Biographical Roster of the Fifty-One Members and a Composite Diary of Their Activities from All Known Sources.* 1970. Reprint, Lincoln: Bison Books, University of Nebraska Press, 2002.

skin canoes   See BULL BOATS.

skins and pelts   See BEAVERS; FUR TRADE; OTTERS.

Smith's River (Smith River)

By July 15, 1804, the expedition had completed the laborious PORTAGE around the GREAT FALLS and were following the MISSOURI RIVER southwest toward THREE FORKS. From that point, they had been told, a river would take them to the foot of the CONTINENTAL DIVIDE. Following their usual practice, MERIWETHER LEWIS and WILLIAM CLARK named features along the river as they came into view. On their journey up to the Great Falls, they had named the creeks, rivers, and bluffs they had passed after incidents that had occurred or after members of the expedition party. Although they continued to do this, they also remembered they were representatives of the U.S. government. For this reason, after leaving the area of the Great Falls, Lewis and Clark named the next two rivers they came to after members of President THOMAS JEFFERSON's cabinet: Secretary of the Navy Robert Smith (1757–1842) and Secretary of War HENRY DEARBORN.

Of Smith's River, on the left bank of the Missouri, Lewis wrote: "in honour of Mr Robert Smith the Secretary of the Navy we called [it] Smith's River. This stream meanders through a most lovely valley to the S.E. for about 25 miles

when it enters the ROCKY MOUNTAINS and is concealed from our view." Today called the Smith River, it rises in the Little Belt Mountains and runs southwest toward White Sulphur Springs, Montana, before turning due north to the Missouri River, which it joins at today's Ulm, Montana.

See also DEARBORN RIVER; NOMENCLATURE, GEOGRAPHICAL.

Further Reading

Fifer, Barbara, and Vicky Soderberg. *Along the Trail with Lewis and Clark.* Great Falls, Mont.: Montana Magazine, 1998.

smoking ceremonies

In front of the cheifs a plac of 6 feet diameter was clear and the pipe of peace raised on (forked) sticks (about 6 or 8 inches from the ground) under which there was swans down scattered. On each side of this circle, two pipes, the (two) flags of Spain 2 & the flag we gave them in front of the grand chief. . . . The great chief then rose with great state . . . and then with great solemnity took up the pipe of peace & after pointing it to the heavins, the 4 quarters of the globe & the earth, he made some disertation, lit it and presented the stem to us to smoke.

When the principal chief spoke with the pipe of peace he took in one hand some of the most delicate parts of the dog which was prepared for the feast, and made a sacrifice to the flag. After a smoke had taken place, & a short harangue to his people, we were requested to take the meal . . . We smoked for an hour (till) dark. . . .

—William Clark, September 26, 1804

As MERIWETHER LEWIS and WILLIAM CLARK were to discover, the ritual of smoking had great significance to the Indians. It was not only an integral part of formal meetings, it also played a role in ceremonial and festive occasions. In the expedition's JOURNALS, smoking ceremonies are described in connection with several different types of encounters with Indians, from simple introductory meetings to official councils.

The pipes used in smoking ceremonies are today often called peace pipes, or, from the French, calumets. Indians, however, called them sacred pipes because of their ritual importance. In describing the actions of the TETON LAKOTA INDIANS (Teton Sioux) chief above, Clark noted that the pipe was pointed first to the heavens, then to the four quarters of the planet, and finally to the earth. By doing this, offerings of smoke were made to those mystical beings that the Indians regarded as God. In addition, by sharing the pipe, smokers were joined in a spiritual bond.

Sacred pipes were especially important among the PLAINS INDIANS. Their long (up to five feet) stems were usually made from ash or sumac, and the bowl was often made from a red-colored stone called catlinite, or pipestone, although soapstone was sometimes used. The pipes were decorated with feathers, beads, fur, and horsehair. While TOBACCO was the

The calumet, or peace pipe, was an essential part of diplomatic meetings with Indians. The Mandan presented Lewis and Clark with this ceremonial pipe. *(Peabody Museum, Harvard University, N29638)*

most common substance smoked, other plants were sometimes used as well.

Having observed the importance of smoking ceremonies to the Indians the expedition met, Clark took care in his journals to describe in detail the ritual and protocol involved. In doing so, he made it possible for others who came after him to know what to expect in formal encounters with Indians of the GREAT PLAINS.

Further Reading
Paper, Jordan. *Offering Smoke: The Sacred Pipe and Native American Religion.* Moscow: University of Idaho Press, 1988.
Ronda, James P. *Lewis and Clark among the Indians.* Lincoln: University of Nebraska Press, 1984.
Warner, Sky. "The Sacred Pipe." Available on-line. URL: http://www.ouachitalk.com/sacred.htm. Downloaded on April 10, 2002.

Snake Indians   See SHOSHONE INDIANS.

Snake River
The Snake River rises in Jackson Lake, Wyoming, south of Yellowstone National Park. It flows southwest into Idaho, where it

then turns northwest and becomes the boundary with Oregon up to today's Clarkston and Lewiston. Here the river turns due west to join the COLUMBIA RIVER at present-day Pasco, Washington. For the Lewis and Clark Expedition, the Snake would be the penultimate river they would travel before finally reaching the PACIFIC OCEAN.

By early October 1805, the CORPS OF DISCOVERY had made their arduous and dangerous crossing of the BITTERROOT MOUNTAINS, had met the NEZ PERCE INDIANS, and had begun to make CANOES at CANOE CAMP (near today's Orofino, Idaho). On October 7 they set off down the CLEARWATER RIVER, which soon proved treacherous when they came to 15 rapids; one canoe sank, though luckily it was in waist-deep water. They reached the junction with the Snake River on October 10.

The expedition's journey down the Snake was characterized by a laconic comment from PATRICK GASS on the matter that concerned him most. As a carpenter, he noted on October 11 that "there is no wood of any kind to be seen except a few small willows along the shore so that it is with difficulty we can get enough to cook with." He noted also that though FISH was plentiful all the way down the river, "Most of our people having been accustomed to meat, do not relish the fish, but prefer dog meat; which, when well cooked, tastes very well."

For the next five days, the corps's journey down the Snake was eventful and hazardous. A canoe was overturned and stores were lost, while the constant rapids meant portaging was often necessary. They reached the junction with the Columbia on October 18. Gass wrote: "We arrived at the great Columbia river, which comes in from the northwest. . . . The country all round is level, rich and beautiful, but without timber."

On their return journey in 1806, MERIWETHER LEWIS and WILLIAM CLARK realized that it would be too hazardous to try and take canoes up the Snake River. After passing The Dalles, they managed to procure some packhorses and followed the Columbia upstream, arriving on April 27 at today's Wallula, Washington. Here they met the WALLA WALLA INDIANS, who sold them more horses and told them of a shortcut across country that avoided the Snake River. On April 30 the expedition left the Walla Walla and headed northwest for the junction of the Snake and the Clearwater. They reached it on May 4, met Chief TETOHARSKY of the Nez Perce, and, on his advice, crossed the Snake just below the junction, and rode up the banks of the Clearwater, leaving the Snake River behind them.

Further Reading

Fifer, Barbara, and Vicky Soderberg. *Along the Trail with Lewis and Clark.* Great Falls, Mont.: Montana Magazine, 1998.

MacGregor, Carol Lynn, ed. *The Journals of Patrick Gass, Member of the Lewis and Clark Expedition.* Missoula, Mont.: Mountain Press Publishing Company, 1997.

Moulton, Gary E., ed. *Atlas of the Lewis and Clark Expedition.* Revised ed. Lincoln: University of Nebraska Press, 1999.

snow   See WEATHER.

soup, portable

In making his PREPARATIONS FOR THE EXPEDITION, MERIWETHER LEWIS was aware that although there would be HUNTING and FISHING along the trail, there would also be times when they would run short of FOOD. Thus, he planned for extra provisions that could be brought along on the journey. These included flour, cornmeal, sugar, coffee, salt, dried apples, lard, and biscuits, but he knew even more would be needed. On April 15, 1803, as he traveled east from HARPERS FERRY, Lewis wrote to General William Irvin, superintendent of military stores in Philadelphia, asking him to purchase several items for the expedition—the first of which was portable soup:

> *Portable Soup, in my opinion, forms one of the most essential articles in the preparation [for the expedition], and fearing that it cannot be procured readily in such quantities as is requisite, I . . . take the liberty to request that you will procure two hundred pounds of it for me. . . . I have supposed that the soup would cost about one dollar pr lb; should it however, come much higher*

then quantity must be limited by the sum for $250 as more cannot be expended.

Lewis eventually procured 193 pounds of portable soup, paying $289.50 for it, the largest amount he paid for any provision. He was clearly enthusiastic about it, and this has led to conjecture that he had used it before, perhaps during his travels as army paymaster. Another suggestion is that the soup was a recognized army-issue item, although if this were the case it is likely Lewis would simply have asked General Irwin to supply him from army stocks rather than purchase it.

Although dried soup was known in Britain in the 1750s and was used by Americans during the Revolutionary War, the recipes of the time were usually based on meat and produced something resembling the bouillon cubes of today. However, historian Stephen Ambrose has described the expedition's portable soup as consisting of beans and other dried vegetables. It may have been carried as a paste or simply in dried vegetable form and was made into a liquid by mixing it with water or melted snow.

In May 1804 the "canesters" of soup were loaded onto the keelboat at CAMP DUBOIS and carried up the MISSOURI RIVER with other nonperishables. It is not known if any was consumed during the winter of 1804–05 at FORT MANDAN. The first significant mention of it in the JOURNALS does not come until the CORPS OF DISCOVERY was on the most difficult stretch of their journey, making their way over the perilous BITTERROOT MOUNTAINS. On September 14, 1805, at their camp on the LOCHSA RIVER, Sergeant PATRICK GASS wrote: "[N]one of the hunters killed anything except for 2 or 3 pheasants; on which, without a miracle it was impossible to feed 30 hungry men and upwards, beside some Indians. So Capt. Lewis gave out some portable soup, which he had along, to be used in cases of necessity. Some of the men did not relish this soup. . . ." Sergeant JOHN ORDWAY made a similar note: "[We] had nothing to eat but Some portable Soup . . . We being hungry for meat as the Soup did not Satisfy we killed a fat colt which eat verry well at this time."

The following day saw soup and a handful of parched CORN as their only food, while at the midday meal on the 16th there was again soup. Another colt killed in the evening provided them with some meat, but on the 18th Lewis reported, "We dined & suped on a skant proportion of portable soup, a few canesters which, a little bears oil and about 20 lbs of candle from our stock of provision, the only resources being our guns and packhorses. . . ." On the 19th Ordway wrote that they ate "the verry last morcil of our provisions except a little portable soup." The following day they ate a horse's carcass left for them by Clark, who had gone on ahead, and on the 22nd they finally came off the mountain and were met by the NEZ PERCE INDIANS, who gave them roots and dried fish to eat.

There is one further mention of the soup. Lewis and WILLIAM CLARK retained at least some of it for the return journey the following year. On May 26, 1806, Clark still had some left and was able to administer it as a medicine to a Nez Perce while they were encamped on the CLEARWATER RIVER.

Further Reading

Ambrose, Stephen E. *Undaunted Courage: Meriwether Lewis, Thomas Jefferson, and the Opening of the American West.* New York: Simon and Schuster, 1996.

Cutright, Paul Russell. *Lewis & Clark: Pioneering Naturalists.* Lincoln: University of Nebraska Press/Bison Books, 1989.

MacGregor, Carol Lynn, ed. *The Journals of Patrick Gass, Member of the Lewis and Clark Expedition.* Missoula, Mont.: Mountain Press Publishing Company, 1997.

South West Point   See RECRUITING.

Spain

By the time of the Lewis and Clark Expedition, the days of Spain's glory and great explorations were long over. In 1519 Hernán Cortes conquered Mexico; within 15 years Francisco Pizarro had taken Peru. By 1540 the Spaniards had sailed up the Gulf of California and discovered the Grand Canyon. By 1609 they had explored from South Carolina across the continent to California, reached the PLATTE RIVER, and established Santa Fe. Their collective exploits have been called the most remarkable feat of conquest in the history of the world.

While much of Spain's success as explorers and conquerors rested on greed for the gold and silver they found, it was its dependence on these minerals that contributed to its gradual decline during the next 200 years. The Spanish possessions in the Americas were not colonies to provide land and farms for new settlers from Europe (as the English colonies became). They were instead royal provinces, kept under rigid control to provide wealth for the Spanish Crown, and even Spaniards needed permission to travel there. Fervent Catholics, the Spanish placed as much importance on converting the Native population to Christianity as they did to the gold and silver on which the country relied, and they fought hard to protect their territories from outside influences.

In the late 17th–early 18th centuries, Spain lost its position of primacy in Europe to FRANCE, and by the end of the French and Indian War (1754–63), the Spanish were happy to accept the terms of the Treaty of Paris (1763). France lost CANADA to GREAT BRITAIN, and, as compensation for losing Florida, Spain acquired the LOUISIANA TERRITORY. The territory was secretly ceded back to France in 1800, although Spain still maintained practical control over it. Apart from some 40,000 Creoles and their slaves on the lower reaches of the MISSISSIPPI RIVER, the population of Louisiana comprised French merchants and traders at settlements up and down the river and small Spanish garrisons scattered between New Orleans and ST. LOUIS.

The sale of Louisiana to the United States, though straightforward in intent, left one important question unanswered. The territory was described as those lands drained by the Mississippi and its tributaries, which included the Red River and Arkansas River. Both of these ran into areas the Spanish had claimed as New Mexico more than two centuries before. Thus, the western boundaries of the Louisiana Territory fell into dispute, and although the United States had a good legal case, they were in no position to enforce their rights. Further, the Spanish had founded settlements up the Pacific coast to San Francisco and beyond and had laid claim to the coastline up to and including the OREGON TERRITORY. As soon as MERIWETHER LEWIS and WILLIAM CLARK crossed the CONTINENTAL DIVIDE at LEMHI PASS, they were, in Spanish eyes, on Spanish soil.

In December 1802 President THOMAS JEFFERSON informed Spanish minister Carlos Martínez de Yrujo of an expedition he hoped to send to the West Coast, with "no other view than the advancement of the geography." Perhaps not surprisingly, Martínez viewed with skepticism Jefferson's explanation that the party would only be mapping territory, something that could benefit both nations. He subsequently refused to give Lewis a Spanish passport, although France and Great Britain did so.

Although the Lewis and Clark Expedition was a small one, the Spanish viewed it with considerable alarm. The CORPS OF DISCOVERY was a unit of the U.S. Army, traveling across the continent with the approval of the U.S. government. From the Spanish point of view, they were the forerunners of hundreds more Americans who would cross the continent to occupy the Oregon Territory and then move south down the Pacific coast to take over Spanish ports and settlements.

Urged on by their American informant, arch conspirator and general JAMES WILKINSON, Spain decided to take action. Four parties of Spanish soldiers were sent north from Santa Fe to intercept the expedition but were unable to do so, probably because of the distance involved (nearly 1,000 miles). The closest they came was, apparently, at the PLATTE RIVER, arriving there a month after the expedition had passed through the area. It was not until the expedition returned east that Lewis and Clark learned of the Spanish attempt to stop them.

In 1806 another party sent by President Jefferson to explore the Red River was intercepted and firmly turned back at Spanish Bluff in Texas. It was to be another 30 years before Spain gave up its claims and the terms of the LOUISIANA PURCHASE were at last fulfilled.

See also EXPLORATION, EARLY; RED RIVER EXPEDITION.

Further Reading

Brebner, John B. *The Explorers of North America 1492–1806.* New York: Macmillan, 1933.

DeConde, Alexander. *This Affair of Louisiana.* New York: Charles Scribner, 1976.

Marshall, Thomas Maitland. *A History of the Western Boundaries of the Louisiana Purchase, 1819–1841.* Berkeley: University of California Press, 1914.

Morison, Samuel Eliot. *Oxford History of the American People.* New York: Oxford University Press, 1965.

specimens   See ARTIFACTS AND SPECIMENS.

Spirit Mound

In late August 1804, after the expedition had met the OTOE (Oto) and MISSOURI INDIANS, they proceeded up the MISSOURI RIVER and passed the location of present-day Sioux City, South Dakota. On August 23 Private JOSEPH FIELD shot the expedition's first BUFFALO, a source of FOOD they were to rely on until they reached the CONTINENTAL DIVIDE nearly a year later. Though the party was apprehensive of the TETON LAKOTA INDIANS (Teton Sioux), whom they knew were not far up the river ahead of them, stories they had heard of a "Hill of Little Devils" took them away from the river on August 25.

Called by the Sioux (Dakota, Lakota, Nakota) *Paha Wakan,* the Spirit Mound was feared by Indians who believed it was occupied by "little people," or spirits who would kill any human beings who approached it. MERIWETHER LEWIS and WILLIAM CLARK were told it was "the abode of little deavels . . . they are in human form with remarkably large heads and about 18 inches high, armed with sharp arrows, with which they are very skillful . . . This has inspired all the neighboring nations, Sioux, Mahas, and Otoes, with such terror that no consideration could tempt them to visit the hill."

The captains and 10 of their men were tempted enough to follow the Whitestone River north to what is now Vermillion, South Dakota, and then turn north for eight miles to reach the mound. Except for some small holes on the top of the hill, the party found nothing, although they enjoyed "the delightful prospect of the plain . . . enlivened by large herds of buffalo feeding at a distance." The conical hilltop also abounded in INSECTS, which attracted large numbers of swallows, causing Clark to note that "one evidence which the Inds give for believing this place to be the residence of Some unusisal Sperits is that they frequently discover a large assemblage of Birds about this Mound is in my opinion a Suffecent proof to produce in the Indian mind a confident belief of all the properties which they ascribe it."

Although Lewis and Clark had estimated the Spirit Mound to be about 70 feet tall, it actually rises some 120 feet from the prairie on a roughly rectangular base. As Lewis noted: "The only thing characteristic in this hill is its extreme symmetry . . . would induce a belief that it was artificial." It is probable that Lewis, perhaps unknowingly, identified another the cause of the Indians' superstition about the mound. Later in the journey, he and Clark saw rocks and banking along the river so regular in form that they thought they were humanmade. It is likely that the Indian had come to believe the Spirit Mound was a prehistoric tumulus and, as is common in undeveloped societies, attributed supernatural powers to those they thought had built it.

Today, although the mound is privately owned, it is open to the public.

Further Reading

Fifer, Barbara, and Vicky Soderberg. *Along the Trail with Lewis and Clark.* Great Falls, Mont.: Montana Magazine, 1998.

Lewis, Meriwether, and William Clark. *The History of the Lewis and Clark Expedition.* Edited by Elliott Coues; 4 vols., 1893, Harper. Reprinted in 3 vols., New York: Dover Publications, 1979.

MacGregor, Carol Lynn, ed. *The Journals of Patrick Gass, Member of the Lewis and Clark Expedition.* Missoula, Mont.: Mountain Press Publishing Company, 1997.

Square Butte   See FORT MOUNTAIN.

squirrels   See ANIMALS, NEW SPECIES.

Station Camp

By November 8, 1805, the CORPS OF DISCOVERY had reached the estuary of the COLUMBIA RIVER and, because of the many islands on the southern side, were making their way in dugout CANOES along the river's north bank. The WEATHER had turned bad, and they spent two miserable nights of wind and rain beside present-day Gray's Point (dubbed "Dismal Point") at the western end of Gray's Bay before managing to force their canoes through the high waves to a spot on the eastern side of POINT ELLICE ("Point Distress") on November 10. Conditions there were even worse, and the constant rain rotted their CLOTHING while the high winds put them and their canoes in danger.

On November 13 JOHN COLTER, ALEXANDER WILLARD, and GEORGE SHANNON managed to take a small Indian canoe around Point Ellice, and Colter returned overland the next day to report there was a better campsite on that side. Subsequently, MERIWETHER LEWIS took a small party of four men to search for the location, north of CAPE DISAPPOINTMENT, where he and WILLIAM CLARK had been told that trading ships sometimes came. Unfortunately, no ships were then in the area.

On November 15, during a break in the weather, Clark took the remaining party in canoes around Point Ellice and proceeded some way into today's Baker Bay, which Clark called Haley's Bay. There, near Chinook Point, they found a reasonable campsite on the beach, as Colter had said, and were at last able to dry their clothing and equipment and find game to eat. Clark named the site Station Camp, and as the party awaited Lewis's return, they shot some DEER, GEESE, and game birds. After Lewis joined them on November 17, having seen no sign of ships or traders, it became clear to both captains that they needed to decide where to spend the winter. While Clark took a party of men to view Cape Disappointment and retrace his cocaptain's exploration up the coast, Lewis learned what he could of local conditions from the CHINOOK and the CLATSOP INDIANS who came to visit them and to TRADE.

On November 24, two days after the return of Clark and his party, the captains held a meeting to discuss where the corps should spend the winter. Their choices were threefold: They could move back upriver to find better SHELTER; they could stay on the north side of the river; or they could move to the south side of the estuary, near the Clatsop, where the HUNTING would possibly be better. The discussion concluded with a vote. Sergeant PATRICK GASS described it in his journal: "At night the party were consulted by the Commanding Officers, as to the place more proper for winter quarters; and the most of them were of the opinion, that it would be best, in the first place, to go over to the south side of the river, and ascertain whether good hunting ground could be found there."

It is significant that every member of the party had a say in this decision, even SACAGAWEA and YORK. As Gass noted, the majority elected to look for a campsite on the south side, and the following day, November 25, they began to paddle their canoes up the Columbia until they were able to safely cross the river. Finally, on December 7, they arrived at the site where they would build FORT CLATSOP, their winter quarters.

Station Camp had served its purpose well. It had provided shelter, a respite from the constant wind and rain, and enough FOOD to keep the expedition going. Most significant, it became the site of what some historians feel is the first-known occasion where an Indian woman and a slave had been allowed to vote.

See also DEMOCRACY ON THE EXPEDITION.

Further Reading

Duncan, Dayton. "The Vote: 'Station Camp,' Washington." *Columbia* 15, no. 1 (Spring 2001). Available on-line. URL: http://www.wshs.org/lewisandclark/vote.htm. Downloaded on July 12, 2002.

MacGregor, Carol Lynn. *The Journals of Patrick Gass, Member of the Lewis and Clark Expedition.* Missoula, Mont.: Mountain Press Publishing Company, 1997.

Stoddard, Amos (1762–1813) *civil and military commander of Upper Louisiana*

On March 9, 1804, in ST. LOUIS, MERIWETHER LEWIS and WILLIAM CLARK attended ceremonies marking the formal transfer of Upper Louisiana from SPAIN to FRANCE and then, the following day, from France to the United States. The man designated by President THOMAS JEFFERSON to receive the transfer was Captain Amos Stoddard of the U.S. Artillery, who was named the territory's first American commandant as well as acting governor.

Stoddard was born in Woodbury, Connecticut, had trained as a lawyer, and was an artilleryman during the American Revolution. Following the war he returned to his law practice and served for a time in the Massachusetts legislature. He reenlisted in the army in 1798 and was made a captain in the Second Artillery. He was posted at KASKASKIA in 1803 when Lewis and Clark arrived there to recruit men for their expedition. Through him they also requisitioned 75 pounds of gunpowder as well as a container for it.

Stoddard became good friends with the two captains, who were present when he "took possession of Upper Louisiana in the name of the French Republic on the 9th day of March; and on the next day, I assumed the country and Gov-

ernment in the name of the United States." He was to be the territory's acting governor until September 1804 when a formal government was put into place. In May that year, as the expedition was about ready to depart up the MISSOURI RIVER, Lewis officially authorized him to act as agent for the explorers until their return. Specifically, Stoddard was to conduct financial transactions "which the nature of the service may in your judgment and at your discretion be deemed necessary." To this end, Lewis wanted him to oversee arrangements for getting a delegation of OSAGE INDIANS to Washington to meet President Jefferson. He was also to pay the ENGAGÉS when they returned to St. Louis the following year as well as anybody who came to the city bearing a chit from Lewis. Finally, Stoddard was to forward any LETTERS for Lewis to President Jefferson.

Stoddard was among those who saw the expedition off from ST. CHARLES on May 21, 1804. He subsequently saw to the departure of the Osage delegation for Washington while also carrying out his role as acting governor. During that six-month period he is credited with keeping peace and reassuring the territory's inhabitants that they would benefit under the new government's regime. On October 1 William Henry Harrison of Indiana Territory became governor, also on a temporary basis.

In spring 1805 a number of OTOE (Oto) INDIANS arrived in St. Louis, sent by Lewis to visit Jefferson as the Osage had done. By this time General JAMES WILKINSON had come to assume the governorship, and he objected to both the size of the Otoe delegation and the expense it would take to get them to Washington. Believing that Lewis had overstepped his authority and impinged on the War Department's funds, Wilkinson nevertheless appointed Stoddard to take charge of the Otoe's tour, noting that "[e]very unnecessary expense should be carefully avoided."

As other Indians continued to arrive in the city, the tour was delayed until 45 Indians from 11 nations had been gathered. In October 1805 the party left St. Louis, arriving in Washington in January 1806. There they met the president, who told them, "My children, we are strong, we are numerous as the stars in the heavens, & we are all gun-men." How much this impressed the Indians is uncertain. In any event, Stoddard saw to their safe return to St. Louis a few weeks later.

Stoddard maintained his friendship with Lewis despite extended periods during which the latter did not write. On September 22, 1809, he heard from the troubled explorer, now governor of the territory and mired in debt: "I hope you will . . . pardon me for asking you to remit as soon as is convenient the sum of $200 which you have informed me you will hold for me." Stoddard sent the requested money, but less than three weeks later Lewis killed himself.

Stoddard himself was killed during the War of 1812 at the siege of Fort Meigs. A year prior to his death, he had published *Sketches, Historical and Descriptive, of Louisiana.* In 1829 the new county of Stoddard in Missouri was named after him.

Further Reading

Ambrose, Stephen E. *Undaunted Courage: Meriwether Lewis, Thomas Jefferson, and the Opening of the American West.* New York: Simon and Schuster, 1996.

Hudson, Mary A. "Amos Stoddard and the Territory of Missouri." From *The Heritage of Missouri.* Available on-line. URL: http://www.rootsweb.com/~mostodd2/stod-settlers/amos-stod.htm. Downloaded on March 3, 2002.

Stoddard, Amos. *Sketches, Historical and Descriptive of Louisiana.* 1812. Reprint, New York: AMS Press, 1973.

storage   See CACHES.

Sulphur Springs   See SACAGAWEA SPRING.

Sun River   See MEDICINE RIVER.

supplies and equipment

Though several lists exist of the FOOD, supplies, equipment, and baggage MERIWETHER LEWIS AND WILLIAM CLARK took on their expedition, there appears to be no complete, all-inclusive inventory. It is possible that one still exists somewhere, but if Clark, a meticulous man in many ways, took such a schedule with him, he would have had little use for it after the expedition transferred their depleted baggage into CANOES at FORT MANDAN.

While certain items are well known—for example, the IRON-FRAME BOAT, the PORTABLE SOUP, and Lewis's airgun (see FIREARMS)—the sheer weight of baggage and numbers of items they took still evoke initial surprise. What should never be forgotten, however, are the factors that make the Lewis and Clark Expedition unique in the history of exploration: they were expected to fulfill the roles of soldiers, watermen, frontiersmen, hunters, explorers, navigators, surveyors, mapmakers, diplomats, botanists, zoologists, mineralogists, paleontologists, and ethnologists.

Considered from this point of view, the quantity of stores the expedition took upriver from CAMP DUBOIS assumes a more reasonable aspect. As a military unit, they took their uniforms, in which they were to parade at formal COUNCILS WITH INDIANS, as well as working CLOTHING. As explorers, they took such standard items of equipment as tentage, tarpaulins, mosquito nets, lanterns, FISHING equipment, cooking equipment, and, presumably, metal plates and mugs as well as spoons for eating. Knowing they would have to make canoes and build themselves winter quarters, they took tools including handsaws, hatchets, chisels, and adzes. Firearms and other WEAPONS were necessary for HUNTING and self-defense.

One list of 25 items ranges from a chronometer, quadrant, sextant, surveyor's chains, and spirit level to microscopes, compasses, and at least four volumes of astronomical tables for use in the explorers' work as navigators, surveyors, and mapmakers. Another list includes BOOKS on botany, mineralogy, a four-volume dictionary, and a two-volume edition of Linnaeus (on the classification of plants).

As diplomats on a mission of peace to the known and unknown Indian nations they would meet, they packed at least 50 types of GIFTS. One list begins with 12 pipe tomahawks and 47^1/$_2$ yards of red flannel, then ranges through 27 dozen "Pocket Looking Glasses," brass kettles, 500 "Broaches" to "4600 Needles, assorted" and "2800 Fish Hooks," finishing with 1152 "Moccasin Awls."

Although Lewis and Clark selected fit, hardy, healthy young men for the expedition, they knew that medical supplies were essential. Some 47 items are known to have been carried, including powdered Peru bark, cloves, cinnamon, laudanum, and a set of medical and dental instruments, not to mention 50 dozen of Dr. BENJAMIN RUSH's "Bilious Pills."

Lewis spent a total of $2,324 on gear for the expedition. Much of the equipment was bought for him by ISRAEL WHELAN in PHILADELPHIA, and when it was all assembled, Lewis calculated it weighed about 3,500 pounds. He employed William Linnard to take it by wagon from Philadelphia to HARPERS FERRY, collect the firearms there, and then take the load down to PITTSBURGH. In the event, Linnard found that the extra load was too heavy, and Lewis had to contract with another wagoner to collect the weapons and equipment from Harpers Ferry.

Finally, there was food. Although Lewis and Clark must have been told repeatedly of the plentiful game they would find on the GREAT PLAINS, they were good army officers who followed a golden rule—never let your soldiers go hungry. When Lewis and Clark realized the expedition's numbers would have to be doubled, they made provision accordingly.

Later in the expedition, Clark provided an excellent indication of the party's appetite, calculating that it needed four DEER or one BUFFALO to feed them for one day. With this in mind, it is difficult to criticize the seven tons of food Clark loaded onto the KEELBOAT in May 1804. It included such staples as CORN, flour, and pork (which kept remarkably well even after it had spent months buried in a CACHE).

Altogether, it was a heavy load to drag, row, and pole up the MISSOURI RIVER for thousands of miles and then take through the ROCKY MOUNTAINS to the PACIFIC OCEAN. But the result justified the captain's prudence. The portable soup may not have been popular, but along the LOLO TRAIL it was all they had left. Dress uniforms may seem ostentatious, but they were appropriate for formal councils with Indian chiefs, and they proved their worth on the way home when exchanged for HORSES along the banks of the COLUMBIA RIVER. The spare clothing was exhausted, but deer and ELK skin proved an adequate substitute. The medical supplies paid for food for the party when Clark doctored dozens of NEZ PERCE INDIANS.

With hindsight, Lewis and Clark planned their supplies extraordinarily well. The iron-frame boat was a failure, and they realized they should have brought more blue beads, which they had been told were the most popular item of TRADE goods among Indians. But aside from those two items, they were justified in what and in how much they carried so far for so long.

It is doubtful if any of the expedition had an item of uniform clothing left when they came back to St. Louis after 28 months away. But it should be noted that they came back as good soldiers should, with their rifles and enough powder and ammunition to turn around and do it again.

See also HAY, JOHN.

Further Reading

Bedini, Silvio A. "The Scientific Instruments of the Lewis and Clark Expedition." *Great Plains Quarterly* 4, no. 1 (1984): 54–69.

Burroughs, Raymond Darwin, ed. *The Natural History of the Lewis and Clark Expedition.* East Lansing: Michigan State University Press, 1995.

Cutright, Paul Russell. "Lewis has successfully outfitted the Expedition." From *Contributions of Philadelphia to Lewis and Clark History.* Available on-line. URL: http://www.lewisand clarkphila.org/philadelphia/philadelphiacutright37.html. Updated on August 13, 2001.

Hawke, David Freeman. *Those Tremendous Mountains: The Story of the Lewis and Clark Expedition.* New York: W. W. Norton & Company, 1998.

Jackson, Donald. "Some Books Carried by Lewis and Clark." *Bulletin of the Missouri Historical Society* 16 (1959): 3–13.

Jefferson National Expansion Memorial. "The Lewis and Clark Journey of Discovery: Medical Supplies of the Lewis and Clark Expedition." Available on-line. URL: http://www.nps.gov/jeff/LewisClark2/CorpsOfDiscovery/Preparing/Medicine/Medicine.htm. Downloaded on April 11, 2002.

Jeffrey, Joseph D. "Meriwether Lewis at Harpers Ferry." *We Proceeded On* 20 (November 1994).

National Geographic. "Lewis and Clark Expedition Supplies." Available on-line. URL: http://www.nationalgeographic.com/lewisandclark/resources.html. Downloaded on May 18, 2003.

PBS Online. "Lewis and Clark: To Equip an Expedition." Available on-line. URL: http://www.pbs.org/lewisandclark/inside/equip.html. Downloaded on May 18, 2001.

Swooping Eagle   See OLD TOBY.

T

Tabeau, Pierre-Antoine (1755–1820) *fur trader, explorer*

Early in October 1804, the Lewis and Clark Expedition arrived at the villages of the ARIKARA INDIANS on the MISSOURI RIVER. Among the Arikara were two traders, JOSEPH GRAVELINES and Pierre-Antoine Tabeau, both of them multilingual and both important sources of information about the upper Missouri and its Indians. MERIWETHER LEWIS and WILLIAM CLARK had already anticipated meeting Tabeau at some point in their journey, having been told previously that there was a "Mr. Tebaux" who could give them "much information in relation to that country."

Tabeau had acquired his knowledge from personal experience. Born in Montreal, he had entered the FUR TRADE as an engagé in 1776 and gradually moved west, living first in Illinois and then in Missouri. In 1795 he joined an expedition up the Missouri River headed by RÉGIS LOISEL, a partner in the Missouri Company. (Lewis and Clark had met Loisel in LA CHARETTE, and he too had provided them with useful information.) Still working for Loisel when Lewis and Clark met him, Tabeau was at that time was preparing a journal of the prior expedition, which was later published. Whether the information he gave the captains added significantly to what they already knew is unclear, although he was certainly able to augment their existing knowledge and gave them more particulars on the TETON LAKOTA INDIANS (Teton Sioux) and YANKTON NAKOTA INDIANS (Yankton Sioux), whom they had encountered recently, as well as the Arikara.

Prior to the captains' council with the Arikara, Tabeau came ahead to warn them of the delicate balance of power that existed among the chiefs of the three Indian villages, indicating they should all be treated with equal respect. Despite his advice, Lewis and Clark insisted on according one of the chiefs greater honors than the other two, in their belief that there should always be just one leader overall. This resulted in tensions between the captains and the two "lesser" chiefs, although in subsequent meetings the Arikara said they would consider making a trip to Washington to meet President THOMAS JEFFERSON. Prospects for the trade network that Lewis hoped to establish were uncertain due to the Arikara's trading partnership with the more hostile Teton Lakota, enemies of the MANDAN and the HIDATSA INDIANS, but the Arikara at least seemed willing to discuss it.

When the expedition left the villages, Gravelines and an Arikara chief accompanied them to the Mandan-Hidatsa villages as part of a plan to forge a peaceful alliance among those nations. After Gravelines returned downriver, he and Tabeau continued to correspond with Lewis and Clark. During the winter of 1804–05 at FORT MANDAN, the explorers wrote, asking for any news the traders could pass on and, after some Sioux attacked members of their party, asking Tabeau and Gravelines to intercede with the Arikara on their behalf. Late in February 1805, Gravelines arrived at Fort Mandan with a letter from Tabeau advising that the Arikara were amenable to friendly relations with the Mandan and the Hidatsa and were in fact even considering moving north to KNIFE RIVER region. While this was welcome news, the captains were nonetheless uneasy about a peace being maintained.

After Fort Mandan, Tabeau seems to disappear from expedition records, although he remained in the area. His legacy can be found in Taboo Settlement and Tabo Creek in Lafayette County, Missouri, both of which are named after him.

Further Reading

Ambrose, Stephen E. *Undaunted Courage: Meriwether Lewis, Thomas Jefferson, and the Opening of the American West.* New York: Simon and Schuster, 1996.

Ronda, James P. *Lewis and Clark among the Indians.* Lincoln: University of Nebraska Press, 1984.

Tabeau, Pierre-Antoine. *Tabeau's Narrative of Loisel's Expedition to the Upper Missouri.* Edited by Annie Heloise Abel. Translated by Rose Abel Wright. Norman: University of Oklahoma Press, 1939.

Tetoharsky (unknown–unknown) *Nez Perce chief*

When the CORPS OF DISCOVERY reached WEIPPE PRAIRIE and met the NEZ PERCE INDIANS in September 1805, they were welcomed, fed, and given assistance in building CANOES for the next stage of their journey. By October 7 they were ready to set off down the CLEARWATER RIVER, which would take them to the SNAKE RIVER, from there to COLUMBIA RIVER, and finally to the PACIFIC OCEAN. Along the way they knew they would meet many Indian nations, some of whom had never before encountered white men. For that reason, two Nez Perce chiefs, TWISTED HAIR and Tetoharsky, offered to accompany the corps downriver. Twisted Hair also agreed to look after the expedition's horses that winter.

The two chiefs proved helpful as the expedition negotiated the dangerous rapids on the Clearwater and Snake Rivers. On October 14, just before they reached the confluence of the Snake and Columbia Rivers, Tetoharsky and Twisted Hair went on ahead to speak to the WANAPAM and YAKAMA (Yakima) INDIANS who lived in that area and were, like the Nez Perce, Sahaptian speakers. Reassured that the white explorers coming down the river were friendly and peaceful, the Wanapam and Yakama lined the riverbanks to see the expedition when they arrived and subsequently visited them in their camp. Thanks to the two chiefs, the expedition had a similar experience with the WALLA WALLA INDIANS.

Tetoharsky and Twisted Hair continued to act as advance men and interpreters for MERIWETHER LEWIS and WILLIAM CLARK down the Columbia as far as a village of WISHRAM AND WASCO INDIANS just below The Dalles. Grateful for their services, which had done so much to pave the way for the expedition, Lewis and Clark presented the two chiefs with medals and enjoyed a parting smoke with them before they left to return to their own villages by the Clearwater.

During the return journey several months later, on May 4, 1806, the corps had gone some three miles up the west bank of the Snake when, according to PATRICK GASS, "we met with one of our old chiefs who had come down with us last fall; . . ." It was their friend Tetoharsky, and he advised them to cross the river, "as the best road is on the north side." The route he recommended took them quickly back to the Clearwater and to Twisted Hair's village. Before long the explorers had met CUT NOSE and BROKEN ARM as well.

While Tetoharsky receives no further mention in the JOURNALS, his importance to the expedition is clear. As interpreters, guides, and mediators, he and Twisted Hair had made it possible for the Lewis and Clark expedition to establish friendly relations with the Indians of the upper Columbia.

Further Reading

Ambrose, Stephen E. *Undaunted Courage: Meriwether Lewis, Thomas Jefferson, and the Opening of the American West.* New York: Simon and Schuster, 1996.

Ronda, James P. *Lewis and Clark among the Indians.* Lincoln: University of Nebraska Press, 1984.

Teton Lakota Indians (Teton Sioux)

THOMAS JEFFERSON had instructed MERIWETHER LEWIS to deal with the Indians he would meet "in a most friendly and conciliatory manner." As they traveled up the MISSOURI RIVER in 1804, Lewis and WILLIAM CLARK held councils with the OTOE (Oto), MISSOURI, and YANKTON NAKOTA INDIANS (Yankton Sioux) that, if not very productive, were at least friendly. Then, in late September that year, they met the Teton Lakota Indians (Teton Sioux), and for the first time Jefferson's directive was put to the test.

Sometimes collectively called Lakota after the largest subgroup, the Sioux were once Woodland Indians who had moved west in the mid-1700s and were now spread throughout the GREAT PLAINS. (The name *Sioux* was derived from the French version of a Chippewa word in Algonquian used for their enemies, literally "adders," a type of snake. This was not what the people called themselves, and so Dakota, Lakota, or Nakota is more proper.) There were four branches of the Sioux nation— Teton (Lakota), Santee (Dakota), Yankton (Nakota), and Yanktonai (Nakota). Of these the Teton (Lakota) were the largest and included seven subgroups: the Brulé (Sicangu), Hunkpapa, Itazipco (Sans Arc), Miniconjou, Oglala, Oohenonpoa (Two Kettle), and Sihasapa. The Teton inhabited a large stretch of territory that extended as far as the Black Hills region in western South Dakota and into eastern Montana and Wyoming. While the Dakota and Nakota had adopted more settled ways, the Teton Lakota became the epitome of the PLAINS INDIANS: seminomads who lived in TIPIS, hunted BUFFALO, and were fierce warriors often feared by other nations.

On September 23, 1804, three Teton teenagers swam across the Missouri to the expedition's camp below BAD RIVER and informed them of two large bands of Brulé Teton Lakota upriver. The captains instructed the boys to tell the Teton chiefs that they wished to hold a council with them. The following day, as the expedition proceeded upriver, they met JOHN COLTER, who had been HUNTING and reported that his horse had been stolen. When the captains spotted five Teton Lakota on the riverbank, they issued a scolding, telling the warriors (falsely) that the stolen horse had been intended as present for the Teton chief, and they would talk to no Teton until it was returned. (The JOURNALS do not indicate if this was done.)

On September 25, 1804, at the mouth of the Bad River, Lewis and Clark held a council with the Teton chiefs BLACK BUFFALO, THE PARTISAN, and Buffalo Medicine. Communications were difficult since their only capable Sioux interpreter, PIERRE DORION, had stayed behind with the Yankton Nakota downriver as a diplomatic measure. While PIERRE CRUZATTE could speak some Sioux, his translating skills were negligible, and even the capable GEORGE DROUILLARD had difficulty conveying the captains' words to the Teton Lakota, who may have chosen not to understand them.

The captains made the first of several mistakes when they designated Black Buffalo as "first chief," giving him superior presents and honors. They did not know that Black Buffalo and The Partisan were engaged in a power struggle and each had hoped to use the expedition to his advantage. Affronted by the favoritism given to Black Buffalo, The Partisan subsequently sought to stir up trouble. Another mistake the captains made was in assuming they could interest the Teton in their proposed ST. LOUIS-based trading network, which was a direct threat to the Teton's control of the TRADE along the middle and upper Missouri.

Consequently, Lewis's standard speech regarding trade and peace made little impression on the Teton. Disgusted with the quality of the GIFTS they had received, their interest centered on the goods on the keelboat and PIROGUES. They expected the expedition to pay them a bigger tribute before they would allow it to continue upriver. Lewis and Clark attempted to divert the chiefs by inviting them aboard the keelboat, where they were given some whiskey. It was when they returned to shore that the trouble started. As the pirogue landed, three warriors seized the bowline, while another wrapped his arms around the mast. When The Partisan began to threaten him, Clark drew his sword and Lewis ordered the guns on the keelboat to be made ready. Along the riverbanks, Indians fitted arrows to their bows and raised their muskets. As the situation was about to explode, Black Buffalo stepped forward, took the bowline, and ordered the warriors away from the pirogue, although it was some time before he himself stopped arguing with Clark.

During the next two days the expedition camped near Black Buffalo's village and joined in festivities including a demonstration of the Lakota SCALP DANCE. But Lewis and Clark failed to make any progress in their diplomatic efforts; the Lakota clearly were not going to give up their position as the feared middlemen of the Missouri.

On the evening of September 27, as The Partisan and one of his warriors were accompanying the captains back to the keelboat, a cable broke, causing both the pirogue and the keelboat to swing wildly. Clark shouted out instructions to regain control of the boats, but this in addition to The Partisan's yells caused alarm on shore, where it was believed that an attack by OMAHA INDIANS was underway. Tensions remained high throughout the night.

By the morning of Friday, September 28, the captains were determined to leave, although they allowed the chiefs on board

The Teton Lakota dominated a significant area of the Great Plains. Their aggressive reputation was amply demonstrated during their encounter with Lewis and Clark in September 1804. This 1833 engraving depicts a Teton Lakota horse race. *(National Archives Still Pictures Branch [NWDNS-111-SC-92837])*

the keelboat one more time. As they were returned to shore, there was a repetition of the previous incident as some warriors grabbed the pirogue's bowline, The Partisan threatened to detain the expedition, and Black Buffalo interceded. Only after the captains gave some TOBACCO to the warriors holding the bowline was it released and the expedition was able to proceed upriver.

There was still one more encounter with the Teton to come. On August 30, 1806, as the expedition were returning down the Missouri, a large number of Teton Lakota formed along the riverbank. Clark had RENÉ JESSAUME shout to the Indians that they were "bad people" and "if any [came] near our camp we should kill them certainly." After repeated threats from Clark, many of the Teton retreated, although some returned the insults. Later a warrior, believed to be Black Buffalo, came to the riverbank and invited the captains to cross the river. They ignored him, upon which he went to a nearby hilltop and struck the ground with the butt of his gun three times. "This I am informed is a great oath among the Indians," Clark reported.

Earlier that year, Lewis had given considerable thought to the problem of the Teton Lakota and had written to HUGH HENEY, asking his assistance in convincing them that cooperation with the Americans' trading scheme was in their best interests. Lewis wrote that the Lakota should understand the United States would "not long suffer her citizens to be deprived of the free navigation of the Missouri by a few comparatively feeble bands of Savages." Heney never received the letter, and the Teton continued to control Missouri River traffic for some time. They were, however, finally overcome by the inexorable migration of white settlers into the West, which disrupted the way of life of all Plains Indians.

Throughout the 1800s the Teton Lakota were often at the center of Plains resistance against the U.S. government. They were also the victims of brutal massacres, the most famous being that at Wounded Knee in 1890, which signaled the end of the wars in the West. Today many Dakota, Lakota, and Nakota of all bands are settled on reservations in several U.S. states and in Canada, while others have made their homes in a number of U.S. cities.

Further Reading

Ambrose, Stephen E. *Undaunted Courage: Meriwether Lewis, Thomas Jefferson, and the Opening of the American West.* New York: Simon and Schuster, 1996.

Hawke, David Freeman. *Those Tremendous Mountains: The Story of the Lewis and Clark Expedition.* New York: W. W. Norton & Company, 1998.

Ronda, James P. *Lewis and Clark among the Indians.* Lincoln: University of Nebraska Press, 1984.

Waldman, Carl. *Encyclopedia of Native American Tribes.* Revised ed. New York: Checkmark Books, 1999.

Teton River   See BAD RIVER.

Thompson, David (1770–1857) *surveyor, explorer, mapmaker*

While not confirmed, it is believed that among the MAPS taken along on the Lewis and Clark Expedition was one that MERIWETHER LEWIS had copied from a chart depicting the Great Bend of the MISSOURI RIVER. The original had been created by the British explorer and geographer David Thompson and would have been a valuable resource for the expedition. It was Thompson whose explorations of the upper Missouri in the 1790s had formed the conclusion that the river's headwaters might lead to a passage across the ROCKY MOUNTAINS—something that the CORPS OF DISCOVERY hoped to prove—and it was Thompson's surveys on which Lewis and WILLIAM CLARK depended most for accuracy as they prepared to enter otherwise unknown territory.

Born in London, England, as a child Thompson proved himself remarkably adept in math and quickly learned navigational techniques. When he was only 14 years old, the HUDSON'S BAY COMPANY hired him as an apprentice. He was subsequently sent to North America, where he helped to transcribe the manuscript describing the voyages of explorer Samuel Hearne. During the winter of 1789–90 at Fort Cumberland, Thompson met Philip Turnor, from whom he learned surveying and astronomy in addition to receiving a sextant, telescope, and nautical almanacs. There followed several years of frustrated attempts to do surveying work for the Hudson's Bay Company, until he left in 1797 to go work for the NORTH WEST COMPANY. That year he surveyed the southwest boundary of the Great Lakes to meet conditions specified in the Jay Treaty of 1794. This was followed by numerous other surveying expeditions in Canada and the northern sections of the LOUISIANA TERRITORY. It was during this time that he surveyed the northern source of the Mississippi River (1798) and created the map copied by Lewis and Clark.

By 1801 Thompson had become one of many who hoped to find a NORTHWEST PASSAGE to the PACIFIC OCEAN. That year he tried but failed to follow the Ram River across the continent. After the Lewis and Clark Expedition, the North West Company wanted to know whether the COLUMBIA RIVER could be used for its own trading purposes. Thompson was given the mission of surveying the area, and in June 1807, after traversing down Blaeberry River, he reached Kootenay Lake, which he did not realize until later was the headwaters of the Columbia. During the next three years his men traded furs while he surveyed the area and studied its FLATHEAD (Salish) INDIANS. In 1810–11, again on a mission for his employers, he looked for a land route from the company's base camp in the mountains to the Columbia. Blocked along the way by the Piegan BLACKFEET INDIANS and abandoned by most of the men who had accompanied him, Thompson did not arrive at Fort Astoria, Oregon, until July 15, 1811. However, he had succeeded in finding a route between Montreal and the Pacific and in the process had surveyed the entire length of the Columbia from its source to its mouth. (After the Treaty of 1847 that established the Canadian-U.S. border, Thompson's route fell into U.S. territory.)

Thompson officially retired in 1812 but continued to do some surveying work, in particular determining the southern border of Canada for the International Boundary Commission. In 1814 he finished work on a huge map depicting the Northwest between the Pacific Ocean and Lake Superior. The following year he bought a farm at Williamston, Ontario, where he lived out his life with his wife.

See also EXPLORATION, LATER.

Further Reading

Allen, John Logan. *Passage Through the Garden: Lewis and Clark and the Image of the American Northwest.* Urbana: University of Illinois Press, 1975. Reprint ed.: New York: Dover Publications, 1991.

Lewis, Meriwether. *David Thompson and the Lewis and Clark Expedition; An Unpublished Account of the Lewis and Clark Expedition Written by Captain Meriwether Lewis and Copied by David Thompson of the North West Company.* Vancouver, B.C.: Library's Press, 1959.

Smith, James K. *David Thompson: Fur Trader, Explorer, Geographer.* Toronto: Oxford University Press, 1971.

Thompson, David. *Columbia Journals.* Edited by Barbara Belyea. Seattle: University of Washington Press, 1998.

———. *Travels in Western North America, 1784–1812.* Edited by Victor G. Hopwood. Toronto: Macmillan of Canada, 1971.

Wood, W. Raymond. "David Thompson at the Mandan-Hidatsa Villages, 1797–1798: The Original Journals." *Ethnohistory* 24 (1977): 329–342.

Thompson, John B. (unknown–unknown)
private in the permanent party

Very little is known about Private John Thompson, not even what his middle initial "B" represents. He apparently had lived in Indiana Territory, where he had been a surveyor, and this skill probably came in useful during the expedition, enabling him to assist as needed in making ASTRONOMICAL OBSERVATIONS and in the creation of MAPS. Officially enrolled in the corps on January 1, 1804, he also performed cooking chores throughout the journey. On June 28, 1804, he served on the panel for the COURT-MARTIAL of Privates JOHN COLLINS and HUGH HALL, who were found guilty of drinking without permission while Collins had been on duty.

Although he was a dependable member of the permanent party, Thompson received very little mentions in the expedition's JOURNALS. On October 9, 1805, Captain WILLIAM CLARK noted that one of the CANOES had been damaged during a passage through some rapids on the COLUMBIA RIVER, and Private Thompson "was a little hurt." At the beginning of July 1806, he was left at the GREAT FALLS with HUGH McNEAL and SILAS GOODRICH to prepare for the PORTAGE around the falls while MERIWETHER LEWIS and some others went to explore the MARIAS RIVER.

Apparently nothing is known about Thompson's whereabouts and activities following the expedition. Clark, who had previously noted that Thompson had been "a valuable member of our party," listed him as "killed" by 1825–28.

Further Reading

Clarke, Charles G. *The Men of the Lewis and Clark Expedition: A Biographical Roster of the Fifty-One Members and a Composite Diary of Their Activities from All Known Sources.* 1970. Reprint, Lincoln: Bison Books, University of Nebraska Press, 2002.

North Dakota Lewis & Clark Bicentennial Foundation. *Members of the Corps of Discovery.* Bismarck, N.Dak.: United Printing and Mailing, 2000.

PBS Online. *Lewis and Clark: Inside the Corps of Discovery:* "Lesser Known Members of the Corps." Available on-line. URL: http://www.pbs.org/lewisandclark/inside/lesser.html. Downloaded on May 18, 2001.

Three Forks

During the expedition's stay at the villages of the MANDAN INDIANS in the winter of 1804–05, the HIDATSA INDIANS gave MERIWETHER LEWIS and WILLIAM CLARK much valuable information on what they would find on their journey along the MISSOURI RIVER. They learned of the YELLOWSTONE RIVER and the MEDICINE RIVER and were told that some 140 miles beyond, the Missouri would divide into three nearly equal branches at a place called Three Forks. The most northern of these three rivers, the Hidatsa told Lewis, "is navigable to the foot of a chain of high mountains that formed the ridge dividing the waters of the Atlantic from those of the PACIFIC OCEAN."

On July 25, 1805, Clark and four men were walking along the banks of the river ahead of the CANOES, trying to find the SHOSHONE INDIANS, whom SACAGAWEA had told them frequented the area. That morning they came to Three Forks. Clark wrote: "A fine morning, we proceeded on a fiew miles to the three forks of the Missouri those three forks are nearly of a Size, the North fork appears to have the most water and must be Considered as the one best calculated for us to assend. Middle fork is quit[e] as large about 90 yards wide, the South fork is about 70 yds. wide & falls in about 400 yards below the middle fork."

Clark left a note stuck in a stick at the junction and took his party along the northern (southwest) fork, encamping some miles upstream. Despite feeling extremely ill that night ("with high fever & akeing"), he led the group southeast the following day to investigate the middle fork. He rejoined Lewis and the rest of the party the next day (July 27) at the Three Forks. Lewis himself had arrived at the junction earlier in the day, seen Clark's note, and explored and written a description of the area.

Because of Clark's illness (thought today to be Colorado tick fever), the party stayed at Three Forks for three days. Realizing that game was growing scarce and would become even harder to find as they went on into the mountains, the captains sent out hunters to get as much meat as they could. The rest of the party, as PATRICK GASS reported, "were employed in

Lewis and Clark named the Three Forks of the Missouri "Gallitin's river," "Maddison's river," and "Jefferson's River." They correctly decided to follow the Jefferson, the northernmost fork, which eventually led them to Lemhi Pass and the Shoshone Indians. *(Montana Historical Society, Helena)*

airing the baggage, dressing skins and hunting. Our squaw [Sacagawea] informed us that it was at this place she had been taken prisoner by the Grossventers 4 or 5 years ago."

Lewis recounted the same story, adding, "she does not, however, show any distress at these recollections, or any joy at the prospect of being restored to her country. . . ." He went on: "We begin to feel considerable anxiety with rispect to the Snake [Shoshone] Indians. If we do not find them or some other nation who have horses I fear the successful issue of our voyage will be very doubtful."

On July 30 the expedition left Three Forks to travel up the northernmost fork of the river, which Lewis agreed with Clark was the correct branch of the Missouri to follow. It was not until August 9, however, that it occurred to the captains to name the three branches. Clark had no argument with Lewis's choices. The southeast fork (or southernmost fork) was dubbed "Gallitin's river," in honor of Secretary of the Treasury ALBERT GALLATIN; the middle fork was named "Maddison's river," after Secretary of State JAMES MADISON; and the southwest fork (or northernmost fork), which they had been traveling along, was given the name "Jefferson's River in honor [of] that illustrious personage THOMAS JEFFERSON President of the United States." It was four days later that Lewis and a small party finally met the Shoshone.

The following year, after the captains had split the returning expedition into two parties, Clark and his group came back to Three Forks, arriving there on July 13, 1806. After a midday meal, Sergeant JOHN ORDWAY and the nine men took the canoes down the Missouri to the GREAT FALLS, while Clark and the rest of the party rode south to the Yellowstone River.

Three Forks today is the point where the Missouri River officially begins. To Lewis it was a critical landmark in the exploration of a new nation. He wrote: "believing this to be an essential point in the geography of this western part of the Continent I determined to remain at all events untill I obtained the necessary data for fixing it's latitude Longitude &c."

Further Reading

Cutright, Paul Russell. *Lewis & Clark: Pioneering Naturalists.* Lincoln: University of Nebraska Press/Bison Books, 1989.

Fifer, Barbara, and Vicky Soderberg. *Along the Trail with Lewis and Clark.* Great Falls, Mont.: Montana Magazine, 1998.

Moulton, Gary E., ed. *Atlas of the Lewis and Clark Expedition.* Revised ed. Lincoln: University of Nebraska Press, 1999.

ticks   See INSECTS.

Tillamook Indians (Killamook Indians)

As MERIWETHER LEWIS and WILLIAM CLARK were to discover, the Pacific Northwest contained the densest concentration of Native Americans on the entire continent. During their journey down the COLUMBIA RIVER, they encountered numerous Indian nations, and when they settled in for the winter at FORT CLATSOP, they had many Indian neighbors, most of them subgroups of the CHINOOK INDIANS. At some distance from the fort were the Tillamook, whom the captains initially thought were a related nation, since they could speak Chinookian. However, the Tillamook were actually Salishan speakers who shared some similarities with the many other coastal tribes.

Archaeologists have placed the Tillamook, or Killamook, Indians on the Oregon coast as early as 1400. Their name has been translated as "Land of Many Waters," and this certainly described the area in which they lived, between the Nehalem and Salmon Rivers and along the PACIFIC OCEAN, extending inland to the CASCADE MOUNTAINS. They were the largest Salish group on the coast south of the Columbia River (other Salishan nations were located as far north as British Columbia). Like most coastal Indians, they were distinguished by their custom of flattening their babies' heads. They lived in large wood houses and were skillful builders and navigators of CANOES.

The nation's name was often cause for confusion; they are mentioned in the expedition's journals as *Kilamox, Killamuck, Cal la' mox,* and *Callemex.* At the time of the expedition, the Tillamook population was estimated to be around 2,200; Lewis and Clark mentioned 50 Tillamook houses with a population of 1,000, although they never traveled further south than the village of Necost. Certainly they were able to identify several Tillamook towns around Tillamook Bay, and some Tillamook lived with a few CLATSOP INDIANS in a village at the mouth of the Necanicum River.

The expedition's encounters with the Tillamook were few but memorable. In early January 1806 Lewis and Clark learned of a beached whale on the coast, some 35 miles to the south. Anxious to see it and obtain some blubber, Clark assembled a party (including SACAGAWEA) and proceeded to the spot, arriving on January 8. Unfortunately, he had arrived too late; as PATRICK GASS described it, "The natives had taken all the meat off its bones, by scalding and the other means, for the purpose of trade." Clark had to bargain with the Tillamook to obtain 300 pounds of blubber as well as several gallons of oil.

The following night, January 9, while Clark and his party were visiting with some Tillamook and Clatsop by the Necanicum River, Private HUGH MCNEAL was invited by a Tillamook man to enjoy a woman's sexual favors. In fact, the man planned to kill McNeal and take his blanket. The unsuspecting private went along, ignoring the efforts of a friendly Chinook woman to warn him of the plot. The woman then began to call for help. Hearing the commotion across the river, Clark sent Sergeant NATHANIEL PRYOR and four men to provide assistance. It was not needed; the frightened McNeal returned safely, although his Tillamook attacker escaped.

With his usual conciseness, Patrick Gass summed up this encounter: "The Indians, who live up there are another of nation, and call themselves the Callemex nation. They are a ferocious nation: one of them was going to kill one of our men, for his blanket; but was prevented by a squaw of the Chinook nation, who lives among them, and who raised an alarm." Appropriately, Clark later dubbed the Necanicum "McNeal's Folly Creek."

Like all the coastal Indians, the Tillamook were adversely affected by the arrival of settlers in the years following the expedition. Disease took such a toll that by 1849 they numbered only 400, and by 1900 they were down to 200. Some still live in Tillamook County, Oregon.

Further Reading
Ronda, James P. *Lewis and Clark among the Indians.* Lincoln: University of Nebraska Press, 1984.
Sauter, John, and Bruce Johnson. *Tillamook Indians of the Oregon Coast.* Portland: Binfords and Mort, 1974.

Timm Mountain   See MOUNT HOOD.

tipis (tepees)

Like the feather-bonneted warrior on horseback, the tipi has become a popular symbol of the American Indian. Both, however, were used by only a minority of Native Americans, the PLAINS INDIANS, whose resistance to white incursions in the 19th century is so often portrayed in books or on film.

The tipi was only one of 11 forms of SHELTER developed by Indians across North America. These range from the pueblo still in use in the Southwest to igloos in the Far North, and they include such variations as the plankhouse, earth lodge, wickiup, hogan, pithouse, longhouse, grass house, and wigwam. Some ethnologists believe tipis came into common use on the GREAT PLAINS in the 18th century when the nations there acquired HORSES. It was the horse that enabled the Plains Indians to become fully nomadic and follow the BUFFALO they hunted. The tipi, light and portable, was the ideal form of shelter for such people.

The normal type of tipi was a conical tent with a pole frame and a covering of hides. Three or four poles, about 25 feet long, were placed in the ground, leaning inward, and the ends were tied together about four feet from the top. Other poles were then placed against these, forming a rough circle about 15 feet in diameter, and buffalo hides sewn together made the cover. The doorway, by tradition, faced east.

The CORPS OF DISCOVERY saw tipis for the first time in the villages of the YANKTON NAKOTA INDIANS (Yankton Sioux) on August 29, 1804. Sergeant NATHANIEL PRYOR wrote that the lodge he had seen "was handsum made of Buffalow Skins Painted different Colour, all compact & handSomly arranged, their Camps formed of a Conic form Containing about 12 or 15 persons each and 40 in number."

When the explorers reached the MANDAN INDIANS on October 26, 1804, they found static, stockaded villages that included solidly built earth lodges. This very different form of shelter reflected the Mandan's history. They were farmers—growers of crops who lived in settled communities, although they hunted buffalo as well. Whether they used tipis themselves, perhaps while out buffalo hunting, is not known.

However, when TOUSSAINT CHARBONNEAU was engaged as interpreter with his wife SACAGAWEA at the Mandan villages, he appears to have acquired a tipi for the journey. This proved a useful addition to the expedition because it solved the problem of a young woman and baby traveling with a party of soldiers. Whether the idea came from MERIWETHER LEWIS, WILLIAM CLARK, or Charbonneau himself is not known. Whosever idea it was, from the day they left FORT MANDAN on

The tipi, made from animal hides with a pole frame, provided a portable home for the nomadic Plains Indians. *(Library of Congress, Prints and Photographs Division [LC-USZ62-1745])*

April 7, 1805, it became the practice for the two captains, GEORGE DROUILLARD, Charbonneau, Sacagawea, and the baby Pomp to share the same accommodation, as Lewis wrote that day:

> Capt Clark myself the two interpreters and the woman and child sleep in a tent of dressed skins. This is in the Indian stile, formed of a number of dressed buffalo skins sewed together with sinues. It is cut in such a manner that when foalded it forms the quarter of a circle, and is left open at one side here it may be attatched or loosened at pleasure by strings which are sewed to its sides for the purpose.
>
> To erect this tent, a parsel of ten or twelve poles are provided, fore or five of which are attatched together at one end, they are then elevated and their lower extremities are spread in a circular manner to a width proportionate to the demention of the lodge; in the same position orther poles are lent against those, and the leather is then thrown over them forming a conic figure.

It is not known how long the tipi remained in use. Was it carried around the GREAT FALLS? Did it travel over the CONTINENTAL DIVIDE? All that is known for sure is that when Lewis paid Charbonneau on their return to the Mandan villages 16 months later, the payment included a charge for the tipi.

Further Reading

Moulton, Gary E., ed. *The Journals of the Lewis and Clark Expedition.* 13 vols. Lincoln: University of Nebraska Press, 1983–2001.

Ronda, James P. *Lewis and Clark among the Indians.* Lincoln: University of Nebraska Press, 1984.

tobacco

Along with ALCOHOL, tobacco was an important component of the SUPPLIES AND EQUIPMENT brought along on the Lewis and Clark Expedition. Seven of the permanent expedition members did not smoke, but to the remainder, tobacco was important for morale and relaxation. Furthermore, MERIWETHER LEWIS and WILLIAM CLARK knew that it held a symbolic importance to the Indians they were to meet and would be among the GIFTS the chiefs would expect. It is probably for this reason that Clark bought 136 pounds of tobacco at ST. CHARLES in May 1804 to add to whatever was left of the 130 rolls of pigtail tobacco that are known to have been brought from PHILADELPHIA.

As with whiskey, tobacco seems to have been used sparingly by the party. At FORT CLATSOP on Christmas Day 1805, they still had remaining 12 carrots (rolls) of tobacco, of which Lewis doled out half to the smokers of the party. On March 26, 1806, three days after leaving Fort Clatsop, Lewis announced that their stock was down to a few carrots. It was after this that the smokers followed the custom of the CHINOOK INDIANS and began to use the inner bark of the red willow and bearberry trees as a substitute, while those who chewed rather than smoked made do with wild crabapple bark. When Clark's party reached CAMP FORTUNATE and the BEAVERHEAD RIVER on July 8, 1806, where they had cached stores of tobacco the year before, he recorded that his men "scarcely gave themselves time to take off their saddles before they were off to the deposit."

The expedition seems to have first tried Indian tobacco (*Nicotiana quadrivalvis*) when they met the ARIKARA INDIANS in October 1804. Both Captain Lewis and Sergeant PATRICK

GASS commented on it; Gass's journal entry of October 10, 1804, notes that it "answered for smoking, but not for chewing." Lewis recognized it as a species of tobacco he was used to and collected specimens to be sent back to President THOMAS JEFFERSON, who was able to cultivate it at MONTICELLO. Later in their journey, at Fort Clatsop, Lewis noted that the Chinook Indians smoked the dried, crumbled leaves of the bearberry, though these were sometimes mixed with their own species of tobacco.

As so often depicted in paintings and films later, the ritual of smoking together was an integral part of formal meetings among Indian nations. Lewis and Clark appreciated this very well, and their notes contain several accounts of smoking as a mandatory prelude to any COUNCILS WITH INDIANS. It was during the winter of 1804–05 in the MANDAN villages that Clark recorded the symbolic significance of tobacco to the Indians. He described the importance they paid to the protocol of formal meetings, the ritual of smoking together, the order of seating, and even the necessity of placing a BUFFALO robe over the shoulders.

See also SMOKING CEREMONIES.

Further Reading

Cutright, Paul Russell. *Lewis & Clark: Pioneering Naturalists.* Lincoln: University of Nebraska Press/Bison Books, 1989.

Mussulman, Joseph. "Critical Shortages." From *Discovering Lewis and Clark: Fort Clatsop.* Available on-line. URL: http://www.lewis-clark.org/FTCLVIRTUAL/pl_nico1.htm. Downloaded on March 10, 2002.

Ronda, James P. *Lewis and Clark among the Indians.* Lincoln: University of Nebraska Press, 1984.

Toby　See OLD TOBY.

trade

The issue of trade had two meanings for the Lewis and Clark Expedition. On a larger scale, there was the trading network that MERIWETHER LEWIS and WILLIAM CLARK were seeking to establish as part of their MISSION OBJECTIVES. In the early 1800s, Indians along the MISSOURI RIVER had a complex but effective system of trade that involved many different nations, who generally came to the villages of the MANDAN INDIANS or the ARIKARA INDIANS to conduct their business. Even nations hostile to each other would suspend their enmity at certain times of the year to gather and trade for necessary goods. The TETON LAKOTA INDIANS (Teton Sioux), for example, depended on the Arikara for CORN and other agricultural goods, while in return they supplied BUFFALO meat and European trade goods.

The presence of British and French-Canadian traders at the villages added another dimension to this trading network. What they desired most were furs (see FUR TRADE), which the Indians were happy to supply in exchange for all sorts of items, especially firearms. With the American acquisition of the LOUISIANA TERRITORY, THOMAS JEFFERSON hoped to break this pattern and draw the Indians into trade with a U.S. network based in ST. LOUIS. This became one of the primary points Lewis and Clark made in their COUNCILS WITH INDIANS.

To persuade the Indians to break off relations with the British and French and do business with the United States, Lewis and Clark brought along some 26 bags of GIFTS to be distributed to chiefs and headmen. The primary purpose of the presents was to show diplomatic goodwill, but the captains also wanted to demonstrate the quality of the goods the Indians would get if they did business with the Americans. In essence, the gifts were equivalent to "free samples." Unfortunately, this sometimes backfired. Often the Indians found what the expedition had to offer was of poor quality or not what they wanted. Many were more interested in the speed with which they could obtain trade goods, no matter what the nationality of the provider. Others found such items as needles, scissors, and mirrors useless; what they wanted most were guns.

Nevertheless, the captains handed out their presents in councils, and only when the expedition began to run low on FOOD did they start turning to their supply of gifts as a source of trade goods. In time it was not trade with the United States that was the issue, it was their own survival. This situation began as early as the winter of 1804–05 at FORT MANDAN, when food was low. JOHN SHIELDS set up a makeshift forge and began to repair guns and tools and to make battle-axes for the Mandan and HIDATSA, who provided bushels of CORN in return. It was the first but not the last time that services would be bartered for necessities.

Other items were bartered as well. In August 1805, when the expedition met the SHOSHONE INDIANS, one of the captains' highest priorities was obtaining HORSES to make the journey over the BITTERROOT MOUNTAINS. On August 18 Lewis made his first trade, as he noted in his journal: "I soon obtained three very good horses. for which I gave an uniform coat, a pair of legings, a few handkerchiefs, three knives and some other small articles the whole of which did not cost more than about 20$ in the U' States. the Indians seemed quite as well pleased with their bargin as I was." One of the privates also obtained a horse "for an old checked shirt a pair of old legings and a knife."

Soon, however, the Shoshone realized just how desperate the expedition was for horses, and their prices went up. On August 29 Clark was forced to give "my Pistol 100 Balls Powder & a knife" for just one horse. By the time the expedition left the Shoshone, they had horses, but as Clark noted, "nearly all [had] Sore Backs [and] several [were] Pore, & young." In the end, James Ronda has written, the Shoshone demonstrated themselves to be far superior to the Americans at Yankee trading.

The expedition continued to pay high prices for food and horses for several months. Their supply of trade goods dwindled so severely during the winter at FORT CLATSOP that men were using ribbons to purchase sexual favors from the CHINOOK women, and Lewis was forced to steal a CANOE from the

CLATSOP INDIANS when he could not get one at an affordable price. Even the most helpful Indians they met were unwilling to give them something for nothing. When Chief YELLEPT of the WALLA WALLA INDIANS gave Clark a fine horse, it was apparently not to be considered a gift; he wanted a kettle in return. Unable to comply, Clark instead "gave him my Swoard, 100 balls & powder and some small articles of which he appeared perfectly satisfied."

The corps traded anything in which Indians seemed to be even remotely interested. When they reached the NEZ PERCE in June 1806, it was discovered that the brass buttons on uniform coats were "an article of which these people are tolerably fond." Buttons—including those of the two captains—were immediately cut off and exchanged for bushels of roots. Clark's skills as a doctor were also traded for food. On some days he had a constant stream of Nez Perce patients at his "clinic," but it helped to keep the expedition from starving.

Only after reaching the GREAT PLAINS, where game was available again, did the expedition no longer have to trade with Indians. But there is a poignant reminder of the straits in which they found themselves in an item in Lewis's expense account, submitted after their return:

> One Uniform Laced Coat, one silver Epaulet, one Dirk, & belt, one hanger & belt, one pistol & one fowling piece, all private property, given in exchange for Canoe, Horses &c. for public service during the expedition—$135.

Further Reading

Ambrose, Stephen E. *Undaunted Courage: Meriwether Lewis, Thomas Jefferson, and the Opening of the American West.* New York: Simon and Schuster, 1996.

Ronda, James P. *Lewis and Clark among the Indians.* Lincoln: University of Nebraska Press, 1984.

translation   See INTERPRETATION.

Travelers' Rest (Travellers Rest)

On September 1, 1805, the CORPS OF DISCOVERY was making its way north along the LEMHI RIVER under the guidance of OLD TOBY, who had agreed to take them over the BITTERROOT MOUNTAINS. They had hoped to find a route directly west of LEMHI PASS, where they had previously crossed the CONTINENTAL DIVIDE, but the SALMON RIVER had proved impossible to follow either by water or on foot. The SHOSHONE INDIANS had advised them the only possible route to the PACIFIC OCEAN was to go due north and then strike west through the mountains along the LOLO TRAIL.

The expedition followed the Lemhi River to the north fork of the Salmon River and then followed that upstream over LOST TRAIL PASS and down into the BITTERROOT RIVER valley. At ROSS'S HOLE near today's Sula, Idaho, they met the FLATHEAD (Salish) INDIANS, who greeted them hospitably, shared what little FOOD they had with them, and, more important, exchanged several of the worn-out HORSES that the explorers had purchased from the Shoshone. After the Flathead left on September 6 to join their Shoshone allies in hunting BUFFALO on the plains, the explorers continued north beside the Bitterroot River. Traveling was slow, and the hunters found little game to kill.

On September 9 the corps arrived at the junction of Lolo Creek and the Bitterroot, near today's Lolo, Idaho. This, Toby told them, was where they would turn west and begin their crossing of the Bitterroot Mountains. MERIWETHER LEWIS decided to spend a day HUNTING for food to take with them; the hunters brought in four DEER, a BEAVER, and three GROUSE. They left their camp, which Lewis named Travellers Rest, on September 11, traveling west along Lolo Creek. In front of them was the most arduous and dangerous part of their journey.

It was to be nine months before the expedition returned to Travelers' Rest. Guided by some NEZ PERCE INDIANS, they came back down from the Lolo Trail on June 30, 1806; as WILLIAM CLARK wrote: "Descended the mountain to Travellers rest leaveing those tremendious mountanes behind us—in passing of which we have experienced Cold and hunger of which I shall ever remember."

They rested at Travelers' Rest for three days while they planned the splitting of the expedition into two parties. Lewis was to take one group and ride due east to explore the MARIAS

Travelers' Rest is at the junction of Lolo Creek and the Bitterroot River near present-day Lolo, Idaho. The expedition rested here before their arduous crossing of the Bitterroot Mountains on their western journey and on their return in 1806. *(Library of Congress, Prints and Photographs Division [Haer, Mont,32-LOLO.V,1-1])*

RIVER. Clark would take the remainder and go south to the YELLOWSTONE RIVER. Along the way, each was to detach small groups to carry out specific missions, and the aim was for all the groups to meet at the mouth of the Yellowstone more than 500 miles away.

With hindsight it was a hazardous, almost foolhardy plan, with five parties scattered across the whole of Montana from just below the Canadian border down to the edge of today's Yellowstone National Park. As it turned out, fortune was on their side (see COINCIDENCES AND CHANCE ON THE EXPEDITION), although it was to be five weeks before they were reunited.

When they left Travelers' Rest for the last time on July 3, 1806, Clark wrote: "I took My leave of Capt. Lewis and the indians at 8 AM Set out with [19] men interpreter Shabono [TOUSSAINT CHARBONNEAU] & his wife & child." Sergeant PATRICK GASS's entry for the day is written in his normal laconic style: "We . . . collected our horses and set out. Captain Lewis and his party went down Clark's river, and Captain Clark with the rest of the party went up it."

Further Reading

Ambrose, Stephen E. *Undaunted Courage: Meriwether Lewis, Thomas Jefferson, and the Opening of the American West.* New York: Simon and Schuster, 1996.

Fifer, Barbara, and Vicky Soderberg. *Along the Trail with Lewis and Clark.* Great Falls, Mont.: Montana Magazine, 1998.

Moulton, Gary E., ed. *Atlas of the Lewis and Clark Expedition.* Revised ed. Lincoln: University of Nebraska Press, 1999.

trees

Although MERIWETHER LEWIS and WILLIAM CLARK discovered many new plants and trees on their journey, the success of their mission depended on just one type of tree: the cottonwood, a form of poplar whose seeds have cottonlike hairs. Lewis's first description of the cottonwood, written early in the expedition near LA CHARETTE, was slightly dismissive: " . . . the Cottonwood . . . is so abundant in this country . . . this tree arrives at a great size, grows extremly quick the wood is of a white colour, soft spungey and light, PIROGUES are most usually made from these trees, the wood is not durable nor do I know any other valuable purpose which it can answer except that just mentioned."

Despite Lewis's opinion, it is no exaggeration to say that without the cottonwood it is doubtful the explorers could have gone much beyond the villages of the MANDAN INDIANS. Accustomed to the well-wooded eastern states, both Lewis and Clark were surprised at the lack of trees on the GREAT PLAINS. On September 3, 1804, PATRICK GASS wrote in his journal: "There is no timber in this part of the country; but continued prairie on both sides of the river." Until they reached the headwaters of the MISSOURI RIVER below the CONTINENTAL DIVIDE, the explorers were to see very few trees, and these comprised small willows beside the river bottoms with occasional stands of cottonwood.

It was during their winter at FORT MANDAN (1804–05) that members of the CORPS OF DISCOVERY began to appreciate how useful the cottonwood tree could be. They built the fort out of it; made tables, benches, and beds from it; and found it provided excellent firewood. They also learned that the bark provided an excellent substitute for grass for the Mandan's HORSES. The six CANOES built at the fort for the onward journey were all made from the cottonwood, as were the wheels and frames the explorers constructed later to PORTAGE the canoes around the GREAT FALLS.

Such was the explorers' dependence on cottonwoods as the only source of shade and firewood that they became natural nighttime campsites. Yet the stands of cottonwood along the river were often miles apart. When the IRON-FRAME BOAT proved to be a failure at the Great Falls, the captains sent out hunters to look for trees big enough to use for canoes. They found just two cottonwoods some eight miles away and felt themselves fortunate that they did not have to travel further.

In 1806, when Clark made his return journey down the YELLOWSTONE RIVER, it took four days' travel to find suitable trees for canoes. Even then, the result was two cottonwood dugouts only 16–18 inches deep and 18–24 inches wide, far too unstable and dangerous for a party of 13 that included SACAGAWEA and her baby. Clark therefore improvised yet again and joined the canoes with planks tied across to form a crude but stable catamaran. Improvisation and ingenuity were major features of the expedition's success, but on at least five occasions these would have been of no avail without the cottonwood.

From a botanical point of view, Lewis and Clark were the first if not to discover then certainly to describe more than two dozen tree species and subspecies. Both men were accustomed to the woodlands of the eastern United States and the trees that grew there. Based on the little information they had on climatic conditions by the PACIFIC OCEAN, it seems probable they expected to encounter similar species of trees and plants there. As it turned out, they found a very different climate and, consequently, many trees new to them. Of the 26 new trees they noted, all but two come from areas west of the Continental Divide. The Douglas fir had already been discovered and described by Archibald Menzies, who had accompanied the GEORGE VANCOUVER expedition in 1793. However, Lewis provided a detailed description of this tree as well, and he and Clark were the first to describe accurately the grand fir, subalpine fir, three types of maple (vine, Rocky Mountain, and bigleaf), three alders (white, red, and Sitka), the Oregon ash, the Sitka spruce, and four types of pine (whitebark, lodgepole, ponderosa, and western white).

Members of the expedition were particularly struck by the enormous size of certain trees on the western seaboard. Lewis recorded that the Sitka spruce "grows to imence size . . . we have found them as much as 36 feet in the girth . . . frequently rise to the hight of 290 feet, and one hundred and twenty or 30 of that hight without a limb."

Lewis also noted, with some admiration, the many uses the CLATSOP INDIANS made of the different types of trees. While

The expedition came to depend on cottonwood trees such as these, just about the only trees to be found in the otherwise timberless Great Plains. *(National Archives Still Pictures Branch [NWDNS-412-DA-14707])*

members of the expedition found that the bark of the Oregon crabapple formed a substitute for chewing TOBACCO, Lewis wrote that the Indians used it to split other timber and firewood and even to hollow out canoes: "I have seen the natives drive the wedges of this wood into solid dry pines which it cleft without fracturing or injuring the wedge in the smallest degree." He remarked as well on the many uses the CHINOOK INDIANS found for the western red cedar, which they employed for building their houses and boats and making bowls, plates, and spoons. They used the bark to make roofs for their houses, while from the bark fibers they made hats, nets, cord lines, and ropes.

Although President THOMAS JEFFERSON and horticulturalists William Hamilton and Bernard McMahon all raised plants successfully from the seeds Lewis brought back with him, perhaps the most direct arboreal link with the expedition stems from a package Lewis sent to Jefferson before the expedition had even left CAMP DUBOIS. In March 1804, along with other specimens, he sent the president a box containing cuttings of the Osage orange from trees owned by PIERRE CHOUTEAU. A small row of trees grown from these cuttings can still be seen in the cemetery of St. Peter's Episcopal Church in PHILADELPHIA.

See also PLANTS, NEW SPECIES.

Further Reading

Arno, Stephen F. *Northwest Trees.* Seattle, Wash.: The Mountaineers, 1977.

Cutright, Paul Russell. "Lewis and Clark and Cottonwood." *Bulletin of the Missouri Historical Society* 22 (October 1965): 35–44.

————. *Lewis & Clark: Pioneering Naturalists.* Lincoln and London: University of Nebraska Press, 1969.

trout   See FISH, NEW SPECIES.

Tuttle, Ebenezer (1774–unknown) *private in the temporary party*

The only record of Private Ebenezer Tuttle is provided by Charles G. Clarke in his roster of the expedition. Tuttle was born in New Haven, Connecticut, stood 5'7" tall, and had brown hair, blue eyes, and a fair complexion. Prior to entering the army, he had been a farmer. He was recruited at KASKASKIA for the first part of the expedition up the MISSOURI RIVER to FORT MANDAN. He returned to ST. LOUIS with the KEELBOAT party under the command of Corporal RICHARD WARFINGTON in April 1805.

Further Reading

Clarke, Charles G. *The Men of the Lewis and Clark Expedition: A Biographical Roster of the Fifty-One Members and a Composite Diary of Their Activities from All Known Sources.* 1970. Reprint, Lincoln: Bison Books, University of Nebraska Press, 2002.

Twisted Hair (Walammottinin)

(unknown–unknown) *Nez Perce chief*

After the CORPS OF DISCOVERY completed their arduous crossing of the BITTERROOT MOUNTAINS in September 1805, they became first guests and then neighbors of the NEZ PERCE INDIANS. Before their arrival, some of the Nez Perce had discussed killing the starving and exhausted explorers, but others chose to feed and welcome them. This was certainly the attitude taken by Chief Twisted Hair, whom WILLIAM CLARK described as "a Chearfull man with apparant siencerity." His Nez Perce name, Walammottinin, meant "hair or forelock bunched and tied." Like other Nez Perce, he was possibly influenced by the counsel of WATKUWEIS, a woman in his band who had lived among Canadian traders and regarded all white people favorably. More likely, however, he was aware that friendly relations with the soldiers would be advantageous in obtaining the guns and other TRADE goods his people desired.

About 65 when MERIWETHER LEWIS and Clark met him, Twisted Hair was the only chief of importance present in the Nez Perce villages at that time; BROKEN ARM and CUT NOSE were both away on raids and would not meet them until the expedition's return the following spring. Although communication was difficult, because none of their party could speak Nez Perce, the captains were still able to obtain valuable information from Twisted Hair about the country west of them, which he drew on a whitened ELK skin. If he was accurate, Clark calculated that they were about 10 days away from the falls of the COLUMBIA RIVER and perhaps two weeks from the PACIFIC OCEAN.

With major chiefs absent and the expedition anxious to be on its way, Lewis and Clark decided to leave most of its diplomatic and ethnographic work with the Nez Perce until the following spring. Nevertheless, they held a council with Twisted Hair and other chiefs on September 23; it was hampered by language difficulties and there is no indication of what, if anything, the meeting accomplished.

It was at this time that almost the entire corps began to suffer from dysentery, probably due to their abrupt change in diet. While this seriously weakened them, Clark still went ahead with finding timber for building CANOES, assisted by Twisted Hair and his son, who also showed the stricken corps members a less laborious way to make canoes by burning out the centers of logs. Ten days later, with five canoes completed, the expedition was ready to go on. Twisted Hair agreed to look after the expedition's HORSES during the winter, with the understanding that they would be collected the following spring.

On October 7, still slowly recovering, the expedition loaded their canoes and set off down the CLEARWATER RIVER. With them were Twisted Hair and TETOHARSKY, a younger Nez Perce chief, both of whom had agreed to act as guides and intermediaries with the Sahaptian-speaking Indians downriver, relatives of the Nez Perce. They also proved helpful in negotiating the dangerous rapids of the Clearwater and SNAKE Rivers. On October 14 they went ahead to the confluence of the Snake and COLUMBIA Rivers, near which bands of WANAPAM INDIANS and YAKAMA (Yakima) INDIANS lived, to assure those nations that the white explorers who were coming were friendly and peaceful. By the time the expedition arrived at this junction, it was crowded with Indians who gave them a warm welcome. After spending four days there, the expedition proceeded down the Columbia, with their Nez Perce guides again paving the way, resulting in a friendly greeting from Chief YELLEPT of the WALLA WALLA INDIANS.

Twisted Hair and Tetoharsky accompanied the expedition down the Columbia as far as a village of WISHRAM AND WASCO INDIANS just below The Dalles. They would go no further, as they were now in Chinookan territory, where the Indians were potentially hostile, both to them and to the Americans. Grateful for their services, Lewis and Clark presented the two chiefs with medals and enjoyed a parting smoke with them before they left.

They would not meet again until May 1806, when, as the expedition was returning up the Clearwater, they encountered Tetoharsky, who offered to take them to Twisted Hair's village. On May 8 they finally met Cut Nose, who joined them as they proceeded upriver. Two days later they were reunited with Twisted Hair, but to the captains' surprise he behaved very coolly toward them. Suddenly he and Cut Nose began to argue violently. It took some time and separate meetings with the two chiefs for Lewis and Clark to sort out the problem, which primarily had to do with their horses. Twisted Hair claimed that when Cut Nose had returned to the Nez Perce the previous autumn, he had attempted to take control of the horses out of jealousy and spite. Cut Nose, however, claimed that Twisted Hair had abused the captains' trust in him and allowed some of his warriors to ride the horses too hard. Twisted Hair admitted that he may have neglected the horses a bit and that some were missing. Consequently, Lewis and Clark gave him only part of the promised payment for his service, the rest to be tendered when he had recovered and returned all the horses. As it turned out, some of them did show signs of having been ridden too hard, but the captains diplomatically chose not to make an issue of this.

During the weeks in May and early June that the expedition stayed with the Nez Perce, they invited members of Twisted Hair's family to camp with them, hoping to use them as guides over the LOLO TRAIL to the other side of the Bitterroots. However, there is no indication that the previously cooperative Twisted Hair provided any assistance in this respect, and in the end the expedition had to bargain for the guides they finally got elsewhere. Nevertheless, Twisted Hair had been of great help to the expedition and was always remembered as an important friend and ally.

Further Reading

Ambrose, Stephen E. *Undaunted Courage: Meriwether Lewis, Thomas Jefferson, and the Opening of the American West.* New York: Simon and Schuster, 1996.

Ronda, James P. *Lewis and Clark among the Indians.* Lincoln: University of Nebraska Press, 1984.

Two Medicine River

Two Medicine River is the southern of two forks that combine at the head of the MARIAS RIVER near present-day Browning, Montana. It was the setting for the CORPS OF DISCOVERY's only fatal encounter with Indians.

On the expedition's return journey in 1806, while WILLIAM CLARK took some of the party south from TRAVELERS' REST to explore the YELLOWSTONE RIVER, MERIWETHER LEWIS and 11 men rode straight across country to their old camp above the GREAT FALLS of the MISSOURI RIVER. After losing some of their HORSES there, Lewis decided to take only three men to explore the Marias River, leaving the others behind to conduct the PORTAGE around the falls.

On July 16 Lewis left the Great Falls with GEORGE DROUILLARD, JOSEPH FIELD, and REUBIN FIELD. They reached the Marias on the 19th and came to its north fork (today's Cut Bank Creek) on the 21st. Taking this fork, Lewis found the next day that it headed due west and not up to the Canadian border as he had hoped. He decided to camp there and tried to take ASTRONOMICAL OBSERVATIONS, but the WEATHER was too cloudy for him to do so. On July 26 the party turned south from the campsite Lewis had named CAMP DISAPPOINTMENT and, traveling overland, arrived at the south fork of the Marias, Two Medicine River, that afternoon.

On the hills above the river, they met eight BLACKFEET INDIANS who, after smoking a pipe with them, agreed to camp

It was near Two Medicine River that the expedition's only violent encounter with Indians took place. This woodcut, from the 1810 version of Patrick Gass's journal, is an inaccurate depiction of the incident. *(Library of Congress, Prints and Photographs Division [LC-USZ62-19231])*

with the explorers on the banks of the river. Fully aware of the fierce reputation of the Blackfeet, Lewis took first watch before handing over to Reubin Field. Early the following morning, the captain was awakened by a shout to find one Indian had grabbed the rifles of the Field brothers while another had snatched his rifle and Drouillard's. In the ensuing scuffle, Reubin Field fatally stabbed the Indian who had stolen his rifle while Lewis and Drouillard recovered their FIREARMS. Lewis then spotted two other Blackfeet trying to drive off their horses. He chased after them on his own, cornered them among some rocks, and as one aimed his musket, Lewis fired, fatally wounding the Indian in the belly.

Having retrieved their horses as well as four of the Blackfeet's, the soldiers rode south away from Two Medicine River as fast as they could. They went more than 50 miles before they stopped for an hour and then covered another 50 miles before they eventually halted for the night. After three hours of sleep, on the morning of July 28, they rode on again, and in one of the COINCIDENCES AND CHANCE ON THE EXPEDITION, they saw JOHN ORDWAY and their CANOES coming down the Missouri. An hour later, PATRICK GASS and his party on horseback joined them, and the reunited group took to the canoes, leaving Two Medicine River and the Blackfeet far behind.

The site of what is now called the Two Medicine Fight has been marked and fenced and can be visited today.

Further Reading

Ambrose, Stephen E. *Undaunted Courage: Meriwether Lewis, Thomas Jefferson, and the Opening of the American West.* New York: Simon and Schuster, 1996.

Cutright, Paul Russell. *Lewis & Clark: Pioneering Naturalists.* Lincoln: University of Nebraska Press/Bison Books, 1989.

Moulton, Gary E., ed. *Atlas of the Lewis and Clark Expedition.* Revised ed. Lincoln: University of Nebraska Press, 1999.

Ronda, James P. *Lewis and Clark among the Indians.* Lincoln: University of Nebraska Press, 1984.

Werner Wilbur P. "Disaster at Montana's Two Medicine River Fight Sight." *We Proceeded On* 6, no. 3 (August 1980): 12–13.

Umatilla Indians

In October 1805, after a wretched crossing of the BITTER-ROOT MOUNTAINS and a welcome respite with the NEZ PERCE INDIANS, the Lewis and Clark Expedition began the last stage of its westward journey. From the CLEARWATER RIVER, they canoed down to the SNAKE RIVER and arrived at the confluence of the Snake with the COLUMBIA RIVER on October 16. Two Nez Perce guides, TWISTED HAIR and TETO-HARSKY, had traveled ahead of the expedition to bring news of the explorers' coming, and as a result numerous WANAPAM and YAKAMA (Yakima) INDIANS thronged the riverbanks at the Snake-Columbia junction. As the expedition proceeded downriver, they met the WALLA WALLA INDIANS, who greeted them warmly. After the Walla Walla, however, the river Indians' curiosity and welcome changed to fear and suspicion, a new atmosphere that became noticeable once the expedition reached the Umatilla River and met the Indians after whom it was named.

The Umatilla were Sahaptian-speaking PLATEAU INDI-ANS who had long occupied ancestral territory along the Columbia in what is now southern Washington and northern Oregon. They lived in rush-mat houses and were primarily fishers, although they also subsisted on small game and roots, especially the bulbs of the CAMAS ROOT. Unlike the other Plateau Indians the expedition had met, though, they were not quick to strike up friendly relations with the explorers.

The CORPS OF DISCOVERY entered Umatilla territory on the afternoon of October 19, and as they approached the Umatilla villages, they noticed the Indians' haste to hide, even abandoning their houses. While WILLIAM CLARK was walking on shore with a small party that included SACAGAWEA, he shot a CRANE, an incident that apparently confirmed the Indians' dread of the soldiers. As Clark explained it to NICHOLAS BIDDLE years later, "The alarm was occasioned by their thinking that we were supernatural and came down from the clouds." Unaware of this at the time, it took him a while to allay the Indians' fears. With GEORGE DROUILLARD, REUBIN FIELD, and JOSEPH FIELD, he went to visit a village of Umatilla, where all the doors of the mat house were firmly shut. Pushing his way into the first house, he found 32 Umatilla cowering before him "in the greatest agutation." This scene was repeated in the other lodges, and it was not until hands were shaken and GIFTS were offered that the Indians calmed down. Twisted Hair, Tetoharsky, and Sacagawea all assisted in reassuring the Umatilla that the white men were peaceful. It later came out that Clark's shooting of the crane—they had never before heard a gun—had been the primary factor in their fear: "These shots . . . a few light clouds passing, the fall of the birds and our immediately landing and coming towards them convinced them that we were from above."

The expedition left the Umatilla on friendly terms, but as they continued down the Columbia, they encountered an even higher level of fear and distrust and sometimes actual hostility. Nevertheless, the groundwork they laid with the Umatilla enabled those Indians to became key participants in the FUR TRADE that later developed in the area. Like other Plateau Indians, they resisted white efforts to force them off their lands, leading to the Cayuse War of 1847–50 and the

The Umatilla lived along the Columbia in dwellings such as this one. This photograph was taken in the vicinity of Beacon Rock ca. 1903. *(Library of Congress, Prints and Photographs Division [LC-USZ62-117238])*

Yakima War of 1855–56. In 1853 the Umatilla Reservation was established near Pendleton, Oregon, close to their ancestral lands. Today the Umatilla share this land with the Cayuse and the Walla Walla as the Confederated Tribes of the Umatilla Reservation.

Further Reading

Ronda, James P. *Lewis and Clark among the Indians.* Lincoln: University of Nebraska Press, 1984.
Waldman, Carl. *Encyclopedia of Native American Tribes.* Revised ed. New York: Checkmark Books, 1999.

V

Vancouver, George (1757–1798) *explorer*

When MERIWETHER LEWIS and WILLIAM CLARK finally reached the COLUMBIA RIVER in October 1805, they were finally able to refer to MAPS to guide them to the PACIFIC OCEAN. The maps had been published by George Vancouver, an English navigator and explorer who had sailed on Captain James Cook's second and third voyages (see EXPLORATION, EARLY).

Vancouver had entered the Royal Navy at the age of 13, and in just a few years' time was serving with Cook. In 1791 he determined to conduct his own exploration and survey of the American northwest coast. By this time, hopes were fading that a NORTHWEST PASSAGE could be found north of CANADA, and the object was to find a series of connecting rivers across the North American continent. Vancouver specifically wanted to find a large river that discharged into the Pacific Ocean.

Vancouver left England in April 1791 with 100 men aboard two ships, the *Chatham* and his flagship, the *Discovery.* A year later they arrived off the California coast, and thereupon, as the expedition sailed north from Cape Mendacino to Cape Flattery, Vancouver recorded latitudes and charted features of the coastline. Despite this attention to detail, however, he somehow missed the mouth of the Columbia River.

On April 29, 1792, Vancouver encountered the southbound U.S. ship *Columbia Rediviva,* commanded by ROBERT GRAY. Gray informed Vancouver that he had recently discovered a large river but had been unable to cross the bar; he was now heading back to it to make a second attempt. Vancouver doubted that Gray's river was worth investigating and contin-

ued north. Gray, meanwhile, succeeded in his second try at crossing the bar into the mouth of the river and proceeded about 20 miles in before turning around. He claimed it for the United States and named it the Columbia River, after his ship.

Vancouver went on to discover and explore Puget Sound, which was named after Peter Puget, one of his lieutenants. He also explored the coastline of British Columbia and circumnavigated what is now Vancouver Island. On June 4 he landed and formally laid claim to the entire region around present-day Everett, Washington, for GREAT BRITAIN.

Later Vancouver visited the Spanish Captain Juan de la Bodéga y Quadra at Nootka on Vancouver Island for negotiations regarding conflicting claims between SPAIN and Britain. There he learned that Captain Gray had been to Nootka and left a chart showing the location of the newly discovered Columbia River. Vancouver hastened to the area, arriving there in October 1792. Although the *Discovery* was too large to cross the sandbar, the *Chatham,* commanded by Lieutenant William Broughton, was able to make the passage easily. On Vancouver's instructions, Broughton proceeded to sail 100 miles up the Columbia River, charting features along the way and naming landmarks such as MOUNT HOOD. Broughton made it as far as present-day Portland before turning back; he named this area Point Vancouver in honor of his commander.

It was the maps produced from this surveying expedition that Lewis and Clark brought with them and used 13 years later. Vancouver spent two more years charting the Pacific coastline, arriving back in England in 1795 after mapping 1,700 miles of shoreline. He was preparing an account of his exploration at the time of his death three years later. His

George Vancouver, an English explorer, had sailed with Captain James Cook and continued his work in charting the northwest coast of America, including the Columbia River. *(Washington State Historical Society, Tacoma)*

brother and Peter Puget finished the book, which was published in 1798 and also used as a resource for Lewis and Clark. Vancouver's charts and his landing near Everett, however, strengthened the British claim to lands in the Pacific Northwest and became a factor in the dispute over OREGON TERRITORY, which was not resolved until 1846.

Further Reading

Anderson, Bern. *Life and Voyages of Captain George Vancouver, Surveyor of the Sea.* Toronto: University of Toronto Press, 1966.

Fisher, Robin, and Hugh Johnston, eds. *From Maps to Metaphors: The Pacific World of George Vancouver.* Vancouver: University of British Columbia, 1993.

Large, Arlen J. "Vancouver's Legacy to Lewis and Clark." *We Proceeded On* 18, no. 1 (1992).

Vancouver, George. *A Voyage of Discovery to the North Pacific Ocean and Round the World, 1791–1795.* Reprint, New York: Da Capo Press, 1968.

venereal disease　　See MEDICINE AND MEDICAL TREATMENT; SEX DURING THE EXPEDITION.

voyageurs　　See ENGAGÉS.

Walla Walla Indians (Walula Indians)

In October 1805, as the Lewis and Clark Expedition canoed down the SNAKE RIVER toward its confluence with the COLUMBIA RIVER, the NEZ PERCE chiefs TWISTED HAIR and TETOHARSKY went ahead of them to let Indians nations downriver know that white men were coming in peace. As a result, by the time the CORPS OF DISCOVERY reached the Columbia, the riverbanks were crowded with curious Indians who subsequently came to visit them. Just past the Walla Walla River, in what is now Washington State, Twisted Hair and Tetoharsky advised MERIWETHER LEWIS and WILLIAM CLARK that Chief YELLEPT of the Walla Walla Indians would be visiting them.

The Walla Walla, whose name means "little river," were Sahaptian-speaking relatives of the Nez Perce. They had long lived in their territory along the lower Walla Walla River and near the junction of the Snake and Columbia Rivers. Like other PLATEAU INDIANS in the area, they lived primarily on a diet of salmon supplemented by roots and small game. They were enthusiastic about meeting the expedition, and after visiting the captains on the evening of October 18, about 20 Walla Walla, including Yellept, camped nearby.

The following day a council was held with Yellept and two other Walla Walla chiefs as well as another chief who was either a Cayuse or an UMATILLA. The captains spoke of their "friendly intentions towards our red children" and presented some GIFTS. Impressed and curious, Yellept asked the explorers to stay longer so that more of his people could see them, but the need to push on to the PACIFIC OCEAN was too great, so Lewis and Clark refused politely but promised they would stay longer when they returned in the spring.

The captains kept their promise, arriving back in Walla Walla territory on April 27, 1806. Yellept greeted them and invited them to his village, a settlement of 15 lodges located on the north bank of the Columbia about 12 miles below the river's junction with the Snake. The expedition stayed here for the next three days, and on the second night there was a large party to which a number of YAKAMA (Yakima) INDIANS were invited. To everybody's delight, PIERRE CRUZATTE played his fiddle while soldiers and Indians danced. At one point more than 500 Indians—men, women, and children—began to sing and dance in a large circle, most of them standing in one place and jumping up and down to the music of the drums and rattles, while some men went into the center "and danced in a circular manner sidewise." It was a joyous evening.

The expedition's stay with the Walla Walla was both enjoyable and helpful. Thanks to a SHOSHONE captive who could be brought into the chain of INTERPRETATION, the captains were able to communicate easily with Yellept, and consequently they obtained some valuable information, in particular learning of a shortcut across the northern bend of the Snake River that would save them some 80 miles on their route back to the Nez Perce. They also obtained a number of HORSES, which were badly needed and much appreciated.

Lewis and Clark did, however, pay a high price for the Walla Walla's hospitality. On April 28 Yellept presented Clark with "a very elegant white horse" but then startled the captain when he asked for a kettle in return. Clark gave the chief his sword plus some ammunition instead. The following morning two Walla Walla chiefs gave a horse to each of the captains; in return, Lewis wrote, "we gave them sundry articles and among

353

others one of my case pistols and several hundred rounds of ammunition." The pistol had been Lewis's personal property. The Indians also requested and received medical services from Clark.

On the morning of April 30 the expedition left "these friendly honest people the Wollahwollahs . . ." and proceeded upriver. On the evening of the 31st, three teenage Walla Walla boys arrived at their camp to return a steel trap that had been left behind. Lewis praised them and in his journal summed up his opinion of their people: "I think we can justly affirm to the honor of these people that they are the most hospitable, honest, and sincere people that we have met with in our voyage."

The Walla Walla's friendly relations with white men would continue into the 1850s, until they, like other nations in the area, were tricked out of their lands by Washington Territory governor Isaac Stevens. They participated in the Yakima War of 1855–56 and with other nations engaged in attacks on white settlers until they were finally defeated in 1858. Thereafter they moved with the Umatilla and the Cayuse Indians to the Umatilla Reservation in Oregon, where the combined nations live today as the Confederated Tribes of the Umatilla Reservation.

The expedition's relations with the Walla Walla Indians were friendly. Some 50 years later the Walla Walla were forced off their lands by Washington Territory governor Isaac Stevens. This picture of Chief Peo Peo Mox Mox (a double agent during the Yakima War of 1855–56) was done by Gustav Sohon during Stevens's treaty tour of 1855. *(Washington State Historical Society, Tacoma)*

Further Reading

Ambrose, Stephen E. *Undaunted Courage: Meriwether Lewis, Thomas Jefferson, and the Opening of the American West.* New York: Simon and Schuster, 1996.

Ronda, James P. *Lewis and Clark among the Indians.* Lincoln: University of Nebraska Press, 1984.

Waldman, Carl. *Encyclopedia of Native American Tribes.* Revised ed. New York: Checkmark Books, 1999.

Wanapam Indians (Wanapum Indians)

In mid-October 1805, as the CORPS OF DISCOVERY were making their way down the SNAKE RIVER, MERIWETHER LEWIS and WILLIAM CLARK sent their NEZ PERCE guides, TWISTED HAIR and TETOHARSKY, on ahead of the expedition to advise the Indians downriver of their coming. Like the Nez Perce, the nations who lived around the confluence of the Snake and the COLUMBIA RIVERS were Sahaptian-speaking PLATEAU INDIANS, which enabled Twisted Hair and Tetoharsky to carry out their mission successfully. By the time the corps arrived at the rivers' junction on October 16, throngs of YAKAMA (Yakima) and Wanapam Indians were there to see the white explorers, who received a warm and curiosity-filled welcome.

That evening the expedition was visited by a delegation of some 200 Wanapam, whom they referred to in the JOURNALS as the Sokulk. Led by their chief, Cutssahnem, the Indians made a grand entrance, singing and beating on small drums as they came into the camp. The captains smoked with Cutssahnem and then held a council, but their problems with the language made communication difficult. Through GEORGE DROUILLARD, the American message was first conveyed in sign language to Twisted Hair and Tetoharsky, who then translated to the Wanapam, but whether the translation was accurate could not be determined. However, if the verbal message declaring their "friendly disposition to all nations" did not impress the Wanapam, the GIFTS certainly did. Cutssahnem was presented with a large medal, a handkerchief, and a shirt, while lesser chiefs were given smaller medals. The Americans then purchased eight dogs (for FOOD), some dried salmon, and dried horsemeat from the Indians.

The following day Lewis did more trading and also spent some time with Cutssahnem and several other Indians studying their vocabulary. Meanwhile, Clark visited some of the Wanapam and the Yakama fishing villages and then returned to camp to record his observations about their housing, clothing, ornamentation, medical ailments, and dental habits. "Those peoples appears to live in a State of comparative happiness," he wrote, also noting that "they take a great[er] share [in the] labor of the woman, than is common among Savage tribes, and as I am informed [are] content with one wife."

In the course of their short visit among the Wanapam and Yakama, both captains added much to the expedition's ethnographical knowledge. Their talks with the chiefs also allowed them to gain valuable data about the geography of the area. Using charcoal on a skin, Cutssahnem drew them a map depicting "the rivers and Tribes above on the great river and its waters on which he put great numbers of his nation and friends." After nearly three days resting and gathering information, the expedition set off downriver, where they would meet Indians who would treat them with suspicion and hostility, quite unlike the warm and friendly Wanapam.

At that time the Wanapam numbered about 2,500 and dwelt in the Columbia Basin from the mouth of the Yakima River to the Saddle Mountains. They participated in the later FUR TRADE that developed in the area, but like other Plateau Indians they were adversely affected by the migration of white settlers into the West. They refused to sign an 1855 treaty ceding their lands to the U.S. government, but because they were in a more remote location than other Plateau Indians, they were left alone. Many moved onto the Yakima Reservation and retained land by Priest Rapids, but their numbers were depleted by epidemics. In 1943 the government took over their lands for use in connection with the Manhattan Project, and they were forced to move. By this time there were only a dozen full-blooded Wanapam left. Today about 100 people of Wanapam descent are struggling to reclaim their culture, reviving the traditions of their ancestors and keeping their history alive.

Further Reading
Ronda, James P. *Lewis and Clark among the Indians.* Lincoln: University of Nebraska Press, 1984.

wapato (broad-leaved arrowhead)

On November 4, 1805, the CORPS OF DISCOVERY was on the final stage of its journey down the COLUMBIA RIVER. Just downstream from today's Portland, Oregon, they came to a large SKILLOOT Indian village where, as PATRICK GASS reported, "We got some dogs and roots from the natives. The roots are of a superior quality to any I had before seen; they are called whapto; resemble a potato when cooked, and are about as big as a hen egg."

The expedition had previously noted the importance of the BITTERROOT to the SHOSHONE INDIANS and the bread the NEZ PERCE made from CAMAS ROOTs. The wapato was the favorite vegetable of the nations they met on the COLUMBIA RIVER. These "roots," as Gass called them, were the staple vegetable of the explorers during their time at FORT CLATSOP, although the nearest grew some 15 miles upstream. WILLIAM CLARK wrote: "This root they call Wap-pa-to to which the Chinese cultivate in great quantities called the Sa-git-ti-folia or common arrow head (we believe it to be the Same) it has an agreeable taste and answers very well in place of bread. we purchased about 4 bushels of this root and divided it to our party."

The variety *Sagittaria latifolia,* which Clark correctly identified, is one of about 30 species of aquatic herbs of the waterplantain family, so named because the leaves are arrow shaped. The bulb of the plant is the size of a hen's egg and, when roasted, tastes much like a potato. It grows in shallow water or swampy ground, and Indian women gathered it by walking into the water and loosening the bulbs with their feet. These floated to the surface and were then collected in boats. Lewis said it was so enjoyed by the coastal nations that they would dispose of valuable property to obtain the roots.

The wapato root played its part in the vote the expedition held at STATION CAMP on November 24, 1805. Camped in severe discomfort west of POINT ELLICE on the north side of the Columbia estuary, the captains gave everyone the chance to have a say on whether they should move camp elsewhere for the winter. A majority voted to move to the south side of the estuary, mainly because the Indians had said game and timber were plentiful there. Unusually for the time, both YORK and SACAGAWEA also took part (although some historians feel Sacagawea's vote was not counted in the "official" tally). Sacagawea supported the south bank because, Clark reported, she was "in favour of a place where there is plenty of Potas [Wapato roots]."

Further Reading
Ambrose, Stephen E. *Undaunted Courage: Meriwether Lewis, Thomas Jefferson, and the Opening of the American West.* New York: Simon and Schuster, 1996.
Cutright, Paul Russell. *Lewis & Clark: Pioneering Naturalists.* Lincoln: University of Nebraska Press/Bison Books, 1989.

Warfington, Richard (Richard Worthington, Richard Worbington, Richard Warvington)

(1777–unknown) *corporal in the temporary party*
The only corporal on the expedition, Richard Warfington was recruited for just the first leg of the journey up the MISSOURI RIVER. A native of Louisburg, North Carolina, he was officially transferred to the CORPS OF DISCOVERY from the Second Infantry on May 14, 1804. He was specifically hired as a member of the temporary party to accompany the expedition to its winter quarters and then to command a return party to ST. LOUIS the following spring with reports, MAPS, LETTERS, and JOURNALS, as well as ARTIFACTS AND SPECIMENS to be delivered to President THOMAS JEFFERSON in Washington.

On May 14, 1804, the first leg of the expedition's journey began when the KEELBOAT, PIROGUES, and CANOES set out from CAMP DUBOIS up the Missouri. Warfington initially commanded one of the canoes, with six men paddling. He later took charge of the white pirogue. The following spring the keelboat was made ready, and Warfington was given command of it after receiving detailed instructions from Captain MERIWETHER LEWIS on getting through TETON LAKOTA INDIAN (Teton Sioux) territory and delivering the boat's contents. Traveling with Warfington were JOSEPH GRAVELINES, a Frenchman who was to be the boat's pilot; MOSES REED and JOHN NEWMAN, both of whom had been expelled from the expedition; Privates JOHN DAME, JOHN BOLEY, EBENEZER TUTTLE, and ISAAC WHITE, all members of the temporary party; and three of the ENGAGÉS. They later picked up an ARIKARA INDIAN chief, whom Gravelines was to take to Washington to meet President Jefferson. (The chief died during the journey.)

On April 7, 1805, Lewis noted in his journal: "We gave Richard Warfington, a discharged corporal, the charge of the barge and crew, and confided to his care likewise our dispatches to the government, letters to our private friends, and a number of articles to the President of the United States." The keelboat arrived in St. Louis that summer, and the shipment for Jefferson was delivered to him on August 12.

Warfington's army enlistment had technically expired in August 1804, but he carried out his mission with distinction, for which Lewis later praised him in a report to Secretary of War HENRY DEARBORN, also recommending that the corporal receive the rewards given to the members of the permanent party. After arriving in St. Louis and ensuring the delivery of the shipment to Washington, Warfington rejoined his old military unit. There is no record of his whereabouts after this.

Further Reading

Clarke, Charles G. *The Men of the Lewis and Clark Expedition: A Biographical Roster of the Fifty-One Members and a Composite Diary of Their Activities from All Known Sources.* 1970. Reprint, Lincoln: Bison Books, University of Nebraska Press, 2002.

Wasco Indians   See WISHRAM AND WASCO INDIANS.

Watkuweis (unknown–unknown) *Nez Perce woman*

Although they were a resourceful and hardy group of frontiersmen, on more than one occasion the CORPS OF DISCOVERY had to rely on Native American women for their survival. The most famous example of this is SACAGAWEA, who not only saved them from starvation by finding edible foodstuffs in the wild but also ensured their safety with her presence on the expedition; seeing her, the Indians they met knew that theirs was a peaceful mission and therefore did not attack them. However, the story of Watkuweis demonstrates another instance when the corps owed their lives to an Indian woman.

In September 1805, after their perilous crossing of the BITTERROOT MOUNTAINS, the corps arrived at WEIPPE PRAIRIE, where they encountered the NEZ PERCE INDIANS. Weak with hunger and exhausted by their trek over the mountains, they were more vulnerable than at any other point on the expedition. (They would be more so later, after eating roots and dried fish and then coming down with dysentery.) The Nez Perce, who had never before encountered white men, were now were faced with a weak and bedraggled group of them. It would have been an easy matter to kill them and take possession of their guns, ammunition, and TRADE goods, thus ensuring the Nez Perce's dominance over other nations, and several of the warriors advocated doing just that.

It was an old woman named Watkuweis who stopped them. Her name meant "Returned from a Faraway Country," and it was an apt description, given her history. As a girl she had been captured by a band of Indians (probably BLACKFEET) and taken to CANADA, where she was sold to a white trader, who showed her great kindness. She was, in fact, consistently treated well, and after she finally managed to return to her people, she retained nothing but good memories of her years among the whites. Thus, according to Nez Perce oral tradition, as the warriors were discussing the explorers' fate, Watkuweis

stepped forward and said, "These are the people who helped me. Do them no hurt."

Neither MERIWETHER LEWIS nor WILLIAM CLARK ever knew the important role Watkuweis played in their survival at that moment. James Ronda has noted that the warriors had other valid reasons for sparing the explorers' lives and lending them assistance, chiefly the recognition that cooperating with the white men would have greater advantages in trade and obtaining guns than killing them would do. All the same, Watkuweis surely made an impression, as a Nez Perce named Many Wounds later recalled: "She told history about the whites and every Nez Perce listened . . . told how the white people were good to her, treated her with kindness. That is why the Nez Percés never made harm to the Lewis and Clark people. . . . We ought to have a monument to her in this far West. She saved much for the white race."

See also WOMEN ON THE EXPEDITION.

Further Reading

Duncan, Dayton, and Ken Burns. *Lewis & Clark: The Journey of the Corps of Discovery.* New York: Alfred A. Knopf, 1998.

Ronda, James P. *Lewis and Clark among the Indians.* Lincoln: University of Nebraska Press, 1984.

Watlala Indians

As MERIWETHER LEWIS and WILLIAM CLARK discovered, the Indians who lived along the lower section of the COLUMBIA RIVER were very different from those who lived further upriver, near its confluence with the SNAKE RIVER. Whereas the WALLA WALLA, the WANAPAM, and the YAKAMA (Yakima) INDIANS who lived well above CELILO FALLS AND THE DALLES were friendly and helpful, the CORPS OF DISCOVERY found that, with some exceptions, those who lived below this point on the river could be neither friendly nor trustworthy. Such was the case with the Watlala Indians.

The Watlala were a band of CHINOOK INDIANS who lived near the WILLAMETTE RIVER in the Cascades area of the COLUMBIA RIVER GORGE. Very little is known of the history of this group, and little has been written about them apart from what is in the expedition's JOURNALS. What is known is that they resented the presence of outsiders in their territory who did not pay tribute, and rather than welcome the explorers, they plagued them with harassment and petty thefts. Lewis was to write of them: "These are the greatest thieves and scoundrels we have met with."

The expedition first encountered the Watlala in early November 1805. Sergeant JOHN ORDWAY recorded what happened when they met again on April 9, 1806: "we crossed over to the North Side & halted at a village of the Wa-cla-lah [Watlala] nation where we bought 5 or 6 fat dogs. found Capt Clarks pipe tommahawk which was Stole from him last fall, below Quick Sand River. we took it from them. they Signd that they bought it below and appeared to be highly afronted at our taking it but were afraid to Show it. . . ." In fact, it was a

SKILLOOT INDIAN who had stolen the tomahawk the previous fall; JOHN COLTER recovered it in a Watlala lodge.

During the return journey, the difficult PORTAGE upstream past the Cascades was made even more difficult for the corps by the Watlala, who crowded and delayed them, stole goods whenever the opportunity presented itself, and even threw stones. On April 11, 1806, several men threatened to rob JOHN SHIELDS, who drew his knife on them. They were not prepared to fight, however, and they fled. That same evening three Watlala stole Lewis's dog SEAMAN. The outraged captain sent three men after the thieves with orders to kill if necessary, but fortunately the Indians released the dog and ran away. Although a Watlala chief hastened to assure Lewis and Clark what the thieves had done was "not the wish of the nation," the captains issued orders to shoot any Indians caught trying to steal expedition property. Thereafter their problems with the Watlata Indians eased enough for them to continue with the portage relatively undisturbed.

In the years following the expedition, with the influx of white settlers, the population of the Watlala dropped significantly. Eventually what few remained joined the WISHRAM AND WASCO INDIANS and moved to the Warm Springs Reservation in Oregon.

Further Reading

Ronda, James P. *Lewis and Clark among the Indians.* Lincoln: University of Nebraska Press, 1984.

weapons

Although FIREARMS played a vital part in the success of the expedition, several other types of weapons are mentioned in the JOURNALS. As well as the archaic ESPONTOON that MERIWETHER LEWIS and WILLIAM CLARK carried and put to good use, the lists of SUPPLIES AND EQUIPMENT at the beginning of the expedition included "18 Tomahaws" and "15 Scalping Knives & belts." Since these appear in the list of supplies for the party of one officer, one sergeant, and 12 men originally authorized by CONGRESS, it is fair to assume that the intention was to issue one knife to each member of the expedition. The difference between hunting knives and the "Scalping Knives" that were apparently issued to the expedition is still a matter for conjecture.

Knives were second only in importance to rifles for the expedition. They killed game for FOOD whenever they could, and Clark noted that they needed four DEER or one BUFFALO a day to feed the party. This may seem a remarkable amount of meat to modern eyes, but no more remarkable than the butchering and meat-dressing skills every man seemed to possess. Throughout the expedition the journals tell of single individuals killing animals and birds of every description and eating it for their evening meal. A good knife was clearly an essential adjunct.

Although some Indian nations in North America had developed metalworking skills, these were mainly in soft metals like gold, silver, and copper and for decorative purposes. Iron working had been brought in by Europeans, and sharp-edged, durable metal knives were highly desirable items among the nomadic and seminomadic nations whom Lewis and Clark expected to meet. Among the lists of Indian GIFTS the expedition took with them, therefore, were 15 dozen knives as well as 4,600 needles and 2,800 fishhooks.

The 12 pipe tomahawks Lewis procured for Indian presents were standard gifts used by traders and trappers to gain the Indians' goodwill. Originating as a basic war club, the tomahawk developed into a war-axe, and for many nations an elaborate, highly decorated tomahawk gave its owner prestige. It is not known when the pipe tomahawk was developed. By the time of Lewis and Clark, the hollow stick with a small axe-head balanced by a pipe bowl on the other side was common. However, the "18 Tomahaws" listed among the expedition's arms appear to have been military equipment because they were issued from the Public Store. They are not described as pipe tomahawks, but when the expedition was visited by SKILLOOT INDIANS during their journey down the COLUMBIA RIVER, WILLIAM CLARK complained on November 4, 1805, that one of them "Stold my pipe Tomahawk which They were Smoking with." Since this had belonged to CHARLES FLOYD and Clark had kept it to return to Floyd's parents, he must have been particularly annoyed. It is cheering to know that, on their return journey in April 1806, JOHN COLTER spotted it in a WATLALA Indian lodge and returned it to Clark.

The journals make occasional mention of Indian weapons. The Skilloot, for instance, were described as being fully armed with war-axes, spears, and bows. In March 1804, before the expedition left CAMP DUBOIS, Lewis sent THOMAS JEFFERSON a box of botanical specimens, including slips of the Osage orange tree. His letter included a note: "So much do the savages esteem the wood of this tree for the purpose of making their bows, that they travel many hundred miles in quest of it."

While Lewis and Clark noted the Indians' horsemanship often, their markmanship with bows and arrows received little attention. One exception is noted during the corps's time with the NEZ PERCE INDIANS in May 1806. The explorers and Indians held foot races, shooting matches, and horse races. The journals recorded with admiration how the Nez Perce, controlling their horses only with their knees, could hit a rolling target with their arrows while at full gallop.

One unusual addition to the armory of the MANDAN INDIANS came from Private JOHN SHIELDS. During the winter of 1804–05 at FORT MANDAN, food was short. Shields, a blacksmith, set up a forge and repaired such metal tools as the Mandan possessed, including hoes and axes. When he had satisfied this need, he began to make war-axes, which proved extremely popular and brought in bushels of CORN from eager customers. On February 5, 1805, Lewis noted:

> *A number of the Indians come with corn for the blacksmith, who being now provided with coal [charcoal] has become one of our greatest resources for procuring grain. They seem particularly attached to a battle-axe, of a very inconvenient figure. It is made wholly of iron, the blade*

extremely thin and from seven to nine inches long; it is sharp at the point and five or six inches on either side, whence the edges converge toward the eye, which is circular. . . . the blade itself being not more than an inch wide; the handle is straight and 12 or 15 inches long; the whole weighs about a pound. The length of the blade, compared with the shortness of the handle, renders it a weapon of very little strength, particularly as it is always used on horseback.

Despite Lewis's criticisms, the war-axes were very popular with Shields's customers. It is reported that he saw some of his Fort Mandan axes in the possession of the Nez Perce on the other side of the CONTINENTAL DIVIDE some 14 months later.

The last category of weapons, swords, ranks with the espontoons as a seemingly inappropriate item of equipment to take on such an arduous journey of exploration. It should be remembered, however, that Lewis and Clark were army officers leading a military unit. The dress uniforms and other CLOTHING they took with them were to emphasize to the Indians they met that they were representatives of the American government. During the early part of the journey, parades were held before formal COUNCILS WITH INDIANS, and officers and men wore full dress. This is why, during the confrontation with the TETON LAKOTA INDIANS (Teton Sioux) on September 25, 1804, Clark wrote: ". . . his [THE PARTISAN's] justures [gestures] were of such a personal nature I felt myself Compeled to Draw my sword, at this motion Capt. Lewis ordered all under arms in the boat. . . ."

Clark's sword may or may not have been a factor in resolving the situation with the Teton Lakota, but it proved its usefulness later in the expedition. By April 1806, during the return journey, the expedition had exhausted their trade goods. When Chief YELLEPT of the WALLA WALLA INDIANS presented Clark with "a very elegant white horse," he made it clear he wanted a kettle in return. Unable to meet this request, Clark gave him his sword plus some powder and ball instead.

Further Reading

Ambrose, Stephen E. *Undaunted Courage: Meriwether Lewis, Thomas Jefferson, and the Opening of the American West.* New York: Simon and Schuster, 1996.

Lewis, Meriwether and William Clark. *The History of the Lewis and Clark Expedition.* Edited by Elliott Coues; 4 vols., 1893, Harper. Reprinted in 3 vols., New York: Dover Publications, 1979.

weasels   See ANIMALS, NEW SPECIES.

weather

The journey of the CORPS OF DISCOVERY across thousands of miles of unknown territory presented them with many tests of their courage and fortitude: hard physical labor, HOSTILE ENCOUNTERS with Indians; hunger; ILLNESSES AND INJURIES; and, not least of all, the weather, which was the one thing they could not control. For 28 months they had to cope with bitter cold, extreme heat, high winds, rain, snow, and hail. Not surprisingly, therefore, observations on the weather appear constantly in the JOURNALS. MERIWETHER LEWIS also maintained tables that logged the weather, day by day, for each month of the expedition.

Fine weather was often noted, but it was the adverse conditions that the journal writers were more likely to record. During the winter of 1804–05 at FORT MANDAN, the temperature averaged 4° above zero in December, 3.4° below in January, and 11.3° above in February, making an average of 4° above zero for the entire winter. The corps arrived at the villages of the MANDAN INDIANS in late October 1804, and by November 12 ice had begun to form on the MISSOURI RIVER. By December 8 the thermometer was registering well below zero, and there were several cases of frostbite. On December 17 the journals noted it was "colder than any we had yet experienced, the thermometer at sunrise being 45 degrees below zero." Consequently, Lewis and WILLIAM CLARK ordered that the sentry be relieved every 30 minutes.

Different conditions would prevail after the expedition left Fort Mandan in April 1805. They were barely two weeks into their journey on the GREAT PLAINS when they found themselves slowed and sometimes stopped by high winds. The problem was the lack of TREES, as Lewis noted: "There is scarcely any timber to brake the wind in this quarter & the country on both sides being level plains, wholly destitute of timber, the wind blows with astonishing violence." In the eight days from April 18 to 25, the expedition was completely unable to move for two entire days and partially immobilized on two others. Clark noted that "we cant move when the wind is high with[out] great risque, and [if] there was no risque the winds is generally a head and often to violent to proceed. . . ." The winds also drove particles of sand from riverbanks and sandbars into their faces, resulting in numerous cases of inflamed eyes, which Lewis treated with a special eyewash.

On June 27, 1805, as the party was in the last stages of its PORTAGE around the GREAT FALLS, a violent thunderstorm suddenly erupted, sending down hail "about the size of pigeon eggs and not unlike them in form," according to Clark. The hailstones were "driven with violence almost incredible. When they struck ground they would rebound to the height of ten or twelve feet and pass twenty or thirty before they touched again. . . . Capt. Lewis weighed one of those hailstones, which weighed three ounces and measured seven inches in circumference; . . . I am convinced if one of those had struck a man on his naked head it would certainly have fractured his skull."

Sergeant JOHN ORDWAY described the need to take shelter: ". . . a hard Shower of rain and hail came on of a Sudden So I got under a Shelving rock on one Side of the creek where a [I] kept dry through the heardest of it. hard thunder. large hail the creek rose So high in a fiew minutes that I had to move from the dry place and proceeded on. the wind blew So high that the hail cut verry hard against me and I could hardly keep my feet. . . . cloudy all night. Some buffalow came down the River dead."

On June 29 Clark, YORK, TOUSSAINT CHARBONNEAU, and SACAGAWEA were approaching the falls when they saw another storm coming on and took refuge under some rocks in a ravine. However, Clark noted, "The rain fell like one volley of water falling from the heavens and gave us time only to get out of the way of a torrent of water which was pouring down the hill into the river with immense force." The water rose so quickly that they would have drowned had not Clark been able to lead Charbonneau and Sacagawea out of the ravine and up to the top of a hill. Here they met a distressed York and others in the party who had abandoned their portage loads when the storm hit. Clark wrote of these men that they were "much bruised, and some nearly killed. One knocked down three times, and others without hats or anything on their heads bloody and complained very much." Clark lost several items in the flood, including his compass, though it was found the next day.

Snow was the prevailing factor in the corps's crossings of the BITTERROOT MOUNTAINS. In September 1805, during their torturous, 11-day passage across the LOLO TRAIL, snow and fallen timber continually obstructed their path. On September 14 Clark noted that it "rained and snowed & hailed the greater part of the day all wet and cold." Two days later PATRICK GASS wrote: "The snow fell so thick, and the day was so dark, that a person could not see to a distance of 200 yards. In the night and during the day the snow fell about 10 inches deep." That same day Clark observed that the "men [were] all wet cold and hungary." The only advantage the snow had was that when melted and mixed with their dried PORTABLE SOUP, the starving explorers at least had some FOOD.

The following year, on June 10, 1806, the expedition set out from CAMP CHOPUNNISH to make their return crossing of the Bitterroots. The NEZ PERCE INDIANS had warned them that it was too soon and they should wait until the snows on the

This page from Lewis's weather diary for January 1805 records temperatures and other details, including the thickness (three feet) of the ice on the Missouri River. *(American Philosophical Society)*

mountain had melted some more. Lewis and Clark stubbornly pressed ahead, only to find the Nez Perce had been right; in some places the snow was 10 feet deep. They had to wait another two weeks on WEIPPE PRAIRIE before they were final able to cross the Lolo Trail.

The most depressing time for the corps was undoubtedly their winter at FORT CLATSOP in 1805–06. From the moment they arrived at the PACIFIC OCEAN in November 1805, the journals are replete with references to the "Disagreeable weather," as Ordway described it. Conditions were almost always "Rainy & wet" or "Wet and rainey." Entry after entry makes reference to "Wind and Rain," "hard rain," "moderate showers of rain," and so on. Throughout the 141 days that the expedition spent at Fort Clatsop, only 12 were free of rain, and of those only half saw any sunshine. Not surprisingly, there many cases of colds and flu.

The constant rain was discouraging for another reason. For the entire first month at the fort, Lewis was unable to make any ASTRONOMICAL OBSERVATIONS. On February 28, 1806, he wrote: "I am mortified at not having it in my power to make more celestial observations since we have been at Fort Clatsop, but such has been the state of the weather that I have found it utterly impracticable."

On March 23, 1806, two journalists provided different perspectives of their happy departure from Fort Clatsop. William Clark wrote: "at this place we had wintered and remained from the 7th of Decr. 1805 to this day and have lived as well as we had any right to expect, and we can say that we were never one day without 3 meals of some kind a day either pore Elk meat or roots, notwithstanding the repeated fall of rain which has fallen almost constantly since we passed the long narrows. . . ." Sergeant PATRICK GASS put it more succinctly: ". . . at 1 o'clock left fort Clatsop. The afternoon was fair, . . ."

Further Reading

Duncan, Dayton, and Ken Burns. *Lewis & Clark: The Journey of the Corps of Discovery.* New York: Alfred A. Knopf, 1998.

Hawke, David Freeman. *Those Tremendous Mountains: The Story of the Lewis and Clark Expedition.* New York: W. W. Norton & Company, 1998.

Large, Arlen. "'It Thundered and Lightened': The Weather Observations of Lewis and Clark." *We Proceeded On* 12, no. 2 (May 1986).

Moulton, Gary E., ed. *The Journals of the Lewis and Clark Expedition.* 13 vols. Lincoln: University of Nebraska Press, 1983–2001.

Weippe Prairie

On September 11, 1805, the Lewis and Clark Expedition left TRAVELERS' REST and began what was to be the most arduous and difficult part of their journey. The previous month they had reached the SHOSHONE INDIANS, from whom they had procured HORSES, and reconnoitered the SALMON RIVER, which proved to be an impassable route through the mountains. This left them no choice but to take the Shoshone's advice and go north up the BITTERROOT RIVER valley and then west along the LOLO TRAIL. To make the crossing over the BITTERROOT MOUNTAINS, they had enlisted the services of a Shoshone guide named OLD TOBY, who now led them from Travelers' Rest onto the trails.

The next 11 days were spent struggling for 160 miles up and down the mountains' precipitous slopes and valleys, picking their way through the brush and fallen trees that impeded every yard of the way. Snow falls slowed them even further, and there was no game; three of their HORSES had to be killed to stave off starvation. On September 18 WILLIAM CLARK took six of the best hunters and went ahead to try and find FOOD. Passing over today's Sherman Peak, he saw to his delight a stretch of grassland in the distance. It took his party another day and a half to reach it, but on September 20 he rode down to Weippe Prairie, where MERIWETHER LEWIS and the main party joined him two days later. Here they were greeted and fed by the NEZ PERCE INDIANS.

Weippe is the Nez Perce word for "very old place." Today Weippe Prairie surrounds modern Weippe, Idaho, southeast of Orofino. At the time of the expedition, it was part of Nez Perce lands. The Indians initially considered killing the explorers but instead decided to welcome them and gave them CAMAS ROOTs and dried salmon. The outcome of this abrupt change in diet for the meat-eating corps (and perhaps due to bacteria in the fish) was severe gastroenteritis in most of the men, and it was not until a week later that they were able to start to build CANOES for their journey down the CLEARWATER RIVER, leaving the Nez Perce behind them on October 6, 1805.

The expedition returned to Weippe Prairie, albeit briefly, on their return journey in 1806. They spent nearly a month with the Nez Perce, refurbishing their equipment and making pack saddles for the horses the Nez Perce had tended for them through the winter; and they waited for the snow to melt on the mountains ahead of them. On June 10, ignoring the warnings of the Nez Perce, the party left CAMP CHOPUNNISH and rode up the steep slopes to their old camp site on the Weippe Prairie. They spent four days here before attempting the Lolo Trail on the morning of June 15, only to find the Nez Perce had been right. Up to 10 feet of snow made travel almost impossible, and without the INDIAN GUIDES they needed, they had no alternative but to return to Weippe Prairie. Not until June 24, with five Nez Perce to guide them, did they finally leave it behind.

With the exception of the PACIFIC OCEAN, Weippe Prairie was probably the most welcome sight the explorers saw on the journey westward. Today descendants of the Nez Perce Indians who greeted them so kindly 200 years ago still live along the CLEARWATER RIVER and still dig for camas roots on Weippe Prairie.

Further Reading

Ambrose, Stephen E. *Undaunted Courage: Meriwether Lewis, Thomas Jefferson, and the Opening of the American West.* New York: Simon and Schuster, 1996.

Cutright, Paul Russell. *Lewis & Clark: Pioneering Naturalists.* Lincoln: University of Nebraska Press/Bison Books, 1989.

Fifer, Barbara, and Vicky Soderberg. *Along the Trail with Lewis and Clark.* Great Falls, Mont.: Montana Magazine, 1998.

Moulton, Gary E., ed. *Atlas of the Lewis and Clark Expedition.* Revised ed. Lincoln: University of Nebraska Press, 1999.

Weiser, Peter (Peter Wiser) (1781–unknown)
private in the permanent party

Private Peter Weiser (also spelled Wiser in some sources) was born on October 3, 1781, in Tulpehocken, Pennsylvania, the son of John Philip and Barbara Weiser. One of the lesser-known members of the CORPS OF DISCOVERY, he officially enlisted in the expedition on January 1, 1804, and served as a cook, quartermaster, and hunter. In February 1804, at CAMP DUBOIS, he and three other men defied Sergeant JOHN ORDWAY's orders to mount guard duty and instead headed to a local whiskey shop to get drunk. Captain MERIWETHER LEWIS had been away when this happened, but upon his return he took swift action, confining the four men to their quarters for 10 days.

Weiser seems to have made no substantial contributions to the expedition aside from being part of the COURT-MARTIAL that tried JOHN NEWMAN for mutiny in October 1804. He was one of the permanent party who traveled all the way to the PACIFIC OCEAN and back, and when the expedition split into two groups during the return, he went with Captain WILLIAM CLARK. Like the other men on the expedition, he had a landmark named after him. In his case it was a tributary of the SNAKE RIVER in western Idaho; it is still the Wiser River today, and the town of Wiser, Idaho, is also named after him.

Following his discharge from the corps, Weiser went to work as a fur trader for MANUEL LISA. His movements become difficult to trace after this. He was recorded as being at Fort Raymond in July 1808, and he was seen on the SNAKE RIVER and in the THREE FORKS area in 1808–10, during which time he presumably also crossed the CONTINENTAL DIVIDE. By 1828 Clark had listed Weiser as "killed," but the date and place of his death are not known. One theory is that he was part of the group (including GEORGE DROUILLARD) that was killed by BLACKFEET INDIANS at Manuel Lisa's trading post at Three Forks in 1810. Other sources, however, indicate that he may have died as late as 1828.

Further Reading

Clarke, Charles G. *The Men of the Lewis and Clark Expedition: A Biographical Roster of the Fifty-One Members and a Composite Diary of Their Activities from All Known Sources.* 1970. Reprint, Lincoln: Bison Books, University of Nebraska Press, 2002.

North Dakota Lewis & Clark Bicentennial Foundation. *Members of the Corps of Discovery.* Bismarck, N.Dak.: United Printing and Mailing, 2000.

PBS Online. *Lewis and Clark: Inside the Corps of Discovery:* "Lesser Known Members of the Corps." Available on-line. URL: http://www.pbs.org/lewisandclark/inside/lesser.html. Downloaded on May 18, 2001.

Welsh Indians

The legend of the "Welsh Indians" is one that has intrigued many over the centuries, including THOMAS JEFFERSON. As with the LOST TRIBES OF ISRAEL, little if any conclusive evidence has come to light that would indicate the Welsh Indians do exist, but the theory is still believed by many. Indeed, MERIWETHER LEWIS and WILLIAM CLARK hoped to find the mythical Indians among the nations they would meet on their journey, as indicated from several references in the expedition's JOURNALS. It should also be noted that verification of the legend would have enabled the British government to counter Spanish claims to discovering the New World.

The origin of the legend lies in Welsh folklore and was promulgated in a 15th-century Welsh poem. This recounted the story of a minor Welsh prince, Madog Ab Owain Gwynedd (Madoc), who sailed with 10 ships and 300 men to land in the West about A.D. 1170 and never returned. The story was repeated in the book *Brut y Tywysogion* (translated in 1584) and became popular in England when Robert Southey wrote his poem "Madoc." The belief was that Prince Madoc had landed at present-day Mobile, Alabama; returned to Wales to report his discovery; and then went back to the New World with a large party of colonists and disappeared into the continent. Although it has been suggested that this party were the founders of the Mayan and Aztec civilizations, the more popular theory has come to concentrate on the MANDAN INDIANS as Madoc's most likely descendants.

While it seems strange to modern eyes, many educated Americans of the 18th and 19th centuries gave credence to the legend. Jefferson, a leading thinker of the day, certainly discussed it with MERIWETHER LEWIS when planning the expedition. It was also widely enough known for Sergeant JOHN ORDWAY to write of the expedition's first meeting with the FLATHEAD (Salish) INDIANS in September 1805: "These natives are well dressed, decent looking Indians; light complexioned . . . they have the most curious language of any we have seen before. . . . They talk as though they lisped or have a bur on their tongue. . . . We suppose they are the Welch Indians, if there is any such." Sergeant PATRICK GASS described them as "the whitest Indians I ever saw."

The widespread popularity of the legend and its association with the Mandan almost certainly began with the American William Bowles. Late in the 18th century he traveled to London and gave a series of lectures in which he claimed to be an Indian, a descendant of the Madoc party (Madocians). Such was the enthusiasm he aroused that a number of Welshmen raised funds to send JOHN EVANS to North America to investigate the theory. He reached the Mandan villages in 1796 and spent the winter there, but as Clark wrote, Evans "went as high as the Mandans in 1796–7 and . . . returned with a conv[iction] that there were no Welsh Indians."

Despite this and despite the later realization that the Flathead's language was so different because they came from a tribal group different from the SHOSHONE INDIANS, the legend of the Mandan's descent from Europeans still has its adherents. In 1966 writer Gene Jones went even further, suggesting in an article published in *Real West* that they were descendants of the Vikings. In the United Kingdom there are still many folklorists who give the legend considerable credence. They quote a Welsh missionary captured by Indians in the late 17th century who escaped death when he prayed in Welsh. His words were immediately recognized by his captors, who conversed with him, treated him as an honored guest, and returned him to where they had captured him.

In 1995–97, the Welshman Tony Williams carried out a further study of the legend and claimed that the Mandan still used many words of Welsh, built their houses on the design of medieval Wales, and copied the Welsh coracle for their light, portable, skin-covered BULL BOAT. He furthermore claimed that a Mandan historic scroll painting of 1907—which depicts the lineage of the tribal "corn-priest" who came from an unknown land to show the Mandan how to farm—had chronological markers giving a date that coincided with Madoc's disappearance.

While these findings are merely corroborative rather than conclusive, it would be unwise to dismiss the Madoc legend as pure myth. Archaeologists and historians long derided as equally absurd the theory that the Vikings had reached America; this is now an accepted fact. Folklore may exaggerate, but it should not be ignored.

Further Reading

Duncan, Dayton, and Ken Burns. *Lewis & Clark: The Journey of the Corps of Discovery*. New York: Alfred A. Knopf, 1998.

Jones, Gene. "The Mandan Indians, Descendants of the Vikings." *Real West* 9, no. 47 (May 1966): 31–32.

Kimberly, Howard. "Madoc: Were the Welsh the First European Americans?" Madoc 1170 website. Available on-line. URL: http://www.madoc1170.com/home.htm. Updated on February 7, 2001.

Pugh, Ellen. *Brave His Soul: The Story of Prince Madog of Wales and His Discovery of America in 1170*. New York: Dodd, Mead & Company, 1970.

Williams, David. *John Evans and the Legend of Madoc, 1770–1779*. Cardiff: University of Wales Press, 1963.

Werner, William (unknown–unknown) *private in the permanent party*

One of the least-known members of the CORPS OF DISCOVERY, Private William Werner served primarily as a cook. He was probably born in Kentucky; there is no record of any army service prior to his joining the expedition late in 1803 (he was officially enrolled as of January 1, 1804). He was a DISCIPLINE problem during the winter of 1803–04 at CAMP DUBOIS, and for a brief period after the expedition began its journey up the MISSOURI RIVER, those problems continued. During the layover in ST. CHARLES in May 1804, Werner and Privates HUGH HALL and JOHN COLLINS were court-martialed for being absent without leave. Hall and Werner were sentenced to 25 lashes on their bare backs, while Collins received 100 lashes. Thereafter Werner caused no further trouble, and later that year he sat on the panel for the court-martial of Private JOHN NEWMAN for mutiny.

Early in January 1806, Werner was part of the party that accompanied Captain WILLIAM CLARK to see a beached WHALE. Unfortunately, the TILLAMOOK INDIANS had already stripped the whale of its blubber by the time they got there. Later that same month Werner and THOMAS HOWARD were sent to get some salt from the SALTWORKS, as it was needed for the preservation of meat brought back to FORT CLATSOP by the expedition's hunters. Foul weather and a bad road combined to delay their return to the fort until some five days later.

When the corps was split into two parties during the return journey in 1806, Werner was included in MERIWETHER LEWIS's group. Following the expedition's return, he became an Indian agent for William Clark for a short period. Clark later believed that Werner settled in Virginia, where he was reported to be around 1828. However, the date and place of his death are unknown.

Further Reading

Clarke, Charles G. *The Men of the Lewis and Clark Expedition: A Biographical Roster of the Fifty-One Members and a Composite Diary of Their Activities from All Known Sources*. 1970. Reprint, Lincoln: Bison Books, University of Nebraska Press, 2002.

North Dakota Lewis & Clark Bicentennial Foundation. *Members of the Corps of Discovery*. Bismarck, N.Dak.: United Printing and Mailing, 2000.

PBS Online. *Lewis and Clark: Inside the Corps of Discovery:* "Lesser Known Members of the Corps." Available on-line. URL: http://www.pbs.org/lewisandclark/inside/lesser.html. Downloaded on May 18, 2001.

westward expansion

In 1803 the population of the United States was more than 5.3 million. The nation was still young, still rural, and still in the early stages of its growth. Although most people of that era never traveled more than 25 miles from their homes in their lifetimes, others were beginning to feel the pull of the West, and migrations to the valleys of the OHIO RIVER and MISSISSIPPI RIVER were already taking place. Since independence was declared in 1776, four more states had been added to the Union, the latest being Ohio on March 1, 1803. Just six weeks later, FRANCE offered to sell the LOUISIANA TERRITORY west of the Mississippi to the United States, an offer President THOMAS JEFFERSON accepted immediately. The LOUISIANA PURCHASE more than doubled the size of the young nation and allowed for its eventual expansion across the continent to the Pacific coast. The gateway to the West had been opened.

Certainly Jefferson foresaw a period of American expansion, but neither he nor anyone else could have imagined the speed and scale with which it unfolded over the next nine decades. Once the Louisiana Purchase had been agreed, two important tasks had to be considered: exploring and mapping the new territory, which was already under way, and dealing with the Indians who lived within its boundaries. Jefferson was not worried about the possible interference of foreign governments in the American march westward; FRANCE and GREAT BRITAIN in particular were preoccupied with the Napoleonic War, and as he noted to JAMES MADISON, "we should have such an empire for liberty as she has never surveyed since the creation: & I am persuaded no constitution was ever before so well calculated as ours for extensive empire & self-government."

Jefferson's Indian policy, however, may have been too simplistic. In his mind U.S. citizens and those Indians who could be civilized would live in the area east of the Mississippi—at that time the demarcation line of the frontier—while the remaining Indians would live in the West on what amounted to a large reservation. To this end, he wanted to remove Indians from the East and send them west, while at the same time moving non-Indians then west of the Mississippi to the East. This proved impossible to implement. Even before the Lewis and Clark Expedition returned from their historic journey to the West Coast, the first wave of American fur trappers and traders had begun to travel up the MISSOURI RIVER and to advance to the ROCKY MOUNTAINS.

Once begun, the tide could not be stemmed, although it flowed slowly at first. ZEBULON PIKE and later Stephen Long had described the western plains as a vast desert, which did not attract settlers in much numbers. Instead, it was the fur-trapping and exploring MOUNTAIN MEN who were the first pioneers of the American West, opening routes to the Pacific coast that others would follow. When in 1842 the U.S. government began to issue land grants in the OREGON TERRITORY, which was then jointly occupied by the United States and Great Britain, the initial trickle of migration became a flood during the next three decades.

Americans were spurred on to move west by the words of John L. O'Sullivan, who in 1845 wrote that it was "our manifest destiny to overspread the continent allotted by Providence for the free development of our yearly multiplying millions." (The term *manifest destiny* would subsequently be used to justify American expansion outside the continent as well.) In 1846–47 the first of the great Mormon treks began, and during the next 22 years some 70,000 Mormons migrated to Salt Lake City. After gold was discovered in California in 1848, miners and fortune seekers joined farmers, ranchers, and merchants in moving west to make new lives. In all, between 1840 and 1870 more than 350,000 settlers traveled overland by way of the OREGON TRAIL, Mormon Trail, Santa Fe Trail, and other routes.

Meanwhile, the United States was expanding its boundaries. Florida had already been added to the nation in 1819 and would become a state in 1845. That same year Texas, which had won its freedom from Mexico in 1836, also became a state. The following year saw the signing of the Oregon Treaty, which settled the border of the U.S.-Canadian border at the 49th parallel and added 522 million acres to the country. In 1848 the Treaty of Guadalupe Hidalgo ended the U.S.-Mexican War and added a further 500,000 square miles of territory, including the future states of California, Nevada, and Utah. Finally, on December 30, 1853, the Gadsden Purchase established the current boundaries of the continental United States with the acquisition of 29,644 square miles in the southernmost sections of what is now Arizona and New Mexico. The country now truly extended from coast to coast, just 50 years after the Louisiana Purchase, and as each new territory was acquired, settlers poured in.

Throughout these years of non-Indian migration, the Native Americans of the GREAT PLAINS and the Pacific Coast were ravaged by disease, forced to give up their lands, and removed to reservations. As they suffered the breaking of one treaty after the next, confinement to the most arid lands in the West, and the loss of their way of life, many nations engaged in armed resistance against the U.S. government. The wars for the West ended with the infamous massacre at Wounded Knee in 1890. That same year the U.S. Census Bureau declared the frontier to be officially closed. Americans had fulfilled their destiny.

See also EFFECTS AND INFLUENCES OF THE EXPEDITION; EXPLORATION, LATER.

Further Reading

Ambrose, Stephen E. *Undaunted Courage: Meriwether Lewis, Thomas Jefferson, and the Opening of the American West.* New York: Simon and Schuster, 1996.

Billington, Ray Allen, and Martin Ridge. *Westward Expansion: A History of the American Frontier,* 6th ed. Albuquerque: University of New Mexico Press, 2001.

Colorado Migration Project. "Westward Expansion." Available online. URL: http://www.americanwest.com/pages/wexpansi.htm. Downloaded on May 24, 2001.

Goetzmann, William. *Exploration and Empire: The Explorer and the Scientist in the Winning of the American West.* New York: Alfred A. Knopf, 1966.

Hebard, Grace Raymond, and E. A. Brininstool. *The Bozeman Trail: Historical Accounts of the Blazing of the Overland Routes in the Northwest, and the Fights with Red Cloud's Warriors.* Lincoln: University of Nebraska Press, 1990.

Horsman, Reginald. *Expansion and American Indian Policy, 1783–1812.* East Lansing: Michigan State University Press, 1967.

Montgomery, M. R. *Jefferson and the Gun-Men: How the West Was almost Lost.* New York: Crown Publishers, 2000.

Waldman, Carl. "Wars for the West." In: *Atlas of the North American Indian.* Revised ed. New York: Checkmark Books, 1999, pp. 147–182.

Weuche (La Liberator, Handshake, The Shake Hand) (unknown–unknown) *Yankton Nakota chief*

Among the first Native Americans the Lewis and Clark Expedition met as they traveled up the MISSOURI RIVER were the YANKTON NAKOTA INDIANS (Yankton Sioux) in late August 1804. Less than two weeks earlier they had held a council with the chiefs of the OTOE (Oto) and the MISSOURI INDIANS. The outcome was mixed, partly due to the Otoe's and the Missouri's disappointment with their GIFTS and partly due to the insistence of MERIWETHER LEWIS and WILLIAM

CLARK that one chief for each nation be designated "first chief." This was a non-Indian concept to which they stubbornly held despite the affront it gave to other chiefs. In the case of the Yankton Nakota, it was Weuche whom they named first chief.

The council with the Yankton took place on August 30, 1804 at CALUMET BLUFF. The corps had prepared by wearing their full dress uniforms, running up a flag, and firing the bow swivel gun on the KEELBOAT. The Nakota also came in full regalia, and four musicians led the chiefs into camp with great ceremony. Lewis delivered the speech he had given to the Otoe and the Missouri and would present to other nations' chiefs: They now had a "great white father" in Washington (THOMAS JEFFERSON) who desired peace among the Indian nations and wished them to enter into TRADE with the ST. LOUIS merchants, and he invited the Yankton chiefs to go and meet the president in Washington. The chiefs listened intently and then gave the response the captains were to hear often in their dealings with Indians: They would think it over and let the Americans know in the morning.

The presentation of gifts followed, and Weuche was given a military coat trimmed with red lace as well as a military cocked hat and an American flag; other chiefs were given medals. To what extent the Yankton were offended by this apparent favoritism is not recorded. In the morning, when they gave their responses, it was Weuche who spoke first. His primary concern was the issue of trade and the ability to get the guns and ammunition that the Yankton desperately needed for their survival; this was an issue that other chiefs also touched on in their replies. Weuche made special note of his people's poverty and the need for a source of trade goods—those on the keelboat had impressed him, and he wanted to help himself immediately, something the captains refused to allow. Nevertheless, the chief was pointed in his remarks regarding the expedition's gifts, noting that something more than medals and beads were needed.

Weuche was astute enough to realize that acknowledging the new U.S. government and going to Washington in the spring would be to his advantage, so he offered to organize a delegation from the Nakota and other nations. He stipulated, however, that the interpreter PIERRE DORION accompany the delegation. The captains agreed readily to this suggestion and subsequently left Dorion with the Yankton. As to the Lewis and Clark plan for intertribal peace, while the chief concurred this was desirable, he also thought such matters were best left to the Indians themselves.

Weuche's response to Lewis and Clark was that of many of the chiefs they met. He wanted something more substantial than what they were offering, and their failure to achieve agreement to their plans for peace and trade was a reflection of their inability to understand the problems of the Indians with whom they were dealing.

Further Reading

Ronda, James P. *Lewis and Clark among the Indians.* Lincoln: University of Nebraska Press, 1984.

whale

The CORPS OF DISCOVERY found the winter of 1805–06 at FORT CLATSOP uncomfortable and depressing. The weather was wet for weeks on end, making firewood impossible to dry out properly; there was no whiskey to be had; and only ELK to be hunted and killed for FOOD. Though it was good to have meat, eating elk at every meal, enlivened only by dogmeat traded from the CLATSOP INDIANS, was tedious.

On December 27, 1805, the Clatsop told the captains of a beached whale on the shore some distance to the south. Bad weather prevented WILLIAM CLARK from setting out at once, and on January 3 he wrote that the Clatsop had brought to the fort "a Small quantity of fresh blubber, this blubber they informed us they had obtained from their neighbours the Cal la' mox who inhabit the coast to the S.E. near one of their villages a whale had recently perished. this blubber the Indians eat and esteem it excellent food." On January 5 ALEXANDER WILLARD and PETER WEISER returned from the SALTWORKS, confirming the news of the whale and bringing some blubber with them.

A party led by Clark finally set out on January 6 and reached the beached whale two days later, at the mouth of Ecola Creek, just above present-day Cannon Beach, Oregon. To their disappointment, the whale had already been stripped by the TILLAMOOK INDIANS, but Clark managed to secure some 300 pounds of blubber and several gallons of oil. It was not as much as he had hoped to cull but enough to introduce a rare moment of whimsy into his journal: "Small as this stock is I prise it highly, and thank providence for directing the whale to us; and think him much more kind to us than he was to jonah, having Sent this monster to be Swallowed by us in Sted of Swallowing of us as jonah's did."

Clark estimated the whale carcass to be some 105 feet long (probably an overestimate), and naturalists now believe it was either a great gray whale or a blue whale, the largest of the whale family. He also noted the Indians' method to render down the blubber, "boiling whale in a trough of about 20 gallons with hot stones, and the oyle they put into a canoe." MERIWETHER LEWIS made notes regarding the blubber after it was eaten: "It was white & not unlike the fat of Poark, tho' the texture was more spongey and sometimes coarser. I had a part of it cooked and found it very pallitable and tender, it resembled the BEAVER or dog in flavour."

Somewhat surprisingly, among the party that spent four days traveling to and from the site of the beached whale was SACAGAWEA, who had asked to go. Clark was reluctant to let her come with them but eventually agreed. Her plaintive appeal still touches a chord after 200 years: "She observed that She had travelled a long way with us to See the great waters, and that now that monstrous fish was also to be Seen, She thought it very hard that She could not be permitted to See either (She had never yet been to the Ocian)."

Further Reading

Amacker, Mary Ann. "Captain Clark and Party's Journey over Tillamook Head (Clark's Point of View) to the Site of the Beached

Whale at Ecola Creek." Available on-line. URL: http://www.nps.gov.focl/whale1.htm. Downloaded on May 25, 2001.

Burroughs, Raymond Darwin, ed. *The Natural History of the Lewis and Clark Expedition.* East Lansing: Michigan State University Press, 1995.

Cutright, Paul Russell. *Lewis & Clark: Pioneering Naturalists.* Lincoln: University of Nebraska Press/Bison Books, 1989.

Whelan, Israel (1752–1806) *purveyor of public supplies*

During the last three weeks of May and the first week of June 1803 in PHILADELPHIA, MERIWETHER LEWIS consulted the specialists to whom THOMAS JEFFERSON had sent him for advice and tutelage—BENJAMIN SMITH BARTON, ANDREW ELLICOTT, ROBERT PATTERSON, BENJAMIN RUSH, and CASPAR WISTAR. While Lewis learned from these scientific luminaries, he also visited Israel Whelan, a man who, like JOHN HAY, was to play an important, if often overlooked, part in the success of the Lewis and Clark expedition.

Whelan, a Philadelphia merchant, had been appointed purveyor of public stores by President John Adams, and it was to him that Lewis came with a list of more than 200 items to be purchased for the expedition. Whelan had already had warning of Lewis's arrival by way of a War Department directive, instructing him to provide whatever Lewis wanted. Even more persuasive was the draft for $1,000 that came with it.

Among the long list of SUPPLIES AND EQUIPMENT that Lewis commissioned Whelan to procure was the PORTABLE SOUP that the expedition carried over the CONTINENTAL DIVIDE and ate on the LOLO TRAIL two years later. A hundredweight of pigtail TOBACCO was to be bought as well as more than 1,000 moccasin awls. Whelan also found for Lewis more than 50 different types of GIFTS for Indians and most of his camp equipment, mathematical instruments, and medical supplies.

Records still exist showing many of the suppliers Whelan used. The portable soup came from François Baillet of 21 North Ninth Street; the 130 rolls of pigtail tobacco were supplied by Thomas Leiper of 12 High Street. A large order for awls, augers, and gimlets were met by Harvey and Worth of 62 North Front Street, while Gillaspy & Strong of 103 South Second Street provided the medical and surgical supplies.

Apart from Lewis's famous air rifle, there has always been one item to stir the interest of FIREARMS enthusiasts. Lewis was very proud (and with reason) of the leaden canisters he had made to carry powder for the rifles. They kept the powder dry in the most adverse conditions and were so made that the lead canister, when melted down, provided just the right number of balls for the powder the canister had contained. There is still argument as to whether this was an accepted practice of the time or a new idea of Lewis's, but perhaps it was the idea of the man who supplied Whelan with the canisters: George Ludlan, plumber, of 96 South Second Street, Philadelphia.

Although Whelan did well by Lewis and the expedition, his role in the PREPARATIONS FOR THE EXPEDITION is often unnoticed in written accounts. He has, however, another claim to fame. While few Americans remember Israel Whelan of Philadelphia, purveyor of public supplies, many remember him as Whelan, the "Fighting Quaker" who forsook the precepts of his religion to fight with the colonial forces in the American Revolution, became a friend of George Washington, and rose to the rank of commissary-general.

Further Reading
Cutright, Paul Russell. *Contributions of Philadelphia to Lewis and Clark History.* Philadelphia: Philadelphia Chapter Lewis and Clark Trail Heritage Foundation, 2001. Also available on-line. URL: http://www.lewisandclarkphila.org/philadelphia/philadelphiacutright conten.html. Updated on October 15, 2001.

whiskey See ALCOHOL.

White, Isaac (1777–unknown) *private in the temporary party*

Information is scanty on Private Isaac White. Born in Holliston, Massachusetts, he was 5'7½" tall and had sandy hair and a fair complexion. He was recruited at KASKASKIA for the first part of the expedition up the MISSOURI RIVER to FORT MANDAN. He returned to ST. LOUIS with the KEELBOAT party under the command of Corporal RICHARD WARFINGTON in April 1805. There is otherwise no record of him.

Further Reading
Clarke, Charles G. *The Men of the Lewis and Clark Expedition: A Biographical Roster of the Fifty-One Members and a Composite Diary of Their Activities from All Known Sources.* 1970. Reprint, Lincoln: Bison Books, University of Nebraska Press, 2002.

White Bear Islands

When the CORPS OF DISCOVERY reached the GREAT FALLS of the MISSOURI RIVER on June 16, 1805, they realized that they were going to have to carry their CANOES and supplies around not one set of waterfalls but five. It soon became evident that the PORTAGE was going to be an agonizingly slow and difficult process that involved the party dragging everything across some 18 miles of rough ground covered with PRICKLY PEARS. Thus, two camps were set up. The lower portage camp was at PORTAGE CREEK (now named Belt Creek), just east of modern Great Falls, Montana. For the upper camp, after WILLIAM CLARK conducted a careful reconnaissance, a spot on the south bank, some three miles west of the MEDICINE RIVER, was chosen. (While this lengthened the already long portage, the banks nearer the falls were too difficult and unsafe for the expedition's purposes.) This camp lay opposite three small islands in the river, and since the area was soon discovered to be infested with grizzly BEARS, one of whom chased JOHN COLTER into the river, the corps named them White Bear Islands.

After several days of preparations, the portage began on June 22. To transport the canoes, a crude-wheeled frame had been constructed by cutting down the only large cottonwood tree in the area. Sawing it crossways in sections, the men had made rough wheels and cut the mast of one of the PIROGUES into sections to act as axles. Each canoe was then placed on this frame and dragged overland, while the men's moccasins were cut to shreds by the dried, churned-up earth and the ever-present prickly pears.

While Clark and the majority of the party labored up and down the portage route, Lewis and three men set about building the collapsible, IRON-FRAME BOAT that had been transported to this point. It took until July 2—a total of 10 days—for the portage to be completed. On that day, perhaps to celebrate the conclusion of their arduous portage, they launched a concerted attack on one of the islands in the river and killed a large grizzly they found there. Two days later they celebrated the Fourth of July by dancing to PIERRE CRUZATTE's fiddle and enjoying the last ration of whiskey they were to have for more than a year.

Meanwhile, work continued on the collapsible boat, but it was not until July 9 that it became clear that the boat would never float without a proper sealant. Fortunately, about 20 miles away the men found some cottonwood TREES that were big enough to be made into canoes. As at Portage Creek, some equipment and baggage were put into CACHES, including the rough wheels that had brought the baggage across the portage. The expedition finally left White Bear Islands on July 13, 1805, nearly a month after they had first arrived at the Great Falls.

A year later, on July 11, 1806, Meriwether Lewis, PATRICK GASS, and eight men arrived back at the site on horseback. Gass's JOURNALS illustrate succinctly how much the members of the expedition had learned and how quickly they could overcome minor problems: ". . . and having gone eight miles, came to the Missouri at the Bear islands, nearly opposite our old encampment. Here our hunters, in a short time, killed five buffaloe; and we saved the best of the meat; and of the skins made two canoes to transport ourselves and baggage across the river." By this stage in the journey, killing BUFFALO, skinning them, and using the skins to make BULL BOATS was so commonplace to Gass that he did not feel it worth any particular mention, except to say the bull boats "served the purpose very well."

While many of the botanical specimens the corps had left in the cache were spoiled, the crude cottonwood wheels and the map of the Missouri that Lewis and Clark had drawn were safe. Though disappointed that the specimens had been lost, Lewis kept to the complex and, in many respects, almost foolhardy plan he had agreed on with Clark. Having already split the expedition into three groups, it was now to be split into four (and later five). Lewis and three men would take some horses and go north to explore the MARIAS RIVER. Sergeant Gass and five men were to wait at White Bear Islands for JOHN ORDWAY and his men who were coming down the Missouri River in canoes that had been left at THREE FORKS. Meanwhile, Clark and the remainder of the party were making their way down the YELLOWSTONE RIVER from where he sent NATHANIEL PRYOR and three men off in another direction, making the fifth split of the party.

This daring decision to divide the expedition into so many parts demonstrates the confidence Lewis and Clark had in their men and exemplifies their extraordinary LEADERSHIP. Captains, sergeants, and privates all trusted each other implicitly. As Stephen Ambrose writes in *Undaunted Courage: Meriwether Lewis, Thomas Jefferson, and the Opening of the American West*, ". . . they had become a family. They could recognize each other at night by a cough, or a gesture; they knew each other's skills, and weakness, and habits, and background . . . where they came from, what their parents were like, what dreams they had. . . ."

And they looked after each other. At White Bear Islands, a worried Lewis would not leave on his exploration of the Marias until GEORGE DROUILLARD had returned safely from his pursuit of the Indians who had stolen some of their HORSES. He trusted the men whom he was leaving at the Great Falls to conduct the portage and to carry out their instructions without hesitation or fear. He told Gass how long to wait for Ordway to arrive at the falls, how long to wait for him (Lewis) at the mouth of the Marias, and where to meet Clark (at the mouth of the Yellowstone). Gass's journals describe this prosaically: "Captain Lewis informed us, that should his life and health be preserved he would meet us at the mouth of Maria's river on the 5th of August."

The captains' trust in their men was completely justified. Ordway and his men came down the river to join Gass's party on July 19. By July 26 they had taken all the canoes and baggage overland down past the falls and had left White Bear Islands behind them. They dug out the pirogue from its hiding place at the lower end of the falls, resumed their journey, and met Lewis and his party just two days later, near the mouth of the Marias, as they had arranged. In due course the entire expedition was reunited and heading down the Missouri River for ST. LOUIS.

Depending on the height of the water, one of the White Bear Islands can still be seen today, although changes of the river's course have made it part of the shore just north of Sand Coulee Creek and south of present-day Great Falls, Montana.

Further Reading

Ambrose, Stephen E. *Undaunted Courage: Meriwether Lewis, Thomas Jefferson, and the Opening of the American West.* New York: Simon and Schuster, 1996.

Fifer, Barbara, and Vicky Soderberg. *Along the Trail with Lewis and Clark.* Great Falls, Mont.: Montana Magazine, 1998.

MacGregor, Carol Lynn, ed. *The Journals of Patrick Gass, Member of the Lewis and Clark Expedition.* Missoula, Mont.: Mountain Press Publishing Company, 1997.

Moulton, Gary E., ed. *Atlas of the Lewis and Clark Expedition.* Revised ed. Lincoln: University of Nebraska Press, 1999.

White Cliffs See MISSOURI BREAKS.

Whitehouse, Joseph (ca. 1775–unknown)
private in the permanent party

Although the captains and sergeants of the Lewis and Clark expedition kept JOURNALS, it was not usual for privates to do so as well. Joseph Whitehouse and ROBERT FRAZIER were two who did, although only Whitehouse's made it into print. He was born in Fairfax County, Virginia, and moved to Kentucky with his family when he was about nine years old. He enlisted in the U.S. Army in 1798 and was posted at FORT MASSAC when MERIWETHER LEWIS recruited him for the expedition. He became a member of the permanent party as of January 1, 1804.

Whitehouse appears to have been a corporal when he first joined the CORPS OF DISCOVERY, for this is how WILLIAM CLARK refers to him in a journal entry dated December 26, 1803. However, during the winter of 1803–04 at CAMP DUBOIS, he and some other men were expelled from the corps for disorderly conduct. He was later readmitted and assigned to the permanent party, but thereafter he is referred to as a private. He apparently excelled at making buckskin CLOTHING and sometimes employed his skills to provide tailoring services to the other men. He also made moccasins for Captain Clark as a Christmas present in 1805.

Whitehouse began to write his journal on May 14, 1804, the day the expedition set off from Camp Dubois on the MISSOURI RIVER, and continued it to November 6, 1805. During that time he recorded events and places largely covered in other journals but providing his own perspective as an enlisted man. When, on April 13, 1804, a PIROGUE piloted by TOUSSAINT CHARBONNEAU nearly capsized, quick thinking on the parts of PIERRE CRUZATTE and SACAGAWEA saved the disaster that nearly resulted. Whitehouse recorded the episode and noted: "Some of the papers and nearly all the books got wet, but not altogether spoiled." He also provided vivid descriptions of the Indians the corps met, detailing their appearance and ceremonies. He noted of the FLATHEAD (Salish) that they were "the likelyest and honestst Savages we have ever yet Seen" and made a valiant attempt to render in writing their strange language, which he described as a "brogue."

In early August 1805, as the expedition struggled up the rapid waters of the JEFFERSON RIVER, Whitehouse was nearly killed in an effort to keep his dugout canoe from being swamped. Caught for a time between the bottom of the boat and the riverbed underneath, he finally reached a deeper point where he could allow the boat to pass over him. Lewis later wrote, "Had the water been two inches shallower, it must inevitably have crushed him to death."

Following the expedition, Whitehouse received double pay and a land warrant, which he sold to GEORGE DROUILLARD (who later made a significant profit on it). Although he had started out the expedition committed to the military and to an ambition to see the country, afterward he left the army and fell into a wastrel life, accumulating a number of debts. When the War of 1812 broke out, he rejoined the army but deserted in 1817. Thereafter his whereabouts are unknown, nor is it recorded where and when he died. Some 100 years after the expedition, though, Whitehouse came back into public notice when scholar Reuben Gold Thwaites found his journal and published parts of it. In 1997, a more complete version of the Whitehouse journal was published by Gary Moulton; it includes a more recently discovered paraphrased text that extends the journal to April 2, 1806.

Further Reading
Clarke, Charles G. *The Men of the Lewis and Clark Expedition: A Biographical Roster of the Fifty-One Members and a Composite Diary of Their Activities from All Known Sources.* 1970. Reprint, Lincoln: Bison Books, University of Nebraska Press, 2002.

North Dakota Lewis & Clark Bicentennial Foundation. *Members of the Corps of Discovery.* Bismarck, N.Dak.: United Printing and Mailing, 2000.

PBS Online. *Lewis and Clark: Inside the Corps of Discovery:* "Private Joseph Whitehouse." Available on-line. URL: http://www.pbs.org/lewisandclark/inside/jwhit.html. Downloaded on May 18, 2001.

Wilkinson, James (1757–1825) *U.S. Army general, informant for the Spanish*

In April 1806, as the CORPS OF DISCOVERY was returning from the Pacific coast, another expedition organized by WILLIAM DUNBAR set out to explore the Red River. Their mission was aborted, however, when the Spanish military intercepted them in July 1806 and ordered them to turn back. It was later learned that SPAIN had made a similar attempt to stop the Lewis and Clark party but had failed to find them. Even more shocking—but perhaps not surprising—was the identity of the man who had informed the Spanish authorities of the U.S. explorations: General James Wilkinson, undoubtedly the most notorious of all the public figures connected with the expedition.

Wilkinson was born into a merchant-planter family in Calvert County, Maryland. A medical student when the American Revolution broke out, he joined the colonial forces and was commissioned a captain, serving under Benedict Arnold and Horatio Gates before being brevetted a brigadier general and appointed secretary of the Board of War in 1778. When his role in the Conway Cabal—a plot to supplant George Washington as the U.S. Army's commander—was revealed, he was forced to resign his commission. He was subsequently appointed clothier general to the army, failed in that role, tried his hand at farming, and for a short period served in the Pennsylvania legislature.

In 1784 Wilkinson moved to Kentucky, where he began to agitate for the separation of that territory from Virginia. An amoral man who sought personal gain at any cost, in 1787 he established connections with authorities in New Orleans and won a trading monopoly in exchange for swearing allegiance to the Spanish governor. His monopoly was later rendered ineffective when Spain opened up trade on the MISSISSIPPI RIVER, but he continued to foment discontent in the territory and to receive payments from the Spanish for information serving their interests.

For financial reasons Wilkinson rejoined the army, and again he rose rapidly through the ranks, being made a brigadier general under General Anthony Wayne in March 1792. Still a Spanish informant, he attempted unsuccessfully to discredit Wayne. After Wayne's death, Wilkinson was given command of the southern frontier in 1798, but by this time he had become the subject of harsh criticism for his land deals, speculation in army contracts, and apparent association with the Spanish. Despite his scheming and duplicity, he nonetheless retained his public position and joined with William C. C. Claiborne in formally taking possession of the LOUISIANA PURCHASE for the United States in 1803. The following year, however, he entered into a conspiracy with Aaron Burr to invade Mexico.

It was not until after his death that research in the Spanish archives showed the extent of Wilkinson's betrayal of his country. In March 1804 he sent a message to Madrid from New Orleans reporting that an expedition headed by MERIWETHER LEWIS was about to ascend the MISSOURI RIVER in an attempt to cross the continent to the PACIFIC OCEAN. He suggested a course of action for the Spanish: "An express ought immediately to be sent to the governor of Santa Fe, and another to the captain-general of Chihuaga [Chihuahua], in order that they may detach a sufficient body of chasseurs to intercept Captain Lewis and his party, who are on the Missouri River, and force them to retire or take them prisoners." Anxious to prevent an American invasion of their territory, Spain acted on Wilkinson's suggestion, and the governor of New Mexico sent out four military parties to intercept the expedition. While they never got close to Lewis and Clark, they did succeed in stopping the RED RIVER EXPEDITION in 1806.

In spring 1805 President THOMAS JEFFERSON appointed Wilkinson governor of LOUISIANA TERRITORY, in which capacity he dispatched ZEBULON PIKE on two exploratory missions. (It should be noted that during the second expedition Pike and his men were captured by the Spanish, but Wilkinson apparently had no connection to this.) He also arranged the passage of a delegation of Indians to Washington under the command of Captain AMOS STODDARD and sent American troops to guard a disputed area between eastern Texas and Western Louisiana. However, after proving vastly unpopular as governor—in part due to his tendency to grant trading licenses with abandon and foment disputes over land titles—Wilkinson was removed from office in May 1806 and sent back to the southern frontier. By this time it seemed likely the Burr conspiracy was about to be exposed, so Wilkinson attempted to save himself by turning on Burr warning President Jefferson of a plot to invade Mexico and suggesting that troops should be posted in New Orleans. Typically, he then advised Mexico's viceroy of the invasion and demanded money to prevent it. He subsequently declared martial law in New Orleans and arrested as many Burr associates as he could locate.

Burr himself was arrested in Mississippi Territory and consequently put on trial for treason. Wilkinson was the chief witness against his former friend but only barely escaped prosecution himself. Publicly reviled, with few supporters (oddly, one was Jefferson), he was brought before a court of inquiry but was acquitted six months later. Jefferson then sent him back to New Orleans to discuss a possible alliance with Spanish authorities in Havana and Pensacola. This time Wilkinson's scheming and intrigues resulted in a court-martial ordered by JAMES MADISON, who by that time (July 1811) had become president. On December 25, 1811, Wilkinson was found not guilty, but suspicion still surrounded him.

His continued survival was remarkable but did not last. After resuming command of New Orleans, he was commissioned a major general in 1813 and sent to the Canadian frontier, where his attempt to launch an attack on Montreal resulted in disaster. Relieved of his command, he was ordered to Washington, where, after quarreling with U.S. diplomat John Armstrong, he was once again tried and acquitted but discharged from the service. Thereafter he moved to a plantation near New Orleans, where he wrote the three-volume *Memoirs of My Own Times,* published in 1816. He supported the 1820 Stephen Long expedition, and in 1821 he went to Mexico to obtain a land grant in Texas. He died, however, before fulfilling the conditions of the grant and was buried in Mexico City, leaving behind a reputation for deceit and betrayal.

Further Reading

Ambrose, Stephen E. *Undaunted Courage: Meriwether Lewis, Thomas Jefferson, and the Opening of the American West.* New York: Simon and Schuster, 1996.

Clark Daniel. *Proofs of the corruption of Gen. James Wilkinson, and of his connexion with Aaron Burr, with a full refutation of his slanderous allegations in relation to the character of the principal witness against him.* Freeport, N.Y.: Books for Libraries Press, 1970. Reprint, Arno Press, New York, 1971.

Hay, Robson and M. R. Werner. *The Admirable Trumpeter: A Biography of General James Wilkinson.* Garden City, N.Y.: Doubleday, Doran & Company, Inc., 1941.

Montgomery, M. R. *Jefferson and the Gun-Men: How the West Was almost Lost.* New York: Crown Publishers, 2000.

Wilkinson, James. *Memoirs of My Own Times.* Reprint ed. New York: AMS Press, 1973.

Willamette River (Multnomah River)

When the CORPS OF DISCOVERY made their way down the COLUMBIA RIVER in November 1805, their course followed the river's north bank. Consequently, as they passed what is now Portland, Oregon, on November 4, the islands on their left hid the mouth of the Willamette River from their view. Not until their return from FORT CLATSOP, as they made their way back up the Columbia, were they told by some WATLALA INDIANS on April 2, 1806, that a large river entered the Columbia from the south. Even though they had passed it, WILLIAM CLARK turned back four miles or so to explore this river. He took with him seven men and a Watlala guide who had been hired with the gift of a burning-glass.

The party went 10 miles up what the Indians called the Multnomah River, which Clark reported was "deep enough for a Man of War or Ship of an Burthen." He also noted the names of the Indian nations living along the river, writing on April 7: "I prevailed on an old Indian to mark the Multnomah River down on the sand, which he did, and it perfectly corresponded with the sketch given me by sundry others, with the addition of a circular mountain which passes this river at the falls and connects with the mountains of the seacoast. He also laid down the Clackamas, passing a high conical mountain near its mouth on the lower side and heading in MOUNT JEFFERSON, which he laid down by raising the sand as a very high mountain and covered with eternal snow."

Clark was also informed that the river flowed all the way north from California. Because of this, he believed it might be the elusive NORTHWEST PASSAGE, going across Oregon and what is now northern Utah. In fact the Willamette rises in southern Oregon and flows north parallel to the coastline for a sufficient distance to give credence to the Indians' belief regarding its course. The Willamette rises due north of Crater Lake and journeys up to the Columbia for some 300 miles, joining several other rivers along the way. In the years following the expedition, the Willamette Valley became the final destination of many pioneers traveling the OREGON TRAIL.

Further Reading

Cutright, Paul Russell. *Lewis & Clark: Pioneering Naturalists.* Lincoln: University of Nebraska Press/Bison Books, 1989.

Moulton, Gary E., ed. *Atlas of the Lewis and Clark Expedition.* Revised ed. Lincoln: University of Nebraska Press, 1999.

Schmidt, Thomas, and Jeremy Schmidt. *The Saga of Lewis & Clark into the Uncharted West.* New York: DK Publishing, 1999.

Willard, Alexander Hamilton (1778–1865)
private in the permanent party

Along with JOHN SHIELDS and WILLIAM BRATTON, Alexander Hamilton Willard was one of the expedition's blacksmiths; he was also a gunsmith and became one of the few members of the CORPS OF DISCOVERY to have survived to an advanced age. At 5'10" tall, he boasted a fine physique and dark features. Born in Charlestown, New Hampshire, he later moved to Kentucky, where he enlisted in the army in 1800. On January 1, 1804, he was officially enrolled in the Corps of Discovery. (In the detachment orders of April 1, 1804, listing the members of the permanent party, his name is given as Williams, an apparent error.)

Although a reliable soldier overall, Willard made a number of errors during the expedition. The most grievous was falling asleep while on sentry duty during the night of July 11–12, 1804. This was technically punishable by death, for which reason Captains MERIWETHER LEWIS AND WILLIAM CLARK conducted Willard's COURT-MARTIAL alone. The private was charged with "Lying down and Sleeping on his post whilst a Sentinal." Although Willard pled guilty to lying down, he denied having fallen asleep. He was found guilty on both counts, however, and was sentenced to 100 lashes for four days.

During the winter of 1804–05 at FORT MANDAN, FOOD became scarce and it was necessary to barter with the MANDAN and the HIDATSA INDIANS for corn. As TRADE goods were running short, John Shields built a forge and, with Willard and Bratton, repaired metal tools, pots, and knives for the Indians, in addition to making arrowheads, axes, and hide scrapers to be used as TRADE items.

One night in August 1805 the expedition camped by a small creek that was a tributary of the BEAVERHEAD RIVER (in present-day Montana). Captains Lewis and Clark dubbed it Willard's Creek, a name it would retain for some 60 years before being renamed Grasshopper Creek. What they did not know then was that the area was rich with minerals other than the ones they had noted, and it would later become a major mining site for gold seekers.

In November that same year, Willard was among those dispatched by Lewis to scout out territory around the COLUMBIA RIVER to find a suitable location for what would become FORT CLATSOP. On the night of November 14, Willard and GEORGE SHANNON, who were out HUNTING, made camp with five CHINOOK INDIANS. When they awoke the following morning, they discovered the Indians had stolen their rifles. It was only the appearance of Lewis and others on the scene that enabled them to get their rifles back.

Late in December, Willard and PETER WEISER were assigned to help set up the SALTWORKS some 15 miles south of Fort Clatsop. When the two returned in early January, they brought with them some blubber and news of a WHALE that had been beached. An excited Clark headed to the site with a party of men and SACAGAWEA, only to find the whale had already been stripped by TILLAMOOK INDIANS.

Willard seemed to have bad luck with HORSES. While the expedition made its torturous crossing of the BITTERROOT MOUNTAINS in September 1804, he managed to lose his horse and was sent back to find it. He came back late in the day without the animal. The following April, as the corps traveled up the Columbia on its return journey, Willard failed to obey Lewis's order that all horses be hobbled; consequently, his wandered off during the night of April 19. The captain was furious, noting in his journal that he "reprimanded [Willard] more severely for this peice of negligence then had been usual" for him.

Following the expedition, Willard became a government blacksmith, in which role he provided services to a number of Indian nations. In 1807 he married Eleanor McDonald, with whom he had 12 children; one of his sons was named Lewis and another Clark. Following service in the War of 1812, he resumed his trade as a blacksmith in Missouri but eventually moved to Wisconsin, living there from 1824 to 1852. Very few photographs exist of expedition members, but there is one of Willard with his wife, probably taken late during this period.

In 1852 he migrated with his family to the gold fields of California, where he lived until his death at the age of 87. The only member of the Corps of Discovery to outlive him was Sergeant PATRICK GASS. Alexander Willard is buried in Franklin, California, near Sacramento.

Further Reading

Clarke, Charles G. *The Men of the Lewis and Clark Expedition: A Biographical Roster of the Fifty-One Members and a Composite Diary of Their Activities from All Known Sources.* 1970. Reprint, Lincoln: Bison Books, University of Nebraska Press, 2002.

North Dakota Lewis & Clark Bicentennial Foundation. *Members of the Corps of Discovery.* Bismarck, N.Dak.: United Printing and Mailing, 2000.

Wilson, Alexander (1766–1813) *weaver, peddler, schoolteacher, poet, ornithologist*

After the expedition, when MERIWETHER LEWIS returned to PHILADELPHIA in April 1807, he set about making arrangements for the disposition of ARTIFACTS AND SPECIMENS that he and WILLIAM CLARK had brought back or sent back from the West. Many of these were placed in the museum of CHARLES WILLSON PEALE, who also painted the two explorers. Lewis hired FREDERICK PURSH to catalog and draw the PLANT specimens, and in connection with the expected publication of the expedition's JOURNALS, he commissioned artists to produce paintings of some of the BIRDS, ANIMALS, and Indians the expedition had encountered. For the bird portraits, he turned to an unusual man: Alexander Wilson.

Best known today for his innovative nine-volume *American Ornithology* (or *Birds of America*), Wilson was born in Paisley, Scotland. At the age of 13 he was apprenticed to a weaver but later became a traveling peddler. On his journeys around Scotland, he began to compose dialect poems of a wry, humorous nature, depicting the life of the Scottish poor. When he sided with the weavers in a dispute they were then having with their employers, his poetic satires led to charges of libel, which landed him in prison.

Wilson emigrated to New Castle, Delaware, in 1794, arriving with nothing but a gun and the clothes on his back. He became a teacher in New Jersey before moving to Philadelphia as a schoolmaster. It was here he met William Bartram (1739–1823), the eminent naturalist and friend of BENJAMIN SMITH BARTON and THOMAS JEFFERSON. Bartram learned of Wilson's interest in ornithology and encouraged him in his ambition to produce an illustrated book on American birds. Although he had no formal training in drawing or painting, he soon taught himself to do so and in 1808 produced the first volume of his nine-volume masterwork. *American Ornithology* was the first inclusive study of the birds of the United States.

After Lewis died, Wilson wrote of his meeting with the explorer in 1807: "It was the request and particular wish of Captain Lewis made to me in person that I should make drawings of each of the feathered tribe as had been preserved, and were new." Even before the expedition's return, Jefferson had written to Wilson about the magpies that had been included in the shipment sent back from FORT MANDAN in 1805. One magpie had survived the trip, and after it died CHARLES WILLSON PEALE mounted it; Wilson used it as a model for a drawing in his book.

Wilson described and made drawings of three of the bird skins Lewis and Clark brought back in 1806: the western tanager (*Piranga ludoviciana,* then the Louisiana tanager), Lewis's woodpecker (*Asyndesmus lewis*), and Clark's nutcracker (*Nucifraga columbiana,* then Clark's crow). All three appear together in an engraving on Plate XX in Volume III of *American Ornithology.* His original sketches of the latter two birds now reside in the Academy of Natural Sciences in Philadelphia; that of the western tanager has been lost. The skin of Lewis's woodpecker can still be seen in Harvard's Museum of Comparative Zoology.

Wilson died in 1813, leaving his masterwork unfinished. His friend and colleague, the naturalist George Ord (1781–1866), completed the last two volumes and reissued the book in augmented form in 1824–25.

Further Reading

Cutright, Paul Russell. *Lewis & Clark: Pioneering Naturalists.* Lincoln: University of Nebraska Press/Bison Books, 1989.

Ord, George. *Sketch of the Life of Alexander Wilson.* Philadelphia: H. Hall, 1828.

Wilson, Alexander. *Birds of America.* 9 vols. Philadelphia: Bradford & Innskeep, 1808–1814.

———. *The Life and Letters of Alexander Wilson.* Edited by Clark Hunter. Philadelphia: American Philosophical Society, 1983.

Wilson, Alexander, and Charles Lucien Bonaparte. *American Ornithology; or The Natural History of the Birds of the United States.* Edited by Robert Jameson. Edinburgh: Constable & Co., 1831.

Windsor, Richard (unknown–unknown) *private in the permanent party*

Private Richard Windsor's only real claim to fame on the Lewis and Clark Expedition was that he came close to being the second man to die during the journey. Nothing is known of when or where Windsor was born. He was recruited for the CORPS OF DISCOVERY from the army post at KASKASKIA and was officially enrolled on January 1, 1804. With his skills as a woodsman, he became one of the corps's best hunters.

Early in June 1805, Windsor was among the men chosen by MERIWETHER LEWIS to join him on a scouting mission to locate the GREAT FALLS of the MISSOURI RIVER. The WEATHER turned rainy, creating slippery conditions on the terrain. On the morning of June 7, as they passed along the face of a bluff, Lewis slipped and nearly fell down a treacherous precipice but caught himself with his ESPONTOON. Behind him, however, Windsor had actually fallen and was lying on his stomach, his right arm and leg dangling out over the precipice. "God, God, captain, what shall I do?" the private cried out, shaken with fear. Equally alarmed but calm, Lewis directed Windsor to use his knife to dig a hole in the face of the precipice to give him a foothold, which (with his moccasin removed) enabled him to crawl forward and out of danger.

Other than this incident, Windsor receives very little mention in the expedition's JOURNALS. Following the corps's return, he continued to serve in the army until 1819, after which he apparently settled in Illinois. By 1829 he was reported as living on the Sangamon River in Illinois, but his whereabouts after this are unknown.

Further Reading

Clarke, Charles G. *The Men of the Lewis and Clark Expedition: A Biographical Roster of the Fifty-One Members and a Composite Diary of Their Activities from All Known Sources.* 1970. Reprint, Lincoln: Bison Books, University of Nebraska Press, 2002.

North Dakota Lewis & Clark Bicentennial Foundation. *Members of the Corps of Discovery.* Bismarck, N.Dak.: United Printing and Mailing, 2000.

PBS Online. *Lewis and Clark: Inside the Corps of Discovery:* "Lesser Known Members of the Corps." Available on-line. URL: http://www.pbs.org/lewisandclark/inside/lesser.html. Downloaded on May 18, 2001.

Wisdom River (Big Hole River)

In early August 1805, as the expedition proceeded up the JEFFERSON RIVER, MERIWETHER LEWIS chose to walk on shore with a small party, soon pulling ahead of WILLIAM CLARK and the others in CANOES. Every member of the CORPS OF DISCOVERY could see the mountains in front of them and knew that to cross those rocky hills they would need HORSES, which could only be obtained from the so-far elusive SHOSHONE INDIANS. On August 3 Lewis and his men arrived at the point where, like the MISSOURI RIVER behind them, the Jefferson split into three forks. He made a detour up each to decide which was the main stream and, correctly, decided to follow the middle river.

Before he made his decision, however, Lewis gave names to the other two rivers. While he and Clark had named most of the rivers they had encountered after people, now, as a keen Mason, he chose tenets of Masonry for his nomenclature. Thus, he named the river to the south the Philanthropy (now the Ruby River) and the one to the north the Wisdom (now the Big Hole River). (He had already named the Philosophy River downstream.) He traveled some 15 miles up the Wisdom before turning back to the river junction and leaving a note for Clark wedged in a stick on the bank. He then set off up the middle stream, which he continued to call the Jefferson but is now the BEAVERHEAD RIVER.

When Clark arrived two days later, the stick and the note had gone, probably taken by a BEAVER. Thinking Lewis had

Now called the Big Hole River, the northernmost branch of the Jefferson was named Wisdom by Lewis, who was a Freemason, after one of the tenets of Masonry. *(Library of Congress, Prints and Photographs Division [LC-USF34-064999-D])*

gone up the Wisdom, Clark and his canoe party struggled up that river for nine laborious miles before GEORGE DROUILLARD and PATRICK GASS, who had been sent north by Lewis to look for the Shoshone, came across them and told them of their mistake. The party turned around, and while the journey up the river had been slow and arduous, the passage back down to the forks was even more difficult. In the swift stream, one of the canoes overturned, and some equipment was lost. Clark and his group rejoined Lewis at the junction of the three rivers on the same day, August 6, 1805, and after another day there they set off up the Beaverhead.

A year later, on the return journey, Clark was to travel down the Wisdom River valley again. From TRAVELERS' REST, Lewis and a few selected men headed east to WHITE BEAR ISLANDS, while Clark and the remainder set off south back to CAMP FORTUNATE. This time, however, they turned east to cross the CONTINENTAL DIVIDE at present-day Gibbons Pass. They rode down into what is now the Big Hole Valley, reaching a point on the Wisdom River just north of modern Jackson, Montana, on July 6, 1806. Following the river for some miles, they then turned due south on a short cut across the hills that SACAGAWEA showed them, taking them back to their CACHES at Camp Fortunate by July 8.

See also NOMENCLATURE, GEOGRAPHICAL; ROSS'S HOLE.

Further Reading

Cutright, Paul Russell. *Lewis & Clark: Pioneering Naturalists.* Lincoln: University of Nebraska Press/Bison Books, 1989.

Fifer, Barbara, and Vicky Soderberg. *Along the Trail with Lewis and Clark.* Great Falls, Mont.: Montana Magazine, 1998.

Wiser, Peter   See WEISER, PETER.

Wishram and Wasco Indians

When MERIWETHER LEWIS and WILLIAM CLARK were gathering information on the COLUMBIA RIVER from the NEZ PERCE INDIANS, they were mistakenly told there were non-Indian traders in the area of CELILO FALLS AND THE DALLES. But as James Ronda writes in *Lewis and Clark among the Indians,* "there were, in fact, no white traders in the territory so jealously guarded by Wishram and Wasco Indian middlemen."

The area of The Dalles on the Columbia River (on the present-day border of Oregon and Washington) was the hub of a vast Indian FISHING and trading network in the Pacific Northwest equivalent to the trading system of the PLAINS INDIANS (see MANDAN INDIANS). This network extended from the Pacific coast to Nez Perce territories and included Chinookian, Salishan, and Sahaptian nations along the Columbia and its tributaries, although there were also links to the Middle Missouri system via the SHOSHONE INDIANS. At The Dalles, the Wishram occupied the north bank of the river, while the Wasco lived in villages along the south side. There were fishing villages of several nations from here up to Celilo Falls, although it was the primary Wishram village,

The Wishram and the Wasco were middlemen in the complex trading system centered on The Dalles on the Columbia River. These Wishram Indians were photographed by Edward Curtis. *(Washington State Historical Society, Tacoma)*

Nixluidix (meaning "trading place"), that served as the main center for trade. When the CORPS OF DISCOVERY visited this village on October 24, 1805, Clark recorded seeing 107 stacks of salmon, which he estimated to weigh more than 10,000 pounds; this was just one example of the many sorts of goods that were traded in the village.

While trading lasted through three salmon runs, from spring through autumn, the major trade fair at The Dalles took place in the fall and attracted Indians from numerous nations. Goods brought for trade included meats, roots, and berries as well as agricultural products, skins, HORSES, clothing, blankets, beads, and guns. It has been estimated that at peak trading time, some 3,000 Indians crowded the area, not only to trade but to socialize. The Wishram and the Wasco Indians—two related nations who were considered the easternmost of the Chinook—acted as the primary intermediaries with the other nations. Although Lewis and Clark arrived at The Dalles after the major trading was over, they still managed to witness enough to describe a significant amount of activity and the goods that were traded in addition to providing details of the unique FISHING methods they observed.

Having already experienced some tension and hostility with some Chinook Indians on the lower Columbia, when the captains heard rumors that the expedition might be attacked, they were on their guard. Yet when Clark visited the Wishram village of Nixluidix, he was greeted warmly and invited into one of the 20 large wooden houses there, which he later described in detail. The expedition's carpenter, PATRICK GASS, also approved of the Wishram houses, describing them as "tolerably comfortable." (Each house contained three Wishram families.) The captains' council with the Indians consisted primarily of passing out medals and other GIFTS and encouraging them to make peace with the Nez Perce.

In the years following the expedition's visit, the trading focus was to switch from FISH to furs as British and American traders entered the area. As was the case for so many Indians along the Columbia, the Wishram and the Wasco way of life changed gradually and then became permanently altered when, in 1855, Washington governor Isaac Stevens tricked them into ceding their lands. That year both nations moved to the Warm Springs Reservation in Oregon along with what remained of the WATLALA INDIANS. Some of their descendants are associated with the Warm Spring Tribal Council. The population of the Wasco continued to be tracked for a number of years, with 260 reported in 1945.

Further Reading

Rhonda, James P. *Lewis and Clark among the Indians.* Lincoln: University of Nebraska Press, 1984.

Wistar, Caspar (1761–1818) *physician*

In spring 1803, during the time that MERIWETHER LEWIS spent in PHILADELPHIA prior to the expedition, he met a number of leading scientists and savants for instruction and technical advice. One of these was Dr. Caspar Wistar, a medical professor with whom Lewis discussed fossils and PREHISTORIC ANIMALS. Like many of his time, including THOMAS JEFFERSON, Wistar believed it was possible that beasts like mastodons still roamed the prairies. It was his hope that Lewis would bring back proof of this.

Born in Philadelphia, Wistar graduated from the College of Philadelphia (now the University of Pennsylvania) in 1782 and then went to Edinburgh University, where he received his M.D. four years later. He returned to the College of Philadelphia and began to teach chemistry and physiology; he succeeded BENJAMIN RUSH as professor of chemistry in 1789. After 1792, however, his teaching focused primarily on anatomy, and he assumed that chair at the college's medical school. He was reported to be a superb and popular teacher.

In 1787 Wistar became a member of the AMERICAN PHILOSOPHICAL SOCIETY, through which he met THOMAS JEFFERSON. The two became regular correspondents and scientific collaborators, serving together on an advisory panel for CHARLES WILLSON PEALE's museum as well as on a society committee to assemble a mastodon skeleton. By this time Wistar had become the nation's leading expert on American fossils, and when he and Jefferson discovered the bones they named *Megalonyx,* it was Wistar who correctly identified it as a giant ground sloth.

Wistar was delighted when he received the news of the LOUISIANA PURCHASE, recognizing immediately its value to the young nation. He wrote to Jefferson: "Altho no one here appears to know the extent or price of the cession, it is generally considered as the most important and beneficial transaction which has occurred since the declaration of Independence, & next to it, more like to influence or regulate the destinies of our Country." When Jefferson wrote asking Wistar's assistance in instructing Meriwether Lewis, he was proud to accept.

In Jefferson's letter to Lewis providing the expedition's MISSION OBJECTIVES, he included the instruction to search for fossilized remains of animals like mastodons, which he believed may still exist in the western regions of the continent. Wistar agreed with this and focused on it during his time with Lewis, urging the explorer to watch out for signs of the animals and to investigate exposed areas on bluffs along the MISSOURI RIVER that might contain fossils. Word had also been received of a discovery of mammoth bones at Big Bone Lick, near Cincinnati. Wistar hoped the site could be visited, and in fact Lewis stopped there during his journey from PITTSBURGH to CLARKSVILLE later that year.

Like others who had consulted with Lewis, Wistar provided a questionnaire of points he wished the explorer to pursue on the expedition. Unfortunately, he sent it to Jefferson in July 1803, after Lewis had already departed, and though his cover letter exists today, his list of "abstract queries" have disappeared. Wistar also wrote to Jefferson in October 1803 regarding information he had received that the Spanish had sent a party of Indians to the PACIFIC OCEAN by way of the MISSOURI RIVER and that they had returned within two years after successfully reaching the coast. From Jefferson's point of view, this was good news, even though it may have been apocryphal.

In 1811 Wistar published *A System of Anatomy for the Use of Students of Medicine,* the first American textbook on anatomy. Vice president of the American Philosophical Society for 20 years, he succeeded Jefferson as its president in 1815, and during his three years in that capacity, he maintained a weekly open house for members of the society and visiting scientists. The "Wistar Parties" became so popular that they continued even after his death in 1818. It is a measure of the esteem in which Wistar was held that the English botanist Thomas Nuttall named a vine for him. It is known today as the wisteria.

Further Reading

Cutright, Paul Russell. *Contributions of Philadelphia to Lewis and Clark History.* Philadelphia: Philadelphia Chapter Lewis and Clark Trail Heritage Foundation, 2001. Also available on line. URL: http://www.lewisandclarkphila.org/philadelphia/philadelphiacutright conten.html. Updated on October 15, 2001.

Hosack, David. *Tribute to the memory of the late Caspar Wistar, M.D.: professor of anatomy, &c. in the University of Pennsylvania, president of the American Philosophical Society for the Promotion of Useful Knowledge, &c.* New York: Printed by C.S. Van Winkle, 1818.

wolves

Although wolves were common across the United States at the time of the Lewis and Clark Expedition, the difference between the gray wolf of the plains and those on the Atlantic seaboard was obvious to the explorers. They correctly identified the gray wolf as a separate subspecies, using the word *large* to distinguish the wolf from the coyote, which they called the small wolf. The party first saw the plains gray wolf on May 30, 1804, near present-day Leavenworth, Kansas, and then often through the journey. On May 5, 1805, above the YELLOWSTONE RIVER, MERIWETHER LEWIS noted that "[t]he large woolf found here is not as large as those of the Atlantic states. They are lower and thicker, shorter leged . . . We scarecely see a gang of buffaloe without observing a parsel of these faithfull shepherds on their skirts in readiness to take care of the maimend wounded. The large wolf never barks, but howls as those of the atlantic states do."

On February 20, 1806, at FORT CLATSOP, Lewis noted another factor: "The large brown wolf is like that of the Atlantic States and are found only in the woody country on the PACIFIC OCEAN imbracing the mountains which pass the Columbia between the GREAT FALLS and rapids of the same." He drew the inference that the wolves along the maritime wooded areas of the United States had developed differently from those in the central open plains and was probably correct in his observations, even if his conclusions are now arguable.

Wolves and COYOTES played a vital part in the ecology of the GREAT PLAINS. By eliminating the weaker, sick, and older animals on whom they preyed, they acted as excellent scavengers and helped to prevent overpopulation among many species. Because humans were then rare in the plains wolves' habitat, the explorers found them comparatively docile. On May 29, 1805, above the MUSSELSHELL RIVER, Lewis wrote: "[W]e saw a great many wolves in the neighborhood of those mangled carcases [BUFFALO], they were fat and extremely gentle, Capt. C. who was on shore, killed one of them with his ESPONTOON."

During the entire journey, only one occasion was recorded of a wolf attacking a human. On August 8, 1806, WILLIAM CLARK wrote: "[T]he night after the horses had been stolen a Wolf bit Sgt. Pryor [NATHANIEL PRYOR] thrugh the hand when asleep, and this animal was so vicious as to make an attempt to seize Winsor [RICHARD WINDSOR], when Shannon [GEORGE SHANNON] fortunately Shot him."

Overall, the expedition saw little to fear from wolves. They knew them, and when necessary they killed them, but they had to take precautions against them as efficient scavengers since they found the wolves would take any animal the explorers killed unless it was kept out of their reach.

Further Reading

Burroughs, Raymond Darwin, ed. *The Natural History of the Lewis and Clark Expedition*. East Lansing: Michigan State University Press, 1995.

Cutright, Paul Russell. *Lewis & Clark: Pioneering Naturalists*. Lincoln: University of Nebraska Press/Bison Books, 1989.

women on the expedition

Although SACAGAWEA was the only woman to accompany the CORPS OF DISCOVERY across the continent and back, there were several others associated with the expedition, some of whom played a part in its successful outcome. All, of course, were Indian women.

The extent of Sacagawea's importance to the success of Lewis and Clark's mission cannot be underestimated. Although young, she possessed an intelligence and level-headedness that helped the corps on more than one occasion, from saving valuable items that had fallen from a PIROGUE into the river's currents to finding roots, berries, and wild vegetables to eat. MERIWETHER LEWIS and WILLIAM CLARK relied on her to provide INTERPRETATION services even after they had left her people, the SHOSHONE INDIANS, behind them. Though not employed as a guide, she provided valuable information on the landmarks, telling the captains when they were in Shoshone country and guiding Clark to the YELLOWSTONE RIVER on the return journey in 1806. Most important, she was, as Clark described her, a "token of peace" to the Indian nations they met, her presence assuring them the expedition was not hostile.

As the wife of TOUSSAINT CHARBONNEAU, Sacagawea's position was respected by the men on the expedition; the captains ensured this by having her and Charbonneau share their sleeping quarters. This did not mean the men were celibate; far from it. Many formed attachments to Indian women, especially during the winters at FORT MANDAN and FORT CLATSOP. In some nations women were prostituted by their husbands, either for profit or to gain some of the white men's "medicine" through sexual contact. On other occasions normal affections were involved. When the expedition was a few miles upriver from Fort Mandan in early April 1805, Lewis wrote, a MANDAN Indian arrived with "a woman who was extreemly solicitous to accompany one of the men of our party, this however we positively refused to permit."

Private HUGH MCNEAL's friendship with a CHINOOK woman saved his life. On the night of January 9, 1806, while Clark and a small party were visiting with some TILLAMOOK and CLATSOP by the Necanicum River, McNeal went off for an assignation with a woman arranged by a Tillamook man. The Indian was planning to kill McNeal and take his blanket, but a Chinook woman who knew the private and was aware of the plot attempted to warn him. When he ignored her, she raised an alarm in the village, thwarting the intended murder.

Twice during the expedition, women proved important in initial encounters with Indians. The first such occasion was in August 1805 when Lewis and Clark were searching for the SHOSHONE INDIANS. Lewis and a small party had gone ahead, traveling overland while Clark and the others came up the BEAVERHEAD RIVER in CANOES. On August 11 they encountered a mounted Shoshone warrior who rode off when they attempted to approach him. Two days later they met an Indian man and two women, all of whom retreated at their approach, but a short time after that they came to three woman, one elderly, the other two a teenager and a 12-year-old girl.

The teenager ran away, but the frightened girl and the old woman remained and sat on the ground with their heads bowed as Lewis approached them. Not until he showed them his white skin and gave them some beads, mirrors, moccasin awls, and paint did they relax. Communicating in sign language through GEORGE DROUILLARD, he then had the teenager recalled and asked the women to lead him to their people.

They had gone just two miles when a Shoshone war party rode up. Lewis laid down his rifle and, picking up a flag, followed the old woman toward the warriors. The woman spoke to the chief, CAMEAHWAIT, making it clear that there was nothing to be afraid of and excitedly showing the presents she had received. This broke the tension, and Cameahwait proceeded to welcome the explorers warmly. The outcome could have been different. Believing that BLACKFEET INDIANS had invaded their territory, Cameahwait and his men would have attacked the explorers without hesitation had not the old woman effectively saved their lives.

The story of WATKUWEIS is one of the favorite tales to come out of the expedition, though it is not recounted in any of the JOURNALS. After the expedition had completed its brutal crossing of the BITTERROOT MOUNTAINS and reached the NEZ PERCE INDIANS, some warriors considered killing the exhausted and starving explorers for their FIREARMS and trade goods.

Watkuweis, an elderly woman who had once lived among Canadian traders, stopped them, saying, "These are the people who helped me. Do them no hurt." Though Clark mentions seeing this old woman, he and Lewis were apparently unaware of her role in their fate. Her story has come down through the years via Nez Perce legend.

Further Reading

Ambrose, Stephen E. *Undaunted Courage: Meriwether Lewis, Thomas Jefferson, and the Opening of the American West.* New York: Simon and Schuster, 1996.

Clark, Ella E., and Margot Edmonds. *Sacagawea of the Lewis and Clark Expedition.* Berkeley: University of California Press, 1979.

Hagen, Cecil. "Liberated Women? . . . Not Those Lewis and Clark Met on Their Way." *Pacific Northwesterner* 25, no. 2 (1981): 17–25.

Ronda, James P. *Lewis and Clark among the Indians.* Lincoln: University of Nebraska Press, 1984.

Wood River   See CAMP DUBOIS.

Y

Yakama Indians (Yakima Indians, Waptailmin Indians, Cutsahnim Indians, Chimnapam Indians)

In October 1805, after a brief stay with the NEZ PERCE INDI-ANS, the CORPS OF DISCOVERY began the last stage of their westward journey to the PACIFIC OCEAN. Leaving CANOE CAMP on October 7, they set off down the CLEARWATER RIVER on their way to the SNAKE RIVER and finally the COLUMBIA RIVER. Accompanying them were two Nez Perce chiefs, TWISTED HAIR and TETOHARSKY, who went ahead of the expedition to advise the Indians downriver—relations of the Nez Perce—that white men were coming in peace. Shortly before the expedition reached the confluence of the Snake and the Columbia Rivers, on October 16 the corps met five Indians coming upriver, probably Yakama (Yakima) Indians. They were given TOBACCO, which they smoked with Captains MERI-WETHER LEWIS and WILLIAM CLARK, and then hurried back to their village to share the news. By the time the corps reached the Columbia, scores of Yakama and WANAPAM INDIANS were lining the riverbanks, eager to see the strange-looking white men in their CANOES.

Like the Nez Perce, the Yakama (then often known as Yakima) were a Sahaptian-speaking people of the Plateau culture. They had long occupied territory along the Yakima River, a tributary of the Columbia that was named after them, in the southeastern part of what is now Washington State. Their Sahaptian name means "the pregnant ones"; they also called themselves the Waptailmin, or "narrow river people," after the narrow area of the Yakima River where their primary village was situated. Lewis and Clark called them the Cutsahnim or Chimnapam. Like other Indians in the region, the Yakima's diet con-sisted primarily of salmon, supplemented by roots, berries, nuts, and small game.

After arriving at the junction of the Snake and Columbia rivers, Lewis and Clark set up camp and welcomed delegations of Wanapam and Yakama. They wanted the Indians to be aware of "our friendly disposition to all nations, and our joy in Seeing those of our friendly Children around us." Medals and GIFTS were distributed, and Clark visited various fishing villages and made notes on the Indians and their cultures, an important contribution to the expedition's ETHNOGRAPHY. A council was held on October 18, and from their talks with the chiefs, Lewis and Clark obtained much valuable information on what lay ahead of them. Two maps were provided of the territory along the Columbia and its Indians; one was drawn for them by an unnamed Yakama chief.

In April 1806, during the expedition's return journey up the Columbia, they again met the Yakama, a large number of whom had been invited to a feast hosted by Chief YELLEPT of the WALLA WALLA INDIANS. Like many in the upper Columbia area, the Yakama were a happy, friendly nation, and they enjoyed good relations with the American and British traders who followed the expedition into their territory. In the 1850s, however, they and other PLATEAU INDIANS fell victim to what was in effect chicanery on the part of the Washington Territory governor Isaac Stevens. Persuaded to sell their lands on the basis of having two–three years to relocate, Stevens declared their territory open to non-Indian settlement less than two weeks after the agreement was signed. This led to outbreaks of violence and what is now called the Yakima War, a series of raids and battles that also involved the Walla Walla, the

A group of Yakama (Yakima) Indians (although not those shown here) were the first to greet the expedition as they approached the junction of the Snake and the Columbia Rivers. *(Washington State Historical Society, Tacoma)*

Cayuse, and the UMATILLA INDIANS. The war continued on an off-and-on basis into 1858, after which the Yakama accepted defeat and moved to the Yakima Reservation beside Yakima, Washington, as did the Wishram, the Wanapam, the Palouse, and the Klickitat Indians. Yakama activism today centers around attempts to regain fishing runs that were lost when the Bonneville, Grand Coulee, and Dalles dams were built, effectively destroying a way of life for the Yakama and other river Indians.

Further Reading

Relander, Click (Now-Tow-Look). *Strangers on the Land: A Histori- ette of a Longer Story of the Yakima Nation's Efforts to Survive Against Great Odds.* Yakima, Wash.: Franklin Press, 1962.

Ronda, James P. *Lewis and Clark among the Indians.* Lincoln: Univer- sity of Nebraska Press, 1984.

Waldman, Carl. *Encyclopedia of Native American Tribes.* Revised ed. New York: Checkmark Books, 1999.

Yankton Nakota Indians (Yankton Sioux)

While there are four branches of Sioux Indians and subgroups or bands in each branch, the Lewis and Clark Expedition met only two bands: the Brulé of the TETON LAKOTA INDIANS

(Teton Sioux) and the Yankton Nakota (Yankton Sioux). Each encounter was strikingly different in tone and in what MERI- WETHER LEWIS and WILLIAM CLARK were and were not able to accomplish.

It was the friendly Yankton Nakota they met first. Of the four main groupings of Sioux, only the Yankton Nakota had just one subgroup or band—also called Yankton. Like other Sioux (a term not preferred by the people themselves; it was derived from an insulting name in the language of an enemy tribe), they had originally been Woodland Indians who had lived along the upper MISSISSIPPI RIVER. In the mid-1700s they moved west when Europeans began to invade their territory and their enemies began to acquire guns. The Yankton finally settled along the MISSOURI RIVER in what is now southwestern Minnesota, southwestern Iowa, and southeastern South Dakota. Although classified as PLAINS INDIANS, they did not become seminomads as other Dakota, Lakota, and Nakota did but instead retained their agricultural characteristics, living in earth lodges in permanent villages and growing crops. When they acquired HORSES, they started to hunt BUFFALO, but otherwise they were a settled, peaceful community of Prairie Indians.

On August 27, 1804, as the CORPS OF DISCOVERY moved slowly up the Missouri, Lewis ordered that a PRAIRIE

FIRE be lit to signal the Yankton of their presence. Near the mouth of the James River, they met three teenage Yankton boys who informed them of a large band camped further up the James. While Sergeant NATHANIEL PRYOR and interpreter PIERRE DORION were dispatched to invite the chiefs to a council, the expedition moved up the Missouri a short way and set up camp on the west side of the river near present-day Gavins Point Dam, Nebraska. They named the site CALUMET BLUFF.

To his embarrassment and delight, Pryor was accorded a grand welcome at the Yankton camp and had to decline their efforts to carry him in on a painted buffalo robe. He was impressed by their TIPIS, of which he wrote a description, and he and Dorion were treated to a feast that night. The following day they brought some 70 Yankton back to the Missouri, where they set up camp on the east side of the river. Lewis sent over some CORN, TOBACCO, and iron kettles as presents. The following morning, August 30, the Indians crossed over to Calumet Bluff and, dressed in full regalia, entered the camp with great ceremony, the Yankton chiefs following four musicians. The soldiers wore their dress uniforms as well, a flag was raised, and the KEELBOAT's bow gun was fired in salute.

In the council that followed, Lewis gave his standard speech to Indian nations. He informed the chiefs that they now had a new "father" (THOMAS JEFFERSON) who wanted all nations to live together in peace and also wished them to visit him in Washington. Lewis also spoke of the trading prospects with the merchants in ST. LOUIS and the desire to bring the Dakota, Lakota, and Nakota into the new American TRADE network. The speech lasted most of the day, and when it was done the chiefs indicated they would give their response in the morning. There followed the presentation of GIFTS, with Chief WEUCHE, who had been designated "first chief" by the captains, receiving a red-laced coat, military cocked hat, and American flag; the "lesser" chiefs received medals. After the council ended, there were demonstrations of Yankton warriors' skills with bow and arrows, and that evening campfires were built around which the Yankton danced and sang songs that proclaimed their merits as warriors. In his journal, Sergeant JOHN ORDWAY described the ceremony, noting that the singers always began "with a houp and hollow and ended with the same." Impressed expedition members threw gifts of tobacco, knives, and bells to the dancers, and Clark described the Yankton as "a Stout bold looking people (the young men hand Som) & well made."

The following morning the Yankton chiefs gave their replies to the captains' message of peace and trade. Most of the replies stressed the same note: The Yankton needed guns and ammunition more than medals and beads, and they wanted a reliable source for trade goods. Weuche was particularly vehement on this point as he emphasized the poverty of his people and the need for immediate relief. Aware, however, that good relations with the new U.S. government would be beneficial to his people, he offered to organize a delegation of Yankton and other nations to go to Washington, provided Pierre Dorion could stay and assist in that venture. The captains agreed to this.

The last chief to speak, Arcawechar (Half Man), proved to be prophetic on the subject of the peace among Indian nations that Lewis and Clark were proposing. Agreeing that such a peace was desirable, he nevertheless pointed out that "those nations above will not open their ears, and you cannot I fear open them." The captains would discover the truth in these words when they went on to visit the Teton Lakota.

During their return journey down the Missouri in late August 1806, the expedition met some old friends from the Yankton Nakota. To their delight, Lewis and Clark learned that a Yankton delegation had indeed gone to Washington, although whether it included Weuche is unclear. Today the descendants of the Yankton and other bands of Dakota, Lakota, and Nakota live on a number of reservations in North, Dakota, South Dakota, and several other states. Many also now live in urban areas of the United States.

Further Reading

Ambrose, Stephen E. *Undaunted Courage: Meriwether Lewis, Thomas Jefferson, and the Opening of the American West.* New York: Simon and Schuster, 1996.

Hawke, David Freeman. *Those Tremendous Mountains: The Story of the Lewis and Clark Expedition.* New York: W. W. Norton & Company, 1998.

Ronda, James P. *Lewis and Clark among the Indians.* Lincoln: University of Nebraska Press, 1984.

Waldman, Carl. *Encyclopedia of Native American Tribes.* Revised ed. New York: Checkmark Books, 1999.

Yellept (Yelleppit) (unknown–unknown)
Walla Walla Indian chief

By October 18, 1805, the CORPS OF DISCOVERY had journeyed down the CLEARWATER RIVER to the SNAKE RIVER and were on the last stage of their westward journey, heading down the COLUMBIA RIVER toward the PACIFIC OCEAN. Just after passing the mouth of the Walla Walla River in what is now Washington State, they stopped for the night, and here they were visited by about 20 WALLA WALLA INDIANS who set up camp nearby. Their chief was a man whom Clark described as "a bold handsom Indian, with a dignified countenance about 35 years of age, about 5 feet 8 inches high and well perpotioned." This was Yellept.

On the morning of October 18, MERIWETHER LEWIS and WILLIAM CLARK held a council with Yellept, two other Walla Walla chiefs, and another chief who may have been either a Cayuse or an UMATILLA. Translation was difficult, although the chiefs seemed to understand and be pleased by the captains' message of TRADE with other white men who would come after them. There followed the presentation of GIFTS, and Yellept was presented with a medal, a handkerchief, and a string of wampum. Even though the expedition's supplies of gifts and trade goods were by then dwindling, Yellept was still impressed enough to ask Lewis and Clark to stay longer in his territory.

They could not do this but promised that they would visit him the following spring.

True to their word, in late April 1806, as the expedition was proceeding back up the Columbia, they were greeted by Yellept and a small party of Walla Walla, and the captains accepted the chief's invitation to stay in his village. This was a settlement of 15 lodges on the Columbia's north bank, some 15 miles below the river's junction with the Snake. The village contained a population of about 150 and—of great interest to the captains—a large number of HORSES, which they badly needed and subsequently obtained.

The expedition's stay with the Walla Walla was a festive occasion as well as fortunate in many ways. Yellept proved himself a generous host, bringing the explorers firewood and FISH, and on the second day he presented Clark with "a very eligant white horse." To Clark's surprise, however, the chief then asked for a kettle in return. This not being possible, "I gave him my Sword, 100 balls & powder and some small articles of which he appeared perfectly satisfied." (The following day Lewis gave up his personal pistol, 100 rounds of ammunition, and some other small articles in exchange for two horses that other Walla Walla chiefs presented to him and Clark.)

It transpired that there was a SHOSHONE woman being held captive by the Walla Walla, and she was immediately enlisted to provide translation services, making communication much easier than it had been the previous fall. Yellept was happy to answer the explorer's questions, and he provided useful information about the country along the Columbia and Snake Rivers; in particular he told them of a shortcut that would save them 80 miles on their journey back to the NEZ PERCE INDIANS. Lewis and Clark were equally forthcoming in their answers to his questions, and, according to Lewis, "fully satisfied all their enquiries with rispect to ourselves and the objects of our pursuits." Clark also pleased the Walla Walla by providing medical services.

In all, the expedition stayed three days with the Walla Walla. If Yellept had had his way, they would have stayed even longer, but on April 30 they finally took their leave of "these friendly honest people the Wollahwollahs . . ." and their chief. Lewis and Clark left knowing they had enlisted an enthusiastic participant in the new American trading system they had proposed. Like other Indians they had met, however, Yellept's interest was not so much in dealing with the Americans specifically as in obtaining quality trade goods. In July 1811, when British explorer DAVID THOMPSON visited the Walla Walla, Yellept encouraged him to stay longer, just as he had done with Lewis and Clark, and also asked him to build a trading post at the junction of the Snake and Columbia Rivers. He remained a good friend to non-Indians for many years.

Further Reading

Ambrose, Stephen E. *Undaunted Courage: Meriwether Lewis, Thomas Jefferson, and the Opening of the American West.* New York: Simon and Schuster, 1996.

Ronda, James P. *Lewis and Clark among the Indians.* Lincoln: University of Nebraska Press, 1984.

Yellowstone River

The Yellowstone River (from the French *Roche Jaune*) flows 670 miles from today's Yellowstone National Park to the northeast before meeting the MISSOURI RIVER near present-day Williston, North Dakota (just east of the border with Montana). On April 25, 1805—three weeks after leaving the villages of the MANDAN INDIANS—MERIWETHER LEWIS and three men walking on shore ahead of the main party on the river reached the mouth of the Yellowstone. Lewis measured the width and the depth of the river mouth and sent JOSEPH FIELD 10 miles upstream with instructions to, among other things, look out for the yellow stones from which it was assumed the river got its name. (None were found, and the origin of the name is still a matter of conjecture.)

Lewis had been told by the HIDATSA INDIANS that the Yellowstone (which they called Elk River) ran close to the Missouri in its upper reaches. This may have tempted him to consider using it as a route to the west, but THOMAS JEFFERSON had emphasized that the Missouri River was to be followed as far as possible. Consequently, it was not until the following year that WILLIAM CLARK was to travel and explore the Yellowstone.

Apart from their confrontation with the TETON LAKOTA INDIANS (Teton Sioux) in September 1804, the explorers had encountered no hostility from Indians on their way west, and this was certainly a factor in their minds when they planned the return journey. With hindsight, their scheme was daring—almost foolhardy. When they made their way back across the BITTERROOT MOUNTAINS to TRAVELERS' REST in July 1806, the expedition split into two. They were later to split into five separate parties, hundreds of miles apart, but the captains were confident their men were capable of acting responsibly on their own. This confidence was to be completely justified.

While Lewis and one group rode east to the GREAT FALLS, Clark and the remainder rode 150 miles south back to CAMP FORTUNATE. Here they retrieved the CANOES they had left the year before and traveled down the BEAVERHEAD RIVER and JEFFERSON RIVER to THREE FORKS. Clark then detached Sergeant JOHN ORDWAY and nine men, who took the canoes downriver to meet Sergeant PATRICK GASS and his group at Great Falls. The two sergeants would PORTAGE the canoes around the falls, meet Lewis and his party at the mouth of the MARIAS RIVER, and then proceed down the Missouri.

With the remaining 10 men, SACAGAWEA, and her little boy Pomp, Clark rode south to the Yellowstone, reaching it on July 15 near present-day Livingston, Montana. Anxious to find large enough TREES with which to build canoes, the soldiers found that while game was plentiful, timber was scarce. Not until July 19, near today's Park City, Montana, did Clark find two cottonwoods that were so narrow that the resulting dugouts had to be lashed together for stability.

On July 24 Clark and half the party embarked to travel down the Yellowstone. Meanwhile, Sergeant NATHANIEL PRYOR and three men were detached to ride directly across country to the Mandan villages, about 250 miles away. The following day, the captain and his party came to POMPY'S TOWER, where Clark carved his name on the soft sandstone;

On the return journey in 1806, while Lewis explored the Marias River, Clark traveled down the Yellowstone. This view of the river was taken from the top of Pompy's Tower, east of Livingston, Montana. *(Montana Historical Society, Helena)*

it can still be seen today. A few miles downstream, he made an unusual, almost nostalgic note in his journal: "I take my leave of the view of the tremendous chain of Rocky Mountains white with Snow in view of which I have been Since the 1st of May last."

The journey down the river was fast and uneventful, except for the mosquitoes that plagued them. Such was the discomfort these INSECTS caused them that when they reached the Missouri on August 3, Clark decided to go on, traveling downstream until they were free of this pest four days later. He had not seen Lewis for a month, and their agreement had been to meet at the mouth of the Yellowstone, but the mosquitoes made that impossible.

As they made their way slowly down the Missouri, they were joined on August 8 by Nathaniel Pryor and his three men, whom Clark had sent off to ride to the Mandan villages 14 days before. Two days into their journey, all their horses had been stolen, probably by CROW INDIANS. Pryor and his group had followed the thieves for five miles but realized they had little chance of catching them. They then walked north back to the Yellowstone, killed two BUFFALO, made themselves BULL BOATS, and followed Clark downstream. On August 12 Lewis and his men arrived, and the expedition was reunited after five weeks and a journey of nearly 1,000 miles by Clark and 500 miles by Lewis.

Although Clark's exploration of the Yellowstone attracts little attention in analyses of the expedition, it was more worthwhile than Lewis's dramatic journey up the MARIAS RIVER. Clark conscientiously recorded what he saw; charted

the river, its tributaries, and its landmarks on MAPS that were to remain in use for 40 years; and noted the game and wildlife that flourished there. It is still possible to follow his route down the Yellowstone today. Unlike the COLUMBIA RIVER, the Missouri, or the other rivers the expedition explored, there are no dams blocking the Yellowstone. At the time of writing, it is the longest free-flowing river in the United States.

Further Reading

Cutright, Paul Russell. *Lewis & Clark: Pioneering Naturalists.* Lincoln: University of Nebraska Press/Bison Books, 1989.

Fifer, Barbara, and Vicky Soderberg. *Along the Trail with Lewis and Clark.* Great Falls, Mont.: Montana Magazine, 1998.

Heidenreich, C. Adrian. "The Native Americans' Yellowstone." *Montana: The Magazine of Western History* 35 (autumn 1985): 56–67.

Moulton, Gary E., ed. *Atlas of the Lewis and Clark Expedition.* Revised ed. Lincoln: University of Nebraska Press, 1999.

Newby, Rick. "The Yellowstone River." From *Discovering Lewis and Clark: Clark on the Yellowstone.* Available on-line. URL:http://www.lewis-clark.org/CLARK-YELLOWSTONE/YELLOWSTONE/yr_submenu.htm. Downloaded on February 28, 2002.

Osgood, Ernest S. "Clark on the Yellowstone 1806." *Montana: The Magazine of Western History* 18, no. 3 (1968): 9–29.

Wood, W. Raymond, and Gary E. Moulton. "Prince Maximilian and New Maps of the Missouri and Yellowstone Rivers by William Clark." *Western Historical Quarterly* 12 (1981): 372–386.

York (unknown–ca. 1832) *slave, member of the expedition*

Those Indians wer much astonished at my Servent. They never Saw a black man before. All flocked around him & examined him from top to toe.

—William Clark

The son of slaves known as Old York and Rose, York was an African-American slave who had been willed to WILLIAM CLARK in 1799; they had known each other since childhood. Throughout the expedition, York acted as a full member of the CORPS OF DISCOVERY and was given the duties—and privileges—of any other soldier. Yet despite his service to Clark and to the corps, he was rewarded not with his freedom but with continued slavery until, years later, Clark finally granted him what he desired most.

York was living with Clark in CLARKSVILLE, Indiana Territory, when MERIWETHER LEWIS arrived there on October 15, 1803, and it was from that point when many consider the expedition to have really started. Although York was described as Clark's "manservant," Clark's journal entry of December 26

that same year commented on "corporals Whitehouse and York sawing with the whipsaws." This showed that early on York was working with the enlisted men rather than serving Clark exclusively. Later journal entries indicate that he carried a rifle—unusual for a slave—and that he was treated as a trusted member of the corps.

York's complexion, which was very dark, was a source of amazement to the Indians they met, who had never seen a man of his color before; the HIDATSA chief ONE EYE even tried to wipe the blackness off his skin. His size and strength were also fascinating, and the ARIKARA INDIANS among others believed him to be possessed of special powers. He also had a good sense of humor; when Arikara children followed him, then ran screaming when he turned around, he put on an act for them, saying he was a man-eating bear or a cannibal. He often danced for the expedition's Indian hosts, with Private PIERRE CRUZATTE providing the music on his fiddle.

While all Indians tended to like him, Indian women seemed especially enamored of York. In an 1814 interview, Clark described his slave's frequent absences from camp when-

York was a curiosity to many of the Indians the corps met. In this 1908 painting by Charles M. Russell, Hidatsa chief One Eye is trying to rub the blackness off York's skin. *(Montana Historical Society, Helena)*

ever the expedition was within the vicinity of an Indian village. York was apparently in demand as a sexual partner, and he was happy to oblige. Indeed, once an Indian warrior stood guard while his wife slept with York, in the belief that he would attain some of the black man's spiritual power through the sex act.

On November 19, 1805, the corps arrived near the mouth of the COLUMBIA RIVER, where they would spend the winter. A decision needed to be made about where they would build their fort, and the captains opted to put it to a vote on November 24. All expedition members voted—including SACAGAWEA and York. It was a remarkable moment, for never before had a slave or a woman (much less a Native American woman) voted in any form in the United States, although Sacagawea's vote was not included in the final tally as recorded in Clark's journal entry for that date. What York's choice was is not known, but ultimately the corps elected to build FORT CLATSOP on the south side of the river.

Like all other expedition members, York had a landmark named after him: York's Dry River, now Custer Creek, a tributary of the YELLOWSTONE RIVER. In every respect he was an equal of the other men in the expedition. Yet when they returned to non-Indian civilization, he reassumed his role as slave and was given neither the pay nor the land awarded to other men on the expedition. With his service to the corps thus overlooked, he became increasingly recalcitrant and insolent. Surprisingly, Clark could not understand this behavior, writing to his brother in December 1808, "I did wish to do well by him [York]. But as he has got Such a notion about freedom and his emence Services, that I do not expect he will be of much Service to me again." Just a few months later, in a letter written from ST. LOUIS, Clark noted that he had had to give York "a severe trouncing" after refusing to allow him to live near his wife, a slave in Louisville. Harsh though Clark's attitude may seem to modern eyes, it was a sign of the time he lived in and the upbringing of thousands like him.

Clark eventually relented and hired his slave out to a master in Louisville. Finally, some 10 years after the expedition, after being badgered about it relentlessly, he granted York his freedom. York went on to make a living hauling freight between Nashville, Tennessee, and Richmond, Kentucky. He loved to relate stories about his adventures with the expedition, and many of his tales became extremely tall over the years. Although some claim that York lived and died among the Indians of the ROCKY MOUNTAINS, in truth he died of cholera in Tennessee sometime around 1832. On January 17, 2001, President Bill Clinton named him honorary sergeant, regular army.

Further Reading

Betts, Robert B. *In Search of York: The Slave Who Went to the Pacific with Lewis and Clark.* Boulder, Colo.: Associated University Press, 1985.

Duncan, Dayton, and Ken Burns. *Lewis & Clark: The Journey of the Corps of Discovery.* New York: Alfred A. Knopf, 1998.

Hall, Brian. "The Slave Who Went with Them." *Time,* July 8, 2002. Available on-line. URL: http://www.time.com/time/2002/lewis_clark/york.html. Downloaded on July 11, 2002.

Worsham, Alison. "The Placement of York: Where a Black Man Fit in the Hierarchy of the Corps of Discovery." Available on-line. URL: http://www.artsci.wustl.edu/~sjboyd/lc/allison.htm. Downloaded on January 10, 2002.

Appendix A
TRIBES THE EXPEDITION ENCOUNTERED

Note: The names of tribes with an entry in this book are set in **boldface**.

Alsea Indians
Amahami Indians (Anahami, Ahaharway, Wattasoon)
Arikara Indians (Sahnish)
Assiniboine Indians
Bannock Indians
Blackfeet Indians
Cathlamet Indians (Kathlamet)
Cayuse Indians
Chehalis Indians (Chilwitz, Chiltz)
Cheyenne Indians
Chinook Indians
Clackamas Indians
Clatskanie Indians
Clatsop Indians
Cowlitz Indians
Crow Indians (Absaroka)
Flathead Indians (Salish)
Gros Ventre Indians (Atsina)
Hidatsa Indians (Minitari, Minnetaree)
Kickapoo Indians
Klickitat Indians (Klikitat)
Kootenai Indians (Kootenay, Kutenai)
Mandan Indians
Missouri Indians (Missouria)

Multnomah Indians
Nez Perce Indians (Sahaptin, Shahaptin)
Omaha Indians
Osage Indians
Otoe Indians (Oto)
Palouse Indians (Palus)
Pawnee Indians
Quinault Indians
Shoshone Indians
Siletz Indians
Siuslaw Indians
Skilloot Indians
Tenino Indians
Teton Lakota Indians (Teton Sioux)
Tillamook Indians
Umatilla Indians
Umpqua Indians
Wahkiakum Indians (Wahkiaku)
Walla Walla Indians (Walula)
Wanapam Indians (Wanapum, Sokulks)
Wasco Indians (Kiksht)
Wishram Indians (Wishham, Tlakluit)
Yakama Indians (Yakima)
Yankton Nakota Indians (Yankton Sioux)

Appendix B
MAPS

Note: See also maps throughout the Chronology section.

1. United States, 1802
2. Route of the Lewis and Clark Expedition, August 1803–September 1806
3. Fort Mandan and Neighboring Mandan and Hidatsa Villages, November 1804–April 1805 and August 1806
4. Great Plains Indian Culture Area
5. Portage around the Great Falls, June–July 1805
6. Bitterroot Mountains (Lolo Trail), September–October 1805 and May–July 1806
7. Plateau Indian Culture Area
8. Fort Clatsop and Its Indian Neighbors, 1805–1806
9. Campsites and Selected Sites near the Mouth of the Columbia River, November 15, 1805–March 23, 1806
10. Natural History Sites along the Route of the Lewis and Clark Expedition, August 1803–September 1806

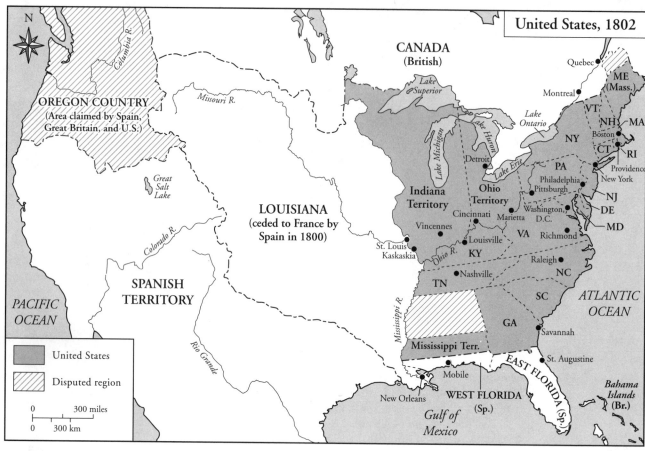

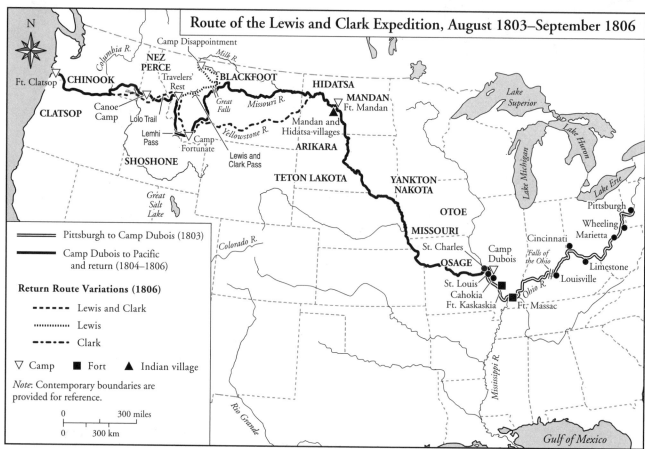

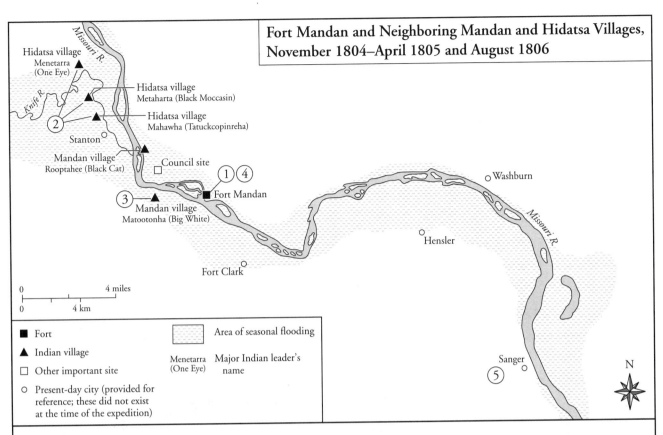

Fort Mandan and Neighboring Mandan and Hidatsa Villages, November 1804–April 1805 and August 1806

Hidatsa village
Menetarra
(One Eye)

Hidatsa village
Metaharta (Black Moccasin)

Hidatsa village
Mahawha (Tatuckcopinreha)

Stanton

Mandan village
Rooptahee (Black Cat)

Council site

Fort Mandan

Mandan village
Matootonha (Big White)

Fort Clark

Washburn

Hensler

Sanger

Missouri R.

Knife R.

Missouri R.

0   4 miles
0   4 km

◼ Fort

▲ Indian village

☐ Other important site

○ Present-day city (provided for
   reference; these did not exist
   at the time of the expedition)

☐ Area of seasonal flooding

Menetarra
(One Eye)   Major Indian leader's
            name

N

1. ". . . half a mile lower down the river, began to clear a place for a camp and fort. We pitched our tents and laid the foundation of one line of huts."

—Patrick Gass, November 2, 1804

2. "The Indians in all the towns and camps treated Captain Lewis and the party with great respect, except one of the principal chiefs . . . Horned Weasel, Who did not chuse to be seen by the Capt., and left word that he was not at home, &c."

— William Clark, November 27, 1804

3. ". . . went up to the 1st village of Mandans to dance . . . carried with us a fiddle & a Tambereen & a Sounden horn, . . . So we danced in different lodges until late in the afternoon. then a part of the men returned to the fort. the remainder Stayed all night in the village."

—John Ordway, January 1, 1805

4. "About five o'clock this evening, one of the wives of Charbonneau was delivered of a fine boy. . . . her labor was tedious and the pain violent. . . . he administered two rings of [rattlesnake] to the woman, broken in small pieces with the fingers, and added to a small quantity of water. . . . she had not taken it more than ten minutes, before she brought forth."

—Meriwether Lewis, February 11, 1805

5. "We do not go on so rapidly as we did higher up the river: but having lashed our small canoes together, we go on very safe and can make fifty or sixty miles a day. Captain Lewis is getting much better and we are all in good spirits. . . . and we proceeded on, . . ."

—Patrick Gass, August 19, 1806

Note: Original spelling and punctuation have been retained from journal entries.

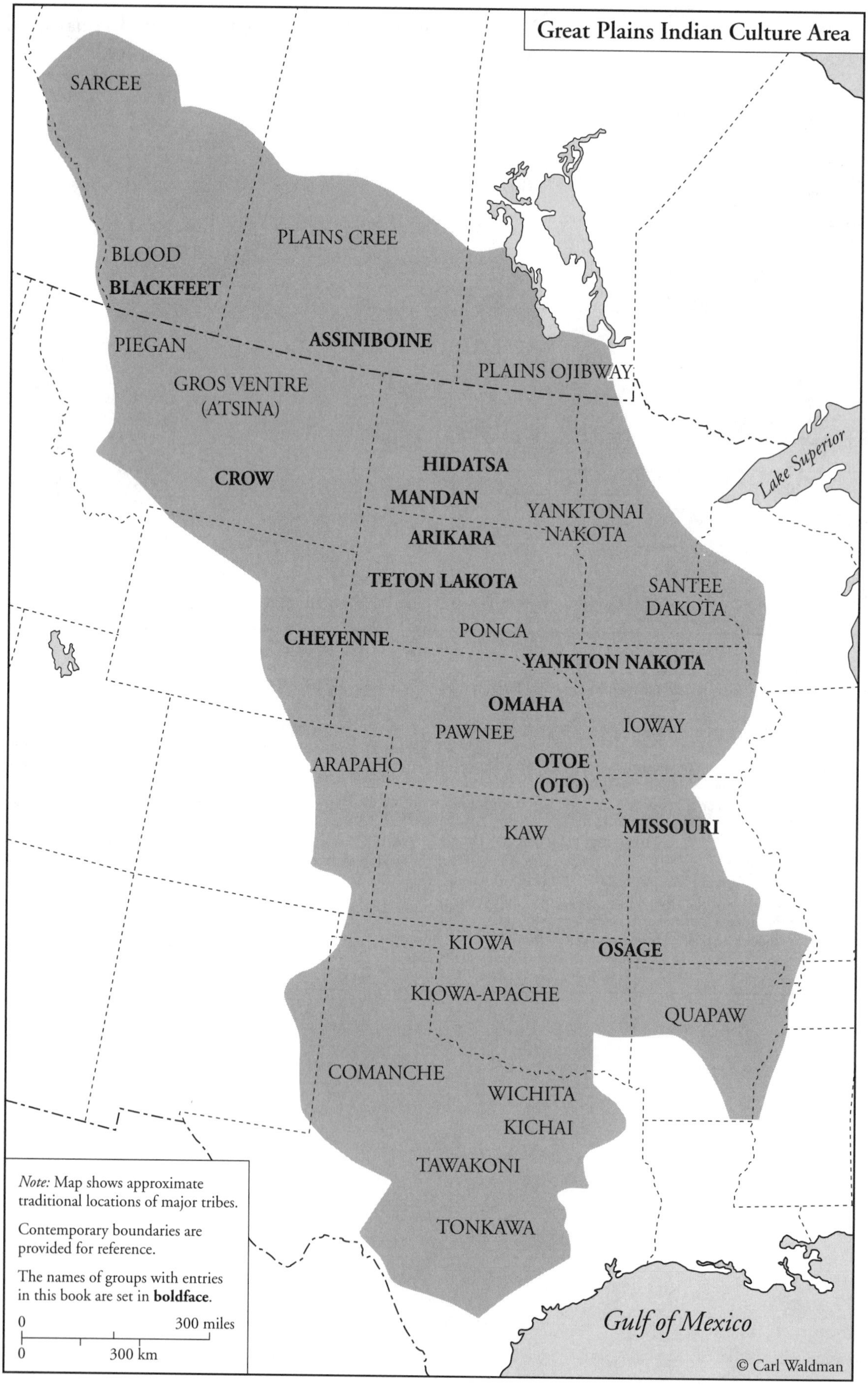

Great Plains Indian Culture Area

SARCEE

PLAINS CREE

BLOOD
BLACKFEET

PIEGAN

ASSINIBOINE

PLAINS OJIBWAY

GROS VENTRE
(ATSINA)

Lake Superior

HIDATSA

CROW

MANDAN

YANKTONAI
NAKOTA

ARIKARA

TETON LAKOTA

SANTEE
DAKOTA

CHEYENNE

PONCA

YANKTON NAKOTA

OMAHA

PAWNEE

IOWAY

ARAPAHO

OTOE
(OTO)

KAW

MISSOURI

KIOWA

OSAGE

KIOWA-APACHE

QUAPAW

COMANCHE

WICHITA

KICHAI

TAWAKONI

TONKAWA

Gulf of Mexico

Note: Map shows approximate traditional locations of major tribes.

Contemporary boundaries are provided for reference.

The names of groups with entries in this book are set in **boldface**.

0	300 miles
0	300 km

© Carl Waldman

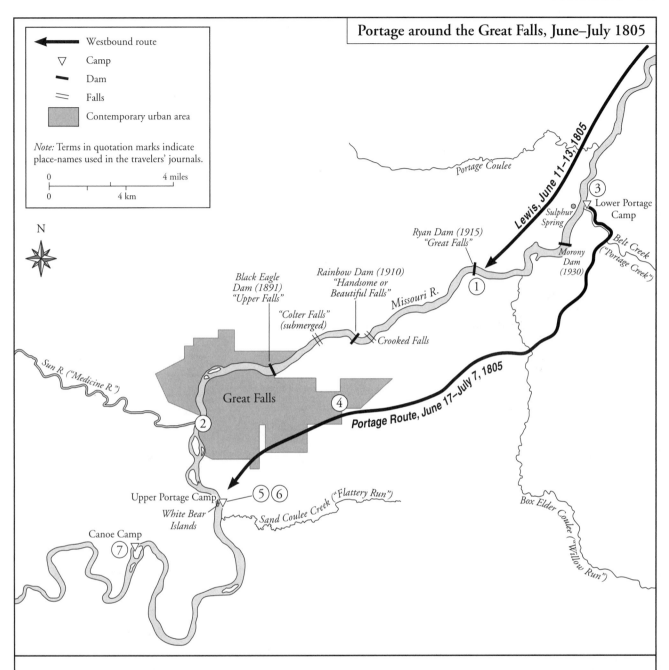

Portage around the Great Falls, June–July 1805

Westbound route
▽ Camp
▬ Dam
⸗ Falls
Contemporary urban area

Note: Terms in quotation marks indicate place-names used in the travelers' journals.

0 — 4 miles
0 — 4 km

N

Portage Coulee

Lewis, June 11–13, 1805

Sulphur Spring

③ Lower Portage Camp

Belt Creek ("Portage Creek")

Ryan Dam (1915) "Great Falls"

Morony Dam (1930)

Rainbow Dam (1910) "Handsome or Beautiful Falls"

Black Eagle Dam (1891) "Upper Falls"

Missouri R.

①

"Colter Falls" (submerged)

Crooked Falls

Sun R. ("Medicine R.")

Great Falls

②

④

Portage Route, June 17–July 7, 1805

Box Elder Coulee ("Willow Run")

Upper Portage Camp ▽

⑤ ⑥

White Bear Islands

Sand Coulee Creek   *("Flattery Run")*

Canoe Camp ▽

⑦

1. "I wished for the pencil of Salvator Rosa, a Titian, or the pen of Thomson, that I might be enabled to give to the enlightened world some just idea of this truly magnificent and sublimely grand object which has, from the commencement of time, been concealed from the view of civilized man."
   —Meriwether Lewis, June 13, 1805

2. ". . . a large white, or reather brown bear had perceived and crept on me within twenty steps before I discovered him. In the first moment I drew up my gun to shoot, but at the same instant recolected that she was not loaded . . . "
   —Meriwether Lewis, June 14, 1805

3. "The Indian woman verry bad, & will take no medisin what ever . . . If she dies it will be the fault of her husband as I am now convinced."
   —William Clark, June 16, 1805

4. "At every halt these poor fellos tumble down and are so much fortiegued that many of them are asleep in an instant. In short, their fatiegues are incredible . . . yet no one complains. All go with cheerfullness."
   —Meriwether Lewis, June 23, 1805

5. "It being the 4th of Independence we drank the last of our ardent Spirits except a little reserved for Sickness."
   —John Ordway, July 4, 1805

6. "Therefore for want of tar or pitch we had, after all our labour, to haul our new [iron-frame] boat on shore, and leave it at this place."
   —Patrick Gass, July 9, 1805

7. "About 11 o'clock we set out from this place, which we had called Canoe Camp."
   —Patrick Gass, July 15, 1805

Note: Original spelling and punctuation have been retained from journal entries.

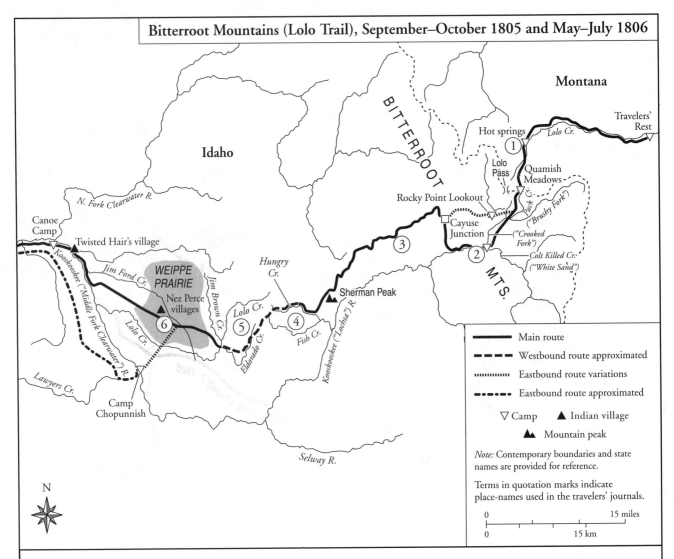

Bitterroot Mountains (Lolo Trail), September–October 1805 and May–July 1806

Main route

Westbound route approximated

Eastbound route variations

Eastbound route approximated

▽ Camp   ▲ Indian village

▲▲ Mountain peak

Note: Contemporary boundaries and state names are provided for reference.

Terms in quotation marks indicate place-names used in the travelers' journals.

0 — 15 miles

0 — 15 km

1. "When we had gone 2 miles, we came to a most beautiful warm spring, the water of which is considerably above the blood-heat; and I could not bear my hand in it without unpleasantness."
—Patrick Gass, September 13, 1805

2. ". . . encamped opposit a Small Island at the mouth of a branch on the right side of the river. . . . Here we were compelled to kill a colt for our men & selves to eat for the want of meat & we named the south fork Colt Killed Creek, . . ."
—William Clark, September 14, 1805

3. "Some of the men without Socks, wrapped rags on their feet, and loaded up our horses and Set out without anything to eat and proceeded on. Could hardly See the old trail for the Snow."
—Joseph Whitehouse, September 16, 1805

4. "Encamped on a bold running creek passing to the left which I call *Hungery* Creek as at that place we had nothing to eate."
—William Clark, September 18, 1805

5. "The men are becoming lean and debilitated, on account of the scarcity and poor quality of the provisions on which we subsist . . . We have, however, some hopes of getting soon out of this horrible mountainous desert . . ."
—Patrick Gass, September 19, 1805

6. "At 12 miles descended the mountain to a leavel pine counttry. Proceeded on . . . to a small plain in which I found main Indian lodges. Those people gave us a small piece of buffalow meat, some dried salmon beries & roots. . . . They call themselves *Cho pun-nish* or *Pierced noses.*"
—William Clark, September 20, 1805

Note: Original spelling and punctuation have been retained from journal entries.

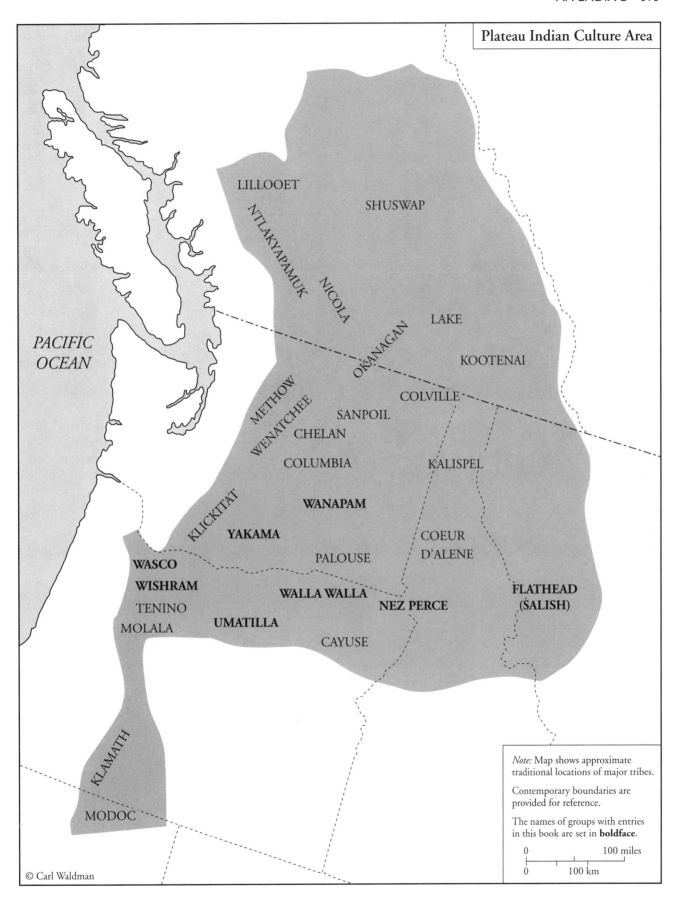

Plateau Indian Culture Area

PACIFIC OCEAN

LILLOOET
SHUSWAP
NTLAKYAPAMUK
NICOLA
OKANAGAN
LAKE
KOOTENAI
COLVILLE
METHOW
WENATCHEE
SANPOIL
CHELAN
COLUMBIA
KALISPEL
KLICKITAT
WANAPAM
YAKAMA
COEUR D'ALENE
PALOUSE
WASCO
WISHRAM
WALLA WALLA
FLATHEAD (SALISH)
TENINO
NEZ PERCE
MOLALA
UMATILLA
CAYUSE
KLAMATH
MODOC

Note: Map shows approximate traditional locations of major tribes.

Contemporary boundaries are provided for reference.

The names of groups with entries in this book are set in **boldface**.

0   100 miles

0   100 km

© Carl Waldman

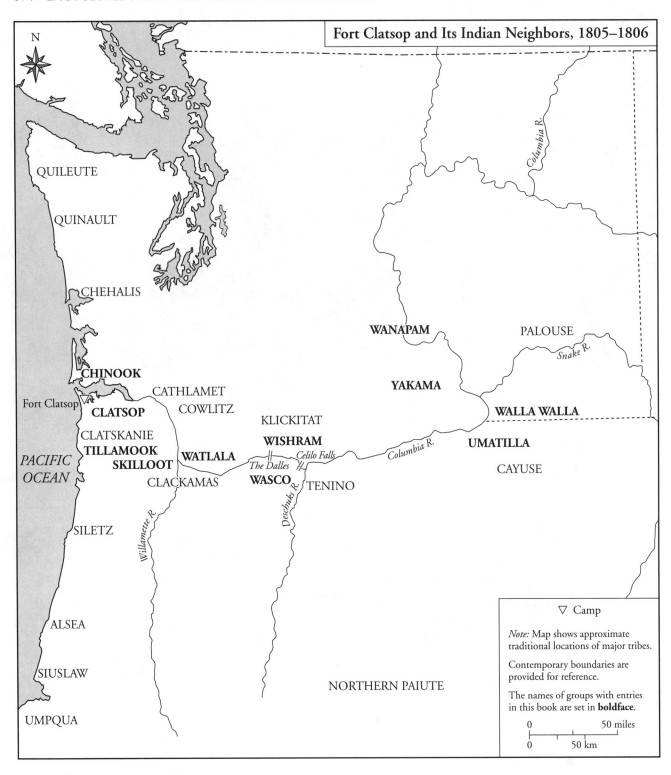

Fort Clatsop and Its Indian Neighbors, 1805–1806

N

QUILEUTE

QUINAULT

CHEHALIS

CHINOOK

Fort Clatsop

CLATSOP

CATHLAMET

COWLITZ

KLICKITAT

CLATSKANIE

TILLAMOOK

SKILLOOT

WATLALA

WISHRAM

Celilo Falls

The Dalles

WASCO

TENINO

CLACKAMAS

PACIFIC OCEAN

SILETZ

Willamette R.

Deschutes R.

Columbia R.

WANAPAM

PALOUSE

Snake R.

YAKAMA

WALLA WALLA

UMATILLA

CAYUSE

ALSEA

SIUSLAW

NORTHERN PAIUTE

UMPQUA

▽ Camp

Note: Map shows approximate traditional locations of major tribes.

Contemporary boundaries are provided for reference.

The names of groups with entries in this book are set in **boldface**.

0   50 miles

0   50 km

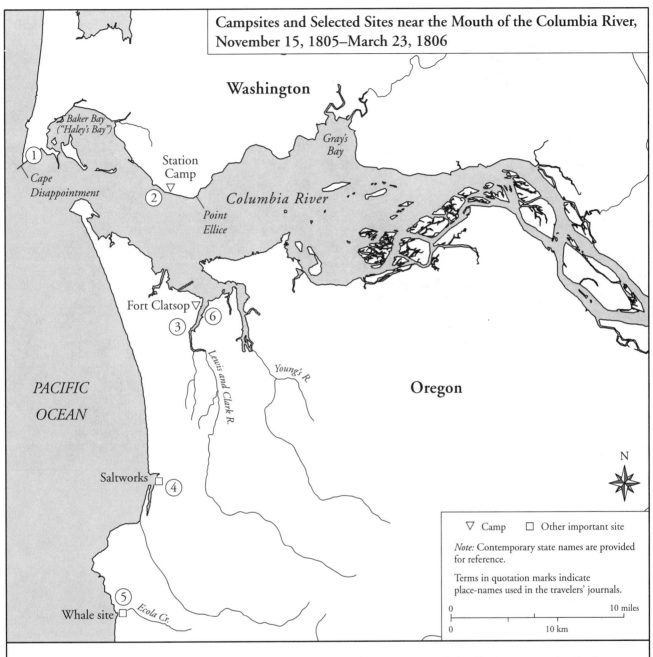

Campsites and Selected Sites near the Mouth of the Columbia River,
November 15, 1805–March 23, 1806

1. "Here I found Capt. Lewis name on a tree. I also engraved my name,
   & by land the day of the month and year, as also several of the men."
   —William Clark, November 18, 1805

2. "In the Evening our Officers had the whole party assembled in order to
   consult which place would be the best, for us to take up our Winter
   Quarters at. The greater part of our Men were of opinion; that it
   would be best, to cross the River, . . . "
   —Joseph Whitehouse, November 24, 1805

3. "at day light this morning we we[re] awoke by the discharge of the
   fire arms of all our party & a Selute, Shoute and a Song which the
   whole party joined in under our windows, after which they retired to
   their rooms were Chearfull all the morning."
   —William Clark, December 25, 1805

4. "About noon Captain Clarke with 14 men came to the saltmakers camp,
   in their way to the place where the large fish had been driven on shore,
   some distance beyond this camp."
   —Patrick Gass, January 7, 1806

5. "I . . . thank providence for directing the whale to us; and think him
   much more kind to us than he was to jonah, having Sent this monster to
   be Swallowed by us in Sted of Swallowing of us as jonah's did.
   —William Clark, January 8, 1806

6. "the rain Seased and it became fair. about meridian at which time we
   loaded our canoes & at 1 P.M. left Fort Clatsop on our homeward bound
   journey. at this place we had wintered and remained from the
   7th of Decr 1805 to this day, and have lived as well as we had any right
   to expect, . . ."
   —John Ordway, March 23, 1806

Note: Original spelling and punctuation have been retained from journal entries.

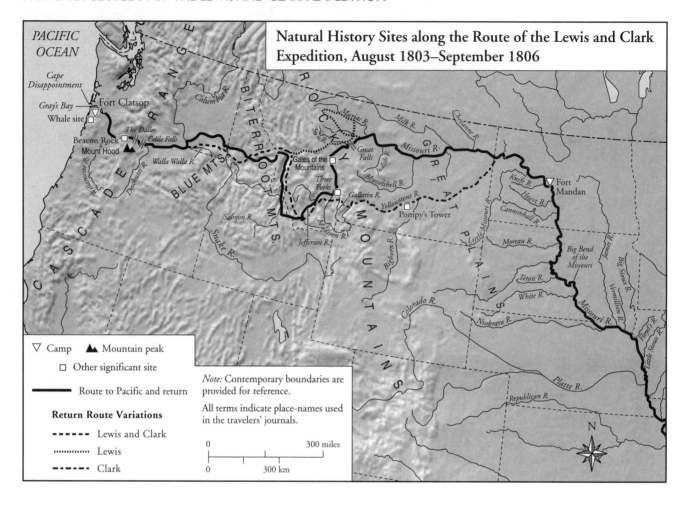

Natural History Sites along the Route of the Lewis and Clark Expedition, August 1803–September 1806

PACIFIC OCEAN

Cape Disappointment
Gray's Bay — Fort Clatsop
Whale site
Beacon Rock
Mount Hood
The Dalles
Celilo Falls
Columbia R.
Walla Walla R.
Deschutes R.
CASCADE RANGE
BLUE MTS.
BITTERROOT MTS.
Snake R.
Salmon R.
Jefferson R.
Madison R.
Three Forks
Gates of the Mountains
Gallatin R.
Great Falls
Sun R.
Marias R.
Milk R.
Cheyenne R.
Missouri R.
Judith R.
Musselshell R.
Yellowstone R.
Pompy's Tower
Bighorn R.
Colorado R.
ROCKY MOUNTAINS
GREAT PLAINS
Little Missouri R.
Knife R.
Heart R.
Cannonball R.
Fort Mandan
Big Bend of the Missouri
Moreau R.
Teton R.
White R.
Niobrara R.
James R.
Big Sioux R.
Vermillion R.
Floyd's R.
Little Sioux R.
Missouri R.
Platte R.
Republican R.

N

△ Camp ▲▲ Mountain peak
□ Other significant site

——— Route to Pacific and return

Return Route Variations

- - - - Lewis and Clark
·········· Lewis
- · - · - Clark

Note: Contemporary boundaries are provided for reference.

All terms indicate place-names used in the travelers' journals.

0   300 miles

0   300 km

Bibliography

BOOKS AND ARTICLES

The following bibliography is divided by topics for ease of use. This combines books, printed articles, and on-line articles. Some may appear under more than one heading. At the end there is a list of recommended websites for further information.

General Information

Allen, John Logan. *Passage Through the Garden: Lewis and Clark and the Image of the American Northwest.* Urbana: University of Illinois Press, 1975. Reprint, New York: Dover Publications, 1991.

Ambrose, Stephen E. *Undaunted Courage: Meriwether Lewis, Thomas Jefferson, and the Opening of the American West.* New York: Simon and Schuster, 1996.

Appleman, Roy E. *Lewis and Clark: Historic Places Associated with Their Transcontinental Expedition (1804–06).* Washington, D.C.: U.S. Department of the Interior, National Park Service, 1993.

Bakeless, John E. *Lewis & Clark: Partners in Discovery.* Mineola, N.Y.: Dover, 1996.

Chidsey, Donald Barr. *Lewis and Clark: The Great Adventure.* New York: Crown, 1970.

Chuinard, Eldon G. "The Actual Role of the Bird Woman." *Montana: The Magazine of Western History* 26, no. 3 (1976): 18–29.

Cutright, Paul Russell. *Lewis & Clark: Pioneering Naturalists.* Lincoln: University of Nebraska Press/Bison Books, 1989.

Duncan, Dayton, and Ken Burns. *Lewis & Clark: The Journey of the Corps of Discovery.* New York: Alfred A. Knopf, 1998.

Eide, Ingvard Henry. *American Odyssey: The Journey of Lewis and Clark.* Chicago: Rand McNally, 1969.

Hawke, David Freeman. *Those Tremendous Mountains: The Story of the Lewis and Clark Expedition.* New York: W. W. Norton & Company, 1998.

Jackson, Donald. *Thomas Jefferson & the Stony Mountains: Exploring the West from Monticello.* Norman: University of Oklahoma Press, 1993.

Lavender, David. *The Way to the Western Sea: Lewis and Clark Across the Continent.* New York: Harper and Row, 1988.

Ronda, James P. *Finding the West: Explorations with Lewis and Clark.* Albuquerque: University of New Mexico Press, 2001.

———, ed. *Voyages of Discovery: Essays on the Lewis and Clark Expedition.* Helena: Montana Historical Society Press, 1998.

Schmidt, Thomas and Jeremy Schmidt. *The Saga of Lewis & Clark into the Uncharted West.* New York: DK Publishing, 1999.

Biographical Information

CORPS OF DISCOVERY

Anderson, Irving W. "The Sacagawea Mystique: Her Age, Name, Role and Final Destiny." *Columbia* 13, no. 3 (Fall 1999). Available on-line. URL: http://www.wshs.org/lewisand clark/sacagawea.htm. Downloaded on July 12, 2002.

———. "Sacajawea?—Sakakawea?—Sacagawea? Spelling—Pronunciation—Meaning." Available on-line. URL: http://www.lewisandclark.org/pages/sactext.htm. Downloaded on March 26, 2001.

Appleman, Roy E. "Joseph and Reubin Field, Kentucky Frontiersmen of the Lewis and Clark Expedition and Their Father, Abraham." *Filson Club Quarterly* 49, no. 1 (1975): 5–36.

Archambault, Alan, and Marko Zlatich. "Corps of Volunteers for North Western Discovery, 1804–1806." *Military Collector and Historian* 44 (winter 1992): 176.

Bakeless, John E. *Lewis & Clark: Partners in Discovery.* Mineola, N.Y.: Dover, 1996.

Betts, Robert B. *In Search of York: The Slave Who Went to the Pacific with Lewis and Clark.* Boulder, Colo.: Associated University Press, 1985.

Bratton, Steve. "William E. Bratton of Lewis and Clark Fame." *The Bratton Bulletin,* Vol. 5, Issue 1, October–December 1995. Available on-line. URL: http://www.gendex.com/~guest/69751/BrattonHomePage/br09011.htm. Updated on February 6, 2000.

Brown, D. Alexander. "The Mysterious Death of a Hero." *American History Illustrated* 5, no. 9 (1971): 18–27.

Butterfield, Bonnie "Spirit Wind-Walker." *Sacagawea: Captive, Indian Interpreter, Great American Legend: Her Life and Death.* ©1998, 2000. Available on-line. URL: http://www.geocities.com/CollegePark/Hall/9626/NativeAmericans.html. Downloaded on March 15, 2002.

Clark, Ella E., and Margot Edmonds. *Sacagawea of the Lewis and Clark Expedition.* Berkeley: University of California Press, 1979.

Clarke, Charles G. *The Men of the Lewis and Clark Expedition: A Biographical Roster of the Fifty-One Members and a Composite Diary of Their Activities from All Known Sources.* Reprint, Lincoln: Bison Books, University of Nebraska Press, 2002.

Colter-Frick, Ruth. "Forty-Four Years with John Colter: Colter, U.S. Mounted Ranger." *Yellowstone Net Newspaper.* Available on-line. URL: http://www.yellowstone.net/newspaper/news090998.htm. Posted on September 9, 1998.

———. "Forty-Four Years with John Colter: John Colter's Estate." *Yellowstone Net Newspaper.* Available on-line. URL: http://www.yellowstone.net/newspaper/news100998.htm. Posted on October 9, 1998.

Dawson, Jan C. "Sacagawea: Pilot or Pioneer Mother?" *Pacific Northwest Quarterly* 83, no. 1 (1992): 22–28.

Dillon, Richard. *Meriwether Lewis: A Biography.* Santa Cruz: Western Tanager, 1988.

Everley, Steve. "Web Site Dedicated to the History and Memory of Sgt. Charles Floyd 1782–1804." Available on-line. URL: http://www.sgtfloyd.com/default.htm. Updated on October 2, 2001.

Field, Eugene A., and Lucie C. Field. "The Ancestry of Joseph and Reubin Field of The Lewis and Clark Expedition The Corps of Discovery." Available on-line. URL: http://www.luciefield.net/ancjr.html. Updated on January 5, 2001.

Fisher, Vardis. *Suicide or Murder?: The Strange Death of Governor Meriwether Lewis.* Reprint, Denver, Colo.: Alan Swallow Co., 1962; Reprint, 1993.

Forrest, Earle E. "Patrick Gass, Carpenter of the Lewis and Clark Expedition." *Bulletin of the Missouri Historical Society* 4 (July 1948): 217–222.

Hall, Brian. "The Slave Who Went with Them." *Time* (July 8, 2002): p. 60. Available on-line. URL: http://www.time.com/time/2002/lewis_clark/york.html. Downloaded on July 11, 2002.

Harris, Burton. *John Colter: His Years in the Rockies.* Lincoln: University of Nebraska Press, 1993.

Hebard, Grace Raymond. *Sacagawea: Guide and Interpreter of Lewis and Clark.* Reprint ed. Mineola, N.Y.: Dover Books, 2002.

Howard, Helen Addison. "The Mystery of Sacagawea's Death." *Pacific Northwest Quarterly* 58, no. 1 (1967): 1–6.

Hunsaker, Joyce Badgley. *Sacagawea Speaks: Beyond the Shining Mountains with Lewis & Clark.* Helena, Mont.: Falcon Publishing Co., 2001.

———. "Who Was Sacagawea?" *Time* (July 8, 2002): pp. 56–57.

Jackson, Donald. "Call Him a Good Old Dog, but Don't Call Him Scannon." *We Proceeded On* 11, no. 3 (1985).

Jacob, John G. *The Life and Times of Patrick Gass, Now Sole Survivor of the Overland Expedition to the Pacific, under Lewis and Clark, in 1804–5–6.* Wellsburg, Va.: Jacob & Smith, 1859.

Jefferson National Expansion Memorial. "The Lewis and Clark Journey of Discovery: Corps of Discovery—The Others." Available on-line. URL: http://www.nps.gov/jeff/LewisClark2/CorpsOfDiscovery/TheOthers/Others.htm. Downloaded on April 11, 2002.

Johnston, Ed. "The Life and Times of John Colter." Available on-line. URL: http://www.edjohnston.com/edsci/colter1.htm. Downloaded on September 16, 2001.

Jones, Landon Y. "Iron Will." *Smithsonian* 33, no. 5 (August 2002): pp. 96–107.

Kessler, Donna J. *The Making of Sacagawea: A Euro-American Legend.* Tuscaloosa: University of Alabama Press, 1996.

Lange, Robert. "The Expedition's Brothers—Joseph and Reuben Field." *We Proceeded On* 4, no. 3 (July 1978): 15–16.

———. "George Drouillard (Drewyer)—One of the Two or Three Most Valuable Men on the Expedition." *We Proceeded On* 5, no. 2 (May 1979): 14–16.

———. "John Shields: Lewis and Clark's Handyman: Gunsmith–Blacksmith–General Mechanic for the Expedition." *We Proceeded On* 5, no. 3 (July 1979): 14–16.

———. "Private George Shannon: The Expedition's Youngest Member—1785 or 1787–1836." *We Proceeded On* 8, no. 3 (July 1982): 10–15.

———. "William Bratton—One of Lewis and Clark's Men." *We Proceeded On* 7, no. 1 (February 1981): 8–11.

Loos, John L. "William Clark: Indian Agent." *Kansas Quarterly* 3, no. 4 (1971): 29–38.

Mountain Men and the Fur Trade (Research Center): "Accounts of John Colter's Escape from the Blackfeet." From various contemporary sources. Available on-line. URL: http://alt.xmission.com/~drudy/mtman/html/colter.html. Downloaded on May 20, 2001.

Mussulman, Joseph. "My Boy Pomp: About That Name." From *Discovering Lewis and Clark: Clark on the Yellowstone.* Available on-line. URL: http://www.lewis-clark.org/CLARK-YELLOWSTONE/POMPSTOWER/yr_pomp1.htm. Downloaded on February 28, 2002.

Nielsen, Quig. "Sacagawea of the Lewis and Clark Expedition." Available on-line. URL: http://www.thehistory.net.com/WildWest/articles/1999/1299_text.htm. Downloaded on May 23, 2001.

North Dakota Lewis & Clark Bicentennial Foundation. *Members of the Corps of Discovery.* Bismarck, N.Dak.: United Printing and Mailing, 2000.

Osgood, Ernest Staples. "Our Dog Scannon—Partner in Discovery." *Montana: The Magazine of Western History* 26, no. 3 (1976): 8–17.

Ottoson, Dennis R. "Toussaint Charbonneau, a Most Durable Man." *South Dakota History* 6, no. 2 (1976): 152–185.

PBS Online. *Lewis and Clark: Inside the Corps of Discovery.* Available on-line. URL: http://www.pbs.org/lewisand clark/inside/index.html. Downloaded on May 18, 2001.

Pringle, Lawrence. *Dog of Discovery: A Newfoundland's Adventures with Lewis and Clark.* Honesdale, Penn.: Boyds Mills Press, 2002.

Rogers, Ken. "The Engages: Who were the unnamed French watermen?" *The Bismarck Tribune.* Available on-line. URL: http://www.ndonline.com/tribwebpage/features/ lewisclark/2001/engages.html. Downloaded on February 16, 2002.

Skarsten, M.O. *George Drouillard: Hunter and Interpreter for Lewis and Clark and Fur Trader, 1807–1810.* Glendale, Calif: A. H. Clark Co., 1964.

Smith, James S., and Kathryn Smith. "Sedulous Sergeant, Patrick Gass: An Original Biography by Direct Descendants." *Montana The Magazine of Western History* 5, no. 3 (summer 1955): 20–27.

Sonneborn, Liz. *Pomp: The True Story of the Baby on the Sacagawea Dollar.* Available on-line. URL: http://pomp story.home.mindspring.com/. Downloaded on May 22, 2001.

Steffen, Jerome O. *William Clark: Jeffersonian Man on the Frontier.* Norman: University of Oklahoma Press, 1977.

Talbot, Margaret. "Searching for Sacagawea." *National Geographic* 203, no. 2 (February 2003): 68–85.

Wagner, Chad, and Denny Wesney. "Meriwether Lewis: A Portrait of an American Explorer and Hero." Available on-line. URL:http://www.wfu.edu/Academic-departments/ History/newnation/lewis/lewisdex.htm. Downloaded on January 10, 2002.

Woodhouse, Leighton. "Who Killed Meriwether Lewis?" For Salon Ivory Tower. Available on-line. URL: http:// www.salon.com/it/feature/1999/03/22feature.html. Posted on March 22, 1999.

Worsham, Alison. "The Placement of York: Where a Black Man Fit in the Hierarchy of the Corps of Discovery." Available on-line. URL: http://www.artsci.wustl.edu/ ~sjboyd/lc/allison.htm. Downloaded on January 10, 2002.

Yater, George H. "Nine Young Men from Kentucky." *We Proceeded On.* Lewis and Clark Trail Heritage Foundation Publication No. 11, May 1992: 3.

OTHERS

American Council of Learned Societies. *Dictionary of American Biography.* "Allen, Paul." New York: Charles Scribner's Sons, 1928.

Anderson, Bern. *Life and Voyages of Captain George Vancouver, Surveyor of the Sea.* Toronto: University of Toronto Press, 1966.

Bakeless, John E. *Background to Glory: The Life of George Rogers Clark.* Lincoln: University of Nebraska Press, 1992.

———. *Daniel Boone: Master of the Wilderness.* Reprint, Lincoln: University of Nebraska Press, 1989.

Business Leader Profiles for Students. "Nicholas Biddle." Gale Research, 1999. Available on-line. URL: http:// on-line.valencia.cc.fl.us/ckillinger/AMH2010/ AMH2010.Biddlebio2.htm. Downloaded on January 10, 2002.

Clark, Daniel. *Proofs of the corruption of Gen. James Wilkinson, and of his connexion with Aaron Burr, with a full refutation of his slanderous allegations in relation to the character of the principal witness against him.* Freeport, N.Y.: Books for Libraries Press, 1970. Reprint ed.: Arno Press, New York, 1971.

Connor, Seymour V. "Sibley, John (1757–1837)." Handbook of Texas On-line. URL: http://www.tsha.utexas.edu/ handbook/on-line/articles/view/SS/fsi2.html. Downloaded on February 6, 2002.

Daniells, Roy. *Alexander Mackenzie and the North West.* Toronto: Oxford University Press, 1971.

Daniel Stowe Botanical Garden. "André Michaux: Explorer, Collector, Botanist." Available on-line. URL: http://www. michaux.org. Downloaded on January 20, 2002.

Davis, Nancy M. "Andrew Ellicott: Astronomer . . . Mathematician . . . Surveyor." Lewis and Clark Heritage Trail Foundation, Philadelphia Chapter. Available on-line. URL: http://www.lewisandclarkphila.org/philadelphia/ philadelphiaellicott.html. Downloaded on February 7, 2002.

DeRosier Jr., Arthur H. "William Dunbar, Explorer." *Journal of Mississippi History* 25 (July 1963).

Dictionary of American Biography. "Henry Dearborn." Available on-line. URL: http://www.hampton.lib.nh.us/hampton/ biog/henrydearborn1.htm. Updated on December 22, 1999.

Douglas, Walter Bond. *Manuel Lisa. With hitherto unpublished material, annotated and edited by Abraham P. Nasatir.* New York: Argosy-Antiquarian, 1964.

Faragher, John Mack. *Daniel Boone: The Life and Legend of an American Pioneer.* New York: Henry Holt, 1992.

Fisher, Robin, and Hugh Johnston, eds. *From Maps to Metaphors: The Pacific World of George Vancouver.* Vancouver: University of British Columbia, 1993.

Foley, William E. "The Lewis and Clark Expedition's Silent Partners: The Chouteau Brothers of St. Louis." *Missouri Historical Review* 77, no. 2 (1983): 131–146.

Foley, William E., and C. David Rice. *The First Chouteaus: River Barons of Early St. Louis.* Urbana: University of Illinois Press, 2000.

Govan, Thomas Payne. *Nicholas Biddle: Nationalist and Public Banker, 1786–1844.* Chicago: University of Chicago Press, 1959.

Graveline, Paul. "Joseph Gravelines and the Lewis and Clark Expedition." *We Proceeded On* 3, no. 4 (October 1977): 5–6.

Hay, Robson, and M. R. Werner. *The Admirable Trumpeter: A Biography of General James Wilkinson.* Garden City, N.Y.: Doubleday, Doran & Company, Inc., 1941.

Hosack, David. *Tribute to the memory of the late Caspar Wistar, M.D.: professor of anatomy, &c. in the University of*

Pennsylvania, president of the American Philosophical Society for the Promotion of Useful Knowledge, &c. New York: Printed by C.S. Van Winkle, 1818.

Hudson, Mary A. "Amos Stoddard and the Territory of Missouri." From *The Heritage of Missouri.* Available on-line. URL: http://www.rootsweb.com/~mostodd2/stod-settlers/amos-stod.htm. Downloaded on March 3, 2002.

Jackson, Donald. *The Journals of Zebulon Montgomery Pike with Letters and Related Documents.* 2 vols. Norman: University of Oklahoma Press, 1966.

Jefferson, Thomas. *Jefferson: Writings: Autobiography/Notes on the State of Virginia/Public and Private Papers/Addresses/Letters.* New York: Library of America, 1984.

Ketcham, Ralph. *James Madison: A Biography.* Charlottesville: University of Virginia Press, 1990.

Kuralt, Charles. "Tribute to the Noted French Botanist Andre Michaux." Grandfather Mountain, August 28, 1994. URL: http://www.grandfather.com/museum/michaux/CKmichaux.htm. Downloaded on January 20, 2002.

Laroque, François. *The Journal of François Larocque.* Reprint, Fairfield, Wash.: Ye Galleon Press, 1981.

Madsen, Axel. *John Jacob Astor: America's First Millionaire.* New York: Wiley, 2001.

Marshall, Thomas Maitland. *The Life and Papers of Frederick Bates.* St. Louis: Missouri Historical Society, 1926.

Mathews, Catherine Van Cortland. *Andrew Ellicott: His Life and Letters.* Alexander, N.C.: WorldComm, 1997.

McDonald, Forrest. *The Presidency of Thomas Jefferson.* Lawrence: University Press of Kansas, 1998.

McLaughlin, Jack. *Jefferson and Monticello: The Biography of a Builder.* Reprint ed. New York: Henry Holt, 1990.

Mussulman, Joseph. "François-Antoine Larocque." From *Discovering Lewis and Clark: Clark on the Yellowstone.* Available on-line. URL: http://www.lewisclark.org/CLARK-YELLOWSTONE/LAROCQUE/am_laroc-mmenu.htm. Downloaded on February 28, 2002.

Oglesby, Richard E. *Manuel Lisa and the Opening of the Missouri Fur Trade.* Norman: University of Oklahoma Press, 1963.

Ord, George. *Sketch of the Life of Alexander Wilson.* Philadelphia: H. Hall, 1828.

Pugh, Ellen. *Brave His Soul: The Story of Prince Madog of Wales and His Discovery of America in 1170.* New York: Dodd, Mead & Company, 1970.

Pursh, Frederick. *Journal of a Botanical Excursion in the Northeastern Parts of the States of Pennsylvania and New York during the year 1807.* Edited by William. M. Beauchamp. Port Washington, N.Y.: I. J. Friedman, 1969.

Reveal, James L. "Frederick Traugott Pursh (1774–1820)." From *Discovering Lewis and Clark: A Nomenclatural Morass.* Available on-line. URL: http://www.lewis-clark.org/REVEAL/bo_purs1.htm. Downloaded on March 1, 2002.

Rush, Benjamin. *The Autobiography of Benjamin Rush; His "Travels through life" Together with his Commonplace Book*

for 1789–1813. Edited with introduction and notes by George W. Corner. Princeton, N.J.: Published for the American Philosophical Society by Princeton University Press, 1948.

Savage Jr., Henry, and Elizabeth J. Savage. *André and François André Michaux.* Charlottesville: University of Virginia Press, 1986.

Sellers, Charles Coleman. *Charles Willson Peale.* New York: Scribner, 1969.

———. *Mr. Peale's Museum: Charles Willson Peale and the First Popular Museum of Natural Science and Art.* New York: Norton, 1980.

Smith, James K. *David Thompson: Fur Trader, Explorer, Geographer.* Toronto: Oxford University Press, 1971.

Stein, Susan R. *The Worlds of Thomas Jefferson at Monticello.* New York: Harry N. Abrams, 1993.

Stevens, John Austin. *Albert Gallatin: An American Statesman.* New York: AMS Press, 1998.

Stokesbury, James L. "John Jacob Astor: A Self-Invented Money-Making Machine." Available on-line. URL: http://www.thehistorynet.com/AmericanHistory/articles/1997/12972_text.htm. Downloaded on May 15, 2001.

Terrell, John Upton. *Zebulon Pike: The Life and Times of an Adventurer.* New York: Weybright and Talley, 1968.

Van Noppen, John James, and Ina Woestemeyer Van Noppen. *Daniel Boone, Backwoodsman: The Green Woods Were His Portion.* Boone, N.C.: Appalachian Press, 1966.

Williams, David. *John Evans and the Legend of Madoc, 1770–1779.* Cardiff: University of Wales Press, 1963.

Wilson, Alexander. *The Life and Letters of Alexander Wilson.* Edited by Clark Hunter. Philadelphia: American Philosophical Society, 1983.

Worster, Donald. *A River Running West: The Life of John Wesley Powell.* New York: Oxford University Press, 2001.

Exploration on the Expedition

Allen, John Logan. "Lewis and Clark on the Upper Missouri: Decision at the Marias." *Montana: The Magazine of Western History* 21, no. 3 (1971): 2–17.

Amacker, Mary Ann. "Captain Clark and Party's Journey over Tillamook Head (Clark's Point of View) to the Site of the Beached Whale at Ecola Creek." Available on-line. URL: http://www.nps.gov.focl/whale1.htm. Downloaded on May 25, 2001.

Discovery Writers. *Lewis & Clark in the Bitterroot.* Stevensville, Mont.: Stoneydale Press Publishing Co., 1999.

———. *Lewis & Clark on the Upper Missouri.* Stevensville, Mont.: Stoneydale Press Publishing Co., 2000.

Erickson, Vernon. "Lewis and Clark on the Upper Missouri." *North Dakota History* 40, no. 2 (1973): 34–37.

Howard, Ella Mae. *Lewis and Clark's Exploration of Central Montana.* Great Falls, Mont.: Lewis and Clark Interpretative Association, 1993.

Mussulman, Joseph. "Nathaniel Pryor's Mission." From *Discovering Lewis and Clark: Clark on the Yellowstone.*

Available on-line. URL: http://www.lewisclark.org/ CLARK-YELLOWSTONE/PRYOR/yr_pryor- mmenu.htm. Downloaded on February 28, 2002.

———. "Ocean in View." From: *Discovering Lewis and Clark: The Extent of Our Journey.* Available on-line. URL: http://www.lewis-clark.org/FTCCOLUMBIA/fc_stac1. htm. Downloaded on March 10, 2002.

Osgood, Ernest Staples. "Clark on the Yellowstone 1806." *Montana: The Magazine of Western History* 18, no. 3 (1968): 9–29.

Ronda, James P. *Finding the West: Explorations with Lewis and Clark.* Lincoln: University of Nebraska Press, 2001.

Saindon, Bob. "The River Which Scolds at all Others: An Obstinate Blunder in Nomenclature." *Montana: The Magazine of Western History* 26, no. 3 (1976): 2–7.

Simon-Smolinski, Carol. "The Corps of Discovery on the Clearwater River." *Idaho's Northwest Passage.* Available on-line. URL: http://www.idahonwp.org/togo/bmc/lc_ clear.htm. Downloaded on February 10, 2002.

Wells, Merle. "Lewis & Clark's Water Route to the Northwest: The Exploration That Finally Laid to Rest the Myth of a Northwest Passage." *Columbia* 8, no. 4 (Winter 1994/95). Available on-line. URL: http://www.wshs.org/ lewisandclark/water_route.htm. Downloaded on July 12, 2002.

Campsites, Route, and Trails

Appleman, Roy E. "Lewis and Clark: The Route 160 Years After." *Pacific Northwest Quarterly.* 57 (January 1966).

———. "The Lost Site of Camp Wood: The Lewis and Clark Winter Camp, 1803–04." *Journal of the West* 7, no. 2 (1968): 270–274.

Cavan, Seamus. *Lewis and Clark and the Route to the Pacific.* New York: Chelsea House, 1991.

Duncan, Dayton. "The Vote: 'Station Camp,' Washington." *Columbia* Magazine 15, no. 1 (Spring 2001). Available online. URL: http://www.wshs.org/lewisandclark/vote. htm. Downloaded on July 12, 2002.

Ehrenberg, Ralph. "Mapping on the Trail." *Route Mapping on the Lewis and Clark Expedition.* Available on-line. URL: http://www.edgate.com/lewisandclark/mapping_on_trail. html. Downloaded on March 1, 2002.

Fanselow, Julie. *The Traveler's Guide to the Lewis and Clark Trail.* Helena, Mont.: Falcon Press, 1994.

Fifer, Barbara, and Vicky Soderberg. *Along the Trail with Lewis and Clark.* Great Falls, Mont.: Montana Magazine, 1998.

Henrikson, Stephen E. "This Place of Encampment." *American History Illustrated* 20, no. 5 (1985): 22–33.

Lankiewicz, Donald P. "The Camp on Wood River: A Winter of Preparation for the Lewis and Clark Expedition." *Journal of the Illinois State Historical Society* 75, no. 2 (1982): 115–120.

Mayer, Robert W. "Wood River, 1803–1804." *Journal of the Illinois State Historical Society* 61, no. 2 (1968): 140–149.

National Park Service. "Lewis and Clark at Wood River 1803–1804, Part II." Available on-line. URL: http://
www.nps.gov/jeff/L&cWood2.htm. Downloaded on September 14, 2001.

———. "A moment in history: The Salt Works, Seaside, Oregon." Available on-line. URL: http://www.seasurf.com/ ~kirkham/saltwork.html. Downloaded on February 28, 2002.

Peebles, John J. "On the Lolo Trail: Route and Campsites of Lewis and Clark." *Idaho Yesterdays* 9, no. 4 (1965): 2–15; and 10, no. 2 (1966): 16–27.

———. "Rugged Waters: Trails and Campsites of Lewis and Clark in the Salmon River Country." *Idaho Yesterdays* 8, no. 2 (1964): 2–17.

———. "Trails and Campsites in Idaho." *Lewis and Clark in Idaho.* Boise: Idaho Historical Series No. 16 (December 1966).

Plamondon, Martin. *Lewis and Clark Trail Maps: A Cartographic Reconstruction.* Pullman: Washington State University Press, 2000.

Rasmussen, Jay. "Report on the 1997 Archaeological Excavations at Fort Clatsop." *Lewis and Clark on the Information Superhighway.* Available on-line. URL: http://www. lcarchive.org/fcexcav.html. Downloaded on February 10, 2002.

Rogers, Ken. "Fort Mandan Winter: on the banks of a river of ice." *The Bismarck Tribune.* Available on-line. URL: http:// www.ndon-line.com/tribwebpage/features/lewis clark/2001/winter.html. Downloaded on January 29, 2002.

Ronda, James P. "A Most Perfect Harmony: Life at Fort Mandan." *We Proceeded On* 14, no. 4 (February 1987).

Salter, Cathy Riggs. "Lewis and Clark's Lost Missouri: A Mapmaker Re-creates the River of 1804 and Changes the Course of History." *National Geographic* 201, no. 4 (April 2002): 89–97.

Schmidt, Thomas. *National Geographic Guide to the Lewis & Clark Trail.* Washington, D.C.: National Geographic, 1998.

Space, Ralph S. *The Lolo Trail: A History and a Guide to the Trail of Lewis and Clark,* 2d ed. Missoula: Historic Montana Publications, 2001.

Woolworth, Alan R. "New Light on Fort Mandan: A Wintering Post of the Lewis and Clark Expedition to the Pacific, 1804–1806." *North Dakota History* 55, no. 3 (1988): 3–13.

Supplies, Equipment, Gifts, Provisions, and Boats

The Bead Site. "The Beads of Lewis and Clark." Available online. URL: http://www.thebeadsite.com/FRO-LaC.htm. Downloaded on February 10, 2002.

Bedini, Silvio A. "The Scientific Instruments of the Lewis and Clark Expedition." *Great Plains Quarterly* 4, no. 1 (1984): 54–69.

Boss, Richard C. "Keelboat, Pirogue, and Canoe: Vessels Used by the Lewis and Clark Corps of Discovery." *Nautical Research Journal* 38, no. 2 (1993): 68–87.

Cutright, Paul Russell. "Lewis and Clark Indian Peace Medals." *Missouri Historical Bulletin* 24, no. 2 (1968): 160–167.

———. "Lewis has successfully outfitted the Expedition." From *Contributions of Philadelphia to Lewis and Clark History*. Available on-line. URL: http://www.lewisandclarkphila.org/philadelphiacutright37.html. Updated on August 13, 2001.

Fort Clatsop National Memorial. "Candle Making." Available on-line. URL: http://www.nps.gov/Focl/candles3.htm. Posted on April 30, 1999.

Fritz, Harry. "Store Room." From *The Lewis & Clark Expedition: A Western Adventure—A National Epic*. Available on-line. URL: http://www.lewis-clark.org/te_cache.htm. Downloaded on February 21, 2002.

Hunt, Robert R. "Gills and Drams of Consolation: Ardent Spirits on the Lewis and Clark Expedition." *We Proceeded On* 17, no. 3 (February 1991).

Jackson, Donald. "Some Books Carried by Lewis and Clark." *Bulletin of the Missouri Historical Society* 16 (1959): 3–13.

Jefferson National Expansion Memorial. "The Lewis and Clark Journey of Discovery: Food." Available on-line. URL: http://www.nps.gov/jeff/LewisClark2/CorpsOfDiscovery/Preparing/Food/Food.htm. Downloaded on April 11, 2002.

———. "The Lewis and Clark Journey of Discovery: Indian Presents and Trade Goods." Available on-line. URL: http://www.nps.gov/jeff/LewisClark2/CorpsOfDiscovery/Preparing/Gifts/Gifts.htm. Downloaded on April 11, 2002.

———. "The Lewis and Clark Journey of Discovery: Medical Supplies of the Lewis and Clark Expedition." Available on-line. URL: http://www.nps.gov/jeff/LewisClark2/CorpsOfDiscovery/Preparing/Medicine/Medicine.htm. Downloaded on April 11, 2002.

———. "The Lewis and Clark Journey of Discovery: Peace Medals." Available on-line. URL: http://www.nps.gov/jeff/LewisClark2/CorpsOfDiscovery/Preparing/PeaceMedals/PeaceMedals.htm. Downloaded on April 11, 2002.

Jeffrey, Joseph D. "Meriwether Lewis at Harpers Ferry." *We Proceeded On* Vol. 20 (November 1994).

Lentz, Gary. "Captain Lewis's Air Rifle." *Washington State Chapter Lewis and Clark Trail Heritage Foundation January 2000 Newsletter*. Available on-line. URL: http://www.lcarchive.org/wa_n0100.html. Downloaded on January 10, 2002.

Lewis-Clark.org. "Portable Inkwell." From *Discovering Lewis and Clark*. Available on-line. URL: http://www.lewis-clark.org/FTCLVIRTUAL/te_inkwl.htm. Downloaded on March 10, 2002.

Mussulman, Joseph. "Bull Boats: Float Craft on the Middle Missouri." From *Discovering Lewis and Clark: Clark on the Yellowstone*. Available on-line. URL: http://www.lewis-clark.org/CLARK-YELLOWSTONE/YELLOWSTONE/in_bull-boat.htm. Downloaded on March 1, 2002.

———. "Critical Shortages." From *Discovering Lewis and Clark: Fort Clatsop*. Available on-line. URL: http:// www.lewis-clark.org/FTCLVIRTUAL/pl_nico1.htm. Downloaded on March 10, 2002.

———. "A Neighborly Gift." From *Discovering Lewis and Clark*. Available on-line. URL: http://www.lewis-clark.org/FTCCOLUMBIA/fc_ngift.htm. Downloaded on March 19, 2002.

National Geographic. "Lewis and Clark Expedition Supplies." Available on-line. URL: http://www.nationalgeographic.com/lewisandclark/resources.html. Downloaded on May 18, 2003.

PBS Online. *Lewis and Clark: To Equip and Expedition*. Available on-line. URL: http://www.pbs.org/lewisandclark/inside/equip.html. Downloaded on May 18, 2001.

Russell, Carl P. "The Guns of the Lewis and Clark Expedition." *North Dakota History* 27 (1960): 25–34.

Stanton, Lucia C. "Jefferson Indian Peace Medal." *Monticello* (Resources). Available on-line. URL: http://www.monticello.org/resources/interests/peace_medal.html. Updated on April 27, 2001.

Journals and Letters

Abrams, Rochonne. "A Song of the Promise of the Land: The Style of the Lewis and Clark Journals." *Missouri Historical Society Bulletin* 32, no. 3 (1976): 141–157.

Barth, Gunther. "Timeless Journals: Reading Lewis and Clark with Nicholas Biddle's Help." *Pacific Historical Review* 63, no. 4 (1994): 499–519.

Bergon, Frank, ed. *The Journals of Lewis and Clark*. Reprint ed. New York: Penguin, 1995.

Bolas, Deborah W. "Books from an Expedition: A Publications History of the Lewis and Clark Journals." *Gateway Heritage* 2, no. 2 (1981): 30–35.

Butler, James Davie, ed. *The New Found Journal of Charles Floyd, a sergeant under Captains Lewis and Clark*. Worcester, Mass.: Press of Charles Hamilton, 1894.

Clark, William, and Jonathan Clark. *Dear Brother: Letters of William Clark to Jonathan Clark*. New Haven, Conn.: Yale University Press, 2002.

Cutright, Paul Russell. *A History of the Lewis and Clark Journals*. Norman: University of Oklahoma Press, 2000.

———. "Meriwether Lewis and the Marias River." *Montana: The Magazine of Western History* 18, no. 3 (1968): 30–43.

Furtwangler, Albert. *Acts of Discovery: Visions of America in the Lewis and Clark Journals*. Urbana: University of Illinois Press, 1993.

Jackson, Donald. *Letters of the Lewis and Clark Expedition, with Related Documents, 1783–1854*. Urbana: University of Illinois Press, 1979.

———. "The Race to Publish Lewis and Clark." *Pennsylvania Magazine of History and Biography* 85, no. 2 (1961): 163–177.

Jefferson, Thomas. "President Jefferson writes to Reuben Lewis." *Lewis & Clark in North Dakota*. Available on-line. URL: http://dorgan.senate.gov/lewis_and_clark/jef1.html. Downloaded on January 17, 2002.

Jones, Landon Y. *The Essential Lewis and Clark.* New York: The Ecco Press, HarperCollins, 2000.

Lewis, Meriwether. *David Thompson and the Lewis and Clark Expedition; an unpublished account of the Lewis and Clark Expedition written by Captain Meriwether Lewis and copied by David Thompson of the North West Company.* Vancouver, B.C.: Library's Press, 1959.

Lewis, Meriwether, and William Clark. *The History of the Lewis and Clark Expedition.* Edited by Elliott Coues; 4 vols., 1893, Harper. Reprinted in 3 vols., New York: Dover Publications., 1979.

———. *History of the Expedition under the Command of Captains Lewis and Clark, to the Sources of the Missouri, thence across the Rocky Mountains and down the River Columbia to the Pacific Ocean: Performed during the Years 1804–5–6 by Order of the Government of the United States.* Prepared for the press by Paul Allen; in two volumes. Philadelphia: Bradford and Inskeep; New York: Abm. H. Inskeep, 1814. Reprints: New Amsterdam Book Company, New York, 1902; Lippincott, Philadelphia, 1961.

Lewis, Meriwether, et al. *The Journals of Lewis and Clark.* Edited by Bernard Devoto. Boston: Mariner Books, 1997.

MacGregor, Carol Lynn. "The Role of the Gass Journal." *We Proceeded On* 16, no. 4 (November 1990): 13–17.

———, ed. *The Journals of Patrick Gass, Member of the Lewis and Clark Expedition.* Missoula, Mont.: Mountain Press Publishing Company, 1997.

Moulton, Gary E., ed. *The Journals of the Lewis and Clark Expedition.* 13 vols. Lincoln: University of Nebraska Press, 1983–2001.

———. *The Journals of the Lewis and Clark Expedition: The Journals of John Ordway, May 14, 1804–September 23, 1806, and Charles Floyd, May 14–August 18, 1804.* Lincoln: University of Nebraska Press, 1996.

———. "The Missing Journals of Meriwether Lewis." *Montana: The Magazine of Western History* 35, no. 3 (1985): 28–39.

Quaife, Milo M., ed. *The Journals of Captain Meriwether Lewis and John Ordway: Kept on the Expedition of Western Exploration, 1803–1806.* Madison: State Historical Society of Wisconsin, 1916.

Thwaites, Reuben G., ed. *Original Journals of the Lewis and Clark Expedition, 1804–1806; printed from the original manuscripts in the library of the American philosophical society and by direction of its committee on historical documents, together with manuscript material of Lewis and Clark from other sources, including note-books, letters, maps, etc., and the journals of Charles Floyd and Joseph Whitehouse, now for the first time published in full and exactly as written.* 8 vols. New York: Dodd, Mead, 1904–05.

———, ed. *Original Journals of the Lewis and Clark Expedition Atlas.* Scituate, Mass: Digital Scanning, Inc., 2000.

Other Aspects of the Expedition

American Philosophical Society. "Treasures of the APS: Lewis and Clark's Specimens as Sketched by Charles Willson Peale." Available on-line. URL: http://www.amphilsoc. org/library/exhibits/treasures/pealecw.htm. Downloaded on March 1, 2002.

Chuinard, Eldon G. *Only One Man Died: The Medical Aspects of the Lewis and Clark Expedition.* Glendale, Calif.: A. H. Clark Co., 1979.

Criswell, Elijah H. *Lewis and Clark: Linguistic Pioneers.* Columbia: University of Missouri Press, 1940.

Cutright, Paul Russell. "Jefferson's Instructions to Lewis and Clark." *Bulletin of the Missouri Historical Society* 22, no. 3 (1966): 303–320.

———. "Meriwether Lewis Prepares for a Trip West." *Bulletin of the Missouri Historical Society* 23, no. 1 (October 1966).

Fent, Cindy. "Some Medical Aspects of the Lewis and Clark Expedition." *North Dakota History* 53, no. 1 (1986): 24–28.

Fields, Wayne D. "The Meaning of Lewis and Clark." *Gateway Heritage* 2, no. 2 (1981): 2–7.

Gill, Larry. "The Great Portage: Lewis and Clark's Overland Journey Around the Great Falls of the Missouri River." *We Proceeded On* 1, no. 4 (fall 1975): 6–9.

Gottfred, A. "Lewis & Clark: A Canadian Perspective." *Northwest Journal* 11: 1–13. Available on-line. URL: http://www.northwestjournal.ca/XI1.htm. Downloaded on February 27, 2002.

Hunt, Robert R. "The Blood Meal: Mosquitoes and Agues on the Lewis and Clark Expedition." *We Proceeded On* 18, no. 3 (May and August 1992).

———. "Crime and Punishment on the Lewis and Clark Expedition." *Military Collector and Historian* 41 (summer 1989): 56–65.

———. "The Espontoon: Captain Lewis's Magic Stick." *We Proceeded On* 16, no. 1 (February 1990): 12–18.

———. "Merry to the Fiddle: The Musical Amusement of the Lewis and Clark Party." *We Proceeded On* 14, no. 4 (November 1988).

Jefferson, Thomas. Jefferson's Confidential Letter to Congress. From *Thomas Jefferson and the Lewis and Clark Expedition.* Available on-line. URL: http://www.monticello.org/ jefferson/lewisandclark/l&c_congress_letter.html. Downloaded on January 10, 2002.

———. Jefferson's Instructions to Meriwether Lewis. From *Thomas Jefferson and the Lewis and Clark Expedition.* Available on-line. URL: http://www.monticello.org/jefferson/ lewisandclark/l&c_lewis_letter.html. Downloaded on January 10, 2002.

———. *Message from the President of the United States Communicating Discoveries Made in Exploring the Missouri, Red River and Washita, by Captains Lewis and Clark, Doctor Sibley, and Mr. Dunbar: with a statistical account of the countries adjacent.* Washington, D.C.: A. & G. Way, printers, 1806.

Jefferson National Expansion Memorial. "The Lewis and Clark Journey of Discovery: What did the men who went west with Lewis and Clark wear?" Available on-line. URL: http://www.nps.gov/jeff/LewisClark2/CorpsOf Discovery/Preparing/Clothing/Clothing.htm. Downloaded on April 11, 2002.

Jones, Landon Y. "Leading Men: Commanding, cooperative, confident, complementary—Why Lewis and Clark were perfectly cast as co-CEOs." *Time* (July 8, 2002): 54–57. Available on-line. URL: http://www.time.com/time/ 2002/lewis_clark/lcaptains.html. Downloaded on July 11, 2002.

Kyle, Robert. "Bargains Galore at Lewis & Clark's Yard Sale." Maine Antique Digest, November 1997. Available on-line. URL: http://www.maineantiquedigest.com/ articles/lewi1197.htm. Downloaded on February 10, 2002.

Lange, Robert. "$2,500.00 vs. $38,722.25—The Financial Outlay for the Historic Enterprise." *We Proceeded On* 1, no. 2 (February 1975): 17–18.

Large, Arlen. "'Additions to the Party': How an Expedition Grew and Grew." *We Proceeded On* 16, no. 1 (February 1990): 4–11.

———. "All in the Family: The In-House Honorifics of Lewis and Clark." *Names* 42, no. 4 (1994): 269–277.

———. "Fort Mandan's Dancing Longitude." *We Proceeded On* 13, no. 1 (February 1987).

———. "'It Thundered and Lightened': The Weather Observations of Lewis and Clark." *We Proceeded On* 12, no. 2 (May 1986).

———. "Lewis and Clark: Part Time Astronomers." *We Proceeded On* 5, no. 1 (February 1979).

Lewis & Clark in North Dakota. "Report to Congress." Available on-line. URL: http://dorgan.senate.gov/lewis_and_ clark/message.html. Downloaded on May 17, 2001.

Loos, John L. "William Clark's Part in the Preparation of the Lewis and Clark Expedition." *Bulletin of the Missouri Historical Society* (July 1954).

Merritt, James, et al. "Shooting the Moon (and the Sun and Stars): Lewis and Clark as Celestial Navigators." *We Proceeded On* 27, no. 4 (November 2001).

Moulton, Gary E. "A Note on the White Pirogue." *We Proceeded On* 12, no. 2 (May 1986): 22.

Mussulman, Joseph. "In Greatest Harmony: 'Medicine Songs' on the Lewis and Clark Trail." *We Proceeded On* 23, no. 4 (August 1997).

———. "Music on the Trail." From *Discovering Lewis and Clark*. Available on-line. URL: http://www.lewis-clark. org/MUSIC/mu_mmenu.htm. Downloaded on March 19, 2002.

Nicandri, David. "The Independence Hall of the West." Washington State Historical Society. Available on-line. URL: http://www.wshs.org/lewisandclark/independence_ hall.htm. Downloaded on July 12, 2002.

Paton, Bruce C. *Lewis and Clark: Doctors in the Wilderness.* Golden, Colo.: Fulcrum Publishing, 2001.

Peck, David J. *Or Perish in the Attempt: Wilderness Medicine in the Lewis & Clark Expedition.* Helena, Mont.: Farcountry Press, 2002.

Preston, Richard S. "The Accuracy of the Astronomical Observations of Lewis and Clark." *APS Proceedings,* June 2000. Available on-line. URL: http://www.aps-pub. com/proceedings/jun00/Preston.pdf. Downloaded on February 10, 2002.

Rasmussen, Jay, comp. "Old Newspaper Accounts Regarding Lewis and Clark." *Lewis and Clark on the Information Superhighway.* Available on-line. URL: http://www.lcarchive. org/newspapers.html. Updated on May 24, 2000.

———, comp. "Visual Resources and Artifacts." *Lewis & Clark on the Information Superhighway.* Available on-line. URL: http://www.lcarchive.org/visualresources.html. Updated on November 6, 2001.

Rogers, Ken. "Heart and Sole: Expedition Members Placed One Tender Foot in Front of the Other." *The Bismarck Tribune.* Available on-line. URL: http://www.ndonline. com/tribwebpage/features/lewisclark/2001/sole.html. Downloaded on February 21, 2002.

———. "A Life Saver: Espontoon: Lewis' Trusty Pike." *The Bismarck Tribune.* Available on-line. URL: http://www. ndonline.com/tribwebpage/features/lewisclark/2001/saver. html. Downloaded on February 21, 2002.

———. "Roughing It: Give Me Shelter." *The Bismarck Tribune.* Available on-line. URL: http://www.ndon-line.com/ tribwebpage/features/lewisclark/2001/rough.html. Downloaded on February 16, 2002.

Ronda, James P. "'A Knowledge of Distant Parts': The Shaping of the Lewis and Clark Expedition." *Montana: The Magazine of Western History* 41, no. 4 (1991): 4–18.

Seelye, John. "Beyond the Shining Mountains: The Lewis and Clark Expedition as an Enlightenment Epic." *Virginia Quarterly Review* 63, no. 1 (1987): 36–53.

Slosberg, Daniel. "Instruments of the Expedition." *Cruzatte! Study Guide.* Available on-line. URL: http://www. cruzatte.com/studyguide/5_instruments.html. Downloaded on February 19, 2002.

Stein, Joel. "Have You Ever Tried Ashcakes?" *Time* (July 8, 2002): 74–76. Available on-line. URL: http://www.time. com/time/2002/lewis_clark/lcuisine.html. Downloaded on July 11, 2002.

Werner Wilbur P. "Disaster at Montana's Two Medicine River Fight Sight." *We Proceeded On* 6, no. 3 (August 1980): 12–13.

Wesselius, Allen "Doc." "A Lasting Legacy: The Lewis and Clark Place Names of the Pacific Northwest." *Columbia:* Part I, 15, no. 1 (spring 2001); Part II, 15, no. 2 (summer 2001); Part III, 15, no. 3 (fall 2001); Part IV, 15, no. 4 (winter 2001). Available on-line. URL: http://www. wshs.org/lewisandclark/lc-articles.htm. Downloaded on July 12, 2002.

Will, Drake W. "Lewis and Clark: Westering Physicians." *Montana: The Magazine of Western History* 21, no. 4 (1971): 2–17.

———. "The Medical and Surgical Practice of the Lewis and Clark Expedition." *Journal of the History of Medicine and Allied Sciences* 14, no. 3 (1959): 273–297.

Young, F. G. "The Higher Significance in the Lewis and Clark Expedition." *Quarterly of the Oregon Historical Society* 6, no. 1 (March 1905).

Indians: Ethnology, History, and Specific Nations

Andrist, Ralph K. *The Long Death: The Last Days of the Plains Indians.* Norman: University of Oklahoma Press, 2001.

Cash, Joseph H., and Gerald W. Wolff. *The Three Affiliated Tribes (Mandan, Arikara, and Hidatsa).* Phoenix: Indian Tribal Series, 1974.

Catlin, George. *Letters and Notes on the Manners, Customs, and Conditions of the North American Indians; Written during Eight Years' Travel (1832–1839).* Reprint, New York: Dover Publications, 1973.

Chapman, Carl H. *The Origin of the Osage Indian Tribe.* New York: Garland Pub., Inc., 1974.

Clark, W. P. *The Indian Sign Language.* Lincoln: University of Nebraska Press, 1982.

Criswell, Elijah H. *Lewis and Clark: Linguistic Pioneers.* Columbia: University of Missouri Press, 1940.

Denig, Edwin Thompson. *The Assiniboine.* Edited by J. N. B. Hewitt. Norman: University of Oklahoma Press, 2000.

Drucker, Philip. *Indians of the Northwest Coast.* New York: McGraw-Hill, 1955.

Edmunds, R. David. *The Otoe-Missouria People.* Phoenix: Indian Tribal Series, 1976.

Emerson, William Dana. *Indian Corn.* Wilmington: Scholarly Resources, 1978.

Ewers, John C. *The Blackfeet: Raiders on the Northwestern Plains.* Norman: University of Oklahoma Press, 1958.

———. "Plains Indian Reactions to the Lewis and Clark Expedition." *Montana: The Magazine of Western History* 16 (January 1966): 2–12.

Fahey, John. *The Flathead Indians.* Norman: University of Oklahoma Press, 1974.

Foley, William E., and C. David Rice. "The Return of the Mandan Chief." *Montana: The Magazine of Western History* 29, no. 3 (1979): 2–15.

Gasque, Thomas J. "Lewis and Clark's Onomastic Assumptions." *Midwestern Folklore* 21 (spring–fall 1995): 30–38.

Hagen, Cecil. "Liberated Women? . . . Not Those Lewis and Clark Met on Their Way." *Pacific Northwesterner* 25, no. 2 (1981): 17–25.

Heidenreich, C. Adrian. "The Native Americans' Yellowstone." *Montana: The Magazine of Western History* 35 (autumn 1985): 56–67.

Jackson, Donald. "Lewis and Clark among the Oto." *Nebraska History* 41 (1960): 237–248.

Jefferson National Expansion Memorial. "The Lewis and Clark Journey of Discovery: Native Peoples." Available on-line. URL: http://www.nps.gov/jeff/LewisClark2/TheJourney/NativePeoples.htm. Downloaded on April 11, 2002.

Jones, Gene. "The Mandan Indians, Descendants of the Vikings." *Real West* 9, no. 47 (May 1966): 31–32.

Josephy, Alvin M., Jr. *The Nez Perce Indians and the Opening of the Northwest.* New Haven: Yale University Press, 1965.

Kartunnen, Frances. *Between Worlds: Interpreters, Guides and Survivors.* New Brunswick: Rutgers University Press, 1994.

Kawashime, Yasuhide. "Forest Diplomats: The Role of Interpreters in Indian–White Relations in the Early American Frontier." *The American Indian Quarterly* 13, no. 1 (winter 1989): 1–14.

Lewis & Clark in North Dakota. "Personal Profiles: Profile of Three Chiefs." Available on-line. URL: http://www.ndlewisandclark.com/profiles.html. Downloaded on February 2, 2002.

Lowie, Robert H. *The Crow Indians.* Lincoln: University of Nebraska Press, 1983.

Madsen, Brigham D. *The Lemhi: Sacagawea's People.* Caldwell, Idaho: Caxton Printers, 1979.

Majors, Harry M., ed. "Lewis and Clark Among the Sayleesh Indians: Ross Hole, September 4–5, 1805." *Northwest Discovery* 7, no. 32–33 (1987): 126–246.

McBeth, Kate. *The Nez Perces Since Lewis and Clark.* 1908. Reprint, Moscow: University of Idaho Press, 1993.

Meyer, Roy W. *The Village Indians of the Upper Missouri: The Mandans, Hidatsas, and Arikaras.* Lincoln: University of Nebraska Press, 1977.

National Park Service. "Knife River Indian Villages: National Historic Site." Available on-line. URL: http://www.nps.gov/knri/overview.htm. Downloaded on April 14, 2002.

Nichols, William. "Lewis and Clark Probe the Darkness." *American Scholar* 49, no. 1 (1979/80): 94–101.

Paper, Jordan. *Offering Smoke: The Sacred Pipe and Native American Religion.* Moscow: University of Idaho Press, 1988.

PBS Online. *Lewis and Clark: The Native Americans.* Available on-line. URL: http://www.pbs.org/lewisandclark/native/index.html. Downloaded on May 18, 2001.

Peabody Museum of Archeology and Ethnology, Harvard University. "The Ethnography of Lewis and Clark." Available on-line. URL: http://www.peabody.harvard.edu/Lewis_and_Clark/default.html. Downloaded on March 22, 2002.

Pioneer Middle School. "The Wenatchee Valley Plateau Indian Culture." Available on-line. URL: http://pio.wsd.wednet.edu/SAMMgrant/NativeAm/homepage.shtml. Updated on September 14, 2001.

Prucha, Francis Paul. *Indian Peace Medals in American History.* Norman: University of Oklahoma Press, 1995.

Ray, Verne F. "The Chinook Indians in the Early 1800s." In *The Western Shore: Oregon Country Essays Honoring the American Revolution.* Edited by Thomas Vaughan, pp. 121–150. Portland: Oregon Historical Society, 1976.

———. *Lewis and Clark and the Nez Perce Indians.* Washington, D.C.: The Westerners, 1971.

Ray, Verne F., and Nancy O. Lurie. "The Contributions of Lewis and Clark to Ethnography." *Journal of the Washington Academy of Sciences* 44 (1954): 358–370.

Rees, John E. "The Shoshoni Contribution to Lewis and Clark." *Idaho Yesterdays* 2 (1958): 2–13.

Relander, Click (Now-Tow-Look). *Strangers on the Land: A Historiette of a Longer Story of the Yakima Nation's Efforts to Survive Against Great Odds.* Yakima, Wash.: Franklin Press, 1962.

Ronda, James P. "'A Chart in His Way': Indian Cartography and the Lewis and Clark Expedition." *Great Plains Quarterly* 4, no. 1 (1984): 43–53.

———. *Lewis and Clark among the Indians.* Lincoln: University of Nebraska Press, 1984.

———. "Exploring the Explorers: Great Plains Peoples and the Lewis and Clark Expedition." *Great Plains Quarterly* 13, no. 2 (1993): 81–90.

Ruby, Robert H., and John A. Brown. *The Chinook Indians: Traders of the Lower Columbia River.* Norman: University of Oklahoma Press, 1976.

Saindon, Bob. "The Lost Vocabularies of the Lewis and Clark Expedition." *We Proceeded On* 3 (1977): 4–6.

Sappington, Robert Lee. "Lewis and Clark Expedition Among the Nez Perce Indians: The First Ethnographic Study in the Columbia Plateau." *Northwest Anthropological Research Notes* 23 (1989): 1–33.

Sauter, John, and Bruce Johnson. *Tillamook Indians of the Oregon Coast.* Portland, Oreg.: Binfords and Mort, 1974.

Stewart, Frank Henderson. "Hidatsa Origin Traditions Reported by Lewis and Clark." *Plains Anthropologist* 21, no. 72 (1976): 89–92.

Stewart, Hilary. *Indian Fishing: Early Methods on the Northwest Coast.* Seattle: University of Washington Press, 1977.

Trenholm, Virginia, and Maurine Carley. *The Shoshonis: Sentinels of the Rockies.* Norman: University of Oklahoma Press, 1964.

Waldman, Carl. *Encyclopedia of Native American Tribes.* Revised ed. New York: Checkmark Books, 1999.

———. "Wars for the West." In *Atlas of the North American Indian.* Revised ed. New York: Checkmark Books, 1999, pp. 147–182.

Wallace, Anthony F. C. *Jefferson and the Indians: The Tragic Fate of the First Americans.* Cambridge, Mass.: Harvard University Press, 2001.

Warner, Sky. "The Sacred Pipe." Available on-line. URL: http://www.ouachitalk.com/sacred.htm. Downloaded on April 10, 2002.

Washington State University. "Lewis and Clark Among the Indians of the Pacific Northwest. Excerpts from the Journals of the Expedition of the Corps of Discovery: Flora and Fauna (recorded at Fort Clatsop)." Available on-line. URL: http://www.libarts.wsu.edu/history/Lewis_Clark/LCEXP_Flor.html. Downloaded on May 20, 2001.

Wells, Merle. "The Importance of 'Old Toby.'" Lewis & Clark in Idaho. Available on-line. URL: http://idptv.state.id.us/lc/oldtoby.html. Downloaded on May 25, 2001.

Wood, W. Raymond. "David Thompson at the Mandan-Hidatsa Villages, 1797–1798: The Original Journals." *Ethnohistory* 24 (1977): 329–342.

Writers' Program, Montana. *Land of Nakoda; the story of the Assiniboine Indians. From the tales of the Old Ones told to First Boy (James L. Long), with drawings by Fire Bear (William Standing).* Helena, Mont.: State Pub. Co., 1942. Reprint, AMS Press, New York, 1975.

Natural History

Academy of Natural Sciences. "The Lewis and Clark Herbarium." Available on-line. URL: http://www.acnatsci.org/lewis&clark/. Downloaded on May 17, 2001.

Arno, Stephen F. *Northwest Trees.* Seattle, Wash.: The Mountaineers, 1977.

Beavers: Wetland and Wild Life. "The Beaver (Castor Canadensis)." Available on-line. URL: http://www.beaversww.org/beaver.html. Downloaded on December 10, 2001.

Botkin, Daniel B. *Our Natural History: The Lessons of Lewis & Clark.* New York: Putnam, 1995.

Brooklyn College, City University of New York. "Dinosaur History: William Clark." Available on-line. URL: http://academic.brooklyn.cuny.edu/geology/chamber/clark.html. Downloaded on February 26, 2002.

Burroughs, Raymond Darwin, ed. *The Natural History of the Lewis and Clark Expedition.* East Lansing: Michigan State University Press, 1995.

Calverley, Dorthea. "The Beaver: Foundation of the Fur Trade." Available on-line. URL: http://www.calverley.ca/Part%2002%20-%20Fur%20Trade/2-001.html. Downloaded on December 10, 2001.

Chisholm, Colin. "Undaunted Botany." *Sierra* Magazine. (May/June 2002): 47–49.

Cutright, Paul Russell. "Lewis and Clark and Cottonwood." *Bulletin of the Missouri Historical Society* 22 (October 1965): 35–44.

———. *Lewis & Clark: Pioneering Naturalists.* Lincoln: University of Nebraska Press/Bison Books, 1989.

———. "Meriwether Lewis: Botanist." *Oregon Historical Quarterly* 69 (June 1968): 148–170.

———. "Meriwether Lewis: Zoologist." *Oregon Historical Quarterly* 69 (June 1968).

———. "The Odyssey of the Magpie and the Prairie Dog." *Missouri Historical Society Bulletin* 23, no. 3 (1967): 215–228.

Dary, David A. *The Buffalo Book: The Full Saga of the American Animal.* Athens, Ohio: Swallow Press/Ohio University Press, 1989.

Flores, Dan. "The American Bison." From *Discovering Lewis and Clark.* Available on-line. URL: http://www.lewis-clark.org/bison/bison_flores-history.htm. Downloaded on March 21, 2002.

Graves, Russell A. *The Prairie Dog: Sentinel of the Plains.* Lubbock: Texas Tech University Press, 2001.

Jameson, Ronald J. "Translocated Sea Otter Populations off the Oregon and Washington Coasts." Available on-line. URL:

http://biology.usgs.gov/s+t/SNT/noframe/pn175. htm. Downloaded on April 14, 2001.

Johnson, Morris D., and Joseph Knue. *Feathers from the Prairie: A Short History of Upland Game Birds.* 2d ed. Bismarck: North Dakota Game and Fish Dept., 1989.

Knue, Joseph. *Big Game of North Dakota: A Short History.* Bismarck: North Dakota Game and Fish Dept., 1991.

McNamee, Thomas. *The Grizzly Bear.* New York: Viking Penguin, 1990.

Meehan, Thomas. "The Plants of Lewis and Clark's Expedition Across the Continent, 1804–1806." *Proceedings of the Academy of Natural Sciences of Philadelphia.* January–March 1898.

Moring, J. R. "Fish Discoveries by the Lewis and Clark and Red River Expeditions." *Fisheries* 21 (July 1996): 6–12.

Nickerson, Roy. *Sea Otters: A Natural History and Guide.* San Francisco: Chronicle Books, 1989.

Osgood, Ernest Staples. "A Prairie Dog for Mr. Jefferson." *Montana: The Magazine of Western History* 19, no. 2 (1969): 54–56.

Phillips, H. Wayne. *Plants of the Lewis and Clark Expedition.* Missoula, Mont.: Mountain Press Publishing, 2003.

Quinn, C. Edward. "A Zoologist's View of the Lewis and Clark Expedition." *American Zoologist* 26 (1986): 299–306.

Reid, Russell, and Clell G. Gannon. "Birds and Mammals Observed by Lewis & Clark in North Dakota." *North Dakota History* 66, no. 2 (1999): 2–14. Jamestown, N.Dak.: Northern Prairie Wildlife Research Center Home Page. Also available on-line URL: http://www.npwrc.usgs.gov/resource/2000/bmam/bmam.htm. Downloaded on May 20, 2001.

Rossi, Linda, and Alfred E. Schuyler. "The Iconography of Plants Collected on the Lewis and Clark Expedition." *Great Plains Research* 3, no. 1 (1993): 39–60.

Schafer, Shaun. "Prairie Fires Designed to Help Nature." IM-Diversity Daily News, Associated Press. Available on-line. URL: http://www.imdiversity.com/Article_Detail.asp?Article_ID=6612. Downloaded on February 28, 2002.

Schullery, Paul. *Lewis and Clark Among the Grizzlies: Legend and Legacy in the American West.* Guilford, Conn.: Globe Pequot Press, 2002.

Setzer, Henry W. "Zoological Contributions of the Lewis and Clark Expedition." *Journal of the Washington Academy of Sciences* 44 (November 1954).

Tobin-Schlesinger, Kathleen. "Jefferson to Lewis: The Study of Nature in the West." *Journal of the West* 29, no. 1 (1990): 54–61.

Van Wormer, Joe. *The World of the Pronghorn.* Philadelphia: Lippincott, 1969.

Walcheck, K. C. "Birds Observed by Lewis and Clark in Montana, 1805–06." *Proceedings of the Montana Academy of Science* 29: 13–29.

Wilkinson, Todd, and Paul Rauber. "Lewis & Clark's America: The Corps of Discovery Left Us a Blueprint for a Wild West." *Sierra* (May/June 2002): 42–46.

Wilson, Alexander. *Birds of America.* 9 vols. Philadelphia: Bradford & Innskeep, 1808–14.

Wilson, Alexander, and Charles Lucien Bonaparte. *American Ornithology; or The Natural History of the Birds of the United States.* Edited by Robert Jameson. Edinburgh: Constable & Co., 1831.

Geography and Mapping

Allen, John Logan. "Geographical Knowledge and American Images of the Louisiana Territory." *Western Historical Quarterly* 2 (April 1971).

———. *Passage Through the Garden: Lewis and Clark and the Image of the American Northwest.* Urbana: University of Illinois Press, 1975. Reprint, New York: Dover Publications, 1991.

American Rivers. "The Rivers of Lewis and Clark." Available on-line. URL: http://www.americanrivers.org/lewisclark/default.htm. Downloaded on February 10, 2002.

Botkin, Daniel B. *Passage of Discovery: The American Rivers Guide to the Missouri of Lewis and Clark.* New York: Berkley Publishing Group, 1999.

Clawson, Roger. *Pompeys Pillar: Crossroads of the Frontier.* Billings, Mont.: The Prose Works, 1992.

Dietrich, William. *Northwest Passage: The Great Columbia River.* Seattle: University of Washington Press, 1996.

Dryden, Cecil. *The Clearwater of Idaho.* New York: Carlton Press, 1972.

Ehrenberg, Ralph. "Mapping on the Trail." *Route Mapping on the Lewis and Clark Expedition.* Available on-line. URL: http://www.edgate.com/lewisandclark/mapping_on_trail.html. Downloaded on March 1, 2002.

Ellet, Charles. *The Mississippi and Ohio Rivers.* New York: Arno Press, 1970.

Furdell, William J., and Elizabeth Lane Furdell. *Great Falls: A Pictorial History.* Norfolk, Va.: Donning Co., 1987.

Harris, Stephen L. *Fire and Ice: The Cascade Volcanoes.* Revised ed. Seattle: The Mountaineers, Pacific Search Press, 1980.

Hawke, David Freeman. "William Clark and the Mapping of the West." *Gateway Heritage* 10, no. 3 (1989–90): 4–13.

Heidenreich, C. Adrian. "The Native Americans' Yellowstone." *Montana: The Magazine of Western History* 35 (Autumn 1985): 56–67.

Hulbert, Archer Butler. *Waterways of Western Expansion: The Ohio River and Its Tributaries.* New York: AMS Press, 1971.

Johnsgard, Paul A. *The Platte: Channels in Time.* Lincoln: University of Nebraska Press, 1984.

Lang, William L., and Robert C. Carriker, eds. *Great River of the West: Essays on the Columbia River.* Seattle: University of Washington Press, 1999.

Larson, Ron. *Upper Mississippi River History: Fact, Fiction, Legend.* Revised ed. Winona, Minn.: Steamboat Press, 1998.

Lower, J. Arthur. *Ocean of Destiny: A Concise History of the North Pacific, 1500–1978.* Vancouver: University of British Columbia Press, 1978.

Moulton, Gary E., ed. *Atlas of the Lewis and Clark Expedition.* Revised ed. Lincoln: University of Nebraska Press, 1999.

Mussulman, Joseph. "Pompy's Tower." From *Discovering Lewis and Clark: Clark on the Yellowstone.* Available on-line. URL: http://www.lewis-clark.org/CLARK-YELLOWSTONE/POMPSTOWER/yr_pomp-remark-able.htm. Downloaded on February 28, 2002.

National Geographic Atlas of Natural America. Washington, D.C.: National Geographic Society, 2000.

National Park Service. "Knife River Indian Villages: National Historic Site." Available on-line. URL: http://www.nps.gov/knri/overview.htm. Downloaded on April 14, 2002.

Naval Meteorology and Oceanography Command. "Pacific Ocean." Available on-line. URL: http://oceanographer.navy.mil/pacific.html. Updated on May 30, 2001.

Newby, Rick. "The Yellowstone River." From *Discovering Lewis and Clark: Clark on the Yellowstone.* Available on-line. URL: http://www.lewis-clark.org/CLARK-YELLOWSTONE/YELLOWSTONE/yr_submenu.htm. Downloaded on February 28, 2002.

Nicandri, David, and Gary Lentz. "Lewis & Clark and the Mountain of Mystery." Washington State Historical Society. Available on-line. URL: http://www.wshs.org/lewisandclark/mountain-of-mystery.htm. Downloaded on July 12, 2002.

Peterson, Nick. "Umatilla County's Hat Rock a significant site on Lewis and Clark's route." *East Oregonian.* Available on-line. URL: http://www.eastoregonian.com/stories/99/apr/01/story1.html. Posted on April 1, 1999.

Reid, Robert L. *Always a River: The Ohio River and the American Experience.* Bloomington: Indiana University Press, 1991.

Saindon, Bob. "The River Which Scolds at all Others: An Obstinate Blunder in Nomenclature." *Montana: The Magazine of Western History* 26, no. 3 (1976): 2–7.

Salter, Cathy Riggs. "Lewis and Clark's Lost Missouri: A Mapmaker Re-creates the River of 1804 and Changes the Course of History." *National Geographic* 201, no. 4 (April 2002): 89–97.

Schwantes, Carlos A. *Columbia River: Gateway to the West.* Moscow: University of Idaho Press, 2000.

Space, Ralph S. *The Clearwater Story: A History of the Clearwater National Forest.* Missoula, Mont.: Forest Service, ISDA; Orofino, Idaho: Clearwater Historical Society, 1980.

USDA Forest Service. "Beaverhead-Deerlodge National Forest Southwest Montana: Lemhi Pass National Historic Landmark." Available on-line. URL: http://www.fs.fed.us/r1/bdnf/virtualtours/lemhi-pass/virtual-lemhi-pass.html. Downloaded on May 20, 2001.

———. "Clearwater National Forest, Idaho." URL: http://www.fs.fed.us/r1/clearwater/. Updated on February 27, 2002.

Vestal, Stanley. *The Missouri.* Lincoln: University of Nebraska Press, 1996.

Webb, Walter Prescott. *The Great Plains.* Lincoln: University of Nebraska Press, 1981.

Wood, W. Raymond. "The John Evans 1796–97 Map of the Missouri River." *Great Plains Quarterly* 1 (1981): 39–53.

———. "William Clark's Mapping in Missouri, 1803–1804." *Missouri Historical Review* 76, no. 3 (1982): 241–251.

Wood, W. Raymond, and Gary E. Moulton. "Prince Maximilian and New Maps of the Missouri and Yellowstone Rivers by William Clark." *Western Historical Quarterly* 12 (1981): 372–386.

Cities and Towns

Baldwin, Leland D. *Pittsburgh: The Story of a City, 1750–1865.* Pittsburgh: University of Pittsburgh Press, 1970.

Billon, Frederic. *Annals of St. Louis in Its Early Days under the French and Spanish dominations, 1764–1804.* Reprint, New York: Arno Press, 1971.

Cutright, Paul Russell. *Contributions of Philadelphia to Lewis and Clark History.* Philadelphia: Philadelphia Chapter Lewis and Clark Trail Heritage Foundation, 2001. Also available on-line. URL: http://www.lewisandclarkphila.org/philadelphia/philadelphiacutrightconten.html. Updated on October 15, 2001.

Foley, William. "St. Louis: The First Hundred Years." *Bulletin of the Missouri Historical Society* 34, no. 4, Pt. 1 (July 1978).

Lorant, Stefan. *Pittsburgh: The Story of an American City.* 5th ed. With contributions by Henry Steele Commager et al. Pittsburgh: Esselmont Books, 1999.

Muhly, Frank. "Firm Foundations in Philadelphia: The Lewis and Clark Expedition's Ties to Philadelphia." Lewis and Clark Heritage Trail Foundation, Philadelphia Chapter. Available on-line. URL: http://www.lewisandclarkphila.org/philadelphia/philadelphiafrankmuhly.html. Downloaded on February 7, 2002.

Taylor, Troy. "Curse of Kaskaskia: The Strange Fate of the First State Capitol of Illinois." *History and Hauntings of Illinois.* Available on-line. URL: http://www.prairieghosts.com/kaskaskia.html. Downloaded on April 5, 2002.

Town of Clarksville, Indiana. "Clarksville History." Available on-line. URL: http://town.clarksville.in.us/home/history.html. Downloaded on February 13, 2002.

Fur Trade, Traders, and Trappers

Alwin, John A. "Pelts, Provisions, and Perceptions: The Hudson's Bay Company Mandan Indian Trade, 1795–1815." *Montana: The Magazine of Western History* 29 (1979): 16–27.

Bryce, George. *The Remarkable History of the Hudson's Bay Company, Including That of the French Traders of Northwestern Canada, and of the North-west, XY, and Astor Fur Companies.* 2d ed. New York: B. Franklin, 1968.

Davidson, Gordon Charles. *The North West Company.* New York: Russell & Russell, 1967.

Foley, William E. "The Lewis and Clark Expedition's Silent Partners: The Chouteau Brothers of St. Louis." *Missouri Historical Review* 77, no. 2 (1983): 131–146.

Irving, Washington. *Astoria: or, Anecdotes of an Enterprise Beyond the Rocky Mountains.* 1836, Reprint edited by Edgeley W. Todd. Norman: University of Oklahoma Press, 1964.

MacKay, Douglas. *The Honourable Company: A History of the Hudson's Bay Company.* Freeport, N.Y.: Books for Libraries Press, 1970.

Maguire, James H., Peter Wild, and Donald A. Barclay, eds. *A Rendezvous Reader: Tall, Tangled, and True Tales of the Mountain Men, 1805–1850.* Salt Lake City: University of Utah Press, 1997.

Newman, Peter C. *Caesars of the Wilderness.* Markham, Ontario: Viking, 1987.

Oglesby, Richard E. *Manuel Lisa and the Opening of the Missouri Fur Trade.* Norman: University of Oklahoma Press, 1963.

O'Meara, Walter. *The Savage Country.* Boston: Houghton Mifflin, 1960.

Rich, E. E. *The Fur Trade and the Northwest to 1857.* Toronto: McClelland and Stewart, 1967.

Scofield, John. *Hail, Columbia: Robert Gray, John Kendrick and the American Fur Trade.* Portland: Oregon Historical Society, 1993.

Wood, W. Raymond, and Thomas D. Thiessen. *Early Fur Trade on the Northern Plains: Canadian Traders Among the Mandan and Hidatsa Indians, 1738–1818.* Norman: University of Oklahoma Press, 1985.

Exploration (Other Than Lewis and Clark)

American Philosophical Society. "Treasures of the APS: Jefferson Proposes a Scientific Expedition." Available on-line. URL: http://www.amphilsoc.org/library/exhibits/treasures/michaux.htm. Downloaded on January 10, 2002.

Anderson, Bern. *Life and Voyages of Captain George Vancouver, Surveyor of the Sea.* Toronto: University of Toronto Press, 1966.

Avalon Project at the Yale Law School. "Jefferson's Letter to George Rogers Clark." Available on-line. URL: http://www.yale.edu/lawweb/avalon/jefflett/let21.htm. Downloaded on January 10, 2002.

Barclay, Donald A., James H. Maguire, and Peter Wild, eds. *Into the Wilderness Dream: Exploration Narratives of the American West, 1500–1805.* Salt Lake City: University of Utah Press, 1994.

Brebner, John B. *The Explorers of North America 1492–1806.* New York: Macmillan, 1933.

Canadian Arctic Profiles. "Exploration of the Northwest Passage." *Arctic Canada,* Vol. 1, 3d ed., 1982. Available on-line. URL: http://collections.ic.gc.ca/arctic/explore/intro.htm. Downloaded on January 25, 2002.

Carver, Jonathan. *The Journals of Jonathan Carver and Related Documents, 1766–1770.* Edited by John Parker. St. Paul: Minnesota Historical Press, 1976.

Coalwell, Christine. "Jefferson's Library: Exploring the Americas at Monticello." From *The Author of Our Enterprise: Thomas Jefferson and the Lewis and Clark Expedition.* Available on-line. URL: http://www.monticello.org/jefferson/lewisandclark/libraryofamerica.html. Downloaded on January 21, 2002.

Coues, Elliott, ed. *The Explorations of Zebulon Montgomery Pike.* 3 vols. New York: Harper, 1895.

Daniells, Roy. *Alexander Mackenzie and the North West.* Toronto: Oxford University Press, 1971.

Delgado, James P. *Across the Top of the World: The Quest for the Northwest Passage.* New York: Checkmark Books, 1999.

Flores, Dan K. "Red River Expedition." Handbook of Texas Online. Available on-line. URL: http://www.tsha.utexas.edu/handbook/on-line/articles/view/RR/upr2.html. Downloaded on February 6, 2002.

———, ed. *Jefferson and Southwestern Exploration: The Freeman and Custis Accounts of the Red River Expedition of 1806.* Norman: University of Oklahoma Press, 1984.

Goetzmann, William. *Army Exploration in the American West.* 2d ed. Lincoln: University of Nebraska Press, 1979.

———. *Exploration and Empire: The Explorer and the Scientist in the Winning of the American West.* New York: Alfred A. Knopf, 1966.

Hart, Stephen Harding, and Archer Butler Hulbert, eds. *Zebulon Pike's Arkansaw Journal: In Search of the Southern Louisiana Purchase Boundary Line (interpreted by his newly recovered maps).* Edited, with bibliographical resumé, 1800–1810. Westport, Conn.: Greenwood Press, 1972.

Haycox, Stephen W., et al. *Enlightenment and Exploration in the North Pacific 1741–1805.* Seattle: University of Washington Press, 1995.

The Illustrated Lower Columbia Handbook. "Exploration." Available on-line. URL: http://www.lowercolumbiahandbook.com/explorers.cfm. Downloaded on March 25, 2002.

Jackson, Donald. *Thomas Jefferson & the Stony Mountains: Exploring the West from Monticello.* Norman: University of Oklahoma Press, 1993.

Jefferson, Thomas. *Message from the President of the United States Communicating Discoveries Made in Exploring the Missouri, Red River and Washita, by Captains Lewis and Clark, Doctor Sibley, and Mr. Dunbar: with a statistical account of the countries adjacent.* Washington, D.C.: A. & G. Way, printers, 1806.

Large, Arlen. "Vancouver's Legacy to Lewis and Clark." *We Proceeded On* 18, no. 1 (1992).

Mackenzie, Sir Alexander. *Voyages from Montreal through the Continent of North America to the Frozen and Pacific Oceans in 1789 and 1793, with an Account of the Rise and State of the Fur Trade.* 2 vols.; Reprint, New York: AMS Press, 1973.

Maritime Museum of British Columbia. "European Exploration on the Northwest Coast." Available on-line. URL: http://mmbc.bc.ca/source/schoolnet/exploration/ee_nwc.html. Downloaded on April 10, 2002.

Moring, John. *Men with Sand: Great Explorers of the North American West.* Helena, Mont.: Twodot Books, 1998.

Pathfinders and Passageways: The Exploration of Canada. Available on-line. URL: http://www.nlc-bnc.ca/2/24/index-e.html. Updated on December 7, 2001.

Pethick, Derek. *First Approaches to the Northwest Coast.* Vancouver: J. J. Douglas, 1976.

Powell, John Wesley. *The Exploration of the Colorado River and Its Canyons.* Reprint, Washington, D.C.: National Geographic Books, 2002.

Pugh, Ellen. *Brave His Soul: The Story of Prince Madog of Wales and His Discovery of America in 1170.* New York: Dodd, Mead & Company, 1970.

Rollins, Philip Ashton, ed. *The Discovery of the Oregon Trail: Robert Stuart's Narratives of His Overland Trip Eastward from Astoria in 1812–13.* New York: Edward Eberstadt, 1935.

Schwantes, Carlos, ed. *Encounters with a Distant Land: Exploration and the Great Northwest.* Moscow: University of Idaho Press, 1994.

Tabeau, Pierre-Antoine. *Tabeau's Narrative of Loisel's Expedition to the Upper Missouri.* Edited by Annie Heloise Abel. Translated by Rose Abel Wright. Norman: University of Oklahoma Press, 1939.

Thompson, David. *Columbia Journals.* Edited by Barbara Belyea. Seattle: University of Washington Press, 1998.

———. *Travels in Western North America, 1784–1812.* Edited by Victor G. Hopwood. Toronto: Macmillan of Canada, 1971.

University of Virginia. "Exploring the West from Monticello." Available on-line. URL: http://www.lib.virginia.edu/exhibits/lewis_clark/home.html. Downloaded on March 27, 2002.

Vancouver, George. *A Voyage of Discovery to the North Pacific Ocean and Round the World, 1791–1795.* New York: Da Capo Press, 1968.

Walker, Dale. *Pacific Destiny: The Three Century Journey to Oregon Country.* New York: Forge Books, 2000.

Wilson, Gaye. "The American Philosophical Society and Western Exploration." From *Thomas Jefferson and the Lewis and Clark Expedition.* Available on-line. URL: http://www.monticello.org/jefferson/lewisandclark/aps.html. Downloaded on January 10, 2002.

———. "Jefferson's Long Look West." From *Thomas Jefferson and the Lewis and Clark Expedition.* Available on-line. URL: http://www.monticello.org/jefferson/lewisandclark/l&c_essay.html. Downloaded on January 10, 2002.

Wood, W. Raymond. *Prologue to Lewis & Clark: The Mackay and Evans Expedition.* Norman: University of Oklahoma Press, 2003.

Zimmerman, Emily. "The Mountain Men: Pathfinders of the West." University of Virginia American Studies Project. Available on-line. URL: http://xroads.virginia.edu/~HYPER/HNS/Mtmen/home.html. Downloaded on March 14, 2002.

History and Expansion

Aldrich, John. *Why Parties? The Origin and Transformation of Political Parties in America.* Chicago: University of Chicago Press, 1995.

Avalon Project at the Yale Law School. "The Louisiana Purchase, 1803 and Associated Documents." Available on-line. URL: http://www.yale.edu/lawweb/avalon/diplomacy/france/fr1803m.htm. Updated on February 1, 2002.

Billington, Ray Allen, and Martin Ridge. *Westward Expansion: A History of the American Frontier.* 6th ed. Albuquerque: University of New Mexico Press, 2001.

Brigham, David R. *Public Culture in the Early Republic: Peale's Museum and Its Audience.* Washington, D.C.: Smithsonian Institution Press, 1995.

Colorado Migration Project. "Westward Expansion." Available on-line. URL: http://www.americanwest.com/pages/wexpansi.htm. Downloaded on May 24, 2001.

DeConde, Alexander. *This Affair of Louisiana.* New York: Charles Scribner, 1976.

DiLeo, Juliet, et al. "Government and the Louisiana Territory." Available on-line. URL: http://www.artsci.wustl.edu/~lschwarz/finalhome.html. Downloaded on March 3, 2002.

Dunbar, William. *Documents Relating to the Purchase and Exploration of Louisiana.* Boston: Houghton, Mifflin & Co., 1904.

Fanning, Susan. "Keelboats Once King of River." American Local History Network. Available on-line. URL: http://www.usgennet.org/usa/wi/county/eauclaire/history/ourstory/vol3/keelboats.html. Updated on April 27, 2000.

Frontier Heritage Alliance. "Travel the Bozeman Trail." (Includes history of the trail and pass.) Available on-line. URL: http://www.bozemantrail.org/index.htm. Downloaded on January 10, 2002.

Hebard, Grace Raymond, and E. A. Brininstool. *The Bozeman Trail: Historical Accounts of the Blazing of the Overland Routes in the Northwest, and the Fights with Red Cloud's Warriors.* Lincoln: University of Nebraska Press, 1990.

Hitchcock, Ripley. *The Louisiana Purchase & the Exploration Early History and Building of the West.* Reprint, Scituate, Mass: Digital Scanning, Inc., 2001. Also available on-line. URL: http://www.usgennet.org/usa/topic/preservation/history/louis/cover.htm. Downloaded on March 13, 2002.

Horsman, Reginald. *Expansion and American Indian Policy, 1783–1812.* East Lansing: Michigan State University Press, 1967.

Hudson, Mary A. "Amos Stoddard and the Territory of Missouri." From *The Heritage of Missouri.* Available on-line. URL: http://www.rootsweb.com/~mostodd2/stodsettlers/amos-stod.htm. Downloaded on March 3, 2002.

Illinois Department of Natural Resources. "Fort Massac History: Chronology." Available on-line. URL: http://dnr.state.il.us/lands/landmgt/PARKS/R5/from_history.htm. Downloaded on January 26, 2002.

Kawashime, Yasuhide. "Forest Diplomats: The Role of Interpreters in Indian-White Relations in the Early American Frontier." *The American Indian Quarterly* 13, no. 1 (winter 1989): 1–14.

Keogh, Xavier F. "The American Federal Interpreter and How the West Was Won." *Proteus* VII: 3 (summer 1998). Available on-line. URL: http://www.najit.org/proteus/keogh. html. Downloaded on May 23, 2001.

Kimberly, Howard. "Madoc: Were the Welsh the First European Americans?" Madoc 1170 website. Available on-line. URL: http://www.madoc1170.com/home.htm. Updated on February 7, 2001.

Kukla, Jon. *A Wilderness So Immense: The Louisiana Purchase and the Destiny of America.* New York: A. A. Knopf, 2003.

Marshall, Thomas Maitland. *A History of the Western Boundaries of the Louisiana Purchase, 1819–1841.* Berkeley: University of California Press, 1914.

Mattes, Merrill J. *The Great Platte River Road: The Covered Wagon Mainline via Fort Kearney to Fort Laramie.* Lincoln: Nebraska State Historical Society, 1969.

Montgomery, M. R. *Jefferson and the Gun-Men: How the West Was almost Lost.* New York: Crown Publishers, 2000.

Morison, Samuel Eliot. *Oxford History of the American People.* New York: Oxford University Press, 1965.

Nasatir, A. P., ed. *Before Lewis and Clark: Documents Illustrating the History of the Missouri, 1785–1804.* 2 vols. St. Louis: St. Louis Historical Documents Foundation, 1975.

Nichols, Roger L. "The Army and Early Perceptions of the Plains." *Nebraska History* 56, no. 1 (1975): 121–135.

Oregon Blue Book. "Oregon History–Columbia Plateau." Available on-line: URL: http://bluebook.state.or.us/cultural/history/history03.htm. Downloaded on April 4, 2002.

Prucha, Francis Paul. *Indian Peace Medals in American History.* Norman: University of Oklahoma Press, 1995.

Rodriguez, Junius P., ed. *The Louisiana Purchase: A Historical and Geographical Encyclopedia.* Santa Barbara, Calif.: ABC-CLIO, 2002.

Ronda, James P. *Thomas Jefferson and the Changing West.* St. Louis: Missouri Historical Society Press, 1997.

Ross, Alexander. *Adventures of the First Settlers on the Oregon or Columbia River.* 1849. Reprint edited by Milo M. Quaife. Chicago: Lakeside Press, 1922.

Shoemaker, Floyd. "The Louisiana Purchase, 1803." *Missouri Historical Review* 48 (October 1953).

Stoddard, Amos. *Sketches, Historical and Descriptive, of Louisiana.* 1812. Reprint, New York: AMS Press, 1973.

Thwaites, Reuben G. *How George Rogers Clark Won the Northwest and Other Essays in Western History.* New York: Arno Press, 1978.

Trinklein, Mike, and Steve Boettcher. "The Oregon Trail." Available on-line. URL: http://www.isu.edu/~trinmich/Oregontrail.html. Downloaded on January 15, 2002.

Utley, Robert M. *A Life Wild and Perilous: Mountain Men and the Paths to the Pacific.* New York: Henry Holt and Co., 1997.

Wallace, Anthony F. C. *Jefferson and the Indians: The Tragic Fate of the First Americans.* Cambridge, Mass.: Harvard University Press, 2001.

Miscellaneous

Carvalho, David N. *Forty Centuries of Ink.* New York: B. Franklin, 1971.

Fussell, Betty. *The Story of Corn.* New York: Knopf, 1992.

Gottfried, J. "The Well-Dressed Explorer." Available on-line. URL: http://www.northwestjournal.ca/sample.html. Downloaded on February 28, 2002.

History of Paper. Available on-line. URL: http://www.mead.com/ml/docs/facts/history.html. Downloaded on April 14, 2002.

Leepson, Marc. *Saving Monticello: The Levy Family's Epic Quest to Rescue the House that Jefferson Built.* New York: Free Press, 2001.

Licht, Daniel S. *Ecology and Economics of the Great Plains.* Lincoln: University of Nebraska Press, 1997.

Nova Online. "Lost Tribes of Israel." PBS Companion Website. Available on-line. URL: http://www.pbs.org/wgbh/nova/israel/. Created February 2000; downloaded on February 20, 2002.

Russell, Carl P. *Firearms, Traps & Tools of the Mountain Men.* Albuquerque: University of New Mexico Press, 1977.

Snow, Jan. "Lewis and Clark in the Museum Collections of the Missouri Historical Society." *Gateway Heritage* 2, no. 2 (1981): 36–41.

Wheelock, Mary E. *Paper: Its History and Development.* Chicago: American Library Association, 1928.

RECOMMENDED WEBSITES

There are thousands of websites devoted to Lewis and Clark. The following are among the best. See also individual on-line articles in the bibliography above.

Bibliography of the Lewis and Clark Expedition (Compiled and Annotated by Lance Gillette)
http://www.olypen.com/gillde/lance/bibliographies/lewis.htm#Primary

Discovering Lewis and Clark
http://www.lewis-clark.org/

Exploring the West from Monticello (University of Virginia)
http://www.lib.virginia.edu/exhibits/lewis_clark/home.html

The Journals of Lewis and Clark (University of Virginia)
http://xroads.virginia.edu/~HYPER/JOURNALS/toc.html

The Journals of the Lewis and Clark Expedition (University of Nebraska Press, Center for Great Plains Studies, UNL Libraries Electronic Text Center)
http://lewis and clarkjournals.unl.edu/

Lewis and Clark in North Dakota (Senator Byron Dorgan)
http://dorgan.senate.gov/lewis_and_clark/contents.html

The Lewis and Clark Journey of Discovery (Jefferson National Expansion Memorial; National Park Service, U.S. Department of the Interior)
http://www.nps.gov/jeff/LewisClark2/HomePage/HomePage.htm

Lewis and Clark: The Journey of the Corps of Discovery
(PBS On-line)
http://www.pbs.org/lewisandclark/index.html.

Lewis and Clark National Historic Trail (National
Park Service)
http://www.nps.gov/lecl/

Lewis and Clark on the Information Superhighway
(Compiled by Jay Rasmussen)
http://www.lcarchive.org/index.html

The Lewis and Clark Trail
http://lewisandclarktrail.com/index.html

Lewis and Clark Trail Heritage Foundation, Inc.
http://www.lewisandclark.org/index.htm

Lewis and Clark Trail Heritage Foundation—
Philadelphia Chapter
http://www.lewisandclarkphila.org/

National Geographic.com: Lewis & Clark website.
http://www.nationalgeographic.com/lewisandclark.

On the Trail: Lewis and Clark in Montana
http://lewisandclark.state.mt.us/discovery.shtm

Pacific County Friends of Lewis and Clark website.
http://www.lewisandclarkwa.com/pages/home.html

U.S. Department of the Interior Bureau of Land
Management: Idaho. Lewis and Clark Historical Articles
URL: http://www.id.blm.gov/lc/index.htm

Washington State Historical Society: Lewis and Clark website.
URL: http://www.wshs.org/lewisandclark/index.htm

Entries by Subject

ANIMALS

animals, new species
antelope
bears
beavers
buffalo
coyotes
deer
elk
foxes
horses
jackrabbits
otters
prairie dogs
prehistoric animals
rattlesnakes
sheep and goats
wolves

ASPECTS OF THE EXPEDITION

alcohol
artifacts and specimens
astronomical observations
caches
candles
clothing
coincidences and chance on the expedition
costs of the expedition
councils with Indians
democracy on the expedition
discipline
effects and influences of the expedition
ethnography
hostile encounters
hunting

illnesses and injuries
interpretation
leadership
maps
medicine and medical treatment
mission objectives
navigation
news reports of the expedition
nomenclature, geographical
organization of the expedition party
payments and rewards
portage
preparations for the expedition
recreation on the expedition
recruiting
religion
route of the expedition
sex during the expedition
shelter
skills on the expedition
supplies and equipment
trade
weather
women on the expedition

BIRDS

artifacts and specimens
birds, new species
cranes
curlews
geese and brants
gulls
Wilson, Alexander

BOATS

bull boats
canoes

iron-frame boat
keelboat
pirogues

BOOKS, JOURNALS, AND LETTERS

Allen, Paul
Biddle, Nicholas
books on the expedition
ink
journals
letters
paper

CAMPS AND CAMPSITES

Camp Chopunnish
Camp Disappointment
Camp Dubois
Camp Fortunate
Camp White Catfish
Canoe Camp
Fort Clatsop
Fort Mandan
Fort Rock Camp
Station Camp
White Bear Islands

CITIES, TOWNS, AND OTHER PLACES

Clarksville
Fort Massac
Harpers Ferry
Kaskaskia
La Charette
Monticello
Philadelphia

SCIENCE AND SCIENTISTS

American Philosophical Society
animals, new species
astronomical observations
Barton, Benjamin Smith
birds, new species
Dunbar, William
Ellicott, Andrew
ethnography
fish, new species
maps
Patterson, Robert
prehistoric animals
Pursh, Frederick
Rush, Benjamin
Wistar, Caspar

SUPPLIES, EQUIPMENT, AND GIFTS

alcohol
books on the expedition
clothing
espontoon
firearms
food
gifts
ink
oilcloth
paper
peace medals
tobacco
weapons

TRADE AND TRADERS

Astor, John Jacob
Chouteau, Auguste, Sr.
Chouteau, Pierre, Sr.
Evans, John
fur trade
Gravelines, Joseph
Hay, John
Heney, Hugh
Hudson's Bay Company
Larocque, François Antoine
Lisa, Manuel
Loisel, Régis
MacKenzie, Charles
North West Company
Tabeau, Pierre-Antoine
trade
Whelan, Israel

TRAILS AND PASSES

Bozeman Pass
Lemhi Pass
Lewis and Clark Pass
Lolo Trail
Lost Trail Pass
Oregon Trail

WEAPONS

espontoon
firearms
Harpers Ferry
weapons

Index

Page numbers in **boldface** indicate main entries. Page numbers in *italics* indicate photographs. Page numbers followed by *m* indicate maps. Page numbers followed by *c* indicate chronology entries.